THE MOVIE MAKERS

A VINEYARD BOOK

THE MOVIE
MAKERS

by
Sol Chaneles
and
Albert Wolsky

OCTOPUS BOOKS

Vineyard Books Staff *for* The Movie Makers

Project Director
Albert R. Leventhal

Managing Editor
Regina Grant Hersey

Contributing Editor
Jack B. Long

Research Director
Jane Quinson

Editors
J.P.V. Bowles
Paula Dranov
Lucille Ogle
Ellen Schachter

Copy Editors
Robert Myer
Margaret Wiener

Paris Editor
Evelyne Duval

London Editors
Carmen Callil
Barbara Crosby

Art Director and Designer
Jos. Trautwein

Production Director
Helen Barrow

Business Manager
Cecilia Waters

This edition first published 1974 by
Octopus Books Limited
59 Grosvenor Street,
London W 1 X 9DA

Produced by VINEYARD BOOKS, Inc.
159 East 64 Street, New York, N.Y. 10021
© *1974 Vineyard Books, Inc.*

ISBN 0 7064 0387 8

Printed in the United States of America

ACKNOWLEDGMENTS

The number of individuals who gave unsparingly of their time and energy to help make this book possible could very well supply the human material for a mob scene in a latter-day remake of Cecil B. De Mille's *The Ten Commandments*.

Our particular thanks are extended to those private collectors who opened their archives, gave valuable suggestions and lent their expertise to the venture: Gene Andrewski, Jack and Paula Klaw Kramer, Mark Ricci, Art Maillet, Ernest Burns and Lois Smith. Our deepest thanks go as well to Tom Golberg of the Walt Disney organization and to Richard Lawton, whose books on films and film-making are already on their way to becoming classics.

We are grateful to the motion-picture production and distribution companies, great and small, who helped us to locate and obtain the photographic material that runs through these pages: Allied Artists, Warner Brothers Pictures, 20th Century–Fox Film Corporation, Metro-Goldwyn-Mayer, Inc., RKO Radio Pictures, Columbia Pictures, Paramount Pictures, Republic Pictures, United Artists, Screen Gems, Avco-Embassy Pictures, Samuel Goldwyn Productions, the J. Arthur Rank organization, the Walter Reade organization, National General Pictures, Walt Disney Productions, Lopert Films, Inc., Brandon Films, Hanna-Barbera Productions, Inc., Kingsley International, Janus Films, the Walter Lantz organization, First National, Fox Film Company, Universal and Universal-International. Thanks go as well to the three major television networks, CBS-TV, NBC-TV and ABC-TV.

We are deeply in debt as well to the capable and highly cooperative staff of the Research Division of the Lincoln Center Library for the Performing Arts in New York, whose guidance and assistance helped our work beyond measure. Finally, our thanks go to the experts and movie buffs alike who gave their time (often evenings and weekends) to speed the project along: Janine Chaneles, Paula Dranov, Michelle Patrick, Claudie Grandberg, Nancy Trichtor, Ellen Schachter, Barbara Treckor, Jane Quinson, Mindy Shirn, Janet Scharf, Barbara Sher, Alan Becker, Harry Curtis, William Oric and P. R. De Olivira.

If any individual or organization which contributed visual material has not been acknowledged and thanked, our sincere apologies—and the assurance that the error was inadvertent and will be corrected in future editions.

THE EDITORS

FOREWORD

It took a team of more than thirty individuals to bring this book into being. A separate volume might well be written about the running debate, lasting for months, as to who should be included in these pages and who left out. Readers, some of whom will disagree with the standards established, may well be interested in a summary of how and why certain decisions were made.

The first 1,500 entries presented no problem. Then the arguments began and were eventually resolved as outlined here. Some of the pioneers of the early days—when films were ground out in a few days—were passed over in favor of those who came along a bit later and did the same sort of thing better. Thus, Flora Finch and John Bunny, the first thin and fat comedians, respectively, gave way to more polished performers—Chaplin and Keaton, Ben Turpin and Harry Langdon, Mack Swain and Harold Lloyd.

Sarah Bernhardt, the "Divine Sarah," who dominated the European stage for decades, was reluctantly omitted since her brief appearance in films was made when she was an octogenarian and far from her peak. Equally, Bronco Billy Anderson, who appeared in the first "full-length" film, *The Great Train Robbery*, was passed over in favor of more proficient gunslingers, such as William S. Hart, who came along several years later.

While virtually all of the "stars" of the 20's are included, even though for some the duration of stardom lasted little longer than the life of a butterfly, many supporting actors of the silent era were omitted. Some of these hard-working players appeared in scores of films. The parts they played, however, were almost always in third-rate films and almost always the same—looking evil standing at the bar in Western saloons; the pal or rival of the film's lead player; bank clerks, stenographers, or dance-hall girls, etc. On the other hand, all of the authentic character actors who added dimension to the roles they played, from Claude Gillingwater to Tully Marshall, are, of course, included.

The era of the talkies has relatively few omissions, and particular attention is paid to players who began in television and went on to motion pictures, and vice versa—a reasonable enough decision, the editors believe, since more and more original films are being made for TV release.

The biggest problem, as one might expect, was the selection of "new faces" from recent years. The decline of the big studios, which for decades spent millions to promote and build up durable stars with box-office appeal, created an entirely new situation that is continuing to change with dizzying speed. Better pictures, many of them brilliantly directed and independently produced, bring new actors and actresses of "star" proportions into the headlines almost on a weekly basis. In the old days it took years before a Ronald Colman or a Merle Oberon became a true star. Nowadays, the new faces of four or five years ago—from Jon Voight and Liza Minnelli to Dustin Hoffman and Glenda Jackson and Al Pacino—became stars overnight. Today, they are veterans, watching from their own private summits as a Linda Blair makes a first appearance in *The Exorcist* and with it a Golden Globe Award and headlines around the world.

In these pages, therefore, we have included those young actors and actresses who have made more than one or two films and who we feel have a bright future ahead of them. Undoubtedly, there are some grievous omissions, and for these we apologize in advance. On the other hand, we do not apologize for the omission of Linda Lovelace and other ladies and gentlemen of the porno scene—not because we are particularly prudish but because this book is about good actors and actresses, and an inner voice tells us that there is several million light-years' difference between the performances in *Deep Throat* and those in *The Sound of Music* or, for that matter, *Last Tango in Paris*.

As for directors, the editors do not share the opinion of a number of critics who feel that nothing very new or exciting is being done these days, that the basics, from close-ups to fade-outs, date back to D.W. Griffith and that when the great directors of the 1930–1960 era—Ford, Capra, Vidor, Carol Reed, Raoul Walsh and a dozen or more others—retired or died there were no new young and trained professionals to take their place. This school of thought contends, in effect, that the chase scene in *The French Connection* is an overdramatized Keystone Cop comedy and that *Clockwork Orange* contains nothing that was not done better a half century ago in the surrealist *The Cabinet of Dr. Caligari*. To us this is a little like asking why Neil Simon doesn't write plays like *King Lear* or claiming that we don't make triumphal arches the way the Romans used to do. To our way of thinking there are dozens of directors today—from Truffaut, Kubrick, Rohmer, Altman, Peckinpah, Lumet, Bertolucci, Scorsese, Bogdanovich, Friedkin—who are innovative, imaginative and highly creative. And so all of these gentlemen, plus many more, are included in the later segment of the book.

Finally, producers—who were once defined as men who knew what they wanted but couldn't spell it—are not included. There were several reasons for this decision. First, the giants of the olden days—Goldwyn, Fox, Zukor, Selznick, Mayer, and the rest of them—are gone, along with the massive studios they operated. They were truly dinosaurs, funny ones for the most part, and their place has been taken by producing units that, in general, change from picture to picture. Secondly, the producer, as the money man, was invariably the heavy in the scene—cutting the budget, grabbing the credit, an idiot with a whim of iron, the enemy and adversary of director and actor alike.

All of the above was, for the most part, untrue. Someday a great book will be written about the Goldwyns and Laemmle and Thomas Ince and others. Their role, however, was the business end of the industry and as such does not really belong in a book of this sort. Just how bright some of them were is indicated by an interchange many years ago between Erich von Stroheim and Irving Thalberg, the brilliant young boss of the vast MGM lot.

Von Stroheim was a good but wildly extravagant director, and the cost of each successive production aged Metro executives perceptibly. On one occasion Thalberg saw some rushes from *The Merry Widow*—an endless scene showing close-ups of a baron's footwear, including boots, shoes, slippers, etc.

"What in hell is all that?" Thalberg demanded.

"I want to make it clear that this man is a shoe fetishist," Von Stroheim explained.

"And you," Thalberg snapped, "are a footage fetishist!"

Ah, well, here is our big book. We hope it gives you many happy hours.

THE EDITORS

BUD ABBOTT (1898–1974)

He was born in Asbury Park, New Jersey, but grew up within earshot of the Coney Island roller coasters. After a number of unsuccessful years in the theatre, he teamed-up with Lou Costello, and the duo promptly became one of filmdom's biggest boxoffice attractions.

Abbott invariably played straight-man to squeaky-voiced Costello in a succession of custard-pie comedies—with Costello on the receiving end of the pie.

After a score or more movies, the team broke up in 1957, following which Abbott joined forces with Eddie Foy, Jr. Eventually he attempted a solo comeback in Las Vegas, but it failed to come off and Abbott retired. **Highlights:** *Buck Privates* (1941), *In Society* (1944), *Time of Their Lives* (1946), *Abbott and Costello Meet Frankenstein* (1948), *Abbott and Costello Meet the Killer* (1950), *Abbott and Costello Meet the Invisible Man* (1951), *Dance With Me Henry* (1956).

JOHN ABBOTT (1905–   )

Although John Abbott appeared in over 40 films, the only one he considered worthy of mention was *The Woman in White* (1948) in which he played the frightening Frederick Fairlie.

The British actor, who played his full share of oddball characters, was replaced as the lead in *He Who Gets Stabbed* and recast as the hero's father. Abbott explained, "They wanted a romantic lead and I am definitely not it." **Highlights:** *The Return of the Scarlet Pimpernel* (1938), *Jane Eyre* (1943), *The Merry Widow* (1952), *Gambit* (1966).

WALTER ABEL (1898–   )

He said that he could never remember a time in his life when he did not want to act. In high school he worked as a part-time usher at the Metropolitan Opera House in his native St. Paul. Then he attended the American Academy of Dramatic Arts, and subsisted on $17.50 a week.

When he first began acting, he took on serious roles. Later he switched to comedy. "Let who will go in for serious drama," he said, "I'm for the livelier life and the fatter paychecks."

Abel's first screen role was in the motion picture version of a big Broadway success, *Liliom* (1930). **Highlights:** *The Three Musketeers* (1935), *Green Light* (1937), *Men With Wings* (1938), *Wake Island* (1942), *The Kid From Brooklyn* (1946), *Raintree County* (1957).

EDDIE ACUFF (1902–1956)

The Midwestern actor worked in stock companies before going to Hollywood. Early in his career, he appeared with Bogart in the film version of Robert Sherwood's play *The Petrified Forest* (1936) and later added to the general confusion of *Hellzapoppin* (1941). Acuff also added to the merriment in a number of *Blondie* films and turned up in a *Dr. Kildare* film or two. **Highlights:** *The Golden Arrow* (1936), *Four Daughters* (1938), *The Boys From Syracuse* (1940), *Blondie Goes Latin* (1941), *Dr. Kildare's Victory* (1942).

EDIE ADAMS (1929–   )

As the wife of the talented Ernie Kovacs, she generally took a backseat to him in night-club acts and on television shows until he died in an automobile accident in 1962.

On her own she became highly successful as a nightclub performer and in television. Her first stage role came when she was chosen by producer George Abbott to play the role of Eileen in a revival of *Wonderful Town*, which was based on *My Sister Eileen*, a best-selling book. Movie roles followed. **Highlights:** *It's a Mad, Mad, Mad, Mad World* (1963), *Love With the Proper Stranger* (1963), *The Best Man* (1964), *The Honey Pot* (1967).

Bud Abbott invariably suffered whilst Lou Costello and his cigar subjected him to endless indignities.

Edie Adams and Cliff Robertson in The Best Man.

NICK ADAMS (1931–1968)

Adams' movie career began in 1950 after he hitchhiked from his Jersey City home to Hollywood where he played several bit parts in Warner productions. His chance for a bigger, better role in John Ford's *Mister Roberts* (1955) came while he was in the Coast Guard. Determined to keep the part, Adams arranged to make the movie while on leave.

Until he starred in the successful television series, *The Rebel*, Adams was perhaps better known as a friend of the young Hollywood stars—James Dean, Elvis Presley, Natalie Wood, Robert Wagner—than as an actor in his own right. However during his brief career, he made over 15 movies. **Films include:** *Somebody Loves Me* (1952), *No Time for Sergeants* (1958), *Pillow Talk* (1959), *Young Dillinger* (1965).

LUTHER ADLER (1903–   )

Adler had acting in his blood, coming from a distinguished family of performers which at one time had 17 of its members active in the theatre. He made his stage debut at the age of seven and by the time he was 17 he managed and acted in his own touring company. Adler achieved stardom after joining the Group Theater and appearing in several Clifford Odets plays—most notably, in the title role of *Golden Boy* (1937).

On screen, Adler played notorious, villainous or criminal types in a series of character parts that included Hitler and Mussolini —two of his eight roles in *The Magic Face* (1951). In addition to stage and screen performances, he also made a number of appearances on television dramatic shows. **Highlights:** *Saigon* (1948), *House of Strangers* (1949), *The Last Angry Man* (1959), *Cast a Giant Shadow* (1966), *The Brotherhood* (1968).

RENÉE ADORÉE (1898–1933)

French-born Renée Adorée was a woman of contrast and many talents. Before launching her movie career, she traveled across Europe with a circus troupe appearing as a toe dancer, an acrobat, an equestrienne, and a clown. When she made her movie debut, she had command of five languages, but had spent not one day of her life in school.

Adorée appeared in more than 20 films; her most famous role was that of Melisande in *The Big Parade* (1925) in which she starred with John Gilbert. **Highlights:** *Man and a Maid* (1922), *Tin Gods* (1926), *Mr. Wu* (1927), *Call of the Flesh* (1930).

IRIS ADRIAN (1913–   )

The blonde actress was seen most often in character roles playing parts that ranged from gun molls to secretaries. A typical role was as Two-Gun Gertie in *Roxie Hart* (1942) in which she coped with lines like "Got a butt, Buddy?"

Iris was dancing with the Ziegfeld Follies at 17 and recalls those days. "The girls were beautiful. Young girls are always beautiful. When you grow older you may be beautiful in another way, but you don't attract gangsters any more." **Highlights:** *Stolen Harmony* (1935), *Road to Zanzibar* (1941), *The Paleface* (1948), *The Odd Couple* (1968).

BRIAN AHERNE (1902–   )

The American ideal of the charming Englishman, he was forced to study ballet by his actress mother until he rebelled. He did, however, agree to study acting and made his London stage debut at the age of 12.

He was a great success in the theatre, in silent films and early talkies. In 1930, he was invited by Katharine Cornell to appear with her as Robert Browning in *The Barretts of Wimpole Street*, an association which he repeated in *Romeo and Juliet* and *Saint Joan*, all to great critical acclaim.

He made his American film debut in *Song of Songs* (1933) with Marlene Dietrich, but perhaps his best role was Emperor Maximilian in *Juarez* (1939).

Aside from acting, he developed into a very successful licensed airplane pilot. Aherne was married to Joan Fontaine for several years. **Highlights:** *Sylvia Scarlett* (1935), *My Son, My Son!* (1940), *My Sister Eileen* (1942), *A Night to Remember* (1943), *Titanic* (1953), *The Swan* (1956), *Rosie* (1968).

PHILIP AHN (1911–   )

Born in Los Angeles, the son of a Korean revolutionary who died in a Japanese prison

With the advent of talkies young Brian Aherne made a suave, sleek and ultra-sophisticated leading man.

camp, Ahn began his movie career while trying to get work as a movie extra to support his mother and to pay for his college tuition. An interview with Lewis Milestone got him a role in *Anything Goes* (1936).

After Pearl Harbor, he was much in demand for such wartime Oriental roles as a Chinese in *The Story of Dr. Wassell* (1944). He developed into one of the screen's more popular "bad guys." **More than 200 films include:** *The General Died at Dawn* (1936), *The Keys of the Kingdom* (1944), *Love Is a Many-Splendored Thing* (1955), *Never So Few* (1959).

ANOUK AIMÉE (1932–   )

Born either Françoise Sorya or Françoise Dreyfus (experts disagree), she named herself after the character she played in one of her early films. The dark-eyed beauty turned in stunning performances in *La Dolce Vita* (1961) and won an Academy Award nomination five years later for *A Man and a Woman*. She has also acted in a number of French films which only a small portion of English and American moviegoers have been privileged to view. **Credits include:** *The Golden Salamander* (1951), *Lola* (1962), *8½* (1963), *The Appointment* (1969), *Justine* (1969).

ANNA MARIA ALBERGHETTI (1936–   )

Star of *Carnival*, the Best Broadway Musical of 1961, the vocal and dramatic abilities of Miss Alberghetti were recognized early in her life for, by the time she was ten, she was hailed as a child prodigy. Born of Italian parents on the Greek island of Rhodes, the star quickly won leading parts in films as diverse as Gian-Carlo Menotti's *The Medium* and the entertaining silliness of Jerry Lewis' *Cinderfella*. She has appeared in lead roles of such T V musical specials as *Kismet*. **Highlights:** *Here Comes the Groom* (1951), *Ten Thousand Bedrooms* (1957).

LUIS ALBERNI (1887–1962)

Perhaps the most popular portrayer of explosive and highly agitated Italian types, he amused the English speaking world but not Italians. Alberni was actually a native of Spain who turned to comedy after a performance in *Hamlet* produced laughter from the audience. He came to the United States in 1914 and after more than a decade on the Broadway stage made his film debut in *Santa Fe Trail* (1930).

As an excitable Latin he appeared in scores of films. **Films include:** *One Night of Love* (1934), *Love Me Forever* (1935), *A Bell for Adano* (1945), *Captain Carey, U.S.A.* (1950).

EDDIE ALBERT (1908–   )

An enormously talented performer who is equally at home in dramatic or musical settings, he is credited with being the inventor of the toy bird that drinks water in perpetual motion and an aerial torpedo that was widely used in World War II.

While Albert never became a top ranked star, his performances were almost always flawless. Typical was his recent portrayal of the wealthy non-permissive father in *The Heartbreak Kid* (1972) which brought him an Academy Award nomination. He was also the star of the *Green Acres* television series. **Films include:** *Brother Rat* (1938), *Bombardier* (1943), *The Teahouse of the August Moon* (1956), *The Sun Also Rises* (1957), *The Longest Day* (1962).

Anouk Aimée in Justine, *made nearly two decades after she began giving talented performances in both English and French language films.*

Eddie Albert, in his leading-man days, with Loretta Young in Perfect Marriage *(1947).*

FRANK ALBERTSON (1909–1964)

Albertson began his film career as a prop boy in 1922. Through the years he has played everything from leading roles to comedy and character parts, mostly as a juvenile.

His last role was as the mayor in *Bye Bye Birdie* (1963) and he may also be remembered as the boorish brother in *Alice Adams* (1935). **Highlights:** *A Connecticut Yankee* (1931), *Room Service* (1938), *The Hucksters* (1947).

JACK ALBERTSON (c.1910–   )

From a young age in his native Lynn, Massachusetts, he loved the theatre and often appeared with his sister in local amateur theatricals. It was much later, however, that "he got in show business for good." In the interim he worked in an industrial plant, a shoe factory, and on a freighter. Coming to New York during the Depression, he slept in subways on winter nights and on park benches in summer months. He worked in vaudeville initially and later in burlesque with Phil Silvers. "At first I was scared to death," he said, "I had all the charm of a stopped-up sink; it took me years to feel relaxed on stage." His first legitimate role was in *Waiting for Godot* (1957). Afterwards, playwright Frank Gilroy asked him to do *The Subject Was Roses* on Broadway. "I wasn't sure I had the capacity to do it," said Albertson, who still was anything but sure of himself. However, Albertson won a Tony for his performance on stage and an Oscar for the screen version (1968). **Other films:** *Man of a Thousand Faces* (1957), *Period of Adjustment* (1962), *A Tiger Walks* (1964), *How to Murder Your Wife* (1965), *Justine* (1969), *Rabbit, Run* (1970).

HARDIE ALBRIGHT (1903–   )

The son of Scottish vaudevillians, Albright came to the United States at the age of ten. While in college, he was discovered by actress Eva LeGallienne and by the 30's he was playing leading film roles.

Albright was the long-suffering Reverend Dimmesdale in the sound version of *The Scarlet Letter* (1934) and also appeared in *The Pride of the Yankees* (1942), with Gary Cooper as Lou Gehrig. **Highlights:** *So Big* (1932), *Cabin in the Sky* (1932), *Three Cor-

nered Moon* (1933), *Angel on My Shoulder* (1946), *Ski Patrol* (1951), *Mom and Dad* (1957).

LOLA ALBRIGHT (1925–   )

Although she appeared in a dozen or more films she has made vastly more television appearances, notably as the female pal of Craig Stevens in the adventure of private-eye Peter Gunn. An accomplished actress, she has played supporting roles in films and has often been compared to Barbara Stanwyck. **Credits include:** *Champion* (1949), *The Tender Trap* (1955), *Kid Galahad* (1963), *Where Were You When the Lights Went Out?* (1968), *The Impossible Years* (1968).

ALAN ALDA (1936–   )

His first on-stage appearance was in the arms of his acting father, Robert Alda, during rehearsals. His earliest success came 20 years after the diaper period, doing imitations of John F. Kennedy. Alda won a starring role in *Paper Lion* (1968) playing George Plimpton. It was a part which tested not only his acting ability, but also his athletic prowess. The up-and-coming actor has a successful television career, notably in *M*A*S*H*.

Of his life and career in Hollywood, he quotes Gertrude Stein: "There's no there there." **Films include:** *Gone Are the Days* (1963), *The Moonshine War* (1970).

ROBERT ALDA (1914–   )

Born Alphonso Giovanni Giuseppe Roberto d'Abeuzzo Alda, he had planned to be an architect. While studying at New York University he occasionally worked for amateur theatrical productions, sometimes he got small parts through agents at a fee of $1.50 a show. These were the 30's and show business seemed more promising than his original chosen career. He worked in nightclubs, resort hotels, stock companies and appeared in some films. After spending 19 years in show business including six in burlesque, he got his first chance on Broadway and became known to the public when he created the role of a gambler in the original production of *Guys and Dolls* for which he won a Tony Award. **Some of his films are:** *Rhapsody In

Robert Alda clutches Andrea King while Peter Lorre appears unflustered by The Beast With Five Fingers *(1946). For Alda, it was a far cry from singing "Luck Be a Lady . . ." in* Guys and Dolls *on Broadway some years later.*

Blue (1945), *Cloak and Dagger* (1946), *Beast With Five Fingers* (1946), *Tarzan and the Slave Girl* (1950), *Mr. Universe* (1951), *Beautiful but Dangerous* (1958), *Imitation of Life* (1959), *Cleopatra's Daughter* (1960).

BEN ALEXANDER (1911–1969)

He started his film career at the age of three in DeMille's *Each Pearl a Tear,* and by the age of seven, appearing in D.W. Griffith's *Hearts of the World,* the child actor received critical praise. One reviewer called him "the precocious child who arouses laughter, tears, and applause," and Griffith himself said he was "the most wonderful child actor the screen has ever known."

In the 30's he was a radio announcer on such shows as *Queen for a Day, Father Knows Best,* and *The Charlie McCarthy Show.*

By the time he appeared in the *Dragnet* series on television as Jack Webb's partner, he was wealthy from his investments and competent as ever. **His movies include:** *Penrod and Sam* (1923), *All Quiet on the Western Front* (1930), *Stage Mother* (1933), *Man With a Shadow* (1958).

KATHERINE ALEXANDER (1901–   )

Though she couldn't even find the stage door for her first theatrical job, Katherine Alexander became an accomplished actress. During the 30's she specialized in sisterly roles, to Melvyn Douglas in *She Married Her Boss* (1935), to Norma Shearer in *The Barretts of Wimpole Street* (1934), and to Joel McCrea in *Splendor* (1935). She portrayed generally sympathetic figures throughout her career. **Highlights:** *The Painted Veil* (1934), *That Certain Woman* (1937), *The Hunchback of Notre Dame* (1939), *The Vanishing Virginian* (1942), *John Loves Mary* (1949).

ELIZABETH ALLEN (1916–   )

The English leading lady brought her Shakespearean training to the Hollywood screen and was seen most often as a sensitive, well-born heroine. Her bearing was so elegant that producers felt the 5' 6" actress gave the impression of being too tall.

After her debut in 1931, Miss Allen ap-peared in British and American productions for the next 25 years, including such classics as *David Copperfield* (1934) and *Camille* (1936). **Highlights:** *Alibi* (1931), *A Tale of Two Cities* (1936), *Went the Day Well* (1942), *48 Hours* (1944), *The Heart of the Matter* (1954).

GRACIE ALLEN (1902–1964)
See **Burns and Allen**

WOODY ALLEN (1935–   )

Great comedians almost always portray little men attempting to cope with the trappings of a civilization that is a bit too much for them, and Woody Allen is no exception. His insecurities—physical, sexual and emotional—are truly of monumental proportions. One has only to watch the opening scene of *Play It Again, Sam* (1972)—in which a balding, wizened, misty-eyed Woody gazes enraptured at the on-screen Bogart-Bergman love scene—to understand why this former gag writer has become the funniest performer of the 70's.

Like Chaplin, Allen writes, directs and acts in his own films. His versatility is prodigious, his humor wildly imaginative and completely unpredictable. Even the blackest sequence —as when TV announcer Howard Cosell, acting his usual unflappable and pompous self, interviews a Central American dictator who has just been gunned down on the steps of his capitol—is capable of reducing an audience to helpless laughter. **Films include:**

The brilliant and innovative Woody Allen encountered police interference in Take the Money and Run.

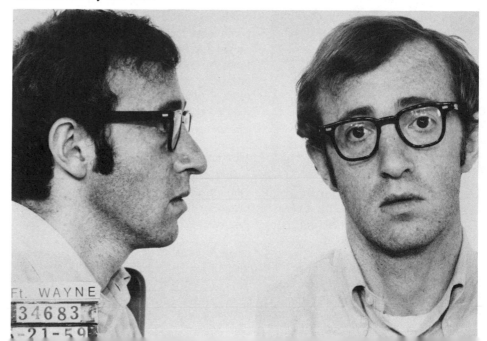

In mid-career, June Allyson starred with James Stewart in The Stratton Story.

In Hangover Square *Sara Allgood attempted to charm Laird Cregar and was murdered for her efforts.*

What's New, Pussycat? (debut, 1965), *Casino Royale* (1967), *Take the Money and Run* (1969), *Bananas* (1971), *Everything You Always Wanted to Know About Sex* (1972), *Sleeper* (1973).

SARA ALLGOOD (1893–1950)

Ireland's esteemed Miss Allgood was one of her country's foremost actresses long before her first silent film appearance in 1918. Her career progressed from leading, often tragic roles to sweet and lighthearted comedy roles at the end of her life. Nominated for an Academy Award for Best Supporting Actress for her performance in *How Green Was My Valley* (1942), many of her admirers were disappointed that so uncompromising an artist was not given proper recognition. During her last years, there were additional disappointments including long periods without movie or stage work. Most of her roles were those of the stern, loving but yet uncompromising mother. **Highlights:** *Blackmail* (1930), *Juno and the Paycock* (1930), *Jane Eyre* (1943), *Mother Wore Tights* (1948), *Cheaper by the Dozen* (1950).

CLAUDE ALLISTER (1891–1970)

A worried expression, a general air of uncertainty and fluttery fingers were trademarks Claude Allister used to personify the "silly Englishman" on stage and screen.

Born in London, he made his American debut on Broadway in Molnar's *The Play's the Thing* (1926), after appearing on the London stage and touring extensively with his own company. After his movie debut in England in *Bulldog Drummond* (1929), he continued to alternate between films and stage in both countries. **More than 60 films include:** *Reaching for the Moon* (1930), *Dracula's Daughter* (1936), *Captain Fury* (1939), *Charley's Aunt* (1941), *Kiss Me Kate* (1953).

JUNE ALLYSON (1917–   )

Bronx-born Ella Geisman pretended she was two years older and at the age of 15 landed her first job in a Broadway chorus line. Nearly ten years later, as Betty Hutton's understudy, she was given a chance to play the star role in *Best Foot Forward* (1941). A successful career was assured after she repeated her performance in the film version (1943).

Allyson's husky voice combined with her fresh and uncomplicated personality to endear her to audiences and until the late 50's she starred in two or three pictures a year, generally as a true-blue girlfriend or dedicated wife. As film scripts became more sophisticated, however, her all-American-girl style went out of fashion. She retired from films in 1960 but more recently reappeared on stage in *Forty Carats* (1970).**Films include:** *Two Girls and a Sailor* (1944), *Little Women* (1949), *Executive Suite* (1954), *The Glenn Miller Story* (1954), *The Shrike* (1955), *My Man Godfrey* (1957), *Stranger in My Arms* (1959).

DON ALVARDO (1900–   )

The Latin leading man of the 20's appeared in many films with foreign settings, including a silent version of *Carmen* (1926). Peru was the scene of *The Bridge of San Luis Rey* (1929) and it was Spain for *The Devil Is a Woman* (1935). Later he played character roles. **Highlights:** *Drums of Love* (1927), *The Battle of the Sexes* (1928), *Rio Rita* (1929), *Morning Glory* (1933), *The Big Steal* (1950).

With his fork poised in mid-air, Leon Ames joins Rosemary DeCamp and Van Johnson in peering at a very beautiful Elizabeth Taylor. From The Big Hangover *(1950)*.

DON AMECHE (1908–   )

Once dropped by Texas Guinan from her vaudeville act because he was "too stiff," his voice made him a national favorite in many popular radio shows of the 1930's. It was this voice, once described by a critic as a "butterscotch baritone," that led to a contract with 20th Century–Fox. Making his debut in *Sins of Man* (1936), he became a star in *Ramona* (1936). Thereafter, he appeared in film biographies, light comedy and in musicals, and was for a number of years one of the 25 top box-office attractions.

In the 50's, with the decline of his film career, he returned to the stage to appear in such musicals as Cole Porter's *Silk Stockings* and on television. **More than 40 films include:** *Alexander's Ragtime Band* (1938), *The Story of Alexander Graham Bell* (1934), *That Night in Rio* (1941), *Heaven Can Wait* (1943), *Wing and a Prayer* (1944), *Sleep, My Love* (1948).

LEON AMES (1903–   )

The movie father of such luminaries as Judy Garland, Elizabeth Taylor, Doris Day, Lana Turner and Margaret O'Brien he once said "all as sweet as sugar until the director says, 'Action!' And then they'll cut your throat with a dull saw . . . the actress at work is a killer shark."

Before turning to the stage he was a sailor, lumberjack, shoe salesman, detective, personnel manager, and a barn storming flier. At 23 he got his first part in stock, making his Broadway debut 11 years later.

He made his screen debut in *The Murders in the Rue Morgue* (1932) but it wasn't until *Meet Me in St. Louis* (1944) that his career as a screen father began in earnest. In the 50's and 60's he branched out into television playing in *Life With Father* (1954) and *Father of the Bride* (1962) series. **More than 50 films include:** *The Lady in the Lake* (1946), *Little Women* (1949), *Peyton Place* (1957), *From the Terrace* (1960), *On a Clear Day You Can See Forever* (1970).

EDDIE ANDERSON (1905–   )

Although he is best remembered as the throatily funny Rochester on the Jack Benny Radio Show, he was also a film actor of some

stature. In 1936 he won national attention as Noah in *Green Pastures*, and then he went on to make *You Can't Take It With You* (1938). Before his role as Benny's faithful valet-chauffeur-cook, he was a song-and-dance man in an all-black revue. **Films include:** *Gone With the Wind* (1939), *Tales of Manhattan* (1942), *The Meanest Man in the World* (1943), *Cabin in the Sky* (1943), *It's a Mad, Mad, Mad, Mad World* (1963).

Don Ameche (left) has a tug-of-war with Tyrone Power in Love Is News *(1937)*, while George Sanders looks on paternally.

16

Judith Anderson, as the sinister housekeeper of Manderley, menaces Joan Fontaine in the prize-winning thriller, Rebecca.

The beautiful Bibi Andersson, one of the stars of Ingmar Bergman's The Seventh Seal.

DAME JUDITH ANDERSON (1898–   )

When she was a little girl she saw Nellie Melba in her native Australia, and decided to become a great stage actress. She achieved her goal and was, after Melba, the second Australian actress to receive the Most Excellent Order of the British Empire in 1960.

Anderson was a successful stage actress when she came to the United States to appear on Broadway and she remained so, starring in many stage classics—*Strange Interlude, Mourning Becomes Electra, Three Sisters, Medea, Macbeth.* Although she made her movie debut in *Blood Money* (1933), it was her role as Mrs. Danvers in *Rebecca* (1940) that made her world famous in films as the personification of evil. She has since appeared in many sinister film rôles, but the stage has remained her main career. At the age of 71 she played *Hamlet* in a cross-country tour. **Films include:** *King's Row* (1942), *Laura* (1944), *Specter of the Rose* (1946), *The Ten Commandments* (1956), *Cat on a Hot Tin Roof* (1958), *A Man Called Horse* (1969).

RICHARD ANDERSON (1926–   )

For nearly 25 years he's played roles ranging from light-headed and -hearted romantics to doomed air pilots, in pictures as different as *The Student Prince* (1954) and *Compulsion* (1959). Along with 30 or more films, his activities have extended to television and the Broadway stage, where he made his debut in *The Highest Tree* in the late 40's. **Some of his films are:** *Twelve O'Clock High* (1950), *Across the Wide Missouri* (1951), *Escape from Fort Bravo* (1954), *Paths of Glory* (1957), *The Long, Hot Summer* (1958), *Seven Days in May* (1964), *Seconds* (1966).

WARNER ANDERSON (1911–   )

Recognized as a solid supporting actor, Warner Anderson was a child actor in silent motion pictures. His stage debut was as the grandson in the Broadway production of *Maytime* (1917) and soon after that he toured the country with Laurette Taylor in *Happiness*. His first movie, starring Charles Ray and Mabel Taliaferro, was made in 1915 when Anderson was four years old. As an adult he worked in burlesque, vaudeville, movies, plays, radio and television. **Films include:** *Destination Tokyo* (1944), *Command Decision* (1948), *Destination Moon* (1950), *The Caine Mutiny* (1954), *The Blackboard Jungle* (1955), *Rio Conchos* (1964).

BIBI ANDERSSON (1936–   )

One of the many fine Swedish actresses whose gemlike beauty and acting talents flowered most fully in Ingmar Bergman's early films, she was at the top of her form in the mystical (and magnificent) *Wild Strawberries* (1959). A year before that she had been equally impressive in *The Seventh Seal*, another of Bergman's enigmatic triumphs.

Andersson, alas, has been less fortunate in her English language films. Her debut was in *Duel at Diablo* (1966), a Western with racial overtones which did poorly with both critics and the box office. *Persona* came in 1967, and Andersson-addicts keep hoping that another Bergman will come along soon.

URSULA ANDRESS (1936–   )

The Swiss-born beauty's film assets were first noticed, and undoubtedly whistled at, while she was vacationing in Rome. Thereafter she appeared in Italian films before making her initial English language film success as one of James Bond's exquisitely ungowned female friends.

To an interviewer who commented that her screen image was "unabashedly nude" she replied sharply: "When I pose in the nude it's strictly art." And who's to say her nay? **Films include:** *The Loves of Casanova* (1954), *What's New, Pussycat?* (1965), *The Blue Max* (1966), *Casino Royale* (1967), *Southern Star* (1969).

DANA ANDREWS (1909–   )

Lantern-jawed and exuding an air of unrelenting honesty, he was a popular leading man and then supporting actor in action films made over a span of 30 years. Andrews was born in a small town in Mississippi, the son of a Protestant minister, and began his career with a 12-word part in *The Westerner* (1938). Thereafter, as a star, he usually fought against long odds—as the innocent victim of a lynch mob in *The Ox-Bow Incident* (1943) or the embattled sergeant in *A Walk in the Sun* (1945). Perhaps his best performance was that of the restless veteran in *The Best Years of Our Lives* (1946).

He also appeared on Broadway in *Two for the Seesaw* in 1959 and several years later in *The Captains and the Kings*. In the mid-60's he was president of the Screen Actors Guild. **Highlights:** *Kit Carson* (1940), *Tobacco Road* (1941), *Berlin Correspondent* (1942), *Wing and a Prayer* (1944), *Laura* (1944), *State Fair* (1945), *Edge of Doom* (1950), *The Loved One* (1965), *Ten Million Dollar Grab* (1968).

HARRY ANDREWS (1911–   )

English-born Harry Andrews already had made his way in the theatre before he started working in films. His first stage appearance was as a young boy in *Rip Van Winkle* and later on he began being largely identified with Shakespearean roles at Stratford and the Old Vic. As a screen actor, tough-looking Andrews has appeared in a great number of films, usually in hardboiled roles. **Credits include:** *Moby Dick* (1956), *The Devil's Disciple* (1959), *Sands of the Kalahari*

Dana Andrews and Gene Tierney in one of the best suspense films of the 40's, Laura.

(1965), *The Charge of the Light Brigade* (1968), *The Night They Raided Minsky's* (1968), *The Mackintosh Man* (1973).

JULIE ANDREWS (1935–   )

The charmer, thought of by millions of children in the 60's as Mary Poppins, was born in Walton-on-Thames and began her career in British music halls. She first became known to Broadway in *The Boy Friend* (1954) and soared to stardom two years later as the original and irresistible Eliza in *My Fair Lady*. For reasons which will probably forever lie buried in the arcane archives of Hollywood, Julie Andrews was passed up in favor of Audrey Hepburn when *Lady* went into film production.

Walt Disney shrewdly cast her as the magical nanny in *Mary Poppins*—a role which brought her the Academy Award as Best Actress of 1964 and turned the movie into one of the top box office favorites of all time. Less than a year later Andrews starred in *The Sound of Music*, a musical which in less than seven years grossed $75,000,000 and was fighting *Gone With the Wind* for the position of biggest moneymaker of all time. **Films include:** *The Americanization of Emily*

Four years after Mary Poppins, *Julie Andrews came down to earth in* Star!

An eyeball to eyeball confrontation between Evelyn Ankers and Basil Rathbone in Sherlock Holmes and the Voice of Terror.

Annabella and Tyrone Power guard his pipe whilst staring soulfully in Suez.

(1940), *The Saxon Charm* (1948), *The Premature Burial* (1962).

PIER ANGELI (1932–1971)

Born in Sardinia, twin sister of Marisa Pavan, she later moved with her family to Rome and studied art. Introduced to director Leonide Moguy at the home of a friend, she appeared in two of his films made in Italy in 1949 and 1951. MGM signed her for the starring role in *Teresa* (1951) after one of the co-authors discovered her in Rome where he had been searching for an actress to play the title role. The reviews were ecstatic; she was compared to Garbo. Co-starring with leading actors, she made films in the U.S. and in Europe, but her career was uneven and had many gaps. In 1971 she died, an apparent suicide. **Some of her films:** *The Devil Makes Three* (1952), *The Silver Chalice* (1954), *Somebody Up There Likes Me* (1956), *The Battle of the Bulge* (1965).

EVELYN ANKERS (1918–   )

''Her screams still ring in my ears,'' one reviewer said of the most persecuted heroine in films who somehow always managed to look cool and unruffled. Known to moviegoers as the ''Queen of Horrors,'' Evelyn Ankers was born in Chile of British parents, and lived all over South America. After she went to England, she entered and won five separate beauty contests. Progressing from small parts in a few British films, she came to Hollywood and, beginning with *Hold That Ghost* (1941), she made almost 30 features in four years. After her marriage to Richard Denning, she retired in the late 40's and has made infrequent appearances since. **Films include:** *The Wolf Man* (1941), *The Ghost of Frankenstein* (1942), *The Mad Ghoul* (1943), *Son of Dracula* (1943), *The Frozen Ghost* (1945).

MORRIS ANKRUM (1896–1964)

Seen in many films for 25 years as a lawyer, judge or Western villain, Ankrum, a former associate professor of economics, never lost his interest in the legitimate stage. He directed Blanche Yurka in *Electra*, founded repertory companies in Washington and Stanford, and became a director during

(1964), *Thoroughly Modern Millie* (1967), *Star!* (1968), *Darling Lili* (1969).

ANDREWS SISTERS

For the historic record, there were three of them: Laverne (1915–1967); Maxene (1918–   ) and Patricia (1920–   ). They were an enormously popular singing trio long before The Supremes were out of diapers and their hit records induced Hollywood to cast them in 17 non-classic films between 1940 and 1948. **Films include:** *Argentine Nights* (1940), *Follow the Boys* (1944), *Road to Rio* (1947), *Melody Time* (1948).

HEATHER ANGEL (1909–   )

Her sweetness and fragile loveliness caused her to be plagued throughout her career with saccharine, simpering roles she never quite escaped. Born in England, the daughter of an Oxford don, she was trained at the Old Vic, danced, sang, trouped the Orient, and had a brief film career before coming to the United States to appear opposite Leslie Howard in *Berkeley Square* (1933). She eventually drifted into character parts, occasionally returning to the stage. **Films include:** *Orient Express* (1934), *The Informer* (1935), *Pride and Prejudice*

many of his Hollywood years at the Pasadena Playhouse. **Films include:** *Tales of Manhattan* (1942), *The Harvey Girls* (1945), *Good News* (1947), *The Damned Don't Cry* (1950), *Vera Cruz* (1954), *The Most Dangerous Man Alive* (1961).

ANNABELLA (1909–   )

Named Suzanne Charpentier, she took her professional name from Edgar Allan Poe's "Annabel Lee" and with *Le Million* (1931), directed by René Clair, she became the toast of Europe. Coming to the attention of Hollywood, she made her U.S. debut in *Caravan* (1934) with Charles Boyer but it was inauspicious and she returned to Europe.

She appeared in *Wings of the Morning* (1937) in England and again was re-imported. This time her career improved. While making *Suez* (1938) she met and married her co-star, Tyrone Power. Until her retirement in the late 40's, she continued to make infrequent films and appeared on the New York stage, most effectively in *No Exit* (1946). **Films include:** *Le Quatorze Juillet* (1933), *Hotel Du Nord* (1938), *Bomber's Moon* (1943), *13 Rue Madeleine* (1946).

ANN-MARGRET (1941–   )

Swedish-born sex symbol Ann-Margret started in show business in Las Vegas singing with a band. She was spotted by George Burns who used her in his act and she later appeared on television with Jack Benny. The role of Bette Davis' daughter in *A Pocketful of Miracles* (1961) followed, along with singing parts in some screen musicals. In 1964 the Theatre Owners of America voted her "Star of the Year" and she was 8th-ranked at the box office.

Huge publicity campaigns did not always succeed in bringing her critical acclaim, but her recent appearance in *Carnal Knowledge* (1972) was well-received. **Other films are:** *State Fair* (1962), *Bye, Bye, Birdie* (1963), *Viva Las Vegas* (1964), *Once a Thief* (1965), *Stagecoach* (1966).

SUSAN ANSPACH (1944–   )

An expert linguist with a college degree in philosophy and credentials attesting that she was a Campus Queen at the age of 17, Anspach seems destined for even more glittering laurels in the years to come.

She came to motion pictures from the world of television where she performed in such non-classics as *The Nurses*, *The Defenders* and *The Patty Duke Show*. Her first film appearance, a brilliant performance in *Five Easy Pieces* (1970), represented a jump forward of several light years. Then, co-starring with George Segal as the distaff side of *Blume in Love* (1973) she not only created a memorable screen characterization but indicated that, as a completely liberated woman of the 70's with a lingering attachment for what used to be referred to as "old-fashioned romance," even better things are to come.

ROSCOE "FATTY" ARBUCKLE (1887–1933)

The 250-pound comedian was the unlikely and tragic victim of Hollywood's first scandal. It happened in 1921 when he was at the height of his career: a bit-player named Virginia Rappe died following a party at a San Francisco hotel which Arbuckle had attended. Although he was cleared of all manslaughter charges in three separate trials, the third of which harshly criticized the State for bringing him to trial in the first place, a venomous press and an irate public combined to ring down the curtain on his career.

Born in Kansas, Arbuckle had been in show business (mostly vaudeville) from boyhood on and appeared as early as 1907 in one- and two-reelers. In 1913 Mack Sennett paid him $3 a day to be the *fat* Keystone cop in *In the Clutches of the Gang* and after that he went on to become part of a company which included Ford Sterling and, later, Charlie Chaplin. With Mabel Normand he made a series of historic comedies, e. g., *Mabel and Fatty's Wash Day*.

In 1917 Joseph Schenck set him up in his own company where he went on to write, direct, produce and act in comedies like *His Wedding Night* (1918). Two years later Famous Players-Lasky gave him the same freedom, plus $7,000 a week, to do the same job for them. Then tragedy struck. When death came, he was still trying to make a comeback.

Ann-Margret, one of Sweden's gifts to the film world.

Fatty Arbuckle (right) and fellow Keystone Cops in one of their early efforts, In the Clutches of the Gang.

*Alan Arkin, who can handle any sort of role, here orders his son Luis (Ruben Figueroa) to get into a skiff and start rowing. The movie—*Popi.

Today, Arbuckle comedies seem archaic and unfunny, but back in the naive days when a fat man dressed in a girl's dress wowed audiences, the public loved them. **Highlights:** *Moonshine* (1918), *The Life of the Party* (1920).

EVE ARDEN (1912–   )

She took her last name from a cold cream jar and through the 40's and early 50's she saved many a movie with her biting sarcasm and caustic wit.

Cast invariably as a brassy dame with a heart of gold, the best friend of the heroine, she grew up in California and made several film appearances as Eunice Quedens before going to New York and appearing in musicals and the Ziegfeld Follies. Returning to Hollywood as Eve Arden, she appeared in *Stage Door* (1937) and *Ziegfeld Girl* (1941) and became firmly established, appearing in more than 70 films. Since 1952 she has appeared in television series, notably as the very popular *Our Miss Brooks*. **Some of her films:** *Mildred Pierce* (1945), *The Voice of the Turtle* (1947), *One Touch of Venus* (1948), *Anatomy of a Murder* (1959), *Sergeant Deadhead* (1965).

ALAN ARKIN (1934–   )

Apart from being a wonderful actor, he is a folk singer, composer, expert photographer and director. Arkin made his New York stage debut with the Second City troupe from Chicago and went on to win a Tony Award for his role in *Enter Laughing*, where he met his actress-author wife, Barbara Dana.

His film debut was in the uproarious *The Russians Are Coming, the Russians Are Coming* (1966) and he won Academy Award nominations both for this and for his performance as Singer, the deaf-mute in *The Heart Is a Lonely Hunter* (1968).

Arkin presently alternates screen appearances with directorial jobs for stage and screen productions. **His films include:** *Wait Until Dark* (1967), *Popi* (1969), *Catch-22* (1970), *Last of the Red Hot Lovers* (1972), *Freebie and the Bean* (1974).

RICHARD ARLEN (1899–   )

Arlen arrived in Hollywood in 1920 and worked as an apprentice technician and later as an extra. He got his big break in 1927 when director William Wellman cast him in the silent film, *Wings*, with Clara Bow and Charles (Buddy) Rogers. It was the first film to get the Academy's Best Picture Award.

Under contract with Paramount for 25 years, he appeared as a leading man to such popular players as Bebe Daniels, Louise Brooks and Mary Brian. Successfully progressing from silents to talkies, he became particularly noted for his virile portrayals of "outdoor" men. **His many films include:** *Feel My Pulse* (1928), *The Virginian* (1929), *Three-Cornered Moon* (1933), *Power Dive* (1941), *Law of the Lawless* (1964) *Fort Utah* (1967).

ARLETTY (1898–   )

A celebrated actress of the French stage and screen, her haunting and mocking performance in *Les Enfants du Paradis* (1944) made her internationally known. Born in France, she was a short-hand typist, artists' model and singer before making her stage debut in operettas. She was alternating between stage and screen when she achieved her first major film success in *Hotel du Nord* (1938). Adept at portraying world-weary, sophisticated women, she had a tremendous personal success as Blanche du Bois in the French stage version of *A Streetcar Named Desire*. **Highlights:** *La Guerre des Valses*

Bette Davis guards pearls and gloves as George Arliss clenches a fist in The Man Who Played God.

(1933), *Le Jour Se Leve* (1939), *L'Amour Madame* (1952), *Huis Clos* (1954), *La Gamberge* (1962).

GEORGE ARLISS (1868–1946)

Called "Mr. Arliss" by everyone on the set including the director, he was always engaged to bring tone, dignity, and aristocratic hauteur to the films in which he appeared. Known for his gallery of historical roles, he won an Academy Award for Best Actor in *Disraeli* (1929), probably his most famous role.

Arliss was born in England and appeared in amateur theatricals before becoming a distinguished actor on the London stage. He toured the United States with Mrs. Patrick Campbell for a "limited" stay and remained for 20 years, playing Voltaire, Richelieu, Wellington, Hamilton and, of course, Disraeli on both stage and screen. Of his acting technique he once said, "You must feel power from within . . . The eye is the most important powerful medium of expression that an actor has." **Distinguished films:** *The Green Goddess* (1923), *Alexander Hamilton* (1931), *The Man Who Played God* (1932), *House of Rothschild* (1934), *Cardinal Richelieu* (1935), *Dr. Syn* (1937).

PEDRO ARMENDARIZ (1912–1963)

Born in Churubusco, Mexico, his father was a Mexican, his mother an American. He was already a star in Mexico when he began making movies in the U.S. and Europe. He won international recognition for his starring role in Steinbeck's *The Pearl* (1948) and in 1952 he achieved his greatest fame for his role in *Border River* for which he won Mexico's equivalent of an Academy Award. Often called "the Cosmopolitan Actor," Pedro Armendariz lived in a dozen capitals, and was easily identifiable by his massive physique and expansive personality. He committed suicide after learning that he had cancer and only one more year to live. **Films include:** *Isle of Passion* (1941), *Maria Candelaria* (1943), *The Fugitive* (1947), *Maclovia* (1948), *Fort Apache* (1948), *Three Godfathers* (1949), *Tulsa* (1949), *We Were Strangers* (1949), *The Torch* (1950), *El Bruto* (1952), *Lucretia Borgia* (1953), *The*

Sombreroed Pedro Armendariz makes friends with Gilbert Roland in The Torch *(1950).*

Conqueror (1956), *Manuela* (1957), *From Russia With Love* (1964).

HENRY ARMETTA (1888–1945)

Born in Palermo, Sicily, Armetta stowed away on a ship bound for Boston at age 14. Police took him into custody but an Italian barber befriended him and taught him his trade. His natural talent for comedy soon brought him to the stage and in 1929 he came to Hollywood. He appeared in more than 200 films and his portrayals of the excitable, gesticulating Italians were familiar to movie fans everywhere. In 1935, out of 9,000 Hollywood players he ranked 4th in the number of hours before the camera. Audiences easily recognized him but few knew his name. **Films include:** *Strangers May Kiss* (1931), *The Unholy Garden* (1931), *The Man Who Reclaimed His Head* (1934), *The Big Store* (1940), *A Bell for Adano* (1945).

LOUIS ARMSTRONG (1900–1971)

The beloved "Satchmo," one of the greatest of all jazz musicians, was born on the Fourth of July at the turn of the century in

Satchmo always played what his fans wanted—his trumpet and himself.

Robert Armstrong, flanked by Joan Blondell and Glenda Farrell, shoots from the hip in The Kansas City Princess *(1934).*

Sig Arno being quietly throttled while Rosalind Russell looks on approvingly.

New Orleans, at that time a center of racism devoted to the concept of white supremacy. Reared in the ghetto, he was in a reformatory by the age of 12—and it was there that he learned to play the trumpet, an instrument that helped him to become an internationally honored and respected citizen of the world.

Satchmo's first major appearance on stage was in *Hot Chocolates*, a 1929 revue in which he introduced Fats Waller's ''Ain't Misbehavin','' a jazz classic that has lived through the years. Thereafter he made thousands of appearances on stage, in nightclubs and hotels, on radio and television but, lamentably, very few movies.

As his fame grew, his appearances in cities around the world came to resemble triumphal processions. When he died uncounted millions, from New Orleans to Novasibersk, mourned the passing of a black man who had become an international symbol of grace and goodwill among all men. **Highlights:** *Pennies From Heaven* (1936), *Every Day's a Holiday* (1937), *Dr. Rhythm* (1938), *Cabin in the Sky* (1943), *The Glenn Miller Story* (1954), *The Five Pennies* (1959), *High Society* (1956).

ROBERT ARMSTRONG (1896–1973)

Best known for his role in *King Kong* (1933), his interest in show business started in college when he wrote sketches for a school theatrical. Later he worked in vaudeville and silent movies and a bit on Broadway. He starred in more than a hundred adventure movies—action-packed gangster films, Westerns, and war movies. He retired at age 72. **Films include:** *The Main Event* (1927), *The Most Dangerous Game* (1932), *Son of Kong* (1934), *G-Men* (1935), *Blood on the Sun* (1945), *Sea of Grass* (1947), *The Paleface* (1948), *Mighty Joe Young* (1949), *Las Vegas Shakedown* (1955).

JAMES ARNESS (1923–)

Starting in advertising, this remarkably tall actor (6'6") got his first movie job as one of Loretta Young's brothers in *The Farmer's Daughter* (1947). In 1951 he played a role in *The Thing*. Parts were hard to find because leading actors didn't want a taller supporting actor in the picture. He is best remembered as Marshal Dillon, the role he created for the long running TV series *Gunsmoke*. He is the brother of another well-known television actor, Peter Graves. **Other films:** *Battleground* (1949), *Them* (1954), *The Sea Chase* (1955).

SIG ARNO (1895–)

Although he wanted to be a dramatic actor, Arno became one of Germany's top comedians in the 1920's. With the rise of Hitler, he left, wandered around Europe, and came to the United States in 1939, unable to speak one word of English.

Feeling that, with a language barrier, movies would be easier to tackle than plays, he went to Hollywood where he was cast almost always as a comic waiter or butler. In the 1950's he returned to the stage and appeared most notably with Helen Hayes in *Time Remembered*, as a waiter again. In recent years he has returned to acting in Germany. **Some of his films include:** *Pandora's Box* (1928), *The Great Dictator* (1940), *Up in Arms* (1944), *A Song to Remember* (1945), *The Toast of New Orleans* (1950).

EDWARD ARNOLD (1890–1956)

A polished and persuasive actor, he was a popular man and star in supporting roles for more than 20 years. Portly and highly professional, he played heroes and villains with equal grace—press lords and financiers, crooked politicians and ambassadorial types, wealthy fathers and hard-bitten executives.

His childhood was miserable. Orphaned, he was a newsboy on New York's lower East Side before taking a job in a meat market. He was picked up as a truant, forced to undergo some schooling, and began his theatrical career by appearing in some 40 two-reelers in the days of silents. Turning to the stage, a major role in *Whistlin' in the Dark* led to a contract with Universal Studios in 1932. **Films include:** *Rasputin and the Empress* (1932), *Crime and Punishment* (1935), *The Toast of New York* (1937), *You Can't Take It With You* (1938), *Mr. Smith Goes to Washington* (1939), *Dear Ruth* (1947), *Command Decision* (1948), *Living It Up* (1954), *The Ambassador's Daughter* (1956).

George Raft grabs Edward Arnold who grabs Claire Dodd in a tense moment from Dashiell Hammett's The Glass Key *(1935).*

CHARLES ARNT (1908–)

A master at playing snoops or suspicious characters, he seems to have been born old. Coming from the New York stage, he always played character roles older than himself, helped no doubt by the fact that he was an expert at make-up. **Some of his many films include:** *Ladies Should Listen* (1934), *Blossoms in the Dust* (1941), *Miss Susie Slagle's* (1946), *Wabash Avenue* (1950), *Sweet Bird of Youth* (1962).

GEORGE K. ARTHUR (1900–)

Born in Scotland, he was a successful theatrical performer in Europe when Charles Chaplin advised him to go to California and try the movies. The suggestion was a good one, and for upwards of ten years he played supporting roles (generally as a comedian) in a score or more pictures. **Credits include:** *Salvation Hunters* (1925), *Irene* (1926), *The Last of Mrs. Cheyney* (1929), *Oliver Twist* (1933), *Rip Tide* (1934).

JEAN ARTHUR (1908–)

When she emerged as a top-ranking star in the early days of talkies, Jean Arthur played feminist roles decades before Women's Lib entered the vocabulary. The cracked- and

A cuddly, pajama-clad Jean Arthur won an Oscar nomination for her role in The More the Merrier.

In Mr. Smith Goes to Washington, *Jean Arthur had a hard time convincing a naive but idealistic James Stewart of the pitfalls existing in the nation's capital, even in pre-Watergate times.*

After Ginger Rogers, Fred Astaire danced with Rita Hayworth in several films. Here they are in You'll Never Get Rich *(1941).*

throaty-voiced young lady was a new and captivating type of film heroine—an honest, no-nonsense girl, civilized but unpretentious, city-bred but not over sophisticated, who told her men exactly what she thought. On screen she was invariably durable and resilient, pursuing a career that quite often happened to be journalism. Great directors, among them Ford, Capra and Howard Hawks, liked to work with her—and she never let them down.

New York-born Gladys Georgianna Greene was a photographer's model while still in school and played in silent movies —mostly in comedies and third-rate Westerns—for ten years, beginning with John Ford's *Cameo Kirby* in the early 20's. Convinced that she couldn't act, she quit films and spent several years with stock companies and on Broadway before taking another crack at Hollywood. Her big break came in John Ford's *The Whole Town's Talking* (1935), a genuinely funny comedy in which Edward G. Robinson played the dual roles of gangster and timid clerk.

Thereafter, while she quarreled bitterly with studios about scripts, she rewarded her directors with sparkling performances in a dozen hit movies, ranging from the Oscar-winning *You Can't Take It With You* (1938) and *Mr. Deeds Goes to Town* (1936) to *Mr. Smith Goes to Washington* (1939) and *The More the Merrier* (1943), for which she received an Oscar nomination.

In real life Jean Arthur was an extremely shy individual who hated the spotlight. Studious by nature, she has, since retirement, occasionally taught drama courses at Vassar College. **Other Highlights:** *The Ex-Mrs. Bradford* (1936), *The Plainsman* (1936), *Only Angels Have Wings* (1939), *The Devil and Miss Jones* (1941), *Shane* (1953).

ELIZABETH ASHLEY (1939–   )

Beginning her career as a high fashion model, she won, among other citations, the Tony Award for her enormously comic Broadway performance in *Take Her, She's Mine*. She began in movies at the top, drawing a starring role in the film adaptation of Harold Robbins' *The Carpetbaggers* (1964).

Born Elizabeth Cole in Baton Rouge, Louisiana, she renamed herself after the rather pallid character Leslie Howard portrayed in *Gone With the Wind*. **Among her other films:** *Ship of Fools* (1965), *The Third Day* (1965), *The Solid Gold Kidnapping* (1974).

FRED ASTAIRE (1899–   )

After his first screen test, a studio report read "Can't act, slightly bald. Can dance a little." This foremost dancer of stage and screen started performing with his sister Adele at the age of five in vaudeville. They were topliners for years and eventually took Broadway by storm in such shows as *Lady Be Good* (1924), *Funny Face* (1927), and *The Band Wagon* (1931).

When Adele married in 1932 and retired, Fred turned to Hollywood and made his debut in a small role in *Dancing Lady* (1933) but it was his "Carioca" number with Ginger Rogers in *Flying Down to Rio* (1933) that triggered his popularity and began a famous succession of classic musicals.

A stickler for detail, a champion worrier and a fastidious worker, he received a special Academy Award in 1949 for his contribution to dance. Since the early 60's he has been seen mainly as a straight actor in films as well as in T V specials. **Highlights:** *The Gay Divorcee* (1934), *Top Hat* (1935), *Ziegfeld Follies* (1946), *Blue Skies* (1946), *Easter Parade* (1948), *Daddy Long Legs* (1955), *On the Beach* (1959), *Finian's Rainbow* (1968).

NILS ASTHER (1902–   )

Swedish-born Nils Asther was brought to Hollywood in 1927 to play in *Topsy and Eva* with the Duncan Sisters. He played in many silent movies, twice as leading man to Garbo, but his accent and imperfect English prevented him from getting as many roles in talkies. He went to England, returned to Hollywood in 1934, and was signed immediately. He has appeared in numerous films, generally in suave character parts. **Films include:** *Sorrell and Son* (1927), *Letty Lynton* (1932), *The Bitter Tea of General Yen* (1933), *The Hour Before the Dawn* (1945), *That Man from Tangier* (1953).

The boys in the chorus wore top hats and carried canes, too, but Fred Astaire was always out there in front—the greatest song-and-dance man the movies have ever known.

MARY ASTOR (1906–   )

Born in Quincy, Illinois, Lucille Langehanke was brought to New York in 1920 by her German-born father who wanted to see his offspring turned into another Mary Pickford. A number of smallish parts brought her to the attention of John Barrymore who chose her as his leading lady in *Beau Brummel* (1924). She at once became a Hollywood name.

A woman of intelligence who played every role given her with taste and keen insight, she easily made the transition to sound pictures, but throughout her career deliberately elected to play supporting roles rather than lead parts. In her memoirs she explained why she turned down a starring contract with RKO: "Once

Nils Asther pledges undying love to Joan Crawford in Letty Lynton *(1932).*

Mary Astor shares a tense moment with Humphrey Bogart in a World War II melodrama Across the Pacific *(1942).*

your name *goes above* the title of a picture, it must never come down or your prestige is gone.''

Selected by Bette Davis to play a bitchy role in *The Great Lie* (1941), Mary Astor was perhaps the only screen performer to steal a picture from the great Davis, a feat for which she won the Academy Award as Best Supporting Actress of the year. During the 50's, however, parts came to her less frequently and she turned to the stage and television. In 1961, however, she received ecstatic notices for her performance in *Return to Peyton Place*.

Her memoirs, written in 1959 and disclosing a turbulent off-stage life, were a success and she followed them with two novels, the last of which, *A Place Called Saturday*, was published in 1969. **More than 100 films include:** *The Man Who Played God* (1922), *The Bright Shawl* (1923), *Dodsworth* (1926), *The Prisoner of Zenda* (1937), *The Maltese Falcon* (1941), *Across the Pacific* (1942),

Meet Me in St. Louis (1944), *Youngblood Hawke* (1964), *Hush, Hush, Sweet Charlotte* (1964).

ROSCOE ATES (1892–1962)

A graduate of Warren (Ohio) Conservatory where he studied violin, Ates started out as a concert violinist but soon became a comedian in vaudeville, particularly well known throughout his stage and screen career for his nervous stutter. Said Ates: ''This stutter began in vaudeville. I forgot a line and in trying to remember it I started stuttering. The audience thought it was a gag and so I kept it up.'' **His films include:** *The Champ* (1931), *Alice in Wonderland* (1933), *Gone With the Wind* (1939), *Captain Caution* (1940), *The Errand Boy* (1961).

RICHARD ATTENBOROUGH (1923–   )

A Charlie Chaplin film viewed at age 12 in Cambridge, England, where he was born, prompted Attenborough to choose an acting career. He won a scholarship to the Royal Academy of Dramatic Arts and made his first professional stage appearance in *Ah, Wilderness* (1941). His film debut was *In Which We Serve* (1942). Thereafter he had many character roles, often playing the role of a coward. He was particularly memorable as a teen-age thug in *Brighton Rock* (1947). In 1964 he was voted Best Actor (an English award) for his performances in *Guns at Batasi* and *Seance on a Wet Afternoon*. He directed *Oh, What a Lovely War* (1969) and *Young Winston* (1972). **His many films include:** *Stairway to Heaven* (1946), *The Lost People* (1949), *Private's Progress* (1955), *I'm All Right, Jack* (1959), *Doctor Doolittle* (1967).

LIONEL ATWILL (1885-1946)

British-born Lionel Atwill began his acting career on the London stage in 1905 and for ten years appeared in Ibsen roles. In 1915 he came to Broadway and repeated his stage successes. His first film was *The Silent Witness* (1932) in which he played the lead role.

He remained in Hollywood and made numerous films, generally playing supporting parts, Teutonic villains, slick seducers, mad doctors or the like. **His many films include:** *The Mystery of the Wax Museum* (1933),

A smiling Lionel Atwill presents what looks like either a wedding cake or an atomic bomb to a group of admirers in Mr. Moto Takes a Vacation *(1939). Peter Lorre, at the far right, looks properly inscrutable.*

Captain Blood (1935), *The Great Waltz* (1938), *The Hound of the Baskervilles* (1939), *Sherlock Holmes and the Secret Weapon* (1942), *House of Dracula* (1945).

MISCHA AUER (1905–1967)

Mischa Ounskowsky came to the United States from Russia in the early days of the revolution. His angular frame first appeared on the Broadway stage but by 1928 he was in Hollywood playing comic bit parts as mad scientists, Russian noblemen or cocky butlers. A master at zany character parts, his best performance was most probably in *My Man Godfrey* (1936). **His many films include:** *100 Men and a Girl* (1937), *You Can't Take It With You* (1938), *Lady in the Dark* (1944), *A Royal Scandal* (1945), *Arrivederci, Baby* (1966).

JEAN-PIERRE AUMONT (1913–)

He made his debut in English films in *Dark Eyes* (1938), but he is probably best remembered for the World War II espionage thriller *Assignment in Brittany* (1943). An attractive personality combined with great acting ability have made him a star of stage and screen in France, but he has not been particularly lucky in the assignments given him in the United States. **Credits include:** *The Cross of Lorraine* (1943), *Lili* (1953), *John Paul Jones* (1959), *Five Miles to Midnight* (1963), *Day For Night* (1973).

GENE AUTRY (1907–)

Unlike other makers of film Westerns, he never resorted to violence to resolve a conflict between the good guys and the bad. Gene Autry's portrayals of cowpunchers, sheriffs, frontier marshals and range riders showed that a soft voice, amiable character, sweet reasonableness and a song on the lips at the drop of a ten-gallon hat could iron out even the worst clash between cowboys and the cattle rustlers.

On many occasions, motivated by causes which remain obscure, he dropped everything to sing a song to an on-screen audience of one—his horse Champion. Millions of young fans loved the Sagebrush Troubadour, however, and he set a standard of cowboy sartorial elegance that is imitated by one to seven-year-old guntoters to this day. **Among his films are:** *In Old Santa Fe* (1934), *Tumbling Tumbleweeds* (1935), *Git Along, Little Dogies* (1937), *Back in the Saddle* (1941), *Goldtown Ghost Riders* (1953).

FRANKIE AVALON (1940–)

He began his performing career playing the trumpet and then started to sing in his father's night club for teenagers. At 17, he became one of America's most popular singers and in 1960 appeared in his first film, *Guns of the Timberland*.

Said Avalon, "Look, I was a star when I was seventeen. I mean I knew from nothing. In the old days they had vaudeville, stock, burlesque, lots of ways to learn the business before they hit it big. Me, I had to learn the business after I became a star." **Films include:** *Beach Party* (1963), *Muscle Beach Party* (1964), *Bikini Beach* (1964), *Beach Blanket Bingo* (1965), *How to Stuff a Wild Bikini* (1967).

FELIX AYLMER (1889–)

A distinguished stage actor in England, British-born Felix Aylmer became president of British Actors Equity Association in 1950. He has also appeared on Broadway several times. A leading supporting actor in films since 1933, he generally played the part of a

Richard Attenborough confronts Jack Hawkins in Guns at Batasi *(1964).*

Joan Blondell and Bing Crosby prepare to wage war on a contemplative Mischa Auer, who apparently goofed. The picture was East Side of Heaven *(1939).*

28

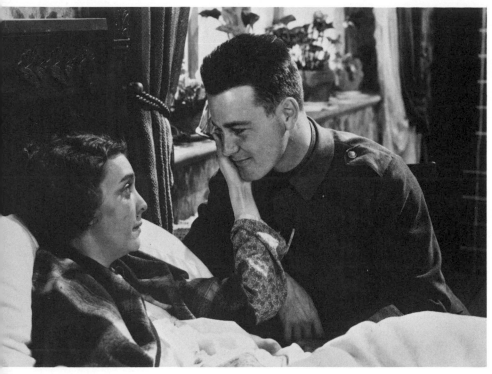

*Lew Ayres and Zasu Pitts in what may well be the greatest war picture ever made—*All Quiet on the Western Front, *filmed more than forty years ago.*

chestra instead. After one bit part in a silent film, he was chosen to play opposite Greta Garbo in her last silent picture, *The Kiss* (1929). That led him to the lead role, a young German soldier, in what may well be the finest war picture ever made, *All Quiet on the Western Front* (1930).

The Lewis Milestone classic made him a great star, but the scripts he was thereafter given were, with few exceptions, second rate. One of those exceptions was *Holiday* (1938), in which he played Katharine Hepburn's hard drinking brother; another was *Young Dr. Kildare* (1938) in which Ayres set a medical standard that was handed down through the years. He played in eight of the Kildare epics.

It is interesting to note that Ayres was the first motion picture star to register as a conscientious objector in World War II. Although he served as a medic and chaplain's aide it hurt him at the box office and when the war ended jobs were few and far between. In recent years, however, he has been making a comeback—a good thing, for he is an enormously capable actor. **Films include:** *East Is West* (1930), *State Fair* (1933), *The Last Train From Madrid* (1937), *Johnny Belinda* (1948), *Advise and Consent* (1962), *The Carpetbaggers* (1964), *Battle for the Planet of the Apes* (1973).

schoolmaster, banker, or bishop. In 1944 he starred in *Mr. Emmanuel*. **Among his many films are:** *The Wandering Jew* (1933), *Victoria the Great* (1937), *Quo Vadis* (1951), *Becket* (1964), *Hostile Witness* (1968).

AGNES AYRES (1896–1940)

Agnes Ayres began her acting career in the early days of movies as an extra at the Essanay Studio in Chicago. From there she went to Vitagraph and co-starred with Edward Earle in 25 silent film versions of O. Henry stories. She skyrocketed to fame opposite Rudolph Valentino in *The Sheik* (1921), but failed to survive the talkies and retired. **Her many films include:** *Forbidden Fruit* (1921), *The Affairs of Anatol* (1921), *The Awful Truth* (1925), *The Donovan Affair* (1929).

LEW AYRES (1908–   )

After studying medicine at the University of Arizona, Minneapolis-born Lew Ayres decided to play banjo and guitar with an or-

CHARLES AZNAVOUR (1924–   )

The son of Armenian actors who settled in Paris and opened a restaurant, French character-actor Charles Aznavour started his career as a cabaret singer. He became very well known as a popular vocalist before becoming a film star. He received the Golden Lion Award at the Venice Film Festival for his role in *Tomorrow Is My Turn* (1962). He continues to write and sing his songs while appearing in films. Marcel Pagnol said of him: "Aznavour is the only writer who can say in a three-minute song what it has taken many writers of plays three acts to say." **Highlights:** *La Tete Contre Les Murs* (1958), *Shoot the Piano Player* (1960), *Le Passage du Rhin* (1961), *Cloportes* (1965), *Candy* (1968), *The Adventurers* (1969), *The Games* (1969).

![B](film strip logo with letter B)

LAUREN BACALL (1924–   )

Her way of walking, it was said, suggested that there must have been "a panther in her family tree." For years she was cast in sultry, feline roles.

Born Betty Jane Perske in New York City, she rose to stardom in her first featured screen appearance, *To Have and Have Not* (1944). Legend has it that Director Howard Hawks saw her picture on the cover of *Harper's Bazaar* and decided to cast her opposite Bogart in the Hemingway story. In any event Bacall's husky voice intoned the line that was to make her famous: "If you want anything, all you have to do is whistle. You know how to whistle, don't you? You just put your lips together and blow."

The same film also marked the beginning of the romance between Bogie and Betty. They married a year later and became one of Hollywood's most influential couples, both on screen and off.

Four years after Bogart's death in 1957 she married Jason Robards, Jr. Later divorced from him, she continued her film career and in 1970 scored on Broadway in *Applause*. **Film highlights:** *The Big Sleep* (1946), *Key Largo* (1948), *Young Man With a Horn* (1950), *How to Marry a Millionaire* (1953), *Written on the Wind* (1956), *Harper* (1966).

JIM BACKUS (1913–   )

Although known off-screen as one of the funniest men in Hollywood, Backus was forever cast in serious roles. The reason, he explained, is "the curse of a sad face and cow-brown eyes. To them I must look like a St. Bernard. They did everything but put a keg of brandy around my neck." He spent years in pictures as the perennial best friend

Lauren Bacall and Humphrey Bogart in the film that brought them together— To Have and Have Not *(1944).*

before trying outright comedy. One role which he could not attribute to his appearance was the voice of Mr. Magoo in UPA cartoons. **Films include:** *Rebel Without a Cause* (1955), *It's a Mad, Mad, Mad, Mad World* (1963), *Where Were You When the Lights Went Out?* (1968).

IRVING BACON (1893–1965)

A bespectacled character actor who was in constant demand for nearly 40 years beginning with his debut in talkies in *The Good-bye Kiss* (1928), he was usually cast in solid citizen roles or as a comic type. He rarely appeared in less than seven or eight pictures per year. **Highlights:** *Million Dollar Legs* (1932), *Private Worlds* (1935), *Grapes of Wrath* (1940), *Meet John Doe* (1941), *State of the Union* (1948), *The Glenn Miller Story* (1954), *Dakota Incident* (1956).

HERMIONE BADDELEY (1906–   )

The British comedienne made her stage debut as a mad boy at the age of eight, was a

Jim Backus played the role of James Dean's father in Rebel Without a Cause *(1955).*

Hermione Baddeley and Tommy Steele in The Happiest Millionaire.

star by the time she was 15 and in recent years has played madcap roles or middle-aged eccentrics in a limited number of films. George Bernard Shaw once suggested that she change her name from Miss Baddeley to Miss Goodeley—a tribute to her fine performances.

While most of her time has been spent on stage, she has also made television appearances—often being interviewed, for she is a sparkling conversationalist. On screen, she gave a particularly memorable supporting performance as the blowzy music mistress in *Room at the Top* (1959). **Films include:** *Brighton Rock* (1947), *Quartet* (1948), *The Unsinkable Molly Brown* (1964), *Mary Poppins* (1964), *The Happiest Millionaire* (1967).

PEARL BAILEY (1918–   )

The highly versatile entertainer, acclaimed around the world for her bubbling, chatty effervescence, captivated Broadway audiences several years ago in the all-black version of *Hello, Dolly!* As far back as 1954, however, she appeared in a notable musical, *Carmen Jones*, and in 1959 in the Gershwin classic *Porgy and Bess*.

Ebullient Pearl has turned in fine dramatic performances in such sober films as *All the Fine Young Cannibals* (1960).

Highlights: *Variety Girl* (1947), *St. Louis Blues* (1957), *The Landlord* (1969).

FAY BAINTER (1892–1968)

Although she made her stage debut in her native Los Angeles at the age of six and her Broadway debut in 1912, it wasn't until she was 41 that Bainter first appeared on the screen in *This Side of Heaven* (1934) beginning a screen career that included many sympathetic mothers, long suffering wives, and wise aunts. Her performance in *Jezebel* (1938) won her the Academy Award for Best Supporting Actress. Her last screen appearance was in *The Children's Hour* (1962) for which she received an Academy Award nomination as Best Supporting Actress. **Highlights:** *Quality Street* (1937), *White Banners* (1938), *Daughters Courageous* (1939), *Our Town* (1940), *Woman of the Year* (1942), *The Human Comedy* (1943), *State Fair* (1945), *The Secret Life of Walter Mitty* (1947), *June Bride* (1948).

CARROLL BAKER (1931–   )

She skyrocketed to stardom as a poor Southerner's child-wife in Tennessee Williams' *Baby Doll* (1956), a film which left its impact on Hollywood standards.

Thereafter, the sexy blond star was often cast as other sexy blond stars. She played a Harlow type in a toned-down version of *The Carpetbaggers* (1964) and played Harlow herself in *Harlow* (1965). **Films include:** *Bridge to the Sun* (1961), *Something Wild* (1961), *Station Six-Sahara* (1964), *Jack of Diamonds* (1967).

DIANE BAKER (1938–   )

Her mother, Dorothy Harrington, had acted with the Marx Brothers, but Diane preferred to play it straight. She made her debut as the sister in *The Diary of Anne Frank*

Fay Bainter (right) in a typical supporting role of her long career—with star Bette Davis in June Bride *(1948), with Betty Lynn and Marjorie Bennett.*

(1959) and appeared regularly thereafter, usually in so-so films.

She is candid about the roles she chose to accept and said of one film, "It's the kind of picture I wouldn't go to see even if I weren't involved in it." **Films include:** *Journey to the Center of the Earth* (1959), *Nine Hours to Rama* (1963), *The Prize* (1963), *Marnie* (1964), *Krakatoa* (1968).

STANLEY BAKER (1928–   )

The highly competent Welsh actor began his film career as a teenager in 1941 and, once the war had ended, usually found himself cast as a tough, menacing or rather sinister individual. He played Henry Tudor to Olivier's *Richard III* (1956) but more often appeared in tales of adventure or in such unlikely B epics as *Sodom and Gomorrah* (1962). In recent years he has co-produced his own films. **Credits include:** *Undercover* (1941), *The Good Die Young* (1954), *The Guns of Navarone* (1961), *Sands of the Kalahari* (1965), *Accident* (1966).

WILLIAM BAKEWELL (1908–   )

For a while when he was an extra, he managed to look like a perennial juvenile. With the passing of time and the emergence of talking pictures he graduated into better roles, but in nearly 40 films never quite managed to achieve stardom. **Films include:** *The Heart Thief* (1927), *All Quiet on the Western Front* (1930), *Spirit of Notre Dame* (1931), *Three-cornered Moon* (1933), *Cheers for Miss Bishop* (1941), *Davy Crockett, King of the Wild Frontier* (1954).

LUCILLE BALL (1910–   )

Although her talents as a comedienne and serious actress graced more than 50 films, many of which were of the B-minus variety, it is her television work that will best identify her to future generations. Married to producer-actor Desi Arnaz for 20 years, Lucille and the Desilu team created the *I Love Lucy* series that far outlasted the marriage and set a pattern for television comedies of domestic life that has been endlessly imitated.

A native of Jamestown, New York, Lucille Ball set out for New York at the age of 15 and a career in the theatre. After she was dis-

missed from a drama school as "too shy and reticent" she spent years modeling, dancing and playing bit parts in mostly second-rate films. At long last her friend Carole Lombard introduced her to Damon Runyan who helped her land the key role, that of a crippled and high-keyed actress, in his story *The Big Street* (1942). Playing opposite Henry Fonda, the bellhop in love with her, she drew rave notices but, alas, stardom didn't bring her the good scripts she deserved.

Everything else she did turned to gold. As the major stockholder in Desilu, as a motion picture producer, as the creator and owner of television series which succeeded *I Love Lucy*, Ball, with her energy and shrewd judgment, produced financial bonanzas.

Best of all, at least one of her recent pictures, *Yours, Mine, and Ours* (1968), in which she and Henry Fonda played the widow and widower with an endless number of children between them, proved to be one of the most amusing films she ever made. **Other highlights:** *Having Wonderful Time* (1938), *Room Service* (1938), *Easy to Wed* (1946), *Sorrowful Jones* (1949), *The Long, Long Trailer* (1950), *The Facts of Life* (1960), *Mame* (1974).

A studio photograph of Carroll Baker, the sexy blonde star who often played sexy blonde stars.

A young Lucille Ball shared theatre ambitions and living quarters at the "Footlights Club" with Katharine Hepburn and Ginger Rogers in the 1937 classic, Stage Door. *The screen version of the Edna Ferber–George S. Kaufman play was widely considered to be an improvement on the original.*

MARTIN BALSAM (1919–   )

Because he lends enormous credibility to his character roles, Martin Balsam is known on stage, screen and television as an actor's actor. He made his debut in *On the Waterfront* (1954) and appeared in a number of tour-de-force roles after that. A decade later he gave an Academy Award-winning performance for Best Supporting Actor in *A Thousand Clowns* (1965), one of the most light-hearted films of his career. **Notable credits are:** *Twelve Angry Men* (1957), *Marjorie Morningstar* (1958), *Psycho* (1960), *Breakfast at Tiffany's* (1961), *Cape Fear* (1962), *Little Big Man* (1970), *Summer Wishes, Winter Dreams* (1973).

ANNE BANCROFT (1931–   )

A brilliant actress whose stage presence and polished professionalism caused her to be labeled "a female Brando," Bancroft wasted her talents during the 50's in such gaudy nonsense as *Demetrius and the Gladiators* (1954).

She was born Anna Maria Italiano in the Bronx and the stage was her first love. After such film beauties as *Gorilla at Large* (1954) she returned (understandably) to Broadway and created a sensation as Annie Sullivan in *The Miracle Worker*. Preparing for the role of Helen Keller's teacher, she attached adhesive to her eyes, wore dark glasses for two days, and learned the manual alphabet for the blind. In 1962 her long neglected acting talents became apparent to even the most myopic movie producer when she repeated the Sullivan role on the screen and received for it the Academy Award as Best Actress of the year. More recently, as the restless Mrs. Robinson, she seduced Dustin Hoffman in *The Graduate* (1967) and has starred in television specials.

In 1964 Miss Bancroft married perhaps the funniest writer of our day, Mel Brooks of 1000-year-old-man fame. **Other films:** *Don't Bother to Knock* (debut, 1952), *Walk the Proud Land* (1956), *The Pumpkin Eater* (1964), *The Slender Thread* (1965).

Anne Bancroft as the memorable Mrs. Robinson is unzipped by Dustin Hoffman in The Graduate, *one of the best screen tragi-comedies of our time (1967).*

GEORGE BANCROFT (1882–1956)

The big, craggy actor was popular on Broadway years before he became one of Hollywood's favorite two-fisted heros in silents and early talkies. He was not only a portrayer of good guys, however. His scowl, snarl and football-player build combined to make him a highly convincing villain and for some years he met his just reward in such diverse locations as a gangster hangout and a Western gulch. **Films include:** *Pony Express* (1925), *Underworld* (1927), *Mr. Deeds Goes to Town* (1936), *Angels With Dirty Faces* (1938), *Stagecoach* (1939), *The Bugle Sounds* (1942).

TALLULAH BANKHEAD (1903–1968)

There has never been anyone quite like her. Tallu's flamboyance, on and off screen, was legendary. The daughter of an eminent Southern congressman, she maintained she could never root for a team called the Yankees.

Though she was acclaimed for her stage role in *The Little Foxes*, other performances were less than monumental. John Mason

Brown wrote of *Antony and Cleopatra*: "Miss Bankhead barged down the Nile last night as Cleopatra—and sank."

Tallulah Bankhead acted in occasional films from 1918 on and is well remembered for her electric performance in Hitchcock's *Lifeboat* (1943). She was also successful as a radio and television personality. **Films include:** *Tarnished Lady* (1931), *Faithless* (1932), *A Royal Scandal* (1945), *Die! Die! My Darling* (1965).

LESLIE BANKS (1890–1952)

After a distinguished stage career, Banks unsuccessfully tried his luck with English silent films before going to Hollywood. There he was a resounding success as the villain in *The Most Dangerous Game* (1932).

His trademark, a half-glad, half-mad expression, was the result of an injury he suffered which left one side of his face paralyzed. **Films include:** *The Man Who Knew Too Much* (1934), *Jamaica Inn* (1939), *Fire Over England* (1939), *The Big Blockade* (1942), *Henry V* (1944), *Your Witness* (1950).

VILMA BANKY (1903–   )

The Hungarian actress was a popular vamp of the 20's, one of the hardy band of exotic femmes fatales first popularized by Theda Bara. She reached the pinnacle of stardom playing opposite Rudolph Valentino in *The Eagle* (1925) and *Son of the Sheik* (1926), which proved to be the great lover's last film.

Though discovered and brought to the screen by Sam Goldwyn, her star faded with the advent of the talkies. **Highlights:** *The Dark Angel* (1926), *The Winning of Barbara Worth* (1928).

IAN BANNEN (1928–   )

A lively, long-chinned Scot, Bannen appeared in a number of stage and screen roles. A critic once remarked that his temperament was better suited to contemporary works than to Shakespeare. Bannen, it seemed, imbued Hamlet with more neuroses than the traditional ones. **Notable films:** *Private's Progress* (1955), *Macbeth* (1959), *Station Six Sahara* (1963), *The Flight of the Phoenix* (1965), *Lock Up Your Daughters* (1969).

Tallulah Bankhead, an ultra-dynamic personage on screen and off, doesn't appear to register with Charles Laughton in Devil and the Deep *(1932).*

THEDA BARA (1890-1955)

She was born in the shadow of the Sphinx, weaned on serpents' blood, and had occult powers. Her name was an anagram for Arab Death, and her seductive powers drove men mad.

All of the above must have seemed puzzling to Theodosia Goodman's relatives in Cincinnati, Ohio, particularly the Baranger side of the family whose name she borrowed. Be that as it may, she became the screen's first Sex Queen, brought a new word—vamp—into the language, and appeared in films that created as big a stir in her day as *Deep Throat* and *Last Tango* did in ours. "Kiss me, my fool," she commanded in *A Fool There Was* (1914), her first smash hit. When the drunken, drug-addicted and expiring victim

Theda Bara, wearing what appears to be 60 or 70 pounds of costume jewelry, sights another luckless male who will succumb to her wiles.

34

George Barbier, in a typical supporting role, with Richard Whorf, both playing theatrical types in Yankee Doodle Dandy *(1942).*

Brigitte Bardot spent a great deal of her time on screen entering and leaving bathtubs and beds. This time it was a bathtub.

did so, one could hear the sharp intake of breath in movie houses around the world.

Watching a Theda Bara seduction scene today is somewhat less exciting than viewing the courtship of two landlocked salmon. Her sexual responses were confined to back-arching, couch-lolling, arm-waving plus long soulful glares at the audience through mascara ringed eyes.

By the time "normalcy" returned to the United States in 1919, Theda Bara had turned out four or more pictures each year, almost always playing the vamp, siren, unfaithful wife or murderess. By then her style of dramatics had given way to more sophisticated techniques and, despite a few feeble attempts at a comeback, the gasps that had attended her appearances had turned to giggles. During the last years of her life, a sad time, she continued to advertise in Hollywood trade papers that she was "at liberty." **Films include:** *Carmen* (1915), *The Eternal Sappho* (1916), *Camille* (1917), *Cleopatra* (1918), *Madame Dubarry* (1918), *When a Woman Sins* (1918), *When Men Desire* (1919).

GEORGE BARBIER (1865–1945)

Though he had prepared for a career in the pulpit, Barbier realized his true calling was the theatre. During his 50-year career he played roles ranging from Shakespearean to modern comedy. His career also included behind-the-scenes work as a set painter, property man and stage manager. He is familiar to audiences as the nervous, chubby, cigar-smoking magnate. **Films include:** *The Smiling Lieutenant* (1931), *The Man Who Came to Dinner* (1941), *Song of the Islands* (1942), *Yankee Doodle Dandy* (1942).

BRIGITTE BARDOT (1934–   )

At the age of 23 she announced: "I shall leave the screen at 25 when my beauty begins to fade." At 40 she is still around, possibly because she has become a better actress and is still smashing to look at.

She was the cover girl on *Elle*, a leading French women's magazine, at the age of 15. Her film career began when director Marc Allegret saw her picture and had his assistant,

Roger Vadim, get in touch with the "prim-looking" adolescent. A zealous publicity campaign by Vadim, who became the first of her three husbands, turned her into a celebrity overnight.

The Bardot style—her walk, her pout, her long blond hair, her mode of dress and undress—all of these helped to make her, over a period of some years, filmdom's number one sex symbol. It was, however, her magnificent body, all of which moviegoers were privileged to see unencumbered by clothing, that helped most of all.

Some unkind wit said that Bardot was part Lolita, part Mae West, and he wasn't far off the mark. **Films include:** *And God Created Woman* (1956), *The Devil is a Woman* (1958), *Dear Brigitte* (1965), *Shalako* (1968).

LYNN BARI (1916–   )

Because she was painfully shy, her mother sent her to dramatic school. By the mid-30's, Lynn Bari was having her screams and shrieks dubbed in for stars who weren't strident enough. She made her movie debut in the chorus of *Dancing Lady* (1933) starring Joan Crawford. Bari once said: "You learn a great deal opening doors for other people, kicking your heels in the line of a chorus, being a 'meanie' and the 'other woman' while most of the plum parts go to the other girls." **Films include:** *Return of the Cisco Kid* (1939), *Kit Carson* (1940), *Blood and Sand* (1941), *The Bridge of San Luis Rey* (1944), *Margie* (1946), *The Young Runaways* (1968).

LEX BARKER (1919–1973)

In 1948, with *Tarzan's Magic Fountain*, Lex Barker joined the number of actors who at one time or another have played the jungle hero. After five films he went in search of other roles.

With his blond hair, rugged physique and jungle experience, he landed various adventurer parts in minor films. One of his more interesting roles was that of a washed-up ex-Tarzan actor in *La Dolce Vita* (1961). **Films include:** *Battles of Chief Pontiac* (1952), *The Price of Fear* (1956), *The Girl in the Kremlin*

(1957), *Code 7 Victim 5* (1963), *A Place Called Glory* (1966), *Shatterhand* (1968).

BINNIE BARNES (1906–   )

London-born Binnie Barnes, who at different times worked as a milkmaid, a nurse, and ballroom dancer, was once known as Texas Binnie in a cowgirl rope-twirling act which she devised based solely on her experience with American films.

Her role as Katherine Howard in *The Private Life of Henry VIII* (1932) brought her to Hollywood, where she went on to play a great variety of character roles, both serious and comic. She was married to film producer Mike Frankovich for 30 years. **Films include:** *The Last of the Mohicans* (1936), *Three Smart Girls* (1937), *The Adventures of Marco Polo* (1938), *Holiday* (1938), *The Man From Down Under* (1943), *If Winter Comes* (1947), *The Trouble With Angels* (1966), *Forty Carats* (1973).

VINCE BARNETT (1902–   )

Barnett was lured away from a career in aeronautical engineering to "stand-in" for his father Luke, a well-known comedian. Soon a professional in his own right, he became known for his depictions of second-string gangsters and other down-and-out types. **Some of his more than 200 films:** *Scarface* (1932), *A Star Is Born* (1937), *The Killers* (1946), *Brute Force* (1947), *The Human Jungle* (1954).

ROBERT BARRAT (1891–   )

Robert Barrat might have been a professional fighter but for an unexpected invitation to join the cast of a musical comedy. He decided to give up the ring and to fight it out on the screen, often as a snarling bad man.

He played innumerable surly characters during a career which began in the silent era. **Films include:** *The Picture Snatcher* (1933), *The Last of the Mohicans* (1936), *The Adventures of Mark Twain* (1944), *Tall Man Riding* (1955).

JEAN-LOUIS BARRAULT (1910–   )

The distinguished French actor studied art in his youth, but turned to the theatre when he

Lynn Bari, always an interesting actress, is here sandwiched between a milk-drinking Victor McLaglen and a suave George Montgomery in China Girl *(1943).*

was accepted as a scholarship student at the Theatre de L'Atelier. Too poor to rent a room, he slept in the wings of the stage.

During his apprenticeship he learned the art of mime, a skill with which he would later enchant audiences in *Les Enfants du Paradis* (1945). **Films include:** *La Symphonie Fantastique* (1942), *La Ronde* (1950), *La Testament du Docteur Cordelier* (1961), *The Longest Day* (1962), *Chappaqua* (1967).

Binnie Barnes appears to realize that Pat O'Brien's sweet smile belies the gun in his pocket, and so does Frank McHugh, in 'Til We Meet Again *(1940). But does George Brent?*

Wendy Barrie was the girl friend when George Sanders played The Saint *in the '30's series of thrillers.*

MONA BARRIE (1909—   )

A movie scout discovered the tall, blue-eyed Australian actress and brought her to Hollywood where she plowed through a number of minor roles. For a time she was coupled with Gilbert Roland as a new romantic team, but when that didn't work, she was cast in shady-lady parts.

Mona Barrie commented, "Some days I get so wrapped up in my movie characterizations that I feel uncomfortable without a pistol, bludgeon or bottle in my hand." **Films include:** *A Message to Garcia* (1936), *Storm Over Lisbon* (1944), *Plunder of the Sun* (1953).

WENDY BARRIE (1912–   )

Wendy Barrie was lunching at the Savoy, in London, one day when she was offered an opportunity for the screen test that launched her career. She played the role of Jane Seymour in *The Private Life of Henry VIII* (1933) and in several other British films before going to Hollywood. She was there ten days when she had a studio contract. After appearing in some 30 films, but never quite reaching stardom, Miss Barrie switched over to radio and television. **Films include:** *The Hound of the Baskervilles* (1939), *A Date*

With the Falcon (1941), *It Should Happen to You* (1954).

EDGAR BARRIER (1906–1964)

On stage in *The Magnificent Seven* he portrayed Justice Louis Brandeis and subsequently received many letters from the latter's friends and acquaintances who wished to comment on the actor's fine performance. Said Barrier: "If I suffered from any lack of vanity my mail at the Royale would fix that up in a jiffy." **Films include:** *Flesh and Fantasy* (1943), *A Game of Death* (1945), *Macbeth* (1948), *To the Ends of the Earth* (1948), *Cyrano de Bergerac* (1950), *Princess of the Nile* (1954), *Irma la Douce* (1963).

ETHEL BARRYMORE (1879–1959)

The female member of The Royal Family of Broadway—a term used to describe John, Ethel and Lionel Barrymore—appeared in relatively few films rather late in her career, almost always as a kind-hearted but crotchety matriarch who, as David Shipman put it, "dispensed wisdom with a trowel."

Her days of greatness were in the theatre. Pictures of her taken around the turn of the century disclose that she was a great beauty. By the time her motion picture career began, however, she was a haughty and impressive russet-haired figure who overwhelmed interviewers by her majestic presence. Actually she was a baseball fan and extremely witty.

Her outstanding film achievement was in *None but the Lonely Heart* (1944), for which she received an Oscar as Best Supporting Actress. **Other credits include:** *Our Mrs. McChesney* (1918), *Rasputin and the Empress* (1932), *Portrait of Jennie* (1948), *Young at Heart* (1954).

JOHN BARRYMORE (1882–1942)

"Prince John" and "The Great Profile" were just two of the tags that writers attached to the youngest of the three Barrymores. Broadway performances in heavy dramas like *The Jest* and *Hamlet* caused him to be regarded as the greatest actor of his day, a reputation that is hardly borne out by watching the films he made. In tragic parts he displayed a distinct tendency towards eye-

Ethel Barrymore was Cary Grant's mom back in 1944 when RKO filmed None but the Lonely Heart *from Richard Llewellyn's novel. Screenplay and direction were by Clifford Odets.*

rolling and scenery chewing; in comic roles he hammed it up outrageously.

His film debut was in *An American Citizen* (1917) but it was as the schizophrenic *Dr. Jekyll and Mr. Hyde* (1920) that he turned himself into one of the highest paid performers of all time. Then, in 1922, he played another role in which scowling and a great deal of facial movement were acceptable– that of *Sherlock Holmes*.

He had been billed in *Don Juan* (1926) as "The Greatest Lover of All Time," and this reputation carried on after talkies arrived. Barrymore helped it along mightily by a succession of off-screen marriages and love affairs, all of which ended unhappily.

All three Barrymores appeared together in *Rasputin and the Empress* (1932) and he played with Lionel in the highly successful *Dinner at Eight* at around the same time. In 1934 he gave one of his best performances, aided by Carole Lombard, as the flamboyant movie producer in *Twentieth Century*.

John Barrymore had a drinking problem throughout his acting career and by the late 30's he was in and out of clinics for alcoholics. His old friends have said that he wanted his life to end. He did several parodies of himself and his drinking-wenching habits, notably in one of his last films, *The Great Profile* (1940). When he died in 1942 he was penniless. **Other films include:** *The Man From Blankleys* (1930), *Grand Hotel* (1932), *A Bill of Divorcement* (1932), *Topaze* (1933), *Counsellor-at-Law* (1933), *Playmates* (1942).

LIONEL BARRYMORE (1878–1954)

The first-born of the three Barrymores never appeared in starring roles but played in far more pictures than the other two combined. His vocal delivery, midway between a drawl and a snarl, along with a dour facial expression, caused him to be cast again and again as a crotchety senior citizen who, underneath a gruff exterior, concealed a heart of gold. Although he was a big man, four inches over six feet, later-day audiences never realized it, for arthritis combined with an automobile accident in 1938 crippled him badly and from that point on his screen appearances were in his wheelchair.

Lionel Barrymore and Mickey Rooney, two of MGM's reliables, often appeared together and are posed here examining a model of a schooner used in Captains Courageous *(1937).*

Profile meets profile as John Barrymore, playing Mercutio, duels with the devilish Tybalt, played by Basil Rathbone, in MGM's lavish production of Romeo and Juliet. *Leslie Howard is Romeo.*

Richard Barthelmess and (you'll never guess) Mary Astor in The Bright Shawl.

Alan Bates, one of England's most versatile young stars, in Georgy Girl *(1966).*

It was in 1938 that he made his initial appearance as Dr. Gillespie, advisor to *Young Dr. Kildare*. Kildare pictures went on and on through the years and Barrymore's impact on them was so great that the later ones bore such titles as *Dr. Gillespie's Criminal Case* (1943).

Lionel won an Oscar in 1931 for his work in *A Free Soul* (1931). He was particularly sinister as the lecherous monk in *Rasputin and the Empress* (1932). It should also be noted that, before and after the Gillespie era, he appeared in a great many of the top pictures of the 30's and 40's. **Some of his more than 100 films:** *Alias Jimmy Valentine* (debut, 1928), *Grand Hotel* (1932), *Night Flight* (1933), *Treasure Island* (1934), *David Copperfield* (1935), *The Voice of Bugle Ann* (1936), *Captains Courageous* (1937), *You Can't Take It With You* (1938), *As Thousands Cheer* (1943), *Duel in the Sun* (1946), *Key Largo* (1948), *Main Street to Broadway* (1953).

RICHARD BARTHELMESS
(1895–1963)

One of the greatest of the early stars of silent films, he admirably survived the coming of sound until his retirement in 1942. Barthelmess exuded innocence and total honesty in the roles he played and, as a defender of the basic verities, gave some of the best performances of his time.

Born in New York, he worked in the theatre from his college days and played his first important role in *War Brides* (1916). In 1919 he began an association with Lillian and Dorothy Gish and under the direction of D. W. Griffith made two all-time classics: *Way Down East* in which he rescues Lillian from the cold and *Tol'able David* (1922) in which he wins one of the best fights ever filmed.

Once talkies arrived, he did a beautiful job in a film that was way ahead of its time, *The Last Flight* (1931), and made a marvelously craven husband to Rita Hayworth in *Only Angels Have Wings* (1939). **Other highlights:** *Broken Blossoms* (1919), *The Bright Shawl* (1923), *The Enchanted Cottage* (1924), *The Dawn Patrol* (1930), *The Man Who Talked Too Much* (1940), *The Spoilers* (1942).

FREDDIE BARTHOLOMEW
(1924–   )

At the age of ten Freddie Bartholomew played the title role in *David Copperfield* (1935) and held his own with such stars as Lionel Barrymore, Basil Rathbone, and W.C. Fields. He was widely praised in *Little Lord Fauntleroy* (1936), and by the middle 30's rivaled Jackie Cooper and Dickie Moore as the most popular child star.

When he grew older he retired from the screen and became an advertising executive. **Films include:** *Lloyds of London* (1936), *Captains Courageous* (1937), *Tom Brown's School Days* (1940), *Swiss Family Robinson* (1940), *A Yank at Eton* (1942), *St. Benny the Dip* (1951).

JAMES BARTON (1890–1962)

James Barton worked his way from burlesque to "B" pictures, generally appearing as grumpy characters given to drink. He was not a man to mince words, having already uttered some of the earthiest lines ever heard in a Broadway theatre.

Though his film credits were not as memorable, he did appear with some top stars, including Bing Crosby in *Here Comes the Groom* (1951) and Gregory Peck in *Yellow Sky* (1948). **Highlights:** *Captain Hurricane* (1935), *Lifeboat* (1943), *The Time of Your Life* (1948), *Golden Girl* (1951), *Quantez* (1958).

RICHARD BASEHART (1914–   )

He made his screen debut in *Cry Wolf* (1947) after careers in radio, theatrical productions and local politics. Appearances in more than 20 films have enabled him to play a wide variety of roles with equal facility. He has been relentlessly honest in some, a treacherous double-crosser in others. In all roles his screen image has been highly convincing. **Films include:** *He Walked by Night* (1948), *La Strada* (1954), *Moby Dick* (1956), *The Satan Bug* (1965), *Chato's Land* (1972).

ALBERT BASSERMAN (1867–1952)

One of Germany's foremost actors and possessor of the Iffland Ring, token of preeminence on the German stage, Basserman came to the United States in 1939 as a refugee. He had gone into voluntary exile in 1934 in Switzerland because of his wife, Elsa Schiff, a non-Aryan actress who played opposite him for years.

He began his Hollywood career before he could understand English in *Dr. Ehrlich's Magic Bullet* (1940) and continued to portray men of dignity with sympathy and insight. **Films include:** *Foreign Correspondent* (1940), *The Moon and Sixpence* (1942), *Madame Curie* (1943), *Since You Went Away* (1944), *Rhapsody in Blue* (1945), *The Red Shoes* (1948).

ALAN BATES (1934–)

Born in Derbyshire, England, Bates attended the Royal Academy of Dramatic Arts. He began his performing career on the stage, appearing in such notable plays as *The Crucible* (1956), *Look Back in Anger* (1956), and *Long Day's Journey Into Night* (1958). He made his screen debut in *The Entertainer* (1960) and pursued his movie career in a number of excellent films, first becoming popular for his portrayal of the trapped husband in *A Kind of Loving* (1962). His performance in *The Fixer* (1968) won him an Academy Award nomination. Bates has continued to alternate between stage and screen, recently appearing in the successful play, *Butley* (1972). **Films include:** *Whistle Down the Wind* (1962), *The Caretaker* (1963), *Zorba the Greek* (1964), *Nothing but the Best* (1964), *Georgy Girl* (1966), *Far From the Madding Crowd* (1967), *Women in Love* (1970), *The Go-Between* (1971), *A Day in the Death of Joe Egg* (1972).

FLORENCE BATES
(1888–1954)

Florence Bates will be remembered by millions as the domineering Mrs. Van Hopper (the employer of Joan Fontaine) in the unforgettable opening scenes of *Rebecca*, Alfred Hitchcock's classic of 1940. She was then 52 and making her film debut—but her life to that point had perhaps been more interesting and varied than any of the later screen fictions she appeared in. Born Florence Rabe, she had in turn been a musical prodigy, the first woman lawyer in Texas, an

Florence Bates (right) looks slightly bemused as Ingrid Bergman addresses herself to a couple of veranda dowagers in Saratoga Trunk, *as John Warburton and Gary Cooper look on.*

antique dealer, land developer, and bakery owner. In 1935, she accompanied a friend to the Pasadena Playhouse and ended up reading for the role of Miss Bates in a stage adaptation of Jane Austin's *Emma*. She not only won the part but took the character's name for her own. In her more than 50 films, she invariably played addled, gossipy, haughty, or downright mean ladies. **Films include:** *Kitty Foyle* (1940), *The Chocolate Soldier* (1941), *The Moon and Sixpence* (1942), *Kismet* (1944), *Saratoga Trunk* (1945), *Cluny Brown* (1946), *I Remember Mama* (1948), *A Letter to Three Wives* (1948).

ALAN BAXTER (1908–)

Alan Baxter has proven to be a versatile and solid actor in a long career in films and on

Albert Basserman played Marie and Pierre Curie's academic friend, Prof. Jean Perot, in Madame Curie *with Greer Garson and Walter Pidgeon.*

the stage. Beginning as a leading man in the 40's, he graduated to more mature roles, notably as colonels and business executives, with occasional excursions into villainy. Equally adaptable in the theatre, it was said of his part in the long-running stage hit, *Voice of the Turtle*, ''Baxter made himself at home in the extremely comfortable living room, bedroom and kitchenette setting at the Morosco Theatre.'' **Films include:** *Mary Burns, Fugitive* (1935), *Abe Lincoln in Illinois* (1940), *Winged Victory* (1944), *End of the Line* (1956), *This Property Is Condemmed* (1966).

ANNE BAXTER (1923–)

Anne Baxter was born in Michigan City, Indiana, the granddaughter of Frank Lloyd Wright. After some stage work on Broadway and in summer stock, she progressed to Hollywood where she was turned down for the title role in *Rebecca* because she looked more like the daughter than the wife of the leading man. She had to play a whole series of wholesome, girl-next-door types before she won an Oscar for portraying a tragic figure in *The Razor's Edge* (1946).

Several years later, she played the part of the ruthless understudy in *All About Eve* (1950). Since then filmgoers have seen her as a nightclub singer, saloon keeper, dance hall girl, and, of all people, Nefertiti. **Films include:** *The Magnificent Ambersons* (1942), *The Ten Commandments* (1956), *A Walk on the Wild Side* (1962).

WARNER BAXTER (1893–1951)

A delicately trimmed mustache above gleaming white teeth caused him at one time to be likened to a Valentino without a horse. That wasn't quite an accurate statement because Baxter's first starring appearance as the Cisco Kid in *In Old Arizona* (1929), the first all-talking Western, was full of horses. For this performance Baxter received an Oscar for Best Actor, the second ever presented.

Warner Baxter with Myrna Loy in Broadway Bill, *one of the fastest and funniest Capra films of the early 30's.*

He made this breakthrough after years of stage and screen work and remained an extremely popular leading man for more than a decade before switching to character roles. Two of his many performances are still dear to the hearts of old movie buffs: with Myrna Loy in Frank Capra's 1934 classic *Broadway Bill* and as the bone weary but imperious stage director who tells Ruby Keeler to go out on the stage and come back a star, in *42nd Street* (1933). **Films include:** *The Great Gatsby* (1926), *Stand Up and Cheer* (1934), *Prisoner of Shark Island* (1936), *Lady in the Dark* (1944), *State Penitentiary* (1950).

JOHN BEAL (1909–   )

The clean-cut actor seemed perfect as *The Little Minister* (1935), though the film was a disaster for another of its stars, Katharine Hepburn. Several years later Beal appeared in the spooky comedy *The Cat and the Canary* (1939), and then in other less amusing horror films. **Highlights:** *Les Miserables* (1939), *My Six Convicts* (1952), *Remains to Be Seen* (1953), *The Vampire* (1961).

THE BEATLES: George Harrison (1943–   ), John Lennon (1940–   ), Paul McCartney (1942–   ), Ringo Starr (1940–   ).

The members of the talented rock quartet were all born in Liverpool, England, and were performing in amateur bands and school musical groups early in their teens. Harrison, Lennon, and McCartney teamed up as a trio, the Moondogs, in 1959. In 1960, they were joined by Starr, and the Beatles were born. After appearing all over Europe, they came to the fore in the United States in 1964, making appearances on the *Ed Sullivan Show* and a cross-country tour. They were an incredible success.

The Beatles were not just a singing group; they were a cult. Teenagers of both sexes adopted their distinctive, long (for that time) hairstyle. Their records were bought by millions of adoring fans. In 1964, the group won two Grammy awards—as Best Performing Vocal Group and Best New Artists.

Their charismatic talents were utilized in three campy, successful movies and a televi-

The mop-topped Beatles were made Members of the British Empire by their Queen in 1967. Here Paul McCartney, George Harrison, John Lennon, and Ringo Starr merrily display their medals.

sion film, *The Magical Mystery Tour* (1967). All featured their songs and their appealing, if iconoclastic, personalities. Whether or not the Beatles would have maintained their popularity or their creative excellence as a group is a moot point. Before the group broke up, they had already put their artistic stamp on a whole decade. **Films include:** *A Hard Day's Night* (1964), *Help!* (1965), *The Yellow Submarine* (voices, 1968).

ROBERT BEATTY (1909–   )

A craggy-featured Canadian, Beatty has appeared most frequently in British crime films, though his career took him to sea in *Captain Horatio Hornblower* (1951), to the jungle in *Tarzan and the Lost Safari* (1957), and to who knows where in *2001: A Space Odyssey* (1968). **Films include:** *Odd Man Out* (1946), *Something of Value* (1957), *Where Eagles Dare* 1969).

WARREN BEATTY (1937–   )

At the age of six he wanted to be President, at seven he was willing to settle for the Governorship of Georgia, at eight he decided on

42

Warren Beatty, with Faye Dunaway and Michael J. Pollard in the background, nears the end of the long, murderous road the trio traveled together in Bonnie and Clyde.

Louise Beavers and Bobby Breen are flanked by Alan Mowbray (left) and Henry O'Neill in this scene from Rainbow on the River (1937). In those days, a black actor's chances of escaping roles as household servants or tap dancers were minimal.

an acting career as did his famous sister Shirley MacLaine.

He began his career with a triumphant performance in *Splendor in the Grass* (1961), and although he had much more charm and wasn't nearly as sullen, critics referred to him as the new James Dean. He continued to turn in good performances in a number of so-so films and it wasn't until he played the genial but murderous Clyde to Faye Dunaway's Bonnie (1967) that he became recognized as one of the outstanding actors of our day. **Some of his other films are:** *All Fall Down* (1962), *Lilith* (1964), *The Only Game in Town* (1969), *McCabe and Mrs. Miller* (1971).

LOUISE BEAVERS (1902–1962)

Portraying the plump, southern, Negro maid—a popular stereotype of the 30's—was a problem for Miss Beavers. She wasn't fat and had to constantly gain weight, she did not have a Southern accent and had to develop one, and for her most important screen role—Aunt Delilah, a flapjack genius in *Imitation of Life* (1934)—she had to be taught how to mix the batter.

She made her film debut in *Coquette* (1929) and increased her popularity as the star of the *Beulah* television series in the 1960's. **Films include:** *Brother Rat* (1938), *Reap the Wild Wind* (1942), *Mr. Blandings Builds His Dream House* (1948), *All the Fine Young Cannibals* (1960).

SCOTTY BECKETT (1929–1968)

His was a tragic life. A popular child actor and then a successful juvenile actor in the 30's and 40's, he ran afoul of the law and was arrested on several occasions for possession of drugs and drunken driving. He made his movie debut at three in *Gallant Lady* (1933), became part of the *Our Gang* series for two years, and continued to other roles such as Garbo's son in *Conquest* (1937). His biggest juvenile role was as the teen-aged Al Jolson in *The Jolson Story* (1946). In *Battleground* (1949) he finally played a grown-up part. Beckett died in 1968 in a Hollywood rest home, probably of an overdose of barbiturates. **Films include:** *Dante's Inferno* (1935), *Anthony Adverse* (1936), *The Escape* (1939), *King's Row* (1942).

REGINALD BECKWITH (1908–1965)

Though he often portrayed badgered or timorous little men, Beckwith played a hero's role during the Second World War. From the secret radio station in France, he attacked the Nazis on a program called "The Voice of the Night." The British actor was also a playwright. **Films include:** *Scott of the Antarctic* (1948), *The Runaway Bus* (1954), *The Horse's Mouth* (1958), *The Thirty-nine Steps* (1959), *The Password Is Courage* (1962), *Mister Moses* (1965).

DON BEDDOE (1891–   )

Often cast as a sheriff, reporter or policeman, Don Beddoe is best known for his friendly, slightly startled look. Once he even played a leprechaun. He made his debut during the silent era and when pictures started talking, he started talking, too. He made his sound debut in *There's Always a Woman* (1938). **Films include:** *Golden Boy* (1939), *The Best Years of Our Lives* (1946), *Saintly Sinners* (1962), *Jack the Giant Killer* (1962), *The Impossible Years* (1968).

ALFONSO BEDOYA (1904–1957)

Mexican-born Bedoya is best remembered as Gold Hat, the laughing bandit in *The Treasure of Sierra Madre* (1948), his Hollywood debut. A veteran of more than 100 Mexican and American films, he specialized mostly in sinister, bad-man roles. **Highlights:** *The Streets of Laredo* (1949), *The Black Rose* (1950), *Sombrero* (1952), *The Big Country* (1958).

JANET BEECHER (1884–1955)

The daughter of the German Consul to Chicago, Janet Beecher originally came to New York in the early 1900's with the intention of studying art, but she was soon swept into films. As befits someone with her background, she played proper mothers and other ladylike roles until her retirement in 1943. **Films include:** *Gallant Lady* (1934), *The Dark Angel* (1935), *Bitter Sweet* (1940), *Reap the Wild Wind* (1942), *Silver Queen* (1943).

NOAH BEERY (1884–1946)

Noah Beery, who had a long career as a screen villain in both silents and talkies, was a

Noah Beery and Jetta Goudal back in the days when villains wore earrings and screen sirens always appeared to lapse into a semi-catatonic state. The film was The Great Chase.

between-the-acts hawker at the old Gillis Theatre in Kansas City, Missouri, when his booming voice caught the ear of an actor. He recommended that Beery take singing lessons which led first to the stage and eventually to a screen career. Half-brother of the famous Wallace Beery, his favorite role was the hard-boiled army sergeant in *Beau Geste* (1926). **Films include:** *The Mark of Zorro* (1920), *The Four Feathers* (1929), *She Done Him Wrong* (1933), *The Bad Man of Brimstone* (1938), *This Man's Navy* (1945).

NOAH BEERY, JR. (1916–   )

He always felt that being the son and nephew of well-known actors was a mixed blessing. While producers and directors expected him to resemble Wallace and Noah, Sr., he managed to escape being typecast, perhaps because he never could look particularly villainous in films. Starting as a child actor in the silent days, his first important role which brought him critical recognition came

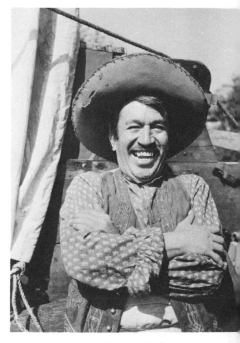

Mexican actor Alfonso Bedoya in Man in the Saddle.

Wallace Beery, with Marie Dressler, engaged in an hilarious love-hate relationship in Min and Bill *and the pair scored again in* Tugboat Annie.

Ed Begley appeared with Michael Caine in Billion Dollar Brain *(1967).*

when he played a doomed aviator in *Only Angels Have Wings* (1939). **Films include:** *Of Mice and Men* (1940), *Gung Ho!* (1944), *Red River* (1948), *The Story of Will Rogers* (1952), *Inherit the Wind* (1960), *Incident at Phantom Hill* (1965).

WALLACE BEERY (1886–1949)

He was at his best playing out-and-out villains or lovable rogues and is probably best remembered for his performances with Marie Dressler in *Min and Bill* (1930) and *Tugboat Annie* (1933).

The big, shuffling actor, whose gravelly voice often sounded as though he was speaking baby-talk, was the son of a Kansas City policeman. As the story goes, Beery ran away from home to tend elephants in a circus. He played on Broadway soon after the turn of the century and made his first film appearances in 1913 as a thickheaded Swedish maid in the *Swedie* series. Briefly married to Gloria Swanson, he was a Hun who tried to rape Blanche Sweet in *The Unpardonable Sin* (1919) and played the equally bad Magua in *The Last of the Mohicans* (1921).

After innumerable silents, perhaps his best performance came early in the era of sound when he led the prison uprising in *The Big House* (1930). He was a complete monster in that one but turned almost saccharine the following year when he shared with Fredric March the Oscar for Best Actor for his performance as the rogue who befriended Jackie Cooper in *The Champ*. His portrayal left audiences around the world dissolved in tears. He was quite wonderful, also, as Pancho Villa in *Viva Villa* (1934) and (again with Jackie Cooper) as Long John Silver in *Treasure Island* (1934).

Beery remained among the top money making stars for some years and was still going strong when he died of a heart attack after making *Big Jack*, his last film. **Other highlights:** *Hell Divers* (1931), *Grand Hotel* (1932), *Dinner at Eight* (1933), *Ah! Wilderness* (1936), *The Man From Dakota* (1940), *The Mighty McGurk* (1946).

ED BEGLEY (1901–1970)

When Begley played on stage opposite Paul Muni in *Inherit the Wind,* Muni had it written into his contract that if Begley stopped playing William Jennings Bryan, Muni himself would stop playing Darrow. As Muni explained, "I didn't see Ed Begley playing opposite me, I saw Bryan."

Begley's film roles, however, have been generally less histrionic. He has often played harassed or pretentious characters. Begley came to films after many successful years on the stage and was awarded Hollywood's top honor as Best Supporting Actor for *Sweet Bird of Youth* (1962). **Films include:** *The Great Gatsby* (1949), *Twelve Angry Men* (1957), *The Unsinkable Molly Brown* (1964), *Wild in the Streets* (1968).

HARRY BELAFONTE (1927–   )

Among his occasional films is *Carmen Jones* (1954), a contemporary version of the Bizet opera, with an all-black cast. Belafonte played Don José, modernized as an Army sergeant.

His calypso singing style has been popularized on television and records, as has his trademark—a low-cut shirt. **Highlights:** *Island in the Sun* (1957), *The World, the Flesh and the Devil* (1958), *Odds Against Tomorrow* (1959), *The Angel Levine* (1969).

BARBARA BEL GEDDES (1922–   )

The blonde, pertly pretty actress is not often seen, but makes her rare appearances on stage and screen worth waiting for. Highly discretionary in the selection of her scripts, Bel Geddes has limited her "visibility," perhaps unwisely at times.

Bel Geddes began her performing career on stage with a stock company. She made her Broadway debut at the age of 20 in *Out of the Frying Pan*. Thereafter she alternated between Broadway, stock and USO appearances. Following her successful stage role in *Deep Are the Roots* she was called to Hollywood and made her film debut in *The Long Night* (1947). This film was followed with the very successful *I Remember Mama* (1948).

In 1950 she returned to the stage (making occasional forays back to Hollywood) and to such productions as *The Moon Is Blue, Cat on a Hot Tin Roof,* and her great success *Mary, Mary*. In between, Bel Geddes has also made an occasional appearance on television. **Films include:** *Panic in the Streets*

Ralph Bellamy presents his case to Carole Lombard in Fools for Scandal *in 1938. As usual, he was rejected.*

(1950), *Fourteen Hours* (1951), *Vertigo* (1958), *Summertree* (1971).

JAMES BELL (1891–   )

During a career of more than 30 years, he played just about every type of supporting role in the actors' handbook: good guys and bad guys, leathernecks and detectives, zombie hunters and generals. **Films include:** *I Am a Fugitive From a Chain Gang* (1942), *My Friend Flicka* (1943), *The Sea of Grass* (1947), *The Glenn Miller Story* (1954), *Huck* (1956), *Twilight of Honor* (1963).

MADGE BELLAMY (1903–   )

When only 17, Madge Bellamy appeared on the stage with William Gillette in *Dear Brutus* and was billed as "The Most Beautiful Girl on Broadway." Her fragile features and ethereal look disguised an iron will.

She was signed to films by Thomas Ince in 1918 and in 1923 starred in the first screen version of *Lorna Doone*. Her days as a Hollywood star were relatively brief. Bellamy gave as the reason:"I wanted too much money, and when it was not forthcoming, I quit." **Her films include:** *The Riddle Woman* (1918), *Bertha, the Sewing Machine Girl* (1927), *Mother Knows Best* (1928).

Jean-Paul Belmondo and Claudia Cardinale in a pensive mood. The picture, La Viaccia, *was made in 1962.*

RALPH BELLAMY (1904–   )

As a young film actor, Ralph Bellamy was always the one who never got the girl. He extended this role to parody in *His Girl Friday* (1941). Later he grew into more substantial roles. In 1959, Bellamy left Hollywood to act on Broadway in *Sunrise at Campobello* and the following year he starred as Franklin Delano Roosevelt in the film version. Twice president of Actors Equity, he was drafted for a third term, not unlike the character he immortalized in *Campobello*. **Films include:** *Surrender* (1929), *The Awful Truth* (1937), *Boy Meets Girl* (1938), *The Court Martial of*

Robert Benchley, one of America's funniest writers, loved acting as well. This scene is from Three Girls About Town *(1941), with Joan Blondell.*

Billy Mitchell (1955), *Rosemary's Baby* (1968).

JEAN-PAUL BELMONDO (1933–   )

The French actor moved on screen with the alert slouch of a boxer. He was, in fact, an amateur boxer, and even had his nose broken, but not while he was in the ring.

With his laconic speech and battered face, Belmondo was catapulated to fame as the alienated gangster in *Breathless* (1961). He wasn't content just being the major anti-hero of the 60's; he chose to play several fast-moving comedy roles, notably in *That Man From Rio* (1964), a literal catalogue of suspense clichés. **Memorable films:** *Two Women* (1961), *Is Paris Burning?* (1966), *Mississippi Mermaid* (1969), *The Inheritor* (1973).

ROBERT BENCHLEY (1889–1945)

He was an outstanding dramatic critic, author of what are perhaps the funniest essays written in this century, and one of the leaders of the Thanatopsis Club, the group that included Dorothy Parker and George S. Kaufman and which, from its poker-playing headquarters in New York's Hotel Algonquin, managed to have a substantial impact on the American theatre.

Harvard educated, Benchley made his Broadway debut in *The Music Box Revue* (1923) doing a monologue he wrote himself. Later he wrote, directed and acted in a wildly funny succession of movie shorts. One of them, *How to Sleep* (1935), in which he managed to assume sleeping postures that had never before been dreamed of, won the Academy Award as Best Short Subject of the year.

Benchley's glorious sense of the absurd caused him to appear in many films, almost always as a well-meaning bumbler. **Credits include:** *Dancing Lady* (1935), *Foreign Correspondent* (1940), *The Major and the Minor* (1942), *I Married a Witch* (1942), *The Bride Wore Boots* (1946).

WILLIAM BENDIX (1906–1964)

William Bendix once said, "I didn't go to high school, so how could I be a doctor or a lawyer? I was a semi-pro in baseball, a semi-pro in football and got the gate as a grocery clerk. I can't sing, I can't dance, I can't play an instrument, what's left but acting?'' His first break after a spotty theatrical career came in Saroyan's *The Time of Your Life* (1939) leading to his film debut as a funny, shadow-boxing barkeep in *Woman of the Year* (1942). It was his role as the hired killer in *The Glass Key* (1942), however, which established him on the screen.

For 24 years he alternated between comic and dramatic roles. Simultaneously, he created the part of Chester Riley which he played on both radio and television for almost ten years. **His more than 50 films include:** *Lifeboat* (1943), *The Hairy Ape* (1944), *A Bell for Adano* (1945), *The Time of Your Life* (1948), *Detective Story* (1951), *Dangerous Mission* (1954), *For Love or Money* (1963).

RICHARD BENJAMIN (1938–   )

Living for a time in the career shadow of his beautiful and talented wife, Paula Prentiss, Benjamin achieved stardom with his role in *Goodbye, Columbus* (1969). Playing a lower-middle-class librarian against Ali MacGraw's spoiled and rich Radcliffe snob, he struck a responsive chord in movie audiences. Skinny and unglamourous, with a nasal, rather unpleasant voice, Benjamin presented a figure with whom the ''common man'' could identify. He used these characteristics again to create another memorable, if less likeable, character in *Diary of a Mad Housewife* (1971)—in which his portrayal of the whining, social-climbing husband made most viewers abhor the character but admire the actor. His movie roles thus far have established Benjamin as an intelligent and sensitive actor. **Films include:** *Catch-22* (1969), *Portnoy's Complaint* (1972), *The Last of Sheila* (1973), *Westworld* (1973).

CONSTANCE BENNETT (1905–1965)

The oldest of the three Bennett sisters (Joan follows this entry and Barbara had but a short career) began her movie activities in 1922 and was starred at the age of 19 with Lewis Stone in *Cytherea*. With the introduction of sound she became one of the screen favorites in the United States and England at a then record-breaking salary of close to $40,000 a week.

During the period she was billed as ''the highest paid actress in the world'' her picture

Rough, tough, but mostly warm-hearted Bill Bendix's presence lent a great deal to every movie he played in. This one was Lifeboat.

material was pretty bad, a notable exception being the now forgotten *What Price Hollywood?* (1932), an early version of *A Star Is Born*. She was a Hollywood waitress who became a leading lady in that one, but in other films she usually was a kept woman, a hooker or a spy.

In the late 30's Hollywood discovered that she was excellent at comedy. She made a great hit as Cary Grant's co-ghost in *Topper* (1937) and scored again with Brian Aherne in *Merrily We Live* (1938).

Her career ebbed and in the 50's she had only small screen parts, and supplemented her career with television appearances, a night club act and tours in such hit plays as *Auntie Mame* and *Toys in the Attic*. Her career also included several business ventures and five husbands. **Some other films:** *Common Clay* (1930), *Moulin Rouge* (1934), *Ladies in Love* (1936), *Topper Takes a Trip* (1938), *Two-Faced Woman* (1941), *Centennial Summer* (1946), *As Young As You Feel* (1951), *Madame X* (1966).

Philip Roth's novel Goodbye, Columbus *was transformed into one of the top pictures of the late 60's and a sparkling performance by Richard Benjamin (here with Ali MacGraw) helped immeasurably.*

Joan Bennett, with George Raft, in House Across the Bay *(1940) in one of her brunette glamour roles.*

JOAN BENNETT (1910–)

The youngest of actor Richard Bennett's three acting daughters was a highly professional performer throughout a career that lasted more than 30 years. She began in ingénue roles, played heroines, femmes fatales, and ended up in comedy, making an amusing wife to Spencer Tracy's *Father of the Bride* (1951).

She began her film career as an extra in *The Divine Lady* (1928) and went on to play lead roles before becoming a star. Adept at comedy and tragic roles alike, she was distinctly handicapped by an endless succession of third-rate scripts—a good example being *Maybe It's Love*, a 1931 epic with Joe E. Brown and the All-American Football Team. When a good picture came along, such as Fritz Lang's *The Woman in the Window* (1944), in which she played the siren who converted Edward G. Robinson from a professor to a murderer, her performance was beyond reproach.

Like that of sister Constance, her off-screen life was somewhat tumultuous. She became a mother at 16 and had her first divorce at 18. Big headlines came her way in 1951 when her third husband, producer Walter Wanger, shot her agent whom she was talking to in a Hollywood parking lot. Thereafter only small film roles came her way though she did appear on stage and television. **Films include:** *Bulldog Drummond* (1929), *Little Women* (1933), *Mississippi* (1935), *Valley of the Giants* (1938), *The Song of Bernadette* (1943), *Duel in the Sun* (1946), *Johnny Belinda* (1948), *The Big Country* (1958), *A Big Hand for the Little Lady* (1966), *House of Dark Shadows* (1970).

JACK BENNY (1894–)

As virtually everyone knows, he was born Benny Kubelsky in Waukegan, Illinois, never passed the age of 39, drives an extremely ancient Maxwell, is the stingiest man alive, and was a disaster in movies.

The last of these statements, although part of Jack's comic routine, does not conform to the facts. He made more than 20 movies and in several both Benny and the film were great—with Carole Lombard in *To Be or Not to Be* (1942) and in the same year with Ann Sheridan in *George Washington Slept Here*.

It is true that Benny, whose place in both radio and television Halls of Fame is secure, appeared to prefer films least as a mode of expression. His first great success came on the vaudeville stage and his deadpan build up of his own character—part coward, part miser, part violin virtuoso—seems to register best via television or a live audience. **Films include:** *The Hollywood Revue of 1929* (debut), *Medicine Man* (1930), *Buck Benny Rides Again* (1940), *The Horn Blows at Midnight* (1945), *Beau James* (1957), *A Guide for the Married Man* (1967).

MARISA BERENSON (1947–)

The granddaughter of the late fashion designer, Elsa Schiaparelli, and grandniece of the late Bernard Berenson, the world's foremost authority on Renaissance art, Miss Berenson has a style all her own. Among other achievements, *Vogue* magazine chose her in 1970 as its first nude model. An accomplished linguist, she played sensitive, timid,

Jack Benny's violin playing always had surprising effects on his listeners. He is greeted with mixed emotions by (l. to r.) Gracie Allen, Louis Da Pron, Mary Boland, and George Burns in College Holiday *(1936).*

delicate, but highly perceptive young women in her first motion picture appearances, and was warmly received by the critics and public alike. **Highlights:** *Death in Venice* (1972), *Cabaret* (1972), *Everything-Plus* (1974), *How to Make It in a Man's World* (1974).

CANDICE BERGEN (1946–)

The daughter of ventriloquist Edgar Bergen, her first important role was as the beautiful lesbian in Mary McCarthy's *The Group* (1966). She was featured in several films of the late 60's before her major part as one of the luckless women in *Carnal Knowledge* (1971), Jules Feiffer's tragi-comedy of American mores. The talented Bergen is also a photo-journalist and dramatist. **Films include:** *The Sand Pebbles* (1966), *The Day the Fish Came Out* (1967), *Live for Life* (1967), *The Magus* (1968), *The Plot* (1970).

POLLY BERGEN (1919–)

A woman of many talents, Polly Bergen is known for her light and pleasing personality. She has been variously a hillbilly singer, a teletype operator, a model, and a waitress.

Though best known for her radio and television work, she has to her credit several Dean Martin–Jerry Lewis movies. **Films include:** *Warpath* (1951), *Cape Fear* (1962), *The Caretakers* (1963), *Move Over, Darling* (1963), *Kisses for My President* (1964), *A Guide for the Married Man* (1967).

INGRID BERGMAN (1915–)

The second of the great Swedish stars was, like Garbo, born in Stockholm. A print of one of the early movies she made there, *Intermezzo*, caused David Selznick to bring her to the United States for a remake under the title *Intermezzo, A Love Story* (1939). The film, with Leslie Howard as the famous musician who conducts an illicit love affair with a young pianist, overnight made Bergman the hottest property in moviedom.

Her healthy good looks, intelligence, charm and unaffected sexuality—combined with a very considerable acting talent—made her the top box office attraction. One hit picture followed another: *Casablanca* in 1942, *For Whom the Bells Toll* a year later, *Gaslight*, which brought her the Academy Award as Best Actress in 1944, *Spellbound*

Candice Bergen in The Magus. *The weird creature behind her is not Charlie McCarthy.*

which resulted in a similar presentation from the New York critics in 1945.

Then with bewildering suddenness, the roof fell in. She had gone to Italy to make a film for director Roberto (*Open City*) Rossellini, fallen in love and candidly admitted that she was soon to bear his baby. Even though she asserted that her former marriage was long since washed up, and was quickly wedded to Rossellini, the public which had so venerated Bergman furiously rejected her and the film, *Stromboli,* which she had been making.

During the next six years she had a dreadful time. The marriage collapsed and the few films she made abroad were flops. It wasn't until she made *Anastasia* (1957) in England that she was welcomed back into the fold by her fans. Bergman was given both the Academy Award and the New York Critics Award for her performance as the supposedly living daughter of Tsar Nicholas of Russia.

Ingrid Bergman's beauty shines twice in this bit from perhaps her most popular role in surely one of the most popular movies of all time, Casablanca.

Elisabeth Bergner was another of Hollywood's imports from Europe as Hitler ascended in Germany. Miss Bergner was not always properly used, but invariably excellent.

Films include: *Rage in Heaven* (1941), *Spellbound* (1945), *Saratoga Trunk* (1945), *Notorious* (1946), *Joan of Arc* (1948), *Indiscreet* (1958), *The Yellow Rolls-Royce* (1965), *Cactus Flower* (1969).

ELISABETH BERGNER (1900–   )

Elisabeth Bergner was Germany's most popular actress before she left to make films in France and England. She was in England shooting *Catherine the Great* (1934) when Hitler came to power and she didn't return to Germany.

The actress was utterly unfamiliar with the social and working patterns of Hollywood. It was said when she first arrived in the film capital, ''her gamine ways make you want to adopt her straight off.'' When asked the secret of great acting she replied, ''I wish I knew.'' **Films include:** *Escape Me Never* (1935), *As You Like It* (1936), *A Stolen Life* (1939), *Paris Calling* (1942).

MILTON BERLE (1908–   )

As a child actor, Berle appeared in the silent *Perils of Pauline* series, but he spent more time on the vaudeville stage under the watchful eye of his stage mother, who more often than not sat in the audience supplying strategic laughter and applause.

He said of his Hollywood career, ''They used me for everything but what I was suited for. I had to get out before they cast me as Fred Astaire's dancing partner—with curls.'' Thereafter ''Uncle Miltie'' reigned as the king of television in that medium's earliest days. **Films include:** *New Faces of 1937*, *Sun Valley Serenade* (1941), *Margin for Error* (1943), *Always Leave Them Laughing* (his autobiography, 1949), *It's a Mad, Mad, Mad, Mad World* (1963), *The Oscar* (1965), *For Singles Only* (1968).

TURHAN BEY (1920–   )

Until loyal fans started complaining, the tall, handsome, exotic-looking Turkish actor was invariably killed off in the middle of the action. He was thereafter cast in more life-preserving roles. Bey arrived in Hollywood with a price on his head after he fought as a mercenary soldier in the Turkish Army on the side that lost. Later, he returned to Vienna, his birthplace, and became a photographer. **Highlights:** *Footsteps in the Dark* (debut, 1941), *Dragon Seed* (1944), *Adventures of Casanova* (1948), *Song of India* (1949).

CHARLES BICKFORD (1889–1967)

After going through an early repertoire of vocations as an engineering student, logger, carnival barker and, if it can be called a vocation, vagabond in China, Bickford landed a job with a Boston stock company and began a theatrical career that stretched well over a half-century. Cecil B. DeMille brought him to Hollywood and he made his debut in *Dynamite* (1929), an early talkie.

In short order Bickford was recognized as one of moviedom's great stand-by performers, capable of taking on almost any sort of role on short notice and bringing to it a complete feeling of reality. **More than 100 films include:** *Anna Christie* (1930), *The Song of Bernadette* (1943), *Johnny Belinda* (1948), *A Star Is Born* (1954), *Days of Wine and Roses* (1963).

THEODORE BIKEL (1924–   )

The portly actor once said, ''It isn't true that a man can do only one thing well, this is a fallacy in our thinking; specialization has many disadvantages.'' Apparently taking his

Milton Berle looks highly clean-cut in this shot with Joan Davis in Sun Valley Serenade.

own advice to heart, Bikel plays roles which rarely resemble each other. He has been as old as 83 in one film and as young as 25 in another. He is a guitarist and singer of great talent and can convincingly portray many nationalities. **Film credits include:** *The African Queen* (1952), *The Defiant Ones* (1958), *The Blue Angel* (1959), *My Fair Lady* (1964), *The Russians Are Coming, The Russians Are Coming* (1966), *Sweet November* (1968), *Darker Than Amber* (1970).

HERMAN BING (1899–1947)

Bing built a career on his thick German accent which he used whenever necessary after he emigrated from Germany in the 20's. First a comedian, Bing became an adept dialectician. He mastered several accents which he used to give dimension to his generally overwrought characters.

A technician as well as a performer, Bing once worked as an assistant to the distinguished director F. W. Murnau. **Films include:** *Dinner at Eight* (1933), *Call of the Wild* (1934), *The Great Ziegfeld* (1936), *Maytime* (1937), *Where Do We Go From Here?* (1945).

JULIE BISHOP (1917–   )

Born Jacqueline Brown in Denver, she changed her name to Jacqueline Wells and faked a Texan accent in order to play cowgirls. Losing enthusiasm for cattle handling, she left Hollywood to perform in summer stock. On returning to Hollywood, she became Julie Bishop and began a new career as a leading lady.

She was said to have "an almost perfect shoulder line" and "all the physical requirements of the modern medusa." **Films include:** *Alice in Wonderland* (1933), *The Bohemian Girl* (1936), *The Nurse's Secret* (1941), *Rhapsody in Blue* (1945), *Sands of Iwo Jima* (1949), *Westward the Women* (1952), *The High and the Mighty* (1954), *The Big Land* (1957).

JACQUELINE BISSET (1945–   )

As has happened to film beauties before, the sumptuous physical dimensions of this British-born actress of French descent were, at times, a hindrance rather than a help. Her

Charles Bickford in a characteristically sympathetic role in Johnny Belinda, *flanked by Lew Ayres and Jane Wyman. Agnes Moorehead and Hume Cronyn are in the background.*

movie debut was in Polanski's *Cul de Sac* in which she was cast as a non-speaking sex symbol. Next she played Giovanna Goodthighs in *Casino Royale* (1967), nomenclature which tells the whole story. Finally, playing lead roles opposite Steve McQueen and Frank Sinatra, producers discovered both her voice and her natural ability and, under more recent direction by François Truffaut, she appears headed for the top. **Other films:** *The Detective* (1968), *Airport* (1969), *The Thief Who Came to Dinner* (1973), *Day for Night* (1973).

GUNNAR BJÖRNSTRAND (1909–   )

The Swedish actor was a member of the troupe of actors who appeared regularly in Ingmar Bergman's films. Though remembered for his role as the cold, analytical novelist in *Through a Glass Darkly* (1961), he was not always a picture of gloom. One writer described Björnstrand in *Winter Light* (1962) as "elegantly stiff, yet slightly droll." He has done some comedy roles as well. **Films include:** *Frenzy* (1944), *The Naked Night* (1953), *Smiles of a Summer Night* (1955), *The Seventh Seal* (1956), *Wild Strawberries* (1959), *Persona* (1966).

KAREN BLACK (1943–   )

Her first appearance in *Five Easy Pieces* (1970) brought her the New York Film Critics Award as Best Supporting Actress, along with an Academy Award nomination. That overnight success brought her the role of "Monkey" in the film adaptation of Philip Roth's *Portnoy's Complaint* (1972). Of the part she said, candidly, "I was sure it was a winner when I read the script . . . it's so dirty." She was wrong, for the film was a bust. Miss Black, however, found her services more in demand than ever. **Other films include:** *Born to Win* (1971), *Drive, He Said* (1971), *Cisco Pike* (1973).

SIDNEY BLACKMER (1898–1973)

He was often seen in serials back in the dawn of movies, often as one of the dangers Pearl White faced in *The Perils of Pauline*. With talkies his services were much in demand and he appeared in nearly 100 films, usually as a city slicker, suave con-man or soft spoken army officer or medico. In *This Is My Affair* (1937) he played Theodore Roosevelt, the first of 14 films in which he played the inimitable Teddy. Perhaps his greatest triumph was on Broadway in 1950 in *Come Back, Little Sheba*.

He entertained lavishly in private life and one of his enemies described him as "the sort of person who rehearses his conversation and repeats it with graceful accuracy." **Films include:** *Little Caesar* (1931), *The Count of Monte Cristo* (1934), *Duel in the Sun* (1947), *High Society* (1956), *Rosemary's Baby* (1968).

JANET BLAIR (1921–   )

A former band singer, Miss Blair won rave reviews in the role of Rosalind Russell's slightly madcap younger sister in *My Sister Eileen* (1942), and in fact, Miss Russell insisted she be given star billing. Nothing later quite matched that role, however, and she found herself playing a series of bland ingenue parts, only somewhat livened by her singing and dancing. "All I got were princess parts," she complained. "A girl gets awful tired of being a princess all the time." **Films include:** *Two Yanks in Trinidad* (1942), *Tonight and Every Night* (1945), *The Fabulous Dorseys* (1947), *Burn, Witch, Burn* (1962).

ROBERT BLAKE (1934–   )

He began his career as a child performer in the *Our Gang* films of the 30's and it wasn't until he played the mass murderer Perry Smith in the film version of Truman Capote's grisly documentary *In Cold Blood* (1967) that he achieved his first popular success.

The high spot of Blake's career to date came when he played the title role in *Tell Them Willie Boy Is Here* (1970), directed by Abraham Polonsky, one of the brilliant technicians who for years had been banished from Hollywood as a result of the McCarthy witch-hunts. **Other credits:** *Pork Chop Hill* (1959), *The Purple Gang* (1960), *This Property Is Condemned* (1966), *Electra Glide in Blue* (1973).

CLARA BLANDICK (1881–1962)

Though few will remember her name, Clara Blandick has been seen by millions over the years as Dorothy's (Judy Garland's) Aunt Emily in *The Wizard of Oz* (1939)—and she also played Aunt Polly in the 1930 movie version of *Tom Sawyer*. Earlier she had portrayed the screen's first dual-personality role in *A Woman* (1908). Then came the roles as sensible aunts, servants, mothers, and grandmothers in a career that spanned 40 years of film making. At the age of 81, she committed suicide. **Films include:** *The Easiest Way* (1931), *One Foot in Heaven* (1941), *Life With Father* (1947), *Love That Brute* (1950).

SALLY BLANE (1910–   )

She was born Elizabeth Jane Young, the sister of Loretta, and made her screen debut at the age of eight in a film called *Siren of the Sea*. She was already a full-fledged ingénue in *The Collegians* (1927), her first adult role. By the 30's, Sally was playing strenuous roles in forgettable Westerns and retired at the end of the decade. **Films include:** *Fools for Luck* (1928), *Shanghai Love* (1931), *I Am a Fugitive From a Chain Gang* (1932), *A Bullet for Joey* (1955).

JOAN BLONDELL (1909–   )

In the glittering prosperity that preceded the Wall Street crash of 1929, Joan Blondell almost despaired of a permanent career on stage or screen and took such unlikely jobs as that of clerk in a New York bookshop. Less than two years later, as the world depression deepened, she set what must be a Hollywood record by appearing in 32 pictures in 27 months and freely admitted she was "Warner Brothers' work horse."

Christened Rosebud Blondell (her sister's given name was Lover) by a somewhat sentimental mother, she came from a family of vaudevillians and appeared on stage with them in her early years. Bit parts in Broadway plays were few and far between and it wasn't until she landed a lead role in *Penny Arcade* that a Warner scout noticed her and offered a Hollywood tryout, along with another youngster in the same cast, a stocky little actor named James Cagney. Her screen debut in 1930 was in *Office Wife* and while she did little but look saucy and waggle her rear end attractively as she crossed the screen, it proved enough to elicit whistles and other signs of approval from audiences and to convince Warners that they had something pretty good.

While she never was a great star, Blondell remained among moviedom's most popular featured players for a good 12 years. A complete professional, she almost always played loyal, breezy, fast-talking and slightly cynical blondes in films that ranged from *Public Enemy* (1931) to *Cry Havoc* (1943). It was said that she never once gave a bad performance.

After marriages to three husbands—photographer George Scott Barnes, singing star Dick Powell and entrepreneur Mike Todd—she found herself nearly penniless, her looks gone and her services no longer in demand. With great courage she fought back via television, off-Broadway stage productions and small parts in movies like *The Cincinnati Kid* (as a card-dealer, 1965) and *The Phynx* (1970). Her first novel, which was highly praised, was published in 1973. **More than 100 films include:** *Union Depot* (1932), *Footlight Parade* (1933), *Three Men on a Horse* (1937), *A Tree Grows in Brooklyn* (1944), *The Blue Veil* (Academy Award nomination, 1951), *Will Success Spoil Rock Hunter?* (1958), *Support Your Local Sheriff* (1971).

Joan Blondell shows her latest bauble to Ginger Rogers in Broadway Bad *(1933), a typical early show-biz movie.*

CLAIRE BLOOM (1931–   )

As a young schoolgirl in England she saw Norma Shearer play Juliet, went home, and proceeded to memorize every line Shakespeare had written for the Veronese maiden.

Her dedication to acting has never flagged. As Charles Chaplin, who cast her as the dancer in his 1952 production, *Limelight*, said, "Claire has distinction, enormous range, and underneath her sadness there is a bubbling humor, so unexpected, so wistful."

In recent years the huge-eyed and talented brunette has played a wide variety of taxing roles with sensitivity and perception. **Films include:** *Richard III* (1956), *Look Back in Anger* (1959), *The Chapman Report* (1962), *The Spy Who Came in From the Cold* (1965), *Three Into Two Won't Go* (1969), *A Doll's House* (1973).

ERIC BLORE (1887–1959)

Rarely appearing without a tray or a clothes brush, he played the gentleman's gentleman,

Claire Bloom had a role she could sink her teeth into in A Doll's House.

54

The hanger is the inevitable clue to Eric Blore's role as a gentleman's gentleman, played in a score of movies.

the butler, the waiter—all with pained tolerance and comic exasperation.

Blore came to the United States in 1923 from his native London to appear in an Irene Bordoni vehicle, but it was his role on Broadway as the waiter in *The Gay Divorcee* with Fred Astaire which led to his screen debut when he recreated the role in 1934. At one point he appeared in as many as 26 movies in two years. **More than 70 films include:** *Top Hat* (1935), *It's Love I'm After* (1937), *Sullivan's Travels* (1942), *The Moon and Sixpence* (1942), *Holy Matrimony* (1943), *Kitty* (1946), *Love Happy* (1950).

BEN BLUE (1901–   )

A rubber-limbed comedian, Ben Blue started in vaudeville in 1916 and made his first film in 1926. He was known off-screen for his avocations; that of nightclub owner and heavy gambler. In addition, his relationships with the other sex and the Internal Revenue Service received wide publicity. **Films include:** *College Rhythm* (1933), *For Me and My Gal* (1942), *My Wild Irish Rose* (1947), *It's A Mad, Mad, Mad, Mad World* (1963), *The Russians Are Coming, the Russians Are Coming* (1966), *Where Were You When the Lights Went Out?* (1968).

MONTE BLUE (1890–1963)

Monte Blue's experience as a miner, cowboy, and lumberjack prepared him for the rough and tumble life on the movie lot. In 1926 it was reported that he single-handedly saved several extras' lives by averting a train wreck, and in 1932, he rescued a young actress from a burning set.

He started his career as a script clerk and stunt man and appeared in Griffith's *Intolerance* in 1915. Though a popular silent star, he abandoned films for a time with the advent of talkies, which he felt were "trash." But he soon changed his mind and resumed a film career that was to span four decades. **Films include:** *Affairs of Anatol* (1921), *Lives of a Bengal Lancer* (1935), *Dodge City*

A troubled Dirk Bogarde leans on a tombstone in this scene from Darling, *with Julie Christie.*

(1939), *The Mask of Dimitrios* (1944), *Apache* (1954).

ANN BLYTH (1928–   )

Ann Blyth began her film career singing and dancing along with Donald O'Connor, though she is best remembered for her dramatic role in *Mildred Pierce* (1945) as Joan Crawford's undeserving daughter. During the late 50's she appeared in several show business biographies. **Highlights:** *Chip Off the Old Block* (1943), *The Great Caruso* (1951), *Rose Marie* (1954), *The Helen Morgan Story* (1957), *The Buster Keaton Story* (1957).

BETTY BLYTHE (1893–1972)

Betty Blythe was acting on stage in New York when one day she went to visit the old Vitagraph studios in Brooklyn and was cast in her first film.

She became a leading silent star, best known for her performance in *The Queen of Sheba* (1921). In 1964 she came out of retirement to play an extra in *My Fair Lady*. **Films include:** *Chu Chin Chow* (1925), *The Girl From Gay Paris* (1927), *Eager Lips* (1930), *Tom Brown of Culver* (1932), *Misbehaving Husbands* (1940).

ELEANOR BOARDMAN (1898–   )

One of Hollywood's true-life Cinderella girls, she was selected out of more than a thousand entries as the likeliest new screen personality and went on to become a leading lady in the 20's and the wife of director King Vidor.

If for no other reason she must be remembered for her brilliant performance in what many still believe to be the best silent picture ever made—*The Crowd* (1928). **Other films include:** *Souls for Sale* (1923), *Three Wise Fools* (1923), *Memory Lane* (1926), *The Squaw Man* (1931).

DIRK BOGARDE (1920–   )

The versatile British actor has appeared in some 40 films in such varying roles as artist, gangster, suicide, and prison escapee. Bogarde won wide acclaim for his etched-in-acid performance in *The Servant* (1963).

He is a careful craftsman. For his role as Franz Liszt in *Song Without End* (1960), he spent over 100 hours learning the fingering to piano music. **Films include:** *Esther Waters* (debut, 1947), *Darling* (1965), *Accident* (1967), *The Fixer* (1968), *The Damned* (1969), *Death in Venice* (1971).

HUMPHREY BOGART (1899–1957)

The most legendary of all Hollywood's legends wasn't handsome. His eyes appeared to have a myopic squint. His voice rasped and his clothes never seemed to quite fit him. Yet women adored him—perhaps because he was tough but courteous, perhaps for other reasons. Men did too—perhaps because they identified with him and his particular approach to life. Whatever the reasons of either sex, Humphrey Bogart's place in the Pantheon of movie greats is secure. As Pauline Kael said several years ago: "There isn't an actor in American films today with anything like his assurance, his magnetism or his style."

He was born in New York and his wealthy parents weren't happy when he took to the stage in 1920. Neither was critic Alexander Woollcott, who wrote of one of his first roles: "(he) . . . is what is usually and mercifully described as inadequate." Nonetheless, assignments in both films and plays came with relative ease and he made his first major appearance on Broadway in 1935 as Duke Mantee, the itchy-fingered gangster in Robert Sherwood's *The Petrified Forest*. The play's star, Leslie Howard, convinced Warner Brothers to cast him in the same role in the film version and he drew ecstatic notices. With unique short-sightedness, however, Warners withheld starring parts from him and Bogart is quoted by Richard Gehman as saying that he was shot, hanged, electrocuted or jailed in 29 of his first 34 pictures. "I played more scenes writhing around on the floor than I did standing up."

His big breakthrough came in 1941 when George Raft turned down the role of an aging gangster in *High Sierra* because he didn't want to die in the end. Director Raoul Walsh gave the part to Bogart. A bit later another Raft turndown caused John Huston to cast Bogie as Sam Spade in *The Maltese Falcon* and at long last he reached the top of the Hollywood ladder. With Ingrid Bergman, and aided mightily by Claude Rains, he made

Humphrey Bogart's most famous early role was as Duke Mantee in The Petrified Forest, *and here he menaces Bette Davis and Leslie Howard in the roadhouse where all the action takes place.*

The African Queen *(1951) co-starred Humphrey Bogart with Katharine Hepburn. Both played their unlikely roles superbly, with relish and wit, and Bogart won the Academy Award.*

Mary Boland struggles with a smiling Charles Laughton in Ruggles of Red Gap, *a picture that literally had audiences rolling in the aisles in 1934.*

Ward Bond is best remembered as seen above—as a capable, no-nonsense Westerner.

the historic *Casablanca* (1943) which won the Academy Award as Best Picture of the Year and made him one of filmdom's top box-office drawing cards.

With a new leading lady, Lauren Bacall, Howard Hawks filmed *To Have and Have Not* in 1944 and the lady who urged Bogart to "whistle" soon became his fourth wife. In short order the couple became Hollywood's equivalent of a royal couple.

An Oscar for the Best Actor of the Year came in 1952, along with Great Britain's Picturegoer Award, when Bogart played the alcoholic navigator who woos and wins Katharine Hepburn in *The African Queen*. Then, two years later, came perhaps his greatest performance, as psychotic Captain Queeg in the film version of Herman Wouk's *The Caine Mutiny*.

In 1957 Humphrey Bogart died of throat cancer. "There will never be anybody like him," John Huston said at his funeral. He was probably right. **Some other films:** *A Devil With Women* (1930), *Love Affair* (1932), *Two Against the World* (1937), *They Drive by Night* (1940), *Across the Pacific* (1942), *The Big Sleep* (1946), *Key Largo* (1948), *We're No Angels* (1955), *The Harder They Fall* (1956).

MARY BOLAND (1882–1965)

In 1954 critic Walter Kerr wrote of her performance in *Lullaby* on Broadway, "She has lost not an ounce of that brazen, badgering and triumphant witlessness which was always her fiercest glory."

At that point Mary Boland had been playing daffy ladies for 35 years. After a brief flurry in silent films she returned to the screen in the 30's to star with Charlie Ruggles in a number of highly successful comedies, notably *Ruggles of Red Gap* (1934). **Highlights:** *The Women* (1939), *People Will Talk* (1951).

JOHN BOLES (1895–1969)

John Boles was discovered by Gloria Swanson while he was singing in a Broadway operetta and appeared with her in his first film, *The Loves of Sunya* (1927).

He was a popular star of 30's musicals before turning to such dramatic roles as the undependable father in *Stella Dallas* (1937). **Highlights:** *The Desert Song* (1930), *Back Street* (1932), *Curly Top* (1935), *Thousands Cheer* (1943), *Babes in Baghdad* (1952).

RAY BOLGER (1904–   )

The lanky rubber-legged dancer and musical comedy star immortalized himself in two roles—the Scarecrow who desperately wanted a brain in *The Wizard of Oz* (1939) and in female garb as Charley's Aunt in the stage and screen versions of *Where's Charley?* (1952).

Highly affable and popular with his fellow players, Bolger once entered a boxing ring while Sugar Ray Robinson and Sidney Miller were engaged in a mock fight. Robinson playfully motioned Bolger to join the fun. The agile dancer did—and, inadvertently, was knocked out. **Films include:** *The Great Ziegfeld* (1936), *Sunny* (1941), *The Harvey Girls* (1946), *April in Paris* (1952), *Babes in Toyland* (1961), *The Daydreamer* (1966).

WARD BOND (1904–1960)

The husky actor began his career as a stock villain in "B" Westerns. Eventually he moved on to better films, often playing a likable roughneck in pictures directed by his lifelong friend John Ford. In the late 50's Bond was back in the saddle as the capable

wagonmaster of the television series *Wagon Train*. **Highlights:** *The Informer* (1935), *Tobacco Road* (1941), *They Were Expendable* (1945), *My Darling Clementine* (1946), *Mister Roberts* (1955).

BEULAH BONDI (1892–)

Before she retired, Beulah Bondi built a considerable repertoire of elderly ladies. Though some of her characters were out of sorts, she was the picture of patience and tact as the displaced mother in *Make Way for Tomorrow* (1937).

Her debut in *Street Scene* (1931) was the first of more than 40 films. **Highlights:** *Rain* (1932), *Our Town* (1940), *Watch on the Rhine* (1943), *The Snake Pit* (1948), *The Big Fisherman* (1959).

PAT BOONE (1934–)

Pat Boone owes his success to his clean-cut image, pleasant manner and good voice. His first screen kiss, or his refusal to deliver one, caused something of a furor.

Boone made his mark as a teenage idol with his mild-manner singing and his white buck shoes. His film debut was as the sunny youth in *Bernadine* (1957). **Films include:** *April Love* (1957), *State Fair* (1962), *Goodbye Charlie* (1965), *The Perils of Pauline* (1967).

RICHARD BOONE (1917–)

A producer once said of him, "I guess I'll need boxing gloves to work with Richard Boone. He's the unbeatable combination of an artist and an intelligent, educated man and a tough hombre." After some training in the Navy and the Actors Studio, Boone made his film debut in *The Halls of Montezuma* (1951). He has become well known as a rugged-character type, particularly in his television series, *Have Gun, Will Travel*. **Films include:** *Return of the Texan* (1952), *The Robe* (1953), *The Alamo* (1960), *A Thunder of Drums* (1961), *The Night of the Following Day* (1969), *Little Big Man* (1970).

SHIRLEY BOOTH (1907–)

Shirley Booth already had a successful stage and radio (*Duffy's Tavern*) career when she created a sensation in the play *Come Back, Little Sheba*. It was said of her perfor-

mance as the dowdy ex-flapper, "she doesn't act, she lives on stage." In 1953 she won an Oscar for her role in the film version and at the Cannes Film Festival was proclaimed "the best actress in the world."

Since she could hardly leave films at that point, Shirley Booth played several more screen roles before beginning her television antics as *Hazel*, the wise-cracking maid. **Films include:** *About Mrs. Leslie* (1954), *Hot Spell* (1958), *The Matchmaker (1959)*.

OLIVE BORDEN (c. 1908–1947)

Olive Borden earned $1500 a week at the peak of her career in 1927, though she died penniless 20 years later. The actress was one of Fox's major stars, appearing in such films as *The Monkey Talks* (1927) and *Pajamas* (1927), but her association with the studio ended abruptly when she refused a salary cut.

A wistful and thinner-than-Hazel Shirley Booth won universal raves for her touching performance in Come Back, Little Sheba.

Ray Bolger in perhaps his best-known role, the Scarecrow in The Wizard of Oz. *His rubber legs and mobile face were great assets. Jack Haley was the Tin Woodman, and Judy Garland, of course, was Dorothy.*

Ernest Borgnine as Marty the butcher pleads with a wistful Betsy Blair who played his girl friend in Marty.

Timothy Bottoms and Liza Minnelli, two then-rising stars, in The Sterile Cuckoo *(1969).*

She ended her career in several films for other studios, the last being *The Social Lion* (1930). **Highlights:** *The Happy Warrior* (1925), *The Secret Studio* (1927), *The Joy Girl* (1927).

VEDA ANN BORG (1915–1973)

This actress was beginning a promising Hollywood career when a serious car accident in 1939 left her literally without a face. Three years later, however, after more than ten plastic surgery operations, she made a comeback in 1942 and continued in scores of films, often playing a wise-cracking, good-natured tart. **Films include:** *San Quentin* (1937), *Two Yanks in Trinidad* (1942), *Forgotten Women* (1949), *Guys and Dolls* (1955), *The Alamo* (1960).

ERNEST BORGNINE (1917–)

The thickset actor first won attention as the sadistic sergeant in *From Here to Eternity* (1953). He had been playing heavies for years before he won wide acclaim as the shy, lonely butcher in Paddy Chayefsky's television drama, *Marty*. The screen re-creation of this role won Borgnine an Academy Award for Best Actor in 1955.

He became immensely popular as Commander McHale in the long-running television series *McHale's Navy* and saw late 60's action in *The Dirty Dozen* (1966) and *The Wild Bunch* (1969). **Other highlights:** *China Corsair* (debut, 1951), *Johnny Guitar* (1954), *Jubal* (1956), *The Flight of the Phoenix* (1965), *Ice Station Zebra* (1968).

HOBART BOSWORTH (1867–1943)

Born just two years after the close of the Civil War, he was a stage favorite for more than 30 years before making his screen debut in *Oliver Twist* (1916). A kind-faced, white-haired gentleman with vast camera presence, he almost always played *important* roles —ministers and judges, industrialists and police captains. He had no trouble converting to talkies and at the time of his death had been an actor for nearly 70 years. **Highlights:** *Vanity Fair* (1923), *The Big Parade* (1925), *A Woman of Affairs* (1929), *Dirigible* (1931), *Lady for a Day* (1933), *Steamboat Around the Bend* (1935), *Sin Town* (1942).

TIMOTHY BOTTOMS (1950–)

It is unlikely that the following conversation could have taken place prior to 1970:

First Movie Producer: "I'm making a great film—all about the law school curricula and a kid who has trouble passing his exams."

Second M.P.: "Oh, wow!"

It is indeed a tribute to the intelligence of today's film makers and the growing sophistication of audiences that a film like *The Paper Chase* (1973) was produced.

Bottoms' first recognition came with his stunning portrayal of Eugene Gant in the 1971 television dramatization of Thomas Wolfe's fine novel *Look Homeward, Angel*. The following year, working under the direction of Peter Bogdanovich, the full range of his ability helped to make *The Last Picture Show* (1972) one of the finest movies of that season. Along with actors like Robert De Niro, Jeff and Beau Bridges and Al Pacino he is now high on the list of exciting young leading men of the 70's. **Other films:** *Love and Pain and the Whole Damn Thing* (1973), *The White Dawn* (1974).

CLARA BOW (1905–1965)

As befitted a Brooklyn girl who was born into a poverty stricken household and grew up to be a teen-age receptionist, her movie roles were almost always waitresses, shop girls or similar menial professions. Movie goers identified with her and to countless female adolescents her cupid-bow lips, bangs, flat chest and hyper-active, bouncy body represented the last word in sexual allure. Although she practiced her come-hither wiles on assorted males in dozens of pictures, Clara was actually on the uptight side, and reacted in horror whenever her screen virginity was even mildly threatened.

Winner of a beauty contest, her first appearance was as a boy in *Down to the Sea in Ships* (1923). B. P. Schulberg took her on and in 1925 released no less than 14 Clara Bow epics bearing such titles as *Parisian Love* and *The Primrose Path*. Her fame grew and reached its peak when she became the "It" girl, starring in the screen version of Elinor Glyn's appallingly bad novel of the same name. "It" meant what Hayworth, Monroe and Raquel Welch possessed in later days and Clara became world famous. More wild party pictures followed (*wild* meant lots of jazz, gin and ruining table tops by dancing on top of them) which culminated in 1929 with *The Saturday Night Kid*. In that year she was the Number One box-office draw.

Her career collapsed with startling suddenness. She was tangled up in an alienation of affections action, charged with failure to pay Nevada gambling debts and a counter-suit brought by a secretary (whom Clara had charged with embezzlement) alleged that drugs and drinks had played a big part in her life. After the trial her films flopped miserably and she married cowboy star Rex Bell and retired to his ranch. A comeback attempt a few years later failed and thereafter she had gained too much weight to take on parts that were occasionally offered her. **Films include:** *Black Oxen* (1924), *Dancing Mothers* (1926), *Wings* (1928), *The Wild Party* (1929), *Her Wedding Night* (1930), *Call Her Savage* (1932).

LEE BOWMAN (1914–   )

Lee Bowman dropped out of law school in his last year and started acting. He made his debut in *Three Men in White* (1936) and often challenged screen morality as the playboy or the "other man." He never lost his flair for politics, however. In 1969, he was hired by a GOP congressional committee to polish the radio and television style of Republican congressmen as well as to advise Republicans "at all levels." **Films include:** *I Met Him in Paris* (1937), *The Impatient Years* (1944), *Smash-up* (1948), *Double Barrel Miracle* (1955), *Youngblood Hawke* (1964).

STEPHEN BOYD (1928–   )

The Irish actor first gained attention playing a German spy in *The Man Who Never Was* (1956). But he is probably best known as the treacherous Roman, Messala, who was ultimately bested in the spectacular chariot race by *Ben Hur* (1959).

Boyd was also featured in *Fantastic Voyage* (1966) as the hero of a journey through the human body. **Highlights:** *Island in the Sun* (1956), *Jumbo* (1962), *The Oscar* (1966), *The Bible* (1966), *Shalako* (1968).

WILLIAM BOYD (1898–1972)

Boyd's long but not too varied career started in 1919, when his rugged physique and graying hair brought him to the attention of Cecil B. DeMille. His first noteworthy role was the lead in *The Volga Boatman* (1926) and when the talkies arrived his pleasant speaking voice helped him survive the transition to sound.

In 1935 he was cast as Hopalong Cassidy, a part he played exclusively from that time, both on the screen and on television. It was reported that Boyd so identified with the role he would not say, "I am going on tour," but rather, "Hoppy is going on tour." **More than 80 films include:** *Why Change Your Wife?* (1919), *King of Kings* (1927), *Yankee Clipper* (1928), *The Spoilers* (1930).

CHARLES BOYER (1897–   )

He will always be known for the line "Come-wiz-me-to-the-Casbah" even though it didn't come out quite that way in *Algiers* (1938). In any event it was that picture which made him the screen's great lover of his day and (along with Cagney, Bogart, Chevalier and Cary Grant) among the most imitated male screen stars that ever lived.

Born in southern France he had studied acting at the Paris Conservatoire and was a European stage and screen actor for many years before a first disastrous encounter with Hollywood and its film makers in the early 30's. It wasn't until he appeared with Claudette Colbert in *Private Worlds* (1935) that audiences began to take notice of him. Thereafter, he proved that he was a skilled comedian (*Tovarich*, 1937) as well as a brilliant dramatic performer as Napoleon to Garbo's Countess Walewska in *Conquest* (1937).

For ten years after *Algiers* he remained a big star, perhaps his best performance that of the husband who drives Ingrid Bergman almost to insanity in *Gaslight* (1944). Boyer left Hollywood in 1948 and returned, minus toupee, in 1951. Thereafter he divided his time among television, stage appearances and character portrayals in French, British and

The earliest personification of "It" with a capital "I" was Clara Bow. In this pose she is more coy and less rambunctious than on the screen.

Admirers and detractors alike called them "bedroom eyes"—but here they gaze out upon the desert in Garden of Allah *as Charles Boyer embraces his beautiful co-star, Marlene Dietrich (1936).*

The truth of Peter Boyle's Joe *was instantly recognizable in the 1970 film that brought the actor fame.*

American films. His accent has remained unchanged. **His many films include:** *Red-Headed Woman* (1932), *Shanghai* (1935), *Love Affair* (1939), *The Constant Nymph* (1943), *Flesh and Fantasy* (1943), *Arch of Triumph* (1948), *Barefoot in the Park* (1967), *The April Fools* (1969).

PETER BOYLE (1936–   )

Though he had appeared on stage and in films for some time, Boyle did not become well-known until 1970 when he played the title role in *Joe*. His portrayal of the blue-collar, conservative, chauvinistic "hero" was done with such sensitivity, understanding and control that he won ecstatic critical acclaim. Peter Boyle is a "new face" who assuredly is going to leave his mark on the films of the future. **Credits:** *The Candidate* (1972), *Slither* (1972), *Kid Blue* (1973), *Steelyard Blues* (1973).

EDDIE BRACKEN (1920–   )

Bracken made his film debut in *Too Many Girls* (1940) and three years later gave a fine performance in Preston Sturges' farce *The Miracle of Morgan's Creek* (1944).

During the next decade, he appeared frequently in character parts, often as the shy country bumpkin in lightweight films. Later he acted on stage and television. **Films include:** *The Fleet's In* (1941), *Sweater Girl* (1942), *Hail the Conquering Hero* (1944), *Fun on a Weekend* (1947), *The Girl From Jones Beach* (1949), *A Slight Case of Larceny* (1953).

ALICE BRADY (1892–1939)

While remembered for the zany, Malapropian characters she portrayed on the screen, in 1931 she created the part of Lavinia in O'Neill's *Mourning Becomes Electra*, one of the great performances of the American Theatre.

She made her Broadway debut in 1911 in an operetta, *The Balkan Princess*, but bored with the limitations of singing, she went on to dramatic roles and made her screen debut in her father's production, *As Ye Sow* (1914). She continued to alternate with great success between stage and screen.

After an absence of ten years from the screen, she returned to make her first talkie, *When Ladies Meet* (1933). She continued to play comedy until almost the end of her career when she created the dramatic part of Mrs. O'Leary in *In Old Chicago* (1937), winning an Academy Award for Best Supporting Actress. Her last screen appearance was in *Young Mr. Lincoln* (1939), filmed while she was dying of cancer. Of the 78 films she made, 52 were silent. **Films include:** *The Gay Divorcee* (1934), *My Man Godfrey* (1936), *Three Smart Girls* (1937), *100 Men and a Girl* (1937), *The Joy of Living* (1938).

MARLON BRANDO (1924–   )

Perhaps the first of the "anti-stars," Brando was a thorn in Hollywood's side practically from his arrival in Tinsel Town for his film debut in *The Men* (1950). Surly toward interviewers, iconoclastic toward the Hollywood establishment, and difficult on set—Brando won no popularity contests in the film capital. Despite these personality minuses, his acting prowess has kept him on top during a more than 20 year career.

Brando's mumbling speech and intense characterization in the film version of *A Streetcar Named Desire* (1952) captivated audiences and critics alike. Two years later, the young Brando won the Academy's Best Actor Oscar for his role in *On the Waterfront* and mesmerized audiences with his gang leader in *The Wild One.*

Playing a variety of roles, Brando has been by turn a singing gambler in *Guys and Dolls* (1955), a Japanese interpreter in *The Teahouse of the August Moon* (1956), a Nazi in *The Young Lions* (1958), and an army officer with homosexual tendencies in *Reflections in a Golden Eye* (1967). Brando's career has had about as much variety in the quality and success of his films; many were unqualified winners, but some (notably *The Fugitive Kind, One-Eyed Jacks,* and *A Countess From Hong Kong*) were box office poison.

The 60's saw a diminution of Brando's film-giant status and it was believed (perhaps hoped) by some that his reign was over. 1972 and *The Godfather* belied this belief. As the aging head of a gangland family, Brando was superb. His portrayal of Don Corleone was perhaps the highlight of his career and won for him his second Oscar. True to his old style, Brando shocked and horrified the Hollywood establishment by sending a beautiful American Indian girl (*cum* speech) to accept his award and lobby for Indian rights. In *Last Tango in Paris* (1973) the actor again surprised his public by appearing (often sans clothes) as an aging American widower who loves . . . and loves . . . and loves a young, sexy French girl. The explicit film created a furor and long box-office lines. It received mixed reviews, but Brando, as always, received almost unanimous praise and the Film Critics' Circle Award. **Highlights:** *Viva Zapata* (1952), *Julius Caesar* (1953), *Sayonara* (1957), *Mutiny on the Bounty* (1962), *The Ugly American* (1963).

PIERRE BRASSEUR (1903–)

Pierre Brasseur studied at the Paris Academy of Design during his youth and began his working career as a cartoonist. Lured from the graphic arts first by the stage and later, in the mid 20's, by the screen, Brasseur went on to distinguish himself as a fine actor over his more than 50-year career.

In addition to being an actor, Brasseur is a playwright of some note. **Highlights:** *Quai des Brumes* (1938), *Les Enfants du Paradis* (1944), *Il Bell' Antonio* (1960).

ROSSANO BRAZZI (1916–)

In his American debut as Professor Bhaer in *Little Women* (1949), Brazzi knew so little English he didn't fully understand the script. But he had improved significantly in *Three Coins in the Fountain* (1954) and was an immediate success.

Though generally cast in romantic roles, he resented playing the lover. In Italy he had done enough swashbuckling to qualify as the Latin Douglas Fairbanks. **Films include:** *The Barefoot Contessa* (1954), *South Pacific* (1958), *The Light in the Piazza* (1962), *Woman Times Seven* (1967).

After winning a second Academy Award for The Godfather *(1972), Marlon Brando played in* Last Tango in Paris, *a brilliant, controversial film by Bernardo Bertolucci (1973).*

Marlon Brando as Terry Malloy in the unforgettable On the Waterfront *written by Budd Schulberg and directed by Elia Kazan. The film brought an Oscar to Brando. The woman is Eva Marie Saint.*

Walter Brennan peers into Gary Cooper's tobacco pouch in a scene from The Westerner. *Brennan started playing old men superbly when he was in his thirties and just went right on.*

EDMOND BREESE (1871–1936)

He could be funny, he could be mean, he could lead his troop through fearsome dangers and he could turn into a gorgeous foil for the Marx Brothers. A product of the Broadway stage, he appeared in nearly 50 pictures over a film career that lasted for less than 11 years. **Highlights:** *Marriage Morals* (debut, 1923), *All Quiet on the Western Front* (1930), *Platinum Blonde* (1931), *Mata Hari* (1932), *Duck Soup* (1933), *Broadway Bill* (1934).

EL BRENDEL (1896–1964)

He was on the vaudeville stage by the age of 13, playing comic German characters which he switched to Swedes during World War I. He and his wife, as Brendel and Bert, were well known as a vaudeville team in the early 20's. Although he had been in pictures since 1926, it was not until he played in the early talkie, *The Cock-eyed World* (1929), that he gained the public's attention. **Films include:** *The Campus Flirt* (1926) *Wings* (1927), *Happy Landing* (1928), *Little Miss Broadway* (1938), *The Beautiful Blonde from Bashful Bend* (1949).

WALTER BRENNAN (1894–   )

The three-time Academy Award winner for Best Supporting Actor and veteran of over 100 films, not counting extra and bit roles, once said: "I'm not good copy. I've been married to the same wife for nearly 40 years."

Descended from early New England settlers, he got his first big break in the early 30's and won his first Academy Award for his supporting role in *Come and Get It* (1936), winning again in *Kentucky* (1938) and *The Westerner* (1940).

During his long career he had specialized in playing backwoodsmen, cracker barrel philosophers, and seedy old swamp characters. For six years he appeared on television in *The Real McCoys* series (1957–1963). **Highlights:** *Barbary Coast* (1935), *The Adventures of Tom Sawyer* (1938), *Sergeant York* (1941), *Pride of the Yankees* (1942), *To Have and Have Not* (1944), *Red River* (1948), *Bad Day at Black Rock* (1955), *Rio Bravo* (1958), *The One and Only, Genuine, Original Family Band* (1968).

EVELYN BRENT (1899–   )

The American silent star made several early pictures in Great Britain. Her major film was *Underworld* (1927), often considered the first to portray gangsters as heroes. Brent played George Sanders' moll, and as such projected the kind of intriguing image later perfected by Marlene Dietrich. She appeared rarely after 1930. **Highlights:** *Sybil* (1921), *Silk Stocking Sal* (1924), *Queen of Diamonds* (1926), *Madonna of the Streets* (1930), *The Golden Eye* (1948).

GEORGE BRENT (1904–   )

Brent was a rebel secret service man after the Irish rebellion and had to leave his country when a leader was killed. He arrived in New

York and played in a Broadway show along with another unknown, Clark Gable. Brought to Hollywood about 1930, he appeared in a series of ''B'' pictures. Brent's first suave and sophisticated role was with Ruth Chatterton in *The Rich Are Always With Us* (1932). He later became a leading man in many Bette Davis movies. **Films include:** *42nd Street* (1933), *The Painted Veil* (1934), *Jezebel* (1938), *Dark Victory* (1939), *The Old Maid* (1939), *Tomorrow Is Forever* (1945), *Montana Belle* (1952).

JEAN-CLAUDE BRIALY (1933–   )

The French actor made a great number of films in the 50's, appearing in many French historical dramas. He is best known in the United States for *Le Beau Serge* (1958) and *Les Cousins* (1958). More recently, he appeared in the critically popular *Claire's Knee* (1971) as a fussy diplomat. **Credits include:** *Paris Belongs to Us* (1962), *La Ronde* (1964), *King of Hearts* (1967), *The Bride Wore Black* (1968).

MARY BRIAN (1908–   )

During her film career sweet-faced Mary Brian played Wendy in *Peter Pan* (1924) and appeared in the classic western *The Virginian* (1930). She also starred with Adolphe Menjou and Pat O'Brien in *The Front Page* (1930). She more or less retired in the late 30's. **Highlights:** *Beau Geste* (1927), *Shanghai Bound* (1928), *Ever Since Eve* (1934), *Navy Bound* (1937), *The Dragnet* (1948).

FANNY BRICE (1891–1951)

One of the world's best-loved comediennes, Fanny Brice was more active offscreen than on, though some of her funniest routines were parodies of film stars like Theda Bara. On radio she was the annoying but enormously popular Baby Snooks.

She first gained public notice for her torch song ''My Man'' and later appeared in the silent film of the same title. Her infrequent films were generally concerned with show business, notably *Ziegfeld Follies* (1944) and *The Great Ziegfeld* (1936), in which she played herself. The life story of Fanny Brice has inspired several movies, most recently *Funny Girl* (1968).

Evelyn Brent looks as if she is seven-eighths under water, but she is really projecting her brand of early femme-fatalism for the silent screen camera.

BEAU BRIDGES (1942–   )

The older son of Lloyd Bridges has been recognized, with his brother and good friend Jeff, as one of the most gifted new faces of the 70's. In 1969 he won critical acclaim for his winning, comic performance in *Gaily, Gaily* and won the lead role in *The Landlord* in 1970. Concerned with the quality of the scripts he accepts, he was among many actors who turned down the top role in *Love Story* (which finally went to Ryan O'Neal). Despite the financial failure of his earlier films, his appeal and talent undoubtedly will bring him future success. **Films include:** *Force of Evil* (debut, 1948), *The Red Pony* (1949), *For Love of Ivy* (1968), *Child's Play* (1972), *Hammersmith Is Out* (1972), *Loving Molly* (1974).

Beau Bridges played the earnest young man setting off for the big city (Chicago) in Gaily, Gaily, *made from Ben Hecht's story.*

It is apparent that Lloyd Bridges and Gary Cooper were not seeing eye-to-eye in High Noon, *and it was, as usual, Cooper who prevailed.*

JEFF BRIDGES (1950–)

Among the growing number of second generation actors from Hollywood's leading dynasties, Jeff Bridges is one of the sons of celebrated Lloyd Bridges. His characterization of a "drifter" in *Bad Company* was a highlight of the 1972 New York Film Festival. Some critics have hailed young Bridges as a modern Wallace Beery. His characterization in *The Last Picture Show* (1972) won him an Oscar nomination, and his performance in *The Last American Hero* (1974) has received critical acclaim.

LLOYD BRIDGES (1913–)

Equally at home on the range or under water, Lloyd Bridges played standard melodrama for years. He won acclaim as the hotheaded young deputy who infuriated Gary Cooper in *High Noon* (1952). Mainly a TV actor in recent years, the film work of the Bridges family has been taken on by sons Jeff and Beau. **Films include:** *Here Comes Mr. Jordan* (1941), *Home of the Brave* (1949), *The Sound of Fury* (1951), *The Rainmaker* (1956), *The Dating Game* (1968).

BARBARA BRITTON (1923–)

Though she generally played second leads and appeared in only a few, but very good, movies, Barbara Britton gave fine, lively performances. She is perhaps better known for the 50's television series, *Mr. and Mrs. North*, in which she starred with Richard Denning. **Highlights:** *Wake Island* (debut, 1942), *The Virginian* (1946), *The Spoilers* (1955).

HELEN BRODERICK (1891–1959)

The mother of Broderick Crawford was a Broadway favorite for many years, brightening comedies and musicals with her caustic humor and ability to sing, dance, or do almost anything else required of her. In movies, often working with topnotch performers like Victor Moore, she was fated to be cast in third-rate productions of second-rate screenplays. When a good one came along, i.e., *Top Hat* (1935), she was marvelous. **Other films:** *Fifty Million Frenchmen* (1931), *Love on a Bet* (1936), *Meet the Missus* (1937), *Father Takes a Wife* (1941), *Because of Him* (1946).

JAMES BROLIN (1940–)

The handsome, six-foot-four actor is best known as Dr. Kiley on the *Marcus Welby* television series. Brolin has expressed his desire to crack this "Mr. Clean" image and try more challenging work. He made his film debut in 1965 in *Von Ryan's Express* and recently broke from his doctor image as a participant in *Westworld* (1973), in which he acquitted himself well in his comedy role. In addition to acting, he hopes to write, direct and produce films in the future.

J. EDWARD BROMBERG (1903–1951)

Hungarian-born, his varied range of character parts included Spaniards, South Americans, Egyptians, Germans, Russians, Frenchmen and even a Hungarian. He claimed to have also played a dog.

A veteran of more than 45 films, he came to Hollywood from the New York stage and made his debut in *Under Two Flags* (1936). **Highlights:** *Seventh Heaven* (1937), *Rebecca of Sunnybrook Farm (1938), Suez* (1938), *The Mark of Zorro* (1940), *Lady of Burlesque* (1943), *Tangier* (1946), *Guilty Bystander* (1950).

BETTY BRONSON (1906–   )

After several years in minor roles, she was "discovered" and given the title role in *Peter Pan* (1924), an assignment she played to the hilt. She never reached that pinnacle again, although she did appear in *Ben Hur* (1927), an epic that cost over $4,000,000 to produce, and in Al Jolson's *The Singing Fool* (1927), the movie's historic transition from silents to sound that turned Hollywood topsy-turvy. **Other films:** *Are Parents People?* (1924), *The Cat's Pajamas* (1927), *Medicine Man* (1930), *The Yodelling Kind From Pine Ridge* (1937).

CHARLES BRONSON (1920–   )

Born in Scooptown, Pennsylvania, the rugged looking, dark-haired actor has appeared in many films, mostly in supporting roles. Whether cast as a half-breed Indian, hired killer, tough cop or veteran soldier, Bronson always turns in an effective and convincing performance. He has also appeared in numerous television roles as special guest star. More recently he was seen in *The Valachi Papers* (1972) and *The Stone Killer* (1973). **Credits:** *Drum Beat* (1954), *Never So Few* (1960), *The Magnificent Seven* (1960), *The Great Escape* (1963), *The Sandpiper* (1965), *The Battle of the Bulge* (1965), *The Dirty Dozen* (1967), *Tell Them Willie Boy Is Here* (1970), *Chato's Land* (1972), *The Mechanic* (1972).

CLIVE BROOK (1887–   )

Looking as though he had just emerged from one of London's more exclusive men's clubs, the British actor played leads and supporting roles for more than 40 years. On most occasions his film behavior was exemplary but in some instances, such as *Underworld*

Helen Broderick in a scene from Rage of Paris *with (left to right) Louis Hayward, Douglas Fairbanks, Jr., and Danielle Darrieux (1938).*

(1927), he turned out to be one of society's renegades. In one notable role, as Captain Harvey in *Shanghai Express*, he forgot his manners and fell in love with the less than virginal Shanghai Lily. But, since Lily was played by Marlene Dietrich, who can blame him? **Some 80 films include:** *Woman to Woman* (1924), *Interference* (1928), *Sherlock Holmes* (1932), *Convoy* (1941), *The List of Adrian Messenger* (1963).

HILLARY BROOKE (1916–   )

Born Beatrice Peterson on Long Island, Brooke spent a great deal of her time in the movies registering fear and dismay for, with few exceptions, she was generally cast as a lady fated to face the unpleasant. Her 14 years in films did, however, include a sprinkling of comedies. In the 50's she appeared as the cool, kind neighbor and love interest on *The Abbott and Costello Show*. **Highlights:**

Edward Brophy appeared in nearly 100 movies in supporting roles.

Sherlock Holmes and the Voice of Terror (1942), *Jane Eyre* (1944), *Ministry of Fear* (1945), *Road to Utopia* (1946), *Invaders from Mars* (1953), *The Man Who Knew Too Much* (1956).

LOUISE BROOKS (1900–)

She looked just like any flapper, with bobbed hair, bangs, and a svelte figure, but soon after she appeared in *A Girl in Every Port* (1928), Louise Brooks was invited to star in European films. *Pandora's Box* (1929) and *Diary of a Lost Girl* (1930), both made in Germany, depicted the sordid lives of fallen women. A critic of *Pandora's Box* wrote, "We now know that Louise Brooks is a remarkable actress endowed with uncommon intelligence, and not merely a dazzlingly beautiful woman." **Highlights:** *It's the Old Army Game* (1926).

EDWARD BROPHY (1900–1960)

A critic said of his performance as Ditto Beoland in *The Last Hurrah* (1958), "It is Brophy climbing the Skeffington staircase to pay his last respects to his idol that makes the final fadeout so affecting." A short, round-faced man with a high-pitched voice, bulging eyes and mobile features, Brophy often played tough, cigar-puffing characters. With his ever-present bowler hat, he could portray with equal skill a gangster or a valet. In fact he was cast as Goldie, the inept valet, in the *Falcon* series of the 40's. **Films include:** *The Champ* (1932), *The Thin Man* (1934), *Wonder Man* (1945).

JIM BROWN (1936–)

A magnificent athlete who holds a number of football records that may never be broken, he left the Cleveland Browns (the team was not named after him, but it might well have been) to pursue a movie career. Brown soon proved that he could cope with dialogue and action almost as adeptly as he could handle a football, and unlike so many other professional athletes, has shown that he is not a flash in the pan. His initial appearance was in *Rio Conchos* (1964) and almost all of his films have been on the violent side, with Brown taking it almost as often as he dished it out. He was particularly impressive in one of the most action-packed dramas of our time, *The Dirty Dozen* (1967). **Other films:** *Dark of the Sun* (1968), *The Split* (1968), *Ice Station Zebra* (1968), *Black Gunn* (1972).

JOE E. BROWN (1892–1973)

His trademark was his incredible mouth, referred to as the "Great Open Space." "I'll open my mouth until my stomach shows if people think it's funny," he once remarked.

Brown ran away to join the circus at the age of nine and later performed as an acrobat. The skills he learned were put to good use. In 1918 he made his Broadway debut, but it was a decade before he "went Hollywood." His movie style was broad slapstick, usually at his own expense. After a number of supporting roles as a comic, he was starred in his own comedies. **Films include:** *Crooks Can't Win* (debut, 1928), *Elmer the Great* (1933), *A*

Jim Brown's pistol handling does not seem to bother Raquel Welch in this scene from 100 Rifles.

Midsummer Night's Dream (1935), *Show-boat* (1951), *Some Like It Hot* (1959), *It's a Mad, Mad, Mad, Mad World* (1963).

JOHN MACK BROWN (1904–   )

An All-American back at the University of Alabama (a school that still produces outstanding players) voted handsomest man in the school, Brown naturally gravitated to Hollywood. In short order he made a name for himself playing opposite Mary Pickford in *Coquette* (1929) and for some years thereafter was a popular leading man in talkies—almost always honorable and looking as though he had just emerged from an Arrow collar ad. **More than 200 films include:** *The Bugle Call* (debut, 1927), *Our Dancing Daughters* (1928), *Billy the Kid* (1930), *Wells Fargo* (1937), *Ride 'Em Cowboy* (1942), *Short Grass* (1951).

TOM BROWN (1913–   )

For a long time Tom Brown suffered from one of the occupational hazards of the former juvenile—he couldn't get a chance to act because of his youthful appearance.

He played clean-cut roles from 1929 and, as nature took its course, won a "heavy" part in *Big Town Czar* (1939).

His films include: *Three Cornered Moon* (1933), *Anne of Green Gables* (1934), *In Old Chicago* (1938), *Margie* (1941), *Duke of Chicago* (1949), *The Quiet Gun* (1957).

CORAL BROWNE (1913–   )

A very versatile actress, Coral Browne played the role of Lady Macbeth on stage in Old Vic productions as well as the role of Vera Charles, the cynical and tippling actress-friend of Auntie Mame in the movie. **Films include:** *Auntie Mame* (1958), *The Roman Spring of Mrs. Stone* (1961), *Dr. Crippen* (1964), *The Killing of Sister George* (1968).

NIGEL BRUCE (1895–1953)

Although best remembered as Dr. Watson in the Sherlock Holmes series, the Mexican-born but English-educated Bruce appeared in more than 50 other film roles.

Beginning on the London stage in 1920, he came to Hollywood in 1934, making his

Nigel Bruce looks worried as he observes John Dall reporting to his tutor, Bette Davis, in The Corn Is Green *(1945).*

debut in *Coming-Out Party* and starting a long career, usually as the stuffy, well-meaning, upper-class bumbler. He appeared in the first full length film made in Technicolor, *Becky Sharp* (1935). It was in *The Hound of the Baskervilles* (1939) that he portrayed Dr. Watson for the first time, a role he repeated 13 more times. **Films include:** *The Scarlet Pimpernel* (1935), *Charge of the Light Brigade* (1936), *Kidnapped* (1938), *The Rains Came* (1939), *Rebecca* (1940), *Suspicion* (1941), *Lassie Come Home* (1943), *Limelight* (1952).

VIRGINIA BRUCE (1910–   )

She was discovered while on a visit to a movie studio and subsequently appeared in a couple of films: *Fugitives* (1929) starring Madge Bellamy and *Blue Skies* (1929) star-

Virginia Bruce, with nice wide shoulders to match Robert Livingstone's, consults with him on travel plans in Brazil *(1944).*

Victor Buono often plays the smiling menace, as in the campy Whatever Happened to Baby Jane?

ring Helen Twelvetrees. Feeling that she was getting nowhere, Bruce went to Broadway as a Ziegfeld girl and after two shows returned to Hollywood. Her roles improved and during the filming of *Downstairs* (1932) she met and married John Gilbert. After a two-year retirement, a daughter and a divorce, she came back to Hollywood and finally began getting better parts, such as her role in *The Great Ziegfeld* (1936).

Since her retirement, Bruce has appeared occasionally on television. **More than 45 films include:** *The Mighty Barnum* (1934), *Metropolitan* (1935), *Born to Dance* (1936), *Flight Angel* (1940), *Pardon My Sarong* (1942), *The Night Has a Thousand Eyes* (1948), *Strangers When We Meet* (1960).

NANA BRYANT (1888–1955)

During a career that spanned more than 50 years, Bryant was rarely unemployed. Starting in stock while still in high school, she went on to Broadway, films and television. She had appeared on Broadway for ten years

in musicals and comedies before coming to Hollywood for her debut in *A Feather in Her Hat* (1935). **Highlights:** *Pennies From Heaven* (1936), *The Adventures of Tom Sawyer* (1938), *The Corsican Brothers* (1942), *Song of Bernadette* (1944), *Harvey* (1951).

YUL BRYNNER (c. 1915–)

Brynner is reputed to be the offspring of a Manchurian father and Gypsy mother. In his early days he was a traveling minstrel who sang ballads and, until he met with a serious accident, a high flyer on the trapeze. Later he joined a repertory company in Paris and became its stage manager as well as an actor with the troupe.

Brynner had pretty much given up the stage and was living in New York and working as a television producer when a chance to play the King in the Rodgers and Hammerstein adaptation of *Anna and the King of Siam* came along. His close friend Bil Baird, eminent puppeteer and expert on Oriental modes and manners, helped him to perfect his walk and swagger and, the moment *The King and I* opened, he became a top star. A few years later he received the Academy Award as Best Actor in the screen version (1956). **Other films include:** *Port of New York* (debut, 1950), *Anastasia* (1956), *The Brothers Karamazov* (1958), *The Magnificent Seven* (1960), *Taras Bulba* (1962), *The Return of the Seven* (1966).

EDGAR BUCHANAN
(1902–)

Before becoming an actor, Edgar Buchanan was a practicing dentist. Turning to films, he became adept as a character actor. In one of his early movies, *Arizona* (1940), the 37-year-old Buchanan played a 70-year-old judge. He appeared in Westerns in portly roles, both comic and villainous. At various times, Buchanan was called upon to play cowboys and all types of avuncular figures, but never once a dentist. **Films include:** *My Son Is Guilty* (1940), *Penny Serenade* (1941), *The Best Man Wins* (1948), *Cheaper by the Dozen* (1950), *Shane* (1953), *Welcome to Hard Times* (1967).

HORST BUCHHOLZ (1933–   )

Berlin-born Buchholz began performing at an early age, making stage appearances at the Berlin Metropole in 1947. He made his screen debut in *Marianne, My Youthful Love* (1955) and his English-language film debut in *Tiger Bay* (1959), turning in a fine, sensitive performance opposite Hayley Mills. His film roles since have ranged from the romantic, *Fanny* (1961), to the comic, *One, Two, Three* (1961), to the violent, *The Magnificent Seven* (1960). **Films include:** *Confessions of Felix Krull* (1957), *Nine Hours to Rama* (1963), *Marco the Magnificent* (1965), *Cervantes* (1966).

VICTOR BUONO (1938–   )

"I felt like an altar boy invited to the Ecumenical Council in Rome," the San Diego born Victor Buono said of his film debut in *Whatever Happened to Baby Jane?* (1962) with Bette Davis and Joan Crawford. The 300-pound actor came from theatre and television and since his debut has been seen regularly in all three media. **Films include:** *The Strangler* (1964), *The Greatest Story Ever Told* (1965), *Hush . . . Hush, Sweet Charlotte* (1965), *Beneath the Planet of the Apes* (1969).

BILLIE BURKE (1885–1970)

The widow of Florenz Ziegfeld is probably best remembered as the good witch of the East in *The Wizard of Oz* (1939) but her role in *Dinner at Eight* (1933) in which *The New York Times* called her "the personification of an anxious hostess at one moment and subsequently a deeply disappointed woman" was one of the less stereotyped parts in her long line of empty-headed, society-matron roles.

On stage since early childhood, she first appeared on the screen in *Peggy* (1916). She was paid $300,000 to do the picture and went on to make a number of popular but forgettable photoplays. It wasn't until much later that her name became synonymous with elderly fluttery matrons. She also saw herself portrayed on screen by Myrna Loy in *The Great Ziegfeld* (1936). In the late 50's she appeared in a few cameo parts and some television shows, retiring at last after 60 years in show business. **Film credits:** *A Bill of Divorce-*

Yul Brynner played Dmitri in MGM's The Brothers Karamazov *in 1958 and Maria Schell was Grushenka.*

ment (1932), *Becky Sharp* (1935), *Topper* (1937), *The Man Who Came to Dinner* (1942), *Father of the Bride* (1950), *The Young Philadelphians* (1959).

LESTER ALVIN "SMILEY" BURNETTE (1911–1967)

A plump man, he made 81 movies playing Gene Autry's comic sidekick. He was also Roy Rogers' pal in seven films. One of the top 10 money-making Western actors in the 1940's, he said of himself: "I came to Hollywood 29 years ago, I've been featured in 71 movies but nobody in Hollywood knows me. Even my movie fans don't know me. All they know is Ole Frog in a battered black hat."

"It's My Lazy Day," "My Home Town," and "Hominy Grits" are among over 300 songs he composed. Many of his compositions were used in movies in which he played.

Burnette often appeared with Charles Starrett in the *Durango Kid* series. On television he portrayed the railroad engineer in the

Billie Burke at the mid-point in her long movie career—from 1916 to 1960. She died in 1970.

A young and sinister, and thinner, Raymond Burr confronts the hapless Montgomery Clift in A Place in the Sun, *another re-make of Theodore Dreiser's* An American Tragedy.

Gracie Allen garbed as a Grecian goddess still looks like Gracie Allen in this scene from College Holiday, *with George Burns.*

Petticoat Junction series. All in all, Burnette made nearly 200 Westerns. **Films include:** *Border Patrolman* (1936), *Boots and Saddles* (1937), *Manhattan Merry-Go-Round* (1937), *The Stadium Murders* (1938), *Under Western Stars* (1938).

GEORGE BURNS (1896–   ) and GRACIE ALLEN (1902–1964)

Their fame rested on their radio and television performances, for which they remained American favorites for many years, but they did make a number of pictures over the years. In most of these films they repeated the routine they had originated in vaudeville with George acting as straight man, attempting with vast patience to unravel wife Gracie's malapropisms, topsy-turvy and featherbrained approaches to life's little problems.

Off screen, Grace Ethel Rosalie Allen was a quiet woman not at all given to gags while her cigar chomping husband, George Nathan Birnbaum Burns, was and is recognized as one of the true wits in show business—a high priest of the ad lib and a brilliant master of ceremonies for any occasion.

Following Gracie's death, George continued to make television appearances and appeared without her in several pictures. **Their films include:** *The Big Broadcast* (1932), *International House* (1933), *The Gracie Allen Murder Case* (1939), *Mr. and Mrs. North* (1941), *Two Girls and a Sailor* (1944).

RAYMOND BURR (1917–   )

To most viewers he will always be Perry Mason, television's nimble-witted attorney, who won every court case he tried. Quite a number of real-life lawyers objected to him because his inevitable success made them, in their court efforts, look somewhat ridiculous. Indeed, one judge in North Carolina refused to attend a Bar Association meeting because Burr was the featured speaker.

In his early Hollywood appearances, he was generally cast in unpleasant roles—as a murderer, psychopath, gangster, or cattle rustler. After many years of depravity, his image did an about face and he has remained a good guy ever since. He also starred in another successful television series, *Ironside*. **Films include:** *Desperate* (1947), *A Place in the Sun* (1951), *Rear Window* (1954), *Crime of Passion* (1957), *Mr. P. J.* (1968).

ELLEN BURSTYN (1932–   )

Here's a new twist to the classic story of how movie stars get discovered. Burstyn had done some acting on Broadway and a few featured roles in films, but her big break came when producer Joseph Strick heard her give a political speech in California. He was impressed by her eloquence and offered a starring role opposite Rip Torn in *Tropic of Cancer* (1970).

Her performance led to the role of Donald Sutherland's wife in *Alex in Wonderland* (1970). Reviewers were enthusiastic and so was director Peter Bogdanovich. He asked Burstyn to choose whichever of the three women's roles she preferred in *The Last Picture Show* (1971). She decided to play Lois

Farrow and her brash but sympathetic portrayal won her the New York Film Critics Award as the Best Supporting Actress of the Year and an Academy Award nomination as Best Supporting Actress.

Burstyn was born in Detroit but left at age 18, first to model in Texas and then to work as a dancer in Montreal. Eventually, she went to New York where she did some television commercials, appeared as a "regular" on the Jackie Gleason Show and won her first Broadway role opposite Sam Levene in *Fair Game*.

Among Burstyn's screen credits is the role of actress Chris MacNeil in the box-office smash hit *The Exorcist* (1974). **Films include:** *Goodbye Charlie* (1964), *For Those Who Think Young* (1964), *The King of Marvin Gardens* (1972).

RICHARD BURTON (1925–   )

The son of a Welsh coal miner, Richard Burton is alleged to have once vowed: "By heaven, I'm going to be the greatest actor, or what's the point of acting?"

Whether he ever made the remark or ever achieved his goal are equally debatable. Some of his performances have been memorable. Others—and his Antony to Elizabeth Taylor's *Cleopatra* (1963) is as good an example as any—have more than a touch of ham added to the acting recipe.

Burton's rise to the top came slowly. Playing mostly roles from Shakespeare, he starred with the Old Vic company and made his screen debut in the Welsh film *The Last Days of Dolwyn* (1949). His first appearances in American films, including his debut in *My Cousin Rachel* (1952), were in secondary roles. By the time his romance with Taylor hit the front pages, however, he had already achieved stardom.

One reason for the difficulty in assessing Burton as an actor is the oceans of publicity evoked by his marriage to, consequent adventures with, separations from and reconciliations with Elizabeth Taylor. Their meanderings around the world, their opulent gifts to one another, their appearances or non-appearances together, their ups and downs—all of these front page items tended somehow to obscure what they did from time to time in front of motion picture cameras. To

Richard Burton and Elizabeth Taylor gave performances as Antony and Cleopatra that were the most highly publicized of all time, but surely not the best. Their personal entanglements may have had something to do with it.

this non-appraisal should be added a postscript: in some of his films, notably *Becket* (1964), Burton was superb. **Other films include:** *The Robe* (1953), *The Spy Who Came in From the Cold* (1965), *Who's Afraid of Virginia Woolf?* (1966), *Boom* (1968).

MAE BUSCH (1897–1946)

In the 20's, she was a leading lady in silent films, being directed by such luminaries as Erich von Stroheim in *The Devil's Pass Key* (1920) and *Foolish Wives* (1921). In the 30's and with the advent of sound, she was a comic foil for Laurel and Hardy in some of their two-reeler comedies. **Films include:** *Alibi* (1929), *Scarlet Dawn* (1932), *Cheating Blondes* (1933), *Beloved* (1934), *Women Without Names* (1940).

FRANCIS X. BUSHMAN (1883–1966)

He was the first screen idol of the fans, often co-starring with his wife, Beverly Bayne, in the placid days that preceded America's entry into World War I. By the

Charles Butterworth unhappily cuddles his voluptuous "secretary" (Marion Martin).

mid-20's his career had been eclipsed by the emergence of a new generation of male movie stars but he made a considerable comeback in a supporting role to Ramon Novarro in the spectacular *Ben Hur* (1926). Thereafter he appeared occasionally in small parts, his last when he had reached the age of 82. **Films include:** *The Magic Wand* (1912), *Romeo and Juliet* (1916), *The Lady in Ermine* (1927), *Hollywood Boulevard* (1936), *Sabrina* (1954), *The Ghost in the Invisible Bikini* (1966).

CHARLES BUTTERWORTH
(1897–1946)

His wizened and pointy face and balding pate combined with an on-stage aura of mouselike timidity and overwhelming diffidence to make him one of the funniest comedians of his day. Butterworth's specialty was a monologue, delivered before a mythical rotary-type group of clubmen, in which he began with vast assurance and gradually bogged down in a hopeless morass of contradictions and *non sequiturs*.

After college Butterworth was a newspaper reporter and appeared in such Broadway musicals as *Helen of Troy, New York* before making his screen debut in *The Life of the Party* (1930). **Films include:** *Love Me Tonight* (1932), *The Night Is Young* (1934), *Baby Face Harrington* (1935), *This Is the Army* (1943), *Follow the Boys* (1944).

RED BUTTONS (1919–   )

Schooled in the knockabout tradition of burlesque comedy, Red Buttons has said of himself, "I'm a little guy and that's what I play all the time—a little guy and his troubles." After years of near-obscurity (he had a one-word part in *13 Rue Madeleine*) he made a breakthrough in *Sayonara* in 1957 and won an Oscar for his appealing performance in the role of Sergeant Kelly. **Films include:** *Five Weeks in a Balloon* (1962), *The Longest Day* (1962), *Harlow* (1965), *They Shoot Horses, Don't They?* (1969).

SPRING BYINGTON (1893–1971)

She once said of her early years: "that's the wonderful thing about innocence, or ignorance; you aren't a bit frightened because you just don't know enough to be." Born in Colorado, Byington appeared in stock and on Broadway for more than 20 years before making her screen debut as Marmee in *Little Women* (1933).

She appeared in scores of films, usually cast as a scatter-brained and pleasant maternal type. In 1954 she starred in the *December Bride* television series as well as on the *Laramie* series. **More than 90 films include:** *You Can't Take It With You* (Oscar nomination, 1938), *Roxie Hart* (1942), *Heaven Can Wait* (1943), *Dragonwyck* (1946), *It Had to Be You* (1947), *In the Good Old Summertime* (1949), *Please Don't Eat the Daisies* (1960).

Spring Byington, the mother in Little Women, *surrounded by her daughters: Jean Parker as* Beth, *Joan Bennett as* Amy, *Katharine Hepburn as* Jo, *and Frances Dee as* Meg.

James Caan was seen by millions in his role as Sonny in The Godfather, *a movie that broke box-office records. Left to right: Al Pacino, Marlon Brando, James Caan, and John Cazale.*

JAMES CAAN (1939–   )

In 1972 he appeared in two diverse roles that marked the turning point of his career. He was hotheaded Sonny in *The Godfather* and the touching Brian Piccolo in the television movie *Brian's Song*. These roles combined to bring him critical recognition.

For 12 years he had studied, acted in off-Broadway plays, understudied on Broadway and appeared in a series of indifferent movies until he was hired by Francis Ford Coppola who had directed him in *The Rain People* (1969). **Some of his films are:** *Lady in a Cage* (debut, 1964), *El Dorado* (1967), *Games* (1967), *Rabbit, Run* (1970), *Slither* (1973), *Cinderella Liberty* (1973).

BRUCE CABOT (1905–1972)

A handsome, square-visaged man with a somewhat saturnine look, he played outdoor roles in nearly 100 pictures from the early days of sound to his death in 1972. He followed the paths of evil on many occasions and was an outlaw, a bank robber and a general all-around badman in a large percentage of his films. He played heroes as well and usually got his girl without too much trouble, although in his most famous picture, *King Kong* (1933), the gravest sort of obstacles were in his path. Anyone who studied the situation realized that rescuing a damsel from the fingertips of a multi-ton monster clinging to the topmost tower of the Empire State Building wasn't a job for amateurs—or even for professional movie heroes.

Most of Cabot's film vehicles were of the "B" variety. They moved along crisply, however, and Cabot gave all of himself to the parts assigned him. As a result, one often sees

Bruce Cabot (l.) was one-third of this frightened trio in the classic King Kong—*the others were Fay Wray and Robert Armstrong.*

A down-and-out James Cagney gets some sympathy from Gladys George in The Roaring Twenties *(1939).*

Cabot films on nighttime television (usually late nighttime), most of them dating back to the mid-30's. **Film credits include:** *Roadhouse Murder* (1932), *Redhead* (1934), *The Last of the Mohicans* (1936), *The Badman of Brimstone* (1938), *Dodge City* (1939), *Sorrowful Jones* (1949), *Cat Ballou* (1965), *The Green Berets* (1968).

SEBASTIAN CABOT (1918–)

Early jobs as a garage mechanic, chauffeur and cook somewhat mysteriously equipped him to play bearded exquisites in films, gentlemen of intuition and taste who, one instinctively knew, could distinguish a 1949 St. Estephe from a 1951 Médoc at ten paces. Born in England, he played cameo roles in more than a score of films including that of father Capulet in *Romeo and Juliet* (1954). The following year he made *Kismet* in Hollywood and since then has appeared in supporting roles. In recent years, however, the portly actor has been seen more often in television series such as *Checkmate* and *A Family Affair*. **Film credits include:** *Secret Agent* (1936), *They Made Me a Fugitive* (1947), *Ivanhoe* (1952), *The Family Jewels* (1965).

SID CAESAR (1922–)

New York-born Caesar studied saxophone and clarinet and began his performing career as a musician in various bands and orchestras. After World War II, he found his true niche in comedy and toured the theatre and nightclub circuit.

Caesar made his film debut in *Tars and Spars* (1946), but television was the medium that provided the best showcase for his comic talents. He was the viewers' favorite with Imogene Coca in *Your Show of Shows* (1950–1954) and starred in *Caesar's Hour* (1954–1957) and *Sid Caesar Invites You* (1958), as well as making appearances on many variety shows.

Caesar also made stage appearances, starring in the Broadway musical *Little Me* (1962). **Film credits:** *The Guilt of Janet Ames* (1947), *It's a Mad, Mad, Mad, Mad World* (1963), *A Guide for the Married Man* (1967).

JAMES CAGNEY (1904–)

His staccato delivery and outrageous pugnacity brought his own special brand of dynamism to every role Cagney played. The combination made him the most exciting gangster-hoodlum ever portrayed on film. He also proved, in melodramas and comedies, that he was one of the top notch actors in movie history.

Born on New York's East Side, he briefly attended Columbia University, but the low estate of the family fortunes obliged him to take jobs (among others) in pool halls and as a waiter in a restaurant. He drifted into vaudeville and then bit parts in Broadway productions, once as an unlikely chorus girl. Better roles followed and one of these—a craven murderer in *Penny Arcade* (1929)—brought him a Hollywood tryout along with another unknown from the same cast, Joan Blondell.

After several modest appearances in so-so Warner Brothers efforts, William Wellman promoted him to the lead in *Public Enemy* (1931). The picture was a smash, not only because of the historic scene where Mae Clarke gained immortality by having Cagney push half a grapefruit in her face, but mostly because of the brilliance of Cagney's performance as the big shot hoodlum whose bullet-

James Cagney is handkissed by Ruth Donnelly and arm-squeezed by Mary Brian in a scene from Hard to Handle *(1933).*

ridden body ends up where it began, in a city slum.

The gangster pictures that followed—from *Smart Money* (1931) to *G-Men* (1935)—were equally successful and, although made with small budgets, have dated very little and remain almost as exciting today as when they were first made. In scores of other films, ranging from his sensitive portrayal of Bottom in *Midsummer Night's Dream* (1935) to his vibrant George M. Cohan in *Yankee Doodle Dandy* (1942), he proved a master of song and dance along with his acute sensitivity to dialogue. *Angels With Dirty Faces* (1938) and *Yankee Doodle Dandy* both brought him the New York Film Critics' Award for Best Actor, and the George M. Cohan performance brought him the Academy Award as well.

A shy and retiring man, he withdrew from pictures in the early 60's. Since that time he shunned the limelight, raised cattle and lived close to nature, finally emerging from seclusion in March 1974 to appear on television to accept homage paid by the world of entertainment to a great actor who made great films. **Highlights of a brilliant career:** *The Crowd Roars* (1932), *Winner Take All* (1932), *Lady Killer* (1934), *Ceiling Zero* (1936), *Each Dawn I Die* (1939), *Strawberry Blonde* (1941), *13 Rue Madeleine* (1947), *A Lion Is in the Streets* (1953), *Love Me or Leave Me* (1955), *Man of a Thousand Faces* (1957), *One, Two, Three* (1962).

MICHAEL CAINE (1933–   )

Once called "England's most popular bachelor," this engaging leading man decided to become an actor after working briefly as a construction hand. "I didn't realize at the time," Caine later admitted, "that there are plenty of actors who are worse off than laborers." His first big break came when he replaced Peter O'Toole in the successful play *The Long and the Short and the Tall*. This eventually led to a feature role in *Zulu* (1963), but it was as Harry Palmer, the British secret agent in *The Ipcress File* (1965), that he had his first major screen success. He again appeared as Palmer in *Funeral in Berlin* (1966) and in *Billion Dollar Brain* (1967) but neither were box-office hits. In *Alfie* (1965), his por-

Louis Calhern comforts Dorothy McGuire in Invitation *(1952).*

trayal as the amorous Don Juan was received with critical acclaim and his superb performance in *Sleuth* (1973) won him an Oscar nomination for Best Actor. **Major credits:** *Gambit* (1966), *The Magus* (1968), *The Last Valley* (1971).

LOUIS CALHERN (1895–1956)

He starred and played supporting roles in innumerable Broadway and road company productions and managed to appear in more than 70 films, beginning with silents in 1921 and concluding with his death from a heart attack during the filming of *The Teahouse of the August Moon* (1956).

Calhern, a highly popular man off stage and screen, was usually cast as a villain. It was easy for him to look haughty and nastily aristocratic, and his sneer carried with it an aura of complete believability. He was particularly effective as the crooked lawyer in *The Asphalt Jungle* (1950) with Marilyn Monroe doing a fine job as his mistress. On occasions he was cast in comedy roles, which he handled as deftly as he did bad-men assignments. **His films include:** *Stolen Heaven* (1931), *The Gorgeous Hussy* (1936), *The*

Michael Caine is representative of the new breed of English movie stars—here in The Magus.

A showdown seems imminent between Rory Calhoun (l.) and Dean Jagger in Red Sundown, *and the bartender looks leery.*

Life of Emile Zola (1937), *Notorious* (1946), *The Magnificent Yankee* (1951), *Rhapsody* (1954), *The Blackboard Jungle* (1955), *High Society* (1956).

RORY CALHOUN (1922–   )

Born Francis Timothy Durgin in Los Angeles, Calhoun made his screen debut in *Something for the Boys* (1944). The pleasant, dependable actor played innumerable cowboy roles in films and on television (starring in *The Texan* series). Off the range, Calhoun was featured in a variety of films including *With a Song in My Heart* (1952), *How to Marry a Millionaire* (1953) and *Requiem for a Heavyweight* (1962). He also gave an outstanding performance with Jeff Chandler in *The Spoilers* (1955), a film remembered chiefly for its spectacular fistfight. **Highlights:** *River of No Return* (1954), *The Hired Gun* (1957), *Black Spurs* (1965), *Dayton's Devils* (1968).

JOSEPH CALLEIA (1897–   )

He made his early appearances under the somewhat complex name of Joseph Spurin Calleia, but the middle name soon vanished as he assumed roles of ultimate villainy in films like *Public Hero Number One* (1935). Born in Malta and educated in England, he

was a successful (but not very highly paid) singer in London music halls and on the concert stage before becoming an actor. It was his appearance in Maxwell Anderson's *Winterset* (1935) that brought him to Hollywood's notice. He was most always a badman in films, but when opportunities came he did a beautiful job in less grisly parts. **His films include:** *After the Thin Man* (1939), *Juarez* (1939), *Golden Boy* (1939), *The Glass Key* (1942), *For Whom the Bell Tolls* (1943), *The Littlest Outlaw* (1955), *Touch of Evil* (1958), *Cry Tough* (1959).

CAB CALLOWAY (1908–   )

Born Cabell Calloway in Rochester, New York, this lawyer's son left a pre-law course at Chicago's Crane College to work as a drummer, and wound up singing with Louis Armstrong's Chicago band. In 1929, he formed his own group. Subsequent nightclub appearances led to film and stage roles, including a three-year stint as Sportin' Life in *Porgy and Bess* (1950), a role which had originally been inspired by and created for Calloway back in 1935. **His film appearances include:** *The Big Broadcast* (1932), *Stormy Weather* (1943), *St. Louis Blues* (1958), *The Cincinnati Kid* (1965), *A Man Called Adam* (1966).

PHYLLIS CALVERT (1915–   )

English-born Calvert made her stage debut at seven with Ellen Terry and was dancing in musicals at the age of 16 when an injury turned her to a career as a dramatic actress. She made her film debut in *They Came by Night* (1940) after an extensive stage career. Her role as a schizophrenic in *Madonna of the Seven Moons* (1944) brought her to Hollywood in 1947 where she made a few films such as *My Own True Love* (1949) before returning to England. In recent years Calvert has appeared on the stage, on screen, and on television. **Films include:** *Fanny by Gaslight* (1944), *The Magic Bow* (1947), *The Woman With No Name* (1950), *Indiscreet* (1958), *Oscar Wilde* (1960), *Oh, What a Lovely War* (1970).

CORINNE CALVET (1926–   )

"I married for love and I was divorced for

love," said the five-times-married, five-times-divorced Calvet. "The one who lost out was always me." From co-starring roles in the 50's with Dean Martin, James Cagney, Alan Ladd and Danny Kaye, Calvet's career went into decline in the 60's. In 1971 she admitted that to support her three children she had tried unsuccessfully to gain work as a restaurant hostess, an airline stewardess and a window dresser.

Originally an actress in French films, Calvet reached to stardom after her arrival in the United States in 1949. She had made less than 20 films when her career faded. **Highlights:** *Rope of Sand* (1949), *What Price Glory?* (1952), *The Far Country* (1955), *Apache Uprising* (1965).

GODFREY CAMBRIDGE (1933–   )

Born in New York City, Cambridge studied drama after graduating from Hofstra College. He made his first stage appearance in the off-Broadway production *Take a Giant Step* (1956). He followed this appearance with roles in such Broadway successes as *The Detective Story* and *Purlie Victorious*, and in 1961 won an Obie for his role in Genet's *The Blacks*.

In 1959, he made his film debut in *The Last Angry Man*. In addition to his nightclub, stage and screen roles, Cambridge frequently appears on television. **Films include:** *The Busy Body* (1967), *The President's Analyst* (1967), *Bye, Bye, Braverman* (1968), *The Night the Sun Came Out* (1969), *Cotton Comes to Harlem* (1970).

DYAN CANNON (1937–   )

She was Miss West Seattle of 1955 and ten years later became the fourth Mrs. Cary Grant. Her whistle-evoking natural endowments have at least partially obscured her true potential as an actress, and she has been seen too often as the bored, unhappy, neglected lady planning to make up for lost time in a stranger's bed. Equally maladroit was the sequence in *Such Good Friends* (1972) in which Miss Cannon is obliged to undergo sexual fantasies about an unclad Burgess Meredith, with particular ineptitude shown in the camera angles of his rear-end. Not that we have any quarrel with Mr. Meredith's

posterior—it's just that he acts much, much better from the front. **Credits:** *Bob & Carol & Ted & Alice* (1969), *Doctors' Wives* (1971), *The Last of Sheila* (1973), *The Burglars* (1974).

JUDY CANOVA (1916–   )

This comedienne and singer made her first Broadway appearance in *Calling All Stars* (1934), a musical revue in which she played a hillbilly singer. So successful was her performance that Canova was subsequently typecast in similar roles in several motion pictures. She made her film debut in *In Caliente* (1935) and continued her film career over a 25-year period. A veteran of vaudeville and radio, witty Canova was once engaged to Edgar Bergen but broke the engagement because she "didn't want to play second fiddle to a dummy." **Film highlights:** *Going Highbrow* (1935), *Artists and Models* (1937), *Sis Hopkins* (1941), *Chatterbox* (1943), *The Adventures of Huckleberry Finn* (1960).

Judy Canova often played the country girl in the big city, as seen here in Scatterbrain.

Godfrey Cambridge (r.) scored with James Coburn, who played the title role, in The President's Analyst.

Tall headdress and free-floating earrings are not needed to enhance the beauty of Capucine.

CANTINFLAS (1917–)

Perhaps the best-known and most-loved star to emerge from Mexico's film industry, almost all of Cantinflas' movies have been comedies in Spanish and little seen outside Latin America. But he will always be remembered for his wonderfully funny portrayal (in English) of Passepartout, the indefatigable manservant, to David Niven's Phileas Fogg in *Around the World in 80 Days* (1956). **Other English-language film credits:** *Neither Blood nor Sand* (1941), *Romeo and Juliet* (1944), *Pepe* (1960).

EDDIE CANTOR (1892–1964)

Born Edward Israel Iskowitz, the complete vaudevillian, with his banjo eyes, dancing feet and enthusiastic vocal delivery, became an immensely popular stage and burlesque performer. Florenz Ziegfeld once claimed to have paid him the highest salary ever given to a comedian. After a couple of silent films Cantor left the lights of Broadway permanently for the silver screen in the early 30's. He is best known for a succession of musicals in which he was forever surrounded by phalanxes of Goldwyn Girls. In later years he appeared on radio and television. **Highlights:** *Kid Boots* (1926), *Special Delivery* (1927), *Whoopee* (1930), *Roman Scandals* (1933), *Strike Me Pink* (1936), *Thank Your Lucky Stars* (1943), *If You Knew Susie* (1948).

CAPUCINE (1933–)

Born Germaine Lefebvre Capucine in Toulon, France, she was a top model in Paris (spotted on a sightseeing tour by a commercial photographer) before launching her acting career. Her classic features have enhanced the few films in which she has appeared, but she has not as yet been given an opportunity to display her acting talents. **Films include:** *Song Without End* (1960), *A Walk on the Wild Side* (1962), *The Pink Panther* (1964), *The Seventh Dawn* (1964), *What's New, Pussycat?* (1965), *The Honey Pot* (1967), *The Queens* (1968).

CLAUDIA CARDINALE (1939–)

"She moves like a pagan poem of love; her child's head on a seductively curved and carved woman's body," rhapsodized one journalist in 1961. Cardinale, the daughter of a Sicilian laborer, has been lauded for her "earthy" appeal. Born in Tunis, Tunisia, she was 18 when elected "the most beautiful Italian girl in Tunis." The prize, a trip to the Venice Film Festival, led to Cardinale's appearance in numerous Italian magazines, attracting the attention of film producers. She made her film debut in *I Solito Ignoti* (1958). **Film highlights:** *The Big Deal on Madonna Street* (1960), *Rocco and His Brothers* (1961), *8½* (1963), *Cartouche* (1964), *The Pink Panther* (1964), *The Professionals* (1966), *Blindfold* (1966), *The Queens* (1968), *The Red Tent* (1971).

HARRY CAREY (1878–1947)

The man who epitomized the Western hero as early as 1911 in countless silent films and whom Will Rogers once called "the greatest cowboy in pictures" learned how to ride a horse from mounted policemen in his native New York City. With the advent of sound, his

Eddie Cantor looks apprehensive about the bread being offered by a swami in Strike Me Pink. *That's George Raft in between.*

career began to slip, but he bridged the gap as leader of the expedition in *Trader Horn* (1931). In the 40's, after more than 32 years in films, he made his Broadway debut. His son, Harry Carey, Jr., played a leading part in John Ford's *Three Godfathers* (1949) which was dedicated to the memory of Harry Carey who acted in 26 Ford films. **Almost 400 films include:** *The Outcasts of Poker Flat* (1919), *Barbary Coast* (1935), *Mr. Smith Goes to Washington* (1939), *They Knew What They Wanted* (1940), *Duel in the Sun* (1947).

HARRY CAREY, JR. (1921–   )

Son of the silent film cowboy, Harry Jr. followed in his father's footsteps as a featured player in two of the finest John Ford Westerns, *She Wore a Yellow Ribbon* (1949) and *The Wagonmaster* (1950). Carey also appeared in the glittery romp *Gentlemen Prefer Blondes* (1953), with Marilyn Monroe as the lady whose best friends are diamonds. **Highlights:** *Pursued* (1947), *Mister Roberts* (1955), *The Great Imposter* (1961), *Bandolero* (1968).

JOYCE CAREY (1898–   )

Born Joyce Lawrence in London, England, Carey led a doubly successful life with careers as actress, under the Carey banner, and as playwright, under the *nom de plume* Jay Mallory. Until she came into her own as an actress, she was a supporting player to the famed Jane Cowl in most of her performances, and often performed in supporting roles with Noel Coward and Gertrude Lawrence. She made her stage debut in America in Coward's *Easy Virtue* (1935). After several inconsequential silent films, she dedicated herself to the stage for a decade until, through the magnetic appeal of Noel Coward, she returned to the screen. **Highlights:** *In Which We Serve* (1942), *Blithe Spirit* (1945), *Brief Encounter* (1946), *Cry, the Beloved Country* (1952), *A Nice Girl Like Me* (1969).

MACDONALD CAREY (1913–   )

The actor who once described himself as "sort of everyman's Everyman, the perfect middle-class type" has played all-around nice guys in most of his more than 35 features. Born in Iowa, he sang in musicals and

One of Harry Carey's typical roles was that of the veteran frontiersman in The Spoilers *with John Wayne in 1942.*

Claudia Cardinale appeared with Marcello Mastroianni in Il Bell' Antonio *in 1962.*

Macdonald Carey seems about to draw the wrath of Fred MacMurray as he gazes at Paulette Goddard in Suddenly It's Spring *(1947).*

Gilbert & Sullivan operettas and toured in tabloid versions of Shakespearean plays until he got his first big stage role opposite Gertrude Lawrence in *Lady in the Dark* (1941). It was a fortuitous production, for it brought him, as well as Danny Kaye and Victor Mature, to Hollywood. In addition to his more than 20-year screen career he has also appeared extensively on television. **Films include:** *Shadow of a Doubt* (1943), *Dream Girl* (1948), *The Great Gatsby* (1949), *Stranger at My Door* (1956), *Blue Denim* (1959), *Broken Sabre* (1965).

RICHARD CARLE (1876–1941)

The balding, bespectacled Carle was a stage actor in the United States and Britain before coming to films in 1916. Among his credits are *One Night in the Tropics* (1940), Abbott and Costello's first comedy. During his 26-year career Carle made more than 60 films. **Highlights:** *Zander the Great* (1925), *The Fleet's In* (1928), *George White's Scan-*

dals (1934), *Ninotchka* (1939), *New Wine* (1942).

MARY CARLISLE (1912–   )

Boston-born Carlisle was four when her father died and she and her mother moved to Hollywood. It was a fortunate move, for at age 14, while lunching in a studio commissary, she was noticed and offered a screen test. Delaying her movie career until she finished school, she began making films at 16, appearing in 18 films in 18 months. Typecast as the ideal college girl and campus queen of the 30's, Carlisle reached her height of popularity in the three movies made with Bing Crosby, *College Humor* (1933), *Double or Nothing* (1937) and *Doctor Rhythm* (1938). In 1942, she married and retired from the screen. **Highlights:** *Justice for Sale* (1932), *The Sweetheart of Sigma Chi* (1933), *Dance, Girl, Dance* (1940), *Baby Face Morgan* (1942).

RICHARD CARLSON (1912–   )

In his early films Carlson played the college-hero type—student or professor—the coeds' delight, and then went on to play the guy who did not get the girl until he graduated to stronger character roles. His first movie part was as Janet Gaynor's kilted lover in *The Young in Heart* (1938). He left Hollywood soon after his debut to act on Broadway, returning later to resume his screen career.

A man of varied interests, the Minnesota-born actor also wrote short stories and novels, and in the 50's he began directing films such as *Riders to the Stars* (1954) while continuing his acting career. **Credits include:** *The Little Foxes* (1941), *White Cargo* (1942), *King Solomon's Mines* (1950), *It Came From Outer Space* (1953), *Kid Rodelo* (1966), *The Valley of Gwangi* (1969).

HOAGY CARMICHAEL (1899–   )

Hoagland Howard Carmichael was born in Bloomington, Indiana. Best known as a songwriter, he once said of his most famous tune: "I had no idea what 'Stardust' meant, but I thought it would make a gorgeous title." Noted for his free improvisation on the keyboard, Carmichael claims he inherited his calling from his ragtime pianist mother. The composer of such classics as "Rockin'

Chair'' and "The Nearness of You,'' Carmichael has sung his own compositions and acted in several films. **Film highlights:** *To Have and Have Not* (1944), *The Best Years of Our Lives* (1946), *Young Man With a Horn* (1950), *Belles on Their Toes* (1952).

TULLIO CARMINATI (1894–1971)

The former Italian aristocrat pursued a European stage career before he arrived in Hollywood to appear in such silents as *The Bat* (1926), a chiller with Louise Fazenda. He later starred with Grace Moore in *One Night of Love* (1934), one of the first films to achieve a top quality mix of sound and picture in its operatic sequences. In 1963 he played a character role in *The Cardinal*. **Film credits:** *Moulin Rouge* (1934), *Roman Holiday* (1953), *El Cid* (1961).

MORRIS CARNOVSKY (1897–   )

It can be said that he began his acting career in his father's St. Louis grocery store, for he recalls that "Once, I amazed a customer by bursting forth from behind the counter with: 'Tea? Indeed, sirrah, cased in papyrus and scented with the pungence of the Orient!' '' He made his Broadway debut in *God of Vengeance* (1932) and was one of the original members of the Group Theatre in the 30's. Closely linked to the plays of Clifford Odets, he appeared in such stage hits as *Waiting for Lefty* (1935), *Awake and Sing* (1935) and *Golden Boy* (1937).

He made his movie debut as Anatole France in *The Life of Emile Zola* (1937) and continued to alternate between stage and screen, playing parts that varied from gangster roles to broad comedy until he was blacklisted during the McCarthy era in 1951. After some difficult and lean years, he returned to play the role of Shylock in *The Merchant of Venice* in the American Shakespeare Festival and was given film roles again in the early 60's. **Films include:** *Tovarich* (1937), *Rhapsody in Blue* (1945), *Our Vines Have Tender Grapes* (1945), *Saigon* (1948), *Cyrano de Bergerac* (1950), *A View From the Bridge* (1962).

MARTINE CAROL (1921–1967)

Carol, born Maryse Mourer in Basque Country, France, was a sex symbol in postwar French films and one of the first stars to appear semi-clad on screen. In the more than 40 movies she made from 1942 to 1961, the actress took "innumerable baths, had wine poured over her bare torso, and otherwise disported herself.'' Hailed as the Gallic rival of Marilyn Monroe, one of Carol's last remarks was, "For me, at the age of 46, hell is over.'' **Film highlights:** *The Wolf Farm* (1957), *Caroline Cherie* (1950), *Lola Montes* (1954), *Austerlitz* (1960), *Money, Money, Money* (1962).

SUE CAROL (1908–   )

The leading actress, born Evelyn Lederer in Chicago, Illinois, appeared in mainly forgettable films during her ten-year career. A 1928 Wampas Star, she played in such jazz-age epics as *Girls Gone Wild* (1929) and *Dancing Sweeties* (1930), one of the many dancing films of the epoch. She retired in the late 30's to become an actors' agent. Probably her best-known protegé was Alan Ladd, whom she married in 1942. **Highlights:** *Soft Cushions* (1927), *Graft* (1931), *Secret Sinners* (1934), *A Doctor's Diary* (1937).

LESLIE CARON (1931–   )

When she returned to France not long ago, she remarked that "Hollywood is an inappropriate place for an actress of 40." Her departure was a great loss, for she gave some of the most delightful performances in film history.

Born in Paris, at the age of 17 she created a sensation as the Sphinx in David Lichine's ballet, *La Rencontre*. Gene Kelly saw her perform and persuaded Vincente Minnelli to cast her opposite him in one of the Gershwin classics, *An American in Paris* (1951), a film that won six Academy Awards.

As an actress, singer, and perhaps the best female dancer in film history, Caron was irresistible in *Lili* (1953) for which she received an Academy Award nomination for Best Actress, and at the very top of her form as the puzzled and virtuous young lady who is being converted into a mistress in *Gigi* (1958), another Minnelli film which captured nine Academy Awards. While *Gigi* marked the peak of her career, she did receive her second

An elegant young Leslie Caron sips champagne in Gigi, *one of the top films of the 50's and certainly one of the prettiest.*

John Carradine played a simple dirt-farmer in The Grapes of Wrath *and it was one of his best roles, perfectly played.*

Leo Carrillo is whisked off by Jean Arthur in If You Could Only Cook *(1935).*

major British award and second Academy nomination as the pregnant French refugee in *The L-Shaped Room* (1963). **Films include:** *The Story of Three Loves* (1953), *Daddy Long Legs* (1955), *Fanny* (1961), *Promise Her Anything* (1966), *Chandler* (1971).

MARY CARR (1874–1973)

Early in her career, she played leading roles on the legitimate stage, but having raised six sons and daughters of her own, film producers relentlessly cast her in mother roles over nearly four decades. She was invariably sweet and understanding, even though her film offspring were from time to time hoodlums or murderers. To the time of her death she remained as maternal and loving as ever. **Credits include:** *Mrs. Wiggs of the Cabbage Patch* (1919), *Over the Hill to the Poorhouse* (1920), *Hogan's Alley* (1925), *Jesse James* (1927), *Kept Husbands* (1931), *Change of Heart* (1934), *Friendly Persuasion* (1956).

JOHN CARRADINE (1906–)

Tall, gaunt and sinister-looking, Carradine was a cadaverous figure in tatters doing Hamlet in full voice on Hollywood Boulevard in the late 20's and early 30's. Known as the "Bard of the Boulevard" he was rivaling Garbo as a tourist attraction when he came to the attention of Cecil B. De Mille, who began using his compelling voice with its pure diction off-camera to lead mob cries and read oratorical statements in his epics.

Once saying "I don't care how mean or despicable I am as long as the roles keep coming," he finally began to appear on camera in the early 30's and became one of the screen's busiest supporting players, playing in film classics such as *The Grapes of Wrath* (1940). In later years he turned to playing the sinister butler or evil assistant in horror films, and is still active on the screen. **More than 200 films include:** *Les Miserables* (1935), *Stagecoach* (1939), *The Ten Commandments* (1956), *Billy the Kid vs Dracula* (1966), *The Astro Zombies* (1968), *Myra Breckinridge* (1970), *Thieves Like Us* (1974).

LEO CARRILLO (1880–1961)

Los Angeles-born Carrillo made his film debut in *Mr. Antonio* (1929). Thereafter, the Spanish-American actor often played affable Western and Mexican character roles. Carrillo was Wallace Beery's lieutenant in *Viva Villa!* (1934), a stirring biography of the Mexican revolutionary, and he appeared again some 15 years later in the inevitable *Pancho Villa Returns* (1950). **Highlights of more than 75 films:** *Hell Bound* (1931), *The Broken Wing* (1932), *History Is Made at Night* (1937), *Riders of Death Valley* (1941), *Top Sergeant* (1943), *The Fugitive* (1947).

JOHN CARROLL (1908–)

Often a leading man, never a star, John Carroll, who was born in Mandeville, Louisiana, pleased audiences with his clean-cut good looks and excellent voice. He played leading roles in a number of films of the 40's at the time when musicals were in flower. After *Susan and God* (1940), he joined a more earthy crew of the Marx Brothers in *Go West* (1941). Carroll also appeared with Abbott and Costello in *Rio Rita* (1942) and in the Air Force drama *Flying Tigers* (1942). **Highlights:** *Fiesta* (1947), *The Flame* (1948), *Decision at Sundown* (1957), *Plunderers of the Painted Flats* (1959).

LEO G. CARROLL (1892–1972) ·

This polished British actor was perhaps best known for his television series portrayals of Cosmo Topper in *Topper* and of Mr. Waverly, the spymaster, in *The Man From U.N.C.L.E.* During an acting acreer that began with grammar school Gilbert and Sullivan productions, the droll, urbane Carroll played countless character roles in legitimate theatre, films and television. Late in life, looking back over his career, Carroll once said, "It's brought me much pleasure of mind and heart." **Highlights of more than 40 films:** *Sadie McKee* (1934), *The Barretts of Wimpole Street* (1934), *Rebecca* (1940), *The House on 92nd Street* (1945), *The Swan* (1956), *One Spy Too Many* (1966).

MADELEINE CARROLL (1906–)

A product of West Bromwich, not exactly one of the key towns on the itinerary of visitors to England, her cool beauty made her far and away the most popular British female film star during the 30's. Her English film debut was in *The Guns of Loos* (1928) and her peaches-and-cream charm kept her working around the clock in British plays and movies for the next five years. Her first American-made film was John Ford's *The World Moves On* (1934) with Franchot Tone, and while the world moved, the movie was a flop and didn't.

More glamorous than ever, Carroll rose to the top level of stardom as the harried but heroic heroine of two fine Hitchcock suspense classics: *The Thirty-nine Steps* (1935) and *Secret Agent* (1936). Thereafter, audiences loved her in films as varied as *The General Died at Dawn* (1936) with Gary Cooper to *My Son, My Son!* (1940) with Brian Aherne. With the spread of the war in 1942 she left Hollywood for more than three years of solid war work, a sacrifice which won her a Legion of Honor award from the French government.

She appeared in several additional films in the late 40's but since then has retired from the movie world and divided her time between Paris and London. **Credits include:** *Young Woodley* (1930), *Lloyds of London* (1936), *The Prisoner of Zenda* (1937), *Café Society* (1939), *One Night in Lisbon* (1941), *The Fan* (1949).

NANCY CARROLL (1906–1965)

Born Nancy Lahiff in New York, her first stage appearances came in her early teens in Shubert musicals. Her first important film chance came in 1928 when she appeared with Buddy Rogers in the screen version of the wildly popular Broadway success, *Abie's Irish Rose*. The vivacious redhead starred in more than 20 films before her retirement in the late 30's. While Nancy Carroll was an intelligent and sparkling performer, many of her pictures were on the dreary side and have stood up rather badly with the passage of years. **Other credits:** *The Dance of Life* (1929), *Laughter* (1930), *Child of Manhattan* (1933), *The Kiss Before the Mirror* (1933), *That Certain Age* (1938).

JACK CARSON (1910–1963)

The bulky ''comedy actor''—his own term in preference to comedian—was born in Canada but grew up in Milwaukee. Carson attended Carleton College in Minnesota

Madeleine Carroll comforts Tyrone Power in Lloyds of London, *the picture that gave Power his first starring role.*

Jack Carson, playing the studio publicity man, is being pushed out by James Mason in A Star is Born.

John Cassavetes and Mia Farrow look cheerful enough in this early scene with Ruth Gordon in Rosemary's Baby; *the peculiar stuff came later.*

JOHN CASSAVETES (1929–)

This fine actor/director has appeared in a number of mediocre films. In 1962, on his way to Dublin (to play a gambler in a minor drama, *The Western Boy*) via London he was asked by the National Film Theatre to show a film he had made in New York with the Variety Arts Studio, an actor's workshop he had founded. Cassavetes had directed the film *Shadows* (1959) with incisiveness, truthfulness and sympathy. Although not a box-office success, it made its mark both in England and in the U.S. and made a name for Cassavetes as a director. Following this, Cassavetes acted in and directed films such as *Faces* (1968), which again got critical recognition but was too brutally frank for general public acceptance. Recently he directed *Minnie & Moscowitz* (1971) starring his wife, Gena Rowlands. **Major performances include:** *Taxi* (1954), *Edge of the City* (1957), *The Dirty Dozen* (1967), *Rosemary's Baby* (1968), *Husbands* (director and star, 1970).

JEAN-PIERRE CASSEL (1932–)

An athletic, cavorting, comically-serious Casanova is the part generally given French actor Cassel. Most of his work in films has been done under the direction of Philippe de Broca, who, it has been said, sees much of himself in both the real life and movie characters of Cassel. The popular French film star was a find of Gene Kelly, who launched him in *The Happy Road* (1956). Cassel has also made stage appearances, generally in wistful farces like *The Joker*. **Highlights:** *The Love Game* (1960), *The Five-Day Lover* (1961), *The Elusive Corporal* (1962), *Is Paris Burning?* (1966), *The Discreet Charm of the Bourgeoisie* (1972), *Baxter* (1973).

WALTER CATLETT (1889–1960)

A florid performer with a marvelous talent for appearing exasperated, he created unforgettable characters like the crooked politician caught in the act, the tobacco-chewing cowpuncher and scatterbrained judge pounding his gavel and yelling "I want order in this Court!" He started his career as an opera singer, switched to dramatic roles and to mu-

where he "majored in football" before beginning his career in vaudeville. Famous for his double-takes and sheepish grins on screen, the actor was also active on stage and in television. "When I arrived in Hollywood," Carson liked to recall, "the cameraman looked at me and said, "Gosh, we'll need two cameras for this test." **Highlights of over 70 films:** *The Bride Came C.O.D.* (1941), *Arsenic and Old Lace* (1944), *Mildred Pierce* (1945), *A Star Is Born* (1954), *Cat on a Hot Tin Roof* (1958), *King of the Roaring Twenties* (1961).

ANTHONY CARUSO (c. 1913–)

Caruso played a good many secondary roles during his 30 years in films. He was seen most often as a belligerent character, often of Italian background. His first major film role was as a gangster in Tyrone Power's *Johnny Apollo* (1940). **Highlights:** *Objective Burma* (1945), *The Iron Mistress* (1952), *The Badlanders* (1958), *Young Dillinger* (1965), *Nobody Loves Flapping Eagle* (1970).

sicals before making his screen debut in *Second Youth* (1924). He gave comic cameo performances in hundreds of films such as the memorable jail scene in *Bringing Up Baby* (1938). Off-screen he had a predilection for gambling and, although he claimed to have earned more than 2 million dollars, he rarely had any money. **Films include:** *Palmy Days* (1931), *Back Street* (1932), *Mr. Deeds Goes to Town* (1936), *Up in Arms* (1944), *The Inspector General* (1949), *Friendly Persuasion* (1956).

PAUL CAVANAGH (1895–1960)

The English stage actor came to films in the late 20's and thereafter played several debonair roles and many more as a menace of some kind. Cavanagh appeared in a number of second-rate chillers, but did turn up now and again in "classics" like *Humoresque* (1946). **Highlights:** *A Bill of Divorcement* (1932), *Tarzan and His Mate* (1934), *Captains of the Clouds* (1942), *Shadows on the Stairs* (1943), *House of Wax* (1953), *Francis in the Haunted House* (1956).

HOBART CAVANAUGH (1887–1950)

For nearly 20 years on screen he was henpecked, cowed or generally nervous. Every once in a while, Cavanaugh departed from his repertoire of husbands, clerks and bookkeepers to play the villain, as in *Horror Island* (1941). **Highlights:** *I Cover the Waterfront* (1933), *Captain Blood* (1935), *Cain and Mabel* (1936), *Kismet* (1944), *You Gotta Stay Happy* (1948), *A Letter to Three Wives* (1949), *Stella* (1950).

GINO CERVI (1901–)

The Italian actor, whose film career spanned more than 30 years, starred in *Four Steps in the Clouds* (1948), the landmark comedy about the misadventures of a young man trying to return home. Cervi was perhaps best known in the U.S. for his role as mayor of the small town in the *Don Camillo* series (1951–1956). **Highlights:** *Frontier* (1934), *Fabiole* (1947), *The Naked Maja* (1959), *Becket* (1964).

GEORGE CHAKIRIS (1934–)

Born in Norwood, Ohio, Chakiris attended the American School of Dance before making his film debut in *West Side Story* (1961), for which he received the Academy Award for Best Supporting Actor. Through the 60's he appeared in several action and suspense films before he was back dancing again, this time with Gene Kelly in *The Young Girls of Rochefort* (1968). **Highlights:** *Diamondhead* (1963), *Is Paris Burning?* (1966), *The Big Cube* (1969).

Walter Catlett was one of the most durable and comical of Hollywood's supporting cast reliables.

Suave and bemedalled, Paul Cavanagh has stepped into Claudette Colbert's drawing room in Tonight Is Ours *(1933).*

One of Richard Chamberlain's best movie roles was in The Madwoman of Chaillot *and he made the most of it.*

This studio still of Jeff Chandler was made to publicize his role in Iron Man *(1951).*

RICHARD CHAMBERLAIN
(1935–   )

Ignored by Hollywood until he became popular as the lead in the *Dr. Kildare* television series in 1961, he once asserted that he didn't know how to act until he went to England to learn his craft. He thereafter became the first American actor to play Hamlet in England since John Barrymore, and has steadily been changing his image from the boyish-looking clean-cut American of *Joy in the Morning* (1965) to such personalities as Byron in *Lady Caroline Lamb* (1973). He has also appeared quite successfully in a number of television dramas such as *The Last of the Belles* (1974). **Films include:** *Petulia* (1968), *The Madwoman of Chaillot* (1969), *Julius Caesar* (1970), *The Three Musketeers* (1974).

MARGE (1923–   ) and GOWER (1921–   ) CHAMPION

This husband and wife dancing team first appeared together at a club in Montreal in 1947. Previously, each had pursued separate dancing and performing careers. Marge was

the daughter of Ernest Belcher, a Hollywood ballet master. She studied under him, and in her teens taught ballet and made bit appearances in films. Her screen debut was made in *Sorority House* (1939). She went from films to the stage, securing good roles in *Portrait of a Lady* (1942) and *Dark of the Moon* (1945).

Gower Champion began his career at 15 by winning a dance contest. Quitting school, he and his teenage partner went to New York and appeared in clubs and on Broadway. After a stint in the Coast Guard, Champion returned home to find that his former partner had retired. When he completed the filming of *Till the Clouds Roll By* (debut, 1946), he began to search for a replacement. Marge Belcher was suggested to him as a likely substitute.

Marge and Gower were married in October of 1947. In 1950 they made their first joint film appearance in *Mr. Music* and thereafter made several pictures throughout the 50's. When Marge retired in 1960, Gower began a successful career as a stage director, working on such hits as *Bye, Bye, Birdie* (1960), *Hello, Dolly!* (1964), *I Do, I Do* (1966), and *Irene* (1973). In 1973, the couple was divorced. **Credits include:** *Show Boat* (1951), *Lovely to Look At* (1952), *Jupiter's Darling* (1955).

CHICK CHANDLER (1905–   )

The versatile actor played in a wide variety of films, including comedy, science fiction, Westerns and war drama. One of his best-known films is *Swanee River* (1939), the biography of Stephen Foster. **Highlights:** *Alexander's Ragtime Band* (1938), *Mother Wore Tights* (1947), *Family Honeymoon* (1949), *Battle Cry* (1955), *The Naked Gun* (1956).

GEORGE CHANDLER (1905–   )

His face is familiar to most movie and television watchers, for his roles have included reporters, taxi drivers, hotel clerks, radio operators, salesmen, policemen, ticket takers, mailmen and panhandlers. His first featured role, as Ginger Rogers' husband in *Roxie Hart* (1942), came 12 years after his screen debut in *The Light of the Western Stars*. **Movies include:** *Nothing Sacred* (1937), *It Happened Tomorrow* (1944), *The*

Paleface (1948), *The High and the Mighty* (1954), *Dead Ringer* (1964).

HELEN CHANDLER (1909–1968)

She played leading roles in several films before her abrupt retirement in the mid-30's. Helen Chandler starred with Bela Lugosi in *Dracula* (1931), which proved to be one of the most long-lived horror films ever made. She also appeared in *Outward Bound* (1930), an unusual story about a shipload of people who come to realize they are dead. **Highlights:** *The Music Master* (1927), *The Last Flight* (1931), *Christopher Strong* (1933), *Long Lost Father* (1934), *It's a Bet* (1935).

JEFF CHANDLER (1918–1961)

The silver-haired actor was a successful radio star before coming to films. Spotted by Dick Powell, he was signed to a long-term contract even before his first picture, *Johnny O'Clock* (1947), was completed.

One of Chandler's most popular roles was as Cochise, the Apache chief in *Broken Arrow* (1950), a film which set new standards for its sympathetic portrayal of Indians. His penchant for action films led to several memorable bouts, notably in *The Spoilers* (1955) and in *Iron Man* (1951), which happened to be about boxing. **Highlights:** *The Battle at Apache Pass* (1952), *Jeanne Eagels* (1957), *Thunder in the Sun* (1959), *Return to Peyton Place* (1961), *Merrill's Marauders* (1962).

LON CHANEY (1883–1930)

''The Man of a Thousand Faces'' was born in Colorado Springs, the son of deaf-mute parents, a fact which may have had a strong psychological influence in determining the grotesque roles he made famous as one of the great stars of silent pictures. In his early days he worked in a theatre owned by his brother and then became a comedian and song-and-dance man in third-rate road companies.

The shape of things to come became apparent when he played an ultra-hairy primitive man in *The Lion, the Lamb, and the Man* (1917), but it wasn't until he played the bogus cripple in *The Miracle Man* (1919), a picture which also made stars of Betty Compson and Thomas Meighan, that he took the country by storm.

Lon Chaney scared the wits out of his audiences in scenes such as this one from Phantom of the Opera *with Mary Philbin.*

In the years that followed he caused audiences to scream, faint or grip their chair seats as he played the lame, the halt and the blind, gangsters, mad scientists and a Chinese laundryman. His most famous role was Quasimodo, the hideously deformed hunchback in *The Hunchback of Notre Dame* (1923) who elicited audience sympathy. Thereafter, he starred in more monster roles, as a crippled bishop and tragic circus clown and, most effectively, as a ventriloquist who played a diabolical old harridan in *The Unholy Three* (1925) and as the acid-scarred musician in *The Phantom of the Opera* (1925).

The outrageous makeups and outfits he had to squeeze into made his last years physical torture; he suffered from aching bones, acute

Lon Chaney, Jr., in his best-known and most sympathetic role, as Lennie in Of Mice and Men, *is shown here with Betty Field.*

headaches and eye strain. A revised talkie version of *The Unholy Three* was nearing completion when he died of throat cancer. **Other Highlights:** *Oliver Twist* (1922), *He Who Gets Slapped* (1924), *The Road to Mandalay* (1926), *Laugh, Clown, Laugh* (1928), *West of Zanzibar* (1928), *Where East Is East* (1929).

LON CHANEY, JR. (1907–1973)

Born Creighton Chaney in Oklahoma City, the son of the illustrious actor, he resisted an acting career at first and it was not until he gained recognition on his own that he changed his name to Lon Chaney, Jr.

During his career he turned down dozens of offers to re-create his father's roles and in his youth worked as a butcher boy, plumber, fruit picker and boilermaker. While he did play monster roles such as the Wolf Man, his most

notable performance was as Lennie in *Of Mice and Men* (1940) which made him a star. **More than 100 films include:** *Bird of Paradise* (1932), *Accent on Youth* (1935), *Jesse James* (1939), *The Ghost of Frankenstein* (1942), *House of Dracula* (1945), *Not as a Stranger* (1955), *Buckskin* (1968).

CHARLES CHAPLIN (1889–   )

Many decades have passed since motion picture critics, along with connoisseurs of related arts, gave us to understand that Chaplin was not only the greatest film comedian of all time but a post-Renaissance master whose genius extended to the ballet, the art of pantomime and to the innermost workings of the human soul. It is with considerable trepidation, therefore, that one respectfully suggests that over the years there were other comedians—Buster Keaton, W.C. Fields, Jacques Tati and Woody Allen, to name a few—whose performances often approached, sometimes equalled, and on occasions surpassed those of The Little Tramp. For example, there was Jacques Tati's encounter with a garden hose in *M. Hulot's Holiday* and W. C. Fields in *The Dentist* probing cautiously with a stethoscope to determine where, if at all, a human mouth lurked behind the monstrously overgrown beard of his patient.

Chaplin was born in a sleazy section of South London. At the age of five, with his mother in an infirmary and his father dead, he sang his first song on stage and went on to become a successful music hall comedian. In 1913, on tour in the United States, he accepted a $150 a week offer to join the Keystone company and such early favorites Ford Sterling, Mack Swain, Mabel Normand, Fatty Arbuckle and Chester Conklin. In 1914 he made 35 films (mostly one-reelers) at an average cost per film of $1000. Today most of them seem repetitious and unfunny, but it was at this time that Chaplin switched to the derby and cane, minute mustache and waddling gait, frock coat and baggy pants that were to become famous worldwide.

In short order Chaplin began to write and direct his films, often playing with Mabel Normand, but more notably with Marie Dressler in his first six-reeler, *Tillie's Punctured Romance* (1914)—a film which made his leadership in the world of movies secure.

In the years that followed he went to Essanay (at $1240 a week plus bonuses) then to Mutual ($10,000 a week plus $150,000 bonus); finally to First National ($150,000 for each two-reeler!). Of the scores of films made in this era, many with Edna Purviance (one of his many female favorites whom he failed to marry) several stand out—*The Floorwalker* (1916), *Easy Street* (1919), *Shoulder Arms* (1918) plus the classic six-reeler with Jackie Coogan, *The Kid* (1921), and a four-reeler, *The Pilgrim* (1923).

In the early 20's, along with Douglas Fairbanks and Mary Pickford, he organized United Artists and it was under this banner that his greatest films were produced. These included *The Gold Rush* (1925), an arctic saga immortalized by the Cordon Bleu care with which Chaplin prepared and ate a boiled shoe with shoelace trimmings and performed the ballet of the breakfast rolls played to the tune of "The Oceana Roll"; *City Lights* (1931), with a stone drunk Harry Myers who recognized Charlie only when under the influence; and the wildly funny *Modern Times* (1936) with Chaplin again playing the exploited and put-upon Tramp, but this time at the mercy of a mechanized society. All of these were silents, for Chaplin was the last producer to succumb to pictures that talked.

After two more films—the brilliant lampoon of fascist dictatorships, *The Great Dictator* (1940), in which he played both a Jewish barber and Hitler to Jack Oakie's Mussolini; and the more controversial *Monsieur Verdoux* (1947)—he left the United States and went to live in Switzerland with his fourth wife, Oona, daughter of playwright Eugene O'Neill. Throughout his career his divorces and rumored extra-curricular activities with other ladies had drawn him bad publicity. A baseless paternity suit, combined with his espousal of liberal causes in the McCarthy era, hurt him badly. When he announced that his new picture, *Limelight* (1952), would first be shown abroad, he was told that he might not be granted a re-entry visa. He decided not to ask for one. During his long, self-imposed exile he lived happily with Oona, raised a delightful family, made only two pictures and wrote his memoirs, which, unhappily, turned out to be a smashingly dull and egocentric volume.

After nearly 25 years abroad, like his own Little Tramp walking alone into the twilight of a dying day, Chaplin returned to the United States to receive a thunderous ovation and a special Academy Award for his massive contribution to motion pictures. **A few of his other films:** *The Face on the Barroom Floor* (1914), *The Tramp* (1915), *The Fireman* (1916), *A Woman of Paris* (he directed Edna Purviance in this film, which is allegedly a masterpiece though no one has seen it for nearly 50 years, 1923) *The Circus* (1928), *A King in New York* (1957), *The Countess from Hong Kong* (1967).

EDWARD CHAPMAN (1901–   )

A former bank clerk, the British character actor made his stage debut in 1924. He launched his film career in 1930 in Alfred Hitchcock's *Juno and the Paycock*. **Among his movies are:** *Ships With Wings* (1942), *Bhowani Junction* (1956), *School for Scoundrels* (1960).

Charles Chaplin's "Everyman"— The Little Tramp.

Monsieur Verdoux was a brilliant and total change of pace for Chaplin, but was unpopular on first release and then withdrawn. It has since become a "cult" favorite.

Cyd Charisse in a tough dance sequence with Fred Astaire.

CYD CHARISSE (1923–   )

The long-limbed brunette beauty was one of Fred Astaire's last dancing partners in films, but aside from that distinction her career was studded with ill fortune. She was born Tula Ellice Finklea in Amarillo, Texas, and after studying ballet for a year was given a job with the Ballet Russe. She married her ballet teacher, Nico Charisse, but the union was short-lived, and in the late 40's, she divorced Charisse and married actor-singer Tony Martin. She switched to motion pictures and received parts, all of them anonymous, in such musicals as *Ziegfeld Follies* (1946) and *The Harvey Girls* (1946).

When important roles came along, there was always something that prevented her from accepting them. Pregnancy and then childbirth eliminated her from playing opposite Gene Kelly in *An American in Paris*, and the role went to Leslie Caron. Prior to that, her opportunity to star with Fred Astaire and

Playing the long-suffering female, as usual, Ruth Chatterton appeared in Sorrel and Son *with Fredric March in 1930.*

Judy Garland in *Easter Parade* (1948) vanished when she broke her leg and the part went to Ann Miller instead.

A break finally came her way when Gene Kelly cast her in *Singin' in the Rain* (1952). The following year she played opposite Fred Astaire in *The Band Wagon* (1953), a picture which is believed to contain one of Astaire's top performances. One more important film, *Silk Stockings* (1957), a version of Garbo's *Ninotchka*, was her last musical. Although it didn't live up to *The Band Wagon* in quality, there was one memorable solo number by Charisse in which she discarded her severe and mannish Russian cottons in favor of silks and satins. During the 60's she occasionally appeared in dramatic roles and supplemented her screen appearances with nightclub and summer theatre work. **Her credits include:** *Mission to Moscow* (debut, 1943), *Till the Clouds Roll By* (1946), *East Side, West Side* (1949), *Sombrero* (1953), *Brigadoon* (1954), *Black Tights* (1962), *Assassination in Rome* (1967).

SPENCER CHARTERS (1878–1943)

The gentle-looking character actor often played harmless country fellows well endowed with horse sense. In pictures from the early 20's to the 40's, Charters appeared in John Ford's *Mr. Deeds Goes to Town* (1936) with the "pixilated" Gary Cooper, in *Jesse James* (1939) with Tyrone Power, and in *Tobacco Road* (1941). **Highlights:** *Little Old New York* (1923), *Janice Meredith* (1924), *Whoopee* (1930), *Twenty Thousand Years in Sing Sing* (1933), *Banjo on My Knee* (1936), *In Old Chicago* (1938), *Juke Girl* (1942).

ILKA CHASE (1905–   )

Although she is basically known as an author of successful novels and social commentaries, she has had an extensive stage and film career as an actress. She began as a child model for *Vogue* magazine, which her mother edited, and appeared in many Broadway plays, most notably the original production of *The Women*.

On the screen, she specialized in playing elegant and sardonic women in such films as *Now, Voyager* (1942). **Some of her other**

films include: *Paris Bound* (1929), *Miss Tatlock's Millions* (1948), *The Big Knife* (1955), *Ocean's Eleven* (1960).

RUTH CHATTERTON (1893–1961)

One of the most popular actresses on Broadway in the 20's, and a director of several plays as well, she accompanied her then-husband Ralph Forbes when he went West to defend the desert stockade in Paramount's *Beau Geste* (1926). Emil Jannings saw a stage performance by her on the coast and cast her as a no-good wife in *Sins of the Fathers* (1929). With the coming of sound the following year her stock soared and by 1931 readers of fan magazines were voting her the "finest actress" of the year.

A fine actress she was indeed, but the films she played in were almost invariably dreadful. She nearly always played a mature and put-upon female, a woman deceived, a constant sufferer who was called upon to make some of the most idiotic lines ever written sound believable—a feat she almost accomplished. Perhaps her best script and performance was as the insular, non-responsive wife of Walter Huston in *Dodsworth* (1936). Two years later, bored with bad scripts, she abandoned films and returned to her first love, the stage. Not entirely, however, for she also was an accomplished novelist and one of her books, *Homeward Borne*, became a best seller. **Film credits include:** *Madame X* (1929), *The Magnificent Lie* (1931), *Female* (1933), *Lady of Secrets* (1936), *The Rat* (1938).

VIRGINIA CHERRILL (1908–   )

Discovered by Chaplin, she was the enchanting blind flower girl in *City Lights* (1931). The film made her an overnight star, but sound pictures were in and her high-pitched voice and nasal Midwestern accent did not fit her features. She never managed to equal her first success.

Born in Illinois, a farm girl, she went to Hollywood as a result of a beauty contest and there met Chaplin. In 1933 she became Cary Grant's first wife, but they were divorced two years later. She remarried three more times and retired in 1936. She now lives in San

Two smiles and four hands convey the message before bursting into song—Maurice Chevalier and Jeanette MacDonald in Love Me Tonight.

Diego. **Films include:** *Delicious* (1931), *Charlie Chan's Greatest Case* (1933), *What Price Crime?* (1935), *Troubled Waters* (1936).

MAURICE CHEVALIER (1888–1972)

He spent much of his career fighting with producers who insisted on casting him in debonair and coy roles, yet it was as such a Gallic charmer and gay boulevardier that he became an authentic superstar with a score or more hugely successful films to his credit. Born in Paris in the same year the Eiffel Tower came into existence, he worked in cafes and music halls, ending up in the Folies Bergères as dancing partner to Mistinguette, the star whose celebrated legs were insured for some millions of francs. He was wounded and captured by the Germans in World War I. After the war, he was moderately successful in Paris and London, but it wasn't until he sang "Every little breeze seems to whisper Louise. . ."in Paramount's *Innocents of Paris* (1929) that he skyrocketed to stardom. The same year, his second American film, *The Love Parade* with Jeanette MacDonald, set a new standard for musicals, and his accent, crinkly-eyed wink and sly smile were imitated in every corner of the world. Thereafter, working with directors as different as Lubitsch, Cukor, Mamoulian and René Clair, Chevalier always remained Chevalier—a carefree, vivacious performer who had once told an interviewer: "There are 10,000 ways of loving. The main thing is to chose one that goes best with your age."

During the Second World War he sang for German occupation forces, and as a result his career diminished greatly until it was revealed that he had been attempting to help Jewish friends escape the Nazi occupation and had been working with the French Underground. Thereafter he confined himself to French films and spectacularly successful stage appearances until his reappearance in the movie *Gigi* (1958), as an aging Parisian man-about-town. *Gigi* brought him a special Oscar. After his 80th birthday and shortly before his death, Chevalier was still wowing audiences with his television and nightclub routines, and still playing the role he always hated—that of a

gay and insouciant Parisian heart-breaker. **Highlights of his career:** *The Big Pond* (1930), *Playboy of Paris* (1930), *Love Me Tonight* (1932), *The Merry Widow* (1934), *J' Avais Sept Filles* (1954), *Count Your Blessings* (1959), *Fanny* (1961), *A New Kind of Love* (1963), *Monkeys Go Home* (1967).

MADY CHRISTIANS (1900–1951)

Though essentially a stage star, the Austrian actress appeared in several films of unusual quality. She was seen in the perennially popular love story *Seventh Heaven* (1937) and in Arthur Miller's searing drama *All My Sons* (1948).

Perhaps she felt most at home in the highly romantic *Letters From an Unknown Woman* (1948), the story of an indifferent pianist and a twice-wronged woman, elegantly staged in old Vienna. Black-listed as a Communist sympathizer in the hysterical McCarthy era, her career was destroyed. **Highlights:** *The Runaway Princess* (1929), *Escapade* (1935), *Heidi* (1937), *Address Unknown* (1944).

JULIE CHRISTIE (1940–   )

Born in Assam Province, India, the daughter of a tea planter, Christie attended school in England and began her drama studies in 1958. The beautiful English actress was a member of the Birmingham Repertory Group and the Royal Shakespeare Theatre. She made her film debut in *Crooks Anonymous* (1963) and since that time has given fine performances in a number of notable films, such as *Billy Liar* (1963), *Dr. Zhivago* (1965) and *Far From the Madding Crowd* (1967). In 1965 she won Best Actress awards from the British Film Academy and the Motion Picture Academy of Arts and Sciences for her brilliant performance in *Darling*. **Films include:** *Young Cassidy* (1965), *Fahrenheit 451* (1966), *Petulia* (1968), *In Search of Gregory* (1969), *The Go-Between* (1971), *Don't Look Now* (1973).

BERTON CHURCHILL (1876–1946)

In films from the mid-20's, the Canadian character actor was seen in hundreds of roles, often as a blustery, small-town citizen or a strict parent. He was the banker aboard the John Ford *Stagecoach* (1939) who turned out to be an embezzler on the side. **Highlights:**

Maurice Chevalier sings "I Remember It Well" with Hermione Gingold in Gigi.

Tongues of Flame (1924), *Scandal for Sale* (1932), *I Am a Fugitive From a Chain Gang* (1932), *Madame Butterfly* (1933), *Judge Priest* (1934), *Dimples* (1936), *Saturday's Children* (1940).

EDUARDO CIANNELLI (1884–1969)

Before becoming one of Hollywood's most menacing and expert villains, he was a doctor in his native Italy and an opera singer at La Scala. After World War I, he was a familiar figure on Broadway in operettas and in plays such as *Yellow Jack, The Front Page* and *St. Joan* with Katharine Cornell.

He made his screen debut in *Reunion in Vienna* (1933), a role he also created on the stage. He again repeated his stage role in the movie version of *Winterset* (1936). In his more than 24 years in Hollywood, he appeared in scores of films. **Highlights:** *Gunga Din* (1939), *Foreign Correspondent* (1940), *For Whom the Bell Tolls* (1943), *Houseboat* (1958), *The Brotherhood* (1968).

DIANE CILENTO (1933–)

Although she was already an established actress before her marriage, Cilento frequently is identified in the public mind as the wife (now former wife) of actor Sean Connery of James Bond fame.

Cilento broke with her family's medical tradition—father is in tropical medicine, mother in gynecology—to go on the stage. She began studying acting after her family moved to New York from their native Australia. After a stint at the American Academy of Dramatic Arts, she went to London to attend the Royal Academy of Dramatic Arts. Later, she joined the Manchester Library Theatre in England.

She scored her first success on the New York stage opposite Michael Redgrave in *Tiger at the Gates*. Cilento's performance earned her the New York Drama Critics Award and a nomination for a Tony.

One of her more famous film roles was as the sexy, tousled peasant who coos "Tom" through the bushes at Albert Finney in *Tom Jones* (1963), for which she was nominated for an Academy Award for Best Supporting Actress. In addition to acting, Cilento has written two books, *The Manipulator* and *The Hybrid*. **Films include:** *The Passing*

Stranger (1954), *Passage Home* (1955), *The Woman for Joe* (1956), *The Admirable Crichton* (1957), *The Naked Edge* (1961), *I Thank a Fool* (1962), *The Third Secret* (1964), *Rattle of a Simple Man* (1964), *The Agony and the Ecstasy* (1965), *Hombre* (1967), *Negatives* (1968).

DANE CLARK (1913–)

Although Bernard Zanville, later Dane Clark, had a law degree from St. John's, legal jobs were scarce during the Depression. Clark worked on a road gang and tried boxing and modeling before turning to the theatre. Cast as the tough-guy leading man of the 40's he was still playing pugnacious toughs in the 50's and 60's. Clark once said of his television roles, "Eugene O'Neill this ain't. It's television . . . and a good place to visit but not to stay." **Major films include:** *Destination Tokyo* (1944), *A Stolen Life* (1946), *The Toughest Man Alive* (1955), *Murder by Proxy* (1955), *Whistle* (1967).

In a tense scene in Fahrenheit 451, *Julie Christie with Oskar Werner.*

Eduardo Ciannelli is restrained by Victor McLaglen, as Douglas Fairbanks, Jr. and Cary Grant look on rather apprehensively in Gunga Din.

Poor Mae Clarke. Here she is having her ears tugged by James Cagney in Lady Killer—*a year before it was a grapefruit in the face from the same gent in* Public Enemy.

FRED CLARK (1914–1968)

Making his movie debut as a detective in *The Unsuspected* (1947) after extensive theatre experience, Clark played a series of stuffy businessmen, disreputable officers, corrupt newspaper columnists before becoming firmly typed in comic roles that called for exasperated and frustrated characterizations.

He alternated between stage and screen, but became best known as the next door neighbor in a perpetual state of uncontrolled indignation in the *Burns and Allen* television comedy series. **More than 50 movies include:** *Ride the Pink Horse* (1947), *Sunset Boulevard* (1950), *Dreamboat* (1952), *The Solid Gold Cadillac* (1956), *Bells Are Ringing* (1960), *Skidoo* (1968).

PETULA CLARK (1932–   )

A vastly popular singer in the United States, England and France, Clark's records are "big sellers" in over 14 countries. She is a two-time winner of Grammy Awards for "Downtown" and for "I Know a Place."

Born in Epsom, near London, she was a movie star at the age of 12 (with her debut in *A Medal From the General*)—considered to be England's Shirley Temple—and by the time she was 21 she was hailed as Britain's "Miss Television."

Clark has been leading lady and co-star of such male notables of filmdom as Peter O'Toole, Peter Ustinov and Alec Guinness. Her remarkable voice, vibrant personality and presence combine to make outstanding performances. **Highlights:** *London Town* (1946), *Vice Versa* (1948), *The Card* (1952), *Finian's Rainbow* (1968), *Goodbye, Mr. Chips* (1969).

MAE CLARKE (1916–   )

To her dismay, and although she made more than 85 films, she is best remembered as the girl who had a grapefruit pushed in her face by James Cagney in *The Public Enemy* (1931). Starting in amateur theatricals in Atlantic City, Clarke sang in nightclubs and eventually ended up in the chorus lines of musicals before traveling to Hollywood. Since the 40's she has been playing bit parts in films and has been appearing regularly on television. **Highlights:** *The Front Page* (1931), *Waterloo Bridge* (1931), *Lady Killer* (1934), *Not as a Stranger* (1955), *Ask Any Girl* (1959), *Thoroughly Modern Millie* (1967).

GEORGE CLEVELAND (1886–1965)

Known to television fans as the benevolent Gramps of *Lassie* (1955–65), Cleveland had been playing the type for years on film. He arrived in Hollywood in 1904, well before some of the film pioneers got there, and played in some 150 comedies, Westerns and dramas. **Highlights:** *Ghost Town Riders* (1938), *The Spoilers* (1942), *Sunbonnet Sue* (1945), *The Wistful Widow of Wagon Gap* (1947), *Untamed Heiress* (1954).

MONTGOMERY CLIFT (1920–1966)

Clift's screen stardom dated from his first two films, both made in 1948—*The Search*, a modest, near-documentary film done by Fred Zinnemann about the plight of Europe's homeless children following World War II, and Howard Hawks' great Western, *Red River*, in which he played John Wayne's rugged-but-gentle foster son. His acting career, however, had begun long before on the New York stage: at the age of 15 he had achieved Broadway billing in *Jubilee*.

His portrayals of restless, tortured characters were perhaps not far from his real life. Slight in build, with a sensitively handsome and rather gaunt face, he was a brilliant actor whose personal life was troubled by depressions and alcoholism. In 1949 he played the passionate but disappointing suitor in Henry James' *The Heiress* (opposite Olivia de Havilland); then came the unfortunate George Eastman in *A Place in the Sun* (1951—opposite his good friend Elizabeth Taylor), and the proud young Corporal Prewitt in *From Here to Eternity* (1953). By 1961 when he was cast in *The Misfits* (the last picture ever made by both Clark Gable and Marilyn Monroe) he had suffered a bone-shattering automobile accident and his battered face proved perfect for the role of the sad and lonely rodeo rider. Clift died in 1966. **Other film credits:** *Raintree County* (1957), *The Young Lions* (1958), *Lonelyhearts* (1959), *Suddenly, Last Summer* (1959), *Freud* (1962), *The Defector* (1966).

COLIN CLIVE (1898–1937)

The British actor remained in Hollywood after going there to film the World War I drama *Journey's End* (1930). He played several choice roles during the 30's including Mr. Rochester in *Jane Eyre* (1934) and the doctor who created the monster in *Frankenstein* (1931). Clive, generally cast in somber parts, was featured with Katharine Hepburn in *Christopher Strong* (1933), the tragic story of a woman pilot. **Highlights:** *Lily Christine* (1932), *Bride of Frankenstein* (1935), *Clive of India* (1935), *History Is Made at Night* (1937).

E. E. CLIVE (1879–1940)

A veteran of 1,159 plays before he made his film debut, Clive was noted for his screen portrayals of sour-faced butlers, fluent cockneys, and harrumphing dukes and earls. E.E. Clive died in 1940 while holding a cup of tea in his hands.

Born in Wales, he made his stage debut at the Drury Lane but achieved his greatest success in this country when he formed his own

In Our Man Flint *(1966) Lee J. Cobb played a character of roughly his own real age—a rare occurrence. He played William Holden's father in* Golden Boy, *for example, though he is only seven years older.*

repertory company in Boston at the Copley Theatre in 1916. He remained there for 14 years, operating a very successful company and appearing in 301 plays.

In 1930 he went to Hollywood and started another company, but after making his film debut in *The Invisible Man* (1933), he devoted himself exclusively to motion pictures. **More than 50 films include:** *The Bride of Frankenstein* (1935), *The Charge of the Light Brigade* (1936), *Camille* (1937), *Raffles* (1940).

LEE J. COBB (1911–   )

One of the finest actors of his day, Cobb's portrayal of Willie Loman, a luckless drummer beaten in mind and body, in Arthur Miller's prize-winning *Death of a Salesman* (1949), caused movie producers to clamor for his services. Unfortunately they have chosen to cast him most of the time in unpleasant or unrewarding roles.

Typical was his role in *Twelve Angry Men* (1957) in which he leads the efforts of a jury to railroad a presumably innocent youth to his death, his motive being (shades of Willie

Whether in cleric's garb or judge's robes or pin-striped banker's suit, Charles Coburn always seemed just right.

Lew Cody often seemed the epitome of suave worldliness, with thin mustache and double-breasted vest.

Loman) guilt for the manner in which he raised his own son.

"The character actor is gratified very few times," the burly and impressive Cobb commented. "So far I have come close to that feeling only twice in Hollywood, in *The Brothers Karamazov* (1958) and *On the Waterfront* (1954)." **Other films include:** *Golden Boy* (1939), *Men of Boys Town* (1941), *The Man in the Gray Flannel Suit* (1956), *Exodus* (1960), *Mackenna's Gold* (1969).

CHARLES COBURN (1877–1961)

They were always billed as Mr. and Mrs. Coburn in a long string of Broadway successes during the early decades of this century. Charles Coburn repeatedly refused to accept film offers since his wife was not included in the propositions that came his way from Hollywood. After her death, however, he decided to make the westward trek and made his film debut in *Boss Tweed* in 1933. For 27 years thereafter, he lent his cherubic presence and British-appearing ways (he was actually born in Macon, Georgia) as a supporting actor in nearly 100 films. Coburn affected a monocle, but it didn't prevent him from playing any kind of role—benevolent father, haughty aristocrat, butler, friend of the family—to which he brought a distinguished quality of his own. In *The More the Merrier* (1943) Coburn received an Academy Award for Best Supporting Actor of the year. **Highlights of Coburn's career are:** *Yellow Jack* (1938), *Idiot's Delight* (1939), *Road to Singapore* (1940), *The Lady Eve* (1941), *Knickerbocker Holiday* (1944), *Colonel Effingham's Raid* (1946), *Monkey Business* (1952), *Around the World in 80 Days* (1956), *The Remarkable Mr. Pennypacker* (1959), *Pepe* (1960).

JAMES COBURN (1928–   )

With his amiable and graceful manner, Nebraska-born Coburn made a specialty of playing engaging young desperados before he turned in his chaps for more sophisticated trappings. His first film was *Ride Lonesome* (1959). His later films tend to be more of the cloak-and-dagger type, with fast action and an occasional bizarre touch. **Highlights:** *The Magnificent Seven* (1960), *Charade* (1963),

A High Wind in Jamaica (1965), *What Did You Do in the War, Daddy?* (1966), *In Like Flint* (1967), *The President's Analyst* (1967), *Harry in Your Pocket* (1973), *The Last of Sheila* (1973).

STEVE COCHRAN (1917–1965)

"My face always aroused suspicion," he once said. It stood him in good stead, however, during a screen career in which he usually played handsome, tough, virile heavies. The one notable exception was his sensitive performance in Antonioni's *Il Grido* (1957), which was released in the United States in 1962. Before making his debut in *Wonder Man* (1945), he worked as a railway hand, cowpoke and department store detective. A discovery of Mae West, he appeared with her in the 1949 revival of *Diamond Lil*. He died on his yacht while sailing off the California coast. **Credits include:** *The Best Years of Our Lives* (1946), *White Heat* (1949), *The Desert Song* (1953), *I, Mobster* (1958), *Mozambique* (1966).

ANN CODEE (1890–1961)

She and her husband of 50 years, Frank Orth, played all over the world as a vaudeville team before pioneering the first talking comedy shorts. The seventh generation in a European theatrical family, she played middle-aged roles after leaving the French stage to make movies in America. **Among her films are:** *Under the Pampas Moon* (1935), *The Other Love* (1947), *Kiss Me Kate* (1953), *Daddy Long Legs* (1955), *Kings Go Forth* (1958).

LEW CODY (1884–1934)

A medical student who decided to switch to the theatre, Lew Cody's meticulously-clipped mustache and somewhat heavily-lidded eyes fitted him superbly as an on-screen seducer of fragile young maidens. From time to time he was given a comedy role or that of a charming man of the world, but he really excelled in dastardly doings.

Cody, a native of New Hampshire, went before the camera as early as 1915, but it wasn't until 1919 that his services were eagerly sought. Beginning with *Don't Change Your Husband* in 1919, he played leading or supporting roles. He was seen in 45 films prior to his death in 1934. He was married for some years to Mabel Normand, whose demise preceded his. **A few of his credits:** *Souls for Sale* (1923), *Husbands and Lovers* (1924), *Exchange of Wives* (1925), *Adam and Evil* (1927), *A Woman of Experience* (1931), *Wine, Women and Song* (1934).

CLAUDETTE COLBERT (1907–   )

The effervescent, lovely-looking superstar was born Lily Chauchoin in Paris but came to New York at the age of six. She wanted to be an actress and by the mid 20's was a leading lady in a string of plays produced by Al Woods. The only problem with this was that Mr. Woods, who had made a lot of money around the turn of the century producing such ten-twenty-thirty melodramas as *Bertha, the Sewing Machine Girl* and *Nellie, the Beautiful Cloak Model*, had fallen on evil days and the vehicles given Claudette—*e.g., A Kiss in a Taxi* (1925)— were for the most part pretty ghastly affairs. *The Barker* (1927) with Walter Huston and her first husband, Norman Foster, was a hit, however, and in the same year she made her first movie, the Capra-directed *For the Love of Mike*.

Stardom came with the talkies—*Young Man of Manhattan* (1930) and *The Smiling Lieutenant* (1931) in which she turned Miriam Hopkins over to Chevalier with perhaps the weirdest lyric ever written into a popular song: "You've got to jazz up your lingerie . . . " Conceivably carried away by this somewhat enigmatic sex fantasy, Claudette was soon seen bathing in asses' milk as Nero's wicked consort Poppaea in De Mille's *Sign of the Cross* (1932). Except for *Cleopatra* two years later, Colbert thereafter swore off sex siren roles and turned to what she was best at—comedy.

A hint of things to come was *Three-Cornered Moon* (1933), a charmer which was followed by a film that revolutionized comedy-making for all time, Colbert and Gable in *It Happened One Night* (1934). As the haughty runaway heiress she won the Academy Award for Best Actress. Gable and Capra carried off the Best Actor and Director Oscars.

More fine comedies, with Colbert as one of

Claudette Colbert in Cecil B. DeMille's Sign of the Cross.

Hollywood's highest paid stars, followed —*She Married Her Boss* (1935), *Tovarich* (1937), *It's a Wonderful World* (1939), *The Palm Beach Story* (1942) and many others. There were also some stunning melodramas —John Ford's *Drums Along the Mohawk* (1939), to name just one.

In the mid 50's Colbert returned to the stage and television. She and Boyer played

A formidable actress and drama coach, Constance Collier is here tricked out for her role in Kitty *(1946).*

for nearly a year on Broadway in *The Marriage-Go-Round,* and Colbert, Coward and Bacall had a fine time with television's *Blithe Spirit.* Nowadays Mrs. Pressman (she was married to her second husband, Dr. Joel Pressman, for more than three decades) divides her time between homes in New York and the West Indies. **Other films include:** *Manslaughter* (1930), *I Cover the Waterfront* (1933), *The Gilded Lily* (1935), *Midnight* (1939), *Since You Went Away* (1944), *Sleep, My Love* (1948), *Parrish* (1961).

NAT "KING" COLE (1919–1965)

The "King" once said, "Some singers use words to call attention to their voice; I do it the other way around." The words of the songs he made popular are as warmly remembered as his casual, gentle presence. Among his triumphs were his own television show and invitations to sing at Buckingham Palace and the White House. The smoother-than-silk artist was a favorite of black and white audiences and his records sold in the tens of millions. His few movie appearances were centered around his singing. **Credits include:** *The Blue Gardenia* (1953), *St. Louis Blues (1958), Night of the Quarter Moon* (1959), *Cat Ballou* (1965).

CHARLES COLEMAN (1885–1951)

The cherubic-looking Australian actor became known as Hollywood's Butler, a role which he played in more than 100 films. One of his best performances was as the family retainer in *Three Smart Girls* (1936), the first Deanna Durbin feature film. **Highlights:** *Becky Sharp* (1935), *Free and Easy* (1941), *The Runaround* (1946), *Never Say Goodbye* (1946).

CONSTANCE COLLIER (1878–1955)

A sixth-generation actress, born while her mother was on tour, she made her stage debut at three as a fairy in *A Midsummer Night's Dream* and her London debut at fifteen as a "Gaiety Girl." Wanting to become a serious actress, she progressed from ingénue roles to Shakespearean heroines. Arriving in the United States in 1908, she appeared in many

Broadway plays, including her own adaptation and direction of *Peter Ibbetson* (1917) with John Barrymore. Her movie debut was in *Intolerance* (1916).

Constance Collier will be remembered in films as the jaded but engaging grande dame, as in *Kitty* (1946). Ill health curtailed her screen activities, but she was active in her last years as a drama coach and had among her students such luminaries as Katharine Hepburn and Marilyn Monroe. **Films include:** *Macbeth* (1916), *The Bohemian Girl* (1923), *Wee Willie Winkie* (1937), *Susan and God* (1940), *The Perils of Pauline* (1947), *An Ideal Husband* (1948), *Rope,* (1948).

WILLIAM COLLIER, SR. (1866–1944)

Veteran of 60 years on stage and screen, he was one of Broadway's greatest farceurs, appearing with Weber and Fields, Lillian Russell and in musicals produced by George M. Cohan and George White. His first notable stage success was in *The City Directory* (1892) in which he built up a walk-on part to one of the major characters. He subsequently helped write many of the plays in which he appeared.

As early as 1916 he was in Hollywood where he appeared in early Mack Sennett comedies and remained to play character comedy roles. A son, William Collier, Jr., born in 1902, also had a successful film career playing in over fifty films. **Some of his films include:** *Plain Jane* (1916), *The Cheaters* (1934), *Josette* (1938), *Thanks for the Memory* (1938), *Invitation to Happiness* (1939), *There's Magic in Music* (1941).

JOAN COLLINS (1933–   )

"England is wonderful for someone who likes gracious living; but for someone young and ambitious, give me America." So announced London-born Joan Collins when she went to Hollywood in the early 50's. The actress, who made her stage debut in *A Doll's House* (1946), subsequently appeared in a number of poor British films, in one of which she had only one line—"I forgot my lipstick." **Film Highlights:** *The Girl in the Red Velvet Swing* (1955), *Rally 'Round the Flag, Boys!* (1958), *Seven Thieves* (1960), *Road to Hong Kong* (1962).

RAY COLLINS (1890–1965)

His first acting job was at the age of 14, when he organized and starred in his own stock company in Vancouver. After that came vaudeville, Broadway and radio. His film debut was in *Citizen Kane* (1941), and more than 75 movies followed. Most movie-goers remember him as a business executive, policeman or military officer. **Among his films are:** *The Magnificent Ambersons* (1942), *The Bachelor and the Bobby-Soxer* (1947), *Dreamboat* (1952), *Never Say Goodbye* (1956), *Touch of Evil* (1958).

RONALD COLMAN (1891–1958)

Countless millions of females, over a span of 40-odd years, dreamed of strolling hand-in-hand with Ronald Colman into some sunlit Shangri-La. His screen charm, his voice that caressed, his patent honesty, his inner strength and nobility—all of these combined and supplemented each other to make him the movies' dream lover to end dream lovers.

Born in Surrey, he was invalided out of the London Scottish Regiment in the First World War and as early as 1918 starred in a London production of *Damaged Goods*. His first major film appearance was as leading man to Lillian Gish in *The White Sister* (1923) and in the years that followed he starred in some of the top hits of that era: notably *The Dark Angel* (1925), *Stella Dallas* (1925) and in the initial filming of the swashbuckling saga of the French Foreign Legion *Beau Geste* (1926). He co-starred in several pictures with Vilma Banky, and they became a tremen-dously successful box-office team.

The arrival of sound raised Colman over-night to the top of the ladder as a male star. It was the Colman voice that did it and within hours after *Bulldog Drummond* (1929) opened, long queues stood before box offices on two continents.

For more than 20 years thereafter Colman's particular brand of romantic understatement resulted in hugely popular films. They brought him four Oscar nominations and a Best Actor award, somewhat mysteriously, for one of his lesser efforts, *A Double Life* (1948). In that one he played an actor whose off-stage impulse to play Othello had lethal consequences for Shelley Winters. It was films like *Arrowsmith* and *Cynara* (1931 and 1932), however, along with costume dramas like *A Tale of Two Cities* (1935) and *The Prisoner of Zenda* (1937), which his millions of fans remember best. Plus, of course, the epic of a modern Utopia, also released in 1937, *Lost Horizon*. Near the end of his life he frequently appeared on the Jack Benny television show with his wife, Benita Hume. **Other highlights:** *Clive of India* (1935), *Under Two Flags* (1936), *The Talk of the Town* (1942), *Random Harvest* (1942), *The Late George Apley* (1947), *Around the World in 80 Days* (1956).

Ronald Colman, looking disheveled and somewhat rueful, in a quieter moment of A Tale of Two Cities.

Ronald Colman has that worried look but Myrna Loy is cool and collected in The Devil to Pay *(1930).*

Chester Conklin in the middle of an indescribable situation typical of early Keystone shorts.

JERRY COLONNA (1904–   )

Before his film debut in *52nd Street* (1937), he was a professional trombonist with a penchant for mimicking opera singers. His assets were a walrus mustache, trick eyes and a voice that could hold notes for as long as 75 seconds. Colonna, who was a fixture in Bob Hope movies and radio shows, first started his comic imitations of opera stars as a youngster when his brother, manager of the Boston Opera House, gave him free entry to the gallery. "I thought the singing was funny," he said. **His movies include:** *College Swing* (1938), *Road to Singapore* (1940), *Road to Rio* (1948), *Andy Hardy Comes Home* (1958).

BETTY COMPSON (1897–1974)

A native of Beaver City, Utah, the stunning blonde broke into movies via comedy roles. A single role, the female lead in *The Miracle Man* (1919), turned her into one of the most popular stars of the "Roaring Twenties." It was the same film that first showed Lon Chaney monstrously contorting his body to play a bogus cripple and was a sensation in its day.

In dozens of silents thereafter, Compson played more traditional roles, many of them in such minor epics of the Jazz Age as *The Fast Set* (1924). More important, she was one of the few silent actresses who survived the coming of sound. She switched to character roles in the 40's. **Other credits:** *Prisoners of Love* (1921), *The Little Minister* (1921), *The Female* (1924), *The Barker* (1928), *Laughing Irish Eyes* (1936), *Here Comes Trouble* (1948).

JOYCE COMPTON (1907–   )

A character actress in the 20's and 30's, she starred in some 50 films, playing minor but significant roles and mostly typecast as the dumb blonde. She will be remembered playing the role of the nurse in the film *Magnificent Obsession* (1935). **Highlights:** *What Fools Men* (1925), *Three Rogues* (1931), *Only Yesterday* (1933), *Top of the Town* (1937), *Blues in the Night* (1941), *Jet Pilot* (1957).

CHESTER CONKLIN (1888–1971)

Starting in 1912 as one of Mack Sennett's original Keystone Cops, his bushy mustache and rimless spectacles became a familiar sight in many silent films. With the advent of sound, the former circus clown's career was reduced to occasional small parts in such films as Chaplin's *Modern Times* (1936). In later years he worked as a department store

Santa Claus and in the late 50's retired to a Hollywood home for indigent performers. But in 1965, at the age of 77, he eloped with a 65-year-old bride. **Sound films include:** *Swing High* (1930), *Every Day's a Holiday* (1938), *The Great Dictator* (1940), *Knickerbocker Holiday* (1944), *The Perils of Pauline* (1947), *The Beautiful Blonde From Bashful Bend* (1949).

SEAN CONNERY (1930–   )

The vigorous Scotsman has become something of a cult figure as super-spy James Bond. As the intrepid 007, Connery has blazed his way through a number of Ian Fleming tales, obliterating sinister enemies with ultra-sophisticated violence, all the while enjoying extraordinary success with the ladies. As one critic observed, "Connery's conquests seem to reflect the triumph of wardrobe over wit, and his women almost invariably succumb with all the spontaneity of mechanical dolls."

In addition to his film appearances, Connery made his stage debut in *South Pacific* (1953) and has appeared on television in such specials as *Anna Christie* and *The Crucible*. **Highlights:** *Darby O'Gill and the Little People* (1959), *Doctor No* (1963), *From Russia With Love* (1964), *Marnie (1964), Goldfinger (1964), You Only Live Twice* (1967), *Shalako* (1968), *The Anderson Tapes* (1971).

WALTER CONNOLLY (1887–1940)

His short hours as a bank clerk allowed him to concentrate on acting, and he became one of the stage and screen's most versatile actors. His roles varied from senile watchmen to prosperous businessmen to suave Europeans.

He is perhaps best remembered for his portrayal of an editor in *Nothing Sacred* (1937), in which he threatened to take out Fredric March's heart and "stuff it like an olive." **Among his movies are:** *The Bitter Tea of General Yen* (1933), *It Happened One Night* (1934), *Fifth Avenue Girl* (1939), *The Great Victor Herbert* (1939).

WILLIAM CONRAD (1923–   )

Conrad began his performing career as a trumpet player with his hymn-singing wife, Marianne, as evangelists in the Detroit slums. Moving on to Hollywood, he had a lively movie career with over 50 credits. In 1971 he began a new career on television, as the fat-and-fifty private-eye, *Cannon*. The show was remarkably successful and the chunky, gourmet/gourmand Cannon became an off-beat hero. In addition to his acting, Conrad has also directed and produced a number of films. **Highlights:** *The Killers* (1946), *Sorry, Wrong Number* (1948), *Johnny Concho* (1956), *The Ride Back* (1957).

HANS CONRIED (1917–   )

His success at playing Nazi heavies typecast him so that he had trouble finding straight roles. "So, in order to eat, I had to become a comedian," he said. He enjoyed success as a dialectician and a straight man to comedians, but heavies remained his forte. In Westerns, he said, he was "never the working heavy—the coarse fellow who opens the gate to let the

Betty Compson's beautiful face attracted fans for many years.

Sean Connery's tie went askew only when James Bond was in some kind of fix, as he obviously is here. Jack Lord plays the menace.

rustlers in. I was the town heavy—the impeccably attired villain with the fancy waistcoat.'' **Among his 100 films are:** *Dramatic School* (debut, 1938), *My Friend Irma* (1949), *Bus Stop* (1956), *The Patsy* (1964).

FRANK CONROY (1890–1964)

When he announced to his family his acting intentions, his father got him a job with a Shakespeare company and sent him money for over a year ''while I was learning to hold a spear. . . . I believe there is no better training for a young actor than wrestling with the small parts in Shakespeare,'' he said. He

Richard Conte is defended by Edward G. Robinson in this scene from House of Strangers *(1949).*

switched from Shakespeare to Hollywood in the early 30's, where he became famous for rolling his eyes and for playing domestic tyrants. **His movies include:** *Grand Hotel* (1932), *Call of the Wild* (1935), *The Ox-Bow Incident* (1943), *The Last Mile* (1959).

RICHARD CONTE (1915–   )

Richard Conte came to films in the mid-40's during the time of many World War II pictures. Later he switched to gangster films and continued to play the type. Even when he was on the right side of the law, his characters had a cynical edge. During his active career Conte has appeared in a good many urban crime films. **Highlights:** *Guadalcanal Diary* (1943), *A Bell for Adano* (1945), *A Walk in the Sun* (1946), *Call Northside 777* (1948), *New York Confidential* (1955), *I'll Cry Tomorrow* (1956), *Who's Been Sleeping in My Bed?* (1963), *Tony Rome* (1967).

TOM CONWAY (1904–1967)

A British actor of Russian descent, Tom Conway made his first film appearance in *Sky Murder* (1940). In 1942 he took over from his brother, George Sanders, the starring role in the *Falcon* series. After starring in films and early television programs, Conway's career faded in the 50's. In 1965 he was found penniless and ill in a cheap hotel room in Venice, California. News of his situation brought help from many entertainers but he wasn't well enough to work and he died in 1967. **Major performances include:** *Cat People* (1942), *One Touch of Venus* (1948), *Death of a Scoundrel* (1956).

JACKIE COOGAN (1914–   )

There were millions of damp handkerchiefs in the world in those pre-tissue days when Charles Chaplin and Jackie Coogan concocted a brilliant mixture of laughter and tears in *The Kid* (1921). Five-year-old Jackie, with his enormous eyes and cherubic features beneath an oversized cap set askew on his head, was irresistible as an orphaned waif while Chaplin, making his first non-slapstick film, was magnificent fending off crooks and do-gooders in his effort to raise the tiny foundling as his own son and into what some critics referred to as a Junior Tramp.

Lamentably, Little Jackie's first picture

Two pairs of saucer eyes in Old Clothes—*Jackie Coogan with Joan Crawford.*

marked the peak of his career. He was very good indeed as a seven-year-old *Oliver Twist* (1922), but by the time he was all of 16 and making films like *Tom Sawyer* (1930) and *Huckleberry Finn* (1931) the Hollywood machinery that nearly always puts the skids under child superstars was operating.

Coogan vanished almost completely from the Hollywood scene until the late 50's. Since then, happily, jobs have been a bit easier to find both in movies and in television. **Credits include:** *Old Clothes* (1925), *Kilroy Was Here* (1947), *High School Confidential* (1958), *John Goldfarb, Please Come Home* (1965).

DONALD COOK (1900–1967)

His stage career was marked by such successes as *Paris Bound* (1927), *Claudia* (1941) and *Foolish Notion* with Tallulah Bankhead (1945). After a long tour with Bankhead in *Private Lives*, a revival that delighted audiences across the country (1948), he starred in *The Moon Is Blue* (1951). His film career was mainly a series of second features on double bills. He had the distinction, however, of playing the man who finally assassinated Pancho Villa, an old friend, in *Viva Villa!* (1934). **Highlights:** *The Man Who Played God* (1932), *Show Boat* (1936), *Bowery to Broadway* (1944), *Patrick the Great* (1945), *Our Very Own* (1950).

ELISHA COOK, JR. (1902–   )

On stage, his small, thin frame made it possible for him to play the 16-year old hero of O'Neill's *Ah! Wilderness* at the age of 31. On screen, his earnest face, thin black hair combed back and eyes like black saucers staring for concentration made him adept at playing nervous neurotics, most notably as Wilmer in *The Maltese Falcon* (1941). **More than 50 films include:** *Phantom Lady* (1944), *The Big Sleep* (1946), *The Great Gatsby* (1949), *Shane* (1953), *One-Eyed Jacks* (1961), *Rosemary's Baby* (1968), *El Condor* (1970).

GARY COOPER (1901–1961)

Although a few unfair critics claimed that he had only two looks—a stern one and a not so stern one—almost everyone else feels he was among the all-time greats, and more than

a few experts maintain he was the greatest star of all time. His father was a judge in cowboy country—Helena, Montana. Cooper had planned to be an artist, but jobs were hard to find, and his ability to ride a horse landed him a job as an extra in Valentino's *The Eagle* (1925) and a chance to die in Ronald Colman's arms in *The Winning of Barbara Worth* (1926). His first lead role came with Clara Bow in *Children of Divorce* (1927).

By the time he played the aviator role with Colleen Moore in the saccharine *Lilac Time* (1928) he was well-known, but true stardom awaited the opening of *The Virginian* (1929), his first all-talking picture in which his dialogue was confined mostly to "yups" and "nopes."

For 30 years thereafter "Coop" played in more hit pictures (good ones, too) than any other performer. He was always a good guy, a laconic idealist, in pictures that ranged from *Morocco* (1930) to *City Streets* (1931); *A Farewell to Arms* (1932) to *Lives of a Bengal Lancer* (1935); *Mr. Deeds Goes to Town* (1936) to *The Plainsman* (1937); *Sergeant York* (1941) to *For Whom the Bell Tolls*

Gary Cooper's wartime love in Today We Live *was Joan Crawford (1933).*

Gary Cooper (note the modern hair style) inspects Sigrid Gurie while Ferdinand Gottschalk inspects both of them. The film: Adventures of Marco Polo *(1938).*

(1943), and from *High Noon* (1952) to *Love in the Afternoon* (1957).

Cooper twice won the Academy Award as Best Actor, for *Sergeant York* and *High Noon*, while *Friendly Persuasion* (1956) won the Grand Prix at Cannes. **More than 80 films include:** *The Texan* (1930), *The Devil and the Deep* (1932), *Design for Living* (1933), *The General Died at Dawn* (1936), *The Cowboy and the Lady* (1938), *The Pride of the Yankees* (1942), *Saratoga Trunk* (1945), *Springfield Rifle* (1952), *Ten North Frederick* (1958), *The Wreck of the Mary Deare* (1959).

GEORGE A. COOPER (1913–)

The British character actor who has played many a spiteful type in his day has recently turned up in rather lively settings, from the earthy, 18th century England of *Tom Jones* (1963) to the modish London of *The Strange Affair* (1968). **Highlights:** *Miracle in Soho* (1956), *Violent Playground* (1958), *Hell Is a City* (1961), *Nightmare* (1964), *Life at the Top* (1965).

GLADYS COOPER (1888–1971)

"I am just a ham actress," she said—a statement which anyone who saw her joyously ebullient performance as 'enry 'iggins' mother in *My Fair Lady* (1964) will hotly deny.

Cooper is believed to have made her stage debut early in the century as a Gaiety Girl, a member of the most glamorous chorus line in Europe. She appeared in more musicals before going on to dramatic roles, and during World War I she was far and away the number one pin-up girl of British fighting men in all parts of the Empire.

She went to Hollywood for three days in the early 30's and extended her visit to more than 25 years. Her first appearance in British talkies came in *Dandy Donovan* (1931). In the years that followed, movie goers will recall her superb performances in such films as *Rebecca* (1940), *Kitty Foyle* (1941), and above all, her outstanding portrayal of the stiff, austere, and somewhat oblique Lady Hamilton in *That Hamilton Woman* (1941). For her performance in *Now, Voyager* (1942) she received an Academy Award nomination.

Married to actor Philip Merivale in 1937, she varied her movie roles with stage appearances, most notably in *The Chalk Garden*, and in the 1960's, after appearing in the television *Rogue* series, she was made a Dame of the British Empire. Her zest and joy for life are perhaps best exemplified by her answer to a reporter who asked her when she would retire. "Retire? Whatever for?" she said in 1971. "Who cares how old I am? Who cares how long it was since I first played Peter Pan?" Her fine performances insured her a permanent spot in motion picture annals. **Films include:** *The White Cliffs of Dover* (1944), *Mrs. Parkington* (1944), *Green Dolphin Street* (1947), *The Bishop's Wife* (1947), *Separate Tables* (1958), *The Happiest Millionaire* (1967).

JACKIE COOPER (1922–)

His mother was playing piano on the vaudeville circuit and his grandmother's mode of baby-sitting was to get him jobs as a movie extra at the age of four. "People often ask me what I did until then," Cooper commented.

Jackie Cooper in a scary scene from Treasure Island *with Wallace Beery.*

At six he became a member of the Our Gang group and when he was nine Paramount cast him as *Skippy*, based on one of the more popular comic strips of the day. Overnight his tow-headed freshness and petulant overshot lower lip made him a star and brought him an Academy Award nomination. Metro took him over and he had two smash successes with Wallace Beery: as pal of a prizefighter in trouble, *The Champ* (1931), and as Long John Silver's nemesis (but secret friend), playing Jim Hawkins in *Treasure Island* (1934).

He had earned $100,000 a year when he was nine and was spending nearly as much when he was 14 and jobless. Without any formal education to speak of, he enlisted in the Navy when war came but flunked out of the Notre Dame training program. He got a job playing drums for the troops in the South Pacific but before leaving the States married a girl he had known in Hollywood. It didn't last and Cooper said something which summarizes the tragedy suffered by so many child stars, before and after him: "I feel I might have married June just so someone might care I was going overseas."

The story has a happy ending. With film jobs few and far between and another marriage come and gone, he took to drinking. His salvation was nearly three years of psychoanalytical treatment in New York and a third marriage, to Barbara Kraus, an advertising executive. In the 50's he made a few successful Broadway appearances and played lead roles in television series, *The People's Choice* and *Hennesey*. In the 60's he became vice-president of Columbia's television subsidiary, Screen Gems, and since 1969 has produced films for TV and become a motion picture director.

He lives in California with his wife and three children, no one of whom, he insists, will be a child actor. **Other films:** *Peck's Bad Boy* (1934), *Streets of New York* (1939), *The Love Machine* (1971), *Chosen Survivors* (1973).

MELVILLE COOPER (1896–1973)

Although his 50-year career ranged from butler to king, he once said of himself "I've been bossed about as a valet, secretary or handyman, until I've developed a sort of screen servant complex." Born in England, he made his stage debut at Stratford-on-Avon in 1914, his film debut in *The Private Life of Don Juan* (1934) and his Broadway debut in 1935. **Some of his films include:** *The Scarlet Pimpernel* (1935), *Rebecca* (1940), *Pride and Prejudice* (1940), *Father of the Bride* (1950), *The Story of Mankind* (1957).

ROBERT COOTE (1909–   )

When he was 16, he dropped out of school to join a stock company, becoming the fifth generation in his family to be lured by acting.

The British character actor has played a wide variety of roles since his film debut in *Sally in Our Alley* (1931). **Films include:** *Gunga Din* (1939), *The Ghost and Mrs. Muir* (1947), *The Prisoner of Zenda* (1952), *A Man Could Get Killed* (1966), *Prudence and the Pill* (1968).

Gladys Cooper was Laurence Olivier's no-nonsense but kind sister in Rebecca. *Here she and husband Nigel Bruce have come to meet Max de Winter's new wife, Joan Fontaine.*

Melville Cooper, *usually shy but eager to please, in an early film role.*

ELLEN CORBY (1913–   )

Seen recently as the grandmother in the television series *The Waltons*, she has been an established character actress in films since her screen debut in *The Dark Corner* (1946). Born in Racine, Wisconsin, she appears most often as crusty, tough housekeepers and maids. Perhaps her most memorable film role was the aunt in *I Remember Mama* (1948), which earned her an Academy Award nomination. **More than 70 films include:** *Madame Bovary* (1949), *Shane* (1953), *Vertigo* (1958), *The Caretakers* (1963), *A Quiet Couple* (1968).

WENDELL COREY (1914–1968)

He came to the screen from the Broadway stage and made his film debut in *Desert Fury* (1947) playing a weak hood. Graduating to more sympathetic roles, he became the solid, dependable, but slightly colorless second lead of more than 40 films. One of his professional honors was being elected as President of the Academy of Motion Picture Arts and Sciences. He was also active in television. **Films include:** *No Sad Songs for Me* (1950), *Rear Window* (1954), *The Rainmaker* (1956), *Blood on the Arrow* (1964), *Buckskin* (1968).

Ricardo Cortez shares carnival time with Irene Dunne in Symphony of Six Million *(1932). One hopes she didn't get mustard on those nice white gloves.*

LLOYD CORRIGAN (1900–   )

He came to Hollywood as a screenwriter for Paramount in the 20's, wrote the first of the Fu Manchu scripts and wrote and directed the last one. His first acting part was in *The Splendid Crime* in 1925. **Some other films:** *The Great Man's Lady* (1942), *The Bandit of Sherwood Forest* (1946), *Cyrano de Bergerac* (1950), *The Manchurian Candidate* (1962).

BUD CORT (1950–   )

Though appearing in other movies, Cort's first starring role was in *Harold and Maude* (1971). He was effectively cast as a 15-year-old discontented with his own environment who finds momentary happiness with his octogenarian, eccentric "lover," humorously played by Ruth Gordon. He has also appeared in *M*A*S*H.* (1970) and *Brewster McCloud* (1970).

VALENTINA CORTESA (1925–   )

Italian-born Valentina Cortesa began her screen career at age 15 in *La Cens Della Beff* (1941). Although she went on to win supporting roles in several films, she was little known outside her own country until she played the lead in the English *The Glass Mountain* (1950). She then appeared in several international films but eventually returned to Italy. In 1952 she won the Venice Film Festival award for her performance in *Women Without Names* and again in 1957 for her role in *Anici*. She married actor Richard Basehart in 1956. **Films include:** *Thieves' Highway* (1949), *Shadow of the Eagle* (1951), *The House on Telegraph Hill* (1951), *The Barefoot Contessa* (1954), *Barabbas* (1962), *Juliet of the Spirits* (1965), *The Legend of Lylah Clare* (1968).

RICARDO CORTEZ (1899–   )

Born Jacob Kranz, his big film break came when he was hired as a threat to Valentino. This led to exotic Latin lover roles, a name change and a birthplace listed as Vienna. He made his debut in *Sixty Cents an Hour* (1923), and in 1926 became Garbo's first American leading man in *The Torrent*. His first sound film was *The Lost Zepplin* (1930).

Playing mostly gangsters in sound films, he began to direct a few films in the late 30's and since the mid-40's has been seen infrequently on the screen—*The Last Hurrah* (1958) being his most recent film. **Films include:** *Argentine Love* (1924), *Volcano* (1926), *The Maltese Falcon* (1931), *I Am a Thief* (1935), *Shadow of a Doubt* (1935). *The Locket* (1947), *Bunco Squad* (1950).

DOLORES COSTELLO (1905–)

The daughter of actor Maurice Costello (1877-1950) and the sister of actress Helene (1904-1957), she is reputed by old-timers to have been one of the most beautiful women ever to appear on screen. Her 20-year career began with *Lawful Larceny* (1923) and it extended well into the era of talkies. One of her last and best performances was in *The Magificent Ambersons* (1942) as the long-suffering widow whose son refuses to allow her to wed an automobile enthusiast.

Her father had once broken the ironclad rule of early cinema by announcing, "I am an actor, and I will act, but I will not build sets and paint scenery." Dolores was more easy-going, and generally, looking very beautiful, played sweet and non-exacting roles. Probably one of her more trying offscreen performances was as wife to John Barrymore in a marriage of short duration. **Film credits include:** *The Sea Beast* (1926), *Third Degree* (1927), *Madonna of Avenue A* (1929), *King of the Turf* (1939), *This Is the Army* (1943).

LOU COSTELLO (1906–1959)

Chubby, appealing Costello was the dominant half of the Abbott and Costello comedy team that kept America laughing for several decades. Their comedy consisted mainly of broad slapstick and cross-conversation —their "Who's on first" routine became famous. They made their film debut in *One Night in the Tropics* (1940) and followed that with the well-remembered *Buck Privates* (1941), distinguished by the Andrews Sisters' rendition of the classic, "Boogie Woogie Bugle Boy." They appeared on their own successful television series in the 50's. In 1957 the team split up. **Highlights:** *Rio Rita* (1942), *Pardon My Sarong* (1942), *Abbott and Costello Meet Frankenstein* (1948),

Abbott and Costello Meet the Invisible Man (1951), *Dance With Me, Henry* (1956).

JOSEPH COTTEN (1905–)

A Virginian, Cotten exemplified, in the theatre, films and on television, the legendary qualities of Virginians: elegance, an aristocratic flair, ruthless honesty and a sharp edge of cynicism. His southern drawl was retained or dropped depending on the requirements of the role he played. Fortunately for his devoted fans, Cotten's attempt at business (the Tip Top Salad Company) failed early in his young manhood and he turned to acting. In 1931 Cotten made his first real breakthrough in the theatre when he won leading roles in plays such as *Absent Father, Accent on Youth* and *The Postman Always Rings Twice*. Though none of these was especially memorable, during this time Cotten made a big step forward when he met Orson Welles. When Welles formed the famed Mercury Theatre, he called upon Cotten to play the lead in the then "contemporary" version of *Julius Caesar*. This was followed by successful radio and theatre work and the making of the classic *Citizen Kane* (1941). After filming Welles' *The Magnificent Ambersons* (1942), Cotten entered into a long and brilliantly productive relationship with David O. Selznick.

In recent years Cotten has played in numerous television movies and has made periodic appearances on the stage. **Highlights of a more than 40-year career:** *Shadow of a Doubt* (1943), *Love Letters* (1945), *Duel in the Sun* (1947), *Portrait of Jennie* (1949), *The Third Man* (1950), *The Steel Trap* (1952), *The Angel Wore Red* (1960), *Hush . . . Hush, Sweet Charlotte* (1965), *Petulia* (1968), *Tora! Tora! Tora!* (1970).

GEORGE COULOURIS (1903–)

Long known for his portrayals of screen villains, he was always attracted to roles of menace, for he delighted in making audiences interested in him even while arousing their opposition.

Born in England, he made his Old Vic debut in 1926 before coming to the United States in 1929 and appeared in many plays,

Joseph Cotten, with Jennifer Jones made up to look like a half-breed in Duel in the Sun.

George Coulouris did not often appear in Westerns, but here he is in California *with Ray Milland (1947).*

Tom Courtenay makes friends with a pooch in King Rat *(1965).*

including *Watch on the Rhine*, for which he re-created his part in the 1943 screen version. Starting with *Christopher Bean* (1933), he remained in Hollywood until the 1950's, when he returned to England. There he has remained active in English films. **Some of his films are:** *All This and Heaven, Too* (1940), *Citizen Kane* (1941), *For Whom the Bell Tolls* (1943), *Mr. Skeffington* (1944), *None but the Lonely Heart* (1944), *An Outcast of the Islands* (1951), *King of Kings* (1961), *Arabesque* (1966).

TOM COURTENAY (1937–   )

The spare English actor often appears as a young man with problems. Courtenay gave a memorable performance as the mixed-up delinquent in *The Loneliness of the Long Distance Runner* (1962) and as the fanatic Strelnikow in *Doctor Zhivago* (1965). He blithely governed his private world in *Billy Liar* (1963), though as one critic put it, "His (Billy's) imagination is even sloppier than his environment." His is a rare ability to portray even the most antisocial, atypical characters with sympathy and clarity. **Highlights:** *King and Country* (1964), *Operation Crossbow* (1965), *The Night of the Generals* (1967), *A Dandy in Aspic* (1968), *Otley* (1969).

JEROME COWAN (1897–1972)

A versatile, lanky character actor with a pencil-thin mustache and plastered-down hair, he has been seen in more than 140 films—portraying impeccably dressed businessmen, fast-talking reporters or agents, lawyers, detectives, and gangsters, almost all of them with a bit of larceny in their hearts.

Beginning his career as an emcee in vaudeville (hired mainly because of his extensive wardrobe) he appeared in a number of Broadway plays before making his screen debut in *Beloved Enemy* (1936). His detective role in *The Maltese Falcon* (1941) and as one of Bette Davis' suitors in *Mr. Skeffington* (1944) were typical of the variety of parts he played. He also appeared often on television. **A few of his films include:** *The Hurricane* (1937), *The Miracle on 34th Street* (1947), *The West Point Story* (1950), *Pocketful of Miracles* (1961), *Penelope* (1966).

SIR NOEL COWARD (1899–1973)

One of the most talented theatrical artisans of this century, he was an actor, composer, director, original author, producer and screenwriter. His wit and charm made friends in every level of society, and such plays as *Private Lives* (1930), *Calvacade* (1931), *Bittersweet* and *Design for Living* (both 1933), plus *Blithe Spirit* (1941) and others, continue to be restaged and show little sign of being dated. Coward appeared in fewer than ten movies, but to each one he imparted a charm and conviction that were uniquely his own. Perhaps the best of these was *The Scoundrel* (1935). The tale of an unscrupulous book publisher, it conveyed a mood of total reality. While his forte was comedy, his performance in *In Which We Serve* was a splendid propaganda effort for the British Navy when it was in its deepest trouble in 1942. *Private Lives*, his most popular play, reached the screen (1931) but with Norma Shearer and Robert Montgomery playing the roles Coward had originally created for himself and Gertrude Lawrence on the stage —one of Broadway's memorable events. Perhaps his best work as a screenwriter was the poignant screenplay of *Brief Encounter* (1946). **Some of his films include:** *Around the World in 80 Days* (1956), *Our Man in Havana* (1960), *Paris When it Sizzles* (1964), *Bunny Lake Is Missing* (1965), *Boom!* (1968).

LARRY "BUSTER" CRABBE (1907–   )

Like Lex Barker and Johnny Weissmuller, Crabbe played Tarzan, making his debut in a mildly impressive *King of the Jungle* (1933). For the most part, however, the bulky barrel-chested star of "B" pictures preferred the American outdoors. He was featured in scores of Westerns, usually as a cowboy with problems, but, on occasions, as an Indian—a good one. Of one thing audiences could be certain—when Crabbe walked into a saloon a fight was virtually certain to ensue.

Lest it be thought that Crabbe was typecast, it should be added that as *Flash Gordon* (1936) he single-handedly, without benefit of horse or lariat, prevented a collision between Earth and another planet. In the early 50's his

As he often was, Jerome Cowan is the man in the middle—in this picture between hand-kissing Fred Astaire and Ginger Rogers in Shall We Dance? *(1937).*

television series *Captain Gallant of the French Foreign Legion* was popular. **Scores of films include:** *Nevada* (1936), *Buck Rogers* (1939), *Last of the Redmen* (1947), *Arizona Raiders* (1965).

JAMES CRAIG (1912–   )

The rugged leading actor has appeared in films for more than 35 years. Since his debut in *Thunder Trail* (1938), Craig has played in comedies, Westerns and dramas. His best role was as the Faustian character in *The Devil and Daniel Webster* (1941), also shown as *All That Money Can Buy*. **Highlights:** *Kitty Foyle* (1941), *The Human Comedy* (1943), *Kismet* (1944), *While the City Sleeps* (1956), *Hostile Guns* (1967), *The Doomsday Machine* (1973).

JEANNE CRAIN (1925–   )

Born in Barstow, California, in the Mojave Desert, she played walk-on child roles prior to her formal screen debut in *The Gang's All*

Buster Crabbe was often backed against a wall, but invariably fought his way out of his predicament.

110

Here (1943). She achieved a considerable degree of popularity with screen fans, for the most part playing either "sophisticated" roles, which in Hollywood parlance can be translated to mean sexy-sultry ladies who more or less know the score, or "the girl next door." In short, she was versatile. Most of the time she was cast in second-rate films, or worse, but when a good one like *A Letter to Three Wives* (1949) came along, she proved that she was a first-rate performer. **Other films in her career were:** *Home in Indiana* (1944), *State Fair* (1945), *Margie* (1946), *Pinky* (1949), *Cheaper by the Dozen* (1950), *The Joker Is Wild* (1957), *Hot Rods to Hell* (1967).

FRANK CRAVEN (1875–1945)

"Whenever they need a boob," he used to say, "they send for Craven." He started his film career as a writer, after a successful stage career, by selling Fox his play *The First Year.* Later he made his film-acting debut in *The Very Idea* (1929). His best known role was as the kindly stage manager of *Our Town* (1940) which he had played on the stage as well. **Other films are:** *State Fair* (1933), *Barbary Coast* (1935), *The Richest Man in Town* (1941), *In This Our Life* (1942), *Through Different Eyes* (1943), *The Right to Live* (1945).

BRODERICK CRAWFORD (1910–   )

No movie hoodlum was ever nastier to his film mistress than Crawford was to Judy Holliday in *Born Yesterday* (1950). Equally, few actors have put on as engaging a performance as Crawford has when given a non-meany part to play.

The son of Broadway stars Helen Broderick and Lester Crawford, he early attempted to avoid a theatrical career, but the lure of studio cameras finally won him over. Usually he played heavies until his electrifying performance as the southern demagogue based on Huey Long in *All the King's Men* (1949), adapted for the screen from Robert Penn Warren's brilliant novel of the same name, brought him the Academy Award as Best Actor of the Year.

Beginning with his debut in *Woman Chases Man* (1937) he has appeared in nearly 100 films, an unfortunate percentage of which

have been in the "B" rather than the "A" category. One of his problems may be that his burly build and ultra-positive personality do not lend themselves to many starring roles. He did star, however, on the television series *Highway Patrol*. **Credits include:** *Beau Geste* (1939), *Broadway* (1942), *The Time of Your Life* (1948), *Anna Lucasta* (1949), *Night People* (1954), *A House Is Not a Home* (1964), *The Vulture* (1967).

JOAN CRAWFORD (1908–   )

Her mouth was too wide, her shoulders too broad and her facial expressions almost ludicrously limited. Over a span of 50 years critics have been obliged to eat these unkind remarks, one by one, as the shrewd, talented, ambitious and grimly determined Crawford rose to the top of the Hollywood ladder, securely enthroned among Hollywood's Olympians.

Born in San Antonio, Texas, she used her stepfather's name, Billie Cassin, in her early years. She worked in a laundry and took other ignoble jobs to help pay her school tuition and in 1924 landed a job in the back row of a New York chorus line. She was good enough to get a Hollywood tryout and, as Lucille LeSueur, she doubled for Norma Shearer in *Lady of the Night* (1925), her first film effort. A contest held by *Photoplay* decided that her new name should be Joan Crawford (she hated it at first) and Joan Crawford she was forever after.

Chorus girl, jazz baby, shop girl, clothes horse, socialite, tragedienne—these, roughly speaking, cover most of her roles in nearly 140 films. Her first big breakthrough came as a turned-on flapper in one of the last of the silents, *Our Dancing Daughters* (1928), and she was the first tap-dancer audible to audiences in *Hollywood Revue of 1929,* a film, incidentally, that introduced a great song —"Singin' in the Rain."

Hit movies followed in rapid succession: *Dance, Fools, Dance* (1931), *Grand Hotel* (1932), *The Women* (1939), *A Woman's Face* (1941) and many, many more. In 1945, several years after stars like Garbo and Norma Shearer had retired, Joan won an Oscar as Best Actress of the Year, playing a crafty but sexy business woman in *Mildred Pierce*. During the next 15 years her roles varied from the suicidal socialite in *Humoresque* (1946)

A studio picture of Jeanne Crain; note the fashionable 40's footwear to complement her bathing suit.

to a red-headed publishing big shot in *The Best of Everything* (1959).

With her career theoretically ended, Joan and Bette Davis began entirely new careers with their brilliantly horrifying performances in *Whatever Happened to Baby Jane?* (1962). As Hedda Hopper said several years ago: "It certainly won't be Crawford's fault if she doesn't make another 50 films before she dies."

Crawford is equally active off-screen. Widowed by the death of her fourth husband, Alfred Steele, who was Chairman of the Board of the Pepsi Cola corporation, she has spent a vast amount of time as a supersaleswoman and ambassadress for that already hugely successful corporation. **Other films include:** *Untamed* (1929), *Rain* (1932), *The Last of Mrs. Cheyney* (1937), *Above Suspicion* (1943), *Flamingo Road* (1949), *Goodbye, My Fancy* (1951), *The Caretakers* (1963), *Berserk!* (1968), *Trog* (1970).

LAIRD CREGAR (1916–1944)

His immense bulk—more than 300 pounds—and his distinctive voice made him a very popular character portraying usually sinister men much older than himself until he died at 28 following an operation.

A descendant of John Wilkes Booth, he decided that the only way to get attention was to star in a play and he convinced a moneyed friend to stage *Oscar Wilde*. Appearing in the title role, he was signed almost immediately by 20th Century–Fox, for whom he worked almost exclusively and was seen most notably as Jack the Ripper in *The Lodger* (1944). **His films include:** *Blood and Sand* (1941), *This Gun for Hire* (1942), *The Black Swan* (1942), *Heaven Can Wait* (1943), *Hangover Square* (1945).

JOSEPH CREHAN (1884–1966)

In a long and active film career Crehan's face, walk and authoritative toughness made him a living synonym of law and order. Perhaps more than any other Hollywood actor, he played frontier sheriffs and big city, brash cops. **Highlights of over 75 films:** *Sleeper's East* (1933), *Vinegar Tree* (1934), *The Roaring Twenties* (1939), *Stanley and Livingstone* (1939), *The Foxes of Harrow* (1948), *Ringside* (1949).

Joan Crawford counsels Geraldine Brooks in Possessed *(1947).*

RICHARD CRENNA (1927–   )

Crenna is perhaps best known for his television work, notably his roles as Walter Denton in the long-running *Our Miss Brooks* series and as Luke in *The Real McCoys*. He was a popular child star on radio in the 30's and began in films in the 50's. **Film credits:** *The Pride of St. Louis* (1952), *Over-Exposed* (1956), *John Goldfarb, Please Come Home* (1965), *The Sand Pebbles* (1966), *Wait Until Dark* (1967), *Star!* (1968).

LAURA HOPE CREWS (1880–1942)

Best remembered as the fluttery Aunt Pittypat in *Gone with the Wind* (1939), she gave deft and witty character portrayals in films in the 30's and early 40's. She was born in San Francisco, and began as a child actress on the stage. Later she toured with John Drew and Herbert Tree. She first came to Hollywood in the early days of the talkies as an elocution coach for Norma Talmadge and for a while was an associate producer whose main func-

Typical of Joan Crawford's beautifully-groomed-but-sinister lady roles was the one in Flamingo Road *(1949).*

Donald Crisp listens as Basil Rathbone proposes a toast to David Niven and Errol Flynn (looking downright surly) in The Dawn Patrol *(1938).*

Hume Cronyn in bow tie watches as June Allyson greets Jackie (Butch) Jenkins backed up by Van Johnson in The Bride Goes Wild *(1948).*

tion was to find suitable stage plays for pictures and to train actors for talkies. **Some of her films include:** *The Silver Cord* (1933), *Escapade* (1935), *Camille* (1937), *Thanks for the Memory* (1938), *The Blue Bird* (1940), *One Foot in Heaven* (1941).

DONALD CRISP (1880–1974)

Born in Scotland, he served in the Boer War. Coming to New York, he first appeared in opera and theatre. In 1911 he joined D.W. Griffith for whom he worked both as an actor and assistant. In *Birth of a Nation* (1915), he both played General Grant and directed the battle scenes. When he was refused screen credit for his efforts, he left Griffith and went on to direct his own films, such as *The Navigator* (1924) with Buster Keaton.

His film career, which encompassed more than 364 productions, spanned close to 60 years. He won an Academy Award for Best Supporting Actor for *How Green Was My Valley* (1941). **His credits include:** *Broken Blossoms* (1919), *Mutiny on the Bounty* (1935), *Jezebel* (1938), *National Velvet* (1944), *Bright Leaf* (1950), *Spencer's Mountain* (1963).

RICHARD CROMWELL (1910–1960)

The gentlemanly actor, prominent in the 30's, starred in the sound remake of *Tol'able David* (1930), the story of a young farm boy who routs a Goliath-like and malevolent enemy.

Cromwell played a featured role in *Jezebel* (1938), the Bette Davis saga of a scheming Southern lady. He also appeared in *Young Mr. Lincoln* (1939), the John Ford film about Lincoln's formative years. **Highlights:** *Emma* (1932), *Tom Brown of Culver* (1932), *Lives of a Bengal Lancer* (1935), *Baby Face Morgan* (1942), *Bungalow 13* (1948).

HUME CRONYN (1911–   )

His acting career began when he was ten years old, when he put on an impromptu theatre production. "It was pure living in a dream world," he said, "which was much richer, much gayer, and much more delightful than the world I really lived in." Cronyn's dream world expanded when Alfred Hitchcock gave him his first film role in *Shadow of a Doubt*, (1943). Since then, the Canadian-born actor and his talented actress-wife, Jessica Tandy, have appeared on both stage and screen. His range includes Albee, Shakespeare, Chekhov, Thurber and Coward. **Movies include:** *Lifeboat* (1944), *People Will Talk* (1951), *Sunrise at Campobello* (1960), *There Was a Crooked Man* (1970).

BING CROSBY (1904–)

If show business people ever decided to offer a Decathlon Award rather than an Oscar for overall achievements, the great Bing would probably win it in a walk. He sold more records than anyone else (over 325,000,000) and ''White Christmas'' alone is close to the 40 million mark. For 15 years he was among the top radio favorites and for nearly as long was the top motion picture star or close to it. He was a hugely successful businessman on the side, and even the annual golf tournament that bears his name is among the most glamorous and prestigious of such events in the world of sports.

He studied at Gonzaga University in his native Washington and first came to attention as one of a trio of Paul Whiteman's Rhythm Boys. Early records and radio performances quickly turned him into the first of the teen-age idols, antedating Sinatra, Presley and the Beatles, and his appearance at New York's Paramount Theatre nearly caused that solidly built structure to be ripped apart brick by brick.

Crosby was a crooner in *The Big Broadcast* (1932), and every picture he made was a success, playing both comedy and serious drama. In 1940 came *Road to Singapore* with Bob Hope and Dorothy Lamour. It was a perfect casting job and the trio went down a number of highly amusing ''roads'' together. Meanwhile two great films, *Holiday Inn* (1942) and *Going My Way* (1944), made Bing the most popular actor in Great Britain and the United States—a spot he clung to for many years. *Going My Way*, the tale of two priests, brought Oscars to both Crosby and Barry Fitzgerald (the acerbic old cleric), and claimed both the New York Film Critics and Academy awards for Best Film of the Year. In 1945, working with Ingrid Bergman, he made the equally successful *The Bells of St. Mary's*.

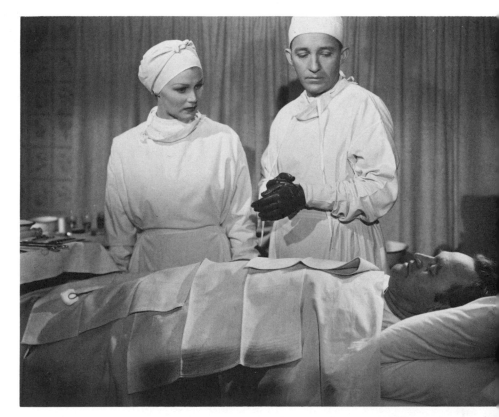

Bing Crosby had Joan Caulfield as his nurse in Welcome, Stranger *(1947). Barry Fitzgerald is their patient.*

As the years rolled by Crosby continued to make pictures, but fewer of them as his other interests broadened and developed. Nowadays one sees him on television from time to time, often as a co-announcer pointing out the terrors of the Pebble Beach Golf Course which one sees in the background. (P.S.: He and Bob Hope are still close friends.) **Other films include:** *Mississippi* (1935), *Pennies From Heaven* (1936), *Birth of the Blues* (1941), *Blue Skies* (1946), *Riding High* (1950), *White Christmas* (1954), *The Country Girl* (1954), *The Road to Hong Kong* (1962), *Stagecoach* (1966).

ROLAND CULVER (1900–)

A portrayer of impeccable British types, the London-born Culver was a veteran of World War I with no aims in life until he joined an amateur theatrical group. A first-class comedian, he has appeared in scores of films both in England and the United States since making his debut in 1932. His most memorable Hollywood role was perhaps in

Before the going got rough, Richard Cromwell looked splendidly shiny in uniform in Lives of a Bengal Lancer.

114

Constance Cummings is in rather glum contrast to an exuberant Margaret Rutherford in Blithe Spirit. *Rex Harrison is non-committal.*

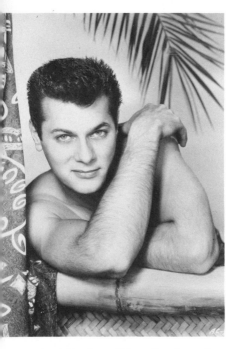

A studio shot of Tony Curtis—when short hair was okay even in an exotic setting.

adults in *Beach Party* (1963). During the 50's he starred in a highly successful television series. **Highlights:** *So Red the Rose* (1935), *Saboteur* (1942), *How to Be Very, Very Popular* (1955), *The Carpetbaggers* (1964), *Stagecoach* (1966).

FINLAY CURRIE (1878–1968)

After his first important role in *The Good Companions* (1933), he played a variety of dour Scotsmen, villains, saintly Biblical characters and strong-minded old men. His best-known role, however, was as Magwitch in *Great Expectations* (1947).

A law student who switched to music and became a professional organist, he first visited the United States with the Livermore Minstrels, a small stock company. His theatre career paralleled his movie work, and his last stage role was at the age of 87. **Films include:** *Treasure Island* (1950), *The Mudlark* (1950), *Quo Vadis* (1951), *Ben Hur* (1959), *Billy Liar* (1963), *Bunny Lake Is Missing* (1965).

TONY CURTIS (1925–   )

Almost too handsome for his own good, he escaped pretty-boy parts only after he proved his ability to play exacting dramatic roles. Curtis' talents began to be recognized when he played the corrupt press agent in *Sweet Smell of Success* (1957) and again the following year as an escaping prisoner shackled to fellow convict Sidney Poitier in *The Defiant Ones* (1958).

It is to be regretted that less-than-starring roles came his way in the 60's, for, in films like *Some Like It Hot* (1959), with Marilyn Monroe and Jack Lemmon, he proved that he was equally adept at comedy. **Credits:** *City Across the River* (debut, 1949), *Trapeze* (1956), *Operation Petticoat* (1959), *40 Pounds of Trouble* (1963), *The Boston Strangler* (1968).

CYRIL CUSACK (1910–   )

Born in South Africa and educated in Dublin, he followed the family stage tradition. He spent 14 years as an actor and producer with the Abbey Theatre in Dublin before his British film debut in *Odd Man Out* in 1947. His American debut came four years later

To Each His Own (1946) with Olivia de Havilland. **Films include:** *On Approval* (1945), *Dead of Night* (1946), *The Yellow Rolls-Royce* (1965), *Fragment of Fear* (1971).

CONSTANCE CUMMINGS (1910–   )

The American-born actress went to Britain soon after her film debut in 1931. She appeared in many amusing films, notably *Blithe Spirit* (1945), Noel Coward's spooky comedy. **Highlights:** *Movie Crazy* (1932), *Glamour* (1934), *John and Julie* (1957), *The Battle of the Sexes* (1960), *A Boy Ten Feet Tall* (1965).

ROBERT CUMMINGS (1908–   )

The buoyant, never aging leading man has breezed through a number of light comedies since his debut in 1935. Two of his serious roles were the hero of the small-town drama *Kings Row* (1942) and Grace Kelly's romantic interest in *Dial M for Murder* (1954). Cummings also appeared as one of the archaic with *Soldiers Three*. **His movies include:** *Floods of Fear* (1958), *The Waltz of the Toreadors* (1962), *The Spy Who Came in From the Cold* (1965), *Fahrenheit 451* (1966).

ZBIGNIEW CYBULSKI (1927–1967)

One of the few Polish stars to be recognized by English-speaking audiences, Cybulski had a brief (13-year) and somewhat uneven career. He began performing with a repertory group and later was co-founder of a student theatre which gained a wide following. Turning to films, he gained small roles in a number of pictures after his debut in *A Generation* (1954). Within three years he worked himself into a lead role in *Wrecks* (1957).

In the West, Cybulski's *Ashes and Diamonds* (1958) is perhaps his best known film—in art cinemas, at least. During his career he appeared in German, Swedish, French and international productions. Cybulski starred in modern tragedies and in rare comedies, and often returned to the stage. Despite his versatility he lacked consistency—many of his performances were below the artistic levels he had previously attained—and thus he never received the international recognition that otherwise might have been his. At the age of 40, he died under a moving train which he was attempting to board. **Credits:** *See You Tomorrow* (1960), *L'Amour a Vingt Ans* (1962), *Jowita* (1967).

Robert Cummings laughs it up in My Geisha *(1962), but Yves Montand looks less amused.*

LIL DAGOVER (1897–   )

American audiences became familiar with Dagover as the glamourous heroine in a number of German-made silent films in the late 20's. Her first American film was *The Woman From Monte Carlo* (1931). At that time a critic referred to Dagover as "Warners' own entry in the Garbo-Dietrich race." In 1958, in reviewing the German film, *The Big Barrier*, an American critic asserted that the dark, lissome actress was "still one of the screen's great beauties" who "outshines much younger competition" in her portrayal of an impractical widow. **Film highlights:** *The Cabinet of Doctor Caligari* (1919), *Tartuffe* (1926), *The White Devil* (1929), *Das Maedchen Irene* (1937), *The Big Barrier* (1958).

ARLENE DAHL (1924–   )

The green-eyed redhead from Minneapolis never attained stardom but sandwiched in 26 films between jobs as a copywriter and an assistant lingerie buyer in her youth and as a beauty columnist and vice-president of one of the largest advertising agencies in the country after her more or less formal retirement from Hollywood.

She worked for the Dayton Company and Marshall Field and Company after leaving school, came to New York and combined modeling with small parts in Broadway productions. "I wore more on my head then than they wear all over now," she said, commenting on her chorus-girl role at the Latin Quarter. Warners "discovered" her, cast her in two films and then permitted her to move to MGM where she made eight pictures, almost always with Red Skelton, almost always

highly unfunny. Thereafter, with other studios, she appeared in a succession of low-budget adventure films, none of them quite as eventful as the five marriages and four divorces which ran concurrently with her film career.

In the 60's she made nightclub and television appearances plus a few movies and in 1972 did a good job replacing Anne Baxter in the Broadway hit *Applause!* She is still active in half a dozen enterprises and must have meant it when she said: "I ended up in Hollywood where I never wanted to be in the first place, but I never considered those Hollywood years as anything but marking time." **Credits include:** *Life With Father* (1947), *The Bride Goes Wild* (1948), *Caribbean* (1952), *Sangaree* (1953), *Journey to the Center of the Earth* (1959), *The Land Raiders* (1969).

DAN DAILEY (1917–   )

The son of a New York Hotel owner, he appeared in vaudeville and burlesque, and when jobs weren't available, worked as a golf caddy, shoe salesman, interior decorator and grocery clerk. In 1934 he signed with an entertainment troupe on a South American cruise ship. After this stint Lorenz Hart, a composer and producer (with Richard Rodgers) of musicals, spotted him and gave him a part in *Babes in Arms* (1937), which ran for a year on Broadway. Success and a film career followed. **Numerous film credits:** *The Mortal Storm* (debut, 1940), *Mother Wore Tights* (1947), *Give My Regards to Broadway* (1948), *When My Baby Smiles at Me* (1948), *Call Me Mister* (1951), *The Wayward Bus* (1957).

MARCEL DALIO (1900–   )

His finest pictures were made many years ago when he appeared in such classics as *Grand Illusion* (1938) with Jean Gabin and as the star of Jean Renoir's masterpiece, *Rules of the Game* (1939). Nowadays, as a part of the Hollywood community, he is most often to be seen in supporting roles—dandies, hotel managers (or assistant hotel managers), as a caterer at posh parties and the like. In such films he is usually called Henri, Zizi, Lizki, etc.—a considerable comedown for an actor

A very beautiful Arlene Dahl clings to Van Heflin, whose deshabille *is somewhat less fortunate, in* Woman's World *(1954).*

as talented as Dalio, but no matter what role is assigned to him, one can be certain that he will play it to the hilt. **Credits include:** *The Song of Bernadette* (1944), *The Snows of Kilimanjaro* (1952), *Pillow Talk* (1959), *The 25th Hour* (1967), *The Great White Hope* (1970).

JOHN DALL (1918–1971)

His screen debut, playing with Bette Davis in *The Corn Is Green* (1945) earned him an Academy Award nomination, promising a noteworthy film career. Although he had good roles and interesting films thereafter, he never quite made it to the top.

His Broadway debut was in *The Eve of St. Marks* in 1941 and, three years later, his performance in *Dear Ruth* resulted in a Hollywood contract. In the 50's, however, he returned to Broadway and for the next ten years appeared in a wide variety of major dramatic television shows. **His screen credits include:** *Something in the Wind* (1947), *Another Part of the Forest* (1948), *Rope* (1948), *The Man Who Cheated Himself* (1951), *Spartacus* (1960).

LILI DAMITA (1906–)

Born in Paris, she succeeded Mistinguette as the star of the Casino de Paris Revue at the age of 14. After making her screen debut in Berlin, she was discovered by Samuel Goldwyn and brought to Hollywood to co-star with Ronald Colman in *The Rescue* (1928).

Like many other European imports, she was touted as the "new Garbo". She married Errol Flynn for a spell, made several films a year and in 1935 abandoned Hollywood to return to France. **Hollywood films include:** *The Bridge of San Luis Rey* (1929), *The Match King* (1932), *This Is the Night* (1932), *Brewster's Millions* (1935).

DOROTHY DANDRIDGE (1923–1965)

Often described as the most striking black singer since Lena Horne, Dandridge also won recognition as an actress and was nominated for an Academy Award for her performance in *Carmen Jones* (1954).

She got an early start in show business, performing in a tumbling, singing and dancing act with her mother and sister when she

Even though her legs are not showing, it is indeed Betty Grable to whom Dan Dailey is making winsome advances. The picture: My Blue Heaven *(1950).*

In the earlier days it was fashionable for the object of men's passions to look the other way as the lovemaking hotted up. Ronald Colman is the aggressor, Lili Damita the lady looking into outer space, and the film was The Rescue.

The beautiful and talented Dorothy Dandridge in Carmen Jones, *one of her infrequent but brilliant screen appearances. The boy at the wheel of the jeep is Harry Belafonte.*

was only five. The family moved from Cleveland to Hollywood in the 30's and Dorothy made her screen debut at the age of 13 in *A Day at the Races* (1937). She also worked on radio in the *Beulah* shows of the 30's and 40's.

Her career came to a halt for several years during her first marriage in the 40's, but she returned to show business after a divorce in 1951. She sang with Desi Arnaz' band and appeared in a Tarzan picture, *Jungle Queen* (1951). Her appearances with Arnaz helped make her a star on the nightclub circuit before she was cast in *Carmen Jones*. The film helped increase her drawing power as a nightclub performer, and she made appearances in Europe and South America as well as in the United States. Although she commanded a high salary, Dandridge had money troubles during this period and losses through bad investments forced her into bankruptcy in 1963.

This reversal also affected her career, but according to her manager things were improving just before her premature death in 1965. **Films include:** *Bahama Passage* (1942), *Island in the Sun* (1956), *Porgy and Bess* (1959), *Moment of Danger* (1960).

KARL DANE (1886-1934)

The advent of sound finished off Dane's brief career as a silent screen comic. Once a studio carpenter, Dane became an overnight star for his performance as the gangly, tobacco-chewing doughboy in *The Big Parade* (1925). The Danish-born actor's heavy foreign accent made his voice unsuitable for talking pictures, and he joined the ranks of actors thrown out of work at the end of the 20's. After his money ran out, Dane went back to carpentry, then took a job as a mechanic and finally tried operating a hot-dog stand in Hollywood. When that venture failed, the despondent Dane committed suicide. **Films include:** *Baby Mine* (1928), *Circus Rookies* (1928), *Trial of '98* (1928), *Speedway* (1929), *Montana Moon* (1930).

HENRY DANIELL (1894–1963)

A character actor of great range, Daniell appeared in more than 100 films which included many cinematic classics, such as *The Great Dictator* (1940) and *The Philadelphia Story* (1940). His performance as Baron de Varville in *Camille* (1937) was termed "brilliant"—one of the few compliments given the actors (Garbo excepted) in this production. His career spanned all sorts of roles—doctors, lawyers, society gentlemen, even parts in horror flicks. His face is one swiftly recognized by film buffs for he seemingly appeared in all memorable pictures of the 40's. Prior to his screen career, Daniell appeared on Broadway in the 20's and early 30's. **Highlights:** *Madame X* (1937), *All This and Heaven, Too* (1940), *Watch on the Rhine* (1943), *Jane Eyre* (1944), *The Body Snatcher* (1945), *Song of Love* (1947), *The Man in the Gray Flannel Suit* (1956), *The Sun Also Rises* (1957), *The Chapman Report* (1962).

BEBE DANIELS (1901–1971)

Playing one of the princes in her father's

stock-company version of *Richard III* at the age of three, she was billed as The World's Youngest Shakespearean Actress. By the time she signed a contract with DeMille and then Paramount she was all of 18 and already had made more than 200 films—some Westerns but for the most part two-reel comedies with Snub Pollard and young Harold Lloyd (with whom, incidentally, she won several dancing contests).

Throughout the 20's, the pert Dallas-born beauty (her ancestry was half Scottish, half Spanish) appeared in scores of silents, mostly comedies. She played jazz babies, manicurists, a mine-owner, a sheikess, or, if you will, female sheik, and dozens of other roles, some of them male impersonations (*Señorita*, 1927). Throughout this period she held her position (after Gloria Swanson and, for a spell, Pola Negri) as the studio's most popular star.

With the advent of talkies, Paramount lost interest in her (as they did many of their high-salaried silent stars) and RKO starred her in one of the first big musicals where her warm soprano helped make *Rio Rita* (1929) a huge success. She continued to make films for some years more—old-timers will recall her role as the temperamental actress who broke a leg in *42nd Street* (1933), thus giving Ruby Keeler her chance to "go out there" and come back a star—but by the mid-30's both she and her husband, Ben Lyon, were finding it harder and harder to get decent parts. Both thereupon moved to England where vaudeville appearances and a smash revue entitled *Haw Haw!* made them national favorites. *Hi, Gang!*, a radio show and later movie, with Vic Oliver, helped cheer up Britishers during the Blitz her work throughout the war for British and American servicemen brought Daniels the U.S. Medal of Freedom. After the war she and Lyon returned briefly to Hollywood but they were homesick for Piccadilly and returned to England for more work on British radio and television, this time with their son and daughter. When Bebe died all Britain mourned. **Her credits include:** *Male and Female* (1919), *The Affairs of Anatol* (1921), *Nice People* (1922), *Monsieur Beaucaire* (1924), *The Campus Flirt* (1926), *A Kiss in a Taxi* (1927), *Lawful Larceny*

Henry Daniell, one of the screen's outstanding character actors, with Garbo in Camille, *one of the great lady's less successful ventures.*

(1930), *Reaching for the Moon* (1930), *Silver Dollar* (1932), *Counsellor-at-Law* (1933), *The Return of Carol Dean* (1939).

HELMUT DANTINE (1918–)

The former Austrian cavalry officer was born and trained as a diplomat in Vienna before emigrating to the United States in the late 30's. During the war he was typecast in a series of films as a cruel Nazi officer—in real life he had been imprisoned by the Nazis during the German invasion of Austria. Of Dantine's portrayals of German officers, one critic wrote in 1943: "They have transformed the movies' arch German villain from a pasteboard caricature to a subtler, more lifelike, and therefore more horrifying character." More recently Dantine has turned to directing films. **Film highlights:** *Mrs. Miniver* (1942), *Mission to Moscow* (1943), *Hotel Berlin* (1945), *War and Peace* (1956), *Operation Crossbow* (1965).

An admirer drapes a hunk of jewelry around the neck of Bebe Daniels, one of the best-loved stars of the 20's, in Treachery on the High Seas.

Hollywood usually did wrong by France's talented Danielle Darrieux, but she nevertheless managed to steal the 1951 M G M musical, Rich, Young and Pretty. *Here she is with Wendell Corey.*

BOBBY DARIN (1936–1973)

When he embarked on his singing career in the late 50's, Darin made no secret of the fact that he wanted to be a millionaire and a show-business legend by his 25th birthday. He almost made it—by then he had come a long way from his poor childhood in the Bronx via a series of hit records.

Darin's first big break was his recording of "Splish Splash," a 1958 hit that sold 100,000 records in three weeks and established him as a teenage singing idol. He scored an even bigger success with his 1960 recording of "Mack the Knife." That one sold two million records and won Darin Grammy Awards for the best song and as the best new singer of the year.

By then, the former Walden Robert Cassotto—he said he found the name Darin in a phone book—was being sought by Hollywood. His first film role was in *Come September* (1960) with Rock Hudson, Gina Lollobrigida and Sandra Dee. At this time, Darin had achieved much of what he said he would. He was a nightclub star with $2 million in film contracts and he was married to starlet Sandra Dee.

During the 60's in Hollywood, Darin alternated between light and serious roles. His performance as the young, shell-shocked soldier in *Captain Newman, M.D.* (1964) with Gregory Peck and Angie Dickinson won him an Academy Award nomination for Best Supporting Actor.

Throughout his life, Darin had been plagued with heart trouble, and in 1971, he underwent open-heart surgery to replace two defective valves. His illness slowed him down some, but he remained active as a performer until 1973 when he entered a Los Angeles hospital for another operation, this one to repair damage to the artificial heart valves. Darin died following the surgery. **Films include:** *Too Late Blues* (1961), *Pressure Point* (1962), *That Funny Feeling* (1965), *Gunfight at Abilene* (1967), *Stranger in the House* (1967), *The Happy Ending* (1969).

LINDA DARNELL (1923–1965)

Burned slightly when she was playing Tuptim in *Anna and the King of Siam* (1946), she expressed her recurring fears of fire—a chilling irony since she died in a Chicago suburb blaze 19 years later.

Making her debut in *Hotel for Women* (1939), she was invariably cast in sweet ingenue roles in such ventures as *Blood and Sand* (1941), until she managed to escape to meatier and sexier roles such as the much publicized *Forever Amber* (1947). **More than 50 films include:** *Summer Storm* (1944), *Fallen Angel* (1946), *My Darling Clementine* (1946), *A Letter to Three Wives* (1949), *This Is My Love* (1954), *Black Spurs* (1965).

JAMES (JIMMY) DARREN (1936–   )

A teenage-idol and popular singing star, Darren never quite shook his image as the boyfriend in *Gidget* (1959) and a series of beach-party films he made in the early 60's. Darren first went to Hollywood in 1954 at the age of 17 and hung around Schwab's drugstore for months hoping to be discovered. When that didn't work, he tried a more realistic approach, returning to his native Philadelphia and commuting to New York to study with drama coach Stella Adler.

He actually was "discovered" when a Screen Gems executive spotted him waiting for an elevator in a Manhattan office building.

That chance encounter led to a Hollywood contract and his debut in *Rumble on the Docks* (1956). Darren's singing career got a boost when he recorded the title song for *Gidget* (1959). He followed that up with a number of hits, including "Goodbye Cruel World" which ranked third on the recording charts for some weeks in 1961.

Darren repeatedly tried to change his teen-hero image in a series of films in the 60's, including *The Guns of Navarone* (1961). In 1966, he starred in the television series *Time Tunnel*. **Films include:** *Operation Mad Ball* (1957), *Let No Man Write My Epitaph* (1960), *Diamond Head* (1963), *Lively Set* (1964).

DANIELLE DARRIEUX (1917–   )

The Bordeaux-born actress is considered one of the great actresses of the French stage and screen, in a career spanning 40 years, beginning with her debut at 14 in *Le Bal* (1931). Her most notable films were made before the outbreak of World War II and Americans remember her particularly for her wonderful portrayal of the doomed young Maria Vetsera to Charles Boyer's Prince Rudolph in *Mayerling* (1937). Strong accusations of collaboration with the Nazis reduced her film assignments in Europe after the War, but as time went by and memories faded she resumed an active career, and in 1970 she replaced Katharine Hepburn in the title portrayal of Coco in the Broadway musical. In 1971, however, Ophul's feature documentary film *The Sorrow and the Pity* showed Darrieux smilingly on her way to entertain Nazi troops, and the controversy resumed. **Highlights include:** *I Give My Life* (1941), *Alexander the Great* (1956), *Pot Bouille* (1958), *Rouge et Noir* (1958), *Loss of Innocence* (1961), *The Young Girls of Rochefort* (1968).

FRANKIE DARRO (1917–   )

In motion pictures since the age of three, one of Darro's interesting young roles was in *The Public Enemy* (1931), in which he played the tough kid who later grows up to be James Cagney. In 1933 a critic observed that the young actor had assumed many of the Cagney

Seemingly fresh from his hairdresser, an elegant George Sanders offers his wrist to Linda Darnell in Forever Amber, *a screen version of Kathleen Windsor's best-seller about life and lust in London back in the bad old days.*

Frankie Darro is restrained by a number of hands in this scene from On the Spot.

Jane Darwell, hefty but competent as always, in Brigham Young. *Linda Darnell and Tyrone Power are the venturesome pioneers at the left.*

mannerisms. In his adult career Darro was cast primarily in character roles and after serving in the Navy during World War II he re-emerged as a Hollywood stunt-man and a regular on the *Red Skelton Show*. **Film highlights:** *So Big* (1925), *Long Pants* (1927), *The Circus Kid* (1928), *The Mayor of Hell* (1933), *Little Men* (1935), *Juvenile Court* (1938), *Across the Wide Missouri* (1951).

JANE DARWELL (1880–1967)

Wanting to be a circus performer, she compromised when her family objected and made her acting debut in a Chicago stock company and her first movie appearance in 1914. It wasn't until the 30's that her ample figure and empathetic face made her a popular mother type in countless films. She crowned her career as Ma Joad in *The Grapes of Wrath* (1940), a role that she was given at the insistence of Henry Fonda and which won her an Academy Award for Best Supporting Actress. **Hundreds of films include:** *Jesse James* (1939), *Gone With the Wind* (1939), *All That Money Can Buy* (1941), *Caged* (1950), *The Last Hurrah* (1958), *Mary Poppins* (1964).

HOWARD DA SILVA (1909–   )

One of Broadway's finest character actors, he played in early radio dramas, in the Mercury Theatre's exciting production of *The Cradle Will Rock* and jumped into his first important movie role as the bartender in *The Lost Weekend* (1945) who tried, ineffectu-

Looking stern and strong, Howard da Silva as he appeared in Unconquered *(1947).*

ally, to cope with Ray Milland's hankering for alcohol. His exciting performance in the Broadway production of Rodgers and Hammerstein's *Oklahoma* (1943) caused his services to become greatly in demand and Hollywood directors, noting his flat broken-nosed and vaguely pugnacious appearance, almost always cast him as a criminal menace. Actually, da Silva was a true intellectual, and highly vocal to boot: during the era of McCarthy he was outspoken in his contempt for Hollywood witch hunts and witch hunters, an attitude that caused a distinct cooling off in his relationships with the cowardly studios and producers who in the 50's treated even mildly liberal opinions like edicts handed straight down from the Kremlin.

In the 60's, happily, da Silva returned in films like *David and Lisa* (1962) and, a few years later, with Candice Bergen and Ring Lardner, Jr., was among the first Americans to be included in a cultural exchange group visiting Chairman Mao's China. **Credits include:** *Abe Lincoln in Illinois* (1940), *The Sea Wolf* (1941), *The Outrage* (1964), *Nevada Smith* (1966).

CLAUDE DAUPHIN (1904–   )

Dauphin was a well-known French actor of stage and screen before he made his first English-language film, *English Without Tears* (1943). His acting career began in 1930, when he was working as a set designer at the Odéon Theatre in Paris. An actor became ill and Dauphin, stage-struck, memorized his lines in several hours and performed without a rehearsal. A lieutenant in the French tank corps during World War II, Dauphin escaped to England after the fall of France. **Film highlights:** *The Affair Lafont* (1939), *Little Boy Lost* (1953), *Phantom of the Rue Morgue* (1954), *Tiara Tahiti* (1963), *The Visit* (1964), *Is Paris Burning?* (1966), *Two for the Road* (1967), *Barbarella* (1968).

HARRY DAVENPORT (1866–1949)

This character actor began his career at the age of five, when he appeared in a stage production of *Damon and Pythias* in his native Philadelphia. A member of one of the theatre's most illustrious families, Davenport traced his lineage back to Jack Johnson, famous Irish actor of the 18th century. In the course of a career which spanned over three-quarters of a century, Davenport, in addition to numerous stage roles, appeared in over 100 films. **Film highlights:** *The Life of Émile Zola* (1937), *Gone With the Wind* (1939), *The Hunchback of Notre Dame* (1940), *Kings Row* (1942), *The Enchanted Forest* (1945), *Little Women* (1949).

MARION DAVIES (1897–1961)

Such adulation was lavished on each of her new pictures by the Hearst Press (on orders from the boss) that a California wit once said that if an earthquake should suddenly send Los Angeles sliding into the sea, the Hearst headline would read: HOLLYWOOD VANISHES: MARION NEVER LOOKED LOVELIER.

Born Marion Cecilie Douras in Brooklyn, she went directly from a Westchester County Convent into Broadway chorus lines as early as 1913. Experts disagree, but it was either in *Queen of the Movies* (1914) or the *Ziegfeld Follies* (1916) that William Randolph Hearst first saw her and, so legend has it, attended every performance for two months, buying two tickets per night—one for himself and one for his hat. Even if the hat story is apocryphal, there is no doubt that the relationship between the 17-year-old fledgling actress and the 51-year-old press lord lasted more than 35 years and that they were as much in love with one another when Hearst died in 1951 as they had been in those remote days when a society still suffering from a bad Victorian hangover continued to profess that adultery was just one step down the ladder from first-degree murder.

Since divorce and remarriage weren't in the cards for Hearst, he determined to make Marion the biggest star in the land. To do this he established Cosmopolitan Pictures and released through Adolph Zukor and MGM a series of handsomely mounted costume dramas so loaded with Ruritanian castles and corny subtitles as to totally obscure Davies' natural talents and genuine flair for comedy. While the Hearst papers wrote MARION DAVIES SOARS TO NEW HEIGHTS, the spirits of movie house owners sunk to new lows since only one film, *When Knighthood*

Harry Davenport, one of filmdom's old reliables, exchanges pleasantries with Rosalind Russell in Tell It to the Judge.

After escaping a succession of horrendous costume dramas, Marion Davies proved that she was a far better actress than had been suspected. Here she is, blonde and a bit frilly, with Jean Parker in Operator 13 *(1934).*

Young Marion Davies, the way W. R. Hearst liked to see her pictured. Marion's principal problem was how not to get tangled and fall down the stairs.

Ossie Davis, actor, writer and intellectual, as he appeared in the 1969 film Sam Whiskey.

Was in Flower (1922), managed to make money. Dozens of books have been written telling how Hearst hired Louella Parsons to push Marion's career, the sad fate that overcame monstrosities like *Janice Meredith* (1924) and *Beverly of Graustrak* (1926) and the problems directors and leading men had filming kissing scenes with Hearst looming menacingly in the background.

Late in her career she finally got a few chances to show, as Marilyn Monroe did years later, what a fine comedienne she really was. In films like *The Patsy* (1928) and *Show People* in the same year, she was bright, funny and an excellent mimic. Hearst grudgingly permitted her to make these and a few other non-spectaculars, but he adamantly refused to let her be hit in the face with a custard pie in *Show People,* which was more or less the story of Gloria Swanson's rise from slapstick to stardom.

Marion Davies retired from film-making a few years after the birth of talkies. When Hearst's empire fell on evil days, she was a big help to him financially, and when he died at the age of 88, they were together in their Beverly Hills mansion: his body was removed before Marion, who had been under sedation-plus-alcohol, awoke, and the Hearst family never allowed her to see him before interment.

She married for the first time late in 1951, shunned the spotlight thereafter, and died in September, 1961, after a long bout with cancer, which she fought with exemplary courage and high spirits.

A final word: In Orson Welles' great picture, *Citizen Kane,* Dorothy Comingore played the bland and untalented but aspiring opera singer, mistress of the newspaper king. Nearly everyone who knew the *real* Marion Davies will disagree with this portrait. In truth, she was a fine lady—warm, witty, intuitive and kind. **Other films:** *The Belle of New York* (1919), *Yolande* (1924), *The Red Mill* (1927), *The Cardboard Lover* (1928), *Bachelor Father* (1931), *Peg O' My Heart* (1933), *Going Hollywood* (1933).

BETTE DAVIS (1908–   )

Hard-working, single-minded and uniquely talented, ten Oscar nominations only begin to tell the story of the lady who may well be the best American-born actress in film history. She was born Ruth Elizabeth Davis in Lowell, Massachusetts, and after attending a school for actors, played in stock and with the Provincetown Players. After a Broadway debut (*Broken Dishes*, 1929), she passed the second of two screen tests and was signed by Universal and almost played the daughter in the movie version of *Strictly Dishonorable*. When the studio bosses met her, however, they opined she had "as much sex-appeal as Slim Summerville" but, since she was under contract anyway, gave her minute parts in films like *Bad Sister* (1931) and *Waterloo Bridge* (1931). Switching to Warner Brothers (she was now a blonde and had learned many tricks of the trade) she played her first leading role opposite George Arliss in *The Man Who Played God* (1932) and more than one critic pointed out that she had extraordinary talents.

Davis' big breakthrough came when she fought like a tiger to get the leading feminine role in RKO's screen adaptation of W. Somerset Maugham's fine novel *Of Human Bondage* (1934). Directed by John Cromwell, her performance of Mildred, the sullen, sluttish and avaricious waitress who entraps a crippled medico (Leslie Howard) was widely hailed as perhaps the best portrait of a nasty woman ever filmed. In a moment of creative genius, Warners next decided to cast her in an item entitled *The Case of the Howling Dog* but she gave them a pointblank refusal, just one of many conflicts she battled out with the Brothers over the years. She was good with Paul Muni in *Bordertown* (1935) and for her work as an ex-actress turned alcoholic in *Dangerous* (1935) she was awarded the Oscar that should have gone to her for *Of Human Bondage*.

More good movie performances—*The Petrified Forest* (1936) and *Kid Galahad* (1937) are just two examples—followed and then, under William Wyler's direction she made *Jezebel* (1938), which brought her a second Oscar and worldwide acclaim.

By the end of the 30's Davis supplanted Deanna Durbin (!) as the most popular female star of the day. A critic wrote of her "No one is as good as Davis when she is bad."

For the next quarter of a century the pattern was unchanged—more fights with studios and producers, more and more great performances, more and more awards and medals. No matter what part she played—historical personage in *The Private Lives of Elizabeth and Essex* (1939); murderess in *The Little Foxes* (1941); mistress of comedy in *The Man Who Came to Dinner* (1942); tragedienne in *Hush . . . Hush, Sweet Charlotte* (1964)—her greatness shone on the screen for all to see.

In her autobiography written in 1962, *The Lonely Life*, Davis lucidly reveals her feelings about actors, directors, producers and theatrical careers in general. It's well worth reading. **Other Davis highlights:** *Dark Victory* (1939), *Now, Voyager* (1942), *Mr. Skeffington* (1944), *The Corn Is Green* (1945), *All About Eve* (1950), *The Virgin Queen* (1955), *What Ever Happened to Baby Jane?* (1961).

JOAN DAVIS (1908–1961)

At the age of three she performed at church benefits and at the age of six she flopped at a local amateur contest only to return a week later with a funny routine that won her a vaudeville engagement. Her first movie role was in 1934 as a hillbilly in a Mack Sennett short, *Way Up Thar*. After more than 40 films, she switched to radio and television, starring in the successful series, *I Married Joan*. In 1955 she retired, saying she was "worn out." **Some of her movies are:** *My Lucky Star* (1938), *Sun Valley Serenade* (1941), *She Gets Her Man* (1945), *The Traveling Saleswoman* (1949).

OSSIE DAVIS (1917–   )

Although Davis is more identified in the public mind with acting, he prefers to think of himself primarily as a playwright. Married to frequent co-star Ruby Dee, Davis made his Broadway stage debut in the title role of *Jeb* (1946). His film debut came in 1950 in Fox's *No Way Out*. Davis wrote the popular *Purlie Victorious* (1961), a play which he describes as a "Non-Confederate Romp Through the Cotton Patch." Says Davis of integration and the arts; "There are too many things in Negro culture that I don't ever want to see lost. If I'm told I can come into the Big House so long as I leave my old possessions at the door, well,

Bette Davis with Warren William in one of her less heralded romantic films, Satan Met a Lady *(1936).*

The First Lady of the American screen in what was perhaps her best-known film, The Private Lives of Elizabeth and Essex.

Sammy Davis, Jr., perhaps the most versatile and talented song-and-dance man of the recent era.

Doris Day, suffering from a virulent attack of galloping cold cream, as she appeared in That Touch of Mink *(1962).*

I'm just gonna stay right outside.'' **Film highlights:** *The Joe Louis Story* (1953), *The Cardinal* (1963), *Shock Treatment* (1964), *A Man Called Adam* (1966), *The Scalphunters* (1968).

SAMMY DAVIS, JR. (1925–   )

In a recent exciting and extremely moving television spectacular, Sammy Davis, Sr. explained why young Sammy was dancing on stage at the age of three instead of playing with other kids in Harlem. Young Sammy, while regretting that he never had a chance to play baseball, seemed generally happy about those early days and the warmth between the old trouper and the younger one was the high spot of the show.

Sammy, Jr. fooled his father by not becoming a dance specialist. He's wonderful at it, of course, but he's also one of the outstanding singers, comedians and dramatic actors of our day. Davis claims that Sinatra taught him phrasing and breathing, and Bogart convinced him to discard his eye patch after an accident resulted in the loss of his left eye. Be that as it may, he has excelled in too many areas for the onlooker to concede more than one percent of his success to anyone or anything beyond his own inherent talents.

Away from the stage, screen, TV camera or recording studio Davis has taken vigorous, dramatic and sometimes highly controversial stands on issues of the day. One of the first famous blacks to marry a white (May Britt), at a time when ''that sort of thing wasn't done,'' he also caused a vast amount of puzzled head-shaking when he converted to Judaism. Whatever Sammy does, however, he does with conviction and flair. Altogether, his contribution to inter-racial understanding has been enormous. **Film credits include:** *The Benny Goodman Story* (debut, 1956), *Anna Lucasta* (1959), *Porgy and Bess* (1959), *Pepe* (1960), *Johnny Cool* (1963), *Sweet Charity* (1968), *Man Without Mercy* (1969).

DORIS DAY (1924–   )

Even when cast in ''naughty'' parts, as in *Pillow Talk* (1959), Cincinnati-born Doris Kappelhoff always managed to look inexora-

bly virginal and clean-scrubbed. She is quoted as saying (Hear! Hear!) ''Decency on the screen is very important to me. I'm really not with some of the downbeat pictures being made these days.''

An automobile accident forced her to give up a planned career as a dancer and she became a singer—an extremely good one—instead. It was while she was performing at Barney Rapp's Little Club in her home town that Rapp changed her name to Day, and in so doing helped a star to be born.

Her film debut was in *Romance on the High Seas* (1948) and she hasn't gone out of fashion since then. She's a fine comedienne, a convincing dramatic actress, and a delight to listen to. **Highlights:** *Young Man With a Horn* (1950), *April in Paris* (1952), *Calamity Jane* (1953), *Young at Heart* (1955), *Love Me or Leave Me* (1955), *The Man Who Knew Too Much* (1956), *Please Don't Eat the Daisies* (1960), *Glass Bottom Boat* (1966), *Where Were You When the Lights Went Out?* (1968).

LARAINE DAY (1919–   )

For a girl whose screen behavior was almost always predictable, she astonished her fans by marrying (and staying married for 12 years) to Leo Durocher, the most combative baseball player and manager in the history of the sport. So far as one knows, that was the only non-peaceful move ever made by the wholesome Mormon lass who starred in more than 30 pictures between 1937 and her virtual retirement in 1960.

Her family moved to California from Utah when she was ten and she made her screen debut in *Stella Dallas* (1937) as Laraine Johnson. Several years later, with her name changed, she was starred by MGM in at least seven Dr. Kildare pictures plus many others, always playing the sympathetic, true-blue and, of course, all-American girl; the kind of woman every right-thinking Mom wanted her daughter to grow up to be. **Credits include:** *Calling Dr. Kildare* (1939), *My Son, My Son* (1940), *Journey for Margaret* (1942), *The Story of Dr. Wassell* (1944), *Tycoon* (1947), *The High and the Mighty* (1954), *The Third Voice* (1960), *House of Dracula's Daughter* (1972).

JAMES DEAN (1931–1955)

Dean began his brief but memorable career by winning a dramatic contest while in high school. He joined a theatre group while in UCLA and succeeded in landing bit parts in two films. This "suceess" encouraged him to go to New York where he made his Broadway debut in *See the Jaguar*. Television roles followed as well as another play, and he was "discovered" by Elia Kazan who signed him for *East of Eden*.

Dean became not only an actor of note, but a cult. His youthful fans cast him in a hero's mold, and his sullen, difficult, iconoclastic personality became an object of admiration. His death, a result of an automobile accident in 1955, was the cause of nationwide mourning—equalled only by the flood of tears shed for Valentino. **Credits:** *Fixed Bayonets* (1951), *Has Anybody Seen My Gal?* (1951), *Rebel Without a Cause* (1955), *Giant* (1956).

ROSEMARY DE CAMP (1913–   )

Since her debut in *Cheers for Miss Bishop* (1941), she has been seen in a variety of sister and mother roles always played with great warmth and understanding.

Her placid screen presence belies her early nomadic life as the daughter of a mining engineer. While she did some stage work, she became well established as a radio actress and was a familiar mainstay on the *Dr. Christian* series. She also worked on television doing commercials and appearing in the television series, *The Bob Cummings Show*. **Some of her films include:** *Yankee Doodle Dandy* (1942), *Nora Prentiss* (1947), *Look for the Silver Lining* (1949), *Strategic Air Command* (1955), *13 Ghosts* (1960).

YVONNE DE CARLO (1922–   )

Her first screen test was for the role of a "wolf girl" in a Universal Pictures epic. She was turned down, but while sitting in the casting office, a producer saw her and gave her the starring role in *Salome, Where She Danced* (1945). Prior to her acting career, De Carlo had appeared as a nightclub dancer. In 1971 she was featured in the Broadway musical, *Follies*. **Films include:** *Brute Force* (1947), *Scarlet Angel* (1952), *The Captain's*

Laraine Day, who almost always played Good Girls, in what for her was a madly seductive posture. The film: Bride by Mistake *(1944).*

Paradise (1953), *Passion* (1954), *A Global Affair* (1964), *The Power* (1968).

PEDRO DE CORDOBA (1881–1950)

Seen often on the screen as a sympathetic priest with a Spanish accent, he was born in New York City of a Cuban father and a French mother. His impressive bass voice enabled him to pursue an operatic career before turning to the stage in 1902. In 1915, after a succession of classic roles, he appeared by night in a Greek drama and by day in a silent film farce with Geraldine Farrar. His deep voice allowed him to make a smooth transition from silent to sound films. **Highlights:** *New Moon* (1919), *When Knighthood Was in Flower* (1922), *The Crusades* (1935), *The Light That Failed* (1939), *For Whom the Bell Tolls* (1943), *The Beast With Five Fingers* (1946), *Comanche Territory* (1950).

FRANCES DEE (1908–   )

She had been doing walk-ons for a year as a film extra when she was spotted by Maurice Chevalier in the studio commissary. This led to her first big role opposite him in *Playboy of Paris* (1930). In 1933, she starred with Buster Crabbe in *King of the Jungle*, appeared in *Little Women* (1933) with Katharine Hepburn and began her long (by Hollywood standards)

James Dean, whose style caused a revolution in motion picture studios, at the height of his all too brief career.

Sidney Poitier, Claudia McNeil and Ruby Dee in the 1961 film version of Lorraine Hansberry's prize-winning Raisin in the Sun.

Sandra Dee and Troy Donahue in one of the dramatic moments (there weren't too many of them) in A Summer Place *(1959).*

marriage to Joel McCrea. **Highlights:** *Becky Sharp* (1935), *So Ends Our Night* (1941), *I Walked With a Zombie* (1943), *Bel Ami* (1947), *Gypsy Colt* (1954).

RUBY DEE (1924–   )

The Cleveland-born, lovely black actress was graduated from Hunter College in 1945. Apprenticed at the American Negro Theatre, she made her professional stage debut in *Jeb* (1946), and appeared on Broadway in such successes as *Raisin in the Sun* (1959) and *Purlie Victorious* (1961). She later re-created both roles for the screen. Dee made her movie debut in *The Jackie Robinson Story* (1950) and has, since that time, continued to give moving performances. In 1968 she appeared in *Up Tight*, a film for which she had written the screenplay. Married to actor Ossie Davis, Dee and her husband are devoted to the broader involvement of blacks in the arts. They were the recipients of the Frederick Douglass award of the New York Urban League in 1970. **Highlights:** *No Way Out* (1950), *Go, Man, Go* (1954), *Edge of the City* (1957), *The Balcony* (1963), *Gone Are the Days!* (1963), *The Incident* (1967), *Black Girl* (1972).

SANDRA DEE (1942–   )

"I was a junior Doris Day for years," she said, after making a string of movies about the girl next door. Before her movie career, Alexandra Zuck was anything but the girl next door. At 13, she was one of New York's top teen-aged models, making an average of $100,000 a year.

In the late 50's and early 60's she played in numerous teenage-type movies that met with bad reviews from the critics. In 1970 she said she'd like to re-enter films, playing more mature roles. **Among her films are:** *The Reluctant Debutante* (1958), *Gidget* (1959), *Imitation of Life* (1959), *Tammy Tell Me True* (1961), *That Funny Feeling* (1965), *Rosie!* (1968).

DON DEFORE (1917–   )

Born in Cedar Rapids, Iowa, DeFore attended the University of Iowa and later studied at the Pasadena Community School Theatre. He began his performing career in stock and made his Broadway debut in *Where*

Do We Go From Here? (1939). His film debut came in 1941 when he appeared in *We Go Fast*. That picture marked the beginning of a more than 30-year film career. DeFore is also familiar to television audiences, notably for his role in the long-running *Hazel* series. **Highlights:** *The Human Comedy* (1943), *A Guy Named Joe* (1943), *My Friend Irma* (1949), *A Girl in Every Port* (1952), *The Facts of Life* (1961).

GLORIA DE HAVEN (1924–   )

The daughter of two vaudeville and silent-film stars, she got her first featured role at 16 in *Susan and God*. Although Metro was grooming her to be another Lana Turner, she quit to marry actor John Payne. When the marriage failed she went back to making movies, but never found her "glamour-girl" roles satisfying. In the 50's she moved from screen to stage and television. **Films include:** *Two Girls and a Sailor* (1944), *Summer Holiday* (1948), *Three Little Words* (1950), *So This Is Paris* (1955).

OLIVIA DE HAVILLAND (1916–   )

The sensitive and delicate-looking star has appeared in as varied a list of roles and most probably given as many superlative performances as all but the top four or five all-time greats. Born in Tokyo of English parents, she and her sister, Joan Fontaine, both began their distinguished screen careers in the mid-30's. Movie-goers saw de Havilland first in *Alibi Ike* (1935) although she had previously played in Max Reinhardt's film production of *A Midsummer Night's Dream* which was released a bit later on.

Early in her career she was constantly called upon to look lovely and permit herself to be rescued (usually by Errol Flynn) in such swashbucklers as *Captain Blood* (1935), *The Charge of the Light Brigade* (1936) and as the somewhat vapid Maid Marian in *The Adventures of Robin Hood* (1938). After more Flynn heroics she was cast as Melanie in *Gone With the Wind* (1939) and succeeded in making that perhaps too-sweet, and rather pallid Southern lass into a three-dimensional and highly sympathetic human being.

Despite a running feud and law suits against Warner Brothers (her efforts helped

Don Defore (right) plays a riotous game of gin rummy with Robert Cummings in You Came Along *(1945). The happy kibitzers are Lizabeth Scott and Charles Drake.*

Olivia de Havilland, looking lovely as always, with Errol Flynn in one of the many swashbucklers they did together. This one was They Died With Their Boots On *(1941).*

Another sensitive performance by De Havilland, with honors shared by Montgomery Clift, was in the screen adaptation of Henry James' novel, The Heiress.

One of the few actresses who deserved the most-beautiful-woman-in-the-world title was Mexican star, Dolores Del Rio.

the acting profession mightily) her films kept getting better and better. She won an Oscar nomination for *Hold Back the Dawn* (1941) but lost the award that year to her sister Joan. *To Each His Own* (1946) brought her the first of her Oscars as Best Actress of the Year and the sensitivity of her performance in the historic *The Snake Pit* (1948) won her the New York Critics' award. Just one year later in *The Heiress* she captured both a second Oscar and, once again, the Critics' Best-of-the-Year trophy.

So it went over the years. As a favor to her friend Bette Davis she appeared in *Hush . . . Hush, Sweet Charlotte* (1964) when Joan Crawford was taken ill. More recently she made one of her few mistakes, appearing in the somewhat more than mildly repulsive *The Adventurers* (1969). She has also been superb in several television dramatic presentations. **More than 40 films include:** *Anthony Adverse* (1936), *Dodge City* (1939), *The Private Lives of Elizabeth and Essex* (1939), *They*

Died With Their Boots On (1941), *My Cousin Rachel* (1952), *Libel* (1959), *Light in the Piazza* (1962), *Lady in a Cage* (1964).

ALBERT DEKKER (1905–1968)

"Politics would be all right if I were a bad actor. But I'm a good actor and I like the job of acting," he said upon completion of a two-year term in the California legislature as an assemblyman. Making his Broadway debut with Alfred Lunt in *Marco's Millions* (1927), Dekker appeared on the stage until his screen debut in *The Great Garrick* (1937). During a screen career which spanned more than 30 films, he specialized in mostly villainous or Western roles and made frequent stage and television appearances. To the shock of the industry, he committed suicide in 1968 by hanging himself. **Highlights:** *Marie Antoinette* (1938), *Once Upon a Honeymoon* (1942), *Cass Timberlane* (1947), *East of Eden* (1955), *Middle of the Night* (1959), *Come Spy With Me* (1967).

ALAIN DELON (1935–   )

The French actor with the pretty face was born in a Paris suburb to parents who soon separated. His early life was a sad, unstable one, as he was shunted from home to home. When he was 17 he served in the French army in Indo-China. After the end of his army service, he went to Paris where he became the friend of some actors.

A trip with his friends to the Cannes Film Festival turned out to be a fortuitous journey. There he was noticed by a film maker and cast in *Quand la Femme s'en Mêle* (1958). His career has been extremely variable with as many low spots as high. In 1969 it seemed as if his film making was at its end. The murder of his body guard brought forth a tide of rumors about the actor's supposedly immoral/illegal private life. Surprisingly, the furor died down and Delon resumed his up-again-down-again position in filmdom. **Credits:** *Christine* (1959), *L'Eclisse* (1962), *The Leopard* (1963), *The Yellow Rolls-Royce* (1964), *Is Paris Burning?* (1966), *Borsalino* (1970), *The Assassination of Trotsky* (1972), *Scorpio* (1973).

DOLORES DEL RIO (1905–   )

One of the great beauties of the films, the Mexican leading lady was "discovered" at a party in her own home by Hollywood director Edwin Carewe who offered her a contract.

She made her debut in *Joanna* (1925), and continued to look lovely and act creditably in many films. After *Journey Into Fear* (1943), unhappy over the quality of her scripts and a fading romance with Orson Welles, she left California saying: "I wish to choose my own stories, directors and cameramen. I can do that better in Mexico."

She did just that and became one of Mexico's reigning stars for several decades, but more recently has returned from time to time to perform in Hollywood-made productions.

English language credits include: *What Price Glory?* (1926), *Evangeline* (1929), *Bird of Paradise* (1932), *Madame Du Barry* (1934), *Lancer Spy* (1937), *The Fugitive* (1947), *Cheyenne Autumn* (1964), *More Than a Miracle* (1967).

WILLIAM DEMAREST (1892–   )

A show-business veteran with more than 70 years of service behind him, he was a vaudevillian who played, of all instruments, the cello; a Broadway performer and television star; a film producer and character actor in more than 100 films, almost always portraying a dour-faced, acerbic misanthrope who underneath that forbidding exterior concealed a heart of (you guessed it) gold.

Like many other film stars he was born in the midwest but raised in New York. Apart from starring as Uncle Charley in the television series *My Three Sons*, Demarest has appeared in scores of films and received an Oscar nomination for his role in *The Jolson Story* (1946). **Other film credits include:** *The Jazz Singer* (1927), *Rosalie* (1938), *Mr. Smith Goes to Washington* (1939), *The Miracle of Morgan's Creek* (1944), *It's a Mad, Mad, Mad, Mad World* (1963), *That Darn Cat* (1965).

CATHERINE DENEUVE (1943–   )

Like so many actresses before her, she has been billed as "the world's most beautiful woman"—and in Deneuve's case the claim comes very close to justification. One of France's leading performers who also has international box-office appeal, she is almost equally appealing in a film classic like *Belle de Jour* (1966), or appearing on American television to implore American manhood to buy a certain French perfume for their girlfriends at Christmastime.

Deneuve made her film debut as a teen-ager playing the sister of Françoise Dorléac—her sister in real life as well, who was later killed in an automobile accident. By the time Deneuve was 24 she had made 23 films with such outstanding European directors as Luis Buñuel, a total that included several American pictures that were distinctly less memorable than the beautiful *The Umbrellas of Cherbourg* (1964). **Other credits:** *Repulsion* (1965), *Benjamin* (1968), *Mayerling* (1969), *The April Fools* (1969), *The Mississippi Mermaid* (1969), *Tristana* (1970).

ROBERT DE NIRO (1943–   )

De Niro performed for over five years in a series of off-Broadway plays that were plainly flops. In a few minor film appearances, however, he established enough credibility to get the principal role in a low-budget

Alain Delon assumes an Errol Flynnish pose in Rene Clement's film Purple Noon *(1961).*

William Demarest, whose skeptical facade enlivened countless movies, is here flanked by Betty Hutton and Diana Lynn in the highly amusing film The Miracle of Morgan's Creek.

Robert De Niro, one of the most exciting and talented new screen stars.

Even though it was written by Neil Simon, a surefire producer of hits, The Out-of-Towners did nothing to enhance the reputation of Sandy Dennis. Here she is in a scene from that film, accompanied by a five-o'clock-shadowed Jack Lemmon.

film that became an outstanding artistic and commercial success. In *Bang the Drum Slowly* (1973) De Niro played the part of a dying baseball player with such sensitivity and realism that one felt he was well on his way to be numbered among the new acting greats. The feeling was justified when he followed *Drum* with another success, his taut portrayal in *Mean Streets* (1973), for which he won the Film Critics' Circle Award. **Main credits:** *Hi, Mom* (1970), *The Gang That Couldn't Shoot Straight* (1971).

RICHARD DENNING (1914–   )

Born Louis Albert Denninger in Poughkeepsie, New York, Denning has acting credits for screen, stage, radio and television. He made his film debut in *Hold 'Em Navy* (1937) and throughout the 40's and 50's made numerous adventure, mystery and action films, many of "B" quality. He then turned to television, starring in such series as *Mr. and Mrs. North, The Flying Doctor* and *Karen*. More recently, he appeared on *Hawaii Five-O* in the role of governor of the island state. **Film credits:** *Her Jungle Love* (1938), *The Farmer's Daughter* (1940), *North West Mounted Police* (1940), *The Glass Key* (1942), *Scarlet Angel* (1952), *The Lady Takes a Flyer* (1958).

SANDY DENNIS (1937–   )

Sandy Dennis is a promise unfulfilled. After her first two successful films, *Who's Afraid of Virginia Woolf?* (1966) and *Up the Down Staircase* (1967), Dennis typecast herself with her fluttering hands, hesitant speech and facial mugging.

Born in Nebraska, Dennis first appeared on stage in a Lincoln local production of *The Rainmaker*. Going on to summer stock, she finally reached Broadway in the very successful *Any Wednesday* which she followed with another hit, *Barefoot in the Park*. These two plays once again brought her to Hollywood (she had already been there in 1961 for a small part in *Splendor in the Grass*). She made *Woolf* and *Staircase* winning the Oscar for Best Supporting Actress for the former. She followed these with the box-office hit, *The Fox* (1968), but thereafter made mediocre films and has yet to make a comeback. **Films**

include: *A Touch of Love* (1969), *The Out-of-Towners* (1970), *The Only Way Out Is Dead* (1971).

REGINALD DENNY (1891–1967)

Son of a five-generation theatrical family, he was born in England and made his stage debut at the age of seven. Although he first appeared on the New York stage in 1911, it wasn't until after World War I that he settled in the United States, starring in many silent film comedies.

With the advent of sound, he went into character roles—usually playing stiff-upper-lip Britishers. Although he essayed a wide variety of parts, he was always best remembered for his comic roles. **More than 200 films include:** *The Iron Trail* (1921), *Oh, Doctor* (1925), *Skinner's Dress Suit* (1926), *Anna Karenina* (1935), *Rebecca* (1940), *Love Letters* (1945), *Around the World in 80 Days* (1956), *Cat Ballou* (1965).

JOHN DEREK (1926–   )

Both his parents were in pictures—his father as a producer-director and his mother as an actress—so it was natural for young Derek to study acting after high school. He was enrolled at David O. Selznick's studio school until he was drafted in the late 40's. Derek returned to Hollywood after his two years in the service and made his screen debut in *Knock on Any Door* (1949). His dark good looks made him a fan magazine hero in the 50's, but his career never kept pace with his publicity. Derek was cast in a string of routine action films until Cecil B. DeMille chose him to play Joshua in *The Ten Commandments* (1956). He followed that one up with another big budget picture, *Exodus* (1958), but his fortunes in Hollywood seemed on the decline. Derek underwent another publicity blitz after his marriage to actress Ursula Andress in 1957. They were later divorced. During the early 60's, he attempted to establish himself in Europe. He returned to the United States disillusioned but determined to take another crack at Hollywood. **Films include:** *Mask of the Avenger* (1951), *Adventures of Hajji Baba* (1954), *The Flesh Is Weak* (1955), *Nightmare in the Sun* (1964), *Once Before I Die* (1966), *Childish Things* (1969).

VITTORIO DE SICA (1902–)

The Italian actor-director is a true talent, deserving credit for both his film specialties. As an actor, De Sica has appeared in more than 40 films since his debut in 1933, including such successes as *A Farewell to Arms* (1958), *The Angel Wore Red* (1960), and *The Amorous Adventures of Moll Flanders* (1965). Perhaps his greatest fame stems from the films he directed, such as *The Bicycle Thief* (1949), which won a special Academy Award, *Two Woman* (1961), *Boccaccio '70* (1962), *Yesterday, Today, and Tomorrow* (1964), *Woman Times Seven* (1967), and his most recent success *The Garden of the Finzi-Continis* (1972). De Sica is of the "neo-realistic" school, the post-war cinematic movement in Italy which broke away from the traditional "escapist" format in film. **Highlights:** *Scandal in Sorrento* (1957), *The Gold of Naples* (1957), *The Bigamist* (1958).

ANDY DEVINE (1905–)

He made his film debut as a romantic lead in silent movies in the 20's, portraying a baseball player in *The Collegians*. When talkies arrived, his expanding girth and unique voice made the Arizona-born actor much in demand for supporting comic roles, more often than not in Westerns and war pictures.

His debut in talkies was in 1931 in *The Spirit of Notre Dame* and he followed it up by appearing in well over 150 films in the next four decades plus innumerable radio and television appearances—most notably as a sidekick of Buck Benny and Wild Bill Hickok. **A few highlights:** *A Star Is Born* (1937), *Stagecoach* (1939), *When the Daltons Rode* (1940), *Sudan* (1945), *The Red Badge of Courage* (1951), *The Man Who Shot Liberty Valance* (1962), *How the West Was Won* (1963), *The Ballad of Josie* (1968).

COLLEEN DEWHURST (1926–)

Born in Montreal, Canada, Dewhurst studied at the American Academy of Dramatic Art and made her first professional appearance in the play, *The Royal Family* (1946). She has appeared on Broadway in numerous plays, among them *Desire Under the Elms* (1952), *Camille* (1956), and *A Moon for the*

Vittorio de Sica, a well-known actor before he became a top director, still takes an occasional turn before the cameras. This jovial scene, with Edward G. Robinson (r.), is from The Biggest Bundle of Them All *(1968).*

Andy Devine's husky bullhorn voice was featured in innumerable movies. He is shown here with Mrs. Phil Harris—alias Alice Faye—and Tyrone Power in In Old Chicago *(1938).*

For more than two decades Colleen Dewhurst has never quite received the recognition she deserved, as one of the best actresses of her time. Here she is as Monique in the 1971 film The Last Run.

The late Brandon de Wilde, Ethel Waters and Julie Harris in a notable film adaptation of a notable play, The Member of the Wedding.

Misbegotten (1973). Dewhurst's vast talents have been universally recognized as various awards attest, including two Obies (1957 and 1963) and a Tony (1961). She has appeared extensively on television, and though her film-credit list is short, her performances were long on artistry. She has made the papers not only for her performing talents, but also for her off-again/on-again marriage to actor George C. Scott, which recently ended in divorce. **Films include:** *The Nun's Story* (1959), *Man on a String* (1960), *A Fine Madness* (1966).

BRANDON DE WILDE (1942–1972)

The gifted child star was well on his way to becoming an outstanding movie personality when he died in a car accident in 1972. He had made his stage debut when he was seven years old in Carson McCullers' *The Member of the Wedding*, and played the same role in the film version (1952). He was lauded at the time for having the "magnetic personality of a real performer." **His movies include:** *Shane* (1953), *Blue Denim* (1959), *Hud* (1963), *In Harm's Way* (1965).

BILLY DE WOLFE (1907–1974)

His parents had hoped he would become a Baptist minister, but their son worshipped vaudeville and worked for 50 cents a night in the local theatre. After the show one evening, De Wolfe went on stage and practiced his gynmastics. The leader of an acrobatic group chanced to see him and offered the star-struck youngster a job. He took the name William De Wolfe from the theatre manager who had told him that his real name, Bill Jones, would not do for a "star."

De Wolfe's distinctive, lisping voice, mustachio, and comic talents are familiar to movie and TV audiences alike. **Credits include:** *Dixie* (1943), *Blue Skies* (1946), *Dear Ruth* (1947), *Lullaby of Broadway* (1951), *Call Me Madam* (1953), *The Queen and I* (1969).

ANGIE DICKINSON (1936–   )

Born in Kulm, North Dakota, she planned to become a secretary until friends entered her in a beauty contest which she won. That victory led to the films and she played small parts for a time, making her debut in *Lucky Me* (1954). Howard Hawks, who had discovered Carole Lombard, Rita Hayworth and Lauren Bacall, noticed Dickinson and signed her to a starring role in *Rio Bravo* (1959). This film brought her good reviews and she has worked steadily since in rather unexceptional films and on television.

In 1965, Dickinson married Bert Bacharach and over the years they have become one of the most glittering couples in the entertainment world. **Highlights:** *The Sins of Rachel Cade* (1961), *Captain Newman, M.D.* (1964), *The Chase* (1966), *Point Blank* (1967), *Fuzz* (1969).

MARLENE DIETRICH (1901–   )

With the possible exception of a few Renaissance masterpieces auctioned off by Sotheby's and a case of 40-year-old Château Mouton-Rothschild, she is perhaps Europe's most prized export to America of the century. She is wise. She is beautiful. She is enigmatic. She is elusive. She is witty. She is the epitome of glamour. She is, in short, the one and only Marlene, of whom a critic wrote: "I can only say that she makes Reason totter on her throne."

Maria Magdalena von Lösch was born in Berlin, Germany, and had appeared in at least a dozen plays and German films when Josef von Sternberg saw her perform in a revue, *Zwei Kravatten*, in 1929. At Emil Jannings' request von Sternberg cast her in the historic *Blue Angel* (1930), in which Marlene played fast and loose with the affections of an aging Jannings. As Lola-Lola, her combination of top-hat, black silk stockings and snow-white thighs above them, transformed her into a dynamically new type of vamp—several million light-years removed from the Theda Baras and Pola Negris of earlier years. When she straddled a chair to sing "Falling-in-love-again," enough energy was generated among audiences to light up a whole city.

More von Sternberg films followed: *Morocco* (which was released simultaneously with the English-language version of *The Blue Angel*) was equally sensational, and employed the same theme. She was a nightclub girl, Adolphe Menjou was an older man, Gary Cooper a member of the French Foreign

Typical Billy De Wolfe elegance and humor are represented in this scene with Doris Day from Lullaby of Broadway.

Angie Dickinson barely tolerates the restraining grip of Peter Finch in a scene from The Sins of Rachel Cade.

For at least a decade after her debut, studio photographers were constitutionally unable to photograph Dietrich without featuring her legs. Here is one of the screen's immortals as she appeared in Seven Sinners.

Destry Rides Again *gave Marlene Dietrich the chance to match comic wits with the likes of Mischa Auer. She played her role with gusto, and the film was a great hit.*

Legion who not only won her love but convinced her that settling down in the Sahara was the thing to do.

Although Dietrich averaged only about one film a year (she and von Sternberg parted company in 1935), many of them were so highly publicized and a few of them so good that it seemed like more. The weak ones —and many of her scripts read as though they had been dashed off by writers who had learned their trade through correspondence schools—were forgotten when a good one came along like *Destry Rides Again* (1939), in which she played her comedy role to the hilt.

Violently anti-Nazi, Dietrich refused a direct command from Hitler to return to Germany and during the war spent much of her time entertaining Allied fighting men overseas. She made a number of French films and then, in 1948, and again cast as a cabaret entertainer, she did a bang-up job in *A Foreign Affair*. Her last important film was *Judgment at Nuremberg* (1961) but since then she has made many nightclub appearances and given concerts in every corner of the globe. Her first return to Germany, which had been awaited with considerable apprehension, turned out to be a huge success before packed and appreciative houses. **Films include:** *Shanghai Express* (1932), *Desire* (1932), *Angel* (1937), *Seven Sinners* (1940), *Witness for the Prosecution* (1958).

DUDLEY DIGGES (1879–1947)

Born in Dublin, Digges, a member of the original Abbey Players, made his Broadway debut with the celebrated Minnie Maddern Fiske in 1904. Beginning with his appearance in *Bonds of Interest* in 1919, when the Theatre Guild was formed, the actor played more than 3,500 times for that organization alone before his death in 1947. His most famous stage role was that of Gramps, a character he created in *On Borrowed Time* (1939). Between 1929 and 1947, in addition to his stage work, Digges also made more than 50 films. **Film highlights:** *Condemned* (1929), *Outward Bound* (1930), *The Maltese Falcon* (1931), *The General Died at Dawn* (1936), *The Searching Wind* (1946).

BRADFORD DILLMAN (1930–   )

San Francisco-born Dillman made an impressive reputation for himself on Broadway well before his successes as a leading man in films and on television. He received enthusiastic reviews for his role in the Broadway production of O'Neill's *Long Day's Journey Into Night* (1959), a year after his film debut in *A Certain Smile*. For a long while, his fresh, handsome youthfulness, kept him in young roles. More recently, however, his varied characterizations have extended to villains and heavies. **Highlights:** *Compulsion* (1959), *A Rage to Live* (1965), *The Bridge at Remagen* (1969), *The Way We Were* (1973).

ALAN DINEHART (1886–1944)

He played many supporting roles during the 30's and 40's, often portraying a bluff businessman. He appeared in more than 65 films in a 13 year period, often making as many as nine and ten films a year. **Films include:** *Wicked* (1932), *Lawyer Man* (1933), *Dante's Inferno* (1935), *This Is My Affair* (1937), *Hotel for Women* (1939), *Girl Trouble* (1943).

CHARLES DINGLE (1888–1956)

Born in Wabash, Indiana, Dingle made his dramatic debut as Denver Dan Peabody, a 65-year-old gambler in the play *Forgiven*. Innumerable roles in stock and repertory followed, and by the age of 17 Dingle was an established leading man. His most famous stage role was that of Benjamin Hubbard in the New York performance of *The Little Foxes* (1939). When Dingle portrayed the same role on screen, the *Times* film critic, Bosley Crowther, called him "a perfect villain in respectable garb." **Film highlights:** *The Little Foxes* (1941), *Unholy Partners* (1941), *Cinderella Jones* (1946), *Call Me Madam* (1953), *The Court-Martial of Billy Mitchell* (1955).

RICHARD DIX (1895–1945)

Like Ronald Colman, he was one of the few leading men whose career grew and prospered after the advent of talkies. Born Ernest Carlton Brimmer in St. Paul, Minnesota, he

One of innumerable scenes from innumerable movies in which everyone stops eating. In this instance it is Bradford Dillman, making his debut in A Certain Smile, *along with* . . . ???

Richard Dix, a big star of early talkies, almost always wore a look of lantern-jawed intensity. In this scene with Madge Evans from Transatlantic Tunnel *he is apparently figuring out what number to enter in the ship's pool.*

abandoned medical school at the state university to take to the stage and landed on Broadway after serving in the First World War. He was a reliable performer and during the 20's played cowboys, Indians, playboys and newspaper reporters. Old-timers will also recall that he played in the second or rather modern sequences of DeMille's massive 1923 epic, *The Ten Commandments*.

Dix made his talkie debut in 1929 in *Nothing but the Truth* but was at the top of his form playing opposite Irene Dunne in the film adaptation of Edna Ferber's *Cimarron* (1931). He was always at his best playing Westerns—somehow they seemed to fit his slightly grim and lantern-jawed visage. *West of the Pecos* (1934) and *Man of Conquest* (1939), the story of Sam Houston, were especially interesting.

Just before his death after a series of heart attacks, he had concluded four or five pictures in the series that began with *The Whistler* (1944). **Other credits:** *Souls for Sale* (1923),

The Vanishing American (1925), *Sporting Goods* (1928), *The Lost Squadron* (1932), *Stingaree* (1934), *The Ghost Ship* (1943), *The Thirteenth Hour* (1947).

IVAN DIXON (1931–   )

Born in New York City, the son of a war hero, Dixon, who graduated from North Carolina College, started his acting career as a stunt man and stand-in for Sidney Poitier. He says of his early years as an actor: ''You had to be nuts to stay an actor when there were two (black) roles and both of them played by Poitier.'' His most important film role to date had been as Duff in *Nothing but a Man* (1964). More recently Dixon has been seen in a number of television specials, in addition to appearing as a regular in CBS's *Hogan's Heroes*. **Film highlights:** *Something of Value* (1957), *Porgy and Bess* (1959), *A Raisin in the Sun* (1961), *A Patch of Blue* (1965).

CLAIRE DODD (1908–1973)

Richard Watts, Jr. reviewing *Gambling Lady* (1934) wrote: ''Miss Dodd, who is one of this department's favorite heroines, is, as you know, invariably assigned to the role of a shallow and discomfited villainess and again she handled it with a vividness worthy of better things. I suspect that she is one of the most unappreciated of the screen's potentially important figures.''

Signed by Ziegfeld while still in her teens, Dodd appeared on Broadway in *Smiles* (1930) with Marilyn Miller before going to Hollywood to begin a career which included 45 films in which she generally played seductresses, murdered mistresses, scheming blondes and treacherous blackmailers. **Highlights:** *Hard to Handle* (1933), *Babbitt* (1934), *The Pay-off* (1935), *The Singing Kid* (1936), *In the Navy* (1941).

TROY DONAHUE (1937–   )

The tall, blue-eyed blond was born Merle Johnson, Jr. in New York City. His youthful good looks served as an opening wedge to a film career. He made his screen debut at age 20 in *Man Afraid* and for ten years after that appeared with regularity in light-hearted and-headed films. He has made recent ap-

The late Claire Dodd, a good actress given bad roles, in a scene with William Gargan from one of her last films, In the Navy.

pearances on television but the need for good-looking but light-weight film actors seems to have diminished with the influx of realistic, finely wrought films which require stronger, more meaningful performances. **Highlights:** *This Happy Feeling* (1958), *A Summer Place* (1959), *Parrish* (1961), *Susan Slade* (1961), *Those Fantastic Flying Fools* (1967).

ROBERT DONAT (1905–1958)

Although he made but one picture in America and relatively few in his native England, he was without question one of the finest performers of his generation, equally adept at comedy and drama. His career was blighted by a chronic illness, asthma, which kept him off screen in the later years of his life and eventually caused his early death.

Donat began his career playing with repertory companies, moved on to the London stage and was then discovered by Alexander Korda who cast him as an Oxford undergraduate in *Men of Tomorrow* (1932). He played Culpepper, the luckless lover of Charles Laughton's fourth wife in *Henry VIII* (1933), and then starred in *The Count of Monte Cristo* (1934), a very good film indeed. There followed what most experts feel was the best thriller ever made, Hitchcock's *The Thirty-Nine Steps* (1935) and René Clair's altogether charming comedy, *The Ghost Goes West* (1936), in which Donat played both the ghost who tries to prevent an American millionaire from moving his castle to the U.S.A., and the venerable ghost's modern descendant.

Illness slowed down his career during the next few years but in 1938 *The Citadel* was a success and the one that followed, *Goodbye, Mr. Chips* (1939) not only won Donat the Oscar and Picturegoer Medal for Best Actor of the Year but was, almost certainly, one of the highest-praised films of the decade.

Refusing Hollywood offers, he chose to make *The Young Mr. Pitt* as a contribution to the war effort. Thereafter he made a few films and stage appearances, but oxygen tanks had to be kept in the wings since he was fading rapidly. His last picture assignment, as a Chinese mandarin in Ingrid Bergman's *The Inn of the Sixth Happiness* (1958) contained

A tense scene from The 39 Steps, *believed by many to be the best thriller ever made. Here Robert Donat attempts to cheer up Madeleine Carroll when things look blackest.*

the closing screen line: ''We shall not see each other again, I think.'' He was dead a few weeks later. **Other films:** *Sabotage* (1936), *The Adventures of Tartu* (1943), *Perfect Strangers* (1945), *Vacation From Marriage* (1946), *The Winslow Boy* (1950).

LUDWIG DONATH (1907–1967)

Born in Vienna, Donath graduated from the Royal Academy of Music and Dramatic Arts there. He made his stage debut in his hometown as Lysander in *A Midsummer Night's Dream*. Donath is noted for his versatility, having played a variety of roles from classical drama to musical comedy. With the German occupation of Austria, Donath migrated to the United States and made his film debut in *The Strange Death of Adolph Hitler* (1943). In addition to having appeared in nearly 50 films and numerous stage productions, Donath has made a number of television appearances. **Film highlights:** *The Jolson Story* (1946), *To the Ends of the Earth*

Brian Donlevy, who played lead and supporting roles in a great many better-than-average pictures, is here shown in The Glass Key.

(1948), *The Fighting O'Flynn* (1949), *The Great Caruso* (1951), *Sins of Jezebel* (1954).

BRIAN DONLEVY (1903–1972)

An unkind critic once said of the Irish-born actor that he always looked as though he were standing in a hole and could only emerge from it if you wound him up and got the clockwork moving. The impression, one suspects, came from his large square face and broad, broad shoulders, which combined to give him a military bearing plus a certain stiffness of movement that went with it.

Donlevy played innumerable leading roles on stage and screen—good newspaper men and bad Western outlaws, frontiersman and Marine officers, killers and police lieutenants. While he was villainous more often than not, he was also adept at comedy.

His debut was in *Mother's Boy* (1929), a title which hardly forecast the sterner stuff that was to come. He made nearly 100 pictures during his career. **Some of his best films:** *Jesse James* (1939), *Destry Rides Again* (1939), *The Great McGinty* (1940), *Hold Back the Dawn* (1941), *The Glass Key* (1942), *The Virginian* (1946), *Kiss of Death* (1947), *A Cry in the Night* (1956).

RUTH DONNELLY (1896–   )

She once said of her four-year association with George M. Cohan: "I learned to talk fast from him. He never let anything lag. Kept things moving. That was valuable to me when I came to Hollywood." Born in Trenton, New Jersey, she made her Broadway debut at the age of 16 in the chorus of *Quaker Girl*. She landed in Hollywood 20 years later and became noted as the wise-cracking girl friend with the instant retort, making as many as 15 features in 1934 alone. **More than 100 films include:** *Transatlantic* (1931), *Mr. Deeds Goes to Town* (1936), *Mr. Smith Goes to Washington* (1939), My Little Chickadee (1940), *The Bells of St. Mary's* (1945), *The Snake Pit* (1948), *Autumn Leaves* (1956).

ANN DORAN (1913–   )

The movie actress was once told that owls brought good luck. When she was out of work, she bought an owl and immediately found a job. "It soon came about that every time I got an owl I got a job." By 1967 she had 567 owls and was starring in television's *National Velvet* series. **Some of her movies are:** *Blondie* (1938), *Air Force* (1943), *The Snake Pit* (1948), *Rebel Without a Cause* (1955), *Where Love Has Gone* (1964).

DIANA DORS (1931–   )

Born Diana Fluck in Swindon, England, Dors was considered "Britain's Marilyn Monroe" by American columnists in the 50's, when the super-bosomy blond actress was cast in a number of sexpot roles. Reporters, one of whom referred to the actress as "the one with the libidinous lip," were delighted with Dors' publicity stunts. In 1955, for example, the actress, clad in a mink bikini, skimmed down Venice's Grand Canal on the prow of a gondola. More recently, after a period of absence from films, Dors was praised by a critic for having ripened into "a fine actress with a knowing comedy touch." **Film highlights:** *I Married a Woman* (1956),

Ruth Donnelly, a specialist in wise cracks (as they were then known) here arbitrates an interchange between two super wise-guys, Dick Powell and James Cagney. The film: Footlight Parade *(1933).*

Value for Money (1957), *The Unholy Wife* (1958), *There's a Girl in My Soup* (1970).

FIFI D'ORSAY (1907–   )

Movie audiences thought she was a genuine Parisienne during her heyday in the early 30's, but actually, she was born in Montreal. D'Orsay wasn't in demand for very long. She made her movie debut with Will Rogers in *They Had to See Paris* (1930) and starred in several other films until the fad for Parisian pictures ended in 1932.

D'Orsay claims she took her last name from a bottle of French perfume and adopted the nickname Fifi because that's what the other girls called her when she was in the chorus of the Greenwich Village Follies in the 20's. She had to do something about a name. Her own—Angelina Yvonne Cecile Lussier D'Sablon—was a bit long for a marquee.

For years, D'Orsay has been trying to change her image. She says she only went along with the story that she was French for publicity purposes. She was stuck with it though, and perhaps because of it, never regained the kind of popularity she enjoyed during her brief years as a top box-office attraction.

During World War II, D'Orsay made more than 2,000 personal appearances entertaining troops. Her movie career did survive to some extent—she was cast in supporting roles from time to time, most recently in *The Art of Love* (1965). D'Orsay lives in Hollywood. **Films include:** *Hot for Paris* (1930), *Just Imagine* (1931), *Silk Stockings* (1932), *Accent on Youth* (1945), *Wild and Wonderful* (1963).

GABRIELLE DORZIAT (1880–   )

This French-born stage star did not make her American screen debut until 1953, when she played the role of the mother superior in *Little Boy Lost*. In fact, although Dorziat began her stage career in France in 1913, it was not until 1935 that she consented to act in a French film, as she considered cinema an "upstart form." It was the French director Anatole Litvak who finally convinced her to try films, casting her in the role of the empress in his *Mayerling* (1937). **Film highlghts:** *La*

It's a bit difficult to tell which of the two is behind bars, but it is obvious that Diana Dors and Rod Steiger are not overly pleased with one another. The films was The Unholy Wife *(1957), so perhaps it was Diana who was incarcerated.*

Fin du Jour (1939), *Les Parents Terribles* (1948), *Les Espions* (1957), *Germinal* (1963).

KIRK DOUGLAS (1916–   )

"My life is a 'B' script," he said. "I'd never make it as a picture—too corny." Douglas should have known, for he was no stranger to "B" scripts, along with a number of good ones that came his way. The actor known for the cleft in his chin, manner of vocal delivery that appears to emanate from between clenched teeth, and powerful bodily musculature was born Issur Danielovitch in Amsterdam, New York, and made his first screen appearance in *The Strange Love of Martha Ivers* (1946). In at least 50 films over the next 25 years he was three times nominated for an Academy Award and thrice voted the worst actor of the year by the Harvard Lampoon—a contradiction not as weird as it seems, for (like the little girl with a curl) when he was good he was very, very good and when

Gabrielle Dorziat, making her film debut at the age of 57 in Mayerling. *The willowy French actress had begun her career before the outbreak of World War I.*

Kirk Douglas, who was in some pretty tight spots in his long career, finds it necessary to react with extreme violence in this "action-packed" sequence from Indian Fighter *(1955).*

he was bad—vide *Spartacus* (1960)—he was horrid. It is also interesting to note that, while never becoming one of the top stars, he has remained consistently popular with movie goers, good pictures or bad. **Credits include:** *A Letter to Three Wives* (1948), *Champion* (1949), *The Glass Menagerie* (1950), *Detective Story* (1951), *Lust for Life* (1956), *Paths of Glory* (1957), *Seven Days in May* (1964), *Cast a Giant Shadow* (1966), *A Lovely Way to Die* (1968).

MELVYN DOUGLAS (1901–)

The son of concert pianist Edouard Hesselberg was born in Macon, Georgia, and had been acting on stage for more than ten years when he enjoyed his first Broadway success, playing opposite his wife-to-be, Helen Gahagan, in *Tonight or Never* (1931). That sent him straight to Hollywood and an extended series of films in which he was miscast in romantic roles, playing against such luminaries as Gloria Swanson and Greta Garbo (in *As You Desire Me,* 1932). With the passing of time he developed into a highly popular leading man but his true flair was sophisticated comedy and it was in films like *Ninotchka* (1939), again with Garbo, and *Mr. Blandings Builds His Dream House* (1948), with Myrna Loy, that he was at his best.

Like his congresswoman wife, who was the celebrated victim of a particularly venomous campaign waged by Richard Nixon in California early in Nixon's career, Douglas was concerned with national issues and was the first actor to be a delegate to a national convention—that of the Democrats in 1940. During World War II he enlisted as a private, emerged as a major and conceded that he preferred the army to movies. Nonetheless, he has continued to make pictures, along with television appearances and Broadway performances, winning a Tony Award for *The Best Man* (1960). Back to films again, he won an Oscar for Best Supporting Actor of the Year in *Hud* (1963). **Nearly 60 films include:** *Counsellor-At-Law* (1933), *She Married Her Boss* (1935), *The Gorgeous Hussy* (1936), *Theodora Goes Wild* (1936), *The Shining Hour* (1939), *The Sea of Grass*

(1947), *Billy Budd* (1962), *The Americanization of Emily* (1964), *The Candidate* (1972).

PAUL DOUGLAS (1907–1959)

Although he wanted to be an actor from
childhood, Philadelphia-born Douglas didn't
get his first big part until 1946, when he was
almost 40 years old. When Garson Kanin cast
the stage version of *Born Yesterday*, he
looked for an actor to play Harry Brock, an
uncouth, chiseling scrap dealer. When Kanin
saw Douglas he felt the actor was perfect for
the part.

His stage appearance led to his film debut
in Mankiewicz' classic, *A Letter to Three
Wives* (1949). In this picture, Douglas
handed in an expert performance opposite
Linda Darnell as her wealthy, but unloved,
spouse. His brief acting career spanned al-
most 25 films. **Films include:** *Fourteen
Hours* (1951), *When in Rome* (1952),
Executive Suite (1954), *The Solid Gold
Cadillac* (1956), *The Mating Game* (1959).

BILLIE DOVE (1900–   )

The Ziegfeld Follies were Dove's route to
Hollywood in the 20's. She was an artist's
model who Ziegfeld first noticed in a photograph. He hired Dove to dance and to pose
sitting in a hoop during Follies' big production numbers. When Hollywood decided to
make a picture about the Follies, Dove was
one of the dancers who won a role. That first
featured part in *Dolly of the Follies* (1922)
with Constance Talmadge led to some leading
roles in silent films. Although Dove did a few
talking pictures, she never really adjusted to
sound and retired from the screen when she
married rancher Robert Kenaston. She lives
in Palm Springs, California, and occasionally
does a small film part, as in *Diamondhead*
(1962). **Films include:** *Beyond the Rainbow*
(1922), *Wanderer of the Wasteland* (1928),
The Black Pirate (1926), *One Night at
Susie's* (1928), *Painted Angel* (1930),
Blondie of the Follies (1932).

TOM DRAKE (1919–   )

If ever an actor was type cast, it was Drake.
The picture that did it was *Meet Me in St.
Louis* (1944) with Judy Garland. Drake

As urbane an actor as ever lived, Melvyn Douglas sternly subjects Joan
Blondell to close-up inspection. The film, made more than 35 years ago, is
The Amazing Mr. Williams.

Paul Douglas, whose career was all too short, is here shown in a scene from
Forever Female *(1953). The lady is Catherine Crowley.*

Marie Dressler, a fantastic actress and an extremely funny lady, shown here as a super-dowager with Madge Evans in Dinner at Eight—*a far cry from* Tillie's Punctured Romance.

played the basketball player Garland fell in love with in the movie—the one she meant when she sang "The Boy Next Door."

Drake first tried to break into motion pictures in 1940 after several Broadway appearances. He landed one minor part before giving up and returning to New York. It was as the juvenile lead in the Broadway comedy *Janie* (1942) that Drake first made his mark. MGM spotted him and signed him during a talent search for actors who looked like they belonged in movies about small town American life.

He made his screen debut as Van Johnson's pal in *Two Girls and a Sailor* (1944). Most of his films were light comedies, although he did play the role of the adult Robert Shannon in *The Green Years* (1946) with Charles Coburn. Another high point was his role as the army sergeant who turned Lassie into a war killer in *Courage of Lassie* (1946). Elizabeth Taylor played the girl who "saved" Lassie after the war and turned her into a nice, gentle collie again.

Drake's career was on the downgrade in the late 40's after MGM failed to renew his contract. He did play supporting roles in a few films like *Mr. Belvedere Goes to College* (1949), and his old friend Elizabeth Taylor got him roles in two of her pictures, *Raintree County* (1957) and *The Sandpiper* (1960). But even supporting roles were fewer and far between in the 60's. He did some television in the 70's, including episodes of *Mannix*, *Marcus Welby, M.D.*, and *Owen Marshall*. **Films include:** *Mrs. Parkington* (1944), *This Man's Navy* (1945), *Words and Music* (1948), *The Great Rupert* (1950), *Sudden Danger* (1955), *The Singing Nun* (1966), *The Spectre of Edgar Allan Poe* (1973).

LOUISE DRESSER (1879–1965)

She came to Hollywood in 1923, after 22 years in light opera, musical comedy and vaudeville. In 1928, she won an Academy Award nomination for *A Ship Comes In*, but she became best known as the crotchety, understanding wife of Will Rogers in seven of his films. She retired from acting in 1937, but continued her interest in the film industry and was one of the founders of the Motion Picture Country House and Hospital for indigent actors. **Some of her films include:** *The Goose Woman* (1925), *The Eagle* (1925), *Not Quite Decent* (1929), *State Fair* (1933), *The Scarlet Empress* (1934), *Maid of Salem* (1937).

MARIE DRESSLER (1869–1934)

She was born Leila von Koerber in a remote Canadian town, was a chorus girl in light operas by the time she was 13, and played Mrs. Malaprop on Broadway at the age of 26. During the early years of this century she was far and away the most popular comedienne both in England and the United States and, on a visit to Los Angeles, Mack Sennett persuaded her to make a film version of one of his plays, *Tillie's Nightmare*. She was to be supported by two players named Charles Chaplin and Mabel Normand and it was to be the first comedy ever to run a full six reels. The 1914 production, re-christened *Tillie's Punctured Romance*, proved as funny and as successful as Sennett had promised.

After a few more silents, two of them variations on the Tillie theme, Dressler (after becoming a leading crusader in the fight to establish Actors Equity) found that the bottom had fallen out of her career. Almost destitute for a while, a turn in her fortunes didn't really arrive until the talkies, although she appeared in a number of fairly successful comedies with Polly Moran. Finally she landed the part of Marthy in Garbo's *Anna Christie* (1930). She turned to comedy and the public loved her craggy, jutting-jawed mixture of humor and sentiment. She leaped to stardom with Wallace Beery in *Min and Bill* (1930), a gorgeous performance that brought her the Oscar for Best Actress of the Year and placed her as number one on audience's popularity lists. She won the Picturegoer's Gold Medal for *Emma* (1932) and clicked again as an indomitable old woman who said of her husband, Wallace Beery, in *Tugboat Annie* (1933): "He never struck me except in self-defense."

The most beloved star on the lot, she died of cancer after a brief illness in 1934. **Other credits include:** *Caught Short* (1930), *Prosperity* (1932), *Dinner at Eight* (1933), *The Late Christopher Bean* (1933).

ELLEN DREW (1915–   )

A discovery of William Demarest, the actor who was then an agent, while working behind an ice cream counter in Hollywood, she appeared in 25 films under her real name—Terry Ray. As Ellen Drew in *Sing, You Sinners* (1938), her career picked up and she began to play light leading roles, often secretaries and Western gals in more than 40 films. **Films include:** *Geronimo* (1940), *My Favorite Spy* (1942), *Johnny O'Clock* (1947), *Man in the Saddle* (1951), *Outlaw's Son* (1957).

HOWARD DUFF (1913–   )

Born in Bremerton, Washington, Duff frequently appeared with his wife, Ida Lupino, on the radio in the 50's, and later they had their own television series, *Mr. Adams and Eve.* Duff made his film debut in *Brute Force* (1947) and subsequently starred in several ''B'' films as a tough detective or cop. He has appeared recently on television dramatic shows. **Credits include:** *The Naked City* (1948), *Johnny Stool Pigeon* (1949), *Women's Prison* (1955), *While the City Sleeps* (1956), *Boy's Night Out* (1962).

PATTY DUKE (1946–   )

Born in New York City, Duke is a graduate of Quintano's School for Young Professionals. Professional she is indeed. In her late 20's, she is a veteran of stage, television, and the screen. Duke made her Broadway debut at 13 as Helen Keller in *The Miracle Worker* and in 1962, she won an Academy Award for Best Supporting Actress for her film recreation of this role. She starred in the television series, *The Patty Duke Show,* from 1963 to 1964 and has appeared frequently in TV movies and on dramatic shows. Her adult talents (which are of vast scope) have yet to be utilized to their full advantage. One would hope that in the future Duke will be able to break from the sodden termagant roles in which she has recently been cast. **Other credits:** *The Goddess* (debut, 1958), *Happy Anniversary* (1959), *Billie* (1965), *Valley of the Dolls* (1967), *Me, Natalie* (1969).

KEIR DULLEA (1939–   )

The public first noticed Dullea in a big way when he played the psychotic David in *David*

Howard Duff, who apparently is designing a rocket in Spaceways.

Patty Duke rose to prominence as young Helen Keller in The Miracle Worker. *She is shown here with Anne Bancroft, who played her teacher, Annie Sullivan.*

and Lisa (1962). His performance won him the Best Actor award at the San Francisco Film Festival and a nomination for Britain's equivalent of the Academy Award.

Although it made his name, *David and Lisa* wasn't Dullea's first picture. A year earlier, he had made his debut as the baby-faced killer in *The Hoodlum Priest* (1961).

Dullea, a product of New York's Neighborhood Playhouse and the Actors Studio, had been performing for several years off-Broadway, in summer stock and on daytime television before getting his movie break. His first off-Broadway role was in *Season of Choice* with Betsy von Furstenberg. Dullea

Keir Dullea, a "new face" that has been around for more than a decade, was particularly impressive in DeSade. *He is shown here with Senta Berger.*

continues to act on stage. He played the lead as the blind boy in *Butterflies Are Free* on Broadway in 1970. **Films include:** *Bunny Lake Is Missing* (1965), *2001: A Space Odyssey* (1967), *DeSade* (1969).

DOUGLAS DUMBRILLE (1890–1974)

A durable movie villain who portrayed mobsters, corrupt politicians and unsavory lawyers with great suavity, he made his screen debut in *His Woman* (1931). Born in Canada, he came to films with an extensive stage background including a Broadway debut as Banquo in *Macbeth*. By way of a complete reversal, he appeared recently in *The Petticoat Junction* television series. **Some of his films include:** *Crime and Punishment* (1935), *Mr. Deeds Goes to Town* (1936), *The Big Store* (1941), *Julius Caesar* (1953), *The Ten Commandments* (1956).

MARGARET DUMONT (1890–1965)

High-toned, high-browed, high-bosomed, she stood tightly-girdled and imperturbably clutching her lorgnette whilst being the target for assorted insanities wreaked upon her by the Marx Brothers, generally Groucho.

She was born in Brooklyn and began her career as a singer. After appearing on Broadway with George M. Cohan and the mad Marxes she made her screen debut, as did they, in one of the talkies first comedies, *The Cocoanuts* (1929). Although she appeared in scores of films thereafter, often with other comedians such as W.C. Fields and Jack Benny, it was her one-sided love affairs over the years with Groucho that transformed her into a cult. Almost always cast as a rich dowager, she beamed tolerantly upon him, with equal warmth, as the mustached one attempted to separate her from a Rembrandt painting or asked her to wash out a pair of socks for him. She was, in short, the stateliest and most wonderful comic foil ever. **Credits include:** *Animal Crackers* (1930), *Duck Soup* (1933), *A Day at the Races* (1937), *The Big Store* (1941), *Never Give a Sucker an Even Break* (1941), *Diamond Horseshoe* (1945), *Auntie Mame* (1958), *What a Way to Go!* (1964).

FAYE DUNAWAY (1941–   )

Faye Dunaway began her acting career as one of the original members of the Lincoln Center Repertory Company and appeared in a number of off-Broadway productions, such as *Hogan's Goat*. Her stunning performance as Bonnie Parker, the gun-toting companion of Warren Beatty in *Bonnie and Clyde* (1967), won her an Oscar nomination for Best Actress. The following year she turned in another fine performance as a detective hot on the trail of Steve McQueen in *The Thomas Crown Affair* (1968). During the course of the film the pursuer and the pursued meet in one of the most publicized screen kisses in film history. **Other credits:** *The Happening* (1967), *Doc* (1972).

JAMES DUNN (1905–1967)

Whenever he was given an opportunity, in a worthwhile role, he proved that he was a very good actor indeed. Unfortunately, the smiling, cheerful, and eternally optimistic performer was usually relegated to second rate musical comedies and improbable melodramas. Dunn's screen debut was in *Bad Girl* (1931), but it wasn't until he appeared in Shirley Temple's first feature film, *Stand Up and Cheer* (1934) that demand for his services increased markedly. Nearly ten years more passed before he played Johnny Nolan in *A Tree Grows in Brooklyn* (1945). The quality of his acting was then recognized and he received an Oscar for best supporting role of that year. **Credits include:** *The Daring Young Man* (1935), *Mysterious Crossing* (1937), *That Brennan Girl* (1946), *Killer McCoy* (1948), *The Oscar* (1966).

JOSEPHINE DUNN (1906–   )

When Paramount set up an acting school in New York, Josephine Dunn was one of the first to enroll. She was a former Ziegfeld Follies girl who had made several Broadway appearances before deciding to try her luck on the screen. Her first part was in a school graduation picture *Fascinating Youth* (1926). During her Hollywood years in the early 30's, Dunn often was cast in "tough mama" roles, despite her youth and glamor. Her greatest screen success was with Al Jolson in *The*

What the Dark Lady of the Sonnets was to Shakespeare, Margaret Dumont was to the Marx Brothers. Here Groucho passionately declaims the depth of his emotion to an overtly suspicious (but rapidly melting) Miss Dumont.

The scene has a Bonnie and Clyde look, but Faye Dunaway's allies in this take from Oklahoma Crude *(1973) are George C. Scott and John Mills.*

Irene Dunne and Cary Grant combined forces to make The Awful Truth, *one of the funniest comedies of its era. That was the film, remember, when Cary, ostensibly returning from a business trip to Florida, threw his wife, as a homecoming gift, an orange—with California stamped on it. Or was it the other way around?*

Singing Fool (1928). Although she made both silent and sound movies, Dunn never really caught on in Hollywood, therefore, she resumed her stage career. **Films include:** *A Man's Man* (1929), *Big Time* (1929), *Two Kinds of Women* (1932).

MICHAEL DUNN (1935–1973)

Only a shade over three-feet tall, Dunn was becoming a giant of an actor before his untimely death—rumored to be suicide—in a London hotel during the filming of his final film. His portrayal of a courageous dwarf, filled with love of life and optimism in spite of a sea of folly that surrounded him, brought laughter and warm wisdom to the bitter message of *Ship of Fools* (1965). **Highlights:** *Junior Miss* (debut, 1945), *Mother Wore Tights* (1947), *No Way to Treat a Lady* (1968), *Madigan* (1968), *Boom!* (1968).

IRENE DUNNE (1904–   )

Her regal appearance and classic beauty were highly deceptive for she was one of the outstanding comediennes of her time. Born in Louisville, Kentucky, she was graduated from the Chicago College of Music and in short order was singing and acting in touring companies and Broadway shows of the 20's. After playing Magnolia in the road company of *Show Boat* she was signed up by RKO and, through the efforts of Richard Dix, given the co-starring role with him in *Cimarron* (1931), a Western epic that won the Oscar for Best Picture of the Year and brought Dunne an Oscar nomination.

For years thereafter she was known as a four-handkerchief girl, for she was almost always cast in lachrymose parts in films like *Back Street* (1932) and *The Silver Cord* (1933), along with such Kern musicals as *Sweet Adeline* (1935) and *Roberta* (1935) which did permit spots of levity.

Then, mixed in with drama, came the comedies: *Theodora Goes Wild* (1936), and in 1937 one of the best ever filmed, Columbia's *The Awful Truth* with Cary Grant.

She continued to make outstanding films—*Love Affair* (1939) with Charles Boyer is one example—into the early 50's. Thereafter, except for an occasional television appearance, she retired but in 1956 she became an alternate delegate to the U.N. Assembly. She was married to the same husband, Dr. Francis Griffin, for nearly 40 years, until his death in 1965. Almost every actor and director who performed with her felt she was the most charming and unassuming actress with whom they had ever worked. **Credits include:** *Leathernecking* (debut, 1930), *Ann Vickers* (1933), *Magnificent Obsession* (1935), *My Favorite Wife* (1940), *The White Cliffs of Dover* (1944), *Life With Father* (1947), *I Remember Mama* (1948), *It Grows on Trees* (1952).

MILDRED DUNNOCK (1906–)

With an amazing voice capacity for so fragile a person, a small-featured face and expressive eyes (all belying a tremendous inner strength), Dunnock achieved the peak of her career on Broadway as the mother in *Death of a Salesman* (1949), a role she recreated on the screen and television.

She worked for years in stock, little-theatre groups and Broadway flops that closed out of town until she was cast as Miss Ronberry in *The Corn Is Green* (1940), leading to a distinguished stage career and to her film debut in the same role in 1945. **She has appeared memorably in:** *Kiss of Death* (1947), *Viva Zapata!* (1952), *Baby Doll* (1956), *The Nun's Story* (1959), *Sweet Bird of Youth* (1962), *Behold a Pale Horse* (1964), *7 Women* (1966).

JIMMY DURANTE (1893–)

The tired old Laugh-Clown-Laugh theme really applies to one of the best-loved comedians of the century. As a little boy in New York his associates would say: "Look, it's the big-nosed kid!" Commenting on the appendage that made him famous, Jimmy said ". . . Even if they said nothin', I'd shrivel up and think they was sayin' 'What an ugly kid! What a monster!' And then I'd go home and cry."

The Schnozz, laughing through his tears, teamed up with Lou Clayton and Eddie Jackson and made their Broadway debut in Ziegfeld's *Show Girl* (1929). In the same year, with Prohibition still the law of the land, they performed an act that was to make them famous, at a long-forgotten Broadway night-

Mildred Dunnock listens only slightly to Karl Malden in the film version of Tennessee Williams' play Baby Doll. *He played Archie to Carroll Baker's* Baby Doll.

Cantinflas pointedly calls attention to Jimmy Durante's proboscis problem in Pepe *(1960).*

Deanna Durbin the way she looked when 101 Men and A Girl *was produced, one of the pictures that made her the number one box-office attraction.*

Dan Duryea, either drunk or extremely tired, in one of his infrequent roles where he wasn't playing the villain.

club christened *Les Ambassadeurs*. It was here that the trio dismantled pianos and performed the most frenzied and frenetic routine ever to convulse an audience.

Although Durante made nearly 40 films, Hollywood generally managed to miscast him. Almost always he sparkled in nightclub acts, Broadway revues and, for two decades or more, television. It wasn't until the mid-40's that he was given a decent role in *It Happened in Brooklyn* (1947). Thereafter, except for *The Great Rupert* (1950), highlights in his film career are hard to find. He more than made up for a disappointing camera career, however, with numerous on-stage triumphs. **Film credits include:** *Roadhouse Nights* (1930), *Hell Below* (1933), *Joe Palooka* (1934) *You're in the Army Now* (1941), *The Milkman* (1951), *Jumbo* (1962), *It's a Mad, Mad, Mad, Mad World* (1963).

DEANNA DURBIN (1921–   )

She made only 21 pictures in a 12-year film career, but during four of those years she was far and away the most popular female star in Britain and, as a super-wholesome ingenue, mesmerized American audiences to nearly the same extent. In truth, she loathed Hollywood, hated show business generally, and told Eddie Cantor, who had paved the way to success by getting her to sing on his radio show, that the Durbin screen personality "never had any similarity to me, not even coincidentally."

Born in Winnipeg, Canada, her parents moved to Los Angeles where her fine singing voice caused her to be cast in a short with Judy Garland. She was dismissed after a few months, so Hollywood legend has it, because Louis B. Mayer said: "Drop the fat one." The "fat one" he had in mind was Judy!

Joe Pasternak at Universal took her on and her radio fame and her performance helped to make *Three Smart Girls* (1937) an overnight smash success. In her next film, Leopold Stokowski and his entire symphony orchestra (it was a Depression year and musicians have to eat, too) played opposite her, and *One Hundred Men and a Girl* (1937) also hit the jackpot. Then, in 1941, she made perhaps her best picture of all with Charles Laughton, *It Started With Eve*.

Her public remained loyal to her but, unlike Judy Garland (who was equally unhappy but for different reasons), Deanna was given weaker and weaker scripts. She wanted to quit as early as 1942, but it was wartime and she felt she could best serve the cause by entertaining servicemen. Finally, at the age of 27, she did retire for good and all. **Durbin films include:** *Three Smart Girls Grow Up* (1939), *The Amazing Mrs. Holliday* (1943), *Hers to Hold* (1943), *Christmas Holiday* (1944), *Up in Central Park* (1948), *For the Love of Mary* (1948).

DAN DURYEA (1907–1968)

Re-creating his stage role, he made his screen debut as the evil, weak Cousin Leo in *The Little Foxes* (1941). However, it was in his menacing role in *Woman in the Window*

Ann Dvorak is shown here in a film that drew fans to the box office, The Crowd Roars.

(1945), that he established himself as one of the screen's most popular heels.

He made his Broadway debut in *Dead End* (1935) and although he occasionally played other types of roles in nearly 60 films and over 75 television shows, his tight-lipped delivery and sneer typecast him as the arch villain. **Films include:** *None but the Lonely Heart* (1944), *Scarlet Street* (1946), *Another Part of the Forest* (1948), *This Is My Love* (1954), *The Bounty Killer* (1965), *The Flight of the Phoenix* (1966).

ROBERT DUVALL (1931–   )

Duvall has been working steadily on television, the stage and in films for a number of years, appearing on such series as *Route 66* and *The FBI* and in such off-Broadway productions as *A View From the Bridge* (1965). He was not truly recognized as a fine actor, however, until his 1972 portrayal of Tom O'Hagan in *The Godfather*. Duvall did a masterful job of depicting the mild-mannered, head counsel for the mob. It is to be hoped that the recognition he received for this role will lead to greater use of this talented performer. **Credits:** *To Kill a Mockingbird* (1963), *The Chase* (1966), *True Grit* (1969), *Joe Kid* (1973).

ANN DVORAK (1912–   )

Through almost 60 films, she has appeared frequently as sirens in melodramas and dance hall girls in Westerns. The daughter of vaudevillians, convent educated, she made her debut in *The Hollywood Revue* (1929), but it was *Scarface* (1932) that launched her film career.

She spent the years of World War II in England driving ambulances, working in canteens and entertaining in army camps. Resuming her career when she returned to this country, she made her last screen appearance in *The Secret of Convict Lake* (1951). **Some of her films include:** *Three on a Match* (1932), *Stronger Than Desire* (1939), *The Long Night* (1947), *The Walls of Jericho* (1948), *A Life of Her Own* (1950).

The "consignilieri" in The Godfather *in another role. Here Robert Duvall stars as a man battling the syndicate in* The Outfit.

CLINT EASTWOOD (1930–   )

He had already appeared in bit parts on film and had had the lead in the *Rawhide* television series when he went to Italy to make *A Fistful of Dollars* (1967), the first of a series of "spaghetti Westerns" filmed in Italy and Spain. He came back to the United States an international star and one of the biggest box-office draws in recent years.

The former lumberjack and swimming instructor spent his early years in the Depression accompanying his father all over the West Coast. After a hitch in the army, courses at Los Angeles City College, and marriage, he made a screen test for Universal which led to his slow, but sure, film career.

Eastwood continues to play in Westerns and detective films, usually of a bloody and violent nature. In 1971, landing a part originally earmarked for Frank Sinatra, Eastwood appeared in the title role of *Dirty Harry*, one of the most brutal films ever produced; and two years later, he made an equally violent sequel, *Magnum Force*. About the only peaceful role he ever portrayed on film was Lee Marvin's rival in *Paint Your Wagon* (1969). In 1971, Eastwood made his directorial debut with *Play Misty for Me* and in 1973 directed *Breezy*. **Films include:** *Revenge of the Creature* (1955), *Never Say Goodbye* (1956), *For a Few Dollars More* (1967), *The Good, the Bad and the Ugly* (1967), *Hang 'Em High* (1968), *Where Eagles Dare* (1969), *Two Mules for Sister Sara* (1970), *The Warriors* (1970), *Joe Kidd* (1972).

BUDDY EBSEN (1908–   )

Although most people know him as the star of the long-running television series *The Be-*

Deputy Clint Eastwood emphatically tells his story to the court in Hang 'Em High.

verly Hillbillies, he was a reliable second-string comic in many film musicals of the 30's and later emerged as a character actor.

Ebsen started out in show business as a dancer, but has since played many Western roles, including the best friend of Fess Parker's *Davy Crockett* (1955). Directors told him, "When we put you in buckskin you're the perfect Western type." Recently he has turned to detective work on his television series *Barnaby Jones*. **Some of his movies are:** *Banjo on My Knee* (1936), *Breakfast at Tiffany's* (1961), *Mail Order Bride* (1964).

MAUDE EBURNE (1875–1960)

The petite character actress usually played wry or waspish matrons. One of her best-known roles was with Charles Laughton in *Ruggles of Red Gap*. Before films, she appeared on Broadway with stars like Will Rogers. **Her scores of pictures include:** *The Bat Whispers* (1931), *The Guardsman* (1932), *The Suspect* (1944), *The Prince of Peace* (1951).

NELSON EDDY (1901–1967)

Born in Providence, Rhode Island, of a musical family, Eddy began singing soprano parts in his church choir. Still in his teens, he joined the Savoy Opera Company and made his professional operatic debut with the Philadelphia Civic Opera Company. He was discovered by an MGM scout while he was singing in a Los Angeles concert and, as a result, made his film debut in *Broadway to Hollywood* (1933). His real break came when he was co-starred for the first time with Jeanette MacDonald in *Naughty Marietta* (1935). The two became "America's Sweethearts." They made eight films together over a period of seven years.

In 1942, Eddy left Metro and his co-star to freelance. He made some rather forgettable pictures and finally retired from films altogether. In the 60's he toured the nightclub circuit, collapsing and dying from a stroke after a performance in 1967. **Highlights:** *Rose Marie* (1936), *Sweethearts* (1938), *I Married an Angel* (1942), *Phantom of the Opera* (1943).

BARBARA EDEN (1934–   )

Tucson-born Eden has had a limited film career, but the fact that she is curvaceous, blonde and beautiful has enabled her to keep in the public eye. Her films are generally in the comic or adventure genre and are best forgotten. She has had a successful television career, recreating Marilyn Monroe's role in the television series *How to Marry a Millionaire* (1958), and more recently starring in the *I Dream of Jeannie* (1965–69) series. **Credits:** *A Private's Affair* (debut, 1959), *All Hands on Deck* (1961), *Five Weeks in a Balloon* (1962), *The Seven Faces of Dr. Lao* (1964), *Ride the Wild Surf* (1964).

ROBERT EDESON (1868–1930)

Cecil B. De Mille persuaded Edeson to give up a promising stage career in 1914 to go to Hollywood. Edeson was already established as a respected tragedian in the theatre when De Mille convinced him that movies were the wave of the future.

The actor came from a theatrical family and made his professional debut on a dare in 1886. He was working at the time at the old Park Theater in Brooklyn when one of the actors in *Fascination* became ill and couldn't perform. Edeson went on in his place and that was the beginning of a career that spanned more than 40 years. His most famous theatrical role was in Richard Harding Davis' *Soldiers of Fortune*, and he was also a smash hit on Broadway in *Strongheart*.

He had a long and varied career in Hollywood, acting in silent films, including *The Prisoner of Zenda* (1922). Edeson was a dialogue director and character actor at Fox when he died in 1930 of heart disease. **Films include:** *Triumph* (1924), *The Little Wildcat* (1929), *Marianne* (1929), *Danger Lights* (1930), *Swing High* (1930), *The Lash* (1931).

CLIFF EDWARDS (1895–   )

"Ukelele Ike" Edwards made his film debut in *Marianne* in 1929 and spent the next decade making light entertainment films. His place in film history, however, was not secured until his voice was discovered by Walt Disney and immortalized as Jimminy Cricket's in the Disney cartoon feature *Pinocchio* (1939). **Some of his other movies are:** *Saratoga* (1937), *Gone With the Wind* (1939), *She Couldn't Say No* (1941), *The Falcon Strikes Back* (1943).

JAMES EDWARDS (1922–1970)

His role as the sensitive black soldier in *Home of the Brave* (1949) was the pivotal part of his career. One of the early films to deal with racial bigotry, it was hailed as a breakthrough in its day.

Born in Indiana, he had appeared on Broadway, most notably in another controversial vehicle—*Deep are the Roots*—before making his screen debut in *The Set Up* (1949). In recent years, he was seen regularly on television. **Some of his films include:** *The Member of the Wedding* (1952), *The Phoenix City Story* (1955), *Men in War* (1957), *The Sandpiper* (1965).

VINCE EDWARDS (1928–   )

Brooklyn-born Vincent Edward Zoino started his acting career in college shows at

A "Russian" Nelson Eddy whooped it up without Jeanette MacDonald in Balalaika *(1939).*

A wide range of emotions are displayed in this scene from De Mille's King of Kings *(1927)—including those of Robert Edeson (center, with beard) and H. B. Warner in the title role (arm upraised at right).*

the University of Hawaii. Later attending the Academy of Dramatic Arts, Edwards made his Broadway debut in the chorus of *High Button Shoes*. He followed this appearance with other stage performances, road-show productions and television work. It was on television that he became widely known for his role as the hirsute doctor, *Ben Casey* (1961-1966). He made his film debut in *Mr. Universe* (1951), and, following that, made some rather forgettable "B" flicks. **Highlights:** *The Killing* (1956), *City of Fear* (1958), *The Victors* (1963), *The Devil's Brigade* (1968), *The Desperadoes* (1969).

RICHARD EGAN (1921–)

Once believed to be the likely successor to Clark Gable's image and popularity, he made scores of movies but remained one notch below the superstar category.

After making *Underwater* (1955) with Jane Russell, he was offered a two-picture-

Ever-brooding, Vince Edwards stares into the still camera.

a-year contract at Fox. In the years that followed he played cowboys, GIs, skin divers, alcoholics, Spartan kings, and Sandra Dee's father in *A Summer Place* (1959). **Among his other movies are:** *Demetrius and the Gladiators* (1954), *Love Me Tender* (1956), *Pollyanna* (1960), *The Big Cube* (1969).

SAMANTHA EGGAR (1939–)

London-born Eggar made her film debut at the age of 25 in *Dr. Crippen* (1963), and her career took off apace. Inexplicably, however, after her first burst of success, the talented actress seems to be left in the wake of her British sisters—Christie, Miles, George. Her biggest success to date was her deft and moving performance opposite Terence Stamp in *The Collector* (1965). **Credits:** *Young and Willing* (1964), *Walk, Don't Run* (1966), *The Molly Maguires* (1970).

SALLY EILERS (1908–)

Born Dorothea Sally Eilers in New York City, she blossomed from a homely girl in grade school to "the most beautiful girl in Hollywood," according to Florenz Ziegfeld.

While having lunch with her friend, Carole Lombard, on the Mack Sennett lot, she was offered the lead in *The Goodbye Kiss* (1928). Three years later Fox signed her to a long-term contract. Overnight success came with *Bad Girl* (1931). Her more than 20-year career included almost 60 films. **Pictures include:** *Quick Millions* (1931), *State Fair* (1933), *Strike Me Pink* (1936), *Stage to Tucson* (1951).

ANITA EKBERG (1931–)

Complaining that Hollywood producers "figured I was a sex type," the beautiful Swedish-born actress fled to Rome and established her acting talents in such films as *La Dolce Vita* (1961) and *Boccaccio '70* (1962).

Before entering films, she was a model in Stockholm and Miss Sweden in the Miss Universe contest. She made her movie debut as a Chinese girl in *Blood Alley* (1955), and her first important part was as Princess Helene in *War and Peace* (1956). **Films include:** *Back From Eternity* (1956), *Sign of the Gladiator* (1959), *4 for Texas* (1963), *Woman Times Seven* (1967).

Sally Eilers discusses life and love with Richard Arlen from her side of the diner counter in She Made Her Bed *(1934).*

JACK ELAM (1916–)

During the 40's, Elam was one of the highest-salaried auditors in Hollywood, but "I was finally nipped by the acting bug. Casting directors told me I had a face that reflected evil, that I could put it to more rewarding use by closing my books and becoming a villain-actor."

Since then, he has played in over 100 movies and as many television shows, but never as the hero. "When you look like me," he said, "you just can't be a hero." **Some of his films are:** *Vera Cruz* (1954), *The Man From Laramie* (1955), *Gunfight at the OK Corral* (1957), *Once Upon a Time in the West* (1969).

JOHN ELDREDGE (1904–1960)

After becoming interested in drama at the University of California, he went to New York and landed stage parts in *Goodbye Again* and *The Dark Tower*. When the latter was made into a movie, *The Man With Two Faces* (1934), he repeated his Broadway role and won a long contract with Warners.

He generally appeared as someone's weakling brother, or as a bland schemer, and it has been said that his most impressive trait was the restraint he showed in his roles. **Some of his movies are:** *Mr. Dodd Takes the Air* (1937), *Blossoms in the Dust* (1941), *Backlash* (1947), *The First Traveling Saleslady* (1956).

FLORENCE ELDRIDGE (1901–)

Brooklyn-born Eldridge made her Broadway debut at the age of 17 in *Rock-a-Bye Baby* and played exclusively on the stage until her film debut nine years later in *The Studio Murder Case*. Though her list of picture credits is short, she made a lasting impression on filmgoers with her memorable performances.

Primarily a stage actress, she won the New York Drama Critics' Best Actress award for her performance in *Long Day's Journey Into Night* (1956). Married to actor Fredric March since 1927, she and her husband live in semi-retirement in New Milford, Connecticut. **Credits:** *Les Miserables* (1935), *Mary of Scotland* (1936), *Another Part of the Forest* (1948), *Inherit the Wind* (1960).

JAMES ELLISON (1910–)

His early desire was to become a lawyer, but lack of funds caused him to turn to Hollywood. Ellison usually played secondary characters in a long list of Westerns, war and adventure films. He made his debut in *The Play Girl* (1932), and made over 20 pictures in the next ten years. Included in his credit list are such classics as *The Plainsman* (1937) and *Charley's Aunt* (1941). **Highlights:** *Reckless* (1935), *Annapolis Salute* (1937), *Dixie Dugan* (1943).

ISOBEL ELSOM (1893–)

It was once said of her character portrayals that she was a woman who could give the Madwoman of Chaillot lessons in aristocratic wackiness.

Long on the British stage and in silent films, Elsom came to the United States in 1926 to appear on Broadway. She then alternated between stage and screen until she settled in Hollywood after appearing in *Ladies in Retirement* (1941) and remained playing character roles. **Credits include:** *Of Human Bondage* (1946), *The Ghost and Mrs. Muir* (1947), *Escape Me Never* (1947), *Désirée* (1954), *My Fair Lady* (1964).

FAYE EMERSON (1917–)

Thrice-married Emerson was born in Louisiana, lived in Illinois for a time, and grew up in California. She was offered film contracts by Paramount and Warners after her performance in the San Diego Municipal Theatre production of *Here Today* (1941). Choosing Warners, Emerson made her film debut in *Bad Men of Missouri* (1941) and went on to make more than 20 pictures in the next 12 years.

She made her television debut in 1948 and, from that time until her retirement in 1963, was one of the most popular and sought-after personalities on that medium. **Credits:** *The Nurse's Secret* (1941), *Between Two Worlds* (1944), *The Mask of Dimitrios* (1944), *Hotel Berlin* (1945), *Main Street to Broadway* (1953).

This crazy mixed-up costume adorned Anita Ekberg in Way . . . Way Out *(1966).*

Faye Emerson was almost the only woman to appear in Warner Brothers' wartime epic, Air Force *(1943).*

HOPE EMERSON (1898–1960)

She was six feet, two inches tall and weighed more than 190 pounds. Her role as a sadistic prison matron in *Caged* (1950) typified her screen career and led her once to say, "For 20 years I did comedy. When I came to Hollywood I got into a rut killing, choking people and playing jail matrons."

Born in Iowa, she made her Broadway debut as an Amazon in *Lysistrata* (1930), her radio debut with Jimmy Durante as "Toodles Bong-Snook" and her television debut as Mother in the *Peter Gunn* series. **Some of her films include:** *Cry of the City* (1948), *Adam's Rib* (1949), *Copper Canyon* (1950), *The Lady Wants Mink* (1953), *All Mine to Give* (1958).

GILBERT EMERY (1889–1945)

A former reporter, World War I ambulance driver and diplomat, Emery came to Hollywood by way of the stage. He made his sound film debut in 1929 in *Behind That Curtain*. Best known for his character acting, he was also a novelist and a playwright. His more than 25-year screen career included 57 films—adventures, comedies, war and horror films. **Highlights:** *A Farewell to Arms* (1932), *Gallant Lady* (1933), *The Life of Emile Zola* (1937), *Nurse Edith Cavell* (1939), *The Brighton Strangler* (1945).

JOHN EMERY (1905–1964)

Once classified as belonging to the "profile school of acting," Emery was usually cast in films as the suave rake, or the villain with a mustache.

Born in New York City of a sixth-generation theatrical family, he made his Broadway debut in 1923. A leading man for many years before appearing on the screen, he was married to Tallulah Bankhead for four years during which time they appeared together in a disastrous Broadway production of *Antony and Cleopatra* (1937). **Some of his films are:** *Here Comes Mr. Jordan* (1941), *Spellbound* (1945), *The Woman in White* (1948), *Ten North Frederick* (1958), *Youngblood Hawke* (1964).

LEIF ERICKSON (1911–   )

He said he heard himself described as a "blond Adonis" so many times that it made his stomach turn. Someone once said he was too good looking to be believable. Despite his good looks and the fact that he made more than 100 movies, he has remained quite inconspicuous.

He was discovered by a movie talent scout while playing the trombone for the Olsen and Johnson comedy team, and made his film debut in *Wanderer of the Wasteland* (1935). In 1937 he was Greta Garbo's leading man in *Conquest*, but thereafter usually played in mysteries, comedies, adventures and horror films of "B" quality. **Highlights:** *College Holiday* (1936), *Sorry, Wrong Number* (1948), *On the Waterfront* (1954), *Tea and Sympathy* (1956), *Mirage* (1965).

LEON ERROL (1881–1951)

Small, with a bald pate and a skeleton that seemingly could disintegrate like melting gelatin, he was the master of nervous twitches and frantic gestures.

Born in Australia, he made his Broadway debut in 1911 in the Ziegfeld Follies and

Leif Erickson was heralded as a "new screen find" by Paramount in 1935 when the studio released this portrait of his debut in Wanderer of the Wasteland.

continued to appear in many subsequent editions. He began his film career in 1924 in two-reeler comedies and made the transition to sound pictures with great ease, appearing most notably in the *Mexican Spitfire* (1940) and the *Joe Palooka* film series of the 40's. **Highlights include:** *Alice in Wonderland* (1933), *Never Give a Sucker an Even Break* (1941), *Higher and Higher* (1944), *Footlight Varieties* (1951).

STUART ERWIN (1903–1967)

Famous for his sad eyes, droopy expression and amusing voice, comedian Erwin often played the hero's best friend or just an average guy. California-born, he attended the University of California and then played on the Hollywood stage. He made his film debut in *Mother Knows Best* (1928), a movie he also directed. His talkie debut was made in *The Trespasser* (1929) and in the next 25 years he made over 80 pictures. His big break came when he was called to replace Lee Tracy in *Viva Villa!* (1934). That film brought attention to his acting proficiency.

In addition to stage and film, in the 50's Erwin had his own TV show with his wife, June Collyer—*The Trouble With Father* (later *The Stu Erwin Show*). **Credits:** *Sweetie* (1929), *International House* (1932), *Three Men on a Horse* (1935), *Our Town* (1940), *Blondie for Victory* (1942), *Father Is a Bachelor* (1950), *Main Street to Broadway* (1953), *Son of Flubber* (1964).

DALE EVANS (1912–)

Frances Octavia Smith was born—as one might expect—in Texas. The Queen of the Cowgirls was married twice before being hitched to her present husband and long-time riding and roping companion, Roy Rogers. Evans' film career began in 1942 with *Orchestra Wives* and lasted for nine years, during which time she made 41 films, the majority being horse operas.

In addition to her film career, Evans appeared (astride her horse Buttermilk) on television's popular *Roy Rogers Show* in the 50's. **Credits:** *Girl Trouble* (1942), *The Yellow Rose of Texas* (1944), *Song of Arizona* (1946), *Trigger, Jr.* (1950), *Pals of the Golden West* (1951).

Stuart Erwin (right) faces some unknown horror in Make Me a Star *(1932). The diminutive gent with the large camera and his ladyfriend are unnamed.*

Plastered with medals, Dame Edith Evans poses with Giulietta Masina, Katharine Hepburn and Margaret Leighton in The Madwoman of Chaillot.

Madge Evans, sitting in a bistro with Robert Young in Paris Interlude *(1934).*

DAME EDITH EVANS (1888–)

Primarily known as a brilliant stage performer, this British actress has appeared in numerous films which attest to her magnificent talents. Studying acting at night, working as a milliner by day in her teens, Evans turned to professional acting in her 20's and by 1918 was "on tour." She soon became well-known for her portrayals, particularly in the plays of Shakespeare and Chekhov.

In 1948, at the age of 60, Evans launched her film career with *The Queen of Spades*. The following year she made *The Last Days of Dolwyn*, the film in which Richard Burton made his debut. During her 22-year film career, Evans won two Oscar nominations —for *Tom Jones* (1963) and *The Whisperers* (1967). For the latter film she also won the New York Film Critics Circle Award for Best Actress. **Highlights:** *The Importance of Being Earnest* (1952), *Look Back in Anger* (1959), *The Nun's Story* (1959), *The Madwoman of Chaillot* (1969), *David Copperfield* (1970).

MADGE EVANS (1909–)

She made her first picture at the age of five, became a child star of the silent screen at the age of seven and was a has-been by 12 when she reached the gawky age. With the advent of sound, she returned as the beautiful heroine of such films as *Dinner at Eight* (1933). She retired in 1939 after her marriage to Pulitzer playwright Sidney Kingsley. **Some of her films include:** *The Sign of the Cross* (1914), *Classmates* (1924), *What Every Woman Knows* (1934), *David Copperfield* (1935), *Pennies From Heaven* (1936).

MAURICE EVANS (1901–)

The "canny Welshman with a handsome face, soulful brown eyes and a mellifluous baritone voice" has had a long, distinguished acting career with roles running the gamut from Hamlet on Broadway to an ape in *Planet of the Apes* (1968) on the screen.

Tom Ewell, in yet another remake of State Fair *(1962), drew Alice Faye as his co-star, in her one and only "comeback" performance.*

He was a leading man at the Old Vic in London when he was brought to this country in 1935 to play Romeo to Katharine Cornell's Juliet. Occasionally in British films since the early 30's, he made his U. S. debut in *Kind Lady* (1951) and has appeared in many prize-winning TV specials such as *The Taming of the Shrew*. **His films include:** *White Cargo* (1930), *The Story of Gilbert and Sullivan* (1953), *Androcles and the Lion* (1953), *The War Lord* (1965), *Rosemary's Baby* (1968).

CHAD EVERETT (1939–)

A man of many talents, Everett has directed and acted in films, made an album (*All Strung Out*), starred on television, and written a book (*A Toast to Shelby*). Born Raymon Lee Cramton in South Bend, Indiana, Everett graduated from Wayne State University and began as an actor with Warner Brothers, later moving on to MGM. He made his screen debut in *Claudelle Inglish* (1961), and thus far has made few and undistinguished films. His real claim to fame is his starring role in the television series *Medical Center*. **Credits include:** *The Chapman Report* (1962), *The Singing Nun* (1966), *The Impossible Years* (1968).

TOM EWELL (1909–)

Pre-law student Tom Ewell was asked unexpectedly by a traveling stock company to replace a cast member who "was taken suddenly drunk one Sunday morning." He went on stage with only eight hours' notice and stayed with the company two years. Soon after landing in New York, he made his debut on Broadway in *They Shall Not Die* (1934). The film version of *The Seven Year Itch* with Marilyn Monroe (1955) established him as a top comic actor and thereafter he has been appearing regularly on stage as well as in films.

Reputed to be modest, Ewell has been quoted as saying: "I'm no comedian. I'm an actor who manages to do the wrong thing and come off looking funny. That is —sometimes." **Highlights:** *Adam's Rib* (1949), *Finders Keepers* (1951), *The Lieutenant Wore Skirts* (1956), *Tender Is the Night* (1962).

ALDO FABRIZI (1905–)

Fabrizi worked as a mail boy, coachman, jockey, piano tuner and streetcar conductor. However, it was his job as a fruit peddler in his native Rome, where he would tell stories and imitate popular actors, that led to his theatrical career and eventually to his moving performance as the compassionate priest in Rossellini's *Open City* (1945). This performance made him internationally famous.

One of Italy's leading character actors, Fabrizi started his professional career in vaudeville and over the years branched out into directing and writing. **Films include:** *To Live in Peace* (1947), *Flesh Will Surrender* (1950), *Of Life and Love* (1958), *Three Bites of the Apple* (1967).

DOUGLAS FAIRBANKS (1883–1939)

Along with Mary Pickford and Charles Chaplin, he was one of the trio who dominated the film world in the days of silents, a converted stage performer whose flashing grin and astonishing acrobatic feats are still mistily recalled by aging filmgoers in all parts of the world. The story has it that D.W. Griffith watched him vault a hedge in New York's Central Park and urged him to enter motion pictures. In any event, his debut in *The Lamb* (1915) was under Griffith's aegis.

In 1919, with Pickford, Chaplin and Griffith, Fairbanks helped form United Artists and it was this company that released the romantic spectacles which spread his name and fame. In 1920 he married Pickford and it was in Pickfair, a Camelot-type structure of massive proportions, that America's Sweetheart and the bounding, leaping, chandelier-swinging Fairbanks held court. A

coronary attack abruptly ended his career at the age of 57. **More than 30 film classics include:** *The Americano* (1916), *The Mark of Zorro* (1920), *The Three Musketeers* (1921), *Robin Hood* (1922), *The Thief of Baghdad* (1924), *The Black Pirate* (1926), *The Taming of the Shrew* (with Pickford, 1929), *The Private Life of Don Juan* (1934).

DOUGLAS FAIRBANKS, JR. (1909–)

He could be just as swashbuckling and athletic as his famous father but he preferred not to be imitative and, in truth, had little of the passion for a film career that characterized Douglas, Sr. Born and raised in New York City, Fairbanks was offered a movie role when he was only 13, but his first picture was a resounding flop. He had a few smallish roles in silent films of the late 20's; but when he appeared in his first talkie, *A Woman of Affairs* (1929), he became recognized as a skillful performer in his own right. "Garbo Talks!" was, incidentally, the way that film was ballyhooed.

Throughout the 30's he turned in fine performances in films as varied as *Dawn Patrol* (1930), *Outward Bound* (1930), *The Prisoner of Zenda* (1937), *Having a Wonderful Time* (1938) and *Gunga Din* (1939). He served for four years in World War II, emerging as a lieutenant commander in the U. Ś. Navy. He continued to make films from time to time, but by the end of the 40's, except for infrequent appearances, he retired to run his own television film producing unit and to devote himself to other business interests. **Other credits include:** *Little Caesar* (1931), *Catherine the Great* (1934), *The Joy of Living* (1938), *The Young in Heart* (1938), *Sinbad the Sailor* (1947), *State Secret* (1950).

PETER FALK (1927–)

He went straight from a job with the Connecticut Budget Bureau to the stage, television, and movies. His film debut was in *Wind Across the Everglades* (1958). Later he was nominated for an Academy Award for Best Supporting Actor for his role in *Murder, Inc.* (1960).

Equally well known in the theatre and on television, particularly for the *Columbo* TV

Aldo Fabrizi in his famous portrayal of the priest in Open City.

The one, the only Douglas Fairbanks.

Janet Gaynor comforts Charles Farrell in Seventh Heaven.

series, he often appears in "Brooklynesque" parts. **Films include:** *The Balcony* (1963), *The Great Race* (1965), *Luv* (1967), *Pocketful of Miracles* (1969).

FRANCES FARMER (1915–1970)

Her placid and delicate beauty on the screen belied a history of alcoholism and nervous breakdowns that led to her confinement in mental hospitals from 1942 to 1950.

Making her screen debut in *Too Many Parents* (1936), she appeared in a dozen films and in the stage version of *Golden Boy* (1937) before her retirement. In the 50's she was rediscovered working as a hotel receptionist and she returned to the screen in *The Party*

Glenda Farrell looks a little distracted, so Frank McHugh grabs up the champagne glass in this scene from Havana Widows, *a typical film flimsy of the 30's.*

Crashers (1958). She continued to make appearances in television. **Films include:** *Come and Get It* (1936), *The Toast of New York* (1937), *South of Pago-Pago* (1940), *Son of Fury* (1942).

WILLIAM FARNUM (1876–1953)

He became an overnight star in his first movie, *The Spoilers*, famous for its fight scene, in 1914. A handsome matinee idol of silent films, he was one of the highest paid actors of the era, but he lost his fortune in the stock market crash of 1929.

By the 30's his popularity had waned, and he was forced to play bit parts. When *The Spoilers* was remade in 1942, he played only a minor role. **Among his many movies are:** *Les Miserables* (1917), *If I Were King* (1920), *Jack and the Beanstalk* (1952).

CHARLES FARRELL (1901–   )

He decided to become a film actor when his father opened a movie theatre on Cape Cod in Massachusetts. However, his first brush with show business was as valet to Little Billy, a vaudeville midget.

He made his way to Hollywood and got his first job there as an extra in Pola Negri's *The Cheat* (1923). Paramount gave him important roles in *Old Ironsides* (1926) and in *The Rough Riders* (1927) before he was offered the starring role by Fox Studio in *Seventh Heaven* (1927) with Janet Gaynor, a movie which established him as a star. Gaynor and Farrell became one of Hollywood's most successful romantic teams. In early television days he appeared for many years in the popular *My Little Margie* series. **Films include:** *Street Angel* (1928), *Sunny Side Up* (1929), *Delicious* (1931), *The First Year* (1932), *Night and the City* (1950), *The Sheriff of Fractured Jaw* (1958).

GLENDA FARRELL (1904–1971)

Best remembered as the dizzy, fun-loving, gum-chewing blonde who wisecracked her way through scores of movies, she made her debut in *Little Caesar* (1931).

Born in Oklahoma, she acquired a stock and Broadway background as a young actress before moving on to Hollywood. In more than 120 films she managed to soften even her most hard-boiled characterizations with wry wit. In the 50's she made a comeback in character parts and appeared often on television, winning an Emmy in 1963 for Best Supporting Actress. One of her last appearances was as the grandmother in the Broadway production of *Forty Carats* (1969). **A few of her films include:** *I Am a Fugitive From a Chain Gang* (1932), *Gold Diggers of 1935* (1935), *Johnny Eager* (1942), *Susan Slept Here* (1954), *Middle of the Night* (1959), *The Disorderly Orderly* (1964).

MIA FARROW (1946–)

Daughter of director/producer/writer John Farrow and actress Maureen O'Sullivan, the petite, auburn-haired Farrow had show business in her blood. She made her professional debut in New York City in the play *The Importance of Being Earnest* (1964). She gained national recognition for her role of Allyson on the television series *Peyton Place* and world-wide attention when she married Frank Sinatra, divorced him, bore Andre Previn twins and later married him (in 1970).

Farrow was a "personality" in her teens, but was not considered a serious actress until her fine performance in *Rosemary's Baby* (1968). For this role she won the Best Actress Award of the French Academy. **Credits:** *Guns at Batasi* (1964), *A Dandy in Aspic* (1968), *Secret Ceremony* (1968), *John and Mary* (1969), *The Great Gatsby* (1974).

GEORGE FAWCETT (1861–1939)

A plump character actor, Fawcett was at his best and funniest playing rather simpleminded millionaires. His career spanned a 14-year period and nearly 100 pictures, ending in 1931. **Films include:** *Hearts of the World* (1918), *Sentimental Tommy* (1921), *West of the Water Tower* (1923), *The Merry Widow* (1925), *The Private Life of Helen of Troy* (1927), *The Four Feathers* (1929), *A Woman of Experience* (1931).

ALICE FAYE (1912–)

Blonde and blue-eyed, she had been on stage since the age of seven as a dancer, band singer, and actress when she recreated her Broadway role in the filmed version of *George White's Scandals* (1934). Three

years later in such films as *Alexander's Ragtime Band* (1938) she was the reigning queen of Hollywood musicals.

Once married to Tony Martin, she married Phil Harris in 1941 and her leave of absence to have a child gave Betty Grable her break. Faye retired after playing a dramatic role in *Fallen Angel* (1946) and appeared in only one film since, *State Fair* (1962). She also made occasional television appearances. In 1974 she returned to the theatre in a revival of the musical *Good News*. **More than 30 films include:** *In Old Chicago* (1938), *Rose of Washington Square* (1939), *Tin Pan Alley* (1940), *Week-End in Havana* (1941), *The Gang's All Here* (1943).

FRANK FAYLEN (1907–)

A former pantomimist, clown, song-and-dance man, and acrobat, he has made over 250 movies since his film debut in 1936. Playing everything from the town doctor to the town drunk, he used to boast he could play

Mia Farrow in a scene with Robert Redford from The Great Gatsby *(1974).*

Alice Faye listens intently as Helen Westley peeps through the keyhole in Lillian Russell *(1940). Miss Faye played the title role.*

Frank Faylen ogles Betty Hutton as she ogles his bejeweled clam shell in
The Perils of Pauline *(1947).*

*Louise Fazenda is here attended by two gentlemen, one of whom is Dick
Powell and the other unknown, in* Colleen *(1936).*

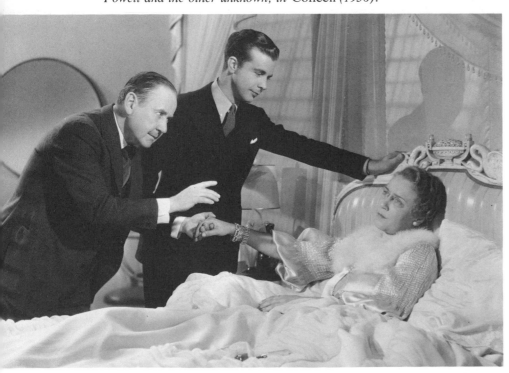

nine out of ten parts ever written. His most
famous part was the four-minute-and-20-
second role of a male nurse in *Lost Weekend*
(1945). **Films include:** *The Grapes of Wrath*
(1940), *Road to Rio* (1948), *Riot in Cell
Block 11* (1954), *Funny Girl* (1968).

LOUISE FAZENDA (1895–1962)

Born in Indiana, she began as an ingénue in
stock but her hoydenish manner and sense of
humor made her unsuitable for serious drama.
After making her screen debut in 1913 in a
one-reel comedy she went on to become a
Mack Sennett Bathing Beauty along with
Bebe Daniels and other stars-to-be—but she
was always the funny one. Until 1921 almost
all her films were with Sennett, mainly two-
reelers. She was known as the queen of
custard-pie comedy. A voice that matched her
personality carried her from silents to the
sound era, making her twice as loony and
amusing in such films as *No, No, Nanette*
(1930) and *Alice in Wonderland* (1933).

Married to producer Hal B. Wallis for 35
years, she made her last film appearance in
The Old Maid (1939). **Films include:**
Abraham Lincoln (1924), *Cuban Love Song*
(1931), *Colleen* (1936).

FRITZ FELD (1900–   )

Whether he was playing an indignant
maître d', a psychiatrist, or a foreign spy, his
trademark was always the "pop," a sound
which he made by bringing his palm with a
quick movement to his rounded mouth.

The German character actor made 30 silent
movies, in which he usually played the
heavy, before going on to his more famous
roles as a psychiatrist in *Bringing Up Baby*
(1938), Anatole of Paris in *The Secret Life of
Walter Mitty* (1947), and a waiter in *The
Patsy* (1964). **Some of his more recent films
are:** *Caprice* (1967), *Barefoot in the Park*
(1967), *Hello, Dolly!* (1969).

LESLIE FENTON (1903–   )

The Liverpool-born actor dropped out of
Ohio State University to go to Hollywood. He
first attracted attention in a juvenile part in
The Goose Hangs High (1925).

His first important portrayal was a young
soldier who goes berserk in *What Price*

Glory? (1926). Among his many roles, he was seen as a gangster, a stool pigeon, a dope addict and a moral weakling. He also directed a number of pictures, including *Lulu Belle* (1948). **Films include:** *Lady Killer* (1934), *The Golden Fleecing* (1940), *There's a Future in It* (1943), *The Redhead and the Cowboy* (1951).

ELSIE FERGUSON (1883–1961)

At one time called "the most beautiful girl on the American and British stage," she achieved recognition in the theatre before going to Hollywood.

Her first important movie role was in *Barbary Sheep* (1917). From 1918 to 1927 she was one of America's most popular leading ladies in silent melodramas about the upper classes. When she came out of retirement in 1933 to play in *Outrageous Fortune*, she was paid as much as $9,000 a week. In the 40's and 50's she appeared occasionally in character parts. **Films include:** *His Parisian Wife* (1919), *A Society Exile* (1919), *Lady Rose's Daughter* (1920).

FRANK FERGUSON (1899–   )

Familiar to television audiences as the storekeeper in the original *Peyton Place*, Ferguson has had an extensive career as a character actor—usually in comic bit parts. His motion picture and television credits number more than 600. **Films include:** *This Gun for Hire* (1942), *The Miracle of the Bells* (1948), *Abbott and Costello Meet Frankenstein* (1949), *Elopement* (1951), *Johnny Guitar* (1954), *Raymie* (1960).

FERNANDEL (1903–1971)

This rubber-faced French comedian learned his art while working as a longshoreman on the waterfront in Marseille, where he encountered all kinds of characters, many of whom were later reproduced in his more than 150 movies. He made his stage debut at five, vaudeville in his teens and his stopover on the Marseille waterfront led him to the Paris movie studios, where he made his debut opposite another French comedian, Raimu. In 1939, Frenchmen voted Fernandel, whom they had nicknamed "Horseface," their most popular screen star. His one serious film,

Murders, was a failure. **Films include:** *The Red Inn* (1954), *The Sheep Has Five Legs* (1955), *The Virtuous Bigamist* (1959), *My Wife's Husband* (1965).

JOSÉ FERRER (1912–   )

He was enormously successful on the stage—in *Charley's Aunt*, *Cyrano de Bergerac*, *Othello* and other plays—before coming to movies.

His film debut was in *Joan of Arc* in 1948, where he played the weak and treacherous Dauphin, with Ingrid Bergman in the title role. The film version of *Cyrano* won him an Academy Award in 1950. Other famous roles include Toulouse-Lautrec in *Moulin Rouge* (1953).

An accomplished writer and painter, Ferrer said that in order to work himself up for an emotional scene once, he had to imagine that he had killed every member of his family. **Films include:** *Anything Can Happen* (1952), *The Caine Mutiny* (1954), *I Accuse!* (1958), *Lawrence of Arabia* (1962), *Ship of Fools* (1965), *Enter Laughing* (1967).

José Ferrer gave a splendid performance as Cyrano de Bergerac *in 1950.*

One of Fernandel's most popular roles was as the priest in The Little World of Don Camillo *(1953).*

Edwige Feuillere lives up to the title of her 1956 film, Adorable Creatures, *in this scene with Daniel Gelin.*

Frayed, sun-bleached overalls were almost the inevitable costume for Stepin Fetchit, who was cast in scores of stereotyped "darky" roles that Hollywood was criticized for.

MEL FERRER (1917–)

Once called "the nerve in perpetual motion," this handsome leading man came to Hollywood after stints as a writer of children's books, a dancer on Broadway, and a radio writer, producer and director.

His first important role was as a black physician who passes for a white in *Lost Boundaries* (1949). He also played a toreador in *The Brave Bulls* (1951) and a morose puppeteer in *Lili* (1953). **Notable films:** *Scaramouche* (1952), *War and Peace* (1956), *The Sun Also Rises* (1957), *El Greco* (1965).

STEPIN FETCHIT (1902–)

Born Lincoln Theodore Perry, he was the first black actor to make a big hit in Hollywood, mainly by playing the popular stereotype of his day. He became widely known in the 20's and 30's for his slow, molasses-like movements and rolling eyes in such films as *In Old Kentucky* (1927). His voice was equally infectious and his success in talkies was assured. He was a comic in a number of Will Rogers' vehicles. **Films include:** *Stand Up and Cheer* (1934), *On the Avenue* (1937), *Bend of the River* (1952), *The Sun Shines Bright* (1954).

EDWIGE FEUILLÈRE (1907–)

Feuillère's low, haunting voice, enigmatic smile and authoritative presence combine to suggest great beauty. Since her stage debut in 1930 and her film debut a year later, she has been one of the most prominent French actresses of stage and screen.

A member of the famed Comédie Française, she is a veteran of more than 40 films, a highlight of which was her brilliant performance as Nastasia in Dostoyevsky's *The Idiot* (1948).

The accomplished actress alternated between stage and screen throughout the 60's and in 1969 made her television debut. **French films include:** *Topaze* (1935), *Sans Lendemain* (1940), *L'Aigle a Deux Têtes* (1948), *Le Blé en Herbe* (1953), *Aimez-vous les Femmes?* (1964), *Clair de Terre* (1970).

BETTY FIELD (1918–1973)

Born in Boston, she got her first break when she was signed by Gilbert Miller for the London company of *She Loves Me*. Returning to the United States, she appeared in a succession of George Abbott hits, including *Room Service* and *What a Life*, and made her screen debut when the latter play was filmed in Hollywood in 1939.

Her superb performance as Mae in *Of Mice and Men* (1940) established her as a powerful dramatic actress and she appeared through the years both in films and on Broadway. Later, she played character roles, often portraying sympathetic mothers. **Highlights:** *Kings Row* (1942), *Flesh and Fantasy* (1943), *The Southerner* (1945), *The Great Gatsby* (1949), *Bus Stop* (1956), *Birdman of Alcatraz* (1962).

VIRGINIA FIELD (1917–)

She was first "heard" on the screen dubbing American films into French and German. London-born of a theatrical family, she was sent to Paris at the age of nine and at 13 was playing on stage in French.

In 1936, after appearing on Broadway in *Victoria Regina*, she went to Hollywood and made her debut in *Lloyds of London* (1936). Never really typecast, she has played a wide gamut of roles both in films and on stage. She was married for a time to Paul Douglas. **Films**

include: *The Primrose Path* (1935), *Waterloo Bridge* (1940), *The Perfect Marriage* (1947), *The Explosive Generation* (1962).

GRACIE FIELDS (1898–)

She started her career at the age of seven, singing in a moving picture theatre, and in her teens on the streets for pennies. By the 30's, she was acknowledged to be Britain's greatest comedienne. Fields had already appeared on the vaudeville stage in New York when she made her screen debut in *Sally in Our Alley* (1931). She alternated between stage and screen appearances until the war years when she almost made a separate career out of entertaining British and American troops. Beginning with *Holy Matrimony* (1943), she worked for a time in Hollywood. Since the mid-50's she has been semi-retired—running a very successful hotel on Capri. In 1960 she wrote her autobiography, *Sing As We Go*. **Films include:** *Queen of Hearts* (1936), *Shipyard Sally* (1940), *Molly and Me* (1945), *Paris Underground* (1945).

STANLEY FIELDS (1880–1941)

Before he became a gravel-voiced screen heavy, legend has it, he used to sing in the choir of Trinity Church and sell newspapers on Times Square. He was also a fairly good prize fighter, they say, until Bennie Leonard broke his nose. The resulting disfigurement appealed to casting directors looking for ferocious villains—and so a screen thug was born. His first screen portrayal of a gangster was in *Little Caesar* (1930). **Films include:** *Island of Lost Souls* (1933), *Kid Millions* (1934), *Way Out West* (1937), *New Moon* (1940), *The Adventures of Marco Polo* (1965).

W.C. FIELDS (1879–1946)

Anyone who ever watched the immortal Fields sight a pool-table shot with a cue warped at a 20-degree angle will appreciate Kenneth Tynan's evaluation: "He played straight-man to a malevolent universe which had singled him out for destruction." Nearly everything—dogs, children, mothers-in-law, inanimate objects of all sizes and shapes —frustrated and persecuted him. His raspy,

misanthropic responses turned a dozen or more of his films into the more delicious high spots in motion picture history. Today his battered top hat, his bulbous nose, his dislike for children and his fondness for the bottle have become part of a cult, properly so, for his talents were unique.

Born in Philadelphia of a British father, he ran away from a miserable home life at the age of 11 and in short order became a juggler in an amusement park. He perfected his routines in vaudeville, made a huge hit in the Ziegfeld Follies and in 1923 floored Broadway audiences in the musical *Poppy*. Under the direction of D. W. Griffith, he made his first film appearance in *Janice Meredith* (1924). His first sound film was *The Gold Specialist* (1930), a two-reeler, which he followed with a number of other shorts, among them *The Dentist* (1932), which some film buffs contend is the funniest picture ever made.

Betty Field, as she appeared with Fredric March in Tomorrow the World *(1944).*

"Cutting my way through a wall of solid flesh . . ." was the way W. C. Fields described his relationship with the American Indian—until one of them appeared on the scene, at which point the hatchet was promptly buried. Here he is as a startled sheriff in My Little Chickadee.

Peter Finch as Boldwood in Thomas Hardy's Far From the Madding Crowd *(1967), a story of passions and problems in a small British farming community.*

Albert Finney, still in his thirties, has been turning in first-rate performances in films over a period of nearly 15 years.

One of his most memorable roles was that of Mr. Micawber in *David Copperfield* (1935). Fields usually ad-libbed his way through films (most of which he wrote himself). He commented that the only lines he ever followed precisely were those of Charles Dickens. **Highlights:** *Million Dollar Legs* (1932), *Tillie and Gus* (1933), *Man on the Flying Trapeze* (1935), *You Can't Cheat an Honest Man* (1939), *My Little Chickadee* (with Mae West, 1940), *Never Give a Sucker an Even Break* (1941).

PETER FINCH (1916–)

Peter Finch was born in London and raised in France. He lived for a time in India and later worked in Australia at such diverse jobs as waiter, journalist and comedian before he began his acting career. From vaudeville he moved to bit parts in the theatre and small roles in grade "B" Australian-made films. His first large role was as the delinquent son in *Mr. Chedworth Steps Out* (1938). While touring Australia, Laurence Olivier noticed Finch and subsequently helped him get to London, where he dazzled theatre audiences under Olivier's management.

His first film lead was in *Elephant Walk* (1954) in which he was cast at the suggestion of Vivien Leigh. In 1959 Fred Zinnemann chose him to star in *The Nun's Story* with Audrey Hepburn and this film earned him the reputation of a literate and poised actor. **Other films include:** *Girl With Green Eyes* (1964), *The Pumpkin Eater* (1964), *Judith* (1965), *Far From the Madding Crowd* (1967), *Sunday, Bloody Sunday* (1971), *England Made Me* (1973), *Lost Horizon* (1973).

ALBERT FINNEY (1936–)

British-born Albert Finney chose an acting career at the suggestion of his headmaster, who thought that he had done well in the school's plays. He enrolled in a two-year course at the Royal Academy of Dramatic Arts and after graduation began to work with the Birmingham Repertory Theatre. His portrayal of Henry V caught the attention of Charles Laughton and resulted in his first appearance in the West End. He once told an interviewer: "I don't give a damn whether I

am a star or not . . . I just want to have a go—to act and to mean what I say, joking or serious." He married actress Anouk Aimée in 1970. **Films include:** *The Entertainer* (1960), *Saturday Night and Sunday Morning* (1961), *Tom Jones* (1963), *The Victors* (1963), *Night Must Fall* (1964), *Two for the Road* (1967), *Charlie Bubbles* (1968), *Scrooge* (1970), *Gumshoe* (1971).

BARRY FITZGERALD (1888–1961)

The diminutive Irish actor was touring America with the Abbey Theatre when director John Ford convinced him to reproduce his stage role in *The Plough and the Stars* (1937) for the movies. He stayed to play irascible or whimsical Irish roles in countless films.

Sean O'Casey once called him "the greatest comic actor in the world." The man who didn't become a professional actor until the age of 42 won an Academy Award for Best Supporting Actor for *Going My Way* in 1944. **Over 30 films include:** *Bringing Up Baby* (1938), *How Green Was My Valley* (1941), *Two Years Before the Mast* (1946), *The Catered Affair* (1956).

GERALDINE FITZGERALD (1914–)

"Most of my film career was lousy with dignity," she once said, but her moods on screen have been varied—long-suffering as the wife of a psychopathic murderer in *Uncle Harry* (1945), courageous but shifty as a secret agent in *O.S.S.* (1946), sweet and drunk in *So Evil My Love* (1948), and cold and cunning in *Ten North Frederick* (1958).

Her Hollywood career started when talent scouts noticed her in Orson Welles' Mercury Theatre production of *Heartbreak House* and signed her with Warners. She was cast with Bette Davis in *Dark Victory* (1939) and became an overnight success.

In 1971 she received laudatory reviews for her New York stage role in O'Neill's *Long Day's Journey Into Night*. She has also made several television appearances. **Films include:** *Wuthering Heights* (debut, 1939), *Watch on the Rhine* (1943), *Wilson* (1944), *The Pawnbroker* (1965), *Rachel, Rachel* (1968).

PAUL FIX (1902–)

His wry, lugubrious features are well known to movie goers, because he has played hundreds of cameos since his film debut in 1922 in a Western with Tom Mix.

Born in Dobbs Ferry, New York, he also worked as a screen writer and appeared in numerous John Wayne films. **Some of his more recent movies are:** *To Kill a Mockingbird* (1963), *Shenandoah* (1965), *El Dorado* (1967), *Day of the Evil Gun* (1968).

JAMES FLAVIN (1906–)

His first feature film was *King Kong* (1933), and after that he was usually the tough-talking detective, Marine sergeant, policeman, sailor or politician in his over 400 films.

While making a cowboy picture, he said, it was only his cavalry training at West Point that saved him from getting a broken leg or a skull fracture when his horseback-jump from a cliff to a river didn't turn out too well. **Films include:** *Cloak and Dagger* (1946), *Mister Roberts* (1955), *The Last Hurrah* (1958), *Cheyenne Autumn* (1964), *In Cold Blood* (1967).

RHONDA FLEMING (1923–)

Los Angeles-born Fleming was sent by her mother to singing and dancing lessons in hope that she would end up in show business. That hope was realized when Fleming was spotted by a talent agent as she was walking in Beverly Hills. The red-headed 17-year-old got a contract with Twentieth Century–Fox as a result of that walk.

Her first important role was as a nymphomaniac in *Spellbound* (1945). Despite the singing and dancing lessons, she had only two musical roles—in *A Connecticut Yankee in King Arthur's Court* (1949) and in *The Great Lover* (1949). She has also made numerous appearances on television. **Films include:** *The Spiral Staircase* (1946), *Inferno* (1953), *Gunfight at the OK Corral* (1957), *Home Before Dark* (1959), *The Big Circus* (1959), *The Revolt of the Slaves* (1961).

JAY C. FLIPPEN (c.1898–1971)

His show-business career began when he ran away from home at the age of 15 to join a

Barry Fitzgerald looks less crotchety than usual as he is fussed over by Veronica Lake (yes, indeed) and Joan Caulfield in The Sainted Sisters *(1948).*

Rhonda Fleming interrogates Don Beddoe in a scene from Bullwhip *(1958), a Western of B-plus proportions.*

Jay C. Flippen (right) gives a "so what?" look to Connie Francis as she is introduced to him and to Barbara Nichols by Jim Hutton in Looking For Love *(1964).*

minstrel show. He passed through vaudeville and radio on his way to films.

After his role as the warden in *Brute Force* in 1947, he appeared regularly in films, sometimes as the heavy and sometimes as a comic. **Among his many films:** *Flying Leathernecks* (1951), *The Wild One* (1953), *Cat Ballou* (1965), *Firecreek* (1968).

ERROL FLYNN (1909–1959)

Like John Barrymore, he lived his private life publicly and to the hilt. Like Barrymore, he was an old man at 40 with (friends who loved him say) a will to die. As an actor, critics delighted to pan almost every one of more than 50 films which starred him but nowadays there is a fast-growing school which maintains he was the most charming and entertaining swashbuckler (Fairbanks, Sr., included) who ever climbed a mizzenmast.

He was born in Tasmania, is alleged to have pursued professions as varied as diamond smuggling and tropical bird hunting, and made his film debut in the Australian picture *In the Wake of the Bounty* (1933). He went to London to act with a repertory company, appeared in one dreadful film but was offered a contract which took him to Hollywood and a few minor supporting roles. When Robert Donat was unable to play the title role in *Captain Blood* (1935) Warners took a chance on Flynn and, aided by exquisite-looking Olivia de Havilland, he became a star. The two of them teamed up again in *The Charge of the Light Brigade* (1936) and the financial results made the Warners very happy indeed.

The third, and best, of the Flynn–de Havilland films was the gorgeous and exciting *The Adventures of Robin Hood* (1938), which made Flynn one of the 10 most popular male actors. Some of his other films in this period (also with Olivia) were *Dodge City* (1939) and the madly inaccurate (historically) portrait of Custer, *They Died With Their Boots On* (1941).

His later years were almost a photocopy of Barrymore: lawsuits (he had been acquitted of

Errol Flynn (right) and David Niven in the 1938 remake of Howard Hawks' epic of World War I fliers, Dawn Patrol.

statutory rape as early as 1940); publicized divorces; heavy drinking; a gaudy affair with a teenager. Ironically, one of his last decent roles was playing a drunken John Barrymore in *Too Much Too Soon* (1958). He died of a heart attack late in 1959. **Other films include:** *The Prince and the Pauper* (1937), *The Private Lives of Elizabeth and Essex* (1939), *Virginia City* (1940), *Gentleman Jim* (1942), *Edge of Darkness* (1943), *Never Say Goodbye* (1946), *The Sun Also Rises* (1957), *The Roots of Heaven* (1958).

NINA FOCH (1924–)

The cool, comely blonde cost MGM a great deal of money by catching chicken pox during the filming of *An American in Paris* (1951). As she put it, ''They plastered my face with make-up an inch thick and the spots still showed. I was a mess.''

Born in Holland, she studied to be a concert pianist, but after seeing her first Broadway play, she decided to become an actress. Trying to get work on the New York stage, she was spotted by a Hollywood talent scout and made her film debut in *The Return of the Vampire* (1944). Seven years later, after 20 films in which she played mainly sophisticated roles, she returned to the stage in *King Lear*. Since, she has appeared on both coasts and has been seen regularly on television in dramatic roles. **Films include:** *A Song to Remember* (1945), *The Guilt of Janet Ames* (1947), *Johnny Allegro* (1949), *Executive Suite* (1954), *The Ten Commandments* (1956), *Spartacus* (1960).

HENRY FONDA (1905–)

One of the few actors who makes every role he plays (even in television commercials) completely believable, he has been a top-ranking star through nearly all of the years that elapsed since he, along with Marlon Brando's mother, began acting with the Omaha Community Playhouse in the mid-20's. He was born in Grand Island, Nebraska, and the flat Midwest twang that never left him was first heard on Broadway stages in the early 30's in dramas like *Forsaking All Others* (1933). Walter Wanger signed him up and his first starring role in films was with Janet Gaynor in *The Farmer Takes a Wife* (1935).

Only Nina Foch seems happy with the situation as Jean Simmons offers a cold collation to Laurence Olivier and Peter Ustinov in Spartacus *(1964).*

Henry Fonda gave a memorable performance in Zanuck's production of Grapes *of* Wrath. *He is shown here with Ma and Pa Joad (Jane Darwell and Russell Simpson) in one of the more moving sequences of John Steinbeck's classic.*

170

Another early Fonda film was Jezebel, *with Bette Davis as the wicked lady in question.*

Out of his scores of pictures Fonda was proud of only a few: *Young Mr. Lincoln* (1939), *The Grapes of Wrath* (1940), *Lady Eve* (1941), *The Ox-Bow Incident* (1943), *My Darling Clementine* (1946). In addition, he made two other outstanding films: *Mister Roberts* (1955), starring in the screen version of the play he had appeared in for nearly 1,700 performances on Broadway, and *12 Angry Men* (1957) which he spotted as a television play. The latter was a critical success and a financial failure although nowadays it is making up for lost time by television showings. It was a perfect role for Fonda, who, cast as a thoughtful, even-tempered, fair-minded architect, convinces 11 other members of a jury that the man they have voted to execute for murder is innocent. One by one, confronted with Fonda's logic, they vote for acquittal—the last holdout being Lee

J. Cobb, who also turned in one of his best performances.

Over the years Fonda has alternated film making with starring appearances in such Broadway stage hits as *The Caine Mutiny Court Martial* and has done considerable work in television, including *The Deputy* series in the 50's. **Other films include:** *Jezebel* (1938), *Jesse James* (1939), *The Male Animal* (1942), *War and Peace* (1956), *The Longest Day* (1962), *Fail Safe* (1964), *The Battle of the Bulge* (1965), *Yours, Mine and Ours* (1968), *The Cheyenne Social Club* (1970), *Ash Wednesday* (1973).

JANE FONDA (1937–   )

The famous actor's famous daughter won an Academy Award for *Klute* (1971), and many thought she should have won one for her stunning performance in *They Shoot Horses, Don't They?* in 1969.

Joshua Logan gave her her first role in *Tall Story* (1960) when she was 22. She also scored on the stage in *There Was a Little Girl* (1960). While married to French director Roger Vadim, she starred in the sexy *Barbarella* (1968) before leaving her husband and that image behind. Her outspokenness for liberal causes has often made her front page news. **Films include:** *The Chapman Report* (1962), *Cat Ballou* (1965), *Hurry Sundown* (1967), *Barefoot in the Park* (1967), *Steelyard Blues* (1973).

PETER FONDA (1939–   )

Growing up in a Hollywood home, the son of actor Henry Fonda once said, "I wish I could have lived in a more stable home, played in a sandbox—things like that."

After graduating from the University of Omaha, he was a Broadway actor before making his film debut in *Tammy and the Doctor* in 1963. He also played in *The Wild Angels* (1966) and *The Trip* (1967) before skyrocketing to success with *Easy Rider* (1969). As he describes it, the movie was about an American conception of freedom rather than the codes of hippies, motorcyclists or the alienated young. **Films include:** *The Victors* (1963), *Lilith* (1964), *Man Without Mercy* (1969).

Jane Fonda, perhaps the cutest crusader for causes on record, here glares at Donald Sutherland in Klute, *a performance that won her an Academy Award.*

JOAN FONTAINE (1917–)

Born Joan de Beauvoir de Havilland in Tokyo a year after sister Olivia, she changed her name to Fontaine following her mother's divorce and remarriage. In her teens she began playing smallish roles under the name Joan Burfield (why, we don't know) and made her film debut, with no positive results at all, in *No More Ladies* (1935). As Joan Fontaine she went back on stage, was signed by RKO and appeared in a dozen films with results that can most kindly be described as negative, even though her work in films like *The Women* (1939) was first rate.

The Hollywood story has it that she was planning to abandon her movie career, when, sitting next to David Selznick at a dinner party, she urged him to cast Margaret Sullavan in his forthcoming Hitchcock-directed *Rebecca* (1940). "Why don't you test for it?" said Selznick, or words to that effect. She did and overnight became one of Hollywood's top stars. The following year, as Cary Grant's edgy wife in another Hitchcock thriller, *Suspicion*, she not only won the Oscar for Best Actress but the New York Critics' Award as well.

Over the years she had her share of fights with the Hollywood powers-that-were. Most of her objections were justified, for she was constantly being loaned to outside studios to play trashy roles in trashy screen plays. She received Oscar nominations for *Rebecca* and *The Constant Nymph* (1943) and played her parts superbly whenever given half a chance. She has made television appearances, appeared on Broadway in *Tea and Sympathy* (1954) and nowadays makes her home in New York. **Other films include:** *This Above All* (1942), *Jane Eyre* (1944), *Frenchman's Creek* (1944), *The Emperor Waltz* (1948), *Flight to Tangier* (1953), *Island in the Sun* (1957), *Tender Is the Night* (1962), *The Devil's Own* (1967).

RICHARD FORAN (1910–)

New Jersey-born Dick Foran studied geology and worked for a while as a railroad yard guard before a producer spotted him in the audience of a Hollywood nightclub in the early 30's. He signed with Warners and played singing cowboys and then straight and

Peter, the third Fonda, reached stardom overnight with his role in Easy Rider.

Joan Fontaine and Laurence Olivier made Rebecca *nearly 35 years ago. The screen adaptation of Daphne Du Maurier's novel remains a landmark among cinematic thrillers.*

Glenn Ford and Rita Hayworth in Gilda *(1946), a better than average suspense yarn with a South American setting.*

Paul Ford, as funny in films as he was on television, rallies his phalanx of war veterans to do battle against Reds in The Russians Are Coming, The Russians Are Coming!

comic roles. He often portrayed the good guy who doesn't get the girl. **Films include:** *Shipmates Forever* (1935), *Horror Island* (1941), *Guest Wife* (1945), *Taggart* (1964).

MARY FORBES (1880–1964)

Born in New York, she was a model before beginning a long and successful stage career in 1910. Forbes was almost 50 when she went to Hollywood; but after her debut in *Sunny Side Up* (1929) she stayed on to play mainly haughty society ladies and dowagers in scores of films. **Films include:** *A Farewell to Arms* (1932), *Les Miserables* (1935), *The Awful Truth* (1937), *The Adventures of Sherlock Holmes* (1939), *Two Tickets to London* (1942), *The Picture of Dorian Gray* (1945), *The Ten Commandments* (1956).

RALPH FORBES (1902–1951)

A British leading man who began his career on the stage, he said his film parts progressed from "a smoothie who gets the girl to the buffoon who doesn't."

Even though his mother, Mary Forbes, was one of England's most celebrated stars, his parents wanted him to make the Navy his career. However, he began acting in amateur theatricals and went on to make over 50 movies. His American debut was in the silent film *Beau Geste* (1926). **Some of his pictures are:** *The Green Goddess* (1930), *Bachelor Father* (1931), *The Barretts of Wimpole Street* (1934), *Mary of Scotland* (1936), *The Private Lives of Elizabeth and Essex* (1939), *Frenchman's Creek* (1944).

GLENN FORD (1916–   )

He came with his parents from Quebec to Hollywood at the age of seven. "It was different in those days," he recalls. "Why, I can remember Aimee Semple McPherson (the evangelist) walking into the ocean and Charlie Chaplin making films on Venice Pier." Stage work, mostly in touring companies, preceded his film debut in *Heaven With a Barbed Wire Fence* (1939).

A versatile actor, he was starred in over 70 films which include comedies, dramas and outdoor adventures. He has also starred on the television series *Cade's County*. From 1943 to 1959 he was married to dancer-actress Eleanor Powell. **Some of his films are:** *Undercover Man* (1949), *Follow the Sun* (1951), *The Blackboard Jungle* (1955), *The Teahouse of the August Moon* (1956), *The Gazebo* (1960), *The Courtship of Eddie's Father* (1963), *Day of the Evil Gun* (1968).

PAUL FORD (1902–   )

He was 37 years old and the father of five when he could no longer resist the desire to act. Beginning in stock, he went on to radio and then to Broadway, getting his major break in *The Teahouse of the August Moon* as Colonel Purdy—a part he re-created in the 1956 screen version.

His portrayals of pompous men and bombastic bumblers have been seen since in many plays and films. He became best known, however, as the harassed Colonel Hall in the *Sergeant Bilko* television series. **Some of his credits include:** *The Matchmaker* (1958), *Advise and Consent* (1962), *The Music Man* (1962), *Never Too Late* (1965), *The Russians Are Coming, the Russians Are Coming* (1966), *The Comedians* (1967).

WALLACE FORD (1897–1966)

Born Samuel Jones, he was raised in a London orphanage and foster homes before he ran away to join a vaudeville troupe at the age of 11. He later teamed up with a hobo named Wallace Ford, and when the chum was killed beneath a railroad car, he took over the name and made it famous.

Ford first gained his fame on the stage, and then made over 200 movies. His impact was first felt in *Possessed* (1931), with Joan Crawford. **Some of his many other films include:** *Freaks* (1932), *The Mummy's Hand* (1940), *The Green Years* (1946), *A Patch of Blue* (1965).

JOHN FORSYTHE (1918–   )

Though he is probably best known as a television actor, notably as a comedy straightman in his role as the bewildered and beleaguered *Bachelor Father* in the long-running series, Forsythe has played a number of varied roles in pictures ranging from light comedy to war films to dramas like *Madame*

Wallace Ford, adjusting his bow tie in She Couldn't Take It *(1935), is watched approvingly by a superslick George Raft.*

X (1966) in which he gave a sensitive performance as the politico/husband. **Films include:** *Destination Tokyo* (1944), *The Glass Web* (1953), *Escape From Fort Bravo* (1954), *The Trouble With Harry* (1955), *In Cold Blood* (1967).

NORMAN FOSTER (1900–   )

The movie roles for this Indiana-born actor varied from the naive innocent to the wise-cracking reporter. He was, in fact, a reporter before coming to New York in search of a better newspaper job and ending up on Broadway. His film debut was in an early talkie, *Gentlemen of the Press* (1929).

He played opposite his wife, Claudette Colbert, on both stage and screen, before they were divorced. He then married Sally Blane, Loretta Young's sister.

After he directed and played in *I Cover Chinatown* in 1936, he received a contract as a director and, in addition to "B" movies, directed Orson Welles' *Journey Into Fear* (1943) and *Rachel and the Stranger* (1948),

Preston Foster, who once upon a time managed to look like half a dozen other leading men, whispers sweet nothings into Joan Fontaine's ear in You Can't Beat Love *(1937).*

starring Loretta Young. **Among his films are:** *Young Man of Manhattan* (1930), *State Fair* (1933), *Tell It to the Judge* (1949), *Davy Crockett* (1956), *The Nine Lives of Elfego Baca* (1959), *The Merry Wives of Windsor* (1966).

PRESTON FOSTER (1902–1970)

He portrayed both dashing heroes and rugged villains for over 30 years in over 100 films. Born in New Jersey, the former shipping clerk, bus driver, and professional wrestler started as an opera singer before turning to acting. His appearance in *Two Seconds* (1931) led him to success in Hollywood, where he re-created his role in the screen version in 1932. However, he had appeared in an earlier film, *Follow the Leader*, in 1930.

One of the early Hollywood actors to become a TV star, playing in the *Waterfront* series (1954), he subsequently made over 100 TV films. **Films include:** *The Informer* (1935), *Geronimo* (1940), *Guadalcanal Diary* (1943), *The Big Night* (1952), *Destination 60,000* (1957), *You've Got to Be Smart* (1968).

SUSANNA FOSTER (1924–   )

Born Susan DeLis Flanders Larson in Chicago, the blonde opera singer of films in the 40's devised her professional name by combining Stephen Foster and his song "Oh Susannah."

Singing since the age of three, she was heard in her teens by Mary McCormick, who recommended her to a movie studio. Groomed in the studio school for two years, she made her debut at 15 in *The Great Victor Herbert* (1939). But she is best known for the remake of *Phantom of the Opera* (1943) opposite Claude Rains. She retired from the screen in the mid-40's. **Films include:** *There's Magic in Music* (1941), *Top Man* (1943), *This Is the Life* (1944), *Frisco Sal* (1945), *That Night With You* (1945).

DOUGLAS FOWLEY (1911–   )

He was living in a tent in back of the Fox studios in Hollywood when he was discovered singing in a beer garden for two dollars a week and meals.

Since his 1934 debut in *The Gift of Gab*, he has played in hundreds of pictures. In the 1962 production of *Barabbas* he played eight different roles, including a hunchback, a gladiator, and a beggar. His most famous role was as the Hollywood director in *Singin' in the Rain* (1952). **Films include:** *Alexander's Ragtime Band* (1938), *The Hucksters* (1947), *The High and the Mighty* (1954), *The Good Guys and the Bad Guys* (1969).

EDWARD FOX (1937–   )

A handsome, energetic, precise actor and leading man, Fox won the British Academy Award as Best Supporting Actor for his performance as Lord Trimingham in *The Go-Between* (1971). Prior to his acting career, Fox was a successful professional dancer, appearing with Magris Chaney. **Films include:** *Morgan* (1966), *Oh! What a Lovely War* (1969), *The Day of the Jackal* (1973).

Preston Foster slaps the cuffs on jewel-thief Brian Donlevy as Miriam Hopkins watches in this scene from Heliotrope Harry.

JAMES FOX (1939–   )

Born in London, England, into a theatrical family, James Fox was signed for a small role when he visited a movie set with his father. In 1966 Michael Short described him as "the young leading man with polish, a type not seen much since Leslie Howard's and Ronald Colman's day."

In 1973 it was reported that Fox, having "discovered religion," had given up acting and had become an active member of an international religious organization. **Films include:** *The Magnet* (1950), *The Servant* (1963), *Those Magnificent Men in Their Flying Machines* (1965), *King Rat* (1965), *The Chase* (1966), *Thoroughly Modern Millie* (1967), *Duffy* (1968), *Isadora* (1968), *Arabella* (1969).

VICTOR FRANCEN (1888–   )

Suave, distinguished looking, he was a familiar continental figure in Hollywood spy dramas during the 40's, after making his local debut in *Hold Back the Dawn* (1941).

Born in Belgium, he began acting at 15 in small suburban theatres until he was discovered in Lyon by Lucien Guitry and toured with his company throughout South America. Returning to Paris, he began to establish himself as a leading actor in such plays as *Cyrano de Bergerac*. Two of the plays he wrote at that time were produced by Sarah Bernhardt. Before coming to Hollywood he made 25 French films, beginning in the 20's. **Films include:** *Après l'Amour* (1931), *La Fin du Jour* (1939), *Passage to Marseilles* (1944), *Hell and High Water* (1954), *Fanny* (1961), *Top-Crack* (1966).

ANTHONY FRANCIOSA (1928–   )

New York-born Franciosa was once a doorman at the Roxy Theatre. When he was 18 years old he went to the YMCA for free mambo lessons, but ended up reading for a play. He won a scholarship to the Dramatic Workshop and made his way to Broadway. His role in *A Hatful of Rain* led to his film debut in 1957 in *A Face in the Crowd*, as a ruthless young man. He is equally at home on stage, in the movies, and on TV, where he has appeared frequently. **Films include:** *Wild Is*

Anthony Franciosa and Eva Marie Saint in A Hatful of Rain *(1957), the movie version of the role he had played on Broadway.*

James Fox worriedly faces up to the fact that the extortion racket has perils all its own. The picture was Performance *(1970) and the chap leaning on the chairback is Mick Jagger.*

the Wind (1957), *The Long Hot Summer* (1958), *The Pleasure Seekers* (1964), *The Sweet Ride* (1968), *Across 110th Street* (1972).

ANNE FRANCIS (1930–   )

This actress-director, the former heroine of the television series *Honey West*, began her career at the age of five as a magazine cover model. At seven she was working in radio soap operas and when she was 11 she played on Broadway with Gertrude Lawrence in *Lady in the Dark*. She made her film debut in a Mickey Rooney movie, *Summer Holiday* (1948), at 17. Cast as the delinquent in *So Young, So Bad* (1950), she rendered a performance which led to a Hollywood contract.

After directing a "Movie of the Week" episode for television, Francis explained, "Ida Lupino proved that a woman could be a competent director, breaking the ice for us." **Highlights:** *A Lion Is in the Streets* (1953), *The Blackboard Jungle* (1955), *Forbidden Planet* (1956), *Funny Girl* (1968), *Pancho Villa* (1972), *The Sting* (1973).

KAY FRANCIS (1903–1968)

She was a star in more than 60 pictures, most of them terrible, but ranked high in popularity for more than a decade. Probable reasons were (a) her beauty; (b) her ultra-chic mode of dressing which set a pattern for women's clothing on two continents; (c) a semi-lisp—"Kay Fwancis is gwacious . . . "; (d) finally, if given a chance, as in *British Agent* (1934) with Leslie Howard, she could be a very good actress indeed.

She began her career on Broadway and, as a sultry siren playing with Walter Huston in *Gentlemen of the Press* (1929), was offered a picture contract. Her debut, as Kay instead of Katherine Francis, was that of a scheming vamp who was totally overwhelmed by the Marx Brothers in their first crack at screen madness in *The Cocoanuts* (1929).

Stardom came to her gradually after a long series of dramatic roles in which she drove men mad with her wiles or played forgiving wives. Finally, Hollywood discovered that she could play comedy and in her last picture for Paramount, *Strangers in Love* (1932), she

Kay Francis' sculptured hairdo in I Found Stella Parish *(1935) left the critics cold but hairdressers in a complete tizzy.*

and Fredric March made a fine combination.

Her pictures kept coming at a rate of three or four a year, and with them one of the highest salaries in the business. Unfortunately most of them were based on dreadful screenplays and in the early 40's she left her then studio and continued to make films for others, interrupting her schedule to work for the USO and men in the fighting services. Finally, after some appearances in stock she closed her acting career around 1950. When she died of cancer in 1968 most of her fortune of nearly $2,000,000 was left for training guide dogs for the blind. **Credits include:** *The Virtuous Sin* (1930), *Twenty-Four Hours* (1931), *One Way Passage* (1932), *The White Angel* (1936), *Stolen Holiday* (1937), *Little Men* (1940), *Charley's Aunt* (1941), *Divorce* (1945).

WILLIAM FRAWLEY (1887–1966)

Although he is best remembered for his ten-year stint as the exasperated neighbor with the gravelly voice on the *I Love Lucy* television series, he made over 100 films. Before his screen debut in *Surrender* (1931), Frawley had a long career as a song-and-dance man in vaudeville and on Broadway. He was seen through his extensive film career mainly in comic roles as cigar-chewing gangsters, drunks, and bumbling policemen. **Films include:** *Moonlight and Pretzels* (1933), *Bolero* (1934), *Roxie Hart* (1942), *Miracle on 34th Street* (1947), *Monsieur Verdoux* (1947), *Rancho Notorious* (1952), *Safe at Home* (1962).

PAULINE FREDERICK (1885–1938)

One of the early stars of the silent movies, almost all of her successful pictures appeared before the advent of sound. However, she scored heavily in one of the first "all-talkies," *On Trial* (1928). Like so many of the silent film favorites, she often turned out four or more pictures in a single year. Her last appearance was in *Thank You, Mr. Moto*, one of the "B"-grade efforts of 1938. **Films include:** *Bella Donna* (debut, 1915), *Resurrection* (1918), *Madame X* (1920), *Let Not Man Put Asunder* (1924), *This Modern Age* (1931), *Ramona* (1936).

MONA FREEMAN (1926–)

She called herself "the female Andy Hardy," and it seemed she couldn't stop playing the part of a teenager, even after she was a wife and a mother.

Born in Baltimore, Maryland, she was working as a model in high school when Howard Hughes signed her to a contract and then sold her contract to Paramount. Her young-looking face wasn't always an asset. She was taken out of *Double Indemnity* in 1944 because she photographed too young. **Films include:** *Junior Miss* (1945), *Black Beauty* (1946), *Jumping Jacks* (1952), *Battle Cry* (1955), *The World Was His Jury* (1958).

PIERRE FRESNAY (1897–1973)

Born in Paris, he acted with the Comédie Française and the French National Theatre, playing over 80 roles, before his important role in *Grand Illusion* (1938). Following the picture's success, he was swamped with offers to play parts similar to the disdainful Captain Boeldieu, but instead he accepted roles as a convict, student, doctor, lawyer, architect, sailor, journalist, saint, and police inspector.

For his part in *La Valse de Paris* (1949), the biography of Offenbach, he learned to sing, conduct and play eight bars of a waltz on the cello. Married to the outstanding French actress Yvonne Printemps, he directed her in *Le Duel* (1939). **Among his films are:** *Marius* (1933), *The Man Who Knew Too Much* (1935), *Fanny* (1948), *Monsieur Vincent* (1948), *The Ostrich Has Two Eggs* (1960).

GERT FROBE (1912–)

The German character actor played General von Choltitz in *Is Paris Burning?* (1966), the officer who refused Hitler's order to burn Paris.

The turning point in his career came with *Goldfinger* (1964), a picture in which he won the role after being spotted as a child-murderer in *It Happened in Broad Daylight* (1960). Most of his film roles have been those of villainous men. **Films include:** *He Who Must Die* (1958), *The Longest Day* (1962), *Those Magnificent Men in Their Flying Machines* (1965), *Chitty Chitty Bang Bang* (1968).

Long before he became Lucille Ball's TV neighbor, William Frawley was a top Hollywood supporting actor. He is shown here with Lee Tracy in the 1934 cops and crooks film, The Lemon Drop Kid.

Pierre Fresnay and Jean Gabin in René Clair's 1938 masterpiece, Grand Illusion, *which had to do with life in a German prisoner-of-war camp circa 1917.*

MARTIN GABEL (1912–   )

A versatile performer, Philadelphia-born Gabel has appeared on stage, screen and television. He began as a stage actor, making his professional debut on Broadway in *Man Bites Dog* (1933). His other stage appearances include *Three Men on a Horse, Dead End,* and *Baker Street.*

His film career began in 1951 when he made his debut in *Fourteen Hours.* Since that time Gabel has appeared in mysteries and comedies of less than classic quality.

In recent years, he made frequent appearances with his lovely wife, Arlene Francis, on television's *What's My Line?* **Credits:** *M*

Jean Gabin sees nothing to smile about in this scene from Stormy Waters *(1946). Madeleine Renaud does.*

(1951), *The Thief* (1952), *Marnie* (1964), *Lord Love a Duck* (1966), *Divorce American Style* (1967), *There Was a Crooked Man* (1969).

JEAN GABIN (1904–   )

One of the most popular actors of the French cinema, Gabin created a character type which remained consistent throughout his long film career. His portrayals of world-weary, fatalistic men in the lower echelons of life have a real vitality and truthfulness about them.

The son of music-hall entertainers, Gabin worked as a manual laborer before entering show business in the chorus of the Folies Bergère. He made his film debut in *Chacun sa Chance* (1930), and in the early 30's played in many movies examining the low-life of Paris. Gabin was often cast as a petty crook, but also appeared as a basically honest outcast from society. His films during the late 30's, especially those directed by Jean Renoir, brought him world-wide attention. He continued to develop his image as a rugged, independent victim-hero, sometimes forced by circumstances to commit murder, often the victim of murder himself.

In 1940 he came to America to star in *Moontide* (1942). This and another American film were not successful, and Gabin left Hollywood to join the Free French forces fighting the Nazis.

His parts in post-war films were similar to his earlier roles, but he was allowed, in some, to mellow a bit. **His credits include:** *Pépé le Moko* (1937), *La Grande Illusion* (1937), *Le Plaisir* (1951), *French Cancan* (1954), *Un Singe en Hiver* (1962), *Le Chat* (1971).

CLARK GABLE (1901–1960)

The "King" of filmdom and its most popular male actor for two decades was singularly modest in his public pronouncements. "I can't act worth a damn," he said. "When I die they'll put on my tombstone 'He was lucky—and he knew it.'" He was wrong, for today, 14 years after his death, none of the new crop of super-hardboiled leading men has come close to replacing him. Like Bogart, he was unique.

William Clark Gable was born in Cadiz, Ohio. Eager to become an actor, he left school at 16, played in stock companies and married a former actress named Josephine Dillon. Dillon was 17 years older than Gable, and taught him to act, helped him get jobs as an extra in films like Clara Bow's *Plastic Age* (1926) and land Broadway parts in plays like *Machinal*. Although friends like Lionel Barrymore tried hard to help him, he made several bad screen tests, and it wasn't until he played a heavy in *The Painted Desert* (1931) that his services were eagerly sought. He made 12 films in 1931 and by the time the last one, *Hell Divers*, was released, fans were lining up at box offices to see him perform.

Metro, whose two big stars—Gilbert and Novarro—were at the end of the road, was delighted with this new type of movie hero, a real he-man to male audiences, and a magnetic, tough but also gentle romantic hero to women. After *Red Dust* (1932) with Harlow and Mary Astor, he became one of the most popular male stars. Then, to punish him for refusing to play a gigolo in a Joan Crawford movie, Metro farmed him out to Columbia. Claudette Colbert was also being similarly punished. Gloomily they followed Frank Capra's directions, and a film called *It Happened One Night* (1934) emerged. It made movie history, was Best Picture of the Year, brought Oscars to both of them plus the British Picturegoer Best Actor Medal for Gable. The film's bare-chested Gable also wrecked the men's undershirt business for years to come.

Night was just the beginning of a series of successes. As Fletcher Christian in *Mutiny on the Bounty* (1935) he appeared unmustached for the last time, and two of the films that followed—*Wife vs. Secretary* (1936), with Jean Harlow and Myrna Loy, and *San Francisco* (1936) with Jeanette MacDonald—were smash hits and paved the way for his tie-up with Spencer Tracy in *Test Pilot* (1938), for his sparkling work with Norma Shearer in *Idiot's Delight* (1939), and then for his, perhaps, most famous role of Rhett Butler in one of the most successful pictures ever made, *Gone With the Wind* (1939).

Around this time Gable had married, for the third time, the beautiful and bright Carole

Gable and Crawford in Chained *(1934). Because Gable was bored with stereotyped and gigolo roles, Metro "punished" him by farming him out to Columbia to make a picture called* It Happened One Night.

Lombard. It appeared to be a perfect match, but Lombard was killed in an air crash returning from a War Bond selling tour. Gable left the screen for three years' service in the Army Air Corps.

In the late 40's films like *Command Decision* (1948) were highly successful but after that his box office receipts faded and when Gable's contract ($520,000 a year) expired in 1954, it was not renewed. He made a number of other films but he was aging noticeably when he accepted the lead role in *The Misfits* (1961), a screen play Arthur Miller had written for his wife, Marilyn Monroe. It was a doomed enterprise: Gable, Monroe and Montgomery Clift, the three top stars, died within a few years after it was completed, Gable just two months after the shooting had stopped. Gable never saw his only child, John Clark, who was born to Gable's fifth wife,

And here are Colbert and Gable (also 1934) in the famous hitchhiking sequence from the comedy that proved a landmark in cinematic history.

The lushly stunning Eva Gabor, with James Franciscus in Young-blood Hawke *(1964).*

The great Garbo in one of her best films, Queen Christina.

Kay Spreckels. **Other Gable films:** *Strange Interlude* (1932), *Night Flight* (1933), *Forsaking All Others* (1934), *Saratoga* (1937), *Boom Town* (1940), *The Hucksters* (1947), *Mogambo* (1953), *Run Silent, Run Deep* (1958), *It Started in Naples* (1960).

EVA GABOR (1924–   )

Born in Budapest, Hungary, into a family of seemingly ageless beauties and educated mostly by governesses, she always knew she wanted to be an actress. At 15 she enrolled in acting classes but her parents forced her to withdraw.

At 17 she rebelled and went to Hollywood. An agent "discovered" her there in a dentist's office and got her a $75-a-week contract and her film debut in *Forced Landing* (1941).

The sister of Zsa Zsa Gabor, Eva achieved her greatest public success as Eddie Albert's citified wife in the *Green Acres* television series. **Her films include:** *Royal Scandal* (1945), *Don't Go Near the Water* (1957), *The Truth About Women* (1958).

ZSA ZSA GABOR (1923–   )

Noted more for her beauty and personality than for her screen roles, this Hungarian-born actress appears frequently on television talk shows on which her décolletage, carefully maintained accent, and stories of her many husbands entertain millions of viewers.

Gabor was asked in 1965 whether or not she intended to begin playing character roles. "I may be a character," she retorted, "but I do not play character parts. No! I am a glamorous celebrity who never stops talking."

Gabor began her film career in 1952 with *Lovely to Look At* and made several romantic comedies thereafter. **Highlights:** *Moulin Rouge* (1953), *Lili* (1953), *Pepe* (1960), *The Boys' Night Out* (1962), *Arrivederci, Baby!* (1966).

RICHARD GALLAGHER (1896–1955)

Gallagher first became interested in show business when he was a law student. He began to write stories and vaudeville sketches as a study break. Abandoning law, he spent five years as a singer and dancer in vaudeville before starting a film career.

He made his film debut in *New York* (1926). The next year he went to Hollywood, appearing in many early talkies. **Among his films:** *The Racket* (1928), *It Pays to Advertise* (1931), *Polo Joe* (1937), *Zis Boom Bah* (1942), *The Duke of Chicago* (1950).

RITA GAM (1929–   )

A very competent actress, Gam has not often been given screen vehicles equal to her talents. She made her film debut in *The Thief* (1952) and made some rather undistinguished films thereafter. In 1962, however, she appeared in Sartre's *No Exit* and for this performance won the Berlin Best Actress Silver Bear Award.

The one-time wife of director Sidney Lumet, Gam made her stage debut in *A Flag Is Born* (1948) and later appeared in the hit *There's a Girl in My Soup* (1967). **Film Credits:** *Night People* (1954), *King of Kings* (1961), *Klute* (1971), *Such Good Friends* (1971).

GRETA GARBO (1905–   )

The lady who virtually all critics agree was one of the screen's greatest stars began her career lathering men's faces in a Stockholm barber shop. She ended it somewhat abruptly in 1941 and for the past 23 years, as she put it, "I suppose I'm just drifting."

Innumerable writers have ravished dictionaries in many languages attempting to find phrases to describe the secret of Garbo's genius. Words and terms like charisma, inner fire, enigmatic mystique, elusive beauty, etc., etc. have been tossed about as loosely as confetti at a society wedding. Miraculously, she made but 27 films (three of them in Sweden) and not one ranks in quality with screenplays like *The Little Foxes* or, for that matter, *It Happened One Night*.

Born in Stockholm of what used to be called "peasant stock," she always yearned to be an actress. After appearing as a mannequin and in two commercial films for a department store where she worked, she got a small part in *Peter the Tramp* (1922) and then enrolled in the Royal Academy of Dramatic Arts. Mauritz Stiller, Sweden's top director and the man who was to play a key part in her life, changed her name from Gustafsson to Mona Gabor and then to Greta Garbo and gave the plump 17-year-old a part in *The Saga of Gösta Berling* (1924). Thinning down a bit, she made another movie for Stiller the following year. Louis B. Mayer appeared on the scene and signed both Garbo and Stiller to come to Hollywood. Mayer's parting words to Stiller (whom apparently he wanted more than Garbo) were, "Tell her that in America men don't like fat women."

In typical Hollywood fashion, Metro elected to have Monta Bell rather than Stiller direct Garbo's first American film, *The Torrent* (1926). She stole the picture from under Ricardo Cortez' nose. Then, when Stiller couldn't get along with Antonio Moreno, star of Garbo's second film, *The Temptress* (1926), he left Metro, made a few films for Paramount and returned to Sweden, where he died, a broken man, in 1928.

Garbo, still mourning over Stiller's departure, made *Flesh and the Devil* (1927) with John Gilbert, and the Garbo/Gilbert team became filmdom's top romantic stars. The duo starred again in *Anna Karenina*, which the studio retitled *Love* (1927). Originally the same brilliant title-changers had christened it *Heat* but had second thoughts when they considered how GRETA GARBO IN HEAT would look on movie marquees.

"Garbo Talks!" was the ad slogan for *Anna Christie* (1930). Like Chaplin she had avoided talkies at first but as Anna and "dat old devil sea" she was magnificent. More hits followed, each a bigger success than its predecessor. For *Queen Christina* (1933), one of the best, she rejected Olivier and insisted on John Gilbert, possibly in a last-ditch effort to save his waning career. *Anna Karenina*, this time with the Tolstoy title happily intact, came in 1935 and *Ninotchka* (1939), her first comedy (Garbo Laughs!), was a triumphant and genuinely amusing portrayal of a robot-like Russian Communist who gradually succumbs to the siren calls of sex and Paris. *Two-Faced Woman* (1941) was her last film.

Astonishingly, she never won an Oscar al-though nominated four times—for *Anna Christie, Romance, Camille* and *Ninotchka*. Finally, the Academy awarded her a special Oscar for her "unforgettable screen performances." That was in 1954, 13 years after her last film, and the lady who said the famous line, "I want to be alone" to John Barrymore in *Grand Hotel* (1932) didn't show up to receive the award. Nancy Kelly accepted it for her.

Garbo has lived in New York for many years and from time to time is spotted, sans makeup and unglamorously garbed, by keen-eyed movie buffs. She never married although the publicized list of her "intend-eds" is most impressive—John Gilbert, Gaylord Hauser, Leopold Stokowski, Cecil Beaton, Aristotle Onassis, George Schlee, et cetera. While books have been written about her by Beaton and others, she is reputed to have turned down offers running into seven figures for her memoirs. **Other Garbo films:**

Rita Gam added considerable sex appeal to a doorway in The Thief— *a film without dialogue.*

The sixth movie remake of Camille *(Bernhardt did it first in 1912) starred Garbo and Robert Taylor. Here she is, looking extremely beautiful. The dowager is Laura Hope Crews and the young man at right is Rex O' Malley.*

Reginald Gardiner, one of the smoothest of British comedians, plays dog-sitter in a Gracie Fields film, Molly and Me *(1945).*

Ava Gardner, one of Hollywood's great beauties and, during much of her career, an underrated star.

A Woman of Affairs (1929), *Inspiration* (1931), *Susan Lenox—Her Fall and Rise* (1931), *Romance* (1932), *Mata Hari* (1932), *As You Desire Me* (1932), *The Painted Veil* (1934), *Camille* (1937).

REGINALD GARDINER (1903–   )

After graduating with honors from the Royal Academy of Dramatic Arts in London, he toured the provinces for two years before settling into the West End in plays, musicals, and revues. During that time he introduced his monologues (about trains, wallpaper, ships and lighthouses) which were to become famous later.

Beatrice Lillie brought him to New York where he did revues. Later he went to Hollywood under contract to MGM, and played supporting roles in films like *Born to Dance* (1936), and Judy Garland's first starring film, *Everybody Sing* (1938). His 33-year career included more than 50 films. **Credits include:** *The Great Dictator* (1940), *The Man Who Came to Dinner* (1942), *Halls of Montezuma* (1951), *Mr. Hobbs Takes a Vacation* (1962).

AVA GARDNER (1922–   )

"I never had any ambitions to be anything but dead in those days," she said of her early life as one of six children of an impoverished tenant farmer in Grabtown, North Carolina. Maybe the name of the town inspired her, for she fought her way up to become one of the screen's leading ladies. For more than 30 years she has acquitted herself admirably in more than 50 films, a large proportion of which were inferior examples of the screenplay writers' art.

After high school and secretarial courses she arrived in New York. Photographs of the green-eyed beauty taken by her brother-in-law were seen by the MGM people, who sent her to the Coast on a munificent $50-a-week contract. She was then only 18 and it took two years more before she got her first bit part in a Norma Shearer film, *We Were Dancing* (1942). Around that time the first of her marriages, to top-ranked star Mickey Rooney, came and went. "Our lives were run by a lot of other people," she said. "We didn't have a chance."

It wasn't until she played the nightclub singer in *The Hucksters* (1947) that she attained star billing. Coincident with unsuccessful marriages to bandleader Artie Shaw (his fifth) and to Frank Sinatra, she was good in *Show Boat* (1951), most impressive in *The Snows of Kilimanjaro* (1952) and excellent with Grace Kelly and Clark Gable in *Mogambo* (1952). Later, in another Hemingway story, she made an extremely effective Lady Brett Ashley in *The Sun Also Rises* (1957).

An independent, gutsy lady, she has continued to appear in films even though reduced to an "also starring" category. **Films include:** *Joe Smith, American* (1942), *The Killers* (1946), *One Touch of Venus* (1948), *The Barefoot Contessa* (1954), *On the Beach* (1959), *Seven Days in May* (1964), *The Night of the Iguana* (1964), *Mayerling* (1968), *The Life and Times of Judge Roy Bean* (1972).

JOHN GARFIELD (1913–1952)

A fine actor, he was an early version of what James Dean became later (a sullen exile from society) but in Garfield's case it was through no fault of his own.

Garfield was a product of the New York slums who won a scholarship to the Ouspenskaya Drama School and later joined The Group Theatre. Clifford Odets, a close friend, wangled a part for him in *Golden Boy*, his play about a poor boy who couldn't decide whether to fight or to play a violin, and this led Garfield straight to Hollywood and a role in *Four Daughters* (1938).

The pictures in which he played weren't very good material, and in a great many of them he was a convict who, almost always, had been turned from the straight and narrow by our modern society. As the Jewish soldier in *Gentleman's Agreement* (1947) he was excellent as, indeed, he was in *The Sea Wolf* (1941) and *Force of Evil* (1948).

During the McCarthy era he was asked to supply names of his friends in Hollywood who he believed to have Communist sympathies. He refused and, although no accusations were leveled against him, he found himself blacklisted and jobless. He was scheduled to play the lead in a revival of

Golden Boy on Broadway when he died suddenly—from a heart attack or suicide the real cause of death has never been determined. **Credits include:** *They Made Me a Criminal* (1939), *Saturday's Children* (1940), *Tortilla Flat* (1942), *Pride of the Marines* (1945), *Body and Soul* (1947), *The Breaking Point* (1950).

EDWARD GARGAN (1902–1964)

The brother of William Gargan, Edward began his career as a musical comedy actor on Broadway and went to Hollywood in 1930. His roles were mostly those of a comedy cop or prizefighter's manager. **His films include:** *Wake Up and Live* (1937), *Thanks for the Memory* (1938), *Spring Parade* (1940), *The Bullfighters* (1945), *Cuban Fireball* (1952).

WILLIAM GARGAN (1905–   )

A fiery Irishman from Brooklyn, Gargan began his acting career on the New York stage. He made his film debut in *The Misleading Lady* (1932).

In his early films, Gargan was cast in "good guy" roles; later he became a character actor, often cast as a detective. His tough-guy tone of voice was perfect for his role as detective Martin Kane in a popular television series.

In 1960, he was forced to retire from films because of cancer and the removal of his larynx. He learned to speak again and has toured for the American Cancer Society.

In 1967 The Screen Actors' Guild awarded him its annual award for fostering the finest ideals of the acting profession. **His films include:** *Rain* (1932), *They Knew What They Wanted* (1941), *Miss Annie Rooney* (1942), *The Bells of Saint Mary's* (1945).

BEVERLY GARLAND (1926–   )

Born in California, Beverly Garland played leading roles in "B" pictures of the late 40's and early 50's. Like many other actresses of this period, she turned to television, where her career was quite successful. She appeared in many serials and had a leading role opposite Fred MacMurray in the popular series *My Three Sons*. In 1953, she

John Garfield, a prototype of the non-heroes who came years later, roughs up Claude Rains slightly in Daughters Courageous *(1939).*

was nominated for an Emmy Award. **Her film credits include:** *D.O.A.* (1949), *The Glass Web* (1953), *The Joker Is Wild* (1957), *Twice Told Tales* (1963).

JUDY GARLAND (1922–1969)

"She is a great artist," Philip Oakes said of her. "She is Judy. She is the very best there is."

The savage irony is that her private life, from infancy to death, was a modern tragedy, a living nightmare compounded by insecurities, reasonless terrors, and endless hours of work in which her body was sustained by "diets" in which the main ingredients were tranquilizers and drugs.

Frances Gumm's parents were traveling vaudevillians. Her earliest years were pretty well summed up in a line from one of her most plaintive songs—"I was born in a trunk . . . in Pocatello, Idaho . . . "—although in Judy's case it was Grand Rapids, Minnesota. She was performing on stage at the age of three, and in the years that followed she and her two older sisters covered the country,

William Gargan reluctantly takes leave of Myrna Loy in a drama of the air, Night Flight *(1933).*

shepherded by Ma Gumm, performing a second-rate vaudeville act of their own. Her mother hired an agent for Judy, who impressed two of Louis B. Mayer's henchmen with her ability. Mayer heard her sing and, without a screen test, signed her up. Later Judy said she had never signed anything. "Nobody asked me," she said. "That should be the title of my life: *Nobody Asked Me.*"

Judy and another youngster, Deanna Durbin, who was also 14, made a two-reeler together in 1936. It was called *Every Sunday* and Hollywood legend has it that Mayer, after viewing the final version, said: "Let the fat one go." He meant Judy but his minions decided he meant Deanna, who was forthwith released and went on to fame and fortune at Universal. Mayer's blood pressure rose sharply but MGM went on to give Judy singing roles in pictures like *Love Finds Andy Hardy* (1938). Notices were good and audiences began to write Judy fan letters.

Unable to cast Shirley Temple (she belonged to 20th Century–Fox) in the role,

Judy Garland had just reached the age of 24 when she made Till the Clouds Roll By.

Judy Garland as Dorothy in the never-to-be-forgotten classic, The Wizard of Oz *(1939).*

MGM gave Judy the part of Dorothy in *The Wizard of Oz* (1939), a picture that has probably given more pleasure (thanks to television) to more people than any other film in motion picture history. Judy received a special Oscar, became permanently identified with one of the Arlen-Harburg songs, "Over the Rainbow," and the following year was voted, after Bette Davis, the most popular female star. She was already beginning to rely on pep pills and sedatives, however, and began to make surreptitious visits to a psychiatrist at the suggestion of Joe Mankiewicz, at that time a screenwriter. Ma Gumm found out, told Mayer, and abruptly the medical treatments stopped, Mankiewicz left MGM and Judy became alienated from her mother, whom she described as "the real-life Wicked Witch of the West . . . [She] . . . was no good for anything except to create chaos and fear."

Judy made more films with Mickey Rooney (at that point the number one male star) and then came such blockbusters as *For Me and My Gal* (1942), in which Gene Kelly made his debut; *Meet Me in St. Louis* (1944), an enormous box-office hit; *The Harvey Girls* (1946); and, with Astaire, *Easter Parade* (1948). By now she was in poor shape mentally, but when the former head of the U.S. Bureau of Narcotics suggested she be given a year off for hospital treatments, the studio was firm—the plan wouldn't work. "We've got 14 million invested in her, and she's at the top of her box-office right now."

When her second marriage to director Vincente Minnelli broke up, she attempted suicide. In 1953 she married Sid Luft, an ex-test pilot, who persuaded her to attempt a concert tour. It was a huge success and Judy seemed well on the road to recovery when she contracted with Warners for *A Star Is Born* (1954). The picture was a smash; she won an Oscar nomination, but her health had left her. The last 15 years of her life were more of the same: Roles in pictures like *Judgment at Nuremberg* (1961), which brought her another Academy nomination, and a historic Carnegie Hall concert in the same year alternated with long stretches when she could do no work at all, sunk in depressions that lasted for weeks on end. In 1963 her television show was launched, but playing at the same time as *Bonanza*, it didn't make the grade. In June 1969, her fifth husband, Mickey Deans, found her in their London flat, dead from an "accidental" overdose of barbiturates. **Other films include:** *Babes in Arms* (1939), *Strike Up the Band* (1940), *Girl Crazy* (1943), *Till the Clouds Roll By* (1946), *In the Good Old Summertime* (1949), *I Could Go on Singing* (1963).

JAMES GARNER (1928–)

A former traveling salesman, oil field worker, carpet layer and Korean War veteran, Oklahoma-born James Baumgarner got his first show-business job when producer Paul Gregory gave him a non-speaking role in the stage play *The Caine Mutiny Court Martial*.

Garner achieved great popularity on the *Maverick* television series and, after his film debut in *Toward the Unknown* (1956), became well known to filmgoers as well. His engaging, humorous, somewhat bumbling style plus his all-American good looks combined to promote him as the "new Cary Grant." This image failed to stick, however. Although he has made many good films, Garner has also accepted roles in many "B" flicks as well—of the kind that do not make stars. One would hope that the studios will be kinder to him in the future. **Credits:** *Cash McCall* (1960), *The Children's Hour* (1962), *The Great Escape* (1963), *The Americanization of Emily* (1964), *Grand Prix* (1966), *Support Your Local Sheriff* (1968).

PEGGY ANN GARNER (1931–)

A child star of the 40's, Garner began her professional career as a model at the age of four. Her mother thought she was "star material," and brought her to Hollywood. She made her debut in *Little Miss Thoroughbred* (1938), cutely lisping "Now I lay me down to sleep . . ." in an orphanage scene.

She was only 13 when she was cast as Francie in *A Tree Grows in Brooklyn* (1945). The movie was a big hit, and Peggy Ann Garner was a star. She won a special Academy Award for "the outstanding child actress of 1945." She finally graduated to

James Garner disposes of a hired gun who was about to kill him in Support Your Local Sheriff. *The girl is Joan Hackett and the deputy Jack Elam.*

teenage roles, including the highly successful *Junior Miss* (1945). After her film career began to falter she made her Broadway debut in *The Man*. She has appeared in road company productions, on television dramatic shows, and from time to time in films. **Other film credits include:** *Jane Eyre* (1944), *Teresa* (1951), *Black Widow* (1954), *The Cat* (1967).

BETTY GARRETT (1919–)

One of the most appealing "supporting actresses" of the 40's, Betty Garrett added a touch of humor, wit and humanity to many films. She was often cast as the female star's best friend, and at times provided welcome relief from the more serious aspects of a film.

She received a dance scholarship after graduating from high school, and later joined Martha Graham's dance company. She also

Peggy Ann Garner's performance in A Tree Grows in Brooklyn *won her a special Academy Award.*

Greer Garson and Robert Donat in Goodbye Mr. Chips, *a film that evoked sobs and tears around the globe.*

Vittorio Gassman took readily to light hearted roles. Here he is in The Easy Life.

appeared in nightclubs and musical revues. Her break came when she was an understudy for Ethel Merman in *Something for the Boys* (1943). When Merman got sick, Garrett filled in and her performance made a successful career certain. She made her film debut in *The Big City* (1948), cast as a wise-cracking, fun-loving young woman, the type of role she would continue to play. She has appeared on television and has toured in plays in the United States and Britain. **Among her movies are:** *Take Me Out to the Ball Game* (1948), *On the Town* (1949), *My Sister Eileen* (1955), *The Shadow on the Window* (1957).

GREER GARSON (c.1908–)

Some say she was born in 1908, some say 1914, but all historians agree that it happened in County Down, Ireland, and that she was a prominent figure on the London stage by the mid-30's. Thinking he was going to see a musical, Louis B. Mayer went to see her in *Old Music* (1938) and even though there was no music, he liked Garson well enough to sign her up.

Arriving in Hollywood, she drew a check for $500 a week, got no assignments and was about to return to London when director Sam Wood gave her a part in a Robert Donat film that was going to be made in London. It was called *Goodbye, Mr. Chips* (1939), and although Garson died early in the film, her performance was exciting enough to bring her an Oscar nomination.

Back in Hollywood, with Norma Shearer and Greta Garbo still ruling the roost, she found it hard to capture important roles and it wasn't until Shearer decided she didn't want to play a mother that Garson accepted a role she didn't care much about either. Under the brilliant direction of William Wyler *Mrs. Miniver* (1942) was a smash success both in America and Britain and brought Garson the Oscar for Best Actress of the year. Although some critics called the film a phoney, millions disagreed and it made Garson a top star.

More hits followed until she had acquired a total of seven Oscar nominations and won the British Picturegoer Medal for three years in a row. She was now listed as one of the top ten movie stars, and her hits included *Random Harvest* (1942), *Mrs. Parkington* (1944), and *The Valley of Decision* (1945).

After that her luck turned and the parts she played were so ladylike, so long-suffering, so utterly noble that one wit noted: "Lassie is Greer Garson with fur."

She made 25 films in all, but after the years of the big hits she had no luck at all and pretty much retired in 1955. Five years later she appeared in *Sunrise at Campobello* and won her seventh Academy nomination playing young Eleanor Roosevelt. Since then she has performed on television from time to time, appeared in several other films and is one of a distinct minority violently pro-Louis B. Mayer. **Other films:** *Remember* (1939), *The Youngest Profession* (1943), *Madame Curie* (1943), *Adventure* (1945), *Julie Misbehaves* (1948), *Julius Caesar* (1953), *The Happiest Millionaire* (1967).

VITTORIO GASSMAN (1922–)

A native of Genoa, Italy, Gassman studied at Rome's Academy of Dramatic Arts and became a respected stage performer. He made his film debut in *Preludio d'Amore* (1946), and made several films which did little to enhance his reputation. However, his theatre fame brought him to the attention of American film-makers. He made several films for American studios, but his first real popularity came when he turned to comedy in the Italian production *I Soliti Ignoti* (1958). Both Italian and American producers learned to utilize his comedic talents, and he made popular films in both countries. He has used much of his film earnings to subsidize his work in the theatre, which he prefers. **His film credits include:** *Bitter Rice* (1948), *Big Deal on Madonna Street* (1960), *The Easy Life* (1963), *Woman Times Seven* (1967).

MARJORIE GATESON (1900–)

Gateson attended the Brooklyn Conservatory of Music and began her performing career in operetta, making her debut in *Dove of Peace*. She followed this performance with successful dramatic stage work and in the 30's went to the West Coast and Hollywood. She made her film debut in *The Beloved Bachelor* (1931) and remained in Hollywood long enough to make almost 100 films.

With the rise of television's popularity, Gateson turned her attention to that medium, appearing as Mother Barbour on *One Man's*

Family (1949-1952) and, since 1956, playing Grace Tyrell on the TV soap *The Secret Storm*. **Film credits:** *Husband's Holiday* (1931), *Society Girl* (1932), *Let's Fall in Love* (1934), *Wife vs. Secretary* (1936), *The Man I Marry* (1936), *Back Street* (1941), *No Time for Love* (1943), *The Caddy* (1953).

JOHN GAVIN (1934–)

Los Angeles-born Gavin graduated from Stanford University in 1952, served in the USNR (1952–1955) and began his performing career with his film debut in *Four Girls in Town* (1957). He has appeared in a wide variety of pictures, but it is surprising that this extremely handsome, competent actor has not been used more frequently. **Credits:** *A Time to Love and a Time to Die* (1958), *Imitation of Life* (1959), *Psycho* (1960), *Midnight Lace* (1960), *Romanoff and Juliet* (1961), *Back Street* (1961), *Thoroughly Modern Millie* (1967).

JANET GAYNOR (1906–)

The first woman to win an Academy Award decided to try her luck in pictures because she didn't like working as a bookkeeper in a shoe store or as an usherette in a theatre. Gaynor made the right decision. Within five years of her first film walk-on, she was a star and was being billed as the successor to Mary Pickford. Her Academy Award came within that period, too—for three films in 1927-28: *Seventh Heaven*, *Sunrise* and *Street Angel*.

After some small parts in two-reelers, Gaynor got her first break in *The Johnstown Flood* (1926) and her first movie contract. The next year, she hit the big time, playing a Parisian streetwalker in *Seventh Heaven* (1927) with Charles Farrell. Both the film and its stars did so well at the box office that Gaynor and Farrell were co-starred many times over the next few years as ''America's Favorite Lovebirds.''

Gaynor filmed both musicals and dramatic pictures and, true to her image as Pickford's successor, did a remake of *Tess of the Storm Country* (1932). She rebelled, however, when 20th Century–Fox tried to cast her in *Rebecca of Sunnybrook Farm* (1932) and another actress did that Pickford remake.

She remained a top star through most of the 30's in such films as *State Fair* (1933) with

Marjorie Gateson shows what the well-dressed dowager wore in 1937. The picture was Turn Off the Moon.

another box-office great, Will Rogers, and *Small Town Girl* (1936) with Robert Taylor.

By the end of the 30's, however, the studios seemed to be losing interest in Gaynor. Although she was still offered some big parts, including *A Star Is Born* (1937) with Fredric March, her salary was being reduced and she was being asked to share billing with other movie queens of the day. After *The Young in Heart* (1938) with Douglas Fairbanks, Jr., Gaynor married MGM dress designer Adrian and announced her retirement. Her only role since then has been as Pat Boone's mother in *Bernadine* (1957). She still lives in Hollywood with ''no regrets'' about quitting. **Films include:** *Two Girls Wanted* (1927), *Sunny Side Up* (1929), *The Man Who Came Back* (1931), *One More Spring* (1935), *Three Loves Has Nancy* (1938).

MITZI GAYNOR (1930–)

A vivacious, effervescent addition to movie musicals, Mitzi Gaynor is the daughter

Mitzi Gaynor followed Mary Martin's footsteps closely in the film version of South Pacific. *She tried hard but the production totally lacked the oomph of the Broadway production.*

One of the top silent stars, Janet Gaynor made a hugely successful comeback with Fredric March in A Star Is Born.

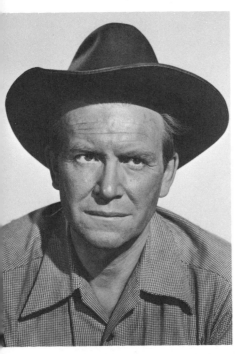

A botanist by preference, Will Geer has done a fine job in films as well, notably Westerns.

of a dancer and at the age of 12 was a member of the ballet corps of the Los Angeles Civic Light Opera. Her first screen role in *My Blue Heaven* (1950) brought rave notices, some of which outshone those of the star, Betty Grable. She was given roles in several of the big musicals of the period, including starring parts in two. But the time of the big song-and-dance spectacles of Hollywood was over, and she had to settle for whatever parts were available. Some, like her portrayal in *Anything Goes* (1956), demonstrated her dancing skill and charm. What should have revitalized her career, the leading role in *South Pacific* (1958), was marred by bad direction and weak co-stars. Although she continues to make films, Gaynor has entered other media, including theatre stock work, nightclub engagements, and television specials. **Some of her films are:** *Golden Girl* (1951), *There's No Business Like Show Business* (1954), *The Joker Is Wild* (1957), *For Love or Money* (1963).

BEN GAZZARA (1930–   )

An actor of substance, Gazzara has appeared on stage, screen and television. He is most famous, perhaps, for his video series, *Run for Your Life*. A member of Actors Studio, Gazzara reached Broadway as the star of a student production, *End As a Man* (1953). It was this same vehicle, retitled *The Strange One*, that brought him to Hollywood in 1957.

Though he aspires to be a serious actor, Gazzara has permitted himself to be cast in a series of lightweight films such as *The Passionate Thief* (1961), *The Young Doctors* (1961), and *Convicts 4* (1962). In 1970, a film came along which proved that Gazzara had what it takes. Under the direction of John Cassavetes, his performance in *Husbands* was unanimously acclaimed. Unfortunately, the film was a bit too sophisticated for the ordinary movie goer and was not a box-office hit. **Film credits:** *Anatomy of a Murder* (1959), *A Rage to Live* (1966), *The Bridge at Remagen* (1969).

WILL GEER (1902–   )

Born in Frankfort, Indiana, Geer moved about a bit for his education, attending Col-

umbia University in New York City, the University of Chicago, and Oxford. He studied botany at the University of Chicago as well as acting, and it has been a life-long toss-up which of the two interests he prefers.

Before his film debut in *The Misleading Lady* (1932), Geer acted on stage with the Sothern and Marlowe Shakespearean Repertory Company. Though his film credits are short, his career has spanned 34 years.

In private life he is an avid gardener, growing all of the 400 plants mentioned in Shakespeare's plays. In addition, he is the author of a book on the 1,000 plant references in Shakespeare. **Films include:** *Lust for Gold* (1949), *Broken Arrow* (1950), *Tall Target* (1951), *Seconds* (1966), *Bandolero!* (1968).

JUDY GEESON (1948–   )

Born in London, Judy Geeson attended the Corona Stage School simply because it was close to her home. She soon discovered that she liked acting, and made her stage debut at the age of nine. Her professional debut was made on television in 1960, and she went on to play small roles, both in plays and on television. She left school at 15 and received many parts from the B.B.C., including starring roles in several popular series.

Geeson's first film part was in *To Sir With Love* (1966) where the petite, honey-blonde actress played a cynical schoolgirl who becomes the star pupil. **Her other film credits include:** *Prudence and the Pill* (1966), *Three into Two Won't Go* (1969), *10 Rillington Place* (1972).

LEO GENN (1905–   )

London-born Genn studied at Cambridge and became a lawyer, but turned to acting when a girl friend invited him to join an amateur theatrical group. His appearances with this group led to the legitimate stage and later to films.

He made his film debut in *Jump for Glory* (1937), and though he did not make numerous screen appearances, his career spanned 30 years. In addition to his stage and screen work, Genn narrated radio programs, notably the commentary on the coronations of George VI (1937) and Queen Elizabeth II (1953). **Among his films:** *Henry V* (1946), *The*

Snake Pit (1948), *Lady Chatterley's Lover* (1956), *Moby Dick* (1956), *The Longest Day* (1962), *Circus of Fear* (1967).

GLADYS GEORGE (1900–1954)

Her parents were actors, and Maine-born Gladys Clare made her first appearance on stage with them at the age of three. She became so popular that they changed the name of the show from "The Three Clares" to "Little Gladys George & Co."

She appeared in many silent films and made her first sound feature, *Straight Is the Way,* in 1934. However, it was only after *Valiant Is the Word for Carrie* (1936) that her film career really took off.

She considered herself a character actress and often turned down ingénue roles for serious parts. **Her long list of movies includes:** *The Roaring Twenties* (1939), *The Way of All Flesh* (1940), *The Maltese Falcon* (1941), *The Best Years of Our Lives* (1946), *Flamingo Road* (1949), *It Happens Every Thursday* (1953).

SUSAN GEORGE (1950–   )

Another of the increasing number of talented British beauties, George made her first film at the age of four, appeared in a West End production of *Sound of Music* at 12, and "retired" (to hairdressing) at 15. Back in films soon after, she made *Spring and Port Wine* (not released in the U.S., 1969). Her career has had, to date, only one high point—*Straw Dogs* (1971). In this Peckinpah thriller, George starred with Dustin Hoffman as a couple terrorized by local toughs. Her fine performance in *Dogs* placed her on the list of bright new female stars. **Credits:** *Billion Dollar Brain* (1967).

STEVE GERAY (1904–   )

Signed by the National Theatre of Hungary directly from drama school, Geray had a long distinguished career in Berlin, Vienna, Paris and London before coming to this country in 1941 and establishing himself as a fine character actor. Best remembered for his role as the adoring but betrayed husband in *The Moon and Sixpence* (1942), he usually portrayed weak, pathetic and mild-mannered men. **Some of his films include:** *Dance Band*

Leo Genn looks on compassionately as Olivia de Havilland lives through one of her fantasies in the powerful and disturbing film classic The Snake Pit.

(1936), *The Mask of Dimitrios* (1944), *Gilda* (1946), *The Big Sky* (1952), *Call Me Madam* (1953), *Count Your Blessings* (1959).

HOOT GIBSON (1892–1962)

Gibson spent his childhood in the American West and was one of the few movie cowboys to have experienced, in part, the type of life he portrayed in the movies. He had a great sense of showmanship, and during his movie career often performed in rodeos and carnival shows.

Gibson made his debut in *Shotgun Jones* (1915), and played in many one- and two-reelers in the teens and early 20's. He skyrocketed to fame in *Action* (1921), and thereafter produced his own films which were good-humored and light in mood. Later, he played small roles in more sophisticated cowboy dramas. **Credits:** *Hazards of Helen* (1915), *The Cactus Kid* (1919), *Surefire* (1924), *Powdersmoke Range* (1953), *Ocean's Eleven* (1961).

Susan George, a bright new British face, clings to her husband, Dustin Hoffman, in Straw Dogs.

Sir John Gielgud, one of Britain's great actors, as he appeared in Warner Brothers' Assignment to Kill *(1969).*

WYNNE GIBSON (1899–   )

At 14, Gibson ran away from home to join a road show. Although her parents objected to her ambition to become an actress, she was allowed to pursue her career. After several months with a road company, she appeared on the New York stage and had roles in many musicals.

Pert, red-headed, with a winning talent for comedy, Wynne Gibson made over 30 movies in 13 years. Making her film debut in *Nothing but the Truth* (1920), she went on to play leading roles that demonstrated both her light acting touch and her ability to play more serious roles. **Her films include:** *I Give My Love* (1934), *Gangs of New York* (1938), *Café* Hostess (1940), *The Falcon Strikes Back* (1943).

SIR JOHN GIELGUD (1904–   )

Tall, and graced with a commanding presence, Gielgud is one of the foremost interpreters of Shakespeare of our time. Descended on his mother's side from the famous theatrical family, the Terrys, Gielgud became interested in acting as a young man. He studied at Lady Benson's School and received a scholarship to the Royal Academy of Dramatic Arts in 1921.

Gielgud's voice is perhaps his greatest asset, and it carries easily and beautifully, maintaining the melody of Shakespeare's verse. His interpretation of Hamlet, a role which he has performed innumerable times, is masterful.

Although his greatest work has been in the theatre, Gielgud also has appeared in several films. His first talkie was *Insult* (1932). He was knighted in 1953 for his services to the English stage. **His film credits include:** *The Prime Minister* (1940), *Julius Caesar* (1955), *Richard III* (1956), *The Barretts of Wimpole Street* (1957), *Saint Joan* (1957), *Becket* (1964), *Oh! What a Lovely War* (1969).

BILLY GILBERT (1894–1971)

Until 1929, Gilbert enjoyed a moderately successful career as both producer of burlesque shows and as a comedy singer in musical sketches. At the urging of Stan Laurel (of the Laurel and Hardy comedy team) Gilbert began writing situations and gags for them. Soon, he was also in constant demand for small comic parts (especially excitable Italians), and became a memorable patsy for Laurel and Hardy, the Marx Brothers and the Three Stooges.

In 1937 he created the character, voice and the immortal sneeze of Sneezy in Walt Disney's *Snow White and the Seven Dwarfs*. Thereafter, many of his movie roles were built around an expected, volcanic sneeze. **Highlights of more than 110 films:** *Noisy Neighbors* (1929), *Million Dollar Legs* (1932), *Sutter's Gold* (1936), *Destry Rides Again* (1939), *Five Weeks in a Balloon* (1962).

JOHN GILBERT (1897–1936)

A romantic star of the silent film era, Gilbert was born into an acting family and from a young age longed to get into the movies. He began as a low-paid extra, mostly in Westerns, graduated into playing second male leads, and found his place portraying the

Billy Gilbert is seen here as one of a quartet of distinctive and highly talented supporting players who all appeared in Sandy Is a Lady *(1940). From left to right: Mischa Auer, Gilbert, Eugene Pallette, Edgar Kennedy.*

romantic leads with some of Hollywood's most popular actresses. His physical attributes were certainly to his advantage —especially at a time when Valentino was *the* movie idol. Gilbert, too, was dark, Latin-looking and had deep, expressive eyes.

In the early 20's Gilbert made many films with most of the big movie companies, and after his appearance in the very popular *Cameo Kirby* (1923) he was recognized as potential star material. He played parts requiring compassion and understanding, but was equally able to play semi-villainous roles. His characterization of the average doughboy in King Vidor's fine *The Big Parade* (1925) launched him into new popularity. In the late 20's the studios delighted in co-starring him with Greta Garbo, especially when rumors of an off-stage romance boosted box-office appeal tremendously.

Gilbert is unfortunately best remembered by some as the silent star who could not make it in the talkies. His voice was thin, almost effeminate, and his talkies lacked the success of his silent films. **His films include:** *The Count of Monte Cristo* (1922), *La Boheme* (1926), *Love* (1927), *Desert Nights* (1929), *Queen Christina* (1933).

CONNIE GILCHRIST (1904–   )

Inspired by her actress mother, Gilchrist developed a liking for the theatre at an early age. She made her stage debut at age 16 in London and subsequently toured France in repertory. Later she managed theatrical companies in the U.S. and appeared both on Broadway and in a number of films. **Credits include:** *Hullabaloo* (1940), *Tortilla Flat* (1942), *A Letter to Three Wives* (1949), *Little Women* (1949), *The Man in the Gray Flannel Suit* (1956), *The One With the Fuzz* (1969).

JACK GILFORD (1919–   )

Jack Gilford, blessed with a touch of absurdity, is often cast as the "little man," beset and confused by the troubles of those around him. His doleful face belies an instinct for comedy and the absurd.

Gilford was born and brought up in Brooklyn, New York, and first performed as a comedian at the Bronx Opera House in 1934. He toured in vaudeville during the 30's, and appeared in many productions on Broadway. He made his film debut in *Hey Rookie!* (1953). When *A Funny Thing Happened on the Way to the Forum* (1966) was made into a movie after a very successful Broadway run, Gilford re-created his role in the film version. **His other films include:** *Main Street to Brooklyn* (1953), *Enter Laughing* (1967), *The Incident* (1967), *Catch-22* (1969), *They Might Be Giants* (1970).

CLAUDE GILLINGWATER
(1870–1940)

Born in St. Louis, Gillingwater began his acting career in the Midwest, making his stage debut in 1892. He came to New York where he established a long and successful relationship with producer David Belasco and performed in many of his productions. A

John Gilbert and Eleanor Boardman in Wife of a Centaur (1925).

Jack Gilford, closely followed by Zero Mostel, in the 1966 version of a play Plautus had written in ancient Rome nearly 2,000 years earlier—A Funny Thing Happened on the Way to the Forum.

When crotchety millionaires were needed, Claude Gillingwater was always available. This shot is from The Poor Little Rich Girl *(1936).*

Lillian Gish is comforted by Ronald Colman in The White Sister.

talented writer as well, Gillingwater starred in his own plays from 1913-1917.

He was featured in several silent movies, and his work in the talkies demonstrated his talents as a comedian and character actor. Gillingwater was a fine dialectician, and this added another dimension to his performances. He made 27 talking pictures. **Films include:** *Daddy Long Legs* (1931), *Baby Face Harrington* (1935), *Top of the Town* (1937), *Café Society* (1939).

VIRGINIA GILMORE (1919–)

Gilmore arrived in Hollywood to see Sam Goldwyn and refused to be put off—when she was denied admission at the studio, she simply went to see Goldwyn at home. He was impressed with her persistent attitude, but not with her appearance. She was turned over to the Hollywood beauty specialists, was given a new haircut, braces for her teeth, and told to return in a year. When she returned, she was voted, in a publicity stunt, the actress who had the most beautiful legs in Hollywood, surpassing even Marlene Dietrich's. But it was her youth and coquettish charm that played the more important role in her success. After a prolific film career, Gilmore appeared in several Broadway light comedies. **Over 40 films include:** *Manhattan Heartbeat* (1940), *Swampwater* (1941), *Pride of the Yankees* (1942), *Wonderman* (1946).

HERMIONE GINGOLD (1897–)

She seems to delight in playing slightly grotesque, eccentric characters, and is well-suited to this. Her lisping, expressive voice suggests second and even third meanings to every line she utters. She began her career at 17 as a dramatic actress, appearing at Stratford-on-Avon and with the Old Vic. But her first musical revue proved to her and her audiences that comedy was her true métier.

Gingold appeared as a stage comedienne in England and began making films there in 1936. When she came to New York in 1954 in the play *Almanac*, she was a critical success, and she has remained in this country ever since. She is perhaps best known for her portrayal of the grandmother in *Gigi* (1958). Still active, Gingold's most recent appearance was on Broadway in *A Little Night Music* (1973).

Some of her films are: *Pickwick Papers* (1952), *Around the World in 80 Days* (1956), *Bell, Book and Candle* (1958), *The Music Man* (1961), *Munster Go Home!* (1966).

ETIENNE GIRARDOT (1856–1939)

He was born in London of French parents. His father, Gustave Girardot, was a portrait painter and for a while Girardot thought he might follow in his father's footsteps. However, success in amateur theatre led him to the stage. His first London success was in *The Yellow Dwarf* (1883) and for the next three years Girardot often did as many as 15 parts a week in various Shakespearean productions. He came to the U.S. in 1893 and was successful on Broadway in *Charley's Aunt*. He continued appearing regularly on the stage and also in films after his successful screen debut in 1933. **His films include:** *20th Century* (1934), *Clive of India* (1935), *The Longest Night* (1936), *There Goes My Heart* (1938), *The Hunchback of Notre Dame* (1940).

DOROTHY GISH (1898–1968)

More lively and outspoken than her sister Lillian, Dorothy Gish was also a fine actress. She started acting in repertory companies at the age of four. When Dorothy was 14, she and Lillian auditioned for D.W. Griffith. It may have been one of the strangest auditions in film history, as Griffith chased the young girls with a pistol, testing their reactions and expressions. Their responses were apparently considered appropriate, for both sisters became members of the Griffith company.

Her film debut was in *An Unseen Enemy* (1912), and although she never became as famous as her older sister, she acted well and sensitively in many succeeding Griffith films. Her career faltered when talkies came in, but she did return to films occasionally later. **Among her many films are:** *Remodeling Her Husband* (1920), *Orphans of the Storm* (1922), *Our Hearts Were Young and Gay* (1944), *The Whistle at Eaton Falls* (1951), *The Cardinal* (1963).

LILLIAN GISH (1896–)

She has been called the greatest actress of the American silent film era, and certainly was the most popular and respected film actress of her time. Although the parts she played seem melodramatic and old-fashioned to the modern filmgoer, her talent and her intuitive understanding of her roles are still memorable.

Gish made her stage debut at the age of five, and she, her sister Dorothy, and their mother toured in repertory companies. While touring, they met Mary Pickford, who brought Lillian and Dorothy to the D.W. Griffith studios. In order to tell them apart, Griffith had Lillian wear a blue ribbon and Dorothy a red one. They made their joint film debut in *An Unseen Enemy* (1912) and became members of the Griffith company, playing a variety of roles in many one- and two-reelers.

In 1915 Griffith made one of the most influential movies in film history—the tradition-breaking, 12-reel *The Birth of a Nation*. Lillian Gish, the perfect, fragile Griffith heroine, was the star and it brought her world fame. She continued with Griffith, playing delicate, innocent women with vibrancy and appeal. Her work with other directors was equally successful, and she created fine portraits in such films as *La Boheme* (1926) and *The Scarlet Letter* (1927). Her last movie during this period was the talkie *One Romantic Night* (1930). She returned to the New York stage and toured with plays both here and in Britain. She has performed on television, on stage, and has returned now and then to films, generally playing gentle old ladies. **Her many films include:** *Intolerance* (1916), *Broken Blossoms* (1919), *Orphans of the Storm* (1922), *The White Sister* (1923), *Duel in the Sun* (1947), *Orders to Kill* (1958), *The Comedians* (1967).

GEORGE GIVOT (1903–)

Givot is a talented impersonator and dialectician who developed his skills in vaudeville. His appearances on Eddie Cantor's radio show developed his characterization of a "Greek Ambassador of Good Will." His mangling of the English language into a Greek-sounding dialect delighted millions of movie and radio fans. Because of the versatility of his dialects, there has been much speculation about his origins; the truth is rather commonplace—he was born in Chicago and

raised in Omaha. **Some of his movies are:** *Conquest* (1937), *Marie Walenska* (1938), *Du Barry Was a Lady* (1943), *Riff-Raff* (1947), *Miracle in the Rain* (1956).

JACKIE GLEASON (1916–)

The rotund comedian is probably more famous for his bus driver, Ralph Kramden, on the television series *The Honeymooners* than he is for his motion pictures. But Gleason did appear on the screen relatively frequently during the 60's, most notably as Minnesota Fats in *The Hustler* (1961).

A show-business veteran, Gleason had first tried to break into motion pictures during the early 40's while he was still a stand-up nightclub comic. He gave up on Hollywood after a few bit parts in "B" pictures and returned to New York in time to get in on what was the ground floor in television.

The Brooklyn-born comic soon was a familiar fixture on TV screens across the nation and the characters he created became

Jackie Gleason in a dramatic role in Gigot.

Dorothy (left) and Lillian Gish, soon to be caught up in the terrors of the French Revolution, as they appeared in Orphans of the Storm *(1922). It was another D.W. Griffith triumph that extended the frontiers of film-making.*

equally famous. He was the swaggering Reggie Van Gleason III, the sympathetic Joe, the Bartender, the pathetic Poor Soul, and of course Kramden. Eventually, the skit "The Honeymooners" featuring Gleason as Kramden, Audrey Meadows as his wife, Alice, and Art Carney as his neighbor became a television series in its own right.

After his starring role in *The Hustler* with Paul Newman, Gleason continued to appear in motion pictures in both comedy and dramatic roles. He has said he prefers drama to comedy and has signed a new television contract to act in three dramas a year after September 1974. **Films include:** *Blood Money* (1962), *Gigot* (1962), *Requiem for a Heavyweight* (1962), *Soldier in the Rain* (1963), *Skidoo* (1968), *How to Commit Marriage* (1969), *Don't Drink the Water* (1969).

JAMES GLEASON (1886–1959)

Gleason was born in a theatrical boarding house in New York City. His parents had a touring company; therefore, his education was intermittent, for he often played child parts in the family productions. He appeared later in two silent films and in 1925 co-authored and acted in *Is Zat So?* which ran for three years on Broadway, on tour and abroad. Following this success the gaunt and talented character actor went to Hollywood and played a vast number of roles. In September 1927 Gleason became the first man in movies to sign a four-way contract when he joined Republic as a writer, producer, actor and director. In 1938, he appeared in *The Higgins Family* and four subsequent episodes in the same series with his wife Lucille and his son, Russell. **More than 100 films include:** *A Free Soul* (1931), *West Point of the Air* (1935), *My Gal Sal* (1942), *Arsenic and Old Lace* (1944), *A Tree Grows in Brooklyn* (1945), *The Life of Riley* (1949), *What Price Glory?* (1952), *The Last Hurrah* (1958).

RUSSELL GLEASON (1906–1945)

He was born in Portland, Oregon, but because his parents, Lucille and James Gleason, were then both repertory performers, he spent much of his childhood traveling. They encouraged him to become an actor, and he began performing in plays with them at quite a young age. He began his film career in 1929, and went on to play in over 20 movies during the 30's and early 40's. He died in a tragic accident—a fall from a hotel window—at the age of 39. **His films include:** *Strange Cargo* (1929), *The Shady Lady* (1929), *All Quiet on the Western Front* (1930), *Private Jones* (1933), *Hitchhike to Heaven* (1936), *Down on the Farm* (1938), *Young as You Feel* (1940), *The Adventures of Mark Twain* (1944).

PAULETTE GODDARD (1911–   )

Although Chaplin is always given credit for making her a star, her performances in films like *Nothing but the Truth* (1941) and *Kitty* (1946) lead one to suspect that she might well have made it on her own.

A native of New York's Great Neck, Long Island, she left school in Manhattan early and was a Ziegfeld girl at the age of 14. After parts in musicals like *Rio Rita*, she married, divorced, and signed a contract with film-maker Hal Roach. The story has it that she met Chaplin on Joseph Schenck's yacht in 1932, that he dissuaded her from investing her alimony in a hopeless film venture, bought her contract from Roach, caused her blonde hair to revert to its normal brunette color —and promptly proceeded to cast her as his co-star in *Modern Times*. It couldn't have been quite that prompt because the film wasn't released until 1936, at which point she had become the third Mrs. Chaplin. The picture was one of the funniest of the Chaplin epics and Paulette was exactly right as his waif-like companion. After testing out for and almost getting the Scarlett O'Hara role in *Gone With the Wind*, she was starred for the first time with Bob Hope in *The Cat and the Canary* (1939). The next year, not long before she and Chaplin split up, she appeared with him in *The Great Dictator*.

During the next five years Goddard became one of the most popular female stars, helped along by films like De Mille's *Reap the Wild Wind* (1942). In the late 40's a succession of weak films pointed her career downward and, although she continued in films until the mid-50's, her later efforts were in the weakest sort of "B" pictures. In 1958, married to novelist Erich Maria Remarque (*All Quiet on*

The versatile James Gleason played one of his infrequent non-comedy roles in What Price Glory?

the Western Front, etc.), she retired, except for one Italian film which she appeared in in the mid 60's. **Other credits:** *The Women* (1939), *Northwest Mounted Police* (1940), *Hold Back the Dawn* (1941), *So Proudly We Hail!* (1943), *Duffy's Tavern* (1945), *Anna Lucasta* (1949), *The Unholy Four* (1954).

MINNA GOMBELL (1892–1973)

After graduating from college, Gombell was determined to become an actress, very much against her parents' will. A bit part on Broadway, stock roles and another Broadway part confirmed her talents and the fact that she had made the right career choice. In 1930 she went to Hollywood and landed character parts in many films. **Credits:** *Sob Sister* (1931), *The Thin Man* (1934), *The Hunchback of Notre Dame* (1940), *High Sierra* (1941), *The Best Years of Our Lives* (1946), *I'll See You in My Dreams* (1951).

THOMAS GOMEZ (1905–1971)

Gomez began his acting career at 18 when he won a city-wide contest by reading 20 lines of Falstaff's speech from *King Henry IV*. His prize was a scholarship to Walter Hampden's Dramatic School.

His dramatic studies led to Broadway and appearance with the Lunts. He made his screen debut in *Sherlock Holmes and the Voice of Terror* (1942) and thereafter played mainly villains or detectives.

In private life he was an expert on Benjamin Franklin, Enrico Caruso and handmade bicycles, of which he owned one of America's finest collections. **Among his many films:** *Phantom Lady* (1944), *Key Largo* (1948), *Macao* (1952), *Trapeze* (1956), *Beneath the Planet of the Apes* (1970).

LEO GORCEY (1915–1969)

Broadway and motion picture audiences knew him as "Spit," the pugnacious wise guy of the Dead End Kids. Gorcey was working as an apprentice in his uncle's New York City plumbers shop when casting began for the original stage version of *Dead End*. His father thought Gorcey should audition because the producers were looking for non-professionals.

Paulette Goddard stares uneasily at nothing in The Cat and the Canary.

Leo Gorcey, the most belligerent of the East Side Kids, entered the prize ring in Pride of the Bowery *(1941).*

The show was a smash hit and the cast, including Gorcey, went to Hollywood to make the movie version. He stayed to film more than 20 Dead End Kids pictures, as well as the Bowery Boys series and, later, the East Side Kids.

In his role as Spit, Gorcey was described by one critic as "the littlest, the one most stunted by cigarette smoking, a venomous expectorator for whom the eye of the enemy was like a flying quail to a huntsman." He was the one who always wore a felt beanie and talked out of the side of his mouth.

Gorcey left Hollywood and settled in northern California 15 years before his death in 1969. **Films include:** *Angels With Broken Wings* (1941), *Maisie Gets her Man* (1942), *Bowery Buckaroos* (1947), *Tell It to the Marines* (1952), *Bowery to Baghdad* (1955), *It's a Mad, Mad, Mad, Mad World* (1963), *The Phynx* (1969).

C. Henry Gordon looks not only villainous but enormously rich as he practices evil in Tarzan's Revenge *(1938).*

The television set appears to be broken as Gale Gordon (l.) joins Paul Newman in staring at nothing in Rally 'Round the Flag, Boys!

C. HENRY GORDON (1874–1940)

His obituaries refer to him as "the most detested actor in Hollywood." This is not a reflection on his personality, but a description of the characters he created in many movies. A fine character actor, Gordon began his career on Broadway, and then came to Hollywood. In his movies he represented cold-blooded, ruthless villainy through his sardonic, suave portrayals of menacing men. His grating voice and his scowling expression enhanced his characterizations. **His films include:** *A Devil With Women* (1930), *Mata Hari* (1932), *Scarface* (1932), *The Charge of the Light Brigade* (1936), *Yellow Jack* (1938), *Kit Carson* (1940).

GALE GORDON (1906–   )

Although he started in show business playing a small part in *The Temptress* (1929), Gale Gordon is most popularly known as a radio and television comedian. He acted in many radio shows of the 30's and 40's and was a major success playing a pompous politician on the *Fibber McGee and Molly Show* of the 40's. He was the envy of other Hollywood comedians when Mary Pickford chose him to be on her New York radio show.

Both in the movies and on television, Gordon is most often cast as a pompous, straight-laced type, with a temper that flares uncontrollably at the foolishness of others. His portrayal of the principal in the movie *Our Miss Brooks* (1956) was a perfect example of his character-type, and he re-created this role in the long-running television series. **His film credits include:** *Pilgrimage Play* (1929), *Here We Go Again* (1942), *A Woman of Distinction* (1950), *Rally 'Round the Flag Boys!* (1958), *Visit to a Small Planet* (1960), *Speedway* (1968).

HUNTLEY GORDON (1897–   )

Born in Canada and educated in England, Gordon's first stage experience was with a Canadian stock company. He later went on to Broadway, where he was noticed by Ralph Ince, who suggested that Gordon enter films. He became a leading man in silent pictures and switched to secondary roles and character parts with the advent of talkies. **Pictures in-**

clude: *Scandal* (1929), *Phantom Express* (1932), *Daniel Boone* (1936), *Mr. Wong in Chinatown* (1939).

MARY GORDON (1882–1963)

Gordon started in films in the 20's, but is most familiar to moviegoers as a middle-aged character actress. A short, plump woman, she often portrayed the mother of the film's leading character. Gordon was born in Scotland, but was often required to play Irishwomen and developed a fine brogue to do this. She is probably best remembered for her characterization of Mrs. Hudson in the Basil Rathbone *Sherlock Holmes* series of 1939–1946. **Her credits include:** *The Irish in Us* (1935), *Pot o' Gold* (1941).

RUTH GORDON (1896–   )

An actress capable of playing roles ranging from satire to tragedy, Ruth Gordon began her acting career when she was quite young. She came to New York to perform on the stage, and also crossed the river to work as an extra in the silents produced in Fort Lee, New Jersey. Although she flunked out of the American Academy of Dramatic Arts, she went on to have a very successful stage career, acting both in New York and London.

She made her debut in the talkies portraying Mary Todd in *Abe Lincoln in Illinois* (1940). Her later movies prove her to be a fine character actress, often cast as an eccentric old lady. She won an Oscar for her role in *Rosemary's Baby* (1968) portraying the ultimate eccentric, a witch in modern-day New York City.

Her innate wit and charm are apparent not only in her many movie roles, but also in the screenplays she has written. She and her husband, Garson Kanin, wrote *Adam's Rib* and other light comedies. **Her credits include:** *Camille* (1915), *Dr. Ehrlich's Magic Bullet* (1940), *Two-Faced Woman* (1942), *Inside Daisy Clover* (1966).

VERA GORDON (1886–1948)

At age 12 she got the part of a 55-year-old mother in her native Russia. In 1904, when Gordon came to the U.S. she continued to land mother roles in the Yiddish theatre. Later

Mary Gordon, inevitably playing a mother role, is here shown with Kay Francis in When the Daltons Rode *(1940).*

Ruth Gordon, a true professional, as she appeared in Whatever Happened to Aunt Alice? *(1969). The lady imbibing the sherry, a fine performer in her own right, is Geraldine Page.*

198

she played in vaudeville in London and in 1917 first appeared on Broadway. She gained popularity for her part in *Humoresque* (1920) and later appeared in a number of other roles. **Films include:** *The Cohens and the Kellys in Paris* (1926), *The Big Street* (1942), *Abie's Irish Rose* (1946).

MARIUS GORING (1912–   )

Born in England, Goring attended universities in Paris, Munich, Frankfurt, Vienna and Cambridge and achieved such proficiency in languages that he was able to play Hamlet in French and the plays of Chekhov and Gogol in German. A distinguished member of the Old Vic, he made his screen debut in *Consider Your Verdict* (1936). Goring went on to appear in many British films, usually as neurotic villains or in fey roles. **Some of his credits include:** *Rembrandt* (1936), *Stairway to Heaven* (1946), *The Red Shoes* (1948), *So Little Time*

Jetta Goudal, a favorite in the long-gone 20's, in Her Man o' War *(1926)*

(1953), *Up From the Beach* (1965), *First Love* (1970).

FERDINAND GOTTSCHALK
(1858–1944)

Born and educated in England, Gottschalk began his acting career in amateur productions, and later joined a stock company which traveled to Canada. There he worked both as an actor and a playwright.

His film career began in the early 20's, and he remained a successful film comedian and character actor through the 30's. He was cast in a variety of roles—dupe, sucker, spineless husband, cheerful reprobate—and to each he brought a good sense of timing and a light approach. **His film credits include:** *Tonight or Never* (1931), *Grand Hotel* (1932), *Gold Diggers of 1933* (1933), *Folies Bergère* (1935), *I'll Take Romance* (1937), *Josette* (1938).

JETTA GOUDAL (1898–   )

When she arrived in Hollywood to act in silent pictures, Goudal was described as an oriental beauty with a certain mysterious charm. Later, as a star of the silent screen she was variously described as "exotic," "unique," and "bizarre."

Goudal was born in Versailles, France, and said that when she first saw actress Sarah Bernhardt in *L'Aiglon* she decided that she too must go on the stage. She studied drama in Paris, Germany and Holland before coming to the United States. Goudal appeared on the American stage in *The Elton Case* and *The Hero* before making her screen debut in a small part in a European production, *Timothy's Quest*.

Her performance as the oriental servant in *The Green Goddess* (1923) made Goudal famous. She played the sultry siren in a series of pictures—all silents. The only sound film in which she appeared was *Business and Pleasure* (1932). **Films include:** *The Bright Shawl* (1923), *Salome of the Tenements* (1925), *Three Faces West* (1926), *White Gold* (1927), *The Forbidden Woman* (1927), *Fighting Love* (1927).

MICHAEL GOUGH (1917–   )

A British actor who has appeared on both stage and screen, Gough made his theatrical debut in London in 1936. His first film was *Blanche Fury* (1948). Gough frequently plays homicidal or ghoulish characters. **Films include:** *The Small Back Room* (1952), *The Man in the White Suit* (1952), *Richard III* (1956), *Horror of Dracula* (1958), *Horrors of the Black Museum* (1958), *The Horse's Mouth* (1958), *The Phantom of the Opera* (1962), *Dr. Terror's House of Horrors* (1965), *Circus of Blood* (1967), *Trog* (1969).

ELLIOTT GOULD (1938–   )

Lacking the glamour of the traditional ''movie star,'' Gould seems real and recognizable to his audience, and thus appropriate to represent the confusion and disillusionment of the late 60's and early 70's. Although he made his film debut in *The Night They Raided Minsky's* (1968), a nostalgic look at vaudeville, his big success came in *Bob & Carol & Ted & Alice* (1969), a ''contemporary'' comedy about wife-swapping. He was thereafter rushed into film portrayals of anxiety-ridden young men trying to find their place in society. In most of his films, his wit and comedic touch have added a dimension to rather stereotyped roles. He has the distinction of being the first American actor to be cast in an Ingmar Bergman film, *The Touch* (1971). **His other films include:** *M*A*S*H* (1970), *Getting Straight* (1970), *Little Murders* (1971), *The Long Goodbye* (1973).

BETTY GRABLE (1916–1973)

''I don't think I ever got a good review and I don't think any of my films did either,'' said the lady whose wartime pin-up portraits, hung from walls in Anzio and Guadalcanal, Bastogne and Burma, meant more to fighting men than all the propaganda leaflets turned out in World War II.

Superficially, Grable was a combination of elaborately coiffed hair, meticulous makeup, big bosom, a slim waistline and long, long, long, beautiful legs—all in all a far cry, indeed, from the natural look of today's film beauties. Despite the critics, she was warm and kind and not nearly as untalented as they said she was.

The young St. Louis-born Grable was taken to California by her mother, and at the age of 14 (after fibbing about her age) she

The highly individualistic Elliott Gould, together with Nina van Pallandt, in The Long Goodbye.

danced in blackface in a forgotten musical, *Let's Go Places*. For the next ten years she played in at least 30 films but never really starred. Her legs, which were eventually insured for $1,250,000—against a mere million for Fred Astaire's—were much commented upon, but precious little appeared in the press about her acting.

With her first Technicolor film, Grable zoomed from tenth on the popularity poll of female stars to close to the top. She was greatly helped by *The Dolly Sisters* (1945) with June Haver and a big money maker, *Mother Wore Tights* (1947).

By the early 50's Grable's career was on the skids and new stars like Marilyn Monroe were moving up to become the gold diggers of a new era. In *How to Marry a Millionaire* (1953) Monroe was billed over Grable and Betty is alleged to have told Marilyn: ''Honey, I've had it. Go get yours. It's your turn now.''

Her dress spread like a peacock's feathers, Betty Grable is here shown as countless millions remember her. The film, logically enough, was Pin Up Girl.

In the mid-50's, while married to trumpeter Harry James, she moved to Las Vegas. In the years that followed, she occasionally appeared on stage, getting good notices in 1969 in London, where she starred in *Belle Starr*. **Films include:** *The Gay Divorcée* (1934), *Pigskin Parade* (1936), *College Swing* (1938), *Million Dollar Legs* (1939), *Tin Pan Alley* (1940), *A Yank in the R.A.F.* (1941), *Four Jills in a Jeep* (1944), *Call Me Mister* (1951), *Three for the Show* (1953).

GLORIA GRAHAME (1925–)

She won an Academy Award nomination as a kindhearted floozie in *Crossfire* (1947) and got the Best Supporting Actress Oscar for her performance as a Dixieland tramp in *The Bad and the Beautiful* (1953), but the rest of her career was an up-and-down affair, with emphasis on the down.

Born Gloria Grahame Hallward in Los Angeles, she acted in high school, in local productions and eventually landed on Broadway. There a talent scout signed her up and sent her back to Hollywood in 1944. In the years that followed, a long list of bad movies were interspersed with secondary roles in a few good ones, such as *The Big Heat* (1953). Almost always she was cast as a vixen, a trollop or an out-and-out bum. Her career was hurt by spats with the studios plus a series of rather ugly divorces. In 1962, she married her former stepson, a Hollywood historian and genealogist, and conclusively proved that she had now become her own mother-in-law.

In recent years she has made a considerable comeback, on stage, in television and movies. **Film credits include:** *Blonde Fever* (debut, 1944), *It's a Wonderful Life* (1946), *The Greatest Show on Earth* (1952), *Oklahoma!* (1955), *The Loners* (1972), *Tarot* (1973).

FARLEY GRANGER (1925–)

Granger made his film debut as a juvenile in *The North Star* (1943). Amazingly enough, he got the part simply by answering a modest ad in a Los Angeles newspaper. At 17, the California-born aspiring actor had already studied with such teachers of drama as Stella Adler, Sanford Meisner and Lee Strasberg. Many juvenile roles followed his debut and after World War II Granger began performing regularly in varied and exacting adult supporting parts. Periodically, he appears in East Coast stage productions. **Highlights:** *They Live by Night* (1947), *Rope* (1948), *Hans Christian Andersen* (1952), *Senso* (1968).

STEWART GRANGER (1913–)

His real name is James Stewart, but he never quite reached the heights of his namesake. Born in London, Granger began his acting career playing small roles at the Old Vic and later got leading parts in repertory companies. He made his film debut in *So This Is London* (1938) and had small parts in other films. When he appeared in starring roles with James Mason, Phyllis Calvert and Margaret Lockwood in a series of romances, Granger became a box-office hit in Britain.

His first American movie, *King Solomon's Mines* (1950), was a great success, and American producers looked forward to the creation of a new, dashing, adventurous film hero. He continued to do his best work in those movies which required much action, and his several attempts at comedy received little critical praise. His later work is mostly in films produced by joint European companies. **His other film credits include:** *The Magic Bow* (1947), *Beau Brummel* (1954), *North to Alaska* (1960), *The Last Safari* (1967).

CARY GRANT (1904–   )

Enormous charm, a unique (but much imitated) mode of speech, a great sense of timing, and a face and body which have miraculously retained their youth are some of the elements that have placed Grant high in the ranks of the superstars. For decades moviegoers entering a theatre to see a Cary Grant film could be virtually certain of one highly significant fact—they were going to have a good time.

He was born in Bristol, England, and his background paralleled that of many stars—a broken home. In his early teens he was involved with a troupe of acrobats who taught him to dance and juggle. He performed in the United States, returned to England to do odd jobs and then, at the ripe age of 16, began to play juvenile roles in Broadway musicals produced by Oscar Hammerstein, father of the fabulous Oscar II of musical fame. He had been born Archibald Leach but he changed part of his name when he played Cary Lockwood in *Nikki*, the Broadway version of the movie *The Last Flight*. That performance led to his movie debut in the highly entertaining *This Is the Night* (1932) with Lili Damita.

For the next five years films like Katharine Hepburn's *Sylvia Scarlett* (1935) and Jean Harlow's *Suzy* in the following year contributed to his growing popularity, but it wasn't until *The Awful Truth* (1937), a very funny comedy that he and Irene Dunne played to the hilt, that real stardom arrived. Thereafter, for nearly 30 years, hit pictures came along with clocklike regularity, and although he never won an ''official'' Oscar, he was presented

Gloria Grahame, adept at playing slatterns, does what's expected of her in Human Desire *(1954).*

Cary Grant and Katharine Hepburn in the ultra sophisticated and highly popular film The Philadelphia Story.

Cary Grant as the young Thomas Jefferson in The Howards of Virginia *(1940).*

with a special one in 1970 for the sheer brilliance of his performances over the years.

It is hard to pick out highlights of his career for his films range from *Gunga Din* (1939) to *The Talk of the Town* (1942); from *Bringing Up Baby* (1938) to *Notorious* (1946); from *The Philadelphia Story* (1940) to *Indiscreet* (1958); from *Destination Tokyo* (1944) to *Charade* (1963).

Grant, who these days is involved with assorted business interests, had four marriages (the last to Dyan Cannon) and an equal number of divorces to his credit. New York's Radio City Music Hall has devoted more time to more of his films than to any other actor's. The words "Cary Grant in . . . " have appeared on the theatre's marquee for a total of 15 months over the years. **Some other films:** *Topper* (1937), *Holiday* (1938), *Only Angels Have Wings* (1939), *Suspicion* (1941), *Arsenic and Old Lace* (1944), *The Bishop's Wife* (1947), *I Was a Male War Bride* (1949), *Kiss Them for Me* (1957), *North by Northwest* (1959), *Walk, Don't Run* (1966).

Pearl Bailey offers consolation, if that's what it's called, to Lee Grant after a drinking bout in The Landlord.

LAWRENCE GRANT (1870–1952)

Grant began his stage career in England in *The Money Spinner* and came to the United States in 1908 with a touring company. He made his film debut in *To Hell With the Kaiser* in 1918 and went on to appear in more than 50 films. **Films include:** *Bulldog Drummond* (1929), *Shanghai Express* (1932), *Nana* (1934), *A Tale of Two Cities* (1936), *The Prisoner of Zenda* (1937), *Dr. Jekyll and Mr. Hyde* (1941), *Confidential Agent* (1945).

LEE GRANT (1929–)

A versatile film actress, Grant seems to have an unlimited range. More concerned with the quality of her acting than with maintaining an "image," she has played various character types of many different ages.

At the age of four, Grant was a member of the ballet corps of the New York Metropolitan Opera, and throughout her childhood continued to study both dance and acting. When she was asked to audition for the lead in the Broadway play *Detective Story*, she demurred, preferring instead to play a smaller but more meaningful role. Her creation of a pathetic shoplifter won her a Critics' Award, and she was brought to Hollywood to re-create her role in the 1950 screen version. Her screen debut brought her a nomination for an Academy Award.

Soon after this, Grant was called before the House Un-American Activities Committee and refused to give testimony. She was subsequently blacklisted and did not make another film for 14 years. She returned to Broadway during this period and became an accomplished stage actress. She has since appeared in films and also makes frequent appearances both on the stage and on television. **Some of her films are:** *In the Heat of the Night* (1967), *There Was a Crooked Man* (1969), *The Landlord* (1970), *Plaza Suite* (1971).

BONITA GRANVILLE (1923–)

She was born in New York, her parents both on the stage. Granville always knew she would be an actress. Her first movie was *Westward Passage* in 1932. She got the role because she looked like Ann Harding and she played her daughter. In 1936 she won

Academy Award nomination for her role in *These Three*. For years thereafter she played "meanies and brats," although from 1938 to 1942 she did star in the *Nancy Drew* detective series. **Credits include:** *The Plough and the Stars* (1937), *Love Laughs at Andy Hardy* (1946), *Guilty of Treason* (1949), *The Lone Ranger* (1956).

CHARLES GRAPEWIN (1875–1956)

After 37 years in vaudeville Grapewin retired to live on his investment dividends in California. Then the bottom dropped out of the stock market in 1929 and economic necessity forced the former Broadway and vaudeville comic back into show business. His lined face and western drawl made him a natural for characters called "Pop."

Among his best-known roles were Grampa in *The Grapes of Wrath* (1940) and Jeeter Lester in *Tobacco Road* (1941). Grapewin was featured in more than 100 movies before he retired for a second time in 1952. **Films include:** *Anne of Green Gables* (1934), *Ellery Queen, Master Detective* (1940), *They Died with Their Boots On* (1942), *The Gunfighters* (1947), *When I Grow Old* (1951).

PETER GRAVES (1925–)

Best known for his starring role in the television series *Mission Impossible*, Graves concentrated on motion pictures during his early days in Hollywood. He came West from Minneapolis to join his brother, actor James Arness, in trying to break into show business. Graves had studied theatre arts at the University of Minnesota and had worked as a musician and as a radio announcer before moving to California.

Graves appeared in several pictures, including *Stalag 17* (1953), before finding greater success on television. Most of his featured roles were in Westerns. **Films include:** *Rogue River* (1950), *Fort Defiance* (1952), *Beneath the Twelve-Mile Reef* (1953), *A Rage to Live* (1965).

RALPH GRAVES (1900–)

During his long career in motion pictures, Graves has worked as an actor, director and screen writer. His first appearances as an

Charles Grapewin played the key role of Jeeter Lester in Erskine Caldwell's Tobacco Road *(1941).*

Fernand Gravet breaks up a clinch between Carole Lombard and Ralph Bellamy in Fools for Scandal.

Kathryn Grayson re-enacting the life of another songstress, Grace Moore, in So This Is Love *(1953).*

actor were in two-reel silent comedies. Director D.W. Griffith spotted him in one of them, *Sporting Life* (1918), and signed Graves to his first contract. The actor was later to play the lead in *War Correspondent* (1932) and to write the narrative for *Born to Be Bad* (1934). **Films include:** *Men Who Have Made Love to Me* (1918), *Out of Luck* (1923), *Eternally Yours* (1939), *Alimony* (1949), *Adventures of Batman and Robin* (1967).

FERNAND GRAVET (1904–1970)

Born in Belgium in a theatre where his parents were performing, Gravet was destined to become a performer. His charm, ease and romantic aura made him one of the best known leading men in France in scores of plays and musicals.

Fluent in English, he made his Hollywood debut in *The King and the Chorus Girl* (1937) but he is best remembered as Johann Strauss in *The Great Waltz* (1938) with Luise Rainer.

The veteran of more than 100 films and 60 plays on both continents, he served in the Free French Army during the war. During his distinguished career he also directed, edited and was co-cinematographer for *The Madwoman of Chaillot* (1969). **Some of his films include:** *Fools for Scandal* (1938), *Four Flights to Love* (1942), *La Ronde* (1950).

KATHRYN GRAYSON (1921–   )

Hollywood lured Kathryn Grayson away from her operatic studies and deflected her ambition to star one day at the Metropolitan Opera. She was only a teenager when producer Louis B. Mayer heard her sing in a music festival and offered her an MGM contract.

In order to prepare for her first screen appearance, the studio insisted on months of drama, elocution and music lessons and, to give her some public exposure, arranged appearances on radio programs. Her screen debut finally came in *Andy Hardy's Private Secretary* (1941), one of a series of Mickey Rooney pictures. Grayson got her first starring role the following year in *Seven Sweethearts* (1942) with Van Heflin.

She then was cast in a series of movie musicals which occasionally gave her the opportunity to sing operatic arias but more frequently displayed her delivering songs like "My Heart Sings" and "Love Is Where You Find It."

Grayson was never very happy in these films, but in 1951 was cast in a role she did like, Magnolia in *Show Boat* with Howard Keel. The two singers were teamed again in *Kiss Me Kate* (1953), but by then Hollywood was losing its taste for screen operetta and Grayson's film career was waning. She did make one more picture, *The Vagabond King* (1956), with Mario Lanza before retiring to care for a daughter born during her second marriage to singer Johnny Johnston. She and Johnston had been divorced in 1951. Although she no longer appears in pictures, Grayson has done some musicals on stage and toured for a while in the road production of *Camelot*. **Films include:** *Rio Rita* (1942), *Anchors Aweigh* (1945), *It Happened in Brooklyn* (1947), *Lovely to Look At* (1952), *The Desert Song* (1953).

Richard Greene (center) acknowledges C. Aubrey Smith's toast in Four Men and a Prayer. *The other young men in John Ford's melodrama are, from the left, David Niven, George Sanders and William Henry.*

LORNE GREENE (1915–)

As Ben Cartwright on television's long-running *Bonanza* series, Greene's face has become as familiar to viewers as his voice was to radio audiences in Canada when he was broadcasting the news in the 40's. Greene made his screen debut in *The Silver Chalice* (1954) and played character roles in several films before *Bonanza* came his way. **Films include:** *Autumn Leaves* (1956), *The Gift of Love* (1958), *The Buccaneer* (1959).

RICHARD GREENE (1918–)

Greene was born in England into a theatrical family—his great-grandfather was one of the first to introduce motion pictures to England. Greene joined a repertory company in his teens and later toured with another theatre group in the British Isles. At the age of 19 he had a successful film debut in *French Without Tears* which then led to a Hollywood contract and a long film career. From 1955, he starred in 165 episodes of the British TV series *Robin Hood*. **His numerous films include:** *Four Men and a Prayer* (1938), *The Hound of the Baskervilles* (1939), *Forever Amber* (1947), *Lorna Doone* (1951), *Sword of Sherwood Forest* (1961).

SIDNEY GREENSTREET (1879–1954)

Born in Sandwich, Kent, England, Greenstreet spent a lifetime in the theatre before his film debut. After graduating from high school he went to Ceylon to learn the tea business from a friend of his family. At night when he had nothing to do he read Shakespeare and memorized a great deal of the Bard's writings. When a terrible drought hit Ceylon, the tea business slumped and he went back to England. His great knowledge of Shakespeare made him very popular with amateur theatrical groups and he decided to study acting. In 1904 he arrived in the United States and began an acting career on the stage.

Under the fine direction of John Huston, Greenstreet (in his film debut at age 62) played the infamous Mr. Guttman in *The Maltese Falcon* (1941), and from then on was recognized as one of film's greatest classical villains. After *Falcon*, he and Peter Lorre starred in several other Bogart hits, in such Hollywood gems as *Casablanca* (1942),

Background to Danger (1943), and *Passage to Marseilles* (1944).

Longing to play in a comedy role, he had his chance in *Pillow to Post* (1945), but the film was not a success. Thereafter, he continued to play sinister parts until he announced his retirement in 1952. **Films include:** *Across the Pacific* (1942), *Conflict* (1945), *The Hucksters* (1947), *The Woman in White* (1948), *Malaya* (1949).

CHARLOTTE GREENWOOD (1893–)

Although motion picture audiences remember her best as Aunt Eller in *Oklahoma!* (1956), the role Charlotte Greenwood really made famous was Letty Proudfoot, heroine of a tour de force of the 30's. Greenwood was already well established as a comedienne on Broadway when she introduced the character of Letty to theatre audiences in 1935. The success of her show *So Long Letty* was formidable. Greenwood's tours with the first "Letty" and its successors were some of the longest and most profitable in theatre history.

Those tours were the culmination of years in vaudeville and the theatre. Greenwood made her stage debut in *The White Cat* in New York in 1905, but she didn't turn to comedy until some time later. She did appear in a film as early as 1918, but it wasn't until *Baby Mine* (1928) that she began accepting comic roles in motion pictures. Since then, she has made more than 40 movies. **Films include:** *Up in Mabel's Room* (1944), *Home in Indiana* (1944), *Peggy* (1950).

JOAN GREENWOOD (1921–)

Considered one of England's finest actresses, Greenwood usually wins good notices even when she appears in poor plays or pictures. She was only 17 when she made her London stage debut after studying at the Royal Academy of Dramatic Arts. She was cast as a child early in her career, playing Wendy in a London stage production of *Peter Pan* and juvenile roles in her first films. She made her screen debut in *John Smith Wakes Up* (1940) but didn't get a starring role as an adult until *Latin Quarter* (1946), a Parisian melodrama.

Later, while under contract to J. Arthur

It was filmdom's great loss that Sidney Greenstreet never appeared on the screen until he was 62 years of age.

Charlotte Greenwood, the delightful rubber-limbed comedienne, as she appeared in Moon Over Miami *(1941).*

Jane Greer takes careful aim in The Big Steal, *a better-than-average melodrama.*

Rank, she appeared opposite Alec Guinness in the delightful Ealing comedy *Kind Hearts and Coronets* (1949). Greenwood later created what is considered the definitive characterization of Gwendolyn in *The Importance of Being Earnest* (1952) and not long afterward went to Hollywood for her first American film, *Moonfleet* (1955), in which she played a villainess. She did several other films in the United States and also appeared on television and on Broadway before returning to London.

Greenwood continued to act on both stage and screen until her marriage in 1959 and subsequent motherhood. While she is still active, she has downgraded her career. She played one of Albert Finney's admirers in *Tom Jones* (1963) and did a Walt Disney picture, *The Moonspinners* (1964), with Hayley Mills. Greenwood also appears often on television in England. **Films include:** *The Gentle Sex* (1942), *The October Man* (1947), *Flesh and Blood* (1950), *Stage Struck* (1957), *Mysterious Island* (1962).

JANE GREER (1924–   )

It was in a newsreel that showed her modeling WAC uniforms that Jane Greer first came to the attention of Hollywood. First, Paramount offered a contract, then reneged, and eventually producer Howard Hughes signed Greer to her first film contract. The same newsreel also caught the eye of bandleader Rudy Vallee, who was to become her first husband.

Greer never did make any movies under contract to Hughes. Eventually, she got her release and signed with RKO. Her first roles were bit parts, often in ''B'' movies. The first big-budget picture Greer made was *Sinbad the Sailor* (1947) in which she played Maureen O'Hara's faithful slave girl.

The same year she got her first star billing opposite Robert Young in *They Won't Believe Me* (1947), a film that has become a suspense classic. Greer often was cast as a sharp-tongued woman of the world, a bad girl, or a gangster's moll. She thought the typecasting worked to her disadvantage and obtained a release from her RKO contract.

Just when her career was beginning to pick up in 1947, Greer married attorney Edward

Lasker and began to devote more time to her husband, and later to her three children, than she did to her career. She remained active, however, in such roles as the mother in *Billie* (1965), the Hollywood version of Broadway's *Time Out for Ginger*. **Films include:** *Two O'Clock Courage* (1945), *The Big Steal* (1949), *The Company She Keeps* (1950), *The Prisoner of Zenda* (1952), *Man of a Thousand Faces* (1957), *Where Love Has Gone* (1964).

JAMES GREGORY (1911–   )

He left a business career on Wall Street to begin acting. Gregory made his Broadway debut in *Key Largo* (1939) and since then has become a familiar face on both motion picture and television screens, usually in the role of a policeman or a heavy. He played Captain Vincent Cronin on the television series *21st Precinct*. **Films include:** *The Frogmen* (1951), *The Young Stranger* (1957), *Two Weeks in Another Town* (1962), *A Rage to Live* (1965), *Clambake* (1968).

ROBERT GREIG (1880–1958)

Some actors seem so entirely appropriate for a certain type of role that they are continually cast that way. Although their names are not familiar to most moviegoers, their faces are. Robert Greig was such an actor. The massive, portly butler in many films, Greig played in both serious drama and in lighthearted comedies. **His credits include:** *Animal Crackers* (1930), *Clive of India* (1935), *Sullivan's Travels* (1941), *The Moon and Sixpence* (1942), *Unfaithfully Yours* (1948).

JOYCE GRENFELL (1910–   )

A journalist and poet before becoming an actress, she was also a commercial artist and an artist's model. At a dinner party she was overheard imitating a lecture she had attended and friends convinced her to go on stage. Success on stage as a comedienne led to a film career which began in 1942 with *The Demi-Paradise*. **Her films include:** *Stage Fright* (1950), *The Belles of St. Trinian's* (1954), *Blue Murder at St. Trinian's* (1958), *The Americanization of Emily* (1964).

NAN GREY (1918–   )

She had not yet given any serious thought to a future career when at the age of 12, quite by chance, a friend of the family brought her to the attention of studio executives. At 16 she was offered a minor role and soon found herself playing leads. **Her films include:** *Babbitt* (1934), *Dracula's Daughter* (1936), *The House of Seven Gables* (1940), *Under-Age* (1941).

VIRGINIA GREY (1918–   )

Despite the fact that she has appeared in more than 80 films, Grey has never caught on in a big way with the public or with the Hollywood studios. She started out in films as a child when she was cast as Little Eva in *Uncle Tom's Cabin* (1927). A few more parts in silent films followed until Grey temporarily left the screen to complete her education.

She reappeared in pictures in the early 30's but only as an extra or in very small parts. It wasn't until *Bad Guy* (1937) with Bruce Cabot that she got her first leading part. That break, however, didn't really help her career, and although she got some publicity by dating Clark Gable for a while, MGM continued to give her minor assignments.

After her MGM contract expired in 1942, Grey was on her own and did win a few good roles in pictures like *Sweet Rosie O'Grady* (1943) with Betty Grable, and *Wyoming* (1947). One of her best assignments came in 1957 when she played a has-been actress in *Jeanne Eagels* (1957), starring Kim Novak.

She continued to act both in motion pictures and in television throughout the 50's, and many of her film parts during this period were in producer Ross Hunter's pictures. Grey and Hunter are good friends and he cast her in a variety of minor roles, including the mother of the bratty child passenger in *Airport* (1970). Grey never married. **Films include:** *Jazz Mad* (1928), *The St. Louis Kid* (1934), *Old Hutch* (1936), *The Big Store* (1941), *The Men in Her Diary* (1945), *Jungle Jim* (1949), *The Forty-Niners* (1954), *The Restless Years* (1958), *Flower Drum Song* (1961), *Rosie* (1968).

ETHEL GRIFFIES (1878–   )

A member of the third generation of an

Virginia Grey and Spencer Tracy talk out their problems in Test Pilot *(1938).*

acting family, Griffies made her stage debut when she was two in a play in which her mother was starring. Successful on the English stage and in silent films, she made her American film debut in *Old English* (1930).

In 1965, she received the Whitbread Anglo-American Theatre Award for her role in *Billy Liar*. At the age of 84 she was playing eight performances a week on the stage in *Write Me a Murder*. **Her more than 100 films include:** *Waterloo Bridge* (1931), *Love Me Tonight* (1932), *Anna Karenina* (1935), *Irene* (1940), *The Horn Blows at Midnight* (1945), *The Birds* (1963).

CORINNE GRIFFITH (1898–   )

A one-time convent student, Griffith began her career as a beauty contest winner. Acting in many silent films, she made only one talkie: *Lily Christine* (1932).

Everybody ate heartily in Tom Jones, *but none more ravenously than Hugh Griffith.*

She became famous for her left profile and 500 newspaper critics once voted her "the most beautiful woman on earth." **Among her films:** *Single Wives* (1924), *Syncopating Sue* (1926), *The Divine Lady* (1929).

HUGH GRIFFITH (1912–   )

One of the most versatile Welsh actors, Griffith has played important roles on both stage and screen in England and America. He made his motion picture debut in *Neutral Port* (1940) shortly after winning a Goro Medal at the Royal Academy of Dramatic Arts in London.

He is considered one of the finest Falstaffs ever to appear on the London stage in *Henry IV*. During his 30-year career in the theatre, Griffith has starred in such serious dramatic productions as *Waltz of the Toreadors* and *Look Homeward Angel*.

In motion pictures, he often is cast in menacing roles or as robust characters—he played the ingénue's lusty father in *Tom Jones* (1963). Griffith won an Academy Award for Best Supporting Actor for his performance in *Ben Hur* (1959). **Films include:** *High Treason* (1950), *I'm All Right, Jack* (1959), *Only Two Can Play* (1960), *Exodus* (1960), *The Counterfeit Traitor* (1962), *Term of Trial* (1963), *How to Steal a Million* (1966), *Oliver!* (1968), *Luther* (1974).

RAYMOND GRIFFITH (1896–1957)

Although Griffith came from a theatrical family and had some theatre experience, his career was launched by chance. He was lying on the beach when a man gave him the choice of being a movie extra or leaving. He stayed and earned $5.00. Afterwards the director offered him a job. His first film was *Fools First* in 1922.

Acting in many silent pictures, Griffith retired with the advent of talkies and became a writer and producer. He wrote many comedies for Mack Sennett. **Among his films:** *The Day of Faith* (1923), *Lily of the Dust* (1924), *Hands Up* (1926), *You'd Be Surprised* (1927).

HARRY GUARDINO (1925–   )

He started out in stage musicals but eventually moved to Hollywood to play supporting roles in light comedies. Guardino made his screen debut in *Houseboat* (1958) with Cary Grant and Sophia Loren. He also has appeared frequently on television. **Films include:** *The Pigeon That Took Rome* (1958), *The Five Pennies* (1959), *Pork Chop Hill* (1959), *Hell Is for Heros* (1962), *Rhino* (1965).

PAUL GUILFOYLE (1902–1961)

A character actor who specialized in playing villains, Guilfoyle usually was killed off before the end of the picture. He began acting in New York after completing drama school and made his Broadway debut in 1925 in *The Green Hat* with Katharine Cornell and Leslie Howard. Guilfoyle went to Hollywood in 1935 and was cast in supporting roles in more than 25 motion pictures. In most of them, the character he was playing came to a bad end—he was alternately strangled, shot, drowned, thrown from skyscrapers, buried by

Paul Guilfoyle looks on as George Sanders clarifies matters for Linda Hayes in The Saint in Palm Springs *(1941).*

landslides or run over by autos. Once, James Cagney stuffed him into an auto trunk to get rid of him in *White Heat* (1949). In addition to acting, Guilfoyle also directed more than 150 television features, including segments of *Lawman, Science-Fiction Theater* and *Highway Patrol*. **Films include:** *Special Agent* (1935), *Winterset* (1936), *The Grapes of Wrath* (1940), *Sweetheart of Sigma Chi* (1946), *Torch Song* (1952), *Julius Caesar* (1953), *Valley of Fury* (1955).

SIR ALEC GUINNESS (1914–)

One of the most popular of England's serious actors, Guinness abandoned a successful stage career to concentrate on films. He studied drama in London before joining John Gielgud's acting company and, later, the Old Vic. Among his first leading roles were the lead in a modern-dress production of *Hamlet* and Herbert Pocket in his own adaptation of *Great Expectations*.

Guinness again played the role of Pocket for his film debut in David Lean's 1947 screen version of the Dickens classic and went on to win wide public recognition a few years later with the famous murder-comedy *Kind Hearts and Coronets* (1949) in which he played eight roles.

Guinness' versatility allowed him to swing from comedy roles—the brains behind the *Lavender Hill Mob* (1951)—to drama; he won a Picturegoer Gold Medal in England for his portrayal of Benjamin Disraeli in *The Mudlark* (1950).

Although he continued to act on stage from time to time, much of Guinness' work was in films. His box-office appeal was strong in both Britain and the United States. He received an Academy Award for Best Actor for his portrayal of the British commander in a Japanese prison camp in *The Bridge on the River Kwai* (1957).

A few years later he again received excellent reviews for the role of the dense commanding officer in *Tunes of Glory* (1960). Not long after this success, however, the critics hooted at *A Majority of One* (1961) in which he played a Japanese businessman and Rosalind Russell was cast as a Jewish matron. That disaster took its toll. Afterwards, Guinness was offered only supporting roles in

Alec Guinness as the immovable, inflexible British officer in The Bridge on the River Kwai. *Confronting him is Sessue Hayakawa as the Japanese commander who lost out in the conflict of wills.*

Alec Guinness as a monstrously ugly Fagin in Oliver Twist *(1951). John Howard Davies played Oliver.*

Edmund Gwenn didn't always play Santa Claus. Here, he remonstrates with Lassie in the 1949 production, Challenge to Lassie.

films and at the same time also was having difficulty satisfying the critics with his stage performances. Despite this slump, Guinness continues to act in the theatre and on screen. **Films include:** *Last Holiday* (1950), *The Captain's Paradise* (1952), *The Swan* (1956), *The Scapegoat* (1959), *Our Man in Havana* (1960), *Lawrence of Arabia* (1962), *Dr. Zhivago* (1965), *The Comedians* (1967), *Brother Sun, Sister Moon* (1973).

SACHA GUITRY (1885–1957)

Born in St. Petersburg, Russia, while his actor father was touring there, he was drawn to the theatre very early in life.

He wrote, acted in and directed more than 100 comedies and histories. His film debut was in *Ceux de Chez Nous* (1915). After World War II he was accused by the Resistance of consorting with the Nazis and barred from the stage and screen, though he was later exonerated. **His films include:** *Le Roman d'un Tricheur* (1936), *Ills Etaient Neuf Célibataires* (1939), *Donne-Moi tes Yeux* (1943), *Napoléon* (1955), *La Vie à Deux* (1957).

EDMUND GWENN (1875–1959)

If he's never remembered for anything else, Edmund Gwenn always will be an audience favorite in his most famous film role —the department store Santa Claus in *Miracle on 34th Street* (1947). The part won him an Oscar for Best Supporting Actor, the culmination of 27 years in motion pictures.

Gwenn had a long and distinguished career in the theatre before he ever began to make movies. He was the son of a British civil servant who didn't approve of acting as a profession. When the young Gwenn announced his intention of going on stage, his father disowned him. That was the beginning of 10 long years in provincial repertory theatre in England before Gwenn got the break he needed.

His luck changed when playwright George Bernard Shaw saw him in an obscure play and offered the role as the chauffeur in *Man and Superman* (1905). The two became close friends and Gwenn was to appear in several Shaw plays on the London stage. His performances in *Major Barbara* and *The Devil's Disciple* made him famous. The list of Gwenn's stage credits alone takes up two full pages in *Who's Who in the Theatre*.

In the 40's, however, Gwenn became primarily a motion picture actor. He moved to Hollywood and appeared in more than 30 films between 1942 and 1958. Always a favorite of the critics, Gwenn won special praise for his performance as the amiable counterfeiter in Alfred Hitchcock's *The Trouble With Harry* (1955). **Films include:** *The Skin Game* (1920), *Anthony Adverse* (1936), *Pride and Prejudice* (1940), *Foreign Correspondent* (1940), *Lassie Come Home* (1943), *The Keys of the Kingdom* (1944).

BUDDY HACKETT (1924–)

Best-known as a stand-up comedian in nightclubs, Hackett has also made numerous stage, screen and television appearances. He began his career as an entertainer at the resort hotels of the Catskill Mountains "Borscht Belt." His professional debut, however, was in his native Brooklyn at the Pink Elephant, where for $40 a week he sang, told jokes and did impersonations. Eventually, an appearance at a Los Angeles nightclub gave Hackett his big break and launched his successful career on the big-time cabaret circuit.

Since the 50's, Hackett has also acted on Broadway (notably in *Lunatics and Lovers* in 1954 and in *I Had a Ball*, 1964) and played in films. One of his earliest film roles was that of the lovelorn Georgia rustic, Pluto, in *God's Little Acre* (1958). In 1962 he appeared as Marcellus Washburn in the film version of the hit Broadway musical *The Music Man* and the following year played Benjy Benjamin in *It's a Mad, Mad, Mad, Mad World*. **Credits include:** *Walking My Baby Back Home* (1954), *All Hands on Deck* (1961), *Everything's Ducky* (1961), *The Wonderful World of the Brothers Grimm* (1962), *Muscle Beach Party* (1964).

JOAN HACKETT (1933–)

The pretty, talented Hackett has been cast in a number of character parts on stage, screen and television. Her distinctive voice and staccato gestures add to her fine portrayals. In 1961 she won the Vernon Rice Award for her performance in the stage production *Call Me by My Right Name* and she received high praise for her title role in the television ver-

sion of *Rebecca*. **Films include:** *The Group* (debut, 1966), *Will Penny* (1968), *Support Your Local Sheriff* (1969), *The Last of Sheila* (1973).

GENE HACKMAN (1931–)

This gifted character actor began his career at the off-Broadway theatre The Premise and went on to do a string of plays in New York (among them *Any Wednesday* with Sandy Dennis) before landing his first screen role in *Lilith* (1964).

Hackman's first recognition from the movie industry came with an Academy Award nomination in 1967 for his fine performance as Buck, Warren Beatty's younger brother, in *Bonnie and Clyde*. The acknowledgment was repeated three years later for his characterization of the long-suffering son in *I Never Sang for My Father* (1970). The public, however, never really noticed Hackman in a big way until his starring role as the hard-bitten, foul-mouthed detective Popeye Doyle in *The French Connection* (1971). His performance in the film won Hackman the Academy Award for Best Actor and secured his reputation.

Hackman has appeared frequently on a variety of TV shows, including: *My Father, My Mother, The F.B.I., The Invaders,* and *The Iron Horse*. **Other films:** *Hawaii* (1966), *The Gypsy Moths* (1969), *Prime Cut* (1972), *Scarecrow* (1973), *The Conversation* (1974).

SARA HADEN (1897–1973)

She was introduced to acting by her actress-mother, Charlotte Walter. After playing a number of parts on the New York stage, Haden made her screen debut in *Spitfire* (1934). Her long list of credits include some 300 films or more in which she usually played the part of a secretary or of a spinster. A 1946 *Herald Tribune* article described her as "the actress with the sarcastic tongue and the visage that can be turned into an ice pack at a moment's notice." **Her films include:** *Music in the Air* (1934), *Magnificent Obsession* (1935), *H. M. Pulham, Esq.* (1941), *Our Vines Have Tender Grapes* (1945), *A Lion Is in the Streets* (1953), *Andy Hardy Comes Home* (1958).

Joan Hackett, as she appeared in Rivals *(1972). The attractive actress is beginning to match her fine TV performances in films.*

Gene Hackman as the hard-nosed cop in The French Connection, *an action-packed performance that won him an Academy Award.*

Alan Hale, a versatile actor who was an inventor, opera singer and osteopath on the side.

JEAN HAGEN (1925–)

After extensive radio experience, Hagen (born Jean Verhagen) worked as an usher on Broadway at the Booth Theatre, where the Hecht and MacArthur play *Swan Song* was playing. It was there her stage career began when she was noticed by the authors and cast in a small role to replace an ailing actress.

Hagen made her screen debut in *Side Street* (1949). However, it was her role as the ''other woman'' in *Adam's Rib* (1949) that established her as a comedienne adept at portraying dumb dames. She alternated comic performances with dramatic roles and appeared for three years on the Danny Thomas TV series before retiring. **Films include:** *The Asphalt Jungle* (1950), *Singin' in the Rain* (1952), *The Big Knife* (1955), *Sunrise at Campobello* (1960), *Dead Ringer* (1964).

WILLIAM HAINES (1900–1973)

Haines is best remembered as the brash young show-off in a number of silent films.

He was discovered via an opportunity contest sponsored by a film magazine and dropped a career as a bond salesman on Wall Street to make his first film, *Three Wise Fools* (1922). After the advent of sound, Haines went on to play more smart-aleck roles before retiring in 1935. He later became one of Hollywood's top interior decorators. **Films include:** *True as Steel* (1924), *Lovey Mary* (1926), *Brown of Harvard* (1926), *Tell It to the Marines* (1926), *Show People* (1928), *Navy Blues* (1930), *Just a Gigolo* (1931), *The Marines Are Coming* (1935).

ALAN HALE (1892–1950)

During his long career, the husky character actor appeared in more than 100 films. He gave a memorable performance as Little John with Errol Flynn in the 1938 *Adventures of Robin Hood* and is well remembered as the merchant seaman aiding and abetting Raymond Massey and Bogart in eluding a German sub in *Action in the North Atlantic* (1943). His movie debut had been long before, however, in 1911, in *The Cowboy and the Lady*, and before that (as Rufus Alan McKahan) he had written obituaries for a Philadelphia newspaper, studied to be an osteopath, and tried an operatic career. (At one time he actually sang with the Metropolitan Opera Company in New York.) During the 20's he combined his acting with work as a sub-director under Cecil B. De Mille. Hale was also an inventor of considerable talent and is credited with developing the sliding theatre seat now in use in most first-class movie houses. His son, Alan Hale, Jr., is well known to TV viewers from such series as *Casey Jones*. **Films include:** *Main Street* (1923), *Sailor's Holiday* (1929), *It Happened One Night* (1934), *Stella Dallas* (1937), *This Is the Army* (1943), *My Wild Irish Rose* (1947), *Rogues of Sherwood Forest* (1950).

BARBARA HALE (1922–)

This Illinois-born former model first appeared in motion pictures in *Higher and Higher* (1943). Through the 40's and 50's Hale was often given leading roles, usually in ''B'' Westerns, comedies, adventure or war

Creighton Hale, a silent star whose career carried over into talkies, watches with interest as C. Henry Gordon points at someone who possibly could be a budding starlet. The film: Hollywood Boulevard.

stories. Since 1957, she has appeared on television as secretary Della Street in the *Perry Mason* series, but has continued to make occasional films. **Films include:** *The Falcon Out West* (1944), *The Window* (1949), *Jolson Sings Again* (1949), *Lorna Doone* (1951), *Seminole* (1953), *Airport* (1969).

CREIGHTON HALE (1882–1965)

Hale (born Patrick Fitzgerald) made his stage debut as an infant with his father, a singer and manager of an Irish touring company. He came to the United States as a member of Gertrude Elliot's company. While on tour, he was noticed by Frank Howell, director for Pathé, who gave him a bit part in a film. He had a featured part in his next film, *The Exploits of Elaine* (1915).

He performed as a leading man or second lead in a great many silents and continued to appear, although in fewer movies, after the advent of the talkies. **Films include:** *The Idol Dancer* (1920), *Orphans of the Storm* (1922), *The Marriage Circle* (1924), *Beverly of Graustark* (1926), *Death From a Distance* (1935), *Hollywood Boulevard* (1936), *The Perils of Pauline* (1947).

GEORGIA HALE (c. 1905–   )

She appeared in only five films over a 17-year period, but her performance in each of them was impressive. Hale made her debut in von Sternberg's first film, *The Salvation Hunters* (1925), but it was her performance as the winsome object of Charles Chaplin's affection in *The Gold Rush* (1925) that brought her to brief prominence. **Credits:** *The Rainmaker* (1926), *The Great Gatsby* (1926), *The Last Moment* (1928).

JONATHAN HALE (1892–1966)

From 1938 to 1959 Jonathan Hale (born Jonathan Hatley) appeared in the *Blondie* series as Mr. Dithers, a role that typecast him as the mildly exasperated businessman he frequently played in other films as well. A native of Ontario and a descendant of Nathan Hale, the American Revolutionary hero, character actor Hale had worked as a consular attaché before making his film debut. He was featured in more than 80 films until his apparent suicide in 1966. **Films include:** *Lightning Strikes Twice* (1934), *Bringing Up Baby* (1938), *Tarnished Angel* (1938), *Joe Smith, American* (1942), *The Steel Trap* (1952), *Jaguar* (1958).

LOUISE CLOSSER HALE (1872–1933)

Chicago-born Louise Closser Hale enjoyed professional triumph in several fields. A writer of travel articles for *Harper's* magazine, the actress also authored several travel guides, as well as a play, *Mother's Millions*. An 1898 graduate of the American Academy of Dramatic Arts, Hale made her stage debut in Detroit in *Old Kentucky* (1894) and went on to achieve fame as a character actress on stage and screen. After World War I, Hale was cast most often in "old lady" roles. **Film highlights:** *Daddy Long Legs* (1931), *Rebecca of Sunnybrook Farm* (1932), *Movie Crazy* (1932), *Today We Live* (1933), *No More Orchids* (1933).

JACK HALEY (1899–   )

Although his Gaelic features came through rather metallically in the role, Jack Haley will always be remembered as the Tin Woodsman who so desperately wanted a heart in *The Wizard of Oz* (1939). And once Judy Garland oiled his joints he gave a wonderful performance.

Haley made his stage debut at the age of six, singing in a church social. He later ran off to Broadway and rose from being an apprentice electrician to prominence on the vaudeville circuit during the 20's. He could sing, dance and give excellent comedy performances and through the 30's and 40's played supporting roles in a great many pictures. In 1970 he emerged from retirement to appear in *Norwood*, a film directed by Jack Haley, Jr. **Credits include:** *Follow Thru* (1930), *Sitting Pretty* (1933), *Rebecca of Sunnybrook Farm* (1938), *Alexander's Ragtime Band* (1938), *People Are Funny* (1945), *Vacation in Reno* (1947).

HUNTZ HALL (1920–   )

Movie audiences often thought that the disreputable Dead End Kids really were a bunch

Louise Closser Hale, a past mistress of the maternal role.

Jack Haley in Pick a Star *(1937), a film which also featured Laurel and Hardy.*

Jon Hall and Dorothy Lamour in one of the placid moments of Hurricane. *The storm raged for 20 minutes on screen.*

of New York hoodlums whose comic shenanigans had paved the way to Hollywood. Nothing could be further from the truth. Huntz Hall (born Henry Hall), who played Dippy, the long-faced dumbbell of the group, already had a string of show business credits to his name when the original *Dead End* became a Broadway smash in 1935. Hall's career began when he was five years old and won a role on the radio program, *Madge Tucker's Children's Hour*. He attended the Professional Children's School in New York and made his stage debut at the old Roxy Theatre on Broadway. After their Broadway success, the "Kids" were brought to Hollywood to repeat the roles they created on stage. Ultimately, they made 28 pictures as the Dead End Kids, 48 as the Bowery Boys and 26 as the East Side Kids. He played in several pictures as an adult, including *Gentle Ben* (1967) and *The Chicago Teddy Bear*

(1971), and has also appeared on television and in nightclubs. **Credits include:** *Angels With Dirty Faces* (1938), *They Made Me a Criminal* (1939), *A Walk in the Sun* (1946), *Fighting Fools* (1947), *Blues Busters* (1948), *Private Eyes* (1950), *The Bowery Boys Meet the Monsters* (1954), *Dig That Uranium* (1956).

JAMES HALL (1900–1940)

Hall (born James Brown) ran away from home as a child to play a Hindu beggar boy with a traveling troupe of players. He was more or less forcibly sent home, but reappeared shortly thereafter in front of the footlights. His first film was *The Campus Flirt* (1926). He made several pictures in the next five years, but his film career ended with the beginning of the talkies. **Credits:** *Hotel Imperial* (1927), *The Canary Murder Case* (1929), *Hell's Angels* (1930), *Sporting Chance* (1931).

JON HALL (1913–   )

He used his real name (Charles Hall Locher) for his movie debut in *Women Must Dress* (1935). He was Lloyd Crane for two 1936 features and finally became Jon Hall in *The Hurricane* (1937), playing his first leading role (as Terangi) opposite Dorothy Lamour.

Hall's early years were spent in his mother's home in Tahiti, where he developed an aquatic prowess which stood him in good stead for his film roles. He was married to singer Frances Langford for 17 years. In recent years he has been involved in business and has appeared infrequently on the screen. **Films include:** *South of Pago-Pago* (1940), *Aloma of the South Seas* (1941), *Arabian Nights* (1942), *Lady in the Dark* (1944), *On the Isle of Samoa* (1950), *Forbidden Island* (1959).

PORTER HALL (1883–1963)

A smallish, mustached character actor, Hall played meanies, skinflints, mortgage foreclosers and sneaks in scores of pictures—an interesting climax for a career that began as a worker in a steel mill and a strolling player with a Shakespearean acting troupe.

John Halliday appears to be accusing Sir Guy Standing of cheating at solitaire in The Witching Hour *(1934).*

From comedy roles in a number of Broadway productions of the 20's he was wooed and won by Hollywood, where, for more than 20 years, he almost invariably played heavies. **Films include:** *The Thin Man* (debut, 1934), *Mr. Smith Goes to Washington* (1939), *Double Indemnity* (1944), *Miracle on 34th Street* (1947), *The Half-Breed* (1952), *Return to Treasure Island* (1954).

THURSTON HALL (1883–1958)

Gaslit Boston's theatre district, top hats, and bawdy back alleys first enticed teen aged Hall away from a comfortable, sheltered home toward the stage. The youngster toured with New England troupes and spent three lean years in England. There he formed a stage company which had sporadic success touring in New Zealand and South Africa.

By the time he was 30, Hall had firmly established his career. He made his film debut as Marc Antony in the 1917 version of *Cleopatra* (with Theda Bara). During the following 40 years, he went on to appear in more than 100 films, mainly costume dramas and comedies. He is, perhaps, best remembered for his numerous portrayals of angry executives. In addition to his film work, Hall maintained his theatre career and eventually also appeared on television. **Film highlights:** *Hooray for Love* (1935), *Design for Scandal* (1942), *The Secret Life of Walter Mitty* (1947), *Affair in Reno* (1957).

JOHN HALLIDAY (1880–1947)

American-born, John Halliday was educated in Scotland and earned a degree from Cambridge University, England, before settling in the United States. Thereafter he often played Englishmen on the stage and then on the screen. He created the role of the Honorable Deronius Willoughby in *Stolen Orders* on Broadway and starred in a long list of plays before moving to Hollywood. Among Halliday's early sound films was *Recaptured Love* (1930) with Fredric March and Merle Oberon. **Films include:** *Bird of Paradise* (1932), *Hollywood Boulevard* (1936), *That Certain Age* (1938), *The Philadelphia Story* (1940), *Lydia* (1941).

CHARLES HALTON (1876–1959)

According to family recollections, Halton wanted to act almost as soon as he learned to talk. By the turn of the century he was well known as a polished and versatile stage performer. Much in demand as a character actor, Halton continued in the theatre until his Broadway performance in Sinclair Lewis' *Dodsworth* (1934) brought irresistible film offers. During the following two decades he appeared in scores of films, usually a sour-faced, unyielding professor, bank clerk, or lawyer. He can be recognized as Farnsworth in Raoul Walsh's *They Drive by Night* (1940), as Mr. Barker in Elia Kazan's *A Tree Grows in Brooklyn* (1945) and as one of the dour elders in William Wyler's *Friendly Persuasion* (1956). **Other films include:** *Sing Me a Love Song* (1936), *H. M. Pulham, Esq.* (1941), *Up in Arms* (1944), *When Willie Comes Marching Home* (1950), *Carrie* (1952).

GEORGE HAMILTON (1940–   )

Hamilton was born in Memphis, Tennessee, and began his performing career when he won a high school acting competition. He went to Hollywood at the age of 18 and soon

Versatile Thurston Hall had a long career supporting the stars, from Theda Bara to Danny Kaye.

George Hamilton perspires a bit under the stern gaze of Michael Rennie in The Power *(1968).*

landed a part in *Crime and Punishment U.S.A.* (1959). Despite his dark good looks, Hamilton has played mainly indifferent roles in undistinguished films. He has also appeared on television, notably in a 1969 series *The Survivors*. **Films include:** *All the Fine Young Cannibals* (1960), *Jack of Diamonds* (1967), *The Power* (1968), *Togetherness* (1969).

Margaret Hamilton, the wicked witch who finally melted, thank goodness, frightens Judy Garland in the classic film The Wizard of Oz.

HALE HAMILTON (1880–1942)

A stage actor who played the title role in the play *Get Rich Quick Wallingford* in the original Broadway version, Hale appeared in motion pictures from the early 20's to 1935. **Films include:** *His Children's Children* (1923), *The Great Gatsby* (1926), *The Great Lover* (1931), *Sitting Pretty* (1933).

MARGARET HAMILTON (1902–   )

Since she entered films in the 30's, sharp-featured Margaret Hamilton has portrayed innumerable brittle spinsters, housekeepers, waitresses and maids. She is most famous, however, as the Wicked Witch of the West in *The Wizard of Oz* (1939). The one-time kindergarten teacher gained her first theatre experience in Ohio with the Cleveland Playhouse group, and later went on to work on Broadway. In 1932 she appeared in *Another Language*, and in 1933 recreated her role in the play for the film version. In recent years, Hamilton has combined her movie work with appearances on television and in the theatre. **More than 75 films include:** *The Farmer Takes a Wife* (1935), *My Little Chickadee* (1940), *Guest in the House* (1945), *State of the Union* (1948), *Rosie!* (1968), *Brewster McCloud* (1970), *The Anderson Tapes* (1971).

MURRAY HAMILTON (1925–   )

Hamilton made his screen debut as Pete Hamilton in *Bright Victory* (1951) and has gone on to appear in numerous supporting roles. He played Irvin Blanchared in *No Time for Sergeants* (1958), Sam Crandall in *The F.B.I. Story* (1959), and Mr. Hamilton in *The Graduate* (1967). In addition to his film roles, this general-purpose actor often is cast in TV dramas. **Movie credits include:** *Seconds* (1966), *No Way to Treat a Lady* (1968), *The Boston Strangler* (1968), *If It's Tuesday This Must Be Belgium* (1969).

NEIL HAMILTON (1899–   )

Massachusetts-born Neil Hamilton began in theatre as a prop boy and played with a New York stock company. He was widely pictured in ads of the 20's as "The Arrow Collar Man" and got into films when D. W. Griffith gave him a small part in *The White Rose*

(1923). His successful performance won Hamilton the male lead in Griffith's *America* (1924), and he soon became one of the more popular male stars of the 20's. After the birth of the talkies, Hamilton's career rapidly declined and he was soon relegated to character roles. He still appears occasionally, though, and in the 60's TV audiences enjoyed him in the *Batman* series. **Over 100 films include:** *Isn't Life Wonderful?* (1924), *The Great Gatsby* (1926), *Beau Geste* (1926), *Hot News* (1928), *Tarzan and His Mate* (1934), *Brewster's Millions* (1945), *Batman* (1966).

WALTER HAMPDEN (1879–1955)

Back in the days when every city had one or more theatres with year-round performances, Hampden (Walter Hampden Dougherty) was a national favorite. The role that made him truly famous was that of the big-nosed, duelling, lyrical, but frustrated, lover in Rostand's *Cyrano de Bergerac*—a part he played more than 1000 times in New York alone. (His first Broadway appearance in the role was in 1923.)

Hampden's silent picture debut was in *Warfare of the Flesh* (1917) and he made his first appearance in sound films as the Archbishop in *The Hunchback of Notre Dame* (1940). A good actor (in the somewhat high-blown tradition of the early years of the century), he continued to perform on stage as well as in films, and died while working on a Hollywood lot. **Film credits:** *Reap the Wild Wind* (1942), *All About Eve* (1950), *Five Fingers* (1952), *Sabrina* (1954), *The Vagabond King* (1956).

RUSSELL HARDIE (1904–1973)

Usually seen in tough-guy roles, Hardie had an extensive career on Broadway, on the screen and on television. He began acting in his native Buffalo, but made his professional stage debut in *The Criminal Code* on Broadway in 1929. Hardie first went to Hollywood in 1933 for a film aptly titled *Broadway to Hollywood*. He was a leading man on the stage opposite such actresses as Mae West and Ethel Barrymore. **Films include:** *Stage Mother* (1933), *The Band Plays On* (1934), *Men in White* (1934), *Sequoia* (1935), *Cop Hater* (1958).

ANN HARDING (1902–   )

Texas-born Harding (Dorothy Gatley) "made history" in high school by assuming the role of Macduff when a male classmate came down with the measles. After attending Bryn Mawr College, she joined the Provincetown Players. There she was discovered and offered a Broadway role in *Like a King* (1921). New York critics first acclaimed her, however, two years later in the play *Tarnished*. Harding made her movie debut in *Paris Bound* (1929) and went on to star in a number of films in the 30's. She disappeared from films for a while after making *Love From a Stranger* (1937), but returned in 1942 and went on to appear in a number of supporting roles as "well-bred" women. **Among her many films:** *Holiday* (1930), *The Animal Kingdom* (1932), *Biography of a Bachelor Girl* (1935), *Eyes in the Night* (1942), *The Man in the Gray Flannel Suit* (1956).

OLIVER HARDY (1892–1957)

Before he teamed up with Stan Laurel in 1927, Hardy had appeared in more than 100 films, mostly as an extra or a bit player in silent comedies. It was producer Hal Roach who matched the rotund Hardy with wiry Stan Laurel for a series of two-reelers. After 10 of these shorts did well, Roach decided to star the pair regularly, and Laurel and Hardy made about 12 films a year for him, starting with *Putting Pants on Philip* (1926) about a kilt-clad Scotsman visiting America.

As one of the most popular comedy acts of both silent and sound pictures, Laurel and Hardy usually were featured in short subjects until 1931 when they made their first full-length film, *Pardon Us*. From then on they interspersed the shorts with feature films. One of the shorts, *The Music Box* (1932), won an Academy Award for Short Subjects (Live Action) Comedy.

In the late 30's a rift developed between the two comics and producer Roach. They broke up and patched things up several times during the next few years, and in 1940 severed their

Walter Hampden, one of the best of innumerable Cyrano de Bergeracs (on stage), played a variety of roles on screen.

Lovely Ann Harding, along with Clive Brook, in Gallant Lady *(1934).*

Oliver Hardy conducts an experiment that is certain to work out disastrously.

Sir Cedric Hardwicke, a fine actor, in The Keys of the Kingdom *(1944).*

ties with Roach but continued as a comedy team. Over the next several years they made eight pictures for big Hollywood studios but were unhappy with the creative limits placed upon them. In the late 40's, the team toured music halls in the United States and Europe. The only film they made together during this period was *Atoll K/Robinson Crusoeland* (1951) in France. Hardy did a film, *The Fighting Kentuckian* (1949), with John Wayne. He died following a heart attack in 1957. **Films include:** *Liberty* (1929), *Pack Up Your Troubles* (1932), *Sons of the Desert* (1933), *The Flying Deuces* (1939), *Great Guns* (1941), *Nothing but Trouble* (1944), *The Bullfighters* (1945).

LUMSDEN HARE (1895–1964)

Leaving his native Ireland for a career in the theatre, Hare performed on stage all over the world before making his film debut in *The Avalanche* (1919). Later, he became a Hollywood regular, appearing in over 60 pictures during his 40-year career. **Films include:** *Charlie Chan Carries On* (1931), *Gunga Din* (1939), *Rebecca* (1940), *Young Bess* (1953), *Count Your Blessings* (1959).

KENNETH HARLAN (1895–1967)

Meteoric stardom came to Harlan in 1916 with his first film, *Betsy Burglar*, in which D. W. Griffith cast him as Constance Talmadge's co-star. Fabulously good-looking and dreamily romantic, Harlan remained one of the industry's most notable and popular matinee idols for about 15 years. With the advent of sound films, Harlan made a relaxed adjustment to a variety of supporting roles. After his retirement in the 40's he became a highly respected restaurant owner and theatrical agent. **Highlights of over 100 films:** *The Beautiful and the Damned* (1922), *Twinkletoes* (1926), *Women Men Marry* (1931), *Penrod and Sam* (1937), *Range War* (1939), *Pride of the Bowery* (1941).

SIR CEDRIC HARDWICKE (1893–1964)

In 1934, this fine British stage actor was knighted for his contribution to English dramatic art; the next year he went to Hollywood, and after that most of his dramatic contributions were to American pictures.

Hardwicke studied at the Royal Academy of Dramatic Arts before making his stage debut in 1912 in the London production of *The Monk and the Woman*. The following year he appeared in a short film and was offered (but rejected) a screen contract. World War I interrupted Hardwicke's career, but after service he returned to the stage in Birmingham, England, playing roles in the plays of George Bernard Shaw. His first major London success was *The Barretts of Wimpole Street* (1930). That hit led to a series of film roles, including *Dreyfus* (1931) and *Orders Is Orders* (1933). In 1935 he went to Hollywood to play the role of Marquess of Steyne in *Becky Sharp*, and thereafter made several more films in England and America before making his Broadway debut in *The Green Light*.

Hardwicke made the transition from leading roles to character parts in the early 40's and often was cast as gruff, middle-aged men. His only major departure from supporting roles came with his performance as the Nazi commander in *The Moon Is Down* (1943), the film version of John Steinbeck's novella. Hardwicke returned to the London stage in 1945 and stayed in England to make several pictures, among them *Nicholas Nickleby* (1947). From the 50's, he appeared in films almost exclusively in cameo roles. **Films include:** *The Lady Is Willing* (1934), *Tudor Rose* (1936), *Stanley and Livingstone* (1939), *Forever and a Day* (1943), *Wilson* (1944), *Sentimental Journey* (1946), *The Desert Fox* (1951), *Richard III* (1955), *Around the World in 80 Days* (1956), *The Pumpkin Eater* (1964).

JEAN HARLOW (1911–1937)

Born Harlean Carpentier in Kansas City, Missouri, Harlow had a tragic life, but a magical, if brief, career. The product of a broken home, she lived with her domineering mother until she was 16 when she eloped with an older man. Her mother broke up the marriage and moved Harlow to Los Angeles, where the young blonde began to look for work in films.

After appearing as an extra in a few films, Harlow got her big break when Howard Hughes cast her as Helen in *Hell's Angels* (1930). Her super-sensual quality in the film created a furor and pushed her toward stardom. During the next seven years, Harlow starred in over 20 films. At first, her tough, hard image successfully carried her through films such as *Public Enemy* (1931) opposite Cagney. Later, however, she was "feminized" in comedies opposite such stars as Gable, Grant, and Tracy.

Harlow's second marriage ended tragically when her husband, Paul Bern, committed suicide two months after their wedding in 1932. Her studio hushed up the case and kept her busy turning out some of her best films. In 1937, Harlow became seriously ill while making *Saratoga*, in which she was starring opposite Clark Gable, and on June 7th of the same year died from uremic poisoning at the age of 26. Harlow left a lasting impression on Hollywood—her platinum-blond hair, sexy

Jean Harlow, Sex Symbol #1 of the troubled 30's.

demeanor, and electric screen personality made her one of film's unmatchable love goddesses. **Highlights:** *Moran of the Marines* (debut, 1928), *Platinum Blonde* (1931), *The Beast of the City* (1932), *Red Dust* (1932), *Dinner at Eight* (1933), *Suzy* (1936), *Personal Property* (1937).

JULIE HARRIS (1925–   )

She first began acting in high school plays and at summer camps near her home town of Grosse Pointe, Michigan. To prepare for what was to become a highly successful career in the theatre she studied at the Perry Mansfield Theatre workshop and at the Yale Drama School. Director Harold Clurman saw her in a student production at the Actors Studio in New York and later cast her in *The Member of the Wedding* (1950), based on Carson McCullers' novel.

Harris' touching performance as Frankie, a shy and sensitive teenager, led a year later to the role of Sally Bowles in John van Druten's adaptation of two Christopher Isherwood Berlin stories, *I Am a Camera*.

Wallace Beery, Clark Gable and a tightly sheathed Harlow (she always was) in China Seas *(1935).*

Julie Harris, best known as a Broadway star, with Burl Ives in East of Eden.

She was now firmly established on Broadway, and in the following years she starred in such plays as *The Lark* (1956), *The Country Wife* (1958), *The Warm Peninsula* (1959), *A Shot in the Dark* (1961), *Forty Carats* (1969) and *The Last of Mrs. Lincoln* (1973). Her performances in *Camera, Lark, Forty Carats* and *Mrs. Lincoln* brought her Tony awards.

Her film credits, unfortunately, are few, though she has been seen on television with some frequency. She made her film debut in *The Member of the Wedding* (1952), recreating her stage role of Frankie. **Films include:** *I Am a Camera* (1955), *East of Eden* (1955), *The Truth About Women* (1958), *The Haunting* (1963), *You're a Big Boy Now* (1967), *Reflections in a Golden Eye* (1967).

PHIL HARRIS (1901–   )

Probably better known for his radio, television and nightclub appearances than for his films, Harris usually portrayed what he calls the "brash, illiterate me" on screen. He entered show business as a bandleader, moved on to musical comedy, and in the 30's starred in a series of short feature films for RKO. He played a memorable character-comic role on Jack Benny's radio program for years (in addition to leading the band). Harris is married to movie-musical star Alice Faye. **Films include:** *Melody Cruise* (1933), *The High and the Mighty* (1954), *The Wheeler Dealers* (1963), *The Cool Ones* (1967).

RICHARD HARRIS (1933–   )

This Irishman's biggest problem in films seems to be his clashes with co-stars. He didn't get along with Marlon Brando while making *Mutiny on the Bounty* (1962) and had the same trouble with Kirk Douglas and Charlton Heston on the sets of other pictures. Publicity about these feuds has tended to build his image as a rebel both on screen and off.

After graduating from college Harris studied at the London Academy of Music and Dramatic Arts. He made his theatre debut in 1956 in *The Quare Fellow*, but it wasn't until his success on the London stage in *The Ginger Man* (1959) that theatre audiences took notice of him.

Harris' first movie was the British production *Alive and Kicking* (1958). His first major film part was in *The Wreck of the Mary Deare* (1959) as the villain opposite Charlton Heston and Gary Cooper.

Harris is probably best known for two films he made in the 60's: the Lindsay Anderson film *This Sporting Life* (1963) and the 1967 screen version of the Broadway hit musical *Camelot*, in which he appeared as King Arthur. Harris' reputation as a rebel was strengthened when he walked out on three pictures he had signed for in 1968, including *Flap*, which later was released with Anthony Quinn in the role Harris was to have played.

In addition to his motion picture work, Harris also has appeared on television and in concert. His recording of "MacArthur Park" sold over a million copies. **Films include:**

Richard Harris, a truculent Irishman, as an unhappy seaman in a film with an unhappy history, the remake of Mutiny on the Bounty.

The Guns of Navarone (1961), *Major Dundee* (1965), *Hawaii* (1966), *Caprice* (1967), *Cromwell* (1970), *A Man in the Wilderness* (1971).

REX HARRISON (1908–   )

Harrison was an established and urbane comedy actor on the stage and on screen in both Britain and the United States when his greatest success, the Broadway musical *My Fair Lady,* came his way in 1956. The show made him an international superstar—he did two years as Henry Higgins on Broadway and one year in the London production. On top of that came the film, which won Harrison an Academy Award, the New York Film Critics Award, and the British Film Academy Award.

Harrison had launched his show business career in London on the stage and did bit parts in British pictures until 1937 when he starred opposite Miriam Hopkins in *Men Are Not Gods* (1937). Harrison didn't go to Hollywood until the mid-40's when he accepted the lead opposite Irene Dunne in *Anna and the King of Siam* (1946). Later, he and his second wife, actress Lilli Palmer, were teamed in several plays and movies, including the play *Bell, Book and Candle*. He and Palmer were divorced in 1957, and Harrison married another actress, comedienne Kay Kendall. They starred in *The Reluctant Debutante* (1958). After Kendall's death from leukemia, Harrison married actress Rachel Roberts. They were divorced, and his fifth marriage was to the former wife of actor Richard Harris.

As befits a superstar, Harrison has done several big-budget pictures—he was Julius Caesar in the Elizabeth Taylor–Richard Burton spectacular *Cleopatra* (1963) and starred in *Doctor Doolittle* (1967). **Films include:** *Major Barbara* (1941), *Notorious Gentleman* (1946), *The Four Poster* (1952), *The Yellow Rolls-Royce* (1965), *Staircase* (1969).

DOLORES HART (1939–   )

During her film-making days in the late 50's and 60's pert Dolores Hart (born Dolores Hicks) starred in a string of movies like *Loving You* (1957) opposite Elvis Presley and

Dolores Hart, who gave up a bright career to become a nun.

Where the Boys Are (1961); consequently, Hollywood was stunned when she gave up a promising film career in 1963 to enter a convent. She broke into pictures at the age of 17 after a friend sent her picture to producer Hal Wallis. He was impressed, signed her to a contract and within 18 months she had made her screen debut. Besides her film work Hart also appeared on Broadway, most notably in *The Pleasure of His Company* (1958). **Films include:** *Wild Is the Wind* (1957), *Lonelyhearts* (1959), *Sail a Crooked Ship* (1962), *Come Fly With Me* (1963).

Rex Harrison, a marvelous Professor Higgins, assesses the potential of Eliza Doolittle (Audrey Hepburn) in the fine film version of a great stage musical, My Fair Lady.

Two-gun Bill Hart, probably the most famous cowboy of them all.

WILLIAM S. HART (1870–1946)

Back in the old days, the high spot in a youngster's week was being taken to "Saturday Matinee at the Movies" where, hopefully, a new Bill Hart picture was being shown.

Hart was the first, and one of the most impressive, of all Western stars, and for more than a decade was one of the top box-office drawing cards. Born in Newburgh, New York, and allegedly raised by a Sioux nurse, Hart appeared on stage from the 1890's and made his film debut in *The Fugitive* (1913).

As a matter of record, Hart had one-and-a-half expressions. Mostly, on horseback or off, he stared fixedly at the camera, slit-eyed,

tight-lipped, and rigidly determined. Audiences didn't mind, though, for "the Look" told them that here was a man of honor, champion of the underdog, who would ride or plunge his way through blazing infernos (he often did) to get the evildoer. The half-expression was almost the same, except for the suspicion of a smile which drew up the corners of his mouth: it was almost as menacing as the non-smile look.

Two-gun Hart retired in 1925, several years before the first talkie. Several years later he published his autobiography, *My Life, East and West*. **Many, many films include:** *The Return of Draw Egan* (1915), *Hell's Hinges* (1916), *Wagon Tracks* (1919), *Wild Bill Hickok* (1923), *Tumbleweeds* (1925).

ELIZABETH HARTMAN (1943–)

Blonde, fragile-looking Hartman was nominated for an Academy Award for her first major movie performance in *A Patch of Blue* (1965). That role was followed by one in *The Group* (1966) in which she turned out a sensitive, touching performance in an otherwise banal film. Though Hartman has appeared in relatively few films, her talent is distinctive and marks her as an actress who will be on the scene in years to come. **Highlights:** *You're a Big Boy Now* (1967), *The Fixer* (1968), *Walking Tall* (1973).

PAUL HARTMAN (1904–)

Hartman made his stage debut as a baby in his father's production of *Girofle-Girofla* at the Tivoli Opera House, San Francisco. Determined to make a career in show business, he left college and worked as a dancer, musician and in mime. At the age of 17, he married Gracie Barrett and together they did a dancing act in vaudeville. Hartman went on to appear frequently and successfully on Broadway in such shows as *Red, Hot and Blue* (1937), *Of Thee I Sing* (1952), and *The Pajama Game* (1955). He made his film debut in *Tatjana* (1927), the beginning of his 40-year screen career. In recent years, he has often been seen on television. **Highlights:** *Inherit the Wind* (1960), *The Longest Day* (1962), *How to Succeed in Business Without Really Trying* (1967), *Luv* (1967).

Elizabeth Hartman, looking wholesome as do most stars of today, with Sheriff Joe Don Baker just before they are ambushed in Walking Tall *(1973).*

LAURENCE HARVEY (1928–1973)

Harvey's performance as the scheming, ruthless climber in Jack Clayton's 1958 film based on the John Braine novel *Room at the Top* made the actor a star. During the rest of his career, he remained in the film world's upper echelons despite virulent criticism heaped on his performances by critics around the world.

He was born Lauruska Mischa Skikne in Lithuania, was raised in South Africa, and after war service in Egypt and Italy sought fame and fortune in England. He was playing bit parts by 1948 and leading roles two years later; and almost the nicest word any reviewer used to describe his work was "inadequate." After a stint in Hollywood, he returned to play the lead role in the British 1954 version of *Romeo and Juliet*.

More lead roles in British-made films followed: *I Am a Camera* with Julie Harris (1955) and *The Truth About Women* (1958). After *Room at the Top*, Hollywood snapped him up and two money-making films, *The Alamo* (1960) with John Wayne and *Butterfield 8* (1960) with Elizabeth Taylor, were sandwiched between a number of disasters. Typical critical comment after *Summer and Smoke* (1961): ". . . he adds another still life to his growing gallery."

In the years that preceded his death late in 1973, he made a number of films for Italian, German-Roumanian and Israeli-French-German production units plus an as yet unreleased Orson Welles film, made in Yugoslavia with Jeanne Moreau. **Other films include:** *Walk on the Wild Side* (1962), *Darling* (1965), *A Dandy in Aspic* (1968), *The Flight Into the Sun* (1972).

LILIAN HARVEY (1907–1968)

As British subjects during World War I in Germany, Harvey and the rest of her family (English mother, German father) were forced to remain in that country, where she attended school. Later, after she became naturalized as a German citizen, Harvey appeared in ballets, revues and musicals.

She was discovered by Robert Eichberg at a revue rehearsal during which she tripped and fell onto a drum in the orchestra pit. Through his help she began her film career,

Laurence Harvey gives a distraught Jane Fonda the Laurence Harvey look in Walk on the Wild Side *(1962).*

making her debut in *Die Kleine von Brummel* (1925). In 1933 she came to the United States and made her first American film, *My Weakness*. She retired in 1939. **Films include:** *Congress Dances* (1935), *Capriccio* (1938), *Serenade Eternelle* (1939).

PAUL HARVEY (1884–1955)

A character actor whose motion picture career spanned 40 years and hundreds of films, Harvey usually was cast as the kindly father or the choleric executive. He started acting in the legitimate theatre on the West Coast in such plays as *Dishonored Lady* and *The Spider* and performed in silent pictures before transferring successfully to talkies. Later in his career, he played such roles as the clergyman who performed the ceremony at Elizabeth Taylor's wedding in *Father of the Bride* (1950). Harvey was a founder of the Screen Actors Guild and remained an active member until his death in 1955. **Films include:** *Handy Andy* (1934), *They Shall Have Music* (1939), *The Late George Apley* (1947), *Three for the Show* (1955).

Signe Hasso, highly dejected, in a scene from Johnny Angel *(1945).*

SIGNE HASSO (1915–)

Hasso got a big publicity build-up when Hollywood imported her from her native Stockholm in 1940. Before that she was a leading lady of the Swedish theatre and had toured Europe in roles from Shakespeare, Molière, Ibsen, Schiller and O'Neill.

Hasso (born Signe Eleonora Cecilia Larson) made her stage debut at the age of 12 in Stockholm and later studied drama on a scholarship to Sweden's Royal Academy. Her first films were made in Sweden, England and Austria. After her arrival in Hollywood, no appropriate screenplay could be found for her American debut, so Hasso went to New York to act on Broadway before appearing as Anya in *Journey for Margaret* (1942) and being offered her first starring role in *Assignment in Brittany* (1943). Later, she played the Dutch nurse Bettina in Cecil B. De Mille's *The Story of Dr. Wassell* (1944). It was De Mille's first Technicolor feature and Hasso, with her red hair and green eyes, was a hit.

Her first love, however, was the theatre, and after filming several pictures in the 40's, she concentrated upon her stage career. She also has appeared frequently on television.

Raymond Hatton in one of scores of comedy roles, in a career that stretched over half a century.

Films include: *The Seventh Cross* (1944), *The House on 92nd Street* (1945), *To the Ends of the Earth* (1948), *A Double Life* (1948), *Crisis* (1950).

HURD HATFIELD (1918–)

A native New Yorker, Hatfield was a student at Columbia University when he won a British drama scholarship and made his professional stage debut in London. Returning to New York, he appeared on Broadway before going to Hollywood to make his first film as Lao San in *Dragon Seed* (1944). The following year, he leaped to prominence in the title role in *The Picture of Dorian Gray*. After making a series of films in the late 40's Hatfield returned to the stage. He has, however, continued to make occasional film appearances. **Credits include:** *The Diary of a Chambermaid* (1946), *Joan of Arc* (1948), *King of Kings* (1961), *Mickey One* (1965), *The Boston Strangler* (1968).

RAYMOND HATTON (1892–1971)

Hatton's first role was the lead in the annual play of the Red Oak (Iowa) one-room schoolhouse. The ten-year-old was captivated by acting and several years later he ran away from home to work in the theatre. He eventually joined a road company and after a number of years settled into a well-established vaudeville repertory group. In 1912 he auditioned for, and was given, a role in Hollywood's first feature film, *The Squaw Man*. One of the most active and versatile movie actors of all time, Hatton brought amusing and lively characterizations to comedies, melodramas, Westerns and all other film genres which drew his interest. **Highlights:** *Male and Female* (1919), *The Affairs of Anatol* (1921), *The Hunchback of Notre Dame* (1923), *We're in the Navy Now* (1926), *Tall in the Saddle* (1944), *In Cold Blood* (1967).

In the pages that follow a few of the many actors and actresses who helped to make screen history are pictured in color. The editors only wish that quality color photographs of the stars of an earlier day existed or that we had come upon better color shots of Cagney, Garbo, Chaplin or other screen immortals at the height of their careers.

Katharine Hepburn

Elizabeth Taylor

226   *Paul Newman*

227

An unusual portrait of Humphrey Bogart

Vivien Leigh as Scarlett O' Hara

228   *John Wayne*

Bette Davis as Queen Elizabeth

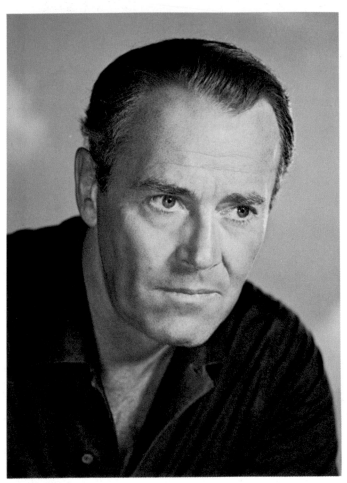

Henry Fonda

Claudette Colbert

Ingrid Bergman

Barbra Streisand in Hello, Dolly!

Liza Minnelli

Richard Burton

Joanne Woodward

Sir Laurence Olivier

George C. Scott

237

238

Marilyn Monroe

Gary Cooper

Marlene Dietrich

Cary Grant

JUNE HAVER (1926–   )

June Haver first appeared on stage at the age of six. At seven she made her debut as a piano soloist with the Cincinnati Symphony Orchestra, at nine she sang on radio, and at the age of 13 she performed as a singer with Dick Jurgens' band. She was spotted in a high school play which led to a 20th Century–Fox contract and her film debut as Maybelle in *The Gang's All Here* (1943).

Her second film, *Home in Indiana* (1944), made Haver a star. She began appearing in musicals, following in the footsteps of reigning star Betty Grable. In 1953 she abandoned Hollywood and her movie career to become a nun. She was unable to complete the probationary period, however, and returned to the West Coast, and in 1955 she married Fred MacMurray. Since then, she has appeared in only a very few TV programs. **Some of her films include:** *The Dolly Sisters* (1945), *I Wonder Who's Kissing Her Now* (1947), *Look for the Silver Lining* (1949), *The Daughter of Rosie O'Grady* (1950), *The Girl Next Door* (1953).

PHYLLIS HAVER (1899–1960)

Hollywood abounds in tales of mothers imposing dreams of film glory on their offspring. Haver, however, was probably the industry's only actress whose grandmother was the controlling force. That indomitable woman brought Haver to Hollywood as a young child and found her some parts in child and juvenile scenes over the next few years. Haver finally entered films as a performer when she was 16—as a Mack Sennett bathing beauty, baring all that was then legally permissable for $12 a week. By 1920, however, Haver was a Mack Sennett comedy star, reigning for almost a decade until her marriage and retirement in 1929. **Highlights:** *A Small Town Idol* (1921), *Up in Mabel's Room* (1926), *The Way of All Flesh* (1927), *Chicago* (1927), *Tenth Avenue* (1928), *Thunder* (1929).

JUNE HAVOC (1916–   )

Her sister, Gypsy Rose Lee, was so famous that Havoc often is thought of only as a minor character in *Gypsy*, the musical biography of the more flamboyant member of the family.

June Haver appeared with William Lundigan in I'll Get By *(1950).*

In fact, Havoc has had a successful stage and screen career of her own and also has won recognition for her autobiography *Early Havoc*, the story of her childhood in vaudeville.

Havoc made her show business debut at the age of two billed as "Baby June" in an act staged by her mother. She was three years old when she made her screen debut, but she wasn't recognized as an actress until much later.

Although Havoc is better known for her work on stage, since 1942 she has appeared in more than 30 films. She was the bigoted secretary in *Gentleman's Agreement* (1947) and the slapstick burlesque performer in *When My Baby Smiles at Me* (1948). She also has

June Havoc submits to a chaste kiss from Jack Oakie in the somewhat less than earth-shaking Hello, Frisco, Hello *(1943).*

Jack Hawkins as he appeared in The League of Gentlemen *(1961).*

Goldie Hawn—the dumb blonde who turned out to be anything but —in Butterflies Are Free.

done television drama and has won Broadway's Donaldson Award for her performance as Montana in Mike Todd's production of *Mexican Hayride* (1944). **Films include:** *The Iron Curtain* (1948), *The Story of Molly X* (1949), *A Lady Possessed* (1951).

JACK HAWKINS (1910–1973)

A stage actor who first scorned films but then decided he preferred them to the theatre, Hawkins was one of Britain's leading box office attractions. He began his acting career on the London stage in *St. Joan* (1924) and later toured with Dame Sybil Thorndike. He came to the United States in 1929 for his Broadway debut in *Journey's End*.

Director Alfred Hitchcock gave Hawkins his first screen role in *The Lodger* (1931). At first Hawkins didn't take films seriously and continued to emphasize his work on the stage. From 1931 until the end of World War II, he appeared in 50 different plays in London and during that period also made 15 motion pictures. After the war, Hawkins began appearing more frequently in films, often playing a solid, reliable British military officer or a thoughtful police inspector. His performance as the interrogator in *The Prisoner* (1955), a film with Alec Guinness about Communist brainwashing in the Balkans, was described as brilliant by the critics.

Hawkins didn't get to Hollywood until 1957 when he went there to promote *The Bridge on the River Kwai*. In 1966, Hawkins' life and career were threatened by cancer of the larnyx. He was operated on and returned to acting—but his speaking voice was impaired and had to be dubbed. Despite the handicap Hawkins remained active in films until his death in 1973. **Films include:** *The Fallen Idol* (1948), *The Cruel Sea* (1953), *Lawrence of Arabia* (1962), *Nicholas and Alexandra* (1971), *Young Winston* (1972).

GOLDIE HAWN (1945–)

When *Laugh-In*, Rowan and Martin's frenzied and maniacal carnival, made its TV debut in 1968 it hit the top of the popularity lists in a very few weeks. It took little longer for the public to decide that this kooky, giggly, highly amusing "dumb" blonde was one of the show's leading assets.

Goldie Hawn was born in Washington, D.C., and made her stage debut with the Virginia Stage Company at the age of 16 as Shakespeare's Juliet. After several years in college, Hawn danced in chorus lines from Puerto Rico to California. Her film debut was a bit part in Disney's unfortunate *The One and Only, Genuine, Original Family Band* (1967). After *Laugh-In* she was given the role of the somewhat oddball little girl in love with Walter Matthau in *Cactus Flower* (1969). Her stunning performance won her the Oscar for Best Supporting Actress, and Director Mike Frankovich, who had spotted her in the first place, moved her up to starring roles. The first of these, played opposite Peter Sellers, was in the warmly satisfying *There's a Girl in My Soup* (1970). **Other films to date:** *$* (1971) with Warren Beatty, *Butterflies Are Free* (1972), *The Sugarland Express* (1974).

SESSUE HAYAKAWA (1890–1973)

This handsome Japanese actor's American career on stage and screen stretched over more than 60 years. Film fans of today will remember him best as the seemingly brutal, but inwardly confused, Japanese prison camp commandant in *The Bridge on the River Kwai* (1957) who is gradually turned suicidal by Alec Guinness' insistence on playing the war strictly by the book.

Hayakawa was a leading man in American silents as early as 1914, playing hero roles at a time when Orientals were almost invariably cast as yellow perils. Good looks and refined mannerisms (he studied at the University of Chicago) equipped him admirably for almost any sort of role. With the advent of talking pictures he switched to character parts and proved an asset to virtually every film in which he appeared. **Films include:** *Typhoon* (1914), *The Tong Man* (1919), *Tokyo Joe* (1949), *The Geisha Boy* (1958), *Hell to Eternity* (1960).

STERLING HAYDEN (1917–)

Born John Hamilton in Montclair, New Jersey, and educated in schools in Massachusetts, Hayden had early turned to the sea. In 1937 he cruised around the world as mate, and was later a captain, until his tall, handsome looks attracted Hollywood scouts.

Sessue Hayakawa, a screen hero of silents, played evil Orientals later in his career. Here he is in Three Came Home.

He made his film debut in *Virginia* (1941) and that same year he played in *Bahama Passage*, displaying to advantage his great physique and sailing knowledge and mostly appearing stripped to the waist in faded dungarees. He also married his leading lady in that film, Madeleine Carroll, though the marriage was short-lived.

Hayden has played a variety of adventurers, cowboys, and strongmen—admittedly for money and not for art, since he prizes his freedom to pursue his own life style and convictions away from the camera. His performance as the more than a little mad American general in *Dr. Strangelove* (1964) brought him high praise from audiences and critics alike. Hayden's non-ghosted autobiography, which pulled no punches in describing the Hollywood scene and is notable for its thoughtful and intelligent writing, was a notable publishing success. His off-screen life has also had its excitement, and Hayden made headlines when he sailed out of the Golden Gate on his 98-foot schooner, *The Wanderer*, with his four children aboard—Tahiti-bound in defiance of a court order granting his ex-wife custody of their children. He has also lived for a time on a Seine river barge in Paris. **Film highlights:** *The Asphalt Jungle* (1950), *The Star* (1953), *Prince Valiant* (1954), *Johnny Guitar* (1954), *The Long Goodbye* (1973).

RICHARD HAYDN (1905–   )

He became famous as the aged, bespectacled Professor Edwin Carp, a character he created early in his career in revues in London. Haydn started in show business as a dancer and appeared in revues in both London and New York before finally accepting a film offer to do *Charley's Aunt* (1941) in Hollywood. **Films include:** *Miss Tatlock's Millions* (1948), *Please Don't Eat the Daisies* (1960), *The Sound of Music* (1965), *The Adventures of Bullwhip Griffin* (1967).

More than three decades after his screen debut Sterling Hayden is still playing lead roles. This one (with Elliott Gould) was in The Long Goodbye.

GEORGE "GABBY" HAYES
(1885–1969)

Born in Wellsville, New York, Hayes was in love with the theatre from his early childhood and appeared in amateur theatricals from the age of eight. In 1902, he ran away from home and high school to join a touring stock company, and later he became a burlesque and vaudeville performer. In the late 20's he arrived in Hollywood, where he got his first film role in *The Rainbow Man* (1929). He was very popular in Westerns, playing Windy in the *Hopalong Cassidy* series and appearing in the Roy Rogers' series of musical Westerns. His gravelly voice, battered hat, and bushy beard were his trademarks. In the early 50's he moved to television and his own evening program, *The Gabby Hayes Show*. **More than 150 films include:** *Riders of Destiny* (1934), *Young*

The voice behind Gabby Hayes's whiskers offered sage advice in countless Westerns.

Buffalo Bill (1940), *Tucson Raiders* (1944), *Albuquerque* (1948), *Caribou Trail* (1950), *Pals of the Golden West* (1951).

HELEN HAYES (1900–   )

Most titles dreamed up by theatrical press agents—"The World's Most Beautiful Body," "The Greatest Lover," etc.—are silly and often untrue. The title given to Helen Hayes, however—"First Lady of the American Theatre"—comes close to the truth.

Born in Washington, D. C. (Helen R. Brown), Hayes was acting by the time she was five and made her Broadway debut at the age of nine in *Old Dutch*. After the opening night of Barrie's *Dear Brutus* (1918) she became the brightest female star in the Broadway firmament, and through the decades that followed her stage career was studded with successes, ranging from *What Every Woman Knows* (1926) to *Victoria Regina* (1935), from *Coquette* (1927) to a part with James Stewart in *Harvey* (1970).

While she appeared in a Vitagraph two-reeler as early as 1910, she consistently took a dim view toward films. In 1928, however, she married screen-writer Charles MacArthur and became pregnant while appearing in *Coquette* and left the play. During the litigation that followed she had what the newspapers referred to as the Act of God baby. Since MacArthur's job was in Hollywood she reluctantly gave up the stage and followed him to the Coast. When MacArthur saw her first film script entitled *Lullabye* he said: "My God, this thing would sink Garbo." But the script was reworked (even though she hated it) and titled *The Sin of Madelon Claudet* (1931). It was a big success and won her the Academy Award for Best Actress of the year. This was followed by two beauties, *Arrowsmith* (1931), playing the wife of Ronald Colman, Sinclair Lewis' idealistic doctor, and as Catherine playing opposite Gary Cooper in the first film version of *A Farewell to Arms* (1932).

Following MacArthur's death in 1956 (and even before) she continued to alternate between stage and screen and, as recently as 1970, she received the Best Supporting Actress Oscar for her role in *Airport*. She has also been active in television, winning an

Helen Hayes consoles Lewis Stone (or was it vice versa?) in The Sin of Madelon Claudet, *a tearjerker that won Hayes an Academy Award.*

Emmy for best actress as far back as 1952. To use a cliché, Helen Hayes is a legend in her own time and, commenting on the slightly dotty-old-lady parts she now plays, she said: "They're loving me more than they ever loved me 20 years ago when I was much better . . ." **Films include:** *Night Flight* (1933), *Another Language* (1933), *My Son John* (1952), *Anastasia* (1956), *Third Man on the Mountain* (1959), *The Further Adventures of the Love Bug* (1973).

LOUIS HAYWARD (1909–)

Born in Johannesburg, South Africa, Hayward went to London at the age of 12. He was educated there with the understanding that he would enter his uncle's shipping business. After a few months in the office, however, Hayward ran away and got a part in a show. He toured, organized his own stock company and also appeared on the London stage. He performed in a few British films before coming to New York in 1935 to appear on stage with the Lunts in *Point Violence*. (His performance won Hayward the New York Critics Award.) He made his U.S. screen debut in *Self-Made Lady* (1932) and went on to make a variety of adventures and romances. Later in his career, Hayward turned to character parts. He has appeared often on television in such programs as *Climax*, *Studio One*, and the *Schlitz Playhouse*. **Films include:** *A Feather in the Hat* (1935), *The Son of Monte Cristo* (1940), *And Then There Were None* (1945), *Fortunes of Captain Blood* (1950), *Duffy of San Quentin* (1945), *The Phynx* (1969).

SUSAN HAYWARD (1919–)

Brooklyn-born Hayward (Edythe Marrener) was one of the virtual unknowns David O. Selznick screen-tested for the role of Scarlett O'Hara. Hayward didn't get the part, but she did land a long-term contract with Warner Brothers. She played in a string of "B" movies before attracting attention as the spoiled beauty in *Adam Had Four Sons* (1941). But even that well-received performance didn't do much for her career.

It wasn't until the critics applauded her in *The Hairy Ape* (1944) with William Bendix that Hayward began getting leads. The films

Louis Hayward gaily prepares to run someone through in The Son of Monte Cristo.

themselves, however, were mediocre, and it took a co-starring role with Gregory Peck in *David and Bathsheba* (1951) and her portrayal of singer Jane Froman in *With a Song in My Heart* (1952) to secure Hayward's place as one of Hollywood's top female stars.

In many of her films she played the tough woman, à la Bette Davis, Joan Crawford and Barbara Stanwyck. Her greatest triumph was as murderess Barbara Graham in *I Want to Live!* (1958), a performance that won her an Oscar and the New York Film Critics Award. Another Hayward landmark was *I'll Cry Tomorrow* (1956), the story of singer Lillian Roth.

She has made a lot of action pictures but did try comedy with James Mason in *The Marriage-Go-Round* (1961) and starred with Bette Davis in *Where Love Has Gone* (1964), the film of the Harold Robbins best-seller.

The coat doesn't come close to fitting, but that is not the reason Susan Hayward looks sulkily at Fred MacMurray and Paulette Goddard in The Forest Rangers *(1942).*

Rita Hayworth, the pin-up queen who deserted films to marry (briefly) an Oriental potentate.

Hayward made her debut on stage in 1968 in the Las Vegas production of the musical comedy *Mame*. **Films include:** *Reap the Wild Wind* (1942), *Smash-Up, the Story of a Woman* (1947), *I Can Get It for You Wholesale* (1951), *Untamed* (1955), *Soldier of Fortune* (1955), *Stolen Hours* (1963), *Valley of the Dolls* (1967), *The Revengers* (1972).

RITA HAYWORTH (1918–   )

If it hadn't been for the late Prince Aly Khan, Rita Hayworth's reign as Hollywood's "Love Goddess" might have lasted a lot longer than it did. Her 1949 elopement to Europe with the Moslem potentate was the turning point in a career that had seen her rise from minor parts in pictures like *Criminals of the Air* (1937) to star stature in *Strawberry Blonde* (1941) and *Affectionately Yours* (1941). Hayworth's allure during her heyday was as the sex symbol epitomized in *Gilda* (1946) when she appeared wearing a clinging black satin dress and elbow-length gloves to sing "Put the Blame on Mame."

Hayworth got her start in show business as a dancer, appearing as her father's partner in nightclubs and resorts, and going by the name of Rita Casino (she had been born Margarita Carmen Cansino). That experience stood her in good stead for a string of musicals she was to do in the 40's. One of them, *Cover Girl* (1944) with Gene Kelly, broke the conventions of backstage musicals and was a box-office smash. Hayworth's personal life (five husbands, including Orson Welles) bolstered her image as a glamour queen, but her career never recovered momentum after she returned to Hollywood when her two-year marriage to Aly Khan had ended. She was able to recapture her old zing only in *Pal Joey* (1957) and, for the most part, has been cast in a series of mediocre pictures since then. **Films include:** *Only Angels Have Wings* (1939), *You'll Never Get Rich* (1941), *Salome* (1953), *Miss Sadie Thompson* (1953), *Fire Down Below* (1957), *Separate Tables* (1958), *The Poppy Is Also a Flower* (1967).

EILEEN HECKART (1919–   )

Heckart has made a place for herself in all three major entertainment media—stage, screen and television. Born in Columbus, Ohio, she graduated from Ohio State University and a short time later began to study at the American Theatre Wing. She made her stage debut with a Broadway walk-on in Thornton Wilder's Pulitzer Prize play *Our Town* (1942). She went on to a bigger and better Broadway role in *The Voice of the Turtle* (1944) and over the years won praise for her performances in such outstanding plays as *Picnic* (1953), *A View From the Bridge* (1956), *Barefoot in the Park* (1965) and *Butterflies Are Free* (1969). In 1958, she won the New York Drama Critics Award for *The Dark at the Top of the Stairs*.

Heckart turned to Hollywood in 1956 with

Miracle in the Rain and thereafter made several films, winning an Academy Award nomination in 1956 for her role in *The Bad Seed*. She has often appeared on television, winning several awards, including an Emmy for *Save Me a Place at Forest Lawn* (1967). **Credits:** *Bus Stop* (1956), *Heller in Pink Tights* (1960), *Up the Down Staircase* (1967), *No Way to Treat a Lady* (1968).

VAN HEFLIN (1910–1971)

He always played either the heavy or the solid citizen who hardly ever got the girl, but he did establish himself as one of the screen's most respected performers.

The Yale Drama School and the Broadway stage were Oklahoma-born Heflin's route to Hollywood. He got his first screen part in 1936 after Katharine Hepburn saw him in a Broadway play and asked RKO to sign him for *A Woman Rebels*. He starred with Hepburn again, this time on the stage, in the original Broadway version of *The Philadelphia Story* (1939). Heflin's screen career got a boost in 1942 when he won an Academy Award for Best Supporting Actor for his portrayal of the alcoholic, Shakespeare-quoting conscience of Robert Taylor in *Johnny Eager*. After a stint as a combat cameraman in the Air Force during World War II, Heflin resumed his acting career and continued to earn praise for a variety of performances —particularly as Brandon de Wilde's homesteader father in *Shane* (1953), as Colonel Huxley in *Battle Cry* (1955), and in *They Came to Cordura* (1959). Heflin also returned to Broadway from time to time, most notably in 1955 as Eddie, the self-destructive longshoreman in *A View From the Bridge*, and in 1964 as attorney Louis Nizer in *A Case of Libel*. He was nominated for an Emmy in 1967 for recreating the Nizer role in a TV production of the play.

Heflin died in July, 1971, following a heart attack, in Hollywood. **Films include:** *Outcasts of Poker Flat* (1937), *The Strange Love of Martha Ivers* (1946), *A Woman's World* (1954), *Patterns* (1956), *Stagecoach* (1966), *Airport* (1970).

O.P. HEGGIE (1879–1936)

The Australian-born character actor began a long career in 1900 when he appeared on stage in *A Message From Mars*. His first appearances in talking pictures were good ones—*The Letter* (1929) and a year later in the popular film version of Rudolf Friml's operetta *The Vagabond King*. **Other credits:** *One Romantic Night* (1930), *Smilin' Through* (1932), *The Count of Monte Cristo* (1934), *The Prisoner of Shark Island* (1936).

BRIGITTE HELM (1907–)

A well-known German actress of the 20's and 30's, Helm (Gisele Eve Schiltenhelm) had a film career that spanned over 40 years. She made her movie debut as a robot in a film classic, Fritz Lang's futuristic fantasy *Metropolis* (1926). During the following few years, she firmly established her screen reputation in her native land. In the 30's, however, she was banned from the German screen by the Nazis because she had married a Jew. As a result, she went to Paris, where she continued her screen work. **Films include:** *The Loves of Jeanne Ney* (1927), *The Blue Danube* (1932), *L'Argent* (1968).

ROBERT HELPMANN (1909–)

A native Australian, Helpmann had an extensive dual career as an actor and ballet dancer, probably best exemplified by his contribution to *The Red Shoes* (1948), for which he choreographed and danced the famous "red shoes" ballet.

A premier danseur, Helpmann made his London debut with the Sadler's Wells Ballet in 1931 and danced most of the great classic ballet roles. As an actor he made his debut in 1937 as Oberon in the Old Vic production of *A Midsummer Night's Dream* and has since continued to act, choreograph and direct both plays and operas. **Films include:** *One of Our Aircraft Is Missing* (debut, 1942), *Henry V* (1946), *Tales of Hoffmann* (1950), *55 Days at Peking* (1963), *The Quiller Memorandum* (1966), *Chitty Chitty Bang Bang* (1968).

DAVID HEMMINGS (1941–)

Born in Guildford, England, Hemmings began his performing career in opera at the age of nine. He later turned to films, making his debut in 1956. For the next ten years Hemmings appeared in a string of mainly "B" pictures. Then, in 1966, his starring role

Eileen Heckart in Butterflies Are Free *(1972), a good film and a fine performance.*

If Van Heflin looks unhappy it's because a lady is hanging from the ceiling in the next room. From Black Widow *(1954).*

Tyrone Power puts the finger on a resplendently gowned Wanda Hendrix in Prince of Foxes.

David Hemmings and a rear view of Vanessa Redgrave in Blow-Up.

in the then controversial, ecstatically reviewed *Blow-Up* catapulted Hemmings to stardom. His portrayal of the amoral, insular photographer in Antonioni's first English-language picture brought the actor wide popularity and critical praise. It also resulted in offers from such directors as Richardson, Vadim and Logan. **Films include:** *No Trees in the Street* (1959), *The Wind of Change* (1960), *Dateline Diamonds* (1965), *Camelot* (1967), *Barbarella* (1967), *The Charge of the Light Brigade* (1968), *Alfred the Great* (1969).

WANDA HENDRIX (1928–   )

Hendrix got her first stage experience as a child actress with the Little Theatre in Jacksonville, Florida. Word of her acting ability soon reached a movie talent scout and Hendrix was brought to Hollywood at 15. She made her screen debut in *Confidential Agent* (1945), and two years later established her status as a leading lady with *Ride the Pink Horse*. Since then, Hendrix has made over 20 films, mainly "B" pictures in which she had the leading role. **Some of her features are:** *Miss Tatlock's Millions* (1948), *Prince of Foxes* (1949), *Boy Who Caught a Crook* (1961), *Stage to Thunder Rock* (1964).

SONJA HENIE (1913–1969)

Attractive, blonde Oslo-born Henie skated her way to stardom, first as the World Figure Skating Champion, then as an Olympic Gold Medal winner, and finally as the leading lady in a string of winter resort films of the late 30's and early 40's.

She decided to convince Hollywood that she ought to be in pictures by renting a rink in Los Angeles and giving producers a first hand demonstration of the style that had made her the darling of the skating world. Her gamble paid off. Producer Darryl Zanuck caught her ice show and signed her to appear in *One in a Million* (1936) with Adolphe Menjou and Don Ameche. It was a hit, and was quickly followed by more of the same—light romances set in snowy surroundings so that Henie could skate a lot. The box-office appeal of her films began to dim in the early 40's and after a few disappointing releases Hollywood gave up on Henie. She, however, continued to pack in the audiences at skating shows. Her annual appearances at Madison Square Garden were sell-outs until 1952, when a dispute between Henie and the management put an end to the shows. Henie retired not long after that. She died of leukemia in 1969. **Films include:** *Happy Landing* (1938), *Second Fiddle* (1939), *Sun Valley Serenade* (1941), *Iceland* (1942), *Wintertime* (1943), *It's a Pleasure* (1945), *Countess of Monte Cristo* (1948), *London Calling* (1968).

PAUL HENREID (1908–   )

Austrian Henreid began his working career in publishing, and his contact with theatre people led to his interest in acting. He studied dramatics at night and started appearing in amateur productions; it was in one such production that he was discovered by Otto Preminger. Subsequent stage successes in Vienna and London led him to Broadway and films.

Henreid's film career began in England, where he lived from 1935 to 1941. Under the name Paul Von Henreid, he gave notable performances in several British films, including *Goodbye, Mr. Chips* (1939), *Night Train to Munich* (1940), and *Under Your Hat* (1940). In 1941, Henreid moved to Hollywood. He made his first American film, *Joan of Paris*, in 1942, and within the same year assured himself a place in Hollywood legend with two roles: Jerry (J.D.) Durrance in *Now, Voyager* and Ingrid Bergman's husband, Victor Laszlo, in *Casablanca*. Since then Henreid has appeared in over 20 films and directed several movies. **Credits include:** *In Our Time* (1944), *Of Human Bondage* (1946), *Operation Crossbow* (1965), *The Madwoman of Chaillot* (1968).

AUDREY HEPBURN (1929–)

Hepburn's trademarks are her fashion-model slimness, her enormous brown eyes and a unique lilt in her voice—traits that have contributed to her enduring image as a ladylike but impish heroine. Belgian-born Hepburn (Edda Hepburn van Heemstra) began her career in England, where she was educated and studied ballet. She landed small roles in several British films, including *The Lavender Hill Mob* (1951). Then a chance encounter with Colette while on location in Monte Carlo won her the lead in *Gigi*, the smash-hit Broadway version of the Colette novel. The role was a bonanza for Hepburn—it catapulated her to stardom and led to her American film debut as Princess Anne in William Wyler's *Roman Holiday* (1953), for which she won an Oscar, the New York Film Critics Award, and the British Film Academy Award.

Hepburn returned to Broadway in 1954 to do *Ondine* where she met and married her co-star, Mel Ferrer. During the late 50's and 60's, she starred in a variety of memorable films, most notably *The Nun's Story* (1959), for which she won a New York Film Critics Award and the British Film Academy's Best Actress Award. Hepburn was chosen over

Julie Andrews to star in the movie version of *My Fair Lady* (1964), one of the industry's biggest box-office successes. She was lauded again for her performance with Albert Finney in *Two for the Road* (1967). Since 1968, however, she has restricted her career to films shot in Italy and Switzerland so she can remain near her second husband, a psychiatrist in Rome. **Films include:** *Sabrina* (1954), *Funny Face* (1957), *Green Mansions* (1959), *Breakfast at Tiffany's* (1961), *The Children's Hour* (1962), *Charade* (1963), *Wait Until Dark* (1967).

KATHARINE HEPBURN (1909–)

It's hard to believe, but 42 years have passed since she made her triumphant debut in films as John Barrymore's daughter in *A Bill of Divorcement* (1932). Since those dimly remembered Depression days Hepburn has never been anything but a star—one of the biggest and most deserving of them all, the only actress ever to receive three Academy Awards plus an unprecedented succession of other acting awards.

Paul Henreid lights his and Bette Davis' cigarettes in Now, Voyager, *a little trick that was much imitated thereafter.*

Audrey Hepburn, who always managed to look cute and chic, with William Holden in the film version of Sabrina.

Young Katharine Hepburn, very beautiful, in Mary of Scotland.

Tracy and Hepburn were both journalists, but a conflict of interests almost wrecked the marriage. The film was Woman of the Year *(1942).*

Stagestruck since childhood, she made her first stage appearance in *The Czarina* (1928) soon after graduation from Bryn Mawr College. By 1932 she was a veteran of Broadway and, as an Amazon Queen, the hit of *The Warrior's Husband*. Once she arrived in Hollywood (she demanded and received a big starting salary from RKO) the 23-year-old product of Hartford, Connecticut, proceeded to raise hell with producers, directors and Hollywood society in general. As the town's *enfant terrible* she went out of her way to be abusive, insulting and generally anti-social. Perhaps because she was such a superb actress, Hollywood swallowed hard—and bore with her.

She received her first Oscar as the young actress in *Morning Glory* (1933) and her fine portrayal of Jo in *Little Women* earned her the Cannes Festival Award in the same year. After her triumph in *Holiday* (1938) with Cary Grant she tried to persuade David O. Selznick to cast her as Scarlett O'Hara in *Gone With the Wind*. Selznick's moment of revenge had come. "I just can't imagine Clark Gable chasing you for ten years," he murmured. She left Hollywood for New York—and a brilliant performance which she later duplicated on film in *The Philadelphia Story* (1939 and 1940).

Hepburn seemed to get better as she got older. One of her top performances, which won her the fifth of eight Oscar nominations, was with her close friend Humphrey Bogart in *The African Queen* (1951). Bogie, who adored her, said, "She talks at you as though you were a microphone." He also said, "I don't think she tries to be a character. I think she is one."

When Spencer Tracy, the love of her life, became ill she semi-retired from films in a desperate effort to nurse him back to health. After his death she received another Academy Award for her role in *Guess Who's Coming to Dinner* (1967), the last film she and Tracy made together. Her third award came for *The Lion in Winter* in 1968 and the year after she starred in the lush Broadway musical *Coco*. Only Hepburn's vitality kept it from being a total disaster. Hepburn was married but once, briefly, and has always guarded her privacy zealously. As becomes the daughter of a mother who was once a leader in suffragette causes, she is, truly, the emancipated woman—in each and every sense of the word. **Films include:** *Alice Adams* (1935), *Mary of Scotland* (1936), *Bringing Up Baby* (1938), *State of the Union* (1948), *The Rainmaker* (1956), *Suddenly Last Summer* (1959), *A Delicate Balance* (1973).

HOLMES HERBERT (1882–1956)

Herbert (born Edward Sanger) started acting on the British stage but came to Hollywood in 1917 to work in motion pictures. After making a number of silents, Herbert went on to appear in scores of sound films. He usually was featured in roles as the soft-spoken English butler, lawyer or clerk. **Films include:** *Gentlemen Prefer Blondes* (1928), *Dr. Jekyll and Mr. Hyde* (1932), *Mark of the Vampire* (1935), *Lloyds of London* (1937), *David and Bathsheba* (1951), *The Brigand* (1952).

HUGH HERBERT (1887–1951)

His trademark was a nervous and frightened "woo woo," which he used to great comic effect in scores of films since his debut in *Caught in the Fog* (1928).

Born in Binghamton, New York, and educated at Cornell University, he began his theatrical career in vaudeville, writing his own routines. He first went to Hollywood as a script writer but remained to appear in more than 125 pictures. **Films include:** *Wonder Bar* (1934), *The Black Cat* (1941), *Hellzapoppin* (1941), *A Song Is Born* (1948).

EILEEN HERLIE (1919–)

Predominantly a stage actress, Herlie scored her first major screen success as Queen Gertrude in Sir Laurence Olivier's production of *Hamlet* (1948). A native of Glasgow, she worked as an understudy in the London theatre and acted with the Liverpool Old Vic before becoming a stage star in England with *The Eagle Has Two Heads* (1946). Herlie appeared on Broadway in *The Matchmaker* (1956), the play upon which the musical *Hello, Dolly!* is based. **Films include:** *Hungry Hill* (debut, 1947), *Gilbert and Sullivan* (1953), *Freud* (1962), *The Seagull* (1968).

JUANO HERNANDEZ (1900–1970)

His powerful presence was first felt on the screen as Lucas Beauchamp in Faulkner's *Intruder in the Dust*, made in 1949 by Clarence Brown. Hernandez was born in Puerto Rico and made his professional debut as an acrobat in Rio de Janeiro in 1922. After trying the boxing ring for a time, he returned to the stage as a singer and was a circus performer, vaudevillian, and translator of MGM films into Spanish before establishing himself as a serious actor. **Films include:** *The Breaking Point* (1950), *Young Man With a Horn* (1950), *The Pawnbroker* (1965).

JEAN HERSHOLT (1886–1956)

Best remembered now as the beloved Dr. Christian in both the popular radio and screen series, Hersholt was also one of the "elder statesmen" of the film community. In a career that embraced silent films, strong dramatic roles in early talkies, and a variety of

No, the patrolman is not thumbing a ride as he removes Hugh Herbert from a Joan Blondell who doesn't want to see him go. The film was Miss Pacific Fleet *(1935), a title one tries to forget but can't.*

Jean Hersholt as the redoubtable Dr. Christian in They Meet Again *(1941). The others are little Anne Bennett, Barton Yarborough and Dorothy Lovett.*

Charlton Heston didn't spare the horses in winning the famous chariot race in the imperishable nineteenth-century story Ben Hur.

led to the creation of the character of the kind and benevolent physician, Dr. Christian, in a series of films that began in 1937 with Hersholt in the title role. **Credits include:** *Greed* (1923), *Stella Dallas* (1925), *Susan Lennox—Her Fall and Rise* (1931), *Grand Hotel* (1932), *Seventh Heaven* (1937), *Run for Cover* (1955).

IRENE HERVEY (1916–   )

A popular leading lady in the 30's and 40's, Hervey first appeared on the screen opposite Franchot Tone in *The Stranger's Return* (1933). Although she never achieved star status, Hervey was much in demand for light films in the 40's. She retired in 1947 to travel with her husband, singer Allan Jones, but returned to the screen after their divorce for roles in such films as *Teenage Rebel* (1956) and *Cactus Flower* (1969). Hervey also has appeared on Broadway, and during the 60's, she played a role in a daytime soap opera in Los Angeles. She is the mother of singer Jack Jones. **Films include:** *East Side of Heaven* (1939), *Destry Rides Again* (1939), *He's My Guy* (1943), *Mr. Peabody and the Mermaid* (1948).

CHARLTON HESTON (1923–   )

The star of some of Hollywood's more flamboyant spectaculars, Heston is best known for his roles in Biblical epics like *The Ten Commandments* (1956) and *Ben Hur* (1959). He got his big break when Cecil B. De Mille spotted him walking across the Paramount lot and tapped him to play the circus manager in *The Greatest Show on Earth* (1952), one of the biggest box-office hits of the 50's. Before that, Heston's acting career had been largely confined to the stage. The Illinois-born actor studied speech at Northwestern University and, after service in the Air Force, had appeared in regional theatre productions with his wife, Lydia Clark. He wound up in New York as a member of Katharine Cornell's company and began appearing on Broadway, notably in a production of *Antony and Cleopatra*. Producer Hal Wallis saw him and brought him to Hollywood for *Dark City* (1950) in which Heston played a crooked gambler. Later he played Andrew Jackson in *The President's*

sympathetic character parts in the 30's and 40's, Hersholt was also a founder of the Motion Picture Relief Fund. For his tireless efforts in behalf of the Fund, he received two special Academy Awards, and the Academy also established the annual Jean Hersholt Humanitarian Award in his honor.

Hersholt made his film debut in his native Denmark in 1906 in *On Walby's Hill* —Denmark's first film effort. In 1914, he came to the United States with a touring company and settled in Los Angeles, where he appeared in silents with such stars as Mary Pickford. With the coming of sound, his foreign accent decreased his popularity for a time and he moved into mature roles, one of these being that of Dr. Defoe, the country doctor who delivered the Dionne quintuplets (in *The Country Doctor*, 1936). This, in turn,

Lady (1953) and was in a number of action films before De Mille tapped him again for the plum role of Moses in *The Ten Commandments*. Heston then seemed almost automatically to be cast in other big budget spectaculars such as *El Cid* (1961) and *Khartoum* (1966) in addition to *Ben Hur*. In real life, Heston often dresses in a tuxedo, however, for he was president of the Screen Actors Guild and has served as an active spokesman for the industry. **Films include:** *The Naked Jungle* (1954), *Touch of Evil* (1958), *The Big Country* (1958), *The Agony and the Ecstasy* (1965), *Planet of the Apes* (1968), *Julius Caesar* (1970), *Skyjacked* (1972).

LOUIS JEAN HEYDT (1905–1960)

He was a City Hall reporter on the old New York *World* in the late 20's when he accidentally landed his first Broadway part. Heydt was waiting in the wings of a New York theatre for a friend when he was asked to read the part of a newsman in the play being rehearsed. He was hired on the spot but didn't take it seriously until the next day when a frantic call from the theatre summoned him to rehearsal. Heydt was hooked and went on to appear in a string of Broadway plays, including *Happy Birthday* opposite Helen Hayes in 1946.

His first notable film was *Test Pilot* (1938) with Spencer Tracy and Clark Gable. After that, he was much in demand for character parts, often playing the role of a man with something to hide. Heydt later appeared frequently on television. He was back in the theatre trying out a new play in Boston when he collapsed and died after a performance in 1960. **Films include:** *Make Way for Tomorrow* (1937), *Each Dawn I Die* (1939), *Dive Bomber* (1941), *The Furies* (1950), *The Wings of Eagles* (1957).

DARRYL HICKMAN (1931–   )

His mother was the movie fan—she named him after Darryl Zanuck—but it was his father who was responsible for young Hickman's film career. In order to sell an insurance policy to Ethel Meglen, Director of the Children's Theater School in Los Angeles, Hickman promised to enroll his son as one of her pupils. Darryl began acting professionally when he was seven and played in some 200 movies as a child star.

His first part was in *The Star Maker* (1939) with Bing Crosby, and he was so popular a child property that at one point he worked on three films simultaneously, *The Human Comedy, Assignment in Brittany,* and *Keeper of the Flame,* all of which were released in 1943.

Hickman's acting career began to slip as he grew up and eventually was eclipsed by that of his younger brother, Dwayne. After graduating from Loyola University and completing his military service, Hickman turned to writing—scripting for such TV shows as *Dick Van Dyke* and *Hawaiian Eye*. Eventually, he joined the daytime network programming staff at CBS. **Films include:** *The Grapes of Wrath* (1940), *Kiss and Tell* (1945), *Prisoner of War* (1954), *Tea and Sympathy* (1956).

DWAYNE HICKMAN (1934–   )

He first followed his older brother, Darryl, into films as a child actor in the 40's, but eventually became better known on television. Hickman, the younger, was featured in juvenile roles in films like *Captain Eddy* (1945) and *The Return of Rusty* (1946). It wasn't until he appeared on television in *The Bob Cummings Show* and starred in *The Many Loves of Dobie Gillis* that he became widely recognized by audiences. On the screen, Hickman often played the eager but slightly brash boyfriend of the ingénue. **Films include:** *The Sun Comes Up* (1949), *Rally 'Round the Flag, Boys* (1959), *Beach Party* (1964), *Cat Ballou* (1965).

RUSSELL HICKS (1895–1957)

Russell Hicks was a director of silents and a bit player in silent classics like *Birth of a Nation* (1915) and *Intolerance* (1916) before his first speaking role in *Happiness Ahead* (1934). He had a long career in character roles on stage, screen and television and played the presiding member of the naval court in *The Caine Mutiny Court Martial* (1954). **Films include:** *The Case of the Howling Dog* (1934), *The Bandit of Sherwood Forest* (1946), *The Big Hangover* (1950).

Wendy Hiller as the crusading Salvation Army lass was a delight in Major Barbara.

Pat Hingle, a highly believable tough guy, in Hang 'Em High.

WENDY HILLER (1912–)

Considered one of England's best stage actresses, Hiller has also acted on the screen since 1937. She scored an instant success in her first appearance on the London stage in *Love on the Dole* (1935) and toured with it in the English provinces and later to New York for the Broadway version. She also married the play's author, Reginald Dow. The following year, Hiller's theatrical reputation was enhanced further when she appeared at the English Malvern Festival in two George Bernard Shaw plays: *Pygmalion* and *Major Barbara*. Once Gabriel Pascal had cleared the way to securing movie rights to the Shaw properties, Hiller was the natural choice of everyone concerned to play the same roles on screen. Her Eliza Doolittle in the film *Pygmalion* (1938) was opposite Leslie Howard, and her co-star in *Major Barbara* (1940) was Rex Harrison. Both pictures were enormously successful on both sides of the Atlantic.

Since then, Hiller has made pictures in both England and the United States. Her first trip to Hollywood was to make *Something of Value* in 1957—and she was quoted as saying, "I was enchanted to go there, and delighted to get away." She added that her daughters thought she had finally truly "arrived" because her co-star was Rock Hudson. She won an Oscar for Best Supporting Actress in *Separate Tables* (1958), playing the innkeeper of the British seaside hotel who sees her lover leave her for another woman. In recent years she has appeared frequently on television. **Films include:** *I Know Where I'm Going* (1947), *An Outcast of the Islands* (1952), *Sons and Lovers* (1960), *Toys in the Attic* (1963), *A Man for All Seasons* (1966), *David Copperfield* (1969).

SAMUEL S. HINDS (1875–1948)

Economic necessity forced Hinds into acting. He had been a successful lawyer, a drama enthusiast and a founder of the famed Pasadena Playhouse before he was wiped out financially in the stock market crash of 1929. He took a $20 job as a bit player in *If I Had a Million* (1932) and launched a new career, usually playing kindly fathers or crooked lawyers. Hinds acted in more than 150 features before his death in 1948. **Films include:** *Little Women* (1933), *She* (1935), *You Can't Take It With You* (1938), *Destry Rides Again* (1939), *The Spoilers* (1942), *The Boy With Green Hair* (1948).

PAT HINGLE (1924–)

His name is not nearly as familiar as his face. Hingle usually plays the heavy—he was Warren Beatty's insensitive, domineering father in *Splendor in the Grass* (1961). A gifted actor, he has had a distinguished career on stage in such plays as *Cat on a Hot Tin Roof* (1955) and *The Dark at the Top of the Stairs* (1960).

After serving in the Navy during World War II, Hingle joined the drama society at the University of Texas because "that's where the prettiest gals could be found." He met his future wife there, played in 25 productions and decided upon acting as a career.

Hingle went to New York in 1949 to study at the Actors Studio. He made his professional stage debut in *End As a Man* (1953) and was tapped by Hollywood for *On the Waterfront* (1954). His career was interrupted in 1959 when he was critically injured in an accident in New York. After his recovery, Hingle continued acting, alternating between screen and stage. **Films include:** *The Strange One* (1957), *The Ugly American* (1963), *Nevada Smith* (1966), *Hang 'Em High* (1968).

ROSE HOBART (1906–)

A Broadway actress who began making movies when she recreated her stage role in *Liliom* in the 1930 screen version of the play, Hobart (Rose Keefer) went on to make more than 35 pictures, first as a leading lady, then as a character actress. **Films include:** *Dr. Jekyll and Mr. Hyde* (1932), *Ziegfeld Girl* (1941), *Nothing but the Truth* (1941), *Song of the Open Road* (1944), *The Farmer's Daughter* (1947).

HALLIWELL HOBBES (1877–1962)

He played the butler in so many movies that he once was asked to start a school for butlers. Hobbes typified the dignified Englishman and was much in demand as an actor in both England and the United States. He acted on the stage in London with such immortals as Mrs. Patrick Campbell and Ellen Terry. Hobbes' American debut was on Broadway in *The Swan* (1923). His first film was *Jealousy* (1929), and he commuted between England and the United States for stage and screen roles until his retirement in 1956. **Films include:** *Charley's Aunt* (1930), *You Can't Take It With You* (1938), *Mr. Skeffington* (1944), *Miracle in the Rain* (1956).

VALERIE HOBSON (1917–   )

After a brief fling with Hollywood in the 30's, the British-born Hobson returned to London to establish herself as a film star of the first rank in England. She had been offered a Hollywood contract after finding early success on the London stage, but the American experience was disappointing—a string of unimpressive movies like *The Werewolf of London* (1935).

Back in England, Hobson landed plum parts in *No Escape* (1937) and *Jump for Glory* (1937). She married producer Anthony Havelock-Allen and, capping a string of solid parts, played Estella in a highly praised version of *Great Expectations* (1946) produced by her husband. She went on to elegant comedy in *Kind Hearts and Coronets* (1949) and later back to the stage in 1953, playing the Gertrude Lawrence role in the British production of *The King and I*. After that, Hobson announced her retirement. She was divorced from Havelock-Allen in 1952 and then married John Profumo, the cabinet minister who was to be the central figure in the celebrated Christine Keeler sex scandal in 1963. Hobson and Profumo are still married. **Films include:** *Drums* (1938), *Contraband* (1940), *The Rocking Horse Winner* (1949), *Background* (1953).

JOHN HODIAK (1914–1955)

Hodiak's acting career began when he turned down an offer to play minor-league baseball and took an unsalaried radio job in Detroit to gain dramatic experience. His first big break came in 1939 in Chicago when he successfully auditioned for the part of L'il Abner in the radio series.

Hodiak was still on radio, working in such series as *The Story of Mary Marlin* and *Ma Perkins*, when a talent scout heard him and arranged an MGM screen test. During the World War II years in Hollywood, Hodiak starred in pictures like *Lifeboat* (1944), Alfred Hitchcock's wartime allegory, and *Marriage Is a Private Affair* (1944) with Lana Turner. Those were the years when many of Hollywood's leading men were in the armed services, and Hodiak—refused by the military because of his hypertension—was in demand. After the war, however, the better scripts began to go to the big stars again, and Hodiak's career suffered. Instead of leads, he was offered supporting roles.

He was married for seven years to actress Anne Baxter, whom he met when they co-starred in *Sunday Dinner for a Soldier* (1945). Hodiak also acted on Broadway and received excellent notices for his portrayal of Lt. Maryk in *The Caine Mutiny Court Martial*. He died of a heart attack in 1955. **Films include:** *A Bell for Adano* (1945), *The Harvey Girls* (1946), *Battleground* (1949), *Across the Wide Missouri* (1951), *Trial* (1955).

DUSTIN HOFFMAN (1937–   )

It isn't widely known that *The Graduate* (1967), the film which brought Hoffman star status, was not his first picture. Hoffman had been trying to break into show business for years before Director Mike Nichols spotted him in an off-Broadway production and cast him as the bewildered young man Anne Bancroft seduces. Not long before he got that break, Hoffman had played a bumbling G-man in an Italian-Spanish cheapie made in Rome. Its English title was *Madigan's Millions* and it was released in the United States in 1968 (after Hoffman became famous).

A native of Los Angeles, Hoffman enrolled at the Pasedena Playhouse before going east to try his luck in New York. He did some television, worked in the Community Theater in Fargo, North Dakota, and almost gave up performing to teach acting when some good off-Broadway roles started coming his way. In 1967, his performance as a middle-aged Russian in *Journey of the Fifth Horse* won him an Obie award as the best off-Broadway actor.

Hoffman has avoided the leading-man

John Hodiak as a morose corporal in Somewhere in the Night *(1946) stares into the same night from the window of a third-rate Broadway hotel.*

Dustin Hoffman, very much on the Indians' side in Little Big Man.

Dustin Hoffman again, this time toting a bag for Stephania Sandrelli in Paramount's recently filmed Alfredo Alfredo *(1973).*

William Holden sports a black eye in the first film to break Hollywood's puritanical code, The Moon Is Blue *(1953).*

both in her native London and on the Broadway stage under the name of Gaby Fay. Holden arrived in Hollywood in 1934 and with a new name became a noted character actress and screen mother of the 30's and 40's. Later on she appeared on television and came out of film retirement in 1958 to appear for the last time as Mrs. Hardy in *Andy Hardy Comes Home*. **Films include:** *Sweethearts* (1938), *Bittersweet* (1940), *Canyon Passage* (1946), *Samson and Delilah* (1949).

WILLIAM HOLDEN (1918–   )

A star for 30 years, Holden (William Beedle, Jr.) was a nice guy on screen and off —capable, unpretentious, workmanlike—in the tradition of Cooper, Gable and Stewart, but with fewer good scripts.

The Illinois-born actor began his film career after his family moved west and he attended Pasadena Junior College. A talent scout spotted him in the part of an 80-year-old, and Holden wound up with a Paramount contract and a two-word part in *Million Dollar Legs* (1939). That same year, however, Columbia made a deal with Paramount for his services and starred him in *Golden Boy*, Clifford Odets' not totally believable play about a youngster torn between two professions he was very good at—boxing and violin playing. For years thereafter (with a break for army service), Holden played what he called "smiling Jim" parts in a long string of so-so comedies and adventure films. Then he played the unsuccessful screen writer in *Sunset Boulevard* (1950) and his career swung into high gear. Three years later his performance as Sefton in *Stalag 17* brought Holden the Oscar for Best Actor, and from 1954 through 1958 he was one of the industry's ten favorites (in 1956 he was number one). His two biggest successes during these years were as the anti-hero in Joshua Logan's *Picnic* (1956) and as Shears in David Lean's *The Bridge on the River Kwai* (1957). His percentage of the gross income of the latter has already mounted close to the three-million-dollar mark.

Holden's last notable performance was as Pike, the leader of the outlaw gang in *The Wild Bunch* (1969). Known to his intimates

syndrome. And despite his youth, he has taken on character roles like the grotesque outcast Ratso Rizzo in *Midnight Cowboy* (1969), the Indian fighter in *Little Big Man* (1971) and Steve McQueen's sidekick in *Papillon* (1973). He is married to Anne Byrne, a dancer. **Films include:** *John and Mary* (1969), *Straw Dogs* (1972), *Alfredo, Alfredo* (1973), *The Rabbi Slept Late* (1974).

FAY HOLDEN (1895–1973)

Fay Holden (Fay Hammerton) is most often remembered by film audiences as Mickey Rooney's mother in the popular ten-year, 15-film Andy Hardy series, which was launched with *A Family Affair* (1937). Her early acting career, however, began in the theatre, and she had an extensive stage career as Golden Holden, he has been living in Switzerland these last few years, keeping an eye on investments on three continents. **His films include:** *Our Town* (1940), *Dear Ruth* (1947), *Born Yesterday* (1950), *The Country Girl* (1954), *The Horse Soldiers* (1959), *Paris When It Sizzles* (1964), *The Revengers* (1972).

JUDY HOLLIDAY (1922–1965)

Judy Holliday (born Judith Tuvim) almost didn't get to recreate her wonderful performance as Billie Dawn in the movie version of her Broadway hit *Born Yesterday* (1950). Columbia originally had Rita Hayworth in mind for the part, and it took the combined persuasive powers of Katharine Hepburn, Spencer Tracy and Ruth Gordon to convince the studio to sign Holliday for the Garson Kanin play. Their confidence was more than justified, for she won an Oscar against the likes of Bette Davis, nominated for *All About Eve*, and Gloria Swanson for *Sunset Boulevard*. Subsequently, Holliday was cast in a variety of movie comedies, almost all of which were successful at the box office. She also starred again on Broadway in a musical written for her by old friends Betty Comden and Adolph Green, *The Bells Are Ringing*, and did the screen adaptation as well (1960).

Holliday was a gifted comic actress, described by actor Jack Lemmon as "intelligent, and not at all like the dumb blonde she so often depicted." She died of throat cancer in 1965. **Films include:** *Adam's Rib* (1949), *The Marrying Kind* (1952), *It Should Happen to You* (1954), *The Solid Gold Cadillac* (1956).

STANLEY HOLLOWAY (1890–   )

After 60-odd years of acting, Holloway became a film immortal (at the age of 74) when he played Eliza Doolittle's begrimed and buoyant father in *My Fair Lady*, one of the biggest box-office successes of all time. He had previously played the gentleman who insisted on getting to the church on time for three years on the New York and London stages in the Lerner/Loewe musical based on George Bernard Shaw's *Pygmalion*.

A long-time British favorite as a

Judy Holliday, a fine comedienne with a voice that combined Brooklynese and baby talk, shown back to back with Dean Martin in Bells Are Ringing.

monologist and a music hall and stage performer, Holloway made his British screen debut in *The Rotter* (1921) and during the next half century appeared in more than 100 films, many of them classics of the screen. He generally played comic characters or sturdy, stubborn bulldog types. **Highlights:** *Brief Encounter* (1946), *This Happy Breed* (1947), *The Lavender Hill Mob* (1951), *The Beggar's Opera* (1953), *Ten Little Indians* (1966).

STERLING HOLLOWAY (1905–   )

He wanted to be a dramatic actor, but his high-pitched, cracking voice and his rather glum face made him a natural comic, cast in dozens of 30's film comedies, and later as a distinctive off-screen voice for characters in such Disney films as *Dumbo* and *Bambi*.

A big hit in the Rodgers and Hart revue *Garrick Gaieties* (1925), he came to Hollywood in the late 20's, making his debut in *Casey at the Bat* (1927). He was filming *Cheers for Miss Bishop* (1941) when his name was picked out of a goldfish bowl and

Sterling Holloway, an easygoing comic and the voice of many of the funniest Disney animals.

Celeste Holm, one of Broadway's favorites and a fine character actress, in Carnival in Costa Rica *(1947).*

That fine character actor, Oscar Homolka, appears here to be using an early primitive listening device.

he became the first actor to be drafted into Army service in World War II. As fate would have it, he was seriously injured when kicked by a horse and promptly discharged. During his almost 50-year acting career, he has made more than 40 movies. **Films include:** *Gold Diggers of 1933* (1933), *Alice in Wonderland* (1933), *Elmer the Great* (1933), *Spring Madness* (1938), *A Walk in the Sun* (1946), *The Beautiful Blonde From Bashful Bend* (1949), *It's a Mad, Mad, Mad, Mad World* (1963).

CELESTE HOLM (1919–)

Holm appeared in six Broadway flops before she created the part of Ado Annie in *Oklahoma!* (1943) and gained her place in show business as a light comedy performer. Born in New York, she had studied ballet as a child before switching to acting. She made her screen debut in *Three Little Girls in Blue* (1946) and won an Academy Award for Best Supporting Actress in *Gentleman's Agreement* (1947). She has continued acting successfully in theatre, films, and more recently on television. **Films include:** *Road House* (1948), *The Snake Pit* (1948), *Come to the Stable* (1949), *All About Eve* (1950), *High Society* (1956), *Bachelor Flat* (1962), *Doctor, You've Got to Be Kidding!* (1967).

PHILLIPS HOLMES (1907–1942)

He played his first film role in *Varsity* (1928) when he was a student at Princeton University. Thereafter, he became a leading man in the early talkies, making more than 30 films in a career that ended just before the outbreak of World War II. A native of Grand Rapids, Michigan, he had planned to become a lawyer but later decided on a film career, making such films as *The Wild Party* (1929), *An American Tragedy* (1931), and *Dinner at Eight* (1933). **Credits include:** *The Return of Sherlock Holmes* (1929), *Nana* (1934), *Housemaster* (1939).

TAYLOR HOLMES (1872–1959)

A stage and silent screen matinee idol, Holmes played the title role in the original *Ruggles of Red Gap* (1918). He came to the screen via vaudeville and the stage and divided his long career between films and the

theatre. As a character actor in his later films, Holmes often played the amiable, but crooked, politician. **Films include:** *One Hour of Love* (1928), *Dinner at Eight* (1933), *Nana* (1934), *Boomerang* (1947), *Father of the Bride* (1950), *The Maverick Queen* (1956).

JACK HOLT (1888–1951)

One of the silent screen's biggest box-office attractions, Virginia-born Holt literally rode his way into films after a stint on western ranches. He began his film career as a stunt rider in action pictures, but was soon getting leads as the strong, romantic hero. He eventually made more than 90 silent and sound features. **Films include:** *The Little American* (1916), *Empty Hands* (1924), *Submarine* (1928), *War Correspondent* (1932), *The Littlest Rebel* (1935), *San Francisco* (1936), *They Were Expendable* (1945), *Across the Wide Missouri* (1951).

TIM HOLT (1918–)

The cowboy hero in a score of low-budget Westerns, Holt also appeared in several more substantial pictures—notably as Lt. Blanchard in John Ford's *Stagecoach* (1939) and as Curtin in John Huston's *The Treasure of Sierra Madre* (1947). He is the son of actor Jack Holt, and made his film debut in 1937. **Films include:** *History Is Made at Night* (1937), *The Magnificent Ambersons* (1942), *His Kind of Woman* (1951), *The Monster That Challenged the World* (1957).

OSCAR HOMOLKA (c. 1900–)

Homolka has had a long international performing career. After studying at the Royal Dramatic Academy in his native Vienna, he made his stage debut in 1918, and subsequently appeared on the stages of Graz, Munich, Berlin, London and New York. He began his film career in the silents of the 20's and later gracefully made the transition to the talkies of the 30's—playing heroes and villains with equal skill and credibility. **His more than 80 films include:** *Ebb Tide* (1937), *Mission to Moscow* (1943), *Anna Lucasta* (1949), *The Seven Year Itch* (1955), *Funeral in Berlin* (1966), *Song of Norway* (1970).

BOB HOPE (1903–)

The ski-jump-nosed comedian who made the song "Thanks for the Memory" his trademark has a fabulous collection of memories to look back upon—an unbroken chain of successes: in films, on radio and television, as a business entrepreneur and an internationally known emcee whose quips camouflaged an underlying seriousness of purpose, even as the author of one of the best-selling books of our time.

Leslie Townes Hope was born in London but left the British Isles at the age of four when his family moved to Cleveland, Ohio. He broke into show business via vaudeville with an act featuring "Songs, Patter and Eccentric Dancing," following an earlier apprenticeship as a boxer, soda jerk and newsboy. His first Broadway appearance was in Jerome Kern's great hit musical *Roberta* (1933), originally christened *Gowns by Roberta*. Critics liked him and he moved on to radio to become hugely popular as a comic. His first film appearance came in Paramount's production *The Big Broadcast of 1938*, in which he and Shirley Ross sang "Thanks for the Memory" for the first time. The duet was such a hit that the song was made the title of another Hope/Ross film later that same year.

During the 40's and 50's, beginning with *The Road to Singapore* (1940), Hope appeared with Bing Crosby in a string of "Road" pictures, several of them very funny, all of them tuneful and good-natured. In these ventures they were ably supported by a sultry, sarong-clad Dorothy Lamour and for a spell the trio were inexorably linked together in the public's mind. In these films, as in another comic classic, *The Paleface* (1948), Hope invariably played the ultra-cowardly hero who was always delighted to have the other fellow (or girl) confront danger.

As time rolled by Hope made fewer films, concentrating on his own TV show, which, beginning in 1952, became a national institution.

From December 8, 1941—the day after Pearl Harbor—a new love affair began, between Hope and the armed forces of the United States. During the next 30 years, through the grim days of World War II, Korea and Viet-

A front view of Bob Hope conceals the ultra-retroussé profile in Critic's Choice *(1963). The screamer is Jessie Royce Landis.*

nam, he and his troupe made dozens of trips overseas to entertain servicemen in every corner of the globe. This dedication to a cause, plus other charitable ventures such as golf's Desert Classic, brought the comedian no fewer than three special Academy Awards plus other kudos far too numerous to list.

Hope combined his wisecracks into print for the first time in 1943 when he wrote *I Never Left Home*, a book about his visits to the armed forces. It sold over a million copies. Later came the highly successful *Have Tux, Will Travel*, a semi-autobiography.

So popular was Hope as a master of ceremonies that, for a time, it was virtually impossible to view any TV ceremony, whether a national convention or an Academy Award presentation, without seeing the familiar large and retroussé nose above the podium. **Films include:** *The Cat and the Canary* (1939), *The Road to Morocco* (1942), *They Got Me Covered* (1943), *Sorrowful Jones*

Long-time favorite Miriam Hopkins talks things over with Ray Milland in the 1937 film Wise Girl.

Dennis Hopper in Easy Rider, *a picture that set a new style for films of the 70's.*

(1949), *The Seven Little Foys* (1955), *Call Me Bwana* (1963), *Boy, Did I Get a Wrong Number* (1966), *How to Commit Marriage* (1969).

MIRIAM HOPKINS (1902–1972)

Georgia-born Hopkins was an established dramatic actress on the legitimate stage when she was signed for *Fast and Loose* (1930), a disastrous film version of the play *The Best People*. She survived that turkey, began to improve on screen and then won raves as Ivy, the drab barmaid, in *Dr. Jekyll and Mr. Hyde* (1932). A series of leading roles followed, and for the next ten years Hopkins remained one of Hollywood's top-ranking stars.

Hopkins was a versatile actress, playing parts ranging from the romantic heroine—in *The Smiling Lieutenant* (1931)—to the good-hearted saloon-keeper—in *Barbary Coast* (1935)—to the ruthless wife—in *A Gentleman After Dark* (1942).

Hopkins left Hollywood from time to time to return to Broadway. When her motion picture career began to dim in the late 40's, she took over Tallulah Bankhead's role in *The Skin of Our Teeth* and concentrated on the stage and summer stock. However, she did continue to make some films, appearing mainly in supporting roles in films like *The Heiress* (1949), *Outcasts of Poker Flat* (1952) and *The Children's Hour* (1962). **Other films include:** *Trouble in Paradise* (1932), *The Story of Temple Drake* (1933), *All of Me* (1934), *Becky Sharp* (1935), *These Three* (1936), *The Old Maid* (1939), *The Mating Season* (1951), *The Chase* (1966).

DENNIS HOPPER (1936–   )

Dennis Hopper was born in Dodge City, Kansas, and raised in San Diego, California. The California acting bug grasped him early and he made appearances on such TV shows as *Medic* and *The Loretta Young Show*. Hopper made his film debut at the age of 19 as Goon in Nicholas Ray's *Rebel Without a Cause*. For the next ten years Hopper appeared in supporting roles, most of which were in Westerns. He was Jordan Benedict II in *Giant* (1956), Billy Clanton in *Gunfight at the O.K. Corral* (1957), and Dave Hastings in *The Sons of Katie Elder* (1965). Hopper's first major starring role, however, did not come until 1969, when he starred with Peter Fonda and Jack Nicholson in *Easy Rider*, which Hopper also co-authored and co-directed. **Other credits include:** *The Story of Mankind* (1957), *Key Witness* (1960), *The Trip* (1967), *Cool Hand Luke* (1967), *The Last Movie* (1971), *Kid Blue* (1973).

HEDDA HOPPER (1890–1966)

Hedda Hopper (Elda Furry) had begun her long career on stage when she met, worked with and married the successful stage actor, DeWolfe Hopper. After their divorce, she kept his name and made her film debut in *Virtuous Wives* (1919). During the next 20 years she appeared in more than 100 films, silents and talkies, generally playing the knowledgable and sophisticated woman of the world.

In 1936, Hopper challenged the reign of Louella Parsons, and began her legendary career as the Hollywood gossip columnist famous for her outrageous hats as well as her sulfuric pen.

Inactive in films for most of the 40's, Hopper twice returned briefly to the studios to play herself: first in *Sunset Boulevard* (1950) and again in *Pepe* (1960). Her son, William Hopper, became well known as Paul Drake in the *Perry Mason* TV series. **Her films include:** *The Snob* (1924), *Wings* (1927), *The Last of Mrs. Cheyney* (1929), *Alice Adams* (1935), *Topper* (1937), *The Women* (1939), *Reap the Wild Wind* (1942).

MICHAEL HORDERN (1911–   )

Usually cast as the world-weary intellectual or official, Hordern, an Englishman, has had a varied dramatic career. He made his debut on the stage in England in 1938 and made his film debut a year later in *The Girl in the News* (1939). Besides appearing in more than 35 British and American films, Hordern has done a lot of television and was voted TV Actor of the Year in 1957. **Films include:** *Passport to Pimlico* (1948), *The Heart of the Matter* (1954), *El Cid* (1961), *The V.I.P.s* (1963), *The Yellow Rolls-Royce* (1965), *The Taming of the Shrew* (1967), *The Bed-Sitting Room* (1969), *Anne of the Thousand Days* (1970).

LENA HORNE (1917–   )

Her great beauty and throaty, insinuating voice have made Horne one of the most popular entertainers since the mid-30's. Horne was establishing her career as a New York nightclub singer when she first received critical acclaim from Hollywood for her performance in *Cabin in the Sky* (1943). Unfortunately, Hollywood in the 40's did not know what to do with a black actress who did not fit into the servant mold. As a result, Horne's film work was largely restricted to appearances in a succession of musicals—doing musical numbers that could be cut out when shown in the South. After the late 50's she did not return to the screen until she played Richard Widmark's wife in *Death of a Gunfighter* (1969). She makes frequent TV appearances and her records continue to be a staple. **Films include:** *The Duke Is Tops* (1938), *Panama Hattie* (1942), *Stormy Weather* (1943), *Two Girls and a Sailor* (1944), *Till the Clouds Roll By* (1946), *Duchess of Idaho* (1950), *Meet Me in Las Vegas* (1956).

EDWARD EVERETT HORTON (1887–1970)

Nobody could do a double-take like Edward Everett Horton. One of the most popular comic character actors of all time, he was in constant demand on stage and screen.

Brooklyn-born Horton launched his career playing in Gilbert and Sullivan productions with a stock company on Staten Island and found work as a screen comedian as early as 1916. He was one of the few silent screen actors who easily made the transition to sound. During a film career that lasted over 50 years, Horton appeared in more than 100 films, invariably as a fuss-budget or twinkly-eyed Scrooge. Some of his best-remembered roles were as Egbert Fitzgerald in *The Gay Divorcée* (1934), Horace Hardwick in *Top Hat* (1935), and Alexander P. Lovett in *Lost Horizon* (1937). His success on screen, however, didn't stunt his theatre career. Horton toured perennially in the straw-hat classic *Springtime for Henry*—playing the role of the philandering bachelor almost 3,000 times. He also was regularly seen on television until his death in 1970. **Sound films include:** *Alice in Wonderland* (1933), *The Man in the Mirror* (1937), *Here Comes Mr. Jordan* (1941), *Arsenic and Old Lace* (1944), *The Story of Mankind* (1957), *Pocketful of Miracles* (1961), *The Perils of Pauline* (1967).

JOHN HOWARD (1913–   )

Howard (born John Cox) was one of Hollywood's most attractive minor leading men in the late 30's and 40's. After graduating Phi Beta Kappa from Ohio's Western Reserve University, Howard appeared on stage in Cleveland. There he was noticed by a Paramount talent scout and soon landed in Hollywood, where he appeared in supporting roles in several minor films. In 1937 his career took a distinct upswing when he landed the part of George Conway (Ronald Colman's younger brother) in *Lost Horizon*—the character who was driven mad by the sudden, horrifying aging of the "young" Margo as they crossed over the border from Shangri-La to the outside world. In that same year, Howard secured the lead in *Bulldog Drummond Comes Back*, and subsequently played the dashing amateur sleuth in seven more films.

Gorgeous Lena Horne, one of the top vocalists of our era, in Cabin in the Sky.

Edward Everett Horton, the face that helped launch a thousand movies (it seemed like that many) in Here Comes Mr. Jordan.

Leslie Howard, one of the film idols of the 30's, along with Heather Angel in the hugely popular Berkeley Square.

He will also be remembered as the stuffy, self-made rich fiancé of Katharine Hepburn in *The Philadelphia Story* (1940). Howard entered the Navy in 1942 and was awarded the Navy Cross and Croix de Guerre for his service. Continuing in movies, mainly "B"'s, he is now often seen on television. **Highlights:** *Disputed Passage* (1939), *The Man From Dakota* (1940), *The High and the Mighty* (1954).

LESLIE HOWARD (1893–1943)

Leslie Howard most often played the kind of men women wanted to take home and care for—sensitive, poetic, gallant, somewhat fragile or world-weary, but usually with strong inner fiber. Perhaps the epitome of this type of role was that of Ashley Wilkes in *Gone With the Wind* (1939). Although Howard did not seek it nor particularly want it, the part was thrust upon him and he played it as perfectly as Clark Gable did his Rhett Butler to the vast satisfaction of millions of fans ever since.

Howard (born Leslie Stainer) began acting in 1918 as therapy for shell shock suffered in World War I, and he quickly established himself in the theatre in his native England. He became a star on the New York stage with a series of hit plays in the 20's, including *The Green Hat* and *Her Cardboard Lover*. Hollywood stardom was equally swift when he repeated his stage role as Tom Prior in the film version of *Outward Bound* (1930). There followed over the years a series of memorable Howard performances in strong and successful films: *Of Human Bondage* (1934, wonderfully well cast with Bette Davis), *The Scarlet Pimpernel* (1935, for which he won the Picturegoers Gold Medal in England), *The Petrified Forest* (1936, again with Bette Davis and bringing Humphrey Bogart's electric presence to the fore), *Romeo and Juliet* (1936, with Norma Shearer; they were both too old, but never mind, it was a handsome and well-crafted production), *Pygmalion* (1938, one of the best, with Wendy Hiller), and *Intermezzo* (1939, with the young Ingrid Bergman, a beautiful weeper of a picture).

War clouds had gathered in Europe when Howard returned to England to make a film and it was cancelled as the war began. He remained at home to work for the war effort and also made three taut war dramas, one of which, *Mister V* (1942), was a modern-dress version of *Pimpernel*. In the middle of the war, en route from Lisbon to London, his airplane and all aboard were lost, presumed to have been shot down by the Germans. **Films include:** *A Free Soul* (1931), *Smilin' Through* (1932), *Berkeley Square* (1933), *The First of Few* (1942), *The Invaders* (1942).

TREVOR HOWARD (1916–   )

With his reputation as one of the world's most effective film actors, Howard has developed a loyal following both in his native Britain and in the United States. Critics are generally enthusiastic about his performances even though they are not quite so generous about some of the pictures he makes.

Howard studied at the Royal Academy of Dramatic Art, and after ten years on the stage, both in London and at Stratford-on-Avon, he made his English film debut in *The Way Ahead* (1944).

Howard scored his first major success as the lead in *Brief Encounter* (1946), David Lean's tender tear-jerker, which was written by Noel Coward. Three years later he confirmed his growing reputation as a distinguished performer with his portrayal of the sarcastic liaison officer in *The Third Man* (1949).

Throughout the late 40's and early 50's Howard combined both stage and screen work, but since the mid-50's he has appeared almost exclusively in films. He went to Hollywood in 1956 for *Run for the Sun* (1956), the first of his many American pictures. Only two years later, he won the British Film Academy's Best Actor Award for his performance in *The Key* (1958) with Sophia Loren and William Holden.

Howard has frequently played British officers—he was the military psychiatrist in *The Man in the Middle* (1964). In the early 70's he was cast most often in supporting roles—the village priest in *Ryan's Daughter* (1970) and Lord Burghley in *Mary, Queen of Scots* (1971). **Films include:** *Green for Danger* (1947), *Odette* (1950), *The Heart of the Matter* (1953), *Moment of Danger* (1960), *Father Goose* (1964), *The Battle of Britain* (1969), *The Night Visitor* (1971), *Something Like the Truth* (1972).

SALLY ANN HOWES (1930–   )

The daughter of Bobby Howes (a musical comedy star of British stage and screen), London-born Sally Ann Howes made her motion picture debut at the age of 13 as the lead in *Thursday's Child* (1943). She went on to make 12 other films in the next seven years.

Although she was a movie star in England before she was 20, she was little known in the United States before she replaced Julie Andrews in the Broadway production of *My Fair Lady*. Her Eliza made Americans aware of her acting ability, blonde good looks and sweet singing voice. Howes has remained in the United States and appeared on stage, screen and television. She was nominated for a Tony Award for her role in the revival of the stage musical *Brigadoon* and won many young hearts with her role in the film *Chitty Chitty Bang Bang* (1968) with Dick Van Dyke. **Credits include:** *Halfway House* (1945), *Dead of Night* (1946), *Nicholas Nickleby* (1947), *Anna Karenina* (1948), *My Sister and I* (1948), *The Admirable Crichton* (1958).

OLIN HOWLAND (1896–1959)

Sarah Bernhardt gave character-actor Howland his first acting job in a production of *La Sourcièrre* in his native Denver. That was the beginning of a long acting career, which eventually included over 40 years in films. After making several silents, Howland went on to play innumerable character parts in sound films until his death. He was also known as Olin Howlin. **Films include:** *Janice Meredith* (1924), *So Big* (1932), *Nothing Sacred* (1937), *This Gun for Hire* (1942), *The Wistful Widow of Wagon Gap* (1947), *Them* (1954), *The Blob* (1958).

ARTHUR HOYT (1876–1955)

Arthur Hoyt invariably played a Casper Milquetoast-type character—the classic timid soul. He came to Hollywood in 1929 after 16 years acting and directing on Broadway. (Previously he had accepted assignments in a number of silents such as the 1925 film *The Lost World*.) For the next 20-some years, Hoyt's meek face, with its trim mustache, apologetic eyes, and horn-rimmed glasses, peeked from the screen in scores of movies. **Films include:** *The Criminal Code* (1931), *American Madness* (1932), *The Devil and the Deep* (1932), *Madame Racketeer* (1932), *A Shriek in the Night* (1933), *Mr. Deeds Goes to Town* (1936), *A Star Is Born* (1937), *East Side of Heaven* (1939), *Mad Wednesday* (1951).

JOHN HOYT (1905–   )

Hoyt (born John Haysradt) is probably most familiar to film audiences for his numerous portrayals of villainous German officers in war movies, and stylish crooks. A Yale graduate, Hoyt appeared in the Ziegfeld Follies, toured nationally with Katharine Cornell, and did nightclub impersonations before

Trevor Howard, the grim-visaged cleric of Ryan's Daughter.

Arthur Hoyt nearly always looked just like this in his scores of movie roles.

launching his film career. **Films include:** *O.S.S.* (1946), *The Desert Fox* (1951), *Julius Caesar* (1953), *The Blackboard Jungle* (1955), *Duel at Diablo* (1966).

ROCHELLE HUDSON (1914–1972)

Eventually a veteran of more than 70 films, Oklahoma-born Rochelle Hudson began her Hollywood career as a popular ingénue of the early and mid-30's—she was Sally Glynn in *She Done Him Wrong* (1933) and Cosette in *Les Misérables* (1935). A protégé of Will Rogers, Hudson played his leading lady in a series of films which included *Mr. Skitch* (1933), *Judge Priest* (1934), and *Life Begins at Forty* (1935). After the 30's she appeared most often in supporting roles; perhaps her most familiar part in later years was that of Natalie Wood's mother in *Rebel Without a Cause* (1955). Never obsessed with her film career, Hudson had joined the Navy in 1941 and later ran a ranch and worked successfully in real estate. Before her death in 1972 she

had also appeared in television. **Credits include:** *Are These Our Children?* (1931), *Imitation of Life* (1934), *Way Down East* (1935), *Men Without Souls* (1940), *Strait Jacket* (1964), *Dr. Terror's Gallery of Horrors* (1967).

ROCK HUDSON (1925–   )

From a bobby-sox idol who got his start in a string of low-budget Westerns, Hudson progressed to top box-office status and a mix of meaty and light comedy roles. He was born Roy Fitzgerald in 1925 in Winnetka, Illinois, and was discovered when he told Hollywood agent Henry Willson that he didn't like his job as a postman.

After his 1948 movie debut in *Fighter Squadron*, Hudson appeared in a string of mainly indifferent films. He got a lot of fan magazine publicity, but seemed just another handsome face until he was chosen to play Elizabeth Taylor's husband in Edna Ferber's *Giant* (1956). His performance led to more good dramatic roles: as Mitch Wayne in *Written on the Wind* (1957), as Lt. Frederick Henry in *A Farewell to Arms* (1958), and in *The Earth Is Mine* (1959). In a change of pace, he did *Pillow Talk* (1959) with Doris Day. The sophisticated light comedy hit earned Hudson the top spot in box-office rankings in the early 60's and prompted Universal to team the pair again for two more pictures: *Lover Come Back* (1962) and *Send Me No Flowers* (1964).

As an established star, Hudson took on a variety of comedy and action film roles. In 1966 he did *Seconds* for director John Frankenheimer, a drama that did not do well at the box office but which displayed another facet of Hudson's abilities. In the 70's, he branched out into television as the Police Commissioner in the popular mystery series *MacMillan and Wife*. **Films include:** *Undertow* (1949), *Magnificent Obsession* (1954), *Bengal Brigade* (1954), *The Tarnished Angels* (1958), *Come September* (1961), *Tobruk* (1967), *Ice Station Zebra* (1968), *Showdown* (1973).

Rock Hudson infuriated Doris Day by wooing and winning countless girl friends by singing the same corny song to each of them in the good-natured Pillow Talk.

LLOYD HUGHES (1897–   )

As a student in Los Angeles, Lloyd Hughes bicycled to studios after school hours to watch

A pretty girl who played pretty girls, Mary Beth Hughes smiles in the Hollywood sunshine.

movies being made. Eventually, a series of small parts led to his first starring role (opposite Mary Pickford) in *Tess of the Storm Country* (1922). Hughes remained a leading man throughout the decade, but his career faded several years after the screen began to speak. **Credits include:** *The Sea Hawk* (1924), *The Lost World* (1925), *Sailors' Wives* (1928), *Moby Dick* (1930), *The Miracle Man* (1932).

MARY BETH HUGHES (1919–   )

A granddaughter of actress Flora Fosdick, who had appeared on the stage with Ethel Barrymore, Mary Beth Hughes played John Barrymore's leading lady in one of her first successful films, *The Great Profile* (1940). She never really hit the top ranks, and even her starring roles were usually in so-so movies. Since 1950 she has been seen only occasionally on screen. **Highlights:** *The Women* (1939), *Dressed to Kill* (1941), *Orchestra Wives* (1942), *Dubarry Was a Lady* (1943), *The Ox-Bow Incident* (1943), *Young Man With a Horn* (1950), *Las Vegas Shakedown* (1955).

HENRY HULL (1890–   )

Henry Hull was born in Kentucky, the son of a newspaper drama critic, and studied to be a civil engineer before turning to acting. He made his stage debut as a black boy in *The Nigger* (1909). By 1916 Hull was a Broadway star and in 1917 started appearing in silent films; in 1924 he appeared in David O. Selznick's first feature film, *Roulette*. He is perhaps best remembered on stage as Jeeter Lester in the Broadway production of *Tobacco Road* (1933). For over four decades, Hull turned in fine performances in scores of pictures; some of the best were *Yellow Jack* (1938), *Jesse James* (1939) and *High Sierra* (1941). He also has worked in television, mainly Western series. **Other films include:** *Great Expectations* (1934), *Stanley and Livingstone* (1939), *My Son, My Son!* (1940), *Lifeboat* (1944), *Inferno* (1953), *The Chase* (1966).

Henry Hull, of Tobacco Road *fame, persuades Joel McCrea in* Colorado Territory *(1949). The lady is Virginia Mayo.*

JOSEPHINE HULL (1884–1957)

Josephine Hull (born Sherwood) started her long acting career in 1902 in Boston and played with touring companies before making her New York stage debut. She played lovable but eccentric old ladies in a host of movies and won an Academy Award for Best Supporting Actress for a role she played both on Broadway and on screen—the harassed sister of Elwood P. Dowd in *Harvey* (1950). Another gem was her performance as Aunt Abby in *Arsenic and Old Lace* (1944), Frank Capra's film version of the Broadway hit. **Other films:** *After Tomorrow* (1932), *Careless Lady* (1932), *The Lady From Texas* (1951).

BENITA HUME (1906–1967)

This British actress, always beautiful and poised, enjoyed a fine stage career before making her screen debut in 1929 in *The Wrecker*. Unfortunately, most of the film roles assigned to her were pretty dreadful,

Marsha Hunt, one of Hollywood's most intelligent and lovely-looking ladies, with an admiring Van Heflin in Seven Sweethearts *(1942).*

such as *Peck's Bad Boy With the Circus* (1939), but she managed to carry them off with a considerable degree of aplomb. She retired from the screen upon her marriage to Ronald Colman, and together they led a quiet private life as prominent members of Hollywood's "British Colony." She is well-remembered during those years, however, for her hilarious appearances with her husband on the Jack Benny radio show. The Colmans played Jack's neighbors, which indeed they really were. **Credits include:** *High Treason* (1929), *Jaws of Hell* (1931), *The Worst Woman in Paris* (1933), *Suzy* (1936), *The Last of Mrs. Cheyney* (1937).

ARTHUR HUNNICUTT (1911–   )

Born in Gravelly, Arkansas (population: 211), Hunnicutt got his early stage experience in medicine shows and circuses and made his New York stage debut as Cabot Yearling, the migratory worker in William Saroyan's *Love's Old Sweet Song* (1941). Noted primarily for his stage work, Hunnicutt has also made a number of movies since his first one, *Wildcat* (1942). He has usually been typecast as a hillbilly. Recently he has performed on television. **Highlights:** *Johnny Come Lately* (1943), *Abroad With Two Yanks* (1944), *Pinky* (1949), *The Big Sky* (1952), *Cat Ballou* (1965), *El Dorado* (1967).

MARSHA HUNT (1917–   )

In the 30's and 40's when she made most of her pictures, Marsha Hunt was known as Hollywood's "youngest character actress." She was a model when she got her first screen contract, but despite her good looks she never rose much above supporting roles. Hunt played the perennial bridesmaid in *These Glamour Girls* (1939), starring Lana Turner, and Lionel Barrymore's granddaughter in *The Penalty* (1941). In the 40's, she broke out of the "B" movies to which she had been relegated early in her Hollywood career and won several leading roles, notably in *Kid Glove Killer* (1942) as Van Heflin's lab assistant and in *Joe Smith, American* (1942) with Robert Young. After her marriage to script writer Robert Presnell, Jr., in 1946 she returned to supporting roles. About the same time, however, she made her Broadway debut in *Joy to the World* and won critical praise for her performance.

When Hollywood began blacklisting liberals during the Senator Joseph McCarthy witchhunt era in the early 50's, Hunt was one of those denied work. When the clouds lifted, she returned to the screen in supporting roles, including that of Brandon de Wilde's mother in *Blue Denim* (1959), and also became familiar to TV audiences as the mother in *Peck's Bad Girl*. In recent years, Hunt has appeared occasionally in films, theatre and television. **Films include:** *Pride and Prejudice* (1940), *Thousands Cheer* (1943), *A Letter for Evie* (1945), *Jigsaw* (1949), *Diplomatic Passport* (1954), *Johnny Got His Gun* (1971).

MARTITA HUNT (1900–1969)

One of England's finest dramatic actresses, Martita Hunt was unknown in the United States until her performance as the mad Miss Havisham in *Great Expectations* (1946). Although she made many films in both England and America, her fame rested largely on her stage performances. Hunt began acting in 1923 and played more than 50 character parts on the London stage and with the Old Vic. Her first theatre appearance in the United States was in *The Madwoman of Chaillot* (1948) for which she won a Tony Award. Hunt went to Hollywood in 1949 to film *Lady Windermere's Fan*, and although she was to return many times for other films, she based her career in England. **Credits include:** *Melba* (1953), *Anastasia* (1956), *Bunny Lake Is Missing* (1965).

IAN HUNTER (1900–   )

South African-born Hunter spent 14 years in Hollywood, usually playing the nice guy—the type who gives up the girl because it's the "only decent thing to do." His theatre career began in 1919 in the London stage production *Jack o' Singles*, and he made his New York debut in 1925 in *School for Scandal*. He played in a variety of British films before going to Hollywood in 1935. He remained in the United States until after World War II, acting in such films as *Strange Cargo* (1940). Hunter was Captain Hook in one of the stage versions of *Peter Pan*. He is now

Martita Hunt as Queen Matilda in Becket *(1964), an outstanding performer in an outstanding cast.*

Ian Hunter and Kay Francis both look mildly guilty (but happy) in Stolen Holiday *(1937).*

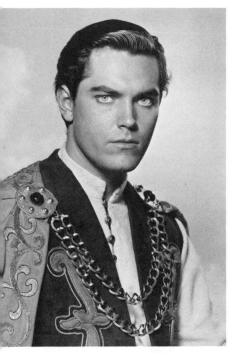

Jeffrey Hunter wears a neo-Egyptian costume in the less than earthshaking Princess of the Nile *(1954).*

Kim Hunter never got the big roles she deserved. This shot is from The Young Stranger *(1957).*

based in London. **Films include:** *Not for Sale* (1924), *A Midsummer Night's Dream* (1935), *Edward, My Son* (1949), *Fortune Is a Woman* (1957), *Guns of Darkness* (1962).

JEFFREY HUNTER (1927–1969)

During his early years in Hollywood, tall, dark-haired, serious-looking Jeff Hunter (Henry H. McKinnies) usually played the All-American boy or somebody's brother in Westerns. But his biggest role unquestionably was as Jesus Christ in *King of Kings* (1961).

A native of New Orleans, Hunter decided to become an actor while he was still in high school. He began his career on radio and in summer stock in Chicago, and made his film debut with Debra Paget in *Fourteen Hours* (1951). His notable roles of the 50's included Frank James in *The True Story of Jesse James* (1957) and Adam Caulfield, the newspaper-reporter nephew of Spencer Tracy in *The Last Hurrah* (1958).

Hunter was married for a time to actress Barbara Rush, and in the 50's they were pictured in fan magazines as a favorite young "ideal" Hollywood couple. Hunter's death in 1969 is something of a mystery—he was found unconscious on the floor of his home and died following emergency brain surgery. **Films include:** *Call Me Mister* (1951), *The Searchers* (1956), *The Longest Day* (1962), *Custer of the West* (1968).

KIM HUNTER (1922–   )

A product of New York's famed Actors Studio, Hunter (born Janet Cole) made her film debut in *The Seventh Victim* (1943) after David O. Selznick discovered her in a Pasadena Playhouse production of *Arsenic and Old Lace*. Although Hunter appeared in several other movies during the 40's, she concentrated on her stage career, eventually landing the Broadway role of Stella in Tennessee Williams' Pulitzer Prize play *A Streetcar Named Desire*. She recreated that role in Elia Kazan's memorable film version of the play and won the Academy Award for Best Supporting Actress for her performance. That success brought Hunter several more substantial roles during the 50's, but since then she has appeared only infrequently on screen. She

has, however, continued her stage work and has made numerous TV appearances. **Films include:** *When Strangers Marry* (1944), *Stairway to Heaven* (1947), *Deadline U.S.A.* (1952), *Storm Center* (1956), *Lilith* (1964), *Planet of the Apes* (1968).

TAB HUNTER (1931–   )

The story goes that somebody told young Arthur Gelien that he ought to be in pictures and that he figured "why not?" He went to Henry Willson (the agent who managed Rock Hudson), was renamed Tab Hunter, squeaked through a screen test and wound up making his 1950 debut in *The Lawless*. Within a short time, the good-looking blond actor became a fan magazine favorite and appeared in a variety of action films like *Track of the Cat* (1954) with Robert Mitchum and Raoul Walsh's *Battle Cry* (1955).

Hunter began to look better to film critics in *Damn Yankees* (1958) with Gwen Verdon, and the next few years brought him several good roles, notably in *They Came to Cordura* (1959) and *The Pleasure of His Company* (1961). About this time, Hunter tried Broadway in the unsuccessful *The Milk Train Doesn't Stop Here Any More*. When Hunter returned to Hollywood, he found his career on the wane. After supporting roles in *Operation Bikini* (1963) with Frankie Avalon and *Ride the Wild Surf* (1965) with Fabian, Hunter went to Europe and appeared in some mediocre pictures. He did, however, land a cameo role in John Huston's *The Life and Times of Judge Roy Bean* (1972). **Films include:** *Gun Belt* (1953), *The Sea Chase* (1955), *Lafayette Escadrille* (1958), *The Fickle Finger of Fate* (1967), *A Kiss From Eddie* (1971).

PAUL HURST (1889–1953)

Most film makers go from acting to directing; Hurst went the other way around. He was a director of silent pictures before making his acting debut in *The Red Raiders* (1927). He played humorous parts in the Monte Hale Western series and acted in both serious and comic roles in more than 90 films before his suicide in 1953. **Films include:** *Shadow of a Doubt* (1935), *Gone With the Wind* (1939),

Caught in the Draft (1941), *Yellow Sky* (1949).

RUTH HUSSEY (1914–   )

Hollywood never really capitalized on Ruth Hussey's talents. She came to Hollywood in the late 30's via Pembroke College in her native Providence, Rhode Island, the University of Michigan's School of Drama, and several years' stage experience. During her early film career Hussey did a series of minor roles until she was upgraded into parts like Robert Young's fiancée in *Northwest Passage* (1940), the Long Island socialite in *Susan and God* (1940) and James Stewart's magazine photographer sidekick in *The Philadelphia Story* (1940). The latter performance won her an Academy Award nomination and several fatter roles, but it was on stage that she won her greatest critical praise, especially in *State of the Union* with Ralph Bellamy in 1945. That role, however, went to Katharine Hepburn on screen. She also toured on stage with *The Royal Family* (1951) and won an Emmy nomination for her TV role in *Craig's Wife* (1955). **Films include:** *H. M. Pulham, Esq.* (1941), *The Uninvited* (1944), *The Great Gatsby* (1949), *Stars and Stripes Forever* (1952), *The Facts of Life* (1961).

WALTER HUSTON (1884–1950)

The adjectives most frequently used to describe Walter Huston's screen performances are "brilliant" and "magnificent." His portrayal of the wise old sourdough in his son John's film *The Treasure of Sierra Madre* (1948) is regarded as a film classic. It won him an Academy Award for Best Supporting Actor and crowned his distinguished 20-year career in Hollywood, mostly in character parts.

Huston was born in Toronto, Canada, and studied engineering and drama. He tried acting first, touring with a stock company and later appearing in vaudeville in New York. Then he married, gave up the stage and took up engineering. In 1909, however, he formed a song and dance act with Bayonne Whipple, who was to become the second of his three wives. Huston spent the next 15 years in vaudeville before his first Broadway appear-

Ruth Hussey looks on disapprovingly as Guy Kibbee offers a smoke to Robert Young in the screen version of John Marquand's fine novel about the Brahmins of Boston's Back Bay, H. M. Pulham, Esquire.

Walter Huston in Howard Hughes's much publicized The Outlaw *(1943). No better actor ever graced the screen than the man who sang "September Song" on Broadway in Kurt Weill's ill-fated* Knickerbocker Holiday.

Walter Huston, flanked by Tim Holt (left) and Humphrey Bogart (right), in a scene from a great movie, The Treasure of Sierre Madre.

ance. Next, he played the lead in *Desire Under the Elms* (1924)—a role which established him as a stage star. He went to Hollywood for his first film role in *Gentlemen of the Press* (1929) and stayed to score success after success in a series of pictures including *The Criminal Code* (1931) and *Beast of the City* (1932). He won a New York Film Critics Award for Best Actor for his portrayal of Sam in William Wyler's much-praised film of the Sinclair Lewis novel *Dodsworth* (1936).

From time to time, Huston returned to the Broadway stage—once to do Kurt Weill's *Knickerbocker Holiday* (1938) in which he sang "September Song." By the 40's his son, John Huston, was a major motion picture director, and the younger Huston cast his father in bit parts in his first two films: Captain Jacoby in *The Maltese Falcon* (1941) and a bartender in *This Is Our Life*. **Films include:**

Abraham Lincoln (1930), *Night Court* (1932). *Rhodes of Africa* (1936), *All That Money Can Buy* (1941), *Mission to Moscow* (1943), *Dragon Seed* (1944), *Duel in the Sun* (1947), *The Furies* (1950).

JOSEPHINE HUTCHINSON (1909–   )

Daughter of actress Leona Roberts, Hutchinson studied acting from the age of ten and made her stage debut in 1920 as a dancer in *The Little Mermaid*. Although most of Hutchinson's career has been centered on the legitimate stage, she also made her share of films, the first of which was *Little Princess* (1917), with Mary Pickford. Most recently, the actress has made numerous TV appearances in such series as: *Gunsmoke, Dr. Kildare* and *Burke's Law*. **Highlights:** *The Melody Lingers On* (1935), *Ruby Gentry* (1952), *North by Northwest* (1959), *Nevada Smith* (1966).

BETTY HUTTON (1921–   )

In the late 40's and early 50's, Michigan-born Hutton (Elizabeth June Thornburg) was one of Hollywood's most valuable musical comedy stars. She played the lead in *Annie Get Your Gun* (1950) and also starred in *The Greatest Show on Earth* (1952), a Cecil B. De Mille spectacular that became one of the industry's biggest box-office hits.

Hutton came to Hollywood via vaudeville and Broadway. She broke into show business as a teenage singer with Vincent Lopez' band and earned a reputation as "The Blonde Bombshell" for her brash and exuberant performances. She was on Broadway in the musical *Panama Hattie* (1940) when Paramount spotted her and offered a screen contract.

After her movie debut in the wartime comedy *The Fleet's In* (1942) with Eddie Bracken, Hutton made a series of GI favorites, usually playing somebody's uninhibited, man-crazy younger sister. The roles earned her a string of nicknames—"The Huttentot," "The Blonde Blitz" and "Bounding Betty." Later she was cast in several musical biographies, playing nightclub singer Texas Guinan in *Incendiary Blonde* (1945) and silent screen heroine Pearl White in *The Perils of Pauline* (1947).

Hutton's motion picture career came to an abrupt halt in 1952 after filming *Somebody Loves Me* (1952), the story of Blossom Seeley. She had married her dance director on the picture, and when Paramount refused her request that her new husband direct her next film, Hutton walked out on her contract. Since then, she has appeared in only one picture, *Spring Reunion* (1957). She appears regularly in nightclubs and stock productions and on television, but seems to have lost much of her earlier audience appeal. **Films include:** *Happy Go Lucky* (1943), *Star Spangled Rhythm* (1943), *The Miracle of Morgan's Creek* (1944), *Red, Hot and Blue* (1949), *Let's Dance* (1950).

JIM HUTTON (c. 1935–)

For a while in the 60's Hutton and Paula Prentiss appeared together on screen so often that movie audiences began thinking of them as a team. They first played in *Where the Boys Are* (1960), Hutton's big break in movies after several years in supporting roles, and went on to make *The Honeymoon Machine* (1961), *Bachelor in Paradise* (1961), etc.

The lanky Hutton got his first movie role while he was serving with the army in Germany. Ironically, one of his first film roles was that of a young Nazi soldier in *A Time to Live and a Time to Die* (1958). After his discharge from the service, he went to Hollywood, where for a time he was described as "a new Jimmy Stewart." **Films include:** *The Horizontal Lieutenant* (1962), *Major Dundee* (1965), *Walk, Don't Run* (1966), *The Green Berets* (1968).

LEILA HYAMS (1905–)

Her parents were professionally known in vaudeville as Hyams and McIntyre and the attractive blonde appeared on stage before making her first film appearance in *Sandra* (1924). One of the first of the talkies, *Alias Jimmy Valentine* (1928), transformed Hyams into a featured player, but her career was a short one, ending in 1936. **Credits include:** *The Bishop Murder Case* (1930), *The Big House* (1930), *Red Headed Woman* (1932), *Ruggles of Red Gap* (1935), *Yellow Dust* (1936).

WILFRID HYDE-WHITE (1903–)

Here's another actor who insists that despite appearances in more than 50 motion pictures, he's primarily a theatre man. Whatever his preference, British character-actor Hyde-White has done a lot of work on the screen during his 50-year career in show business. Hyde-White made his stage debut at age 19 on the Isle of Wight and first appeared in London in 1926 in a play called *Beggar on Horseback*. In 1937, Hyde-White made his screen debut in the British picture *Murder by Rope*. Ten years later, he made his first appearance on Broadway in *Under the County* (1947).

Hyde-White usually is cast in motion pictures as a dignified Englishman, but he frequently softens that image for comedy roles as befuddled fathers (or husbands) and seemingly stern characters with twinkles in their eyes. **Films include:** *The Third Man* (1949), *Gilbert and Sullivan* (1954), *North-West Frontier* (1959), *My Fair Lady* (1964), *The Liquidator* (1965), *Our Man in Marrakesh* (1966), *You Only Live Twice* (1967).

MARTHA HYER (1929–)

Texas-born Martha Hyer got her theatre training at the Pasadena Playhouse. She began appearing in films in her late teens and for over ten years frequently was cast as the nice girl in a string of mainly routine pictures. She was the one who fell in love with Frank Sinatra in *Some Came Running* (1959), a performance that earned her an Academy Award nomination. When she wasn't playing a nice girl, she usually was playing an unsympathetic "other woman." Hyer married producer Hal Wallis in 1966 and, although still active, does not appear in films as frequently as she did in the late 40's and 50's. **Films include:** *The Velvet Touch* (1948), *Sabrina* (1954), *Desire in the Dust* (1960), *The Sons of Katie Elder* (1965), *House of 1,000 Dolls* (1967).

Betty Hutton in Incendiary Blonde *(1945). She looks as though the feathers tickled.*

Martha Hyer, one of a startled trio in Paris Holiday *(1958). The others are Bob Hope and a prognathous-jawed Fernandel.*

RALPH INCE (1887–1937)

The son of John and Emma Brennan Ince (who were well-known in the theatre), Ralph Ince first appeared on the legitimate stage and entered the movies by working on animated cartoons. He soon was given tough-guy parts, and eventually leads in many silent films, usually as a sinister character. He was also interested in directing, and specialized in two- and three-reel movies, making a number of them for the Vitagraph Company. **Films include:** *Chicago After Midnight* (1928), *Little Caesar* (1931), *The Hatchet Man* (1932), *The Big Pay-off* (1933).

FRIEDA INESCORT (1901–   )

Reddish-haired, tall and handsome, Inescort usually was cast in the role of a well-bred woman. She was born in Scotland, the daughter of actress Elaine Inescort, and made her Broadway debut in *The Truth about Blayds* (1922). An energetic, versatile woman, Inescort had dual careers for a time—she spent her days working as a press agent for a publishing company, and her evenings appearing in leading roles on Broadway. After playing a series of intelligent career women in the movies, Inescort was delighted to have the part of a villain in *Tarzan Finds a Son* (1939). **Movie performances include:** *Mary of Scotland* (1936), *Call It a Day* (1937), *Woman Doctor* (1939), *Pride and Prejudice* (1940), *Soldier's Wife* (1944), *The Judge Steps Out* (1949), *The Crowded Sky* (1960).

REX INGRAM (1894–1969)

His compelling physical presence and deep, resonant voice made Rex Ingram the perfect actor to portray De Lawd in the film version of Marc Connelly's play *The Green Pastures* (1936).

His impressive acting career had begun by accident. A Phi Beta Kappa and a graduate of Northwestern Medical School, Ingram had gone to Los Angeles to begin his medical practice, when he was discovered on a street corner by a casting director looking for blacks to play in the first Tarzan movie, *Tarzan of the Apes* (1918), with Elmo Lincoln and Enid Markey. He was subsequently cast in the stereotyped parts available to black actors of the day: cannibals and natives in jungle movies, and porters and butlers in Mack Sennett comedies.

Green Pastures was Ingram's breakthrough movie, and after it, he decided only to take roles that portrayed blacks in a dignified manner. He didn't get another movie role for two years, and often joked that after playing De Lawd there was no place to go but down. Ingram returned to films in *Huckleberry Finn* (1939), and thereafter combined his movie work with his already successful stage career. Two of his many memorable Broadway performances were in *Stevedore* (1934) and *Cabin in the Sky*

Frieda Inescort, looking far more innocent than most members of the jury in Portia on Trial *(1937).*

(1941). **Film credits include:** *The Ten Commandments* (1923), *The Big Parade* (1926), *The Emperor Jones* (1933), *Love in Morocco* (1933), *Cabin in the Sky* (1943), *Dark Waters* (1944), *God's Little Acre* (1958), *Elmer Gantry* (1960), *Hurry Sundown* (1967).

JOHN IRELAND (1915–)

The tough, cynical hero of numerous Hollywood Westerns and some war movies, Ireland began his career as the star of a swimming act featured in a carnival troupe touring his native Canada. He spent several years in summer stock, played on Broadway and made his film debut as Windy in *A Walk in the Sun* (1946). He was nominated for an Academy Award for his performance as Jack Burden in *All the King's Men* (1949).

During the past three decades, Ireland has made over 60 films. **His credits include:** *My Darling Clementine* (1946), *Red River* (1948), *Hurricane Smith* (1952), *Gunfight at the O.K. Corral* (1957), *Spartacus* (1960), *The Fall of the Roman Empire* (1964), *Fort Utah* (1967).

GEORGE IRVING (1874–1961)

A leading man of the New York stage, Irving starred opposite Maude Adams before abandoning the theatre for Hollywood in 1913. Irving, who had studied in New York at City College and the American Academy of Dramatic Arts, began in films as a director. Later, he turned to acting and appeared in character parts in both silent and sound pictures. **Films include:** *Madonna of the Streets* (1924), *Wild Horse Mesa* (1925), *The Port of Missing Girls* (1928), *Craig's Wife* (1928), *Paris Bound* (1929), *Lady with a Past* (1932), *Dangerous* (1935), *Bringing Up Baby* (1938), *Spy Ship* (1942), *Magic Town* (1947).

MARGARET IRVING (c.1900–)

It wasn't easy playing it "straight" with the Marx Brothers, but that was Irving's assignment in her first screen role in *Animal Crackers* (1930). She came to Hollywood from Broadway where she had worked first as a dancer and later as a musical comedy star.

Irving created the role of Clementina in the original stage version of *The Desert Song* (1926). **Films include:** *San Francisco* (1936), *Charlie Chan at the Opera* (1936), *The Outcasts of Poker Flat* (1937), *Wife, Doctor and Nurse* (1937), *The Baroness and the Butler* (1938).

JOSE ITURBI (1895–)

For most of the 40's, Iturbi was Hollywood's resident longhair. A serious musician—conductor, composer and pianist —the Spanish-born artist came to the United States from Europe in 1929 for his American concert debut as pianist with the Philadelphia Orchestra, and was already famous as a flamboyant and temperamental conductor when Hollywood first sought him out.

Iturbi was signed up by MGM and made his movie debut in *Thousands Cheer* (1943) with Judy Garland. He went on to appear (usually as himself) in a series of popular light comedies. The public happily tolerated the classical interludes of his films and relished his lapses into boogie-woogie piano solos. In 1945 he did the soundtrack for *A Song to Remember*, and his recording of a Chopin Polonaise for it sold over a million copies. After a total of seven pictures, Iturbi abandoned films because of criticism from the music world. He returned to Spain as conductor of the Valencia Orchestra and often performed piano duets with his sister, Amparo. After her death in 1969, Iturbi retired, emerging only once to perform with the Rochester (New York) Philharmonic Orchestra. **Films include:** *Adventure in Music* (1944), *Two Girls and a Sailor* (1944), *Anchors Aweigh* (1945), *Holiday in Mexico* (1946), *Three Daring Daughters* (1948), *That Midnight Kiss* (1949).

ROSALIND IVAN (1884–1959)

British-born Rosalind Ivan was sometimes called Ivan the Terrible because of her shrike-like film roles. These elicited enthusiastic hatred from movie audiences —never to more telling effect than in *The Suspect* (1945) in which she drove Charles Laughton to murder.

Rex Ingram, a magnificent performer, as "De Lawd" in Green Pastures.

John Ireland, who specialized in tough roles, makes a properly determined captain in this publicity shot.

*Burl Ives, in his pre-beard period
and as he looked in Walt Disney's*
So Dear To My Heart *(1949).*

BURL IVES (1909–)

A descendant of Illinois farmers, river-boat gamblers and country preachers, Burl Ives (born Burl Icle Ivanhoe) is one of the nation's leading folk singers as well as a powerful dramatic actor whose performance in *The Big Country* (1958) won him an Academy Award for Best Supporting Actor.

Ives began singing with his family and was earning money at the age of four. His first big Broadway break came in *The Boys From Syracuse* (1938) and he made his screen debut in *Smoky* (1946). He has continued to appear on both stage and screen and is a leading television performer. **Films include:** *East of Eden* (1955), *Cat on a Hot Tin Roof* (1958), *Our Man in Havana* (1960), *The Brass Bottle* (1964), *Rocket to the Moon* (1967).

Ivan was trained as a musician and gave her first London recital at the age of ten. Chosen to play in *Candida* by George Bernard Shaw, she later appeared frequently on Broadway with such luminaries as John and Ethel Barrymore. A writer of some note, Ivan translated *The Brothers Karamazov* for the Theatre Guild and was a book reviewer for *The New York Times*. **Films include:** *Scarlet Street* (1945), *The Corn Is Green* (1945), *Johnny Belinda* (1948), *The Robe* (1953), *Elephant Walk* (1954).

ANNE JACKSON (1924–   )

Pennsylvania-born Jackson made her professional stage debut in *The Cherry Orchard* and followed this performance with many Broadway successes, including *Summer and Smoke*, *Major Barbara* and *Luv*. Although she is better known as a stage actress, Jackson has appeared in a number of noteworthy films since her screen debut in *So Young, So Bad* (1950). She and her husband of more than 25 years, Eli Wallach, often perform together on stage, screen and television. **Film highlights:** *The Journey* (1959), *Tall Story* (1960), *The Tiger Makes Out* (1967), *Lovers and Other Strangers* (1970).

Her bittersweet performance in A Touch of Class *won Glenda Jackson the Academy Award for Best Actress. George Segal's performance was also pretty special.*

GLENDA JACKSON (1938–   )

Cool, intense professionalism has been the hallmark of this distinguished British actress. She began her career in amateur productions as a teenager, attended the Royal Academy of Dramatic Art in London on scholarship and went on to tour in provincial repertory for several years. Then, in 1964, she joined the Royal Shakespeare Company. Her first important role came when Peter Brook cast her as Charlotte Corday, executioner of Jean-Paul Marat, in the experimental Old Vic production of the play whose title was shortened to *Marat/Sade*. She was a big hit in London, repeated her success when the play was produced on Broadway and again when she made her screen debut in the 1967 film version.

Since then Jackson has gone on to establish herself as one of the world's most respected and articulate actresses, probably best known for her fiery characterizations of strong, independent women. Her finely etched portraits on stage, screen and television have brought her numerous awards: the New York Film Critics Award and Hollywood's Best Actress Oscar for her Gudrun in Ken Russell's *Women in Love* (1969), the British Film Academy's Best Actress Award for *Sunday, Bloody Sunday* (1971) and two Emmys for her Queen Elizabeth I in the BBC TV series. In 1974 she claimed her second Oscar for her starring role as the chic divorcee entangled with wandering husband George Segal in the hit comedy *A Touch of Class* (1973). **Film credits:** *Negatives* (1968), *The Music Lovers* (1970), *Mary, Queen of Scots* (1972), *The Nelson Affair* (1973).

THOMAS JACKSON (1886–1967)

As an actor on the New York stage, Jackson created the role of detective Dan McCord in the show *Broadway*. In 1929, he repeated his performance in the film version and remained in Hollywood as a supporting actor in pictures like *Little Caesar* (1931). **More than 55 films include:** *The Fall Guy* (1930),

Anne Jackson as she appeared in Columbia Pictures' production The Tiger Makes Out.

Sam Jaffe has a Grand Lama-like look, but this time the film is Rope of Sand *(1949).*

Emil Jannings as the doorman in an outstanding German film of the 20's, The Last Laugh.

Reckless Living (1931), *The Avenger* (1933), *She's No Lady* (1937), *Millionaires in Prison* (1940), *Shady Lady* (1945), *Phone Call from a Stranger* (1952).

RICHARD JAECKEL (1926–   )

Since his debut as a baby-faced Marine in *Guadalcanal Diary* (1943), this native New Yorker has been fighting all sorts of people with an astonishing lack of discrimination —from the Nazis and Japanese in numerous war pictures to Indians and Western baddies. He has escaped only occasionally for roles in pictures like *Come Back, Little Sheba* (1952). **Film highlights:** *Wing and a Prayer* (1944), *Sands of Iwo Jima* (1949), *The Naked and the Dead* (1958), *The Dirty Dozen* (1967), *Devil's Brigade* (1968), *Ulzanas Raid* (1973).

SAM JAFFE (1896–   )

When his name is mentioned, most people say, "Oh, yes, the Grand Lama in *Lost Horizon*." While that 1937 role was his best known, the mildly cadaverous New Yorker has also turned in flawless performances in dozens of other films, in Broadway plays and on television. His range is enormous, from the Inquisitor in *St. Joan* (stage, 1954) to Dr. Zorba in the *Ben Casey* TV series. So far as we know, however, he has played a title role only once—in *Gunga Din*, the 1939 film about Kipling's scrawny little native of India who died to keep the Union Jack flying. **Film highlights:** *We Live Again* (1934), *13 Rue Madeleine* (1947), *Gentleman's Agreement* (1947), *Ben Hur* (1959), *Guns for San Sebastian* (1968).

DEAN JAGGER (1903–   )

During his 40-some years in films, this lantern-jawed, bald character actor from Ohio has appeared in more than 50 supporting screen roles, most often defending or flouting the law. He got his start in show business back in the 20's when he toured the country with sundry stock companies and vaudeville shows. Eventually, he landed in Hollywood, where he found some work in films but no important roles. He therefore abandoned the West Coast to try Broadway. Finally, after several years traveling from one coast to the other, a successful Broadway run aroused the interest of the movie moguls, and his screen career gained momentum. In 1940 he landed the title role in *Brigham Young, Frontiersman,* and in 1949 he won the Academy Award for Best Supporting Actor for his performance as Major Stovall in *Twelve O'Clock High*. Since that time he has continued to appear on screen and in recent years has also become familiar to television audiences. **Credits include:** *Woman from Hell* (debut, 1929), *You Belong to Me* (1934), *Western Union* (1941), *Rawhide* (1951), *White Christmas* (1954), *Bad Day at Black Rock* (1955), *Elmer Gantry* (1960), *Day of the Evil Gun* (1968), *The Kremlin Letter* (1970).

HARRY JAMES (1916–   )

One of the greats of the world of jazz, he made his name playing the trumpet for Benny Goodman, and his own organization has been a fixture in the entertainment world for decades. The much-married James was wed to Betty Grable for more than 20 years and played opposite her in *Springtime in the Rockies* (1942). **Other films include:** *Best Foot Forward* (1943), *Two Girls and a Sailor* (1944), *Carnegie Hall* (1947), *The Benny Goodman Story* (1956), *The Opposite Sex* (1956).

EMIL JANNINGS (1886–1950)

In the years that followed World War I and preceded the advent of Adolf Hitler, German films had a freshness and vitality all their own, and Emil Jannings, who starred in many of those films, was acknowledged to be one of the outstanding, if not *the* outstanding, performer in the world of silent pictures.

Authorities differ as to his place of birth. Some say Switzerland, some the United States. In any event he was in Germany in his infancy and first appeared on stage at the age of ten. He was a member of Max Reinhardt's company before the Great War and in 1918 was persuaded by his friend Ernst Lubitsch to make his film debut in *Madame Dubarry*.

A stocky actor with a masklike countenance that could turn mobile in a split second, Jannings made such films as *The Last Laugh*

(1924) and *Variety* (1925) enormously popular. Later in the decade Lubitsch, who had become one of Hollywood's top directors, persuaded Jannings to come to America. He won the first Best Actor Academy Award ever given for his performances in *The Way of All Flesh* (1928) and *The Last Command* (1928). In Lubitsch's fine film *The Patriot* (1928) some sound was dubbed in, but not Jannings' voice, for he could speak only German.

Returning to Germany, he starred in von Sternberg's *The Blue Angel* (1930) but, as all film addicts know, was overshadowed by a husky-voiced German girl named Dietrich.

During the Hitler regime German films went into a precipitous decline and Jannings appeared in several propaganda pictures. When World War II ended, an inquiry was held into the role he had played in Nazi ventures which ended with his acquittal. Before he could pick up the threads of his career, however, and as he was preparing to play Pope Boniface VIII in a film dealing with the life of that dignitary, he died. **Other films:** *The Eyes of the Mummy* (1918), *Anne Boleyn* (1921), *Waxworks* (1924), *Faust* (1926), *The Young and the Old King* (1935), *Ohm Krüger* (1941).

DAVID JANSSEN (1930–   )

Nebraska-born Janssen (David Meyer) played feature roles in war films and action dramas before being cast as the lead in the TV detective series *Richard Diamond* (1957–1960). Later, Janssen starred in another successful TV series, *The Fugitive*. **Films include:** *Yankee Buccaneer* (1952), *Toy Tiger* (1956), *Ring of Fire* (1961), *Hell to Eternity* (1961), *My Six Loves* (1963), *The Green Berets* (1968), *The Shoes of the Fisherman* (1968), *Where It's At* (1969).

CLAUDE JARMAN, JR. (1934–   )

While attending the fifth grade in his native Nashville, Tennessee, the untrained Claude Jarman, Jr., was chosen by director Clarence Brown to play Jody in *The Yearling* (1946). His fine performance won Jarman a special Academy Award and overnight recognition as a child star. He remained in Hollywood for seven years and appeared in numerous films,

but left the screen at the age of 17. He later tried unsuccessfully to re-establish his career in the 50's. In recent years, Jarman has worked with the film industry in public relations jobs. In 1972, he produced the rock-concert feature *Fillmore*. **Some of his films include:** *High Barbaree* (1947), *The Sun Comes Up* (1949), *Intruder in the Dust* (1949), *Rio Grande* (1950), *Fair Wind to Java* (1953), *The Great Locomotive Chase* (1956).

GLORIA JEAN (1928–   )

Gloria Jean Schoonover made her singing debut at the age of three in Scranton, Pennsylvania, and two years later she had her own radio program, *The Scranton Sirens*. By the time she was 11, Jean was a child star of musical features in New York City. She was

David Janssen, caught betwixt Dina Merrill and Brad Dexter in Twenty Plus Two *(1961).*

Gloria Jean with Alan Curtis and Frank Craven (center) in Destiny *(1945). The dog's name escapes us.*

Allen Jenkins philosophizes as Joan Blondell listens in the enormously funny Three Men on a Horse *(1936).*

"discovered" there by film producer Joe Pasternak, who brought her to Hollywood and cast her in *The Under-Pup* (1939). Soon the impish Jean was the star of musical feature films and hailed as the successor to Deanna Durbin, who had moved on to ingénue roles.

Although she appeared in 21 pictures in the 40's, in such films as *Never Give a Sucker an Even Break* (1941) with W. C. Fields, she was not able successfully to make the transition to adult roles and made only four films in the 50's and 60's. She has since retired. **Credits include:** *If I Had My Way* (1940), *A Little Bit of Heaven* (1940), *Moonlight in Vermont* (1943), *Pardon My Rhythm* (1944), *I'll Remember April* (1945), *Easy to Look At* (1945), *Copacabana* (1947), *There's a Girl in My Heart* (1950), *The Ladies' Man* (1961).

ANNE JEFFREYS (1923–)

Anne Jeffreys began her performing career in opera, but was lured to Broadway to play in *Street Scene*. She subsequently appeared in other productions such as *Kiss Me Kate* and *Three Kisses for Jamie*.

Her first film role was in *I Married an Angel* (1942), and she made several "B" flicks in the 40's before turning to television in the next decade. Jeffries appeared with her husband, Robert Sterling, in the popular TV series *Topper*, and later they played in the *Love That Jill* series. In recent years, Jeffreys has made frequent TV appearances and returned to the stage in a revival of *Kismet*. **Credits include:** *Step Lively* (1944), *Riff-Raff* (1947), *Return of the Badmen* (1948), *Boys' Night Out* (1962).

LIONEL JEFFRIES (1926–)

An English character actor and comedian, Lionel Jeffries specializes in playing rather stiff types, confused and bewildered by those around him. Since his first film appearance in 1952, Jeffries has brightened dozens of pictures. A perfect example of his style is his portrayal of Inspector Parker in the 1963 Peter Sellers film *The Wrong Arm of the Law*. **Other film credits include:** *Lust for Life* (1956), *Please Turn Over* (1961), *Murder*

Ahoy (1964), *Chitty Chitty Bang Bang* (1968).

ALLEN JENKINS (1900–   )

It is not surprising that the hatchet-faced comedian looked Irish, since he was born Al McGonegal. During a long, long career he always played what a critic called "illiterate, illogical, but illuminating mugs." He was a native New Yorker and began as a hoofer in the same chorus line as James Cagney in the 1922 New York production *Pitter Patter*.

His film career began with talkies, in *The Girl Habit* (1931), and subsequently he played elevator boys, gangsters, clerks and the like in nearly 200 movies. More recently, he returned to the stage. **Film credits include:** *Blessed Event* (1932), *42nd Street* (1933), *The Case of the Lucky Legs* (1935), *Brother Orchid* (1940), *Pillow Talk* (1959), *Doctor, You've Got to Be Kidding* (1967).

JACKIE "BUTCH" JENKINS (1937–   )

For five years in the 40's, a kid named Butch Jenkins was an audience favorite as the all-American boy. He had a space between his teeth, freckles and a tousled mop of hair—a marked contrast to the pretty children who usually appeared on screen.

Jenkins was discovered by an MGM talent scout who saw him playing on a Santa Monica, California, beach and was impressed by his high spirits and clowning. He made his debut as Mickey Rooney's younger brother in *The Human Comedy* (1943) and went on to play opposite some of the leading child actresses of the day. He was Elizabeth Taylor's brother in *National Velvet* (1944), Margaret O'Brien's cousin in *Our Vines Have Tender Grapes* (1945) and her sidekick in *The Big City* (1948). In *My Brother Talks to Horses* (1946) he played a boy who could communicate with an equine tipster. Jenkins retired after making 11 pictures. **Films include:** *An American Romance* (1944), *Bud Abbott and Lou Costello in Hollywood* (1945), *Boy's Ranch* (1946), *The Bride Goes Wild* (1948), *Summer Holiday* (1948).

GEORGE JESSEL (1898–   )

The "toastmaster general" of the United States is much more famous for his Broadway and television appearances than he is for his films. He is a supersalesman of bonds for Israel and travels the country delivering his fast line of comic patter as part of his sales pitch.

Jessel, the son of a theatrical manager, made his first stage appearance at the age of nine. During his 60 years in show business, he has written songs, produced 23 films and written several books, including his autobiography, *So Help Me*, published in 1943. **Films include:** *The Other Man's Wife* (1919), *Vitaphone* (1926), *Private Izzy Murphy* (1926), *Lucky Boy* (1929), *Love, Live and Laugh* (1929), *Stage Door Canteen* (1943), *Four Jills in a Jeep* (1944), *The Busy Body* (1967).

Isabel Jewell, looking even blonder than usual, with urbane William Powell in Evelyn Prentice *(1934).*

Glynis Johns soaks nervously in a remake of an earlier film that made history, The Cabinet of Caligari *(1962). The original said Dr. Caligari.*

Ben Johnson, one of several outstanding performers in The Last Picture Show.

ISABEL JEWELL (1910–1972)

From time to time she was starred, but far more often she played brazen hussies, bar girls, gangsters' molls and down-and-out ladies of the street. She hailed from Wyoming cow country and first appeared on Broadway in *Up Pops the Devil* (1930). Not long after that she was so good in *Blessed Event* that she was exported to Hollywood to repeat the role in the 1932 film version.

During a 35-year career she appeared in more than 100 films, some of them very good indeed. **Credits include:** *Counselor-at-Law* (1933), *A Tale of Two Cities* (1935), *Marked Woman* (1937), *Lost Horizon* (1937), *High Sierra* (1941), *Bernadine* (1957).

GLYNIS JOHNS (1923–)

A happy combination of sensuality and innocence, South African-born Johns is at her best when she gives full range to her comic talents. The daughter of Welsh actor Mervyn Johns, she first appeared on the London stage in 1935 and made her English film debut as the hysterical schoolgirl in *South Riding* (1936). The startling and appealing combination of sexy voice and innocent looks later made her a star in *Miranda* (1948). During the following decades she appeared in numerous British films, unfortunately often miscast in melodramas and romances. Johns has also made a handful of American films, mainly light comedies which have proven good vehicles for displaying her comic flair.

Johns now lives in the United States. In 1973 she won a Tony Award for her performance in the long-running Broadway musical comedy *A Little Night Music*. **Film credits include:** *The Card* (1952), *The Court Jester* (1956), *Around the World in 80 Days* (1956), *The Chapman Report* (1962), *Mary Poppins* (1964), *Lock Up Your Daughters* (1969).

BEN JOHNSON (1919–)

An ex-wrangler from Oklahoma, Johnson came to Hollywood in 1940 to deliver 300 horses for a Howard Hughes Western, *The Outlaw,* starring Jane Russell. He stayed —with the horses—becoming a cowboy stunt man and standing in for such Western heroes as Fonda, Wayne, and Cooper. He later appeared in character roles and, in 1971, won an Academy Award for his supporting performance in *The Last Picture Show*. **Highlights of more than 30 films:** *Mighty Joe Young* (1949), *Shane* (1953), *One Eyed Jacks* (1961), *Major Dundee* (1965).

CHIC JOHNSON (1891–1962)

With his partner Ole Olsen, Chic Johnson worked up a vaudeville routine into the frantic Broadway comedy smash hit *Hellzapoppin*. The show, which ran from 1938 to 1941, was turned into an equally hectic movie in 1941, and forever after its veteran show business creators found themselves referred to as the *Hellzapoppin* stars.

The two performers first worked together in Chicago in 1914, when violinist-singer-ventriloquist Olsen and ragtime pianist Johnson decided they would have a better chance as a team than either would doing singles' acts. They were right, and ended up spending almost a half-century together, appearing successfully in vaudeville, on Broadway and in motion pictures. **Film highlights:** *Fifty Million Frenchmen* (1931), *Crazy House* (1943), *See My Lawyer* (1945).

CELIA JOHNSON (1908–)

One of the most respected leading ladies of the London stage, Johnson has appeared in films infrequently but always to the delight of critics. Her performance in the film version of Noel Coward's *Brief Encounter* (1946) won her a New York Film Critics Award.

Johnson attended the Royal Academy of Dramatic Art in London and made her stage debut in *Major Barbara*. She scored her first personal success on stage in the unsuccessful play *Debonair* (1930), and three years later she won raves for her performance in *Wind and the Rain* (1933).

Her appearance as the headmistress in *The Prime of Miss Jean Brodie* (1969) came after a ten-year absence from the screen. **Films include:** *In Which We Serve* (1942), *This Happy Breed* (1944), *The Astonished Heart* (1950), *I Believe in You* (1953), *The Captain's Paradise* (1953), *The Holly and the Ivy* (1954), *A Kid for Two Farthings* (1956).

KAY JOHNSON (c. 1905–)

Kay Johnson was already an established Broadway star when Cecil B. De Mille cast her as the spoiled heiress of his first sound film, *Dynamite* (1929). In 1930, she again starred for De Mille, this time as the bored wife in *Madam Satan* (1930). For several years after this, Johnson continued to be cast in leading roles, but after the mid-30's her career rapidly tapered off. **Films include:** *The Ship from Shanghai* (1930), *This Mad World* (1930), *Billy the Kid* (1930), *The Spoilers* (1930), *Passion Flower* (1930), *The Single Sin* (1931), *American Madness* (1932), *Of Human Bondage* (1934), *Mr. Lucky* (1943).

RICHARD JOHNSON (1927–)

English actor Richard Johnson received his training at the Royal Academy of Dramatic Art in London. He made his stage debut at the Manchester Opera House and later played with Gielgud's repertory group in many Shakespearean roles. After a three-year stint in the British Navy, Johnson returned to the stage, appearing in such plays as *The Madwoman of Chaillot* and *The Lark*. He has been a member of the Royal Shakespeare Theatre and the Royal Shakespeare Company.

In addition to his stagework, Johnson has made several films, usually appearing in supporting roles in "B" or "B+" pictures. **Films include:** *The Haunting* (1963), *The Pumpkin Eater* (1964), *Deadlier Than the Male* (1967), *Oedipus, the King* (1968).

RITA JOHNSON (1912–1965)

Rita Johnson came to Hollywood via Broadway and radio and made her film debut in *London by Night* (1937). During her early film career, Johnson was often cast as the blonde menace or the other woman, but eventually she graduated to more sympathetic roles. In 1948 she was struck on the head by a falling hair dryer and survived an operation to remove blood clots pressing against her brain. After her recovery, she worked sporadically until her death from a brain hemorrhage. **Highlights of more than 50 films:** *Edison, the Man* (1940), *Here Comes Mr. Jordan* (1941), *My Friend Flicka* (1943), *The Big*

Van Johnson turns down Elizabeth Taylor's offer of what looks like caviar but isn't in the MGM picture The Big Hangover *(1950).*

Clock (1948), *Susan Slept Here* (1954), *All Mine to Give* (1957).

VAN JOHNSON (1916–)

With his fresh-faced good looks and sincere expression, Van Johnson was cast in many films as "the boy next door" and his appearances in films during and just after World War II brought thousands of fan letters from infatuated teen-aged girls.

Johnson was born in Rhode Island and began his career on the Broadway stage as a chorus boy. Discovered by Hollywood, he made his debut in a bit part in *Murder in the Big House* (1941) but was soon on the way up at MGM, playing second male leads to some of that company's biggest stars. He did an excellent job in *The Human Comedy* (1943) and really arrived in a sort of "non-war" war picture—as Ted Randall in *A Guy Named Joe* (1943) with Spencer Tracy, Irene Dunne, and Lionel Barrymore. Still flying, Johnson played the real-life hero, Captain Ted Lawson, in *Thirty Seconds Over Tokyo* (1944).

Singing Al Jolson and dancing Ruby Keeler in Go Into Your Dance *(1935).*

As he moved away from semi-juvenile roles, he proved most capable in *State of the Union* (1948) and *The Caine Mutiny* (1954), while continuing to do movie musicals with Esther Williams and June Allyson. In recent years he has developed into an admirable character actor, appearing on the stage as well as the screen. **Other films:** *Miracle in the Rain* (1956), *Wives and Lovers* (1963), *Divorce American Style* (1967), *Company of Killers* (1970).

AL JOLSON (1886–1950)

If assorted anonymous tinkerers had not hit upon a way of synchronizing a sound track with motion picture film, Al Jolson (along with Eddie Cantor and a number of others) would be remembered only as one of a group of second-generation American song-and-dance men who came close to dominating vaudeville and Broadway stages back in the days before the Great Depression. But as things worked out, he achieved a special immortality by starring in the first talking picture, *The Jazz Singer* (1927).

Like so many other Jewish comedians of his day, Asa Yoelson was Russian-born. His family had expected him to become a cantor, but intoning prayers in a synagogue didn't appeal to him, so he ran away from home to join a vaudeville team. A highly emotional performer whose on-stage acrobatics made him look as though he was just on the verge of an epileptic seizure, he rocketed to fame and fortune in blackface. Those were days when ebony makeup surrounding wide fleshy lips combined to create a stereotyped "darky," and no one protested when Jolson, on one knee with white-gloved hands clasped prayerfully above him, implored his dear old mammy to take him back to the unadulterated joys of black life in the sunny South. To the contrary, audiences loved Jolson and his own special tag line—"You ain't heard nothin' yet."

As a Broadway personality and friend of most of Hollywood's pioneer film-makers, Jolson made two early sound shorts for D. W. Griffith. They had little impact, but when the maudlin tear jerker *The Jazz Singer* was released, it became instantly apparent that the world of the film had turned topsy-turvy. Within a few weeks, every studio was feverishly searching for actors who could talk, and the careers of many of the top stars wilted and died overnight.

Jolson went on to make many more pictures, all cast from the same mold. Eventually audiences tired of Swanee River and up-from-the-ghetto themes (which were Jolson's two plot patterns) and stayed away from his films in large numbers. By that time, though, it didn't matter, for Jolson's fame was secure. In 1946 his life was recorded for posterity in *The Jolson Story*, and in that film his own voice was dubbed in for that of Larry Parks, who played the title role. And, as if that wasn't enough, the theme was repeated three years later in *Jolson Sings Again*. **Films include:** *The Singing Fool* (1928), *Mammy* (1930), *Wonder Bar* (1933), *Hallelujah I'm a Bum* (1934), *Rose of Washington Square* (1939), *Swanee River* (1940).

ALLAN JONES (1908–   )

A singer who first found success on Broadway in musical hits like *The Student*

Al Jolson appeared in his famous blackface in The Jazz Singer *with May McAvoy.*

Prince and *Blossom Time*, Jones played some leading roles in motion pictures of the late 30's and 40's. He made his film debut in *Reckless* (1935) and played Gaylord Ravenal opposite Irene Dunne in *Show Boat* (1936). His most memorable film was *The Firefly* (1937) with Jeanette MacDonald. With the Marx Brothers he sang to create interludes that broke up their demented routines.

Jones was the son of a miner of Scranton, Pennsylvania, and sang with his family in a Welsh choral society before winning a music scholarship to Syracuse University. After college, he studied voice in Europe and later made his debut as a soloist with the New York Philharmonic Orchestra. Jones has also been a popular nightclub and recording star whose biggest hit, ''Donkey Serenade,'' became his theme song. He was married for 21 years to actress Irene Hervey and their son is singer Jack Jones. **Films include:** *A Night at the Opera* (1935), *A Day at the Races* (1937), *The Boys from Syracuse* (1940), *One Night in the Tropics* (1940), *True to the Army* (1942), *When Johnny Comes Marching Home* (1943), *Honeymoon Ahead* (1945), *Stage to Thunder Rock* (1963).

BARRY JONES (1893–   )

Barry Jones began his stage career in London in 1921, playing in Shaw repertory. During the following decades he appeared widely in his native England and in America, and after World War II he founded a successful repertory company with an American he had met during the war.

Jones' first film role was Bluntshli in *Arms and the Man* (1931). Usually cast as a shy, diffident man, Jones departed from this type of character to play the slightly mad atomic scientist in the highly successful *Seven Days to Noon* (1950). **Other film credits include:** *Squadron Leader X* (1942), *Dancing with Crime* (1946), *Frieda* (1947), *The Calendar* (1948), *White Corridors* (1952), *Prince Valiant* (1954), *Brigadoon* (1954), *War and Peace* (1956), *The Safecracker* (1958), *A Study in Terror* (1966).

BUCK JONES (1889–1942)

Jones was born in Vincennes, Indiana, and raised on an Oklahoma ranch. He arrived in Hollywood during the 20's and went to work as a double for rough-riding stars. Eventually, his talents as a rider led to stardom. During the 20's and 30's Buck Jones was the hero of millions of young boys who joined the Buck Jones Club, wore Buck Jones cowboy outfits, and carried Buck Jones cap pistols.

He made hundreds of silent and sound features before his death in a tragic Boston nightclub fire that claimed 492 lives. **Films include:** *Straight from the Shoulder* (1920), *Skid Proof* (1923), *Hearts and Spurs* (1925), *Riders of the Purple Sage* (1926), *The Flying Horseman* (1927), *The Lone Rider* (1930), *Border Law* (1932), *The California Trail* (1933), *When a Man Sees Red* (1934), *Boss Rider of Gun Creek* (1936), *Riders of Death Valley* (1941).

CAROLYN JONES (1933–   )

In 1957, six minutes on the screen as the love-starved Greenwich Village bohemian in *The Bachelor Party* earned her an Academy Award nomination for Best Supporting Actress. It also gave her career the boost it needed to transform her from just another actress into a sought-after star.

Texas-born Jones graduated from Pasadena Playhouse only to find the film industry in a slump and acting jobs at a premium. Although things picked up for her the following year when she won roles in *The Big Heat* (1953) and *House of Wax* (1953), Jones subsequently appeared only occasionally in small parts. After *The Bachelor Party*, however, she was able to turn down more roles than she had been offered in all her previous years in Hollywood. She played Marsha, Natalie Wood's man-chasing friend, in *Marjorie Morningstar* (1958) and Frank Sinatra's kooky girlfriend in *A Hole in the Head* (1959). Fearing that she was being typecast in wacky-women roles, Jones attempted to change her image with her straight portrayal in *Ice Palace* (1960).

In addition to her film work, she has appeared on stage and television. In 1964, she played the role of Morticia in the TV series *The Addams Family*. **Films include:** *Road to Bali* (1952), *The Opposite Sex* (1956), *Last Train from Gun Hill* (1958), *A Ticklish Affair* (1963).

Carolyn Jones, with a table setting that may or may not explode.

Jennifer Jones joins hands with Joseph Cotten in the 1949 production Portrait of Jennie.

JENNIFER JONES (1919–   )

Jennifer Jones (born Phyllis Isley) began her acting career as a child—first touring in her parents' stock company and later receiving professional training at the American Academy of Dramatic Arts in New York. In 1939, she married Robert Walker and began appearing in small roles in minor films. Her break came when she attracted the attention of magnate David O. Selznick, who had her carefully schooled in preparation for her "big role." It came in *The Song of Bernadette* (1943), which received five Oscars, including one for Jones for Best Actress.

Thereafter, Selznick devoted himself to finding or creating roles especially for her. She was fortunate in not being stereotyped by her mentor, and performed in a variety of roles. She revealed her comedic talents in *Cluny Brown* (1946), her dramatic abilities in *Madame Bovary* (1949), and her instinct for sensitive characterizations in *Good Morning,*

Miss Dove (1955). Jones and Walker were divorced in 1945; four years later she and Selznick married. **Other film credits include:** *Beat the Devil* (1954), *Love Is a Many-Splendored Thing* (1955), *The Man in the Gray Flannel Suit* (1956), *A Farewell to Arms* (1958), *Tender Is the Night* (1962), *The Idol* (1966).

SHIRLEY JONES (1934–   )

Not many young actresses become overnight stars. Shirley Jones did. The inexperienced hopeful had gone to see an actors' agent during a trip to New York and on the same day was signed by Rodgers and Hammerstein to play Laurey in the road company of *Oklahoma!*. After touring with the show Jones won small roles in *South Pacific* and *Me and Juliet* before being cast, again as Laurey, in the screen version of *Oklahoma!* (1955).

Jones followed up that success with another Rodgers and Hammerstein film hit, *Carousel* (1956). She soon had a reputation in Hollywood as a talented singer ideal for sweet-young-thing roles. She had other ideas, though. She appeared as an alcoholic in the TV film *The Big Slide* and her fine performance led to the role of the prostitute in *Elmer Gantry* (1960). This change-of-pace role surprised Hollywood, freed her from typecasting, and won her an Academy Award for Best Supporting Actress.

During the 60's, Jones appeared frequently in films and on television. In 1970, she won an Emmy nomination for her role in *Silent Night, Lonely Night*. She became further established in the public mind as a TV performer as the mother in the situation comedy *The Partridge Family*, co-starring (among others) her stepson, David Cassidy. She also appeared with husband Jack Cassidy in the successful National Theatre Guild tour of *Wait Until Dark* in 1968. **Jones' films include:** *Two Rode Together* (1961), *The Music Man* (1962), *A Ticklish Affair* (1963), *Bedtime Story* (1964).

DOROTHY JORDAN (1910–   )

An actress who studied at the American Academy of Dramatic Arts in New York,

Shirley Jones as Laurey and Gordon MacRae as Curly in the surrey with the fringe on top, from Arthur Hornblow's production of the famed Oklahoma!

Jordan made her film debut in the 1929 early talkie version of *The Taming of the Shrew* (with additional dialogue by Samuel Taylor!) starring Douglas Fairbanks and Mary Pickford. During the following four years, she made over 20 more films, including a series of pictures like *Devil May Care* (1929) in which she was teamed with heart-throb Ramon Novarro. In 1933, she married Merian C. Cooper, the production chief at RKO, and subsequently appeared only occasionally on screen. **Credits include:** *In Gay Madrid* (1930), *Min and Bill* (1930), *Young Sinners* (1931), *The Lost Squadron* (1932), *The Cabin in the Cotton* (1932).

VICTOR JORY (1902–   )

Jory, born in Dawson City, Alaska, moved to California and studied acting at the Pasadena Playhouse. He soon entered the movies and since 1932 has appeared in over 120 films, mostly Westerns. He has a gloomy, taciturn air about him and is most often cast as a villain. His thin, hard-muscled physique and his championship skill at boxing and wrestling were ideal attributes for the more sinister characters he created in his early films. He has also appeared from time to time on the stage. **Credits include:** *Pride of the Legion* (1932), *Sailor's Luck* (1933), *State Fair* (1933), *Escape from Devil's Island* (1935), *Gone With the Wind* (1939), *The Miracle Worker* (1962), *A Time for Dying* (1969).

ALLYN JOSLYN (1905–   )

A specialist at playing snobs and stuffed shirts, he is a talented comedian who on screen was often engaged to but never married the girl. Before going west he had delighted Broadway audiences in assorted farces and at least once turned serious in *Richard III* with John Barrymore.

His first film was *They Won't Forget* (1937), but it wasn't until his success on Broadway in *Arsenic and Old Lace* (1941) that he became dear to Hollywood's heart. Since then he has appeared in a considerable assortment of films, mostly as insufferable bounders played with subtle humor and insight, the aristocratic nose above his dainty

Allyn Joslyn looks a bit like a young George Arliss as he escorts Gene Tierney front and center in the Lubitsch-directed Heaven Can Wait *(1943).*

mustache looking as though it had sniffed something unpleasant in the air. **Credits include:** *Only Angels Have Wings* (1939), *Junior Miss* (1945), *If You Knew Susie* (1948), *As Young as You Feel* (1951), *The Fastest Gun Alive* (1956).

LOUIS JOURDAN (1919–   )

With his elegance, French accent and dark good looks, Louis Jourdan has spent a good part of his acting years fighting Hollywood's unfailing impulse to cast him as a dashing continental charmer.

Born Louis Gendre in Marseilles, Jourdan attended René Simon's Ecole Dramatique and played small stage roles before being signed up for his first film, *Le Corsaire* (1939). His budding film career was interrupted by the outbreak of the war; and after refusing to act in Nazi propaganda films, Jourdan joined the underground. In 1946, a Hollywood talent scout saw him and sent clips of his works to David O. Selznick. Jour-

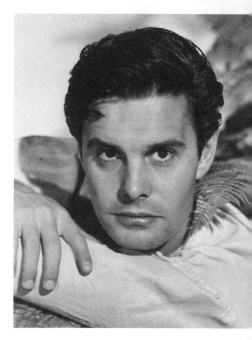

Louis Jourdan being tickled by a stray fern in the 20th Century–Fox production Bird of Paradise *(1951).*

Alice Joyce, apparently fearful of sharing the camera with anyone else, muffles a friend in The Little French Girl *(1925).*

Brenda Joyce shies away from a would-be killer (Lon Chaney) in Pillow of Death *(1946).*

dan was given the role of the guilt-ridden valet in Hitchcock's *The Paradine Case* (1948). After that film, however, Selznick cast him in romantic lead and supporting roles.

Jourdan's biggest film success to date came ten years after his Hollywood debut when he appeared as the bored playboy, Gaston, in the delightful musical *Gigi* (1958). **Film credits include:** *No Minor Vices* (1949), *Madame Bovary* (1949), *Three Coins in the Fountain* (1954), *Julie* (1956), *Can-Can* (1960), *Made in Paris* (1966), *Peau d'Espion* (1967), *A Flea in Her Ear* (1968).

LOUIS JOUVET (1887–1951)

Coupling sardonic wit with a magnetic but menacing exterior, Louis Jouvet was one of the most respected French actors of his generation. He began his career in the French theatre as an actor/director interested particularly in *avant-garde* productions and became one of the leading interpreters of Giradoux, Sartre and Romains.

Jouvet appeared in films as early as 1913, spent the middle part of his acting career in the theatre, and—while still active on stage—once again turned to the screen in *Topaze* (1932). Whether portraying a priest, a petty criminal or a detective, Jouvet brought a cynical charm to his film roles. **His credits include:** *La Kérmesse Heroïque* (1935), *Les Bas Fonds* (1936), *Un Carnet de Bal* (1937), *La Fin du Jour* (1939), *Volpone* (1947).

LEATRICE JOY (1897–   )

She was a star of silent pictures who mostly appeared in the neo-sophisticated drawing-room epics of the day. Her career flourished through the 20's, but after several talkies (*The Bellamy Trial*, 1929, was one) it languished. She left the screen in 1931 but returned to appear in character parts later. **Movie highlights include:** *You Can't Fool Your Wife* (1923), *The Dressmaker from Paris* (1925), *A Most Immoral Lady* (1929), *First Love* (1939), *The Old Swimming Hole* (1940), *Show People* (1967).

ALICE JOYCE (1889–1955)

Joyce was another top-ranking star of the silent era who made only a few pictures after the coming of sound. Her debut was in *The Courage of Silence* (1917), but it was tear-jerkers like *Stella Dallas* (1925) that made her career flourish. **Film highlights:** *Within the Law* (1917), *The Green Goddess* (1923), *Daddy's Gone A-Hunting* (1925), *Beau Geste* (1926), *Dancing Mothers* (1926), *Sorrell & Son* (1927), *Song o' My Heart* (1930), *He Knew Women* (1930).

BRENDA JOYCE (1918–   )

Kansas-born model Brenda Joyce (Betty Leabo) was discovered by Darryl Zanuck, who saw her dazzling smile in a magazine. With her candid beauty and a freshness that made her atypical in Hollywood, Joyce played numerous leading ladies in a series of mostly "B" pictures during the 40's. In 1945, she appeared for the first time as Johnny Weissmuller's Jane in *Tarzan and the Amazons*. Subsequently, she co-starred with him in three more of the Edgar Rice Burroughs tales before transferring her affections to Lex Barker in *Tarzan's Magic Fountain* (1949). **Credits include:** *The Rains Came* (debut, 1939), *Little Old New York* (1940), *Maryland* (1940), *Private Nurse* (1941), *Strange Confession* (1945), *Spider Woman Strikes Back* (1946).

ARLINE JUDGE (1912–1974)

Arline Judge worked her way from nightclub routines, small Broadway parts, radio and vaudeville to her first film role in *Are These Our Children?* (1931). In the early part of her career her youthful, innocent appearance caused her to be cast as baby-faced college girls. However, the much-married Judge eventually graduated to more mature roles in the late 30's. She worked sporadically during the 40's and left the screen early in the next decade. **Credits include:** *Girl Crazy* (1932), *The Age of Consent* (1932), *King of Burlesque* (1936), *Valiant Is the Word for Carrie* (1937), *The Lady Is Willing* (1942), *From This Day Forward* (1946), *Mad Wednesday* (1951).

KATY JURADO (1927–   )

Katy Jurado was born Maria Jurado Garcia into a distinguished Mexican family—her great, great grandfather once owned most of what is now Texas. She was an established leading lady in films south of the border when (with almost no knowledge of English) she made her American film debut in *The Bullfighter and the Lady* (1951).

Sultry, deep-voiced and with a fiery temperament, Jurado had her best part to date in *High Noon* (1952) for which she received an Academy Award nomination. In recent years she has been moving toward character roles, playing mothers to such luminaries as Kirk Douglas and Anthony Quinn—both older than she. For a time she had a syndicated column in Mexican papers as a critic of bullfights and has also written for magazines about her Hollywood career and life. **Some of her films include:** *Arrowhead* (1953), *Broken Lance* (1954), *Trapeze* (1956), *One Eyed Jacks* (1961), *Barabbas* (1962), *Stay Away Joe* (1968).

CURT JURGENS (1912–   )

A versatile movie-maker, Jurgens has worked as an actor, screenwriter, and director, sometimes functioning in all three capacities in the same movie. He was born in Munich and began his career at the Burg Theatre in Vienna. When it was closed by the Nazis in 1944, Jurgens went to work in films. Later, however, he was deported to Hungary and eventually came to the United States.

In his many film appearances both here and abroad, Jurgens often has been cast as either a gentlemanly seducer or a villain. To American audiences, he is probably most familiar as an evil military officer. In 1955 he received the Venice Film Festival Award and in 1957 the French Film Academy Award for Best Actor. **His movie performances include:** *The Royal Waltz* (1936), *The Mozart Story* (1948), *Les Héros Sont Fatigués* (1955), *And God Created Woman* (1957), *The Blue Angel* (1959), *Lord Jim* (1965), *The Threepenny Opera* (1965), *The Battle of Neretva* (1971), *The Mephisto Waltz* (1971).

JAMES R. JUSTICE (1905–   )

This burly Scottish film star has run the gamut of experiences from sports car racing to stage action and movie-making. He is a former journalist and naturalist and the second actor to be elected Lord Rector of Edinburgh University. Since his screen debut in *Fiddlers Three* (1944), Justice, who holds a PhD degree and was once tutor to Prince Charles, has appeared in character roles in some 50 British and American films—a prolific career for a man who once said, "No one is more surprised than I to find myself acting for a living." **Credits include:** *Rob Roy* (1954), *Moby Dick* (1956), *Campbell's Kingdom* (1958), *The Guns of Navarone* (1961), *Act of Mercy* (1961), *Down Among the Dead Men* (1962), *Chitty Chitty Bang Bang* (1968).

Curt Jurgens in the role he played so often—a Nazi officer.

James Robertson Justice was Commander Jensen in the tingling adventure film The Guns of Navarone.

288

MADELINE KAHN (1943–)

After comic performances in only four pictures, Kahn had acquired a coterie of loyal fans and an Academy Award nomination. Although the Oscar nomination came for her performance as Trixie Delight, Ryan O'Neal's floozie in *Paper Moon* (1973), Kahn fans loved her even more as Lili Von Shtupp, the barroom *femme fatale, à la* Dietrich, in Mel Brooks' *Blazing Saddles* (1974).

Kahn was born in Boston and grew up in New York City. She won a drama scholarship to Hofstra University, where she majored in speech therapy since it seemed a more practical profession than acting. After graduation she sang in revues for a few years until parts on Broadway began opening up for her. She was in the Richard Rodgers musical *Two by Two* (1970), starring Danny Kaye, and then switched to drama in the controversial David Rabe play *The Boom Boom Room*. Director Peter Bogdanovich gave Kahn her movie break with the role of Ryan O'Neal's uptight girlfriend who loses out to Barbra Streisand in *What's Up, Doc?* (1972). **Films include:** *From the Mixed-up Files of Mrs. Basil E. Frankweiler* (1973).

MARVIN KAPLAN (1927–)

His pronounced Brooklyn accent wasn't affected, since that New York City borough happened to be his place of origin. He studied acting at the University of Southern California, and the story has it that shortly after graduation he came to the attention of Katharine Hepburn while appearing in a Molière production. Result: the role of court stenographer in the Tracy–Hepburn comedy *Adam's Rib* (1949).

Kaplan is an extremely funny man, his style aided and abetted by his moon face and thick-lensed glasses. He has combined his film career with TV work, and in 1970 he won an Emmy nomination for an appearance in the *Mod Squad* series. Among other less well-known achievements, he was the voice of two prominent television animals—Francis, the talking mule, and Choo Choo in *Top Cat*. **Films include:** *The Reformer and the Redhead* (1950), *I Can Get It for You Wholesale* (1951), *Behave Yourself* (1951), *A New Kind of Love* (1963), *The Great Race* (1965).

ANNA KARINA (1940–)

The almost Tolstoyan name was substituted for her own (Hanne Karin Beyer) when the 18-year-old beauty deserted her native

Anna Karina and Dirk Bogarde show empathy for each other in Justine.

Denmark to model in Paris. Discovered via an advertising film by her future husband, director Jean-Luc Godard, she made her first feature film appearance in 1960 in his *Le Petit Soldat* (U.S., 1967). During the next five years Karina starred almost exclusively in Godard works. She was especially good as the striptease artist who wanted to become a mother in *A Woman Is a Woman* (1961; U.S., 1964), with Jean-Paul Belmondo and Jean-Claude Brialy, and as the pigtailed student who loved a gangster in *Band of Outsiders* (1964). Besides her work with Godard, she has also starred occasionally in other French films and, since the mid-60's, in some American films. **Credits include:** *She'll Have to Go* (1961), *The Stranger* (1967), *Made in USA* (U.S., 1967), *The Magus* (1968), *Before Winter Comes* (1969), *Justine* (1969).

BORIS KARLOFF (1887–1969)

Back in 1931 when the early makers of sound films cast William Henry Pratt as Frankenstein's unphotogenic monster, the London-born actor probably never suspected that he had been typecast beyond hope of redemption. The role he created—of a hulking, shuffling, square-shouldered and square-headed, doughy-faced non-person—not only was imitated in every corner of the globe but also became the basis for an outpouring of cartoons, comic strips and TV comedies. Karloff was invariably hailed with a "Hi, Frankenstein" by fans who obstinately refused to accept the fact that Frankenstein was the creator of the monster, not the thing itself.

Karloff first appeared on stage in a British Columbia stock-company cast and made his initial screen appearance in 1919. Although he appeared in scores of films after the release of *Frankenstein* (1931), he rarely escaped monster roles. As a result, the highly intellectual Britisher played ghouls, mummies who returned to life, or one or another type of walking dead. **Nearly 100 films include:** *Parisian Nights* (1925), *The Unholy Night* (1929), *The Raven* (1935), *Son of Frankenstein* (1939), *Isle of the Dead* (1945), *The Venetian Affair* (1967), *Targets* (1968).

ROSCOE KARNS (1893–1970)

The tough, cynical, hard-boiled comedian with a slightly crooked smile was straight out of Ring Lardner. In real life he came from the then smogless town of San Bernardino, California, and began his career via bit parts with stock companies on the West Coast. News of his performances reached the East, and he made his first Broadway appearance in *Civilian Clothes* (1919).

Although he appeared on screen as early as 1920 in *The Life of the Party*, he didn't really click until talkies arrived. Then, for more than a decade, he played memorable fast-talking, hard-bitten press agents, newspaper reporters, salesmen, etc., in scores of pictures. He was particularly good with John Barrymore and Carole Lombard in *20th Century* (1934). Later in his career, Karns turned to the infant medium of television. In 1950, he starred in *Rocky King, Detective* and in 1958 appeared with Jackie Cooper in the *Hennesey* series. **Credits include:** *Beau Sabreur* (1928), *If I Had a Million* (1932), *It Happened One Night* (1934), *Thanks for the Memory* (1938), *His Girl Friday* (1940), *They Drive by Night* (1940), *Onionhead* (1958), *Man's Favorite Sport?* (1964).

KURT KASZNAR (1913–   )

The Viennese-born actor began appearing on screen after a long and successful career on stage. He made his professional debut at the Salzburg Drama Festival and then worked with Max Reinhardt, who brought him to the United States in a production of *The Eternal Road* (1936). Kasznar decided to stay in New York and was steadily employed on Broadway and in stock companies until he enlisted in the Army in 1941. He was trained as a Signal Corps cameraman and was the first person to photograph Hiroshima and Nagasaki after the atom-bomb attack. He also photographed the Japanese surrender aboard the U.S.S. *Missouri*.

After the war, Kasznar returned to Broadway. Then, in 1952, he made the first of numerous film appearances in *The Light Touch*. In addition to his work on stage and screen, Kasznar starred for two seasons on the TV series *Land of the Giants* (1968–69).

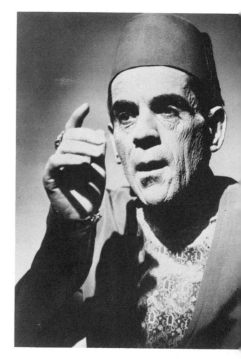

Compared with other makeup jobs, Boris Karloff looked almost like a matinee idol in The Mummy *(1933).*

Kurt Kasznar looks reasonably Parisian as he watched Leslie Caron do the packing in Lili.

Danny Kaye, one of the truly great entertainers, appearing in On the Double *(1961).*

Films include: *Lili* (1953), *My Sister Eileen* (1955), *Anything Goes* (1956), *A Farewell to Arms* (1958), *For the First Time* (1959), *Casino Royale* (1967).

DANNY KAYE (1913–)

Brooklyn-born David Daniel Kaminsky started dancing and singing when he was still in school. He made his professional debut entertaining at the Catskill resort hotels along the upstate New York Borscht Belt circuit —and en route he also met Sylvia Fine, later his wife and the writer of much of his material. A trip to the Orient in 1937 with the A. B. Marcus Show, the Broadway hit *The Straw Hat Revue* (1939) with Imogene Coca and a song called "Tchaikovsky" in *Lady in the Dark* (1941) with Gertrude Lawrence built up his reputation in the United States. Around the same time a sensationally successful appearance at the London Palladium established him as a star in England. The public loved his ease and modesty, his mimicry and double-talking patter songs.

In the United States Sam Goldwyn launched Kaye's career as a comic film star by introducing him to the screen as the disaster-prone Army recruit in *Up in Arms* (1944) with Dinah Shore. Other zany screen romps followed, all successful, some memorable —e.g., *The Secret Life of Walter Mitty* (1947), *The Inspector General* (1949), and *The Court Jester* (1956). Since the early 50's Kaye has been the beloved idol of children around the world, first as the magical storyteller of *Hans Christian Andersen* (1952), then as the much-traveled Ambassador-at-Large for UNICEF. Although his film appearances rapidly dwindled after the 50's, Kaye has continued to make live appearances and in 1970–71 starred on Broadway in Richard Rodgers' *Two by Two*. **Films include:** *Wonder Man* (1945), *A Song Is Born* (1948), *White Christmas* (1954), *Me and the Colonel* (1958), *The Five Pennies* (1959), *The Sound of Laughter* (1963).

STACY KEACH (1941–)

One of the most respected stage actors in the United States, Keach ignored the advice of an agent who told him to limit himself to supporting roles because of a scar that remains after four operations for a hare lip. The son of an actress and an actor, he studied economics, English and drama at the University of California at Berkeley and later did graduate work at the Yale Drama School. His first professional appearances (from 1964) were in Joseph Papp's Shakespeare Festival in New York City's Central Park, but it wasn't until he starred in the off-Broadway political satire *MacBird* that he attracted public attention and began collecting accolades for his performances. *MacBird* brought Obie, Drama Desk, and Vernon Rice awards, and his subsequent performance in *Indians* won him Drama Desk and Tony awards.

Keach made his film debut as the drunken, chess-playing drifter in *The Heart Is a Lonely Hunter* (1968). He was the down-and-out boxer in *Fat City* (1972), and in the film version of John Osborne's play *Luther* (1974) he played the title role. **Films include:** *End of the Road* (1970), *The Traveling Executioner* (1970), *Doc* (1971), *The New Centurions* (1972).

ROBERT EMMETT KEANE
(1893–   )

He appeared in scores of films over a 30-year span, usually sporting a toothbrush mustache, often playing fall guys or roles that fitted his bright, breezy manner.

A veteran of vaudeville and the stage, he once tried to augment the impact of his role in a gangster chiller, *The Spider*, with eerie phosphorescent lights and other spooky gadgets. To his amazement and disappointment, the Chicago audience took it all calmly. It turned out that the bulk of his audience was comprised of Al Capone and some 600 of his cronies and that a rival group of mobsters made up the balance. **Films include:** *Laugh and Get Rich* (1931), *Boys Town* (1938), *The Devil and Miss Jones* (1941), *Fear in the Night* (1947), *Everybody Does It* (1949).

BUSTER KEATON (1895–1966)

There are many Keaton enthusiasts today who judge the master of the deadpan expression to be on a par with, or even superior to, such screen comedians as Charlie Chaplin, Harold Lloyd and W. C. Fields. Regardless of one's personal choice, it is clear that Keaton managed to be extremely funny without resorting to pie-in-the-face routines. Like Chaplin, he played the little man pushed around by society and victimized by the mechanical contrivances of our civilization.

He was born in Kansas to parents who were vaudeville troupers, and by the age of three he had joined their act. His teenage mastery of gymnastics and acrobatics was put to use when he joined Roscoe "Fatty" Arbuckle and his troupe. He made a series of shorts as second man to Arbuckle, but after World War I he branched out on his own.

The Boat (1922) certainly marks one of the high spots in Keaton's career. The most delicious moment comes when the craft, after wrecking the premises in which it was built, slides down into the water and promptly sinks. "Submarine?" Keaton is asked. Pure genius is involved in his solemn shake of the head, "No." On the same high level were two other films of the early 20's: *The Paleface,* in which Keaton chases butterflies and is in turn chased by Indians, and *Cops.* These were followed in the mid-20's by the equally funny *The Navigator* (1924) and *The General* (1927).

With the coming of sound Keaton was teamed with Jimmy Durante in several film disasters. These failures, combined with the break-up of his marriage to the third (and least known) Talmadge sister, Natalie, turned a mild drinking problem into an acute one, and by the early 30's he had become a Hollywood untouchable.

The Keaton story has a happy ending. He abandoned alcohol for many years and by the early 40's began to find bit parts from time to time. In 1950 he enjoyed some TV success on the West Coast and in 1956 delighted his fans with a small but brilliant performance in *Around the World in 80 Days*. By then he had become almost a cult figure, and the old Keaton films were being shown constantly throughout the world. In 1959 he received a special Academy Award for his unique contribution to films, and Eastman House honored him as one of the ten individuals who had done most for the art.

Until his death Keaton continued to appear in films. In 1965 he graced seven pictures with his presence, and in his last year the long, lugubrious countenance added considerably to the merriment of *A Funny Thing Happened on the Way to the Forum*. **Other Keaton films include:** *The Butcher Boy* (1917), *The Cook* (1918), *The Goat* (1921), *The Frozen North* (1922), *Battling Butler* (1926), *Free and Easy* (1930), *Sunset Boulevard* (1950), *It's a Mad, Mad, Mad, Mad World* (1963), *Film* (1965).

DIANE KEATON (1946–   )

One of today's most attractive young stars, she grew up in Santa Ana, California, and early on elected to study acting in New York City. After playing in summer stock in upstate New York, she got her first big break in the tradition-shattering 1968 Broadway production of *Hair,* a musical that shocked some, delighted many and ran on and on and on. The following year she landed her first Broadway starring role, playing opposite the prodigious Woody Allen in his hit comedy *Play It Again, Sam.* That success brought movie offers, and Keaton made her screen debut as the would-be divorcée in *Lovers and*

Nearly half a century after he became a pioneer screen comic, the stern-visaged Buster Keaton appeared in A Funny Thing Happened on the Way to the Forum.

292

Diane Keaton makes a highly pleasant companion for a defrosted Woody Allen in Sleeper, *a comic epic of the world of tomorrow.*

Lila Kedrova and Julie Andrews looking extremely somber in Torn Curtain *(1966).*

Other Strangers (1970). Since then she has starred opposite Woody Allen in two of his films—the 1972 film version of *Sam*, and *Sleeper* (1973), in which she played Woody's 21st-century dream girl. She also played Al Pacino's wife, Kay, in the 1972 blockbuster *The Godfather*.

LILA KEDROVA (1918–)

The Russian-born Kedrova moved to Paris as a child and remained to become a leading actress of stage and screen. Over the years she has appeared in plays that ranged from *A Taste of Honey* and *The Brothers Karamazov* to, more recently, *Cabaret*. She won the French Film Critics Award for her performance as a drug addict in *God Bless You*.

Although her appearances in English-language films have been limited, she won international attention and an Oscar for Best Supporting Actress as Madame Hortense in *Zorba the Greek* (1964). That role came her way after Simone Signoret turned it down, and director Michael Cacoyannis set out to find an outstanding replacement. At first he felt Kedrova would have difficulty with the exacting film role, but a highly successful

screen test changed his mind. **Other films include:** *No Way Back* (1955), *A High Wind in Jamaica* (1965), *Penelope* (1966), *The Kremlin Letter* (1969).

HOWARD KEEL (1919–)

Despite a much-ballyhooed American film debut in *Annie Get Your Gun* (1950) and leads in the few Hollywood musicals turned out by the big studios in the 50's, Howard Keel really arrived on the Hollywood scene too late to equal the screen success of fellow actor-singers Gordon MacRae, Mario Lanza and Tony Martin.

Although Keel had long prided himself on his fine voice, he did not appear professionally until he was in his mid-20's when he sang with the American Music Theatre in Pasadena, California. Then in 1945 an audition for Oscar Hammerstein II landed him a part as understudy to the lead in the Broadway hit musical *Carousel* and led to the starring role in the 1947 London production of *Oklahoma!* Both the show and Keel triumphed, and while in England he made his screen debut with a minor part in *The Small Voice* (1948). By the time he returned to the United States, Warner Brothers was casting *Annie Get Your Gun*.

During the next five years Keel was kept busy making a variety of musicals. Some, like *Lovely to Look At* (1952), were "B" pictures, but a few were wonderful throwbacks to the good old days of lavish musical spectacular—e.g., *Show Boat* (1951) and *Seven Brides for Seven Brothers* (1954). In the 60's he appeared in a few Westerns, and for a while he and Kathryn Grayson teamed up as a nightclub act. More recently Keel has kept active in summer stock. **Films include:** *Callaway Went Thataway* (1951), *Kismet* (1955), *The Big Fisherman* (1959), *Armored Command* (1961), *The War Wagon* (1967), *Arizona Bushwhackers* (1968).

RUBY KEELER (1909–)

She was the founding mother of the "you're-going-out-there-and-you're-coming-back-a-star" school of Hollywood musicals, for it was to Keeler that Warner Baxter, as an overwrought stage director, delivered his imperishable injunction. The film was the famous *42nd Street* (1933) and with it Keeler tap-danced her way to fame and fortune on screen and off.

At least ten virtue-will-triumph screen musicals followed, the last of them (and her last film as well) being *Sweetheart of the Campus* (1941). For nearly 30 years she was forgotten and then, in the early 70's, delighted Broadway audiences by making a triumphant comeback in the revival of *No, No, Nanette!*.

Keeler was born in Nova Scotia (Halifax) and for a time was married to another virtue-will-triumph performer, Al Jolson. **Films include:** *Gold Diggers of 1933* (1933), *Flirtation Walk* (1934), *Shipmates Forever* (1935), *Ready, Willing and Able* (1937).

GEOFFREY KEEN (1918–)

He followed in the footsteps of his father, British stage actor Malcolm Keen, when he decided on a theatrical career. After studying at the Royal Academy of Dramatic Arts he joined the Old Vic, making his professional acting debut in Bristol in *School for Scandal* and his first appearance on the London stage in *The Winter's Tale*. Since his screen debut in 1946 he has played character parts in more than 50 British and American films. Keen also has continued to act on stage in London and has appeared on Broadway in *Ross* and Terence Rattigan's *Man and Boy* (1963). **Films include:** *Odd Man Out* (1947), *The Fallen Idol* (1949), *Treasure Island* (1950), *Cry, the Beloved Country* (1952), *Genevieve* (1954), *The Man Who Never Was* (1956), *Sink the Bismarck!* (1960), *No Love for Johnny* (1961), *Dr. Zhivago* (1965), *Born Free* (1966), *Berserk* (1968).

HARVEY KEITEL (1939–)

A veteran of summer stock and television, Keitel made his motion picture debut in a college-produced film, Martin Scorsese's *Who's That Knocking at My Door?* (1967). A few years later he came to the attention of the public and the critics in Scorsese's highly praised *Mean Streets* (1973), a drama set in Manhattan's Little Italy. Keitel has appeared in off-Broadway productions of *The Caine Mutiny Court Martial* and *A View From the Bridge*. He is a member of the Actors Studio in New York. **Credits:** *Alice Doesn't Live Here Anymore* (1974).

BRIAN KEITH (1922–)

Although he is better known as the lead in the TV series *A Family Affair* and *The Little People*, Keith has also played supporting roles in dozens of films during the past two decades.

Keith made his film debut when he was only four years old but didn't seriously begin his acting career until he had completed a stint in the Marines during World War II. His first professional adult appearances were with the American Theatre Wing, the stock company that played veterans hospitals. He then found work in motion pictures and, later, enduring popularity as a television actor. He is the son of actor Robert Keith. **Films include:** *Arrowhead* (1953), *The Young Philadelphians* (1959), *The Parent Trap* (1961), *The Russians Are Coming, the Russians Are Coming* (1966), *Reflections in a Golden Eye* (1967), *With Six You Get Eggroll* (1968).

IAN KEITH (1899–1960)

His long screen career never did bring Keith the success he found on the legitimate stage as the star of both classical and modern dramas. After studying at the American Academy of Dramatic Arts he made his professional debut at the Comedy Theatre in New York in 1917 and acted with stock companies until he won a part in the Broadway production of *The Silver Fox* (1921). Although Keith did appear in silents—he co-starred with Gloria Swanson in *Manhandled* (1924)—he was better known for his roles in sound films. He played De Rochefort in *The Three Musketeers* (1935) and the mad actor Vitamin Flintheart in the Dick Tracy film series. In addition to his work on screen, Keith continued to star on stage, appearing opposite Helen Hayes in *Mary, Queen of Scotland*, as Luigi in *Laugh, Clown, Laugh* and in the 1958 production of *Edwin Booth*. **Films include:** *Convoy* (1927), *The Divine Lady* (1929), *The Sign of the Cross* (1932), *Queen Christina* (1933), *The Sea Hawk* (1940), *Nightmare Alley* (1947), *Prince of Players* (1955), *The Ten Commandments* (1956).

ROBERT KEITH (1896–1966)

This durable actor (his career spanned half a century) made his stage debut back in 1914 in a St. Charles, Illinois, stock production of

Ruby Keeler, who tap-danced her way to stardom, in Sweetheart of the Campus *(1941), a film made long before beards came in and bras went out.*

Brian Keith looks as if something unpleasant is about to happen in Dino *(1957).*

Cecil Kellaway peers out of the background as Richard Widmark and Dean Stockwell confront each other in Down to the Sea in Ships *(1949).*

Ultra-realism in film-making today, as portrayed by Sally Kellerman and James Caan in Slither.

Got a Match? For the next seven years he toured the United States with a variety of repertory companies until he finally made it to Broadway as Ralph Armstrong in *The Triumph of X* (1921). He continued to perform on stage through the mid-20's and also wrote a play, *The Tightwad*, which ran briefly in New York in 1927. Two years later, however, he abandoned the theatre to go to Hollywood as a dialogue writer for Universal and Columbia. After four years and minor roles in a few films, Keith returned to the East to resume his stage career. His Broadway successes over the following 15 years included roles in Eugene O'Neill's *The Great God Brown* and *Mister Roberts* (1948), in which he played Doc.

In the late 40's and 50's Keith returned to the screen in such films as *My Foolish Heart* (1950), *The Wild One* (1953) and *Guys and Dolls* (1955). He is the father of actor Brian Keith. **Films include:** *Bad Company* (1931), *Boomerang* (1945), *Fourteen Hours* (1951), *Tempest* (1959), *Cimarron* (1961).

CECIL KELLAWAY (1893–1973)

In scores of movies, character actor Kellaway played lovable, twinkly-eyed old gentlemen, including the family priest and Spencer Tracy's golfing partner in *Guess Who's Coming to Dinner?* (1967), the last film for both actors.

Kellaway was born in South Africa and began his acting career in Australia. He went to Hollywood in 1939 under a writer-actor contract with RKO and remained to appear in more than 40 films. He won an Academy Award nomination in 1948 for his performance as a leprechaun in *The Luck of the Irish*. Kellaway made his Broadway debut in *Greenwillow* (1960). **Films include:** *Wuthering Heights* (1939), *Intermezzo* (1939), *Monsieur Beaucaire* (1946), *The Postman Always Rings Twice* (1946), *Harvey* (1950), *The Shaggy Dog* (1959), *The Cardinal* (1963), *Hush . . . Hush, Sweet Charlotte* (1965), *Fitzwilly* (1967).

SALLY KELLERMAN (1938–)

A husky, sexy voice combined with blond good looks that made male heads snap in her direction guaranteed the young hopeful a foothold in her chosen world of entertainment. She began her career as a singer, worked on television and made her first film appearance in *The Third Day* (1965). Five years later, immortality of a sort came to the California-born actress when she played the much put-upon Major "Hot Lips" Houlihan in Robert Altman's hugely funny *M*A*S*H* (1970). Her performance won her an Academy Award nomination and a starring role in Altman's next film, *Brewster McCloud* (1970).

In recent years, Kellerman, who possesses a flair for both comedy and drama, hasn't been given the sort of scripts she deserves, but there's little doubt that she possesses the talent to stay at the top of the heap. She has also appeared in such TV series as *It Takes a Thief* and *Mannix*. **Credits include:** *The Boston Strangler* (1968), *The Last of the Red Hot Lovers* (1972), *Slither* (1973), *Lost Horizon* (1973).

GENE KELLY (1912–)

Kelly and his brother Fred first performed in their native Pittsburgh, Pennsylvania, in a tap dance on roller skates routine which helped Kelly work his way through college and financed his purchase of two dance studios. His first break in show business came in 1938 when he landed a job in the Broadway chorus of *Leave It to Me!* (He was one of a trio who hovered in the background when Mary Martin sang "My Heart Belongs to Daddy.") Other parts followed, and when he played the role of the heel-hero in *Pal Joey* in 1940, Kelly became a star. He made his movie debut opposite Judy Garland as the dastardly vaudevillian in *For Me and My Gal* (1942), and three years later he received an Oscar nomination for his performance in *Anchors Aweigh*.

One of the true phenomena of motion pictures, Kelly has distinguished himself not only as a screen actor, dancer and singer but also as a choreographer and director of such musical-comedy hit films as *On the Town* (1949) and *Singin' in the Rain* (1952). In 1951 he received an honorary Academy Award in recognition of his multifold talents. **Some of his films include:** *The Cross of Lorraine* (1943), *The Pirate* (1948), *An American in Paris* (1951), *Brigadoon* (1954), *Marjorie Morningstar* (1958), *What a Way to Go!* (1964), *Forty Carats* (1973).

Gene Kelly, one of the all-time greats in film musicals, as he looked in the pleasant and tuneful Anchors Aweigh.

GRACE KELLY (1929–)

From time to time her return to the screen is rumored, but for many years now the public has seen Princess Grace only in photographs, usually snapped on the French Riviera and usually showing her with her husband, Prince Rainier of Monaco, or her children.

She was born into a wealthy Philadelphia family that also possessed considerable athletic prowess and educated at an exclusive girls' school in Germantown, Pennsylvania. After graduation she went to New York to study acting at the American Academy of Dramatic Arts. She made her Broadway debut in *The Father* (1949). Two years later she made her screen debut in *Fourteen Hours* and landed a film contract. As the girl who worried about Gary Cooper's ability to live out the impending onslaught of bad men in *High Noon* (1952) she attained stardom and the following year won the International Press Outstanding Performance of the Year Award for her work in *Mogambo*. Both the Academy Award for

Grace Kelly, in her pre-princess days, poses with a trio that helped to make High Noon *one of the best Westerns ever filmed. From the left they are Lloyd Bridges, Katy Jurado and, of course, the immortal "Coop."*

Best Actress and the New York Film Critics Award came her way for a stunning performance in *The Country Girl* (1954).

One of the most beautiful and talented actresses of her time, Grace Kelly would have undoubtedly taken her place among filmdom's immortals if her marriage had not ended a career of just five years' duration. **Other films:** *Rear Window* (1954), *Dial M for Murder* (1954), *To Catch a Thief* (1955), *High Society* (1956).

NANCY KELLY (1921–)

Nancy Kelly already was a respected veteran of both Broadway and Hollywood when she played her best-known role—the mother in Maxwell Anderson's macabre play *The Bad Seed*, which opened on Broadway in 1954. Kelly's performance brought raves from the critics and won her a Tony Award. She was nominated for an Academy Award

when she recreated the role on the screen the following year.

At the age of one Kelly began modeling. The photogenic child soon was spotted by Hollywood and made dozens of films before she left the screen at age eight. She went to New York, where she appeared on Broadway in A. A. Milne's *Give Me Yesterday* (1931). She left the stage for radio but was back on the boards in 1937 for her first really important role, the teenaged Blossom in *Susan and God* with the Rachel brothers. After this Broadway success she returned to Hollywood as a leading lady in the films of the late 30's and 40's and continued to make stage appearances in such plays as Terence Rattigan's *Flare Path* (1942) and Clifford Odets' *The Big Knife* (1949). **Films include:** *Jesse James* (1939), *A Very Young Lady* (1941), *Show Business* (1944), *Crowded Paradise* (1956).

PATSY KELLY (1910–)

No one made a happier comeback to the stage than the comedienne with the ultra-Irish name who, after years of obscurity, wowed Broadway audiences of the early 70's in two stunning revivals: *No, No, Nanette!* and *Irene*.

She taught tap dancing at the age of 12 and broke into show business with her brother via a vaudeville dance routine at New York's Palace Theatre, the mecca of all entertainers. When stony-faced Zasu Pitts demanded more money from Hal Roach, the producer-director went to New York in search of talent, found Patsy Kelly dancing and clowning it up in *Three Cheers* (1928) and brought her out West. In the 30's she appeared in a successful comedy film series with Thelma Todd and also was seen in scores of pictures, usually as a maid, woiking goil, or best friend to the more glamorous heroine. By the 50's, however, even minor roles were hard to find, and in the 60's only occasional cameo parts came her way. **Credits include:** *Going Hollywood* (1933), *Private Number* (1936), *Ladies' Day* (1943), *Please Don't Eat the Daisies* (1960), *C'mon, Let's Live a Little* (1967).

PAUL KELLY (1899–1956)

The handsome, somewhat serious-visaged leading man grew up in Brooklyn, New York, in the shadow of the old Vitagraph Studio and made his first screen appearance as a drummer boy in a Vitagraph film of 1907. After more than a decade of juvenile roles in Vitagraph epics, he graduated to more substantial parts, and from the mid-20's until his death played a vast number of leads and supporting roles on both stage and screen. He was particularly effective in *Crossfire* (1947), one of the first films that dared to treat a hitherto no-no issue, anti-Semitism. **More than 60 films include:** *The New Klondike* (1926), *Mystery Ship* (1941), *Split Second* (1953), *The High and the Mighty* (1954), *Storm Center* (1956).

PERT KELTON (1907–1968)

A character comedienne best known for her stage and screen performances as Mrs. Marian Paroo in *The Music Man* (1962), Kelton was a vaudeville veteran long before she established herself on Broadway and in motion pictures of the 30's. She made her professional debut at three and first appeared on the New York stage as Maud in *Sunny* (1925). Her first feature film was *Sally* (1929), and during the mid-30's she was a regular performer in Hal Roach comedy shorts. Later in her career she appeared on television's *Cavalcade of Stars* in a Jackie Gleason comedy skit, *The Honeymooners*. Kelton played Gleason's wife, Alice Kramden, the role later made famous by Audrey Meadows when *The Honeymooners* was transformed into a long-running TV series. **Films include:** *Bed of Roses* (1933), *The Bowery* (1933), *Hooray for Love* (1935), *Kelly the Second* (1936), *Women of Glamour* (1937), *Love and Kisses* (1965).

KAY KENDALL (1926–1959)

Kendall was married to Rex Harrison when her burgeoning career as one of the most talented of the young comediennes came to an untimely end with her death from cancer in 1959. Although her film debut was in *Fiddlers Three* (1944), it wasn't until 1954 and *Genevieve* that her beauty and charm were seen at their very best. **Film highlights:** *The Constant Husband* (1957), *Les Girls* (1957), *Once More, With Feeling* (1960).

ARTHUR KENNEDY (1914–)

For more than 30 years Kennedy has been juggling outstanding careers in Hollywood and on Broadway. His initial Broadway success in *King Richard II* and fine appearances in *Life and Death of an American* and *Madam, Will You Walk?* in the late 30's brought him his first film role—James Cagney's brother in *City for Conquest* (1940). He made several more films and then enlisted in the Air Force for the duration of World War II. After demobilization he returned to Hollywood for *Devotion* (1946), the story of the Brontë family. Two Broadway hits by Arthur Miller kept Kennedy in New York from 1947 to 1949. One of them, *All My Sons,* was voted the best American play of the 1946-47 season, and the other, *Death of a Salesman,* won the Pulitzer Prize for Drama and brought Kennedy a 1948 Tony Award for his performance as Biff.

He turned in impressive performances on screen throughout the 50's, earning Academy Award nominations for *Bright Victory*

The beauteous Kay Kendall and her real-life husband, Rex Harrison, flank Angela Lansbury in The Reluctant Debutante *(1958).*

One of Broadway's favorite actors, Arthur Kennedy, as he appeared with Brenda Marshall in Highway West *(1941), a film that didn't live up to the dimensions of the steering wheel.*

298

George Kennedy plays a "good-guy" in . . . tick . . . tick . . . tick.

(1951), *Trial* (1955), *Peyton Place* (1957) and *Some Came Running* (1959). Then in 1961 his stature as a stage actor took on added luster when he replaced Sir Laurence Olivier in the title role of another hit play, *Becket.* In addition to his work on stage and screen, Kennedy has frequently appeared in dramatic productions on television. **Films include:** *High Sierra* (1941), *Strange Alibi* (1941), *Air Force* (1943), *Champion* (1949), *The Glass Menagerie* (1950), *The Girl in White* (1952), *Crashout* (1955), *Twilight for the Gods* (1958), *A Summer Place* (1959), *Elmer Gantry* (1960), *Lawrence of Arabia* (1962), *Anzio* (1968).

EDGAR KENNEDY (1890–1948)

A single comic ploy instantly distinguished him from other comedians—clapping a cupped hand to his brow and rubbing it across his face in a gesture of total frustration. Kennedy entered films in 1913 as one of the frantically active Keystone Cops, and he remained in demand for comedy roles for the rest of his life. His brother, Tom Kennedy, another Keystone funnyman, had a long career playing smallish roles in movies and on television. **Many, many credits include:** *Tillie's Punctured Romance* (1915), *Golden Princess* (1925), *Kid Millions* (1934), *San Francisco* (1936), *A Star Is Born* (1937), *Anchors Aweigh* (1945), *Unfaithfully Yours* (1948).

GEORGE KENNEDY (1925–   )

He tried to claw Cary Grant to death with a steel hook in *Charade* (1963), went after Joan Crawford with an ax in *Strait Jacket* (1964) and won an Oscar when he worked over Paul Newman in *Cool Hand Luke* (1967).

Kennedy had been acting for 34 years before the movies made a villain out of him. He made his professional debut at age two in a road-company production of *Bringing Up Father,* and by the time he was seven he had become America's youngest disc jockey. He enlisted in the Army when he was 17 and served 16 years before returning to civilian life and acting. While he was still in the service, however, he worked as technical adviser for the Phil Silvers TV comedy series *Bilko.*

He went to Hollywood after his release from the Army and made his motion-picture debut in *The Little Shepherd* (1961). Although he initially was typecast as a villain, Kennedy has been playing more sympathetic roles in his recent pictures. **Films include:** *Lonely Are the Brave* (1962), *Mirage* (1965), *Hush . . . Hush, Sweet Charlotte* (1965), *Hurry Sundown* (1967), *The Boston Strangler* (1968), *Airport* (1970), . . . *tick* . . . *tick* . . . *tick* (1970).

MERNA KENNEDY (1909–1944)

A Charlie Chaplin discovery, red-haired, Lita Grey look-alike Kennedy starred opposite the famous comic in his silent *The Circus* (1928). She later signed a Universal contract and played leading roles in several films of the early 30's. Kennedy made headlines in 1934 when she married director-choreographer Busby Berkeley. The marriage lasted just one year, and by the time it ended her screen career had dimmed. Kennedy died of a heart attack at age 35 in 1944. **Films include:** *Red-Haired Alibi* (1932), *Don't Bet on Love* (1933), *Arizona to Broadway* (1933), *I Like It That Way* (1934), *Wonder Bar* (1934).

DORIS KENYON (1897–   )

A leading lady of silent films and the wife of matinee idol Milton Sills, Kenyon successfully made the transition to talking pictures and also established herself off screen as a concert soprano, a poet and an author.

She frequently was paired with Sills in films of the 20's. After he died in 1930, she remained in Hollywood making movies until the end of the decade. **Films include:** *The Pawn of Fate* (1916), *A Girl's Folly* (1917), *The Hidden Hand* (1918), *The Ruling Passion* (1922), *Monsieur Beaucaire* (1924), *The Blonde Saint* (1926), *The Hawk's Nest* (1928), *Alexander Hamilton* (1931), *Voltaire* (1933), *Whom the Gods Destroy* (1934), *The Man in the Iron Mask* (1939).

DEBORAH KERR (1921–   )

Early in her career, the ladylike Britisher came terribly close to being typecast permanently. Movie big shots must have taken one look at her and said something like, "Ah-ha, the perfect actress to play the Countess of Twickenham in *Andy Hardy Visits Bucking-*

ham Palace.'' It wasn't until she played the adulterous Army wife in *From Here to Eternity* (1953), with its then shocking love scene on the beach, that her true abilities as a powerful actress were spotted.

Kerr's next vehicle was the Broadway hit *Tea and Sympathy* (1953), in which she played the teacher's wife who helps a young student prove his manhood. Kerr and her co-star John Kerr (no relation) repeated their roles in the 1956 screen version of the Robert Anderson play. She was at the height of her screen career at the time and landed the much sought-after role of the governess in *The King and I* (1956). Even though her singing voice was dubbed, she earned an Academy Award nomination for her performance. Another nomination followed for her appearance in *Separate Tables* (1958).

In 1960 she married her second husband, writer Peter Viertel, and moved to Switzerland. After that, the demand from Hollywood waned; and although Kerr remained active, many of her movies were light forgettable comedies, such as *The Grass Is Greener* (1960), in which she returned to her lady-of-the-manor image. A notable exception was *The Night of the Iguana* (1964) with Richard Burton and Ava Gardner, in which Kerr played the neurotic spinster, a contrast to the lustier roles of her co-stars. **Films include:** *Major Barbara* (1941), *Vacation From Marriage* (1945), *Black Narcissus* (1947), *Beloved Infidel* (1959), *The Innocents* (1961), *Casino Royale* (1967), *The Arrangement* (1969), *The Gypsy Moths* (1969).

J. M. KERRIGAN (1885–1965)

For years, whenever a part called for a character actor with an Irish brogue, Kerrigan got it. He was born in Dublin, attended Belvedere College there and worked as a newspaper reporter before joining the famous Abbey Players in 1907. He played more than 300 roles during his nine years with the company and in his last year directed one of the first Irish films, *O' Neil of the Glen* (1916).

Kerrigan came to the United States in 1917 to appear with Laurette Taylor in *Out There* and *Happiness*. He made his American screen debut in *Little Old New York* (1923). Among Kerrigan's memorable film roles in later years were the groom in *Black Beauty* (1946) and Rose's father in *Abie's Irish Rose* (1946). **Highlights include:** *Lucky in Love* (1929), *Song o' My Heart* (1930), *The Informer* (1935), *Laughing Irish Eyes* (1936), *Captains of the Clouds* (1942), *The Wild North* (1952), *The Fastest Gun Alive* (1956).

NORMAN KERRY (1889–1956)

Of the movies' heroes and villains of the 20's Kerry had the pointiest, waxiest mustache of them all. A heavy-set, good-looking actor, he was still a student when he appeared in *Manhattan Madness* (1916), an early Douglas Fairbanks film shot in New York. Not long after that, he gravitated to the West Coast and, so the story has it, accompanied a friend who was delivering lumber to a film studio. "Working now?" he was asked. "Not at present," Kerry replied. Next thing he knew he was playing opposite Bessie Barriscale in *The Rose of Paradise*.

Kerry was popular throughout the 20's, notably in Lon Chaney's *The Hunchback of Notre Dame* (1923). But with the advent of sound he, like so many others, saw his career go down the drain. **Films include:** *Soldiers of Fortune* (1919), *The Phantom of the Opera* (1925 silent and 1930 talkie), *The Unknown* (1927), *Bachelor Apartment* (1931).

EVELYN KEYES (1919–   )

When she arrived in Hollywood in the late 30's, Keyes thought her southern accent would prove a disadvantage and worked hard to lose it. She succeeded but ironically had to regain it almost immediately for what proved to be her most famous screen role—Scarlett O'Hara's sister Suellen in *Gone With the Wind* (1939).

Keyes started out in show business as a tap dancer in nightclubs in her home town of Atlanta, Georgia. She rarely had an opportunity to display her dancing ability during her screen career, though it did come in handy much later when she starred in the road-company production of *No, No, Nanette!* (1972).

During her Hollywood career of the 40's and 50's, she most often played "nice girl" parts. One of her finest performances, how-

It was virtually impossible for Deborah Kerr to look unladylike. Here she is, regal as one might wish, with Cary Grant in An Affair to Remember *(1957).*

Norman Kerry, a leading man in silent days, looks waxed to the gills in this studio portrait.

Evelyn Keyes, a shapely near star of the early talkies.

ever, was as the patrolman's wife whom Van Heflin coveted in the gripping melodrama *The Prowler* (1951). Keyes was very much a part of the Hollywood establishment in those days. Her second and third husbands were film directors Charles Vidor and John Huston. In 1958 she became the eighth wife of bandleader Artie Shaw. They appeared together in cameo roles in *Across 110th Street* (1972). **Films include:** *Before I Hang* (1940), *Here Comes Mr. Jordan* (1941), *Flight Lieutenant* (1942), *The Desperadoes* (1943), *The Jolson Story* (1946), *Johnny O'Clock* (1946), *Enchantment* (1948), *The Killer That Stalked New York* (1950), *The Seven Year Itch* (1955), *Around the World in 80 Days* (1956).

GUY KIBBEE (1886–1956)

During the 30's it seemed as though the balding, moon-faced actor was in every film that was produced—comedies, Westerns, you name it. There were 50 in the years 1931-36 alone. Not that anyone objected, for he was a highly effective character actor in every role he was given.

At 14 Kibbee worked as a propman with a road show managed by his brother in his native Texas. He broke into show business the day the show's juvenile lead failed to show up and he stepped into the part. Some 20 years later he finally made it to Broadway with a role in the 1930 success *Torch Song*, and the next year he broke into films as the lovable stooge in *Stolen Heaven*. Thereafter, his rotund presence enlivened a host of movies. P.S.: Kibbee's son turned to academics and became Chancellor of the College of the City of New York. **Films include:** *42nd Street* (1933), *Captain Blood* (1935), *Little Lord Fauntleroy* (1936), *Mr. Smith Goes to Washington* (1939), *Our Town* (1940), *Fort Apache* (1948), *Three Godfathers* (1949).

JAN KIEPURA (1902–1966)

Considered Poland's leading operatic tenor by the time he was 21, Kiepura was the toast of European opera houses before British motion pictures like *Farewell to Love* (1930) established him as a film star.

He was born in Sosnowicz and studied law at the University of Warsaw before making his first operatic appearance at the age of 19. He married Hungarian soprano Marta Eggerth while he was filming *My Heart Is Calling* (1935) in Europe, and the two became a popular stage and screen team—particularly when they co-starred in *The Merry Widow*. They first brought the popular operetta to Broadway in 1943 and returned with it in 1957. **Films include:** *My Song to You* (1931), *Be Mine Tonight* (1933), *Give Us This Night* (1936), *Her Wonderful Lie* (1950).

PERCY KILBRIDE (1888–1964)

The lanky, horse-faced comedian was best at portraying laconic New Englanders, and his crisp "Yep," "Nope" and "We need more manure" invariably created a wildly funny effect.

While he did not appear in films until 1933 (*White Woman*), he had been an actor on the legitimate stage long before that and played a vast assortment of roles on Broadway in the 20's and 30's. His performance as a monosyllabic rustic in *George Washington Slept Here* took him back to Hollywood in 1942 to recreate the part on screen. He appeared in a variety of films over the next few years until he finally clicked in *The Egg and I* (1947) as the salty, twangy Pa Kettle. That memorable supporting role resulted in a team-up with Marjorie Main (the film's Ma Kettle) for a succession of highly profitable Universal *Kettle* films. **Credits include:** *Knickerbocker Holiday* (1944), *State Fair* (1945), *Riff-Raff* (1947), *Ma and Pa Kettle* (1949), *Ma and Pa Kettle Back on the Farm* (1951).

VICTOR KILIAN (1898–   )

The dubious character or villain of numerous screen dramas over a 20-year span, Kilian began his film career after he had established himself as a dramatic actor in legitimate theatre. He made his acting debut with a New Hampshire repertory company and first appeared on Broadway in Eugene O'Neill's *Desire Under the Elms* (1924). Other Broadway plays followed until the early 30's when he went to Hollywood for roles in films like *The Wiser Sex* (1932) and *Ramona* (1936). He continued to turn in distinctive performances on screen through the 50's and also returned to Broadway from time to time for plays like *Look Homeward, Angel* (1957). **Films include:** *Air Hawks* (1935), *Boys Town* (1938), *Reap the Wild Wind* (1942), *Spellbound* (1945), *Gentleman's Agreement* (1947), *The Tall Target* (1951).

PHYLLIS KIRK (1930–)

A former model and dancer, Kirk played some leading roles in films of the late 50's but is better known, perhaps, for her TV portrayal of Nora Charles in *The Thin Man* series co-starring Peter Lawford. On screen, she was cowboy(!) Frank Sinatra's leading lady in *Johnny Concho* (1956) and co-starred with Jerry Lewis in *The Sad Sack* (1957). **Films include:** *Our Very Own* (1950), *The Iron Mistress* (1952), *Back From Eternity* (1956), *The Woman Opposite* (1958).

EARTHA KITT (1928–)

Occasionally the sultry-voiced singer takes a break from her flourishing career as a nightclub performer and recording artist to appear in motion pictures. In addition to her screen appearances, Kitt has starred on Broadway in a dramatic role in *Mrs. Patterson* (1954) and, early in her career, played Helen of Troy in an Orson Welles production of *Faust* in Paris.

Kitt's success story has all the elements of melodrama. She was born in rural South Carolina, and her sharecropper father deserted his family when she was still an infant. Her mother died when Kitt was only six, and for two years she and her sister drifted from neighbor to neighbor until an aunt in New York sent for her. At age 16 she won a dance-training scholarship with Katherine Dunham and toured with the troupe, dancing and eventually singing. Her first real break, however, came in Paris. She decided to remain in France after the Dunham troupe completed a European tour and found a job singing in a nightclub. She was an instant success, and soon she was appearing at top night spots in London and Istanbul, and when she returned

Percy Kilbride's New England twang enchants Marjorie Main in The Egg and I, *a film that spawned a flock of subsequent Kilbride–Main appearances.*

Guy Kibbee, a character actor whose services were always in demand, supervises Mickey Rooney's shine-'em-up job, little suspecting that Mickey was none other than Little Lord Fauntleroy.

Jack Klugman appears skeptical as Donald Sutherland attempts the nearly impossible in The Split.

to the United States in 1952 she repeated her European successes.

Kitt made her Broadway debut in the Leonard Sillman revue *New Faces of 1952* and her first screen appearance in *New Faces* (1954). Since then she has retained her popularity as one of the world's foremost vocalists. **Films include:** *St. Louis Blues* (1958), *Anna Lucasta* (1959), *The Saint of Devil's Island* (1961), *Synanon* (1965).

WERNER KLEMPERER (1930–)

The son of conductor Otto Klemperer, he was brought to America in the early days of the Hitler regime. Ironically, his film appearances have almost all been as Germanic types, most conspicuously as Adolf Eichmann in *Operation Eichmann* (1961). His characterizations have not, however, all been for such serious dramas, and in 1965 he made his first telecast as Commandant Klink in the long-running series *Hogan's Heroes*. **Film credits include:** *Death of a Scoundrel* (1956), *Kiss Them for Me* (1957), *Judgment at Nuremberg* (1961), *Youngblood Hawke* (1964), *Ship of Fools* (1965), *Dark Intruder* (1965).

JACK KLUGMAN (1924–)

He is so closely identified with his Emmy Award-winning role as Oscar Madison, the sloppy sportswriter roommate of Tony Randall in the TV comedy series *The Odd Couple*, that audiences frequently forget he is also a fine dramatic actor.

Klugman studied at the Carnegie Institute of Technology and at the American Theatre Wing in New York City before making his New York stage debut in the Equity Library Theatre production of *Stevedore* (1949). A few years later he made it to Broadway as Frank Bonaparte in *Golden Boy*. Film roles followed from the mid-50's—mostly in serious dramas. He was one of the jurors in *Twelve Angry Men* (1957) and the Alcoholics Anonymous member who stood by Jack Lemmon in *Days of Wine and Roses* (1963). He played Ali MacGraw's buffoonish father in *Goodbye Columbus* (1969).

Klugman won a Tony Award for his performance in the Broadway musical *Gypsy*

with Ethel Merman and Emmys for his TV appearances in *Blacklist,* a 1964 drama, and *The Defenders*. **Films include:** *Timetable* (1956), *The Yellow Canary* (1963), *The Detective* (1968), *The Split* (1968).

HILDEGARDE KNEF (or NEFF) (1925–)

As a teenager Knef endured and survived the ravages of World War II to become the first German star to emerge from the rubble of Berlin. Taking a job as a cartoonist for a film company, the beautiful and provocative-voiced Knef (she detested the Hollywood-imposed Neff) soon landed a screen test and bit parts on the stage. Her role in the 1946 film *Murderers Among Us* (U.S., 1948) brought her critical acclaim, and the following year *Film Without Title* (released in the U.S. as *Film Without a Name* in 1950) made her a star and brought her a Hollywood contract. Survival in the Hollywood of the McCarthy era proved difficult, however, and after two frustrating years Knef left, returning only when a definite role was offered. Probably her greatest success in the U.S. was on Broadway in the Cole Porter musical *Silk Stockings* (1955). In recent years she has made stage appearances and become one of Europe's most popular singing and recording stars. Her excellent autobiography, *The Gift Horse*, was a best-seller in Germany and the United States. **Films include:** *Decision Before Dawn* (1951), *The Snows of Kilimanjaro* (1952), *And So to Bed* (1965), *The Lost Continent* (1968).

JOHN FORREST "FUZZY" KNIGHT (1901–)

In dozens of Westerns of the 30's and 40's, Knight provided comic relief as the saddle partner of such cowboy stars as Johnny Mack Brown, Bob Baker, Tex Ritter and Russell Hayden.

He started out in show business as a musician and earned the nickname "Fuzzy" because of his peculiarly soft and mellow singing voice. Knight's early film appearances were in forgettable Paramount musical short subjects. However, he soon established himself as a fine supporting comedian with his role of Ragtime Kelly in the Mae West–Cary Grant favorite *She Done Him Wrong* (1933).

Although he is known primarily for his work in Westerns, he has appeared occasionally in straight dramatic parts. **Films include:** *Moulin Rouge* (1934), *The Trail of the Lonesome Pine* (1936), *Johnny Apollo* (1940), *The Egg and I* (1947), *Down to the Sea in Ships* (1950), *These Thousand Hills* (1959), *Waco* (1966).

SHIRLEY KNIGHT (HOPKINS) (1937–)

An outspoken actress who is openly critical of Hollywood, Knight abandoned a successful motion-picture career to concentrate on more serious roles on stage and television.

She defied her parents' wishes when she left Wichita, Kansas, to go to Hollywood in 1957. Soon after she arrived in California a part in a drama-class production of *Look Back in Anger* brought Knight contract offers from three studios. She signed with Warner Brothers. Her first feature role was in *Ice Palace* (1960) with Richard Burton. The same year, Knight made *The Dark at the Top of the Stairs* and was nominated for an Academy Award for Best Supporting Actress. A second Oscar nomination came two years later for her performance as Heavenly, Paul Newman's childhood sweetheart, in *Sweet Bird of Youth* (1962).

Despite her success, Knight disliked Hollywood and left to appear on the stage in New York and London. She made her Broadway debut in 1964 with Kim Stanley and Geraldine Page in Chekhov's *The Three Sisters*. Later, Knight and her first husband, Gene Persson, moved to London, where he produced and she starred in *Dutchman* (1967). Her performance won her the Volpi Cup at the Venice Film Festival. Knight is now married to British playwright John Hopkins and lives in London. In the last few years she has appeared frequently in TV dramatic productions (many written by Hopkins) in both England and the United States. **Films include:** *The Group* (1966), *Petulia* (1968), *The Rain People* (1969).

DON KNOTTS (1924–)

His nervous twitches, jumpy double-takes and looks of popeyed amazement have helped Knotts carve out a niche for himself in comedy roles, usually as a cowardly but intrepid hero or a dubious sidekick. Knotts graduated from the University of West Virginia before venturing into show business as a nightclub ventriloquist. After a few jobs in Pittsburgh, he went to New York and found work on radio. A Broadway role in *No Time for Sergeants* (1955) led to a lasting friendship with the show's star, Andy Griffith, and from 1960 Knotts appeared as the deputy sheriff on Griffith's long-running TV series. By the time the show went into reruns, he had won five Emmy Awards for his performances. He had originally endeared himself to TV audiences four years earlier as the nervous nail-biting regular on *The Steve Allen Show* (1956-60). His successes on television led to featured roles in several motion pictures, all depicting Knotts as fearful and frazzled as ever. **Films include:** *No Time for Sergeants* (1958), *The Incredible Mr. Limpet* (1964), *The Ghost and Mr. Chicken* (1966), *The Reluctant Astronaut* (1967), *The Shakiest Gun in the West* (1968), *The Love God?* (1969).

PATRIC KNOWLES (1911–)

After four years' acting experience with stock companies in England and Ireland, appearances on the London stage and parts in a few British films, Knowles was recruited for Hollywood by the same talent scout who discovered Errol Flynn.

His first role in an American film was as Flynn's younger brother in *The Charge of the Light Brigade* (1936). Since then Knowles has played second leads in scores of Hollywood features, including *How Green Was My Valley* (1941), *Monsieur Beaucaire* (1946) and *Auntie Mame* (1959). **Credits include:** *The Adventures of Robin Hood* (1938), *A Bill of Divorcement* (1940), *The Wolf Man* (1941), *Lady in a Jam* (1942), *The Bride Wore Boots* (1946), *Ivy* (1947), *Mutiny* (1952), *Band of Angels* (1957), *In Enemy Country* (1968).

Don Knotts of TV fame demonstrates a rare bird call for Edmund O'Brien in The Love God?

The young soldier (Eddie Ryan) is startled to discover that the coffee-server is none other than the President of the United States. Alexander Knox made a fine Woodrow Wilson, and the woman (Mrs. Wilson) in the black boater is Geraldine Fitzgerald.

A genial Clarence Kolb in
Irish Eyes Are Smiling.

ALEXANDER KNOX (1907–)

The high point of Knox's motion-picture career came when he starred as President Woodrow Wilson in the film *Wilson* (1944). He had appeared in only a few films when Darryl Zanuck heard him read the script for *Wilson* and decided he had found the actor who could play the President.

Knox was born in Canada and made his acting debut in Boston in 1929. He then went to England to appear on the London stage and act with the Old Vic. He returned to the United States and appeared on the New York stage before going to Hollywood. In addition to making dozens of films in the 40's, 50's and 60's, Knox has published detective novels under a pen name, and under his own name he has written three novels, including *Bride of Quietness*. He has also written plays. **Films include:** *The Sea Wolf* (1941), *This Above All* (1942), *Sister Kenny* (1946), *The Judge Steps Out* (1949), *The Sleeping Tiger* (1954), *The Longest Day* (1962), *Accident* (1967), *How I Won the War* (1967), *Nicholas and Alexandra* (1971).

CLARENCE KOLB (1875–1964)

Kolb came to the screen after nearly four decades of playing rough-and-tumble comedy in vaudeville, burlesque and operetta. After a short retirement and an abortive attempt to break into films in dramatic roles, he was finally spotted by director Michael Curtiz. Thereafter he made more than 75 films and appeared in scores of TV programs, including the *My Little Margie* series. **Some of his films include:** *Merrily We Live* (1938), *No Time for Comedy* (1940), *Hellzapoppin!* (1941), *Irish Eyes Are Smiling* (1944), *Adam's Rib* (1949), *Man of a Thousand Faces* (1957).

FRITZ KORTNER (1892–1970)

One of Germany's most controversial actors and directors, Kortner also appeared in American and British films. He first found fame as a stage and screen actor in Berlin before World War II but fled Germany after Hitler took power. Kortner spent the war years in the United States.

He returned to Germany in 1947 and continued to provoke controversy for his unorthodox interpretations of classical dramas. He produced and wrote films in Germany, including *The Strange Death of Adolf Hitler* (1943). **Films include:** *Backstairs* (1926), *Three Loves* (1929), *Pandora's Box* (1929), *Abdul the Damned* (1936), *The Hitler Gang* (1944), *The Razor's Edge* (1946), *The Vicious Circle* (1948), *The Last Illusion* (1951).

CHARLES KORVIN (1907–)

A familiar figure in supporting roles—he was the captain in *Ship of Fools* (1965)—Korvin came to Hollywood via Paris, London and then the Broadway stage.

He studied at the Hungarian Academy of Dramatic Arts, played a prominent role in early sound pictures in Hungary, studied at the Sorbonne in Paris and worked as a cameraman and a director on European documentaries before emigrating to the United States.

Korvin began acting under his own name,

Geza Korvin Karpathi, but changed it early in his American stage career. His first Broadway appearance was in *Dark Eyes* (1943), and the following year he went to Hollywood for his American motion-picture debut in *Enter Arsène Lupin* (1944) with Ella Raines. In addition to his work in films, Korvin appears frequently in television dramas and has continued to act on stage. **Films include:** *This Love of Ours* (1945), *Temptation* (1946), *The Killer That Stalked New York* (1951), *Lydia Bailey* (1952), *Sangaree* (1953), *Zorro the Avenger* (1960), *The Man Who Had Power Over Women* (1970).

MARTIN KOSLECK (1907–)

Often typed as a villainous Nazi—he has played Goebbels three times on the screen—Kosleck was born Nicolai Yoshkin in Russia, moved to Germany as a child and had acted extensively on the stage and screen in both Germany and England before coming to the United States in 1932.

A veteran of more than 40 films since *Confessions of a Nazi Spy* (1939), he has also worked steadily in the theatre—notably as the deaf mute in *The Madwoman of Chaillot* (1948). **Other films include:** *Foreign Correspondent* (1940), *The Hitler Gang* (1944), *House of Horrors* (1946), *Something Wild* (1961), *Agent for H.A.R.M.* (1966).

ERNIE KOVACS (1919–1962)

Kovacs' death in an automobile accident ended a screen career filled with promise. A talented comedian who scored heavily in nightclub and TV appearances, he made his film debut in *Operation Mad Ball* (1957). Over the next five years he appeared in nine more films and was well on his way to becoming a major star at the time of his death. He was married to the popular actress-singer-dancer Edie Adams. **Credits include:** *Bell, Book and Candle* (1958), *Our Man in Havana* (1960), *Pepe* (1960), *Sail a Crooked Ship* (1962).

KRIS KRISTOFFERSON (1936–)

The young Rhodes Scholar and winner of four National Collegiate Awards for short-story writing has had an amazing career. The

Ernie Kovacs notes that something is missing on the chessboard, the implication being that Alec Guinness was responsible. The film was the very funny Our Man in Havana.

Kris Kristofferson sings to an attractive Susan Anspach in Blume in Love.

Alma Kruger in a typical "sympathetic" role as she kibitzes a phone call in Dr. Kildare Goes Home *(1940).*

Otto Kruger, who played bad lawyers more often than good ones, with Jacqueline Wells in Counsel for Crime *(1937).*

son of a major general, Texas-born Kristofferson abandoned the military life just before he was scheduled to start teaching English at the United States Military Academy at West Point in order to do what he liked best—sing and compose music.

He went to Nashville, home of country music, and at first found the going tough. His years at Pomona College and Oxford didn't help much, but the fact that he had spent three years in the Army as a helicopter pilot did. He ferried men and supplies via copter to oil fields and off-shore Louisiana rigs until his songs began to find a market. Soon they were being recorded by such top singers as Johnny Cash, and his own vocalizing (in concerts and on records) led to a flurry of film offers.

His first appearance was in the title role of *Cisco Pike* (1971), and since then the flying scholar-singer-composer has turned in several more sterling performances. **Credits include:** *The Last Movie* (1971), *Blume in Love* (1973).

ALMA KRUGER (1872–1960)

Her long acting career had four distinct phases, beginning with her success as a Shakespearean actress in some of the most famous troupes of the early 20th century. When age forced her to abandon roles like Juliet and Lady Macbeth, Kruger retired from the theatre to operate a gift shop and try her hand at real-estate brokerage. She soon returned to the theatre, however, this time as a character actress in such plays as *Daisy Mayme* (1926) and the Eva LeGallienne productions of *Camille* (1931) and *Hedda Gabler*. She then found a third career as an actress in radio dramas and a fourth when director William Wyler was impressed by her performance in *Few Are Chosen* (1935) and offered her work in Hollywood.

Kruger's best-known film role was as Molly Byrd, the head nurse in the *Dr. Kildare* series starring Lionel Barrymore. She also played Empress Maria Theresa in *Marie Antoinette* (1938) and Mrs. Stockton in *Tarnished Angel* (1938). Kruger continued to work in films until ill health forced her to retire in 1947. **Films include:** *These Three*

(1936), *The Man in Blue* (1937), *One Hundred Men and a Girl* (1937), *The Secret of Dr. Kildare* (1939), *Balalaika* (1939), *Saboteur* (1942), *Our Hearts Were Young and Gay* (1944), *Forever Amber* (1947).

OTTO KRUGER (1885–)

Wavy locks, a trim mustache, sleek manners and bedroom eyes combined to make him one of the most convincing movie seducers of them all. Occasionally sympathetic roles came his way, but they were almost always in low-grade films.

Kruger was born in Ohio, played in stock companies and found his proper place on Broadway in 1915 in *The Natural Law*. Despite his diminutive stature he was at his best on stage and remained a popular leading man and supporting actor in legitimate theatre for several decades. Since his first sound film in 1932 (in *The Intruder*), Kruger has made over 65 features. He has also appeared in such TV series as *Climax* and *The Law and Mr. Jones*. **Credits include:** *Turn Back the Clock* (1933), *Treasure Island* (1934), *Seventeen* (1940), *High Noon* (1952), *The Young Philadelphians* (1959), *Sex and the Single Girl* (1964).

NANCY KWAN (1938–)

The daughter of a Chinese architect and a Scottish fashion model, Kwan was educated at a convent in Hong Kong, a finishing school in England and the Royal School of Ballet in London. She made her movie debut opposite William Holden in the title role of *The World of Suzie Wong* (1960) and the following year snagged the part of the Chinese picture bride in the film version of the Rodgers and Hammerstein musical *Flower Drum Song*. Despite its promising start, Kwan's career never gained much momentum, and although she remained active in films through the 60's, most of her roles were in forgettable second features. She is now married to an Austrian hotel keeper and lives in Europe. **Films include:** *Fate Is the Hunter* (1964), *The Wild Affair* (1965), *Arrivederci, Baby!* (1966), *Nobody's Perfect* (1968), *The Girl Who Knew Too Much* (1969).

ALAN LADD (1913–1964)

It was this mild-mannered gentleman's fate to spend most of his nearly 30-year screen career playing stony-faced tough guys in crime melodramas, adventure films and Westerns and to be remembered best for characterizations of what critic Bosley Crowther aptly dubbed "tight-lipped violence."

Ladd was born in Hot Springs, Arkansas, was an outstanding athlete as a teenager in California and got into films at the age of 19 with a bit part in *Once in a Lifetime* (1932). After six discouraging years of minimal film work and various odd jobs, Ladd was taken under the wing of former starlet turned theatrical agent Sue Carol, and his fortune changed. With her determined assistance he began getting some substantial roles, and in 1942 he achieved star status as the psychopathic killer in the low-budget hit *This Gun for Hire*. The film's success also made his leading lady, Veronica Lake, a big drawing card, and the two diminutive performers were immediately cast in a remake of Dashiell Hammett's *The Glass Key* (1942).

Ladd retained his popularity through the 40's and played leads in films which ranged from the crime melodrama *The Blue Dahlia* (1946) and the adventure saga *Saigon* (1948)—both opposite Veronica Lake—to a not too happily received change-of-pace title role in *The Great Gatsby* (1948). His finest performance, however, came after his heyday as the mysterious gunslinger hero of George Stevens' memorable Western about pioneer homesteaders, *Shane* (1953). **More than 50 films include:** *Citizen Kane* (1941), *Lucky Jordan* (1943), *Two Years Before the Mast* (1946), *Appointment With Danger* (1951), *Desert Legion* (1953), *Boy on a Dolphin* (1957), *The Carpetbaggers* (1964).

BERT LAHR (1895–1967)

With his lisping, tremulous vocal delivery somewhere between a gulp and a gargle and his wildly fanciful routines, Lahr was one of America's most popular stage and nightclub comedians for nearly 40 years. He was born Irving Lahrheim and won popularity as a vaudevillian before making his first legitimate-stage appearance in *Harry Delmar's Revels* (1927) and his first film, *Faint Heart* (1931). Surprisingly, Lahr's vast talents did not come across well on screen; his few film roles over the years were usually disappointing. The one exception to this statement is, however, a memorable one. Hidden behind a bewhiskered costume that somehow managed to look exactly like him, Lahr was a magnificent Cowardly Lion in *The Wizard of Oz* (1939)—outwardly totally craven, inwardly prepared to defend Dorothy at all costs. Another Lahr appearance that deserves special mention—his stage performance in the ultra-serious 1966 New York

Alan Ladd surrenders in Warners' The Big Land (1957), a film made late in Ladd's career.

Bert Lahr makes impassioned overtures to a past-mistress of deadpan responses, Virginia O'Brien, in Ship Ahoy *(1942).*

In this studio portrait one sees more of Veronica Lake's face than was usually the case.

Although this old portrait was heavily retouched, Barbara La Marr was indeed a beautiful lady.

production of Samuel Beckett's *Waiting for Godot*. **Other films include:** *Flying High* (1931), *Love and Kisses* (1938), *Always Leave Them Laughing* (1949), *Mr. Universe* (1951), *The Second Greatest Sex* (1956), *The Night They Raided Minsky's* (1968).

ARTHUR LAKE (1905–　　)

For over 15 years the career of this ebullient screen actor was inextricably tied to the antics of a single character—Dagwood Bumstead, the perpetual juvenile and long-suffering husband of Chic Young's *Blondie*. Lake not only played Bumstead (to Penny Singleton's Blondie) in a series of films that appeared at the rate of two a year between 1938 and 1950 but also recreated his role on radio and an ill-fated TV series of 1954.

Born Arthur Silverlake in Corbin, Kentucky, to vaudevillian parents, he made his first stage appearance at the age of three and his film debut before he had turned 13. When his first sound film, *Air Circus*, appeared in 1928 he still looked, and continued to look, like a teenager. **Films include:** *Jack and the Beanstalk* (debut, 1917), *Skinner's Dress Suit* (1926), *Harold Teen* (1928), *Indiscreet* (1931), *Topper* (1937), plus some two dozen *Blondie* films.

VERONICA LAKE (1919–1973)

In 1941 this tiny, husky-voiced screen vamp adopted her legendary "peek-a-boo" hairdo, and over the next few years countless girls spent their time peering myopically out at the world from behind hair that cascaded across half (sometimes a good two-thirds) of their faces.

She was born Constance Ockleman, studied acting in Los Angeles and made her screen debut under the name of Constance Keane in *Sorority House* (1939). After two relatively uneventful short-haired years she clicked with long hair in *I Wanted Wings* (1941), and the following year she became an honest-to-goodness star in *This Gun for Hire*, the first of four films she made with Alan Ladd. For several years after that she enjoyed tremendous popularity. She was almost always presented as a latter-day siren, but devoid of the kiss-me-you-fool quality of a Theda Bara. One always suspected that be-

hind the sensuous façade she was just a nice home-town girl at heart. By the end of the 40's Lake's career was over. She appeared in only two films in the next 20 years, and apart from a few stock-company and British appearances on stage, she supported herself with a variety of menial jobs. Her autobiography, *Veronica*, aroused some interest in her for a spell. **Films include:** *Sullivan's Travels* (1942), *I Married a Witch* (1942), *The Glass Key* (1942), *The Blue Dahlia* (1946), *Saigon* (1948), *Footsteps in the Snow* (1966).

BARBARA LA MARR (1896–1926)

Although she was a screen star for only four years in the early 20's, her beauty was such that for years after La Marr's death it remained the standard against which screen actresses were measured. The former Rheatha Watson first wowed movie audiences in *Cinderella of the Hills* (1921). (She was so remarkably lovely that audiences gasped at close-ups of her face.) She went on to star in a number of silent favorites, including *The Three Musketeers* (1921) with Douglas Fairbanks and Adolphe Menjou and *The Prisoner of Zenda* (1922) with Ramon Novarro. La Marr's private life during this time was a dramatic and tragic one, and the combination of her personal troubles and the strains of stardom soon proved too much for her. She began to drink heavily, gain weight and eventually to neglect her work. Her strength exhausted, she died in 1926. **Film highlights:** *Trifling Women* (1922), *Souls for Sale* (1923), *The White Moth* (1924), *The Heart of a Siren* (1925).

HEDY LAMARR (1913–　　)

When she was still a teenager, Hedwig Kiesler attracted international attention by swimming nude and then dashing off through a forest—still nude—in a picture called *Ecstasy* (1933, U.S. 1940).

After an unhappy marriage to a wealthy manufacturer, the actress fled to England, where she was introduced to MGM's Louis B. Mayer. He renamed her Hedy Lamarr after the most beautiful star he had ever seen, screen siren Barbara La Marr. He took her to Hollywood and cast her in *Algiers* (1938) with Charles Boyer. Lamarr's beauty won raves, and she went on to star with such screen heroes as Robert Taylor and Clark Gable. Lamarr's career began to go downhill soon after Mayer lost interest in her in the early 40's. She continued to make movies but was notorious for choosing unsuitable scripts. By the early 50's her career was virtually in ruins, although she remained in the public eye via her six marriages and divorces and the chronicle she wrote of her life, *Ecstasy and Me*. **Films include:** *Boom Town* (1940), *H. M. Pulham, Esq.* (1941), *Tortilla Flat* (1942), *White Cargo* (1942), *Experiment Perilous* (1944), *Copper Canyon* (1950), *The Female Animal* (1958).

FERNANDO LAMAS (1915–)

Fernando Alvaro Lamas was already the veteran of more than 20 South American and European films as well as numerous stage and radio productions when he made his American screen debut in the MGM musical *Rich, Young and Pretty* (1951). His rich voice and good looks quickly resulted in leads in such films as *The Merry Widow* (1952) and *Rose Marie* (1954). Unfortunately, this Latin lover had come to Hollywood when the popularity of Latin lovers was already on the wane, and despite large budgets and even bigger studio buildups, the productions, and consequently Lamas, were not box-office hits. In the mid-50's he left Hollywood for Broadway and a successful run in *Happy Hunting* with Ethel Merman. In recent years he has appeared on television frequently and made occasional films. Lamas has also tried his hand at directing, with two films and several TV shows to his credit. **Films include:** *Sangaree* (1953), *Dangerous When Wet* (1953), *The Girl Rush* (1955), *The Lost World* (1960), *100 Rifles* (1969).

DOROTHY LAMOUR (1914–)

Dorothy Kaumeyer was a singer on her own radio show in Los Angeles when Paramount signed her up. They wrapped a sarong around her in her very first movie, *The Jungle Princess* (1936), and for the following decade Lamour only rarely escaped appearing as an exotic jungle girl who spoke only in monosyllables.

In 1940 she played Mimi in *Road to Singapore* (1940), the first of the Hope–Crosby–Lamour "Road" spoofs. During the years of World War II she was cast with Hope or Crosby or both in a series of pictures, usually wearing her sarong because the studio convinced her it was good for the morale of the fighting men.

She finally shed her native garb in pictures like *A Medal for Benny* (1945), the film version of John Steinbeck's novel. The movies she made in the late 40's, however, did little for her box-office appeal, and after *Manhandled* (1949) she made only a few pictures until Paramount cast her in Cecil B. De Mille's *The Greatest Show on Earth* (1952). After that, she went back into her sarong and the company of Hope and Crosby for *The Road to Bali* (1953). Lamour then announced her retirement, emerging in 1962 for a brief appearance in *The Road to Hong Kong*. Since then she has made only a handful of films. **Films include:** *Swing High, Swing Low* (1937), *The Hurricane* (1937), *Johnny Apollo* (1940), *Road to Zanzibar* (1941), *Rainbow Island* (1944), *Slightly French*

Hedy Lamarr came a long way from the nude scene in Ecstasy *to parade her lush beauty in* Ziegfeld Girl *(1941).*

Dorothy Lamour, High Priestess of the Sarong, along with a very young-looking Ray Milland in The Jungle Princess *(1946).*

Sergeant Burt Lancaster and Deborah Kerr, as the unhappy wife of an officer, in the (for its day) ultra-torrid lovemaking-on-the-beach scene in From Here to Eternity.

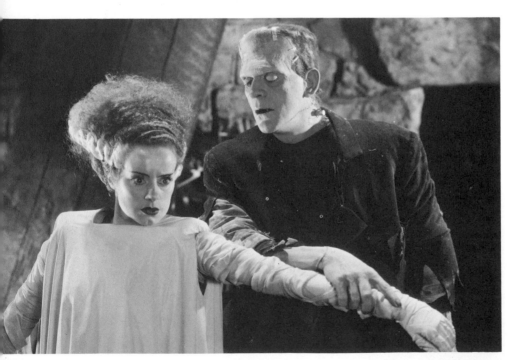

Elsa Lanchester doesn't quite know what hit her as she accompanies Boris Karloff to the altar in Bride of Frankenstein (1935).

(1949), *Donovan's Reef* (1963), *The Phynx* (1970).

BURT LANCASTER (1913–   )

One of Hollywood's biggest names and most solidly established stars, within the first six years of his screen career Lancaster progressed from stereotyped tough-guy and swashbuckler roles to his sensitive performance in the demanding role of the sergeant in *From Here to Eternity* (1953).

After his professional debut in the Broadway production *A Sound of Hunting* (1945), his agent, Harold Hecht, got him a contract with Hal Wallis. He started out playing the brooding ex-prize fighter in *The Killers* (1946) and was soon cast in several other heavyish roles before he and Hecht formed their own production company. Although the enterprise was not successful enough to pose a challenge to the studio-dominated production system in Hollywood, it was the forerunner of other actor-dominated independent companies which did eventually crumple the studio giants.

Meanwhile, Lancaster began tackling more serious roles. He starred opposite Shirley Booth in *Come Back, Little Sheba* (1952), made *The Rose Tattoo* (1955) with Anna Magnani and appeared in *Separate Tables* (1958) with Rita Hayworth, Deborah Kerr and David Niven. In 1960 his fine performance in the title role of *Elmer Gantry* won Lancaster the Academy Award for Best Actor. Other successes followed, notably the title role in a film he particularly wanted to do, *Birdman of Alcatraz* (1962). **Films include:** *All My Sons* (1948), *Ten Tall Men* (1951), *His Majesty O'Keefe* (1954), *Gunfight at the OK Corral* (1957), *The Devil's Disciple* (1959), *The Unforgiven* (1960), *Judgment at Nuremberg* (1961), *The Leopard* (1963), *The Swimmer* (1968), *Airport* (1970), *Valdez Is Coming* (1971).

ELSA LANCHESTER (1902–   )

A veteran of stage and screen in character and comedy roles, English actress Elsa Lanchester has appeared in a broad variety of films, from *The Private Life of Henry VIII* (1933) to *The Bride of Frankenstein* (1935), from *Les Misérables* (1952) to *Blackbeard's Ghost* (1968).

Elizabeth Sullivan began her performing career at age 16 with London's Children's Theatre and in the 20's combined her legitimate-stage career with some film work. It was through her influence that her soon-to-be husband, Charles Laughton, entered the film world in 1928. When Laughton was lured to Hollywood by a Paramount contract in the early 30's Lanchester followed. For the next two decades both Lanchester and Laughton were kept busy in American and British films. They frequently appeared in the same pictures—*Blue Bottles* (1928), *Rembrandt* (1936), *The Big Clock* (1948), *Witness for the Prosecution* (1958). The couple's 33-year marriage was ended by Laughton's death in 1962. Lanchester continues to appear in films in small but spotlighted roles. **Highlights:** *Tales of Manhattan* (1942), *Mary Poppins* (1964), *Me, Natalie* (1969), *Willard* (1971).

MARTIN LANDAU (1933–   )

The tall, serious-looking actor is perhaps best known for his role (opposite his wife, Barbara Bain) in the *Mission Impossible* TV series. Landau studied in New York at the Art Students' League and the Pratt Institute and worked as a staff cartoonist for the New York *Daily News* before deciding on an acting career. He began performing in off-Broadway and summer-stock productions and later appeared in such films as *North by Northwest* (1959) and *Nevada Smith* (1966). **Films include:** *Pork Chop Hill* (1959), *The Gazebo* (1960), *Cleopatra* (1963), *The Greatest Story Ever Told* (1965).

ELISSA LANDI (1904–1948)

Multitalented Elissa Landi was born in Venice and educated in England. By the time she was 20 she had written the first of her three novels, apprenticed in an Oxford repertory company and made her stage debut. She appeared on screen from the late 20's and gained international recognition as the lead in *Underground* (1928, U.S. 1929). She made German, French and British films before going to the United States in 1930 to appear on Broadway. Hollywood then beckoned and

Landi signed a contract with Fox. Fox's publicity build-up did her more harm than good, however, and after several forgettable films and Landi's refusal to do a picture, the studio canceled her contract.

Her screen career revived briefly in the mid-30's, but by the end of the decade she was relegated to ''B'' films and was seen on screen only once in the 40's. **Credits:** *The Parisian* (1931), *Body and Soul* (1931), *The Sign of the Cross* (1932), *The Warrior's Husband* (1933), *The Count of Monte Cristo* (1934), *After the Thin Man* (1936), *The Thirteenth Chair* (1937), *Corregidor* (1943).

CAROLE LANDIS (1919–1948)

Her tasteful animal-skin décolletage and Hollywood-style Cro-Magnon makeup brought whistles from the audiences and stardom to Carole Landis when she appeared opposite cave man Victor Mature in *One Million B.C.*, a fanciful saga of man among the dinosaurs, which was remade by Hammer in 1967 as *One Million Years B.C.*

Before that Frances Lillian Ridste had been a nightclub singer, hula dancer and an early Hollywood sweater girl who first appeared in films as a chorus girl in *Varsity Show* (1937). After her cave-woman success, however, she went on to be featured in upward of 35 films before her untimely death at the age of 29. **Credits include:** *I Wake Up Screaming* (1942), *Four Jills in a Jeep* (1944), *Having Wonderful Crime* (1945), *Out of the Blue* (1947).

JESSIE ROYCE LANDIS (1904–1972)

A veteran of the stage, she made a career of playing bubbly ingénues, Southern belles and venomous wives in dozens of film comedies and dramas before becoming a character actress adept at portraying fussy matrons and mothers in such films as *To Catch a Thief* (1955).

Born in Chicago, she made her stage debut in 1924 and her first film appearance in *Derelict* (1930). **Some of her films include:** *Mr. Belvedere Goes to College* (1949), *The Swan* (1956), *North by Northwest* (1959), *Boys' Night Out* (1962), *Critic's Choice* (1963).

Elissa Landi and a young Paul Lukas in By Candlelight *(1934).*

Jessie Royce Landis at the beginning of her long film career.

Rosemary Lane in Silver Queen *(1943).*

CHARLES LANE (1899–)

Noted for his numerous portrayals of ill-tempered or miserly figures, this veteran character actor appeared as the comic lead's foil in scores of films during his more than 45-year screen career. In recent years Lane has made appearances on a number of TV series, including *Petticoat Junction*. **Film highlights:** *The White Sister* (1923), *Mr. Deeds Goes to Town* (1936), *You Can't Take It With You* (1938), *Ellery Queen and the Perfect Crime* (1941), *Apartment for Peggy* (1948), *What's So Bad About Feeling Good?* (1968).

PRISCILLA LANE (1917–)

The youngest of the Lane sisters to have screen careers, Priscilla Mullican broke into show business as part of a singing act with sisters Rosemary and Lola and made her screen debut with them in *Varsity Show* (1937). The following year the trio, billed as "the picture of American girlhood," attained prominence as the heroines of *Four Daughters* (1938), the film that launched John Garfield on his career. The hit was immediately followed by a sequel, *Daughters Courageous* (1938), and then by *Four Wives* (1939) and *Four Mothers* (1940).

From the late 30's until her retirement a decade later, Lane also appeared in occasional films on her own. Later, she returned to show business as the hostess of a Boston daytime TV show. **Credits include:** *Brother Rat* (1939), *Million Dollar Baby* (1941), *Saboteur* (1942), *Arsenic and Old Lace* (1944), *Bodyguard* (1948).

ROSEMARY LANE (1916–)

The older sister of actress Priscilla Lane never achieved stardom but "supported" many a less able performer. She made her screen debut with sisters Priscilla and Lola in *Varsity Show* (1937). Apart from her other appearances with them, she was cast occasionally as a "slow-moving, dull-witted dame" through the early 40's. **Film highlights:** *Four Daughters* (1938), *Daughters Courageous* (1939), *Always a Bride* (1940), *All by Myself* (1943).

GLENN LANGAN (1917–)

He began his acting career with repertory companies and vaudeville groups before making his Broadway debut in *Swing Your Lady* (1936). His film debut came three years later when he appeared in *The Return of Doctor X* (1939). During the 40's and 50's he played an assortment of leading roles in creepy films like *Dragonwyck* (1946) and the sci-fi picture *The Amazing Colossal Man* (1957). **Film highlights:** *Riding High* (1943), *A Bell for Adano* (1945), *Forever Amber* (1947), *The Snake Pit* (1948), *Mutiny in Outer Space* (1964).

HARRY LANGDON (1884–1944)

"Keaton, Chaplin, Lloyd, Langdon—and the unsung member of the quartet is Langdon," a critic wrote after viewing a Langdon retrospective. The comment, one feels, was entirely valid, for the round and solemn-faced comedian was a very funny man indeed. His deadpan approach to comedy was not unlike

Harry Langdon is about to come up with something startling as his ally, Billy Gilbert, waits apprehensively. The film, one of many Langdon comedies of the 20's, eluded our researcher.

Buster Keaton's—except that Langdon often smiled, twisting the corners of his lips upward in a sweet, almost tragic, expression. Like Chaplin, he played the part of the little man, an outcast subject to the indignities imposed on him by the far more sophisticated world around him. In the end he almost always triumphed.

Langdon came to Hollywood via medicine and minstrel shows, the circus, vaudeville and burlesque. He was spotted by Mack Sennett and made nearly 30 short comedies for him before he switched to Warners for his first feature, *Tramp, Tramp, Tramp* (1926), with Joan Crawford.

Langdon ran into trouble when he decided to direct himself and cranked out three flops in a row. He was off-screen for more than a year before he returned to make short comedies for MGM. Two more features that were box-office losers further reduced Langdon's appeal to the studios. He continued to make shorts and appeared in a few features as a supporting player, but his heyday was over. He was bankrupt by the time he died. **Many credits include:** *Ella Cinders* (1926), *The Strong Man* (1926), *Long Pants* (1927), *See America Thirst* (1930), *Hallelujah, I'm a Bum* (1933), *Zenobia* (1939), *Block Busters* (1944).

HOPE LANGE (1933–)

She was born in Redding Ridge, Connecticut, to show-business parents and first appeared on Broadway at the age of 12 in *The Patriots*. Later an appearance on a television series led to a Hollywood contract and the attention-getting role of Elma in *Bus Stop* (1956). The following year she won an Oscar nomination for her performance in *Peyton Place*. Lange continued to work in films and television through the 60's, and she is well known to TV audiences of the early 70's via *The Ghost and Mrs. Muir* and *The New Dick Van Dyke Show*. **Film highlights:** *The Young Lions* (1958), *The Best of Everything* (1959), *A Pocketful of Miracles* (1961), *Love Is a Ball* (1963), *Jigsaw* (1968).

ANGELA LANSBURY (1925–)

After 20 years of supporting roles on screen and stage—usually as a spiteful or conniving woman, somebody's callous wife or mother —Angela Brigid Lansbury proved a sensation in her first starring role as Patrick Dennis' lovable madcap aunt in the Broadway hit musical *Mame* (1966).

Born in England, Lansbury came to New York in 1940 with her mother and brothers. In short order she had landed a seven-year contract with MGM and made her screen debut with an Academy Award-winning performance as the cockney maid, Nancy Oliver, in George Cukor's *Gaslight* (1944), starring Ingrid Bergman and Charles Boyer.

Over the years Lansbury turned in consistently good performances as a variety of unsympathetic characters, first on screen and later on stage. She made her Broadway debut in 1957 in *Hotel Paradiso* with Bert Lahr and three years later played the floozy mother in *A Taste of Honey*. In films she won an Oscar nomination for Best Supporting Actress as Laurence Harvey's evil mother in *The Manchurian Candidate* (1962). After *Mame*, Lansbury returned to the screen to star opposite Michael York in the black comedy *Something for Everyone* (1970) and appear in a Walt Disney musical, *Bedknobs and Broomsticks* (1971). **Films include:** *National Velvet* (1944), *The Harvey Girls* (1946), *The Long Hot Summer* (1958), *All Fall Down* (1962), *Mister Buddwing* (1966).

MARIO LANZA (1921–1959)

Alfred Arnold Cocozza, the temperamental tenor from Philadelphia, had a brief but highly successful career in films. It began in 1949 with a screen debut opposite Kathryn Grayson in *That Midnight Kiss* and reached its high point two year's later with Lanza's fine performance in the title role of the film biography *The Great Caruso*. Within a few years, however, the combined effect of a swelling waistline and an equally expanded ego had made him a Hollywood untouchable. He tried to revitalize his film career in Italy but continued to punish his body and voice with too much food, alcohol and weight-controlling drugs and died of a heart attack in Rome at the age of 38. **Other films:** *The Toast of New Orleans* (1950), *Because You're Mine* (1952), *Serenade* (1956), *The Seven Hills of Rome* (1958).

Angela Lansbury, a fine actress whose full potential was recognized only in recent years.

Mario Lanza, shaking the rafters with his fine voice in The Great Caruso *(1951).*

Rod La Rocque in The Locked Door *(1930).*

ROD LA ROCQUE (1896–1969)

During his heyday as a silent screen lover during the mid-20's, Chicago-born Roderick la Rocque was compared with Valentino. In 1927, at the peak of his career, he married the equally popular Vilma Banky in a wedding that was one of the most lavish spectacles Hollywood has ever devised. Although he made the transition from silents to sound, his box-office appeal as a leading man quickly diminished, and within a few years he was reduced to occasional character parts. After La Roque left films, he became a real-estate broker and investor and one of the richest men in the film colony. **Some of his films include:** *Stolen Kiss* (1920), *The Ten Commandments* (1923), *Resurrection* (1927), *Let Us Be Gay* (1930), *One Romantic Night* (1930), *The Hunchback of Notre Dame* (1940), *Meet John Doe* (1941).

JACK LA RUE (1903–   )

For a time during the 30's and early 40's La Rue was probably the busiest badman in Hollywood (appearing in three to seven films per year). Although the young Gaspare Biondolillo had played a bellboy in a Norma Talmadge picture filmed back in the dim days when the Vitagraph studio was in Brooklyn, it wasn't until *The Mouthpiece* (1932) that his career gained momentum. Although he played a priest in *A Farewell to Arms* (1932) and again in *Captains Courageous* (1937), on virtually all other occasions he was either murderous or just plain despicable. He was probably at his orneriest as Trigger in *The Story of Temple Drake* (1933).

La Rue pretty much retired from filmmaking in the late 40's but has made a few appearances since—when he is not busy running his Hollywood restaurant. **Credits include:** *Lady Killer* (1934), *Paper Bullets* (1941), *Road to Utopia* (1946), *No Orchids for Miss Blandish* (1951), *Ride the Man Down* (1953), *Robin and the Seven Hoods* (1964).

LOUISE LASSER (c. 1935–   )

Although she has acted on both stage and screen Lasser's face is probably most familiar to Americans as the sympathetic wife on a TV commercial for a cold remedy. She responds with a heartfelt "I know" to each of the symptoms her suffering husband describes.

A native of New York, Lasser first came to public attention when she substituted for Barbra Streisand as Miss Marmelstein in the Broadway musical *I Can Get It for You Wholesale*. She was married for several years to comedian Woody Allen, who cast her (after their divorce) in her first starring film role opposite him in *Bananas* (1971). Before that she had put in brief appearances in two other films with Allen, *What's New Pussycat?* (1965) and *Take the Money and Run* (1969). **Films include:** *Slither* (1973).

TOM LAUGHLIN (1931–   )

Laughlin made his film debut in *Tea and Sympathy* (1956) and periodically appeared in films after that, but it wasn't until he appeared in *Billy Jack* (1971) that audiences and critics took notice. Since then, other important roles have come his way. **Credits:** *South Pacific* (1958), *Tall Story* (1960), *The Born Losers* (1967).

CHARLES LAUGHTON (1899–1962)

So many of his screen performances were masterful that it would be almost impossible to select which of this distinguished Britisher's many roles is most closely identified with him.

Laughton received his training at the Royal Academy of Dramatic Art in London and was well on his way to a successful career on the legitimate stage when he was introduced to films by his future wife, Elsa Lanchester. Although he probably appeared in some silent comedy two-reelers in the late 20's, he won his first screen credit in the early talkie feature *Piccadilly* (1929).

While appearing on Broadway in *Alibi* in the early 30's he accepted his first Hollywood film contract and made his American screen debut in *The Old Dark House* (1932). He won raves for his next film, *The Devil and the Deep* (1932), and proceeded to repeat his success again and again in some of the best movies of the decade. He won an Oscar for his characterization of the King in *The Private Life of Henry VIII* (1933) and the following year gave a memorable performance as

Elizabeth Barrett Browning's domineering father in *The Barretts of Wimpole Street*. In 1935 the New York Film Critics gave him the first of their annual Best Actor awards for his portrayals of Captain Bligh in *Mutiny on the Bounty* and the delightful manservant in the Wild West in *Ruggles of Red Gap*. That same year he also starred with Fredric March in what was probably the best screen version of the Victor Hugo classic *Les Misérables*.

Laughton then returned to England for three years but was back in Hollywood in 1939 for the role of Quasimodo in *The Hunchback of Notre Dame*. During the 40's films diminished slightly in quality, and though he continued to perform until his death, few of his movies had the substance of those of the 30's. Over the years Laughton appeared in a variety of films with Lanchester, and their last joint effort, *Witness for the Prosecution* (1958), brought both husband and wife Oscar nominations. **Other films include:** *Rembrandt* (1936), *Jamaica Inn* (1939), *Tales of Manhattan* (1942), *The Canterville Ghost* (1944), *The Big Clock* (1948), *Hobson's Choice* (1954), *Spartacus* (1960), *Advise and Consent* (1962).

STAN LAUREL (1890–1965)

For more than three decades Stan was the lean, solemn-faced underdog invariably ordered by the rotund Oliver (Hardy) to do whatever work was around—lifting this, opening that, carrying these—and always the results were the same: total but hilarious disaster.

Arthur Stanley Jefferson arrived in Hollywood via music halls in his native England and the vaudeville circuit in the United States. He had his own comedy film series before producer Hal Roach created one of the screen's favorite comedy partnerships when he teamed him with Oliver Hardy for *Putting Pants on Philip* (1926). During the next six years the two men filmed a string of highly successful shorts for Roach at the rate of one a month. In 1931 *Pardon Us* was released as a feature and from then on they made both shorts and features. By the mid-30's, however, a breach had developed between the team and producer Roach, and though things were patched up for a while, they finally

Charles Laughton as the aging but still amorous monarch in the memorable The Private Life of Henry VIII *(1933).*

severed their ties with Roach in 1940 and began making pictures for some of the larger Hollywood studios.

After their film career ended, the two continued to work as a comedy team in music halls. Hardy died in 1957, but Laurel lived long enough to receive Hollywood's long-belated recognition of the team's work in the form of a special 1960 comedy award. **Films include:** *Slipping Wives* (1927), *Sailors Beware* (1927), *Liberty* (1928), *Pack Up Your Troubles* (1932), *Babes in Toyland* (1934), *Bonnie Scotland* (1935), *The Flying Deuces* (1939), *A Chump at Oxford* (1940), *The Bull Fighters* (1945).

JOHN LAURIE (1897–   )

This Scottish-born actor was trained as an architect before making his first stage appearance in 1921. He has played leading parts in a variety of stage productions, from Giradoux to Shakespeare, and has appeared in over 100 films. He has also worked on television in such series as *Tales of Mystery* and *Dad's Army*. **Film highlights:** *Juno and the Paycock* (debut, 1930), *The Thirty-nine Steps*

Stan Laurel and rotund Oliver Hardy in one of their best sequences ever. The picture was Brats.

Peter Lawford and Lassie in MGM's Son of Lassie *(1945).*

(1935), *Farewell Again* (1937), *I Know Where I'm Going* (1946), *Hamlet* (1948), *Hobson's Choice* (1954), *Kidnapped* (1960).

PIPER LAURIE (1932–   )

As the romantic leading lady of costume productions like *Son of Ali Baba* (1952), she seemed the typical 50's starlet. Laurie made her debut in *Louisa* (1950) and later was cast as the ingénue who holds a conversation with Francis, the talking mule, in *Francis Goes to the Races* (1951). Her best screen performance was as Sarah Packard, Paul Newman's crippled girlfriend, in *The Hustler* (1961). She is seen frequently in some of the better TV dramas. **Credits:** *The Prince Who Was a Thief* (1951), *Ain't Misbehavin'* (1955), *Until They Sail* (1957).

PETER LAWFORD (1923–   )

He made his film debut at seven in the British picture *Poor Old Bill* (1930). Several years later when his family visited Hollywood, he played a small part in *Lord Jeff* (1938). Lawford didn't begin making films full time until he completed his education in England and returned to Hollywood. One of his first roles was a pilot in *Mrs. Miniver* (1942), and he continued to play feature parts in a variety of films, including the remake of *Little Women* (1949). In the early 50's his screen career was interrupted by the television series *Dear Phoebe,* in which he starred as an advice-to-the-lovelorn columnist. A second series in 1959, *The Thin Man,* cast Lawford opposite Phyllis Kirk as detectives Nick and Nora Charles. He returned to the screen in the 60's and appears frequently in films, on television, on quiz and talk shows and doing commercials. **Films include:** *Eagle Squadron* (1942), *The White Cliffs of Dover* (1944), *Easter Parade* (1948), *Royal Wedding* (1951), *Exodus* (1960), *Advise and Consent* (1962), *The April Fools* (1969), *They Only Kill Their Masters* (1972).

MARC LAWRENCE (1910–   )

This character actor-director specialized in gunman roles in films of the 30's and 40's. He began his career on the legitimate stage and was featured in the Eva Le Gallienne repertory company. **Film highlights:** *Little Big Shot* (1935), *The Ox-Bow Incident* (1943), *The Princess and the Pirate* (1945), *The Virginian* (1946), *Key Largo* (1948), *The Asphalt Jungle* (1950), *Johnny Cool* (1964), *Krakatoa* (1969).

GEORGE LAZENBY (1939–   )

In 1964 Lazenby left his job as a car salesman in his native Australia to try his luck in London. Before his motion picture debut as James Bond in *On Her Majesty's Secret Service* (1969), however, his sole claim to fame was an appearance in a chocolate commercial on British television. Since then he has made only one film, *The Universal Soldier.*

CLORIS LEACHMAN (1926–   )

After 19 years in films and television as "the actress everyone saw and no one remembered," Leachman finally made the transition from obscurity to fame with an Oscar-winning supporting performance in *The Last Picture Show* (1971).

Cloris Leachman, as the lonely housewife in The Last Picture Show, *exchanges confidences with Timothy Bottoms.*

After a brief stint at Northwestern University Leachman got her first taste of publicity in 1946 as Miss Illinois and eventually as a runner-up in the Miss America pageant. The next stop was New York, where she spent several years acting in TV dramas before her marriage to producer George Englund in 1955. They moved to California, and after that she divided her time between acting in films and television (she was the second of the mothers on the *Lassie* TV series) and raising her five children.

In recent years Leachman has appeared regularly on television as the flighty neighbor, Phyllis, in *The Mary Tyler Moore Show*, and she won a 1972 Emmy for her performances in the comedy series. In 1974 she appeared in the highly acclaimed TV drama *The Migrants*. **Films include:** *Kiss Me Deadly* (1955), *The Rack* (1956), *The Chapman Report* (1962), *Butch Cassidy and the Sundance Kid* (1969), *Lovers and Other Strangers* (1970).

JEAN-PIERRE LÉAUD (1944–)

This appealing French actor made his sensational screen debut at age 14 as the lonely schoolboy in François Truffaut's first feature film, the semi-autobiographical *The 400 Blows* (1959). Since then he has worked almost exclusively with Truffaut (portraying essentially the same character over a period of years and in various guises) and Jean-Luc Godard. **Films include:** *Love at Twenty* (1963), *Le Départ* (1967), *La Chinoise* (1968), *Stolen Kisses* (1969), *Bed and Board* (1971), *Day for Night* (1973).

IVAN LEBEDEFF (1894–1953)

Born in Lithuania, this aristocrat was educated for a diplomatic career in Russia and was a member of the Imperial Dragoons during World War I. After the Bolshevik revolt, Lebedeff took part in the White Russian attempt to recapture Odessa and later became military dictator of the captured city. Eventually, after having worked as a stockbroker in Constantinople and in Berlin, he broke into German films. Moving to this country in 1925, Lebedeff did several films for D. W. Griffith. He made the transition to talkies

easily and appeared in more than a score of pictures in the 30's and 40's. **Film highlights:** *King Frederick* (1922), *The Sorrows of Satan* (1926), *The Gay Diplomat* (1931), *Bombshell* (1933), *China Seas* (1935), *The Snows of Kilimanjaro* (1952).

FRANCIS LEDERER (1906–)

The suave and soulful-looking leading man had a great deal of stage and screen experience in Berlin and Vienna before arriving in Hollywood. It is said that the Czech-born actor learned English in six weeks to prepare for his initial appearance on a London stage, but this tale, one suspects, is almost too good to be true. After appearing on Broadway in *Autumn Crocus* (1932), he journeyed to Hollywood and created a considerable stir by his performance in the romantic comedy *The Pursuit of Happiness* (1934). Thereafter he starred or was featured in a score of films, a few of which were first rate. **Credits include:** *The Gay Deception* (1935), *Confessions of a Nazi Spy* (1939), *The Bridge of San Luis Rey* (1944), *Lisbon* (1956), *Terror Is a Man* (1969).

ANNA LEE (1914–)

Her theatrical career began when she ran away from school in England at the age of 14 to become a bareback rider. After appearing in a number of British and American pictures in subordinate or featured roles, she was starred for the first time in the title role of *My Life With Caroline* (1941). Since then she has added her very considerable talents to more than 20 such films: **Credits:** *King Solomon's Mines* (1937), *How Green Was My Valley* (1941), *The Ghost and Mrs. Muir* (1947), *The Sound of Music* (1965), *In Like Flint* (1967).

BRUCE LEE (1940–1973)

An expert at the ancient Chinese martial art of Kung Fu, Lee literally fought his way to stardom as the hero of a series of action-packed, plot-thin, fight-to-the-finish hit films of the early 70's. Although critics compared them unfavorably to the spaghetti Westerns of an earlier time, these Hong Kong-made, English-dubbed spectacles became some of

Pretty Anna Lee and pretty cockatoo in Bedlam *(1946).*

the most popular and lucrative films of the 70's and spawned a series of spin-offs, including a *Kung Fu* TV series.

Lee was born in San Francisco and grew up in Hong Kong. After studying at the University of Washington he opened Kung Fu academies along the West Coast and trained such actors as Steve McQueen and James Garner. Then, during a visit to Hong Kong, Lee starred in his first Kung Fu picture. That and his subsequent films first found success in Hong Kong, then in Latin America and finally hit the big time in the United States and Europe. In 1973 Lee died in mysterious circumstances. **Films include:** *Fists of Fury* (U.S., 1973), *The Chinese Connection* (U.S., 1973), *Enter the Dragon* (U.S., 1973).

CANADA LEE (1907–1952)

Leonard Canegata was one of the first black actors to lead the fight against Negro stereotypes at a time when Pullman-car conductors were called George and the standard movie script (when blacks were involved) almost inevitably contained lines like "Sho nuf" and "Yassuh!" He had been a jockey, boxer and bandleader without bookings until he joined a theatrical group sponsored by the Depression-born Works Progress Administration. After playing in Orson Welles' stage production of *Hamlet*, Lee made an auspicious film debut in *Lifeboat* (1944).

After just four screen appearances Lee's liberal views resulted in his being blacklisted during the McCarthy-era witchhunts. He died shortly thereafter. **His other films were:** *Body and Soul* (1947), *Lost Boundaries* (1949), *Cry, the Beloved Country* (1952).

CHRISTOPHER LEE (1922–   )

For over two and a half decades this craggy-faced Britisher has been kept busy sending chills up the spines of film and TV audiences alike. He's played most every imaginable demonic figure (notably Dracula) and sinister character (e.g. Fu Manchu) at some point in the course of his more than 100 screen roles and more than 40 TV appearances. Ironically, in Germany, Lee is famous as the hero of a series of Sherlock Holmes

films. **Credits include:** *The Curse of Frankenstein* (1957), *The Horror of Dracula* (1958), *The Face of Fu Manchu* (1965), *The Devil's Bride* (1968), *The Three Musketeers* (1974).

GYPSY ROSE LEE (1914–1970)

Back in the innocent times when a successful striptease routine could be slightly less sexy than a pantyhose commercial in our day, Gypsy was the queen of the burlesque circuit.

Louise Hovick (Gypsy) and her sister, actress June Havoc, began in vaudeville, shepherded by their strong-willed mother, Rose. At 15 she met Tessie the Tassel Twirler in Kansas City and went on to become the best-known stripper of them all. She became Gypsy Rose Lee in the Ziegfeld Follies, but Hollywood was so jittery about public reaction that they cast her with her given name in her first film, *You Can't Have Everything* (1937).

A canny and highly intelligent woman, she wrote books and magazine pieces. *The G-String Murders,* her first mystery story, became a best-seller and was made into a movie, *The Lady of Burlesque* (1943), with Barbara Stanwyck. She technically stopped stripping in the late 30's but made countless farewell appearances thereafter. The Broadway musical *Gypsy* (1959), starring Ethel Merman, was based on her early years. **Films include:** *Ali Baba Goes to Town* (1937), *My Lucky Star* (1938), *Belle of the Yukon* (1945), *Screaming Mimi* (1958), *The Stripper* (1963), *The Trouble With Angels* (1966).

LILA LEE (1905–1973)

The popular screen ingénue and then leading lady of silents began her show-business career at the age of four as "Cuddles" in Gus Edwards' Kiddie Revue, a vaudeville potpourri that was the spawning ground for an astonishing number of later-day screen and stage greats. One of her first screen roles was that of Gloria Swanson's maid in De Mille's *Male and Female* (1919), an adaptation of the popular James M. Barrie comedy *The Admirable Crichton*. Her career flourished through the silent era and into the days of talkies. She made her first talking picture

Ex-strip-queen Gypsy Rose Lee in Belle of the Yukon *(1945).*

Drag in 1929 with Richard Barthelmess and continued to appear on screen until 1936. **Films include:** *Blood and Sand* (1922), *Broken Hearts* (1926), *Honky Tonk* (1929), *The Sacred Flame* (1929), *Woman Hungry* (1931), *False Faces* (1932), *The Ex-Mrs. Bradford* (1936).

ANDREA LEEDS (1914–)

Antoinette Lees' short but highly promising career ended in the early 40's when she retired to devote her attention to her family. She was born in Montana, grew up in Mexico and came to Hollywood to become a screenwriter. Her lovely face led to a screen test and a role in *Come and Get It* (1936). A year later, as the tortured young actress who commits suicide in *Stage Door*, she was cited by many reviewers as the film's outstanding performer. **Other credits:** *The Goldwyn Follies* (1938), *Letter of Introduction* (1938), *Swanee River* (1939), *Earthbound* (1940).

FRITZ LEIBER (1883–1949)

Born in Chicago, Leiber was an outstanding Shakespearean actor as well as a motion picture star. He was a onetime member of the theatrical companies of Sir Philip Ben Greet, Robert Mantell and David Warfield and impresario of his own Shakespearean repertory company. One of the early venturers from stage to films, he made his motion picture debut in 1917 in *Cleopatra*. **Film highlights:** *If I Were King* (1920), *Queen of Sheba* (1921), *A Tale of Two Cities* (1935), *Anthony Adverse* (1936), *The Prince and the Pauper* (1937), *The Hunchback of Notre Dame* (1940), *Humoresque* (1946), *Song of India* (1949).

JANET LEIGH (1927–)

Jeanette Helen Morrison was born in California, entered into the first of four marriages at the age of 15 and played her first leading role in a film (*The Romance of Rosy Ridge*) when she was just 20. She already had a number of featured performances under her belt when she married Tony Curtis in 1951, and when their "idyllic" union was wildly publicized both husband and wife reached a new peak in box-office popularity.

Leigh and Curtis played together in a series of costume dramas, *The Vikings* (1958) being a typical example, but she had nothing to do but look beautiful while he looked as though his Scandinavian regalia was uncomfortable.

It wasn't until she played the terrified victim in *Psycho* (1960) that her ability to act was confirmed, and after her marriage to Curtis ended in 1962 she went on to appear in some good comedies, as well as in superior films like *The Manchurian Candidate* (1962). She was extremely good in a small role, that of Paul Newman's wife, in *Harper* (1966). **Many credits include:** *Little Women* (1949), *Scaramouche* (1952), *My Sister Eileen* (1955), *Touch of Evil* (1958), *Wives and Lovers* (1963), *Bye, Bye, Birdie* (1963), *One Is a Lonely Number* (1972).

VIVIEN LEIGH (1913–1967)

This beautiful British star was born Vivien Mary Hartley in Darjeeling, India, and (according to press releases) was educated in

Janet Leigh and Dick Van Dyke look as though the avian population has already flown the coop in Bye Bye Birdie *(1963).*

Vivien Leigh (left) with Kim Hunter in A Streetcar Named Desire *(1951). Her brilliant portrayal of a faded Southern belle brought Leigh a flurry of fresh awards.*

Two lovers that launched a thousand reruns. Clark Gable as Rhett Butler and Vivien Leigh as Scarlett O'Hara in Gone With the Wind.

An English beauty who is also highly talented and versatile— Margaret Leighton.

England, France and Germany. She reversed the usual actor pattern by appearing in a film, *Things Are Looking Up* (1934), a year before she was first seen by British playgoers in *The Green Sash* in a London suburb. In the West End in 1936 she played opposite Laurence Olivier in the play *Fire Over England*, which brought her overnight fame.

When Olivier heeded the call of Hollywood in 1938, Leigh, who was to become his wife two years later, flew to California to be with him. At the time every newspaper and fan magazine in the United States was full of talk about the most elaborate movie ever to be made, the screen adaptation of Margaret Mitchell's fantastic best-seller *Gone With the Wind*, and speculating on who would play Scarlett O'Hara, the most sought-after screen role in history. Bette Davis wanted the role. So did Katharine Hepburn—desperately. So did scores of other stars and near stars. Leigh got the job, and *Gone With the Wind* (1939)—unlike too many other lush productions that have been wildly ballyhooed before their release only to fall flat on their cinematic faces when they appeared—turned out to be a beauty. Leigh won both the New York Film Critics Award and an Oscar for Best Actress, while Clark Gable's Rhett Butler established him more firmly than ever as a screen immortal. The film itself collected half a dozen other Oscars, and it will probably turn out to be the highest-grossing motion picture ever made.

In 1940 she played opposite Robert Taylor in *Waterloo Bridge*, and the following year she teamed up with Olivier for *That Hamilton Woman*. Illness prevented her from working until she starred in *Anna Karenina* in 1948. She then toured with Olivier and played Blanche Du Bois in the London production of Tennessee Williams' *A Streetcar Named Desire*, also recreating the role in the 1951 screen version with Marlon Brando as Stanley Kowalski. Once again she won the Oscar, the New York Film Critics Award and, this time, the British Film Academy Award as well. She died in 1967 of a recurring illness, tuberculosis. **Other fine Leigh films include:** *Dark Journey* (1937), *Storm in a Teacup* (1938), *Caesar and Cleopatra* (1944), *The Deep Blue Sea* (1955), *The Roman Spring of Mrs. Stone* (1961), *Ship of Fools* (1965).

MARGARET LEIGHTON (1922–)

Despite an auspicious screen debut in the film version of Terence Rattigan's *The Winslow Boy* (1948), this distinguished English stage actress and winner of Broadway's coveted Tony Award for her role in Tennessee Williams' *The Night of the Iguana* (1962) has shied away from film work for most of her acting career.

She made her stage debut in 1938 in the Birmingham Repertory Theatre production of *Laugh With Me*, acted with the Old Vic from 1944 to 1947 and made her Broadway debut with them in 1946. Since then she has appeared in a variety of plays on Broadway, including *Separate Tables* (1956), *Tchin-Tchin* (1962-63) and *The Chinese Prime Minister* (1964).

In her relatively few film appearances she has most often been cast as a rather fragile, elegant and neurotic woman. In recent years she has been seen in character roles, such as the mother in *The Go-Between* (1971) and as Lady Nelson in *The Nelson Affair* (1973). She has also appeared in a number of TV dramas. **Films include:** *Under Capricorn* (1949), *The Holly and the Ivy* (1954), *The Constant Husband* (1955), *The Sound and the Fury* (1958), *The Waltz of the Toreadors* (1961), *Seven Women* (1966).

JACK LEMMON (1925–)

Long thought of as a top comedian, in 1973 Jack Lemmon reminded audiences that he is also a fine dramatic actor with his brilliant, Oscar-winning portrayal of a middle-aged man facing bankruptcy in *Save the Tiger*.

Lemmon's first love was the theatre, and he was trying to establish himself as a dramatic actor on the New York stage when a chance to demonstrate his vast comic talents in a starring role opposite Judy Holliday lured him westward for his film debut in *It Should Happen to You* (1954). The following year, after two musicals, he played Ensign Pulver in *Mister Roberts* (1955), a performance that won him the Academy Award as the year's Best Supporting Actor. Four years later he again earned raves when he costarred with Marilyn Monroe and Tony Curtis in the uproarious *Some Like It Hot* (1959). For that role he was named Best Actor of the Year by the British Film Academy.

After several more comedy hits Lemmon distinguished himself in his "straight" film role as the alcoholic Joe Clay in *Days of Wine and Roses* (1963) with Lee Remick. Despite his fine performance, he was back in comedies for most of the decade. Two of the funniest were with Walter Matthau—*The Fortune Cookie* (1966) and *The Odd Couple* (1968). In 1971 he made his directorial debut with *Kotch,* starring Matthau. Lemmon, a Harvard graduate, is married to actress Felicia Farr. **Films include:** *Phffft* (1954), *My Sister Eileen* (1955), *Operation Mad Ball* (1957), *The Apartment* (1960), *The Notorious Landlady* (1962), *The April Fools* (1969), *The Out-of-Towners* (1970), *Avanti Avanti* (1972).

SHELDON LEONARD (1907–)

For a well brought-up New York boy who graduated from Syracuse University and went to work on Wall Street, Sheldon Bershad was one of the roughest, toughest and most convincing movie gangsters of them all—so good that one sometimes forgot he was equally adept at comedy (particularly gangster comedy) roles.

Leonard first appeared on Broadway in 1930 after the deepening Depression had cost him his Wall Street job and propelled him to the stage. Over the next nine years he was cast in a variety of Broadway roles, most successfully as Pinky in *Having Wonderful Time* (1937), Arthur Kober's very funny play about a summer camp. Leonard's performance was outstanding, and in 1939 he followed the yellow brick road to Hollywood and his first role in *Another Thin Man* (1939). He went on to appear in several dozen movies during the 40's but also turned his attention elsewhere —first to radio (as a script writer and performer) and then, more significantly, to the infant industry of television. Leonard rose rapidly up the TV hierarchy to become one of its leading producer-directors, and after *Pocketful of Miracles* (1961) he gave up acting entirely. His highly successful TV comedy series include: *The Danny Thomas Show, The Andy Griffith Show, Gomer Pyle* and *The Dick Van Dyke Show*. **Film credits include:**

Tortilla Flat (1942), *Lucky Jordan* (1943), *To Have and Have Not* (1944), *The Gangster* (1947), *Stop, You're Killing Me* (1952), *Guys and Dolls* (1955).

BABY LE ROY (1932–)

After a three-year career as Hollywood's favorite toddler, Le Roy Winnebrenner retired from films at the age of four, which must be some sort of record. He was the infant whose winning smile entranced Maurice Chevalier in *A Bedtime Story* (1933), and was the object of W. C. Fields' unconcealed hatred in two films, *Tillie and Gus* (1933) and *The Old-Fashioned Way* (1934). **Films include:** *Torch Singer* (1933), *The Lemon Drop Kid* (1934), *It's a Gift* (1935).

JOAN LESLIE (1925–)

Under her given name of Joan Agnes Theresa Sadie Brodel, she made a debut of sorts in 1927 by walking across a Detroit stage. Some years later she toured the country in dance concerts with her older sisters before Hollywood spotted her and cast her in a small role in George Cukor's *Camille* (1936). Thereafter she played in dozens of films, many of them good ones. Her best roles were in the early 40's, and she was especially good as Velma in *High Sierra* (1941) with Humphrey Bogart. Since her marriage to William Caldwell in 1950 her screen appearances have been few and far between. **Film highlights:** *Sergeant York* (1941), *Yankee Doodle Dandy* (1942), *Rhapsody in Blue* (1945), *Cinderella Jones* (1946), *Born to Be Bad* (1950), *Jubilee Trail* (1954), *The Revolt of Mamie Stover* (1956).

OSCAR LEVANT (1906–1972)

A brilliant pianist, a savage wit and a star of radio's enormously popular quiz show *Information Please*, he also made occasional appearances in films. The swarthy-visaged Levant was a high-octane eccentric who made numerous enemies and gathered a smaller band of devoted admirers during the course of his performing career. He was a close and admiring friend of George Gershwin's and concentrated almost exclusively on Gershwin music. In 1945 Levant played his neurotic, brilliant self in the Gershwin film biography

Having long since proved himself a master of comedy, Jack Lemmon gave a sensitive and perceptive portrayal of an alcoholic in Days of Wine and Roses.

Skipper W. C. Fields about to throw Baby Le Roy overboard in Tillie and Gus *(1933). They were natural enemies.*

Jerry Lewis, with a Bugs Bunnyish look, in one of his own productions, The Nutty Professor *(1961).*

Bea Lillie, the toast of several continents, before she became Lady Peel.

Rhapsody in Blue. **Other credits:** *Kiss the Boys Goodbye* (1941), *Humoresque* (1946), *An American in Paris* (1951), *The Band Wagon* (1953), *The Cobweb* (1955).

SAM LEVENE (1905–)

Since his Broadway debut in *Wall Street* (1927) this Russian-born New Yorker has retained his place as one of Broadway's favorite leading actors. His stage successes span three and a half decades and include *Room Service* (1937), *Guys and Dolls* (1940), *Light Up the Sky* (1948) and, more recently, *Don't Drink the Water* (1968) and *The Sunshine Boys* (1973). He made the first of his screen appearances in 1936, when he repeated his hugely funny stage performance in *Three Men on a Horse*. Levene subsequently recreated his part on both radio and television. Since then he has taken occasional breaks from his work in the legitimate theatre to appear in films and on television. **Credits include:** *After the Thin Man* (1936), *Golden Boy* (1939), *Crossfire* (1947), *The Babe Ruth Story* (1948), *Sweet Smell of Success* (1957), *Slaughter on Tenth Avenue* (1957), *Act One* (1963).

JERRY LEWIS (1926–)

This squeaky-voiced screwball comedian has, on many occasions, proved to be a very funny man indeed. Joseph Levitch first won attention in the 40's when he teamed up with Dean Martin for work in nightclubs and on radio. Their success led to a 1948 appearance on Ed Sullivan's first *Toast of the Town* TV show. The new comedy sensations launched their film career the following year in *My Friend Irma*. Over the next seven years they made a string of box-office hits in which Martin invariably sang and was pretty much a straight man, while Lewis clowned his way through 98 percent of the zaniness. They also spent six of those years as regular featured players on TV's *Colgate Comedy Hour*.

After the team broke up in 1957, Lewis went on to write, direct and star in a dozen films of his own. Although these were all money-makers, many suffered from weak direction and scripts that produced an oversupply of frantic action and plain old mugging.

Lewis also guested on numerous TV shows and became the regular host of the annual TV Muscular Dystrophy telethon. **Films include:** *Scared Stiff* (1953), *Hollywood or Bust* (1956), *The Sad Sack* (1957), *The Bell Boy* (1959), *The Nutty Professor* (1963), *Boeing Boeing* (1965), *Hook, Line and Sinker* (1969).

BEATRICE LILLIE (1898–)

Anyone old enough to remember Beatrice Lillie, Gertrude Lawrence and Jack Buchanan in a stage production called *Charlot's Revue* (1924) is a lucky senior citizen indeed. While all three stars were wonderful, it was Lillie who had audiences rolling (literally) in the aisles when she made her American debut in the show.

This fey and hugely funny lady from Toronto first broke up London audiences in *Not Likely* (1915). Since then the "Queen Bea" has appeared in many shows in New York and London. Among her plays were *At Home Abroad*, *Inside U.S.A.* and *High Spirits*. The stage appearance for which she may best be remembered was *An Evening With Beatrice Lillie* (1952–53), with Reginald Gardiner, which she took on tour in the United States after its New York run.

Her film debut was in *Exit Smiling* (1927). Unfortunately, in subsequent pictures she was never given a chance to display to good effect her clipped and explosively witty monologues. Lady Peel (she was married years ago to Sir Robert) has also made appearances on TV talk shows. **Credits include:** *Show of Shows* (1929), *Are You There?* (1931), *Doctor Rhythm* (1938), *On Approval* (1945), *Around the World in 80 Days* (1956), *Thoroughly Modern Millie* (1967).

ELMO LINCOLN (1889–1952)

It was Otto Elmo Linkenhelter's large chest, rather than his acting ability, that got him his break in Hollywood. When D. W. Griffith learned that the then first-aid man could expand his chest a full six inches the director hired him on the spot. Lincoln made his debut in *Battle of Elder Bush Gulch* (1913) and later played a small role in *Intolerance* (1916). He scored his first big success beating on his magnificent chest in *Tarzan of the Apes* (1918). Lincoln played other Tarzan and he-man roles in the silents, but with the coming of talkies his career declined and he could land only bit parts—often appearing in Gene Autry Westerns. **Films include:** *Birth of a Nation* (1914), *Elmo the Mighty* (1919), *Quincy Adams Sawyer* (1922), *Fashion Row* (1924).

VIVECA LINDFORS (1920–   )

Elsa Viveca Torstens-Dotter Lindfors was born in Uppsala, Sweden, and made her stage debut in Stockholm in a school production of *Ann-Sofi Hedvig* (1937). After several years in Swedish repertory theatre and motion pictures, the actress made her American screen debut in *Night Unto Night* (1947). In 1951 she was honored by the Berlin Film Festival for her screen role in *Four in a Jeep*. Since then she has combined her screen career with work on the stage, most notably in numerous productions of Ibsen and Strindberg plays. In 1974 she appeared in a one-woman off-Broadway show *I Am a Woman*. Lindfors is married to playwright George Tabori. **English-language film highlights:** *No Sad Songs for Me* (1950), *Dark City* (1950), *I Accuse* (1958), *No Exit* (1962), *Coming Apart* (1969), *The Way We Were* (1973).

MARGARET LINDSAY (1910–   )

Deciding that British actresses got the best breaks in Hollywood, Iowa-born Margaret Kies betook herself to England to study. Her natural gift for mimicry served her well, and in short order she had mastered the speech patterns and mannerisms of an upper-class Englishwoman. After a few bit parts she landed a key role in Noel Coward's *Cavalcade* (1933), which 20th Century–Fox was casting exclusively with British performers.

A veteran of scores of films, she often played sympathetic "other women," vaguely mysterious females and, on occasion, comedy. She was also seen in many of the Ellery Queen mystery films. **Credits include:** *Dangerous* (1935), *Jezebel* (1938), *The Spoilers* (1942), *Scarlet Street* (1946), *B.F.'s Daughter* (1948), *Please Don't Eat the Daisies* (1960).

VIRNA LISI (1937–   )

The first view most Americans had of Virna Lisi was an intriguing one when she burst bikini-clad from a cake onto the American screen and into Jack Lemmon's life in *How to Murder Your Wife* (1965). Lisi had appeared in more than two dozen European films before being signed to play the willing wife to Lemmon's unwilling husband in the Hollywood comedy. Though her role was almost purely decorative (she spoke no English in the film), her American debut boosted her stock in Europe, and she returned to Italy to star in *Casanova 70* (1965) with Marcello Mastroianni. Lisi continues to appear in both American and Italian productions. **Credits:** *The Black Tulip* (1963), *Eva* (1965), *Not With My Wife, You Don't!* (1966), *Arabella* (1969), *The Secret of Santa Vittoria* (1969).

JOHN LITEL (1892–1964)

Like so many other actors with stage experience, he slid easily into the Hollywood scene when studios began making talking pictures back in 1929. For more than 30 years thereafter he was featured or played supporting parts in close on to 100 films that covered the widest imaginable range, from *Sister Kenny* (1946) to *Sitting Bull* (1954). A solid performer, Litel appeared as bankers, judges, fathers, Western badmen, plus dozens of other vocations or avocations. **Credits include:** *On the Border* (1930), *The Life of Emile Zola* (1937), *Jezebel* (1938), *Salome, Where She Danced* (1945), *The Sundowners* (1950), *Pocketful of Miracles* (1961).

CLEAVON LITTLE (1939–   )

One of the most talented of today's crop of young actors, Cleavon Little played the black sheriff in *Blazing Saddles* (1974), Mel Brooks' riotous spoof of Western movies and white-man hangups.

Little was born in cowboy country, Chickasha, Oklahoma, but grew up in San Diego, where he attended San Diego State College. After training for the stage in New York, he made his first footlight appearance in a West Coast production of *The Skin of Our Teeth*. He appeared on Broadway with Dustin Hoffman in *Jimmy Shine* (1968) and snagged a

Another Swedish beauty who could act—Viveca Lindfors, here in an early studio publicity photograph.

Margaret Lindsay with (you'll never guess) Vincent Price in The House of the Seven Gables *(1940).*

Harold Lloyd, whose escapes from improbable situations made Houdini look like an amateur.

Tony Award on Broadway for his performance in the musical *Purlie* (1970). **Film credits include:** *What's So Bad About Feeling Good?* (1968), *John and Mary* (1969), *Cotton Comes to Harlem* (1970), *Vanishing Point* (1971).

LUCIEN LITTLEFIELD (1895–1959)

This gifted character actor, noted for his brilliant use of make-up, began his more than 40-year screen career back in 1913. In the 20's he appeared in a number of William S. Hart and Tom Mix Westerns, and in 1926 he played a barber in *The Torrent*, in which Greta Garbo made her American film debut. Surviving the transition from silents to talkies, Littlefield was seen in the first film version of the musical comedy *No, No, Nanette* (1930) and went on to play supporting roles in scores of films. **Film highlights:** *Rose on the Range* (1913), *Babbitt* (1924), *Taxi, Taxi* (1927), *The Cat and the Canary* (1927), *Tom Sawyer* (1930), *Wells Fargo* (1937), *The Little Foxes* (1941), *That Brennan Girl* (1946), *Susanna Pass* (1951), *Pop Girl* (1956).

ROGER LIVESEY (1906–   )

A native of South Wales, Livesey made his first stage appearance at the age of 11 in *Loyalty* at London's St. James Theatre and his screen debut at the age of 14 in *The Old Curiosity Shop*. After several years in repertory touring Newfoundland, the West Indies and South Africa he made his New York stage debut in *The Country Wife* (1936). Livesey played his first adult role in *Lorna Doone* (1935) and went on to combine work as a leading man in films with successful careers on stage and, more recently, in TV dramas. Probably his best screen role was as Wendy Hiller's true love in *I Know Where I'm Going* (1947). **Film highlights:** *Rembrandt* (1936), *49th Parallel* (1941), *The Life and Death of Colonel Blimp* (1945), *Stairway to Heaven* (1946), *The Entertainer* (1958), *Of Human Bondage* (1964), *Oedipus the King* (1968).

MARGARET LIVINGSTON (1902–   )

During her career as a film siren of the 20's, Livingston played home wreckers, conniving women and a whole series of nasty ladies in dozens of films. In one year alone she was murdered on screen 13 times. After her marriage to bandleader Paul Whiteman in 1931 she made one more film, *Call Her Savage* (1937) with Clara Bow, and then retired from the screen. **Films include:** *Divorce* (1923), *Best People* (1925), *American Beauty* (1927), *Bellamy Trial* (1929), *Seven Keys to Baldpate* (1929), *Big Money* (1930), *Smart Money* (1931).

DORIS LLOYD (1899–1968)

Doris Lloyd began her show-business career as a child star on the English stage. She entered films in ingénue roles in the silents and gracefully made the transition to adult roles in the talkies. She was one of the first leading ladies of the *Tarzan* series of the 30's and continued acting, in character roles, until the year before her death. **Films include:** *Charley's Aunt* (1930), *Tarzan, the Ape Man* (1932), *Oliver Twist* (1933), *Clive of India* (1935), *Vigil in the Night* (1940), *Phantom Lady* (1944), *The Time Machine* (1960), *The Notorious Landlady* (1962), *Rosie* (1967).

HAROLD LLOYD (1893–1971)

Back in the silent era this master of visual gags and improbable antics vied with Chaplin and Keaton for the rank of king of the age of comedy.

A native Nebraskan, Lloyd broke into pictures as an extra but soon became Lonesome Luke, the comic hero of more than 100 Hal Roach one- and two-reelers from 1916–17. (Bebe Daniels played his leading lady in the early ones and was replaced by Lloyd's future wife, Mildred Davis.) Luke's screen adventures usually ended with his being pursued by all manner of creatures and things. After Luke, Lloyd created the role of a bespectacled college boy whom he called his Glass character. *In High and Dizzy* (1922) he scaled his first skyscraper, and the perilous adventure was such an audience favorite that Lloyd worked similar stunts into later pictures. One of the most famous was in *Safety Last* (1923).

Lloyd's films generally did better at the box office than those of his rivals Chaplin and Keaton during the 20's, and *The Freshman* (1925) was one of the highest-grossing films of the silent era. After the coming of sound Lloyd appeared in several pictures of the 30's, but only rarely after that. In the 60's he produced two film anthologies of his early work—*Harold Lloyd's World of Comedy* (1961) and *Harold Lloyd's Funny Side of Life* (1966). **Credits include:** *Grandma's Boy* (1922), *Dr. Jack* (1922), *Why Worry?* (1923), *Girl Shy* (1924), *Speedy* (1928), *Feet First* (1930), *Movie Crazy* (1932), *The Cat's Paw* (1934), *The Milky Way* (1936), *Professor Beware* (1938), *Mad Wednesday* (1947).

GENE LOCKHART (1891–1957)

During the course of his 60 years in show business, Lockhart demonstrated his versatility in hundreds of films, TV dramas, plays and in dramatic readings on the college lecture circuit. He had also worked as a singer, a newspaper columnist and a composer ("The World Is Waiting for the Sunrise," with Deems Taylor).

Canadian-born Lockhart made his Broadway debut in 1916 in *Riviera Girl* and later starred in such plays as *Ah! Wilderness* and *Death of a Salesman* (1949). He appeared in films from the mid-30's and was nominated for an Academy Award for his performance in *Algiers* (1938). He frequently played opposite his wife, actress Kathleen (Arthur) Lockhart. The couple's daughter is motion picture and TV actress June Lockhart. **Films include:** *Star of Midnight* (1935), *Something to Sing About* (1937), *Blackmail* (1939), *All That Money Can Buy* (1941), *Going My Way* (1944), *Miracle on 34th Street* (1947), *The Inspector General* (1949), *Rhubarb* (1951), *Androcles and the Lion* (1953), *Carousel* (1956).

JUNE LOCKHART (1925–)

Born into the third generation of a theatrical family, Lockhart made her stage debut at the age of eight in *Peter Ibbetsen* at New York's Metropolitan Opera House, where she was studying ballet. Five years later she appeared with her parents (Gene and Kathleen Lockhart) as one of the Cratchit children in the 1938 MGM film version of Dickens' *A Christmas Carol*.

Lockhart's first major success was on Broadway in 1947 when she starred in *For Love or Money* with John Loder. The hit show made a name for her, and she returned to Hollywood to play a variety of supporting roles. Besides her film and stage work, Lockhart has also appeared frequently on television since the early 50's. She was one of the mothers in the long-running *Lassie* series and appeared from 1965 as Mrs. Robinson in *Lost in Space*. **Films include:** *All This and Heaven, Too* (1940), *Meet Me in St. Louis* (1944), *Keep Your Powder Dry* (1945), *Time Limit* (1957).

MARGARET LOCKWOOD (1916–)

She was the heroine and train companion of the disappearing Miss Froy in one of the best comedy-spy thrillers ever—Hitchcock's *The Lady Vanishes* (1938). Two years later train travel again involved her with spies and suspense when she played a scientist's daughter who keeps an important formula from falling into Nazi hands in *Night Train*.

Born in Karachi, India, Margaret Day received her early education in England and first appeared on stage at the age of 12. She made her film debut in *Lorna Doone* (1935) and within a few years became widely popular as the heroine of escapist films. She has since continued to perform on screen and stage both in England and the United States. **Other films include:** *Dr. Syn* (1937), *The Stars Look Down* (1941), *The Wicked Lady* (1946), *Jassy* (1948), *Cast a Dark Shadow* (1957).

JOHN LODER (1898–)

The son of a British general, Loder (John Lowe) served in the diplomatic corps, failed in business and was down to his last set of tails when he met Alexander Korda and landed a job as a film extra. That chance encounter in 1927 marked the beginning of a long career playing elegant Britishers in both English and American films.

Although Loder's Hollywood films date from *The Doctor's Secret* (1929), the bulk of his U.S. work came in the decade following his move to Hollywood in the late 30's. In 1941 he played Ianto in John Ford's film of *How Green Was My Valley*, and the following year he appeared as Elliott Livingston in

Gene Lockhart, looking dapper and sly, in Hangmen Also Die *(1943).*

Margaret Lockwood and the vanishing Miss Froy (Dame May Whitty) in The Lady Vanishes.

Beautiful Lollobrigida never failed to enhance the films she appeared in—this one Come September.

The untimely death of talented Carole Lombard was a great loss to motion pictures.

the memorable tear-jerker *Now, Voyager*. After these successes, Loder appeared in a variety of films of the mid and late 40's as "the other man," or the sinister but suave menace. By the 50's, Loder's heyday was over. He made fewer and fewer films, and in the early 60's he retired to Argentina. **Films include:** *Her Private Affair* (1930), *Dr. Syn* (1937), *The Hairy Ape* (1944), *Dishonored Lady* (1947), *Gideon of Scotland Yard* (1959).

JACQUELINE LOGAN (c. 1903–   )

A leading lady of silents, this smoky-eyed Texas beauty made her way to Hollywood via the Ziegfeld Follies chorus. During the 20's she starred in more than 40 movies, most memorably perhaps as Mary Magdalene in De Mille's *King of Kings* (1927). After the advent of sound, she made appearances in a few talkies and then went to London to work as a scenario writer and director. When her film *Strictly Business* (1931) proved a hit, she returned to Hollywood for an unsuccessful try at finding similar work there. After that she made a few appearances on Broadway (e.g., *Two Strange Women*), married in 1934 and retired. **Films include:** *The Fighting Lover* (1921), *Burning Sands* (1922), *Salomy Jane* (1923), *If Marriage Fails* (1925), *The Cop* (1928), *The Middle Watch* (1930).

GINA LOLLOBRIGIDA (1928–   )

From the time of her screen debut in 1946, Gina Lollobrigida's well-endowed figure brought her an increasing amount of attention and better screen parts, and before long she was a leading lady of Italian motion pictures. In 1954 her name became a household word throughout Europe and America with the release of *Bread, Love and Dreams*, in which she played a local beauty who creates problems for village police chief Vittorio De Sica. Her first American film, *Beat the Devil*, appeared the same year. After that she continued to make most of her films in Italy, where she remained a big box-office draw, but did accept some American offers. She starred with Frank Sinatra in *Never So Few* (1960) and with Rock Hudson in *Come September* (1961) and *Strange Bedfellows* (1965). **Films include:** *Elisir d'Amore* (1946), *Fanfan La Tulipe* (1951), *A Tale of*

Five Women (1953), *Trapeze* (1956), *Solomon and Sheba* (1959), *Woman of Straw* (1964), *Buono Sera, Mrs. Campbell* (1969), *King, Queen, Knave* (1972).

HERBERT LOM (1917–   )

This versatile Czech actor (Herbert Charles Angelo Kuchacevich ze Schluderpacheru) has proven himself equally adept at playing appealing and nasty characters in both English- and German-language films. He was the title character in the 1962 remake of *The Phantom of the Opera*, played Napoleon at least twice, in *The Young Mr. Pitt* (1943) and *War and Peace* (1956), and was the twitching Chief Inspector Dreyfus in Peter Sellers' *A Shot in the Dark* (1964). **Films include:** *The Seventh Veil* (1945), *The Lady Killers* (1956), *Chase a Crooked Shadow* (1958), *The Big Fisherman* (1959), *Third Man on the Mountain* (1959), *Gambit* (1966), *Villa Rides* (1968).

CAROLE LOMBARD (1908–1942)

Fondly remembered as one of filmdom's most deft comediennes, she met her death in an airplane crash while returning to Hollywood from a war-bond rally in Indianapolis. Just 34 at the time, she was at the peak of a brilliant career.

Jane Alice Peters was 13 when she was cast as Monte Blue's daughter in *A Perfect Crime* (1921). An automobile accident put her out of action for a time, but when she recovered, a series of two-reelers for Mack Sennett sharpened her aptitude for comedy. Her first big part came in 1930 when she appeared with Charles "Buddy" Rogers in the Paramount talkie *Safety in Numbers*. Four years later she starred with John Barrymore in the hugely funny Hecht-MacArthur opus *Twentieth Century* (1934), and the studios realized she had a lot more going for her than long beautiful legs and blond good looks. After *Love Before Breakfast* and *My Man Godfrey* (both 1936) she reached the top of the ladder, and in 1937 she was listed as Hollywood's highest-paid actress.

Most Lombard addicts (and there are still throngs of them around) feel that her finest performances were as the girl who feared she was doomed in *Nothing Sacred* (1937) and opposite Robert Montgomery in *Mr. and*

Mrs. Smith (1941). In 1939, several years after her unsuccessful marriage to William Powell, Lombard married Clark Gable. **Other films include:** *The Arizona Kid* (1930), *No One Man* (1932), *Bolero* (1934), *Swing High, Swing Low* (1937), *Fools for Scandal* (1938), *To Be or Not to Be* (1942).

JULIE LONDON (1926–   )

Nightclub singer London has appeared occasionally in leading roles in motion pictures, but despite her beauty and singing talent, her film career never fully matured. **Films include:** *The Red House* (1947), *The Fat Man* (1951), *The Great Man* (1956), *Saddle the Wind* (1958), *Man of the West* (1958), *The Third Voice* (1960), *The George Raft Story* (1962).

RICHARD LONG (1927–   )

Best known for his work on such TV series as *77 Sunset Strip, Bourbon Street Beat* and *The Big Valley,* Long has also appeared in motion pictures since the mid-40's. **Film highlights:** *Tomorrow Is Forever* (1946), *The Egg and I* (1947), *Criss Cross* (1949), *All I Desire* (1953), *Saskatchewan* (1954), *Follow the Boys* (1963), *Make Like a Thief* (1967).

RICHARD LOO (1903–   )

Born in Hawaii of Chinese parents and educated at the University of California, Loo is a highly polished performer who has been seen in nearly 300 movies during a screen career that has spanned 43 years.

After working for an import-export firm, he went on stage for the first time with a road company of *Hit the Deck* back in 1927. He returned to the business world for a while but began knocking on studio doors when the Hollywood branch of his company closed its doors during the Depression. A few small parts led to his first real break, the juvenile lead in *The Bitter Tea of General Yen* (1933). During the years of World War II Loo played innumerable sinister Japanese officers and was outstanding in films like *The Purple Heart* (1944) and *God Is My Co-Pilot* (1945). Later came pictures like *Soldier of Fortune* (1955), with Clark Gable and Susan Hayward, in which he played a good guy.

Loo remains as busy as ever. In 1974 he

was slated for a new James Bond film and recently had a lot of fun making one of the episodes for the *Kung Fu* TV series. **Other films include:** *Dirigible* (1931), *Love Is a Many-Splendored Thing* (1955), *The Quiet American* (1958), *The Sand Pebbles* (1966).

JACK LORD (1930–   )

Lord is widely known as a successful TV actor and the star of such series as *Stoney Burke* and *Hawaii Five-O*. He is far less well known for his other numerous accomplishments—as an artist whose works claim a place in New York's Metropolitan Museum and London's British Museum, as the creator of several TV series, as a screenplay writer and as an author.

Lord began his performing career in the early 50's in films like *Cry Murder* (1951) and *The Court Martial of Billy Mitchell* (1955). He also appeared a number of times on Broadway, winning the 1959 *Theatre World* award for his performance in *Traveling Lady*. **Film credits include:** *God's Little Acre* (1958), *Man of the West* (1958), *Doctor No* (1963), *The Name of the Game Is Kill* (1968).

MARJORIE LORD (1921–   )

After a series of leading roles in minor films of the 40's and early 50's, Lord scored her biggest success in the late 50's as Danny Thomas' wife in the popular TV series *The Danny Thomas Show*. She first began making movies after her appearance in the Broadway hit *Stage Door* (1936). **Films include:** *Forty Naughty Girls* (1937), *Johnny Came Lately* (1943), *New Orleans* (1947), *Riding High* (1950), *Port of Hell* (1954), *Boy, Did I Get a Wrong Number!* (1966).

SOPHIA LOREN (1934–   )

At the age of 14 Sophia Villani Scicoloni won a beauty contest in Naples, and so her ambitious mother took her to Rome to seek work in the movies. Mother and daughter both found jobs as extras, and Sophia managed to be seen in a few brief roles. Her break came when she met producer Carlo Ponti, who gave her a small part in *Anna* (1950). He then changed her name to Loren, became her mentor and, in 1957, her husband.

Under Ponti's guidance she won more im-

Richard Loo's was perhaps the best-known Oriental face in the movies during the 40's. He alternated between both good- and bad-guy roles.

Sophia Loren and anonymous dove in The Fall of the Roman Empire *(1964).*

His tousled hairdo made Peter Lorre particularly venomous in The Maltese Falcon *(1941). From left to right the others are, of course, Humphrey Bogart as Sam Spade, Mary Astor and Sidney Greenstreet, who is fondling the falcon affectionately.*

portant roles and in 1956 replaced Gina Lollobrigida for the last film in the "Bread and Love" series. By then she had gained international recognition, and offers from Hollywood started to roll in. Her first American movie was *Boy on a Dolphin* (1957) with Alan Ladd. Later that year she went to Hollywood to make a number of films, including *Houseboat* (1958) with Cary Grant.

Back in Italy, she played a more serious role—that of a widow with a teenage daughter in wartime Italy—in *Two Women* (1961), directed by Vittorio De Sica and co-starring Jean-Paul Belmondo. Her performance won her an Academy Award for Best Actress, as well as the Best Actress awards from the Cannes Film Festival and the New York Film Critics. Her Oscar was the first ever to be presented to a performer in a foreign-language film.

Loren's films have since been less impressive, but the Italian beauty continues to hold the admiration of her fans. **Films include:** *Aida* (1954), *Attila Flagello di Dio* (1958), *Desire Under the Elms* (1958), *The Millionairess* (1961), *El Cid* (1961), *Boccaccio '70* (1962), *Yesterday, Today and Tomorrow* (1964), *Judith* (1966), *Man of La Mancha* (1972).

PETER LORRE (1904–1964)

At the very beginning of his long screen career Hungarian Laszlo Löwenstein gave one of his most memorable performances as the psychopathic child-killer in Fritz Lang's *M* (1931; U.S., 1933). His success in the film launched him on a stage and screen career in Berlin that lasted until Hitler's rise to power. At that point he fled first to Austria and then to England, where he played the hired killer in Hitchcock's *The Man Who Knew Too Much* (1935). The next stop was Hollywood, where he made his American screen debut in *Mad Love* (1935).

Lorre soon became one of filmdom's favorite villains. Unlike other heavies, he was a little man, but his shifty-eyed, understated acting style and his striking vocal delivery—a whiny whisper with a querulous Middle European accent—more than made up for his size. He was consistently good—and outstanding in films like *The Maltese Falcon* (1941) and *Casablanca* (1942). Occasionally he was on the right side of the law, notably as the irrepressible Japanese detective in close to a dozen *Mr. Moto* films made between 1937 and 1939.

The quality of Lorre's pictures declined from the late 40's. Although he made *Beat the Devil* (1954) with Humphrey Bogart and Robert Morley, most of his roles in the 50's were small—e.g., the Japanese steward in *Around the World in 80 Days* (1956) and the temperamental movie director in *The Buster Keaton Story* (1957). **Films include:** *Crime and Punishment* (1935), *Secret Agent* (1936), *Think Fast, Mr. Moto* (1937), *The Face Behind the Mask* (1941), *Passage to Marseille* (1944), *The Beast With Five Fingers* (1946), *Rope of Sand* (1949), *The Sad Sack* (1957), *The Raven* (1963).

JOAN LORRING (1926–   )

Born Magdalen Ellis, of English-Russian parentage, Lorring came to the United States from England in 1939. She began her performing career as a radio actress and went on to appear in 40's films, usually as bratty or difficult teenagers. Her portrayal of the nasty Cockney girl in *The Corn Is Green* (1945) is typical of her roles of this period. Tired of being typecast and matured beyond adolescent roles, Lorring returned to radio, studied acting and began appearing on Broadway in such hits as *Come Back, Little Sheba* (1950), for which she won a Donaldson Award. In recent years she has appeared in many TV dramas. **Some of her films include:** *The Bridge of San Luis Rey* (1944), *The Verdict* (1946), *Good Sam* (1948), *Stranger on the Prowl* (1953).

ANITA LOUISE (1915–1970)

Fragile-looking, blond Louise Fremault was a child actress in 20's silents and played lead and supporting roles for nearly two decades after the advent of sound. She had a distinct preference for costume drama and made effective appearances in such dress-up dramas as *Madame Du Barry* (1934), *Anthony Adverse* (1936) and *Marie Antoinette* (1938). Her well-publicized ethereal quality served her in good stead when she played Titania in the 1935 production of *A Midsummer Night's Dream* (a film that featured James Cagney as Bottom). She appeared on a number of TV shows since the 50's, including the series *My Friend Flicka* (1956). For 20 years she was married to Buddy Adler, one of filmdom's ruling production giants. **More than 65 films include:** *What a Man* (1930), *Mississippi* (1931), *The Story of Louis Pasteur* (1936), *Tovarich* (1937), *Casanova Brown* (1944), *The Bandit of Sherwood Forest* (1946).

BESSIE LOVE (1898–   )

After Pickford and the Gish sisters the diminutive Love (Juanita Horton) was probably the most popular star in the years immediately before and after World War I. Like the others she was big-eyed, sweet-faced, demure—and an excellent performer. One of the early high points in her career was in Griffith's stupendous production *Intolerance* (1916).

In 1929 she left sweet roles behind her to become the Charlestoning jazz baby in one of the first (and best) of the early talking-singing musicals, *Broadway Melody*. After roles in a number of other films, she left Hollywood in the mid-30's to live in England and worked in films and theatre. In later years she added her distinctive presence to small parts in a variety

of motion pictures. A good example is her role as the waspish telephone operator in *Sunday, Bloody Sunday* (1971). **Credits include:** *The Village Blacksmith* (1922), *The Lost World* (1925), *Lovely Mary* (1926), *Good News* (1930), *Morals for Women* (1931), *Journey Together* (1946), *Touch and Go* (1956), *Isadora* (1968).

MONTAGU LOVE (1877–1943)

Love's long and successful acting career began strictly by chance when the young London newspaper illustrator paid a visit to a theatrical agent and accepted an unanticipated offer to tour the provinces in a part in *The Lion and the Mouse*. His screen debut also came about by coincidence. Love, visiting New York, went to view a friend's screen test and was offered a job in silent films. He starred with Alice Brady in *Bought and Paid For* (1916), a popular tear-jerker, and continued to play leading roles in silents, often as a would-be seducer. With the coming of sound, Love abandoned motion pictures for a while to appear on Broadway. Later, however, he returned to the screen to play scores of character parts. **More than 100 films include:** *The Gilded Cage* (1919), *Son of the Sheik* (1926), *Don Juan* (1926), *Clive of India* (1935), *The Prince and the Pauper* (1937), *The Prisoner of Zenda* (1937), *Tovarich* (1937), *Gunga Din* (1939), *Tennessee Johnson* (1943).

FRANK LOVEJOY (1914–1962)

When the stock market crashed in 1929, Lovejoy was out of his job as a Wall Street runner (messenger), so he turned to acting. He found his first success on radio and played in more than 4,000 dramatic broadcasts, including *Gangbusters*, *Philo Vance* and *Mr. District Attorney*. He also appeared on Broadway, making his debut in Elmer Rice's *Judgment Day* (1934). Active in films from the late 40's, he frequently played military officers or policemen. Lovejoy was a tough noncom in *Breakthrough* (1950), an iron-jawed colonel in the Korean war picture *Retreat, Hell!* (1952) and an Air Force general in *Strategic Air Command* (1955).

He was highly praised when he returned to Broadway in 1960 to play the unscrupulous

Stunning Anita Louise is stunningly gowned as she plays the luckless Queen in Marie Antoinette *(1938).*

Peering through the fringe of beard and hat is seasoned veteran Montagu Love as he appeared in The Prince and the Pauper *(1937).*

Robert Lowery (left) and sidekick Edward Brophy look equally apprehensive in this scene from a forgotten 30's melodrama.

candidate Joe Cantwell in Gore Vidal's *The Best Man*. On television he starred in *Meet McGraw*. **Films include:** *Home of the Brave* (1949), *House of Wax* (1953), *The Crooked Web* (1955), *Three Brave Men* (1957).

EDMUND LOWE (1892–1971)

This veteran of more than 100 films was first acclaimed for his performance as the outspoken Sergeant Quirt in the silent-screen classic *What Price Glory?* (1926), the film version of the Laurence Stallings–Maxwell Anderson play about trench warfare in World War I.

Lowe appeared in stock-company productions and on Broadway before making his 1919 debut in films. Although he frequently portrayed tough guys on screen, Lowe was also adept at playing the drawing-room Romeo, as he did in *Dinner at Eight* (1933). He appeared on Broadway from time to time during his long film career and was featured in the TV series *Front Page Detective*. **Films include:** *The Silent Command* (1923), *Publicity Madness* (1927), *Dressed to Kill* (1928), *Transatlantic* (1931), *Dillinger* (1945), *The Wings of Eagles* (1957), *Heller in Pink Tights* (1960).

ROBERT LOWERY (1916–1971)

Robert Lowery Hanke began his career as a singer and then turned to acting in little-theatre groups before making his film debut in the late 30's. He appeared in many pictures through the 40's, usually in featured roles. He did, however, play some leads, mainly because of his resemblance to Clark Gable. When Gable went into the service during World War II, Lowery was drafted for films like *Who Is Hope Schuyler?* (1942) and *The North Star* (1943). **Films include:** *Submarine Patrol* (1938), *Young Mr. Lincoln* (1939), *The Dalton Gang* (1949), *The Rise and Fall of Legs Diamond* (1960), *Johnny Reno* (1966).

MYRNA LOY (1905–   )

Few Hollywood stars have gone through as many image changes as Myrna Loy. When she started out in silent films she was typed as a vamp or an Oriental meany. In her early sound pictures she was often a spoiled daughter or a homicidal maniac. In the late 30's the success of the *Thin Man* detective series established her in sophisticated comedy roles, and still later she became the perfect wife and mother as a result of films like *Cheaper by the Dozen* (1950).

Loy's first roles were bit parts in silent films, and she made more than 60 motion pictures before achieving star status. The picture that did it was *Manhattan Melodrama* (1934) with Clark Gable. It became a headline-maker when gangster John Dillinger was shot and killed after leaving the theatre in which he had viewed it. It was a good year for Loy, though. She was teamed for the first time with William Powell in *The Thin Man* (1934)—even though MGM was dubious about allowing them to do comedy and gave a go-ahead to the picture only on condition that it be completed in three weeks. It was, and the rest is history. The film was a huge popular success, and Loy and Powell, who loved working together, went on to co-star in five more *Thin Man* films of the 30's and 40's.

Myrna Loy with Frank Morgan in When Ladies Meet *(1933), a film made during the years when she was making the transition from an evil Oriental to a charming comedienne.*

During World War II Loy bowed out of films to work full time for the Red Cross —although she did make one film, *The Thin Man Goes Home* (1945). After the war she was back on the screen as "perfect mother" in hits like *The Best Years of Our Lives* (1946). In the 50's she did some work in the theatre and on television but rarely appeared in films. **Credits include:** *Pretty Ladies* (1925), *Cock o' the Walk* (1930), *Naughty Flirt* (1931), *The Great Ziegfeld* (1936), *Another Thin Man* (1939), *So Goes My Love* (1946), *Mr. Blandings Builds His Dream House* (1948), *Lonelyhearts* (1959), *The April Fools* (1969).

BELA LUGOSI (1882–1956)

Bela Blasko was an established dramatic actor in his native Hungary before coming to the United States in 1921. He produced plays for the Hungarian community in New York while he learned English and planned for a career on the Broadway stage. However, his performance in *Dracula* in 1927 proved so successful that Hollywood beckoned, and soon Lugosi found himself the star of horror films featuring the nobleman whose favorite drink was human blood, straight.

Although the role made him a star, Lugosi was to regret *Dracula*'s success. He found himself typecast in horror parts and only rarely escaped to appear in straight roles—e.g. *Ninotchka* (1939). Lugosi returned to the stage on the West Coast, starring in a Los Angeles and San Francisco production of *Arsenic and Old Lace* (1943). His career suffered when Hollywood tired of making *Dracula* movies. **Films include:** *Dracula* (1931), *White Zombie* (1932), *The Island of Lost Souls* (1933), *The Mark of the Vampire* (1935), *The Black Cat* (1941), *Return of the Vampire* (1943), *The Body Snatcher* (1945), *Abbott and Costello Meet Frankenstein* (1948).

PAUL LUKAS (1895–1971)

Paul Lugacs became a native of Hungary in a highly dramatic fashion: His mother gave birth to him just as her train was pulling into the Budapest station. He was an early success on the Berlin stage and first appeared on the screen in 1927. In 1928 Adolph Zukor

brought him to the United States to appear with Pola Negri in *Loves of an Actress*.

Lukas was at home in almost any kind of role, sometimes sympathetic but more often slickly villainous. He was the chief baddie in Hitchcock's memorable thriller *The Lady Vanishes* (1938) and several years later starred on Broadway as the quiet, unassuming underground fighter against Nazi rule in Lillian Hellman's *Watch on the Rhine*. He repeated the role in the 1943 film and won the Oscar for Best Actor of the Year. **Other credits in a highly distinguished career:** *Little Women* (1933), *Dodsworth* (1936), *Experiment Perilous* (1944), *The Roots of Heaven* (1958), *Tender Is the Night* (1962), *Lord Jim* (1965).

KEYE LUKE (1904–   )

"Gee, Pop . . ." are the words that immortalized Keye Luke in the minds of Charlie Chan fans. The Chinese-American actor began his film career in *The Painted Veil* (1934) and the following year appeared for the first time as Warner Oland's son in *Charlie Chan in Paris*. Luke made eight more Chan films before Oland's death in 1938. He moved on to substantial roles in *The Good Earth* (1937) and *Across the Pacific* (1942) but in between made more mysteries as Kato, the Green Hornet's faithful servant, in the Green Hornet serials.

In 1942 he appeared as *Dr. Gillespie's New Assistant* and worked in the hospital with Lionel Barrymore in several additional features. By the end of the 40's his career was on the wane, and he found himself back in the Chan series in two low-budget productions with Roland Winters. In the 50's he appeared in only a few "B" movies, but his career was given a boost in 1958 with the start of a three-year stint on Broadway in *The Flower Drum Song*. Recently he has made several TV appearances, notably as Po, the blind monk, in the *Kung Fu* series. **Credits include:** *Sleep, My Love* (1948), *Hell's Half Acre* (1954), *Nobody's Perfect* (1968), *The Chairman* (1969).

JOHN LUND (1913–   )

The handsome, blond Lund began his show-business career as a radio scriptwriter.

Bela Lugosi as Count Dracula, a nobleman who never dreamed of drinking his victims' blood unless dressed in white tie and tails.

Paul Lukas, looking older and grayer than was his wont, is carted off by the Gestapo in Confessions of a Nazi Spy *(1939).*

Ida Lupino at her seductive best in The Man I Love *(1947).*

Paul Lynde is the lawman in The Glass Bottom Boat *(1966).*

He broke into acting on the stage and appeared in such Broadway productions as *The Hasty Heart* (1945). He went to Hollywood in the late 40's to try his luck in films. Though he had good roles in several films—he played Captain John Pringle in *A Foreign Affair* (1948) with Marlene Dietrich, Al in *My Friend Irma* (1949) with Marie Wilson and George Kittredge in *High Society* (1956) with Grace Kelly—he was not able to maintain his leading-man status, and in the late 50's his career took a downward turn. **Credits:** *To Each His Own* (1946), *The Perils of Pauline* (1947), *White Feather* (1955), *If a Man Answers* (1962).

WILLIAM LUNDIGAN (1914–)

In films for 30 years, William Lundigan has become a familiar face in numerous supporting and some starring roles. He began his professional career as a radio announcer but quickly moved to the screen in such films as *The Armored Car* (1937) and *Three Smart Girls Grow Up* (1939). In addition to his film work, Lundigan has appeared frequently on television. In 1954 he was the host of *Climax* and later starred in the *Men Into Space* series. **Credits:** *The Old Maid* (1939), *The Courtship of Andy Hardy* (1942), *Pinky* (1949), *The House on Telegraph Hill* (1951), *Riders to the Stars* (1954), *The Way West* (1967).

IDA LUPINO (1918–)

She was born in England, the daughter of an acting family whose traceable history on stage goes back to medieval Italy, and first made a name for herself in British films of the early 30's. She usually played vapid young things, and when she went to Hollywood in 1934 there was more of the same. The turning point in her career came in 1939 after she played the harridan wife in *The Light That Failed* and quickly followed this with the role of the insane wife in *They Drive by Night* (1940). Finally acknowledged as a first-class dramatic actress, she went on to more demanding roles.

In 1945 she began directing and producing films with her second husband, Collier Young (at that time she was the only woman director in Hollywood). Beginning with *Not Wanted* (1949), she made a series of low-keyed, low-budget, sensitive films. Later, she directed and acted on television. Recently, she returned to the screen for the first time in 17 years in Sam Peckinpah's *Junior Bonner* (1972). **More than 55 films include:** *Her First Affair* (1933), *Peter Ibbetson* (1935), *The Hard Way* (1943), *Road House* (1948), *Beware My Lovely* (1952), *The Big Knife* (1955).

JAMES (JIMMY) LYDON (1923–)

While a student at St. John's Military Academy at Bergenfield, New Jersey, Lydon was selected in a national contest as "the typical American boy." He later worked on Broadway and with the Federal Theatre Project and landed the title role in the stage production of *Tom Sawyer*. He made his screen debut in 1939 in *Back Door to Heaven* and was the star of the popular *Henry Aldrich* series of the early 40's. **Highlights:** *Tom Brown's School Days* (1940), *Little Men* (1940), *Henry Aldrich for President* (1941), *Henry Aldrich, Editor* (1942), *Aerial Gunner* (1943), *Life With Father* (1947), *The Magnificent Yankee* (1951), *Island in the Sky* (1953), *The Last Time I Saw Archie* (1961).

PAUL LYNDE (1926–)

The wisecracking comedian launched his show-business career in New York after graduation from Northwestern University in 1948. Four years later he got his first break on Broadway in Leonard Sillman's revue *New Faces of 1952*. He then did a stint entertaining in nightclubs before winning the role of Kim's harassed father in the Broadway musical *Bye, Bye, Birdie* (1960). His success in the show led to an offer to recreate the role in the 1963 movie version. Since then Lynde has continued to appear in featured comedy on screen. Perhaps his most memorable performance was as the outrageously cheerful, glib cemetery-plot salesman in *Send Me No Flowers* (1964) with Doris Day and Rock Hudson.

Lynde has also appeared frequently on television and starred in his own programs *The Paul Lynde Show* (1972) and *Temperatures Rising* (1973). He is a regular panelist and audience favorite on the popular TV quiz show *The Hollywood Squares*. **Films in-**

clude: *Under the Yum Yum Tree* (1963), *The Glass Bottom Boat* (1966), *How Sweet It Is* (1968).

CAROL LYNLEY (1942–   )

She was a teen-age cover girl before making her motion picture debut in 1958 in *The Light in the Forest*. One other early leading role was as Brandon de Wilde's pregnant girlfriend in *Blue Denim* (1959). After several years in ingénue roles she made the transition to more mature leading lady parts in a variety of mainly forgettable films and TV dramas. **Credits include:** *Holiday for Lovers* (1959), *Return to Peyton Place* (1961), *The Cardinal* (1963), *Under the Yum Yum Tree* (1963), *Harlow* (1965), *Bunny Lake Is Missing* (1965), *The Shuttered Room* (1968), *The Maltese Bippy* (1969), *Norwood* (1970).

DIANA LYNN (1926–1971)

An accomplished pianist, Dolores Loehr broke into films at 13 (using the name Dolly Loehr) as a musician. Three years later she proved herself a gifted comedienne when she appeared with Ginger Rogers and Ray Milland in *The Major and the Minor*. Ironically, in the remake of this film, *You're Never Too Young* (1955), with Dean Martin and Jerry Lewis, she played the Ray Milland role.

Her wry wit was seen in many comedies of the 40's and early 50's. In 1955 she left the screen to appear on stage and television. She was planning to make a comeback in *Play It As It Lays* (1971) when she died from a stroke. **Her many films include:** *They Shall Have Music* (1939), *The Miracle of Morgan's Creek* (1944), *Our Hearts Were Young and Gay* (1944), *My Friend Irma* (1949), *The People Against O'Hara* (1951).

JEFFREY LYNN (1909–   )

A popular leading man of the 30's and 40's, Lynn (Ragnar Lind) alternated between stage and screen in a career spanning more than 30 years. He made his first professional appearance at the Barter Theatre in Abingdon, Virginia, and then played small roles on Broadway and on the road before first appearing in films in the late 30's. After serving in World War II he returned to films and also appeared frequently on stage and on televi-

sion. **Films include:** *Four Daughters* (1938), *Espionage Agent* (1939), *A Child Is Born* (1940), *Million Dollar Baby* (1941), *Whiplash* (1948), *Black Bart* (1948), *A Letter to Three Wives* (1949), *Up Front* (1951), *Tony Rome* (1967).

BEN LYON (1901–   )

His dark good looks and black patent-leather hair parted in the middle helped make him one of the more popular male leads of the silent 20's. When he married Bebe Daniels in 1930, the couple became one of the most popular duos in Hollywood. Lyon began his film career in bit parts as early as 1916 and by 1923 was playing romantic leads. His best-known role in talkies was that of the dashing World War I pilot, playing opposite Jean Harlow, in the super production of its day, *Hell's Angels* (1930).

Lyon served in the U. S. Air Force during World War II, while his wife entertained troops on the battle lines. After the war they settled permanently in England, where they starred with their two children on their own radio show. **More than 80 films include:** *The Great Deception* (1926), *Alias French Gertie* (with Bebe Daniels, 1930), *I Cover the Waterfront* (1933), *The Women in His Life* (1934).

BERT LYTELL (1885–1954)

He began acting in a stock company in Newark, New Jersey, made good on the New York stage and then became one of the most popular leading men of the silent screen. Lytell made a few sound pictures, including the highly successful *On Trial* (1928). After he left Hollywood in the early 30's Lytell resumed his successful stage career. He starred on Broadway with Gertrude Lawrence in Kurt Weill's *Lady in the Dark* and in Kaufman and Hart's *The Man Who Came to Dinner*. During World War II he served as master of ceremonies on the popular radio program *Stage Door Canteen*. For many years Lytell was president of Actors' Equity. **Films include:** *Alias Jimmy Valentine* (1920), *A Message from Mars* (1923), *Lady Windemere's Fan* (1925), *Steele of the Royal Mounted* (1927), *Blood Brothers* (1930), *The Lone Wolf* (1931).

A mildly aggressive Carol Lynley in Once You Kiss a Stranger *(1969).*

Diana Lynn in the pleasant The Miracle of Morgan's Creek *(1943).*

An earlier generation loved it when Jeanette MacDonald and Nelson Eddy sang soulfully at one another. On this occasion the film was Sweethearts.

Tears flooded theatres over the plight of Ali MacGraw and Ryan O'Neal in Love Story.

M

J. FARRELL MacDONALD
(1875–1952)

During a film career that spanned nearly 30 years this former minstrel singer and highly effective character actor played both comic and dramatic roles in well over 100 pictures. (In 1931 alone he made 14 films.) **Some highlights:** *Drifting* (debut, 1923), *The Iron Horse* (1924), *In Old Arizona* (1929), *The Maltese Falcon* (1931), *The Whole Town's Talking* (1935), *Show Boat* (1936), *The Crowd Roars* (1938), *Broadway Limited* (1941), *A Tree Grows in Brooklyn* (1945), *Mr. Belvedere Rings the Bell* (1951).

JEANETTE MacDONALD
(1907–1965)

Best known for the musical spectaculars she made in the 30's with Nelson Eddy, MacDonald first appeared professionally as a chorus girl in the *Demi-Tasse Revue* (1920). This first New York stage bit was followed by several Broadway successes which in turn led to the actress' first screen role in Ernst Lubitsch's *The Love Parade* (1929) opposite Maurice Chevalier.

MacDonald had lead roles in a number of other motion pictures but in the public mind she was inextricably linked with Eddy in a series of "sugar and spice" films, even though she had married actor Gene Raymond in 1937 in one of Hollywood's most publicized weddings. Later in life, when the actress was called upon to defend the MacDonald–Eddy movies, which had become high camp, she declared: "Sentiment, after all, is basic. Without it there is no love, no life, no family." A number of unfriendly souls referred to her as "The Iron Butterfly"—an unfair label, for she was a good singer and an even better comedienne. **Highlights:** *The Vagabond King* (1930), *The Merry Widow* (1934), *Naughty Marietta* (1935), *San Francisco* (1936), *Maytime* (1937), *Sweethearts* (1938), *New Moon* (1940), *The Sun Comes Up* (1949).

ALI MacGRAW (1939–   )

Formerly a fashion model, she became a star overnight as the suburban Jewish princess in the 1969 film version of Philip Roth's comedy of upper-middle-class America, *Goodbye, Columbus*. Since then she starred in the badly reviewed but widely attended *Love Story* (1971). Darkly pretty, New York-born MacGraw is a product of the new school of "natural looking" actresses. She was the protégé, and briefly the wife, of Robert Evans. She is now married to one of America's acting folk heroes and her co-star in *Getaway* (1973), Steve McQueen.

DOROTHY MACKAILL (1904–   )

Born in England, MacKaill first appeared in pictures made in London and Paris. In America her fragile blonde beauty attracted Ziegfeld and from his stage productions she went to Hollywood in the early 20's. During the following 13 years she starred in nearly 40 silents and talkies. Most of these were "B" films, but there were exceptions, among them *Waterfront* (1928). **Her films include:** *Bits of Life* (U.S. debut, 1921), *Chickie* (1925), *The Barker* (1928), *The Great Divide* (1930), *Bulldog Drummond at Bay* (1937).

SHIRLEY MacLAINE (1934–   )

Born in Richmond, Virginia (her brother is actor Warren Beatty), she is one of the most versatile and engaging of today's stars. She can dance, sing and play dramatic or comedy roles with equal conviction. Lamentably, the studios have too often wasted her talents in costly but junky spectacles—e.g., *Can-Can* (1960) and *Irma la Douce* (1963).

MacLaine rose quickly from a Broadway chorus line to the first of three Academy Award nominations as Ginny Goodhead in *Some Came Running* (1958). Her second

Oscar nomination and the British Film Academy award came two years later for her memorable performance opposite (or rather between) Jack Lemmon and Fred MacMurray in Billy Wilder's outstanding tragi-comic *The Apartment*.

When she is not acting, MacLaine is a devout crusader for the cause of women, is active in Democratic political circles and was in the forefront of Vietnam anti-war activities. **Films include:** *The Trouble With Harry* (debut, 1955), *The Matchmaker* (1958), *Two for the Seesaw* (1962), *The Children's Hour* (1962), *The Yellow Rolls-Royce* (1965), *Sweet Charity* (1969), *The Possession of Joel Delaney* (1972).

BARTON MacLANE (1902–1969)

He once said, "I thought an actor should be a man of fine physical build, so I developed my muscles to be able to tear a villain limb form limb." Ironically, during a film career which spanned 45 years and included more than 150 films, he was almost always the rough raspy-voiced badman, convict or desperado felled by the hero.

Born in South Carolina, he was discovered while playing football for Wesleyan University and made one of his first screen appearances in *Quarterback* (1926) with Richard Dix. **Some of his films include:** *Tillie and Gus* (1933), *The Maltese Falcon* (1941), *The Treasure of Sierra Madre* (1948), *Backlash* (1956), *Buckskin* (1968).

DOUGLAS MacLEAN (1890–1967)

A highly engaging leading man of the 20's, he preferred comedy to more serious productions. In addition to his numerous screen appearances, he wrote many of his scripts and produced films via his own production unit. After the emergence of talkies he continued to write and produce for films and later for radio and television. As befitted the son of a minister, MacLean devoted a great proportion of his time to good causes, notably the American Red Cross and the Motion Picture Relief Fund. **His films include:** *The Hun Within* (1918), *Mary's Ankle* (1920), *Seven Keys to Baldpate* (1925), *Hold That Lion* (1926), *The Carnation Kid* (1929).

ALINE MacMAHON (1899–   )

Known for her sensitive character work on stage and screen, she had trained at the Neighborhood Playhouse in New York for three years and had been signed by the Shuberts when she arrived in Los Angeles in a production of *Once in a Lifetime* (1929). Warners signed her to a contract and, beginning with *Five Star Final* (1931), she made 20 pictures for them in four years. Growing restless and wanting parts with more depth, she obtained her release. She continued on a free-lance basis, making films that interested her and playing countless stage roles. **Some of her films include:** *Silver Dollar* (1932), *Ah, Wilderness!* (1935), *Dragon Seed* (1944), *The Search* (1948), *Cimarron* (1961), *All the Way Home* (1963).

FRED MacMURRAY (1908–   )

Born in Kankakee, Illinois, the son of a concert violinist, he was the singer and saxophonist to whom Libby Holman sang "Something to Remember You By" in a 1930 Broadway revue. Legend has it that a Paramount scout spotted him when he doubled as a saxophone player and lead actor in *Roberta* (1933) and signed him. After a few gangster-cop parts he and Ray Milland together rose to stardom when they played lead roles with Claudette Colbert in *The Gilded Lily* (1935).

Over the years MacMurray probably played more genial and relaxed go-getter types than any other screen actor. That was the Hollywood typecasting mind in action and a big mistake it was, too, for when given the chance, MacMurray gave memorable performances in more demanding, hard-edged roles. He made a great villain as the clinical insurance-agent murderer in *Double Indemnity* (1944) and an equally convincing slick philanderer in the Oscar-winning Billy Wilder film *The Apartment* (1960). Unfortunately, these were exceptions, and through the 60's he spent his time appearing mainly in such Disney money-makers as *The Shaggy Dog* (1959). His extremely successful *My Three Sons* series launched his career in television. **Films include:** *Grand Old Girl* (1935), *The Egg and I* (1947), *The Absent-*

Shirley MacLaine, at her most pixyish, in Hot Spell *(1958).*

Irene Dunne is the proud possessor of Fred MacMurray, pin-stripes and all, in Invitation to Happiness *(1939).*

The magnificently explosive Anna Magnani in The Golden Coach *(1954).*

Minded Professor (1961), *The Happiest Millionaire* (1967), *Charley and the Angel* (1973).

GORDON MacRAE (1921–   )

Beginning as a child performing in stock and radio, the New Jersey-born MacRae grew up to become a highly popular singer and actor on television, in the theatre and in nightclubs. He has made a considerable number of movies, originally in roles that called for acting rather than song, but more recently in productions like *Oklahoma!* (1955) and *Carousel* (1956).

He and his former wife, Sheila, had four children, two of whom—Heather and Meredith—have followed their parents in performing careers. **His credits include:** *Look for the Silver Lining* (1949), *Backfire* (1950), *Tea for Two* (1950), *The West Point Story* (1950), *Three Sailors and a Girl* (1953), *The Best Things in Life Are Free* (1956).

GEORGE MACREADY (1909–   )

This native of Providence, Rhode Island, came to Hollywood in 1942 with an impressive stage background that included a Broadway debut in Katharine Cornell's *Lucrece* (1932). He was equally successful on screen and became one of filmdom's favorite arch-villains and the veteran of more than 60 pictures. He has also appeared in 80 some TV shows, including the *Peyton Place* series (1966–68). **Films include:** *Commandos Strike at Dawn* (debut, 1942), *Gilda* (1946), *The Desert Fox* (1951), *Julius Caesar* (1953), *Two Weeks in Another Town* (1962), *The Great Race* (1965).

GUY MADISON (1922–   )

He played a young sailor in a small part in *Since You Went Away* (1944) and it made him a near star overnight. He had just been released from the Navy and his career looked bright and fruitful. After a few more films he drifted primarily into Westerns and has appeared infrequently in recent years. One of the early stars to work in television, he had his own series between 1954 and 1957—*Wild Bill Hickok*. **Some of his films include:** *Till the End of Time* (1946), *The Command* (1954), *The Last Frontier* (1955), *Gunmen From the Rio Grande* (1965), *The Mystery of Thug Island* (1966), *Payment in Blood* (1968).

ANNA MAGNANI (1908–1973)

She had been playing indifferent roles in Italian films for more than ten years when she blazed across the screen in Rossellini's pioneering film about occupied Rome, *Open City* (1945). Her impassioned performance made her an international star, and when she made her American debut in the film version of Tennessee Williams' *The Rose Tattoo* (1955)—in a role originally written for her for the stage but which she declined—she won an Academy Award for Best Actress. In 1957 she was nominated for a second Oscar for her role as a mail-order bride in *Wild Is the Wind*, which was not successful.

Working her way up from the slums of Rome, first as a street and café singer, Magnani became an adept comedienne, often appearing with her friend Aldo Fabrizzi. It was only after *Open City* that she became universally regarded as a great tragedienne. After her Hollywood years, where she had been typecast as a domineering, noisy woman, her career suffered a decline. In the 60's she made only a few films, none of special note. **Films include:** *The Miracle* (1950), *Volcano* (1953), *The Fugitive Kind* (1960), *The Secret of Santa Vittoria* (1969).

GEORGE MAHARIS (1938–   )

Born in New York, Maharis studied acting with Lee Strasberg and made his professional stage debut in 1955 in *Dancing in the Chequered Shade*. He is known primarily for his work in television, having made his debut in that media in the *Mr. Peepers* series (1953). In 1960 Maharis received the Theatre World Award for his role as Jeremy in *The Zoo Story* and in 1962 he received an Emmy for his performance as Buz in *Route 66*. **Major film credits include:** *Sylvia* (1965), *Covenant With Death* (1967), *The Desperadoes* (1969), *The Day of the Landgrabbers* (1969).

MARJORIE MAIN (1890–   )

Born Mary Tomlinson Krebs in Acton, Indiana, this minister's daughter took her last name from the title of Sinclair Lewis' *Main Street*. She made her first stage appearances with the Chautauqua Shakespearean group on the Orpheum Circuit and then worked in stock, vaudeville, radio and Broadway before making her screen debut in *A House Divided* (1932). After fifteen years of supporting roles in several dozen films, the somewhat acerbic lady finally found a niche in film history as Ma Kettle. She first played the character in an Academy Award-winning supporting performance in *The Egg and I* (1947) and went on to make a series of highly successful *Ma and Pa Kettle* pictures over the following decade. (Percy Kilbride played the easygoing Pa Kettle.) **Credits include:** *Music in the Air* (1934), *Dead End* (1937), *Wyoming* (1940), *A Woman's Face* (1941), *Ma and Pa Kettle* (1949), *The Kettles on Old MacDonald's Farm* (1957).

KARL MALDEN (1914–)

Born Malden Sekulovich in Gary, Indiana, Malden studied at the Chicago Art Institute and made his Broadway debut as Barker in *Golden Boy* (1937). Other legitimate theatre roles followed—e.g., in *Gentle People* (1939) and *Key Largo* (1940)—before he broke into films in *They Knew What They Wanted* (1940). For the next decade he combined stage and screen work and won a Best Supporting Actor Oscar when he recreated his stage role as Mitch for Elia Kazan's film version of *A Streetcar Named Desire* (1951). Three years later he was nominated for another Oscar for his performance as Father Berry in *On the Waterfront*. Since then, Malden has continued to turn in fine performances in films. Most recently, he's become well known to TV audiences as the tough protagonist of *The Streets of San Francisco*. **Highlights:** *Decision Before Dawn* (1952), *Baby Doll* (1956), *One-Eyed Jacks* (1961), *Gypsy* (1962), *Hotel* (1967), *Hot Millions* (1968).

MILES MALLESON (1889–1969)

Best known for his role as Canon Chasuble in Wilde's *The Importance of Being Earnest*, Malleson's work in the theatre spanned nearly 60 years. Owing his success partly to his very funny face, Malleson was described by one critic as ''an actor of distinction, an artist of imagination and depth.'' He made his debut in 1911 at Liverpool Playhouse in *Justice*. Malleson also made a substantial contribution to the theatre as a translator of Molière and as a playwright. **Films include:** *Knight Without Armour* (1937), *The Thief of Bagdad* (1940), *The Man Who Never Was* (1956), *The Admirable Crichton* (1957), *I'm All Right, Jack* (1960), *The Magnificent Showman* (1964).

DOROTHY MALONE (1925–)

Born Dorothy Maloney in Chicago, Illinois, Malone began her screen career playing demure, girl-next-door types in Warner Brothers movies of the 40's, but emerged as a more substantial actress in 50's films. In 1956 she won an Oscar for Best Supporting Actress for her portrayal of a loose woman in *Written on the Wind*. She appeared as Constance Mackenzie Carson on the TV soap opera *Peyton Place* (1965–68). **Highlights:** *The Falcon and the Co-eds* (debut, 1943), *The Big Sleep* (1946), *Sincerely Yours* (1955), *Too Much, Too Soon* (1958), *The Last Voyage* (1960), *The Last Sunset* (1961), *Beach Party* (1963).

Karl Malden with Rosalind Russell, who played the strip queen's mother in Gypsy.

Marjorie Main always turned in a good performance, even in forgettable pictures. Here she coyly responds to the advances of J. Carrol Naish in Jackass Mail *(1942).*

Jayne Mansfield and natural endowments in a film titled, as one might expect, The Girl Can't Help It *(1957).*

MILES MANDER (1889–1946)

Mander, the son of a wealthy English manufacturer, had varied careers as a sheep raiser, auto racer, aviator, novelist, playwright, news commentator, scriptwriter and movie director, film studio owner and politician before and during his years as a stage and screen character actor in England and the United States. He first worked in films in the mid-20's in England, and by 1929 he had appeared in the first of several pictures he also wrote and directed (*The First Born*). He remained in England for another six years and then moved to Hollywood. Among Mander's plays produced were *Common People* (1926), *It's a Pity About Humanity* (1931), and *Blessed Are the Rich* (1944). His books include *Albania Today, Oasis, Gentleman by Birth* and *To My Son in Confidence,* the latter a best-seller. **Highlights:** *The Pleasure Garden* (1926), *The Private Life of Henry VIII* (1933), *The Three Musketeers* (1935), *Suez* (1938), *Kidnapped* (1938), *The Little Princess* (1939), *This Above All* (1942), *The Picture of Dorian Gray* (1945).

DAVID MANNERS (1901–)

Before he left his native Halifax, Nova Scotia, the young Rauff de Ryther Duan Acklom changed his name to what proved to be the perfect handle for this portrayer of numerous debonair, well-bred types. One of the first young stage actors to go to Hollywood during the early days of sound, he made his screen debut in *Journey's End* (1930). He went on to appear in more than 35 pictures before resuming his stage career in 1937. In the 50's he turned to writing and has since written three novels. **Films include:** *Kismet* (1930), *Dracula* (1931), *A Bill of Divorcement* (1932), *Torch Singer* (1933), *The Warrior's Husband* (1933), *A Woman Rebels* (1936).

JAYNE MANSFIELD (1933–1967)

When she was poured into tight-fitting satin the super-voluptuous blonde bore a distinct resemblance to Marilyn Monroe, but the resemblance ended abruptly when one watched Mansfield on the screen. Married to strongman Mickey Hargitay, she managed to appear dependent, which in reality she was not. Her life ended in an auto crash in 1967. **Some of her films are:** *Illegal* (debut, 1955), *Will Success Spoil Rock Hunter?* (1957), *The George Raft Story* (1962), *A Guide for the Married Man* (1967).

JEAN MARAIS (1913–)

After several years on stage and some roles in indifferent films, Jean Marais-Villain came to the attention of film audiences in 1943 as the modern-day Tristan of Jean Cocteau's somber film *L'Eternal Retour*. Over the next few years he continued to appear as the leading protagonist in Cocteau's screen essays, most notably as the Beast in *La Belle et La Bête* (1946), in *Les Parents Terribles* (1948) and in the title role of *Orphée* (1950). Since

Fredric March walked away with the Best Actor Award for his portrayal of the medico who turned himself into a monster in Dr. Jekyll and Mr. Hyde.

then, however, most of his screen work has been confined to "B" swashbucklers and spy films. **Credits include:** *L'Epervier* (debut, 1933), *Le Pavillon Brûle* (1942), *L'Aigle à Deux Têtes* (1948), *The Secret of Mayerling* (1951), *Le Testament d'Orphée* (1959), *Austerlitz* (1960), *Peau d'Ane* (1970).

FREDRIC MARCH (1897–)

He is one of the most respected actors of the American stage and screen. His long and distinguished career includes virtually every genre of play, film and television drama. Honors that have come to him include two Academy Awards for Best Actor—for *Dr. Jekyll and Mr. Hyde* (1932) and again for *The Best Years of Our Lives* (1946).

Born in Racine, Wisconsin, Frederick McIntyre Bickel was a recognized stage actor when a Theatre Guild tour of *The Royal Family* brought him to Los Angeles and Adolph Zukor signed him to a five-year contract with Paramount Pictures. He made his debut in *The Dummy* (1929). His film career of more than 65 films ran from light comedy to romantic leading roles to dramatic character parts. He was married to actress Florence Eldridge in 1927 and appeared with her in many films and plays. **Some of his highlights include:** *Manslaughter* (1930), *Design for Living* (1933), *Death Takes a Holiday* (1934), *Les Misérables* (1935), *Anna Karenina* (1935), *A Star Is Born* (1937), *The Adventures of Mark Twain* (1944), *Death of a Salesman* (1951), *Middle of the Night* (1959), *Seven Days in May* (1964), *Hombre* (1967), *The Iceman Cometh* (1973).

MARGO (1918–)

Trained from childhood as a dancer, Maria Marguerita Guadalupe Boldao y Castillo made her professional debut at the age of six in her native Mexico City and worked as a dancer in New York and Los Angeles before being cast in her first screen role as Carmen Brown in Ben Hecht's *Crime Without Passion* (1934). Two years later, she repeated her stage role as Miriamne for the screen version of *Winterset* (1936). She is perhaps best remembered by film audiences, however, as the beautiful young girl who turns into a mummy in the last few moments of *Lost Horizon*

(1937). Once married to Francis Lederer, she has been married to Eddie Albert since 1945. **Other films include:** *The Scoundrel* (1935), *Rumba* (1935), *The Leopard Man* (1943), *Viva Zapata!* (1952), *I'll Cry Tomorrow* (1956), *Who's Got the Action?* (1962).

MONA MARIS (1903–)

The sultry Latin beauty played villainesses in two languages and was almost invariably thwarted at the conclusion of the picture. Her American film career began with *Bondage* (1928) and was interrupted by Spanish-language films like *La Melodia Prohibida* (1933), which never appeared in English but which we take to mean *The Forbidden Melody*. In recent years she has become something of a camp figure—who wouldn't be who made pictures with titles like *One Mad Kiss* (1930), *White Heat* (1934) and *Asegure a su Mujer* (1935), a title which gives precise instruction to all males—*Insure Your Wife*. **Credits:** *The Arizona Kid* (1930), *Secrets* (1933), *Kiss and Make Up* (1934), *Underground* (1941), *My Gal Sal* (1942), *The Falcon in Mexico* (1944), *The Avengers* (1950).

HUGH MARLOWE (1914–)

Born Hugh Herbert Hipple in Philadelphia, Marlowe worked as a radio announcer and then as an actor in England before he made his New York stage debut in 1936 as Donald Drake in *Arrest That Woman*. A year later he was cast by MGM for his first screen role in *Married Before Breakfast*. The actor preferred character roles, believing that "the character actor usually provides the friction they have to have to move the story." **Highlights:** *Meet Me in St. Louis* (1944), *All About Eve* (1950), *Earth Versus the Flying Saucers* (1956), *Elmer Gantry* (1960), *The Birdman of Alcatraz* (1962), *Seven Days in May* (1964).

PERCY MARMONT (1883–)

Now all but forgotten, he played lead roles in a number of highly successful silent movies, but after the advent of sound was seen infrequently and in subordinate parts. Those with long memories will recall him in two of his better characterizations—*Lord Jim*

Margo, the fine Mexican-born actress, in Lost Horizon. *The gentleman halfway out of the picture is Ronald Colman and the hand belongs to Jane Wyatt.*

Jean Marais and Madeleine Sologne in Cocteau's L'Eternal Retour.

Mae Marsh, wide-eyed with anguish, in The Birth of a Nation.

Herbert Marshall worries about his missing daughter (played by Shirley Temple) in Kathleen *(1941).*

(1925) and *Aloma of the South Seas* (1926). **Other films include:** *Turn of the Wheel* (1918), *If Winter Comes* (1923), *The Light That Failed* (1923), *The Shooting of Dan McGrew* (1924), *Mantrap* (1926), *No Orchids for Miss Blandish* (1951), *Lisbon* (1956).

JOAN MARSH (1913–   )

An attractive performer who played secondary roles in a number of extremely good films, she made her talkie debut in the historic *All Quiet on the Western Front* (1930). While her career ended less than 12 years later, she performed extremely well in her several dozen films. **Credits:** *Little Accident* (1930), *Three-Cornered Moon* (1933), *Anna Karenina* (1935), *Idiot's Delight* (1939), *Road to Zanzibar* (1941).

MAE MARSH (1895–1968)

D. W. Griffith once said, "Every motion picture star I've known was made by long training and hard work but Mae Marsh was born a film star as though destiny itself was her acting coach." One of the leading ladies of the silent screen, she is best remembered today for her role as "Little Sister" in Griffith's *The Birth of a Nation* (1915). With the advent of sound, her career faded, yet over the years she returned occasionally to the screen in character and mother roles. **Some of her films include:** *The Sands of Dee* (1911), *Intolerance* (1916), *Polly of the Circus* (1917), *The White Rose* (1923), *Tides of Passion* (1925), *Jane Eyre* (1944), *The Robe* (1953), *Sergeant Rutledge* (1960).

MARIAN MARSH (1913–   )

Born in Trinidad of English, German, French and Irish stock, Violet Krauth moved to Hollywood as a child. During her junior year in high school a screen test led to work as a film extra and then to minor roles until she was suddenly promoted to stardom at 18 when John Barrymore chose her to play Trilby to his *Svengali* (1931). She continued to work in films until the early 40's, when she retired. **Some of her films include:** *The Mad Genius* (1931), *The Eleventh Commandment* (1933), *Crime and Punishment* (1935), *The Black Room* (1935), *Missing Daughters* (1939), *House of Errors* (1942).

BRENDA MARSHALL (1915–   )

Born in Manila and educated in Texas, she studied acting with Maria Ouspenskaya and was playing bit parts on stage when she was spotted and tested by Paramount. Although they turned her down, Warners saw the screen test and hired her as Joel McCrea's co-star in *Espionage Agent* (1939). Over the next decade she appeared in an assortment of films before retiring in the early 50's. She has been married to William Holden since 1941. **Films include:** *The Sea Hawk* (1940), *The Constant Nymph* (1943), *Strange Impersonation* (1945), *The Tomahawk Trail* (1950).

E. G. MARSHALL (1910–   )

This veteran character actor of stage, screen and television began his career in 1932 with radio work in his native Minnesota and made his stage debut the following year with the Oxford Players, a touring repertory company. By 1938 he had made it to Broadway and was playing the first of his numerous legitimate theatre roles—Henry Ontolt in *Prologue to Glory*. His first film appearance was not until 1945, when he was cast in *The House on 92nd Street* by Fox. In later years he frequently appeared in a number of television dramas. In 1963 the actor won an Emmy for his portrayal of trial lawyer Lawrence Preston in *The Defenders* (1960–1966). **Highlights:** *13 Rue Madeleine* (1947), *The Caine Mutiny* (1954), *Twelve Angry Men* (1957), *The Journey* (1959), *Compulsion* (1959), *The Poppy Is Also a Flower* (1967).

HERBERT MARSHALL (1890–1966)

Known as a "drawing room" type throughout most of his career, the immaculate and correct Britisher epitomized gentility in scores of films since his first screen appearance in the English frivolity *Mumsie* (1927).

On stage since 1911, his career was interrupted by World War I. While serving with Ronald Colman in the 14th London Scots Regiment, he lost a leg and was hospitalized for 13 months. He disguised the handicap so well that few knew of it. Marshall came to the United States in the 30's with his then wife, actress Edna Best, and remained to develop successful careers both on stage and in more than 70 Hollywood films, including the superb screen adaptation of Lillian Hellman's *The Little Foxes* (1941). **Other pictures include:** *Trouble in Paradise* (1932), *The Dark Angel* (1935), *A Bill of Divorcement* (1940), *The Moon and Sixpence* (1942), *Duel in the Sun* (1947), *The Virgin Queen* (1955), *The List of Adrian Messenger* (1963), *The Third Day* (1965).

TULLY MARSHALL (1864–1943)

Character actor Tully Marshall Phillips played roles ranging from frontiersman to perpetrators of Oriental skullduggery in upward of 100 films spanning the eras of both silents and talkies. His first appearance was in *The Sable Lorcha* (1915), his last in *Hitler's Madman* (1943). **Other films include:** *The Squaw Man* (1918), *The Hunchback of Notre Dame* (1923), *The Bridge of San Luis Rey* (1929), *Grand Hotel* (1932), *Chad Hanna* (1940), *This Gun for Hire* (1942).

DEAN MARTIN (1917–)

Born Dino Crocetti in Steubenville, Ohio, Martin was a prizefighter, steelworker and eventually a nightclub singer and comedian before becoming an actor. In 1949 he appeared with partner Jerry Lewis in the first of their slapstick, box-office hit films, *My Friend Irma*. When his partnership with Lewis broke up in 1957, Martin's stereotyped image as attractive straight-man and popular singer gradually faded with his success as a dramatic actor in such pictures as *The Young Lions* (1958). More recently he appeared in his own television variety show. **Highlights:** *Sailor Beware* (1952), *Rio Bravo* (1959), *Some Came Running* (1959), *Career* (1959), *Toys in the Attic* (1963), *Robin and the Seven Hoods* (1964), *The Ambushers* (1967), *Bandolero!* (1968), *Showdown* (1973).

MARION MARTIN (1916–)

Statuesque, with a mass of platinum hair, a pout and a voluptuous figure, she was always cast as a not-too-bright chorus girl, a husband stealer or a tough burlesque queen. She made 43 films in 12 years.

Born in Philadelphia but educated in Switzerland, she began her career as an Earl Carroll showgirl before being signed by Ziegfeld, becoming the last of the Follies girls to be

glorified before his death in 1932. Her first notable appearance in films was with Clark Gable in *Boom Town* (1940) and one of her last was again with him in *Key to the City* (1950). **Other films include:** *The Big Store* (1941), *They Got Me Covered* (1943), *Queen of Burlesque* (1947), *Come to the Stable* (1949), *Thunder in the Pines* (1954), *The Mikado* (1967).

MARY MARTIN (1913–)

Broadway leading lady in musical comedy during the 40's and 50's, she made only 11 pictures, and her vast charm did not register as effectively on the screen as it did on the stage. Lamentably, she was never given the opportunity to recreate her roles in *South Pacific* and *The Sound of Music* in films. **Films include:** *The Great Victor Herbert* (debut, 1939), *The Birth of the Blues* (1941), *Night and Day* (1946), *Main Street to Broadway* (1953).

ELSA MARTINELLI (1932–)

This former model and Italian film star was first introduced to American audiences in 1954, when she was discovered by Kirk Douglas and cast in the film *The Indian Fighter*. Since that time she has appeared in a number of Italian and American films, cast opposite such leading men as Anthony Perkins and Marcello Mastroianni. **Highlights:** *Four Girls in Town* (1957), *Stowaway Girl* (1957), *Hatari* (1962), *The Tenth Victim* (1965), *Les Chemins de Khatmandu* (1969).

LEE MARVIN (1924–)

Like so many actors, New York-born Marvin was typecast for years as the rough, tough thug. He broke the mold surrounding him, however, with his role as the sodden but lovable gunslinger in *Cat Ballou* (1965). With this fine performance he displayed his talent for comedy and won the Academy Award as the year's Best Actor. In 1968, he again proved his versatility with his sensitive portrayal of the tragi-comic gold miner in *Paint Your Wagon*. His performance was one of the few things in the film that received critical praise and his unschooled rendition briefly repopularized the song "I Was Born Under a Wandering Star." **Highlights:** *You're in the*

Young "Dino" Martin as he appeared with Jerry Lewis in Jumping Jacks *(1952).*

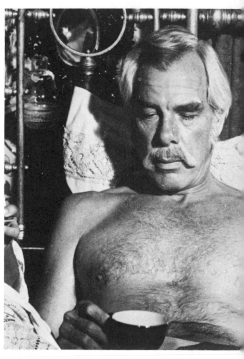

Lee Marvin in contemplative mood in Monte Walsh. *In the film he shared the bed with Jeanne Moreau.*

Groucho, Zeppo and Chico Marx in the days when they were making Go West, *a Western that had many of the same comic ingredients as their earlier, and later, Easterns. The young lady is June McCloy.*

Navy Now (debut, 1951), *The Caine Mutiny* (1954), *Donovan's Reef* (1963), *Ship of Fools* (1965), *The Dirty Dozen* (1967), *Prime Cut* (1972), *Emperor of the North Pole* (1973).

MARX BROTHERS

When the brothers Marx traded success in vaudeville and on Broadway for the silver screen the entire world was vastly enriched.

The father of the five Marxes was an unsuccessful New York tailor known as Misfit Marx. It was their mother, Minnie, who set her heart on putting all of the boys on Broadway. (Undoubtedly the fact that Minnie's brother was Al Shean of the "Oh-Mr. Gallagher-Yes-Mr.-Shean" vaudeville team, a hugely successful duo, helped inspire her.) She got her way, although Gummo (Milton) never appeared in pictures, opening a Hollywood talent agency instead. By 1914 the brothers were perfecting their madness on the vaudeville stage.

CHICO (LEONARD) MARX (1891–1961)
The first-born Marx wore a pointy hat and seedy velvet jacket, had a sly smile and generally helped the plot thicken via his Italian accent. "I tell-a you what, Boss, we take-a the car . . . etc. . . . " Most of his dealings were with Harpo, and when Chico complained of a headache the viewer could be certain that the silent Harpo would promptly present him with a large, dripping haddock.

Chico was famous for his one- and two-finger piano compositions and at one time had a band of his own. He was also a fanatical bridge addict who invented a bidding system.

HARPO (ADOLPH ARTHUR) MARX
(1894–1964) Hailed by many enthusiasts as the great pantomimist of his time, he sported a blond curly wig, battered top hat set jauntily to one side, outrageously baggy clothes and facial features which in a twinkling could convert from rage to a beatific smile. He was an off- and on-screen lecher and the high spots of many of his films came from his endless pursuit of beautiful blondes. Harpo conversed via charade-like activities or by honks on an outmoded automobile horn. Each of his important pictures had the plot interrupted by a harp solo, an instrument he played very well indeed.

GROUCHO (JULIUS HENRY) MARX (1895–   )
With his cigar and heavy-rimmed spectacles, painted-on mustache and half-crouching stride like that of a demented pelican, Groucho is clearly one of the great comic geniuses of our time. Inevitably, as Captain Spalding or Professor Quackenbush or Doctor Something-or-other, he played the phoney with pretensions. Whether voicing wrath ("I'd horsewhip you if I had a horse.") or parental solicitude ("I don't like Junior crossing the railroad tracks on his way to reform school. In fact, I don't like Junior.") or romantic trauma ("Kappelmeister, strike up the violas! My regiment leaves at dawn.") his nasal snarl had the desired effect—that of reducing his audience to helpless laughter.

While many of his lines were written by such masters of comedy as George S. Kaufman and S. J. Perelman, he contributed many of them himself. The high spots in most of his pictures are those in which he wooed Margaret Dumont, who, as the heavily corseted and bejeweled dowager, was alternately dazzled, bewildered or just plain puzzled by his precipitous advances.

Dubbed "Groucho" because of his naturally caustic view of life, the third Marx son wrote books and plays and kept television and radio audiences amused during two decades of quiz shows and comedy appearances.

ZEPPO (HERBERT) MARX (1901–)

The baby of the family didn't seem to have his heart in the entertainment world and appeared only in their first five big movies. He played juvenile lead, straight parts which gave him a chance to sing a love song now and again, a task he performed with modestly successful results. In 1933 he left the team to go into business. **Marx Brothers films include:** *The Cocoanuts* (1929), *Animal Crackers* (1930), *Monkey Business* (1931), *Horse Feathers* (1932), *Duck Soup* (1933). **Without Zeppo:** *A Night at the Opera* (1935), *A Day at the Races* (1937), *Room Service* (1938), *At the Circus* (1939), *Go West* (1941), *The Big Store* (1941), *A Night in Casablanca* (1946), *Love Happy* (1950).

GIULIETTA MASINA (1921–)

The waif-like, appealing Masina was an aspiring stage actress when Federico Fellini, later to be her husband, chose her to play in a series he had written. After they were married in 1943, Masina retired, but later returned to the stage. She was offered her first movie role in 1948, a secondary part in *Senza Pieta*. For her performance she was awarded the Silver Ribbon for Best Supporting Actress. Her seemingly bright career got bogged down in numerous mistress and whore roles, and it wasn't until 1954 that she broke from this mold to play in the internationally acclaimed *La Strada* (U.S., 1956). Masina followed this success with another, *Le Notti di Cabiria* (1956) for which she won the Cannes Film Festival award for Best Actress. Her next memorable performance came in the mid-60's in the masterful *Juliet of the Spirits* (1965). After that, however, her career took a sharp downward turn and she retired from films in 1969. **Highlights:** *Europa '51* (1952), *Il Bidone* (1964), *The Madwoman of Chaillot* (1969).

JAMES MASON (1909–)

A master at portraying introspective roles, he was a star in his native England when his performance in *The Seventh Veil* (1945), followed by his terrifying portrait of the wounded fugitive in *Odd Man Out* (1947), brought him international recognition.

He had studied to be an architect and received his degree at Cambridge but switched to acting instead. He made his screen debut in *Late Extra* (1935) after a few years on the stage and first came to the United States in 1946. After a slow start he established himself in Hollywood first as a leading man, gradually turning into a durable and highly dependable character actor. In 1954 he was nominated for the Academy Award for Best Actor in *A Star Is Born*, playing opposite Judy Garland. **More than 70 films include:** *Madame Bovary* (1949), *The Desert Fox* (1951), *Five Fingers* (1952), *Lolita* (1962), *Georgy Girl* (1966), *The Sea Gull* (1968), *Child's Play* (1972), *The Last of Sheila* (1973), *The Mackintosh Man* (1973).

MARSHA MASON (1942–)

In 1973 this talented newcomer to the screen was cast opposite James Caan in her

James Mason, as the faded and drunken ex-screen idol in A Star Is Born, *inadvertently backhands wife Judy Garland after she has won her Oscar.*

Raymond Massey as Abe Lincoln in the days of the Lincoln-Douglas debates.

Marcello Mastroianni in Sunflower *(1970), one of a number of films he made with Sophia Loren.*

first starring role as the whore in *Cinderella Liberty* (Mark Rydell's tale of a sailor on shore leave), and her superb performance won her a coterie of admirers and an Academy Award nomination. Mason appeared both off and on Broadway from the late 60's and starred in *Cactus Flower* for part of its Broadway run and on tour. **Film credits:** *Beyond the Law* (1968), *Blume in Love* (1973).

ILONA MASSEY (1910–   )

Discovered in Vienna while singing small roles in a small operatic company, she was brought to Hollywood by Metro-Goldwyn-Mayer, which set about training her to be the "singing Garbo," and she made her debut in *Rosalie* (1937).

Born in Budapest of poor parents—her father was a soldier who was captured and sent to Siberia—she worked her way up from menial jobs to singing in Budapest clubs and eventually arrived in Vienna. **Some of her singing and non-singing roles include:** *Balalaika* (1939), *New Wine* (1942), *Frankenstein Meets the Wolf Man* (1943), *Holiday in Mexico* (1946), *Love Happy* (1950), *Jet Over the Atlantic* (1960).

RAYMOND MASSEY (1896–   )

Although he was born in Canada and made his stage debut in London in 1922, he has achieved his greatest successes playing Americans—the title role in *Abe Lincoln in Illinois* (1940) and Dr. Gillespie in the popular *Dr. Kildare* TV series.

He began his career playing end man in minstrel shows and in his early London days did black-face acts in saloons before his formal stage debut. First coming to the United States for the Norman Bel Geddes production of *Hamlet* (1931), he settled in this country in the 30's, alternating between stage and screen. **More than 60 films include:** *The Scarlet Pimpernel* (1935), *Arsenic and Old Lace* (1944), *Possessed* (1947), *East of Eden* (1955), *How the West Was Won* (1963), *Mackenna's Gold* (1968).

MARCELLO MASTROIANNI (1924–   )

Mastroianni had made scores of films in his native Italy after his debut in *I Miserabili*

(1947) when Fellini's *La Dolce Vita* (1959) opened in the U.S.A. in 1961. It made him an international star and the most sought-after interpreter of the modern anti-hero—the man who as lover and mate is often inadequate, ridiculous, tired or just plain bored. He has remained in the forefront ever since and has proved equally adept at both dramatic and comic roles.

Beginning as a clerk, he was first seen by Visconti while performing with a theatrical troupe and was hired for Visconti's own repertory season. This led to other stage work and finally films. **Some of his films include:** *La Notte* (U.S., 1962), *Divorce Italian Style* (U.S., 1962), *8½* (1963), *Marriage Italian Style* (1964), *The Organizer* (1964), *The Tenth Victim* (1965), *The Stranger* (1967), *La Grande Bouffe* (1973).

WALTER MATTHAU (1920–   )

Tall, gruff and with a wry face that can be equally funny or sinister, Matthau began in films playing small but always significant roles as heavies. A New Yorker with a varied stage background, Matthau's film career began to mushroom in the mid-60's and he went from supporting villain to star comedian. After winning the Academy Award for Best Supporting Actor for *The Fortune Cookie* (1966) he went on to recreate his successful Broadway role as the slobbish Oscar in the film version of *The Odd Couple* (1968). In 1971 he was nominated for a best-actor Academy Award for his fine performance in the title role of *Kotch*. **Some of his films include:** *The Kentuckian* (1955), *Lonely Are the Brave* (1962), *Charade* (1963), *Mirage* (1965), *Hello, Dolly* (1969), *A New Leaf* (1970), *Plaza Suite* (1971), *Pete 'n' Tillie* (1972), *Charley Varrick* (1973), *The Laughing Policeman* (1973).

JESSIE MATTHEWS (1907–   )

The dancing, singing, somewhat toothy actress was the toast of London 40 years ago but never achieved great popularity in the United States. Indeed, most of Hollywood's efforts to find a slot for her were futile. Her first film appearance was in *The Beloved Vagabond* (1923) and in the years that followed stage and motion picture roles followed one another in quick succession. She scored outstanding successes in *The Good Companions* (1933) with John Gielgud and in *Evergreen* (1934). After her contract with Gaumont-British ended in the late 30's, she toured, appeared in several "B" films and tried hard but unsuccessfully to reactivate public interest in her. Her last film was *Tom Thumb* (1958). In recent years she has appeared regularly on television. **Films include:** *It's Love Again* (1936), *Head Over Heels in Love* (1937), *Climbing High* (1939).

VICTOR MATURE (1916–   )

Tagged as "A Hunk of Man" in his early films, he made his initial screen impact in *One Million B.C.* (1940) wearing a leopard skin and using dialogue consisting of grunts.

Born in Kentucky, he went to Hollywood at the age of 20. After several years of odd jobs and occasional appearances at the Pasadena Playhouse, he got his first film role in *The Housekeeper's Daughter* (1939). Despite the success of *One Million B.C.*, it wasn't until he appeared on Broadway in *Lady in the Dark* (1941) that his film career took off in earnest. Over the next two decades he starred in dozens of films, mostly "B" epics, adventure sagas or Westerns and only occasionally appeared in more substantial roles—notably as Doc Holliday in Ford's *My Darling Clementine* (1946). **Some of his other films include:** *Kiss of Death* (1947), *Samson and Delilah* (1949), *The Robe* (1953), *The Big Circus* (1959), *After the Fox* (1966), *Head* (1968).

MARILYN MAXWELL (1922–1972)

Maxwell was a band singer and toured the overseas army camps where her blond good looks and breezy manner made her such a favorite with GI's that they wrote to movie studios asking them to give her a break. MGM signed the Iowa-born actress while still on tour and she made her debut in *Stand By for Action* (1942) with Robert Taylor. Always popular, she worked steadily in films, television and on stage but rarely sang on screen. One of her best roles was as the other woman in *Champion* (1949). **Some of her other films include:** *Presenting Lily Mars*

Victor Mature (left) and Reginald Gardiner live it up with girlfriends in Wabash Avenue *(1950).*

Jack Lemmon remonstrates with his sloppy roomie, Walter Matthau, in The Odd Couple.

Mercedes McCambridge and Ben Cooper look grim as they face the foe in Johnny Guitar.

David McCallum, endangered but alert, in a scene from One Spy Too Many.

(1943), *Summer Holiday* (1948), *The Lemon Drop Kid* (1951), *Critic's Choice* (1963), *Arizona Bushwhackers* (1968), *The Phynx* (1970).

KEN MAYNARD 1895–1973)

He was the star rider and roper with Ringling Brothers circus before becoming one of the screen's early Western heroes. A graduate of Virginia Military Institute, the native Texan held a degree as an engineer but preferred to round up bad men on celluloid, liking to base his pictures on actual historical events rather than on fiction. **Credits include:** *The Red Raiders* (1927), *Parade of the West* (1930), *Branded Men* (1931).

VIRGINIA MAYO (1920–)

She was a chorus girl at the Diamond Horseshoe when Sam Goldwyn spotted her blond, luscious good looks and signed her. Cast as pretty decoration in Danny Kaye musicals, she finally managed to break out of this mold with her performance as the greedy wife of Dana Andrews in *The Best Years of Our Lives* (1946). Back to musicals, she emerged once more as a dramatic actress opposite James Cagney in *White Heat* (1949), but again went back to being decorative in musicals and costume adventures—and there she stayed. **Films include:** *Wonder Man* (1945), *Captain Horatio Hornblower* (1951), *The Silver Chalice* (1954), *Fort Dobbs* (1958), *Fort Utah* (1967).

MAY McAVOY (1901–)

Beginning her film career in *Hate* (1917), the bee-stung-lipped actress was a top Hollywood star for a decade. She was a good comedienne and a competent dramatic actress. With the advent of sound she accepted a role in *The Jazz Singer* (1927), the film that turned Hollywood upside down. Thereafter she made several talking films until her retirement in 1929. In the 40's Miss McAvoy returned to films as a contract player at MGM. She has since retired. **Films include:** *Sentimental Tommy* (1921), *Clarence* (1922), *The Enchanted Cottage* (1924), *Ben Hur* (1925), *The Lion and the Mouse* (1928), *No Defense* (1929).

DAVID McCALLUM (1933–)

The small blond Scottish actor is probably best known to the public as Illya Kuryakin in the successful TV spy series *The Man From U.N.C.L.E.* He began acting as a child and later starred on the London stage and directed plays for the British army. In motion pictures he has shown his versatility in varied supporting roles. **Films include:** *Prelude to Fame* (debut, 1950), *Freud* (1962), *The Great Escape* (1963), *The Greatest Story Ever Told* (1965), *One Spy Too Many* (1966).

MERCEDES McCAMBRIDGE (1918–)

Her soft, distinctive voice was heard in countless radio soap operas and mysteries and was familiar to millions when she made her movie debut as the political hatchet-woman in *All the King's Men* (1949) and won an Academy Award for Best Supporting Actress.

Born in Joliet, Illinois, she first worked on radio in Chicago, which was then a soap-opera center. She next went to New York for more radio work and a try at Broadway before beginning her movie career. After a long but successful bout with alcoholism, she devoted much time and effort in educating the public concerning this disease. She made numerous appearances on television from the mid-50's. **Highlights include:** *Johnny Guitar* (1954), *Giant* (1956), *Suddenly, Last Summer* (1959), *Cimarron* (1961), *Run Home Slow* (1965), *Women* (1969).

KEVIN McCARTHY (1914–)

The brother of writer Mary McCarthy, he joined a drama club while attending the University of Minnesota and has been acting ever since. After several years on Broadway he made his film debut recreating his stage role as Biff in the 1951 screen adaptation of Arthur Miller's *Death of a Salesman*. Although basically a stage performer, he has appeared in both leading roles and character parts in close to 20 films of the past two decades and has frequently appeared on television. **Some of his films include:** *Invasion of the Body Snatchers* (1956), *The Misfits* (1961), *The Best Man* (1964), *Mirage* (1965), *Hotel*

(1967), *If He Hollers, Let Him Go* (1968), *Kansas City Bomber* (1972).

PATTY McCORMACK (1945–   )

McCormack was a sensational success as the murderous little witch in *The Bad Seed* (1956) and starred in the television series *Peck's Bad Girl* (1959) with Wendell Corey. Since then her career has diminished, with a few appearances in invariably second- or third-rate pictures. **Credits:** *Kathy O'* (1958), *The Explosive Generation* (1962), *The Mini-Skirt Mob* (1968), *Born Wild* (1968).

ALEC McCOWEN (1925–   )

Long known as a respected stage actor in his native England, the boyish-faced McCowen gained wide recognition in the United States only in the late 60's when he appeared on Broadway in the title role of *Hadrian VII*. He made his stage debut at the age of 14 in a production of Gilbert and Sullivan's *Pinafore* and has appeared occasionally in films since the 50's. **Credits include:** *The Cruel Sea* (1953), *Time Without Pity* (1957), *The Loneliness of the Long Distance Runner* (1962), *The Agony and the Ecstasy* (1965), *The Devil's Own* (1967), *The Hawaiians* (1970).

JOEL McCREA (1905–   )

A native of Los Angeles, he spent several years as a film extra after graduating from Pomona College. Then a fine performance in *The Jazz Age* (1929) and several pictures (*Rockabye*, 1932, and *Bed of Roses,* 1933) with Constance Bennett turned him into one of the most popular leading men of the 30's.

Tall and ruggedly handsome, he bore a decided resemblance to Gary Cooper and, like Cooper, generally played laconic parts. After his great success in the title role of Hitchcock's *Foreign Correspondent* (1940), he turned with increasing frequency to Westerns. While many of these were second-rate, McCrea invariably gave solid perfrormances, and in *Ride the High Country* (1962) he was superlative, teamed with another old-timer, Randolph Scott. During the 50's McCrea was also familiar to television audiences—first as one of the original team on *Four Star*

Playhouse (1952) and then as Marshal Mick Dunbar in the 1959 series *Wichita Town*. A highly successful businessman and rancher, he was married to Frances Dee for over 30 years. **His films include:** *Private Worlds* (1935), *Barbary Coast* (1935), *Dead End* (1937), *Union Pacific* (1939), *The More the Merrier* (1943), *The Virginian* (1946), *Stranger on Horseback* (1955).

HATTIE McDANIEL (1895–1952)

A veteran of more than 40 films, she was the first black performer to win an Academy Award for Best Supporting Actress for her role as Mammy in *Gone With the Wind* (1939).

Born in Kansas, the thirteenth child of a Baptist minister, she made her movie debut in *The Golden West* (1932) after an extensive career as a vocalist on the vaudeville circuit. At the time of her death she was starring as Beulah in the popular TV series. **Some of her films include:** *I'm No Angel* (1933), *Alice Adams* (1935), *Show Boat* (1936), *The Great Lie* (1941), *Reap the Wild Wind* (1942), *Since You Went Away* (1944), *Mr. Blandings Builds His Dream House* (1948).

RODDY McDOWALL (1928–   )

One of the few child actors able to graduate successfully to adult roles, he made his movie debut at the age of eight in his native England in *Murder in the Family* (1936). With the advent of World War II, he emigrated to Hollywood, where he was signed up by 20th Century–Fox in 1940. The following year *How Green Was My Valley* (1941) established him as a major child star.

At 23, eternally typed in teenage roles, he left Hollywood for ten years to work on the stage and in TV until he returned to motion pictures in adult roles. He presently alternates between films and TV. **Some of his more than 50 films include:** *Man Hunt* (1941), *Lassie Come Home* (1943), *The Keys of the Kingdom* (1944), *Cleopatra* (1963), *Planet of the Apes* (1968), *The Poseidon Adventure* (1972).

MALCOLM McDOWELL (1943–   )

Critics thought he was sensational as Mick, the prep-school revolutionary McDowell

Joel McCrea's good looks and reliable performances brought him scores of film roles as the likable good guy. This scene was from The Silver Cord *(1932).*

Hattie McDaniel in The Little Colonel. *She almost always was cast as a Southern "mammy" or a kindly nurse.*

played in his film debut in Lindsay Anderson's *If . . .* (1969), and since then McDowell has scored equally impressive successes in the controversial Stanley Kubrick production of *A Clockwork Orange* (1972) and in *O, Lucky Man!* (1973).

McDowell, the son of a Leeds pub owner, said he always had intended to try acting "if all else failed." First, he helped his father run the pub and then worked for a while as a traveling salesman peddling coffee to English restaurants before deciding to join his girlfriend in studying acting. He progressed from three years with a repertory company on the Isle of Wight to the Royal Shakespeare Company. Then Lindsay Anderson spotted him on television and offered the role in *If . . .*

McDowell has ambitions to direct films "when I've accumulated enough knowledge" and maintains that "if you're semi-coherent, semi-intelligent you could not remain long an actor, unless you're content to let yourself become a monster. That's the only way to survive it." **Films include:**

Figures in a Landscape (1971), *Long Ago Tomorrow* (1971).

SPANKY McFARLAND (1928–   )

Best remembered as the "fat boy" regular of the *Our Gang* comedy series during the 30's and early 40's, George Emmett McFarland appeared in more than 150 feature films and shorts during his 13 years as a child star. Adulthood, however, destroyed his career. In 1957, some 14 years after his last picture, he sought employment with the following ad in a local trade journal: "Childhood (3–16) spent as leader of *Our Gang* comedies. Won't someone give me the opportunity to make a living in the business I love and know so well? Have beanie, will travel." **Other films include:** *Day of Reckoning* (1933), *Kidnapped* (1934), *The Trail of the Lonesome Pine* (1936), *Johnny Doughboy* (1943).

DARREN McGAVIN (1922–   )

This California-born actor was trained at the Neighborhood Playhouse School of Theatre and the Actors Studio in New York City. Although he played supporting roles in a number of films during the 50's and 60's, he is best known as a television actor and the hero of such TV series as *Crime Photographer* (1952), *Mike Hammer* (1958), *Riverboat* (1959), *The Outsider* (1968). **Film highlights:** *Summertime* (1955), *The Man With the Golden Arm* (1955), *Beau James* (1957), *Bullet for a Badman* (1964).

JOHN McGIVER (1913–   )

With his round, round face, balding pate, distinctive nasal speech and comic flair, this delightful character actor has enlivened nearly 20 films with his avuncular presence since his 1957 screen debut in *Love in the Afternoon.*

Although New York-born McGiver was a drama student in college, it wasn't until 1955 at the age of 42 that he gave up teaching to follow an acting career in earnest. Making his way from off-Broadway to television to films, he has worked steadily since. **Some of his films include:** *Breakfast at Tiffany's* (1961), *Mr. Hobbs Takes a Vacation* (1962), *The Manchurian Candidate* (1962), *Fitzwilly* (1967), *Midnight Cowboy* (1969).

Dorothy McGuire, in a typically sympathetic role, comforts a returning GI in Till the End of Time *(1946).*

DOROTHY McGUIRE (1918–   )

This fresh-faced heroine of numerous 40's and 50's films made her stage debut at 13 opposite Henry Fonda in *A Kiss for Cinderella* at the Omaha Community Playhouse in her home town. In 1938 she made her Broadway debut in *Our Town*. Three years later she was featured as the child bride of the hit comedy *Claudia*, and her career soared. After recreating her role with equal success in the 1943 film version of the Rose Franken play, she went on to appear in such films as *A Tree Grows in Brooklyn* (1945), *The Enchanted Cottage* (1945) and *Gentleman's Agreement* (1947), for which she won an Oscar nomination. Other good roles in good films followed through the 50's. In the last decade, however, most of her decreasing number of roles have been in indifferent pictures. **Highlights:** *The Spiral Staircase* (1946), *Three Coins in the Fountain* (1954), *Friendly Persuasion* (1956), *The Dark at the Top of the Stairs* (1960), *Swiss Family Robinson* (1960), *The Greatest Story Ever Told* (1964), *Flight of the Doves* (1971).

FRANK McHUGH (1899–   )

The fast-talking, sharp-voiced comedian comes close to holding a record for the most appearances on stage, screen, radio, and television. He made his stage debut at the age of 11 as a member of his family's stock company in *For Her Children's Sake* and his first Broadway appearance in the hit comedy *The Fall Guy* (1925). He was snapped up in Hollywood's desperate search for actors who could talk and made the first of a vast number of motion picture appearances in *Dawn Patrol* (1930). **More than 100 films include:** *The Front Page* (1931), *A Midsummer Night's Dream* (1935), *Boy Meets Girl* (1938), *Going My Way* (1944), *A Lion Is in the Streets* (1953), *Easy Come, Easy Go* (1967).

KENNETH McKENNA (1899–   )

He first made a name for himself on the Broadway stage shortly after World War I, and then went to Hollywood where he played his first screen role in *Miss Bluebeard* (1924) with Bebe Daniels. After a few more silents he returned to the stage, but the lure of the talkies sent him back to Hollywood to appear in *Pleasure Crazed* (1929) and several other early sound films. His performance in *Men Without Women* (1930) was particularly memorable. After three more years and some work as a director McKenna left the screen. After almost 30 years off-camera, he played some minor roles in the early 60's. **Other credits include:** *A Kiss in the Dark* (1925), *The Man Who Came Back* (1931), *High Time* (1960), *Judgment at Nuremberg* (1961).

LEO McKERN (1920–   )

Australian Leo McKern made his stage debut in his native Sydney in 1924 before going to London to join the Old Vic. He has since appeared extensively on both stage and screen. **Films include:** *All for Mary* (1955), *X the Unknown* (1956), *Time Without Pity* (1957), *The Mouse That Roared* (1959), *Mr. Topaze* (1961), *The Day the Earth Caught Fire* (1962), *A Jolly Bad Fellow* (1964), *Moll Flanders* (1965), *Help!* (1965), *A Man for All Seasons* (1966), *Decline and Fall* (1968).

VICTOR McLAGLEN (1886–1959)

Although he was a veteran of more than 150 films from his debut in *The Call of the Road* (1920) to his last picture, *The Abductors* (1957), he will always be remembered for his brilliant performance as Gypo in John Ford's classic *The Informer* (1935), which won him the Academy Award for Best Actor.

Born in Tunbridge Wells, England, he ran away from home at 14 to enlist in the Life Guards, went to Canada to prospect for gold, worked on a railroad and wandered about the world as a prizefighter and circus performer before being discovered by a film director. Arriving in the United States in 1924, he established himself as a leading screen actor in *What Price Glory?* (1926). Easily bridging the silent-talkies gap, he was active until his death. He was a regular member of John Ford's stock company and was directed by his son, Andrew, in his last film. **Some credits include:** *The Lost Patrol* (1934), *Forever and a Day* (1943), *The Foxes of Harrow* (1947), *The Quiet Man* (1952), *Lady Godiva* (1955), *Around the World in 80 Days* (1956).

Victor McLaglen, tough and talented, in Wee Willie Winkie.

Butterfly McQueen as the jittery house servant at Tara, in Gone With the Wind.

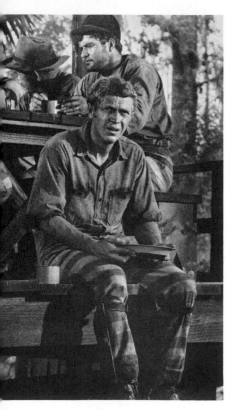

Steve McQueen as a shackled member of a chain gang in Nevada Smith.

HORACE McMAHON (1907–1971)

His craggy face, molded in a football accident at 16, fitted both the mobster and policeman roles he played in more than 125 feature films between 1937 and his death.

A veteran of stock and Broadway before going to Hollywood, he once said of his career, "I was generally a mob boss named Blackie. My pal was always Whitey. If the budget permitted there was a Rocky. Mostly I was behind bars, so often that Western Costumes had a 'Horace McMahon' tag sewn into a convict's striped suit." Oddly enough, he is likely to be best recalled as the older cop in the *Naked City* TV series. **Some of his credits include:** *Rose of Washington Square* (1939), *Birth of the Blues* (1941), *Detective Story* (1951), *My Sister Eileen* (1955), *The Swinger* (1966), *The Detective* (1968).

BUTTERFLY McQUEEN (1911–   )

She became famous as Prissy, the jittery black maid in *Gone With the Wind* (1939), a role which unfortunately typed and identified her for the rest of her career. Born Thelma McQueen in Florida, she was nicknamed Butterfly during her days with a Harlem dance group in the mid-30's. Once asked about her acting talent, she answered, "I used to recite whole books of the Bible forwards and backwards. All I knew as a child was church. It's a love of the theatre that is right out of the church." **Other films include:** *Cabin in the Sky* (1943), *Since You Went Away* (1944), *Mildred Pierce* (1945), *Duel in the Sun* (1947).

STEVE McQUEEN (1930–   )

One of the "anti-stars," McQueen lists with Newman, Hoffman and Redford as one of the top box-office draws. Whether playing the imperturbable Cooler King in *The Great Escape* (1963) or the taciturn cop in *Bullitt* (1968) or the daring bank robber in *The Getaway* (1972), McQueen brings to his roles an inner toughness, a quiet (sometimes almost imperceptible) humor, and a performance that is always technically and artistically interesting.

McQueen's early life smacks of soap opera. Product of a broken home, inmate of a reform school and jack-of-all-trades, McQueen's road to the screen was a rocky one. After a stint at the Actors Studio, he replaced Ben Gazzara in the Broadway production of *A Hatful of Rain*. His fine performance proved to be his entrée into the television world, and in 1958 he starred as bounty-hunter Josh Randall in the TV series *Wanted Dead or Alive*. This brought him to prominence and kicked off his screen career and his meteoric rise to stardom.

Like the other "anti-stars," McQueen prefers a secluded private life, but his marriage in 1973 to his *Getaway* costar Ali MacGraw made national headlines. **Films include:** *The Blob* (1958), *Never Love a Stranger* (1958), *The Magnificent Seven* (1960), *Soldier in the Rain* (1963), *Love With the Proper Stranger* (1963), *Nevada Smith* (1966), *The Sand Pebbles* (1966), *The Thomas Crown Affair* (1968), *Papillon* (1973).

PATRICIA MEDINA (1920–   )

Medina was a leading lady in her native England when she came to the United States in the mid-40's with her then husband, actor Richard Greene. Seen by Louis B. Mayer, he excitedly told her, ". . .only twice have I felt this way about anyone—Greer Garson and Mickey Rooney." To which she allegedly replied: "Greer Garson, I'm flattered, but I don't get the connection with Mickey Rooney." Mayer signed her, but became seriously ill before he was able to do anything about her career. Eventually, she appeared in more than 35 films. Presently married to Joseph Cotten, she still makes TV appearances and occasional films. **Films include:** *The Foxes of Harrow* (1947), *Valentino* (1951), *Botany Bay* (1953), *Mr. Arkadin* (1955), *The Killing of Sister George* (1968).

DONALD MEEK (1880–1946)

Slight, bald and quavery-voiced, he was the personification of the timid soul, the confused Mr. Milquetoast, in hundreds of films after his debut in *Hole in the Wall* (1929). Ironically, off screen the gifted comic was a strong and determined man who served in two wars, toured as an acrobat and loved boxing. Born in Scotland, this stage veteran made 20 films in a single year (1935), including *The Informer*, in which he played one of his first major parts. **Highlights:** *The Merry Widow* (1934), *You Can't Take It With You* (1938), *Stagecoach* (1939), *My Little Chickadee* (1940), *Keeper of the Flame* (1943), *Magic Town* (1947).

RALPH MEEKER (1920–)

This former soda jerk from Minnesota worked on the stage for nearly a decade and won a Theatre World Award for his 1947 performance in *Mister Roberts* before making his film debut in *Teresa* (1951). In addition to his film work, Meeker has made a number of television appearances, the first of which was as Sergeant Dekker in *Not for Hire* (1961). **Highlights:** *Desert Sands* (1955), *Paths of Glory* (1957), *Ada* (1961), *Something Wild* (1961), *The Dirty Dozen* (1967), *The Detective* (1968), *The Anderson Tapes* (1971).

THOMAS MEIGHAN (1879–1936)

Back in the dim, dear days of silents, he was among the five or six most popular leading men. His rugged Irish good looks were first revealed in motion pictures as early as 1915, but it was *The Miracle Man* (1919), in which he played opposite Betty Compson, and *Male and Female,* made in the same year, that transformed him into a top star. Sound pictures brought his career to an end. **Other films include:** *Heart of the Wilds* (1918), *The Easy Road* (1921), *Manslaughter* (1922), *Homeward Bound* (1923), *Blind Alleys* (1927), *Peck's Bad Boy* (1934).

LAURITZ MELCHIOR (1890–1973)

The famous tenor was born in Copenhagen and for a half century was one of the titans of the world of classical music. Late in his career he entered the fields of television and motion pictures. **Film credits:** *Two Sisters From Boston* (1946), *Luxury Liner* (1948), *The Stars Are Singing* (1953).

JOHN MELLION (1933–)

He played the supporting role of Swain in *On the Beach* (1959) and of Bluey in *The Sundowners* (1959), both American pictures filmed in his native Australia. Then Mellion moved to England, where he has continued to work as a character actor in British motion pictures and television. **Films include:** *Offbeat* (1960), *The Valiant* (1961), *Billy Budd* (1962), *The Running Man* (1963), *They're a Weird Mob* (1966).

ADOLPHE MENJOU (1890–1963)

Suave, impeccably dressed, elegantly mustached, he played the insouciant and cynical man of the world in upwards of 100 films. A native of Pittsburgh, Pennsylvania, he learned to speak eight languages and was a film extra as early as 1912, before the motion picture industry moved west. His first Hollywood appearance was in *The Faith Healer* (1921) but full recognition didn't come until Chaplin gave him a key part in *A Woman of Paris* (1923).

For the rest of the silent era he remained popular as a leading man, but with the coming of sound he gradually shifted to character and comedy parts—notably as the hard-bitten city editor in *The Front Page* (1931) and the city slicker to end all slickers in *Little Miss Marker* (1934). **Films include:** *The Sorrows of Satan* (1926), *Morocco* (1930), *A Star Is Born* (1937), *A Bill of Divorcement* (1940), *State of the Union* (1948), *Paths of Glory* (1957), *Pollyanna* (1960).

BERYL MERCER (1882–1939)

During her 16 years in films this British character actress usually played patient, long-suffering and understanding mothers, bringing tears to the eyes of those viewers who liked to indulge in super-sentimentality. More often than not, her movie sons turned out to be rotters. **More than 40 films include:** *The Christian* (debut, 1923), *Mother's Boy* (1929), *The Public Enemy* (1931), *Smilin' Through* (1932), *Night Must Fall* (1937), *A Woman Is the Judge* (1939).

MELINA MERCOURI (1925–)

Although this dynamic Greek actress had been acclaimed by Greek and French theatre audiences for a number of years, she did not become familiar to American audiences until she acted and sang in husband Jules Dassin's popular motion picture *Never on Sunday*

Donald Meek, who almost always played roles that fitted his name, nervously travels westward in John Ford's great film Stagecoach.

Adolphe Menjou, whose aristocratic hauteur usually concealed, at least partially, his talent for comedy.

Melina Mercouri and Maximilian Schell as two members of a gang who planned a marvelously ingenious jewel theft in Topkapi.

Burgess Meredith, with Claire Trevor just managing to get into the picture, seeks light at the end of the tunnel in Street of Chance *(1942).*

(1960). For her earthy performance as a "woman of pleasure," Mercouri won a Best Actress award at Cannes and was nominated for an Oscar. The member of a very old and distinguished Greek family (her father was mayor of Athens), she began her career studying classical Greek tragedy at the Academy of the National Theatre in Athens. In recent years she exiled herself from her native land as a protest against the existing regime. **Highlights:** *Stella* (1957), *He Who Must Die* (1958), *Phaedra* (1962), *Topkapi* (1964), *The Uninhibited* (1968).

BURGESS MEREDITH (1907–   )

His fine sensitive performances and poetic quality made him a great Broadway star from his 1933 role in *She Loves Me Not*, a debut which won him a Drama Critics' Award. Born in Ohio, he worked for a while with Eva Le Gallienne's repertory group and, between film assignments, acted and directed on Broadway. Since he was not the typical leading-man type, Hollywood did not know what to do with him. Thus, his two best film roles were ones he recreated from the Broadway stage—his screen debut, as Mio in *Winterset* (1936), and his portrayal of George in *Of Mice and Men* (1940).

A man of many talents, he not only wrote the screenplay for *Diary of a Chambermaid* (1945) but also co-produced it and starred in it opposite his then wife, Paulette Goddard.

In recent years he has divided his time between films and television—notably as Penguin in the *Batman* series. **Films include:** *Idiot's Delight* (1939), *The Story of G. I. Joe* (1945), *The Man on the Eiffel Tower* (1949), *Advise and Consent* (1962), *Hurry Sundown* (1966), *Such Good Friends* (1972).

UNA MERKEL (1903–   )

Today she is usually remembered for her portrayals of the heroine's flighty best friend in dozens of 30's pictures or for her motherly roles of later years. In fact, the blond Kentuckian got her start in films back in the silent era of the early 20's when her striking resemblance to Lillian Gish brought her to the attention of Charles Ray and led to work as the star's double. Her first substantial role came in 1930 when she played Ann Rutledge in the D. W. Griffith talkie *Abraham Lincoln*. Since then she has appeared in well over 50 films. Her finest performance was probably as Mrs. Winemiller (Geraldine Page's mother) in Tennessee Williams' *Summer and Smoke* (1961). P.S.: She was Dietrich's sparring partner in the celebrated barroom brawl in *Destry Rides Again* (1939). **Films include:** *Private Lives* (1931), *42nd Street* (1933), *The Merry Widow* (1934), *The Bride Goes Wild* (1948), *The Kentuckian* (1955), *Spinout* (1966).

ETHEL MERMAN (1908–   )

George Gershwin told the young Ethel Zimmerman never to take a singing lesson. Who knows what Cole Porter and Irving Berlin told her. Since the Broadway musical *Girl Crazy* (1930), when she stopped the show with "I've Got Rhythm," she has never stopped stopping the show. Although she made her screen debut in *Follow the Leader* (1930), films were never her medium. The screen could not contain her big, brassy voice and exuberant personality. She has been most successful on screen in recreating her stage roles, e.g., *Call Me Madam* (1953). The ex-stenographer from Astoria, Long Island, had to be content to be the long-reigning "Queen of American Musical Comedy." **Films include:** *Kid Millions* (1934), *Anything Goes* (1936), *Alexander's Ragtime Band* (1938), *There's No Business Like Show Business* (1954), *It's a Mad, Mad, Mad, Mad World* (1963).

DINA MERRILL (1925–)

Wife of actor Cliff Robertson, Merrill was born Nedinia Hutton in New York City of millionaire parents (her mother was Mrs. Merriweather Post). She made her film debut in *The Desk Set* (1957) with Tracy and Hepburn. In her film roles she was usually typecast as a cool, pretty blonde socialite. Since her first television appearance on the Kate Smith Show in 1956, Merrill has played in a variety of TV series, including *The Investigators*, *Checkmate* and *Cannon*. **Credits:** *Don't Give Up the Ship* (1959), *Butterfield 8* (1960), *The Sundowners* (1960), *The Young Savages* (1961), *I'll Take Sweden* (1965).

GARY MERRILL (1915–)

Merrill made his stage debut as a spear carrier in Max Reinhardt's *The Eternal Road* (1937), but did not enter films until 1949, when he appeared in *Slattery's Hurricane*. His role in *All About Eve* (1950) led to marriage with Bette Davis. They were subsequently divorced. In addition to his film roles, Merrill worked in radio programs like *Young Dr. Malone* and *Gangbusters* and has appeared on television a number of times. In 1968, he ran for a Republican nomination to Maine's House of Representatives. **Film Highlights:** *Twelve O'Clock High* (1949), *Decision Before Dawn* (1951), *The Pleasure of His Company* (1961), *A Girl Named Tamiko* (1962), *The Power* (1968).

KEITH MICHELL (1926–)

Although he has varied stage experience, particularly in Shakespearean roles, Michell

is probably most widely known for his TV performances in the BBC series *The Six Wives of Henry VIII*. Michell excelled in the demanding role as the King that called for him to portray the monarch first as a robust young ruler and, later, as a dying old man.

Michell began acting in his native Adelaide, Australia, where he made his stage debut in 1947 as Roger in *Lover's Leap*. Later, in England, he trained at the Old Vic and joined the Young Vic to play Bassanio in *The Merchant of Venice* (1950). He continued to appear in Shakespearean roles both in England and in Australia (with the Shakespeare Memorial Theatre Company). He made his American debut as Nestor/Oscar in *Irma La Douce* when it opened in Washington, D.C. Michell has starred in both motion picture and TV dramas. **Films include:** *True as a Turtle* (1957), *Dangerous Exile* (1957), *The Gypsy and the Gentlemen* (1958), *The Hellfire Club* (1961), *Seven Seas to Calais* (1963), *Prudence and the Pill* (1968), *House of Cards* (1968).

TOSHIRO MIFUNE (1920–)

When Akira Kurosawa's *Rashomon* (1950) opened, it established Kurosawa as one of the world's outstanding directors and Mifune, his leading man, as an international star. Mifune has since projected great force and magnetism in a wide variety of roles, but is probably most often remembered for his memorable performance in Kurosawa's spellbinding Academy Award winner *The Seven Samurai* (1954). Born in China, he broke into films by winning a "new faces" contest. Kurosawa saw him, trained him, and their 16 films together represent one of the most fruitful collaborations on record between a director and an actor. Besides being one of Japan's most notable actors, he has directed one feature and made his American debut in *Grand Prix* (1966). **Film highlights:** *The Lower Depths* (1957), *Throne of Blood* (1957), *Yojimbo* (1961), *Hell in the Pacific* (1968), *Tora! Tora! Tora!* (1970).

SARAH MILES (1941–)

The daughter of wealthy British parents, she is noted for her bluntness. After studying at Britain's Royal Academy of Dramatic Art

Ethel Merman, whose voice had a way of raising the rafters and bringing down the house, in Irving Berlin's Call Me Madam.

Gary Merrill and Anne Baxter in a fine film about a conniving climber in show biz, All About Eve.

Ray Milland thoroughly deserved the Oscar he won as a dipsomaniac in The Lost Weekend.

and being cast several times in British repertory, Miles made her first screen appearance in Sir Laurence Olivier's *Term of Trial* (1963) portraying "one of the most enviable roles any girl could ever want." Miles launched a successful film career which has thus far won her two Oscar nominations—one as Dirk Bogarde's amoral girlfriend in *The Servant* (1964) and one for the lead part in David Lean's *Ryan's Daughter* (1970). **Highlights:** *Blow-Up* (1966), *Lady Caroline Lamb* (1971), *The Man Who Loved Cat Dancing* (1973).

VERA MILES (1930–)

Born Vera Ralston in Boise City, Idaho, Miles made her debut in the Janet Leigh/Tony Martin comedy *Two Tickets to Broadway* (1951). Since then, she has given some fine supporting performances in close to 30 films, most of them mediocre, a few—e.g. *So Big* (1953) and *Psycho* (1960)—much better. In recent years, she has been playing fading beauties and mothers of difficult offspring, largely on television dramatic shows. **Credits:** *For Men Only* (1952), *23 Paces to Baker Street* (1956), *The F.B.I. Story* (1959), *The Man Who Shot Liberty Valance* (1962), *Gentle Giant* (1968).

JOHN MILJAN (1893–1960)

The slim, rather daintily mustached actor played supporting roles in more than 100 films and could usually be relied upon to do something extremely mean. He made his screen debut in the 1925 silent *Sackcloth and Scarlet* and 30 years later was still up to his old tricks in *The Pirates of Tripoli* (1955). **Other films include:** *Phantom of the Opera* (1925), *Innocents of Paris* (1929), *The Unholy Three* (1930), *King for a Night* (1933), *The Plainsman* (1937), *The Fallen Sparrow* (1943), *Mrs. Mike* (1950).

RAY MILLAND (1908–)

This outspoken Welsh-born leading man, originally named Reginald Truscott-Jones, served with the Household Cavalry of the British royal family before taking up acting in 1929 in a film called *Plaything*. After three decades and a number of movie successes, including an outstanding Oscar-winning per-

formance in *The Lost Weekend* (1945), Milland retired from the screen during the 60's to concentrate on his television career. A regular on TV from the 50's, Milland had his own show in 1955 and later starred in two series and directed a number of TV dramas. In 1971 the actor returned to the screen as Ryan O'Neal's father in *Love Story* with a performance which was overwhelmingly praised by critics in spite of the bad press generally accorded the film. **145 films include:** *Bought* (1931), *The Gilded Lily* (1935), *Beau Geste* (1939), *The Major and the Minor* (1942), *Lady in the Dark* (1944), *Kitty* (1946), *Dial M for Murder* (1954), *A Man Alone* (1955), *Frogs* (1972).

ANN MILLER (1919–)

Although her name immediately evokes memories of extra fast taps and heel clicks, the long-legged Texan who danced her way to fame in movie musicals had rickets as a child and took ballet and acrobatic lessons to overcome it. She had already made her screen debut in *The Devil on Horseback* (1936) and had done a few other films when she went to Broadway for *George White's Scandals of 1939*, stopped the show and went back to Hollywood as a star. There she remained until recent years, when she reappeared on stage and television. **Films include:** *Room Service* (1938), *Eadie Was a Lady* (1945), *Easter Parade* (1948), *Kiss Me, Kate!* (1953), *The Great American Pastime* (1956).

MARILYN MILLER (1898–1936)

Marilyn Reynolds (her stepfather's name was Miller) was born in Evansville, Indiana, and began her brilliant but too brief career as a toe dancer in musical revues. The fresh, warm and enormously talented singing and dancing star quickly established herself as one of the best-loved and most highly praised American beauties ever to perform on the Broadway stage. Old-timers still talk reverently of Miller in such Ziegfeld hits as *Sally* and *Sunny* and her rendition of such hits of the day as "Look for the Silver Lining."

She made her screen debut in the talkie version of *Sally* (1929). **Other credits include:** *Sunny* (1930), *Her Majesty, Love* (1931).

An enchanting Sarah Miles in Ryan's Daughter *(1970).*

PATSY RUTH MILLER (1904–)

Another leading lady of silents whose career disintegrated soon after the advent of sound, she first appeared on the screen in juvenile roles in films like *Camille* (1915). Her best role came in the early 20's, and old-timers will remember her as the terrified heroine who cringed from Lon Chaney in *The Hunchback of Notre Dame* (1923). Although she continued to make movies into the early 30's, most of her later films were "B"-minus productions. Her only appearance in the last 40 years was in *Quebec* (1951). **Films include:** *Remembrance* (1922), *Daughters of Today* (1924), *So This Is Paris* (1926), *The First Auto* (1927), *Twin Beds* (1929), *Lonely Wives* (1931).

HAYLEY MILLS (1946–)

The London-born daughter of actor John Mills was 12 when film director J. Lee Thompson, who was about to film *Tiger Bay* starring a little boy, saw her amusing herself by doing a burlesque of a television commercial. He promptly changed the film's lead to a little girl. This launched her into a career which included a Disney contract and many juvenile parts through the early 60's. More recently she has made the transition to adult roles, among them stage appearances in Chekhov and Ibsen dramas. **Films include:** *Pollyanna* (1960), *Whistle Down the Wind* (1962), *The Chalk Garden* (1964), *Twisted Nerve* (1968), *Mr. Forbush and the Penguins* (1971).

JOHN MILLS (1908–)

Mills, father of actresses Hayley and Juliet Mills and husband of playwright Mary Hayley Bell Mills, made his stage debut in 1929 when he was cast in the chorus of *The Five O'Clock Girl*. A film debut (*The Midshipmaid*) came four years later for Mills, who is consistently praised by critics for the honesty of his portrayals. After 40 years in starring roles, Mills won his first Oscar for Best Supporting Actor for his character role as Michael, the mute village idiot, in *Ryan's Daughter* (1970). **Highlights:** *The Lash* (1934), *Goodbye, Mr. Chips* (1939), *In Which We Serve* (1942), *Great Expectations* (1946), *War and Peace* (1956), *Tunes of*

Ann Miller as an ingénue and Kenny Baker looking ingenuous in the dimly recalled 1938 production Radio City Revels.

John Mills (left) as a German submarine commander in Above Us the Waves *(1954). The name of the other actor escapes us.*

356

Liza Minnelli, a great star in her mid-20's, as Sally Bowles in Cabaret.

There was never a balancing act like Carmen Miranda's, which may or may not have been a good thing.

Glory (1960), *Dulcima* (1971), *Oklahoma Crude* (1973).

YVETTE MIMIEUX (1942–   )

Throughout her film career, the lovely blonde Californian has given the impression that she might become a top-flight actress if cast in less indifferent roles. Her debut was in *The Time Machine* (1960), and viewers caught a glimpse of her true potential when, two years after that, she played the retarded girl in *The Light in the Piazza*. She has also appeared frequently on television in recent years. **Films include:** *Where the Boys Are* (1961), *Diamond Head* (1963), *Toys in the Attic* (1963), *Joy in the Morning* (1965), *Dark of the Sun* (1968).

SAL MINEO (1939–   )

Born Salvatore Mineo in New York's Bronx County, this casketmaker's son was actually a juvenile street fighter who was expelled from school at nine before he was cast in a series of films as a juvenile delinquent. In 1955 Mineo won an Oscar nomination for his role in *Rebel Without a Cause*, which included a street fight scene. "I wasn't really acting," the actor said after the film was released "I guess I was still running away from those punks in New York." More recently Mineo has turned to producing and directing his own films and plays. In 1969 he restaged and directed *Fortune and Men's Eyes*, a study of prison life. **Highlights:** *Giant* (1956), *Crime in the Streets* (1956), *Exodus* (1960), *The Longest Day* (1962), *The Greatest Story Ever Told* (1964).

LIZA MINNELLI (1946–   )

The daughter of Judy Garland and Vincente Minnelli made her screen debut at the age of two with her mother in *In the Good Old Summer Time* (1949). At the age of 26 she played Sally Bowles in *Cabaret* (1972) and won the Academy Award for Best Actress of the Year. Ironically, she had been turned down for the Broadway version after numerous auditions. In between she worked since the age of 15 in stock, off-Broadway, on Broadway, in supper clubs and on television until she made her adult screen debut in *Charlie Bubbles* (1968). Projecting a combi-

nation of wise innocence, vulnerable toughness and melancholy gaiety, she has made hit recordings and been featured in highly successful TV specials. In 1973, Minnelli's three-week New York concert engagement was sold out within 36 hours. She received standing ovations from the audiences and raves from the critics. **Films include:** *The Sterile Cuckoo* (1969), *Tell Me You Love Me, Junie Moon* (1970).

MARY MILES MINTER (1902–   )

From 1912 to 1923, Mary Miles Minter starred in 52 films. She was the winsome, waif-like type whose popularity for a time almost equalled Mary Pickford's. She was involved in the William Desmond Taylor murder scandal and subsequent legal battles with her mother, and her career failed to survive the publicity. **Films include:** *The Nurse* (1912), *Dimples* (1916), *Anne of Green Gables* (1919), *The Trail of the Lonesome Pine* (1923).

CARMEN MIRANDA (1909–1955)

With *Down Argentine Way* (1940) an outrageous tornado hit the screen. With her bare midriff, platform shoes, and turbaned head (topped by the entire inventory of a fruit store) she sang and sambaed her way to popularity in 20th Century–Fox musicals. She was born in Portugal, but her family moved to Rio de Janeiro when Miranda was three months old. She got her start on a local radio station there, and before long the tiny Brazilian Bombshell was the rage of South America. She was spied by the Shuberts and made her Broadway debut in *The Streets of Paris* (1939). An extremely gifted comedienne, she died of a heart attack at the age of 46. **Films include:** *Weekend in Havana* (1941), *The Gang's All Here* (1943), *Four Jills in a Jeep* (1944), *Something for the Boys* (1944), *Copacabana* (1947), *Scared Stiff* (1953).

ISA MIRANDA (1909–   )

She was one of Italy's most popular film stars and described by D'Annunzio as "the most glamorous woman in the world" when she was imported by Hollywood in the late 30's to make her debut in *Hotel Imperial* (1939). Her talent and value were not appreciated and she soon returned to Europe. A former stenographer and model, she gained her first major success in Max Ophul's *La Signora di Tutti* (1934) and one of her best post-war roles was in *The Walls of Malapaga* (1950), which won her the Cannes Film Festival Award for Best Actress. **Films include:** *Adventure in Diamonds* (1940), *La Ronde* (1950), *Summertime* (1955), *The Yellow Rolls-Royce* (1965).

CAMERON MITCHELL (1918-   )

This minister's son made his first appearance at the age of 20 when he portrayed a 70-year-old professor in *At a Certain Hour* (1938). He subsequently went on to play a number of juvenile roles in the legitimate theatre, eventually making his film debut in 1945 (*They Were Expendable*). Most recently he has appeared in a number of Mexican-made Westerns. **Highlights:** *Death of a Salesman* (1951), *Désirée* (1954), *Carousel* (1956), *The Task of Vengeance* (1971).

GRANT MITCHELL (1875-1957)

This character actor turned to drama only after having tried his hand at newspaper reporting and law. A graduate of Andover, Yale University and Harvard Law School, Mitchell worked briefly as a reporter and practiced law for three years before studying at the American Academy of Dramatic Arts in New York. Although he made his stage debut in 1902 (*Julius Caesar*), Mitchell did not shift to cinema until the early 30's, when talkies were beginning to shake up the movie industry. In Hollywood his high forehead and "disarmingly bland" face won him comic roles as vague, well-meaning little men. Occasionally though he submerged his comic bent to portray bland-looking fiends. **Highlights:** *Three on a Match* (1932), *A Midsummer Night's Dream* (1935), *My Sister Eileen* (1942), *Arsenic and Old Lace* (1944), *It Happened on Fifth Avenue* (1947).

JAMES MITCHELL (1920-   )

He had two film careers. In the early 40's he danced anonymously with such stars as Maria Montez in *Cobra Woman* (1944) and in the production numbers of *Ziegfeld Follies*

Thomas Mitchell as Gerald O'Hara with daughter Scarlett (Vivien Leigh) after Union troops have overrun their plantation in Gone With the Wind.

(1945). Then he came east, made his Broadway debut in *Bloomer Girl* (1945) and as Harry Beaton in *Brigadoon* (1947) danced and sang his way to prominence and a second screen career as a featured player in films like *Colorado Territory* (1949). In later years he appeared on television, most notably as Dr. Hathaway in *Where the Heart Is*. **Films include:** *Border Incident* (1949), *Stars in My Crown* (1950), *Deep in My Heart* (1954), *Oklahoma!* (1955).

THOMAS MITCHELL (1892-1962)

An ex-reporter, Broadway actor and playwright, he became one of the great motion picture character actors, equally at home in comedy and drama. His talent enabled him to inject substance, credibility and power into any role. After his debut in *Craig's Wife* (1936) he appeared in some of the best films of the next 20 years. Mitchell played Scarlett O'Hara's father in *Gone With the Wind* (1939) and won an Academy Award for Best Supporting Actor for his portrayal of the tipsy doctor in *Stagecoach* (1939). **More than 60**

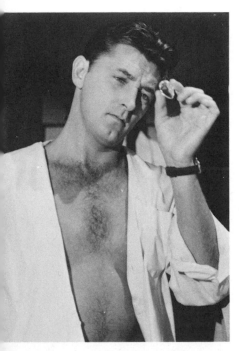

Robert Mitchum appraises a king-sized diamond in Macao.

A hauntingly beautiful shot of Marilyn in her last film, The Misfits.

films include: *Lost Horizon* (1937), *Our Town* (1940), *This Above All* (1942), *Wilson* (1944), *High Noon* (1952), *Pocketful of Miracles* (1961).

ROBERT MITCHUM (1917–   )

A veteran of more than 60 films, this gentle, soft-spoken actor fought his way to stardom, starting with bit parts in Hopalong Cassidy features on through such military epics as *Gung Ho!* (1943) and *The Story of G. I. Joe* (1945). Of his career, the versatile Mitchum pointed out that he has played "everything except women and midgets." Born in Bridgeport, Connecticut, he has mostly been cast as a hard-bitten soldier, cowboy or out-and-out villain. This is probably because of a vaguely belligerent expression and air of one who smells something slightly unpleasant. **Highlights:** *The Human Comedy* (1943), *Thirty Seconds Over Tokyo* (1944), *The Red Pony* (1949), *Track of the Cat* (1954), *The Sundowners* (1960), *Anzio* (1968), *Ryan's Daughter* (1970).

TOM MIX (1880–1940)

This former cowboy and hero of early Western film thrillers fought in the Spanish American War and the Boxer Rebellion and served as sheriff in Kansas and Oklahoma before beginning his show-business career with a Wild West show in 1906. Even during his quarter-century reign as the world's greatest cowboy star, with his famous horse, Tony, Mix never lost his lust for raw action. Once while on location in Arizona he left his movie company to join a local posse trailing a murderer and single-handedly subdued the killer in a fist fight. Mix never used a stand-in for stunts and took delight in inventing progressively more daring feats to perform in his films. Identified with motion pictures from 1910 on, the actor dropped out for a time when talkies arrived, but returned to the screen for a few films in the early 30's. From 1933 until his death in 1940, Mix managed his own circus and Wild West show. **Highlights:** *Treat 'Em Tough* (1918), *Just Tony* (1922), *The Deadwood Coach* (1925), *Dick Turpin* (1925), *Destry Rides Again* (1927), *Terror Trail* (1933).

WILLIAM V. MONG (1875–1940)

He made nearly 50 films, playing a wide variety of character roles in films as different as *Noah's Ark* (1929) and *The Vampire Bat* (1933). His debut was made in *A Connecticut Yankee in King Arthur's Court* (1921). **Other credits include:** *What Price Glory?* (1926), *Gunsmoke* (1931), *The Sign of the Cross* (1932), *Treasure Island* (1934), *Painted Desert* (1938).

MARILYN MONROE (1926–1962)

One of the most publicized and most talked-about luminaries in the history of motion pictures actually appeared in only 22 films, in most of which she gave a something less than overwhelming performance. Her miserable family background, her marriages, her friends in high places, her dazzling blonde beauty with a hint of total vulnerability behind the sensuous facade—all of these combined to make her life and tragic death front-page news around the globe.

Born Norma Jean Baker (or Mortenson) in Los Angeles, the product of a broken home with a family history of mental illness, she first attracted public attention with two appearances in 1950—*All About Eve* and *The Asphalt Jungle*. She instantly became the pin-up queen supreme, whose tiny baby-talk voice and luminous stare perfectly fitted such vehicles as *Gentlemen Prefer Blondes* (1953) and *How to Marry a Millionaire* (1953). It wasn't until *The Seven Year Itch* (1955), however, that she was finally acknowledged to be a talented comedienne who could really *act*. She reached the peak of her career in *Some Like It Hot* (1959), but by that time she was becoming more and more difficult to work with, headed down the tragic road that led to her death from an overdose of sleeping pills. Her last appearance, in *The Misfits* (1961), was roughly handled by critics when it appeared but has since been re-evaluated. **Other films include:** *Clash by Night* (1952), *Bus Stop* (1956), *The Prince and the Showgirl* (1957), *Let's Make Love* (1960).

RICARDO MONTALBAN (1920–   )

Although a talented actor, he rarely managed to escape the "Latin Lover" roles in which Hollywood stubbornly cast him. Born in Mexico City but moving to Los Angeles in his teens, he appeared on the Broadway stage and made films in Mexico before making his Hollywood debut in *Fiesta* (1947). In recent years he returned to the stage and appeared frequently on television. **Films include:** *The Kissing Bandit* (1948), *Battleground* (1949), *Sayonara* (1957), *Madame X* (1966), *Sol Madrid* (1968), *Sweet Charity* (1969), *The Last Three Days of Pancho Villa* (1973).

YVES MONTAND (1921–)

A protégé of Edith Piaf, he began as a singer in small music halls and became one of France's leading popular vocalists. Later he was recognized as a distinguished international star, a master at portraying sensitive and politically committed men. He was born in Italy but moved to France before World War II and first won recognition in Clouzot's *The Wages of Fear* (1952, U.S. 1955). Coming to Hollywood in the early 60's, he was constantly miscast and never able to project the qualities that brought him such acclaim in Europe. In recent years, he was outstanding in two Costa-Gavras films: *Z* (1969) and *State of Siege* (1973). He married Simone Signoret in 1950 and later they appeared in films together. **Films include:** *Etoiles sans Lumière* (debut, 1945), *Les Portes de la Nuit* (1946, U.S. 1950), *The Witches of Salem* (1958), *Let's Make Love* (1960), *My Geisha* (1962), *La Guerre Est Finie* (1966), *L'Aveu* (1970), *Caesar et Rosalie* (1973).

MARIA MONTEZ (1920–1951)

Although she was nearly as popular as Hayworth and Grable as a pin-up girl in wartime barracks, the appalling screenplays she acted in were almost all Arabian Nightmares. Commenting on one of her Scheherazade-type roles, a critic observed: "It should have been called Aladdin and His Wonderful Vamp."

She was born in the Dominican Republic, the daughter of the local Spanish consul. After some theatrical work in Europe she became a New York model. Her stunning face and body brought about her screen debut in *The Invisible Woman* (1941). The films that followed, from *South of Tahiti* (1941) to

Marilyn and her all-girl band, which turned out to have two male musicians. The film was Billy Wilder's very funny Some Like It Hot.

Pirates of Monterey (1947), might well have remained invisible as well.

She and her husband, Jean Pierre Aumont, returned to Europe, where she made a number of French and Italian films, no one of which caused dancing in the streets. She began to diet and to take hot salt-water baths to lose poundage and died of a heart attack while taking one. **Credits include:** *Boss of Bullion City* (1941), *That Night in Rio* (1941), *Bombay Clipper* (1942), *Arabian Nights* (1942), *Cobra Woman* (1944), *The Exile* (1947).

GEORGE MONTGOMERY (1916–)

A former husband of Dinah Shore, Montgomery made his film debut riding astride a silver saddle in *The Cisco Kid and the Lady* (1939). His 26-year movie career spanned a variety of roles in Westerns, romances, adventures and war films. He retired from films to go into the furniture business. **Highlights:**

Yves Montand as he looked playing opposite Ingrid Bergman in Goodbye Again *(1961).*

George Montgomery with Dorothy Lamour in Lulu Belle *(1948), the saga of a lady whose morals were slightly suspect.*

Robert Montgomery, early in his career, along with May Robson and Joan Crawford in Letty Lynton *(1932).*

Stardust (1940), *Roxie Hart* (1942), *Sword of Monte Cristo* (1951), *The Battle of the Bulge* (1965).

ROBERT MONTGOMERY (1904–   )

A leading man in motion pictures for many years, he was too often cast as the sophisticated pursuer of beautiful ladies in lightweight comedies. Intelligent and highly vocal, he showed his full capability as the psychotic killer in *Night Must Fall* (1937), a role Metro had given him as a sort of punishment for his truculence toward studio executives.

Montgomery appeared in stage roles during the 20's and made his film debut in a rah-rah musical entitled *So This Is College* in 1929. Apart from making at least 60 films, he was president of the Screen Actors Guild, played a key role in exposing mobsters who were infiltrating film unions, had a distinguished war record and as television adviser to President Eisenhower helped Ike to improve a somewhat less than overwhelming speaking technique. The versatile actor was also a producer and director of plays, a radio commentator, a social reformer and for years presided over two highly successful television dramatic series. When the Eisenhower administration ended, he turned to the business world and was equally successful as an industrialist and happy at the success of his daughter Elizabeth, who starred in *Bewitched*, a highly successful television series. **Films include:** *Private Lives* (1931), *Night Flight* (1933), *Yellow Jack* (1938), *Mr. and Mrs. Smith* (1941), *Here Comes Mr. Jordan* (1941), *They Were Expendable* (1945), *June Bride* (1948).

RON MOODY (1926–   )

This explosive British actor almost became a school teacher. After obtaining a degree in sociology, he was seen in a London School of Economics revue by Peter Myers and Ronald Cass, who promptly offered him a part in one of their productions. Recognition came quickly for this versatile actor, who is perhaps most familiar to American audiences for his stage (1960) and screen (1968) portrayal of Fagin in the musical *Oliver!* In 1971, the actor wrote and directed his own stage musical,

Saturnalia. **Highlights:** *Follow a Star* (1961), *The Mouse on the Moon* (1963), *Murder Most Foul* (1965).

COLLEEN MOORE (1902–   )

She had been doing well in films for some years when *Flaming Youth* (1923) established her as a reigning movie queen of the Roaring Twenties. Flappers the world round imitated her boyish bobbed hair, her casual gamin look, flat-bosomed and corsetless. Even as they raised the hemlines of their own skirts to the knee and beyond, countless mothers worried whether *their* daughters were, like Colleen Moore, doing these dreadful dances and drinking that awful bathtub gin.

Unfortunately her career did not survive sound and after a few talkies she retired. In 1968 she published her autobiography, *Silent Star*. **Films include:** *So Big* (1925), *Ella Cinders* (1926), *Naughty but Nice* (1927), *Lilac Time* (1928), *Why Be Good?* (1929), *The Power and the Glory* (1933), *The Scarlet Letter* (1934).

DICKIE MOORE (1925–   )

The former child star made his screen debut at the age of two in *The Beloved Rogue* (1927) and was featured in the *Our Gang* film series from 1932 to 1938. At 16, Moore received an award for the best juvenile performance of 1941 for his role in *Sergeant York*. After serving in World War II Moore, in addition to film appearances in character roles, began to produce pictures. His film *The Boy and the Eagle* was nominated for an Oscar in 1950. **Highlights:** *No Greater Love* (1932), *Little Men* (1935), *The Member of the Wedding* (1952), *Eight Iron Men* (1953).

GRACE MOORE (1903–1947)

Like many other of their convictions, the belief of movie magnates that the public wouldn't pay money at the box office to listen to operatic singers fell flat on its face when *Love Me Forever* (1935) made Grace Moore a star. It also dispelled the notion that people who had appeared in the Metropolitan Opera House had, of necessity, ample bosoms and even ampler behinds, for Moore was slim and pleasant to look upon.

Born in Tennessee, she had appeared in such shows as the 1924 *Music Box Revue,* introducing Irving Berlin's "What'll I Do. . ." and appeared in two flop films before she made *One Night of Love* (1934), which brought her an Oscar nomination.

Moore retired from films in 1940. Seven years later she was killed in an air crash at Copenhagen airport. She was semi-immortalized in a film biography of her life, *So This Is Love* (1953), starring Kathryn Grayson. **Other credits:** *A Lady's Morals* (debut, 1930), *New Moon* (1930), *When You're in Love* (1937), *Louise* (1939).

MARY TYLER MOORE (1937–   )

Though she studied to be a dancer, Moore achieved popularity as a television actress. She made her TV debut as a disembodied pair of legs and a sexy voice in the part of the telephone operator, Sam, in the *Richard Diamond* series. She is best known for her role as Laura in the long-running series *The Dick Van Dyke Show* and for her starring role as Mary Richards on the award-winning *Mary Tyler Moore Show.*

Her most notable movie portrayal was that of the "sweet young thing" friend of Julie Andrews' *Thoroughly Modern Millie* (1967). In this role Moore's toothsome smile and feminine prettiness were utilized to the utmost in creating her appealing comic character. **Films include:** *X-15* (debut, 1962), *What's So Bad About Feeling Good?* (1968), *Don't Just Stand There* (1968).

ROGER MOORE (1928–   )

For years Moore starred as the Saint—in the TV series with the same name—a super-sophisticated sleuth who always managed to stumble across murder, intrigue and mayhem in exotic world capitals or at the playgrounds of the very rich. In 1973, however, he attempted to trade in that image for the equally slick but more rough-and-tumble screen status of James Bond in *Live and Let Die* (1973).

Moore was born in London and studied acting at the Royal Academy of Dramatic Art but got his first film break in Hollywood. He appeared in *The Last Time I Saw Paris* (1955) and *Interrupted Melody* (1955) before returning to England for a television series,

Ivanhoe. He made a few more films and did another series, *The Alaskans,* before devoting seven years to playing in *The Saint.* When the series was finally abandoned in 1969, Moore co-produced and starred in still another television intrigue-type show, *The Persuaders.* **Films include:** *The King's Thief* (1956), *Diane* (1957), *The Miracle* (1959), *Gold of the Seven Saints* (1961), *Crossplot* (1969).

TOM MOORE (1885–1955)

He was one of three brothers all of whom enjoyed a considerable degree of success in the era of silents. His brothers were Matt and Owen. Owen for a while was married to Mary Pickford. One of Tom's first appearances was in *The Primrose Ring* (1917). **Films include:** *Big Brother* (1923), *The Song and Dance Man* (1926), *Trouble for Two* (1936), *The Redhead and the Cowboy* (1951).

VICTOR MOORE (1876–1962)

Short and pudgy, with an amiable smile that betrayed total helplessness, he created the prototype for the well-meaning bumbler who always got the worst of everything.

He began his acting career at 17 by brazenly answering a call for tall men to play in *Babes in the Woods.* A veteran of vaudeville and Broadway, his most memorable role was the vice president whose name no one could remember in *Of Thee I Sing.* He began his film career in 1915 and alternated thereafter between Hollywood and the New York stage. **Films include:** *The Clown* (1916), *Swing Time* (1936), *Louisiana Purchase* (1942), *Duffy's Tavern* (1945), *We're Not Married* (1952), *The Seven Year Itch* (1955).

AGNES MOOREHEAD (1906–1974)

One of the top character actresses of the stage and screen, adept at portraying an assortment of strained and neurotic women, she was nominated for the Academy Award four times since her film debut in Orson Welles' *Citizen Kane* (1941). Surprisingly, she never won.

A graduate of the American Academy of Dramatic Arts, she was an established radio actress when Welles chose her as his leading lady for the Mercury Theatre. During a career

Colleen Moore, a bob-haired favorite of silent films, in the 1926 version of a long-lived favorite, Irene.

The late Agnes Moorehead, a superb character actress, in The True Story of Jesse James *(1957).*

Sensitive and seductive, here is Jeanne Moreau in the fairly recent whodunit The Bride Wore Black.

Dennis Morgan as a fast-draw artist in The Gun That Won the West.

that spanned more than 60 films she returned occasionally to the stage and played Endora in the *Bewitched* TV series for five years. **Film highlights include:** *The Magnificent Ambersons* (1942), *Mrs. Parkington* (1944), *Johnny Belinda* (1948), *All That Heaven Allows* (1956), *Hush. . .Hush, Sweet Charlotte* (1964), *Charlotte's Web* (voice only, 1972).

POLLY MORAN (1884–1952)

Years before she played Sheriff Nell in the old Keystone comedies of early silent days, she was internationally famous as a comedienne on vaudeville stages in the United States and in Europe and as a musical-comedy star.

The vivacious and somewhat toothy comedienne moved easily into the new world of talkies in *Caught Short* (1930) and subsequently was teamed with Marie Dressler on several occasions to produce one of the funniest twosomes ever to appear on film. **Films include:** *Reducing* (1931), *The Passionate Plumber* (1932), *Adam's Rib* (1949).

JEANNE MOREAU (1928–   )

Weary-eyed and ultrasensuous, Moreau has few peers today in portraying extreme emotional intensity on the screen. The French actress has often been compared to Bette Davis. The product of a French father and English-Irish mother, she became at 20 the youngest member of the illustrious Comédie Française and made her first screen appearance in *Last Love* (1949). She appeared in a number of pictures with indifferent success and didn't attain international recognition until the Louis Malle film *The Lovers* (1959). She has since worked with the screen's top directors, among them Antonioni, Truffaut, Buñuel and Welles, making both English- and French-speaking pictures. **Films include:** *Démoniaque* (1958), *La Notte* (1960), *Les Liaisons Dangereuses* (1961), *Jules et Jim* (1962), *Viva Maria* (1965), *The Bride Wore Black* (1968), *Monte Walsh* (1970).

MANTAN MORELAND (1901–1973)

A gifted comedian who became best known as the chauffeur, Birmingham Brown, in the *Charlie Chan* series, he would convulse audiences with his gravelly voice, his pop-eyed expression and his trademark line: "Feets, do your stuff." Born in Louisiana, he ran away at 14 to join a circus and was appearing in vaudeville when Joe Louis saw him and helped him land his first movie role. A veteran of more than 100 films, he distinguished himself on Broadway in an all-black revival of *Waiting for Godot* (1957). **Films include:** *Spirit of Youth* (1938), *Cabin in the Sky* (1943), *Pin Up Girl* (1944), *Sky Dragon* (1949), *Rockin' the Blues* (1956), *Enter Laughing* (1967).

ANTONIO MORENO (1889–1967)

Born Antonio Garride Monteagudo in Madrid, Moreno emigrated to New York in 1901 and worked on the legitimate stage before beginning his film career. The actor's dark good looks made him popular as a Latin lover in the 20's, when he was cast opposite such leading ladies as Greta Garbo, Gloria Swanson, Bebe Daniels and Marion Davies. With the advent of the talkies, however, Moreno's heavy Spanish accent caused him considerable difficulty; nonetheless, he went on to make scores of movies, generally cast in supporting roles. The last of the films Moreno made over a 40-year career included several Spanish-language features. **Highlights:** *My American Wife* (1922), *The Exciters* (1923), *The Temptress* (1926), *The Bohemian Girl* (1936), *Seven Sinners* (1940), *Crisis* (1950), *Thunder Bay* (1953), *The Searchers* (1956).

RITA MORENO (1931–   )

Since her 1950 screen debut in *So Young, So Bad* this talented actress and gifted comedienne from Puerto Rico has been cast in every conceivable ethnic role from Mexican to Thai to Rumanian gypsy. Her performance as Anita in *West Side Story* (1961) won her an Academy Award for Best Supporting Actress. Moreno has done some of her best work off the screen in the *Electric Company* TV series and on stage when she won the Chicago Critics' Award for her performance in *The Rose Tattoo* (1969). **Films include:** *Singin' in the Rain* (1952), *Garden of Evil* (1954), *The King and I* (1956), *Summer and Smoke* (1961), *Popi* (1969).

DENNIS MORGAN (1910–   )

Born Stanley Morner in Wisconsin, he had considerable experience as a concert singer before making his screen debut in *I Conquer the Sea* (1936). He was not getting far playing in second-rate pictures until Warner Brothers signed him and renamed him Dennis Morgan. His career picked up and, after being loaned out to RKO for *Kitty Foyle* (1940), he became a popular leading man who even sang in some of his films. **More than 50 pictures include:** *The Hard Way* (1943), *The Desert Song* (1943), *My Wild Irish Rose* (1947), *This Woman Is Dangerous* (1952), *The Gun That Won the West* (1955), *Rogue's Gallery* (1968).

FRANK MORGAN (1890–1949)

He was born Francis Phillip Wuppermann in New York City and took his place in film legend as the humbug wizard in *The Wizard of Oz* (1939). In silent films since 1917, Morgan saw his popularity mushroom with the advent of sound. His robust laughter and unique cracked voice fitted him perfectly for character parts requiring lovable personalities or old rogues. Before making his screen debut in *A Modern Cinderella* (1917) he was a professionally successful boy soprano. Vaudeville and stock eventually led to Broadway in such hits as *Rosalie* (1928) and *The Bandwagon* (1931). A shameless scene stealer, Frank Morgan was also an authority on film acting and wrote articles on the subject. **More than 100 films include:** *Queen High* (1930), *Reunion in Vienna* (1933), *The Great Ziegfeld* (1936), *The Human Comedy* (1943), *Key to the City* (released after his death, 1950).

MICHÈLE MORGAN (1920–   )

Morgan was already an established French film star when she fled Paris in 1940, two days before the beginning of the Nazi occupation. In 1944 a critic described her as an actress with ''a nice honest face that acquires incredible nuances of Gallic oomph once it gets translated into celluloid.'' In 1962 Morgan complained that she had been miscast as well as hurled into second-rate films, likening her fate in American cinema to that of such ac-

tresses as Sophia Loren and Gina Lollobrigida. **Highlights:** *Port of Shadows* (French, 1937), *The Grand Maneuver* (1946), *The Fallen Idol* (1949), *The Vintage* (1957), *There's Always a Price Tag* (1958), *The Mirror Has Two Faces* (1959), *Why Are You So Late?* (1959), *Benjamin* (1968).

RALPH MORGAN (1882–1956)

Morgan was born in New York, brother of Frank and one of 11 children of George Wuppermann, importer of Angostura bitters. Educated at the Trinity School and at Columbia University, Morgan gave up his career as a lawyer to become an actor. He had appeared on the stage for nearly a decade and made occasional films when his Broadway role as Tom Powers in O'Neill's *Strange Interlude* (1931) won him a bid from Hollywood to play in the movie version (1932). In films as in the theatre, Morgan played leads but was most often in demand for his reliable work in supporting roles. **Highlights:** *The Man Who Found Himself* (1925), *Rasputin* (1932), *The*

Michele Morgan, another talented contribution of France to the film-making scene.

Frank Morgan and Elizabeth Taylor, back in the days when Liz was a juvenile actress, Frank Morgan was already a veteran and Lassie was braver than usual, in The Courage of Lassie *(1946).*

Chester Morris as the sleuth and a whispering George E. Stone as his whispering Sancho Panza in Boston Blackie Goes to Hollywood.

The highly engaging Robert Morley, who in recent years has been assuring TV viewers that a certain airline will take good care of them, as he appeared in Oscar Wilde.

Power and the Glory (1933), The Fledgling (1940), Song of the Thin Man (1947), Blue Grass of Kentucky (1950).

MICHAEL MORIARTY (1941–   )

Moriarty catapulted to fame with his first role in the hit film Bang the Drum Slowly (1973). The young actor followed his much praised performance with a starring role in the Broadway drama Find Your Way Home, (1973), which won for him ecstatic notices and a Tony Award for Best Actor. Moriarty began his acting career in summer stock, with the Charles Street Players in Boston and with the Tyrone Guthrie Theatre in Minneapolis. In addition to stage and screen work, he has appeared on television, notably in the TV movie Summer Without Boys (1973). **Film credits:** The Last Detail (1973).

KAREN MORLEY (1905–   )

Popular in the early days of the talkies, she will be remembered as gangster Paul Muni's moll in Scarface (1932). A victim of the House Un-American Activities Committee, Morley was named as a fellow-traveler of the Communist Party in the early 50's and invoked the Fifth Amendment. Her career suffered accordingly. She retired after making nearly 30 pictures, most of them in the adventure category. **Films include:** Thru Different Eyes (1929), Inspiration (1931), Dinner at Eight (1933), Last Train From Madrid (1937), Pride and Prejudice (1940), M (1951), Born to the Saddle (1953).

ROBERT MORLEY (1908–   )

Looking as though he had just stepped out of the pages of a Charles Dickens novel, the portly and enormously talented British actor played comedy and dramatic roles with equal distinction. His transition from stage to screen came in 1938 when he was cast as the doltish Louis XVI in Marie Antoinette. He has appeared in two-score films since then and has written a number of plays, among them the highly successful Edward, My Son. **Films include:** Major Barbara (1940), An Outcast of the Islands (1951), The African Queen (1952), Gilbert and Sullivan (1953), Oscar Wilde (1960), Sinful Davey (1969).

CHESTER MORRIS (1901–1970)

With the coming of sound pictures, New York-born Morris moved from the stage to Hollywood and became one of the film colony's most reliable leading men, mostly in Grade "B" movies. More often than not he played in underworld and prison movies—on both sides of the law. **More than 50 films include:** Alibi (1929), The Big House (1930), Frankie and Johnnie (1936), Smashing the Rackets (1938), Meet Boston Blackie (1941), Secret Command (1944), Unchained (1955).

WAYNE MORRIS (1914–1959)

A native of Los Angeles, he had become a popular lead in such athletic films as Kid Galahad (1937) when his career was interrupted by World War II. After the war, his career failed to flourish as before and it wasn't until he switched to character parts, as in a memorable performance in The Time of Your Life (1948), that he was once more in demand. Active in television, he finally made his Broadway debut in The Cave Dwellers (1957). **Films include:** China Clipper (1936), I Wanted Wings (1941), John Loves Mary (1949), The Master Plan (1955), Paths of Glory (1957).

ARNOLD MOSS (1910–   )

He had earned a master's degree before he decided that teaching was not his goal and joined the Eva Le Gallienne Civic Repertory Theater. Branching out into radio, he also produced and wrote when he was not acting. He made his screen debut in Temptation (1946) and went on to portray sinister characters in scores of pictures. **Films include:** The Black Book (1949), Viva Zapata! (1952), The Fool Killer (1964), Gambit (1966), Caper of the Golden Bulls (1967).

ZERO MOSTEL (1915–   )

Many mimics can imitate James Cagney or Richard Nixon but only Mostel can make one feel he is the authentic African animal. Mostel did it in his Broadway appearance in Ionesco's Rhinoceros.

The Brooklyn-born son of an orthodox Jewish rabbi, Mostel is perhaps best known for his portrayal of Tevye in Broadway's longest-running hit, *Fiddler on the Roof*. He was equally brilliant, however, as a villain in *Panic in the Streets*, nearly 25 years back.

After graduating from college, Mostel worked as a painter under the Works Progress Administration during the Depression and went on to establish himself as a first-rate nightclub and radio comic. Blacklisted during the McCarthy era, he made a triumphant return to the stage in the 60's. **Highlights:** *DuBarry Was a Lady* (1943), *The Enforcer* (1951), *A Funny Thing Happened on the Way to the Forum* (1966), *The Producers* (1968), *The Angel Levine* (1969), *The Hot Rock* (1971), *Rhinoceros* (1974).

ALAN MOWBRAY (1896–1969)

Born in London, he gave his first notable screen performance as George Washington in *Alexander Hamilton* (1931) with George Arliss. He went on to appear in several hundred films, generally in comedy roles as the butler, the aloof headwaiter, the dignified lawyer or the austere doctor.

Arriving in the United States in 1923 after working his way across on a ship, he spent his early New York days sleeping in Central Park, using the Harvard Club to wash and shave and the Automat for free meals—hot water and catsup to make tomato soup. After touring with the Theatre Guild and making his Hollywood debut, the tall, suave and robust character never went back to Central Park. **A few of his many films include:** *Honor of the Family* (1931), *Becky Sharp* (1935), *My Man Godfrey* (1936), *Topper* (1937), *Holy Matrimony* (1943), *Androcles and the Lion* (1953), *The King and I* (1956), *A Majority of One* (1962).

JACK MULHALL (1891–   )

Unusually good-looking, Mulhall spent two years on stage in New York with the West End Stock Company. His first film role was in *Should a Woman Tell?* (1920) and he was a leading man until the coming of sound. Thereafter he played character roles with considerable competence. **Some of his pictures are:** *Dulcy* (1923), *Orchids and Ermine* (1927), *Lady Be Good* (1928), *Waterfront* (1928), *Reaching for the Moon* (1930), *Hollywood Boulevard* (1936), *Cheers for Miss Bishop* (1941), *Sin Town* (1942).

PAUL MUNI (1895–1967)

Of the 23 films this distinguished actor made, five brought him Academy Award nominations and one, *The Story of Louis Pasteur* (1936), a Best Actor Oscar. Born in Austria of parents who were strolling Yiddish players, Muni Weisenfreund arrived in New York as a child and from 1908 to 1925 appeared on stage exclusively in Yiddish-speaking roles. He finally made his English-speaking debut in 1926 and with *Counsellor-At-Law* (1931) he was recognized to be an outstanding Broadway actor. He made his screen debut in *The Valiant* (1929) and three years later, his performance as Al Capone in *Scarface* (1932) turned him into a top Hollywood star. He went on to give many classic performances of great power

The one and only Zero Mostel as a stone-broke and highly sanctimonious denizen of Broadway in The Producers.

When Paul Muni was not Louis Pasteur or Al Capone he made an extremely handsome flight officer. Here he is with Miriam Hopkins in the almost forgotten The Woman I Love *(1937).*

Muni in the film that made him a top star, I Am a Fugitive From a Chain Gang.

and technical skill on both stage and screen. **Films include:** *I Am a Fugitive From a Chain Gang* (1932), *The Good Earth* (1937), *Juarez* (1939), *A Song to Remember* (1945), *The Last Angry Man* (1959).

ONA MUNSON (1906–1955)

She began dancing at the age of four in her native Oregon and had been in vaudeville and on stage when she landed in Hollywood in the early 30's. She is best remembered for roles like Belle Watling in *Gone With the Wind* (1939) and Mother Gin Sling in *The Shanghai Gesture* (1941). **Films include:** *Going Wild* (1931), *Five Star Final* (1931), *The Cheaters* (1945), *The Red House* (1947).

AUDIE MURPHY (1924–1971)

The most decorated American soldier of World War II, Murphy followed James Cagney's promptings, went to Hollywood after the fighting ended and starred in a series of Westerns and war stories in which he portrayed young American heroes much like himself.

In 1955, Murphy re-enacted several of his battle experiences on screen when he starred in *To Hell and Back,* the film version of his autobiography. At that time the actor said he was jolted by "this strange jerking back and forth between make-believe and reality, between fighting for your life and the discovery that it's only a game and you have to do a retake because a tourist's dog ran across the field in the middle of a battle." Murphy was killed in a plane crash in 1971. **Film highlights:** *Beyond Glory* (1948), *Bad Boy* (1949), *The Quiet American* (1958), *A Time for Dying* (1969).

GEORGE MURPHY (1902–)

A competent and engaging song-and-dance star in films of the late 30's and 40's, he later climbed the political ladder as well and was one of California's United States Senators in 1964. A 1925 graduate of Yale University, Murphy danced in nightclubs before making his film debut with Eddie Cantor in *Kid Millions* (1934). For years he was president of the Screen Actors Guild and in 1950 received a special Academy Award for his work in the industry. A conservative Republican, Murphy vociferously defended the Hollywood community during the days of the "Red scare," claiming that the residents of that rather lush town were "normal, hardworking, non-radical citizens." **Highlights:** *Top of the Town* (1937), *You're a Sweetheart* (1937), *Two Girls on Broadway* (1940), *For Me and My Gal* (1942), *Show Business* (1944), *Battleground* (1949), *Walk East on Beacon* (1952).

DON MURRAY (1929–)

Born in Hollywood, the son of a stage director and a former Ziegfeld Follies girl, Donald Patrick Murray worked as theatre usher, waiter, bricklayer and caddie before making his New York stage debut as Ant Number 2 in *The Insect Comedy* (1948). In the 50's he distinguished himself on Broadway with fine performances in *The Rose Tattoo* (1951) and the *Skin of Our Teeth* (1955). The following year he recreated his stage role as Bo Decker for the film version of William Inge's *Bus Stop*. Of all the screen roles he played he is probably best remembered as

George Murphy (left), who was to become moviedom's first United States Senator, points a finger at Ruth Donnelly in Rise and Shine *(1941). The others are Raymond Walburn and Milton Berle.*

Father Charles Dismas Clark in *The Hoodlum Priest*, a film he co-authored and co-produced and which won him the Cannes Film Festival's Humanitarian Award. **Highlights:** *Blood on the Moon* (1948), *Dallas* (1951), *A Hatful of Rain* (1957), *Advise and Consent* (1962), *Happy Birthday, Wanda June* (1971).

JAMES MURRAY (1901–1936)

He gave one of the finest screen performances ever as the downtrodden city clerk in King Vidor's masterful silent *The Crowd* (1928), but the rest of his brief career makes a tragic story. Before Vidor chose him for the role, Murray had been struggling along as a film extra. Only five years and several minor roles after his success, he was out of work and films completely and drinking heavily. Three years later he was found dead in the Hudson River. **Other credits:** *The Shakedown* (1929), *Frisco Jenny* (1933), *Baby Face* (1933).

MAE MURRAY (1885–1965)

This pouting-lipped, platinum blonde waltzed with John Gilbert in von Stroheim's *The Merry Widow* (1925). At 78 she was found wandering the streets of St. Louis, penniless, but well-dressed and slightly senile.

Marie Adrienne Koenig began her show-business career as a dancer in the *Ziegfeld Follies* of 1908, made her film debut in *To Have and to Hold* (1916) and soon became one of the silent screen's leading ladies. In 1931, she married a Georgian prince and walked out on her MGM contract and her film career. **Films include:** *The Mormon Maid* (1920), *Jazz Mania* (1921), *The Gilded Lily* (1921), *Fashion Row* (1924), *Circe the Enchantress* (1927), *Valencia* (1926), *Peacock*

Alley (1931)—a remake of her earlier 20's success.

CLARENCE MUSE (1889–   )

This black actor-director ran the gamut of show business from circus and vaudeville, to radio and, finally, to the stage and screen. Muse was one of the founders of the (old) Lafayette Theatre in New York which served as a springboard for many black actors. An accomplished musician, he was trained for opera by an Italian maestro, but when someone commented that his renditions of black hymns and spirituals sounded like those of a white opera singer, he abandoned formal training. At one time or another Muse has been active as a poet, a playwright, a composer, and an authority on Bantu dialects. Among the songs that he wrote are "When It's Sleepy Time Down South," "I Go Congo" and "Behind the Cabin Door." **Highlights:** *Laughter in Hell* (1933), *So Red the Rose* (1935), *Show Boat* (1936), *Laughing Irish Eyes* (1936), *The Toy Wife* (1938), *Shadow of a Doubt* (1943), *Porgy and Bess* (1959).

CARMEL MYERS (1901–   )

One of the numerous screen sirens to surface in the wake of Theda Bara during the early 20's, she appeared in scores of silents and some early talkies before her career languished in the early 30's. After a minor role in the cumbersome costume drama *Lady for a Night* (1942) she retired from films. During the early years of television, Myers hosted one of the medium's first interview shows. **Films include:** *Sirens of the Sea* (debut, 1916), *The Famous Mrs. Fair* (1923), *Slave of Desire* (1923), *Beau Brummell* (1924), *Babbitt* (1924), *Ben Hur* (1925), *Sorrell and Son* (1927), *Svengali* (1931).

Mae Murray, star of many an ornate romance in the silent era.

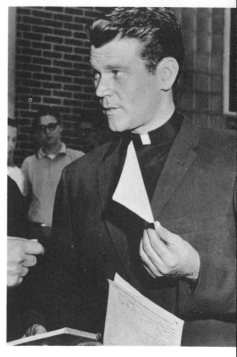

Don Murray as a wearer of the cloth in The Hoodlum Priest *(1961).*

J. Carrol Naish as a sneaky Spaniard in Blood and Sand.

Mildred Natwick as Miss Gravely in Hitchock's suspense comedy The Trouble With Harry.

CONRAD NAGEL (1897–1970)

In the early days of talking pictures, a popular Hollywood command was: "Get Nagel. He can talk." A native Iowan, Nagel made his stage debut in 1914 and his first screen appearance five years later in *Little Women*. He was a popular leading man in silents of the 20's, starring mainly in sophisticated dramas and drawing-room comedies. With the advent of sound his distinctive voice made him a natural choice to become one of the first silent stars to speak in films, and he continued to appear in films over the years as a character actor. He had one of the first panel shows on television. He was one of the founders of the Academy of Motion Picture Arts and Sciences, its early president, and was involved in the creation of the Academy Awards. **Highlights:** *Three Weeks* (1924), *Quality Street* (1927), *East Lynne* (1931), *I Want a Divorce* (1940), *All That Heaven Allows* (1956), *Stranger in My Arms* (1959).

J. CARROL NAISH (1900–1973)

"Hollywood's one-man United Nations" first gained recognition as Loretta Young's Chinese father in *The Hatchet Man* (1932) and went on to play both villainous and sympathetic characters of most every race and nationality (except possibly his own—Irish American) in the course of his long screen career. He was the veteran of more than 200 films as well as numerous radio and TV shows. His best-known role was perhaps Luigi in *Life With Luigi*, which he played on both radio and television. **Films include:** *Good Intentions* (debut, 1930), *The Lives of a Bengal Lancer* (1935), *Blood and Sand* (1941), *Humoresque* (1946), *Clash by Night* (1952), *The Young Don't Cry* (1957).

LAURENCE NAISMITH (1908–   )

British character actor Lawrence Johnson came to films in the late 40's after considerable stage experience, which he put to good use in *The Beggar's Opera* (1952) and in Olivier's *Richard III* (1956). Naismith played in *A Night to Remember* (1958), a movie about the sinking of the *Titanic*, but soon resurfaced in *Sink the Bismarck!* (1960). After several forgettable British films, Naismith appeared in the American film version of *Camelot* (1967). **Films include:** *High Treason* (1952), *Mogambo* (1953), *Jason and the Argonauts* (1963), *The Long Duel* (1967), *A Garden of Cucumbers* (1967).

ALAN NAPIER (1903–   )

Alan Napier-Clavering probably acquired his well-known dignified demeanor during his ten years as a featured player with the Old Vic. In English films from the early 30's, he went to Hollywood in 1940. Since then Napier has spent most of his screen career playing gentlemen and gentlemen's gentlemen, though he did have the opportunity to play one of history's foremost rogues, Captain Kidd. **Films include:** *We Are Not Alone* (1939), *Random Harvest* (1942), *Julius Caesar* (1953), *Journey to the Center of the Earth* (1959), *Marnie* (1964), *The Loved One* (1965).

MILDRED NATWICK (1908–   )

During the early part of her career this highly talented character actress was invariably fated to play women older than herself—the result of a vague quality of eccentricity combined with a high-pitched, cracked and edgy voice. More often than not she portrayed elderly, nasty or slightly fey females. Over the years she has combined her screen career with outstanding Broadway successes in such plays as *Waltz of the Toreadors* and *Barefoot in the Park* and with television appearances that date back to a pioneer TV drama of 1939. **Films include:** *The Long Voyage Home* (debut, 1940),

Yolanda and the Thief (1945), *Cheaper by the Dozen* (1950), *The Trouble With Harry* (1955), *Barefoot in the Park* (1967), *The Maltese Bippy* (1969).

ALLA NAZIMOVA (1879–1945)

One of the great stage actresses of her time, she was an accomplished violinist in her native Russia before she was lured by the footlights and began her studies with Stanislavsky. Nazimova immigrated to the United States in 1905 and quickly established herself as one of the major early interpreters of Ibsen's women on the Broadway stage. For several years during the silent era she had a flourishing screen career, playing leads in such films as *War Brides* (1916), *Camille* (1921), opposite Valentino, and the controversial *Salome* (1923). After that Nazimova worked exclusively on stage until the early 40's, when she returned to the screen as a character actress in such melodramas as *Blood and Sand* (1941) and *In Our Time* (1944). **Films include:** *A Doll's House* (1922), *Escape* (1940), *The Bridge of San Luis Rey* (1944).

ANNA NEAGLE (1904–)

For seven years she set a still unchallenged record as Great Britain's top-drawing female actress, but her genteel charm never brought her the same kind of success on the other side of the Atlantic. Born in a London working-class district, Marjorie Robertson began her career as a chorus girl and climaxed it by becoming a Dame of the British Empire and a four-time winner of England's prestigious Picturegoer Gold Medal Award, twice alongside Laurence Olivier. Critical acclaim for Neagle's films, most of which were made by producer-director Herbert Wilcox (her husband), never matched their British box-office results. Typical is this Graham Greene review: "Miss Neagle looked nice as Queen Victoria, she looks just as nice as Nurse Cavell; she moves rigidly on to the set, as if wheels were concealed under the stately skirt; she says her piece and trolleys out again——rather like a mechanical wonder from the World's Fair." Audiences, however, continued to applaud her versatility in films as diverse as *No, No, Nanette* (1940) and *Forever and a Day* (1943). **Films include:** *Bitter Sweet* (1933), *Nell Gwynn* (1935), *Victoria the Great* (1937), *Nurse Edith Cavell* (1939), *Irene* (1940), *Maytime in Mayfair* (1952), *The Lady Is a Square* (1959).

PATRICIA NEAL (1926–)

An actress of great range and power, she has been given few screen roles worthy of her talent. Patsy Louise Neal was born in Packard, Kentucky, majored in drama at Northwestern University and at the age of 20 won a Tony for her performance on Broadway as the young Regina in *Another Part of the Forest* (1946). She won an Oscar and the British Film Academy Best Actress Award 17 years later for her superlative performance opposite Paul Newman in *Hud* (1963). In the mid-60's she suffered a near-fatal stroke, but through grueling work, continuous struggle and the help of her husband, writer Roald Dahl, she managed to regain speech and movement and to resume her career in motion pictures and television. **Films include:** *John Loves Mary* (debut, 1949), *The Fountainhead* (1949), *A Face in the Crowd* (1957), *Breakfast at Tiffany's* (1961), *The Subject Was Roses* (1968), *Baxter* (1973).

HILDEGARDE NEFF (1925–)
See HILDEGARDE KNEF

POLA NEGRI (1899–)

In 1923 Polish-born Appolonia Chalupek became Europe's first major import to Hollywood. Her widely publicized move came nearly ten years after her screen debut in the Polish film *Love and Passion* (1914) and in the wake of a succession of highly praised appearances in the German films of Ernst Lubitsch. (The best known of these was *Madame du Barry*, made in 1919—and retitled *Passion* for its 1920 American release.)

While fans had flocked to see Negri's German films, they stayed away in droves from the disasters that Hollywood concocted for her. Nor did Negri help her own cause by living a private life as tumultuous and eccentric as those of the characters she played. Her

Patricia Neal, the highly talented actress who survived a terrible illness and resumed her career. Here she is in a 1956 pose.

Pola Negri, a femme fatale *back in the good old days when come-hither looks really meant big doings in Sin City.*

Gene Nelson, who hoofed it with Doris Day in Tea for Two.

outspoken contempt for Hollywood and a widely ballyhooed feud with Gloria Swanson displeased some moviegoers, while her antics at Valentino's funeral (she threw her black-veiled body dramatically across the coffin) caused raised eyebrows from coast to coast.

Somehow Negri managed to survive romances with Chaplin and Valentino, friendships with George Bernard Shaw and Chaliapin, plus a succession of dreadful movies. Her fans were loyal, and now and then a good film (*A Woman of the World,* 1925) proved that she could draw audiences to the box office. After the advent of sound, however, Negri's thick accent sharply curtailed her Hollywood career, and she averaged less than one appearance per decade in English-language films. The most recent of these was in Walt Disney's *The Moonspinners* (1964) as a cheetah-accompanied jewelry expert. **Films include:** *Die Bestie* (1915), *Die Flamme Montmarte* (1920), *The Cheat* (1923), *East of Suez* (1925), *Hotel Imperial* (1927), *Barbed Wire* (1927), *Hi Diddle Diddle* (1943).

BARRY NELSON (1920–   )

Although he started out in show business in 1941 with a long-term contract from MGM, today Nelson is better known for his stage and television work than for his motion picture roles. He appeared in various films throughout the 40's and early 50's but established himself far more successfully as an actor on the legitimate stage in New York. His Broadway credits include *The Rat Race, The Moon Is Blue* and *The Fig Leaves Are Falling.* He also starred in both the stage and screen versions of *Winged Victory* (1944) and *Mary, Mary* (1963). His numerous television roles include leads in such series as *My Favorite Husband* with Joan Caulfield and *Hudson's Bay.* **Film highlights:** *Shadow of the Thin Man* (debut, 1941), *A Guy Named Joe* (1943), *The Beginning of the End* (1947), *The Man With My Face* (1951), *The First Traveling Saleslady* (1956).

GENE NELSON (1920–   )

After his screen debut in *I Wonder Who's Kissing Her Now* (1947), Gene Nelson added

an additional light touch to a variety of already featherweight movie musicals of the 50's. He also appeared in the screen version of that substantial musical monument *Oklahoma!* (1955). After a serious accident, the former dancer and stage star turned his talents to writing and directing and made such films as *Kissin' Cousins* (1964), *Your Cheatin' Heart* (1965) and *The Cool Ones* (1967). In 1971 critics cheered his comeback on the musical stage in Broadway's successful *Follies.* **Film credits:** *Tea for Two* (1950), *Lullaby of Broadway* (1951), *She's Working Her Way Through College* (1952), *So This Is Paris* (1955), *20,000 Eyes* (1961).

CATHLEEN NESBITT (1889–   )

This veteran British character actress began her long and prolific stage career back in the early years of this century, at a time when she was described by her fiancé, the poet Rupert Brooke, as ''incredibly . . . inordinately . . . immortally . . . adorably beautiful.'' She made her London stage debut in 1910 in *The Cabinet Minister* and the following year joined the famous Irish Players. Her first American stage performance came in their New York production of Synge's *Playboy of the Western World.* Since then she has played more than 100 roles on the London and New York stages. Her film roles, though far less numerous, have been distinctive. During the last two decades Nesbitt has also worked on television. She starred for a while in *The Farmer's Daughter* series and most recently was seen as the Countess of Southwold in the highly acclaimed British series *Upstairs, Downstairs.* **Films include:** *The Case of the Frightened Lady* (debut, 1932), *Fanny by Gaslight* (1943), *Nicholas Nickleby* (1947), *Three Coins in the Fountain* (1954), *Desiree* (1954), *Promise Her Anything* (1966), *Staircase* (1969).

ANTHONY NEWLEY (1931–   )

Versatility is Newley's trademark. He is an actor, singer, composer, playwright and lyricist best known in the United States as the star of *Stop the World—I Want to Get Off.* He won a Tony Award for his performance in the Broadway production and made a fortune with his recording of "What Kind of Fool Am I," one of the songs from the show.

Newley, the son of a Hackney shipping clerk, has been in show business since age 14. He made his motion picture debut as the Artful Dodger in *Oliver Twist* (1948) and from then on worked steadily in British films, usually playing character parts. He followed his success in *Stop the World* with another theatrical hit, *The Roar of the Greasepaint, the Smell of the Crowd*, which solidified his reputation as "boy wonder" of Anglo-American show biz. Since then Newley has produced and starred in several films and appeared successfully in nightclubs, on stage and television. He also directed *Summertree* (1971), starring Michael Douglas. **Films include:** *Vice Versa* (1948), *Those People Next Door* (1953), *The Cockleshell Heroes* (1956), *X the Unknown* (1957), *High Flight* (1958), *In the Nick* (1961), *The Small World of Sammy Lee* (1963), *Dr. Doolittle* (1967), *Sweet November* (1968).

PAUL NEWMAN (1925–)

Born in Ohio, Newman attended drama classes at Kenyon College and after some summer stock went on to the Yale School of Drama. New York stage parts led to a Hollywood contract. A slight but perennial pout combined with a general air of sullen insolence made the young Newman one of the most popular of postwar anti-heroes. Like Marlon Brando, whom he once vaguely resembled, he seems at home in almost any sort of role. More often than not he has been seen as the lone and defiant drifter, self-outlawed from society.

Newman's screen meanness perhaps reached its zenith in *Hud* (1963), in which he played the no-account son of a righteous rancher and managed to outrage the moral sense of virtually everyone in the movie. His first appearance was in *The Silver Chalice* (1954) and two years later he rose to stardom as boxer Rocky Graziano in *Somebody Up There Likes Me* (1956). Thereafter he appeared in several films with Joanne Woodward, who became his wife. They continued to work together, and in 1968 Woodward won an Oscar nomination in *Rachel, Rachel*, the first picture directed by Newman.

Newman has a highly magnetic screen personality. He has only to grin to make even the most despicable character seem appealing, and when he turns on his charm full volume he is irresistible to his many fans. **Other films:** *The Long Hot Summer* (1958), *Cat on a Hot Tin Roof* (1958), *The Hustler* (1961), *Cool Hand Luke* (1967), *Butch Cassidy and the Sundance Kid* (1969), *Sometimes a Great Notion,* (1972), *The Life and Times of Judge Roy Bean* (1972), *The Sting* (1973).

ROBERT NEWTON (1905–1956)

The British character actor who made his English stage debut in *Henry IV* (1920) had impressive stage credentials by the time he was an adult. He took over Laurence Olivier's role in the New York production of Noel Coward's *Private Lives* (1931).

During his 20-year screen career, the versatile Newton proved equally adept at portraying massive inefficiency and cunning villainy. He was so exquisitely piratical as Long John Silver in *Treasure Island* (1950) that he was later cast in the 1955 *Long John Silver* TV series. Newton was at his bumbling best as Inspector Fix in his last film, *Around the World in 80 Days* (1956). **Films include:** *Fire Over England* (first major film role, 1937), *Jamaica Inn* (1939), *Odd Man Out* (1947), *The Beachcomber* (1955).

BARBARA NICHOLS (1932–)

The blonde actress has played any number of abused and abusive women since she made her screen debut in the mid-50's. She was notably down-and-out in *Sweet Smell of Success* (1957) and helped drive a sergeant crazy in *The Naked and the Dead* (1958).

On the lighter side she did a bit of singing in *Where the Boys Are* (1961) and a bit of burlesque in *The Scarface Mob* (1960). **Films include:** *Pal Joey* (1957), *The George Raft Story* (1962), *The Loved One* (1965), *The Power* (1968).

JACK NICHOLSON (1936–)

He spent the late 50's and most of the 60's on the fringes of Hollywood, acting in and writing for low-budget films aimed at the teenage market and the drive-ins. Then he wrote the screenplay for *The Trip* (1967), and

Paul Newman in From the Terrace *(1960). He and Joanne Woodward did a fine job in the O'Hara story about marital mixups.*

Robert Newton, as Long John Silver in Treasure Island, *spins a yarn for his young admirer, Bobby Driscoll.*

Jack Nicholson, one of the new generation of brilliant young actors, in the 1974 production of Columbia Pictures' The Last Detail.

Though some may not realize it, David Niven can write as well as he can act. His autobiography was a beauty. Here is the British star in A Shot in the Dark *(1964).*

the focus of his career shifted radically. The film starred Peter Fonda and Dennis Hopper, and the meeting of this trio led to a milestone in Hollywood movie-making when they combined their talents for *Easy Rider* (1969).

Nicholson was cast as a weak, whiskey-soaked, small town Southern lawyer who accompanies Fonda and Hopper on their motorcycle wanderings. His portrayal of a hick discovering freedom with his new found hippie friends struck a responsive chord with moviegoers and helped make the film a huge box-office success.

Easy Rider also brought Nicholson an Oscar nomination and led to his leading role opposite Karen Black in *Five Easy Pieces* (1970), which many critics consider one of the best American films of its time and which brought Nicholson well-deserved recognition as one of America's best film actors. (That same year he tried his hand at directing and made *Drive, He Said.*) His best performance to date was probably as the foul-mouthed Navy lifer in *The Last Detail* (1973). **Films include:** *Cry Baby Killer* (1958), *Studs Lonigan* (1960), *The Raven* (1963), *Ensign Pulver* (1965), *Carnal Knowledge* (1971), *The King of Marvin Gardens* (1972).

LESLIE NIELSEN (1925–)

Best known as a TV actor and the star of such series as *Swamp Fox* and *The New Breed*, blond-haired, blue-eyed Nielsen entered show business as a disc jockey and announcer at a Calgary radio station in his native Canada. He later made his way to a Toronto radio school and eventually to New York, where he began his acting career. He soon found work in live TV dramatic productions and got his first major break with the lead in the successful 1950 series *Suspense*. **His films include:** *The Vagabond King* (1956), *Forbidden Planet* (1956), *Ransom* (1956), *Tammy and the Bachelor* (1957), *Harlow* (1965), *Beau Geste* (1966).

ANNA Q. NILSSON (1894–)

An extremely determined and beautiful girl, she decided to leave her native Sweden to come to America and, after picking beets to earn passage, she arrived in New York at age

14, where she became a celebrated artists' model. By 1911, she had appeared in two-reelers. Later she climbed to stardom in such films as *The Masked Woman* (1922). The advent of sound and a serious horseback riding accident while on location interrupted her career. It was years before she returned to the screen, playing occasional character roles in such films as *The Farmer's Daughter* (1947) and *Sunset Boulevard* (1950). **Films include:** *Barriers Swept Aside* (1915), *Seven Keys to Baldpate* (1917), *One Hour Before Dawn* (1920), *Midnight Lovers* (1926), *The Great Man's Lady* (1942), *Fighting Father Dunne* (1948).

DAVID NIVEN (1910–)

Central Casting listed him as "Anglo-Saxon Type 2008" back in the mid-30's, and this debonair Britisher has been playing impeccably sophisticated Englishmen ever since. He excelled in that sort of role as the unflappable Phileas Fogg in *Around the World in 80 Days* (1956), but won his Academy Award for portraying a flappable character in *Separate Tables* (1958).

Niven's first speaking part was in *Without Regret* (1935). After a score or more appearances over a five-year span his career was interrupted by World War II, in which he served with high distinction before returning to resume his film work. In 1953 he found himself in another battle when he starred with William Holden and Maggie McNamara in *The Moon Is Blue,* the first film to challenge Hollywood's ultra-moralistic production code. Director Otto Preminger refused to excise such terms as "mistress" and "seduction" and, despite heated objections from many quarters, the film proved highly successful.

Over the years Niven has been seen principally in comedy roles, with a few tales of high adventure thrown in, but his overall competence in handling any part assigned him remains unquestioned. His highly successful autobiography, *The Moon's a Balloon* (1972) proved him an extremely literate and clever writer. **Other highlights:** *The Charge of the Light Brigade* (1936), *Dawn Patrol* (1938), *Wuthering Heights* (1939), *Stairway to Heaven* (1946), *The Guns of Navarone*

(1961), *Bedtime Story* (1964), *The Impossible Years* (1968).

LLOYD NOLAN (1902–   )

A superb actor whose portrayal on Broadway of Captain Queeg in *The Caine Mutiny Court Martial* (1953–54) was one of the outstanding stage performances of its time. Nolan made his film debut over 20 years before in 1934. He was typecast in an endless succession of gangster, cowboy and cop roles before his talents were given freer range in *A Tree Grows In Brooklyn* (1945). Since then he has been a character actor *par excellence,* equally adept at comedy or dramatic roles. He has appeared with equal success on TV. **Highlights:** *Stolen Harmony* (1935), *Wells Fargo* (1937), *Bataan* (1943), *A Hatful of Rain* (1957), *Ice Station Zebra* (1968), *Airport* (1969).

MABEL NORMAND (1894–1930)

A former art student and model from Boston Mabel Fortescue made her debut with the Vitagraph Studio in 1910 at $25 a week. Making a hit in Mack Sennett's Keystone Cop comedies, she became highly popular as a slapstick comedienne, and one of Chaplin's preferred leading ladies, with a salary that rose to $5,000 per week. As funny as she was on screen, her off-camera life was a lurid mixture of scandal and tragedy which finally caused her retirement. After spending much time in sanatoriums, she died of tuberculosis at the age of 36. **Films include:** *Barney Oldfield's Race for Life* (1912), *Mickey* (1918), *Sis Hopkins* (1919), *Molly O* (1921), *Suzanna* (1923).

JACK NORTON (1889–1958)

Although numerous actors have spent at least part of their careers typed as gangsters or butlers only Arthur Housman rivalled Norton's record of more than 200 screen appearances as a drunk. The moment he appeared with his blissful smile, weaving across a room or trying to solve the intricacies of a revolving door, he would reduce audiences to helpless laughter. He was sober but twice, in *The Fleet's In* (1942) and *Going My Way* (1944). Off screen, one drink could make him

sick. **Films include:** *The Spoilers* (1942), *Hold That Blonde* (1945), *Blue Skies* (1946), *Mad Wednesday* (1951).

KIM NOVAK (1933–   )

Groomed in the mid-50's as Columbia's replacement for Rita Hayworth, she adopted dumb-blonde mannerisms and acquired a Monroe voice. Pictures such as *Jeanne Eagels* (1957) and *Pal Joey* (1957) helped her develop a screen style of her own. One of her best performances was as the good-hearted gal who saw Frank Sinatra through drug withdrawal in *The Man With the Golden Arm* (1955). **Films include:** *Picnic* (1956), *Bell, Book and Candle* (1958), *The Notorious Landlady* (1962), *Of Human Bondage* (1964), *The Legend of Lylah Clare* (1968), *The Great Bank Robbery* (1969).

RAMON NOVARRO (1889–1968)

One of the great "Latin Lovers" groomed by Hollywood studios in their effort to find another Valentino, Mexican-born Ramon Samaniegos became one of the silent-screen idols of the 20's. After playing bit parts in a succession of indifferent films, he was cast by Rex Ingram as Rupert of Hentzau in *The Prisoner of Zenda* (1922) and he soared to stardom along with his long cigarette holder and monocle. Novarro's forte was costume drama with swashbuckling overtones. He was at his best in films like *Scaramouche* (1923) and in *Ben Hur* (1925) in which his costume consisted mostly of bare skin, decorated by shackles when he suffered in a Roman galley and by bits of neo-Roman armor plate when he triumphed as a charioteer.

With the coming of sound his box-office appeal declined, although his first talking pictures, *The Pagan* (1929) and *Mata Hari* (1932) with Garbo, were acclaimed. Subsequently, he enjoyed a modest degree of success with European audiences and in the 40's made an effort to turn to character parts. **Films include:** *Where the Pavement Ends* (1923), *The Red Lily* (1924), *Thy Name Is Woman* (1924), *The Student Prince* (1927), *Call of the Flesh* (1930), *The Cat and the Fiddle* (1934), *Heller in Pink Tights* (1960).

Lloyd Nolan, being gripped by the arm and hand of George Raft, in She Couldn't Take It *(1935).*

Kim Novak, an interesting actress who starred in a few fine pictures and a lot of so-so ones.

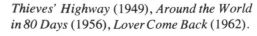

Thieves' Highway (1949), Around the World in 80 Days (1956), Lover Come Back (1962).

Beautiful and talented Merle Oberon played George Sand in A Song to Remember. Cornel Wilde, at the piano, was Frederic Chopin and Stephen Bekassy was Franz Liszt.

JACK OAKIE (1903–)

This tough-talking master of the double-take played supporting comedy roles in scores of films during his 35-year screen career. A native of Sedalia, Missouri, Lewis D. Offield had already appeared in vaudeville and on Broadway when he went West for his screen debut in *Finders Keepers* (1927). He most often appeared on screen as the hero's not too bright friend or someone's beaming brother, but his best performance was probably as Mussolini in Chaplin's *The Great Dictator* (1940). **Films include:** *Million Dollar Legs* (1932), *College Rhythm* (1934), *Little Men* (1940), *It Happened Tomorrow* (1944),

WARREN OATES (1932–)

This native Kentuckian served a long apprenticeship to the leading character roles he is now known for—first with several years of minor roles in hundreds of TV shows in New York and then with more than a decade of equally inconsequential parts in two-bit Westerns in Hollywood. Eventually his craggy face, thin frame, thinning hair and menacing screen presence landed him the role of the bigoted redneck, Deputy Sam Lloyd, in *In the Heat of the Night* (1967), and his career took off. **Some of his films include:** *Private Property* (1960), *Ride the High Country* (1962), *Return of the Seven* (1966), *The Wild Bunch* (1969), *Dillinger* (1973).

MERLE OBERON (1911–)

One of the screen's great beauties, Estelle O'Brien Merle Thompson was born in Tasmania, educated in India and got her first job as a film extra in London at the age of 17. The Oriental-eyed, dark-haired hopeful spent several uneventful years before film magnate Alexander Korda propelled her to stardom when he cast her as Anne Boleyn (to Charles Laughton's King Henry) in *The Private Life of Henry VIII* (1933). She made several other films for Korda, notably *The Scarlet Pimpernel* (1935) with Leslie Howard, and then moved on to Hollywood for her first American film, *The Dark Angel* (1935). Four years later she played opposite Olivier in what is probably her best-known role—Cathy in William Wyler's version of *Wuthering Heights*. That same year she married Korda.

In the years that followed, Oberon's career took a sharp downward turn. She was given wretched scripts (e.g., *The Lodger* in 1944) and gradually disappeared from the limelight. Over the past two decades, however, occasional appearances in films like *Désirée* (1954) have brought her renewed recogni-

Alice Faye gently restrains Jack Oakie from what appears to be a belligerent move in The Great American Broadcast.

tion. **Her films include:** *The Cowboy and the Lady* (1938), *'Til We Meet Again* (1940), *A Song to Remember* (1945), *Hotel* (1967), *Interlude* (1973).

HUGH O'BRIAN (1925–)

Known mostly for his life on the range as television's version of Sheriff Wyatt Earp, O'Brian worked in both theatre and film before appearing on television. He began his acting career in California repertory, choosing the rather odd stage name of Jaffer Gray as a replacement for his own, Hugh J. Krampke. His film debut came soon after in *Never Fear* (1950). He has since played leads in a variety of films, mainly "B" action pictures which exploited his powerfully built, athletic body and standard good looks. **Film credits include:** *Rocketship X-M* (1950), *Red Ball Express* (1952), *Broken Lance* (1954), *Come Fly With Me* (1963), *Ten Little Indians* (1966), *Ambush Bay* (1966).

EDMOND O'BRIEN (1915–)

This solemn-faced, heavy-jawed character actor and sometime leading man is best known for his fine portrayals of tough-looking but nevertheless world-weary men. O'Brien grew up in New York City and began his acting career with the Neighborhood Playhouse. During his early years on Broadway he gained attention in a variety of small Shakespearean roles. After his film debut in *The Hunchback of Notre Dame* (1940), however, he ended up playing heavies in several dozen crime and war non-epics. He returned briefly to Shakespeare in 1953, playing Casca to Brando's Marc Antony in *Julius Caesar,* but was back to standard Hollywood fare the following year with an Oscar-winning performance as the overbearing press agent in *The Barefoot Contessa.* Over the past two decades he has continued to turn in fine performances in a variety of small, meaty parts. In the 60's O'Brien starred in two successful TV series: *Johnny Midnight* (1960) and *Sam Benedict* (1967). **More than 50 films include:** *The Killers* (1946), *White Heat* (1949), *1984* (1956), *The Big Land* (1957), *Birdman of Alcatraz* (1962), *Seven Days in May* (1964), *The Wild Bunch* (1969).

GEORGE O'BRIEN (1900–)

During his 40 years in Hollywood this native San Franciscan probably spent as much film time in the saddle as any of his rough-riding contemporaries. He broke into films during the 20's as a cameraman in Tom Mix films and soon found work as a stuntman and double. His first substantial role was in the early John Ford Western *The Iron Horse* (1924). It was a perfect part for him— juvenile lead, requiring good looks and a muscular physique—and led to a succession of starring roles. The most notable of these came opposite Janet Gaynor in the Academy Award-winning *Sunrise* (1927), the poignant tale about the essential goodness of a sorely tempted man. He kept on riding through the first decade of talkies and in 1939 found his niche in the first of a string of RKO Westerns, the most successful of which was probably *She Wore a Yellow Ribbon* (1949) with John Wayne. **Credits include:** *Riders of the Purple Sage* (1931), *Painted Desert* (1938), *Fort Apache* (1948), *Cheyenne Autumn* (1964).

MARGARET O'BRIEN (1937–)

A native Californian, Margaret O'Brien caused a sensation at the age of five when she played an English war orphan in her second film, *Journey for Margaret,* a low-budget picture that became a huge hit. For the next eight years she reigned as a child star, winning a special Best Child Actress Academy Award in 1944. In 1945 and 1946 she was among the top ten box-office favorites— deservedly, too, for she was a good actress with few of the cutey-pie mannerisms of many child stars. By the early 50's, however, her career came to a standstill, and she made only a few films after that. In recent years she has appeared on TV dramatic shows. **Some of her films include:** *Babes in Arms* (debut, 1941), *Madame Curie* (1943), *Our Vines Have Tender Grapes* (1945), *Meet Me in St. Louis* (1944), *Little Women* (1949), *Glory* (1956), *Heller in Pink Tights* (1960), *Diabolic Wedding* (1971), *Annabelle Lee* (1972).

Five-year-old Margaret O'Brien as a war orphan in Journey for Margaret *(1942).*

Edmond O'Brien in one of at least five thrillers he made in a single year, 1950.

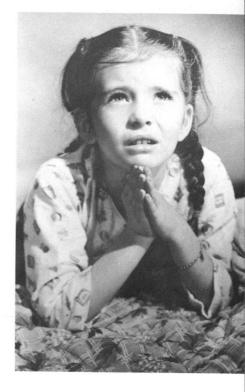

Pat O'Brien as Frank Cavanaugh, football coach and World War II hero, in The Iron Major *(1943).*

PAT O'BRIEN (1899–)

If ever an actor was typecast, it was Pat O'Brien. He has depicted Irish characters of every imaginable kind, from patrolmen, crooks and priests to army men and backroom politicos. Born in Milwaukee to a strict Irish Catholic family, O'Brien attended Marquette Academy. There he met his longtime friend and fellow Irishman Spencer Tracy, and the two went on to attend drama school together. He began his stage career as a song-and-dance man and established himself on Broadway in the 20's. O'Brien's film debut came in 1931 when he recreated his Broadway role as Hildy Johnson for the film version of the Hecht and MacArthur hit *The Front Page*. Over the years he appeared in supporting roles in several scores of pictures and achieved wide popularity as the star of a series of biopics of the 40's, the first of which was *Knute Rockne* (1940), the story of the famous Notre Dame football coach. In the early 50's O'Brien's screen appearances became infrequent. He returned to the stage, launched a nightclub act and also began a successful TV career. In the early 60's he starred as the veteran lawyer, Harrigan, Sr., in the TV courtroom series *Harrigan and Son*. **More than 85 films include:** *Bureau of Missing Persons* (1933), *Angels With Dirty Faces* (1938), *The Fighting 69th* (1940), *Riff Raff* (1947), *The Boy With Green Hair* (1949), *The Last Hurrah* (1958), *Some Like It Hot* (1959).

VIRGINIA O'BRIEN (1922–)

She was the dark-haired beauty who gained tremendous popularity as the deadpan singer in MGM musicals of the 40's. Born in Los Angeles, she made her stage debut in a local production of a shoestring revue called *Meet the People* (1939). Supposedly she was so petrified that she sang her numbers while looking into space, never moving a muscle. It was the genesis of her style as a comedienne. Virtually retired, she occasionally appears in stage revues such as the nostalgic *The Big Show of 1936*, which opened in mid-1972. **Some of her other films include:** *Hullabaloo* (debut, 1940), *The Big Store* (1941), *Panama Hattie* (1942), *Ziegfeld Follies* (1946), *The Harvey Girls* (1946), *Merton of the Movies* (1947).

ARTHUR O'CONNELL (1908–)

A master at portraying gentle confusion, character actor O'Connell began his long performing career on Broadway with a five-year apprenticeship in road shows and three years in vaudeville. In films from the 40's, he won an Oscar nomination when he recreated his Broadway role as Howard Bevans in the 1956 film version of William Inge's simmering small-town tale *Picnic* and another as Parnell McCarthy in the slightly less sensational *Anatomy of a Murder* (1959). **His credits include:** *Open Secret* (1948), *Bus Stop* (1956), *Operation Mad Ball* (1957), *The Great Imposter* (1961), *The Great Race* (1965), *Fantastic Voyage* (1966), *The Power* (1968).

CARROLL O'CONNOR (1923–)

Although Americans find it hard to divorce Carroll O'Connor from his popular image as the stubborn bigot, Archie Bunker, on

Arthur O'Connell confers with Counselor James Stewart in the exciting Anatomy of a Murder *(1959).*

television's *All in the Family,* O'Connor has had a successful career on stage and screen.

O'Connor was born in the United States, educated in Ireland and began his acting career at Dublin's Gate Theatre. He performed on the stages of London, Paris and Edinburgh before returning to the United States.

O'Connor's brusque manner and beefy appearance typecast him to some extent, and in the majority of his films he played tough, blustery parts. In recent years his fine comic talents have been showcased in his TV appearances—in his series and in guest spots. **Film credits include:** *By Love Possessed* (1961), *Lonely Are the Brave* (1962), *What Did You Do in the War, Daddy?* (1966), *Hawaii* (1966), *Point Blank* (1967), *For Love of Ivy* (1968).

DONALD O'CONNOR (1925–)

The breezy, light-of-foot entertainer began his stage career at a tender age in his family's vaudeville act. He made his screen debut in *Sing You Sinners* (1938), played the young Gary Cooper in *Beau Geste* (1939) and went on to dance and sing his way to popularity in buoyant musicals of the 40's.

As an adult actor O'Connor put his vaudeville experience to good use. He often appeared in films that had something to do with show business, notably *Singin' in the Rain* (1952). Beginning with *Francis* (1950), he spent five years as the master of this talking mule star of Universal comedies. During the same period he launched a successful TV career with regular appearances on two seasons of *The Colgate Comedy Hour.* **Credits include:** *When Johnny Comes Marching Home* (1943), *Chip Off the Old Block* (1944), *Yes Sir, That's My Baby* (1949), *Francis in the Navy* (1955), *Call Me Madam* (1953), *There's No Business Like Show Business* (1954), *That Funny Feeling* (1965).

UNA O'CONNOR (1881–1959)

A frail little Irishwoman with enormous eyes reminding one of a hunted animal, she could move audiences to tears or reduce them to helpless laughter. She began her professional career as a member of the famed Abbey Theatre and had gone relatively unnoticed in

Donald O'Connor, flanked by Patricia Medina and Zasu (Colonel Hooker) Pitts, in Francis, *the saga of an equine phenomenon who could talk.*

scores of plays on the London stage when, at the age of 50, Noel Coward cast her in *Cavalcade.* In 1933 she went to Hollywood to repeat her role in the film version and stayed and stayed—portraying Irish or Cockney maids in scores of films. From time to time she escaped this stereotype, as when she played the sorrowing mother in *The Informer* (1935). **More than 50 films include:** *The Barretts of Wimpole Street* (1934), *David Copperfield* (1935), *The Plough and the Stars* (1937), *Orient Express* (1944), *Cluny Brown* (1946), *Witness for the Prosecution* (1958).

DAWN O'DAY See ANNE SHIRLEY

MAUREEN O'HARA (1920–)

The beautiful redheaded Maureen Fitzsimmons made her screen debut in *Jamaica Inn* (1939), fresh out of the Abbey Theatre's acting school in her native Dublin. The following year she attracted considerable attention as the young maiden who cringed from

Una O'Connor, a bewildered housekeeper, in The Bells of St. Mary's *(1945).*

Maureen O'Hara, who lent her decorative presence to many a swashbuckling tale of high adventure.

Charles Laughton's Quasimodo in Clarence Brown's screen version of *The Hunchback of Notre Dame*. For years after she found herself stereotyped as the decorative damsel in distress in an assortment of Westerns and tales of piracy and mayhem. Occasionally, however, she did get more substantial roles, most notably in *How Green Was My Valley* (1941) and in *The Quiet Man* (1952). **Films include:** *Bill of Divorcement* (1940), *Miracle on 34th Street* (1947), *Rio Grande* (1950), *The Long Gray Line* (1955), *The Rare Breed* (1966), *How Do I Love Thee?* (1970), *Big Jake* (1971).

DAN O'HERLIHY (1919–   )

This lithe Irishman received a degree in architecture before pursuing his acting career as a member of the Abbey and Gate Theatres of Dublin. Since his film debut in *Odd Man Out* (1947) he has played numerous character roles and occasional leads on screen. His finest performance was in the title role of *The Adventures of Robinson Crusoe* (1954). He gave a memorable portrayal of the companion-starved, shipwrecked hero of Defoe's classic in a demanding part that left him alone on screen for 60 of the film's 90 minutes and gave him only 800 words of dialogue. Besides his stage and screen careers, O'Herlihy has also appeared frequently on television and in 1963 starred in the series *The Travels of Jamie McPheeters*. **Films include:** *Kidnapped* (1948), *Macbeth* (1950), *Rommel, Desert Fox* (1951), *The Virgin Queen* (1955), *Home Before Dark* (1958), *Imitation of Life* (1959), *Fail Safe* (1964), *100 Rifles* (1969).

DENNIS O'KEEFE (1908–1968)

Vaudeville-trained Edward James Flanagan began in films as an extra (under the name of Bud Flanagan) and worked his way up filmdom's ranks to become a leading man in a host of "B" pictures of the 40's. Although he played no distinguished roles, he was always engaging in lighthearted films like *Topper Returns* (1941) as well as a variety of crime and war movies. In 1959 he was given his own TV comedy program, *The Dennis O'Keefe Show*. **His films include:** *Reaching for the Moon* (debut, 1931), *Bad Man of Brimstone* (1938), *Lady Scarface* (1941), *The Fighting Seabees* (1944), *Mr. District Attorney* (1947), *Walk a Crooked Mile* (1948), *All Hands on Deck* (1961).

WARNER OLAND (1880–1938)

The American screen's best-known Chinaman was, in truth, a Swedish actor who came to America at the age of 13 and had appeared on both stage and screen well before the outbreak of World War I. Although he continued to appear in silents through the 20's, it wasn't until he appeared as the insidious and malevolent arch-criminal Dr. Fu Manchu that he became well known to the public. In the early 30's he turned detective for the first time in the title role of *Charlie Chan Carries On*. He went on to make 15 more Chan pictures in the seven years before his death. **Other films include:** *The Yellow Ticket* (1918), *Don Juan* (1926), *Chinatown Nights* (1929), *The Vagabond King* (1930),

Warner Oland closes in on the guilty person in **Charlie Chan at the Circus** *(1936). The others, left to right, are Keye Luke, Shirley Deane and John McGuire.*

Shanghai Express (1932), *Mandalay* (1934), *The Painted Veil* (1934), *Shanghai* (1935).

EDNA MAY OLIVER (1883–1942)

This Massachusetts-born former singer switched from light opera to comedy when her voice gave out and was an established actress on the legitimate stage when she arrived in Hollywood to make her screen debut in *Icebound* (1924). In great demand throughout the 30's and into the 40's, she was nearly always cast as the lean and sharp-tongued spinster whose lips spoke truths that others avoided. Oliver appeared in some of Hollywood's most prestigious films of the period, probably most memorably as Aunt Betsey Trotwood in *David Copperfield* (1935). **Film highlights:** *Little Women* (1933), *A Tale of Two Cities* (1935), *Romeo and Juliet* (1936), *The Story of Vernon and Irene Castle* (1939), *Pride and Prejudice* (1940), *Lydia* (1941).

SIR LAURENCE OLIVIER (1907–   )

The first actor ever to be created a baron, the director of England's prestigious National Theatre from its inception in 1963 and the man responsible for popularizing Shakespeare for the filmgoing public, Olivier well deserves his reputation as a (if not *the*) towering figure of stage and screen.

He was born in Dorking, England, the son of a clergyman, and began his professional career in 1926 at the Birmingham Repertory Theatre. Within four years he had established himself on the legitimate stages of both London and New York and soon after decided to try his luck in Hollywood. The roles he was offered, however, were undistinguished, and after appearing in such lightweight ventures as *Friends and Lovers* (1931) and *Westward Passage* (1932) and being promised and then removed from the Garbo vehicle *Queen Christina*, he went back to New York to star on Broadway in *The Green Bay Tree*. He then returned to England to do more West End plays, begin his long association with the Old Vic and make several movies for Alexander Korda, among them *Fire Over England* (1937), the first film in which he played opposite his future wife of 20 years, Vivien Leigh. In 1939 Olivier returned to Hollywood, and

Edna May Oliver as Betsey Trotwood gives advice to Madge Evans in MGM's brilliant production of David Copperfield.

this time his fate was different. He played Heathcliffe to Merle Oberon's Cathy in William Wyler's beloved rendition of *Wuthering Heights* (1939) and Maxim de Winter opposite Joan Fontaine in Hitchcock's equally masterful *Rebecca* (1940). He won Oscar nominations for both performances and emerged at the top of the film world with a spate of movie offers. He stayed on to play Mr. Darcy opposite Greer Garson in *Pride and Prejudice* (1940) and Nelson opposite Vivien Leigh in *That Hamilton Woman* (1941) before returning to England to join the war effort.

After more stage work and several light propaganda films, Olivier embarked on the first of his Shakespeare-on-film projects with which he would always be identified. He not only starred in but also produced and directed his 1945 version of *Henry V*. It was a resounding success, brought him the New York Film Critics Best Actor award and a special Oscar. Three years later he repeated the for-

Laurence Olivier, one of the true greats of the stage and screen, in That Hamilton Woman.

Sir Laurence Olivier again, in a tense scene with Sarah Miles in Term of Trial *(1963).*

Pat O' Malley was a fireman and one of Gloria Jean's many uncles in A Little Bit of Heaven *(1940).*

mula with an equally successful *Hamlet* (1948), which brought him both the Best Picture and Best Actor Oscars. The 50's saw him continuing and expanding his by then distinguished stage career, moving increasingly into the areas of direction and production and playing incredibly diverse roles on screen —from kingly guise in another of his Shakespeare vehicles, *Richard III* (1956), to Jennifer Jones's obsessed lover in *Carrie* (1952) and to Marilyn Monroe's Prince in the frivolous *The Prince and the Showgirl* (1957), which he also directed. In 1960 Olivier recreated on screen his role as the down-and-out music hall comic in *The Entertainer* by John Osborne. Despite his fine performance the picture was a flop, and Olivier turned more and more to his work at the National. With the notable exception of *Sleuth* in 1972, his screen appearances are now infrequent and confined mainly to cameo roles. **Other films:** *Murder for Sale* (1930), *As You Like it* (1936), *Spartacus* (1960), *Khartoum* (1966), *Othello* (1966), *The Shoes of the Fisherman* (1968).

MORONI OLSEN (1889–1954)

This tall, broad-shouldered native Utahan possessed a natural air of dignity and authority which stood him in good stead during his long and successful careers on stage and screen. He made his Broadway debut in *Medea* and went on to appear opposite such greats as Katharine Cornell and Helen Hayes. After many years touring the country with his own acting company, he went to Hollywood for his screen debut as Porthos in RKO's 1935 version of *The Three Musketeers*. In the course of the following 19 years he played both villains and good guys in more than 70 pictures. **Films include:** *Kidnapped* (1938), *Rose of Washington Square* (1939), *The Glass Key* (1942), *Father of the Bride* (1950), *The Long, Long Trailer* (1954).

OLE OLSEN (1892–1963)

This Norwegian American comedian worked independently as a violinest, singer and ventriloquist in vaudeville before forming his long-lasting and successful comedy act with Chic Johnson in 1914. He was the straight man in the Olsen and Johnson comedy team and was responsible for devising their biggest success, *Hellzapoppin*, which was presented first in a stage production in California and later as a Broadway hit and as a film (1941). In 1949 Olsen and Johnson starred in their own TV show, *Fireball Fun for All*. **Olsen–Johnson films include:** *Gold Dust Gertie* (1931), *Fifty Million Frenchmen* (1931), *Crazy House* (1943), *See My Lawyer* (1945).

J. PAT O'MALLEY (1904–   )

Irish character actor O'Malley got his start in show business playing in a band and appearing as a comedian on the English stage. He then moved to the United States, appeared on Broadway and did Lancashire and Yorkshire monologues on radio. In Hollywood since the 40's, he has played small roles in a variety of films and has also provided the voices of an assortment of creatures in Disney's animated cartoon features. **Movies include:** *Paris Calling* (1942), *Lassie Come Home* (1943), *The Long, Hot Summer* (1958), *The Cabinet of Caligari* (1962), *A House Is Not a Home* (1964), *Gunn* (1967).

FREDERICK O'NEAL (1905–)

This black character actor spent much of his career on stage but moved to films in the late 40's when Hollywood began turning its attention to racial themes.

O'Neal was featured in the 1957 screen version of Robert Ruark's novel *Something of Value* and later became known to television viewers in the zany police comedy *Car 54, Where Are You?* (1961–62). **Films include:** *Pinky* (debut, 1949), *No Way Out* (1950), *Anna Lucasta* (1959), *Take a Giant Step* (1961), *The Sins of Rachel Cade* (1961), *Free, White and 21* (1963).

RYAN O'NEAL (1941–)

Boyish charm, good looks and naturalness in style have served Ryan O'Neal well in his television and movie career. Born in California, O'Neal spent much of his early childhood traveling with his writer father and actress mother. He first came to public attention with his role as Rodney Harrington in the long-running popular soap opera *Peyton Place*, portraying a decent, honest young man, an image that would remain with him in his early films.

The popular soap-opera movie *Love Story* (1970) exploited O'Neal's ability to suffer poignantly on screen, and the film launched him into stardom. Fortunately, he was not totally typecast, for he was allowed to demonstrate his comedic talents in succeeding films. **Credits include:** *The Wild Rover* (1971), *What's Up, Doc?* (1972), *Paper Moon* (1973), *The Thief Who Came to Dinner* (1973).

TATUM O'NEAL (1963–)

Standing a mere four feet tall, Tatum O'Neal made an impressive debut in *Paper Moon* (1973), winning an Academy Award for Best Supporting Actress. Although she got the job because of her good connections—the star of the movie was her father, Ryan O'Neal—many critics felt she stole the movie and emerged as the real star. Having no acting experience, Tatum let her natural charm and instinct take over and gave an Oscar-winning portrayal of a foul-mouthed, cigarette-smoking but lovable orphan child.

Tatum O' Neal, as the hard-bitten little conniver in Paper Moon, *tours the Bible Belt with Ryan O' Neal, her father in real life.*

BARBARA O'NEIL (1903–)

She made her first appearance at age eight as Mustard Seed in a production of *A Midsummer Night's Dream* in her home town of St. Louis, Missouri. On screen from the 30's, she seemed to make a specialty of portraying disturbed, or at least highly unstable, women. One of her most moving performances was as the neurotic wife in *All This and Heaven Too* (1940), for which she won a Best Supporting Actress Oscar. **Film credits include:** *Stella Dallas* (1937), *Gone With the Wind* (1939), *I Remember Mama* (1948), *Angel Face* (1953), *The Nun's Story* (1959).

SALLY O'NEIL (1908–1968)

This ''baby star'' of the 20's was first featured on screen at the age of 13 in *Sally, Irene and Mary* (1925) and the following year starred in *Mike* (1926). Although she had a rather thin and creaky voice in her first talkie, *On With the Show* (1929), she managed to win

David Opatoshu as the terrorist gang leader in Exodus.

Jennifer O'Neill, an up-and-coming actress of the new school, in The Carey Treatment *(1972).*

substantial roles in a variety of light films through the 30's. **Credits include:** *The Sophomore* (1929), *Hold Everything* (1930), *Salvation Nell* (1931), *The Brat* (1931), *Kathleen* (1938).

HENRY O'NEILL (1891–1964)

During his 28 years as one of Hollywood's foremost character actors, O'Neill was featured in hundreds of movies, usually playing paternal figures. He was a Broadway actor in the 20's and appeared in several Eugene O'Neill—no relation—plays, including *The Hairy Ape* and *The Great God Brown*. O'Neill is credited with introducing actor Paul Robeson to playwright O'Neill—the beginning of a long professional association between the two. O'Neill also is said to have recommended Clark Gable for a stage role that led to Gable's screen career.

After his arrival in Hollywood and a successful screen test, O'Neill was cast in 26 films within ten months. **Films include:** *I Loved a Woman* (1933), *Bordertown* (1935), *The Life of Emile Zola* (1937), *Jezebel* (1938), *'Til We Meet Again* (1940), *Untamed* (1955), *Wings of the Eagles* (1957).

JENNIFER O'NEILL (1948–   )

Soft-spoken and graceful, with almost perfect facial features, O'Neill was one of the most successful fashion models in the United States before she broke into films in the late 60's. Her best performance to date was as the warm, understanding "older woman"—in this case, early 20's—in *Summer of '42* (1971). **Films include:** *For the Love of Ivy* (1968), *Rio Lobo* (1971), *Glass Houses* (1972).

DAVID OPATOSHU (1919–   )

He began his acting career as a teenager playing old men in the Yiddish theatre in New York. Ironically, as Opatoshu got older and more experienced, the characters he played got younger. On Broadway, usually in character parts, he appeared in *Once More With Feeling, Silk Stockings, Me and Molly* and *Flight into Egypt*.

Opatoshu had appeared occasionally in films for more than a decade before landing his favorite screen role—that of the scholarly terrorist leader in *Exodus* (1960). He has also worked extensively in television, appearing in such series as *Name of the Game, Mod Squad* and *Mannix*. **Films include:** *The Brothers Karamazov* (1958), *Cimarron* (1961), *Guns of Darkness* (1962), *Torn Curtain* (1966), *Enter Laughing* (1967), *Death of a Gunfighter* (1969).

FRANK ORTH (1880–1962)

During his 60 years on screen this round-faced, mustachioed character actor most often popped up as a bartender. Originally a vaudeville performer, he appeared in early foreign-language shorts, the *Dr. Kildare* films and played Inspector Farraday in the *Boston Blackie* TV show. **Films include:** *Hot Money* (1936), *His Girl Friday* (1940), *Dr. Kildare's Crisis* (1940), *The Lost Weekend* (1945), *Father of the Bride* (1950), *Here Come the Girls* (1953).

MILO O'SHEA (1925–   )

Dubliner O'Shea had appeared in a number of lightweight, inconsequential films before gaining wide recognition for his masterful portrayal of Bloom in Joseph Strick's controversial film version of Joyce's monumental *Ulysses* (1967). Although he has appeared in several films since, he has concentrated on his stage and television work. **Credits include:** *You Can't Beat the Irish* (1952), *Romeo and Juliet* (1968), *Barbarella* (1968).

MAUREEN O'SULLIVAN (1911–   )

Despite the wide variety of roles she has played, this Irish-born actress will always be known as the female lead of the "You Tarzan, me Jane" pictures. She first entered the jungle with Johnny Weissmuller in 1932 (*Tarzan, the Ape Man*) and recurrently swung from tree to tree for many years thereafter.

Actually, O'Sullivan was a highly capable performer, as she showed in such non-animal films as *A Connecticut Yankee* (1931), *The Barretts of Wimpole Street* (1934) and *David Copperfield* (1935). The widow of John Farrow and mother of Mia, she has appeared infrequently in films in recent years. She appeared on Broadway in the original cast of

Never Too Late and repeated her role in the 1965 screen version. **Some of her other films:** *Song o' My Heart* (debut, 1930), *Strange Interlude* (1932), *Tugboat Annie* (1933), *The Voice of Bugle Ann* (1936), *The Crowd Roars* (1938), *Pride and Prejudice* (1940), *The Phynx* (1970).

PETER O'TOOLE (1932–   )

The handsome Irishman reached stardom with his fourth film in which he played the enigmatic and fascinating T. E. Lawrence in the epic *Lawrence of Arabia* (1962). This film won for the newcomer not only international recognition but also his first Academy Award nomination for Best Actor.

Peter Seamus O'Toole studied at the Royal Academy of Dramatic Art in London. He appeared on stage, acting with the Bristol Old Vic, before making his screen debut in Disney's *Kidnapped* (1959, U.S. 1960). He made two additional movies and then returned to the stage for a season with the Royal Shakespeare Company, receiving much praise for his interpretation of Shylock. Then came *Lawrence*, fame and many film offers. He played several soul-searching roles, including the questing *Lord Jim* (1965) and the weak-willed king in *Becket* (1964). The later film brought the actor his second Academy Award nomination. Since that time O'Toole has continued to distinguish himself on screen and on the British stage. **Credits include:** *The Night of the Generals* (1967), *The Lion in Winter* (1968), *Goodbye Mr. Chips* (1969), *The Ruling Class* (1972), *Under Milk Wood* (1973), *Man of La Mancha* (1973).

MARIA OUSPENSKAYA (1876–1949)

This tiny, dignified woman who carried a cane and wore a monocle is best known as the founder of the School of Dramatic Arts, which profoundly influenced American acting on both stage and screen for more than a quarter of a century. She arrived in the United States from her native Russia with the famed Stanislavsky troupe in 1923. When the group left, she remained behind and began her distinguished English-language acting career at the age of 50. As a rule she played quiet women with a philosophical bent. She made

"Me Jane," alias Maureen O'Sullivan, poses with her jungle family —young Johnny Sheffield, Johnny (Tarzan) Weissmuller and, of course, Cheeta.

Peter O'Toole as the award-winning star of Lawrence of Arabia. *That is Omar Sharif in the background.*

Maria Ouspenskaya as an Indian lady of quality in The Rains Came.

her film debut as the Baroness von Obersdorf in *Dodsworth* (1936), and her roles as Charles Boyer's mother in *Love Affair* (1939) and as the maharani in *The Rains Came* (1939) best exemplified her talents on screen. **Films include:** *Conquest* (1937), *Waterloo Bridge* (1940), *Kings Row* (1942), *A Kiss in the Dark* (1949).

LYNNE OVERMAN (1887–1943)

A pronounced nasal whine characterized this former vaudevillian and Broadway actor's comic style on screen. In between his first film, *Little Miss Marker* (1934), and his last, *The Desert Song* (1943), Overman appeared in more than 50 films. Although he did play a wide variety of character parts, most of them verged on the tough-guy side. **Credits include:** *Broadway Bill* (1934), *Union Pacific* (1939), *Caught in the Draft* (1941), *Roxie Hart* (1942), *Reap the Wild Wind* (1942).

CATHERINE DALE OWEN (1903–1965)

At the height of her Broadway career in 1925 Owen was voted one of the ten most beautiful women in the world. The daughter of Southern aristocrats, she defied her family to go on the stage. Owen studied at the American Academy of Dramatic Arts in New York after attending private schools in Philadelphia and Bronxville, New York. She made her film debut opposite John Gilbert in *His Glorious Night* (1929) and starred in *The Rogue Song* (1930), the film in which baritone Lawrence Tibbett made his first screen appearance. She retired from the stage and motion pictures in 1935 and made only occasional television appearances. **Films include:** *Strictly Unconventional* (1930), *Born Reckless* (1930), *Such Men Are Dangerous* (1930), *Behind Office Doors* (1931).

REGINALD OWEN (1887–1972)

One of the screen's most accomplished character actors and a fine comedian, he appeared in more than 100 films after making his debut in *The Letter* (1929), starring Broadway's Jeanne Eagels. Owen's gallery of characterizations included butlers, diplomats, cripples, giants, thieves, policemen, rich men and beggars. Born in England, he made his local stage debut in 1905, arriving in the United States in the 20's to appear on Broadway before moving to Hollywood. **Films include:** *Of Human Bondage* (1934), *The Earl of Chicago* (1940), *Kitty* (1946), *The Miniver Story* (1950), *Mary Poppins* (1964), *Rosie* (1968).

Reginald Owen was properly nasty in the early segments of A Christmas Carol *(1938). That chap in back of Scrooge is the Spirit of Christmas.*

P

AL PACINO (1940–   )

A star in an era that has no star system, Al Pacino looks exactly like what he is—a born New Yorker, tough, cynical and acutely conscious that pollution exists and Shangri-La does not. Pacino followed his acting training with roles in way-off-Broadway productions and later became a member of the Actors Studio. He won an Obie (1968) and a Tony (1969) for his performances off and on Broadway.

Pacino's first film was *Me, Natalie* in 1968, but it was as Michael Corleone, heir to a Mafia empire in *The Godfather* (1972), that he became a public favorite and an Oscar nominee. To resort to clichés, he was nothing less than sensational in his portrayal of a sensitive and educated youngster who is transformed into a brutal executioner. In *Serpico* (1973) his performance as "the only honest cop in New York" again brought him an Academy Award nomination. **Other film credits:** *Panic in Needle Park* (1971), *Scarecrow* (1973).

GALE PAGE (1918–   )

A native of Spokane, Washington, Sally Rutter got her first acting experience on stage in her home state and made a name for herself soon after as a radio actress and singer with NBC in Chicago. Later, she went to Hollywood for NBC to do a variety of programs, including *Fibber McGee and Molly*. She was teamed with the three Lane sisters in the screen hit *Four Daughters* (their father was Claude Rains) and suddenly found herself with a full-blown screen career. Over the next five years she made four more appearances as the odd sister and also won leading roles on her own. By the mid-40's, however, her career was almost at a standstill and she resumed her radio work, only occasionally returning to the screen in later years. **Films include:** *Crime School* (1938), *Daughters Courageous* (1939), *Four Wives* (1939), *They Drive by Night* (1940), *Four Mothers* (1941), *The Time of Your Life* (1948), *About Mrs. Leslie* (1954).

GENEVIEVE PAGE (1930–   )

This French star of stage and screen has also appeared in occasional English and American films. Her Broadway credits include the lead in Edward Albee's *Tiny Alice*. **Film highlights:** *Foreign Intrigue* (1956), *The Silken Affair* (1957), *Song Without End* (1960), *Michael Strogoff* (1960), *El Cid* (1961), *Youngblood Hawke* (1964), *Grand-Prix* (1966), *Belle de Jour* (1968).

GERALDINE PAGE (1924–   )

Her exceptional work on the New York stage in Tennessee Williams' *Summer and Smoke* (1952) brought Page to the notice of Hollywood producers. The following year she appeared in her first film opposite John Wayne as an aging spinster in *Hondo* (1953). Despite the fact that she got an Oscar nomina-

Al Pacino as the stubbornly honest lawman in Paramount's Serpico.

Genevieve Page adopts a protective attitude toward the Rolls-Royce in The Decline and Fall of a Birdwatcher *(1969).*

Geraldine Page, as a movie star on the skids, in Sweet Bird of Youth.

Jack Palance made a convincing Fidel Castro in Che!.

tion for her work, Hollywood did not seem to recognize her abilities, and she returned to the stage, playing on Broadway, in London and in several road-company productions before she drew Hollywood's attention again, this time for her role in another Williams play, *Sweet Bird of Youth* (1959), in which she played a flamboyant, fading movie star. She repeated her role in the 1962 film version. **Credits include:** *Dear Heart* (1965), *You're a Big Boy Now* (1967), *The Happiest Millionaire* (1967), *Whatever Happened to Aunt Alice?* (1969), *J. W. Coop* (1972).

DEBRA PAGET (1933–   )

During the early 50's, Debralee Griffin was one of Hollywood's most popular ingénues. She was frequently cast in native-girl roles, most notably as the Indian princess who marries James Stewart in *Broken Arrow* (1950). She never advanced much beyond second leads, however, and her greatest claim to screen popularity probably came when she played Elvis Presley's leading lady in *Love Me Tender* (1956). **Films include:** *Cry of the City* (debut, 1948), *Les Miserables* (1952), *Seven Angry Men* (1955), *Tales of Terror* (1962), *The Haunted Palace* (1964).

JANIS PAIGE (1923–   )

Donna Mae Jordan trained as an opera singer but instead became an attractive leading lady with a decided flair for comedy in film musicals. She made her first professional appearance as a member of an opera company in her home town of Tacoma, Washington, and her screen debut in *Hollywood Canteen* (1944). She has made numerous stage appearances and has appeared on television. **Credits include:** *Of Human Bondage* (1946), *Romance on the High Seas* (1948), *Mr. Universe* (1951), *Silk Stockings* (1957), *Please Don't Eat the Daisies* (1960), *The Caretakers* (1963), *Welcome to Hard Times* (1967).

MABEL PAIGE (1880–1953)

A character actress in a great many films during the last ten years of her life, Paige first went on stage at the age of four with her parents, both stock actors. While still a teenager she formed a stock company of her own

and eventually she founded the Paige Theatre in Jacksonville, Florida. **Credits include:** *Someone to Remember* (1943), *Lucky Jordan* (1943), *Murder, He Says* (1945), *If You Knew Susie* (1948), *Johnny Belinda* (1948), *The Sniper* (1952), *Houdini* (1953).

JACK PALANCE (1920–   )

Gaunt features, a tortured air and a rugged physique that attests to his years as a professional prizefighter have all helped to make this native Pennsylvanian a convincing screen menace and dangerous adversary during his more than two decades in films.

Walter Palanuik made his first Broadway appearance in 1949, when he took over the role of Stanley in *A Streetcar Named Desire*. His success landed him his first screen role, that of Blackie, the killer, in *Panic in the Streets* (1950). His outstanding performance immediately distinguished him from the mass of screen heavies, and many of his subsequent portrayals have been marked by unusual psychological insight into the complicated characters he has played. From the early 50's Palance's television credits include a variety of roles in TV specials (notably as the down-and-out Mountain McClintock in *Playhouse 90*'s version of *Requiem for a Heavyweight*) and the lead in the 1963 circus series *The Greatest Show on Earth*. **Film highlights:** *Sudden Fear* (1952), *Shane* (1953), *The Big Knife* (1955), *Barabbas* (1962), *The Professionals* (1966), *The Desperadoes* (1969), *The Horsemen* (1971).

EUGENE PALLETTE (1889–1954)

Back in the days before World War I, this then slim native of Kansas established himself as a leading man on the flickering screen. He appeared with Norma Talmadge in 1916 and played one of the Musketeers in Niblo's 1921 version of *The Three Musketeers* with Douglas Fairbanks. During the 20's, however, his girth developed at a greater rate than his career, and by the time talkies arrived he weighed in at 275 pounds. Although he had literally outgrown his position as a leading man, his distinctive rasping voice and his equally distinctive monolithic body enabled him to find work as a character actor. For two and a half decades the services of the moon-faced, banjo-eyed actor were constantly in demand, and he proved a perfect foil in some of the best comedies and melodramas of his time. **More than 100 talkies include:** *The Love Parade* (1929), *Shanghai Express* (1932), *My Man Godfrey* (1936), *The Adventures of Robin Hood* (1938), *Mr. Smith Goes to Washington* (1939), *Tales of Manhattan* (1942), *Suspense* (1946).

LILLI PALMER (1914–)

Born on a train between Vienna and Berlin to an actress mother, she seems never to have stopped traveling and has been on stage or screen almost her entire life. This international star made her English stage debut at 17. She married Rex Harrison in 1943, and when she appeared opposite him in *The Notorious Gentleman* (1946) she came to Hollywood's attention.

Her first American appearance, opposite Gary Cooper in *Cloak and Dagger* (1946), was well received and established her as a leading woman, equally at home in several languages and the movie studios of the world. **More than 40 films include:** *Thunder Rock* (1944), *Body and Soul* (1947), *The Four Poster* (1952), *The Pleasure of His Company* (1961), *Adorable Julia* (1964), *Madchen in Uniform* (1965), *Sebastian* (1968), *De Sade* (1969).

FRANKLIN PANGBORN (1894–1958)

Pursed lips, nose-in-the-air hauteur and dainty mannerisms resulted in his being cast as a long-suffering floorwalker or hotel clerk who speedily dissolved under stress. Pangborn was also known to millions as a fixture on Jack Benny's radio and TV shows, his trademark being an imperious one-word question: "Ye-e-ess?"

Born in New Jersey, he moved to California to recuperate from shell shock after World War I. He began his acting career on stage and then switched to silent films. He easily made the transition to talkies and appeared in more than 120 pictures. **Credits include:** *Getting Gertie's Garter* (1927), *Design for Living* (1933), *My Man Godfrey* (1936), *A Star Is Born* (1937), *The Bank Dick* (1940), *Now,*

Voyager (1942), *Hail the Conquering Hero* (1944), *Oh, Men! Oh, Women!* (1957).

IRENE PAPAS (1926–)

One of the two internationally celebrated Greek leading ladies of stage and screen, like her countrywoman Melina Mercouri, Papas is now living in political exile from her native land and working to rouse international public opinion against the military regime that rules it.

The daughter of two schoolteachers, she studied classic Greek theatre at the National Academy of Art in Athens. Although she is now known for outstanding performances in screen dramas, she began her professional career at age 16 singing and dancing in variety shows. She then found work in repertory and from 1951 in Greek films.

Not long after her film debut Papas began to make pictures elsewhere in Europe and frequently appeared in Italian productions. In 1964 she confirmed her growing international reputation with her portrayal of the intense, unhappy widow who is stoned to death by villagers in *Zorba the Greek* (1964). Her identification with Greek dissidents was enhanced when she appeared in Costa-Gravas' *Z* (1969) as the wife of a political leader who is assassinated. **Films include:** *Necripolitia* (1951), *The Dead City* (1952), *Tribute to a Bad Man* (1956), *The Guns of Navarone* (1961), *Electra* (1962), *Anne of the Thousand Days* (1970), *The Trojan Women* (1971).

CECIL PARKER (1897–1971)

Britisher Cecil Scwabe decided on a theatrical career after his injuries in World War I upset his original plans to become a surgeon. He made his professional stage debut in *The Merchant of Venice* (1922) ten years before winning his first screen role in *The Silver Spoon* (1932). In the decades that followed, the character appeared in several dozen films as the archtypical well-bred Englishman —pompous, obtuse and often dull. **Screen highlights:** *A Cuckoo in the Nest* (1933), *Caesar and Cleopatra* (1945), *A Man in the White Suit* (1952), *The Ladykillers* (1956), *Indiscreet* (1958), *A Study in Terror* (1966), *Oh! What a Lovely War* (1969).

Lilli Palmer played opposite John Garfield in Body and Soul.

Irene Papas gave a masterful performance in Cacoyannis' production of Zorba the Greek.

Eleanor Parker as the heroine of the screen version of John Van Druten's smash hit The Voice of the Turtle *(1947).*

Jean Parker and Paul Kelly look grim in a film with a grim title, Dead Man's Eyes *(1944).*

CECILIA PARKER (1905–)

The daughter of a British Army officer, Parker was born in Canada, grew up in Los Angeles and started out in films as an extra. Because she could ride, however, she soon found minor roles in Westerns, including *Riders of Destiny* (1933) with John Wayne. The next step was supporting roles (usually as characters much younger than herself) in pictures like *The Painted Veil* (1934) with Garbo and *Ah! Wilderness* (1935). Parker finally found her niche in films as Mickey Rooney's sister in the *Andy Hardy* series. She was 32 when she played the 19-year-old Marian Hardy in the first Hardy film, *A Family Affair* (1937), and continued in this role through the last of the series, *Andy Hardy's Double Life* (1943). She then retired from films but did return to the screen once—for a role in *Andy Hardy Comes Home* (1958). **Films include:** *Women of All Nations* (1931), *The Lost Jungle* (1934), *Naughty Marietta* (1935), *Old Hutch* (1936), *Hollywood Cowboy* (1937), *The Hardys Ride High* (1939), *Seven Sweethearts* (1942).

ELEANOR PARKER (1922–)

This native Midwesterner broke into films via several years in theatre in Cleveland, summer stock and a stint at the Pasadena Playhouse. She first got on screen as an extra in *They Died With Their Boots On* (1941) and went on to play leads in a variety of films of the 40's and 50's. Some fans remember her best as Mildred, the greenish-hued slattern in *Of Human Bondage* (1946), others as the female lead in *Caged* (1950) and still others as opera singer Marjorie Lawrence in the biopic *Interrupted Melody* (1955). In recent years she appeared in supporting roles on screen and in the TV series *Bracken's World*. **Credits include:** *Mission to Moscow* (1943), *The Woman in White* (1948), *Detective Story* (1951), *The Man With the Golden Arm* (1955), *A Hole in the Head* (1959), *The Sound of Music* (1965), *The Oscar* (1966), *Warning Shot* (1967).

JEAN PARKER (1915–)

A demure, sweet, pixyish ingénue, she made her screen debut at 17 in *Divorce in the Family* (1932) and followed that with the ingénue lead opposite the Barrymores in *Rasputin and the Empress* (1932). Born Mae Green in Montana, she and her family moved to Southern California when she was a child. Parker was discovered while still in high school, tested, contracted and continued her education on the MGM lot while playing in pictures. She played unsophisticated roles in scores of films until later in her career when she was able to switch to "hard-boiled roles." She made a telling Broadway debut after her film career was all but over—with Bert Lahr in *Burlesque*. **Some of her films include:** *Little Women* (1933), *Tomorrow We Live* (1942), *One Body Too Many* (1944), *The Gunfighter* (1950), *Apache Uprising* (1966).

SUZY PARKER (1932–)

One of the highest-paid top fashion models of the 50's, this elegant, auburn-haired Texas beauty first appeared on screen (as you guessed it, a model) in *Funny Face* (1957). Within two years she had played Cary Grant's leading lady in *Kiss Them for Me* and Gary Cooper's young love interest in *Ten North Frederick* (1958). Unfortunately, despite Hollywood's campaign to turn her into a star, Parker's acting didn't measure up to her stunning good looks, and she has since appeared in only a few forgettable films. In private life she is married to actor Bradford Dillman. **Films include:** *The Interns* (1962), *Chamber of Horrors* (1966).

LARRY PARKS (1914–)

With the voice of the you-ain't-heard-nothin'-yet comedian dubbed in for his when singing was required, he starred in the title role of *The Jolson Story* (1946) and won an Academy Award nomination for his efforts. Parks had made his first screen appearance only five years before in *Mystery Ship*, and his relatively brief career was laden with "B" scripts and productions. In the early 50's his liberal outlook made him a victim of the McCarthy witchhunts, and it was not until many years had passed that he again appeared on screen. He has pursued his business interests and occasionally made stage appearances with his wife, Betty Garrett. **Films include:** *Canal Zone* (1942), *Reveille With Beverly* (1943), *Down to Earth* (1947), *Gallant Blade* (1948), *Jolson Sings Again* (1949), *Freud* (1962).

ESTELLE PARSONS (1927–)

Her career got off to several false starts before she settled down to acting in the 50's. First there was law school in Boston and some forays into show business as a singer with bands in her native New England. Then she came to New York for a job as production assistant on the original version of NBC-TV's early-morning *The Today Show* and soon found a place on it as a writer, producer and commentator. Besides her TV career, Parsons also established herself as a notable stage actress. She has won two Obies for her performances off Broadway and a Tony nomination for her performance in Tennessee Williams' *The Seven Descents of Myrtle* (1968).

Parsons has appeared in films since the early 60's. She turned in an Academy Award-winning performance in her supporting role as Blanche, Clyde Barrow's hysterical sister-in-law, in *Bonnie and Clyde* (1967) and won an Oscar nomination the following year for another supporting role—in *Rachel, Rachel* (1968). **Films include:** *Ladybug, Ladybug* (1963), *Don't Drink the Water* (1969), *Watermelon Man* (1970), *I Never Sang for My Father* (1970), *I Walk the Line* (1970).

MICHAEL PATE (1920–)

Australian actor Michael Pate frequently has portrayed Indians or villains in Hollywood Westerns. In addition to acting, he has written the screenplays for such films as *Escape From Fort Bravo* (1954) and *The Most Dangerous Man Alive* (1961). **Films include:** *The Strange Door* (1951), *Five Fingers* (1952), *Hondo* (1953), *The Court Jester* (1956), *Congo Crossing* (1956), *The Oklahoman* (1957), *Green Mansions* (1959), *Major Dundee* (1965).

GAIL PATRICK (1915–)

While in school Margaret Fitzpatrick planned to become a lawyer and one day, perhaps, governor of her native Alabama. Instead she entered a motion picture contest on a lark and to her astonishment ended up with a Paramount contract.

In dozens of films, beginning with *If I Had a Million* (1932), the willowy brunette played mostly sophisticated ladies, more often than not other-woman roles. She retired from acting in the late 40's and in recent years has become a highly successful TV producer. Among her credits is the *Perry Mason* series, one of TV's hardiest perennials. **Films include:** *Death Takes a Holiday* (1934), *My Man Godfrey* (1936), *My Favorite Wife* (1940), *Tales of Manhattan* (1942), *Brewster's Millions* (1945), *The Plainsman and the Lady* (1946).

LEE PATRICK (1911–)

Born in New York and educated in Chicago, Lee Patrick became an actress at the urging of George Arliss. She made her screen debut in *Strange Cargo* (1929) and later worked her way through stock, national tours and Broadway before returning to the screen. She has appeared in more than 60 films, usually cast as a hard-bitten blonde with or without a heart of gold. In the early 50's she turned to television as Henrietta Topper, the daffy, hen-pecking wife on the *Topper* series (1953–55) and later (1956-57) appeared on the *Mr. Adams and Eve* series. **A few of her films:** *The Maltese Falcon* (1941), *Now, Voyager* (1942), *Mildred Pierce* (1945), *The Snake Pit* (1948), *Caged* (1950), *Pillow Talk* (1959), *Summer and Smoke* (1961), *The New Interns* (1964).

NIGEL PATRICK (1913–)

He began acting in comedy roles on the London stage in *The Life Machine* (1932) and established his reputation when he played Pa Pennypacker in *The Remarkable Mr. Pennypacker*. Patrick made his motion picture debut in *Mrs. Pym of Scotland Yard* (1939) and has since played leads and supporting roles in numerous British and American films. Patrick has also tried his hand at directing. He appeared on television in the series *Zero One*. **Credits include:** *Noose* (1947), *The Perfect Woman* (1951), *The Pickwick Papers* (1954), *Raintree County* (1957), *The*

Gail Patrick plays Juliet to a highly seductive Jack Romeo Benny in Artists and Models *(1937).*

Estelle Parsons as Clyde's apprehensive sister-in-law in Bonnie and Clyde.

An Oh, wow! shot of John Payne, an Adonis of the 30's, hurling a medicine ball into outer space.

Trials of Oscar Wilde (1960), Johnny Nobody (1965), The Virgin Soldiers (1970), Tales from the Crypt (1972).

ELIZABETH PATTERSON (1874–1966)

During her long career as a character actress Patterson played the mother or aunt of practically every star in Hollywood. She also appeared in more than 100 movies as the housekeeper or the faithful family retainer.

Patterson studied drama in Chicago and first began acting professionally with the touring Ben Greet Players. She joined an Indianapolis repertory company before making it to Broadway. In 1930 she left New York for Hollywood and was featured in *Tarnished Lady* with Tallulah Bankhead and *The Smiling Lieutenant* with Maurice Chevalier. Over the years Patterson occasionally took a break from her kindly (and crotchety) old-lady screen personalities to return to the theatre. She made her last Broadway appearance with Celeste Holm and Robert Preston in *His and Hers* (1954). **Films include:** *The Book of Charm* (1926), *Daddy Long Legs* (1931), *A Bill of Divorcement* (1932), *Dinner at Eight* (1933), *Old Hutch* (1936), *Tobacco Road* (1941), *Intruder in the Dust* (1949), *Pal Joey* (1957).

KATINA PAXINOU (1900–1973)

In her first American film, *For Whom the Bell Tolls* (1943), this Greek actress won an Academy Award for Best Supporting Actress for her portrayal of Pilar, the fiery gypsy. Paxinou began her career as a singer and after some years turned to dramatic roles, eventually becoming one of Europe's outstanding performers. She first came to the New York stage on tour in *Hedda Gabler* when World War II began and a while later went to Hollywood. Directors had great trouble casting her, however, and she eventually returned to her native land, where, with Alexis Minotis, her second husband, she helped establish the Greek National Theatre. Until her death she remained the first lady of the legitimate stage in Greece. **Films include:** *Hostages* (1943), *Confidential Agent* (1947), *Mourning Becomes Electra* (1947), *Mr. Arkadin* (1955), *The Miracle* (1959), *Zita* (1968).

JOHN PAYNE (1912–   )

Fans at first kept confusing his name with John Wayne and his face with Ray Milland's. An extremely good-looking man and a more than competent actor, he became and remained a star for many years. The productions and scripts he played in, however, didn't compare in quality with those that came the way of the other two gentlemen.

Before film appearances Payne had been a crack swimmer, a vocalist, a magazine writer, an actor in summer stock and a Broadway soloist in *At Home Abroad* (1935). His first screen role was in the film version of Sinclair Lewis' *Dodsworth* (1936), and for 20 years thereafter he played lead roles. Payne made a transition to television in the 50's and of late has made a number of guest appearances. In 1974 he made a stage comeback in a revival of the musical *Good News* with Alice Faye. **Many films include:** *Weekend in Havana* (1941), *The Dolly Sisters* (1945), *The Razor's Edge* (1946), *Slightly Scarlet* (1956), *Hidden Fear* (1957), *They Ran for Their Lives* (1968).

Raymond Massey, supported by Rosalind Russell, points a finger at Katina Paxinou in O'Neill's tragic Mourning Becomes Electra.

GREGORY PECK (1916–   )

Variety described his style as "brooding American Gothic." Brooding or not, Peck has all the qualities that one could look for in a hero. He is tall and ruggedly handsome. He is modest and soft-spoken, exuding honesty and what can be best described as worried sincerity. Like Gary Cooper he is an effortless performer, his abilities testified to by four Oscar nominations over a six-year span.

Eldred Gregory Peck, born in La Jolla, California, made it big with his first film appearance in *Days of Glory* (1944) and won an Oscar nomination for his performance as the priest in his next film, *The Keys of the Kingdom* (1944). From then on he was one of the few actors who could pick and choose his parts, becoming at times almost co-producer as well. Sometimes he guessed wrong. "When I'm wrongly cast," he said, "or in a poor script, I sink with the ship." Examples that come to mind include his Captain Ahab in *Moby Dick* (1956) and his starring role in the F. Scott Fitzgerald biopic *Beloved Infidel* (1959). His good pictures, however, outnumber the lemons three or four to one and include *Gentleman's Agreement* (1947), *The Gunfighter* (1950), *The Man in the Gray Flannel Suit* (1956), *The Guns of Navarone* (1961) and *To Kill a Mockingbird* (1963), in which his portrayal of the liberal Southern lawyer, Atticus Finch, won him the Oscar for Best Actor. **Other credits:** *Spellbound* (1945), *The Yearling* (1947), *Twelve O'Clock High* (1950), *Roman Holiday* (1953), *On the Beach* (1959), *Mirage* (1965), *MacKenna's Gold* (1969), *Shoot Out* (1971).

NAT PENDLETON (1895–1967)

The massively built former wrestler, who had won a silver medal in the 1920 Olympics, acted innumerable roles, almost invariably portraying what German critics described as *dumkopfs,* men of highly limited mentality whose dialogue was confined to extremely simple declarative sentences. Predictably, Pendleton began a long career by playing a wrestler in a Broadway production. From there he went on to silent films (e.g., *The Hoosier Schoolmaster* in 1924) and during the talking 30's acted monosyllabically in

Gregory Peck and Joseph Cotten in a fine film that has been seen by untold millions of television viewers, Duel in the Sun.

Abbott and Costello comedies. He was the ambulance driver in the *Dr. Kildare* films, played gangster roles too numerous to mention, plus a wide assortment of muddleheaded good guys. He played a lead role just once: in *Deception* (1933), the tale of a wrestler. His career ended with the early 50's. **Credits include:** *The Sign of the Cross* (1932), *The Thin Man* (1934), *The Great Ziegfeld* (1936), *The Crowd Roars* (1938), *At the Circus* (1939), *Northwest Passage* (1940), *Jail House Blues* (1942), *Death Valley* (1949).

GEORGE PEPPARD (1933–   )

Boyish good looks, inner toughness, self-assurance and an air of sophistication quickly singled him out of the ranks of hopefuls in the movie jungle. Born in Detroit, Michigan, Peppard studied fine arts at the Carnegie Institute of Technology and appeared with a variety of theatre groups before being accepted at the Actors Studio in New York. He soon became a familiar face in TV dramas and appeared in two short-running Broadway plays.

"Hurry or they'll all be dead," Nat *Pendleton appears to be saying to Lew Ayres. The film was* The Secret of Dr. Kildare.

In House of Cards *(1969) George Peppard defends Inger Stevens against a sinister band of international crooks.*

Anthony Perkins and Tuesday Weld make a happy couple in Pretty Poison *(1968).*

His first film, *The Strange One* (1957), an adaptation of Calder Willingham's *End As a Man,* brought him to moviegoers' attention. After several unrewarding films, his talent was again given scope in the male lead in *Breakfast at Tiffany's* (1961) with Audrey Hepburn. There quickly followed *How the West Was Won* (1963), *The Victors* (1963) and a flashy starring role in *The Carpetbaggers* (1964). The scales tipped down again until *The Blue Max* (1966), a film about World War I flying aces, gained critical kudos. He followed this with several forgettable films and is presently ensconced as the star of his own TV series, *Banacek.* **Other films:** *Home From the Hill* (1960), *The Third Day* (1965), *What's So Bad About Feeling Good?* (1968), *The Executioner* (1970), *The Groundstar Conspiracy* (1972).

ANTHONY PERKINS (1932–   )

During his early years on screen in the 50's, the gawky, hunted-looking young New

Yorker seemed to be able to handle effortlessly any role assigned him, playing a paranoid or the friendly lad next door with equal facility. Always, though, he kept his audiences guessing what he was really up to.

The son of stage actor Osgood Perkins, he started his acting career at the age of 15 in a Vermont summer-stock production of *Junior Miss.* Perkins' first film appearance was as Jean Simmons' boy friend in *The Actress* (1953). He soon won plaudits for his performance as the adolescent in *Friendly Persuasion* (1956) and for his portrayal of a confused and troubled professional ball player (Jim Piersall) in *Fear Strikes Out* (1957). He was at his high-tensioned, enigmatic best as the murderous madman in Alfred Hitchcock's 1960 shocker *Psycho.* Other Perkins roles of interest to students of abnormal psychology include the leads in Orson Welles' 1963 version of Kafka's *The Trial* and in *Pretty Poison* (1968), in which he was sinister but not nearly so evil as his partner, Tuesday Weld. For years one of Hollywood's most eligible bachelors, he threw in the sponge in 1973 and married Barinthia (Berry) Berenson, Marisa's sister. **Other films include:** *Desire Under the Elms* (1958), *On the Beach* (1959), *Tall Story* (1960), *Hall of Mirrors* (1969), *Catch-22* (1970), *Play It As It Lays* (1972), *Lovin' Molly* (1974).

BROCK PETERS (1927–   )

His deep, powerful voice won him instant recognition as a soloist with the DePaur Infantry Chorus, and a fierce determination to succeed as an actor sparked a career that has not yet reached its apex.

An off-Broadway play, in which Peters appeared only in shadow, thunderously narrating the story line, brought him critical attention and led to the role of the villainous Army officer in *Carmen Jones* (1954). Later, Samuel Goldwyn picked him to play the brutal Crown in the movie version of Gershwin's *Porgy and Bess* (1959). In *To Kill a Mockingbird* (1963) he brought to life the gentle, goodhearted dirt farmer, Tom Robinson.

Apart from combining appearances in stage productions, television and European films, Peters somehow found time to produce

Five on the Black Hand Side (1973), a warm family comedy that has been hailed as one of the best of the new breed of black films. **His credits include:** *The L-Shaped Room* (1963), *The Pawnbroker* (1965), *Major Dundee* (1965), *The Incident* (1967), *McMasters* (1970), *Lost in the Stars* (1973).

JEAN PETERS (1926–)

The story has it that a Hollywood talent scout saw a picture of this Ohio farm girl in her guise as Miss Ohio State and paved the way to a screen contract. True or not, Jean Peters' freshly scrubbed face and tomboy manner were first seen on screen opposite swashbuckler Tyrone Power in *Captain From Castile* (1947). Other leading roles followed, and in 1955 Peters won an Oscar nomination for her supporting performance in *A Man Called Peter*. Shortly thereafter, with startling abruptness, her career came to a standstill. The explanation for her disappearance can be found in the fact that in 1957 Peters married multi-multimillionaire Howard Hughes, and presumably she simply accompanied him into his highly publicized seclusion. During the later years of the marriage they were separated and finally (in 1971) divorced. In 1972 Peters made a long-awaited performing comeback in a TV production of Sherwood Anderson's *Winesburg, Ohio*. **Films include:** *Deep Waters* (1948), *Viva Zapata!* (1952), *Three Coins in the Fountain* (1954).

SUSAN PETERS (1921–1952)

Suzanne Carnahan started in films while still a student at Hollywood High and spent a good deal of time for the next few years as the official MGM "test girl," appearing in screen tests opposite new male prospects. In spite of this rather dubious start, she was soon considered one of the most promising young actresses on the MGM lot. Her portrayal of Kitty in *Random Harvest* (1942) brought her rave reviews and the Academy Award nomination for Best Supporting Actress.

Peters was paralyzed from the waist down in a hunting accident in 1944. Although she attempted to continue her screen career from a wheelchair, public reaction was negative when she appeared as a ruthless invalid in *The* *Sign of the Ram* (1948). The role was way out of character, for fans preferred her sweet, gentle image from earlier films. She appeared as Laura in a summer-stock production of *The Glass Menagerie* and toured with *The Barretts of Wimpole Street*. **Films include:** *Santa Fe Trail* (1940), *Tish* (1942), *Assignment in Brittany* (1943), *Song of Russia* (1944), *Keep Your Powder Dry* (1945).

DOROTHY PETERSON (1901–)

This kindly-looking character actress spent most of her nearly two decades on screen clad in gingham and one or two aprons and playing somebody or other's mother. On the rare occasions she managed to escape from this typecasting it was almost always to appear as an understanding aunt or a sympathetic nurse, as in *Country Doctor* (1936) and *Dark Victory* (1939). **More than 60 films include:** *Mother's Cry* (debut, 1930), *So Big* (1932), *Freckles* (1935), *Lillian Russell* (1940), *Mr. Skeffington* (1944), *Sister Kenny* (1946).

GÉRARD PHILIPE (1922–1959)

One of the most admired French actors of his generation, Philipe began his stage career in the classical French theatre in productions of Corneille and Racine. In 1947 he came to prominence in the film world as the idealistic romantic youth in *Le Diable au Corps*, the tale of a schoolboy in love with an older woman. He continued in roles that required his characteristic mix of frivolity and melancholy and also performed well in light comedies like *La Beauté du Diable* (1949, U.S. 1952) and even a fast-moving and engaging swashbuckler, *Fanfan la Tulipe* (1951, U.S. 1953). **Other films include:** *Le Ronde* (1950), *Knave of Hearts* (1953), *Le Rouge et le Noir* (1954), *Les Liaisons Dangereuses* (1959).

MACKENZIE PHILLIPS (1960–)

When the casting director for *American Graffiti* (1973) first spotted Phillips singing with an amateur rock band, he thought she was about 20 or 21 but figured she looked young enough to play Carol, the hot-rod-loving teeny bopper who can't convince Paul Le Mat that she's old enough for him.

Brock Peters in the title role in Major Dundee *(1965).*

Gérard Philipe in La Beauté du Diable.

Michel Piccoli maintains complete composure when confronted by Paul Newman and gun in Lady L *(1966). The somewhat startled gentleman on the left is Marcel Dalio.*

It turned out that Phillips was only 13 at the time, but she was a 13-year-old who had been around. Her father is John Phillips, of the former singing group the Mamas and the Papas, and young Mackenzie had met most of the top rock stars of the 60's when she traveled with her father.

After she completed *American Graffiti* Phillips signed for two more films, including one with Gene Hackman and another to be made for television.

MICHEL PICCOLI (1925–   )

In his native France, this versatile actor is a top box-office attraction whether he is appearing on the stage or screen. His more than 60 theatre credits include productions of the Rénaud–Barrault Company and the Théâtre Nationale Populaire, and his work in films has been with some of the world's finest directors. He's made *French Cancan* (1955) and *Diary of a Chambermaid* (1964) for Renoir, *Le Guerre Est Finis* (1967) for Renais, *Topaz* (1969) for Hitchcock and *Belle de Jour*

(1967) for Buñuel. He is married to actress Juliette Greco. **Other films include:** *The Witches of Salem* (1956), *De L'Amour* (1965), *La Curée* (1966), *The Young Girls of Rochefort* (1967), *Un Homme de Trop* (1967), *Dillinger Is Dead* (1968), *La Grande Bouffe* (1972), *Themroc* (1973).

SLIM PICKENS (1919–   )

An expert horseman since his childhood in California, Louis Bert Lindley entered the rodeo circuit while in his teens and eventually became a top rodeo clown. During his more than 25-year career he has appeared in scores of Westerns, notably as a frequent film companion of Rex Allen, the "singing cowboy." In a beautiful bit of self-mockery, Pickens brought his slow, cowboy drawl to the black comedy of *Dr. Strangelove* (1964). Portraying a gung-ho wing commander, Pickens abandons his flight helmet for the familiar Stetson hat as the red alert is sounded. **Films include:** *Rocky Mountain* (1950), *The Sun Shines Bright* (1953), *One-Eyed Jacks* (1961), *Major Dundee* (1965), *Rough Night in Jericho* (1967), *The Getaway* (1972).

MARY PICKFORD (1893–   )

No film star in history, with the possible exception of Shirley Temple, was so adored by filmgoers as Our Mary, "America's Sweetheart." Back in a far more ingenuous day, her every impish gesture, mischievous ploy or waggle of the long, blond and curly locks brought total adulation plus long lines at primitive ticket booths.

Gladys Smith was born in Canada, and as early as 1909 she was appearing in such long-forgotten, flickering epics as *Pippa Passes* and *Her First Biscuits,* the latter a title that causes reason to totter.

In due course she began to work for the great D. W. Griffith and starred in films that were distinctly on the saccharine side but, for their day, remarkably good. When Mary Pickford laughed, audiences laughed with her, and when Mary cried (and she cried a lot) sniffles were audible throughout the theatre. The recipe for her vast success was simple. She was pert. She was cute. She was vitally alive. And when she was cast as the little waif or Cinderella girl (which was almost always) she was completely convincing. In a world that was growing harsher day by day, films like *Rebecca of Sunnybrook Farm* (1917) made mature audiences around the globe recapture, or believe they were recapturing, the innocence of their own youth.

In real life Pickford was an extremely canny business woman. In 1919 Hollywood's Big Four—Chaplin, Fairbanks, Griffith and Pickford—formed United Artists, a vehicle for the distribution of their own films. It was a shrewd move, particularly when films like Pickford's *Little Lord Fauntleroy* (1921), Chaplin's *The Kid* (1921) and Fairbanks' *Robin Hood* (1922), plus dozens more, proved to be enormous money-makers.

The marriage of Queen Mary to King Doug (1920) was front-page news on every continent. During a great part of the 20's anything that happened at Pickfair, the neo-medieval castle where Fairbanks and Pickford held court, was dutifully reported by the press, with even the most trivial happening a subject for dinner-table conversation.

In 1929 Pickford stunned her public by showing her bobbed hair and turning sophisticate in *Coquette*. Fans still liked her, though, and her performance won her one of the earliest Academy Awards. As Kate in *The Taming of the Shrew* (also 1929) Mary was convincing enough, but Fairbanks, who played the tamer, turned out to have a terribly high-pitched voice and wasn't. The famous Pickford–Fairbanks marriage ended in 1935. Soon after, she married Charles (Buddy) Rogers, who had been her leading man in *My Best Girl* (1927).

Now past 80, Pickford has been a recluse for many years. **Some of her other films are:** *Daddy Long Legs* (1919), *Pollyanna* (1920), *Tess of the Storm Country* (1922), *Sparrows* (1926), and her last picture, *Secrets* (1933).

WALTER PIDGEON (1898–   )

This handsome stalwart of Hollywood has almost half a century of screen acting behind him. A veteran of more than 20 silents and 70 talkies, he started his career as a singer in his native Canada. In 1919 he joined the highly respected Copley Players Stock Company in Boston, crossed America with touring companies and established himself in London be-

Mary Pickford, America's Sweetheart, prettily posed with a lapful of posies.

After Mary Pickford played Little Lord Fauntleroy, with Claude Gillingwater as a vulturine nobleman, innumerable small boys were subjected to twin indignities—golden ringlets and velveteen suits—by doting mothers on both sides of the Atlantic.

A somewhat battered Walter Pidgeon in the custody of the Nazis in Man Hunt *(1941).*

The always dependable Zasu Pitts as she appeared in Sing and Like It *(1934).*

fore coming to Broadway, where he played leading roles in operettas and musicals.

He made his film debut in Fannie Hurst's *Mannequin* (1926), and with the advent of sound he was much in demand as a leading man in screen musicals. In 1934, rebelling against being typecast, he returned to the New York theatre and then two years later moved back to Hollywood, where he progressed steadily as a suave and sensitive leading man.

The box-office hit *Blossoms in the Dust* (1941) began his popular association with Greer Garson, and they were teamed up again with equal success for *Mrs. Miniver* (1942), *Madame Curie* (1943) and *The Forsyte Saga* (1949). In recent decades he has been active as a distinguished character actor. **Some of his sound films are:** *Saratoga* (1937), *How Green Was My Valley* (1941), *Design for Scandal* (1942), *Mrs. Parkington* (1944), *If Winter Comes* (1948), *The Bad and the Beautiful* (1953), *Voyage to the Bottom of the Sea* (1961), *Funny Girl* (1968), *Skyjacked* (1972), *The Neptune Factor* (1973).

ZASU PITTS (1898–1963)

Her eyes were huge and plaintive. Her hands fluttered nervously as though they were about to take flight from her body. Her reedy, cracked voice was unmistakable. One of the screen's finest comediennes, she played distraught and harassed ladies for more than 40 years.

What some film addicts don't know or have forgotten is that Zasu Pitts was a magnificent dramatic performer as well. In Erich von Stroheim's silent classic *Greed* (1924) she played the tragic lead role—and gave a subtle, sensitive performance that was a milestone in motion picture history. Audiences, lamentably, always wanted her to be funny. A dramatic sequence in *All Quiet on the Western Front* (1930), for example, had to be reshot after a preview audience laughed at her death scene. Fans preferred to see her as a feather-brained character she popularized in a string of two-reelers made with Thelma Todd in the early 30's. Pitts also appeared with Gale Storm on the *Oh! Susannah* TV series (1956–59). **More than 100 films include:** *The Little Princess* (1917), *The Wedding March* (1928), *No, No, Nanette* (1930), *Ruggles of Red Gap* (1935), *Nurse Edith Cavell* (1939), *Life With Father* (1947), *The Gazebo* (1959), *It's a Mad, Mad, Mad, Mad World* (1963).

DONALD PLEASENCE (1919–   )

This British character actor was perfectly cast in the title role of *Dr. Crippen* (1964), a character who spent his time quietly dismembering bodies and burying the pieces in his back yard. Pleasence seems almost charmingly old-fashioned in his wrongdoing. In later roles his arch-fiend in the James Bond thriller *You Only Live Twice* (1967) and his transvestite husband in *Cul-de-Sac* (1966) added novelty and color to screen wickedness.

Before he began his film career he had already established himself on the London stage. Some of his memorable performances were in *Vicious Circle, Hobson's Choice, The Lark* and *Ebb Tide* (his own play). He won critical raves with his part in Harold Pinter's *The Caretaker,* which he played in London and New York and repeated in the 1963 screen version. **Credits include:** *The Beachcomber* (1955), *1984* (1956), *A Tale of Two Cities* (1958), *Look Back in Anger* (1959), *Sons and Lovers* (1960), *The Great Escape* (1963), *Fantastic Voyage* (1966), *The Night of the Generals* (1967), *Outback* (1970), *The Pied Piper of Hamelin* (1972).

SUZANNE PLESHETTE (1937–   )

This attractive native New Yorker seemed destined for stardom when she began her screen career in the late 50's. An extrovert personality with a natural acting style and a strong booming voice made her an outstanding newcomer, and her fiery manner soon landed her roles as heroine and more as the "other woman." Unfortunately, her arrival in Hollywood coincided with a slump in the industry, and her skill and sex appeal were not enough to make her a star. Like many other actresses of the 60's, Pleshette found it easier to get work on television. She has appeared frequently in starring roles, as well as being a regular on *The Bob Newhart Show,* exercising her comedic talents. **Her films in-**

clude: *The Geisha Boy* (debut, 1958), *Rome Adventure* (1962), *The Birds* (1963), *Youngblood Hawke* (1964), *A Rage to Live* (1965), *Nevada Smith* (1966), *If It's Tuesday This Must Be Belgium* (1969), *Support Your Local Gunfighter* (1971).

CHRISTOPHER PLUMMER
(1927–   )

Trained in the classical theatre, Plummer spent many years playing in Shakespearean productions both in the United States and in his native Canada. He came to the notice of film makers in the late 50's and made a not very successful screen debut in *Stage Struck* (1958). He returned to the stage, gaining world prominence by his performances in New York, London and Canada, and Hollywood again became interested. He was cast as Baron Von Trapp in the immensely successful *The Sound of Music* (1965), but both he and the critics weren't too pleased by his performance.

Since then Plummer has continued to be unlucky in his film roles, and none of his performances has been up to the level he achieves on stage. His most recent Broadway appearance (in *Cyrano*, 1973) brought him a Tony for best actor in a musical. **Films include:** *Inside Daisy Clover* (1966), *Royal Hunt of the Sun* (1969), *Lock Up Your Daughters* (1969), *Waterloo* (1971).

SIDNEY POITIER (1924–   )

Being at the right place at the right time, with the talent and ability to fill an important need in film-making, Poitier became the first actor to create a new screen image of blacks for the filmgoing American public.

Born in Miami of Bahamian parents, he spent part of his childhood in Nassau but returned to Florida in his teens and made his way to New York City. Sleeping on rooftops in summer and in public lavatories in winter, barely surviving on odd jobs, he yearned to become an actor. He began studying at the American Negro Theatre and appeared in plays both on and off Broadway. His clean-cut good looks in an Army documentary film caught the attention of 20th Century–Fox's casting department, and he was given a plum role in *No Way Out* (1950). His appearance as a well-educated and noble physician broke the mold of the movie Negro and had a far-reaching impact on the parts the black actor in Hollywood would eventually get to play. A further success came with *The Blackboard Jungle* (1955), which examined the relations between black and white in America. *The Defiant Ones* (1958) was a study of the individual confrontation between a black and a white man chained together and had much to say about race relations.

Poitier won the 1963 Best Actor Oscar for his performance in the overly sentimental *Lilies of the Field*. In several movies that followed, what had been startling became a cliché, and his image as a loving, understanding man superior in every way to the other characters began to pall. However, *In the Heat of the Night* (1967) allowed Poitier a wider range of emotion, and his honesty and intensity brought him critical plaudits. **Other films include:** *Cry, the Beloved Country* (1952), *Porgy and Bess* (1959), *Raisin in the Sun* (1961), *A Patch of Blue* (1966), *Guess Who's Coming to Dinner* (1967), *To Sir, With Love* (1967), *Buck and the Preacher* (1972).

Christopher Plummer as Baron Von Trapp in the hugely popular The Sound of Music.

Sidney Poitier, who helped smash all motion-picture preconceptions about black actors, as he appeared in The Slender Thread *(1965).*

Michael Pollard looks exactly right for his role in Dirty Little Billie.

Song-and-dance expert Dick Powell with Joan Blondell, whom he later married, in Gold Diggers of 1933.

MICHAEL J. POLLARD (1939–   )

This squat, pudgy-faced actor first caught the public's eye as Kim's boyfriend, Hugo, in the 1961 Broadway musical *Bye, Bye, Birdie.* He then went to Hollywood to play a string of bit parts, most of them exploiting his comic looks. (He's been aptly described in *Newsweek* as looking exactly like Dopey of the Seven Dwarfs.) His fortunes radically changed, however, with the release of *Bonnie and Clyde* (1967). Pollard played the semi-moronic gas-station attendant who joins Warren Beatty and Faye Dunaway on their escapades, and his sensitive performance endeared him to film audiences and brought him an Academy Award nomination for Best Supporting Actor. Thereafter, he commanded a much higher salary and top billing, but his ensuing movies did little to enhance his prestige. **Credits include:** *The Wild Angels* (1966), *The Russians Are Coming, the Russians Are Coming* (1967), *Hannibal Brooks* (1969), *Little Fauss and Big Halsy* (1970), *Dirty Little Billie* (1972).

ERIC PORTMAN (1904–1969)

This distinguished British stage actor began his career in Shakespearean repertory and worked his way up from bit parts to supporting roles. He made his London stage debut in 1924 and became a member of the Old Vic three years later. Portman first appeared on screen in *Murder in the Old Red Barn* (1934, U.S. 1936), and over the following three and a half decades gave occasional but telling performances in a variety of British and American films. His Broadway credits include convincing performances in Terence Rattigan's *Separate Tables* and in Eugene O'Neill's *A Touch of the Poet*. **Film highlights:** *The Prince and the Pauper* (1937), *A Canterbury Tale* (1949), *The Deep Blue Sea* (1955), *The Bedford Incident* 1965), *The Whisperers* (1967), *Deadfall* (1968).

DICK POWELL (1904–1963)

Whenever what seemed like thousands of chorus girls and boys gyrated, in or out of Busby Berkeley films, it was a safe bet that the tenor singing from a spot high above the dancers was Dick Powell.

He learned to sing and to play the piano, banjo and other instruments in his native Arkansas and went on to join the Charlie Davis Orchestra. His first film was *Street Scene* (1931), and within a few years his rich, pleasant, no-nonsense voice had made him one of the singing idols of his time. Audiences liked his wavy hair and dimpled good looks as well, and he somehow managed to make such ultra-extravaganzas as *Goldiggers of 1933, 1935* and *1937* seem almost believable.

An extremely astute gentleman, he sensed that film musicals were on their way out. As the mid-40's approached he stunned reviewers and fans alike by playing the tough private eye in *Murder, My Sweet* (1945) with style and conviction. From then on he specialized in dramatic roles. He later produced and directed his own films and also became a highly successful producer of TV shows, notably *Dick Powell's Zane Grey Theatre*. Of Powell's marriages, the second was to Joan Blondell and the last to June Allyson. **Films include:** *Blessed Event* (1932), *42nd Street* (1933), *Happy Go Lucky* (1943), *Right Cross* (1950), *The Bad and the Beautiful* (1953), *Susan Slept Here* (1954).

ELEANOR POWELL (1912–   )

The whirlwind staccato tap of her dancing shoes carried this Massachusetts-born charmer to film stardom. At 13, on the beach at Atlantic City, she cartwheeled past Gus Edwards, who hired her to join his vaudeville troupe of child performers. Her Broadway debut, at 17, in *Follow Thru,* led to prominent roles in musicals and to her first movie, *George White's Scandals* (1935).

Queen of the tap dancers, she triple-stepped her way through many Hollywood extravaganzas of the 30's and 40's, which provided her with such hand-tailored roles as the desperate victim of spies who tapped out her plight in Morse code in *Ship Ahoy* (1942).

Married to Glenn Ford for 16 years, she retired from pictures in 1951, but after their divorce she made a comeback in nightclubs and TV in the early 60's. **Films include:** *Born to Dance* (1936), the *Broadway Melody* series of 1936, 1938 and 1940, *Lady Be Good* (1941), *Thousands Cheer* (1943), *Sensations of 1945* (1944), *The Duchess of Idaho* (1950).

JANE POWELL (1929–)

In the heyday of screen musicals, Oregon-born Suzanne Burce was taken in hand by Joseph Pasternak, who hoped to create another Deanna Durbin. Although the Pasternak magic did not quite work, Powell did play leads in a number of successful studio-romantic light musicals of the late 40's. Her voice was more than adequate, and she had grace and charm as a dancer.

Her top performance was opposite Howard Keel in *Seven Brides for Seven Brothers* (1954). During the late 50's and early 60's Powell occasionally combined screen appearances with some television work. She most recently appeared in the long-running Broadway hit musical *Irene*. **Films include:** *Song of the Open Road* (debut, 1944), *A Date With Judy* (1948), *Nancy Goes to Rio* (1950), *Royal Wedding* (1951), *Hit the Deck* (1955), *The Female Animal* (1958).

WILLIAM POWELL (1892–)

To millions, Powell, Myrna Loy and the wirehaired Asta made a never-to-be-forgotten combination in the *Thin Man* series of films. Powell was also superb in *My Man Godfrey* (1936), plus a great many other films as well.

A student at New York's American Academy of Dramatic Arts, he had several successful seasons in stock and on Broadway before making his screen debut as the fiendish Professor Moriarty—with John Barrymore in the title role—in *Sherlock Holmes* (1921). Throughout the silent era he was almost always cast as a heavy. All that changed with sound, and he quickly got on the right side of the law in *The Canary Murder Case* (1929) as Philo Vance, the erudite hero of S. S. Van Dine mysteries. Powell's urbane, high-gloss performances in the series managed to make Philo seem almost real.

Powell was at his best in frothy comedies, and he made some beauties with Carole Lombard (who was also his wife for a brief period in the early 30's). In *Manhattan Melodrama* (1934) Powell appeared for the first time opposite Myrna Loy. Hollywood sensed that they were made for each other, and they were immediately cast as Nick and Nora Charles in Dashiell Hammett's fine thriller *The Thin Man* (1934). They again delighted audiences with their brittle repartee and went on to make 11 more films together, five of them *Thin Man* follow-ups. Only Asta, the frisky terrier, was changed.

An Academy Award nomination went to Powell for the Nick Charles role, and a second came his way when he played Flo Ziegfeld in the lush 1936 production *The Great Ziegfeld*. Still a third was for a stunning portrayal of Father in Clarence Day's *Life With Father* (1947), the film version of one of the most popular and long-running plays in Broadway history.

In the early 50's Powell switched to character roles, which he played with the same gracious urbanity he had shown as a star. He retired in the late 50's after a bout with ill health. **Films include:** *Beau Geste* (1926), *Senorita* (1927), *Behind the Makeup* (1930), *The Last of Mrs. Cheney* (1937), *How to Marry a Millionaire* (1953), *Mister Roberts* (1955).

TYRONE POWER (1913–1958)

Born in Ohio to a distinguished theatrical family, Tyrone Power III made his first stage appearance at the age of seven. At eight he made his screen debut in *The Black Panther's Cub* (1921) and appeared as a child actor in a dozen subsequent films.

He first gained major public attention as the romantic interest in *Lloyds of London* (1936), and his appealing good looks and gentle manner quickly endeared him to the distaff side of the audience. A series of leading roles opposite the reigning movie queens of the 30's—Loretta Young, Alice Faye, Norma Shearer, Myrna Loy, Sonja Henie, etc.—and a variety of parts gave him the technique and opportunity for full-fledged stardom, and in the 40's he made a series of commercial successes that established him as a top box-office contender. After his World War II service he returned to Hollywood and resumed his flourishing career, once again demonstrating his versatility in a series of roles as a Western desperado, a bullfighter, a pilot and assorted historical adventurers. He died of a heart attack on the set of *Solomon and Sheba* (1959). **His films include:** *In Old Chicago* (1938), *Marie Antoinette* (1938), *The Rains Came* (1939), *Blood and Sand* (1941), *This Above*

Eleanor Powell tapped up and down the steps of the fountain in Broadway Melody of 1938.

William Powell, as private-eye Nick Charles, confronts a murderous adversary in Song of the Thin Man *(1947).*

Tyrone Power was cast in many costume dramas—perhaps because he could wear the clothes so gracefully in addition to being so handsome. This film was Son of Fury *with Frances Farmer (1942).*

All (1942), *Nightmare Alley* (1947), *Prince of Foxes* (1949), *The Sun Also Rises* (1957), *Witness for the Prosecution* (1958).

STEFANIE POWERS (1942–   )

Growing up in Hollywood with the unlikely name of Taffy Paul, she long planned to be an actress and finally broke into films as a contract player with Columbia Studios, which, perhaps unwisely, dubbed her Powers.

She was cast in a dozen movies within a very short time. Her first important role was playing Lee Remick's teenage sister in *Experiment in Terror* (1962). Unfortunately, as one of the many young, vivacious starlets breaking into movies in the early 60's, she had little opportunity to develop an individual approach or create an image of her own.

Temporary success, however, came on television, and in 1966 she landed the lead in the series *The Girl from U.N.C.L.E.* An attractive, athletically inclined woman, Powers continues to appear in TV dramas and does occasional film work. **Credits include:** *McLintock* (1963), *Palm Springs Weekend*

Lovely Paula Prentiss and a rather bored friend.

(1963), *Die! Die! My Darling* (1965), *Stagecoach* (1966), *Warning Shot* (1967).

PAULA PRENTISS (1939–   )

Shortly after her graduation from Northwestern University Paula Ragusa was whisked off to Hollywood to make her screen debut, as Paula Prentiss, in the unconvincing college comedy *Where the Boys Are* (1961). She went on to play in several youth-oriented comedies opposite Jim Hutton, with whom the studio hoped to team her permanently.

Prentiss is tall, lanky and attractive, and her appeal is more often based on physical kookiness than on the usual Hollywood standard of glamour and sophistication. Her emergence as an individual comedienne was a triumph of hard work and talent over indifferent material. She wisely uses her appearance to create an appealing, self-mocking brand of comedy.

Her horizon has broadened to include appearances on the stage, and for a time she had a TV series, *He and She*, co-starring her husband, Richard Benjamin. **Her film credits include:** *The World of Henry Orient* (1964), *What's New, Pussycat?* (1965), *Catch-22* (1970), *Last of the Red Hot Lovers* (1972), *The Last of Sheila* (1973).

MICHELINE PRESLE (1922–   )

This convent-educated Parisian was one of the European beauties discovered by the camera in the 40's. She came to the United States in 1945, but the language difficulty, an unfamiliar audience and a few less than worthy films sent her back to Paris. An established performer in France, she created a sensation with her torrid love scenes with Gérard Philipe in *Devil in the Flesh* (1949). She still appears in films from time to time, occasionally English or American ones. **Films include:** *Jeunes Filles en Détresse* (1939), *Foolish Husbands* (1948), *Demoniaque* (1958), *If a Man Answers* (1962), *The Prize* (1964), *King of Hearts* (1967), *Peau d'Ane* (1971).

ELVIS PRESLEY (1935–1977)

In the 50's rock-and-roll idol Presley had only to move his hips to evoke shrill screams from his adoring fans. His individualistic vocal delivery, pelvic gyrations and assorted contortions made this talented artist's performances dramatic and electric. He remained at the top of the hit-parade charts for years, and in more than 25 films (many named after his hit song titles) Presley came through as a good-natured and likable young man who was a passable actor.

After his highly publicized induction into the U.S. Army, Presley's standing began to slip. For a time it looked as though he might fade into obscurity, as so many singing stars have done in the past, but as the mid-70's approached Elvis was as popular as ever. In recent years his concert appearances have filled to capacity the largest indoor arenas in America. He still was acknowledged as "the King." **Films include:** *Love Me Tender* (1956), *Jailhouse Rock* (1957), *Kid Galahad* (1963), *Frankie and Johnny* (1966), *Elvis—That's the Way It Is* (1970).

ROBERT PRESTON (1918–   )

This rugged, personable actor can look back on 35 years of success in movies and the theatre. Preston was born in Massachusetts and grew up in California. He began his acting career at the Pasadena Playhouse. After playing in 42 productions there, he was groomed by Paramount as a leading man. In a string of films of the late 30's and 40's, he alternated between playing the hero and the heavy opposite such glamorous ladies as Barbara Stanwyck, Loretta Young, Veronica Lake and Joan Bennett. The most successful of his films were *Beau Geste* (1939), *Northwest Mounted Police* (1940), *Reap the Wild Wind* (1942) and *Wake Island* (1942).

After serving in World War II Preston returned to Hollywood and spent another ten years making films, including *The Macomber Affair* (1947), *The Sundowners* (1950) and *The Bride Comes to Yellow Sky* (1953). During this time, however, his stage career developed at a much more positive pace, and Preston appeared in several Broadway plays until an unusual stage role broadened his horizons. His portrayal of Harold Hill, the smooth-talking con man in *The Music Man,* received critical acclaim from the New York critics, and there was no thought of anyone else recreating the character on film (1962). It was a great personal triumph for Preston.

Although he played parts in several movies after that, they could hardly live up to this ideal Preston role. Today he continues to divide his time between Broadway, television and an occasional film. **His other films include:** *King of Alcatraz* (1938), *Union Pacific* (1939), *This Gun for Hire* (1942), *Blood on the Moon* (1948), *The Dark at the Top of the Stairs* (1960), *How the West Was Won* (1963), *All the Way Home* (1963), *Junior Bonner* (1972).

MARIE PREVOST (1898–1937)

Canadian Marie Bickford Dunn went directly from a *Midnight Follies* chorus line in New York to California's then semi-deserted beaches to frolic with the other Mack Sennett bathing beauties. From the early 20's, however, the ambitious brunette beauty turned to more substantial roles in feature-length silents. She did an outstanding job in comedies like Ernst Lubitsch's seemingly daring *The Marriage Circle* (1924) and also had considerable success in more serious ventures. She was featured in dozens of films before the advent of sound and made a smooth transition to talkies. **Credits include:** *The Beautiful and the Damned* (1922), *The Lover of*

Elvis Presley, without music but with a fancy telephone emerging from a souped-up car—a milieu his fans loved.

A hard-working Robert Preston in Wild Harvest *(1947) rests on a car door. The others are Alan Ladd, Dorothy Lamour and Allen Jenkins.*

Kenneth Harlan didn't dare look at Marie Prevost as he explained just why smoking was injurious to her health. The film was Scott Fitzgerald's The Beautiful and the Damned.

Vincent Price played with a sinister Boris Karloff and an equally sinister Peter Lorre in the sinister film The Raven.

Camille (1924), *The Racket* (1928), *Hell Divers* (1931), *Only Yesterday* (1933), *13 Hours by Air* (1936).

DENNIS PRICE (1915–)

This dependable, dapper British actor is best known for his role in *Kind Hearts and Coronets* (1950), in which he played a vengeful commoner, the ninth in line to inherit a dukedom, who does away with the first eight—all played by Alec Guinness. One of the first films to treat cold-blooded murder in a comic vein, it provided a field day for the two actors.

Price was also seen as the blackmailing publisher in *The Naked Truth* (1958) and was again teamed with Guinness in the moving *Tunes of Glory* (1960). **Other films include:** *A Canterbury Tale* (debut, 1944), *The Magic Bow* (1947), *I'm All Right, Jack* (1960), *A High Wind in Jamaica* (1965), *The V.I.P.s* (1963), *Ten Little Indians* (1966).

VINCENT PRICE (1911–)

During the first half of his career on the stage and in films, Vincent Price spent a good deal of time in attendance at royal courts—Queen Victoria's in the play *Victoria Regina* (1936), Elizabeth I's in *The Private Lives of Elizabeth and Essex* (1939), Catherine the Great's in *A Royal Scandal* (1945) and Louis XIII's in *The Three Musketeers* (1948). His regal bearing, impeccable diction (learned at the University of London) and worldly-wise demeanor belied his birthplace of St. Louis, Missouri. He soon became one of the most prominent of the suave leading men of the 40's, appearing in such successes as *The Song of Bernadette* (1944), *Laura* (1944), *The Keys of the Kingdom* (1944), *Leave Her to Heaven* (1945) and *Dragonwyck* (1946).

After a few years of potboiler movies, his career took a sudden and lucrative turn with *The House of Wax* (1953), a 3-D spectacular that turned him loose to perform a spate of villainies almost unmatched heretofore. There followed a series of commercially successful, low-budget, British-made horror stories, starring Price and directed by Roger Corman. Edgar Allan Poe was their favorite writer, and *The House of Usher* (1960), *The Pit and the Pendulum* (1961), *The Raven*

(1963) and *The Masque of Red Death* (1964) won critical and popular acclaim for Price, who continues turning out literate horror films.

Price himself is a well-rounded man with myriad interests. Having gathered a highly regarded collection of paintings, he frequently lectures on the fine arts. As a respected gourmet cook, he and his wife published a valuable cookbook, *The Vincent and Mary Price Cookbook,* and his autobiography, *I Like What I Know,* has been published. **Other films include:** *Green Hell* (1940), *The Eve of St. Mark* (1944), *Up in Central Park* (1948), *The Ten Commandments* (1956), *House of a Thousand Dolls* (1968), *Dr. Phibes* (1972).

AILEEN PRINGLE (1895–)

The triumph of her career as a vamp of the silent screen came in 1924, when she played leads in two seething Elinor Glynn films—opposite Conrad Nagel in *Three Weeks* and opposite John Gilbert in *His Hour.* Pringle was born Aileen Bisbee in San Francisco and educated in France and England. There she married Sir Charles Pringle and also made her West End debut in *The Bracelet* (1915). She moved to the United States after World War I and made her screen debut in a forgotten silent, *Honor Bound,* with another unknown, Valentino. After almost a decade as one of the box-office queens, her career faltered with the advent of sound and she was relegated to roles in a string of bad Westerns with Lew Cody and forgettable "B" pictures. **Credits include:** *Redhead* (1919), *The Christian* (1923), *Wife of a Centaur* (1924), *Adam and Evil* (1927), *Soldiers and Women* (1930), *Piccadilly Jim* (1936), *The Girl from Nowhere* (1939).

JED PROUTY (1879–1956)

His rotund shape and homey philosophy became familiar to millions of Americans during the 30's and early 40's when he played the father in the more than 12 episodes of the *Jones Family* film series. Born in Boston, Prouty started his professional career in repertory companies and in vaudeville. He went to Hollywood in the 20's and played small roles in hundreds of silents. He had a featured role in MGM's first musical talkie, *The Broadway*

Melody (1929). **His film credits include:** *The Jones Family* (1935), *George White's Scandals* (1935), *The Texas Rangers* (1936), *Roar of the Press* (1941), *Mug Town* (1943), *Guilty Bystander* (1950).

DOROTHY PROVINE (1937–   )

This native of Deadwood, South Dakota, broke into films in the late 50's, played the title role in *The Bonnie Parker Story* in 1958 and Charlestoned her way to a successful TV career as nightclub entertainer Pinky Pinkham in *The Roaring Twenties* TV series of 1960. In a straight dramatic role in *The Wall of Noise* (1963) she remained faithful to the hero in her own fashion, and as the saloon singer in *The Great Race* (1965) she once again combined toughness and tenderness. **Other films include:** *It's a Mad, Mad, Mad, Mad World* (1963), *Good Neighbor Sam* (1964), *Who's Minding the Mint?* (1967), *Never a Dull Moment* (1968).

RICHARD PRYOR (1941–   )

A stand-up comedian who got his start in TV variety shows and in nightclubs, Pryor landed his first substantial screen role in 1968, when he played Stanley X in *Wild in the Streets* with Shelley Winters. He had started his performing career long before that, however, when he sat on drums at age seven at a nightclub in his home town of Peoria, Illinois. Eventually he made his professional debut at a nightclub in Canada and then went to work in New York City coffeehouses before getting his first big break with a spot on *The Ed Sullivan Show*. **Films include:** *The Busy Body* (1967), *The Green Berets* (1968), *Phynx* (1970), *Lady Sings the Blues* (1972), *Dynamite Chicken* (1972).

FRANK PUGLIA (1892–   )

Puglia began his performing career at the age of 15 as a member of an operetta company and later played in vaudeville before being signed by D. W. Griffith for *Orphans of the Storm* (1921). Since then he has crossed the screen in every kind of guise imaginable, including doctors, villains, musical conductors and chiefs of police. **Credits include:** *Ramola* (1924), *Viva Villa!* (1934), *The Mark of Zorro* (1940), *Now, Voyager* (1942), *Casablanca* (1942), *For Whom the*

Bell Tolls (1943), *The Phantom of the Opera* (1943), *Blood on the Sun* (1945), *Cry Tough* (1959), *Girls! Girls! Girls!* (1962).

EDNA PURVIANCE (1894–1958)

Born in Lovelock, Nevada, she made her way to San Francisco to search for a secretary's job and met Charlie Chaplin at a party. Despite a total lack of stage or screen experience, Chaplin engaged her as his leading lady. Beginning with *A Night Out* (1915), she was the golden-haired, innocent ingénue in 35 of his comedies and his partner in a stormy romance. In 1924 unfavorable publicity due to a shooting at her home destroyed her career, but Chaplin kept her on salary for 30 years. She came out of retirement to appear with him in *Limelight* (1952), her last film. **Other films include:** *Sunnyside* (1919), *The Kid* (1921), *The Pilgrim* (1923), *A Woman of Paris* (1923).

DENVER PYLE (1920–   )

He is best remembered as the sheriff who killed Bonnie and Clyde in the 1967 movie of their life and hard times. Pyle's face is also familiar to fans of Westerns, and he has made frequent television appearances, including a continuing role in *The Doris Day Show*. **Films include:** *Man from Colorado* (1949), *To Hell and Back* (1955), *Shenandoah* (1965), *Bandolero* (1968).

Denver Pyle, the sheriff who finally got them, along with Gene Hackman, in Bonnie and Clyde.

Edna Purviance, who played just one serious role (A Woman of Paris), *in a typical role with Charlie Chaplin and the Keystone Cops.*

Randy Quaid in The Last Detail, *a young seaman in deep trouble.*

RANDY QUAID (1953–)

Quaid became interested in acting while a high-school student in Houston, Texas, and began his movie career while a college student. He made his screen debut in *The Last Picture Show* (1972) and was featured in several TV movies. His performance in *The Last Detail* (1973), as the 18-year-old sailor being escorted from Norfolk to a jail in Portsmouth, brought him critical acclaim and an Academy Award nomination for Best Supporting Actor. **Other film credits include:** *What's Up Doc?* (1972), *The Lolla Madonna War* (1972), *Paper Moon* (1973).

JOHN QUALEN (1899–)

Born in Vancouver, Canada, of Norwegian ancestry, John Oleson first gained recognition for his performances as the Swedish janitor in both the Broadway (1929) and screen (1931) versions of Kurt Weill's *Street Scene*. Since then he has appeared in scores of films, usually playing ineffectual or overwhelmed-by-life characters of Scandinavian, German, Italian or French descent. He is probably best remembered as the crazed little man in *His Girl Friday,* the 1940 screen version of the Ben Hecht–Charles MacArthur play *The Front Page*. In addition to his stage and screen work, Qualen has also become familiar to TV audiences. **Credits include:** *Arrowsmith* (debut, 1931), *Counsellor-at-Law* (1933), *Seventh Heaven* (1937), *Casablanca* (1942), *The Fugitive* (1947), *The Man Who Shot Liberty Valance* (1962), *Firecreek* (1968).

ANTHONY QUAYLE (1913–)

This distinguished British actor and director first appeared on stage as straight man to a comic in vaudeville. He made his legitimate-theatre debut with the Old Vic in 1932 and has since acted in Shakespearean roles and other theatre classics. From 1948 to 1956 he managed the Stratford-on-Avon Theatre. He made his American stage debut in 1936 in a revival of *The Country Wife,* and most recently he was seen on Broadway in the long-running *Sleuth* (1970). In films he has given strong, telling performances since appearing in Olivier's *Hamlet* (1948). **Films include:** *The Wrong Man* (1956), *The Guns of Navarone* (1961), *Lawrence of Arabia* (1962), *A Study in Terror* (1966), *Anne of the Thousand Days* (1970), *The Nelson Affair* (1973).

EDDIE QUILLAN (1907–)

This pleasant-faced character actor broke into show business as a member of his family's vaudeville act and began his long, long screen career in comedies. He made 18 two-reelers for Mack Sennett in the silent 20's and was under contract to the Harold Lloyd

Anthony Quayle, right, in Lawrence of Arabia. *Peter O' Toole is the thinker, and the young Arab with the unfriendly look is unknown.*

Corporation during the early talking 30's. From the mid-30's he added more serious roles to his credits, notably as Ellison in *Mutiny on the Bounty* (1935) and as Rosesharn's husband in *The Grapes of Wrath* (1940). Quillan has also appeared on television. **Credits include:** *Big Money* (1930), *Young Mr. Lincoln* (1939), *This Is the Life* (1944), *Brigadoon* (1954), *Move Over Darling* (1965), *Angel in My Pocket* (1969).

ANTHONY QUINN (1916–   )

Born in Chihuahua, Mexico, of a Mexican mother and an Irish father, Anthony Rudolf Oaxaca Quinn came to the United States to escape a revolution. He began working at the age of nine in various odd jobs, including that of a janitor in a drama school, where he got parts in some of the school's plays. A walk-on part in a "B" movie, *Parole* (1936), led to a string of minor roles in other forgettable second features and many supporting roles.

In the early 50's Quinn was offered a contract to appear in a number of Italian films. The first of four were disasters, but the fifth, *La Strada* (1954), was a huge international success, and Quinn returned to Hollywood demanding and receiving starring roles, even though many of the films he made subsequently were less than superior vehicles.

His movie career was the reverse of the usual Hollywood pattern. Most actors go from starring roles to character parts, but Quinn started as a character actor and achieved star status 28 years later in *Zorba the Greek* (1964). Along the road to stardom he picked up two Academy Awards for Best Supporting Actor, in *Viva Zapata!* (1952) and *Lust for Life* (1956).

On Broadway, Quinn replaced Brando in *A Streetcar Named Desire* and also had the male lead in *Born Yesterday* on tour. In 1960 he played opposite Laurence Olivier in *Becket*, and later, in an unusual move, the two men exchanged roles. **Highlights of more than 85 films:** *Union Pacific* (1939), *Blood and Sand* (1941), *The Ox-Bow Incident* (1943), *The Guns of Navarone* (1961), *Requiem for a Heavyweight* (1962), *The Magus* (1968), *The Shoes of the Fisherman* (1968), *Across 110th Street* (1973).

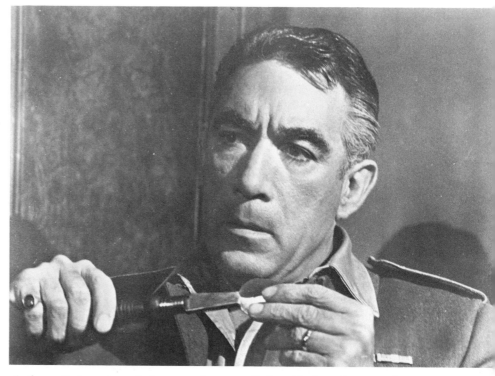

Anthony Quinn, one of the screen's most distinguished performers, in Behold a Pale Horse *(1964).*

The same Anthony Quinn, superbly made up, as Mayor Bombolini in The Secret of Santa Vittorio. *He is greeting Captain Von Prum (Hardy Kruger), who is about to take over the town in the name of the Third Reich.*

CHIPS RAFFERTY (1909–1971)

When the gawky six-foot-six-inch John Goffage made his screen debut as an Irishman in a 1938 picture in his native Australia, he changed his name to Chips Rafferty, an undoubted improvement over the suggestion that he call himself Slab O'Flaherty. Rafferty went on to make a variety of slapstick comedies in Australia. He almost always played a variation of his best-loved character, a lanky, drawling country type called Dinkum, and within a few years he was firmly established as Australia's favorite screen actor. During World War II he was relieved of some of his military duties to appear in morale-booster films, such as *Forty Thousand Horsemen* (1941), a tale of Australian cavalry in the Middle East in World War I, and *The Rats of Tobruk* (1942, U.S. 1951).

Since then Rafferty also appeared in British and American films. In a joint British-American production, *The Overlanders* (1946), he starred as one of the Australian cattlemen who drove their herds across the continent in 1942 to escape an expected Japanese invasion. In *The Wackiest Ship in the Army* (1961) he played an Australian coast watcher. **Films include:** *Dan Rudd, M.P.* (1939), *The Loves of Joanna Godden* (1946), *Bitter Springs* (1951), *Kangaroo* (1952), *King of the Coral Sea* (1954), *The Sundowners* (1960), *They're a Weird Mob* (1966), *Kona Coast* (1968).

FRANCES RAFFERTY (1922–   )

For a few years in the early 40's Rafferty played ingénues in a series of MGM pictures. She generally was cast as an all-American girl—Mickey Rooney's prom date in *Girl Crazy* (1943), Marshall Thompson's girl friend in *Bad Bascomb* (1946). Her most dramatic screen moment came in *Dragon Seed* (1944)—she was murdered.

After her MGM contract expired, Rafferty played leads in several unmemorable pictures. Beginning in 1954, for five years, she played Spring Byington's daughter on the situation-comedy series *December Bride*. Since then she has made only rare screen appearances. **Films include:** *Seven Sweethearts* (1942), *Thousands Cheer* (1943), *The Hidden Eye* (1945), *Abbott and Costello in Hollywood* (1945), *Lost Honeymoon* (1947), *The Shanghai Story* (1954), *Wings of Chance* (1961).

GEORGE RAFT (1895–   )

This leading figure of Hollywood's celluloid underworld during the 30's and 40's once confessed that his early ambition was to become a gangland big shot. He did, but it was for reel rather than for real. Raft landed his first screen role though his mob connections. He was assigned to Texas Guinan's nightclub as "protection" when Guinan helped him get a bit part in her picture *Queen of the Night Clubs* (1929). Small roles as heavies followed until he hit the big time with his performance as gangster Guido Rinaldo to Paul Muni's Al Capone in Howard Hawks' memorable *Scarface* (1932).

He was put under contract by Paramount and cast in a string of mobster roles. The studio did, however, make a brief attempt early on to build him up as a new Valentino. When that didn't work they tried putting his gangster image to use in musicals, and Raft starred in a few, such as *Stolen Harmony* (1935) and *Every Night at Eight* (1935).

He continued to play heavies throughout the 30's and 40's, occasionally teamed with other movie tough guys, notably with James Cagney in *Each Dawn I Die* (1939), with Humphrey Bogart in *They Drive by Night* (1939) and with Edward G. Robinson in *Manpower* (1942). His career began to slip in the late 40's, and since then his screen appearances have largely been confined to second features or to cameo roles—in films like

When he wasn't flipping a half dollar George Raft had an itchy trigger finger. Here he is, complete with arsenal, in Undercover Man.

Around the World in 80 Days (1956), *Some Like It Hot* (1959) and *Casino Royale* (1967). In the 60's Raft was back in his familiar gangster-convict guise in a popular TV commercial as the instigator of a prison food-hall riot who demanded ''Alka-Seltzer, Alka-Seltzer, Alka-Seltzer . . .'' **Credits include:** *Quick Millions* (1931), *Pick-Up* (1933), *The Bowery* (1933), *The Glass Key* (1935), *Background to Danger* (1943), *Follow the Boys* (1944), *Outpost in Morocco* (1949), *Black Widow* (1954), *Jet Over the Atlantic* (1960), *Ocean's Eleven* (1960), *The Upper Hand* (1967), *Skidoo* (1968).

RAGS RAGLAND (1905–1946)

This tall slapstick comedian with a bewildered expression quit school at 14, was a newsboy, film operator and welterweight boxer before joining a traveling show as a comic and beginning his entertainment career. He worked on Minsky's burlesque circuit and in 1938 made his Broadway bow in a revue. Two years later he won a sizable role and popularity on stage in *Panama Hattie* with Ethel Merman. His stage success led to Hollywood offers, and he made his screen debut in *Ringside Maisie* (1941). During the next five years he made more than 20 films, including a remake of the Cross–Carpenter comedy *Whistling in the Dark* (1941) with Red Skelton, the 1942 screen version of *Panama Hattie* and *Anchors Aweigh* (1945). The highly popular comedian died of uremic poisoning at the age of 41. **Other films:** *Du Barry Was a Lady* (1943), *Girl Crazy* (1943), *Her Highness and the Bellboy* (1945), *The Hoodlum Saint* (1946).

RAIMU (1883–1946)

With his equatorial waist, buttony mustache and true clown's genius for pathos, Jules Muraire Raimu was a renowned performer on stage and screen in his native France for several decades before the wide distribution of *The Baker's Wife* (1939) established him everywhere as a memorable screen actor. A native of Toulon, Raimu began his career in music halls and revues and then broke into legitimate theatre, appearing mainly in Feydeau and Guitry plays. He first gained recognition on screen as the café owner in Marcel Pagnol's trilogy: *Marius* (1931, U.S. 1933), *Fanny* (1932, U.S. 1948), *César* (1934, U.S. 1948). **Other films:** *Un Carnet de Bal* (1937, U.S. 1944), *Les Inconnus dans la Maison* (1942), *L'Homme au Chapeau Rond* (1946).

LUISE RAINER (1910–   )

The petite Viennese beauty was already an established stage actress in Vienna and Berlin when she made her first American film, *Escapade* (1935). Outstanding performances in her next two pictures brought her the unique distinction of winning two successive Best Actress Oscars: as Anna Held in *The Great Ziegfeld* (1936) and O-Lan in the screen version of Pearl Buck's bestseller *The Good Earth* (1937). The films that followed proved to be a distinct letdown, and she retired in the early 40's. Rainer was married for a time to playwright Clifford Odets and now lives in London with her present husband, publisher Robert Knittel. **Other credits include:** *Big City* (1937), *The Great Waltz* (1938), *Dramatic School* (1938), *Hostages* (1943).

ELLA RAINES (1921–   )

A graduate of the University of Washington, Ella Wallace Raubes was trying to establish herself on the New York stage when film director Howard Hawks saw her photograph and cast her in *Corvette K-225* (1943). She made a strong impact in her first film and went on to play leads in some good Universal melodramas and war movies over the next four years. By the end of the decade, however, her box-office appeal had gone, and in the mid-50's she retired from the screen. Raines also starred on television in her own series, *Janet Dean, Registered Nurse*. **Screen highlights:** *Phantom Lady* (1944), *Enter Arsène Lupin* (1944), *The Suspect* (1945), *Brute Force* (1947), *The Second Face* (1951), *Man in the Road* (1957).

CLAUDE RAINS (1889–1967)

In his first film he was covered in gauze bandages from head to foot. When the gauze was removed one saw nothing, since the film,

The great Raimu in a great film, The Baker's Wife.

Luise Rainer as Anna Held in The Great Ziegfeld. *Her famous telephone scene in that movie helped clinch her first Oscar.*

Claude Rains in mid-career. The film was Paramount's Song of Surrender *(1949).*

reasonably enough, was H. G. Wells' *The Invisible Man* (1933). Rains is also fondly remembered as the less than honest but secretly anti-Nazi French official who collaborated with Humphrey Bogart in *Casablanca* (1942).

Rains was born in London, first appeared on the legitimate stage at age 11, became a successful stage performer and came to the United States as he neared his fortieth year. His trademark was a trick right eyebrow that could be raised to convey scorn, skepticism, mild amusement or total disbelief.

From the mid-30's Rains was cast in at least three films a year, always suave and mellifluous-voiced and usually sinister. He won an Academy Award nomination for Best Supporting Actor for his performance as a crooked Senator in *Mr. Smith Goes to Washington* (1939). Other nominations were to follow, for *Casablanca, Mr. Skeffington* (1944), in which he played a good-guy role as Bette Davis' husband, and *Notorious* (1946), a Hitchcock film.

Throughout his long career Rains interspersed his screen performances with appearances on stage. He starred in *Darkness at Noon* on Broadway in 1950 and retired after appearing at the Westport Playhouse in *So Much of Earth, So Much of Heaven* in 1965. Rains married seven times. **Films include:** *Crime Without Passion* (1934), *Anthony Adverse* (1936), *Gold Is Where You Find It* (1938), *Four Daughters* (1938), *They Made Me a Criminal* (1939), *Here Comes Mr. Jordan* (1941), *Kings Row* (1942), *Now, Voyager* (1942), *Caesar and Cleopatra* (1944), *The White Tower* (1950), *The Greatest Story Ever Told* (1965).

JESSE RALPH (1864–1944)

Although she was in her mid-60's when she made her screen debut, Ralph proved to be a popular character actress for nearly a decade before she retired at age 75. She had many years of acting experience in the theatre before she went to Hollywood in 1933. Ralph made her stage debut at age 16 and appeared in many Broadway productions, including the 1927 hit *The Road to Rome*. Her screen roles included Peggoty in *David Copperfield*

(1935) and the Irish dowager in *San Francisco* (1936). **Films include:** *Child of Manhattan* (1933), *Captain Blood* (1935), *Camille* (1937), *Café Society* (1939), *They Met in Bombay* (1941).

ESTHER RALSTON (1902–)

An extremely beautiful leading lady in silents and early talkies, Ralston starred in a 1923 serial *The Phantom Fortune* and was at her best in two Herbert Brenon versions of Barrie tales, *Peter Pan* (1924) and *A Kiss for Cinderella* (1925). She also starred as the wronged peasant girl in Von Sternberg's last silent, *The Case of Lena Smith* (1929). **Other credits:** *Old Ironsides* (1926), *The Prodigal* (1931), *After the Ball* (1932), *Hollywood Boulevard* (1936), *Tin Pan Alley* (1940).

JOBYNA RALSTON (1901–1967)

One of the leading actresses of the silent screen, Ralston is best remembered as the leading lady in several of Harold Lloyd's most memorable silent comedies. She came to Hollywood shortly after making her Broadway debut in *Two Little Girls in Blue* (1921). Ralston was considered one of the most beautiful women of her day. In addition to the comedies with Lloyd, she starred in a variety of popular silents, including *Wings* (1927), the first picture to win the Academy Award. **Films include:** *Why Worry?* (1923), *Girl Shy* (1924), *The Freshman* (1925), *For Heaven's Sake* (1926).

VERA HRUBA RALSTON (1921–)

This Czech actress first tasted success as an ice-skating champion who competed in the 1936 Olympics in Berlin and finished second to Sonja Henie. She came to Hollywood with an ice show and, predictably, made her first screen appearance in *Ice Capades* (1941). She married the head of Republic Studios, Herbert Yates, and appeared exclusively in his pictures until her retirement in 1958. **Credits include:** *Storm Over Lisbon* (1944), *Dakota* (1945), *The Plainsman and the Lady* (1946), *Fair Wind to Java* (1953), *Timberjack* (1955), *The Man Who Died Twice* (1958).

Even while skating Vera Hruba Ralston wore glamorous outfits.

MARJORIE RAMBEAU (1889–1970)

She began her 60 years on stage as a leading lady with the title role in a San Francisco stock-company production of *Camille* in 1902 and appeared in silents as early as World War I. Her first sound film was *Her Man* (1930), and over the next three decades she endeared herself to film audiences in a variety of lusty, grand-dame character roles. **Sound highlights:** *Min and Bill* (1930), *Inspiration* (1931), *Man's Castle* (1933), *The Rains Came* (1939), *Tobacco Road* (1941), *Torch Song* (1953), *Man of a Thousand Faces* (1957).

TONY RANDALL (1920–   )

Although he has had a successful career as a screen comedian, Randall is perhaps best known for two characters he portrayed on television: Wally Cox's know-it-all sidekick Harvey Weskitt in *Mr. Peepers* (1952–55) and the fastidious Felix Unger, Jack Klugman's overly domesticated roommate, in *The Odd Couple*.

Randall decided to become an actor back in his home town of Tulsa, Oklahoma, after he saw his first play at age 12. He studied speech and drama at Northwestern University and then moved to New York to enroll at the Neighborhood Playhouse. His first acting jobs were on radio soap operas, and he made his first stage appearance in an adaptation of the 13th-century Chinese fantasy *A Circle of Chalk*. He made his film debut in *Oh, Men! Oh, Women!* (1957) as a patient who falls in love with his analyst's fiancée and followed that with the role of the advertising man who wins a key to the executive washroom in *Will Success Spoil Rock Hunter?* (1957). Two years later he played Rock Hudson's eager rival for Doris Day's affections in *Pillow Talk* (1959). Randall, an opera buff, is a frequent guest on late-night talk shows. **Films include:** *The Mating Game* (1959), *Lover Come Back* (1962), *Boys' Night Out* (1962), *The Brass Bottle* (1964), *The Alphabet Murders* (1966), *Bang! Bang! You're Dead* (1967), *Hello Down There* (1968).

RON RANDELL (1918–   )

This personable Australian began his show-business career in radio at age 14 in his

Alan Hale restrains Marjorie Rambeau from a direct assault on Clarence Kolb in Tugboat Annie Sails Again *(1940).*

native Sydney. Then he joined Australia's respected Minerva Theatre Group and made his stage debut as the juvenile lead in *Journey's End.* Although he appeared in *The Night of Nights* (1939), it wasn't until after he completed his military service in World War II that his screen career took off. His performance in *Pacific Adventure* (1947) as the famed flier Charles Kingford-Smith earned him a Hollywood contract.

In addition to motion pictures, he has appeared on Broadway in *The World of Suzie Wong* and on the London stage in *Sabrina Fair.* Randell has starred in two American television series, *O.S.S.* and *The Vise,* and on British television he has served as the moderator of the quiz program *What's My Line?* **Films include:** *It Had to Be You* (1947), *Kiss Me, Kate!* (1953), *I Am a Camera* (1955), *Beyond Mombasa* (1957), *Gold for the Caesars* (1963).

MIKHAIL RASUMNY (1890–1956)

Born in Odessa, the son of a cantor, he first appeared on stage at 14 touring the Russian

Tony Randall, slightly baffled by circumstances beyond his control, in Hello Down There *(1969).*

provinces and made his movie debut in 1918. By the time he arrived in the United States with the Moscow Art Theatre in 1935, he had acted under Max Reinhardt in Berlin and had also appeared in some 30 German films. He made his Hollywood debut in *Comrade X* (1940) and went on to play character roles in several dozen films. He is perhaps best remembered as Rafael, the lighthearted gypsy guerrilla, in *For Whom the Bell Tolls* (1943). **Some of his character roles:** *Hold Back the Dawn* (1941), *This Gun for Hire* (1942), *Saigon* (1948), *The Kissing Bandit* (1948), *Hot Blood* (1956).

BASIL RATHBONE (1892–1967)

Although he was a popular favorite on stages in Great Britain and the United States for many decades, film addicts will always think of Rathbone as the erudite and eccentric Sherlock Holmes—a role he repeated in no less than 16 films, beginning with *The Hound of the Baskervilles* (1939).

Sherlock Holmes (Basil Rathbone) explains to an admiring Dr. Watson (Nigel Bruce) that something definitely is *wrong with that statue.*

Rathbone, whose hawklike profile was vaguely reminiscent of John Barrymore's, was born in South Africa, first appeared on the British stage in 1911 and made his first screen appearance in England in *The Fruitful Vine* (1921). From 1925 on he was featured, almost always as a villain, in numerous swashbucklers and costume dramas. He was the loathsome Mr. Murdstone in *David Copperfield* (1935), the vicious Captain Levasseur in *Captain Blood* (1935), the sinister Marquis St. Evremonde in *A Tale of Two Cities* (1935) and the evil Sir Guy (who engaged Errol Flynn's Robin Hood in, perhaps, the most exciting sword duel ever filmed) in *The Adventures of Robin Hood* (1938). He loved the stage, however, and returned to it again and again in starring roles. Rathbone used his fine voice to make recordings of classics and toured college campuses to give readings from Shakespeare and Browning. Toward the end of his career he specialized in horror films. **Many, many credits include:** *The Last of Mrs. Cheyney* (1929), *Romeo and Juliet* (1936), *Dawn Patrol* (1938), *The Mark of Zorro* (1940), *Above Suspicion* (1943), *The Last Hurrah* (1958), *Tales of Terror* (1962).

GREGORY RATOFF (1897–1960)

In real life Gregory Ratoff was as flamboyant as the theatrical managers and impresarios he portrayed on screen. The Russian-born actor-director fled his native land during the revolution. He had already received a business education and earned a degree in law before he enrolled in the St. Petersburg Dramatic School.

He first came to the United States when producer Lee Shubert signed the entire cast of the *Revue Russe* in which he was appearing in Paris and made his motion picture debut in *Symphony of Six Million* (1932). During the next 28 years he was to act, direct and write the screenplays for scores of films. **Credits include:** *I'm No Angel* (1933), *Under Two Flags* (1936), *The Corsican Brothers* (1941), *All About Eve* (1950), *Abdullah the Great* (1957), *Once More With Feeling* (1960), *The Big Gamble* (1961).

HERBERT RAWLINSON (1885–1953)

Early in his film career this attractive Britisher rivaled Francis X. Bushman as a matinee idol of the silent screen. Later he became a respected character actor in talkies. Rawlinson launched his show-business career as a boy when he ran away from home to join the circus. He acted in British repertory companies, played one-night stands and appeared in vaudeville before coming to the United States in 1910 as manager of the Belasco Stock Company. Although he did act on the Broadway stage, he was primarily known for his motion picture appearances. **Films include:** *The God of Gold* (1912), *The Sea Wolf* (1913), *Charge It* (1921), *Dark Victory* (1939), *The Swiss Family Robinson* (1940), *Hollywood Boulevard* (1946), *Brimstone* (1949).

ALDO RAY (1926–)

A supporting actor in some good films of the 50's and 60's and the star or second lead in numerous ''B'' adventure and war films, Pennsylvanian Aldo Da Rae made his motion picture debut in *Saturday's Heros* (1951) after serving a hitch in the Navy and spending a year as a constable in Crockett, California. **Credits include:** *Pat and Mike* (1952), *We're No Angels* (1955), *God's Little Acre* (1958), *Nightmare in the Sun* (1964), *The Green Berets* (1968), *Man Without Mercy* (1969).

CHARLES RAY (1894–1943)

At one point during the silent era Ray was the highest-paid performer in Hollywood. He was famous for his roles as a country bumpkin—the shy type who makes good in the big city. Ray had brief experience in stock and vaudeville before he convinced director William Ince to give him a chance in motion pictures. He started out as an extra, then landed supporting roles. For a time he was one of the busiest actors in the business, filming a new picture every nine days. His career collapsed when his film-producing ventures failed, and he was forced to declare bankruptcy in 1925. **Films include:** *Bill Henry* (1919), *The Barnstormer* (1922), *The Girl I Loved* (1923), *The Courtship of Miles Standish* (1923), *Vanity* (1927) *Getting Gertie's Garter* (1927), *Ladies Should Listen* (1934), *A Little Bit of Heaven* (1940).

MARTHA RAYE (1916–)

The comedienne with an ultra-wide mouth and atomic-powered voice has played in many slapstick non-epics and made radio, television and cabaret appearances numbering into the thousands. Her only notable straight role was as the predatory female in Chaplin's *Monsieur Verdoux* (1947). **Films include:** *Rhythm on the Range* (debut, 1936), *Double or Nothing* (1937), *College Swing* (1938), *The Boys From Syracuse* (1940), *Hellzapoppin!* (1941), *Four Jills in a Jeep* (1944), *Jumbo* (1962).

GENE RAYMOND (1908–)

Contrary to popular opinion, Nelson Eddy was *not* married to Jeanette MacDonald; Gene Raymond was—and even starred with her in the 1941 tear jerker *Smilin' Through*. Raymond Guion began his film career shortly after the advent of sound and was featured in the Astaire–Rogers spectacle *Flying Down to Rio* (1933). Over two and a half decades the bland, pleasant-looking actor was kept busy in a string of light musicals and melodramas. From the early 50's he also made frequent appearances on television. **Credits include:** *Personal Maid* (debut, 1931), *Ex-Lady* (1933), *That Girl From Paris* (1937), *The Locket* (1947), *Hit the Deck* (1955), *I'd Rather Be Rich* (1964), *The Best Man* (1964).

RONALD REAGAN (1911–)

Undoubtedly, Reagan's major claim to moviedom fame is the fact that he is the first television and film star ever to be considered a contender for the Presidency of the United States. Most everyone remembers that Reagan appeared on TV's *Death Valley Days* and that the ruggedly handsome Governor of California had a consistently successful film career that lasted over a quarter of a century (1937–1965).

He was born in Tampico, Illinois, and graduated from Eureka College in that state. His first appearance in films was in *Love Is on*

Martha Raye, feathered to a fare-thee-well, in The Farmer's Daughter *(1940).*

Ronald Reagan and Ann Sheridan in Kings Row.

the Air (1937); his last was in *Let the World Go Forth* (1965). In between those dates he was featured or starred in nearly 40 pictures, ranging from Westerns and war films to light comedies. A former president of the Screen Actors Guild, he was also the master of ceremonies of the General Electric TV series. **Films include:** *Cowboy From Brooklyn* (1938), *Dark Victory* (1939), *Knute Rockne* (1940), *Kings Row* (1942), *The Voice of the Turtle* (1947), *John Loves Mary* (1949), *The Last Outpost* (1951), *The Killers* (1964).

ROBERT REDFORD (1937–   )

Early in his motion picture career Redford was known in Hollywood as the actor who turned down choice parts. The opportunity to work with Elizabeth Taylor and Richard Burton wasn't attractive enough to convince him to accept a role in *Who's Afraid of Virginia Woolf?* (1966), and the following year he

Robert Redford and Paul Newman, the two delightfully slick operators in The Sting, *the Academy selection as best film of 1973.*

nixed *The Graduate* because he said he didn't look like a sexually inexperienced college boy.

Redford first made his mark in 1963, on Broadway, playing the young husband in the Neil Simon comedy *Barefoot in the Park*, and he recreated his role in the 1967 screen version. The public really became enthusiastic about him, though, when he appeared as Paul Newman's sidekick in *Butch Cassidy and the Sundance Kid* (1969). His performance as Sundance catapulted Redford to superstar status alongside co-star Newman, and filmgoers were presented with two of America's most handsome actors. The two were teamed again as fellow con men who seek revenge against a big-time racketeer in the Oscar-winning George Roy Hill romp *The Sting* (1973).

The year 1973 was a busy one for Redford. His appearance with Barbra Streisand in *The Way We Were* (1973) was heralded in advertisements for the film as "Redford and Streisand . . . together at last." One critic noted in a review of the picture that "It's good to see Redford with a woman again, after all that flirting with Paul Newman."

At the time, Redford was busy filming the long-awaited remake of F. Scott Fitzgerald's *The Great Gatsby* (1974). Just about every male star in the business had sought the coveted Gatsby role, but director Jack Clayton said he saw a "flash of violence, controlled but tremendous" in Redford and gave him the part. The picture, alas, was panned by many critics. **Films include:** *War Hunt* (debut, 1962), *Inside Daisy Clover* (1966), *The Chase* (1966), *Tell Them Willie Boy Is Here* (1969), *Downhill Racer* (1969), *Little Fauss and Big Halsey* (1971), *The Hot Rock* (1972), *Jeremiah Johnson* (1972), *The Candidate* (1972), *The Great Waldo Pepper* (1974).

LYNN REDGRAVE (1943–   )

Although her famous name didn't hurt, the talented youngest Redgrave didn't really need any help when she launched her acting career. The daughter of Sir Michael Redgrave and sister of Vanessa made her professional debut after studying at England's Central School of

Music and Drama. She played small roles on stage before making her first appearance as the serving girl who screams "rape" in *Tom Jones* (1963), which was directed by her then brother-in-law (Vanessa's ex-husband), Tony Richardson. Redgrave got her big chance in *Georgy Girl* (1966) with Alan Bates and James Mason. Her portrayal of the dumpy girl who takes over her roommate's baby and boyfriend earned her the New York Film Critics Best Actress award.

Since then Redgrave has alternated between stage and screen roles, notably appearing in *The Virgin Soldiers* (1969), a British box-office hit film, and *Black Comedy*, in the West End and on Broadway. In 1974 she starred on Broadway in *My Fat Friend*. **Films include:** *Girl With the Green Eyes* (1964), *Smashing Time* (1967), *Killers of Yuma* (1972), *Every Little Crook and Nanny* (1972), *Everything You Ever Wanted to Know About Sex but Were Afraid to Ask* (1972).

SIR MICHAEL REDGRAVE
(1908–   )

This distinguished-looking Britisher has had a durable career as one of England's best stage and screen actors. He was born in Bristol and embarked on his stage career as a member of the Liverpool Repertory Company (1934–36) after graduating from Cambridge University. He then moved to the Old Vic for two seasons and from there to John Gielgud's company. Already considered a notable serious dramatic actor, he had an equally impressive start in films when he first appeared on screen as the dashing hero of Alfred Hitchcock's comedy-thriller classic *The Lady Vanishes* (1938). Other good roles followed until 1942, when he left the screen for three years to concentrate on his work in the classical theatre. He reappeared in films in 1945 as the British officer in *The Way to the Stars*. After several more films, he went to Hollywood for *Mourning Becomes Electra* (1947) and *The Secret Beyond the Door* (1948). Two years after that, back in England, he scored his first hit in a screen comedy, *The Importance of Being Earnest*. Through the 50's and 60's Redgrave divided

his time between theatre and films as a leading man in the former and more and more as a supporting performer in the latter. Of his various screen performances since then, the finest was probably as the prison warden in *The Loneliness of the Long Distance Runner* (1962). He is the father of actresses Lynn and Vanessa Redgrave. **Film highlights:** *Climbing High* (1939), *Kipps* (1941), *The Man Within* (1947), *Time Without Pity* (1957), *The Hill* (1965), *Oh! What a Lovely War* (1969), *The Battle of Britain* (1969), *David Copperfield* (1970), *The Go-Between* (1971).

VANESSA REDGRAVE (1937–   )

The third of the Redgrave trio is tall, sexy and dedicated to liberal political causes. She is also the most publicized: A marriage and divorce to director Tony Richardson, the birth of a child fathered by actor Franco Nero and a losing campaign to gain a seat in Parliament all made headlines.

Redgrave first appeared on the London stage with her father, Sir Michael Redgrave, in *A Touch of the Sun* (1958) and soon established herself in classical theatre as a member of the Royal Shakespeare Company. Although she appeared in films from the late 50's, it was not until she appeared opposite David Warner in the madcap film *Morgan!* (1966) that she caught the filmgoing public's eye. The following year her status as a movie star was confirmed with the release of Antonioni's hit *Blow-Up*, in which she played the mysterious lady who catches David Hemmings' wandering photographer's eye. Concurrently with those successes Redgrave also broke away from her usual stage roles to give a memorable performance in the West End and on Broadway as the indomitable schoolmistress of *The Prime of Miss Jean Brodie*. In recent years her burgeoning screen career has encompassed leading roles in films as disparate as *Camelot* (1967), *Isadora* (1969) and *The Trojan Women* (1971). **Screen highlights:** *Behind the Mask* (debut, 1958), *Red and Blue* (1967), *The Charge of the Light Brigade* (1968), *The Seagull* (1968), *Oh! What a Lovely War* (1969), *The Devils* (1971), *Mary, Queen of Scots* (1971).

Sir Michael Redgrave nearly three decades ago, in Mourning Becomes Electra.

The brilliant Vanessa Redgrave in The Charge of the Light Brigade.

Donna Reed as she appeared in her Academy Award-winning performance in From Here to Eternity.

Frank Reicher in Never Say Die.

DONNA REED (1921–)

Another fresh-faced pretty American who won a major beauty contest and a film contract with it, Donna Mullenger first appeared on the screen in *The Getaway* (1941) and went on to become a popular leading lady of the 40's. With a few notable exceptions the scripts given her were, to put it mildly, fragile vehicles, but she proved how very, very good she could be by snagging a Best Supporting Actress Oscar for her sizzling performance in *From Here to Eternity* (1953). In the late 50's she largely abandoned motion pictures to become a TV fixture as the oh-so-ladylike mother of *The Donna Reed Show,* a program that remained popular a full decade. **Film credits include:** *Calling Dr. Gillespie* (1942), *See Here, Private Hargrove* (1944), *The Picture of Dorian Gray* (1945), *Green Dolphin Street* (1947), *The Last Time I Saw Paris* (1954), *Pepe* (1960), *Yellow Headed Summer* (1974).

OLIVER REED (1938–)

This tough-looking, burly superstar of films is one of the few successful British actors to start his screen career with no stage experience. The nephew of director Carol Reed, he was born in London, worked for a while as a medical orderly, served in the army and launched himself in films as an extra. Bit parts in pictures like *The Bulldog Breed* (1959), *His and Hers* (1960) and *The Sword of Sherwood Forest* (1961) followed. His tough build and dark, scowling presence soon landed him more important roles as heavies in films like *The Scarlet Blade* (1963). Then director Michael Winner cast him in the comedy-drama *The System* (1964), and Reed spent the mid-60's in a variety of roles on screen and television as slick up-and-coming toughs. Reed finally made it in 1969 with the release of Ken Russell's smash-hit film of D. H. Lawrence's *Women in Love.* In it he co-starred with Glenda Jackson, Alan Bates and Jennie Linden. The association with Russell was a lasting one, and Reed appeared in several of his television ventures and starred opposite Vanessa Redgrave in his torturous *The Devils* (1971). Most recently he's been seen as swashbuckler Athos in Richard Lester's irreverent *The Three Musketeers* (1974).

Films include: *Paranoiac* (1963), *The Trap* (1966), *The Jokers* (1967), *Oliver!* (1968), *Take a Girl Like You* (1970), *The Lady in the Car* (1971), *Sitting Target* (1972).

STEVE REEVES (1926–)

If you think he has enormous biceps, triceps, etc., etc., you're right, for, among other awards, he was a former Mr. America and Mr. World who ultimately captured the Mr. Universe title—and to achieve that goal one simply can't be flabby. Reeves, who never pretended that he was out to capture a Cannes Festival trophy, has specialized in low-budget epics, most of them made in Italy. Almost all are costume dramas of earlier times when cloaks could be discarded to display Reeves' astounding musculature. In these films he has pulled down temples, hurled victims into space like a super shot putter and wooed and won assorted maidens with a display of superhuman strength. Reeves' films are shown over and over on TV screens. **Credits include:** *Hercules* (1959), *The Giant of Marathon* (1960), *Goliath and the Barbarians* (1960), *Hercules Unchained* (1960), *The Thief of Bagdad* (1961), *Duel of the Titans* (1963), *A Long Ride From Hell* (1970).

FRANK REICHER (1875–1965)

A character actor of German origin, Reicher's screen career spanned nearly three decades and included more than 100 roles in films ranging from *Mata Hari* (1932) to *The Secret Life of Walter Mitty* (1947)—plus, of course, the one and only *King Kong* (1933). He remained active in horror, crime and spy films, fantasy and biblical superproductions until he reached his late 70's. **Credits include:** *The Blue Danube* (1928), *Magnificent Obsession* (1935), *Stage Door* (1937), *Underground* (1941), *Hotel Berlin* (1945), *Mr. District Attorney* (1947), *Kiss Tomorrow Goodbye* (1950).

CARL BENTON REID (1893–)

Stage-struck early, Reid was on the road most of his life playing in stock companies and repertory theatres. He finally settled down in California at the age of 60 and became firmly entrenched as a reliable screen character actor during the 50's. Reid had a way of turning up in Westerns, war films and biopics, notably as Ann Blyth's father in *The Great Caruso* (1951) and Clem Rogers in *The Story of Will Rogers* (1952). He also appeared on television in the 60's, notably in the *Amos Burke* and *Secret Agent* series. **Credits include:** *The Little Foxes* (1941), *Lorna Doone* (1951), *Broken Lance* (1954), *The Egyptian* (1954), *The Left Hand of God* (1955), *The Gallant Hours* (1960, *Pressure Point* (1962).

WALLACE REID (1890–1923)

Today his name rarely strikes a responsive chord, but back in the silent era he was one of the great film idols, a highly engaging performer who specialized in rough-and-tumble action pictures. His first screen role was most probably in *The Deerslayer* (1911), and he played the blacksmith in *The Birth of a Nation* (1915). By the early 20's he was a full-fledged star who turned to romantic lead roles, notably with Gloria Swanson in *The Affairs of Anatol* (1921).

Unbeknownst to all but a very few, Reid had become addicted to hard drugs. His sudden death at the age of 31 was mourned around the world. **Other credits:** *To Have and to Hold* (1916), *The Dancing Fool* (1920), *The Dictator* (1922), *Adam's Rib* (1923).

CARL REINER (1922–   )

Not too long ago, when he was a comedy writer living in New Rochelle, New York, Reiner authored a well-written, bittersweet novel. It was called *Enter Laughing* and was turned into a successful play (1963) and a movie (1967) which Reiner acted in, produced and directed. The tall, balding, vastly talented Reiner got his start on Broadway in the late 40's and gained his first popularity as a TV actor in the 50's, featured on both Sid Caesar's enormously successful TV series *Your Show of Shows* (1950–54) and *Caesar's Hour* (1954–58). The programs established Reiner not only as a performer but as a comedy writer as well, and in the 60's he clinched his position as the co-producer, co-writer and occasional performer in *The Dick Van Dyke Show*. First seen on screen in the late 50's, in

more recent years he has shown an increasing interest in films. With his friend and associate Mel Brooks, Reiner also made two hit comedy records, "The 2,000-Year-Old Man" and "The 2,001-Year-Old Man." **Credits include:** *Happy Anniversary* (1959), *The Gazebo* (1960), *The Russians Are Coming, the Russians Are Coming* (1966), *Billy Bright* (1969), *Where's Poppa?* (1970).

LEE REMICK (1935–   )

This highly talented actress started out in show business as a dancer but switched to drama while she was still in school. She was dancing, however, on a TV show when director Elia Kazan noticed her and offered a role in *A Face in the Crowd* (1957). Although it was a small part, she did it well enough to land a contract with 20th Century–Fox and a bigger role in her next picture, *The Long, Hot Summer* (1958). She played the flirtatious, frivolous Southern belle who is married to Anthony Franciosa.

The role that Remick is perhaps most associated with is as Jack Lemmon's wife in *Days of Wine and Roses* (1962). Her performance as the wholesome, naïve girl who begins drinking to keep her husband company and eventually is transformed into a pathetic alcoholic earned critical raves and a nomination for a Best Actress Oscar. In addition to her work in motion pictures, Remick has continued to appear in TV dramas. On Broadway, she created the role of the blind girl in the thriller *Wait Until Dark* (1966). **Films include:** *Anatomy of a Murder* (1959), *Wild River* (1960), *Experiment With Terror* (1962), *The Running Man* (1963), *Baby, the Rain Must Fall* (1965), *No Way to Treat a Lady* (1968), *Sometimes a Great Notion* (1971), *A Delicate Balance* (1973).

DUNCAN RENALDO (1904–   )

His name is most strongly identified with the role he played for years on a popular television series and in feature films, *The Cisco Kid*. The Rumanian-born Renaldo made his film debut during the silent era as Esteban in *The Bridge of San Luis Rey* (1928), and he became a star several years later when he was cast in the African spectacle *Trader Horn* (1931). He began filming the

Steve Reeves defends Georgia Moll in The Thief of Baghdad *(1961).*

Lee Remick, a star of stage, screen and television.

Michael Rennie and Wendy Hiller in Sailor of the King *(1953).*

Fernando Rey, an ultra-suave drug baron in The French Connection.

Cisco Kid series in 1945 and starred in 156 television episodes and 12 feature films as Cisco during a five-year period. **Films include:** *For Whom the Bell Tolls* (1943).

MICHAEL RENNIE (1909–1971)

The epitome of a dashing Englishman, Michael Rennie is probably most widely known as Harry Lime in television's popular *The Third Man* series. With several British films of the 40's to his credit, Rennie arrived in Hollywood at the end of the decade. Within a short time he waited for the end of the world in *The Day the Earth Stood Still* (1951), plumbed the depths of human suffering in *Les Misérables* (1952) and was back home in the British Empire in *The Rains of Ranchipur* (1955). **His credits include:** *The Root of All Evil* (1947), *The Robe* (1953), *Désirée* (1954), *Third Man on the Mountain* (1959), *The Lost World* (1960), *Mary, Mary* (1963), *The Devil's Brigade* (1968).

ANN REVERE (1903–   )

When Hollywood effectively demolished Ann Revere's acting career by blacklisting her during the McCarthy witchhunt of the early 50's, the screen was deprived of one of its finest character actresses. A graduate of Wellesley College, Revere studied acting with the American Laboratory Theatre and appeared in stock and on Broadway in the early 30's before going to Hollywood for the first time to recreate her stage role in the 1934 screen version of *Double Door*. She then returned to Broadway and gave distinguished performances in plays as disparate as *The Children's Hour* (1934), *As You Like It* (1937) and *The Three Sisters* (1939). Then her screen career took off. Between 1940 and 1951 she appeared in 32 films, most often as a stoical type, someone's mother or old-maid aunt or a schoolteacher. She won the Best Supporting Actress Oscar for her portrayal of Elizabeth Taylor's mother in *National Velvet* (1944) and cornered nominations for her performances in *The Song of Bernadette* (1944) and *Gentleman's Agreement* (1947). Her last film was *A Place in the Sun* (1951), in which she played Montgomery Clift's mother. After years without work, Revere won a Best Sup-

porting Actress Tony when she appeared on Broadway in Lillian Hellman's *Toys in the Attic* (1960). **Film highlights:** *The Devil Commands* (1941), *The Gay Sisters* (1942), *The Keys of the Kingdom* (1944), *Dragonwyck* (1946), *Forever Amber* (1947).

FERNANDO REY (1919–   )

In recent years most of Luis Buñuel's films have had one thing in common—fine, incisive performances by Fernando Rey. Born in Spain, he was an architecture student when the Civil War interrupted his studies. He later drifted into acting as a movie extra and dubbed into Spanish for such stars as Tyrone Power and Laurence Olivier. He eventually ended up in Mexico in 1959 to make a movie. Buñuel saw him, and it was the beginning of a relationship that has established Rey as a major actor. **Some of his films include:** *Don Quixote* (1949), *Viridiana* (1962), *Chimes at Midnight* (1967), *The French Connection* (1971), *The Discreet Charm of the Bourgeoisie* (1972).

BURT REYNOLDS (1936–   )

Reynolds, half Italian and half Cherokee Indian, began acting in his native Florida in 1958. He made his first New York stage appearance in a revival of *Mister Roberts* and soon found work on television. He landed a television contract with Universal but walked out after filming 26 episodes of the *Riverboat* series. After that he had trouble finding work and took whatever came his way. Many of those jobs were in pictures like *Angel Baby* (1961) and *Navajo Joe* (1967).

Then in 1972 two events changed everything. The first was his appearance as the nude centerfold in the U.S. edition of *Cosmopolitan* magazine. The second was his Oscar-nomination-winning role in *Deliverance,* the screen version of James Dickey's novel about a group of Atlanta businessmen and the harrowing experiences they have during a weekend canoeing expedition. One critic called the picture ''Reynolds' own deliverance. Overnight he became the Frog Prince of Hollywood.'' **Films include:** *100 Rifles* (1969), *Skullduggery* (1970), *Everything You Always Wanted to Know*

About Sex but Were Afraid to Ask (1972), *Fuzz* (1972), *The Man Who Loved Cat Dancing* (1973).

DEBBIE REYNOLDS (1932–)

She first came to public attention as the "Boop-boop-a-doop girl" when she mouthed the words to Helen Kane's (the original Boop-boop, etc.) rendition of "I Want to Be Loved by You" in *Three Little Words* (1950). The role wasn't Reynolds' first. She had made her debut in a Warner Brothers Bette Davis picture, *June Bride* (1948), after winning a beauty contest and becoming Miss Burbank (Calif.) of 1948. *Three Little Words* brought Reynolds her first fan mail and convinced MGM to cast her in *Two Weeks With Love* (1950) and *Singin' in the Rain* (1952). After that, she was a star, giving bouncy, exuberant performances in a string of musicals and light comedies for the rest of the decade.

By 1960, however, her career was on the skids. Despite the fact that she had demonstrated dramatic talent in *The Catered Affair* (1956), her career in the 60's seemed focused on abortive attempts to recreate her early image, and her screen roles were mainly in such films as Disney's *The Singing Nun*. She was more successful as a nightclub performer and became a Las Vegas headliner before she finally caught the public's eye in the title role of the 1973 Broadway revival of *Irene*. **Films include:** *I Love Melvin* (1953), *Susan Slept Here* (1954), *Tammy and the Bachelor* (1957), *The Pleasure of His Company* (1961), *Mary, Mary* (1963), *The Unsinkable Molly Brown* (1964), *Divorce American Style* (1967), *How Sweet It Is* (1968), *Charlotte's Web* (1972).

MARJORIE REYNOLDS (1921–)

Marjorie Goodspeed began her acting career as a child, and when she grew to leading ladyhood she appeared in several easygoing Bing Crosby productions of the 40's. Then, going the way of many leading ladies, she moved on to television, where for five years (1953–58) she starred as William Bendix's wife, Peg, in the immensely popular *Life of Riley* series. **Films include:** *Holiday*

Inn (1942), *Star Spangled Rhythm* (1942), *Ministry of Fear* (1945), *Heaven Only Knows* (1947), *Models, Inc.* (1952).

ERIK RHODES (1906–)

A tiny waxed mustache, wing collar and bow tie were trademarks of the comedian who seemed to play every room-clerk role going in films of the 30's. He is probably best remembered, however, as the peripatetic Italian, Alberto Beddini, in the Astaire–Rogers classic *Top Hat* (1935). In addition to his screen career, Rhodes has also appeared on stage in musical comedies and more recently on television. **Highlights:** *The Gay Divorcee* (1934), *A Night at the Ritz* (1935), *One Rainy Afternoon* (1936), *Woman Chases Man* (1937), *On Your Toes* (1939).

IRENE RICH (1891–)

This regal-looking actress from Buffalo, New York, first found work in films in 1918 as an extra and went on to establish herself as a silent-screen star in such films as *Beau Brummell* (1924) and *Lady Windemere's Fan* (1925). Her finest performance of the decade was probably as the harsh home-wrecking female in *Craig's Wife* (1928). After the advent of sound Rich's career began to slip, though she did maintain her popularity with a series of pictures in which she played Will Rogers' wife—*They Had to See Paris* (1929), *So This Is London* (1930) and *Down to Earth* (1932). In 1933 Rich made the first broadcast of her national radio program *Dear John*. The program was a hit, and in 1934 Rich gave up Hollywood in favor of a full-time radio career. The show remained on the air for over a decade. (The show's sponsor was Welch's grape juice, and for the entire duration of its run Rich had a second career as a fixture in its advertisements.) Rich returned occasionally to the screen in small roles. **Films include:** *Jes' Call Me Jim* (1920), *Boy of Mine* (1923), *Captain January* (1924), *Beware of Married Men* (1928), *Craig's Wife* (1928), *Wicked* (1931), *The Mortal Storm* (1940), *Joan of Arc* (1948).

ADDISON RICHARDS (1903–1964)

He made his acting debut in *The Pilgrimage Play,* an annual Christmas presentation in

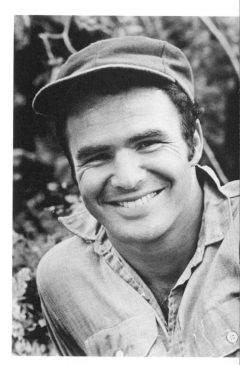

Burt Reynolds as a charming con man in Skullduggery.

Debbie Reynolds and Cliff Robertson, as a wearer of the cloth, in My Six Loves *(1962).*

Los Angeles, and studied at the Pasadena Playhouse before embarking on his long screen career as a character actor in the early 30's. Over the years Richards appeared in more than 160 films, usually in the guise of a professional man. Between 1937 and 1943 he was a fixture in the *Andy Hardy* film series. In addition to his movie work, he appeared extensively on television in shows such as *Wells Fargo, Rawhide, The Real McCoys* and *My Three Sons*. **Film Highlights:** *British Agent* (1934), *Colleen* (1936), *Black Legion* (1937), *Boom Town* (1940), *Texas* (1941), *Air Force* (1943), *Spellbound* (1945), *Davy Crockett* (1950), *Illegal* (1956), *The Oregon Trail* (1959).

ANN RICHARDS (1918–)

She came to the United States at the outbreak of World War II from her native Australia with six local films to her credit, some stage experience, and the skills of a secretarial course her mother insisted she take for "the days when you begin to starve as an actress." Her first American screen appearances were in shorts, but she soon found her way into features and more important roles, including the lead opposite Brian Donlevy in *An American Romance* (1944). She retired from films in the early 50's. **Credits include:** *Random Harvest* (1942), *Love Letters* (1945), *The Searching Wind* (1946), *Sorry, Wrong Number* (1948), *Breakdown* (1952).

SIR RALPH RICHARDSON (1902–)

This distinguished British stage actor has also had a long screen career seesawing between leading and supporting roles. He began his stage career with seven years in touring companies and with the Birmingham Repertory Company before becoming a member of the Old Vic and earning a reputation for himself in Shakespearean roles. He entered films (on the prompting of his friend, Cedric Hardwicke) with a small role in *The Ghoul* (1933). Within a few years he worked his way up to featured roles in films like *Q Planes* (1939) and *The Four Feathers* (1939) and then to starring roles, such as in *The Lion Has Wings* (1939) opposite Merle Oberon and a variety

Sir Ralph Richardson and Katharine Hepburn in Long Day's Journey Into Night.

of morale-boosters made during World War II.

After the war he turned in some of his finest screen performances, first as the butler in the 1948 film version of Graham Greene's *The Fallen Idol*, next recreating his London stage role as the tyrannical father in Hollywood's rendition of *The Heiress* (1950) and finally as the lead in David Lean's *Breaking the Sound Barrier* (1952). For the last performance Richardson collected both the New York Film Critics and the British Film Academy's awards for Best Actor. By the 60's, however, he was back to supporting roles in films like *Exodus* (1960) and *Long Day's Journey Into Night* (1962). Most recently he delighted filmgoers with a multisided performance in Lindsay Anderson's *Oh! Lucky Man!* **Films include:** *Java Head* (1933), *Things to Come* (1936), *South Riding* (1938), *The Volunteer* (1943), *Richard III* (1955), *Dr. Zhivago* (1965), *The Bed-Sitting Room* (1969), *David Copperfield* (1970).

JOHN RIDGELY (1909–1968)

Although he occasionally cropped up in films like *Arsenic and Old Lace* (1944) or *The Greatest Show on Earth* (1952), character actor John Huntingdon Ray spent most of his 15 years in Hollywood movies in gangster tales like *They Made Me a Fugitive* (1939), detective yarns like *The Big Sleep* (1946) and war films like *Destination Tokyo* (1944). In all, he made more than 68 appearances on screen, most of them as a mobster. **Credits include:** *Invisible Menace* (1938), *Brother Orchid* (1940), *The Big Shot* (1942), *Command Decision* (1949), *A Place in the Sun* (1951), *Off Limits* (1953).

STANLEY RIDGES (1892–1951)

This British character actor was one of the best corpses-in-the-closet ever in the 1926 film version of Maxwell Anderson's *Winterset*. He went from a London musical, in which he had been cast by Beatrice Lillie, to Hollywood, where he gave fine, crisp supporting performances in scores of films from the mid-30's through the early 50's. **Films include:** *The Scoundrel* (1935), *Yellow Jack*

(1938), *Sergeant York* (1941), *Possessed* (1947), *The Groom Wore Spurs* (1951).

ELIZABETH RISDON (1887–1958)

This London-born actress began her stage career in England and appeared frequently in the plays of George Bernard Shaw before emigrating to the United States in 1917. She made her film debut in 1919 in *A Star Overnight* and was cast in more than 75 character parts on screen before her retirement in 1956.
Films include: *Crime and Punishment* (1935), *Craig's Wife* (1936), *The Great Man Votes* (1939), *High Sierra* (1941), *Lost Angel* (1944), *The Unseen* (1945), *Mama Loves Papa* (1945), *The Egg and I* (1947), *Life With Father* (1947), *The Milkman* (1951), *Scaramouche* (1952).

THELMA RITTER (1905–1969)

In scores of films, Ritter played the glamour girl's maid or maiden aunt—a sharp-tongued, goodhearted type who was too down to earth to be fazed by anything.

Her long career in show business was punctuated by a series of "retirements." She quit the stage the first time after her actor husband went into advertising during the Depression. A bit part as the mother who upbraids the department-store Santa in *Miracle on 34th Street* (1947) lured her out of her first retirement, and she appeared regularly on screen in character parts through the mid-50's. Her performance as Bette Davis' maid in *All About Eve* (1950) earned her the first of six Academy Award nominations.

Ritter returned to Broadway in *New Girl in Town* (1957) and won a Tony Award for her performance. Then she decided to retire again, but she came back every time she got an offer she considered irresistible. She was Frank Sinatra's disapproving mother in *A Hole in the Head* (1959) and a pioneer woman in *How the West Was Won* (1963). Ritter died following a heart attack in 1969.
Films include: *A Letter to Three Wives* (1949), *Perfect Strangers* (1950), *With a Song in My Heart* (1952), *Rear Window* (1954), *Pillow Talk* (1959), *The Misfits* (1961), *Boeing, Boeing* (1965), *The Incident* (1967), *What's So Bad About Feeling Good?* (1968).

THE RITZ BROTHERS (Al—1901–1966; Jimmy—1903– ; Harry—1906–)

These zany comedians of nightclubs, revues and films formed their brotherly act when the eldest, Al, convinced his two younger brothers to join him on the Keith vaudeville circuit. (They took the name Ritz, they said, from a sign on a laundry across the street from a vaudeville agent's office.) Clad in outlandish costumes, the three mugged, yelled, sang and jumped around at a frantic pace in a routine that brought them enormous success in Broadway revues like *Florida Girl, Vanities* and *Broadway Personalities*.

They made their motion picture debut in *Sing, Baby Sing* (1936) and clowned their way through starring roles in a string of hit comedies of the 30's and early 40's. They

Gravel-voiced Thelma Ritter, with Monty Woolley, in As Young As You Feel *(1951).*

Harry, Al and Jimmy Ritz prepare to overpower a haughty victim in The Sound of Laughter *(1963).*

Jason Robards, Jr., and Martin Balsam, both highly distinguished performers, in A Thousand Clowns.

Cliff Robertson with Claire Bloom in Charly. *The performance won him an Oscar.*

were probably at their collective best in the improbable roles of Aramis, Porthos and Athos in Allan Dwan's uproarious 1939 musical-comedy version of *The Three Musketeers.* **Film highlights:** *One in a Million* (1937), *You Can't Have Everything* (1937), *The Goldwyn Follies* (1938), *The Gorilla* (1939), *Pack Up Your Troubles* (1939), *Everything Happens to Us* (1945).

JASON ROBARDS, JR. (1922–   )

Although he has turned in some fine performances on screen in the past decade, Robards' first love and major success has been as an actor on the legitimate stage.

Robards followed in his famous father's path to an acting career with study at the American Academy of Dramatic Arts in New York. He made his Broadway debut in *Stalag 17* (1951–53). In 1956 he played the role of Hickey in Eugene O'Neill's *The Iceman Cometh.* Under the direction of Jose Quintero, Robards gave a masterful performance and later that year repeated his success in another Quintero-directed O'Neill play, *Long Day's Journey Into Night.* His theatrical reputation secure, Robards made his first foray into films as the Hungarian freedom fighter in *The Journey* (1969). Since then Robards has appeared occasionally in films, most memorably in 1966 when he recreated his 1962 stage role as the weary, workaday-world rebel of *A Thousand Clowns* (1966).

Robards' career was interrupted in 1972 when he was critically injured in an automobile accident in California. After a long recovery, however, he scored another Broadway triumph in the O'Neill drama *A Moon for the Misbegotten* (1974), directed by Quintero and costarring Colleen Dewhurst. He has been married four times, once to actress Lauren Bacall. **Films include:** *By Love Possessed* (1961), *Tender Is the Night* (1962), *Act One* (1963), *Any Wednesday* (1966), *The St. Valentine's Day Massacre* (1967), *Isadora* (1968), *Tora! Tora! Tora!* (1969), *Julius Caesar* (1970).

JASON ROBARDS, SR. (1893–1963)

In his day, Robards Sr. was better known than his son is now. He played in dozens of movies of the 20's and 30's until cataracts cost him his eyesight in 1949. After surgery in 1957 he was able to see again and returned to star on Broadway with his son in *The Disenchanted* (1958).

Robards left his home town of Hillsdale, Michigan, to study acting at the American Academy of Dramatic Arts in New York. He made his professional debut in 1917 in *Turn to the Right* but abandoned the stage to go to Hollywood. He was a success in silent films and explained the ease with which he made the transition to sound this way: "Then talking pictures came in and there I was, right in front of them, an actor who could talk. They grabbed me and I started making one movie after another." Those early sound films included *Abraham Lincoln* (1930) and *Broadway Bill* (1934).

By the mid-40's he was a fading star. **Films include:** *The Crusades* (1935), *On Trial* (1938), *I Stole a Million* (1939), *Riff-Raff* (1947), *Mr. Blandings Builds His Dream House* (1948).

CLIFF ROBERTSON (1925–   )

Clifford Parker Robertson III began his acting career with a summer touring company and was first recognized as a talent when he appeared in the title role of a *Mister Roberts* road production. He left the stage for Hollywood to appear as the second male lead in *Picnic* (1956). His somewhat auspicious start was not a portent of things to come, however, and he marked time for years thereafter making pictures like *Gidget* (1959). In 1963 his first break came when he landed the role of John F. Kennedy in *PT 109*, and five years later he starred in *Charly* and won a Best Actor Oscar for his performance. Robertson has been married for many years to actress Dina Merrill. **Credits include:** *Autumn Leaves* (1956), *The Naked and the Dead* (1958), *The Best Man* (1964), *633 Squadron* (1964), *The Honey Pot* (1967), *Too Late the Hero* (1970), *J. W. Coop* (1972), *Man on a Swing* (1974).

PAUL ROBESON (1898–   )

Paul Robeson, probably the best known black actor of the 20's and 30's, was a familiar face to theatre and concertgoers from the mid-20's. His success on the stage encouraged him to try his luck on the screen. He made a stunning film debut in Eugene O'Neill's *The Emperor Jones* (1933), but the time was not right for a black star of his magnitude to appear with success on screen. His next role was a fairly demeaning one in *Sanders of the River* (1935), playing an African chief. He turned down many stereotype roles, though his role and accompanying song, "Ol' Man River," in *Show Boat* (1936) were memorable parts of that film. He ended his eight-film career on an unfortunate note with his role in the unenlighted black sequence of *Tales of Manhattan*. **Film credits include:** *King Solomon's Mines* (1937), *Dark Sands* (1938), *Proud Valley* (1941), *Native Land* (1942).

AMY ROBINSON (1948–   )

After playing the female lead in *Mean Streets* (1973), Robinson lamented in print in *The New York Times* that starring in a hit film isn't all it's cracked up to be. Her complaint was "I haven't worked since."

Robinson, the daughter of a Trenton, New Jersey, doctor, made her film debut in a small role in *The Long Goodbye* (1973) and appeared in a television movie, *A Brand New Life*, before director Martin Scorsese cast her as Theresa in *Mean Streets*. She had also acted with the La Mama experimental theatre in New York, and as an undergraduate at Sarah Lawrence College she played dramatic roles in student-produced films.

BILL ROBINSON (1878–1949)

Television viewers privileged to view a recent retrospective of early talkies had the great good fortune to watch Bill "Bojangles" Robinson tapping his way up and down a staircase with Shirley Temple in *The Little Colonel* (1935). It was a bright moment in film history, as was Robinson's performance in the last Will Rogers film, *In Old Kentucky* (1935).

Bojangles—the name he was generally known by—was one of the best tap dancers of all time and a long-time favorite on stages from coast to coast. His last film was *Stormy Weather* (1943), a rousing musical with an all-black cast. **Highlights:** *Dixiana* (1930), *Hooray for Love* (1935), *Up the River* (1938), *Rebecca of Sunnybrook Farm* (1938).

EDWARD G. ROBINSON (1893–1973)

For several decades it seemed as if there was no stage or screen role (with the possible exception of juvenile lead) that this stocky, moon-faced actor couldn't handle with grace and conviction. Gangster or gambler, scientist or mature lover, would-be murderer or newspaper executive, Robinson could, and did, make each role he played totally believable.

He was born Emanuel Goldenberg in Rumania, came to the United States at nine and first appeared on stage in New York when he was 20. Over the next decade and a half Robinson concentrated on his theatre career, although he did play in silents from the mid-20's. Then his impact in a single screen appearance prompted him to abandon the stage for 20 years in favor of films. The picture that did it was *Little Caesar* (1931). Robinson was nothing less than electric in the title role of a film that became the prototype for Hollywood gangster yarns for decades. Although his success threatened to typecast him for all time as a mobster, Robinson somehow managed to escape repeatedly in films ranging from *Dr. Ehrlich's Magic Bullet* (1940) to *All My Sons* (1948). The list of films in which Robinson was outstanding could go on and on: *Five Star Final* (1931), *Silver Dollar* (1932), *The Whole Town's Talking* (1934), *A Slight Case of Murder* (1938), *The Woman in the Window* (1945), *Key Largo* (1948).

Off camera, Robinson was an intellectual in the best sense of the word, a connoisseur of fine paintings and a fine raconteur. Amazingly, he never won an Academy Award, but after his death he was awarded an Oscar for his overall contribution to motion pictures. **Other highlights include:** *Night Ride* (1930), *Kid Galahad* (1937), *The Sea Wolf* (1941), *Double Indemnity* (1944), *A Hole in the Head* (1959), *The Prize* (1964), *The Cincinnati Kid* (1965), *Song of Norway* (1969).

Bill "Bojangles" Robinson, the peerless tap dancer, was nearly always cast in a servant role.

Edward G. Robinson, always convincing, always exciting. This shot was from Confessions of a Nazi Spy *(1939).*

Charles "Buddy" Rogers and Nancy Carroll in Follow Thru.

FLORA ROBSON (1902–   )

The distinguished British actress was born in County Durham, England, made her film debut in *Dance, Pretty Lady* (1931) and was well past 30 when she portrayed Queen Elizabeth in *Fire Over England* (1937). The latter film led to her being called to Hollywood for her U.S. debut as Mrs. Read in *Wuthering Heights* (1939). Since then she has given strong character performances in a great variety of roles on both sides of the Atlantic. **Some of her films include:** *We Are Not Alone* (1939), *Saratoga Trunk* (1945), *Caesar and Cleopatra* (1946), *Romeo and Juliet* (1954), *The Shuttered Room* (1968), *Fragment of Fear* (1970).

MAY ROBSON (1864–1942)

Robson's career extended from the gaslit days of the old Bowery theatres to World War II. She was born in Australia, educated in Europe and came to the United States in her early teens. She made her local stage debut in 1883. From the time of her first important screen role—*The Rejuvenation of Aunt Mary* (1927)—she specialized in playing strong-willed, goldenhearted old ladies, perhaps most memorably as Apple Annie in *Lady for a Day* (1933). **More than 50 films include:** *Strange Interlude* (1932), *Alice in Wonderland* (1933), *A Star Is Born* (1937), *Bringing Up Baby* (1938), *Irene* (1940), *Joan of Paris* (1942).

CHARLES "BUDDY" ROGERS (1904–   )

The affable young man from Kansas whose wavy dark hair and ingenuous smile caused him to be tagged "America's Boy Friend" had his first featured role in the late 20's in *Fascinating Youth* (1926) and remained a high-ranking star through the first decade of talkies. He was at his best, with Richard Arlen and Clara Bow, in the last of the super-silents, *Wings* (1927), a saga of World War I pilots which was the first picture ever to win an Oscar.

Rogers was Mary Pickford's leading man in *My Best Girl* (1927) and later became the leading man in her life when they were married. His film career lasted for more than 20 years. **Credits include:** *Abie's Irish Rose* (1928), *Varsity* (1928), *Follow Thru* (1930), *An Innocent Affair* (1948).

GINGER ROGERS (1911–   )

As a flapper in her first film, *Young Man of Manhattan* (1930), Ginger Rogers sang one song and uttered one line: "Cigarette me, big boy." For too long thereafter countless young ladies demanded tobacco with that phrase.

She had sung and danced in vaudeville and on stage and was already an up-and-coming starlet when she danced the Carioca with Fred Astaire in *Flying Down to Rio* (1933). The film proved to be the birth of the most popular dance team since Vernon and Irene Castle in the early years of the century. Astaire and Rogers made more hit films together, the best of them *The Gay Divorcee* (1934) and *Top Hat* (1935). Appropriately enough, the last of the string was *The Story of Vernon and Irene Castle* (1939).

In 1940 Rogers stepped out on her own and won an Oscar for her performance in the title role of *Kitty Foyle*, the ingenuous adolescent

Carole Lombard and May Robson exchange confidences in Lady by Choice *(1934).*

who becomes a worldly businesswoman. From then on she was seen in any number of roles, from comedy to melodrama. Rogers teamed up with Astaire again for *The Barkeleys of Broadway* (1949). Since the 50's she has been popular with television audiences and was delightful as Dolly Levi in the long-running Broadway musical *Hello, Dolly!* She also appeared in Londodon in the late 60's in the musical *Mame*. **Her many films include:** *42nd Street* (1933), *Roberta* (1934), *Lady in the Dark* (1944), *Monkey Business* (1952), *Oh Men! Oh Women!* (1957).

PAUL ROGERS (1917–   )

This British character actor has appeared in films since the early 30's and later embarked on a stage career. Among his credits is his notable comic performance in the comedy-thriller *Our Man in Havana* (1960). Through the 60's he was seen in such films as *Billy Budd* (1962) and the somewhat stolid version of *A Midsummer Night's Dream* (1968). **Credits include:** *Beau Brummell* (1954), *The Trials of Oscar Wilde* (1960), *He Who Rides a Tiger* (1968), *The Looking-Glass War* (1969).

ROY ROGERS (1912–   )

The epitome of the happy-go-lucky cowboy and Gene Autry's only serious rival, Rogers was particularly fortunate in his choice of screen co-stars—Trigger, billed as "the smartest horse in the movies," and Gabby Hayes, the scene-stealing cowboy sidekick.

Rogers (alias Leonard Slye of Cincinnati, Ohio) began his professional career as a singer with the Sons of the Pioneers, a Western-music group, and first rode the Hollywood ranges in *The Old Homestead* (1935). For the next 17 years he was kept extremely busy cleaning up the Old West in 100 Saturday-afternoon-at-the-movies Westerns. After that, he proceeded to do more of the same for another decade on his popular TV series, which co-starred Trigger, wife Dale Evans, sidekick Pat Brady, Bullet and Nellybell the Jeep. **Films include:** *Under Western Stars* (1938), *Lake Placid Serenade* (1944), *My Pal Trigger* (1946), *Apache Rose* (1947), *Son of Paleface* (1952).

Walter Slezak gives an elegantly turned-out Ginger Rogers a sideways look. The film was the amusing Once Upon a Honeymoon *(1942).*

WILL ROGERS (1879–1935)

This cowboy from Oklahoma, whose quips camouflaged a devastating commentary on American politics and the state of the world in general, was one of the most popular actors of his era. He made himself famous on stage and screen twirling a lariat to the accompaniment of a drawling succession of observations on subjects ranging from Calvin Coolidge to bootleg booze, from Tin Lizzies to the Teapot Dome scandals.

Rogers was a fixture of the Ziegfeld Follies and made his first screen appearance as early as 1918 in *Laughing Bill Hyde*. He made a number of delightful talking pictures in the late 20's and 30's, including *Lightnin'* (1930) and a completely captivating 1931 version of Mark Twain's *A Connecticut Yankee in King Arthur's Court*. A favorite of collegians, he lectured on college campuses, and his cracker-barrel philosophy was widely syndicated in newspapers. An early aviation enthusiast, Rogers died in a 1935 plane crash with Wiley Post, one of the first to circumnavigate the globe. His son, Will Jr., did a

The wonderful Will Rogers, sans lariat, sans cowboy suit.

Gilbert Roland and Dorothy Lamour in a 1937 thriller, The Last Train From Madrid.

fine job recreating the humorist in a 1952 biopic, *The Story of Will Rogers*. As recently as 1973 a splendid story of his life was produced by The American Heritage Publishing Company. **Film credits include:** *They Had to See Paris* (1929), *State Fair* (1933), *David Harum* (1934), *Judge Priest* (1934), *In Old Kentucky* (1935).

GILBERT ROLAND (1905–)

Luis Antonio Damaso De Alonso, a darkly handsome, suave Mexican, arrived in Hollywood at the perfect time. Valentino was at the peak of his career, and the studios were waiting with open arms for "Latin lovers." As Gilbert Roland he made his film debut in *The Plastic Age* (1936), and his role opposite Norma Talmadge in *Camille* (1927) catapulted him to fame.

Roland made a successful transition from silents to talkies, but by 1934 the craze for Latin lovers was over. Through the 40's he spent a good deal of time roving with pirates and cowboys and did a brief stint as the third Cisco Kid. In the early 50's he gave two of the finest performances of his career—as Gaucho, the actor, in *The Bad and the Beautiful* (1953), and as the aging toreador in *The Bullfighter and the Lady* (1951). In recent years he has made appearances on a variety of TV Westerns and crime dramas. **His films include:** *The Campus Flirt* (1926), *The Dove* (1928), *She Done Him Wrong* (1933), *Juarez* (1939), *Captain Kidd* (1945), *Any Gun Can Play* (1968).

RUTH ROMAN (1924–)

She was a stage performer who was featured in many so-so films of the 50's, often playing an outwardly tough but inwardly weak female who, more often than not, ended up dead. The first film in which she received much notice was *The Window* (1949). She has been seen many times on television. **Credits include:** *Good Sam* (1948), *Champion* (1949), *Tanganyika* (1954), *The Far Country* (1955), *Great Day in the Morning* (1956), *Love Has Many Faces* (1965).

CESAR ROMERO (1907–)

His experience as a ballroom dancer and Broadway actor made the handsome Latin American performer a perfect candidate for latter-day Valentino–Novarro roles. Romero fooled everybody, however, by proving that he not only was a "Latin lover" but a believable gangster, a convincing cowboy and a good comedian to boot.

His first film was *The Shadow Laughs* (1933), and starting in 1937 he starred in the *Cisco Kid* film series. While Romero spent a lot of screen time south of the border—*Weekend in Havana* (1941) and *Vera Cruz* (1954) are good examples—he also made a suave and often highly amusing leading man in spots ranging from *Coney Island* (1943) to *Prisoners of the Casbah* (1953). He has appeared frequently on television and starred as diplomatic courier Steve McQuinn in *Passport to Danger* (1956). **Film credits include:** *Tales of Manhattan* (1942), *That Lady in Ermine* (1948), *Marriage on the Rocks* (1965), *Batman* (1966), *A Talent for Loving* (1969).

MICKEY ROONEY (1920–)

After nearly 50 years in motion pictures, Rooney has an enormous list of credits. Brooklyn's Joe Yule, Jr., was only six when he made his screen debut as the star of the first of 40 shorts playing the character of, and billed as, Mickey McGuire. Then came several films as Mickey Rooney. As a child Rooney was one of the big studios' hottest properties in pictures like *Captains Courageous* (1937). He matured into teenage roles in *A Family Affair* (1937), playing an awkward adolescent named Andy Hardy. The picture became an audience favorite and so did Rooney as he appeared in episode after episode in the *Hardy* series and in a series of musical films with Judy Garland. In 1939 he was awarded a special Oscar for his personification of youth on the screen.

He obviously couldn't go on as a teenager forever, although his diminutive size helped him continue longer than most. He was 26 when he filmed his last Hardy picture. His first adult role was in *Killer McCoy* (1948). At the time, however, Rooney himself hadn't given up on Andy Hardy and launched a radio series playing the famous teenager. Later he returned to films and as a character actor won an Academy Award nomination for his performance in *The Bold and the Brave* (1956).

He continues to alternate between movies, television and nightclub appearances. Rooney frequently made headlines with his seven marriages, the first to Ava Gardner. **Films include:** *Orchids and Ermine* (1927), *Ah, Wilderness!* (1935), *Boys Town* (1938), *Girl Crazy* (1943), *National Velvet* (1944), *Words and Music* (1948), *Operation Mad Ball* (1957), *Requiem for a Heavyweight* (1962), *The Comic* (1969).

FRANÇOISE ROSAY (1891–   )

Today her classic face, silver hair and smoky voice present the ageless charm of the archetypal French beauty. During her long career the distinguished actress has defied typecasting and has proven herself equally at ease as an elegant and witty burgomaster's wife, a disreputable Moroccan café proprietor, a saintly mother superior or a murderous innkeeper. Born in Paris, Rosay made her stage debut there at 16 and her first film in 1913. Besides starring in some of the classics of the French screen, she has made a variety of American and British films. Rosay is the widow of director Jacques Feyder. **Some of her films include:** *Gribiche* (1925), *Un Carnet de Bal* (1938), *Quartet* (1949), *The Sound and the Fury* (1959), *Up From the Beach* (1965).

GEORGE ROSE (1920–   )

For a while during the 50's this Britisher was one of the busiest character actors in England. He began his professional career by studying voice and landing a job as an offstage singer at the Old Vic. He graduated to speaking parts and by 1948 was appearing in London's West End. He made his screen debut in *Pickwick Papers* (1952) and since that time continues to appear on stage and screen. In 1974 he opened on Broadway with Lynn Redgrave in *My Fat Friend*. **Credits include:** *The Night My Number Came Up* (1955), *The Last Wagon* (1956), *Jack the Ripper* (1960), *Hawaii* (1966), *The Pink Jungle* (1968).

MAXIE ROSENBLOOM (1906–   )

When his ring career ended in the mid-30's, this light-heavyweight champion,

Two of the most talented youngsters in screen history—Judy Garland and Mickey Rooney in Love Finds Andy Hardy *(1938).*

usually affectionately referred to as "Slapsie" Maxie because of his boxing style, turned out to be a fine actor who moidered the English language in dozens of comic toughguy roles. In addition to his screen appearances, Rosenbloom has been seen frequently on television. **Credits include:** *Muss 'Em Up* (1936), *Nothing Sacred* (1937), *The Kid Comes Back* (1938), *Louisiana Purchase* (1942), *Hazard* (1948), *The Beat Generation* (1959).

DIANA ROSS (1944–   )

When it was announced that Diana Ross had been chosen to play Billie Holiday in the film story of the jazz singer's tragic life, many people were skeptical of her ability to handle the difficult role. Ross was a pop singer, and to complicate matters further, the film, *Lady Sings the Blues* (1972), would be her first screen appearance. After seeing the movie, one reviewer wrote, "If there's any justice,

426

Diana Ross and Billy Dee Williams in the film biography of another Billie—Holiday—Lady Sings the Blues.

Katharine Ross, about to flee the altar in favor of Dustin Hoffman in The Graduate.

Diana Ross should be the biggest movie superstar to come along since Barbra Streisand.'' She received an Academy Award nomination for Best Actress for her portrayal.

Ross was born in Detroit and started singing in a church choir. With two other girls, Mary Wilson and Florence Ballard, she formed a singing group called the Supremes, and soon they were at the top of the popular-music charts with such hits as ''Baby Love'' and ''Stop in the Name of Love.'' In 1970 the group split up, and Ross continued on her own as a very successful nightclub and concert headliner. She starred on her own TV special *Diana* in 1971.

KATHARINE ROSS (1942–   )

Born in Hollywood, Ross studied at the San Francisco Workshop and made her rather inauspicious film debut in *Shenandoah* (1965). She followed this with the film blunder *The Singing Nun* (1966), but then landed a substantial part in the now classic *The Graduate*. The film proved to be a showcase for her talent and beauty and led to other major roles. In addition to her acting, Ross has also modeled and done television com-

mercials. **Credits:** *Mister Buddwing* (1966), *Butch Cassidy and the Sundance Kid* (1969), *Tell Them Willie Boy Is Here* (1970), *Get to Know Your Rabbit* (1972).

LILLIAN ROTH (1911–   )

This pert singer was born in Boston, talked with a New York accent, made her first film appearance at five and was a vaudeville headliner at 15. She went directly from a Ziegfeld extravaganza atop the roof of the New Amsterdam Theatre in New York to make her first adult screen appearance in *The Love Parade* (1929) with Maurice Chevalier. After a few successful years, chronic alcoholism caused her retirement. She wrote about it in her best-selling autobiography *I'll Cry Tomorrow,* and Susan Hayward played Roth in a 1955 biopic. As a result of the book and film there was renewed interest in Roth, and she made several television and nightclub appearances in the 50's.

Roth returned to Broadway in 1962 in *I Can Get It for You Wholesale* and later toured with the cast of *Funny Girl*. **Other films include:** *The Vagabond King* (1930), *Animal Crackers* (1930), *Sea Legs* (1930), *Take a Chance* (1933).

RICHARD ROUNDTREE (1942–   )

In the apparently non-stop series of *Shaft* films, Roundtree stars as the chillingly ruthless but incorruptible black detective, among the first of black actors to play lawmen. He began his acting career on the stage as a member of the Negro Ensemble Company, and he starred in a road-company production of *The Great White Hope* before moving to films. In the *Shaft* series he plays a private eye in films that could have been written by Dashiell Hammett and acted in by Bogart or Garfield. In other words, he's very convincing indeed. In 1973 Roundtree and *Shaft* moved to television. **Credits:** *Shaft* (1971), *Shaft's Big Score* (1972), *Charlie One-Eye* (1974).

ALMA RUBENS (1897–1931)

Born Alma Smith, she was another star of the silent screen whose career and life were ended early by drugs. It was with Douglas Fairbanks in *The Half Breed* (1916) that she first won critical and fan applause, although she had been in films back in 1915 (*Intolerance*, etc.). **Film credits include:** *Humoresque* (1920), *Cytherea* (1924), *The Heart of Salome* (1927), *Show Boat* (1929).

CHARLES RUGGLES (1890–1970)

The wistful-looking character actor with a graying mustache and apologetic cough was a tower of strength in upward of 80 films. Charles Sherman Ruggles began his career working with a San Francisco stock company as a teenager and by 1914 was appearing in films and on Broadway. His film career began in earnest with the emergence of sound, and he remained a featured player and near star until his formal retirement in the late 40's. After an absence of 12 years, during which period he appeared on television and won a Tony Award on Broadway for his role in *The Pleasure of His Company* (1958), he returned to the screen and continued to appear in pictures until 1966. **Credits include:** *Gentlemen of the Press* (1929), *Charley's Aunt* (1930), *Ruggles of Red Gap* (1935), *Bringing Up Baby* (1938), *Our Hearts Were Young and Gay* (1944), *Look for the Silver Lining* (1949), *The Pleasure of His Company* (1961), *Follow Me, Boys!* (1966).

SIG RUMANN (c. 1884–1967)

With his thick guttural accent, popping eyes and blustering manner, Siegfried Albon Ruman was to millions of moviegoers the perfect befuddled foreigner, whether Russian, Hungarian or German. Born in Hamburg, Germany, he made his Broadway debut in 1928 and worked steadily on the stage until he went to Hollywood to make his film debut in *The World Moves On* (1934). He reached his peak as a character comedian as Michael Iranoff in *Ninotchka* (1939). His career of more than 90 films also includes his popular portrayal as Schultz in *Stalag 17* (1953). **Some of his films include:** *A Day at the Races* (1937), *To Be or Not to Be* (1942), *A Royal Scandal* (1945), *The Wings of Eagles* (1957), *The Fortune Cookie* (1966).

BARBARA RUSH (1927–)

Pretty Barbara Rush has been used mainly in decorative roles since making her feature

Charlotte Greenwood and Charlie Ruggles plus pooch. They were both very funny in The Perfect Snob.

film debut in *The First Legion* (1951). Born in Colorado, she moved to California as a child and was studying at the Pasadena Playhouse when she was spied by a talent scout and thrown into the starlet pool at Paramount. Over the years she has worked for many of the major studios and has appeared frequently on TV dramatic shows. **Some of her films include:** *Magnificent Obsession* (1954), *No Down Payment* (1957), *The Bramble Bush* (1960), *Strangers When We Meet* (1960), *Come Blow Your Horn* (1963), *Hombre* (1967), *Airport* (1970), *The Man* (1972).

GAIL RUSSELL (1924–1961)

At the time of her marriage to Guy Madison in 1949 she was hailed as the "Star of Tomorrow." But tomorrow never arrived, and after a series of mostly innocuous ingénue roles in the mid-40's, her career declined. Born in Chicago, she was discovered at 17 and made her debut in *Henry Aldrich Gets Glamour* (1943). Beautiful but painfully shy, she developed a drinking problem that she was

Sig Rumann and Myrna Loy in Love Crazy *(1941).*

Jane Russell, Howard Hughes' first film discovery after Jean Harlow, as she appeared in The Outlaw.

never able to overcome. **Some of her 25 films include:** *The Uninvited* (1944), *The Night Has a Thousand Eyes* (1948), *Song of India* (1949), *The Tattered Dress* (1957), *The Silent Call* (1961).

JANE RUSSELL (1921–   )

Ernestine Jane Geraldine Russell was born in Bemidji, Minnesota, studied with Max Reinhardt's Theatrical Workshop and with Maria Ouspenskaya and was a successful model before beginning her screen career. Her film debut was one of the most publicized events in Hollywood history, for she had been selected to appear in the first Howard Hughes production since the legendary tycoon had made film history with Jean Harlow in *Hell's Angels* (1930) and Paul Muni in *Scarface* (1932). He chose Russell, whose prodigious

bosom made girl-watchers gasp in amazement, from scores of models and would-be actresses and not only starred the unknown in *The Outlaw* (1943) but directed the film himself. It was too explicit for its time and was closed by the super-prudish Hays office almost at once. Three years later it was officially released, only to get so-what notices.

Hughes loaned Russell to other studios, and she turned out to be a funny comedienne, spoofing her own sexy image, with Bob Hope in *The Paleface* (1948) and a more than adequate dancer and singer when she was co-starred with Marilyn Monroe in *Gentlemen Prefer Blondes* (1953). **Other films include:** *Young Widow* (1946), *The Las Vegas Story* (1952), *The Revolt of Mamie Stover* (1956), *Fate Is the Hunter* (1964), *Born Losers* (1967).

JOHN RUSSELL (1921–   )

Before he became the star of the TV series *Lawman* (1958) as Marshall Dan Troop, Russell had played second leads in dozens of films, many of them Westerns. He made his screen debut in *Frame-Up* in 1937 and worked steadily for more than 30 years. In addition to *Lawman,* Russell starred in an earlier TV series, *Soldiers of Fortune* (1955). **Films include:** *Jesse James* (1939), *The Bluebird* (1940), *Forever Amber* (1947), *The Fat Man* (1951), *The Sun Shines Bright* (1954), *Rio Bravo* (1959), *Fort Utah* (1967).

ROSALIND RUSSELL (1907–   )

When she first began her film career most of the roles offered her were Myrna Loy rejects. Although she planned to become a serious actress, her forte was comedy, and she was ideal for brittle, sophisticated pictures about women who have what it takes to make it in a man's world.

Russell was born in Connecticut and convinced her reluctant parents to allow her to enroll at the American Academy of Dramatic Arts in New York by telling them she wanted to teach acting. An MGM contract came along, and in her first picture, *Evelyn Prentice* (1934), she appeared with Loy. After that she played one tough woman after another, most notably as the vicious Sylvia

Rosalind Russell, one of the super-catty stars of The Women, *exchanges trivia with Norma Shearer.*

Fowler in *The Women* (1939), for which she won an Academy Award nomination, and as Hildy Johnson, the competitive female reporter in *His Girl Friday* (1940).

She appeared on Broadway in *Wonderful Town* (1953), the musical version of *My Sister Eileen*, and in 1955 scored one of her greatest triumphs in *Auntie Mame*. The show, based on the best-selling Patrick Dennis book, was a smash hit, and Russell also starred in the motion picture version (1958). That success pumped new life into her screen career, and she and her husband, Fred Brisson, produced such films as *A Majority of One* (1962) and *Rosie!* (1968).

During her years in Hollywood Russell has been nominated for the Academy Award five times but has never won. In 1972, however, she received the Jean Hersholt Humanitarian Award from the Academy as a tribute to her work for charities. **Films include:** *The Casino Murder Case* (1935), *China Seas* (1935), *Craig's Wife* (1936), *Fast and Loose* (1939), *My Sister Eileen* (1942), *Sister Kenny* (1946), *Never Wave at a Wac* (1953), *Picnic* (1956), *Gypsy* (1962), *The Trouble With Angels* (1966), *Mrs. Pollifax, Spy* (1971).

ANN RUTHERFORD (1917–   )

Rutherford was singing on a San Francisco radio program when she was noticed by a talent scout and offered a role in her first film, *Waterfront Lady* (1935). She was getting nowhere in "B" Westerns and adventure films when she was hired to play Polly, Mickey Rooney's sweetheart, in *You're Only Young Once* (1938), replacing Margaret Marquis, who had appeared as Polly in the first of the series. Rutherford appeared in 10 more films in the Andy Hardy series while making many other important pictures. In 1939 she was seen as Careen O'Hara in *Gone With the Wind*. She retired in 1950 and only recently returned to the screen in *They Only Kill Their Masters* (1972). **More than 50 films include:** *Love Finds Andy Hardy* (1938), *The Hardys Ride High* (1939), *Pride and Prejudice* (1940), *The Courtship of Andy Hardy* (1942), *The Secret Life of Walter Mitty* (1947), *The Adventures of Don Juan* (1948).

The one and only Margaret Rutherford in Mouse on the Moon *(1963).*

MARGARET RUTHERFORD
(1892–1972)

Of ample build, with bulbous eyes set in deep pouches and a fierce jaw that rested on an accordion chin, she was a comedienne with few peers. She was in her mid-30's before she took up acting seriously and in her late middle age when she attained stardom.

Born in London, Rutherford studied at the Old Vic school and performed at the Old Vic in repertory. She had a perfect sense of timing, and this, coupled with her amusing physique and looks, strengthened her portrayals of a gallery of eccentrics. Her film and stage creation of the medium in *Blithe Spirit* (film, 1945) was one of the best character performances ever, and she became a public favorite.

The role of Miss Marple, Agatha Christie's bike-riding amateur detective, seemed to be created for Rutherford. She played the grimly determined lady with warmth and not a drop of condescension. Rutherford won an Academy Award for Best Supporting Actress in *The V.I.P.s* (1963) and was the one redeeming feature of that movie. **Other film credits include:** *Talk of the Devil* (debut,

Robert Ryan and Ida Lupino didn't see eye to eye in Beware, My Lovely *(1952).*

because he was never given the opportunities he deserved.

Ryan, a keenly intelligent man, was born in Chicago and tried his hand at a number of jobs before he turned to acting. He made an early screen appearance in *Golden Gloves* (1940) and continued to turn in smoothly professional performances until his life ended shortly after completing his last film, *The Iceman Cometh,* in 1973. He was a big success on Broadway (and later on the screen) in *Clash by Night* and returned intermittently to the stage, as late as 1971 in a revival of *Long Day's Journey Into Night*. Politically involved, he was one of the few Hollywood celebrities who actively fought against blacklisting in the era of McCarthyism. **His many screen credits include:** *Crossfire* (1947), *The Set-Up* (1949), *Bad Day at Black Rock* (1955), *The Longest Day* (1962), *Battle of the Bulge* (1965), *The Dirty Dozen* (1967), *The Wild Bunch* (1969).

1936), *Passport to Pimlico* (1949), *The Importance of Being Earnest* (1952), *I'm All Right, Jack* (1960), *Murder, She Said* (1962), *Murder Most Foul* (1965), *A Countess From Hong Kong* (1967).

IRENE RYAN (1902–1973)

After a half century in vaudeville, radio, movies and television she reached the high point of her career as the pipe-smoking, moonshine-making Granny on *The Beverly Hillbillies* TV series, which ran for nine seasons. The comedienne stopped the show cold in Broadway's *Pippin* (1972), for which she won a Tony nomination for Best Supporting Actress in a musical. She was appearing in the show when she was fatally stricken. **Credits include:** *Sarong Girl* (1943), *Diary of a Chambermaid* (1946), *Meet Me After the Show* (1951), *Spring Reunion* (1957).

ROBERT RYAN (1909–1973)

He was a fine actor who played leads and featured parts in dozens of films but never quite achieved true stardom, most probably

Irene Ryan turned in her Granny clothes for her show-stopping performance in Broadway's Pippin.

SABU (1924–1963)

At age 13, Mysore (India) stableboy Sabu Dastagir became an overnight film star when he played the lead in *Elephant Boy*, Robert Flaherty's 1937 screen version of the Kipling story. Sabu's newfound fame took him to England and then to Hollywood, where he appeared in several films, most of them with India as their background. **His credits include:** *The Thief of Bagdad* (1940), *Jungle Book* (1942), *Song of India* (1949), *A Tiger Walks* (1964).

EVA MARIE SAINT (1924–   )

This somewhat brittle blonde from East Orange, New Jersey, began her acting career with work on radio and television in the early 50's. Her fine performance in a TV production of *A Trip to the Bountiful* led to her legitimate-stage debut when she recreated the role for the Broadway production in 1953. Her performance brought her the New York Drama Critics Award and led to her screen debut as Marlon Brando's girlfriend in *On the Waterfront* (1954). She was a sensation in the part, landed an Oscar and seemed to be well on her way to stardom. Numerous Hollywood offers poured in, and she made three films in quick succession—*That Certain Feeling* (1956), with Bob Hope, *A Hatful of Rain* (1957), with Don Murray, and *Raintree County* (1957), with Elizabeth Taylor and Montgomery Clift. She has appeared regularly on screen since then, but has never managed to fulfill her early promise. **Credits include:** *North by Northwest* (1959), *Exodus* (1960), *All Fall Down* (1962), *36 Hours* (1965), *The Sandpiper* (1965), *The Russians*

Are Coming, the Russians are Coming (1966), *The Stalking Moon* (1969), *Loving* (1970), *Cancel My Reservation* (1972).

RAYMOND ST. JACQUES (1930–   )

The black actor, whose experience includes Shakespearean roles in New York, has appeared in several screen dramas set on the streets of the city. He was cast in *The Pawnbroker* (1965), a searing portrait of an embittered shopkeeper, and was later featured in Jules Dassin's *Uptight* (1968). St. Jacques was directed in *Cotton Comes to Harlem* (1970) by the noted black actor Ossie Davis. **His credits include:** *Mister Buddwing* (1966), *The Comedians* (1967), *If He Hollers Let Him Go* (1968).

HOWARD ST. JOHN (1905–1974)

The character actor came to films after almost 25 years on stage. He brought with him a certain distinct bearing which won him roles as a parent, businessman or military officer. His pictures ranged from the breezy *Born Yesterday* (1950) to the horrific *Strait Jacket* (1964). **Films include:** *Undercover Man* (1949), *Counterspy Meets Scotland Yard* (1951), *The Tender Trap* (1955), *Li'l Abner* (1959), *Banning* (1967).

JILL ST. JOHN (1940–   )

The redheaded actress has risen to minor prominence, if not stardom, since her debut in *Thunder in the East* (1952). She appeared in the ineptly fashioned dinosaur tale *The Lost World* (1960) and in the Carol Burnett comedy *Who's Been Sleeping in My Bed?* (1963). St. John has also accepted a number of roles which have effectively disguised her reportedly high intelligence. **Credits include:** *Summer Love* (1958), *Come Blow Your Horn* (1963), *The Liquidator* (1966), *Eight on the Lam* (1967), *Banning* (1967).

S. Z. SAKALL (c. 1884–1955)

Sad eyes, droopy jowls, a distinct accent and the body of a huge overstuffed owl made Hollywood's Cuddles instantly recognizable in his numerous character roles in films of the 40's and 50's.

Eugene Gero Szakall was born in Hungary, became a popular vaudevillian and stage actor

Eva Marie Saint and Don Murray as the drug addict in a fine film version of a fine play, A Hatful of Rain.

Cuddles Sakall as Paul, the butler, in Universal's The Man Who Lost Himself.

George Sanders and Linda Bateson in Village of the Damned.

Telly Savalas requests silence in The Slender Thread *(1965)*.

in Central Europe shortly after the turn of the century and appeared in films as early as World War I. He continued to perform in Europe until the threat of impending war made him immigrate to the United States in 1939. He made his American film debut the following year in *It's a Date* and went on to enliven a host of funny, light pictures and provide comic relief in high-tension melodramas like *Casablanca* (1942). **Many films include:** *Thank Your Lucky Stars* (1943), *Cinderella Jones* (1946), *Whiplash* (1948), *The Student Prince* (1954).

DOMINIQUE SANDA (1952–   )

When her admirers aren't comparing Sanda to Garbo, they're invoking the names of Marlene Dietrich, Lauren Bacall and Deborah Kerr. After less than a dozen films she may well be one of the top international stars of the 70's.

The daughter of a Parisian electrical engineer, she was raised in a strict family but was married at the age of 15. At 17 her marriage was over and she began modeling. Director Robert Bresson, in a search for new faces, signed her for her debut in his film *Une Femme Douce* (1969), and within the next four years she had starred in six other motion pictures. Her performance in *The Conformist* (1970), as Jean-Louis Trintignant's wife, won her rave reviews, and she scored another success a year later in *The Garden of the Finzi-Continis* (1971), the story of a family of wealthy Italian Jews caught in the Fascist net. **Films include:** *First Love* (1970), *Impossible Object* (1972).

GEORGE SANDERS (1906–1972)

Although he starred in *The Saint* and *The Falcon* film series in the early 40's and played Strickland, the hero of *The Moon and Sixpence*, in 1942, the actor who called his autobiography *Memoirs of a Professional Cad* spent most of his 40 years in films playing suave and snobbish roués.

Sanders' ultra-British voice and mannerisms belied the fact that he was born in Russia. He made his stage debut in London while still in his teens and made several films in England before going to Hollywood for

Lloyds of London (1936). After several more British ventures Sanders settled in Hollywood and was starred or featured in scores of films. He gave one of his best performances as the caustic and cynical critic in *All About Eve* (1950) and won a Best Supporting Actor Oscar for the portrayal. In the late 50's he masterminded the *George Sanders Mystery Theatre* on television and continued to work in both media through the following decade. As time went by, however, his roles got smaller and smaller. In 1972 Sanders killed himself, leaving a note that stated he was too bored to go on. **Screen highlights:** *Strange Cargo* (1929), *Nurse Edith Cavell* (1939), *Rebecca* (1940), *Foreign Correspondent* (1940), *The Lodger* (1944), *Forever Amber* (1947), *Call Me Madam* (1953), *A Shot in the Dark* (1964), *The Quiller Memorandum* (1966), *The Kremlin Letter* (1969).

TELLY SAVALAS (1924–   )

Greek American Telly Aristotle Savalas was born in Garden City, New York. A graduate of Columbia University, he fought in World War II and was decorated with the Purple Heart. He made his film debut in *Mad Dog Coll* (1961) and one year later was nominated for an Academy Award for his supporting performance in *Birdman of Alcatraz*. His acting career has spanned a wide film spectrum, including war movies, spectaculars, Westerns and crime flicks. Recently he starred in the television series *Kojak*. **Films include:** *The Young Savages* (1961), *Cape Fear* (1962), *The Greatest Story Ever Told* (1965), *The Battle of the Bulge* (1965), *The Dirty Dozen* (1967), *Buona Sera, Mrs. Campbell* (1968), *A Town Called Hell* (1971).

JOE SAWYER (1908–   )

A familiar face to moviegoers since 1933, Sawyer has appeared in numerous films in supporting roles, usually as a heavy or tough character with a heart of gold. He is, perhaps, best known to TV viewers as Sergeant Biff O'Hara on the long-running *Rin Tin Tin* series. **Credits:** *College Humor* (1933), *Union Pacific* (1939), *About Face* (1942),

Fall In (1943), *Joe Palooka, Champ* (1946), *Fighting Father Dunne* (1948), *It Came From Outer Space* (1953), *North to Alaska* (1960).

JOHN SAXON (1935–)

A Brooklyn boy, Carmen Orrico modeled and studied with drama coach Stella Adler before making his motion picture debut in *Running Wild* (1955). Saxon's dark good looks made him a teenage idol in the 50's, and he found steady work in Hollywood, mostly in Westerns. He appeared sporadically in ''B'' adventure films of the 60's, but more recently he has attempted to make the transition to more serious drama and musical comedy. In 1968 he appeared with Mildred Dunnock in an Oakland National Repertory production of *The Glass Menagerie*. The next year, still out of the saddle and dressed up as a physician, he starred in the TV series *The Bold Ones*. **Films include:** *The Unguarded Moment* (1956), *The Reluctant Debutante* (1958), *Portrait in Black* (1960), *The Unforgiven* (1960), *The Plunderers* (1960), *War Hunt* (1962), *The Cardinal* (1963), *The Deadly Three* (1973).

GIA SCALA (1934–1972)

Born in Liverpool, England, to an Irish mother and an Italian father, the fragile, strikingly beautiful Giovanna Scoglio became far better known for her hard living and flamboyant style than for her acting ability. She emigrated to the United States and grew up in New York City. Scala affected a marked Italian accent on and off the screen, evidently hoping to rival the careers of Loren and Lollobrigida. A talent for publicity found her smoking cigars in public and jumping off a bridge in London, as well as posing for anybody with a camera.

During her career that lasted less than ten years, she gave her best performance as the unhappy wife of a labor organizer threatened by gangsters in the melodrama *The Garment Jungle* (1957). After a number of futile and disheartening attempts to renew her flagging film career, she committed suicide. **Credits include:** *The Price of Fear* (1956), *Four Girls in Town* (1957), *The Angry Hills* (1959), *I Aim at the Stars* (1960), *The Guns of Navarone* (1961).

NATALIE SCHAEFER (1912–)

On screen since the 40's, this native New Yorker has specialized in brittle, arch, comic character roles. Although most of her roles have been in forgettable second features, she has appeared occasionally in more serious ventures like *The Snake Pit* (1948) and *Anastasia* (1956). Schaefer has also made numerous TV appearances, including a three-season stint as the millionaire's (Jim Backus') scatterbrained wife on the *Gilligan's Island* series. **Film highlights:** *Marriage Is a Private Affair* (1944), *Wonder Man* (1945), *Caught* (1949), *Forever, Darling* (1956), *Susan Slade* (1961).

MARIA SCHELL (1926–)

The daughter of a Swiss playwright and a Viennese actress, the multi-lingual Schell decided on an acting career as a child, made her film debut as the young lead in a Swiss film, *Der Steinbruch* (1942), when she was 16 and was playing leads at the State Theatre in Bern at the age of 20. Within short order she established herself throughout Europe as a superb screen actress, and by the time she made her much heralded American screen debut opposite Yul Brynner in *The Brothers Karamazov*, she had 21 films to her credit and a Cannes Film Festival Best Actress Award for her performance in the British-made *The Last Bridge* (1953, U.S. 1957). Schell made two more pictures in America but then returned to Europe to continue her career. Since then, her career has been somewhat overshadowed by that of her actor/director brother, Maximilian. **Films include:** *Angel With the Trumpet* (1949, U.S. 1951), *The Magic Box* (1951, U.S. 1953), *The Heart of the Matter* (1952, U.S. 1954), *Une Vie* (1958), *White Nights* (1961), *Cimarron* (1961), *99 Women* (1969).

MAXIMILIAN SCHELL (1930–)

The handsome, dark-haired Austrian won an Oscar for his portrayal of the defense lawyer for Nazi war criminals in *Judgment at Nuremberg* (1961). It was a remarkable role

Natalie Schaefer as a witness for the prosecution in Dishonored Lady *(1947).*

Maria Schell in her first American-made film, The Brothers Karamazov.

Maximilian Schell in The Condemned of Altona.

for an actor who as a child was forced to flee his native country after the Nazi invasion.

Schell, brother of Maria, acted in the theatre in France, Switzerland and Germany before making his film debut in the German film *Kinder Mutter und ein General* (1955). He made his American acting debut on the Broadway stage and at once attracted the attention of Hollywood. He had a good role and gave a fine performance in *The Young Lions* (1958) with Marlon Brando. Since he was given few film roles that fully utilized his talents, he returned to the European theater, acting, writing and directing. In 1974 he achieved a long-time ambition with the release of *The Pedestrian,* which he wrote, directed, produced and played a small role in, the picture and Schell receiving highly favorable reviews. **Other films:** *Five Finger Exercise* (1962), *The Condemned of Altona* (1963), *Topkapi* (1964), *Counterpoint* (1968), *Paulina 1888* (1972).

JOSEPH SCHILDKRAUT (1895–1964)

In a screen career that spanned 41 years and more than 100 films from *The Song of Love* (1924) to *The Greatest Story Ever Told* (1965), this distinguished son of Austrian actor Rudolph Schildkraut played so many nationalities so convincingly that he earned a permanent place in film history as one of the screen's greatest character actors. He is probably best remembered for his Academy Award-winning performance as Captain Dreyfus in *The Life of Emile Zola* (1937) and for his characterization of Anne's father in *The Diary of Anne Frank* (1959). **Screen highlights:** *Show Boat* (1929), *The Garden of Allah* (1936), *The Man in the Iron Mask* (1939), *The Cheaters* (1945), *Monsieur Beaucaire* (1946).

MARIA SCHNEIDER (1953–)

In 1973 the virtually unknown Maria Schneider drew international attention as the young Parisienne who accepts and then rejects the aging Marlon Brando as her lover in Bertolucci's eyebrow-raising film *Last Tango in Paris.* Schneider broke into show business at age 15 as a dancer in the stage comedy *Superposition* in her native France and then found bit parts in several films. Apart from *Tango,* her only sizable role on screen was as a young existentialist in the 1972 Vadim film *Helle,* which has yet to be released in the United States.

ROMY SCHNEIDER (1938–)

Not long after she first appeared on screen at age 16, Schneider rivaled the appeal of her mother, Austrian movie star Magda Schneider. She was starred in a string of West German musical comedies and light romances and gained notice throughout Europe as Empress Elizabeth of Austria in *Sissi* (1956). Three years later she starred opposite Alain Delon in the first of her several French movies, *Christine* (1959). Despite her popularity, it wasn't until she appeared in Visconti's *Boccaccio '70* (1962) and Welles' *The Trial* (1963) that Schneider won recognition as a notable dramatic actress. By then Hollywood was interested, and she made her American film debut in *The Victors* (1963). Since then her best performances were in *Max et les Ferrailleurs* (1971) with Michel Piccoli and *César et Rosalie* (1972) with Yves Montand and Sami Frey. **Films include:** *Feuerwerk* (debut, 1954), *Robinson Soll Nicht Sterben* (1957), *The Cardinal* (1963), *What's New Pussycat?* (1964),

Maria Schneider, the object of Marlon Brando's superheated affections in Last Tango in Paris.

Triple Cross (1967), *The Assassination of Trotsky* (1972).

PAUL SCOFIELD (1922–   )

One of the world's most distinguished and versatile stage ators, Scofield holds a place with Gielgud and Olivier as one of the foremost interpreters of Shakespeare. He was born in Pierpoint, Sussex, and first performed with the Birmingham Repertory Company (1942–45). By the time he made his first film (appearing as the old man in *That Lady* (1955) with Olivia de Havilland) he was already firmly established as a leading actor on the legitimate stage. Since then Scofield has appeared only occasionally in films but inevitably with distinction. In 1967, when Fred Zinnemann decided to film Robert Bolt's hit play *A Man for All Seasons*, Scofield recreated his stage role as Sir Thomas More and collected an assortment of awards, among them Best Actor Oscar, the British Film Academy's Best Actor Award and the New York Film Critics Award. **Films include:** *Carve Her Name With Pride* (1958), *The Train* (1964), *King Lear* (1969), *Bartleby* (1970), *Scorpio* (1972).

GEORGE C. SCOTT (1929–   )

The feisty, iconoclastic actor of stage and screen is famous not only as a superior talent but also as the first performer to refuse the coveted Oscar award. After graduation from the University of Missouri, Scott did summer stock and ultimately was chosen to .play *Richard III* in the New York Shakespeare Festival of 1957. His performance brought critical raves and an offer from Hollywood. He made his motion picture debut in *The Hanging Tree* (1959) and from then on interspersed his work on the stage with motion pictures. He played supporting parts in his early films, gained an Oscar nomination and better roles for his performance in *The Hustler* (1961) and landed his first starring role in *The List of Adrian Messenger* (1963) as a Scotland Yard detective. After that came *Dr. Strangelove* (1964), in which he played an obtuse Pentagon general.

Practically every star in Hollywood, including John Wayne, wanted to play General Patton when 20th Century-Fox announced plans to film his story. Scott got the role. He received the Academy Award for Best Actor in *Patton* (1969) but refused to accept it. He also won the New York Film Critics Award, which his wife collected for him, saying that it was the only film award Scott thought worth anything. In addition to his continuing success in films, Scott maintains his stage career. **Films include:** *Anatomy of a Murder* (1959), *The Brass Bottle* (1962), *The Flim-Flam Man* (1967), *They Might Be Giants* (1971), *The Hospital* (1971), *The Day of the Dolphin* (1973).

LIZABETH SCOTT (1922–   )

With a voice even huskier than Bankhead's, the former Emma Matzo of Scranton, Pennsylvania, started her Broadway acting career with a job as understudy to Tallulah. Shortly thereafter, the resemblance was noted by starmaker Hal Wallis, who imported Lizabeth Scott to Hollywood with the usual fanfare, as a threat to all the sultry ladies then heating up the screen.

Paul Scofield as Sir Thomas More in A Man for All Seasons, *a performance that won him the Academy Award as Best Actor.*

And another Best Actor who turned his back on Oscar—George C. Scott as Patton. *In this shot James Edwards as Sergeant Meeks adjusts the temperamental general's helmet.*

Zachary Scott uses his own particular brand of persuasion on Georges Metaxa and Victor Francen in The Mask of Dimitrios.

Randolph Scott in the sort of tight spot you knew he would get out of. This time it was Colt .45.

Her sulky look and low voice were definitely not those of the girl next door (even in Scranton), and she embarked on a career of playing tarnished ladies with hearts of gold. Masterminding an elaborate scheme to introduce a fraudulent Edmund O'Brien as a millionaire's long-lost heir in *Two of a Kind* (1951) was one of her minor peccadillos. Occasionally her better nature shone through, as in *Loving You* (1957), when she played an unselfish press agent who touted her ex-husband to success—and remarriage. **Other films include:** *The Strange Love of Martha Ivers* (1946), *Desert Fury* (1947), *The Company She Keeps* (1951), *Bad for Each Other* (1953).

MARTHA SCOTT (1914–   )

The role of Emily in the Broadway production of Thorton Wilder's *Our Town* brought stardom to Martha Scott. She repeated the role and won an Academy Award nomination for it in the 1940 screen version.

She continued to appear on stage, screen, television and radio. On Broadway she starred in *Never Too Late* (1964). Among her screen roles is the mother of the family Hum-

phrey Bogart and cohorts terrorized in *The Desperate Hours* (1955). Scott is married to a Yale University music professor. **Films include:** *The Howards of Virginia* (1940), *Cheers for Miss Bishop* (1941), *One Foot in Heaven* (1941), *So Well Remembered* (1947), *The Ten Commandments* (1956), *Sayonara* (1957), *Ben Hur* (1959).

ZACHARY SCOTT (1914–1965)

He looked like the perfect dashing and mustachioed romantic leading man of the 40's, but, with the notable exception of his fine performance as the sympathetic sharecropper hero of *The Southerner* (1945), his best work in films was done in villainous roles.

Scott was born in Texas and made his professional debut on stage. In the early 40's he was impressive on Broadway in *Ah, Wilderness* and *Yesterday's Magic*. His film debut came in *The Mask of Dimitrios* (1944), in which he played the wicked Dimitrios. After that, Scott's career was confined mostly to Hollywood. He was kept busy in pictures through the mid-50's until he returned to the stage in the Broadway hit musical *The King and I* (1956). Thereafter he appeared on both stage and screen until his death from a malignant brain tumor. **Films include:** *Stallion Road* (1947), *The Unfaithful* (1947), *Born to Be Bad* (1950), *Let's Make It Legal* (1951), *Appointment in Honduras* (1953), *The Young One* (1961), *It's Only Money* (1962).

RANDOLPH SCOTT (1903–   )

When his plea for 24 hours to clean up the town was turned down by the townsfolk in *Blazing Saddles* (1974), black sheriff Cleavon Little says to them, with injured dignity, "You would have given Randolph Scott 24 hours." At which point the entire cast bows its collective head in a moment of silent reverence. That delicious sequence wasn't far off target, since the strong and silent Western star was indeed the ideal of at least two generations of American filmgoers.

Scott began as a straight dramatic actor. His doctor suggested he go west after an illness, so he moved to California, where he shared an apartment with another young hopeful, Archibald Leach, who later became known as Cary Grant. Grant and Scott were wonderful later on in *My Favorite Wife* (1940) as rivals for the hand and heart of Irene Dunne. Grant won.

His film career began in the early 30's in films like *Lone Cowboy* and *Sky Bride* (both 1931), and he was soon featured in dramatic and romantic roles along with shoot-'em-outers. Although he occasionally was allowed to dismount from the saddle—*Roberta* (1935) and *Gung Ho!* (1944) are examples—Scott's Westerns overwhelmingly dominated a career which lasted until his retirement in 1965. His straight-backed dedication to law and order can still be seen on a myriad of television reruns. **Films include:** *Home on the Range* (1935), *The Last of the Mohicans* (1936), *Jesse James* (1939), *Western Union* (1941), *The Spoilers* (1942), *Captain Kidd* (1945), *Canadian Pacific* (1949), *Carson City* (1952), *Ride the High Country* (1962).

ALEXANDER SCOURBY (1908–   )

To millions, this character actor's voice is more familiar than his face or name, for in addition to his numerous appearances on stage and in TV dramas, Scourby has provided the "voice over" in innumerable TV commercials and has made many recordings for the blind. He was born in Brooklyn, attended the University of West Virginia and made his New York debut as the King in Leslie Howard's production of *Hamlet* (1936). Since his motion picture debut in *Affair in Trinidad* (1952) he has made only occasional appearances on screen. Scourby is married to actress Lori March, a long-time regular on the daytime serial *The Secret Storm*. **Films include:** *The Big Heat* (1953), *The Silver Chalice* (1955), *Seven Thieves* (1959), *Confessions of a Counterspy* (1960), *Devil at Four O'Clock* (1961).

JEAN SEBERG (1938–   )

When Otto Preminger decided to film Shaw's *Saint Joan* (1957) he went about it in his inimitable fashion, considering some 18,000 possibilities (or so publicity releases said) before selecting an unknown, fresh-faced Iowa girl, Jean Seberg, for the role. Neither the film nor the actress, however,

George Segal, as a man trailing a murderer, and Eileen Heckart, as his madly solicitous mother, enjoy a brief moment of mirth in No Way to Treat a Lady *(1967).*

lived up to the pre-release fanfare. Since that dubious introduction to the screen, Seberg has rarely managed to capture the attention of either critics or public. Her most successful films were French, and she gave her only really notable performance (opposite Jean-Paul Belmondo) as the offhanded, emotionless American-in-Paris heroine of Godard's *Breathless* (U.S. 1961). **Credits include:** *Bonjour Tristesse* (1958), *The Mouse That Roared* (1959), *Lilith* (1964), *Paint Your Wagon* (1969), *The French Conspiracy* (1973).

GEORGE SEGAL (1934–   )

With an easygoing geniality that is vaguely reminiscent of Cary Grant's in his heyday, Segal has taken a wide assortment of roles in his stride. Although his forte is comedy, best displayed in his performance as the brash young American executive abroad in *A Touch of Class* (1973), he has proven himself equally adept at serious drama (notably in Ingmar Bergman's 1973 TV film *The Lie*).

Segal was born in New York City's suburbia and appeared on stage and television be-

Jean Seberg played a bored (but highly seductive) wife in A Fine Madness *(1966).*

Peter Sellers as the frustrated claimant to Capucine's affections in The Pink Panther.

fore making his screen debut in *The Young Doctors* (1961). Since then he has been an enormously busy actor, appearing in more than 22 films and playing roles that ranged from the young teacher in the harrowing *Who's Afraid of Virginia Woolf?* (1966) and a Japanese prison-camp internee in *King Rat* (1965) to one of the bungling would-be gangsters in *The Hot Rock* (1973). **Films include:** *Act One* (1963), *Ship of Fools* (1965), *The Quiller Memorandum* (1966), *Loving* (1969), *The Owl and the Pussycat* (1970), *Where's Poppa?* (1970), *Blume in Love* (1973).

PETER SELLERS (1925–   )

For a while in the mid-60's British funnyman Sellers was one of the hottest screen actors in the business. A raft of fans loved him in *The Mouse That Roared* (1959) and remained faithful through *I Love You, Alice B. Toklas* (1968). Since then Sellers hasn't scored a big hit.

He started out as a stand-up comic but first earned wide attention in England in the zany radio series *The Goon Show,* which ran for seven years. His first film appearance was with his Goon co-stars, Spike Milligan and Harry Secombe, in *Let's Go Crazy* (1950), but he didn't catch on in pictures until he appeared with Alec Guinness in *Ladykillers* (1956).

After playing three parts in *The Mouse That Roared*, Sellers starred in *I'm All Right, Jack* (1960). It was a big hit, and the British Film Academy voted him the Best Actor of the year. After that Sellers was in demand in both England and the United States. Stanley Kubrick cast him as the detective who pursues James Mason and Sue Lyon in *Lolita* (1962) and then assigned him three roles in *Dr. Strangelove* (1964), in which Sellers played the President of the United States, a British Air Force officer and Strangelove himself. The picture was a box-office smash and has become a classic antiwar fantasy. The same year he delighted audiences as the bungling Inspector Clouseau in *A Shot in the Dark* and in 1965 contributed to the merriment in *What's New Pussycat?* **Films include:** *The Smallest Show on Earth* (1957), *Never Let Go* (1963), *The Pink Panther* (1964), *After the Fox* (1966), *Casino Royale* (1967), *The Magic Christian* (1970), *There's a Girl in My Soup* (1970), *Where Does It Hurt?* (1972).

ANNE SEYMOUR (1909–   )

She comes from a long line of theatre people—a member of the seventh successive generation of Davenports in the acting profession. She made her stage debut with her maternal grandparents when she was 12. In addition to acting, Seymour produced, directed and wrote plays. She was a successful radio actress, appearing with Don Ameche in the *Grand Hotel* radio series.

Seymour began her film career when she was middle-aged and played character parts in several films about political figures. She was Roosevelt's mother, Sara, in *Sunrise at Campobello* (1960) and appeared in *All the King's Men* (1949). **Other film credits include:** *The Whistle at Eaton Falls* (1951), *Man on Fire* (1957), *Home From the Hill* (1960), *Mirage* (1965), *Blindfold* (1966), *Fitzwilly* (1967).

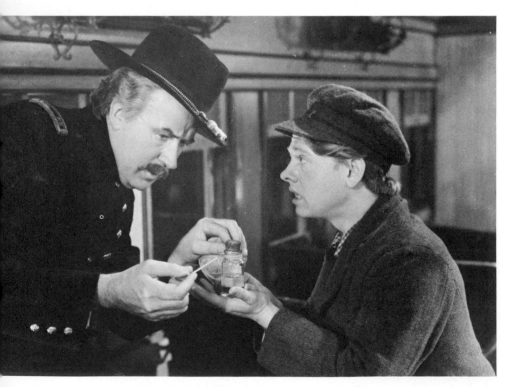

Harry Shannon as a Union officer and Mickey Rooney as an embryonic inventor in Young Tom Edison.

DAN SEYMOUR (1915–   )

Although he was a successful nightclub comedian, Seymour had a habit of turning up in Bogart films as a villain. Perhaps his most famous disagreeable role was as the police chief whose bullying cowardice offsets Bogart's peculiar valor in *To Have and Have Not* (1944). He later appeared in heavyweight crime films. **Credits include:** *Casablanca* (1942), *Key Largo* (1948), *Rancho Notorious* (1952), *Human Desire* (1954), *Beyond a Reasonable Doubt* (1956), *Watusi* (1959).

HARRY SHANNON (1890–1964)

Born Patrick O'Toole in Saginaw, Michigan, Shannon enjoyed a long career in burlesque, vaudeville and on the stage before embarking on a film career in which he played roles of patient, supportive, understanding fathers, uncles, kindly neighbors and countryside wanderers with Confucius-like wisdom. **Major credits:** *Heads Up* (1930), *Young Tom Edison* (1940), *High Noon* (1952), *Executive Suite* (1954), *Written on the Wind* (1957), *Gypsy* (1962).

OMAR SHARIF (1932–   )

Born Michel Shahoub in Alexandria, Sharif is the only Egyptian movie star known outside the Arabic-speaking world and the only film star who is a Life Master in the world of bridge. The dashing mustachioed Sharif had already starred in 21 Egyptian and two French films when David Lean assigned him a supporting role in the 1962 blockbuster *Lawrence of Arabia*. Sharif's performance brought him an Oscar nomination and proved to be the beginning of his career as an international star. The critics weren't kind to Sharif when he starred as Yuri in *Dr. Zhivago* (1965), but the film was a popular one, and subsequently he was in demand for roles that called on him to assume a variety of nationalities, even playing an American Jewish gambler opposite Barbra Streisand in *Funny Girl* (1968). **Films include:** *The Mameluks* (1963), *The Fall of the Roman Empire* (1964), *The Night of the Generals* (1967), *Che!* (1969), *Mackenna's Gold* (1969), *Mayerling* (1969), *The Last Valley* (1971).

Omar Sharif in what would be a difficult situation even for a championship bridge player. The film was Columbia's Genghis Khan *(1965).*

WILLIAM SHATNER (1931–   )

After graduating from McGill University in his native Montreal, Shatner appeared with the Montreal Playhouse, the Canadian Repertory Theatre and the Stratford (Ontario) Shakespeare Festival before venturing to the New York theatre. On Broadway he appeared in *Tamburlaine the Great* (1956), *The World of Susie Wong* (1958) and *A Shot in the Dark* (1958). His film career began as Yul Brynner's youngest brother in *The Brothers Karamazov* (1958). He is probably best known for his role as the commander of the space ship *Enterprise* on the TV series *Star Trek*. **Credits:** *Judgment at Nuremberg* (1961), *The Explosive Generation* (1961), *The Intruder* (1962), *The Outrage* (1964).

MICKEY SHAUGHNESSY (1920–   )

The tough-looking character actor has the bulk of Jackie Gleason and the rubbery face of Red Skelton. Born in New York City, Shaughnessy worked as a longshoreman before he became a nightclub vocalist. He had

Mickey Shaughnessy guards his lunchbox.

Robert Shaw, prepared for action, in Figures in a Landscape *(1971).*

Norma Shearer, for years the unchallenged reigning queen of the American film capital, photographed in 1939.

some stage experience before making his movie debut in *The Marrying Kind* (1952). Although he has played in several serious movies, his forte is comedy. His portrayal of the average sailor in *Don't Go Near the Water* (1957) was highly praised. In *The Sheepman* (1958), a Western spoof, Shaughnessy played the town toughie, and his mugging and scowling to cover wounded dignity was a high spot of the film. **Other credits include:** *From Here to Eternity* (1953), *Jailhouse Rock* (1957), *North to Alaska* (1960), *A House Is Not a Home* (1964), *Never a Dull Moment* (1968).

ROBERT SHAW (1927–   )

Born in Lancashire, England, and a graduate of London's Royal Academy of Dramatic Art, Shaw first established himself in theatre as a member of the Royal Shakespeare Company and the Old Vic. Through the early 50's he appeared in the West End in such notable plays as *Tiger at the Gates* and the *Changeling* and on Broadway in *The Caretaker*, as well as in a dramatization of his own novel, *The Man in the Glass Booth*. In films since the mid-50's, Shaw scored his first great success as Henry VIII in *A Man for All Seasons* (1966). His two most notable performances of the early 70's were as the calculating chauffeur who becomes embroiled with the upper-crust Sarah Miles in *The Hireling* (1972) and as the Scots racketeer who is the "mark" of Paul Newman's and Robert Redford's big con in *The Sting* (1973). In addition to stage and screen careers, Shaw has appeared frequently on television dramas and continues to write novels. **Film highlights:** *The Dam Busters* (debut, 1955), *The Caretaker* (1953), *From Russia With Love* (1964), *The Birthday Party* (1968), *The Royal Hunt of the Sun* (1969), *Figures in a Landscape* (1970).

VICTORIA SHAW (1935–   )

In her early days in Hollywood, Australian leading lady Shaw (Jeanette Elphick) and her then husband, actor Roger Smith, were touted in fan magazines as the ideal young couple —she a budding starlet and he a young, romantic leading man. As things turned out,

however, they split up, and her American screen career consisted largely of secondary parts in indifferent films. **Credits include:** *Cattle Station* (1955), *The Eddy Duchin Story* (1956), *Edge of Eternity* (1960), *The Crimson Kimono* (1960), *Alvarez Kelly* (1966).

DICK SHAWN (1929–   )

Comedian Shawn is best known as a nightclub and television performer, but he has appeared occasionally in motion pictures and on the stage. **Films include:** *Wake Me When It's Over* (1960), *Its a Mad, Mad, Mad, Mad World* (1963), *A Very Special Favor* (1965), *What Did You Do in the War, Daddy?* (1966), *Penelope* (1966), *The Producers* (1968).

NORMA SHEARER (1904–   )

Born in Montreal and trained as a pianist, she began her screen career playing an anonymous extra in *Way Down East* (1920) and retired 22 years later after a long reign as the First Lady of Hollywood. She was not the most beautiful star of her day, nor the best actress. Nonetheless, her canniness and intelligence, combined with patrician good looks and ultra-chic film presence, made her a top box-office draw for nearly ten years. She made a successful transition from the silents to talkies with *The Trial of Mary Dugan* (1929).

Shearer's career was helped mightily by the fact that she was sponsored by Metro's *Wunderkind,* Irving Thalberg, whom she married in 1927. She picked her own scripts, along with leading men like Clark Gable and Robert Montgomery. It is fair to add, however, that she shrewdly chose good scripts and that her fine acting brought her the Academy Award for Best Actress in *The Divorcee* as early as 1930. Four more Oscar nominations followed, the last for *Romeo and Juliet* (1936), which was previewed just before Thalberg's death. She was offered the role of Scarlett O'Hara in *Gone With the Wind* but backed out when polls indicated the public didn't like the idea. She also rejected the lead in *Mrs. Miniver* in 1942, just before her retirement. **Highlights:** *He Who Gets Slapped* (1924), *His Secretary* (1925), *The*

Last of Mrs. Cheyney (1929), *A Free Soul* (1931), *Private Lives* (1931), *The Barretts of Wimpole Street* (1934), *Marie Antoinette* (1938), *Idiot's Delight* (1939), *The Women* (1939), *Her Cardboard Lover* (1942).

MARTIN SHEEN (1940–   )

With his bright blue eyes and Irish good looks Martin Sheen began his acting career performing in off-Broadway plays, spending two years with the Living Theater. His face is familiar to TV audiences, for he appeared in many nighttime serials and also had a featured role in a daytime soap opera. His portrayal of the son in *The Subject Was Roses* on Broadway brought him a Tony nomination, and he recreated the role in the film version (1968). He received high critical praise when he appeared in two major TV dramas: *That Certain Summer* (1973) and *The Execution of Private Slovik* (1974). **Other film credits include:** *The Incident* (1967), *Catch-22* (1969), *Badlands* (1973).

JOHNNY SHEFFIELD (1931–   )

When Johnny Weissmuller discovered Boy in a jungle plane wreck in *Tarzan Finds a Son* (1939), eight-year-old Johnny Sheffield found a place among MGM's ranks of child stars. He went on to appear in seven more episodes of the Tarzan series and then got his own home in the wilds as the star of *Bomba the Jungle Boy* (1949) and subsequent *Bomba* films. In the mid-50's Sheffield quit the movies to attend UCLA and later became a successful investor in California real estate. **Other films include:** *Babes in Arms* (1939), *Knute Rockne—All American* (1940), *Million Dollar Baby* (1941), *Tarzan and the Huntress* (1947).

CYBILL SHEPHERD (1949–   )

This Tennessee beauty was one of the highest-paid models in the United States when she captivated audiences and critics alike with her portrayal of Jacy, the spoiled high-school flirt in Peter Bogdanovich's first film, *The Last Picture Show* (1970). After that success Shepherd entrusted her future to Bogdanovich and at his prompting again took time off from her modeling to appear as the

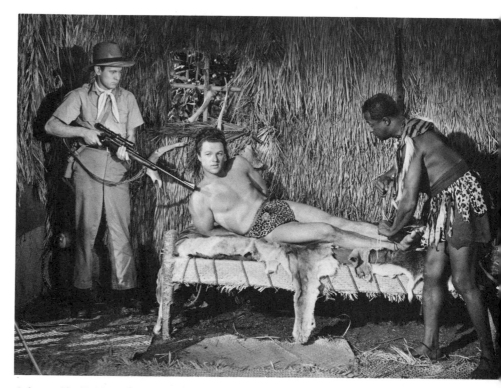

Johnny Sheffield keeps his cool in the face of horrendous dangers, as represented by gun-bearing William Phipps and tier-upper Joel Fluellen. The film was Lord of the Jungle.

Midwestern WASP whom Charles Grodin abandons his bride to pursue in Elaine May's first directing assignment, *The Heartbreak Kid* (1972). In 1974 Bogdanovich starred her in the title role of his screen version of Henry James' *Daisy Miller*.

JOHN SHEPPARD See SHEPPARD STRUDWICK

ANN SHERIDAN (1915–1967)

Tagged "The Oomph Girl" by Warner Brothers, she was a pin-up favorite of the 40's. Sheridan was, however, considerably more than a pretty face atop a fabulous figure. She had warmth and charm, a fine singing voice, and her brassy exchanges with James Cagney in pictures like *Torrid Zone* (1940) proved her a fine comedienne.

Born Clara Lou Sheridan, she won a regional beauty contest in her native Texas and abandoned college in favor of Hollywood. Beginning with a bit part in *Search for Beauty*

Cybill Shepherd as the girl who wanted someone else's bridegroom in The Heartbreak Kid.

Ann Sheridan, one of the most engaging stars of the 40's.

(1934), she appeared in a string of "B" films, more often than not as a fresh outdoor-type American girl. Next she was given slightly wicked roles that gave her more of a chance—with John Garfield, for example, in *They Made Me a Criminal* (1939) and as a tough waitress with Bogart and Raft in *They Drive by Night* (1940). Eventually she escaped hard-boiled roles and did a fine job in musicals—for example, as Norah Bayes in *Shine on Harvest Moon* (1944)—and in bright comedy performances in pictures like *I Was a Male War Bride* (1949) with Cary Grant. Before her death she appeared frequently on TV shows like *Wagon Train* and on the *Pistols and Petticoats* series. **Films include:** *Dodge City* (1939), *Kings Row* (1942), *The Man Who Came to Dinner* (1942), *George Washington Slept Here* (1942), *Nora Prentiss* (1947), *Take Me to Town* (1953), *The Opposite Sex* (1956).

ARTHUR SHIELDS (1900–   )

Bespectacled Irish character actor Shields had already appeared in some early English and Irish silents and established himself in the theatre as a member of the Abbey Players in Dublin before he moved to the United States in the 30's and made his American screen debut in John Ford's *The Plough and the Stars* (1937). Over the following two and a half decades Shields played supporting roles in some 60 films, from melodramas to Westerns. He turned up in several other Ford pictures, including *She Wore a Yellow Ribbon* (1949) and *The Quiet Man* (1952), which featured his brother, Barry Fitzgerald. **Film highlights:** *Drums Along the Mohawk* (1939), *The Long Voyage Home* (1940), *National Velvet* (1944), *The Corn Is Green* (1945), *The River* (1951), *The King and Four Queens* (1956), *The Pigeon That Took Rome* (1962).

JAMES SHIGETA (1933–   )

Hawaiian-born Shigeta often played Japanese roles. He appeared in *Cry for Happy* (1961) with Glenn Ford, in *Nobody's Perfect* (1968) with James Whitmore and in the musical *Flower Drum Song* (1961), which was set in San Francisco's Chinatown. Shigeta was right at home in *Paradise Hawaiian Style* (1966) with none other than Elvis Presley. **His credits include:** *Walk Like a Dragon* (1960), *Bridge to the Sun* (1961).

TAKASHI SHIMURA (1905–   )

This Japanese actor became known in the United States for his performance in Kurosawa's *Rashomon* (1950), the film that popularized Japanese cinema in the West. The story, set in 19th-century Japan, concerns a nobleman and his wife who are attacked by a bandit. The crime is reconstructed four times—by each of the principals and by a witness, a woodcutter played by Shimura. Long a member of Kurosawa's repertory company, Shimura later appeared in the master's other films, notably *Seven Samurai* (1954), *Throne of Blood* (1957), *Sanjuro* (1960), *Yojimbo* (1962).

Shimura has also appeared in Japanese science-fiction thrillers such as *Godzilla* (1956) and *Ghidrah, the Three-headed Monster* (1965). **Other films include:** *The Hidden Fortress* (1958), *The Mysterians* (1959), *Drunken Angel* (1959), *Stray Dog* (1964).

Sylvia Sidney, the star of Dead End *in 1937 and an Academy Award nominee 37 years later. Billy Halop (above) and the other Dead End Kids made their first appearance in the film version of the Sidney Kingsley play.*

ANNE SHIRLEY (1918–)

Dawn O'Day was a child star in the silent era. She changed her name to Anne Shirley with the advent of the talkies. Unlike so many other youngsters who were quickly forgotten, her pert beauty and lively intelligence brought her lead roles in a few years, most notably in the hugely successful screen version of Edna Ferber's *So Big* (1932).

Studios had a penchant for putting Anne Shirley into Anne roles. She was in *Anne of Green Gables* (1934) and in *Anne of Windy Poplars* (1940). Married to writer-director Charles Lederer, she retired in the mid-40's and has been active in local and national causes ever since. **Credits include:** *Stella Dallas* (1937), *Vigil in the Night* (1940), *All That Money Can Buy* (1941), *Murder, My Sweet* (1945).

ANN SHOEMAKER (1895–)

Ann Shoemaker has been playing character roles for more than 30 years. She gave a memorable performance in one of her early films as the nagging mother in the 1935 screen version of Booth Tarkington's *Alice Adams,* a humorous tale of small-town manners. **Films include:** *A Dog of Flanders* (1935), *Stella Dallas* (1937), *The Farmer's Daughter* (1940), *Sunrise at Campobello* (1960), *The Fortune Cookie* (1966).

SYLVIA SIDNEY (1910–)

Few film addicts realized that the aging lady on a fairly recent TV commercial had been one of the most popular actresses of the 30's. It wasn't until she returned to the screen after an absence of nearly 20 years to win an Oscar nomination for her supporting role in *Summer Wishes, Winter Dreams* (1973) that they recognized the star of *An American Tragedy* (1931) and other notable films of that era.

Sidney (Sophia Dosow) began her career on stage as a teenager. Her dark beauty and straightforward acting style were first filmed in *Through Different Eyes* (1929), and by the time of Elmer Rice's *Street Scene* (1932) she had become a star. One of her outstanding performances was with Henry Fonda in *You Only Live Once* (1937), an early version of the Bonnie and Clyde saga which was more a social protest than a glorification of crime.

From the late 40's Sidney's career flagged, and apart from infrequent appearances on television and stage her major artistic work was as the author of several books on needlepoint. **Films include:** *City Streets* (1931), *Madame Butterfly* (1932), *Fury* (1936), *Dead End* (1937), *The Wagons Roll at Night* (1941), *The Searching Wind* (1946), *Les Miserables* (1952), *Violent Saturday* (1955).

SIMONE SIGNORET (1921–)

The epitome of the wise and worldly Frenchwoman, Signoret has aged gracefully from romantic heroines to sensitive characters during her 30 some years in films. She was born Simone Kaminker in Wiesbaden, Germany, and drifted into acting in Paris during World War II.

She made her debut in *Le Prince Charmant* (1942) and did bit parts before being cast as the lead in *Macadam* (1945). From then on she worked steadily in both French and British movies, frequently in prostitute roles. Signoret attracted attention in 1951 with her fine portrayal of a woman in love with the doomed Serge Reggiani in *Casque d'Or*. It won her the British Film Academy's Best Foreign Actress Award, and the London film critics named her Best Actress of the year. A few years later she collected two British Film Academy awards in a row for her performances in *Les Sorcières de Salem* (1957) and *Room at the Top* (1959). Her portrayal of the older woman whom Laurence Harvey loves and leaves in the latter film also won her the first Academy Award ever presented to an actress who had never made a picture in Hollywood. In fact, it wasn't until 1965 that she did go to Hollywood to do *Ship of Fools* for director Stanley Kramer. (She played the romantic countess who has a last fling with Oskar Werner en route to exile.) Since then, Signoret has been cast in character parts in a variety of films, including the housewife who loathes her husband (and he, her) in *Le Chat* (1971) with Jean Gabin. She is married to French actor Yves Montand. **Films include:** *Fantomas* (1947), *Four Days Leave* (1950), *Ombre et Lumière* (1951), *Diabolique* (1954), *The Deadly Affair* (1966), *Games* (1967), *The Seagull* (1968), *L'Aveu* (1970).

Anne Shirley and Tom Brown—two attractive young stars of the early days of talkies—in Anne of Green Gables.

Simone Signoret, sophisticated and sensitive, in the film adaptation of Chekhov's The Seagull.

444

MILTON SILLS (1882–1930)

He died just as talking pictures came into full bloom, but throughout the 20's he was one of the top box-office favorites. Sills was a native of Chicago who had considerable stage experience before he appeared in his first film, *The Rack* (1915). He was tall, ruggedly handsome and at his best as a two-fisted swashbuckler. He appeared in Rafael Sabatini's *The Sea Hawk* (1924), one of the best rough-and-tumble films ever. Sills gave his last fine performance in *The Sea Wolf* (1930) just before his death. **Many other films include:** *The Hell Cat* (1918), *Burning Sands* (1922), *The Spoilers* (1923), *Adam's Rib* (1923), *Madonna of the Streets* (1924), *The Valley of the Giants* (1927), *The Hawk's Nest* (1928), *The Barker* (1928), *His Captive Woman* (1929).

HENRY SILVA (1928–   )

During his two decades in films, Puerto Rican Silva has most often appeared as cruel or menacing figures. Although he has played some leads—e.g., the title role of *Johnny Cool* (1963)—he is known for his fine sup-

Henry Silva, almost always a menace, in Man and Boy *(1972).*

porting performances, most notably as Don Murray's dope pusher, Mother, in *A Hatful of Rain* (1957). **Credits:** *Viva Zapata!* (debut, 1952), *Green Mansions* (1959), *The Manchurian Candidate* (1962), *The Plainsman* (1966), *Never a Dull Moment* (1968).

FRANK SILVERA (1914–   )

Probably Frank Silvera's first well-known role was as Huetra in *Viva Zapata!* (1952), a biography of the Mexican revolutionary played by a young, dynamic Marlon Brando. Their paths crossed again a decade later in *Mutiny on the Bounty* (1962). Something about the rebellious spirit must appeal to him, for he was later seen in the ill-fated *Ché!* (1969). Silvera has also appeared on television, notably on the *Look Up and Live* series. **Films include:** *Fear and Desire* (1953), *Crowded Paradise* (1956), *The Mountain Road* (1960), *Toys in the Attic* (1963), *The Appaloosa* (1966), *Hombre* (1967), *Up Tight* (1968).

PHIL SILVERS (1912–   )

The balding, Brooklyn-born comedian is probably best known for his TV role as Sergeant Bilko, the canny and cunning overseer of a platoon of impossibles, on the *You'll Never Get Rich* series (later called *The Phil Silvers Show*).

A long-time proponent of raucous comedy, Silvers may be remembered as a member of the press in the courtroom satire *Roxie Hart* (1942). In more recent years the former vaudevillian had the opportunity to clown it up with Zero Mostel in *A Funny Thing Happened on the Way to the Forum* (1966). In 1973 his autobiography, *This Laugh Is on Me*, was published. **Credits Include:** *The Hit Parade* (debut, 1941), *Tom, Dick and Harry* (1941), *Where Do We Go From Here?* (1945), *Summer Stock* (1950), *Top Banana* (1954), *It's a Mad, Mad, Mad, Mad World* (1963), *Buona Sera, Mrs. Campbell* (1968).

ALASTAIR SIM (1900–   )

In 1930 the footlights lured Sim away from a spot in his family's Edinburgh tailoring business. Although he began his career in straight dramatic parts on the London stage, he found

Alastair Sim and Jane Wyman whisper at each other in A Kiss in the Dark *(1949).*

fame as a comic in motion pictures. Sim made the switch to screen in *The Private Secretary* (1934). At first his roles were supporting ones in minor films, but he became the critics' favorite when he was featured as Sergeant Bingham in the *Inspector Horleigh* film series about a Scotland Yard detective.

Sim returned to the stage in 1940 to play Captain Hook in *Peter Pan* and did some early television. Then he made the picture that made the big difference in his career, *Green for Danger* (1947). He again played a detective, and this time his reviews were so good that he advanced to star billing. From then on it was clear sailing in role after comic role. Perhaps his best-loved portrayals were in the *St. Trinian* films, in which he played two roles, the regal but crooked headmistress and her equally unscrupulous brother.

After *The Millionairess* (1961) with Sophia Loren, Sim again returned to the theatre. He played with the Old Vic and did two revivals on the London stage—*Too Good to Be True* and *The Magistrate*. He didn't make a movie again until 1972, when he co-starred with Peter O'Toole in *The Ruling Class*. **Films include:** *Wedding Group* (1936), *Sailing Along* (1938), *Let the People Sing* (1942), *Hue and Cry* (1951), *The Happiest Days of Your Life* (1950), *Folly to Be Wise* (1953), *The Belles of St. Trinian's* (1954), *The Green Man* (1957), *The Doctor's Dilemma* (1959), *School for Scoundrels* (1960).

JEAN SIMMONS (1929–   )

Her innocent beauty and sensitive performances made this native Londoner one of Britain's most promising screen ingénues of the 40's. She made her first film—*Give Us the Moon* (1944)—at the age of 14, gave a splendid performance as Estella in David Lean's 1945 version of *Great Expectations* and won an Academy Award nomination for her Ophelia in Olivier's *Hamlet* (1948). Her obvious talent got her through some weak British films over the next few years, and then she moved to Hollywood in the early 50's with her then husband, Stewart Granger, and won renewed acclaim as the adolescent girl in an otherwise forgettable film, *The Actress* (1953).

Beautiful Jean Simmons and handsome Richard Burton in his early Roman, pre-Taylor days. The film was The Robe.

Over the years her beauty matured into elegance, and she brought unusual strength and intensity to her roles, most notably in *Home Before Dark* (1958) as a professor's wife shocked out of her delusions, only to discover they were not delusions at all. She made few films in the 60's but won an Oscar nomination for her role in *The Happy Ending* (1969). **Film credits include:** *Black Narcissus* (1947), *The Robe* (1953), *Guys and Dolls* (1955), *The Earth Is Mine* (1959), *Elmer Gantry* (1960), *Divorce American Style* (1967), *Say Hello to Yesterday* (1971).

MICHEL SIMON (1895–   )

A veteran of more than 60 films, Swiss-born French character actor Simon has played some rather dismal types in his long film career. One of his first important roles was as the anti-social tramp rescued from suicide in Renoir's *Boudu Saved From Drowning* (1932). He was also a stranger framed for a murder in *Panic* (1946) and a guardian of questionable character in *Port of Shadows* (1939). More recently, however, he gave one of his finest performances as the twinkly old-

Simone Simon and James Stewart in a remake of the earlier and beloved Seventh Heaven.

ster in the poignant *The Two of Us* (1968). **Highlights:** *The Passion of Joan of Arc* (1928), *L'Atalante* (1947), *La Beauté du Diable* (1949, U.S. 1952), *Candide* (1962), *Blanche* (1971).

SIMONE SIMON (1914–)

This redheaded, pert native of Marseille with a sexy pout was a movie idol in France during the early 30's. Then Darryl Zanuck picked her up as 20th Century–Fox's rival to Garbo and Dietrich. They billed her as "the Gallic Clara Bow," and she became an overnight star in the United States after her performance in *Girls' Dormitory* (1936).

Her life in Hollywood was not easy. She became embroiled in a much publicized scandal when she accused her secretary of stealing money, and directors and crew claimed that she was difficult to work with. She returned to France to star in Renoir's *Le Bête Humaine* (1939, U.S. 1940), and when the movie was praised she attempted an American comeback. She displayed a fine sense of the macabre in *The Cat People* (1942) but never lived up to the hopes Zanuck had for her. **Other film credits include:** *Seventh Heaven* (1937), *Josette* (1938), *All That Money Can Buy* (1941), *La Ronde* (1950), *Le Plaisir* (1952).

RUSSELL SIMPSON (1880–1959)

After certain basic experiences with acting schools, Broadway and the Alaskan gold rush, Simpson arrived in Hollywood in 1917 bent on breaking into films. He ended up playing in several hundred pictures during the next 40 years, in roles ranging from leading men to minor characters. **Films include:** *The Brand* (1919), *Billy the Kid* (1930), *San Francisco* (1936), *Dodge City* (1939), *The Grapes of Wrath* (1940), *They Were Expendable* (1945), *The Horse Soldiers* (1959).

FRANK SINATRA (1915–)

When, in the spring of 1974, he made a triumphal appearance at a Carnegie Hall concert in New York, it was obvious that the old master had not lost his touch and that he had followed the advice given in one of his most famous songs by remaining young at heart.

Sinatra was born in Hoboken, New Jersey, and began his career as a singer with the Harry James and Tommy Dorsey bands. By the late 30's the emaciated-looking and hollow-cheeked performer had become the idol of millions of screaming bobbysoxers. Hollywood took notice and cast him in his first film, *Las Vegas Nights* (1941). After that came several forgettables and some good musicals with Gene Kelly, among them *Anchors Aweigh* (1945) and *On the Town* (1949). Tough, truculent and enormously talented, Sinatra was not unlike Maggio, the young Italian he played in *From Here to Eternity* (1953). His performance in the film brought him the Best Supporting Actor Oscar and launched him on a series of starring roles in musicals and serious dramas. He made a variety of highly successful films and gave masterful performances on at least two occasions—in *The Man With the Golden Arm* (1955) and in *The Manchurian Candidate* (1962).

We're not sure about this, but we'd guess that Gloria Swanson was trussed and tortured because she wanted to know if Russell Simpson slept with his beard inside the covers or out. The film was Under the Lash *(1921).*

Throughout his career Sinatra has been a controversial figure. His enemies point to his much publicized brawls, his alleged underworld connections and his none too private life and loves. His friends, however, are unflaggingly loyal and deny most or all of the allegations. Hero or villain, there's no doubt that his is one of the great success stories of our time. **Highlights of more than 50 films:** *The Miracle of the Bells* (1948), *Guys and Dolls* (1955), *Pal Joey* (1957), *A Hole in the Head* (1959), *None but the Brave* (1965), *The Detective* (1968), *Dirty Dingus Magee* (1970).

PENNY SINGLETON (1908–)

Dorothy McNulty began her performing career on the Broadway stage, appearing in such plays as *Good News, Walk a Little Faster* and *Hey Nonny, Nonny*. She went to Hollywood to appear in the screen version of *Good News* (1930), and for the next eight years her career was rather undistinguished. Things changed when she became Penny Singleton and appeared in *Blondie* (1938). For the next 12 years she starred in more than 20 adventures of the popular comic-strip character. It so typed her that she rarely ventured far afield. **Films include:** *Swing Your Lady* (1938), *Boy Meets Girl* (1938), *Blondie Goes Latin* (1941), *Young Widow* (1946), *The Best Man* (1964).

RED SKELTON (1913–)

The fiery-haired clown became such a familiar household fixture of radio and television that fans might forget he also starred in a succession of zany comedies during the 40's and early 50's.

At the tender age of ten he is said to have run away from his home town, Vincennes, Indiana, to join a traveling medicine show. He moved on to minstrel shows, burlesque, vaudeville and finally made it to Broadway in 1937. His first film appearance, complete with his doughnut-dunking vaudeville routine, came in the 1938 version of Arthur Kober's funny play about life in a summer camp, *Having Wonderful Time*. He thereafter played the dimwit orderly in two Dr. Kildare films and was starred for the first time as a detective in the Cross–Carpenter crime com-

Frank Sinatra as tough little Maggio, with Donna Reed, in From Here to Eternity.

Lucille Ball, Red Skelton and Gene Kelly in the engaging and tuneful Du Barry Was a Lady.

Alison Skipworth, a very funny comedienne, leers up at Lionel Atwill in The Devil Is a Woman *(1935).*

Alexis Smith manages to look beautiful, hold up the wall and gun down a victim, all at the same time.

edy *Whistling in the Dark* (1941). He repeated the role in two sequels, *Whistling in Dixie* (1942) and *Whistling in Brooklyn* (1944).

In 1953 Skelton launched his TV show and pretty much abandoned motion pictures. The show had an incredible life span of 17 years, and after it was dropped in 1970 Skelton confined his activities to an occasional public appearance. **Films include:** *Lady Be Good* (1940), *DuBarry Was a Lady* (1943), *I Dood It* (1943), *The Show-Off* (1947), *Three Little Words* (1950), *Public Pigeon Number One* (1957), *Those Magnificent Men in Their Flying Machines* (1965).

ALISON SKIPWORTH (1870–1952)

Her ample physique, not unlike that of Margaret Rutherford's, helped to make her a highly engaging performer in 40 films made between 1930 and 1938. She had been on the stage for a long, long time and was masterful at portraying dowagers and duchesses as well as shady matronly ladies. Probably her best-remembered performance was with Charles Laughton in *If I Had a Million* (1932). **Other credits include:** *Raffles* (1930), *Outward Bound* (1930), *Alice in Wonderland* (1933), *Becky Sharp* (1935), *Wide Open Faces* (1938).

WALTER SLEZAK (1902–)

The genial Austrian hadn't planned to become an actor, but he just couldn't help it. First, his father, Leo Slezak, was a world-famous opera star. Then he was noticed by director Michael Curtiz and was cast in the silent extravaganza *Sodom and Gomorrah* (1923). Many years later Leo McCarey offered him the role of the Baron in *Once Upon a Honeymoon* (1942), and Slezak was finally launched on a screen career that involved more than a score of films. He almost always plays comedy roles. He has also appeared occasionally on television. **Credits include:** *Lifeboat* (1944), *Riff-Raff* (1947), *The Pirate* (1948), *The Inspector General* (1949), *Call Me Madam* (1953), *Come September* (1961), *Dr. Coppelius* (1968).

EVERETT SLOANE (1909–1965)

The veteran character actor had played hundreds of radio roles before joining Orson Welles' Mercury Theatre. He appeared in the group's first film venture, *Citizen Kane* (1941), as the irrepressible business manager, Mr. Bernstein, and later played in two other nerve-shattering Welles ventures, *Journey Into Fear* (1943) and *The Lady From Shanghai* (1948). He has also appeared frequently on television. **Credits include:** *The Men* (1950), *The Big Knife* (1955), *Lust for Life* (1956), *Home From the Hill* (1960), *The Disorderly Orderly* (1964).

ALEXIS SMITH (1921–)

Born Gladys Smith in Penticon, Canada, the tall, statuesque blonde made her film debut in *Lady With Red Hair* in 1940 and went on to such Warner Brothers wartime efforts as *Dive Bomber* (1941), *The Dough-girls* (1944) and *Hollywood Canteen* (1944). She played more or less fictional roles in lush film biographies of two enormously popular composers, George Gershwin (*Rhapsody in Blue,* 1945) and Cole Porter (*Night and Day,* 1946), neither movie giving her much more to do than look beautiful. Meatier roles followed, however, and her career on screen lasted into 1959. In recent years she has appeared on Broadway in *Follies* and later in a revival of *The Women.* She is married to

Craig Stevens. **Her credits include:** *Gentleman Jim* (1942), *Of Human Bondage* (1946), *Any Number Can Play* (1949), *The Sleeping Tiger* (1954), *The Young Philadelphians* (1959).

SIR C. AUBREY SMITH (1863–1948)

As long as Sir Aubrey was in the cast, one knew that the sun would never set on the British Empire. His patrician features, Roman nose, bushy graying eyebrows and mustache guaranteed that whatever mischief was brewing at the Khyber Pass would soon be set in order.

A native Londoner and a top-ranking cricket player as a young man, he began his stage career back in 1892, appeared in his first silent in 1915 and was in top form when talking pictures arrived. Thereafter, he played character roles in more than 80 films, many of them the outstanding productions of their day. He even went so far as to help satirize British manners and mannerisms in *Cluny Brown* (1946). Although he obviously did not always play the British colonel, it was as a stiff-lipped military man who prevented the natives from becoming too restless that he is best remembered. **Films include:** *Builder of Bridges* (debut, 1915), *Morning Glory* (1932), *Queen Christina* (1933), *Clive of India* (1935), *Lives of a Bengal Lancer* (1935), *The Four Feathers* (1939), *Rebecca* (1940), *Madame Curie* (1943), *The White Cliffs of Dover* (1944), *Little Women* (1949).

KENT SMITH (1907–   )

Although often thought of as a stage actor, Smith is also familiar to motion picture and TV audiences from dozens of performances in supporting roles. Smith began his career after graduation from Harvard University and was one of the original members of the University Players. Others were Henry Fonda, James Stewart and Margaret Sullavan. He made his Broadway debut in *Men Must Fight* and his first screen appearance in the thriller *Cat People* (1942). His impressive list of stage credits include a 1938 production of Ibsen's *A Doll's House, Bus Stop* (1955) and *What Every Woman Knows* (1954), starring opposite Helen Hayes.

In addition to his other work on television,

C. Aubrey Smith, monocle at the ready, lectures Charlie Ruggles while Myrna Loy adds a distinctly decorative note to the background. The film was the funny Love Me Tonight *(1932).*

he starred in the popular series *Peyton Place*. **Films include:** *Hitler's Children* (1943), *The Spiral Staircase* (1946), *Nora Prentiss* (1947), *Magic Town* (1947), *The Voice of the Turtle* (1947), *Paula* (1952), *Commanche* (1956), *Moon Pilot* (1962), *Youngblood Hawke* (1964), *The Trouble With Angels* (1966), *Games* (1967), *Death of a Gunfighter* (1969).

MAGGIE SMITH (1934–   )

One of today's most popular stage and screen actresses, this red-haired British star is known for her distinctive mannerisms and her electric performances. Her memorable roles range from Desdemona in *Othello* (1965) to Alec McCowan's wacky aunt in *Travels With My Aunt* (1972).

Margaret Natalie Smith was born near London (Ilford) and studied at the Oxford Playhouse Drama School. After several impressive stage appearances she made her

Maggie Smith, voted Best Actress of the year in the title role of The Prime of Miss Jean Brodie, *is backed up by Gordon Jackson (better known as Hudson, the butler in the British-made* Upstairs, Downstairs).

Carrie Snodgress, tied to a status-conscious and prissy mate, in Diary of a Mad Housewife.

Gale Sondergaard as a nasty Oriental in Somerset Maugham's The Letter.

movie debut in *No Where to Go* (1958). Eleven years later she won an Academy Award for Best Actress for *The Prime of Miss Jean Brodie* (1969). Recently she starred opposite her husband, Robert Stephens, in a West End revival of Noel Coward's *Private Lives*. **Credits include:** *The V.I.P.s* (1963), *Young Cassidy* (1965), *The Honeypot* (1967), *Hot Millions* (1968), *Oh! What a Lovely War* (1969).

ROGER SMITH (1932–   )

Known primarily as a TV actor and one of the stars of *77 Sunset Strip* (1958–64) and *Mister Roberts* (1965), Smith made a handful of films in the late 50's and early 60's. His best-known performance was as Rosalind Russell's nephew in *Auntie Mame* (1958). **Credits:** *The Young Rebels* (1956), *Operation Mad Ball* (1957), *Never Steal Anything Small* (1959).

CARRIE SNODGRESS (1945–   )

Snodgress dropped out of college to enroll in the Goodman School of Drama in Chicago and made her professional stage debut there after graduation. She was voted the most promising actress in 1966 and later won the coveted Sarah Siddons Award for her performance as Dorine in *Tartuffe*.

The young actress was noticed by Hollywood and cast in her first film, *Rabbit, Run* (1970), opposite James Caan. Her portrayal of the sodden, slovenly wife was a fine one, but the film received limited release in the United States, and the young actress had to wait for her next film to bring her fame. *The Diary of a Mad Housewife* (1971) not only brought her fame but also an Academy Award nomination for Best Actress. Since *Housewife* she has appeared on television in two made-for-TV movies and on several dramatic programs.

VLADIMIR SOKOLOFF (1889–1962)

The Russian-born actor studied with Stanislavsky before coming to the United States via Germany and France. His training and travel no doubt helped him play character roles of assorted national origins during his 50-year career. Sokoloff appeared in the fam-

ous French film *The Lower Depths* (1936) as well as in such well-known American pictures as *The Life of Emile Zola* (1937). **Films include:** *The Loves of Jeanne Ney* (1928), *Juarez* (1939), *For Whom the Bell Tolls* (1943), *The Magnificent Seven* (1960), *Taras Bulba* (1962).

ELKE SOMMER (1940–   )

This blond, pretty actress first appeared in films at age 18 in her native Germany and made her British screen debut in 1960. Although she made some serious films in her early career, such as *The Victors* (1963) and *The Prize* (1964), she has since gone the way of many sexy beauties into well-forgotten light comedy and bedroom farce. **Credits include:** *Don't Bother to Knock* (1960), *A Shot in the Dark* (1964), *Deadlier Than the Male* (1963), *The Oscar* (1966), *The Wrecking Crew* (1969).

GALE SONDERGAARD (1899–   )

In a 15-year period this striking-looking professor's daughter from Litchfield, Minnesota, made more than 30 film appearances, most often as a mysterious woman with evil intentions. She won the first Oscar ever presented in the Supporting Actress category for her first screen performance in *Anthony Adverse* (1936). Among her many notable portrayals were the sinister Eurasian in *The Letter* (1940) and the King's overlooked wife in *Anna and the King of Siam* (1946). In 1969 she appeared in *Slaves*—after a 20-year absence from films because of the blacklist of so-called Communist sympathizers in the McCarthy era. **Films include:** *The Life of Emile Zola* (1937), *The Black Cat* (1941), *A Night to Remember* (1943), *East Side, West Side* (1949).

ALBERTO SORDI (1919–   )

The Italian comic actor first gained international recognition in *I Vitelloni* (1953) as the foolish member in a group of provincial good-for-nothings. He also starred in *The White Sheik* (1956) as an actor in squalid circumstances who is pursued by a daydreaming young bride. He has since appeared in films in both Europe and the United States. P.S.: Sordi was also responsible for dubbing the voice of Oliver Hardy into Italian. **Credits include:** *The Sign of Venus* (1955), *A Farewell to Arms* (1958), *The Best of Enemies* (1962), *To Bed or Not to Bed* (1963), *Those Magnificent Men in Their Flying Machines* (1965), *Made in Italy* (1967).

ANN SOTHERN (1909–   )

The cheerful and talented native of a small town in North Dakota made her debut as a brunette billed as Harriet Lake in *The Show of Shows* (1929). It wasn't until after she appeared in *Broadway Through the Keyhole* (1933), along with Lucille Ball, that she changed her name to Ann Sothern.

Columbia Pictures signed the now blond Sothern to a term contract in 1934 and starred her in musicals. She had a good singing voice, but for years thereafter her talents were put to use generally in ''B'' pictures, most memorably in the 1939-to-1947 series of ten *Maisie* films in which she starred as the scatterbrained blond detective. In 1949, at long last, she was given a good part in a good picture, *A Letter to Three Wives*.

Sothern quit Hollywood in the early 50's, was hugely successful in two TV series of her own, *Private Secretary* and *The Ann Sothern Show,* and reappeared on screen more than ten years later as charming and competent as ever. **Films include:** *Let's Fall in Love* (1934), *Hotel for Women* (1939), *Brother Orchid* (1940), *Lady Be Good* (1941), *The Blue Gardenia* (1953), *Lady in a Cage* (1964), *Sylvia* (1965), *Chubasco* (1968), *The Killing Kind* (1973).

NED SPARKS (1883–1957)

The Canadian character actor with a unique nasal snarl specialized in ill-tempered roles through the 30's. He was seen often as a cigar-chomping newsman or manager and gave a memorable performance as Happy, the sour henchman of a kindly gangster, in *Lady for a Day* (1933). In 1918 Sparks was a leader of a stage actors' strike which precipitated the formation of Actors Equity. **Films include:** *42nd Street* (1933), *Wake Up and Live* (1937), *Magic Town* (1947).

Ann Sothern and James Craig, along with shaggy dog, in Swing Shift Maisie *(1943).*

ROBERT STACK (1919–   )

He was such a formidable law-enforcement agent in TV's mightily successful *The Untouchables* series that it is hard to believe that Stack's first screen appearance was in the slightly saccharine *First Love* (1939), a film in which Deanna Durbin received from young Mr. Stack her first screen kiss.

Perhaps because he is one of the motion picture colony's most talented athletes (perhaps *the* outstanding amateur) the tall and handsome actor has aged very little over the years. He has appeared in some extremely good pictures, and his notable performances came in such disparate films as *The High and the Mighty* (1954), *Written on the Wind* (1957) and, co-starred with Jean Gabin, *Le Soleil des Voyous* (1967).

Stack's TV credits also include *The Name of the Game* in the late 60's. **Among his films are:** *The Mortal Storm* (1940), *To Be or Not to Be* (1942), *The Bullfighter and the Lady* (1951), *The Last Voyage* (1960), *Is Paris Burning?* (1966), *Story of a Woman* (1970).

Robert Stack as Brigadier General Sibert in Is Paris Burning?

Terence Stamp tries to convince Julie Christie that he loves her. The film was the Hardy classic Far From the Madding Crowd.

Barbara Stanwyck, for 30 years beloved by an army of fans, in the exciting Double Indemnity.

TERENCE STAMP (1940–   )

His motion picture debut in *Billy Budd* (1962) was so well received that for a while Stamp declined film offers because he feared he could not match that initial success. His portrayal of the Christlike Budd won Stamp an Academy Award nomination and a Best Actor award in France. A performance as Iago in a school production of *Othello* brought London-born Stamp enough attention to win him a spot in a repertory company. He spent three years there until actor-director Peter Ustinov began his search for a young man to play Budd. Stamp made another picture that year, *Term of Trial,* released in the United States in 1963.

After a two-year absence from the screen, Stamp accepted the lead in the film version of John Fowles' novel *The Collector* (1965). His performance as the obsessed young man who kidnaps a girl he worships and hides her in his basement until her death won him the Best Actor award at the Cannes Film Festival.

Stamp made his Broadway debut in *Alfie* (1964). A few years later his onetime roommate Michael Caine starred in the screen version. **Films include:** *Modesty Blaise* (1966), *Far From the Madding Crowd* (1967), *Poor Cow* (1967), *Blue* (1968), *Theorum* (1968), *The Mind of Mr. Soames* (1969), *Spirits of the Dead* (1969).

LIONEL STANDER (1908–   )

For more than three decades this raspy-voiced native New Yorker who sounds a bit like a frog in distress has specialized in comedy roles. When the occasion called for it, however, he has also played the complete bastard with equal success. He proved that in Ben Hecht's *The Scoundrel* (1935), a picture about the dangerous shoals of book publishing, and again as the heartless theatrical agent who is Fredric March's enemy in *A Star Is Born* (1937). **Credits include:** *Mr. Deeds Goes to Town* (1936), *Unfaithfully Yours* (1948), *The Loved One* (1965), *Cul de Sac* (1966), *A Dandy in Aspic* (1968), *Pulp* (1973).

KIM STANLEY (1925–   )

One of the most respected leading ladies of the American stage, Stanley (born Patricia Read) has appeared on screen only twice, but both times she was memorable. She made her film debut as the lead in *The Goddess* (1958), the Paddy Chayefsky story about the empty, lonely life of a big movie star, and six years later she won an Academy Award nomination when she returned to the screen as the bizarre medium in *Seance on a Wet Afternoon* (1964).

BARBARA STANWYCK (1907–   )

Her image is that of a woman in charge —the boss lady who is shrewder and more savvy than most of the men she deals with on screen. During her long career she has played villainesses, misunderstood wives, shrews and hard-bitten showgirls but only rarely romantic heroines.

She started out in show business as a dancer but switched to acting when she was cast for a small part on Broadway in *The Noose* (1926). A few years later she followed her first husband, comic Frank Fay, to Hollywood and landed a few small parts. Better roles followed, and after *Illicit* (1930) and *Ten Cents a Dance* (1930) the studios were convinced that she had the makings of a big star. By the time she appeared opposite Adolphe Menjou in *Forbidden* (1932) she was firmly established as one of the top screen actresses of the time. Over the following decade Stanwyck played opposite all of Hollywood's biggest box-office attractions. Her off-screen romance with Robert Taylor was heavily publicized, and when they were teamed in *This Is My Affair* (1937) the ads called it ''the picture the whole world is talking about.'' Stanwyck and Taylor were married in 1939 and divorced in 1952.

She kept turning in solid performances and racked up four Academy Award nominations, including one for her performance in *Double Indemnity* (1944) as a scheming wife who plans to murder her husband and collect his insurance. By the mid-50's, however, fewer good roles came her way. Eventually she turned to television, and her career got a new boost when she starred in her own TV series, *The Big Valley,* for four years in the late 60's. **Films include:** *Miracle Woman* (1930), *Shopworn* (1932), *The Woman in Red* (1935), *The Mad Miss Manton* (1938), *The*

Strange Love of Martha Ivers (1946), *Executive Suite* (1954), *A Walk on the Wild Side* (1962).

MAUREEN STAPLETON (1925–   )

Since she scored her first big success on Broadway as Serafina in Tennessee Williams' *The Rose Tattoo* (1950), Stapleton has been regarded as one of the best actresses of the American theatre.

Stapleton left her home town of Troy, New York, in 1943 to launch her acting career in New York City. After several disappointing years, she joined the Actors Studio and played the first of her numerous Broadway roles in *The Playboy of the Western World* in 1947. Her first film role came 11 years later in *Miss Lonelyhearts* (1959). Stapleton appears occasionally in films and more frequently in TV dramas. **Films include:** *The Fugitive Kind* (1960), *A View From the Bridge* (1962), *Bye Bye Birdie* (1963), *Airport* (1969), *Plaza Suite* (1971).

ROD STEIGER (1925–   )

He has played so many middle-aged heavies on screen and concentrated his formidable talents on so many character parts that audiences frequently are surprised to learn that he is the same age as superstars Paul Newman and Marlon Brando. He began acting after serving with the Navy in World War II and made his professional debut in New York. His arrival on the theatrical scene, however, coincided with the early days of television, and he soon found steady work in video dramas. Steiger's performance in the title role of Paddy Chayefsky's television play *Marty* (1953) led to his first important part in films, as Brando's racketeer brother in *On the Waterfront* (1954). Steiger's performance brought him an Academy Award nomination and increased demands for his services. Steiger, however, was unwilling to sign the long-term contracts that most of the offers carried with them, and the result was almost a decade of work in mainly forgettable films. In the mid-60's, though, all that changed. First there was the role of Joy Boy in *The Loved One* (1965) and then a far better picture that refocused attention on him—*The Pawnbroker* (1965), the story of a guilt-wracked Jewish refugee. His performance brought a second Academy Award nomination and the Best Actor Award at the Berlin film festival. Two years later his portrayal of the bigoted Southern cop in *In the Heat of the Night* (1967) brought him the Oscar and many other awards. Steiger also appeared in *The Illustrated Man* (1970) and *Three Into Two Won't Go* (1970) with his former wife, actress Claire Bloom. **Films include:** *Teresa* (debut, 1951), *The Court Martial of Billy Mitchell* (1955), *Cry Terror* (1958), *The Mark* (1961), *Doctor Zhivago* (1966), *No Way to Treat a Lady* (1968), *Happy Birthday, Wanda June* (1971).

ANNA STEN (1908–   )

When Samuel Goldwyn heard that she had been discovered by Stanislavsky and saw her face in the Russian-made *Karamozof* (1931) he promptly put Anjuschka Stenski Sujakevitch under contract. It was his hope that she could be made into another Garbo. After a crash course in speech training and a vast amount of advance publicity, Sten made her first American screen appearance in the title

Anna Sten as the golden-haired rage of Paris in Nana. *Alas, alas, she never made it in Hollywood.*

Rod Steiger, a top-notch actor, with Joan Collins in Seven Thieves *(1960).*

Henry Stephenson in Rafael Sabatini's tale of derring-do on the high seas, Captain Blood *(1935).*

role of *Nana* (1934). It was, alas, a box-office bust. Two more attempts to make her a star fizzled, and she was finally released. She remained in America and made infrequent appearances in films, stock productions and TV shows. Over the years, however, she did develop another successful career as a painter. **Films include:** *Storm Over Asia* (Russian-made, 1928), *The Wedding Night* (1935), *A Woman Alone* (1938), *So Ends Our Night* (1941), *Soldier of Fortune* (1955), *The Nun and the Sergeant* (1962).

KAREL STEPANEK (1899–   )

This Czech character actor usually played Nazis or other menaces in films following his arrival in England in 1940. Prior to that he was a ballet dancer before turning to acting in Vienna and Berlin under Max Reinhardt, appearing in both Czech and German plays and films. **Films include:** *At Dawn We Die* (1943), *The Fallen Idol* (1949), *Cockleshell Heroes* (1956), *Sink the Bismarck!* (1960), *Before Winter Comes* (1969).

HENRY STEPHENSON (1871–1956)

With his benign expression and clipped mustache, Stephenson appeared in scores of Hollywood films, usually in kindly-old-men roles. Born in Grenada, British West Indies, and educated in England, he made his London stage debut in 1896 and his first New York appearance in 1901. After years of work on the stage and in silent movies, he made his talkie debut when he was past 60. **Films include:** *Red Headed Woman* (1932), *The Animal Kingdom* (1932), *Little Women* (1933), *Little Lord Fauntleroy* (1936), *The Adventures of Sherlock Holmes* (1939), *This Above All* (1942), *Oliver Twist* (1951).

FORD STERLING (1883–1939)

Along with Mack Sennett and Mabel Normand, Sterling helped to create Keystone comedies and appeared as the police chief of the Cops in scores of two-reel comedies. He was discovered by Sennett in 1912 while appearing in musical comedy and had been a circus acrobat before entering vaudeville. Going from straight comedy to character roles, he worked for every major studio between 1920 and 1930, but the advent of sound accelerated his retirement. **Films include:** *Miss Brewster's Millions* (1926), *Casey at the Bat* (1927), *Gentlemen Prefer Blondes* (1928), *Kismet* (1930), *Alice in Wonderland* (1933), *Black Sheep* (1935).

JAN STERLING (1923–   )

Born in New York City of a blue-blood family with an automatic listing in the social register, Sterling has, since making her film debut in *Johnny Belinda* (1948), played a gallery of dumb blondes, tramps and floozies. She made her Broadway debut in *Bachelor Born*, but it wasn't until she replaced Judy Holliday in *Born Yesterday* that her career blossomed. She has also appeared frequently on television. **Films include:** *Caged* (1950), *The Mating Season* (1951), *The High and the Mighty* (1954), *The Harder They Fall* (1956), *The Incident* (1967).

CRAIG STEVENS (1918–   )

A former University of Kansas dental student and amateur boxer, Stevens played in dozens of not very memorable films as a handsome, brainy, brawny hero. However, his characterizations had little impact on the public until his TV success as the smooth, pack-a-punch-a-minute private eye in *Peter Gunn*. **Credits:** *Dive Bomber* (1941), *Since You Went Away* (1944), *Humoresque* (1946), *Gunn* (1967).

INGER STEVENS (1936–1970)

Stevens was a strikingly beautiful Swedish immigrant to New York, and her earliest stage activity was in the chorus line of a New York City nightclub, the Latin Quarter. When she made her film debut in *Man of Fire* (1957) at the age of 22, she was Bing Crosby's youngest leading lady. She appeared in a number of big-budget Hollywood films that enjoyed healthy box-office results, but she did not win much attention until she assumed the lead in the TV series *The Farmer's Daughter* (1963). Stevens committed suicide in 1970. **Films credits:** *Cry Terror* (1958), *The New Interns* (1964), *Madigan* (1968), *Five Card Stud* (1968), *Hang 'Em High* (1968).

ONSLOW STEVENS (1902–   )

The Pasadena Playhouse was Onslow Ford Stevenson's steppingstone to a long career as a character actor of screen and stage. A native of California, he made the first of his numerous film appearances in Universal serials in 1932. After supporting roles in films like *Peg o' My Heart* (1932), *Counsellor-at-Law* (1933) and *The Three Musketeers* (1935), Stevens left Hollywood to try his luck on the New York stage. He made his Broadway debut in *Stage Door* (1936) and later was seen in plays like *Eastward in Eden* and *A Clearing in the Woods* (1957). Over the years Stevens continued to appear regularly in films, mainly "B" horror tales or action pictures. **Credits include:** *When Tomorrow Comes* (1939), *Mystery Sea Raider* (1940), *House of Dracula* (1945), *O.S.S.* (1946), *The Creeper* (1948), *Them* (1954), *All the Fine Young Cannibals* (1960), *The Couch* (1962).

JAMES STEWART (1908–   )

This engaging and talented Pennsylvanian holds a well-deserved and secure place in motion pictures' Hall of Fame, for he has starred in an astonishingly varied list of good films over a period of more than 35 years.

A graduate of Princeton University, Stewart began his acting career as a member of Joshua Logan's University Players, along with such other youngsters as Henry Fonda and Margaret Sullavan. In 1932 he and Fonda went to New York and found bit parts in the theatre. Recommended to MGM by Hedda Hopper, he was tested, signed to a contract and given his first screen role in *The Murder Man* (1935) with Spencer Tracy. By World War II, he had won the New York Film Critics Best Actor award for his performance opposite Jean Arthur in Frank Capra's classic *Mr. Smith Goes to Washington* (1939) and had played in such favorites as *It's a Wonderful World* (1939) and *Destry Rides Again* (1939). A year later he won the Academy Award for Best Actor for his performance as reporter Mike Connor in *The Philadelphia Story* (1940).

When he returned to the screen after a stint in the Air Force, Stewart's successes multiplied—in such Hitchcock thrillers as

James Stewart, who managed to be serious but never mawkish, and funny without turning cute, in No Time for Comedy *(1940).*

Rear Window (1954) and *Vertigo* (1958), in such varied roles as the world's most charming alcoholic in *Harvey* (1950), as the great big bandleader in *The Glenn Miller Story* (1954) and as the hero of a long string of Westerns. Retaining his quality of coolheaded superhonesty, Stewart switched to father and character roles in the 60's. In 1970, at the age of 62, he delighted Broadway audiences in a revival of *Harvey*, and more recently he starred as the laconic lawyer of the TV series *Hawkins*. **Highlights:** *Rose Marie* (1936), *You Can't Take It With You* (1938), *The Shop Around the Corner* (1940), *Call Northside 777* (1948), *Broken Arrow* (1950), *The Man Who Knew Too Much* (1956), *Anatomy of a Murder* (1959), *Mr. Hobbs Takes a Vacation* (1962), *Bandolero!* (1968), *Fool's Parade* (1971).

PAUL STEWART (1908–   )

A native New Yorker, Stewart studied law before turning his attention toward an acting career in the mid-30's. He first found work on stage and then as a radio performer and producer. Between 1934 and 1944 he was heard on thousands of broadcasts, many as a member of Orson Welles' Mercury Theatre of the Air. (He was one of the perpetrators of the

Young Dean Stockwell, with crotchety Lionel Barrymore in the background, in Down to the Sea in Ships *(1949).*

famous *War of the Worlds* broadcast.) Stewart made his screen debut as Raymond in Welles' *Citizen Kane* (1941) and went on to become an expert at portraying sinister characters. He was Zepp in *Mr. Lucky* (1943) with Cary Grant, Captain "Doc" Kaiser in *Twelve O'Clock High* (1949) and Sid Murphy in *The Bad and the Beautiful* (1953).

In the 60's Stewart turned most of his energies toward directing and producing for television, working on such successful series as *Twilight Zone, Peter Gunn, The Defenders* and *Hawaiian Eye*. **Films include:** *The Window* (1949), *Champion* (1949), *The Cobweb* (1955), *In Cold Blood* (1967), *Jigsaw* (1968).

DEAN STOCKWELL (1936–   )

Born in Hollywood of acting parents, Stockwell made his Broadway debut at age six (with his brother Guy) before being tested and signed by MGM and cast in *Valley of Decision* (1945). With a mop of blond curls,

baby-boyish good looks and the ability to sob on request, he quickly became a popular and busy child film star. Although his career seemed over by the time he was 16, Stockwell returned to the screen in the late 50's, most notably recreating his Broadway role in the 1959 film version of *Compulsion*. Since then he has appeared on Broadway and television as well as in occasional films. **Credits include:** *Anchors Aweigh* (1945), *The Green Years* (1946), *Gentleman's Agreement* (1947), *The Boy With Green Hair* (1949), *Sons and Lovers* (1960), *Long Day's Journey Into Night* (1962), *Psych-Out* (1968), *Another Day at the Races* (1973).

GEORGE E. STONE (1903–1967)

Born in Poland, he came to the United States at the age of 14 and broke into show business through the influence of actor William Farnum, who noticed him at his job as a page at the Lambs Club in New York. Work on stage in vaudeville led to work in silents of the 20's and his first notable screen appearance as the sewer rat in *Seventh Heaven* (1927). He soon built up a reputation as a fine character actor, and for more than three decades this small man with the receding hairline and the pencil-thin mustache was kept busy in a wide variety of films, most often playing oppressed little men. He also appeared on television and was a regular on the *Perry Mason* TV series. **Many films include:** *Little Caesar* (1931), *42nd Street* (1933), *Anthony Adverse* (1936), *Guys and Dolls* (1955), *Some Like It Hot* (1959), *Pocketful of Miracles* (1961).

LEWIS STONE (1879–1953)

Lewis Stone's long and prolific acting career began back at the turn of the century in New York, where he was a Broadway matinee idol. In films from 1915, he quickly established himself as a popular leading man of silents and found a place as one of MGM's original contract players when Metro was founded in 1924. Over the years he made a graceful transition from leading-man roles to character parts and appeared with distinction in more than 100 films. He is probably best remembered as the kindly white-haired man

Lewis Stone, a sterling character actor, with Norma Shearer in The Trial of Mary Dugan *(1929).*

with the military bearing who endeared himself to filmgoers as Judge Hardy in the all-
American *Andy Hardy* series of the late 30's
and 40's. **Credits include:** *The Man Who
Found Out* (debut, 1915), *The Prisoner of
Zenda* (1922), *My Past* (1931), *Queen Christina* (1933), *David Copperfield* (1935), *Judge
Hardy's Children* (1938), *State of the Union*
(1948), *All the Brothers Were Valiant*
(1953).

PAOLO STOPPA (1906–   )

The son of a wealthy Roman family,
Stoppa gave up his original plans to enter
medicine or law to become an actor. He
studied at the Eleonora Duse Academy of
Dramatic Art in Rome, began his professional
career as a member of the Wanda Capodaglio
troupe and went on the become one of the
biggest stars of the Italian theatre. Probably
Italy's leading character actor, Stoppa has
appeared in more than 100 films since his
screen debut in *Re Burlone* (1935). After 15
years of popularity in his own country, he
won international acclaim as the villain of De
Sica's *Miracle in Milan* (1950). His success
brought film offers from elsewhere in Europe
and the United States, and in the past two
decades Stoppa has combined his continuing
work in Italian plays and films with notable
appearances in British, French and American
pictures. **Highlights:** *La Beauté du Diable
(1949), The Seven Deadly Sins* (1953), *Gold
of Naples* (1957), *Rocco and His Brothers*
(1961), *The Leopard* (1963), *Becket* (1964),
After the Fox (1966).

GALE STORM (1922–   )

It probably amused producer Jesse Lasky
to discover that his short-lived experiment to
award film contracts to would-be actors on a
radio-audition show would result in the marriage of two winners: Josephine Cottle, a
17-year-old from Houston, Texas, and Lee
Bonnell, a 21-year-old college varsity actor
from South Bend, Indiana. After a brief
movie career, Bonnell went on to become a
successful insurance broker, while his wife,
as Gale Storm, went on to become the leading
lady in a score of interesting, varied and entertaining films, as well as the star of two televi-

sion series, *My Little Margie* and *Oh, Susan-
nah!* **Major credits:** *Tom Brown's School
Days* (1940), *It Happened on Fifth Avenue*
(1947), *Stampede* (1949), *The Underworld
Story* (1950), *The Texas Rangers* (1951),
Woman of the North Country (1952).

SUSAN STRASBERG (1938–   )

The daughter of famed New York dramatic
coach Lee Strasberg, she made her stage
debut off-Broadway at age 14 in *Maya* and
only a few years later landed the lead in *The
Diary of Anne Frank* on Broadway. Her performance as the young Jewish girl in hiding
from the Nazis in war-torn Amsterdam
brought raves, and she was touted as one of
the most promising of young actresses before
she made her screen debut in *Picnic* (1956).
Despite that promising beginning,
Strasberg's film career never went very far,
and she appeared mainly in "B" pictures.
Credits include: *Stage Struck* (1958),
Scream of Fear (1961), *Kapo* (1964), *The
High, Bright Sun* (1965), *The Trip* (1967),
Psych-Out (1968).

ROBERT STRAUSS (1913–   )

This large, heavy-set comedian from the
Bronx first attracted attention on Broadway in
Having Wonderful Time and *Detective Story*.
Shortly after that he participated in a bit of
Dean Martin–Jerry Lewis mayhem when he
made his screen debut as Lardoski in *Sailor
Beware* (1951). Since then he has enlivened
more than 20 films and numerous TV shows.
His most fondly remembered portrayal to date
was probably that of Stosh in Billy Wilder's
screen version of *Stalag 17* (1953). **Credits
include:** *The Bridges at Toko-Ri* (1955), *The
Seven Year Itch* (1955), *The Last Time I Saw
Archie* (1961), *Fort Utah* (1967).

BARBRA STREISAND (1942–   )

Her rise to stardom defies all the rules in
Hollywood's book. Sure, she showed talent
on Broadway, but who ever saw a movie
queen who looked like Streisand? And what
glamour girl ever spoke with a Brooklyn accent? Hollywood risked millions that the
Streisand magic would come across as well
on screen as it had on stage and on her fabul-

*Banjo-eyed Robert Strauss with
Ernie Kovacs in* Wake Me When It's
Over *(1960).*

*While her father smiles, Susan
Strasberg looks somewhat unhappy
in* The Brotherhood *(1958).*

Barbra Streisand and Robert Redford, the Jewish-Wasp duo of The Way We Were *and in real life two of the top-most stars of the 70's.*

box-office charts as the kooky heroine of *What's Up Doc?* (1972). She stayed there with an even bigger hit, *The Way We Were* (1973), in which she starred as Robert Redford's adoring wife in a marriage that couldn't work. **Other films:** *On a Clear Day You Can See Forever* (1970), *The Owl and the Pussycat* (1970), *Up the Sandbox* (1972).

SHEPPARD STRUDWICK (1907–   )

After several years on the legitimate stage, this genial-looking native of North Carolina broke into films in 1938 using the name of John Sheppard. He made his first appearance as Sheppard Strudwick in *Congo Maisie* (1940) and for the next few years alternated between the two names before settling on Strudwick in the mid-40's. Although he starred as the tormented Poe in *The Loves of Edgar Allan Poe* (1942), he spent most of his 20 some years in films playing characters of quiet temperament. His notable roles included that of Adam Stanton in *All the King's Men* (1949) and Anthony Vickers in *A Place in the Sun* (1951). **Film highlights:** *Remember the Day* (1941), *Joan of Arc* (1948), *The Sad Sack* (1957), *The Unkillables* (1967).

GLORIA STUART (1909–   )

Born in Santa Monica, California, Stuart was a leading lady of the screen during a time in the 30's when it was fashionable to be sleek, decorous and demure. Discovered at the Pasadena Playhouse, she was first seen in *Street of Women* (1932) and made over 40 films before she retired in the mid-40's to raise a family. She resurfaced again in the 60's, but this time as an artist with considerable talent. **Film include:** *The Invisible Man* (1933), *Roman Scandals* (1933), *Rebecca of Sunnybrook Farm* (1938), *The Three Musketeers* (1939), *She Wrote the Book* (1946).

MARGARET SULLAVAN (1911–1960)

There still exists a dedicated band of Sullavan addicts who, remembering her in plays like *The Voice of the Turtle* (1943) and films like Molnar's *The Good Fairy* (1935), maintain that she was the finest actress of her time. On stage, and often on screen as well, her

Gloria Stuart in a romantic mood.

ously successful record albums. The gamble paid off, and today Streisand is among the biggest female stars of them all.

Even back in her days growing up in Flatbush, Streisand wanted to be in show business. She made her first singing appearances in Greenwich Village and then landed the role of Miss Marmelstein in the Broadway musical *I Can Get It for You Wholesale* (1962). Streisand stopped the show, and her success brought her the lead in *Funny Girl* (1964), the story of Jewish comedienne and singer Fanny Brice. The show was a hit in New York and London, and Streisand tied with Katharine Hepburn for a Best Actress Oscar when she recreated her role for her screen debut in the equally successful 1968 screen version. Her second film was another musical blockbuster, *Hello, Dolly!*, but this time neither the film nor its star received many favorable comments. After several more disappointing efforts Streisand again got back to the top of the talents imparted to her a unique radiance. It is a lasting tragedy that her career was marred by deafness and some deep uncertainty or misery within herself—a quality that led her into sanitariums and eventually to her death from barbiturates while she was rehearsing a new play, aptly called *Sweet Love Remembered*, in New Haven, Connecticut.

Born in Virginia, she made her early stage appearances with James Stewart and Henry Fonda, who became the first of her four husbands. Hollywood gave her starring roles at once, beginning with her film debut in *Only Yesterday* (1933), but she made things difficult for nearly every director she worked for as well as for the studios that clamored for her services. As a result she made only 16 films.

In 1938 Sullavan won the New York Film Critics Award as Best Actress for her work in *Three Comrades*, and she was superb in *Cry Havoc* (1943). After that she returned to the stage and was an outstanding success in *Sabrina Fair* and several other Broadway shows. In 1956 she was admitted into a sanitarium but was planning a comeback when her life ended on New Year's Day, 1960. **Other films:** *Little Man, What Now?* (1934), *The Shopworn Angel* (1938), *The Shop Around the Corner* (1940), *The Mortal Storm* (1940), *Back Street* (1941), *No Sad Songs for Me* (1950).

BARRY SULLIVAN (1912–)

Sullivan was born in New York and studied law at Temple University in Philadelphia before deciding on an acting career. He played in summer stock and then radio soap operas before establishing himself on Broadway in productions of *Brother Rat, Idiot's Delight* and *The Man Who Came to Dinner*.

He had the tall, rangy look of Western heroes, so when Hollywood beckoned it was to cast him in horse operas. Eventually, however, he progressed to leading roles in dramas. Sullivan appears regularly on television. He played Lt. Barney Greenwald, the defense attorney in the TV production of *The Caine Mutiny Court Martial*, and has been the star of such series as *The Tall Man* and *Harbourmaster*. **Films include:** *Lady in the*

Dark (1944), *Duffy's Tavern* (1945), *The Great Gatsby* (1949), *Payment on Demand* (1951), *The Bad and the Beautiful* (1953), *Queen Bee* (1955), *Light in the Piazza* (1962), *Harlow* (1965), *Intimacy* (1966), *Tell Them Willie Boy Is Here* (1969).

SLIM SUMMERVILLE (1892–1946)

Orphaned at the age of five, Summerville wandered through a series of jobs that included a stint in a coffin factory and arrived in Los Angeles. By 1913 he became one of the famed Keystone Cops. Tall and thin, he was a counterpoint to the fat patrolmen. His comic timing and gift for understatement served him in good stead with the advent of sound, and, beginning with *All Quiet on the Western Front* (1930), he was in great demand as a character actor and comedian. In 1938, 20th Century–Fox reported that his part in *Winner Take All* was his 627th film performance —unlikely, but that was the claim. **Credits include:** *The Front Page* (1931), *Bad Sister* (1931), *Life Begins at Forty* (1935), *Jesse James* (1939), *Tobacco Road* (1941), *The Hoodlum Saint* (1946).

CLINTON SUNDBERG (1919–)

The perennial befuddled clerk or waiter in films of the 40's, Sundberg was a teacher who acted in amateur dramatics until he was spotted by the manager of a stock company. It was the end of teaching and the beginning of his acting career. He has since appeared with regularity on Broadway in such plays as *Room Service, Arsenic and Old Lace* and *Mary, Mary*, as well as continuing his screen career. **Films include:** *Undercurrent* (1946), *Annie Get Your Gun* (1950), *Main Street to Broadway* (1953), *The Birds and the Bees* (1956), *The Wonderful World of the Brothers Grimm* (1962), *Hotel* (1967).

DONALD SUTHERLAND (1934–)

One of the new breed of screen actors, Sutherland made the leap from supporting to leading roles when he was cast as Hawkeye Pierce in *M*A*S*H* (1970). Like co-star Elliott Gould, Sutherland doesn't fit the handsome-leading-man image of Hollywood stars of the past. He was born in Canada and

Again a romantic mood, but this time the lady was Margaret Sullavan and the film was So Red the Rose *(1935).*

Barry Sullivan in Forty Guns *(1957).*

Donald Sutherland as a member of the clergy in Act of the Heart *(1970).*

studied engineering at the University of Toronto before he decided to take acting seriously. He went to England to study at the London Academy of Music and Dramatic Art and later appeared in a British production of *August for the People* with Rex Harrison and Rachel Roberts.

He remained in England, where he made his first film (in the role of a witch), *The Castle of the Living Dead* (1955). Better roles followed after Sutherland's move to Hollywood. He was the fumbling draftee in *The Dirty Dozen* (1968) and, after *M*A*S*H*, Jane Fonda's co-star in *Klute* (1971). In 1973 he was much praised for his portrayal of the psychic father in *Don't Look Now* with Julie Christie. **Films include:** *Die, Die My Darling* (1965), *Interlude* (1968), *Little Murders* (1971), *Steelyard Blues* (1973), *Wet Stuff* (1974).

GRADY SUTTON (1908–   )

His performance as the juvenile comedy heavy in *Laddie* (1935) impressed W. C. Fields, who sought out Sutton and cast him in *The Man on the Flying Trapeze* (1935). Sutton has had a long career in Hollywood playing comic supporting roles. He started out in silent pictures and has made more than 200 screen appearances. His specialty is his characterization of the country bumpkin. **Films include:** *This Reckless Age* (1932), *Only Yesterday* (1933), *Alice Adams* (1935), *The Mad Miss Manton* (1938), *The Great Moment* (1944), *My Wild Irish Rose* (1947), *White Christmas* (1954), *My Fair Lady* (1964), *Myra Breckinridge* (1970), *Support Your Local Gunfighter* (1971).

JOHN SUTTON (1908–1963)

Sutton, born in India, educated in England, came to Hollywood in the 30's and served as a technical adviser on films dealing with British themes. He was soon drafted to play small roles in "B" pictures and later graduated to second leads in better vehicles. **Films include:** *Bulldog Drummond's Revenge* (1937), *A Yank in the RAF* (1941), *Jane Eyre* (1944), *The Golden Hawk* (1952), *The Bat* (1959).

MACK SWAIN (1876–1935)

Film buffs will remember him most vividly as Big Jim McKay, the hulking, walrus-mustached menace in *The Gold Rush* (1925) with whom Charles Chaplin attempts to share his boiled shoe and shoelaces. Earlier he had been seen with Chaplin in *The Pilgrim* (1923).

Swain was a song-and-dance man for 22 years before going to Hollywood, where his whiskers and lush eyebrows made him a prominent fixture in Mack Sennett Keystone comedies. He appeared in virtually all of the two-reelers and went on to play comedy roles in other, longer features. **Films include:** *Hands Up* (1926), *My Best Girl* (1927), *The Locked Door* (1930), *Finn and Hattie* (1931).

GLORIA SWANSON (1898–   )

The tiny, talented, lovely-to-look-at actress had become one of motion pictures' immortals long before most of today's moviegoers were born. After a career that spanned more than 60 years she remained a star whose every public appearance was greeted with applause from audiences who never saw one of the smash-hit silents she made in the days when the movies were in their infancy.

She was 15, with no particular interest in acting, when she was taken by an aunt to the Essanay studio and asked to hand a bouquet to the leading lady of a film that was being made. That insignificant bit led her to Hollywood in 1916, where she appeared in Mack Sennett comedies. "I did my comedies like Duse might have done them," she said. "The more serious I became, the funnier the scene became." She wasn't a Sennett bathing beauty and quit because they wanted to make her one.

Discovered by Cecil B. De Mille, she began to be starred as a woman wronged —wronged, perhaps, but magnificently gowned. In this, the clothes-horse phase of her career, what she wore began to influence women's fashions around the world. Thereafter, beginning with *Male and Female* (1919) to *Sadie Thompson* (1928), she made up to four films a year, which, comedies and drama alike, were almost all box-office successes. Although her first talkie, *The Trespasser* (1929), was a sensation, her career gradually faded. In a moment of genius, she was cast in the role of Norma Desmond in *Sunset Boulevard* (1950), the bitter Wilder–Brackett comedy about an aging movie queen who lives in the past. The picture was made nearly 25 years ago and remains a classic.

In recent years Swanson appeared on Broadway in *Butterflies Are Free*, launched a clothing business, appeared in several less than effective pictures and amiably submitted to television interviews about the life of Hollywood queens, then and now. **A few highlights:** *The Affairs of Anatol* (1921), *Madame Sans Gene* (1925), *The Untamed Lady* (1926), *Tonight or Never* (1931), *Father Takes a Wife* (1941), *3 For Bedroom C* (1952).

BLANCHE SWEET (1896–   )

A heroine of the silent screen, she began her career as a baby appearing in the arms of her actress grandmother. By the time she was 12 she was working with D. W. Griffith and eventually went to Hollywood when the movie industry began to locate there. She made only three talking pictures before retiring from the screen. **Films include:** *The Thousand-Dollar Husband* (1916), *The Unpardonable Sin* (1919), *Anna Christie* (1923), *Singed* (1927), *The Silver Horde* (1930).

BASIL SYDNEY (1894–1968)

While he was far better known as a leading man on the London and New York stages, Britisher Sydney managed to appear in some 20 pictures during the 40 years that followed his film debut in *Romance* (1920). Although he most often was cast as a heavy, he did play Claudius in Olivier's *Hamlet* (1948). **Some of his films include:** *Accused* (1936), *Caesar and Cleopatra* (1946), *Treasure Island* (1950), *Ivanhoe* (1952), *Salome* (1953), *Around the World in 80 Days* (1956), *The Three Worlds of Gulliver* (1960).

Gloria Swanson as she appeared in Elinor Glyn's Three Weeks *(1933).*

A lovely young Blanche Sweet was already a veteran film player when the talkies arrived.

LYLE TALBOT (1904–   )

He snarled and scowled his way to success as an evildoer in many movies of the 30's. Talbot got his first taste of the theatre during his school vacations when he appeared in his father's stock company and he was spotted by a Warner Brothers scout in a Little Theatre Company production. He made his screen debut in *Love Is a Racket* (1932) and went on to appear as second lead or occasionally as the hero in more than 60 films before the end of the decade. In his later career he became a character actor both on the screen and on television in such series as *The Burns and Allen Show* and *December Bride*. **His credits include:** *20,000 Years in Sing Sing* (1933), *I Stand Accused* (1939), *There's No Business Like Show Business* (1954), *Sunrise at Campobello* (1960).

CONSTANCE TALMADGE
(1898–1973)

Like sisters Norma and Natalie, this youngest Talmadge girl from Brooklyn was a star of the silent screen. She first found work in films as an extra back in the days of the Flatbush Vitagraph studio. Her first break came when Griffith cast her as the mountain girl in what was to be one of the screen's classics—*Intolerance* (1916). Eventually she established herself as a top-ranking comedienne in such films as *Wedding Bells* (1921), *East Is West* (1922) and *Heart Trouble* (1924). Probably her most fondly remembered performance was opposite Ronald Colman in *Her Sister From Paris* (1925). She retired from the screen with the advent of talking pictures. **Film highlights:** *Matrimaniac* (1916), *The Honeymoon* (1917), *Happiness a la Mode* (1919), *Lessons in Love* (1921), *The Goldfish* (1924), *Venus* (1929).

NORMA TALMADGE (1897–1957)

A top box office draw in the silent era, she began her professional career posing for colored slides used to illustrate the songs shown in nickelodeons and soon progressed to bit parts in movies made by the fledgling Vitagraph studio in Brooklyn. Her first important role was in the comedy *The Dixie Mother* (1911). When she left Vitagraph she continued to play in comic dramas, notably in the *Belinda* series.

But Talmadge found fame elsewhere. She married Joseph Schenck, who cast her as the long-suffering, elegant heroine in a series of tearful dramas. She became one of the most popular stars of the early 20's, playing in melodramas which allowed her to emote flamboyantly. Talented writers and directors helped Talmadge sustain her image, and in

Norma Talmadge in a soulful moment with Otto Kruger in Du Barry, Woman of Passion.

1927 she gave one of her best performances as the archetypal doomed sufferer in *Camille*. Her career faltered with the coming of sound films, and she retired after making two unsuccessful sound pictures. **Nearly 200 films include:** *The New Moon* (1919), *The Sign on the Door* (1921), *Within the Law* (1923), *Kiki* (1926), *New York Nights* (1930), *DuBarry, Woman of Passion* (1930).

RUSS TAMBLYN (1934–   )

Young Rusty Tamblyn took up dancing when he was five, acrobatics when he was ten and literally tumbled his way into films when he was 14. With two notable exceptions most of his roles have been minor ones. He played the youngest brother in the musical *Seven Brides for Seven Brothers* (1954) and proved such an engaging performer that he was featured the next year in *Hit the Deck* (1955). **Films include:** *Don't Go Near the Water* (1956), *Peyton Place* (1957), *Tom Thumb* (1958), *Cimarron* (1961), *West Side Story* (1961), *How the West Was Won* (1963), *The Haunting* (1963), *Son of a Gunfighter* (1965).

AKIM TAMIROFF (1901–1972)

On screen he was generally unshaven and sweaty; his swarthy features combined with a guttural accent to make him one of the most sinister actors in motion-picture history. Paradoxically, filmgoers often discovered that beneath the grease and grime, the prodigious eating and wine guzzling, there often lurked a chap whose heart was definitely in the right place.

A native of Baku in southern Russia, he came to the United States with the Moscow Art Theatre group in 1923. He stayed in the U.S. and first turned up on the screen in *O.K. America* (1932). During his nearly 40 years in films his enormous versatility brought him two Academy Award nominations for Best Supporting Actor for his performances in *The General Died at Dawn* (1936) and *For Whom the Bell Tolls* (1943). Early in his career Tamiroff generally played heavies; later his outrageous characterizations were largely comedy portrayals. **More than 100 films include:** *The Lives of a Bengal Lancer* (1935), *Anthony Adverse* (1936), *The Way of All Flesh* (1940), *Tortilla Flat* (1942), *Anastasia*

In this rather decorous tableau, Akim Tamiroff is being manacled by Lloyd Nolan before the prone figure of Anna May Wong in Dangerous to Know *(1938).*

(1956), *Topkapi* (1964), *The Great Bank Robbery* (1969).

JESSICA TANDY (1909–   )

Over the years this fine British-born actress has taken occasional breaks from her career on the legitimate stage to appear in films. Tandy first attracted notice shortly after her 1928 London stage debut and has since turned in a variety of memorable performances both in London and her adopted home, New York. Her most famous role was that of Blanche in Tennessee Williams' *A Streetcar Named Desire* (1948), for which she won a Tony.

Although Tandy made her first film appearance in 1932 in *The Indiscretions of Eve*, she did not reappear on screen until 1944, when she made her American film debut opposite her husband and frequent stage co-star, Hume Cronyn, in *The Seventh Cross*. **Credits include:** *Forever Amber* (1947), *A Woman's Vengeance* (1948), *September Affair* (1951), *The Birds* (1963).

Jessica Tandy played Nan Britton in Forever Amber, *in its day considered a risqué film.*

464

Beautiful Lilyan Tashman in the clutches of Irving Pichel in The Road to Reno *(1931).*

The incomparable Jacques Tati in Mon Oncle.

LILYAN TASHMAN (1899–1934)

A onetime Ziegfeld Follies chorus girl, Tashman became a star of silent and sound films, a noted Hollywood hostess and a fashion leader before her death at age 35. She made her motion-picture debut in 1924 and established her screen image the following year when she recreated her Broadway role as the worldly sophisticate in *The Garden of Weeds*.

Tashman's low, throaty voice helped her make a smooth transition to talkies. One of her best performances of the 30's was as Douglas Fairbanks, Jr.'s, mistress in the seething *Scarlet Dawn* (1932). Tashman was married to actor Edmund Lowe of *What Price Glory?* fame. **Films include:** *Experience* (1921), *Manhandled* (1924), *Don't Tell the Wife* (1927), *New York Nights* (1930), *Murder by the Clock* (1931), *Frankie and Johnny* (1934).

JACQUES TATI (1908–   )

The elongated French comedian–director with the stride of an overwrought stork is a master of pantomime, at times comparable to Chaplin at his best, and his films are often compared to American silents. Tati was born in the remote French town of Pecq and found his first success as a music-hall favorite. He broke into films as a scenario writer and soon was appearing in shorts which he produced and directed himself. After World War II filmgoers were treated to the first of his feature-length comic satires, *Jour de Fête* (1947), in which Tati starred (of course) as the befuddled postman obsessed with the dream of efficiency. The film was a hit and collected awards at both the Venice and Cannes film festivals. Then came his riotously funny *Mr. Hulot's Holiday* (1952), which substituted grunts, background noises and remote monosyllables for dialogue in a vignette lampooning life at a French middle-class seaside resort. Quite properly it won the Cannes Grand Prix. Filmgoers still reverently recall Tati's battle with a garden hose and his dramatic struggle with an animal pelt that somehow got stuck in his spurs. His next creation was *Mon Oncle* (1958), an almost savage satire on urban living which won both

an Oscar and the New York Film Critics award for best foreign-language film. After the less successful *Playtime* (1968) Tati scored another hit with *Traffic* (1973), in which he again focused his attention on the little man controlled by the too industrialized, overpowering modern conveniences, this time in the form of the omnipresent automobile. **Credits:** *Sylvie et le Fantôme* (1945), *Le Diable au Corps* (1947).

ELIZABETH TAYLOR (1932–   )

One of filmdom's great beauties, she was a star before she hit her teens and has remained near the top of the heap ever since. While her on-screen performances have ranged from very good to downright terrible, she probably holds the Hollywood record for making headlines. One can only imagine what gossip columnists would have done without her.

The lady known as Liz was born in London, arrived in California at the outbreak of World War II and became an MGM star after the doggy *Lassie Come Home* (1943) and the horsey *National Velvet* (1944). During the following dozen years and via an equal number of films Taylor made an effortless transition to adult roles. She received her first Oscar nomination for *Giant* (1956) and quickly followed that up with three more—for *Raintree County* (1957), *Cat on a Hot Tin Roof* (1958) and *Suddenly, Last Summer* (1959)—before actually capturing an Oscar for *Butterfield 8* (1960). Six years later she won a second Best Actress Academy Award (as well as the New York Film Critics accolade) for a searing performance opposite Richard Burton in *Who's Afraid of Virginia Woolf?*. Between these two successes came the wildly extravagant, star-studded *Cleopatra* (1963), for which she received more than $2,000,000 and met Burton to boot. Her actual performance, however, evokes a line once used about an actor in a Shakespearean role on Broadway: "He played the king as though someone was about to play the ace."

Taylor's career has been interrupted often, by serious illnesses and by marriages to Nicky Hilton; Michael Wilding; producer Mike Todd, who died in an air crash; singer Eddie Fisher, who abandoned Debbie Reynolds to become her bridegroom; and to Richard Burton, for whom she left Eddie Fisher.

Highlights of more than 35 films: *Jane Eyre* (1941), *The White Cliffs of Dover* (1944), *Little Woman* (1949), *Father of the Bride* (1950), *A Place in the Sun* (1951), *Rhapsody* (1954), *The VIP's* (1963), *The Sandpiper* (1965), *The Taming of the Shrew* (1967), *Secret Ceremony* (1968), *Under Milkwood* (1971), *Nightwatch* (1973).

KENT TAYLOR (1907–)

Taylor (Louis Weiss) played lead roles in many low-budget films of the 30's and 40's. He began appearing in features in 1931 and over the past four decades has made more than 50 films. As a hero he gave performances that were a wee bit on the wooden side, but his dark good looks were always a welcome addition to the pictures he played in. In the 50's Taylor turned to television as the star of the *Boston Blackie* series. **Credits include:** *Husband's Holiday* (1931), *Death Takes a Holiday* (1934), *Men Against the Sky* (1940), *Bombers' Moon* (1943), *Slightly Scarlet* (1956), *Harbor Lights* (1964).

ROBERT TAYLOR (1911–1969)

For more than 30 years Taylor (Spangler Arlington Brough) remained one of Hollywood's top stars, progressing from romantic leading man to the hero of Westerns and adventure films. He was one of the few actors who worked under contract to one studio throughout most of his motion-picture career. MGM first signed him in 1934, and he didn't leave the studio until 1959.

Taylor became one of Hollywood's top box-office attractions within two years of his motion-picture debut in *Handy Andy* (1934). His appeal was his dark, romantic good looks. The public loved him in *Magnificent Obsession* (1935) starring opposite Irene Dunne as the playboy who develops a conscience, and in *Camille* (1937) he starred with Greta Garbo. Hollywood then capitalized on his real-life romance with actress Barbara

The youthful Robert Taylor, extremely handsome if not downright beautiful, was often cast in brooding, intense roles.

Elizabeth Taylor, a star whose beauty has never waned.

A grimy Rod Taylor is comforted by his mother, Flora Robson, in Young Cassidy *(1965) after the Easter Uprising.*

Shirley Temple, smartly uniformed as the mascot of the regiment in Wee Willie Winkie.

Stanwyck and co-starred them, to the public's delight, in *This Is My Affair* (1937).

Taylor continued playing romantic leads until World War II and a two-year stint in the Navy interrupted his career. When he returned to Hollywood he was cast opposite Katharine Hepburn in *Undercurrent* (1946). He played a homicidal maniac in the film, one of his few unsympathetic roles. By the 50's Taylor finally escaped his early image as a ladies' man and was cast in a series of big-budget films which included *Quo Vadis* (1951), *Ivanhoe* (1952) and *Valley of the Kings* (1954). Taylor's star had dimmed by the late 50's, but a TV series, *The Detectives* (1959–61), kept him in the public eye. **Films include:** *A Wicked Woman* (1934), *Small Town Girl* (1936), *A Yank at Oxford* (1938), *Waterloo Bridge* (1940), *Johnny Eager* (1942), *The High Wall* (1947), *Quentin Durward* (1955), *Where Angels Go— Trouble Follows* (1968).

ROD TAYLOR (1929–   )

This tall, dark and (you guessed it) good-looking actor made his first screen appearance in his native Australia after a brief experience in the theatre. He then headed for London to pursue his career. En route, however, he made a stopover in Hollywood that turned out to be a permanent detour. His first American film role was in *The Virgin Queen* (1955), and by the following year he was starring in *The Catered Affair* opposite Debbie Reynolds. Since then he has mostly been seen as the second lead in adventure films and light comedies. He was the newspaperman who got entangled with Jane Fonda in the delightful *Sunday in New York* (1964). In 1960 he starred in the TV series *Hong Kong*. **Among his credits:** *The Stewart Expedition* (1951), *Treasure Island* (1954), *The Birds* (1963), *Young Cassidy* (1965), *The Glass Bottom Boat* (1966), *Nobody Runs Forever* (1968), *Zabriskie Point* (1970), *Powder Keg* (1972).

CONWAY TEARLE (1882–1938)

The Brooklyn-born West Point graduate (Frederick Levy) made his mark as an actor in England before becoming a leading man in the early Hollywood silents. He began playing Shakespearean roles in an English touring repertory company in 1901 and eventually was invited by actress Ellen Terry to appear with her as Claudio in *Much Ado About Nothing*. He returned to the United States in 1905 to act on both stage and screen. Tearle successfully moved from silents to talkies and appeared in pictures like *Vanity Fair* (1932) and *Romeo and Juliet* (1938). He was the half brother of British actor Sir Godfrey Tearle. **Films include:** *Virtuous Wives* (1918), *The Forbidden Woman* (1920), *Lilies of the Field* (1924), *The Gold Diggers of Broadway* (1929), *Should Ladies Behave* (1933), *Klondike Annie* (1936).

SHIRLEY TEMPLE (1928–   )

At the peak of her career she was a national institution. In some ways she still is, since no child star ever achieved Temple's enormous success.

She was only four years old when she began playing featured parts in movies like *Red-Haired Alibi* (1932), and by the time she sang "Baby Take a Bow" in *Stand Up and Cheer* (1934) Temple was a public favorite. She could do no wrong through the end of the 30's. She sang "On the Good Ship Lollipop" in *Bright Eyes* (1934), danced with Bill "Bojangles" Robinson in *The Little Colonel* (1935) and *The Littlest Rebel* (1935). She was number one at the box office from 1935 until 1938, and only Louis B. Mayer was paid more than Temple; she got $100,000 per film.

She had to grow up, however, and as she did the public began to lose interest in her. Temple was too famous, however, to slip into obscurity. She made headlines when she ran (and lost) as a Republican candidate for Congress and again, in 1969, when Richard Nixon appointed her a representative to the United Nations. **Films include:** *Our Little Girl* (1935), *Curly Top* (1935), *Wee Willie Winkie* (1937), *Heidi* (1937), *Rebecca of Sunnybrook Farm* (1938), *The Little Princess* (1939), *Miss Annie Rooney* (1942), *The Bachelor and the Bobby-Soxer* (1947), *Mr. Belvedere Goes to College* (1949).

ALICE TERRY (1899–   )

Alice Taafe was a teenaged Hollywood extra when she was spotted by producer-director Rex Ingram. Through him she reached stardom, often appearing as silent-screen idol Ramon Novarro's leading lady. Her career ended with the coming of sound and with her marriage to Ingram. **Films include:** *Not My Sister* (1916), *The Four Horsemen of the Apocalypse* (1921), *The Prisoner of Zenda* (1922), *Mare Nostrum* (1926), *The Garden of Allah* (1927).

TERRY-THOMAS (1911–)

His comic portrayals of upper-crust, pompous Englishmen and stiff-necked British officers have brightened some three dozen British and American films during the past 20 some years.

Born Thomas Terry Hoar-Stevens, this gap-toothed Londoner drifted into films as an extra before winning success as a stand-up nightclub comedian. His first credited film role was in *Helter Skelter* (1949), and he first caught the public's eye as the commanding officer in *Private's Progress* (1956). He was starred but once, as an English professor pursuing and pursued by assorted young coeds in *Bachelor Flat* (1961). Better known are his supporting performances—with Peter Sellers in *I'm All Right, Jack* (1960) and *Tom Thumb* (1958) and as Jack Lemmon's valet in *How to Murder Your Wife* (1965). **Other credits:** *The Green Man* (1956), *The Naked Truth* (1957), *School for Scoundrels* (1960), *The Mouse on the Moon* (1963), *Our Man in Marrakesh* (1966), *The Abominable Dr. Phibes* (1971).

TORIN THATCHER (1905–)

Born in Bombay, India, and schooled in England, Thatcher deserted teaching for the theatre. He studied at the Royal Academy of Dramatic Art in London and was an established stage actor when he made his film debut in *General John Regan* (1934). He has played a variety of roles over the years, including a law counselor in *Witness for the Prosecution* (1958).

Thatcher appears frequently on dramatic radio and TV shows and won the Sylvania award as Best Supporting Actor for his TV performance in *Beyond This Place*. **Other films include:** *Major Barbara* (1941), *The Snows of Kilimanjaro* (1952), *Houdini* (1953), *Love Is a Many-Splendored Thing* (1955), *Hawaii* (1966).

PHYLLIS THAXTER (1921–)

During her 20 years in films Thaxter found a comfortable niche in Hollywood melodramas as somebody or other's wife, mother or daughter who invariably shed tears or fought valiantly to hold them back.

A native of Maine, she came to Broadway via a New England stock company and a Montreal repertory group and in 1940 attracted notice when she replaced Dorothy McGuire as the lead in *Claudia*. From the time of her screen debut as Van Johnson's wife in *Thirty Seconds Over Tokyo* (1944) until a bout with polio in 1952 resulted in a three-year gap in her career, Thaxter was kept busy in Hollywood. She played the tearful bride in *Weekend at the Waldorf* (1945), the daughter who reunited Katharine Hepburn and Spencer Tracy in *The Sea of Grass* (1947) and Margaret O'Brien's mother in *Tenth Avenue Angel* (1948). **Credits include:** *Bewitched* (1945), *The Sign of the Ram* (1948), *No Man of Her Own* (1950), *Springfield Rifle* (1952), *Women's Prison* (1955), *Man Afraid* (1957), *The World of Henry Orient* (1964).

MARSHALL THOMPSON (1926–)

Thompson made his film debut in *Reckless Age* (1944) and for the next 20 years played sedate and sensitive film roles. Then he met the King of the Beasts, and his career took a new turn. After starring in *Clarence, the Cross-Eyed Lion* (1965) Thompson has continued to work with animals—writing, acting, directing and producing wildlife pictures. He also starred with Clarence in *Daktari*, a popular TV series (1966–68). Previously, Thompson was the star of the 1960 *Angel* series with Annie Fargé. **Credits include:** *Homecoming* (1948), *Good Morning, Miss Dove* (1955), *Around the World Under the Sea* (1966).

DAME SYBIL THORNDIKE (1882–)

One of the very great ladies of the British stage, Dame Sybil Thorndike has been worshipped by several generations of theatregoers, among whom must be numbered George Bernard Shaw, who is believed to have written his *St. Joan* with her in mind.

Even the slightest smile reveals Terry-Thomas' natural trademark, his unique front teeth.

Phyllis Thaxter played the wife of the heroic World War II flyer, Captain Ted Lawson (Van Johnson), in Thirty Seconds Over Tokyo.

Gene Tierney in a tense scene with Peter Illing in Never Let Me Go.

She began her professional career as a concert pianist but switched to the footlights, where she found herself completely at home in classic tragedies and modern comedies alike.

Her more important film appearances, beginning with the role of Nurse Edith Cavell in *Dawn* (1928), were largely confined to scipts where her regal bearing and elegant diction could be seen and heard to best effect: Queen Victoria in *Melba* (1953) and the Grand Duchess in *The Prince and the Showgirl* (1957) are good examples. **Other credits include:** *Moth and Rust* (debut, 1921), *Nine Days a Queen* (1936), *Major Barbara* (1941), *Nicholas Nickleby* (1947), *Shake Hands With the Devil* (1959), *Hand in Hand* (1961).

INGRID THULIN (1929–   )

The ravishingly beautiful lady of Bergman's classic *Wild Strawberries* (1957) was later cast by the great Swedish director in a number of startling roles. Thulin was the drab mistress of a cleric in *Winter Light* (1962) and a sorrowful lesbian in *The Silence* (1963). Before joining the Bergman troupe the Swedish actress had appeared in at least 20 films, almost invariably cast as a *femme fatale*. In 1962 she made her American film debut in the rather unsuccessful *The Four Horsemen of the Apocalypse,* and, unlike the silent version's effect on Valentino's career, it did nothing to advance hers. Thulin is active in the Swedish theatre both as a performer and a director. **Film credits include:** *The Magician* (1959), *La Guerre Est Fini* (1966), *The Damned* (1969).

GENE TIERNEY (1920–   )

Hollywood tried to make a big star out of Tierney in the early 40's, but although she was beautiful she didn't have what it took to carry a picture on her own. Tierney was born in Brooklyn and educated in Switzerland. She began acting and appeared on the New York stage but was drawn to Hollywood when offered a part in *National Velvet*. The picture was postponed, so Tierney signed a 20th Century–Fox contract. Critics panned her early screen appearances in *Belle Star* (1941) and *Sundown* (1941), but in *Laura* (1944) she captured the public as the elusive, mysterious lady of a lovely portrait. The next year *Leave Her to Heaven* (1945) brought Tierney her biggest box-office success as a villainess who perpetrates all kinds of evil. She was busy making films through 1955, when she voluntarily entered the Menninger Clinic in Topeka, Kansas, following a nervous breakdown. Tierney returned to films in 1962 playing a Washington hostess in Preminger's *Advise and Consent*. **Films include:** *The Return of Frank James* (1940), *Son of Fury* (1942), *Heaven Can Wait* (1943), *The Razor's Edge* (1946), *The Ghost and Mrs. Muir* (1947), *The Mating Season* (1951), *Never Let Me Go* (1953), *The Left Hand of God* (1955), *Toys in the Attic* (1963), *The Pleasure Seekers* (1964).

LAWRENCE TIERNEY (1919–   )

Tierney has made a specialty of tough-guy roles during his 30 years in motion pictures. He made his debut in *Ghost Ship* (1943) and played his most famous role two years later in *Dillinger* (1945). Tierney's characterization of the sneering killer effectively typecast him. **Films include:** *Step by Step* (1946), *San Quentin* (1947), *Born to Kill* (1947),

Shakedown (1950), *The Hoodlum* (1951), *Singing in the Dark* (1956), *A Child Is Waiting* (1963), *Custer of the West* (1968).

GEORGE TOBIAS (1901–   )

The son of prominent members of the Yiddish Theatre, Tobias has had a long and successful screen career as a character actor known for his versatility in both comic and poignant roles and particularly for his ability to play almost any nationality. He made his acting debut at the age of 15 in Galsworthy's *The Mob* and first appeared on Broadway in O'Neill's *The Hairy Ape*. His characterization of the Russian ballet master in *You Can't Take It With You* brought him to the attention of film-makers, and he went to Hollywood in the late 30's. **More then 65 films include:** *The Hunchback of Notre Dame* (1940), *Sergeant York* (1941), *My Wild Irish Rose* (1947), *Rawhide* (1951), *The Seven Little Foys* (1955), *Marjorie Morningstar* (1958), *The Glass Bottom Boat* (1966).

GENEVIEVE TOBIN (1904–   )

The lively musical-comedy star was part of a sister act at the age of 11. She interrupted her career to finish her schooling in New York and Paris but returned to the stage to become a successful actress, playing in many Broadway hits. After her success in *Fifty Million Frenchmen* she went to Hollywood and made her film debut in *The Lady Surrenders* (1930). Although her stage work was of primary interest to her, she made nearly 40 films. **Credits include:** *Easy to Love* (1934), *Kiss and Make Up* (1934), *No Time for Comedy* (1940), *Queen of Crime* (1941).

ANN TODD (1909–   )

Todd was a member of the Old Vic Company and also performed in comedies on stage before beginning her film career. Her first featured role was in *South Riding* (1938), but it was *The Seventh Veil* (1945) that brought her to film prominence. It was a melodramatic, rather silly film, but it was popular both in England and the United States.

Todd was married to director David Lean, with whom she made several films, including *Passionate Friends* (1948). She came to Hollywood in 1947 to make *The Paradine Case* (1948) directed by Alfred Hitchcock, but she soon returned to England. In recent years Todd has turned to film-making herself, writing, producing and narrating her own documentary films on world travel. **Credits include:** *Keepers of Youth* (debut, 1931), *The Breaking of the Sound Barrier* (1952), *Time Without Pity* (1957), *90 Degrees in the Shade* (1966).

RICHARD TODD (1919–   )

He fought in many cinematic wars, swashbuckled in period pieces, was a plausible Robin Hood in Walt Disney's *The Story of Robin Hood* (1952) but never quite made it to the top of the ladder. Todd was born in Dublin, acted in local repertory and made his first screen appearance in *For Them That Trespass* (1950). Perhaps the film highlight of his career was *The Hasty Heart* (1950), in which he gave a masterful portrayal of a Scottish soldier dying of an incurable disease in a Burmese field hospital. In recent years he has returned to the stage, appearing in such vehicles as *Roar Like a Dove* and *The Marquise*. **His credits include:** *A Man Called Peter* (1955), *Chase a Crooked Shadow* (1958), *The Longest Day* (1962), *Operation Crossbow* (1965), *Asylum* (1972).

THELMA TODD (1905–1935)

She began her career as a vamp of the silent screen in films like *Fascinating Youth* (1926) and *Heart to Heart* (1928) and developed into the wisecracking comic heroine of films of the early 30's. She held her own as the arch blonde who practiced her wiles on Groucho in two Marx Brothers movies, *Monkey Business* (1931) and *Horse Feathers* (1932). In 1935 she was the victim of a bizarre murder. **Credits include:** *Vamping Venus* (1928), *The Maltese Falcon* (1931), *Fra Diablo* (1933), *Two for Tonight* (1935).

SIDNEY TOLER (1874–1947)

Charlie Chan, the philosophical detective, is a perennial movie favorite, and Sidney Toler, who played in 25 Chan adventures, was greatly responsible for his popularity. Although he was the second Chan (he assumed the role after Warner Oland's death), he quickly made the part his own.

Genevieve Tobin competes favorably with the statuary in Kiss and Make Up.

In yet another swashbuckler, Richard Todd had Glynis Johns as his partner.

Sidney Toler, who very creditably followed in Warner Oland's footsteps in the Charlie Chan movies, along with oldest son Sen Yung in Charlie Chan in Honolulu.

Franchot Tone, slightly bruised and disheveled after a scuffle with the forces of crime.

He began his professional career on stage and at one time had 12 stock companies of his own. He wrote plays and appeared in scores of films before starting his career as the Oriental crime fighter. **Credits include:** *Madame X* (1929), *Tom Brown of Culver* (1932), *Blondie of the Follies* (1932), *King of the Jungle* (1933), *The Gorgeous Hussy* (1936), *Charlie Chan in Honolulu* (1938), *A Kid From Kokomo* (1939), *A Night to Remember* (1943), *The Trap* (1947).

ANDREW TOMBES (c. 1891–   )

His droll face and subtle comic touch caused him to be cast most often in supporting roles as harassed or puzzled characters. His long career began on stage; thereafter he became a songwriter and a vaudevillian before appearing in his first significant screen role in *Moulin Rouge* (1933). **Film credits include:** *Hot Money* (1936), *Bedtime Story* (1942), *Reveille With Beverly* (1943), *Frontier Girl* (1945), *The Jackpot* (1950), *How to Be Very, Very Popular* (1955).

FRANCHOT TONE (1905–1969)

"Slim, suave and sophisticated" pretty well sums up the actor who came into prominence in Hollywood drawing-room comedies of the early 30's and rose to stardom in 1935 when he fought off savage mountain tribesmen in *Lives of a Bengal Lancer* and helped send Captain Bligh overboard in *Mutiny on the Bounty*.

Tone came from a wealthy family, was an outstanding scholar at Cornell University and won his first Broadway lead in *Green Grow the Lilacs* (1931). The next year came the first opportunity for him to display his crooked grin and society-smoothie style in *The Wiser Sex*. He continued to be featured or starred for over 20 years but often returned to the stage, where he seemed more at ease. In Ernest Hemingway's *The Fifth Column* (1940), a play about traitors within the gates, he was outstanding.

In 1935 Tone was married to Joan Crawford. It didn't work and proved to be the first of four matrimonial ventures. By the early 50's his film appearances were fewer and farther between, one of his last roles being that of the ill and aging President in *Advise and Consent* (1962). **More than 65 films include:** *Today We Live* (1933), *Bombshell* (1933), *No More Ladies* (1935), *Manproof* (1938), *Five Graves to Cairo* (1943), *Here Comes the Groom* (1951), *La Bonne Soup* (1964), *In Harm's Way* (1965).

REGIS TOOMEY (1902–   )

When he played a policeman one sensed that he was going to die before the film ended, and when he was on the other side of the law the same suspicion lurked. Perhaps it was his smiling, ingenuous face that made directors cast him so many times as an eventual victim.

A native of Pittsburgh, he spent fivvve years on stage in London and New York as a singer before he landed a supporting role in the first all-talkie gangster movie, *Alibi* (1929), with Chester Morris. Since then he has appeared most often walking a beat in more than 150 films. In addition to his film work Toomey has been kept busy with roles in such TV series as *Richard Diamond*, *Burke's Law* (as Detective Sergeant Lester Hart) and *Petticoat Junction*. **Film high-**

lights: *Framed* (1929), *Murder by the Clock* (1932), *G-Men* (1935), *The Big Sleep* (1946), *Show Boat* (1951), *Guys and Dolls* (1955), *Man's Favorite Sport* (1964), *Change of Habit* (1969).

HAYM TOPOL (1935–   )

The producers of the London stage production of *Fiddler on the Roof* were aghast when they met Topol upon his arrival in England. They had hired the Israeli star sight unseen to play the middle-aged Tevye and weren't prepared for the fact that the actor was only 29 at the time. Topol, however, was ready for Tevye and aged himself for the part, scoring an enormous success. Topol since recreated his stage role on the screen (1970). Despite his youth he frequently portrays older characters. He was a 70-year-old Arab sheik in his film debut in *Cast a Giant Shadow* (1965) and an elderly Oriental Jew in *Sallah* (1966). Topol began acting when he was assigned by the Israeli Army to a military theatrical troupe that toured army bases. **Films include:** *Before Winter Comes* (1969), *Public Eye* (1972), *The Boys Will Never Believe It* (1973), *The Growing Up of David Lev* (1973), *Don Quixote* (1974).

RIP TORN (1931–   )

He was born Elmore Torn in Taylor, Texas, and abandoned his original plans to become a rancher in favor of what turned out to be a successful career in the theatre. Since his New York stage debut in *Cat on a Hot Tin Roof* he has won two Obie awards for his off-Broadway performance in Norman Mailer's *Deer Park* (1966) and for his direction of Michael McClure's *The Beard*.

He played the first of his several screen roles in *Baby Doll* (1956) with Carroll Baker. Torn is married to actress Geraldine Page and lives in New York. **Films include:** *Time Limit* (1957), *Pork Chop Hill* (1959), *King of Kings* (1961), *Sweet Bird of Youth* (1962), *The Cincinnati Kid* (1965), *Tropic of Cancer* (1969), *The Rain People* (1969).

ERNEST TORRENCE (1878–1933)

The tall, rawboned character actor was born in Scotland and began his career as a singer (baritone) in musical comedy and comic opera. After his memorable fight with Richard Barthelmess in *Tol'able David* (1921), however, he confined his activities to film-making. His balding head and gaunt features caused him to be cast most often as a villain; yet one of his most exciting performances was as a grizzled scout aiding the pioneers as they made their way west in *The Covered Wagon* (1923), the best picture of its genre until *Stagecoach* came along many years later. Torrence continued to appear in silents and talkies until his death. **Other credits:** *The Hunchback of Notre Dame* (1923), *Peter Pan* (1924), *The King of Kings* (1927), *The Bridge of San Luis Rey* (1929), *Sherlock Holmes* (1932), *I Cover the Waterfront* (1933).

TOTO (1897–1967)

For nearly 50 years Toto was Italy's leading comedian of stage and screen. He was born Antonio Furst de Curtis-Gagliardi in Naples and claimed a noble ancestry stretching back to the year 362. He discovered his talent for comedy and pantomime while serving in the Army during World War I and began appearing on the stage professionally after his discharge in 1919. He later moved to the screen and made numerous films. In 1951 he was awarded the Italian Silver Ribbon for his *Guard and Thieves*. **Films include:** *Fermo con le Mani* (1936), *Toto Le Moko* (1949), *Cops and Robbers* (1953), *Raconti Romani* (1955), *Persons Unknown* (1958), *The Big Deal on Madonna Street* (1960), *Toto of Arabia* (1963), *The Commander* (1967), *The Treasure of San Gennaro* (1968).

AUDREY TOTTER (1918–   )

She first went to Hollywood under a seven-year contract to MGM after five years of success on Chicago and New York radio broadcasts. From her screen debut in *Main Street After Dark* (1944) she was typecast as a bad girl—a meanie, a gun moll, a conniving woman or a murderess. Her image was hardly likely to make her an audience favorite, and once Hollywood abandoned the formula melodramas of the 40's her appearances became less frequent. She had better luck on television and starred in *Cimmaron City* and

Toto, an endearing comedian, in Gold of Naples.

Ernest Torrence, who with equal facility played leering villains and heart-of-gold frontier characters, with Clara Bow in Mantrap *(1926).*

Jean Harlow in a wistful mood and Spencer Tracy in a skeptical one. The film was Libeled Lady (1936).

Our Man Higgins. More recently she was Nurse Wilcox on the television series *Medical Center.* **Films include:** *Bewitched* (1945), *The Postman Always Rings Twice* (1946), *The Set-Up* (1949), *The Sellout* (1951), *Man in the Dark* (1953), *A Bullet for Joey* (1955), *Women's Prison* (1955), *Jet Attack* (1958), *The Carpetbaggers* (1964), *Chubasco* (1968).

LEE TRACY (1898–1968)

On Broadway as the fast-talking, hard-drinking newsman Hildy Johnson who plans to get married but never quite gets around to it in *The Front Page* (1928), he created the model that countless reporters in countless films copied for at least three decades. Tracy himself played a journalist far, far too many times. He was starred as Walter Winchell in *Blessed Event* (1932), played the high-voltage reporter in *Clear All Wires* (1933) and the invincible news hawk, Eddie Haines,

in *Behind the Headlines* (1937). He was a fine actor even when printer's ink was not involved, and he was nominated for an Oscar in one of his last roles—the President of the United States in Gore Vidal's *The Best Man* (1964). **Films include:** *The Big Time* (debut, 1930), *Dinner at Eight* (1933), *Sutter's Gold* (1936), *The Spellbinder* (1939), *High Tide* (1947), *Advise and Consent* (1962).

SPENCER TRACY (1900–1967)

Few film buffs will quarrel with the thesis that Spencer Tracy was one of the finest American actors ever to grace the screen. Completely without affectation, he brought an aura of total honesty to his performances.

Born Spencer Bonaventure Tracy in Milwaukee, Wisconsin, he enlisted in the Navy at the age of 17 and later attended Ripon College. In 1922 he enrolled in the American Academy of Dramatic Arts in New York and, while still a student, was given a small part in the Broadway hit *R.U.R.*, a melodrama in which robots take over the world. More Broadway appearances followed his graduation, but it wasn't until he played the venomous Killer Mears in *The Last Mile* (1930) and was spotted by Director John Ford that his career moved into high gear.

Fox signed him up, and Tracy and Bogart made their joint debut in *Up the River* (1930). He was a success and, predictably, continued to be cast as a gangster until 1933, when he broke the mold with a smashing performance in *The Power and the Glory.*

Tracy's drinking bouts and truculent attitude (he didn't think much of the Fox people) led to endless squabbles with the studio and a switch to MGM in 1935. Working under Irving Thalberg's aegis, he received the first of nine Academy Award nominations (a record for a male) as the priest in *San Francisco* (1936). During the next two years he became the first to win Best Actor Oscars back to back—for performances as the Portuguese fisherman in *Captains Courageous* (1937) and as Father Flanagan in *Boys Town* (1938).

Garson Kanin, who describes in his book the friendship and 25-year love affair between Tracy and Katharine Hepburn, brought the two together for *Woman of the Year* (1942),

Spencer Tracy, Lionel Barrymore and Freddie Bartholomew in the hugely popular but slightly sentimental Captains Courageous.

the first of nine films they made together. Hollywood legend has it that when they first met Hepburn said, ''I fear I may be too tall for you, Mr. Tracy,'' to which Tracy replied, ''Don't worry, Miss Hepburn. I'll cut you down to my size.''

As the years rolled by, Tracy gradually began to play middle-aged roles with the same flawless professionalism he had displayed in the past, in films varying from *State of the Union* (1948) to *Bad Day at Black Rock* (1955), from *The Last Hurrah* (1958) to *Judgment at Nuremburg* (1961).

In his later years Tracy made few films. And although Hepburn tried valiantly to revive his flagging interest in acting and life in general he showed little desire to continue his career. His death from a heart attack came just a few weeks after he and Hepburn played the parents in *Guess Who's Coming to Dinner?* (1967), one of the earlier movies about miscegenation. **Some of Tracy's other films include:** *Riffraff* (1936), *Fury* (1936), *Test Pilot* (1938), *Northwest Passage* (1940), *Adam's Rib* (1949), *Father of the Bride* (1950), *The Old Man and the Sea* (1958), *Inherit the Wind* (1960).

BILL TRAVERS (1922–)

When Travers and his wife, actress Virginia McKenna, went to Africa to make a documentary about lions, they didn't anticipate that the film, *Born Free* (1966), would become one of the most popular animal features in motion-picture history.

Travers was born in Newcastle-on-Tyne in northern England and made his London stage debut in *Cage Me a Peacock* (1949). He made his first screen appearance in a small part in *The Wooden Horse* and became a star when he filmed *Wee Geordie* (1955), the story of a tiny Scotsman who takes a correspondence course in body building and becomes an Olympic champion. **Films include:** *The Square Ring* (1954), *Bhowani Junction* (1956), *The Seventh Sin* (1958), *Gorgo* (1960), *Duel at Diablo* (1966), *Ring of Bright Water* (1969).

HENRY TRAVERS (1874–1965)

By the time this Britisher started making pictures in the 30's, he already had a long career in the theatre behind him. Travers landed his first job in a stock company, spent several years in repertory in England and then signed with a stock company bound for Montreal. Eventually he made his New York debut in the melodrama *The Prince of Peace* and later became a permanent member of New York's Theater Guild company.

Travers first appeared on screen in *Reunion in Vienna* (1933) and went on to portray a series of elderly men in 30's and 40's films. **Screen highlights:** *The Invisible Man* (1933), *On Borrowed Time* (1939), *Dark Victory* (1939), *High Sierra* (1941), *Mrs. Miniver* (1932), *The Moon Is Down* (1943), *Bells of St. Mary's* (1945), *The Yearling* (1947), *The Girl From Jones Beach* (1949).

ARTHUR TREACHER (1894–)

For years Treacher was Hollywood's favorite butler—tall, snooty, impeccably starched but with a soft spot in his heart for the likes of Shirley Temple. He played butlers so often and so well that he was made an honorary member of the Butlers Club of America and eventually established a domestic service, Call Arthur Treacher Service System.

Treacher originally set out to become a lawyer, but after World War I he got himself a job as a chorus boy in a London production and in 1926 went to the United States to appear on stage in *Caesar and Cleopatra*. He eventually went to Hollywood and in the 30's starred in a series of films based on the antics of Jeeves, a butler created by author P. G. Wodehouse.

Television brought him more popularity, first as a guest on talk shows and later as the announcer and alter ego on *The Merv Griffin Show*. Treacher also lent his name to a chain of Arthur Treacher Fish 'n Chips shops. **Films include:** *David Copperfield* (1935), *A Midsummer Night's Dream* (1935), *Heidi* (1937), *National Velvet* (1944), *Countess of Monte Cristo* (1948), *Love That Brute* (1950), *Mary Poppins* (1964).

Henry Travers and anonymous Nazi officer in None Shall Escape *(1944).*

Arthur Treacher, who built a dynasty out of playing a butler in That's the Spirit *(1945).*

Claire Trevor, a beautiful lady and a highly talented performer.

Jean-Louis Trintignant takes aim at a pursuer in Trans-Europe Express.

CLAIRE TREVOR (1909–   )

One of Hollywood's consistently good actresses, she was fated to play a long succession of outwardly tough but inwardly tender ladies—bar girls or saloon keepers, prostitutes or down-and-outers. Considering the limitations imposed on her in good films and the raft of ''B'' pictures she was relegated to between them, Trevor managed to pile up a more than impressive record.

Trevor was born Claire Wemlinger in New York City and gained experience in theatre before making her first film, *Life in the Raw* (1933). She got her first Academy Award nomination when she played Humphrey Bogart's ex-girlfriend turned prostitute in *Dead End* (1937), gave a stunning performance in John Ford's classic *Stagecoach* (1939), which should have brought her a shower of statuary but didn't, and finally landed an Oscar when she appeared as Edward G. Robinson's alcoholic mistress in *Key Largo* (1947). In 1954 she earned yet another nomination as May Holst in *The High and the Mighty*. **Other credits:** *Elinor Norton* (1935), *Five of a Kind* (1939), *Dark Command* (1940), *The Lucky Stiff* (1949), *Lucy Gallant* (1956), *The Stripper* (1963), *How to Murder Your Wife* (1965), *The Capetown Affair* (1967).

JEAN-LOUIS TRINTIGNANT (1930–   )

Until the mid-60's this French star was known only to those British and American filmgoers who didn't mind reading English subtitles. To them he was best remembered as the killer in *Les Liaisons Dangereuses* (1959). The turning point came when he played the racing-car driver who falls in love with Anouk Aimée in Claude Lelouch's *A Man and a Woman* (1966), a film that repeated its enormous success in France throughout the world, boosted Lelouch's reputation and brought Trintignant a series of better roles in more prestigious films.

He was particularly effective as the honest prosecutor in Costa-Gavras' *Z* (1969), the young intellectual in Eric Rohmer's *My Night at Maud's* (1969) and the Italian Fascist in Bernardo Bertolucci's *The Conformist*

(1971). His wife, Nadine Marquand, is a director and Trintignant has worked with her on several pictures, most notably *Mon Amour, Mon Amour* (1967). **More than 45 films include:** *Pechineff* (debut, 1955), *And God Created Woman* (1956), *Les Pas Perdus* (1964), *Is Paris Burning?* (1966), *Trans-Europe Express* (1966), *L'Americain* (1969), *Sans Mobile Apparent* (1971), *L'Attentat* (1972).

ERNEST TRUEX (1889–1973)

When an impoverished Shakespearean actor couldn't pay a bill submitted by Truex's physician father, he offered to take on five-year-old Ernest as a pupil, free of charge. It wasn't long before Truex made his debut in a production of *Hamlet* at the Opera House in Rich Hill, Missouri. After years on stage he tried his luck in films, appearing in such silents as *Come on In* (1918) and *The Night of the Pub* (1920). His first talkie was *Whistling in the Dark* (1933). Because of his small stature Truex frequently was cast as a henpecked husband in screen comedies. He alternated between stage and screen in the 30's and 40's and later became a popular performer on television. **Films include:** *Bachelor Mother* (1934), *His Girl Friday* (1941), *Twilight of the Gods* (1958), *The Man Who Knew Too Much* (1964), *Fluffy* (1965).

FORREST TUCKER (1919–   )

He was fresh out of military service and on vacation in Hollywood when he landed his first motion-picture role in *The Westerner* (1940) with Gary Cooper. He has since been featured in dozens of Westerns, usually as the character who doesn't get the girl. One of his films off the range was *Auntie Mame* (1958), in which he played Mame's (Rosalind Russell's) millionaire husband—the Southern boy with the malicious mama.

Tucker's extensive work on television includes the lead in the *Crunch and Des* series of the 50's and the role of the conniving cavalry sergeant in *F Troop*. **Films include:** *Keeper of the Flame* (1943), *The Yearling* (1947), *The Wild Blue Yonder* (1952), *Pony*

Express (1953), *Trouble in the Glen* (1955), *The Abominable Snowman* (1957), *The Night They Raided Minsky's* (1968), *Barquero* (1969).

SONNY TUFTS (1912–1970)

Perhaps because of his name, perhaps because he was the prototype of all-American college boys of a bygone era, he became a camp figure to a later generation of filmgoers. Tall, blond, husky and a perennial smiler, Tufts came from an old Boston family and attended Yale University back in the good old rah-rah days.

He was a featured player in many films—as a beaming college boy in his early career and as an equally amiable villain later on. His popularity reached its peak during and immediately after World War II. In the late 50's he eased out of films and, except for one comeback appearance in *Town Tamer* (1965), retired to his ranch in Texas. **Films include:** *So Proudly We Hail* (1943), *Swell Guy* (1947), *Easy Living* (1949), *Glory at Sea* (1952), *The Seven Year Itch* (1955), *Come Next Spring* (1956).

TOM TULLY (c. 1902–   )

As one of Hollywood's chief supporting actors, Tully often has been cast as military officers whose bark is worse than their bite. He won an Academy Award nomination for his supporting role as Captain DeVreiss in *The Caine Mutiny* (1954). More recently he became a TV audience favorite in the series *The Lineup* and *San Francisco Beat*.

After three years in the Navy and a year as a salesman Tully went to New York, where he found work on radio by providing the mournful dog's howl that introduced the program *Renfrew of the Mounted*. He then made his Broadway debut in *Dead End* (1936) and subsequently appeared in several productions, including Clifford Odets' *Night Music* (1940). Tully began to concentrate on films in the early 40's and has been active on screen ever since. **Credits include:** *The Lady Takes a Sailor* (1940), *Destination Tokyo* (1944), *Where the Sidewalk Ends* (1950), *Soldier of Fortune* (1955), *Ten North Frederick* (1958), *The Wackiest Ship in the Army* (1961), *Coogan's Bluff* (1968).

FLORENCE TURNER (1888–1946)

Although she was billed as The Vitagraph Girl, Turner also was the first screen actress whose name the viewing public came to know and recognize. She grew up in Brooklyn and went to work in the nearby Vitagraph "studio" in 1907. In those days it took only 48 or 72 hours to crank out a one- or two-reeler, and the young actress, who was paid a munificent $18 a week, acted as wardrobe mistress on the side.

Within a year or so Florence Lawrence began appearing as The Biograph Girl, and, between the two Florences and Biograph/Vitagraph, one can well imagine that considerable confusion resulted. Biograph, incidentally, was D. W. Griffith's company. As for Florence Turner, she continued to appear in non-starring roles until the mid-20's, at which point she retired. **Films include:** *A Dixie Mother* (1910), *The Welsh Singer* (1913), *My Old Dutch* (1914).

LANA TURNER (1920–   )

The legend has persisted that she was discovered sitting at the soda fountain of Schwab's drugstore in Hollywood. In any event the unenthusiastic high-school student first appeared on screen in United Artists' *A Star Is Born* (1937) and first attracted attention with her lavish natural endowments in MGM's Mickey Rooney vehicle *Love Finds Andy Hardy* (1938). Turner was shortly thereafter widely publicized as the Sweater Girl and remained with MGM for a good 18 years.

While critics generally managed to conceal their enthusiasm for her performances, Turner and her films were hugely popular throughout the 40's. In *Honky Tonk* (1941), with Clark Gable, and *Johnny Eager* (1942), with Robert Taylor, she was very good indeed. Her star had dimmed considerably by the time *Peyton Place* (1957) came along, but that box-office success kept it shining a while longer.

Turner was, and is, a Hollywood luminary of a school long vanished—ultra glamorous, seven times married and clearly loving all the trappings that went with fame and fortune. **Other credits include:** *Ziegfeld Girl* (1941), *Slightly Dangerous* (1943), *The Postman*

Forrest Tucker in The Night They Raided Minsky's.

Film history would have been the poorer for it had not Lana Turner dropped in at Schwab's.

Ben Turpin with the look that broke audiences up.

Cicely Tyson helps her son, Kevin Hooks, prepare for life in a distant school in Sounder, *one of the best films of the early 70's.*

Always Rings Twice (1946), *The Bad and the Beautiful* (1953), *Imitation of Life* (1959), *By Love Possessed* (1960), *Madame X* (1966), *The Big Cube* (1970).

BEN TURPIN (1874–1940)

The cross-eyed comedian who became one of Hollywood's slapstick pioneers was first a veteran of vaudeville and burlesque before he began filming comedy shorts with Mack Sennett and Charles Chaplin.

Turpin was born in New Orleans, grew up in New York City and first clowned on stage as part of a vaudeville duo performing for $20 a week. Later, while imitating comic-strip Happy Hooligan on stage, Turpin's eyes accidentally crossed. The audience roared, and crossed eyes eventually became Turpin's trademark. (He had never planned it that way. They kept crossing accidentally due to a medical malfunction and finally became fixed.)

During the heydey of silent comedies of the 20's, Turpin usually portrayed a bumbling character who never could manage to do anything right. He retired soon after the talkies took over. **Films include:** *Uncle Tom's Cabin* (1919), *Small Town Idol* (1921), *Show of Shows* (1929), *Swing High* (1930), *The Love Parade* (1930), *Our Wife* (1931), *Million Dollar Legs* (1932), *Hollywood Cavalcade* (1934).

RITA TUSHINGHAM (1942–   )

This British actress is among the most unlikely-looking of film stars: sharp-featured and plain, with enormous sorrowful eyes. Perhaps her success can be explained by her specialty—making even the most unlikely role believable.

Tushingham attracted immediate acclaim in her first film, *A Taste of Honey* (1961). It is said she got the part (she was in repertory at the time) by answering a newspaper ad in Liverpool, where she had grown up. Her London stage debut came later in *The Kitchen*.

Tushingham maintained her coterie of fans and the interest of critics into the mid-60's via *The Leather Boys* (1963) and *The Girl With Green Eyes* (1964) with Peter Finch and Lynn Redgrave. She scored her greatest success to date when she recreated her stage role in

Richard Lester's 1965 screen version of *The Knack*. **Other credits include:** *A Place to Go* (1963), *Dr. Zhivago* (1965), *The Trap* (1966), *The Bed-Sitting Room* (1969), *The Case of Laura* (1971), *Where Do You Go From Here?* (1972).

HELEN TWELVETREES (1908–1958)

She was born Helen Jurgens in Brooklyn, the daughter of onetime Broadway star Nellie Kelly, and took her professional name from her first husband, actor Charles Twelvetrees. The petite blond actress made her screen debut in *The Ghost Talks* (1929) and during the 30's appeared with such screen heroes as Clark Gable and Robert Taylor. One of her best-known roles was opposite Maurice Chevalier and Baby Le Roy in *A Bedtime Story* (1933). She retired in the 40's. **Films include:** *Millie* (1931), *The Painted Desert* (1931), *Panama Flo* (1932), *Is My Face Red* (1932), *King for a Night* (1933), *Times Square Lady* (1935), *Hollywood Roundup* (1938).

CICELY TYSON (1933–   )

Although Tyson had worked steadily on Broadway and on television, her name was relatively unknown until she played the mother in *Sounder* (1972). Her performance won her an Academy Award nomination and the National Society of Film Critics Best Actress award.

Tyson was born in New York City and grew up in the tenements of East Harlem. After high school she went to work as a secretary but soon decided to take a modeling course. Modeling led to acting, and by 1962 she had won the Vernon Rice Award for her performance in an off-Broadway production of *The Blacks*. The next year she was cast as George C. Scott's secretary on the TV series *East Side, West Side* and later appeared on Broadway in *Tiger, Tiger Burning Bright*. In 1974 Tyson scored another major success in the TV film *The Autobiography of Miss Jane Pittman*. Tyson played Miss Jane from her youth to her old age (110) with incredible skill. **Films include:** *A Man Called Adam* (1966), *The Comedians* (1967), *The Heart Is a Lonely Hunter* (1968).

LIV ULLMANN (1940–   )

The talented Scandinavian actress appears frequently in the films of Ingmar Bergman. She progressed from a small but forceful part as a pregnant wife in *Wild Strawberries* (1957) to such exquisitely complex roles as the mute actress in *Persona* (1966).

In recent years Ullmann has made a two-part film for Swedish director Jan Troell, *The Emigrants* (U.S., 1972) and *The New Land* (U.S., 1973). The first of the two parts brought her an Oscar nomination. In 1973 she appeared in two Hollywood productions, the film version of the successful Broadway play *40 Carats* and the musical remake of *Lost Horizon*. Though neither picture won the critics' compliments, Ullmann was warmly praised for her fine portrayals. **Credits:** *Hour of the Wolf* (1967), *Shame* (1968), *Cries and Whispers* (1972), *Pope Joan* (1972).

LENORE ULRIC (1892–1970)

Though the dark beauty was primarily a stage actress, she did make occasional forays on the screen, often to recreate her stage roles in films such as *Tiger Rose* (1923). She successfully made the transition to talkies and appeared as Olympe in the famous *Camille* (1937) with Greta Garbo. Ulric was once married to Sidney Blackmer. **Credits include:** *Frozen Justice* (1929), *Temptation* (1946), *Two Smart People* (1947).

MIYOSHI UMEKI (1929–   )

Already well known in Japan as a leading lady, Umeki attracted a good deal of attention in her first American film, *Sayonara* (1957). Her performance as the devoted wife of an American GI in occupied Japan brought her the Oscar for Best Supporting Actress and seemed to promise a successful film career. Somehow, though, it never materialized, and after playing the equally devoted and good, sweet young Mei Lei in *Flower Drum Song* (1961) and several other supporting roles in undistinguished films, Umeki disappeared from the screen. She reappeared some six years later on television as housekeeper Mrs. Livingston on *The Courtship of Eddie's Father* series. **Credits:** *Cry for Happy* (1961), *The Horizontal Lieutenant* (1962), *A Girl Named Tamiko* (1963).

MARY URE (1933–   )

Although Mary Ure is best known for her stage work, she has given some distinguished film performances. She was born in Glasgow, studied in London and began her acting career on the stage, appearing in such plays as *Look Back in Anger*, *Duel of Angels* and *The Changeling*. Ure made her screen debut at age 22 in *Storm Over the Nile* (1955) and has appeared infrequently since then in both starring and supporting roles. **Credits include:** *Windom's Way* (1958), *The Luck of Ginger Coffey* (1964), *Custer of the West* (1968), *Where Eagles Dare* (1969).

PETER USTINOV (1921–   )

The dynamic British-born Ustinov has proven himself a man of many talents. Primarily an actor of great scope, he has also won fame as a playright, director and raconteur. He began his stage career as a character actor at the age of 17, made his screen debut in a short, *Hullo Fame* (1940), and nine years later won an Oscar for his supporting role of Batiatus, a Roman slave, in *Spartacus*. He won his second Best Supporting Actor Academy Award for his role as an inept con man in *Topkapi* (1964). He first tried his hand at writing during the mid-40's and has to his credit such plays as *The Love of Four Colonels* and *Romanoff and Juliet* and such screenplays as *Billy Budd* (1962) and *Lady L* (1966), which he also directed.

In addition to his film and stage appearances, Ustinov has been seen occasionally on television, winning an Emmy in 1971 for his gripping performance in *A Storm in Summer*. **Credits include:** *Quo Vadis?* (1951), *Beau Brummell* (1954), *The Sundowners* (1960), *The Comedians* (1967), *Lola Montez* (1968), *Viva Max* (1970).

Liv Ullmann in Warner's recent film, Zandy's Bride *(1974).*

Peter Ustinov as a well-fed Roman slave in Spartacus.

RUDOLPH VALENTINO (1895–1926)

He was a phenomenon in film history— a former waiter, exhibition and tango dancer who became Hollywood's top drawing card (and the prototype for countless future Latin lovers), captivating and holding the adulation of uncounted millions of females. His early death was treated as a national catastrophe.

He arrived in New York from his native Italy at the age of 18 and eventually drifted to Hollywood. Valentino might have remained an anonymous bit player in silents had not screenwriter June Mathis recommended him for the role of Julio in Rex Ingram's forthcoming version of Ibanez' best-seller *The Four Horsemen of the Apocalypse* (1921). It was hard to tell which was the greater hit, the MGM movie or the patent-leather-haired Valentino.

The same year, 1921, saw him make a turbaned appearance in the film with which his name will always be inextricably linked, *The Sheik*. The tempestuous manner in which the dark-hued product of Araby wooed and won ultra-blond Agnes Ayres shocked and delighted legions of movie addicts. Valentino was promptly labeled the greatest lover of all time, and the hit song "The Sheik of Araby" was sung or hummed by a larger percentage of the population than any song in the history of popular music. Valentino was filming a sequel, *The Son of the Sheik* (1926), when he fell ill, contracted peritonitis and, to the stunned anguish of the world, died within a few days at the age of 30. **Other films include:** *Camille* (1921), *The Young Rajah* (1922), *Blood and Sand* (1922), *Monsieur Beaucaire* (1924), *The Eagle* (1925), *Cobra* (1925).

RUDY VALLEE (1901–   )

Back in the days of the Stutz Bearcat he was a national radio idol, a Roaring Twenties preview of Bing Crosby, Frank Sinatra, Elvis Presley and the other great singing stars. His trademark was the University of Maine stein song in which the participants drink to the long-gone happy hours.

His screen debut was in *The Vagabond Lover* (1929). Many musicals followed. But his popularity faded with the years, and it wasn't until he assumed a comedy role in the Pulitzer Prize-winning Broadway musical *How to Succeed in Business Without Really Trying* (1962) that he successfully reappeared in the spotlight. He recreated his stage role in the 1967 film version. **Films include:** *George White's Scandals* (1934), *Gold Diggers in Paris* (1938), *The Palm Beach Story* (1942), *The Bachelor and the Bobby-Soxer* (1947), *The Beautiful Blonde From Bashful Bend* (1949), *The Helen Morgan Story* (1957).

Rudolph Valentino as the dandified and dashing Monsieur Beaucaire *(1924). The admiring aristocrats were, we believe, Paulette Duval and Doris Kenyon.*

ALIDA VALLI (1921–   )

One of Italy's leading female stars by the time she was 20, Alida Maria Allenburger first appeared on screen in light romantic and social comedies of the mid-30's. Her demanding performance in the more serious *Manon Lescaut* (1940) increased her stature in Italy, and her portrayal of the heroine in *Piccolo Mondo Antico* (1941) brought her the Venice Film Festival award and international recognition. She made her American screen debut in *The Parradine Case* (1948) and the following year appeared in her first British film—Carol Reed's thriller *The Third Man* (U.S., 1950), in which she played Joseph Cotten's would-be girlfriend. She was less impressive in subsequent English-language pictures but has continued to perform with distinction in films of France, Spain and Italy. **Her credits include:** *Eugénie Grandet* (1946), *Senso* (1954; U.S., 1968), *Il Gredo* (1957; U.S., 1964), *Ophelia* (1961), *The Spider's Strategy* (1970).

VIRGINIA VALLI (1898–1968)

Born Virginia McSweeney, this silent-screen star first performed on the stages of her native Chicago, where she also began her screen career. At the height of her popularity she played leading roles opposite such stars as William Powell and Ronald Colman. Valli married actor Charles Farrell in 1932 and then retired. The two founded the Racquet Club in Palm Springs, where they lived until her death. **Films include:** *Efficiency Edgar's Courtship* (1917), *The Idle Rich* (1921), *The Black Bag* (1922), *A Lady of Quality* (1923), *The Confidence Man* (1924), *Flames* (1926), *Paid to Love* (1927), *Guilty* (1930).

RAF VALLONE (1916–   )

This handsome Italian star from Turin exudes an air of earthy and sexy strength, which is perhaps why he has been cast so often as a peasant, laborer or in other sub-bourgeois roles. In fact, he was educated at the University of Turin and worked as a newspaper music and film critic before he switched to acting and appeared in *Bitter Rice* (1950), a melodramatic tale of suffering workers.

Vallone adapted, directed and starred in Arthur Miller's *A View From the Bridge* on both French and New York stages and repeated the role in his first English-speaking film (1962). In ensuing American pictures he was generally cast in supporting parts. **Other films include:** *Les Possédées* (1956), *El Cid* (1961), *The Cardinal* (1963), *Harlow* (1965), *Kiss the Girls and Make Them Die* (1967).

LEE VAN CLEEF (1925–   )

From his first appearance on screen as one of the desperados stalking Gary Cooper on his wedding day in *High Noon* (1952), Van Cleef's lean toughness and menacing leer made him a thoroughly believable villain. He has bolstered his career substantially by a series of Italian-made spaghetti Westerns in which he played roles which can only be described as equivocal—neither hero nor villain, a rugged gent with little power of verbal communication who makes his point by violent action and a great deal of it. He was not necessarily on the wrong side of the law, but the right side was not overanxious to claim him either. **Credits include:** *Vice Squad* (1953), *Gunfight at the OK Corral* (1957), *The Young Lions* (1958), *For a Few Dollars More* (1967), *The Big Gundown* (1968), *El Condor* (1970), *Barquero* (1970).

TRISH VAN DEVERE (1944–   )

Marrying actor George C. Scott didn't hurt Van Devere's career, although there's every indication that she would have made it on her own in time. They met while filming *Where's Poppa?* (1970), made *The Last Run* (1971) in Spain and two years later, after their marriage, co-starred in *Day of the Dolphins* (1973).

Van Devere studied at Ohio Wesleyan University and then went to New York to pursue her acting career. She was one of only three applicants admitted to the Actors Studio in 1969.

In addition to her work in films, Van Devere toured the South with the Free Southern Theatre, an integrated troupe that performed for blacks who had never seen live theatre, and helped found the Poor People's Theatre in New York. **Films include:** *One Is a Lonely Number* (1972).

Rudy Vallee, top crooner of the 20's, later turned out to be a fine comedian in such films as Man Alive *(1945).*

Lee Van Cleef, a professional gunman in Day of Anger.

Dick Van Dyke and Sally Anne Howes in Chitty Chitty Bang Bang.

MAMIE VAN DOREN (1933–)

Songwriter Jimmy McHugh spotted Joan Lucille Olander when she was singing in Las Vegas and encouraged her to study drama in preparation of a career in show business. She did, and when she appeared on stage in a Los Angeles production of *Come Back, Little Sheba*, Universal signed her on.

She was immediately recognized as a contender in Hollywood's sex-symbol sweepstakes and for a while was considered a serious rival to stars like Marilyn Monroe. However, after a few touted roles in such films as *Teacher's Pet* (1958), which starred Doris Day and Clark Gable, Van Doren disappeared into the realm of "B" pictures. **Films include:** *Forbidden* (1954), *The Second Greatest Sex* (1955), *Running Wild* (1955), *The Girl in Black Stockings* (1956), *Untamed Youth* (1957), *The Navy Versus the Night Monsters* (1966).

DICK VAN DYKE (1925–)

A TV favorite for many years, the talented dancing-singing star has specialized in domestic-comedy roles in which he is beset on all sides by total disaster. Van Dyke was already popular when he made his screen debut recreating his Broadway role as Albert Peterson in *Bye Bye Birdie* for the 1963 screen version of the musical. A year later, as the chimney sweep in *Mary Poppins*, he made a delightful fantasy companion to Julie Andrews. In a more earthbound role he had it out with Doris Day in *Divorce American Style* (1967). The demands of his TV show, however, have limited his film appearances drastically. **Other credits:** *What a Way to Go!* (1964), *The Art of Love* (1965), *Fitzwilly* (1967), *Chitty Chitty Bang Bang* (1968), *The Comic* (1969), *Cold Turkey* (1971).

PETER VAN EYCK (1913–1969)

The blond German-born actor arrived in the United States in the 30's. After some performing experience as a pianist and on radio he won his first screen role in *The Moon Is Down* (1943) as a Nazi officer who refuses orders to kill Norwegian civilians and the same year played another Nazi in *Five Graves to Cairo* (1943). Van Eyck was rele- gated to "B" pictures for the most part and after almost 20 years in Hollywood was still being given Teutonic roles. He was among the "cast of thousands" in *The Longest Day* (1962), playing the German Lt. Colonel Ocker. Van Eyck returned to Europe to make films from time to time and appeared in such European productions as *The Wages of Fear* (1955) and *The Girl on the Third Floor* (1958). **Credits include:** *The Imposter* (1944), *The Rawhide Years* (1956), *The Spy Who Came in From the Cold* (1965), *Shalako* (1968).

JO VAN FLEET (1922–)

She usually plays an unsavory character, and her forte is embittered, age-worn women who occasionally pack a gun. Born in California, she went to New York and performed with the Neighborhood Theatre on Broadway and on television before making her Oscar-winning film debut as the vinegary madam who turns out to be James Dean's mother in *East of Eden* (1955). The following year she attracted comparable acclaim as Susan Hayward's aggressive mother in *I'll Cry Tomorrow* (1956). She deftly proved her versatility in several other good films of the late 50's, and in *Wild River* (1960) she played an old woman struggling to protect her island home against the combined forces of family, government and the Tennessee River. **Other credits:** *The Rose Tattoo* (1955), *Gunfight at the OK Corral* (1957), *The King and Four Queens* (1957), *Cool Hand Luke* (1967), *I Love You, Alice B. Toklas!* (1968).

PHILIP VAN ZANDT (1904–1958)

The Dutch character actor specialized in villainy during his prolific screen career. Initially, however, his ambitions lay in a different direction. He went to Hollywood at the age of 15, hoping to become a "boy comedian." He did some extra work, went to acting school and moved from touring companies to success in comedies on the Broadway stage. When he returned to Hollywood in 1941 he made his screen debut in *These High Gray Walls*. Although he went on to appear in 30 other screen roles, he is probably best remembered as chief newsman, Mr. Ralston, who presided over the yes-men in the screening room in *Citizen Kane* (1941). **Films include:** *House of Frankenstein* (1944), *April Showers* (1948), *Cyrano de Bergerac* (1950), *Yankee Pasha* (1954), *Around the World in 80 Days* (1956), *The Pride and the Passion* (1957).

VICTOR VARCONI (1896–   )

The Hungarian-born actor (Mihaly Varkonyi) appeared in a number of Hollywood silents, including De Mille's blockbuster *The King of Kings* (1927), and continued his successful career well into the talkie era. Unlike so many other actors Varconi was never typecast and played with equal ease many different roles and nationalities. He was Ladislaw in the musical *Roberta* (1935), Painted Horse in the Western classic *The Plainsman* (1937) and Primitivo in the Spanish war drama *For Whom the Bell Tolls* (1943). While never a star, he was a familiar face in supporting roles to moviegoers throughout the 30's and 40's and to TV movie-rerun aficionados. **Credits:** *Triumph* (1924), *Feet of Clay* (1924), *The Volga Boatman* (1926), *Strange Cargo* (1940), *The Hitler Gang* (1944), *Where There's Life* (1947), *Samson and Delilah* (1949).

NORMA VARDEN (c. 1898–   )

The British character actress moved to the United States and was frequently seen in patrician roles in Hollywood productions. She appeared in comedies, played Mrs. Cunningham in the bizarre Hitchcock thriller *Strangers on a Train* (1951) and was also seen in such dramas as *Random Harvest* (1942) and *Witness for the Prosecution* (1958). **Films include:** *The Iron Duke* (1935), *National Velvet* (1944), *Gentlemen Prefer Blondes* (1953), *The Sound of Music* (1965), *Doctor Doolittle* (1967).

DIANE VARSI (1938–   )

She was all set for a starring career after her first film appearance in *Peyton Place* (1957). Her portrayal of Allison MacKenzie in that super soap opera brought her an Oscar nomination. Then, to the total puzzlement of Hollywood, she began turning her back on her film career and never quite explained why. Varsi refused to help promote the picture and turned down a succession of scripts before agreeing to appear in *From Hell to Texas* (1958) and *Ten North Frederick* (1958). She underwent a nervous breakdown during the filming of the latter but recovered sufficiently to make an appearance as Ruth Evans in *Compulsion* (1959). Since then she has appeared infrequently on screen. **Credits:** *Sweet Love, Bitter* (1967), *Wild in the Streets* (1968), *Bloody Mama* (1970).

ROBERT VAUGHN (1932–   )

Vaughn became famous in 1964 when he first appeared as Napoleon Solo, the super-agent of TV's *The Man From U.N.C.L.E.* He had been acting for years before *U.N.C.L.E.*, making his film debut in *Hell's Crossroads* (1957), but the TV show proved to be the impetus his career needed. He has since appeared in such movies as *The Magnificent Seven* (1960) and *Bullitt* (1968) and starred on British TV series, most recently *The Protectors*. **Credits include:** *The Young Philadelphians* (1959), *The Venetian Affair* (1967), *The Bridge at Remagen* (1969), *Clay Pigeon* (1971).

CONRAD VEIDT (1893–1943)

Veidt was the star of Fritz Lang's surrealist and macabre masterpiece *The Cabinet of Dr. Caligari* (1921), a historic German film produced back in the pre-Hitler days when Berlin came close to becoming the intellectual capital of the film world. The handsome German was born in Potsdam, studied under Max Reinhardt and began his acting career on the stage. He appeared in films as early as 1917 and remained on screen until the year of his death.

He immigrated to England to escape Nazi rule in the 30's and eventually landed in Los Angeles, where his Teutonic accent and chiseled Prussian features made him a perfect U-boat captain or army officer in anti-Nazi films of the early 40's. **Many credits include:** *Waxworks* (1924), *The Passing of the Third Floor Back* (1935), *Dark Journey* (1937), *All Through the Night* (1942), *Casablanca* (1942), *Above Suspicion* (1943).

Norma Varden, a fine character actress, in The Sound of Music.

Conrad Veidt in Nazi Agent, *the type of film and part he was most familiar with.*

Vera-Ellen with an hourglassish figure in Let's Be Happy *(1957).*

LUPE VELEZ (1909–1944)

Her dark Latin beauty and explosive temperament helped this Mexican star graduate from Laurel and Hardy comedies into lead roles, the first of which was opposite Douglas Fairbanks in his hyperactive *The Gaucho* (1927). With the advent of sound she was featured in Tolstoy's *Resurrection* (1931), but studios decided that straight dramatic roles were not for her. Velez was thereafter almost invariably cast as a firebrand in such lesser efforts as *Hot Pepper* (1933) and the *Mexican Spitfire* series, which was first launched in 1940. Her gay and vital exterior in real life proved to be a false facade, for Velez killed herself in 1944. **Credits include:** *Wolf Song* (1929), *Lady of the Pavements* (1929), *The Cuban Love Song* (1931), *Strictly Dynamite* (1934), *Ladies' Day* (1943).

EVELYN VENABLE (1913–)

Venable played opposite such luminaries as Fredric March, Will Rogers and Shirley Temple, but although she was invariably a featured player she never quite became a star. Most often she was a "proper" girl, as in *Alice Adams* (1935), when she played the small-town society lass whom Katharine Hepburn strove to emulate. Her films ranged from Westerns to *Mrs. Wiggs of the Cabbage Patch* (1934). After ten years she had had enough and retired after a final appearance in *He Hired the Boss* (1943). **Other credits:** *Cradle Song* (1933), *Death Takes a Holiday* (1934), *David Harum* (1934), *The Little Colonel* (1935).

VERA–ELLEN (1926–)

The former band singer played sprightly musical leads during her brief film career. She appeared in *On the Town* (1949), in which three sailors on leave in New York burst into song constantly, in the well-known *Call Me Madam* (1953) and in the hearty perennial, *White Christmas* (1954). She retired from the screen in the mid-50's. **Films include:** *Three Little Girls in Blue* (1946), *Words and Music* (1948), *Love Happy* (1950), *Happy Go Lovely* (1951), *Let's Be Happy* (1957).

ELENA VERDUGO (1926–)

In the course of her screen career this Spanish-American actress appeared in several semi-biographical films, including *The Moon and Sixpence* (1942) and *Cyrano de Bergerac* (1950). She also appeared in some fairly exotic adventure dramas and a sprinkling of horror films. She perhaps had her biggest success on television, where she starred on the 1952 *Meet Millie* series and was a regular on the 1963 *The New Phil Silvers Show*. **Her films include:** *Belle Starr* (1941), *House of Frankenstein* (1944), *Song of Scheherazade* (1947), *Thief of Damascus* (1952), *How Sweet It Is* (1968).

FLORENCE VIDOR (1895–)

In 1915 Vidor left her native Texas with her husband, director King Vidor, to try her luck in the infant film industry in Hollywood. Both of them made good. He established himself as a leading director and she became one of the most popular leading ladies of the silent screen. Vidor made her acting debut in *The Yellow Girl* (1915) and subsequently starred in a long list of silent films. However, she and

Scenes like this usually meant that the girl had misbehaved and was going to be put out in the cold. Actually, this is Florence Vidor in Booth Tarkington's story of social life in a small town, Alice Adams *(1923).*

King Vidor went their separate ways. They were divorced, and after her remarriage to concert violinist Jascha Heifetz, Vidor retired from motion pictures. **Her films include:** *Lying Lips* (1921), *Main Street* (1923), *Are Parents People?* (1925), *The Grand Duchess and the Waiter* (1926), *The Patriot* (1928), *Chinatown Nights* (1929).

HELEN VINSON (1907–   )

Born in Beaumont, Texas, Vinson was seen regularly in movies of the 30's and 40's. Although she usually played a cool, aloof, aristocratic lady, one of her first films, *I Am a Fugitive From a Chain Gang* (1932), was noted for its seething social comment. She appeared with Spencer Tracy in *The Power and the Glory* (1933) and in several routine films before playing in the Bob Hope comedy *Nothing but the Truth* (1941), which concerns itself with a man who wagers that he can tell the truth for a day. **Her films include:** *Jewel Robbery* (1932), *Transatlantic Tunnel* (1935), *Torrid Zone* (1940), *The Thin Man Goes Home* (1945).

MONICA VITTI (1931–   )

There are certain elements that immediately identify a film directed by Michelangelo Antonioni during the early 60's—the underlying guilt and consequent inertia of the principals, a general sense of malaise and lack of resolve and the presence of Monica Vitti as a neurotic, middle-class woman in search of an unnamed goal.

Born Maria Luisa Ceciarelli in Rome, Vitti spent her childhood in Milan, attended the Academia d'Arte Dramatica in Rome and appeared on the Roman stage. Her early film roles were in minor comedies like *Ridere Ridere Ridere* (1955) and *Pilliccia di Visone* (1956). Then in 1957 she joined the company of the Teatro Nuovo di Milano. Its director was Antonioni, and the encounter marked the beginning of an association that brought international recognition to both director and actress three years later with the release of Antonioni's much hailed *L'Avventura* (1960). This was followed by other equally successful ventures—*La Notte* (1961), in which Vitti played Marcello Mastroianni's consolation, *L'Eclisse* (1962), in which she

starred opposite Alain Delon, and finally *The Red Desert* (1964).

Between the Antonioni films Vitti appeared in several other Italian and French works. After them Vitti returned to her first love, comedy, displaying a delightful flair in several none too successful French, Italian and American ventures. Her only notable recent performance in a more serious work was in *La Pacifistica* (1971) by Hungarian director Miklós Janscó. **Credits include:** *Le Bambole* (1965), *Modesty Blaise* (1966), *Amore Mio Aiutami* (1969), *Lei* (1972).

MARINA VLADY (1937–   )

One of four sisters who became actresses, Marina de Poliakoff-Baidarov was born in France of Russian ancestry. She started her film career as a child, and by the time she was 16 she had made 11 French and Italian films. Her first major role was in *Avant le Déluge* (1953), and within a few years she was playing leads. Her most notable performances were in the French-made *Crime and Punishment* (1958), Orson Welles' ambitious *Chimes at Midnight* (1967) and Godard's *One or Two Things I Know About Her* (1968). **Other films:** *Cavalcade of Song* (1954), *The Steppe* (1963), *Sweet and Sour* (1964).

JON VOIGHT (1939–   )

The handsome blond actor from suburban New York caused something of a sensation in *Midnight Cowboy* (1969) as Joe Buck, a pleasure-bent youth loose in the seamy underworld of New York City. The film won both Voight and co-star Dustin Hoffman Academy Award nominations and brought Voight the New York Film Critics Circle award.

Voight studied acting at the Neighborhood Playhouse in New York and appeared on television and in stock, off- and on-Broadway productions (winning the Theatre World award for his 1967 Broadway role in *That Summer, That Fall*) before coming before the camera in the mid-60's in two limited-release films. After *Cowboy* Voight appeared in a comic role as Milo Minderbinder in *Catch-22* and was a member of the ill-fated canoe outing in *Deliverance* (1972). In 1974 he ap-

Monica Vitti starred with Richard Harris in Antonioni's Red Desert.

Jon Voight, in the shattering Midnight Cowboy, *is subjected to an impromptu prayer orgy by street-corner evangelist John McGiver.*

peared as the sympathetic teacher of deprived black children in *Conrack*. Though the film got mixed reviews, Voight was universally acclaimed. **Credits include:** *Out of It* (1970), *The Revolutionary* (1970), *The All-American Boy* (1973).

THEODORE VON ELTZ (1894–1964)

His acting career spanned more than 50 years and included extensive work on stage, in films—both silent and sound—and on television. Von Eltz was born in New Haven, Connecticut, where his father, Baron Louis Von Eltz, was a professor of languages at Yale University. He began acting with a New York stock company in 1913 and spent five years touring the United States. He made his Broadway debut in *Prunella* and, after serving in World War I, made his first picture, *Extravagance* (1920), with May Allison. Over the years Von Eltz appeared in scores of films and, on television, starred as Father Barbour on the popular 50's series *One Man's Family*. **Films include:** *Tiger Rose* (1923), *Being Respectable* (1924), *The Four*

Feathers (1929), *The Arizona Kid* (1930), *Private Worlds* (1935), *Magnificent Obsession* (1935), *Topper* (1937), *The Big Sleep* (1946).

GUSTAV VON SEYFFERTITZ (c. 1890–1943)

Although he hailed from Innsbruck, Austria, he played Prussian villains (even when the part didn't call for one) and added his own special brand of skullduggery to some 40 films. He first appeared in *When Knighthood Was in Flower* (1922), survived the coming of sound and ended his film career by playing a particularly venomous German in *Nurse Edith Cavell* (1939). **Films include:** *The Student Prince* (1927), *The Case of Sergeant Grischa* (1930), *Dishonored* (1931), *Queen Christina* (1933), *Mad Holiday* (1936).

ERICH VON STROHEIM (1884–1957)

Hans Erich Maria Stroheim von Nordenwall was much like the Hollywood he first worked in during the long-gone 20's—wildly ornate, hugely ambitious and more than a wee bit ridiculous. His shaven bullet head, monocle, tucked-in chin and ramrod posture combined to make him the perfect movie villain—usually a Prussian officer with bestial impulses, sometimes an un-uniformed meanie with run-of-the-mill carnal instincts. Having said all this, it must be added that his performances stuck in one's mind long after others in a cast had been forgotten and that on at least three occasions—as the ventriloquist in *The Great Gabbo* (1929), as the prison-camp commandant in Renoir's *Grand Illusion* (1938) and as the loyal butler protecting Gloria Swanson's illusions of past glory in *Sunset Boulevard* (1950)—his portrayals came close to excellence.

As a director, Von Stroheim was even larger than life. His tastes were exotic, the cost of his ventures prodigious. He often shot the same scene over and over again, and his films before cutting ran to four hours or more. It was said that the anguished screams of studio bosses who footed the bills could be heard out in the San Fernando Valley. Yet there is no doubt that at least one of the Vienna-born master's films, *Greed* (1923), was an authentic classic. **Film credits include:** *Blind Husbands* (1919), *The Wedding March* (1928), *As You Desire Me* (1932), *Five Graves to Cairo* (1943), *North Star* (1943), *The Great Flamario* (1945).

MAX VON SYDOW (1929–   )

One of the brightest stars in Ingmar Bergman's firmament, he was outstanding in one of the Swedish director's classics—as the gaunt and unforgettable hero, the knight Antonius Block, in *The Seventh Seal* (1956; U.S., 1958).

The son of a scholar and teacher of folklore, Von Sydow first appeared on the stage in 1948 and began making films for Bergman when he was still in his early 20's. His American film debut came many years later, as Jesus Christ in *The Greatest Story Ever Told* (1965).

In addition to his work for Bergman, Von Sydow was particularly impressive in *The Emigrants* (1971; U.S., 1972) and *The New Land* (1971; U.S., 1973), a two-part film co-starring Liv Ullmann and directed by Sweden's Jan Troell that deals with the day-to-day life of an immigrant farm family that travels to and settles in middle America in the 19th century. **Other credits include:** *Wild Strawberries* (1959), *Virgin Spring* (1960), *Winter Light* (1963), *The Reward* (1965), *Hawaii* (1966), *The Touch* (1971), *The Exorcist* (1974).

MURVYN VYE (1913–   )

The heavyset actor went from Yale University to burlesque and then vaudeville, where, for a short spell, he was straight man for Milton Berle. He played the heavy on stage in both *Oklahoma!* and *Carousel* but switched expertly to comedy as the goon in *One Touch of Venus*.

In films he has played widely disparate roles, ranging from a highly amusing Merlin in Bing Crosby's *A Connecticut Yankee in King Arthur's Court* (1949) to a murderous Bugs Moran in *Al Capone* (1959). Vye has also appeared on a variety of TV dramas. **Credits include:** *Golden Earrings* (1947), *Pick-up on South Street* (1953), *The Best Things in Life Are Free* (1956), *Andy* (1965).

There was only one Von Stroheim, ever. Here he is in The Wedding March, *a film he wrote, directed and starred in.*

Max Von Sydow, a brilliant actor, in The Touch.

Robert Walker and Claudette Colbert bid a chaste farewell to each other in Since You Went Away (1944) as Jennifer Jones looks on.

Raymond Walburn, patting a bust of (we think) the Emperor Augustus in Hail the Conquering Hero (1944).

ROBERT WAGNER (1930–   )

Wagner made his film debut fresh from college as a Marine in *Halls of Montezuma* (1951), and for the following decade he spent most of his screen time changing military uniforms with almost monotonous regularity. He finally got demobilized in the 60's and appeared in such films as *The Pink Panther* (1964) and *Harper* (1966). He also starred in the TV series *It Takes a Thief* (1967–68). P.S.: Wagner and starlet Natalie Wood married in 1957. They were divorced, remarried and raised families, were divorced again and married each other for the second time in 1973. **Films include:** *The Frogmen* (1951), *The True Story of Jesse James* (1957), *The Longest Day* (1962), *Don't Just Stand There* (1968).

ANTON WALBROOK (1900–1967)

Walbrook, the son of a circus clown, was born into a family of German performers for three centuries. After studying at Max Reinhardt's drama school, he played his first roles in Vienna, Munich, and Dresden theatres. When Nazi anti-Semitism forced him to leave Germany in the mid-30's, Walbrook settled in England. His best-known movies in the United States were Max Ophul's *La Ronde* (U.S., 1954) and *The Red Shoes* (1948). In 1944, Walbrook refused to appear in a German film, *Dice of Fate*, because the leading lady was a one-time favorite of Goebbels. **Highlights:** *Maskerade* (1934), *The Soldier and the Lady* (1937), *The Queen of Spades* (1949), *Lola Montès* (1955), *I Accuse!* (1958).

RAYMOND WALBURN (1897–1969)

When 16-year-old Walburn left his home in Plymouth, Indiana, to join a stock company he launched an acting career that eventually spanned 54 years and included 87 supporting roles in films of the 30's, 40's and 50's. Pleasant-faced, mustachioed and bug-eyed, he was almost always cast in character comedy parts. His most notable acting role away from films was in the Broadway play *The Show Off*. **Highlights:** *The Count of Monte Cristo* (1934), *The Great Ziegfeld* (1936), *Mr. Deeds Goes to Town* (1936), *Kiss the Boys Goodbye* (1941), *The Spoilers* (1955).

NANCY WALKER (1922–   )

The talented comedienne made her Broadway debut at the age of 19 in *Best Foot Forward* (1941) and appeared on screen for the first time in the 1943 film version. Primarily a stage actress, Walker appeared on Broadway in such hits as *On the Town* (1944), *Pal Joey* (1952) and *Do Re Mi* (1960). Recently she created the character of Mildred, the unconventional, tippling maid on the *MacMillan and Wife* TV series. **Film credits:** *Girl Crazy* (1943), *Broadway Rhythm* (1944), *Lucky Me* (1954).

ROBERT WALKER (1914–1951)

Shyness, charm and lovableness were the chief ingredients of Walker's acting style. He was every mother's son, the clean-cut, good boy next door. After several inconsequential walk-on parts Walker attained star rank in the title role of *See Here, Private Hargrove* (1944), one of the big box-office successes of World War II. He rose to corporal in his next two films. After a few remarkably bad movies in which he starred in roles as composers, he could find only supporting parts in chillers. In his next to last movie, Alfred Hitchcock's *Strangers on a Train* (1951), Walker played the part of an introverted but attractive homicidal maniac. Later that year he committed suicide. **Highlights:** *Bataan* (1943), *Thirty Seconds Over Tokyo* (1944), *Song of Love* (1947), *Vengeance Valley* (1951), *My Son John* (1952).

JEAN WALLACE (1923–   )

A native of Chicago, Wallace started her career at 16 as a showgirl in the Earl Carroll Hollywood Vanities Revue. Her first film role was in Paramount's *Louisiana Purchase* (1941). She has been teamed in films with her actor-director husband, Cornell Wilde. **Highlights:** *You Can't Ration Love* (1944), *Star of India* (1956), *Sword of Lancelot* (1963), *Beach Red* (1967).

ELI WALLACH (1915–   )

Although he has been highly praised for a number of serious film roles, Wallach is best known as a thoroughly accomplished and versatile actor on the legitimate stage. During his long and active theatre career he has only occasionally taken time off to appear in films and has avowed that "movies, by comparison to the stage, are like calendar art next to great paintings." Born in Brooklyn, Wallach studied acting at the Neighborhood Playhouse and later became a member of Actors Studio. He is married to actress Anne Jackson. **Highlights:** *Baby Doll* (film debut, 1956), *The Magnificent Seven* (1960), *The Misfits* (1961), *Lord Jim* (1965), *The Tiger Makes Out* (1967), *A Lovely Way to Die* (1968), *Cinderella Liberty* (1973).

KAY WALSH (1915–   )

This native Londoner gained her first stage experience in London's *West End Revue* and made her New York stage debut in 1930 at the RKO theatres, performing acrobatics during intermissions. Fired from this position for being "too earnest," Walsh returned to England to make a name for herself on the stage as well as in films. **Highlights:** *How's Chances* (debut, 1934), *The Mysterious Mr. Redder* (1940), *Oliver Twist* (1948, U.S. 1951), *The Horse's Mouth* (1958), *Tunes of Glory* (1960), *A Study in Terror* (1966), *The Ruling Class* (1972).

RAY WALSTON (1918–   )

Born in New Orleans, character actor Walston made his stage debut at the Margo Jones Theatre in Dallas. He came to New York in 1945 and since then has appeared in a number of important plays and films. Early in his career he received two prestigious awards for work on Broadway: the Clarence Derwent Award for the best non-featured performance and a New York Drama Critics Circle citation. A veteran of numerous TV dramas, Walston also appeared on the *My Favorite Martian* series. **Highlights:** *Damn Yankees* (1958), *South Pacific* (1958), *The Apartment* (1960), *Wives and Lovers* (1963), *Paint Your Wagon* (1969).

HENRY B. WALTHALL (1878–1936)

A notable leading man of the silent screen, Walthall made his movie debut as a kindly Southern gentleman in *In Old Kentucky* (1909) and went on to appear in more than 100 films. He became identified with portrayals of sensitive, wise and patient fathers and grandfathers. His permanent importance in movie history arises from his appearance as the Little Colonel in D.W. Griffith's Civil War saga *The Birth of a Nation* (1915). **Highlights:** *A Convict's Sacrifice* (1910), *The Raven* (1915), *The Scarlet Letter* (1925), *Abraham Lincoln* (1930), *Viva Villa!* (1934).

SAM WANAMAKER (1919–   )

This actor-director is known primarily for his work on the stage. Born in Chicago, he began his career on the American stage and eventually went on to become one of the most active director-actors in the English theatre during the 50's and the major force in the creation and direction of the Liverpool New Shakespeare Cultural Center. During the 60's Wanamaker returned to the United States to accept a number of stage and screen roles and to direct such TV programs as *The Defenders* series. **Highlights:** *My Girl Tisa* (1948), *Taras Bulba* (1962), *The Spy Who Came in from the Cold* (1965), *Those Magnificent Men in Their Flying Machines* (1965), *The Day the Fish Came Out* (1967)

JACK WARDEN (1925–   )

This former professional boxer and baseball player from Newark, New Jersey, began his acting career after serving as an infantryman during World War II. He first appeared on screen in supporting roles in action and war pictures of the early 50's and

Eli Wallach as the one-eyed corporal in The Good, the Bad and the Ugly *(1967).*

Jack Warden in The Sound and the Fury *(1959).*

H. B. Warner, one of the very first movie stars, in the much, much later Sunset Boulevard *(1950).*

Ethel Waters, a true Great, in The Sound and the Fury *(1959).*

soon established his reputation as a versatile character actor. As one director aptly stated: "Put a bib on him and he could play a baby." In addition to his work in films and on stage, Warden has had an extensive TV career which includes leads in *The Asphalt Jungle* (1961) and *The Wackiest Ship in the Army* (1965). **Highlights:** *From Here to Eternity* (1953), *Edge of the City* (1957), *Twelve Angry Men* (1957), *The Bachelor Party* (1957), *Bye Bye Braverman* (1968), *Who Is Harry Kellerman?* (1971).

H.B. WARNER (1876–1958)

This memorable British actor began his 41-year theatrical career on the London stage when he was seven years old—an expected event, considering that he was preceded on stage by three generations of Warners. During World War I he went on to Hollywood and an equally successful several decades in films. After 1924 Warner performed solely in movies and was one of the most prolific actors in the industry. One of his most notable silent-screen roles was as Christ in De Mille's *King of Kings* (1927). Although his roles grew modest in his later years, his performances were gems of style. **Films include:** *The Beggar of Cawnpore* (1915), *Sorrell and Son* (1927), *Mr. Deeds Goes to Town* (1936), *Lost Horizon* (1937), *You Can't Take It With You* (1938), *The Rains Came* (1939), *Sunset Boulevard* (1950), *The Ten Commandments* (1956).

RUTH WARRICK (1915–   )

A native of St. Louis, Missouri, Warrick began her performing career in the theatre, went on to work as a radio singer and broke into films with a memorable screen debut as Orson Welles' wife in *Citizen Kane* (1941). She has since acted in more than 20 films and has also become a television staple whose credits include the roles of Hannah Cord in *Peyton Place* and Phoebe Tyler in *All My Children*. **Highlights:** *Journey Into Fear* (1943), *Guest in the House* (1944), *Three Husbands* (1950), *Ride Beyond Vengeance* (1966).

ROBERT WARWICK (1878–1965)

Born Robert Taylor Bien in Sacramento, California, Warwick studied singing in Paris

with the intention of embarking on an operatic career. He eventually gave up the plan, however, and turned to the theatre shortly after the turn of the century. After more than a decade of work on the legitimate stage, Warwick abandoned Broadway for Hollywood. He became a silent-screen idol of the 20's, survived the transition from silent cinema to talkies, and when advancing age lessened his appeal as a romantic lead he continued his success in character roles. **Highlights:** *Secret Service* (1919), *The City of Masks* (1920), *The Dark Horse* (1932), *The Life of Emile Zola* (1937), *Gentleman's Agreement* (1947), *Night of the Quarter Moon* (1959).

BRYANT WASHBURN (1889–   )

During the silent teens and 20's, his dimpled, cleft-chinned good looks helped make Washburn something of a matinee idol in a variety of light, romantic Hollywood comedies. After the arrival of sound Washburn continued to play bit parts and to serve as a talent scout for RKO. **Numerous film credits include:** *The Blindness of Virtue* (1915), *Venus in the East* (1918), *The Parasite* (1925), *Swing High* (1930), *Sutter's Gold* (1936), *Gangs Incorporated* (1941), *Two O'Clock Courage* (1945).

ETHEL WATERS (1900–   )

Her singing and acting career extended from performances in vaudeville in the 20's to featured billing in evangelist Billy Graham's televised Crusades of the 70's. In between she became the first black woman to achieve star rank in America and won accolades from the diverse audiences of radio, television, movies, the Broadway stage and concerts.

After more than a decade on the stages of the Southern black entertainment circuit Waters headed north. She made the first of her numerous Broadway appearances in *Africana* (1927) and her film debut two years later in *On With the Show* (1929). Over the years Waters popularized such favorite songs as "Stormy Weather," "Heat Wave" and "Am I Blue." She was twice nominated for an Academy Award—for her role in *Pinky* (1949) and for her performance in *The Member of the Wedding* (1952). **Films include:** *Tales of Manhattan* (1942), *Cabin in the Sky* (1943), *The Long Hot Summer* (1958), *The Sound and the Fury* (1960).

LUCILE WATSON (1879–1962)

Born in Quebec, Canada, Watson was the daughter of Major Thomas C. Watson of the Royal Sherwood Foresters. She was educated in the Ursuline Convent and in 1900 entered the American Academy of Dramatic Arts in New York. She made her New York stage debut in 1902 at the Empire Theatre in *Wisdom of the Wise* and thus launched an acting career that spanned half a century and included 50 some stage roles and many screen parts.

Watson appeared in her first film in 1934 and thereafter was generally cast as an ill-tempered dowager, domineering and acid-tongued. She retired from acting in 1953. **Highlights:** *What Every Woman Knows* (1934), *Waterloo Bridge* (1940), *Watch on the Rhine* (1943), *The Razor's Edge* (1946), *My Forbidden Past* (1951).

MINOR WATSON (1889–1965)

Said Watson of his film career, "I'm a stage actor by heart and by profession. I was a movie actor by necessity and a desire to eat." He made his first stage appearance in 1911 at the Montauk Theatre in Brooklyn, served as an officer in the Pilot Air Service during World War I and made his Broadway debut in 1922.

In the early 30's a lucrative film offer took Watson to Hollywood, where he was typecast in roles of authority—judges, officers, political leaders. He eventually made more than 75 pictures. **Highlights:** *Our Betters* (1933), *Babbitt* (1934), *Boys Town* (1938), *Abe Lincoln in Illinois* (1940), *Yankee Doodle Dandy* (1942), *A Bell for Adano* (1945), *Bright Victory* (1951), *Trapeze* (1956).

DAVID WAYNE (1914–   )

This versatile character actor of stage and screen was born Wayne McKeehan in Traverse City, Michigan, apprenticed with the Eldred Players in Cleveland, Ohio, and made the first of his numerous Broadway appearances in *Escape This Night* (1937). His most notable performances on the legitimate stage were as the leprechaun in *Finian's Rainbow* (1947) and as Sakini in *The Teahouse of the August Moon* (1953). Wayne made his Hollywood debut in *Portrait of Jen-*

Lucile Watson, flanked by Ava Gardner and Melvyn Douglas, in My Forbidden Past *(1951).*

nie (1949). In the early 50's he did a television series called *Norby*. **Highlights:** *Adam's Rib* (1949), *The Tender Trap* (1955), *The Three Faces of Eve* (1957), *The Last Angry Man* (1959), *The Big Gamble* (1961).

JOHN WAYNE (1907–1979)

For more than four decades his craggy presence and nasal drawl have been a source of reassurance to film audiences. With Wayne in charge one knew that the cavalry and/or the Marines would arrive in time, that the lady's virtue would not be sullied, that Right would triumph and that the Pioneer Spirit of this great republic still existed. A titan of the screen, perhaps the biggest box-office attraction in film history, Wayne continued to play romantic leads decades after other stars had turned to character roles—and topped it all off in 1969 when, as the aging one-eyed lawman in *True Grit*, he won the Academy Award for Best Actor.

Born Marion Michael Morrison in Winterset, Iowa, he attended the University of Southern California on a football scholarship and first found work in the film industry as a

John Wayne as he appeared in a fine Western, True Grit.

Young John Wayne, very handsome indeed, with Claire Trevor in the John Ford classic Stagecoach.

Johnny Weissmuller in a classic Tarzan pose. Almost certainly he was calling the elephants for help.

prop man on the Fox lot. Some ten years after his first movie role (a bit part in an early Ford picture) Wayne hit the big time as the Ringo Kid in the Ford classic *Stagecoach* (1939). **Films include:** *The Long Voyage Home* (1940), *Reap the Wild Wind* (1942), *Tall in the Saddle* (1944), *Fort Apache* (1948), *Rio Grande* (1950), *The Quiet Man* (1952), *Hatari!* (1962), *The Longest Day* (1962), *The Green Berets* (1968), *The Cowboys* (1972).

DENNIS WEAVER (1924–   )

Born in Joplin, Missouri, he was a track-and-field athlete in high school and a graduate of the University of Oklahoma when he enrolled in New York's Actors Studio. He headed out to Hollywood in the early 50's, and though touted as a young James Stewart type, he found only supporting roles in a string of Westerns. His luck changed, however, when he was cast as Chester in TV's *Gunsmoke*, a role he played for nine years and which finally made him well known. Later he starred as the Western marshal in New York City in the TV series *McCloud* (from 1970). **Highlights:** *The Raiders* (1952), *Touch of Evil* (1958), *Duel at Diablo* (1966), *Gentle Giant* (1968).

MARJORIE WEAVER (1913–   )

This leading lady of numerous 20th Century–Fox "B" pictures received her early training with a stock company in the early 30's and made her screen debut in *China Clipper* (1936) **Highlights:** *Big Business* (1937), *Young Mr. Lincoln* (1939), *The Mad Martindales* (1942), *We're Not Married* (1952).

CLIFTON WEBB (1893–1966)

The Indiana-born actor (whose real name was Webb Parmelee Hollenbeck) played effete snobs and sophisticated dandies throughout his long career on stage and screen. He will perhaps be best remembered on screen as the ineffably snobbish Mr. Belvedere, housekeeper and babysitter *extraordinaire*, in the hilarious *Sitting Pretty* (1948) and on the stage as one of Gertrude Lawrence's co-stars in the Broadway production of Noel Coward's *Private Lives*. He played in silent pictures as far back as 1921 and ended his career playing heart-of-gold bachelors who, beneath haughty exteriors, spent their time restoring lost dogs to tiny tots or reuniting quarrelsome lovers. **Highlights:** *Polly With a Past* (debut, 1921), *Laura* (1944), *The Razor's Edge* (1946), *Cheaper by the Dozen* (1950), *Mr. Belvedere Rings the Bell* (1951), *The Remarkable Mr. Pennypacker* (1959), *Satan Never Sleeps* (1962).

JACK WEBB (1920–   )

This tough-looking actor with an ominous tone of voice is known principally as the narrator and star of the *Dragnet* TV show, a version of which was released as a movie in 1954. Webb's occasional film appearances include *The Men* (1950), the searing story of a paralyzed veteran. He has had an active career as a producer, director and TV executive. **Highlights:** *Sunset Boulevard* (1950), *You're in the Navy Now* (1952), *The Last Time I Saw Archie* (1961).

JOHNNY WEISSMULLER (1904–)

There were Tarzans (Elmo Lincoln, etc.) before him and Tarzans (Buster Crabbe, etc.) after him, but to most filmgoers and television viewers Weissmuller will always remain the alter ego of Edgar Rice Burroughs' hero.

He held more swimming awards than anyone else until Mark Spitz's performance in the 1972 Olympics but never claimed awards as an actor. Nonetheless, his placid, amiable face carried conviction, and when he swung from limb to limb or thrashed his way across a lake to do battle with a crocodile or two, the viewer felt that he was seeing the real thing. Moreover, he never used a stunt man, performing most of the acts of derring-do himself.

Weissmuller played in a dozen Tarzan films and, unable to shake the call of the jungle, also was the hero in the *Jungle Jim* movies. He played fully dressed roles only once or twice. Weissmuller has retired from the screen and is now the owner of a swimming-pool company. **Films include:** *Tarzan the Ape Man* (1932), *Tarzan and the Amazons* (1945), *Mark of the Gorilla* (1950), *The Devil Goddess* (1955), *The Phynx* (1970).

RAQUEL WELCH (1942–)

Although she has made relatively few pictures, her physical attributes are the most publicized of any actress of her generation. The fabulously endowed winner of numerous beauty pageants has repeatedly declared that she would like to become a serious actress if studios would give her a chance. To date they haven't.

Welch caused low whistles in the audience with her half-clad grunting role in *One Million Years B.C.* (1967). Her first starring part was in *Myra Breckinridge* (1970), in which she competed for attention with another sex goddess, septuagenarian Mae West. Apart from that she was almost always cast as a harlot or a jet-age vamp. **Films include:** *Fantastic Voyage* (debut, 1966), *Bandolero* (1968), *100 Rifles* (1969), *Fuzz* (1972), *The Three Musketeers* (1974).

TUESDAY WELD (1943–)

Weld progressed from fashion modeling as a child to establishing a film model of satanic innocence as a violent and confused teenager in numerous supporting screen roles. Cherubic sluts, angelic unwed mothers, evil and uncontrollable only daughters of sympathetic widowers were her stock in trade in almost 20 movies made in less than 15 years. She has recently attempted somewhat more demanding character roles. Weld has also appeared on television, notably on the *Dobie Gillis* series. **Highlights:** *Rock, Rock, Rock* (debut, 1956), *Rally Round the Flag, Boys!* (1958), *Return to Peyton Place* (1961), *The Cincinnati Kid* (1965), *Pretty Poison* (1968), *Play It As It Lays* (1972).

ORSON WELLES (1915–)

At a time in the 30's when the world apprehensively watched the growth of fascist dictatorships, Welles' ultrarealistic radio broadcast of H.G. Wells' *War of the Worlds*—wherein creatures from Mars overwhelm mankind—caused hysteria and panic among millions of Americans.

As author, director, producer and actor, Welles has always been the focus of controversy. At the age of 22 he set new stan-

Raquel Welch in one of her several million publicity poses.

Orson Welles as the publishing tycoon in Citizen Kane, *one of the most memorable movies ever made. The others are Dorothy Commingore (the mistress) and Ruth Warrick (the wife)*

Mae West with Cary Grant in a typically come-up-'n'-see-me-sometime pose. The picture was She Done Him Wrong.

dards for stage lighting and scenery with his Mercury Theatre production of plays like Marlowe's *Doctor Faustus*, while his motion picture, *Citizen Kane* (1941), which he directed, produced and acted in, created more lawsuits and more talk than any film of its decade. Today *Citizen Kane* is generally considered a screen classic.

Over the years Welles' pictures have ranged from very good to very bad. They have never been routine, which is one reason why today's younger generation has rediscovered him and heatedly debates the virtues and defects of films like *Othello* (1952). **Highlights:** *The Magnificent Ambersons* (1942), *Jane Eyre* (1944), *The Third Man* (1950), *The Long Hot Summer* (1958), *Compulsion* (1959), *Is Paris Burning?* (1966), *Oedipus the King* (1968).

OSKAR WERNER (1922–   )

This stage and screen star was once described by a *Life* writer as "a new kind of movie idol—not a dominant hero but a sensitive, questioning, troubled man." Long acknowledged as one of the finest actors in Europe, Werner won an Oscar nomination and a New York Film Critics Best Actor Award for his performance in *Ship of Fools* (1965).

Born Josef Bschliessmayer in Vienna, he made his acting debut in the one-line role of a fireman in a school play and established his reputation on stage as a member of the Burg Theatre repertory group. Despite his success in films, the actor still prefers the stage and in 1959 he founded his own theatrical company. **Highlights:** *Eroica* (1951), *Jules et Jim* (1962), *Fahrenheit 451* (1966), *The Shoes of the Fisherman* (1968).

MAE WEST (1893–   )

The come-up-and-see-me-sometime lady is one of motion picture's true greats, a talented comedienne and the creator of such classic lines as: "I used to be Snow White but I drifted." "Beulah, peel me a grape." "It's not the men in my life that count, it's the life in my men."

Born in Brooklyn, West first appeared in vaudeville at the age of 14. Later in burles-que, where she was billed as the Baby Vamp, she is credited with being the inventor of a torso-shaking dance, the Shimmy, which became famous the world over. Her Broadway debut in *Sex* (1920), a play she also wrote and directed, created a furor and the show was eventually closed by anti-vice crusaders.

Between 1932 and 1943 the blond, bosomy and brash West swaggered through ten films—almost a caricature of the traditional *femme fatale* and not inappropriately dubbed "the greatest female impersonator of all time." At the age of 77 the lady known as Diamond Lil reappeared on screen in *Myra Breckinridge* and recieved $350,000 for ten days' work. **Highlights:** *Night After Night* (debut, 1932), *She Done Him Wrong* (1933), *Klondike Annie* (1936), *My Little Chickadee* (1940).

HELEN WESTLEY (1879–1942)

This versatile character actress of the stage and screen was born Henrietta Remsen Meserole Manny in Brooklyn and was a descendant of two famous old Dutch families. Although she was active on the New York stage well before World War I, she did not appear in a film until 1934. Many of Westley's screen roles employed her sharp tongue and aquiline features to debunk the movie tradition of "sweet old ladies." **Highlights:** *Moulin Rouge* (1934), *Alexander's Ragtime Band* (1938), *Lillian Russell* (1940), *The Smiling Ghost* (1941).

MICHAEL WHALEN (c. 1907–   )

Although Joseph Kenneth Shovlin wanted to be a musician, his parents convinced him to go into the business world instead. He found a job managing five-and-dime stores near his native Wilkes Barre, Pennsylvania, stuck it out until his father died and went to New York, where he found work with Eva Le Gallienne's repertory company. After several years in stock and some radio work, Whalen headed for Hollywood. He played leading roles in the 30's and later starred in second features. After 16 years in show business Whalen made his Broadway debut in the Agatha Christie thriller *Ten Little Indians* (1944). **Films include:** *Country Doctor*

(1936), *Time Out for Murder* (1938), *Ellery Queen, Master Detective* (1940), *Tahiti Honey* (1943), *Mark of the Dragon* (1951), *She Shoulda Said No* (1957), *Elmer Gantry* (1960).

BERT WHEELER (1895–1968) and ROBERT WOOLSEY (1889–1938)

A comedy star before he was 19, Bert Wheeler was known and loved by vaudeville audiences across the United States. In 1927 he and Robert Woolsey launched Wheeler & Woolsey—one of the most successful teams of zany comics in the entertainment world. Their first performance together in Ziegfeld's staging of *Rio Rita* (1927) brought them to Hollywood for a 1929 film version that set a standard for musical revues for years to come. Wheeler & Woolsey was the first team to shine as stars with the advent of sound films. **Highlights:** *Girl Crazy* (1932), *So This Is Africa!* (1933), *High Flyers* (1938), *Las Vegas Nights* (Wheeler only, 1941).

JESSE WHITE (1919–   )

A familiar figure in films and on television, White specialized in comic roles as an inept gangster or a fast-talking show-biz type. He was born in Buffalo, New York, and worked as a beauty-supply manufacturer, a corset manufacturer and in the jewelry business before making his acting debut in Akron, Ohio.

White was first seen on the New York stage as a vacuum-cleaner salesman in *Sons and Soldiers* (1943) and made his motion-picture debut in *Harvey* (1950). His TV credits include featured roles on the *Danny Thomas Show*, the *Private Secretary* and *That Girl* series. **Films include:** *Death of a Salesman* (1951), *Not As a Stranger* (1955), *The Rise and Fall of Legs Diamond* (1960), *It's Only Money* (1962), *A House Is Not a Home* (1964), *The Reluctant Astronaut* (1967).

PEARL WHITE (1889–1938)

In those dim, remote days when movie audiences excitedly watched the latest episode of *The Perils of Pauline* (1914), Pearl White was the lady about to be cut in half by a buzz saw or run through a rolling mill at the end of the reel.

Serial Queen Pearl White, who escaped a thousand perils, looks as though one of her legs has become detached in this scene from a film made before World War I.

She was a Missouri farm girl who went on the stage at the age of 18. Her voice failed, however, and in 1914 Pathé Frères Studio launched her as America's heroine in the *Perils* serial. Other serials followed (e.g., *The Expolits of Elaine*) and then features. One of the first queens of silents, she performed her own stunts until the studio decided she was too valuable and hired a male stand-in equipped with a blond wig. Her last movie was made in 1921. **Highlights:** *The House of Hate* (1918), *A Virgin in Paradise* (1922).

STUART WHITMAN (1929–   )

Known primarily as the star of action dramas, Whitman was nominated for an Academy Award for his performance as a rehabilitated child molester in *The Mark* (1961). He appeared on the stage and in television in addition to his work in motion pictures. **Films include:** *When Worlds Collide* (1952), *The Story of Ruth* (1960), *Murder Inc.* (1961), *The Comancheros* (1961), *Shock Treatment* (1964), *Those Magnificent Men in Their Flying Machines* (1965), *An American Dream* (1966).

Richard Widmark, usually an aggressor, is on the defensive in The Last Wagon *(1956).*

JAMES WHITMORE (c. 1920–   )

This solid character actor, a familiar personality on both screen and television, made his film debut in *The Undercover Man* (1949). The following year he played the driver for a gang of jewel thieves in *The Asphalt Jungle* (1950). He appeared in several popular 60's films, including *Planet of the Apes* (1968) and the police drama *Madigan* (1968).

In addition to his films, he starred in the TV series *The Law and Mr. Jones* and makes frequent appearances on that medium. In the spring of 1974 his one-man show *Will Rogers' U.S.A.* opened on Broadway. **Highlights:** *Across the Wide Missouri* (1951), *Kiss Me Kate* (1953), *Oklahoma!* (1955), *The Eddie Duchin Story* (1956), *Guns of the Magnificent Seven* (1969), *The Harrad Experiment* (1973).

DAME MAY WHITTY (1865–1948)

Dame Whitty's career spanned 62 years and extended into her 80th year. She was as much at home on British and American stages as she was in movie-production studios in New York, London and Hollywood. Although she appeared in a two-reeler silent film in 1914, her true film debut came in 1937 at the age of 72 when she recreated her stage role in *Night Must Fall*. She often played sweet old ladies who were tough inside, and many filmgoers still fondly remember her as the elusive Miss Froy in Hitchcock's *The Lady Vanishes* (1938). **Films include:** *Mrs. Miniver* (1942), *The White Cliffs of Dover* (1944), *The Sign of the Ram* (1948).

RICHARD WHORF (1906–1966)

Whorf, described as "a protean man of the theatre," was born in Winthrop, Massachusetts, the son of the well-known painter Henry Church Whorf. During his 44-year career he not only established himself as a stage and screen actor but also later directed such films as *Blonde Fever* (1944) and episodes of such well-known TV series as *Rawhide* and *The Beverly Hillbillies*. In addition, Whorf wrote and illustrated a book on the art of applying stage make-up, *Time to Make Up*. **Highlights:** *Midnight* (1934), *Blues in the Night* (1941), *Chain Lightning* (1950).

RICHARD WIDMARK (1914–   )

Widmark was among the screen's leading portrayers of vicious or psychopathic killers during his early years in films. Eventually he managed periodic escapes from crime and appeared in courtroom dramas, Westerns and action melodramas. Box-office interest in Widmark, however, increased when he played a gangster and declined when he was cast as a hero. Therefore, he returned again and again to a career of villainy. **Highlights:** *Kiss of Death* (1947), *Panic in the Streets* (1950), *The Law and Jake Wade* (1958), *Judgment at Nuremberg* (1961), *The Bedford Incident* (1965), *When the Legends Die* (1972).

HENRY WILCOXON (1905–   )

Born in the West Indies, Wilcoxon began his career in British touring companies before going into cinema in England. In 1934 he

Robert Montgomery with Dame May Whitty and Rosalind Russell in the enormously chilling chiller Night Must Fall *(1937).*

went to Hollywood to play Marc Antony opposite Claudette Colbert in his first American film, De Mille's *Cleopatra*. His performance established his reputation in the United States, where he has since worked as actor, director, producer and research expert. **Highlights:** *The Perfect Lady* (1931), *The Crusades* (1935), *Mrs. Miniver* (1942), *The Ten Commandments* (1956), *The Private Navy of Sergeant O'Farrell* (1968).

CORNELL WILDE (1915–   )

Prior to 1945 Wilde acted in a number of mediocre "B" movies, and after 1960 his efforts were primarily devoted to producing and directing movies such as *Beach Red* (1967) and *No Blade of Grass* (1971). In the 15-year interval Wilde acted in more than a score of films of little distinction. The only major exception to the string of forgettables was *A Song to Remember* (1945). This highly inaccurate biography, loosely based on the life of Chopin, was an immense box-office success and made Wilde a star. In other feature films Wilde was cast as Aladdin, Robin Hood, as steadfast romantic lovers or swashbuckling adventurers. **Films include:** *High Sierra* (1941), *The Greatest Show on Earth* (1952), *Edge of Eternity* (1960), *The Naked Prey* (1966).

GENE WILDER (1934–   )

Screen comedian Wilder was born in Milwaukee, Wisconsin, and studied to be an actor at the University of Iowa and then with the Bristol Old Vic. He made his stage debut in the off-Broadway production of *Roots* and went on to win the Clarence Derwent Award as the Dutch hotel valet in *The Complaisant Lover*. He first appeared on screen as the undertaker who gets taken for a joy ride in *Bonnie and Clyde* (1967). Although the role was a small one, his performance was eye-catching and led to the more substantial part of the neurotic accountant in Mel Brooks' *The Producers* (1968). The performance brought Wilder an Oscar nomination. Wilder can play serious roles as well, as he proved by his performance in the 1971 TV production of *Death of a Salesman*. **Films include:** *Start the Revolution Without Me* (1970), *Quackser*

Fortune Has a Cousin in the Bronx (1970), *Two Times Two* (1970), *Rhinoceros* (1974), *Blazing Saddles* (1974).

MICHAEL WILDING (1912–   )

Britisher Wilding began his acting career on the British stage in the 30's. He found bit parts in films late in the decade and within ten years had climbed to brief fame as one of the most popular film stars in England. Recently Wilding gave up acting completely to become a Hollywood agent. **Highlights:** *Tilly of Bloomsbury* (1940), *Carnival* (1946), *Stage Fright* (1950), *The Naked Edge* (1961), *Waterloo* (1970).

WARREN WILLIAM (1896–1948)

A debonair leading man in films and a Broadway matinee idol, William was an audience favorite for more than 30 years. He starred on Broadway in contemporary and classical drama before he began his screen career in the early 30's. Of his numerous screen roles he is probably most fondly remembered as the exceedingly civilized thief of the *Lone Wolf* series. **Films include:** *The Woman from Monte Carlo* (1931), *The Mouthpiece* (1932), *Lady for a Day* (1933), *Imitation of Life* (1934), *Satan Met a Lady* (1936), *The Lone Wolf Spy Hunt* (1939), *The Wolf Man* (1941), *Counter-Espionage* (1942), *The Private Affairs of Bel Ami* (1947).

CINDY WILLIAMS (1948–   )

The year 1973 was a good one for Williams—she filmed four pictures and scored a hit with the public for her role in *American Graffiti* (1973) as the wide-eyed blonde who is delighted when told she looks just like Sandra Dee.

Williams grew up in Van Nuys, California, and majored in drama at Los Angeles City College before she got her first acting break as the teenage wife in the Gene Kelly TV series *The Funny Side*. She made her screen debut in *Drive, He Said* (1971) and played Tooley, an American hippie en route to Nepal via the Orient Express, in *Travels With My Aunt* (1973). **Films include:** *The Killing Kind* (1973), *The Conversation* (1974).

Cornell Wilde as Chopin in A Song to Remember *(1945).*

Michael Wilding in Oscar Wilde's An Ideal Husband.

Emlyn Williams in The Scarf *(1950).*

Esther Williams, swimming champion turned actress, in a lavishly adorned swimsuit.

EMLYN WILLIAMS (1905–)

This eminent Welsh playwright-director-actor had his first resounding stage success in the United States when he starred as the intellectual killer in his own play *Night Must Fall*. Although Williams has appeared in many well-known films, he has achieved international success primarily for his work in legitimate theatre, most notably for his solo presentations of Dickens and the short stories of Dylan Thomas. **Highlights:** *The Case of the Frightened Lady* (debut, 1932), *The Citadel* (1938), *Ivanhoe* (1952), *The L-Shaped Room* (1963), *David Copperfield* (1969).

ESTHER WILLIAMS (1923–)

Like Johnny Weissmuller and Buster Crabbe, she first drew the interest of movie makers because of her outstanding ability as a swimmer featured in Billy Rose's 1939 Aquacade. After a few supporting roles, she became a star in her own right in roles that required posing in a bathing suit, kissing male leads under water and exposing to color film her highly attractive physical characteristics.

Film critics wrote uncomplimentary reviews about Williams' dramatic talents, but producers and exhibitors loved her. She ranks among the biggest box-office attractions of all time. **Films include:** *Andy Hardy's Double Life* (1943), *Thrill of a Romance* (1945), *Million Dollar Mermaid* (1952), *The Big Show* (1961).

GRANT WILLIAMS (1930–)

A leading man of television and occasionally of screen, this native New Yorker is probably best known for his off-screen musical activity. He sang for five seasons with the New York City Opera and is heard on recordings of the Robert Shaw Chorale. Williams also starred in the TV series *Hawaiian Eye* from 1959 to 1963. **Highlights:** *Red Sundown* (debut, 1956), *Written on the Wind* (1957), *The Incredible Shrinking Man* (1957), *PT 109* (1963).

GUINN "BIG BOY" WILLIAMS (1900–1962)

A native of Texas, Williams was a lanky cowboy type who carved a career as a slow-witted figure of comic relief. In the silent 20's he rode the range with the likes of Harry Carey and Tom Mix and later supported talkie Westerners like John Wayne. Williams also played non-cowboy roles occasionally, coining a puzzled squint in his comic roles as a sort of trademark. His most notable straight dramatic performance was as an inmate of an insane asylum in *Private Worlds* (1935). **Highlights:** *Noah's Ark* (1929), *Here Comes the Navy* (1934), *You Only Live Once* (1937), *Dodge City* (1939), *Billy the Kid* (1941), *Bad Men of Tombstone* (1949), *The Alamo* (1960).

HUGH WILLIAMS (1904–1969)

Actor and playwright Williams specialized in portraying the elegant, well-bred Englishman of taste and wit. Born in Sussex and schooled at the Royal Academy of Dramatic Art, Williams made his acting debut in a walk-on part in a London stage play, *The Yellow Jacket* (1922). Never aspiring to classical drama, Williams cultivated a light but sophisticated comic style in both his acting and writing. To the drawing-room comedy, one critic observed, Williams "brought a champagne quality of his own." **Highlights:** *Charley's Aunt* (1930), *David Copperfield* (1935), *Wuthering Heights* (1939), *Khartoum* (1966).

RHYS WILLIAMS (1897–1969)

This Welsh character actor performed on the New York stage in Shakespearean productions before heading for Hollywood and the beginning of a long film career. Williams also appeared in a number of segments of such well-known TV series as *Perry Mason*, *12 O'Clock High* and *The Wild Wild West*. **Highlights:** *How Green Was My Valley* (1941), *The Corn Is Green* (1945), *The Spiral Staircase* (1946), *The Kentuckian* (1955), *The Fastest Gun Alive* (1956), *The Sons of Katie Elder* (1965).

FRED WILLIAMSON (1938–)

The star of so-called "blacksploitation" films such as *The Soul of Nigger Charley* (1973), Williamson was born in Gary, Indiana, grew up in Chicago and played football at Northwestern University. He graduated with a degree in architectural engineering and an offer of a contract with the Kansas City Chiefs. After several years as a pro-football player and as the owner of a Montreal architectural engineering firm, Williamson made his show-business debut on TV's *Laugh-In*. He later got some small acting parts on television before being cast as the pro-football "ringer" in Robert Altman's hit film *M*A*S*H* (1970). Later, he played Diahann Carroll's boyfriend on her TV series *Julia*.

When Hollywood began making movies to appeal exclusively to blacks, Williamson became a star. In 1973 Williamson was signed to star in a series of films about Jefferson Bolt, a black international courier à la James Bond. **Films include:** *Tell Me That You Love Me, Junie Moon* (1970), *The Legend of Nigger Charley* (1972), *Hammer* (1972), *Black Caesar* (1973).

NICOL WILLIAMSON (1940–   )

This Scottish-born actor has an excitable temperament and, as an actor, is noted for his vitality, range and personal magnetism. Williamson began his career with a British repertory company and has appeared on the London stage. His first contact with American audiences was on Broadway in John Osborne's *Inadmissible Evidence* (1965) in a role he later recreated on screen in 1968. He also took over George C. Scott's role in New York in the Neil Simon hit comedy *Plaza Suite* (1969). His unorthodox interpretation of Hamlet on the London and New York stages in 1969 aroused considerable controversy among theatregoers. **Film highlights:** *The Bofors Gun* (1968), *Laughter in the Dark* (1969), *The Reckoning* (1969), *Hamlet* (1970), *The Jerusalem File* (1972).

CHILL WILLS (1903–   )

At 15, Wills left his home in Texas to work as a straight man in burlesque. He eventually (mid-30's) ended up doing vaudeville in New York, where he was spotted by an MGM executive, signed up and given his first film role in *Racketeers of the Range* (1939). Since then he has been cast in various character roles, mostly in Westerns. The actor is noted for his gruff voice and earthy manner. **More**

than 60 films include: *The Westerner* (1940), *Best Foot Forward* (1943), *The Harvey Girls* (1946), *The Sundowners* (1950), *Bronco Buster* (1952), *The Alamo* (1960), *The Rounders* (1965).

LOIS WILSON (1896–   )

The Covered Wagon (1923), in which Wilson starred with J. Warren Kerrigan, was one of the biggest and most lavish of the silent spectaculars and ranks with *The Birth of a Nation* as one of the best. Even the Conestoga wagons were authentic, and the Arapaho Indians thought so highly of the director, James Cruze, that they named him Chief Standing Bear.

Wilson, a pretty and wholesome-looking brunette, planned to teach school in her native Pittsburgh but turned to acting instead. She remained a popular favorite throughout the 20's and went on to play in a number of talking pictures until the end of the 40's. **Other films include:** *Why Smith Left Home* (1919), *Manslaughter* (1922), *Ruggles of Red Gap* (1923), *Icebound* (1924), *The Show-Off* (1926), *The Crash* (1932), *Laughing at Life* (1933), *The Girl From Jones Beach* (1949).

MARIE WILSON (1916–1972)

Early in her career this native Californian established herself as the ultimate in dumb blondes. She played in screen comedies as early as 1936 and became even more widely known via radio and television performances in the 40's and 50's. Many of her films were unfavorably reviewed, but nearly all were box-office successes. Her screen stupidity, however, was carefully assumed, for by most accounts she was an extremely bright and witty lady. **Highlights:** *Satan Met a Lady* (1936), *Shine on Harvest Moon* (1944), *My Friend Irma* (1949), *Never Wave at a Wac* (1953), *Mr. Hobbs Takes a Vacation* (1962).

CLAIRE WINDSOR (1898–1972)

Olga Cronk prepared for her career by studying singing and dancing and by changing her name to Claire Windsor. She entered the film world in 1918 as an extra, was first credited in *To Please One Woman* (1920) and starred in numerous silents before the coming

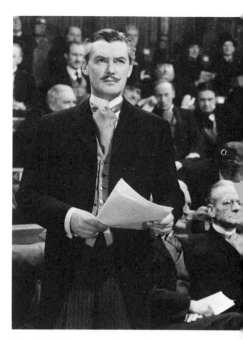

Hugh Williams in Korda's An Ideal Husband *(1948).*

Fred Williamson in bad trouble in Hell Up in Harlem *(1974).*

of talkies and a decreased call for her talents. **Films include:** *Rich Men's Wives* (1922), *Nellie the Beautiful Cloak Model* (1924), *Money Talks* (1926), *Captain Lash* (1929).

MARIE WINDSOR (1923–)

Born Emily Marie Bertelson in Marysvale, Utah, Windsor studied dramatics for two years at Brigham Young University, then went on to Hollywood, where she was accepted as a student by Maria Ouspenskaya. After some stage and radio experience she broke into films. Praised for her ability as well as her personal attractiveness, Windsor nevertheless missed stardom. **Highlights:** *All-American Coed* (1941), *Force of Guilt* (1948), *Dakota Lil* (1950), *The Killing* (1956), *Chamber of Horrors* (1966).

PAUL WINFIELD (1941–)

As one of the new crop of talented black actors, Winfield chooses his roles on the basis of whether or not they diminish the stature of black men. Such parts have been less hard to come by since he won an Oscar nomination for his performance in *Sounder* (1972), a story of Louisiana sharecroppers during the depressed 30's.

Winfield made his first stage appearance in his native Watts, Los Angeles' sprawling black ghetto. Soon he was appearing regularly on such TV reliables as *Mission Impossible*, *Mannix*, *Julia* and *Ironside*. His first screen role was in Sidney Poitier's *The Lost Man* (1969). Since then he has served as artist in residence at three universities —Stanford, Hawaii and California at Santa Barbara—while continuing to turn in admirable appearances in films. **Credits include:** *R.P.M.* (1970), *Brother John* (1971), *Gordon's War* (1973), *Conrack* (1974).

CHARLES WINNINGER (1884–1968)

Winninger, most famous for his role as Cap'n Andy in the Kern and Hammerstein hit Broadway musical *Show Boat* (1927), was the product of a theatrical family that toured as a concert group. He made his stage debut at the tender age of six and worked in vaudeville and Broadway for many years before making the first of his several dozen screen appearances in the early 30's.

In films the character actor played opposite

such stars as Deanna Durbin in *Three Smart Girls* (1937) and Judy Garland in *Little Nellie Kelly* (1940). **Highlights:** *Show Boat* (1936), *Destry Rides Again* (1939), *Coney Island* (1943), *Broadway Rhythm* (1944), *Raymie* (1960).

JONATHAN WINTERS (1925–)

Probably the only comedian who would and could imitate a solitary turtle on a crowded freeway, he is consistently original and consistently way out. His childhood skill at imitations led to a career that has included work in nightclubs, legitimate theatre, films and television. He is a native of Dayton, Ohio. **Highlights:** *It's a Mad, Mad, Mad, Mad World* (1963), *The Loved One* (1965), *The Russians Are Coming, The Russians Are Coming* (1966), *Viva Max!* (1969).

SHELLEY WINTERS (1922–)

Born Shirley Schrift in St. Louis, Missouri, Winters spent several years in vaudeville and on the New York stage before her 1944 screen debut in *Nine Girls*. She has nearly always been cast as an independent tough woman, with roles ranging from brassy madams to abandoned mistresses. Her ability as an actress was never questioned, but stardom has been elusive. She received two Academy Awards for Best Supporting Actress: as Mrs. Van Daan in the touching adaptation of *The Diary of Anne Frank* (1959) and as the mother in *A Patch of Blue* (1965). **More than 50 films include:** *A Double Life* (1948), *The Great Gatsby* (1949), *A Place in the Sun* (1951), *The Big Knife* (1955), *Lolita* (1962), *Alfie* (1966), *Bloody Mama* (1970), *The Poseidon Adventure* (1973).

ESTELLE WINWOOD (1883–)

This versatile English character actress of the stage and a veteran of more than 80 years in show business studied for the theatre at the Lyric Stage Academy in London. She made her American debut at the Little Theatre in New York as Lucilla in *Hush* (1916). Although she appeared on screen occasionally from the early 30's, Winwood is usually associated with her more recent film portrayals of eccentric characters—vague old ladies, alcoholics, madwomen. **Highlights:** *The House of Trent* (1934), *Quality Street* (1937),

Cap'n Andy (Charles Winninger) leads Irene Dunne down the aisle in the famous Show Boat *(1936).*

The Glass Slipper (1955), *The Misfits* (1961), *Camelot* (1967), *Games* (1967), *The Producers* (1968).

GOOGIE WITHERS (1917–)

Her real name was Georgina, but she insisted on retaining the one bestowed on her by an affectionate nurse during her childhood in Karachi. Googie means "dove" in Punjabi and "clown" in Bengali. Dove or clown, Withers has remained one of England's most popular stars and is equally beloved in her adopted Australia. Her first stage role was in *The Windmill Man* (1929), and she went on to become the star of scores of plays that ranged from *The Country Girl* to *The Complaisant Lover*. Withers made her film debut as Miranda in *White Corridors* (1930). One of her most memorable roles was opposite Michael Redgrave in the chilling *Dead of Night* (1946).

Withers and her husband, actor-director John McCallum, moved to Australia in the early 50's. Since then she has appeared in dramatic productions on British television and has alternated between the London and Australian stages. **Films include:** *One of Our Aircraft Is Missing* (1942), *It Always Rains on Sunday* (1949), *Hamlet* (1948), *Derby Day* (1952), *Devil on Horseback* (1954), *Port of Escape* (1955).

GRANT WITHERS (1904–1959)

A onetime reporter on the *Los Angeles Record*, Withers began his 30-year screen career as a leading man in the 20's and 30's. In later life he played character roles (particularly in Westerns) and made occasional television appearances. Withers, once married to Loretta Young, committed suicide in 1959. **Highlights:** *Tiger Rose* (1929), *Hold 'em, Yale* (1935), *A Lady Takes a Chance* (1943), *Tripoli* (1950), *Rio Grande* (1950), *Lady Godiva* (1955).

JANE WITHERS (1926–)

Known today as "Josephine, the lady plumber" in television cleanser commercials, Withers began her show-business career at age two in amateur nights in her home town of Atlanta, Georgia. By the time she was eight she was an established child star

on radio with her own program. She first appeared on screen as Shirley Temple's brattish counterpart in *Bright Eyes* (1934) and soon became one of 20th Century–Fox's biggest child stars of the 30's. Cast as a tomboy in her childhood films, Withers also drew a few adult roles, the most important of which was in *Giant* (1956). **Highlights:** *The Holy Terror* (1937), *Rascals* (1938), *Johnny Doughboy* (1943), *Captain Newman, M.D.* (1964).

CORA WITHERSPOON (1890–1957)

Noted in films for her featured comedy roles, in which she generally played a flighty matron, Witherspoon was born in New Orleans and began her acting career with a stock company at the age of 15. She made her New York stage debut at 20, playing a 70-year-old woman for David Belasco in *The Concert*. Her screen debut was in 1931, and she went on to appear in over 30 motion pictures. In later years she worked in television. **Highlights:** *Peach O' Reno* (1931), *Midnight* (1934), *Madame X* (1937), *Dark Victory* (1939), *The Bank Dick* (1940), *Just for You* (1952).

SIR DONALD WOLFIT (1902–1968)

Heralded as the last of the great actor-managers, Wolfit was born in Nottinghamshire, England. He made his stage debut at 13, performing in a show for wounded soldiers. Having established himself as an outstanding actor, particularly in Shakespearean roles, Wolfit formed his own theatrical company in 1937. During the Battle of Britain he became famous for "lunchtime" performances of Shakespeare at the Strand Theatre during the height of the blitz. Although Wolfit was best known for his work in the classical theatre, he also made a number of motion pictures. **Highlights:** *The Death at Broadcasting House* (1934), *Pickwick Papers* (1954), *Room at the Top* (1959), *Becket* (1964), *Decline and Fall* (1968).

LOUIS WOLHEIM (1880–1931)

After years on the American stage, German-born character actor Wolheim headed for Hollywood shortly after World War I. Dubbed the actor with "the homeliest physiognomy on the screen," he nevertheless

Jane Withers seems to be giving some serious advice to Carl (Alfalfa) Switzer in Wild and Woolly *(1937).*

Shelley Winters had a meaty role in A Double Life, *in which she played opposite the veteran Ronald Colman.*

Eight-year-old child star Natalie Wood, who grew up to be an adult star, poses for a studio shot in 1947.

Joanne Woodward, who invariably gives a fine performance, in A Fine Madness *(1966).*

found a niche playing toughies in numerous silents and early talkies. His most notable performances were as the hard-boiled sergeant in *Two Arabian Knights* (1927) and as the belligerent veteran in *All Quiet on the Western Front* (1930). **Credits include:** *Little Old New York* (1923), *Unseeing Eyes* (1923), *The Racket* (1928), *Condemned* (1929), *Gentleman's Fate* (1931).

ANNA MAY WONG (1902–1961)

Lissome Chinese-American beauty Wong Liu Tsong was the first of Hollywood's Oriental mystery women. She first attracted attention playing opposite Douglas Fairbanks in *The Thief of Bagdad* (1924) and went on to achieve great popularity in the 30's. She appeared also in English and German films, including Europe's first talking picture, *Haitang*. During World War II Wong retired from movies completely and devoted herself to United China relief and USO activities. After spending several years in semi-retirement she appeared in TV dramas. The movie industry's Oriental trend in the late 50's and early 60's resulted in her being recalled to do her last film, *Portrait in Black* (1960). At the time of her death she was preparing for a role in the movie version of *The Flower Drum Song*. **Highlights:** *Red Lantern* (1919), *The Alaskan* (1924), *The Flame of Love* (1930), *Shanghai Express* (1932), *Bombs Over Burma* (1942), *Impact* (1949).

NATALIE WOOD (1938–   )

Petite, with a well-scrubbed, little-girl look, she was one of Hollywood's few child performers to succeed in bridging the gap to an adult movie career. Over the past decade and a half she has given more than competent performances in such diverse roles as the "Jewish princess" in *Marjorie Morningstar* (1958), the gang sweetheart in *West Side Story* (1961) and one of the quartet in *Bob & Carol & Ted & Alice* (1969). **Highlights:** *Tomorrow Is Forever* (1946), *The Bride Wore Boots* (1946), *Miracle on 34th Street* (1947), *The Green Promise* (1949), *Rebel Without a Cause* (1955), *Gypsy* (1962), *This Property Is Condemned* (1966).

DONALD WOODS (1904–   )

Woods made his screen debut in *As the Earth Turns* (1934) and went on to be cast as second romantic lead in a variety of films of the late 30's and 40's. Since the 50's his movie roles have been few, but he has appeared frequently on the legitimate stage and on such TV series as *Wagon Train, Ben Casey, The Rebel* and *Bonanza*. **Highlights of more than 40 films:** *Frisco Kid* (1935), *A Tale of Two Cities* (1935), *I Was a Prisoner on Devil's Island* (1941), *Barbary Pirate* (1949), *Undercover Agent* (1954), *A Time to Sing* (1968).

JOANNE WOODWARD (1930–   )

Two coveted awards reflect the popular reaction to Woodward's distinctive artistry: the Academy Award for Best Actress for her portrayal of the schizophrenic in *The Three Faces of Eve* (1957) and the New York Film Critics Award for her sensitive performance in *Rachel, Rachel* (1968) as a spinster schoolmarm involved in the most important and perhaps the only love affair in her life. Georgia-born Woodward studied at the Neighborhood Playhouse in New York City and made her first professional appearance on television in the early 50's. Some work in the legitimate theatre led to her screen debut in the Western *Count Three and Pray* (1955) with Van Heflin. Since then Woodward has played a dazzling variety of roles, from soul-bared, love-starved loose women to light, sprightly comic parts as in *A New Kind of Love* (1963) co-starring her husband, Paul Newman, to classical American dramas like *The Long Hot Summer* (1958), also with Newman, and *The Sound and the Fury*. In 1973 Woodward was nominated for an Academy Award for her moving performance in *Summer Wishes, Winter Dreams*. **Films include:** *Rally 'Round the Flag, Boys!* (1968), *Winning* (1969), *The Effect of Gamma Rays on Man-in-the-Moon Marigolds* (1972).

MONTY WOOLLEY (1888–1963)

As an actor, Woolley will probably always be best remembered for his stage (1936) and screen (1941) performance in *The Man Who*

Came to Dinner. As Sheridan Whiteside, the man who came for dinner with some Midwesterners while on a lecture tour, broke his leg and stayed for months, he was hilarious. With devilish relish and perfect timing he delivered some of the most acerb witty lines ever written for the screen (by the Epstein brothers from the Kaufman–Hart original) as Whiteside managed to turn an ordinary household into a squirrel cage.

Sent to Yale (class of 1911) to become a lawyer, Woolley was influenced by his college friend, Cole Porter, to partcipate in the Yale Dramatic Society. After service in the Mexican War and World War I, he returned to Yale as a teacher of dramatic writing; among his students were Stephen Vincent Benét and Thornton Wilder. Woolley left the academic life in 1927 to go to Broadway, where he established himself as a successful director before he turned to acting. Woolley played himself in the not very accurate movie biography of Cole Porter (played by Cary Grant), *Night and Day* (1946). **Highlights:** *Young Doctor Kildare* (1938), *The Pied Piper* (1942), *The Bishop's Wife* (1947), *As Young As You Feel* (1951), *Kismet* (1955)

WOOLSEY, ROBERT
See BERT WHEELER

FAY WRAY (1907–)

Forever remembered as the distraught lady clutched in one of King Kong's enormous hands while he clung to the tower of the Empire State Building with the other, Wray actually starred in upward of 50 pictures. Born in Canada, she grew up in Hollywood and became a film extra in the early 20's. In 1926 Erich von Stroheim plucked her from a line of teenage bathing beauties and cast her in the leading role in his lavish *The Wedding March*. Over the next decade Wray played leads in dozens of films, co-starring with the most popular leading men of the day—Gary Cooper, Richard Arlen, Ronald Colman and Fredric March. **Films include:** *Gasoline Love* (1923), *Sea God* (1930), *Viva Villa!* (1934), *Alias Bulldog Drummond* (1935), *Adam Had Four Sons* (1941), *Hell on Frisco Bay* (1956).

TERESA WRIGHT (1918–)

She went to Broadway straight from high school and began her screen career as Bette Davis' daughter in *The Little Foxes* (1941). That brought her an Oscar nomination, as did her appearance in *The Pride of the Yankees* (1942). Her third appearance, in *Mrs. Miniver* (1942), won her the Academy Award for Best Supporting Actress. Married to playwright Robert Anderson, Wright returned to Broadway in 1957 and has been active there for the past several years. **Highlights:** *The Best Years of Our Lives* (1946), *Enchantment* (1948), *The Men* (1950), *The Actress* (1953).

JANE WYATT (1912–)

Wyatt left Barnard College in New York to join the apprentice school of the Berkshire Playhouse at Stockbridge, Massachusetts. This move greatly dismayed the *Social Register*, which promptly dropped her name from its pages. Unperturbed, Wyatt con-

Two wonderful veterans: Monty Woolley and Gracie Fields in Holy Matrimony *(1943).*

No one will ever forget Fay Wray and Bruce Cabot as they look upon the outwardly fearsome but inwardly sentimental King Kong.

Jane Wyman as the unhappy fiancée of an alcoholic in The Lost Weekend *(1945).*

Ed Wynn, once billed as "The Perfect Fool," in the devastating The Diary of Anne Frank *(1959).*

tinued her acting, first on Broadway, then in Hollywood, where her role in *Lost Horizon* (1937) vaulted her to fame. After shuttling between Broadway and Hollywood for a number of years, she finally turned to television, where she became a household staple as Robert Young's wife in the *Father Knows Best* series. **Highlights:** *The Luckiest Girl in the World* (1936), *Gentleman's Agreement* (1947), *Never Too Late* (1965).

JANE WYMAN (1914–   )

Wyman has enjoyed one of the most uniquely diversified careers in movie history. She has performed every conceivable type of lead, supporting, bit and extra role. Her accomplishments in films have been matched by her dramatic successes in television. In 1948 she won both the Academy Award and the British Picturegoer Gold Medal for her performance as the deaf mute in *Johnny Belinda*, co-starring Lew Ayres, Hollywood's best-known M.D. of the 30's and 40's.

Early in her career she was a blues singer and dancer and played the parts of sexy dumb blondes in long-forgotten "B" films. It wasn't until *The Lost Weekend* (1945) that her true talents became generally recognized. Her marriage to Ronald Reagan ended in divorce. **More than 75 films include:** *Smart Blonde* (1937), *Brother Rat* (1938), *Princess O'Rourke* (1943), *The Yearling* (1947), *The Glass Menagerie* (1950), *Magnificent Obsession* (1954), *Pollyanma* (1960), *How to Commit Marriage* (1969).

ED WYNN (1886–1966)

Billed in vaudeville and on the Broadway stage as "The Perfect Fool," the crack-voiced comedian was born Isaiah Edwin Leopold in Philadelphia. His enormously successful stage career was never matched on the screen, but he did make 17 films, if one includes his role in *Alice in Wonderland*, where his voice spoke the sentiments of the Mad Hatter. His final appearance was in another Disney movie, *The Gnome-Mobile* (1967). He was the father of Keenan Wynn. **Films include:** *Rubber Heel* (debut, 1927), *Stage Door Canteen* (1943), *Marjorie Morningstar* (1958), *Mary Poppins* (1964), *That Darn Cat* (1965).

KEENAN WYNN (1916–   )

Wynn is the third link in a four-generation acting family. His grandfather was Frank Keenan, the late stage and silent-film star; his father was Ed Wynn, and his son Ned completes the thespian tree.

In 1942, after appearing in 107 stock-company shows and 21 Broadway plays, Wynn signed a contract with MGM that lasted for 68 movies. He has generally been cast either as a wisecracking comedy sharpie or in straight dramatic roles. **Highlights:** *See Here, Private Hargrove* (1944), *Annie Get Your Gun* (1950), *Dr. Strangelove* (1964), *Once Upon a Time in the West* (1969).

DANA WYNTER (1930–   )

Among the most beautiful of the film ladies, this native Londoner made her screen debut in *The View from Pompey's Head* (1955). She has appeared in relatively few pictures in recent years but has been kept busy on the London stage and in a variety of TV programs. **Other films:** *Something of Value* (1957), *Sink the Bismarck!* (1960), *If He Hollers, Let Him Go* (1968), *Airport* (1970).

DIANA WYNYARD (1906–1964)

Born Dorothy Isobel Cox in London, Wynyard established herself as a leading figure in English drawing-room comedies and the New York theatre before appearing in her first film, *Rasputin and the Empress* (1932). For many Americans, Wynyard's "serene Saxon beauty" typified the well-bred Englishwoman. The actress, who was noted for a range that included Chekhovian, Shakespearean and tragic roles in addition to comic ones, is best remembered for her film role in Noel Coward's *Cavalcade* (1933). **Highlights:** *Reunion in Vienna* (1933), *An Ideal Husband* (1948), *Angel Street* (1952), *Island in the Sun* (1957).

MICHAEL YORK (1942–   )

This fine young British actor from Falmer appeared on stage with the National Theatre before making his first film appearance in *The Taming of the Shrew* (1967). His rise to stardom was almost instantaneous. He gave a delightful portrayal of the apparently innocent, thoroughly Machiavellian social climber after Angela Lansbury's realm in *Something for Everyone* (1970), and his brilliant performance as the young Britisher who shacked up with Sally Bowles in *Cabaret* (1972) convinced critics that he would be a headliner for a long time to come. Most recently he turned swashbuckler as an almost Candidish d'Artagnan in Richard Lester's *The Three Musketeers* (1974). **Other pictures include:** *Accident* (1967), *Strange Affair* (1968), *Romeo and Juilet* (1968), *England Made Me* (1973).

SUSANNAH YORK (1941–   )

This blond, blue-eyed Britisher went straight from the Royal Academy of Dramatic Art in London to the screen as Alec Guinness' daughter in *Tunes of Glory* (1960). The following year her performance as a schoolgirl in Rumer Godden's *The Greengage Summer* (1961) captivated critics and producers alike and landed York her first role in an American film as one of Montgomery Clift's patients in *Freud* (1962).

Undoubtedly the film that brought her her first major success was *Tom Jones* (1963), in which she played the 18th-century squire's daughter who was the object of Albert Finney's affections. After she won rave notices for her West End performance in an

Susannah York and Christopher Plummer spend a night together in Battle of Britain *(1969).*

adaptation of Henry James' *The Wings of the Dove*, she went to Hollywood for a string of so-so pictures. Back in England, her most controversial film role was as the lesbian in *The Killing of Sister George* (1968). In America again she made *They Shoot Horses, Don't They?* (1970) and a couple of other films before being cast by Robert Altman in *Images* (1973), perhaps her best performance to date. She also appeared on American television opposite George C. Scott in a well-received version of *Jane Eyre*. **Films include:** *Loss of Innocence* (1961), *The Seventh Dawn* (1964), *A Man for All Seasons* (1966), *Sebastian* (1968), *Happy Birthday, Wanda June* (1971), *Zee and Company* (1972).

Michael York plays the sitar in The Guru *(1969). Rita Tushingham looks as though she feels he has a long way to go.*

Loretta Young in a comic thriller of long ago, The Man From Blankley's *(1930).*

Robert Young as the newspaper correspondent who heals two war-shocked orphans in Journey for Margaret *(1942).*

CLARA KIMBALL YOUNG (1890–1960)

Young was one of the most famous of the silent screen ladies. She made her film debut in 1912 in *Cardinal Wolsey* and was popular throughout the silent era. She was so popular, in fact, that she formed her own production company and gave Mary Pickford the idea to do likewise. Like so many other stars of her time, Young saw her starring roles shrink to small parts with the advent of the talkies, though she did remain on screen through the 40's. **Credits include:** *My Official Wife* (1914), *The Easiest Way* (1917), *The Forbidden Woman* (1920), *She Married Her Boss* (1935), *Three on the Trail* (1936), *The Roundup* (1941).

GIG YOUNG (1917–   )

Gig Young made his film debut under the name of Byron Barr in the light comedy *Misbehaving Husbands* (1940). He took his present name from that of a character he played in *The Gay Sisters* (1942). Over the past three decades he has appeared in scores of films, plays and TV shows. His broad acting ability won him periodic acclaim as well as two Academy Award nominations for *Come Fill the Cup* (1951) and *Teacher's Pet* (1958). He won an Oscar for his supporting role as the cynical dance-hall emcee in *They Shoot Horses, Don't They?* (1970). **Films include:** *Old Acquaintance* (1943), *The Three Musketeers* (1948), *Only the Valiant* (1951), *Young at Heart* (1955), *That Touch of Mink* (1962), *Strange Bedfellows* (1965), *Lovers and Other Strangers* (1970).

LORETTA YOUNG (1913–   )

Among the most durable of film stars who invariably looked several decades younger than her real age, she made a successful transition from silents to talkies and from talkies to television. Born Gretchen Young in Salt Lake City, Utah, she began acting at four and was a regular studio performer by the time she was 13. She abandoned films in the early 50's but went on to a triumphant career in television, opening each performance by swirling through open doors in flaring skirts. A few years earlier, however, she won an Oscar for her performance in *The Farmer's Daughter*

(1947), **Film credits:** *Laugh, Clown, Laugh* (1928), *Platinum Blonde* (1931), *The House of Rothschild* (1934), *Bedtime Story* (1942), *The Bishop's Wife* (1947), *Because of You* (1952).

ROBERT YOUNG (1907–   )

Young, whose acting career has spanned over 40 years, was born in Chicago and went to Hollywood after a fling at radio. With a voice that had clarity and power, he quickly rose to stardom when the era of talkies began. As a contract player at MGM in the 30's and early 40's Young played romantic leads in more than 100 movies opposite such leading ladies as Katharine Hepburn, Joan Crawford, Margaret Sullavan and Luise Rainer. In the early 50's Young made a successful transition to television as the lead in the popular, long-running series *Father Knows Best* and later as the star of *Marcus Welby, M.D.* **Highlights:** *Strange Interlude* (1932), *Tugboat Annie* (1933), *Spitfire* (1934), *Vagabond Lady* (1935), *The Bride Wore Red* (1937), *Northwest Passage* (1940), *Claudia* (1943), *The Enchanted Cottage* (1945), *Crossfire* (1947), *The Secret of the Incas* (1954).

ROLAND YOUNG (1887–1953)

Born in London, Young started his career in British stage productions and Broadway plays before making his film debut with John Barrymore in *Sherlock Holmes* (1922). Young was noted for his quizzical, humorous portrayals of distracted or vague gentlemen. A personal friend of the late Thorne Smith, who wrote the *Topper* books, Young played the title role in the *Topper* movie series and also in the radio series based on the same character. **Highlights:** *David Copperfield* (1935), *Topper* (1937), *The Philadelphia Story* (1940), *And Then There Were None* (1948), *Let's Dance* (1950).

BLANCHE YURKA (1887–1974)

A leading stage actress of the 20's, Yurka was widely known as an interpreter of Ibsen heroines. Her voice was instantly recognizable by its richness, variety and the sense of authority it conveyed in all roles from light comedy to classic tragedy.

She made her film debut as the blood-thirsty, knitting revolutionary Madame De Farge in the 1935 screen version of Dickens' *A Tale of Two Cities*. Over the following two and a half decades she took occasional breaks from the theatre to play distinctive character parts in some 20 films. **Films include:** *Pacific Rendezvous* (1942), *The Song of Bernadette* (1944), *13 Rue Madeleine* (1947), *Thunder in the Sun* (1959).

MAI ZETTERLING (1925–   )

Born in Västerås, Sweden, Zetterling found her first success on stage in the plays of Strindberg, Ibsen and Anouilh and went on to become one of Sweden's top film stars. Her performance in *Frenzy* (1944) brought international recognition, and between 1947, when she made her English-language screen debut in *Frieda*, and the early 60's she was cast in a number of British films. In 1962 Zetterling tried her hand at directing with a short, *The War Game*. Since then she has achieved substantial recognition as a film-maker and polemicist for women's rights in the Swedish-language features *Loving Couples* (1964), *Night Games* (1966) and *The Girls* (1968). She is married to writer David Hughes. **Highlights:** *Quartet* (1949), *Knock on Wood* (1954), *Only Two Can Play* (1961), *The Main Attraction* (1962).

EFREM ZIMBALIST, JR. (1923–   )

Zimbalist, the son of the concert violinist and opera singer Alma Gluck, began his career as a page for the ABC network after a year at Yale. After acting several years on the New York stage, he made his film debut in 1949 in *House of Strangers*. Although he continued to appear in movies, Zimbalist found his great success as a TV actor and the star of such series as *77 Sunset Strip* and *The FBI*. **Highlights:** *House of Strangers* (1949), *Home Before Dark* (1958), *The Chapman Report* (1962), *The Reward* (1965), *Wait Until Dark* (1967).

VERA ZORINA (1917–   )

Zorina's screen career represents one of the film industry's periodic efforts to enliven their product and broaden its appeal by introducing important talent from other entertainment and performing-arts media. At the time Sam Goldwyn signed her to a contract in 1938, Zorina was already a leading ballerina in performances at London's Covent Garden and at New York's Metropolitan Opera House. **Films include:** *The Goldwyn Follies* (1938), *On Your Toes* (1939), *Louisiana Purchase* (1942), *Star Spangled Rhythm* (1942), *Follow the Boys* (1944).

GEORGE ZUCCO (1886–1960)

Zucco became a Grade-A menace in horror films and such assorted hair-raisers as *The Cat and the Canary* (1939) and *The Mad Ghoul* (1943). The character actor—and a very good one he was, too—was born in England and made his stage debut in Regina, a town in western Canada. He was a well-known actor both in London and New York when he made his first significant film appearance in *The Dreyfus Case* (1931). A long string of supporting roles followed. **Films include:** *Madame X* (1938), *The Hunchback of Notre Dame* (1940), *The Mummy's Tomb* (1942), *The Black Swan* (1942), *Madame Bovary* (1949), *David and Bathseba* (1951).

Mai Zetterling in Night Games.

Vera Zorina, a fine dancer and actress.

Robert Altman's M*A*S*H *(1970)*

M. Antonioni's Blow-Up *(1966)*

Ingmar Bergman's Wild Strawberries *(1957)*

Directors

ROBERT ALDRICH (1918–   ) A high degree of social consciousness and crusading zeal characterized such early films as *Apache* (1954) and *The Big Knife* (1955), while a slicker style and a taste for the macabre marked his works from the time of the grotesque shocker *Whatever Happened to Baby Jane?* (1962). **Highlights:** *The Big Leaguer* (debut, 1953), *Kiss Me Deadly* (1955), *Hush . . . Hush, Sweet Charlotte* (1964), *The Dirty Dozen* (1966), *The Killing of Sister George* (1968), *The Grissom Gang* (1971).

MARC ALLÉGRET (1900–   ) This Swiss-born Frenchman established himself as one of the best film-makers during the first decade of talkies with such memorable works as *Mam'zelle Nitouche* (1931), *Le Lac aux Dames* (1934) and *Les Beaux Jours* (1935). Since World War II most of his movies have been extremely glossy but highly successful ventures. **More than 30 credits include:** *Voyage au Congo* (debut, 1926), *Fanny* (1932), *Gribouille* (1937), *Orage* (1938), *L'Amante di Paride* (1953), *Femmina* (1954), *Un Drôle de Dimanche* (1958), *Le Bal du Comte d'Orgel* (1969).

YVES ALLÉGRET (1907–   ) *Germinal* (1963) is the film with which he is most often associated in the English-speaking world. The younger brother of Marc Allégret, he directed his first film in the early 30's and worked as assistant to Jean Renoir before gaining recognition with *Une si Jolie Petite Plage* (1948), *Dédée d'Anvers* (1947) and *Manèges* (1950). His touch is cynical, almost sardonic. **More than 25 films include:** *Prix et Profit* (1932), *Les Orgueilleux* (1953), *Quand la Femme s'en Mêle* (1958), *Johnny Banco* (1966), *L'Invasion* (1970).

WOODY ALLEN See entry on page 13.

ROBERT ALTMAN (1925–   ) Probably the most intriguing offbeat Hollywood director of the early 70's and the man responsible for one of the cinema's funniest and most successful anti-war movies (*M*A*S*H*, 1970), Altman turned his considerable talents toward commercial films after six years making industrial movies in his home town (Kansas City, Missouri) and more than a decade directing such popular TV series as *Bonanza* and *The Millionaire*. **Credits include:** *Countdown* (1968), *Brewster McCloud* (1970), *McCabe and Mrs. Miller* (1971), *Images* (1972), *The Long Goodbye* (1973), *Thieves Like Us* (1974).

LINDSAY ANDERSON (1923–   ) An influential film critic, the most outspoken founder of Britain's free cinema movement of the 50's and among the most influential and individualistic of British documentarists, Anderson has made three feature films to date—*This Sporting Life* (1963), *If . . .* (1968) and *Oh Lucky Man!* (1973). The first two won Cannes Festival Grand Prix. Besides his work in films Anderson has had an equally successful career as a stage director long associated with London's Royal Court Theatre. **Documentaries include:** *O Dreamland* (1954), *Thursday's Children* (Academy Award, 1954), *Every Day Except Christmas* (Venice Grand Prix, 1957), *The White Bus* (1967), *The Singing Lesson* (1968).

MICHAEL ANDERSON (1920–   ) A native Londoner who broke into films as a bit player at the Elstree Studios and got some of his training as assistant to director Anthony Asquith, Anderson went on to become a specialist in suspense pictures like *Chase a Crooked Shadow* (1958) and *The Quiller Memorandum* (1966). His first feature (co-directed by Peter Ustinov) was *Private Angelo* (1949) and his first resounding success *Around the World in 80 Days* (1956). **Films include:** *The Dam Busters* (1955), *The Wreck of the Mary Deare* (1959), *Shake Hands With the Devil* (1959), *Operation Crossbow* (1965), *The Shoes of the Fisherman* (1968), *Pope Joan* (1971).

KEN ANNAKIN (1914–   ) The director of extravaganzas like *The Longest Day* (1962) and *Those Magnificent Men in Their Flying Machines* (1965), Annakin worked in journalism, the theatre and on documentaries in his native England before making his first feature, *Holiday Camp*, in 1946. **Credits include:** *Miranda* (1949), *The Planter's Wife* (1952), *The Battle of the Bulge* (1965), *The Long Duel* (1967), *The Playroom* (1970).

MICHELANGELO ANTONIONI (1912–   ) A film critic from the late 30's and an assistant director and documentarist from the early 40's, he made his first feature, *Cronaca di un Amore*, in 1950 and found a wide following in his native Italy with the languid and fatalistic *Le Amiche* (1955). In the early 60's he featured Monica Vitti in *L'Avventura* (1960), *La Notte* (1960) and *L'Eclisse* (1962)—a melancholic trilogy on women which secured his international reputation and marked him as a formidable interpreter of the seemingly aimless modern bourgeois world. **Highlights:** *Il Grido* (1957), *The Red Desert* (1964), *Blow-Up* (1966), *Zabriskie Point* (1970).

JACK ARNOLD (1916–   ) A film director with Universal from 1952 and later one of their busiest TV director-producers, this former stage actor was most active in films during the 50's, directing such ghoulish sci-fi tales as *It Came From Outer Space* (1953), *Tarantula* (1955) and *The Incredible Shrinking Man* (1957). His sole excursion outside the realm of ''B''s was the British-made comedy *The Mouse That Roared* (1959). **Credits include:** *The Glass Web* (1953), *The Creature From the Black Lagoon* (1954), *The Revenge of the Creature* (1955), *The Lively Set* (1964).

ANTHONY ASQUITH (1902–1968) The son of a Prime Minister, Asquith brought a new dimension to the British film industry by his skillful direction of contemporary dramas, many of them plays by Terence Rattigan. *The Winslow Boy* (1948) and *The Importance of Being Earnest* (1962) are two of the many highlights of his career. **Other credits include:** *Underground* (1929), *Pygmalion* (1938), *The Way to the Stars* (1945), *The Millionairess* (1961), *The VIP's* (1963), *The Yellow Rolls-Royce* (1964).

CLAUDE AUTANT-LARA (1903–   ) He broke into films as a set and costume designer during the 20's, made several shorts and forgotten features and finally earned wider attention as the director of such delicate love stories as *Le Mariage de Chiffon* (1942) and *Douce* (1942). Five years later he made what remains his best work, *Le Diable au Corps*. With the exceptions of *En Cas de Malheur* (1957) and *Non Uccidere* (1961), most of his later movies have been somewhat stolid versions of literary classics. **Credits include:** *Ciboulette* (1933), *L'Auberge Rouge* (1951), *Le Rouge et le Noir* (1954), *The Count of Monte Cristo* (1961), *The Woman in White* (1965), *Les Patates* (1969).

B

LLOYD BACON (1889–1955) A vaudeville actor during his early days in show business, Bacon played in several Chaplin shorts before directing the first of his numerous two-reel comedies for Mack Sennett in 1921. He is best remembered for lavish Depression-era musicals that were made memorable by the choreography of Busby Berkeley—e.g., *Footlight Parade* (1933), *42nd Street* (1933) and *Gold Diggers of 1937* (1937). **Credits include:** *The Singing Fool* (1938), *A Slight Case of Murder* (1938), *Brother Orchid* (1940), *Action in the North Atlantic* (1943), *The Sullivans* (1944), *The Great Sioux Uprising* (1953).

WILLIAM BEAUDINE (1892–   ) A veteran of more than half a century in films, Beaudine has directed hundreds of movies, from silents like *Sparrows* (1926) through numerous episodes of *The Bowery Boys* during the 40's and 50's to Saturday-afternoon second features like *Lassie's Great Adventure* (1963) and *Billy the Kid Versus Dracula* (1966). **Highlights:** *Penrod and Sam* (1923), *Misbehaving Ladies* (1930), *Kidnapped* (1948), *Westward Ho! the Wagons* (1956).

HARRY BEAUMONT (1893–1966) A director of silents from Hollywood's early days, Beaumont made such popular features as *Beau Brummell* (1924), *Babbitt* (1924) and *Our Dancing Daughters* (1928). He also directed the screen's first musical, *Broadway Melody* (1929), several other early talkies and a handful of lightweight films of the mid-40's. **Credits include:** *A Man and His Money* (1919), *Enchanted April* (1935), *Twice Blessed* (1945), *Up Goes Maisie* (1946), *Maisie Goes to Reno* (1946), *The Show-Off* (1947).

LASLO BENEDEK (1907–   ) His only notable films were made early in his directorial career—a fine 1951 version of Arthur Miller's *Death of a Salesman* and the early Brando vehicle, *The Wild One* (1954). Benedek entered the film industry in Hungary as a cameraman, worked as a script writer in England (1935–37) and as an assistant to Joe Pasternak before directing his first film, *The Kissing Bandit* (1948), in Hollywood. **Credits include:** *Moment of Danger* (1958), *Namu, the Killer Whale* (1966), *Salem Come to Supper* (1970), *The Night Visitor* (1970).

JEAN BENOIT–LEVY (1888–1959) A pioneer of the semi-documentary feature film (he made *Pasteur* with Jean Epstein in 1922), this talented Parisian devoted most of his energies to developing educational films. Besides some 400 educational

shorts produced between 1920 and 1940 in France and his later work for UNESCO, he also made occasional fictional features with Marie Epstein. **Credits include:** *La Maternelle* (1933), *Hélène* (1936), *La Mort du Cygne* (1937), *Altitude 3200* (1937).

INGMAR BERGMAN (1918–   ) His films deal with crises of the human spirit, and the Swedish director is generally ranked with Griffith as one of the greatest innovators and artists in film history. His pictures are heavy with symbolism, mystical in theme and have just one element in common: the camera work is invariably dazzling. Bergman's own company includes such illustrious performers as Max von Sydow, Bibi Andersson, Liv Ullmann and Ingrid Thulin. **A long list of distinguished films includes:** *Crisis* (1945), *Smiles of a Summer Night* (1955), *The Seventh Seal* (1956), *Wild Strawberries* (1957), *The Magician* (1958), *Through a Glass Darkly* (1961), *Persona* (1966), *The Touch* (1972), *Cries and Whispers* (1973).

BUSBY BERKELEY (1895–   ) The acknowledged king of the super-duper musical extravaganza, he came to Hollywood after years on Broadway as a choreographer, producer and impresario. His production numbers, with their mind-boggling stage sets and regiments of chorus girls and boys dancing or swimming with military precision, made classics of such Warner Brothers films as *42nd Street*, *Gold Diggers* of 1933, 1935 and 1937. **Other credits:** *Babes in Arms* (1939), *For Me and My Gal* (1942), *The Gang's All Here* (1943), *Jumbo* (1962).

CURTIS BERNHARDT (1899–   ) A former actor–director of the Berlin theatre, this German-born film-maker came to Hollywood after a year in France (1935) and five (1935–40) in England. Although most of his later career has been spent making heavy melodramas, he did direct the 1945 thriller *Conflict*, starring Humphrey Bogart and Sidney Greenstreet. **Films include:** *Beloved Vagabond* (1937), *Million Dollar Baby* (1941), *The Merry Widow* (1952), *Miss Sadie Thompson* (1953), *Gaby* (1956), *Kisses for My President* (1964).

BERNARDO BERTOLUCCI (1941–   ) The young director of the highly controversial *Last Tango in Paris* (1973) is considered a richly talented film-maker. He first gained notice at age 23 with his second feature, *Before the Revolution* (1964), and has since combined his artistry with a highly developed political and social consciousness. **Credits include:** *La Commare Secca* (debut, 1962), *Partner* (1968), *The Conformist* (1970).

BUDD BOETTICHER (1916–   ) He has a way with Westerns and action pictures that won him a devoted following. He began his busy film career putting his knowledge of bullfighting to use as technical adviser on Mamoulian's 1941 version of Ibanez' *Blood and Sand* and first gained notice as a director with another tale of the bullring, *The Bullfighter and the Lady* (1951). Outstanding is *Seven Men From Now* (1956), the first of three films he made starring Randolph Scott. **More than 30 credits include:** *One Mysterious Night* (debut, 1944), *Seminole* (1953), *The Magnificent Matador* (1955), *Decision at Sundown* (1957), *The Rise and Fall of Legs Diamond* (1960), *A Time for Dying* (1969).

Busby Berkeley's Gold Diggers of 1935 *(1935)*

Bernardo Bertolucci's Last Tango in Paris *(1973)*

PETER BOGDANOVICH (1939–   ) A former film critic and movie devotee, Bogdanovich has directed several notable films, all imbued with the atmosphere of movies of earlier days. After a virtually unnoticed directorial debut with *Targets* (1968), Bogdanovich was hailed as a master by many with his next film, the enormously popular *The Last Picture Show* (1971), a look at life in a dying Texas town. **Other films:** *What's Up, Doc?* (1972), *Paper Moon* (1973), *Daisy Miller* (1974).

SERGE BONDARCHUK (1920–   ) This native Ukrainian first gained prominence after World War II as one of Russia's finest screen actors and the intense hero of such films as *Story of a Real Man* (1948) and *Othello* (1955). He made his debut as a director with *Destiny of a Man* (1959) and won worldwide acclaim for his four-part, eight-hour version of Tolstoy's *War and Peace* (1964–67). **Other credits:** *Waterloo* (1970).

508

Luis Buñuel's The Discreet Charm of the Bourgeoisie *(1972)*

Michael Cacoyannis' Zorba the Greek *(1965)*

Frank Capra's It Happened One Night *(1934)*

FRANK BORZAGE (1893–1962) A onetime coal miner and actor, Borzage began his long film-making career shortly after World War I and came to prominence as a director of gentle, romantic films during the late 20's and 30's. Two of his movies won Academy Awards, the World War I romance *Seventh Heaven* (1927) and the early talkie *Bad Girl* (1932). **Credits include:** *Ashes of Desire* (1919), *Lazybones* (1925), *The River* (1929), *A Man's Castle* (1933), *Little Man, What Now?* (1934), *Three Comrades* (1938), *Till We Meet Again* (1944), *China Doll* (1958), *The Big Fisherman* (1959).

JOHN BOULTING and ROY BOULTING (1914–   ) Since they founded Charter Film Productions in 1937, these twin brothers have been busy sharing the tasks of producing and directing some 35 films ranging from serious dramas to irreverent comedy lampoons. Roy's best work includes the documentaries *Desert Victory* (1943) and *Tunisian Victory* (1944), while John was responsible for *Brighton Rock* (1947), *I'm All Right, Jack* (1959) and *Rotten to the Core* (1965). **Other films:** John—*Journey Together* (debut, 1945), *Seven Days to Noon* (1950), *Heaven's Above* (1963); Roy—*Thunder Rock* (1942), *The Family Way* (1966), *There's a Girl in My Soup* (1970).

ROBERT BRESSON (1907–   ) His films are character studies focusing on the spiritual and reflecting the Catholic concept of redemption through suffering and humiliation. Bresson is one of France's most highly regarded directors, and his pictures, since his early success, *Les Dames du Bois de Boulogne* (1945), have been skilled and graceful illustrations of a style that has changed little over the years. He started out as an assistant director in the 30's and made his first feature film, *Les Anges du Péché*, in 1943. **Films include:** *Au Hasard, Balthasar* (1956), *Pickpocket* (1959), *Mouchette* (1967), *Une Femme Douce* (1969), *Quatre Nuits d'un Rêveur* (1971).

PETER BROOK (1925–   ) Known primarily as one of Britain's leading and innovative theatre directors, Brook has also directed several ambitious film projects, the most successful of them his 1962 version of William Golding's *Lord of the Flies*. **Credits include:** *The Beggar's Opera* (debut, 1952), *Moderato Cantabile* (1960), *Marat/Sade* (1966), *Tell Me Lies* (1967), *King Lear* (1970).

MEL BROOKS (1926–   ) He made his name during the 50's as a TV comedy writer and broke into films via an Academy Award-winning cartoon, *The Critic* (1963). **Credits include:** *The Producers* (1968), *The Twelve Chairs* (1970), *Blazing Saddles* (1973).

RICHARD BROOKS (1912–   ) A broadcaster and journalist in his pre-Hollywood days, Brooks was a script-writer during the 40's before being assigned the dual tasks of writing and directing his first film *Crisis* (1950). He is responsible for a series of well-received hits including *Elmer Gantry* (1960)—he won an Oscar for its screenplay—and the screen adaptations of Tennessee Williams' *Cat On a Hot Tin Roof* (1958) and *Sweet Bird of Youth* (1962). **Films include:** *The Last Time I Saw Paris* (1954), *The Blackboard Jungle* (1955), *The Brothers Karamazov* (1958), *In Cold Blood* (1967), *The Happy Ending* (1969).

CLARENCE BROWN (1890–   ) The director of some of Greta Garbo's most memorable films, Brown started out working on silents as an aide to Maurice Tourner. He soon was directing some of the leading stars of the day, including Rudolph Valentino in *The Eagle* (1925), Norma Talmadge in *Kiki* (1926) and then Garbo in the silent *Flesh and the Devil* (1927). **Films include:** *Anna Christie* (1930), *Anna Karenina* (1935), *Ah! Wilderness* (1935), *Conquest* (1937), *National Velvet* (1944), *The Yearling* (1947), *Intruder in the Dust* (1949), *When in Rome* (1952).

TOD BROWNING (1882–1962) He came to Hollywood as an actor, worked as Griffith's assistant on *Intolerance* (1916) and directed his first film in 1917. Within a short time he found his niche making horror films and went on to establish both Lon Chaney and later Bela Lugosi as household words during his 15-year heyday as the master of the grotesque. **Highlights:** *Jim Bludso* (debut, 1917), *The Wicked Darling* (1919), *The Unholy Three* (1925), *The Blackbird* (1926), *The Unknown* (1927), *Where East Is East* (1929), *Dracula* (1931), *Freaks* (1932), *Mark of the Vampire* (1935), *Miracles for Sale* (1939).

LUIS BUÑUEL (1900–   ) Although a storm of controversy has centered around Buñuel's work from his earliest days as a director, few would question this uncompromising Spaniard's place among cinema's greats. From his first surrealistic and often blasphemous films he provoked equal measures of protest and enthusiasm. He has worked in France, Mexico and the United States, but his films consistently reflect his preoccupation with Spanish cultural heritage. **Films include:** *Gran Casino* (1947), *El Gran Calavero* (1949), *Los Olvidados* (1950), *Susana* (1950), *El* (1952), *La Mort en ce Jardin* (1956), *Nazarin* (1959), *The Young One* (1960), *Viridiana* (1961), *Diary of a Chambermaid* (1964), *La Voie Lactée* (1968).

DAVID BUTLER (1894–   ) A long-time director of Hollywood staples, Butler has made some five dozen films from *High School Hero* (1927) to *C'mon Let's Live a Little* (1967). **Credits include:** *Sunny Side Up* (1929), *The Little Colonel* (1935), *Road to Morocco* (1942), *My Wild Irish Rose* (1947), *Lullaby of Broadway* (1951), *Calamity Jane* (1953).

EDWARD BUZZELL (1897–   ) He started out as a musical-comedy star, went to Hollywood as an actor and ended up a film director whose credits include two Marx Brothers comedies, *At the Circus* (1939) and *Go West* (1941). **Other films:** *The Big Time* (1932), *Ship Ahoy* (1942), *Neptune's Daughter* (1949), *Ain't Misbehaving* (1955).

C

MICHAEL CACOYANNIS (1922–   ) One of Greece's most popular and best directors, Cacoyannis achieved his first international success with *Zorba the Greek* (1965). **Films include:** *Windfall in Athens* (1953), *Stella* (1954), *A Girl in Black* (1955), *Elektra* (1961), *The Trojan Women* (1971).

FRANK CAPRA (1897–   ) The director of fast-paced, sophisticated comedies of the 30's, including the Oscar-winning *It Happened One Night* (1934), Sicilian-born Capra began in films as an assistant for Hal Roach and had his first success when he wrote and directed the first of two Harry Langdon films: *The Strong Man* (1926) and *Long Pants* (1927). **Credits include:** *Ladies of Leisure* (1930), *American Madness* (1932), *The Bitter Tea of General Yen* (1933), *Mr. Deeds Goes to Town* (1936), *Lost Horizon* (1937), *You Can't Take It With You* (1938), *Mr. Smith Goes to Washington* (1939), *Arsenic and Old Lace* (1944), *Here Comes the Groom* (1951).

MARCEL CARNÉ (1909–   ) Carné did his finest work in the late 30's and 40's when he worked in collaboration with Jacques Prévert. Together they made the memorable *Le Jour se Lève* (1939) and the mysterious *Les Enfants du Paradis* (1945). Carné's later films largely differed in style from his early symbolism-heavy works. **Film highlights:** *Jenny* (debut, 1936), *Quai des Brumes* (1938), *Les Visiteurs du Soir* (1941), *Thérèse Racquin* (1953), *Les Jeunes Loups* (1968), *Les Assassins de l'Ordre* (1971).

JOHN CASSAVETES (1929–   ) Best known for his outstanding work as an independent film-maker during the 60's, actor-director Cassavetes has also done several less successful films for Hollywood—e.g., *Too Late Blues* (1961) and *A Child Is Born* (1962). For directorial and performing credits see entry on page 84.

ALBERTO CAVALCANTI (1897–   ) Cavalcanti started out in Paris as the director of avant-garde silents including *Rien que les Heures* (1927) and *En Rade* (1927) and then went to England to work on documentaries and to help develop sound. Later, he directed feature films for Ealing Studios, including *Dead of Night* (1945) with Hamer and *Nicholas Nickleby* (1947). In Brazil he did *O Canto do Mar* (1949) and a few years later was back in Europe doing *Herr Puntila und sein Knecht* (1955), an East German film, and *Les Noces Venitiennes* (1959) in Italy. **Films include:** *They Made Me a Fugitive* (1947), *For Them That Trespass* (1950), *Yerma* (1962).

CLAUDE CHABROL (1930–   ) A prolific director, Chabrol was at the forefront of the "new wave" of French film-makers in the late 50's and early 60's. His films are powerful studies of emotions and relationships. Critics rate *Le Boucher* (1969), the story of a grisly murder in a provincial French town, as Chabrol's best. **Films include:** *Le Beau Serge* (1958), *Les Cousins* (1958), *Le Scandale* (1966), *La Femme Infidèle* (1968), *Les Biches* (1968), *La Rupture* (1970), *Wedding in Blood* (1974).

CHARLES CHAPLIN See entry on page 88.

RENÉ CLAIR (1898–   ) The first film-maker ever admitted to the prestigious French Academy, Clair has worked in both England and the United States, but his best films are those he made in his native land. His career has spanned both the silent and sound eras, and his pictures are distinguished by their visual beauty and his expertise with light comedy. **Films include:** *Sous les Toits de Paris* (1929), *Le Million* (1931), *I Married a Witch* (1942), *Le Silence est d'Or* (1946), *Les Fêtes Galantes* (1965).

JACK CLAYTON (1921–   ) The British producer-director most recently responsible for the lavish Hollywood version of F. Scott Fitzgerald's *The Great Gatsby* (1974), Clayton made his name as director of *Room at the Top* (1958), prototype for a decade of British films. **Films include:** *The Innocents* (1961), *The Pumpkin Eater* (1963), *Our Mother's House* (1967).

RENÉ CLÉMENT (1913–   ) A passion for detail and a devotion to realism characterize Clement's pictures. He started out as a cameraman and documentary film-maker and earned international recognition with his first feature, *La Bataille du Rail* (1945). *Gervaise* (1955), a screen adaptation of Zola's *L'Assommoir*, is considered Clement's masterpiece. **Films include:** *Jeux Interdits* (1952), *The Knave of Hearts* (1954), *Is Paris Burning?* (1966), *Rider in the Rain* (1969).

EDWARD CLINE (1892–1961) Best-remembered as the director of the W. C. Fields classics *My Little Chickadee* (1940), *The Bank Dick* (1940) and *Never Give a Sucker an Even Break* (1941), Cline worked in both silent and sound films and always made comedies. He started out as one of Mack Sennett's Keystone Cops, then directed comedy shorts and some Buster Keaton episodes. **Films include:** *Circus Day* (1923), *Let It Rain* (1927), *Peck's Bad Boy* (1934), *See My Lawyer* (1945), *Bringing Up Father* (1946).

HENRI-GEORGES CLOUZOT (1907–   ) Long known in his native France as a master of psychologically motivated chillers and suspenseful detective stories, Clouzot gained a wide audience in the United States with his grisly *Les Diaboliques* (1955). A few years later he copped an Academy Award as writer and director of *The Truth* (1960). **Other films include:** *Le Corbeau* (1943), *Quai des Orfèvres* (1947), *Manon* (1949), *Le Salaire de la Peur* (1953), *Le Mystère Picasso* (1956).

JEAN COCTEAU (1889–1963) One of the most versatile of France's modern creative talents, Cocteau was a poet, dramatist, novelist, actor, painter and film-maker. His films range in style from the fantasy *La Belle et la Bête* (1946) to the family study *Les Parents Terribles* (1948) to the mythological *Orphée* (1949), which is regarded as his masterpiece. **Other films:** *Le Sang d'un Poète* (1930), *L'Aigle à Deux Têtes* (1947), *Le Testament d'Orphée* (1959).

JACK CONWAY (1887–1952) He got his start with film pioneer D. W. Griffith and went on to direct both silent and sound films. Conway worked principally for MGM. **Credits include:** *The Old Armchair* (debut, 1912), *Viva Villa!* (1934), *A Tale of Two Cities* (1935), *A Yank at Oxford* (1938), *Honky Tonk* (1941), *Julia Misbehaves* (1948).

FRANCIS FORD COPPOLA (1939–   ) He shared an Academy Award with novelist Mario Puzo for their screen adaptation of Puzo's best-seller *The Godfather* (1972). Coppola also directed the fabulously successful box-office hit. **Other films:** *Dementia 13* (1963), *You're a Big Boy Now* (1967), *Finian's Rainbow* (1968), *The Rain People* (1969), *The Conversation* (1974).

ROGER CORMAN (1926–   ) For a while during the 50's this former literary agent turned writer-director-producer was called the king of the

René Clair's The Ghost Goes West *(1936)*

Jack Clayton's Room at the Top *(1958)*

Francis Ford Coppola's The Godfather *(1972)*

Henri Costa-Gavras' Z *(1968)*

George Cukor's The Philadelphia Story *(1940)*

Michael Curtiz' Casablanca *(1942)*

''B''s because he ground out so many horror films and action dramas so fast. Corman's reputation began to improve with *The Fall of the House of Usher* (1960), and since then he has been taken more seriously. **Credits include:** *The Intruder* (1961), *The Wild Angels* (1966), *The St. Valentine's Day Massacre* (1967), *Bloody Mama* (1970).

HENRY CORNELIUS (1913–1958) Although many of his films were indifferent, he did direct two of Britain's most popular comedy hits, *Passport to Pimlico* (debut, 1949) and *Genevieve* (1954). Born in South Africa, Cornelius studied film-making in Germany and France before signing on as an associate producer and writer at Ealing Studios. **Credits include:** *The Galloping Major* (1951), *I Am a Camera* (1955), *Law and Disorder* (1958).

HENRI COSTA-GAVRAS (1933–   ) He made his international reputation as a director with a series of political protest films. He attacked the right-wing military government of his native Greece in *Z* (1968), turned his attention to Communist oppression in Eastern Europe in *The Confession* (1970) and looked at American intervention in South America in *State of Siege* (1973). **Other credits:** *The Sleeping Car Murders* (1965), *Un Homme de Top* (1967), *L' Aveu* (1970).

CHARLES CRICHTON (1910–   ) As a director for England's Ealing Studios during the 40's and 50's, this former film editor turned out a series of successful films, including the perennially popular *Hue and Cry* (1947) and *The Lavender Hill Mob* (1951). He has also directed extensively for television. **Films include:** *For Those in Peril* (1944), *The Titfield Thunderbolt* (1953), *Battle of the Sexes* (1959), *He Who Rides a Tiger* (1965, U.S. 1968).

JOHN CROMWELL (1888–   ) A onetime actor and stage producer, Cromwell directed some of Hollywood's most popular films during the 30's and 40's, including such screen classics as *Of Human Bondage* (1934), *The Prisoner of Zenda* (1937), *The Enchanted Cottage* (1945) and *Anna and the King of Siam* (1946). **Film highlights:** *The Racket* (1928), *Little Lord Fauntleroy* (1936), *Algiers* (1938), *Abe Lincoln in Illinois* (1939), *Dead Reckoning* (1947), *Caged* (1950), *The Goddess* (1958), *A Matter of Morals* (1961).

ALAN CROSLAND (1894–1936) He secured his place in screen history by directing *Don Juan* (1926), the first film with synchronized music, and *The Jazz Singer* (1927), the first talking picture. **More than 30 films include:** *Under the Red Robe* (1923), *The Beloved Rogue* (1927), *Weekends Only* (1932), *The Great Impersonation* (1935).

JAMES CRUZE (1884–1942) A versatile and popular director of silents from 1918, Cruze made his mark with one of the early screen spectaculars, *The Covered Wagon* (1923). Although he directed into the late 30's, he had far less success with sound films. **Other credits:** *Ruggles of Red Gap* (1923), *Hollywood* (1923), *The Pony Express* (1925), *Beggars on Horseback* (1925), *The Great Gabbo* (1929), *Sutter's Gold* (1936).

GEORGE CUKOR (1899–   ) The director of stylish comedies, Cukor is best known for his work on some of Katharine Hepburn's most popular films, including *A Bill of Divorcement* (1932), *The Philadelphia Story* (1940) and *Adam's Rib* (1949). His reputation is as a director especially adept at drawing fine performances from actresses, and he has worked with some of the best—Greta Garbo in *Camille* (1937), Judy Garland in *A Star Is Born* (1954) and Sophia Loren in *Heller in Pink Tights* (1960). Cukor won an Academy Award for directing *My Fair Lady* (1964). **Pictures include:** *Dinner at Eight* (1933), *Little Women* (1933), *David Copperfield* (1935), *The Women* (1939), *Gaslight* (1944), *Born Yesterday* (1950), *Les Girls* (1957), *The Chapman Report* (1962).

IRVING CUMMINGS (1888–1959) During his more than 30 years in Hollywood, Cummings directed a long list of both silent and sound films. He started out as an actor but by the mid-20's was directing such pictures as *The Desert Flower* (1925) and *The Johnstown Flood* (1926). **Films include:** *In Old Arizona* (1929), *Hollywood Cavalcade* (1939), *The Dolly Sisters* (1945), *Double Dynamite* (1951).

MICHAEL CURTIZ (1888–1962) In a long career as a director for Warner Brothers, Curtiz made scores of popular and well-received films, including *Casablanca* (1942), for which he won an Academy Award. He started his film career in his native Hungary and came to Hollywood in the late 20's. He directed most of Erroll Flynn's adventure films in the late 30's, among them *Captain Blood* (1935) and *Angels With Dirty Faces* (1938). **Other Curtiz films include:** *Cabin in the Cotton* (1932), *Front Page Woman* (1935), *The Private Lives of Elizabeth and Essex* (1939), *Yankee Doodle Dandy* (1942), *Passage to Marseilles* (1944), *Mildred Pierce* (1945), *The Jazz Singer* (1952), *White Christmas* (1954), *The Helen Morgan Story* (1957), *The Comancheros* (1962).

D

JULES DASSIN (1912–   ) When Senator Joseph McCarthy was looking for Communists in Hollywood in the early 50's the politically outspoken Dassin left town to film in Europe. Before his departure, however, he had directed shorts for MGM and several features, including one of his best-known works, *Naked City* (1948). Dassin's more recent films have starred his wife, Greek actress Melina Mercouri, and include *Never on Sunday* (1960), *Topkapi* (1964) and *Promise at Dawn* (1970). **Other credits:** *Nazi Agent* (1942), *Brute Force* (1947), *Thieves' Highway* (1949), *He Who Must Die* (1958), *Phaedra* (1962), *Up Tight* (1968).

DELMER DAVES (1904–   ) The popular and patriotic *Destination Tokyo* (1944) was Daves' first film. He was a commercial artist, an engineer and an actor before he became a successful writer-producer-director of films. Among his long list of credits is *Broken Arrow* (1950), one of the first films that allowed Indians to be the good guys. **Other films include:** *Hollywood Canteen* (1944), *Dark Passage* (1947), *3:10 to Yuma* (1957), *Kings Go Forth* (1958), *Parrish* (1961), *Youngblood Hawke* (1964), *The Battle of Fiorita* (1965).

BASIL DEARDEN (1911–1971) Another actor turned director, Britisher Dearden became a specialist in pictures dealing with social issues and was the director of such films as *Sapphire* (1958), which treated a racial theme, and *Victim* (1962), about homosexuality. He started out with Ealing Studios as a director of Will Hay comedies and later collaborated with Michael Relph on producing, directing and writing. **Films include:** *The Blue Lamp* (1951), *The League of Gentlemen* (1959), *Khartoum* (1966), *Assassination Bureau* (1968), *The Man Who Haunted Himself* (1970).

PHILIPPE DE BROCA (1935–   ) A onetime aide to Claude Chabrol and François Truffaut, Paris-born De Broca made his debut as a director with *The Love Game* (1960) and has since demonstrated his adeptness at sophisticated comedy and sexual satire. **Films include:** *The Joker* (1960), *The Five-Day Lover* (1961), *Cartouche* (1964), *The Man From Rio* (1964), *La Poudre d'Escampette* (1970).

ROY DEL RUTH (1895–1961) A onetime gag writer for Mack Sennett, Del Ruth directed silent and sound films ranging from *Wolf's Clothing* (1927) to 30's musicals like *On the Avenue* (1937) and the thriller *Phantom of the Rue Morgue* (1954). His best-known picture is the comedy *Kid Millions* (1934). **Other films include:** *The Maltese Falcon* (1931), *Lady Killer* (1934), *Born to Dance* (1936), *The West Point Story* (1950).

CECIL B. DE MILLE (1881–1959) His name is so firmly identified with multimillion-dollar Biblical extravaganzas like *The Ten Commandments* (1923 and 1956) that it is frequently forgotten that he originally made his reputation with a series of sophisticated silent comedies. De Mille made more than 200 films during his 60-year career in Hollywood, many of them enormously popular. Audiences relished his adept combination of sex, violence, drama and religion. Although critics often dismiss the merit of his films, De Mille was an acknowledged giant of the film industry. **Films include:** *Fool's Paradise* (1921), *King of Kings* (1927), *The Squaw Man* (1931), *The Plainsman* (1937), *The Greatest Show on Earth* (1952).

JACQUES DEMY (1931–   ) The director of the innovative musical, *The Umbrellas of Cherbourg* (1964), in which all the dialogue is sung, French-born Demy makes films that are usually light and eye-pleasing. He made his directorial debut with *Lola* (1960), starring Anouk Aimée. **Credits include:** *La Baie des Anges* (1963), *Les Demoiselles de Rochefort* (1966), *Model Shop* (1968), *Peau d'Ane* (1970).

VITTORIO DE SICA (1902–   ) Actor and director, Italian De Sica is most respected for his post-World War II films—neo-realistic studies of life in war-torn Italy which include the Academy Award winner *The Bicycle Thief* (1949), *Miracle in Milan* (1950) and *Umberto D* (1952). For a decade after the poignant *Two Women* (1960) his films were more commercial and less memorable. **Films include:** *Sciuscià* (1946), *Gold of Naples* (1954), *Yesterday, Today and Tomorrow* (1964), *After the Fox* (1966), *The Garden of the Finzi Continis* (1971).

ANDRE DE TOTH (1900–   ) His most memorable film is *House of Wax* (1953), the first three-dimensional picture from a major studio. Hungarian-born De Toth has worked in Hollywood since he emmigrated from Europe in 1940, making mostly routine films. **Credits include:** *Passport to Suez* (1945), *Springfield Rifle* (1952), *Monkey on My Back* (1957), *Gold for the Caesars* (1962).

WILLIAM DIETERLE (1893–   ) Former actor Dieterle began directing in his native Germany before coming to the United States in the 30's. Early in his Hollywood career he established himself as director of biographical pictures like *The Story of Louis Pasteur* (1936) and *The Life of Emile Zola* (1937). Later he did melodramas—among them *Portrait of Jennie* (1949) and *Elephant Walk* (1954). In the late 50's he returned to Germany. **Other credits:** *Faust* (1926), *Grand Slam* (1932), *Madame Du Barry* (1934), *A Midsummer Night's Dream* (with Max Reinhardt, 1935), *All That Money Can Buy* (1941), *Peking Express* (1951).

EDWARD DMYTRYK (1908–   ) Another victim of the witchhunts conducted by Senator Joseph McCarthy, Dmytryk was fired by RKO because of alleged Communist sympathies. He had started out as a director of suspense features like *Farewell My Lovely* (1944), and after he cleared himself of contempt-of-Congress charges he resumed his career. **Films include:** *Crossfire* (1947), *The Caine Mutiny* (1954), *Raintree County* (1957), *The Young Lions* (1958), *A Walk on the Wild Side* (1962), *Alvarez Kelly* (1965), *Anzio* (1968).

STANLEY DONEN (1924–   ) The co-director of the Gene Kelly musicals, *On the Town* (1949) and *Singin' in the Rain* (1952), Donen later specialized in slick, light comedies—*Once More With Feeling* (1959) and *Surprise Package* (1960). Two of his more recent hits were the popular mystery-comedy-romance *Charade* (1963) and the breezy marital melodrama *Two for the Road* (1967). **Highlights:** *Royal Wedding* (1951), *Seven Brides for Seven Brothers* (1954), *Funny Face* (1957), *The Pajama Game* (1957), *Damn Yankees* (1958), *Arabesque* (1966), *Bedazzled* (1967).

MARK DONSKOI (1901–   ) After more than a decade as a film-maker Donskoi attracted national attention for his brilliant evocation of Tsarist Russia in the trilogy *The Childhood of Maxim Gorki* (1938), *My Apprenticeship* (1939) and *My Universities* (1940). His later notable films include several adaptations of literary works —e.g., *The Rainbow* (1943), *A Village Schoolteacher* (1946) and *At a High Cost* (1959). **Other highlights:** *Mother* (1955), *A Mother's Devotion* (1966), *Chaliapin* (1970).

GORDON DOUGLAS (1909–   ) A onetime comedy writer for Hal Roach who worked on some 30 of the *Our Gang* series, Douglas has a long and varied, if not particularly notable, list of directorial credits dating from 1940. **Films include:** *Saps at Sea* (1940), *I Was a Communist for the FBI* (1951), *The Sins of Rachel Cade* (1961), *Tony Rome* (1967), *In Like Flint* (1967), *Barquero* (1970).

ALEXANDER DOVZHENKO (1894–1956) One of the greats of the Soviet film, Dovzhenko is considered an epic poet of the screen. His most famous film, *Earth* (1930), is a tapestry of life on a collective farm. His style combines realism and fantasy, but much of his work was inhibited by pressures from the Soviet government. **Films include:** *Zvenigora* (1928), *Arsenal* (1929), *Ivan* (1932), *Aerograd* (1935), *Shchors* (1939), *Life in Blossom* (1947).

CARL DREYER (1889–1968) A Danish director rated among the world's best film-makers,

Cecil B. De Mille's The Ten Commandments *(1956)*

Vittorio De Sica's The Bicycle Thief *(1949)*

William Dieterle's The Life of Emile Zola *(1937)*

Sergei Eisenstein's Ivan the Terrible: Part I *(1942–46)*

Federico Fellini's La Dolce Vita *(1959)*

Victor Fleming's Gone With the Wind *(1939)*

Dreyer is revered for *The Passion of Joan of Arc* (1928), one of the most beautiful films in the history of the cinema. **Other films include:** *Leaves From Satan's Book* (1919), *Love One Another* (1922), *Once Upon a Time* (1922), *Master of the House* (1925), *Vampyr* (1932), *Day of Wrath* (1943), *Ordet* (1955), *Gertrud* (1964).

JULIEN DUVIVIER (1896–1967) Although he continued to direct until the year of his death, Duvivier's best work was done in his native France during the mid-30's and includes *La Bandera* (1934), *Le Golem* (1935) and *Pépé le Moko* (1936). **Highlights:** *Le Prix du Sang* (debut, 1919), *La Belle Equipe* (1936), *Tales of Manhattan* (1942), *The Little World of Don Camillo* (1951), *Diabolically Yours* (1967).

ALAN DWAN (1885–) One of the most productive directors in American film history, Dwan has a list of more than 400 screen credits. He began in silents and directed Douglas Fairbanks' popular adventures between 1916 and 1923 and Gloria Swanson comedies, including *Manhandled* (1924) and *Stage Struck* (1925). His sound films are considered more routine, but there are scores of them. **Films include:** *Manhattan Madness* (1916), *Robin Hood* (1922), *The Iron Mask* (1929), *Heidi* (1937), *The Three Musketeers* (1939), *Brewster's Millions* (1945), *Hold Back the Night* (1956), *The Most Dangerous Man Alive* (1961).

E

BLAKE EDWARDS (1922–) He has written, produced and directed, and before making films created the popular TV series *Peter Gunn* and *Mr. Lucky*. Most of Edwards' movies are sophisticated comedies, including *Breakfast at Tiffany's* (1961), *The Pink Panther* (1964) and *A Shot in the Dark* (1964). **Highlights:** *Operation Petticoat* (1959), *The Great Race* (1965), *The Party* (1968), *Wild Rovers* (1971).

SERGEI EISENSTEIN (1898–1948) His contributions to film art are legendary and include the technique of montage—quick cuts or dissolves —which got worldwide exposure in his classic *Battleship Potemkin* (1925). Although he is considered one of the giant creative talents and theorists of the screen, Eisenstein directed only a few films, among them *Strike* (1924), *October* or *Ten Days That Shook the World* (1927), *Alexander Nevsky* (1938), *Ivan the Terrible Part I*, *Ivan the Terrible Part II* (1942–46).

F

JOHN FARROW (1904–1963) He emigrated from his native Australia to the United States, abandoned his career as a research scientist for motion pictures and wrote and directed scores of films, many of them popular action dramas. Farrow and his wife, Maureen O'Sullivan, were the parents of actress Mia Farrow. **Films include:** *War Lord* (1937), *Two Years Before the Mast* (1946), *Hondo* (1953), *John Paul Jones* (1959).

FEDERICO FELLINI (1920–) One of the most imitated and influential of modern directors, Fellini weaves fantasy and reality in films that explore the subconscious and study behavior without drawing conclusions or stating morals. He first worked in films as a scenarist during the 40's, got his first chance to direct in 1950 and won international recognition with *La Strada* (1954). **Credits include:** *Luci del Varieta* (1950), *I Vitelloni* (1953), *Nights of Cabiria* (1956), *La Dolce Vita* (1959), *Boccaccio '70* (1962), *8½* (1963), *Juliet of the Spirits* (1965), *Fellini Satyricon* (1969).

JACQUES FEYDER (1888–1948) He earned a reputation directing such silents as the classic 1928 adaptation of Zola's *Thérèse Racquin*. After a brief stint in Hollywood, where he directed Garbo in *The Kiss* (1929), he returned to his native France. Many of his later films starred his wife, Françoise Rosay, and his best work was *La Kermesse Héroïque* (1935). **Credits include:** *L'Atlantide* (1921), *Crainquebille* (1922), *Carmen* (1926), *Le Grand Jeu* (1934), *Knight With Armour* (1937).

ROBERT FLAHERTY (1884–1951) Although he frequently recorded life in the remote areas of the world as he thought it should be rather than how it was, he still ranks as one of film's great early documentarists. Flaherty's first success was *Nanook of the North* (1921), a study of the Eskimos. **Other credits include:** *Moana* (1925), *Tabu* (1929), *Man of Aran* (1934), *Elephant Boy* (1937), *Louisiana Story* (1948).

RICHARD FLEISHER (1916–) At his best creating violent crime films like *Compulsion* (1959), *The Boston Strangler* (1968) and *10 Rillington Place* (1970), Fleisher has directed such varied pictures as *20,000 Leagues Under the Sea* (1954) and *Doctor Dolittle* (1967). Fleisher began his directorial career in 1940 as production assistant at RKO. **Films include:** *So This Is New York* (1948), *The Narrow Margin* (1952), *The Vikings* (1952), *Che!* (1969), *Tora! Tora! Tora!* (1970).

VICTOR FLEMING (1883–1949) Although his major claim to fame was his award-winning direction of one of the screen's all-time blockbusters, *Gone With the Wind* (1939), Fleming was also responsible for other perennial audience favorites of the 30's and 40's. Fleming worked in silent films as a cameraman and an aide to D. W. Griffith before directing *When the Clouds Roll By* (1919). **Credits include:** *Red Dust* (1932), *Treasure Island* (1934), *Captains Courageous* (1937), *The Wizard of Oz* (1939), *Dr. Jekyll and Mr. Hyde* (1941), *Tortilla Flat* (1942), *Joan of Arc* (1948).

ROBERT FLOREY (1900–) A Parisian who went to Hollywood in 1921 and worked as Erich von Sternberg's assistant, Florey first directed silents and then did the first Marx Brothers comedy, *The Cocoanuts* (1929). After some 30 years in films he turned to directing for television in the 50's. **His films include:** *Le Rouge et le Noir* (1931), *Murders in the Rue Morgue* (1932), *Dangerous to Know* (1938), *Desert Song* (1943), *Johnny One-Eye* (1950).

BRYAN FORBES (1926–) First an actor, then a screenwriter for action films of the 50's, this native Londoner eventually became one of England's top movie and television director-producers. **Credits include:** *Whistle Down the Wind* (debut, 1961), *The L-Shaped Room* (1962),

Seance on a Wet Afternoon (1964), *King Rat* (1965), *The Wrong Box* (1966), *The Whisperers* (1967), *The Madwoman of Chaillot* (1969), *The Raging Moon* (1971).

JOHN FORD (1895–1973) During his 60 years in motion pictures, this masterful director compiled an impressive list of some 200 screen credits. His celebrated Westerns with their endless vistas emphasized themes of loyalty, courage and the pioneer spirit. Born Sean O'Fearna, he occasionally paid tribute to his Irish heritage with films like his *The Informer* (1935), *How Green Was My Valley* (1941) and *The Quiet Man* (1952). The first two of those films won him an Academy Award, as did *The Grapes of Wrath* (1940). **Credits include:** *Stagecoach* (1939), *Fort Apache* (1948), *What Price Glory?* (1952), *Mister Roberts* (1955), *The Last Hurrah* (1958), *Donovan's Reef* (1963), *Seven Women* (1965).

MILOS FORMAN (1932–   ) An acute observer of human foibles, Forman made his name in his native Czechoslovakia with a short, *Talent Competition* (1963), and first attracted international attention with *Loves of a Blond* (1965). **Films include:** *Peter and Paula* (1964), *The Fireman's Ball* (1967), *Taking Off* (1971).

BOB FOSSE (1927–   ) Winner of the Academy Award for the hit musical *Cabaret* (1972), Fosse went to Hollywood in the 50's from Broadway and worked first as a dancer and then as a choreographer and director. **Credits include:** *Give a Girl a Break* (1952), *Kiss Me Kate* (1953), *My Sister Eileen* (1955), *Sweet Charity* (1968).

GEORGES FRANJU (1912–   ) His best features have been eerie studies in terror—e.g., *La Tête Contre les Murs* (1958), *Eyes Without a Face* (1959) and *Judex* (1963). He first came to attention as a documentarist and the maker of the extremely powerful *Le Sang des Bêtes* (1949) and *Hôtel des Invalides* (1952). He also is noted as the co-founder of the invaluable film archives, the Cinémathèque Française. **Films include:** *Le Grand Méliès* (1951), *Thérèse Desqueyroux* (1962), *La Faute de l'Abbé Mouret* (TV, 1970).

JOHN FRANKENHEIMER (1930–   ) Frankenheimer was a successful director of TV dramas (*Studio One* and *Playhouse 90*) before he made his debut as a film director with *The Young Stranger* (1956). He often builds his films around bizarre situations—the brainwashing of a politician in *The Manchurian Candidate* (1962) and accidental nuclear attack in *Seven Days in May* (1964). His early films were considered better than his more recent big-budget efforts. **Films include:** *The Young Savages* (1961), *Birdman of Alcatraz* (1962), *Seconds* (1966), *Grand Prix* (1967), *The Fixer* (1968), *The Gypsy Moths* (1969), *The Horsemen* (1971).

SIDNEY FRANKLIN (1893–   ) A Hollywood pioneer who directed Mary Pickford, Norma Shearer and the Talmadge sisters back in the silent days, Franklin also made some of the big successes of the 30's before moving into the production end of the industry. **Films include:** *Jack and the Beanstalk* (1917), *Private Lives* (1931), *The Barrets of Wimpole Street* (1934), *The Good Earth* (1937), *Goodbye, Mr. Chips* (1939).

WILLIAM FRIEDKIN (1939–   ) A relative newcomer to Hollywood, Friedkin has scored two of the biggest film hits of the 70's. He won an Academy Award for directing *The French Connection* (1970) and was nominated for the record-breaking box-office success *The Exorcist* (1973). **Other screen credits include:** *The Night They Raided Minsky's* (1968), *The Birthday Party* (1968), *The Boys in the Band* (1970).

SIDNEY J. FURIE (1933–   ) A native of Toronto, Furie worked as a writer and director in films and television (e.g., the *Hudson's Bay* series) in Canada before moving to England in 1960 to pursue his career. His two major commercial successes have been *The Ipcress File* (1965), a spy thriller that launched Michael Caine's career, and *Lady Sings the Blues*, a semi-fictionalized account of blues singer Billy Holiday's life, starring Diana Ross. **Other credits:** *A Dangerous Age* (1957), *A Cool Sound From Hell* (1958), *The Young Ones* (1962), *The Leather Boys* (1963), *The Naked Runner* (1967), *Little Fauss and Big Halsey* (1970).

G

TAY GARNETT (1898–   ) He entered the motion-picture industry as a script writer for Hal Roach and directed his first film, *The Spieler*, in 1929. Since the 60's Garnett has concentrated on television. **Screen highlights:** *Her Man* (1930), *One Way Passage* (1930), *The Cross of Lorraine* (1943), *Bataan* (1943), *Mrs. Parkington* (1944), *The Postman Always Rings Twice* (1946), *Wild Harvest* (1947), *Main Street to Broadway* (1953), *The Night Fighters* (1960).

PIETRO GERMI (1914–   ) After more than 15 years as a film-maker Germi finally cashed in at the box office with *Divorce Italian Style* (1961). He has since followed its formula with several far less successful pictures. **Credits include:** *In the Name of the Law* (1949), *Man of Iron* (1956), *Seduced and Abandoned* (1963), *The Birds, the Bees and the Italians* (1965), *Le Castagne Sono Buone* (1971).

LEWIS GILBERT (1920–   ) A former child actor who began his film-making career as a documentarist, Gilbert directed some of the most popular British films of the 60's, including *Alfie* (1965) and *You Only Live Twice* (1967). **Credits include:** *The Little Ballerina* (1947), *The Sea Shall Not Have Them* (1954), *Sink the Bismarck!* (1960), *Greengage Summer* (1961), *The Adventurers* (1970).

JEAN-LUC GODARD (1930–   ) A former film critic with several shorts to his credit, Godard attained instant celebrity with his first feature, *Breathless* (1959). Through the mid-60's he held his place at the forefront of the "new wave" of French film-makers. Over the last few years, however, his Maoist polemics and increasingly diffuse style have made his films more interesting as political treatises than as coherent artistic works. **Credits include:** *Le Petit Soldat* (1960), *Vivre sa Vie* (1962), *Les Carabiniers* (1963), *Le Mépris* (1963), *Bande à Part* (1964), *Alphaville* (1965), *Masculin, Feminin* (1965), *Made in USA* (1966), *La Chinoise* (1967), *Weekend* (1967), *One Plus One* (1968).

MICHAEL GORDON (1909–   ) A director for both stage and screen, Gordon has a varied list of film credits, including the drama *Another Part of the Forest* (1948), the musical *I Can Get It for You*

John Ford's The Informer *(1935)*

Sidney Franklin's The Good Earth *(1937)*

William Friedkin's The Exorcist *(1973)*

D. W. Griffith's The Birth of a Nation *(1915)*

Howard Hawks' Sergeant York *(1941)*

George Roy Hill's Butch Cassidy and the Sundance Kid *(1969)*

Wholesale (1951) and the comedy *Pillow Talk* (1958). In recent years Gordon has concentrated mainly on comedy. **Films include:** *Crime Doctor* (1943), *The Web* (1946), *Boys' Night Out* (1962), *The Impossible Years* (1968).

EDMUND GOULDING (1891–1959) A native Londoner and originally a stage performer, Goulding went to Hollywood as a script writer in the early 20's and made several silents. He directed some of the popular 30's and 40's melodramas that still wrench hearts when they are rerun on late-night TV. **Films include:** *Love* (1928), *Grand Hotel* (1932), *Dawn Patrol* (1938), *Dark Victory* (1939), *Of Human Bondage* (1946), *Mardi Gras* (1958).

ALFRED E. GREEN (1889–1960) Director of the screen's first *Little Lord Fauntleroy* (1921) and another sentimental silent favorite, *Ella Cinders* (1926), Green turned out more than 100 films during his nearly 50 years in Hollywood. **Credits include:** *Disraeli* (1929), *South of Pago-Pago* (1940), *Badlands of Dakota* (1941), *A Thousand and One Nights* (1945), *The Jolson Story* (1946), *The Jackie Robinson Story* (1950), *The Eddie Cantor Story* (1953), *Top Banana* (1954).

DAVID WARK GRIFFITH (1875–1948) Perhaps the single most influential director in the history of American films, Griffith began directing for Biograph in 1908 and took early motion pictures a giant step forward when he adapted contemporary directing and editing techniques and presented them in a dazzling Civil War spectacle, *The Birth of a Nation* (1915). He tried to repeat his triumph with *Intolerance* (1916), but although it is considered a cinema landmark, it never equalled *The Birth of a Nation*'s box-office success. As motion pictures matured, however, and audiences grew in sophistication, Griffith and the films that mirrored his outlook lost ground. He retired in the early 30's. **Films include:** *Enoch Arden* (1911), *Broken Blossoms* (1919), *Way Down East* (1920), *Orphans of the Storm* (1922), *America* (1924), *Abraham Lincoln* (1930).

SACHA GUITRY (1885–1957) As an actor, writer, producer and director of comedy, Guitry enchanted audiences of the 30's—mostly by bringing to the screen adaptations of his own stage work. He was born in St. Petersburg, Russia, but lived and worked in France. **Films include:** *Ceux de Chez Nous* (debut 1914), *Le Roman d'un Tricheur* (1936), *Le Poison* (1951), *La Vie à Deux* (1957).

ALICE GUY-BLACHÉ (1873–1965) In the days before film directing became established as a "man's job," Guy-Blaché worked successfully in her native France and later in the United States. She was secretary to French producer-exhibitor Léon Gaumont and made her first film, *La Fée aux Choux,* at his request in 1896. **Films include:** *Le Voleur Sacrilège* (1903), *Paris la Nuit* (1904), *La Vie du Christ* (1906), *The Dream Woman* (1914), *The Shadows of the Moulin Rouge* (1914).

H

ALEXANDER HALL (1894–1968) He came to Hollywood from Broadway in 1932 and stayed to direct a long list of musicals and comedies. **Credits include:** *Little Miss Marker* (1935), *Limehouse Blues* (1936), *Here Comes Mr. Jordan* (1941), *My Sister Eileen* (1942), *Because You're Mine* (1952), *Forever Darling* (1956).

ROBERT HAMER (1911–1963) The director of such diverse motion pictures as *Dead of Night* (1945) and *Kind Hearts and Coronets* (1949), Hamer worked his way up in films at England's Ealing Studios. Critics seem to prefer the work he did in the 40's to the sophisticated comedies he turned out in the 50's. **Films include:** *Pink String and Sealing Wax* (1945), *It Always Rains on Sunday* (1947), *To Paris With Love* (1955), *School for Scoundrels* (1960).

JOHN HANCOCK (1938–) A newcomer to films, Hancock directed the 1973 hit *Bang the Drum Slowly,* the story about the slow death of a baseball player. The picture introduced Robert De Niro and Michael Moriarty to the screen.

BYRON HASKIN (1899–) A versatile film-maker, Haskin has worked for more than 50 years in filmdom. He directed a few silents, including *Ginsberg the Great* (1926) and *The Siren* (1926), and then worked as a cameraman and on special effects into the mid-40's. He finally returned to directing films, many of them sci-fi "B"'s. **Credits include:** *I Walk Alone* (1947), *Treasure Island* (1950), *Conquest of Space* (1955), *From the Earth to the Moon* (1958), *Robinson Crusoe on Mars* (1964), *The Power* (1968).

HENRY HATHAWAY (1898–) The best of his films are Westerns, and they range from *Wild Horse Mesa* (1932), his first, to the immensely popular *True Grit* (1969)—the picture that won John Wayne an Academy Award. His more than 200 features also include some notable ventures off the range. **Highlights:** *Peter Ibbetson* (1935), *The Lives of a Bengal Lancer* (1935), *The Trail of the Lonesome Pine* (1936), *The House on 42nd Street* (1945), *The Desert Fox* (1951), *How the West Was Won* (1962), *Nevada Smith* (1966), *Airport* (1970).

HOWARD HAWKS (1896–) The list of his screen credits reads like an anthology of audience favorites, ranging from madcap comedy to action drama, musicals and thrillers. Hawks began directing during the silent days and first became known for his action films. **Films include:** *A Girl in Every Port* (1928), *The Dawn Patrol* (1930), *Scarface* (1932), *Viva Villa!* (1934), *Bringing Up Baby* (1938), *His Girl Friday* (1939), *Sergeant York* (1941), *To Have and Have Not* (1944), *Red River* (1948), *Gentlemen Prefer Blondes* (1953), *Hatari* (1962).

STUART HEISLER (1894–) Notable as the director of *The Glass Key* (1942), Heisler worked in Hollywood as a film editor–director from 1914. He was most active in the 40's, making "B" horror stories, mysteries and action-packed adventures. **Credits include:** *The Monster and the Girl* (1941), *Along Came Jones* (1945), *Tokyo Joe* (1949), *I Died a Thousand Times* (1955).

GEORGE ROY HILL (1926–) A former actor and TV director, Hill made his first film, *Period of Adjustment,* in 1962. He is best known for the immensely popular Robert Redford–Paul Newman vehicles *Butch Cassidy and the Sundance Kid* (1969) and *The Sting* (1973). Both pictures copped a slew of Oscars, including Best Director awards for Hill. **Other films:** *Toys in the Attic* (1963), *The World of Henry Orient* (1964), *Hawaii* (1966), *Thoroughly Modern Millie* (1967), *Slaughterhouse Five* (1972).

JAMES HILL (1919–) Active in films from the 40's writer-director-producer Hill scored his biggest success to date with the family feature *Born*

Free (1966). He has also written and directed documentaries and won an Academy Award for *Giuseppina* (1961). **Films include:** *Journey for Jeremy* (1947), *Trapeze* (1956), *A Study in Terror* (1966), *Captain Nemo* (1969).

ARTHUR HILLER (1924–   ) A Canadian-born director who has worked in both films and television since the 50's, Heller's greatest success to date was the tear-jerker *Love Story* (1970). **Other credits include:** *The Careless Years* (1957), *Penelope* (1966), *Tobruk* (1967), *The Tiger Makes Out* (1967), *The Out-of-Towners* (1969), *Popi* (1969), *The Hospital* (1971), *Man of La Mancha* (1973).

ALFRED HITCHCOCK (1899–   ) His style is so distinctive that even the most naïve moviegoer will identify a film as a "Hitchcock" before mentioning the stars, the title or the subject matter. He is the world's acknowledged master of suspense—a specialist in keeping audiences on the edge of their seats. He entered the film industry in his native England at the age of 20, established himself with *The Lodger* (1926) and directed Britain's first sound film, *Blackmail*, in 1929. Before leaving England for Hollywood in 1939 he had already made three of his great thriller classics—*The Man Who Knew Too Much* (1934), *The 39 Steps* (1934), and *The Lady Vanishes* (1938). **Films include:** *Foreign Correspondent* (1940), *Spellbound* (1945), *Dial M for Murder* (1953), *Rear Window* (1954), *To Catch a Thief* (1955), *North by Northwest* (1959), *Psycho* (1960), *The Birds* (1963), *Frenzy* (1972).

WILLIAM K. HOWARD (1899–1954) Noted for several distinctively and dramatically photographed films, Howard is credited with introducing some of the dramatic camera techniques later used by Orson Welles in *Citizen Kane* (1941). **Films include:** *East of Broadway* (1924), *White Gold* (1927), *Scotland Yard* (1930), *Transatlantic* (1931), *Sherlock Holmes* (1932), *Back Door to Heaven* (1939), *Johnny Come Lately* (1943).

H. BRUCE HUMBERSTONE (1903–   ) Active in Hollywood from the early days of sound, Humberstone has made scores of films, most of them musicals and action pictures. **Among his nearly 100 screen credits:** *If I Had a Million* (1932), *The Dragon Murder Case* (1934), *Charlie Chan in Honolulu* (1938), *Lucky Cisco Kid* (1940), *The Desert Song* (1953), *The Purple Mask* (1955), *Madison Avenue* (1962).

BRIAN DESMOND HURST (1900–   ) Irishman Hurst first worked in films with his cousin, John Ford (1928–32). He directed mainly crime films like *Prison Without Bars* (1939) during his early career but later handled such disparate subjects as *Tom Brown's Schooldays* (1951) and *The Playboy of the Western World* (1962). **Credits include:** *Sensation* (1936), *Alibi* (1942), *A Christmas Carol* (1951), *Simba* (1955), *His and Hers* (1960).

JOHN HUSTON (1906–   ) The son of actor Walter Huston, he made his directorial debut with the now classic Bogart vehicle *The Maltese Falcon* (1941), won an Academy Award for his brilliant *The Treasure of Sierra Madre* (1948) and clinched his reputation as one of Hollywood's most prestigious and popular film-makers with *Key Largo* (1948) and *The African Queen* (1952). **Film highlights include:** *The Asphalt Jungle* (1950), *Beat the Devil* (1954), *The Misfits* (1961), *Freud*

(1962), *The Night of the Iguana* (1964), *Casino Royale* (1967), *Fat City* (1972), *The Life and Times of Judge Roy Bean* (1973).

I

KON ICHIKAWA (1915–   ) One of the most respected of Japan's directors, he began his career in films as an animator in 1933. Since World War II he has made more than 50 films covering the gamut of movie genres from comedy and satire to taut drama. **Credits include:** *The Billionaire* (1954), *The Burmese Harp* (1956), *Conflagration* (1958), *The Key* (1959), *Fires on the Plain* (1964), *Tokyo Olympiad* (documentary, 1965), *To Love Again* (1971).

THOMAS INCE (1882–1924) Hollywood pioneer Ince exerted an influence on the fledgling film industry that nearly rivaled that of D. W. Griffith. For a while he directed Mary Pickford and then concentrated on Westerns, helping transform them from costume skits to well-planned films that combined action with plot. He brought to the screen some of the most important silent stars, including William S. Hart, H. B. Warner and Billie Burke. For the last decade of his life Ince turned producer. **His credits as director include:** *Their First Misunderstanding* (1911), *Custer's Last Fight* (1912), *The Battle of Gettysburg* (1913), *The Despoiler* (1915), *Civilization* (1916).

JORIS IVENS (1898–   ) One of the cinema's most respected documentary film-makers, Dutch-born Ivens has worked throughout the world during the course of his 40-some-year career. His films concentrate on the struggle of the ordinary man against the equally harsh rigors of nature and controlling social environments. **His films include:** *The Bridge* (1928), *Rain* (1929), *Komsomol* (1932), *Spanish Earth* (1937), *The 400 Million* (1939), *The First Years* (1949), *The Song of the Rivers* (1954), *Loin du Vietnam* (1967).

J

NORMAN JEWISON (1927– .) Several of the most popular films of the 60's have been the work of this former TV director who has tackled slick, appealing comedies, dramas and musicals. **Highlights:** *The Cincinnati Kid* (1965), *The Russians Are Coming, the Russians Are Coming* (1966), *In the Heat of the Night* (1967), *The Thomas Crown Affair* (1968), *Fiddler on the Roof* (1969), *Jesus Christ Superstar* (1973).

K

JAN KADAR (1918–   ) A Czech director who moved to the United States in 1970, he gained international recognition with *A Shop on Main Street* (1965). That film and his other bittersweet polemics on human rights were made in collaboration with another Czech director, Elmar Klos. **Their credits include:** *Kidnapped* (1952), *Three Wishes* (1958), *Adrift* (1969).

GARSON KANIN (1912–   ) A man of many talents best known for his work as a Broadway

Alfred Hitchcock's The Lady Vanishes *(1938)*

John Huston's The African Queen *(1952)*

Jan Kadar's A Shop on Main Street *(1965)*

515

Elia Kazan's A Streetcar Named Desire *(1951)*

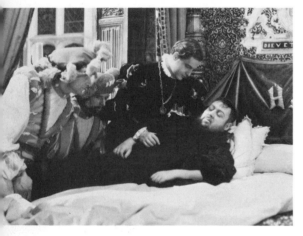

Sir Alexander Korda's The Private Life of Henry VIII *(1933)*

Stanley Kubrick's Dr. Strangelove *(1963)*

way playwright and director, he was George Cukor's favorite screenplay writer during the 40's and 50's and responsible for *Adam's Rib, Born Yesterday, Pat and Mike* and *It Should Happen to You.* He also directed several films, among them the 1945 documentary *The True Glory* (co-director Carol Reed). **Credits include:** *A Man to Remember* (1938), *My Favorite Wife* (1940), *They Knew What They Wanted* (1940), *Tom, Dick and Harry* (1941).

PHIL KARLSON (1908–) A specialist in action films, Karlson spent 20 years in Hollywood in the world of the low-budget ''B''s before landing somewhat more important assignments in the early 50's. **Films include:** *A Wac, a Wave and a Marine* (1944), *Kilroy Was Here* (1947), *The Texas Rangers* (1951), *Five Against the House* (1955), *Hell to Eternity* (1960), *The Silencers* (1966), *Wrecking Crew* (1969), *Ben* (1972).

ELIA KAZAN (1909–) Equally successful as a director of stage and screen, Kazan has an impressive list of film credits dating from the 40's. He won an Oscar for directing *Gentleman's Agreement* (1947) and another for *On the Waterfront* (1954), the third film he and Brando made together. His two films of the 60's were based on his own novels. Kazan was one of the founders of the Actors Studio in New York. **Screen credits include:** *A Tree Grows in Brooklyn* (1945), *A Streetcar Named Desire* (1951), *Viva Zapata!* (1952), *East of Eden* (1955), *America, America* (1964), *The Arrangement* (1969).

BUSTER KEATON See entry on page 291.

WILLIAM KEIGHLEY (1889–) During most of his Hollywood years this former stage actor directed slick, inconsequential films for Warner Brothers. **Highlights of 40 films:** *Babbitt* (1934), *G-Men* (1935), *The Green Pastures* (1936), *Brother Rat* (1939), *The Man Who Came to Dinner* (1942), *George Washington Slept Here* (1942), *The Master of Ballantrae* (1953).

IRVIN KERSHNER (1923–) This former documentarist's first features *Stake Out on Dope Street* (1958) and *The Young Captives* (1959), were about troubled youth and drugs and were considered way ahead of their time. His later films, including *The Hoodlum Priest* (1961) and *The Flim Flam Man* (1967), were distinctive enough to earn him a reputation as a skilled and talented director. **Other films include:** *The Luck of Ginger Coffey* (1964), *A Fine Madness* (1966), *Loving* (1970), *Up the Sandbox* (1972).

HENRY KING (1892–) Although he has spent more than 50 years in Hollywood and directed some of the big box-office successes of the 40's and 50's, King is most respected for his silents, particularly *Tol'able David* (1922), an affectionate look at backwoods America. **A long list of screen credits includes:** *Who Pays* (1916), *Sonny* (1922), *Stella Dallas* (1925), *The Winning of Barbara Worth* (1926), *State Fair* (1933), *The Song of Bernadette* (1944), *Twelve O'Clock High* (1949), *Carousel* (1956), *Tender Is the Night* (1962).

SIR ALEXANDER KORDA (1893–1956) It is generally accepted that the arrival of the Hungarian-born Korda in England in 1930 marked a turning point for British films. He is credited with pumping new life into England's ailing motion-picture industry with such popular films as *Service*

for Ladies (1931) and his all-time great *The Private Life of Henry VIII* (1933). Although Korda's main claim to fame is as a producer, star-maker and founder of London Films and Denham Studios, he continued to direct throughout his career. **Films include:** *Catherine the Great* (1933), *Rembrandt* (1937), *That Hamilton Woman* (1941), *Perfect Strangers* (1945), *An Ideal Husband* (1947).

ZOLTAN KORDA (1895–1961) He followed his older brother Alexander into the film business and directed many of the films produced by Korda's London Films. Zoltan Korda leaned toward action dramas such as *Conquest of the Air* (1936) and *Elephant Boy* (1937). Like his brother, he worked in Hollywood during the World War II years and then returned to London Films. **Among Korda's screen credits:** *Cash* (1932), *Sanders of the River* (1935), *The Jungle Book* (1942), *A Woman's Vengeance* (1948), *Cry the Beloved Country!* (1952), *Storm Over the Nile* (1956).

HENRY KOSTER (1905–) After working his way up in films in his native Germany, Koster went to Hollywood in the mid-30's and has been there ever since. His early assignments included several musicals especially tailored for Deanna Durbin. He made the first Cinemascope spectacular, *The Robe* (1953). He has since directed big-budget comedies, musicals and dramas. **Among his 40 some films:** *100 Men and a Girl* (1937), *Three Smart Girls* (1937), *It Started With Eve* (1941), *The Inspector General* (1949), *Harvey* (1950), *Flower Drum Song* (1961), *The Singing Nun* (1966).

GRIGORI KOZINTSEV (1905–) One of the most important figures in the Soviet cinema, Kozintsev began his career as a dynamic young rebel against dramatic traditions. His first film, an adaptation of Gogol's *Marriage* (1922), created a sensation for its lively innovations. Through the years he has continued to film both classic dramas and realistic studies of contemporary Russian life. Of late he has been concentrating on Shakespeare. **Films include:** *The Adventures of Oktyabrina* (1924), *The Cloak* (1926), *S.V.D.* (1927), *Alone* (1931), *The Maxim Trilogy* (1935,-37,-39), *Pigorov* (1948), *Don Quixote* (1957), *Hamlet* (1964), *King Lear* (1970).

STANLEY KRAMER (1913–) For the past 20 years this concerned producer-director has successfully wrapped his polemics against social injustices in slick, commercially acceptable vehicles. He started out in association with Carl Foreman, producing high-quality hits, including *High Noon* (1952), and directed his first film, *Not As a Stranger,* in 1955. **Screen highlights:** *The Defiant Ones* (1958), *On the Beach* (1959), *Inherit the Wind* (1960), *Judgment at Nuremberg* (1961), *It's a Mad, Mad, Mad, Mad World* (1963), *Ship of Fools* (1965), *Guess Who's Coming to Dinner* (1967), *Oklahoma Crude* (1973).

STANLEY KUBRICK (1928–) Kubrick started out making documentaries in the United States. He worked as screenwriter-director-producer on his first features during the 50's, directed several Hollywood movies and then moved to England, where he scored his first big success with the zany black comedy *Dr. Strangelove* (1963). Five years later his ''philosophical'' sci-fi blockbuster *2001: A Space Odyssey* turned him into a directorial superstar, a position he secured with his 1971 supra-violent adaptation of Anthony Burgess' *A Clockwork Orange*. **Credits include:** *Fear and Desire* (debut, 1953), *The Killing* (1956), *Paths of Glory* (1958), *Spartacus* (1960), *Lolita* (1962).

AKIRA KUROSAWA (1910–   ) A giant of post-World War II Japanese cinema and one of the world's leading directors, Kurosawa drew international attention to the existence of a film industry in Japan with his Venice Grand Prix winner *Rashomon* (1950). His range has been enormous and includes contemporary and period Japanese dramas, adaptations of Western literary classics and tales of the Samurai era. Two of his films have been copied in the West: *The Seven Samurai* (1954) was the basis for *The Magnificent Seven* (1960), while *Rashomon* became *The Outrage* (1961). **Credits include:** *Sanshiro Sugata* (debut, 1943), *The Idiot* (1951), *Ikiru* (1952), *Throne of Blood* (1957), *The Lower Depths* (1957), *Yojimbo* (1961), *Sanjuro* (1962), *Red Beard* (1965), *Dodeska-Den* (1970).

L

GREGORY LA CAVA (1892–1949) A director from the time of silents, he found a niche directing the light comedies of the 30's and early 40's. His sound films starred a galaxy of Hollywood's most popular actresses and are now the regular fare of late-night television. **Credits include:** *Womanhandled* (1926), *Paradise for Two* (1927), *Gabriel Over the White House* (1933), *What Every Woman Knows* (1934), *She Married Her Boss* (1935), *My Man Godfrey* (1936), *Stage Door* (1937), *Lady in a Jam* (1942), *Living in a Big Way* (1947).

FRITZ LANG (1890–   ) One of the two great German directors of the silent era (the other was Murnau), Lang is responsible for at least three screen classics: *Die Nibelungen* (1924), *Metropolis* (1926) and *M* (1931). He fled the Hitler regime in 1933 and worked in France before settling in America in the mid-30's. **His films include:** *Halbblut* (debut, 1919), *Destiny* (1921), *The Spy* (1928), *The Testament of Dr. Mabuse* (1933), *Fury* (1936), *You Only Live Once* (1937), *The Woman in the Window* (1944), *Human Desire* (1954).

WALTER LANG (1936–   ) Lang has had a long career directing Hollywood films, most of them light comedies and musicals. **A long list of credits includes:** *The Satin Woman* (1927), *The Mighty Barnum* (1934), *Tin Pan Alley* (1940), *Sitting Pretty* (1948), *Cheaper by the Dozen* (1950), *Call Me Madam* (1953), *There's No Business Like Show Business* (1954), *The King and I* (1956), *Can-Can* (1960).

DAVID LEAN (1908–   ) Lean entered the film industry as an editor in the late 20's and made the switch to direction in the early 40's on Noel Coward's *In Which We Serve* (1942). Within the decade he established himself as a leading film-maker whose credits included the enormously popular *Brief Encounter* (1946), *Great Expectations* (1946) and *Oliver Twist* (1948). Since then he has won two Academy Awards—for *The Bridge on the River Kwai* (1957) and *Lawrence of Arabia* (1962). **Other films include:** *Blithe Spirit* (1944),

Hobson's Choice (1954), *Dr. Zhivago* (1965), *Ryan's Daughter* (1970).

ROWLAND V. LEE (1891–   ) Another of Hollywood's pioneering directors in the silent era, Lee is best known for his Fu Manchu films and the swashbuckling adventure stories he did after the advent of sound. The fantasy *Zoo in Budapest* (1933) and *The Bridge of San Luis Rey* (1944) are the notable exceptions to his usual fare. **Films include:** *The Mysterious Dr. Fu Manchu* (1929), *The Count of Monte Cristo* (1934), *Cardinal Richelieu* (1935), *The Three Musketeers* (1935), *The Son of Monte Cristo* (1940), *Captain Kidd* (1945).

J. LEE-THOMPSON (1914–   ) Director of action extravaganzas like *The Guns of Navarone* (1961) and suspense films like *Cape Fear* (1962), Lee-Thompson was an actor and playwright before entering the film industry as a writer in the 30's. He turned writer-director in 1950. **Films include:** *Murder Without Crime* (1950), *Yield in the Night* (1956), *Woman in a Dressing Gown* (1958), *Tiger Bay* (1959), *Taras Bulba* (1962), *Mackenna's Gold* (1968).

J. MITCHELL LEISEN (1898–   ) An art director with Cecil B. De Mille for 12 years, Leisen turned film-maker in the early 30's with *Cradle Song* (1933) and *Death Takes a Holiday* (1934). He is best known for his sophisticated comedies and romances. Since the 50's he has been most active directing for television. **Films include:** *Easy Living* (1937), *The Big Broadcast of 1938* (1938), *Midnight* (1939), *Lady in the Dark* (1944), *The Mating Season* (1951), *The Girl Most Likely* (1958), *Spree* (1967).

CLAUDE LELOUCH (1937–   ) His first big international hit was *A Man and a Woman* (1966), a love story that had the mass audience appeal earlier Lelouch films had lacked. He was an amateur film-maker who did a few shorts before making his first feature film, *Le Propre de l'Homme* (1960). **Screen credits include:** *Vivre pour Vivre* (1967), *La Vie, L'Amour, La Mort* (1969), *Le Voyou* (1970), *Happy New Year* (1973).

ROBERT Z. LEONARD (1889–1968) A Hollywood director from the days of World War I, Leonard earned attention with films starring his wife, Mae Murray, in the 20's and was responsible for several of the big musicals and film revues of the 30's and 40's. He directed Fred Astaire's first film, *Dancing Lady* (1933). **Credits include:** *The Restless Sex* (1920), *Jazzmania* (1923), *Fashion Row* (1924), *Susan Lenox* (1931), *Peg O' My Heart* (1933), *The Great Ziegfeld* (1936), *Pride and Prejudice* (1940), *Beautiful but Dangerous* (1958).

MERVYN LE ROY (1900–   ) Movie buffs rate Le Roy's films of the 30's as accurate and artistic mirrors of American mood and melancholy during the Great Depression. He later made some of Hollywood's most popular mass appeal pictures. **Films include:** *Little Caesar* (1931), *I Am a Fugitive From a Chain Gang* (1932), *Gold Diggers of 1933* (1933), *Anthony Adverse* (1936), *They Won't Forget* (1937), *Random Harvest* (1942), *Little Women* (1949), *Quo Vadis?* (1951), *The Bad Seed* (1956), *Gypsy* (1962), *Moment to Moment* (1966).

RICHARD LESTER (1932–   ) The Beatles helped him make his name as director when he filmed their antics in *A Hard Day's Night* (1964)

Fritz Lang's The Big Heat *(1953)*

David Lean's Great Expectations *(1946)*

Mervyn Le Roy's Madame Curie *(1943)*

Anatole Litvak's The Snake Pit *(1948)*

Frank Lloyd's Mutiny on the Bounty *(1935)*

Ernst Lubitsch's Ninotchka *(1939)*

and *Help!* (1965). Although Lester was born in the United States, he has worked mainly in England. Most of his motion pictures have relied heavily on his adeptness at comedy, though their themes are often serious, as in *How I Won the War* (1967). **Films include:** *It's Trad, Dad* (1961), *The Knack* (1965), *A Funny Thing Happened on the Way to the Forum* (1966), *Petulia* (1968), *The Bed-Sitting Room* (1969), *The Three Musketeers* (1974).

HENRY LEVIN (1909–   ) During his three decades in Hollywood Levin has directed some 40 pictures ranging from action adventures to frothy comedy, crime dramas and ghoulish tales. His best film is considered to be the Western, *The Lonely Man* (1957). **Credits include:** *Cry of the Werewolf* (1944), *The Corpse Came C.O.D.* (1947), *Belles on their Toes* (1952), *Bernadine* (1957), *The Wonderful World of the Brothers Grimm* (1962), *The Desperadoes* (1969).

ALBERT LEWIN (1895–1968) A producer for MGM for a decade before he turned to directing, Lewin served as writer-director on some of the most unusual films of the 40's and 50's. **Credits:** *The Moon and Sixpence* (debut, 1942), *The Picture of Dorian Gray* (1944), *The Private Affairs of Bel Ami* (1947), *Pandora and the Flying Dutchman* (1951), *Saadia* (1954), *The Living Idol* (1957).

MARCEL L'HERBIER (1890–   ) Noted for his early work in films as an experimenter in various styles of photography, Parisian L'Herbier later directed historical dramas. He is also the founder of the Institut des Hautes Etudes Cinématographiques, the renowned Paris film-training school. **Best known films include:** *Phantasmes* (1917), *L'Inhumaine* (1923), *Le Mystère de la Chambre Jaune* (1931), *The Last Days of Pompeii* (1949), *Stolen Affections* (1951), *L'Argent* (1968).

ANATOLE LITVAK (1902–   ) Russian-born Litvak got his start as a director in Europe and first attracted attention with *Mayerling* (1936), the romantic story of the Hapsburg prince who shot himself for love. He has been in Hollywood since 1937 and has made such varied films as the comedy *Tovarich* (1938) and the shocking exposé *The Snake Pit* (1948). **Other films include:** *Confessions of a Nazi Spy* (1939), *Sorry, Wrong Number* (1948), *Decision Before Dawn* (1951), *Anastasia* (1956), *The Night of the Generals* (1967).

FRANK LLOYD (1888–1960) He arrived in Hollywood from his native Scotland during the infancy of motion pictures and got his start directing one-reel silents. Later, Lloyd built a reputation for sweeping adventures, including the 1935 version of *Mutiny on the Bounty*. He won two early Academy Awards for *The Divine Lady* (1929) and *Cavalcade* (1933). **Films include:** *Les Misérables* (1918), *Madame X* (1920), *The Sea Hawk* (1924), *Berkeley Square* (1933), *Wells Fargo* (1937), *Lady from Cheyenne* (1941), *The Shanghai Story* (1954).

JOSHUA LOGAN (1908–   ) Logan began making films after earning success as a director on the Broadway stage. He is best known by filmgoers as a specialist in big-budget screen adaptations of Broadway musicals and plays. **Films include:** *Picnic* (1956), *Bus Stop* (1956), *Sayonara* (1957), *South Pacific* (1958), *Fanny* (1961), *Ensign Pulver* (1964), *Camelot* (1967), *Paint Your Wagon* (1969).

JOSEPH LOSEY (1909–   ) One of the most prominent victims of Senator Joseph McCarthy's Communist witchhunt, Losey abandoned Hollywood for England in the early 50's and went on to establish himself as one of the most individual and important contemporary directors. His best work has been done in collaboration with playwright Harold Pinter. **Film highlights:** *The Boy With Green Hair* (1948), *The Servant* (1964), *Modesty Blaise* (1966), *Accident* (1967), *Figures in a Landscape* (1970), *The Go-Between* (1971), *The Assassination of Trotsky* (1972), *A Doll's House* (1973).

ARTHUR LUBIN (1901–   ) Active in films since the mid-50's, Logan has been a specialist in Saturday-afternoon-at-the-movies comedies. The most successful ones were the Abbott and Costello films of the 40's and the *Francis* (the talking mule) series of the 50's. **His pictures include:** *Buck Privates* (1939), *Ali Baba and the Forty Thieves* (1944), *Francis* (1950), *The Thief of Baghdad* (1961), *Hold On!* (1966).

ERNST LUBITSCH (1892–1947) The famed "Lubitsch touch" first emerged in the silent films he made in his native Germany between 1914 and 1922. It was amplified in the more than 20 years he spent in Hollywood. The term itself refers to his penchant for focusing the camera on a seemingly inconsequential object or gesture that was later to prove significant to the plot. **Films include:** *Passion* (1919), *Lady Windemere's Fan* (1925), *Trouble in Paradise* (1932), *The Merry Widow* (1934), *Ninotchka* (1939), *The Shop Around the Corner* (1942), *To Be or Not to Be* (1942), *Cluny Brown* (1946).

GEORGE LUCAS (1945–   ) He scored a commercial and critical success with his second film, *American Graffiti* (1973), a nostalgic look at teenage life and love in a small California town of the 50's. Lucas studied film at the Cinema School at the University of Southern California. His first film was the sci-fi tale *THX 1138* (1971).

SIDNEY LUMET (1924–   ) One of television's most active directors during the 50's, Lumet has had equal success as a director of harsh screen dramas. **Films include:** *Twelve Angry Men* (1957), *Long Day's Journey Into Night* (1962), *A View From the Bridge* (1962), *Fail Safe* (1964), *The Pawnbroker* (1965), *The Hill* (1965), *The Seagull* (1968), *The Anderson Tapes* (1970), *Serpico* (1973).

M

GUSTAV MACHATY (1898–1963) A Czech director who worked for a time in the United States and studied under Erich von Stroheim, Machaty is best remembered for two films considered shockingly erotic by contemporary audiences. One, *Ecstasy* (1932), contained a nude scene that made a young actress, Hedy Lamarr, an international sensation. **Films include:** *The Kreutzer Sonata* (1926), *Erotikon* (1929), *Nocturno* (1934), *Within the Law* (1939), *Jealousy* (1945).

ALEXANDER MACKENDRICK (1912–   ) He has a flair for comedy, which distinguished his early work at England's Ealing Studios and was best displayed in the Alec Guinness vehicles *The Man in the White Suit* (1952) and *The Ladykillers* (1956). Later Mackendrick films have varied, from the incisive *The Sweet Smell of Success* (1957) to the historical drama *Mary, Queen of Scots* (1970). He was born in the United States but has spent most of his life in Britain. **Films include:** *Whisky Galore* (debut, 1948), *Mandy* (1952), *Sammy Going South* (1962), *A High Wind in Jamaica* (1965), *Don't Make Waves* (1967).

KAROLY MAKK (1925–) Hungarian Makk first gained recognition on the international scene with his short *The Imaginary Invalid* (1952) and his feature *Liliomfi* (1954). **Films include:** *Ward No. 9* (1955), *House Under the Rocks* (1958), *His Majesty's Dates* (1964), *Love* (1970).

TERRENCE MALICK (1944–) A new, young talent, Malick achieved recognition in 1973 when his first film, *Badlands,* was selected for the New York Film Festival. The picture is a fictionalized account of mass murderer Charles Starkweather's killing spree through the Midwest in the mid-50's.

LOUIS MALLE (1932–) When his film *Lacombe Lucien* (1973) opened in Paris, it was hailed as a screen masterpiece, and critics rated Malle's achievement as an unsurpassed example of film art. It is the story of French collaborationists during World War II and was made with a cast of unknowns. Malle first established himself among the "new wave" of French directors with his first two feature films, *L'Ascenseur pour l'Echafaud* (1957) and *Les Amants* (1958). **Credits include:** *Zazie dans le Métro* (1960), *Vie Privée* (1961), *Le Feu Follet* (1963), *Le Voleur* (1966), *Dearest Love* (1971).

ROUBEN MAMOULIAN (1898–) Equally successful as a director of stage and screen, Mamoulian has been active in Hollywood since 1929 when he made an inventive early talkie, the strong melodrama *Applause.* During his long career he experimented with every type of film, from crime drama to romantic costumers and rugged action pictures. (In 1935 he made Hollywood's first three-color Technicolor film, *Becky Sharp*.) **Credits include:** *Dr. Jekyll and Mr. Hyde* (1932), *Love Me Tonight* (1932), *High, Wide and Handsome* (1937), *The Mark of Zorro* (1940), *Blood and Sand* (1941), *Summer Holiday* (1948), *Silk Stockings* (1957).

JOSEPH MANKIEWICZ (1909–) Journalism and scriptwriting paved the way for Mankiewicz' extremely successful career in films, first as a screenwriter-producer, then as a director. He won Academy Awards for his screenplays of *A Letter to Three Wives* (1949) and *All About Eve* (1950) and also walked away with Best Director Oscars for both. **Highlights:** *Julius Caesar* (1953), *Guys and Dolls* (1955), *The Quiet American* (1958), *Suddenly, Last Summer* (1959), *Cleopatra* (1963), *There Was a Crooked Man* (1970), *Sleuth* (1972).

DANIEL MANN (1912–) He came to Hollywood from Broadway to direct the screen adaptation of *Come Back, Little Sheba* (1952) and did his best work in the decade that followed. Mann has also directed for television. **Films include:** *About Mrs. Leslie* (1954), *The Rose Tattoo* (1955), *The Teahouse of the August Moon* (1956), *I'll Cry Tomorrow* (1956), *The Last Angry Man* (1959),

Butterfield 8 (1960), *Judith* (1965), *Our Man Flint* (1966), *Willard* (1971).

DELBERT MANN (1920–) An established TV director, Mann won an Academy Award for his first film, *Marty* (1955), an adaptation of a Paddy Chayefsky television play. He followed that with three other memorable films: *The Bachelor Party* (1957) and *Middle of the Night* (1958) from Chayefsky scripts and *Separate Tables* (1958) from the Terence Rattigan play. Mann's later work has ranged from slick Doris Day-Rock Hudson comedies like *Lover Come Back* (1961) to a screen version of *David Copperfield* (1969). **Other credits include:** *Desire Under the Elms* (1958), *The Dark at the Top of the Stairs* (1960), *That Touch of Mink* (1962), *Jane Eyre* (1970).

GEORGE MARSHALL (1891–) Perhaps the most durable of Marshall's films is *Destry Rides Again* (1939), a lively Western that seems to gain in popularity every time it hits a TV late show. Marshall began directing silent Westerns as early as 1917, and his screen credits number in the hundreds. Many of his films are comedies, and most reflect his flair for diverting nonsense. **Films include:** *A Message to Garcia* (1934), *Life Begins at 40* (1935), *You Can't Cheat an Honest Man* (1939), *The Blue Dahlia* (1946), *The Perils of Pauline* (1947), *My Friend Irma* (1949), *Scared Stiff* (1953), *Hook, Line & Sinker* (1969).

ANDREW MARTON (1904–) A Hungarian immigrant who came to Hollywood with Lubitsh in 1923, he began directing in the early days of talkies. He has made some two dozen films, mainly adventure and sci-fi tales. **Credits include:** *Iceberg* (1932), *The Demon of the Himalayas* (1934), *The Secret of Stamboul* (1941), *King Solomon's Mines* (1950), *Green Fire* (1955), *The Crack in the World* (1965), *Africa—Texas Style!* (1967).

PAUL MAZURSKY (1930–) He graduated from small roles in films like *The Blackboard Jungle* (1955) to a successful career as a TV comedy writer and later to work as a scriptwriter and movie producer. He turned writer-director in 1969 and scored a hit with his first film, *Bob & Carol & Ted & Alice* (1969). **Subsequent films include:** *Alex in Wonderland* (1971), *Blume in Love* (1973).

LEO McCAREY (1898–1969) He graduated from scripting and directing Hal Roach comedies during the 20's to directing such classics as the Marx Brothers' *Duck Soup* (1933) and Charles' Laughton's *Ruggles of Red Gap* (1935). McCarey won Academy Awards for two of his 30's comedies, *The Awful Truth* (1937) and *Love Affair* (1939). He also won an Oscar for his work as scenarist on the sentimental Bing Crosby classic *Going My Way* (1944). **Other credits:** *The Kid From Spain* (1932), *Belle of the 90's* (1934), *Six of a Kind* (1934), *The Bells of St. Mary's* (1945), *An Affair to Remember* (1957), *Satan Never Sleeps* (1962).

ANDREW McLAGLEN (1925–) Primarily a director of Westerns, McLaglen worked in television before making some second features. Later he moved up to bigger-budget films. He is the son of actor Victor McLaglen. **Films include:** *Gun the Man Down* (1956), *McLintock* (1963), *Shenandoah* (1965), *The Way West* (1967), *Undefeated* (1969), *Something Big* (1971).

Sidney Lumet's The Pawnbroker *(1965)*

Joseph Mankiewicz' The Barefoot Contessa *(1954)*

Leo McCarey's Going My Way *(1944)*

Lewis Milestone's Of Mice and Men *(1940)*

Vincente Minnelli's Madame Bovary *(1949)*

Mike Nichols' Catch-22 *(1969)*

NORMAN Z. McLEOD (1898–1964) Several of Hollywood's best comedies are the work of McLeod, a former cartoonist and scriptwriter. He got his start as a film-maker, directing the Marx Brothers in *Monkey Business* (1931). One of his most memorable films was *Topper* (1937), the story of a dignified man about town plagued by a couple of zany ghosts only he can see and hear. **Other films include:** *Horse Feathers* (1932), *Alice in Wonderland* (1933), *Little Men* (1940), *The Secret Life of Walter Mitty* (1947), *The Paleface* (1948), *Casanova's Big Night* (1954).

GEORGES MÉLIÈS (1861–1938) His demonstrations that film could be used for entertainment and not simply as a recording device established Méliès as the father of the cinema. He was a magician who first used motion pictures as a means of recording his stage act but soon began experimenting. In 1897 he built the world's first motion-picture studio in France and during the next 16 years made hundreds of films, ranging from Jules Verne science-fiction fantasies to recreations of dramatic moments in history—*L'Affaire Dreyfus* (1899) and *The Coronation of Edward VII* (1902). Méliès also is credited with introducing such camera techniques as stop action, superimposition and the dissolve. **Films include:** *Une Partie des Cartes* (1896), *Voyage to the Moon* (1902), *Baron Munchausen* (1911), *The Conquest of the Pole* (1912).

LEWIS MILESTONE (1895–   ) In the first year of the Academy Awards, Milestone was one of two men singled out by the industry as best directors. He won for his silent comedy *Two Arabian Knights* (1927). A few years later he was to triumph again, this time for *All Quiet on the Western Front* (1930). During the following 30 some years he directed dozens of films. **Credits include:** *The Front Page* (1931), *Of Mice and Men* (1940), *A Walk in the Sun* (1946), *Mutiny on the Bounty* (1962).

JOHN MILIUS (1945–   ) One of the most promising young American directors, Milius achieved recognition in 1972 with his version of the story about that most notorious of gangsters, *Dillinger*.

DAVID MILLER (1909–   ) A onetime film editor, Miller has been directing Hollywood features since 1941. He has made a wide range of pictures, from the zany Marx Brothers *Love Happy* (1950) to the Joan Crawford thriller *Sudden Fear* (1952). **Credits include:** *Billy the Kid* (1941), *Flying Tigers* (1942), *The Story of Esther Costello* (1957), *Captain Newman, M.D.* (1964), *Hammerhead* (1968).

VINCENTE MINNELLI (1913–   ) His early years as a film director were spent pumping a new look and new zest into American musical comedies. He did some of the best musicals of the 40's, including *Meet Me in St. Louis* (1944) and *Ziegfeld Follies* (1945). Still at it more than a decade later, he won an Academy Award for *Gigi* (1958). Minelli's other films have been divided between bright comedies like *Father of the Bride* (1950) and *Designing Woman* (1957) and dramas like *The Bad and the Beautiful* (1953). **Other films include:** *Cabin in the Sky* (1943), *Yolanda and the Thief* (1945), *Brigadoon* (1954), *Some Came Running* (1959), *Bells Are Ringing* (1960), *On a Clear Day You Can See Forever* (1969).

KENJI MIZOGUCHI (1898–1956) An artist whose career spanned both silent and sound eras, Mizoguchi is considered one of Japan's foremost directors. He is best remembered for films that explore the motivations, behavior and social roles of women. Although few of his silents survive, his sound films attest to his mastery. **More than 90 films include:** *City Symphony* (1929), *Osaka Elegy* (1936), *The Story of the Last Chrysanthemums* (1939), *Women of the Night* (1948), *The Crucified Lovers* (1955), *Yokihi* (1955).

ROBERT MULLIGAN (1925–   ) Some of the most popular Hollywood films of the 60's and early 70's were the work of Mulligan, a director who came to motion pictures via radio and television. One of his best was the 1963 screen adaptation of Harper Lee's novel *To Kill a Mockingbird*. **Films include:** *The Great Imposter* (1961), *Love With the Proper Stranger* (1964), *Inside Daisy Clover* (1966), *Up the Down Staircase* (1967), *Summer of '42* (1971).

FRIEDRICH WILHELM MURNAU (1888–1931) His highly stylized silents are considered classics of the early screen. Murnau came to films in 1919 via study with Max Reinhardt and a career as a theatre director in Berlin. He worked principally in his native Germany but made several films in Hollywood. He was an exponent of expressionism, and its influence marks his two most famous films, *Nosferatu* (1922) and *The Last Laugh* (1924). **Other credits:** *Der Knabe in Blau* (debut, 1919), *Janus-Faced* (1920), *Tartuffe* (1925), *Faust* (1926), *Sunrise* (1927), *Our Daily Bread* (1929), *Tabu* (1931).

N

RONALD NEAME (1911–   ) A director of popular English films of the 50's and 60's, Neame is noted for the fine performances he has elicited from his actors and actresses. He started out in films as a cameraman on the first full-length British talkie, *Blackmail* (1929). He first attracted notice as David Lean's cameraman during the 40's and subsequently worked as a producer before making his first film. **Films include:** *Take My Life* (1948), *The Horse's Mouth* (1959), *The Chalk Garden* (1964), *The Prime of Miss Jean Brodie* (1969), *Scrooge* (1970), *The Poseidon Adventure* (1973).

JEAN NEGULESCO (1900–   ) Many of his best-known pictures have been screen romances. His earlier work, however, included such sharp-edged melodramas as *The Mask of Dimitrios* (1944) and *Road House* (1948). **Credits include:** *Johnny Belinda* (1948), *The Mudlark* (1950), *Three Coins in the Fountain* (1954), *A Certain Smile* (1958), *Count Your Blessings* (1959), *The Pleasure Seekers* (1964).

RALPH NELSON (1916–   ) He first made a name as an actor during the 30's and then switched to writing and producing for the Broadway stage and later for television. His first notable film was *Requiem for a Heavyweight* (1962). **Other credits:** *Lilies of the Field* (1963), *Father Goose* (1964), *Charly* (1968), *Soldier Blue* (1970).

JOSEPH M. NEWMAN (1909–   ) In the decade that followed World War II Newman built up a substantial list of action-picture credits, ranging from shoot-em-up Westerns to violent crime stories. **Films include:** *The Outcasts of Poker Flat*

(1952), *Gunfight at Dodge City* (1958), *Tarzan, the Ape Man* (1959), *The George Raft Story* (1961), *Thunder of Drums* (1961).

FRED NIBLO (1874–1948) Director of some of the silent screen's most romantic spectacles, Niblo worked with Douglas Fairbanks and Rudolph Valentino on some of their swashbucklers. He worked for the William Ince studios and later for MGM, where he directed Greta Garbo in *The Temptress* (1926) and *The Mysterious Lady* (1928). His career did not survive the transition to sound. **Films include:** *The Marriage Ring* (1918), *The Mark of Zorro* (1920), *Blood and Sand* (1922), *Camille* (1927), *Ben Hur* (1925 and 1931).

MIKE NICHOLS (1931–) Not many directors get to launch their film careers with screen adaptations of prestigious plays starring such surefire box-office draws as Elizabeth Taylor and Richard Burton. Former nightclub performer turned Broadway director Nichols did just that with *Who's Afraid of Virginia Woolf* (1966). It won an Academy Award for Taylor, and the next year Nichols got his own Oscar for directing the year's biggest hit, *The Graduate* (1967). **Subsequent films include:** *Catch-22* (1969), *Carnal Knowledge* (1971), *The Day of the Dolphin* (1973).

ELLIOT NUGENT (1900–) Comedies are his forte, and Nugent directed scores of them between the 30's and the 50's. He was an actor first, then became a playwright and theatrical producer before launching his career as a director. Among Nugent's screen credits is the 1949 version of F. Scott Fitzgerald's *The Great Gatsby*. **Other films include:** *Life Begins* (1932), *Three-Cornered Room* (1933), *The Male Animal* (1942), *My Outlaw Brother* (1951).

O

MAX OPHÜLS (1902–1957) A former stage actor and director, Ophüls made his first films during the early 30's in his native Germany. His distinctive, opulent work soon attracted attention, and within the decade he was one of Europe's most popular directors. A French citizen from 1938, he worked in Hollywood for a while in the 40's but eventually returned to France. He went on to do his best work there. **Films include:** *The Bartered Bride* (1932), *Liebelei* (1933), *The Exile* (1947), *The Reckless Moment* (1949), *La Ronde* (1950), *Le Plaisir* (1951), *Madame de . . .* (1953), *Lola Montès* (1955).

GERD OSWALD (1916–) This German-born director-producer alternates between work in television and motion pictures. **Films include:** *A Kiss Before Dying* (1956), *Crime of Passion* (1957), *Brainwashed* (1961), *The Agent From H.A.R.M.* (1969), *Bunny O'Hare* (1971).

P

GEORG W. PABST (1885–1967) One of Europe's most influential directors, this native of Bohemia did his best work between 1925 and 1932. He established his reputation with the realistic *The Joyless Street* (1925), a study of middle-class life in post-World War I Vienna; and he created a silent classic with the fantasy *Pandora's Box* (1929). Of his numerous sound films, the most notable were: *Westfront 1918* (1930), *Kameradschaft* (1931) and *The Threepenny Opera* (1931). **Other credits:** *Der Schatz* (debut, 1923), *Secrets of a Soul* (1926), *L'Atlantide* (1932), *Don Quixote* (1933), *The Trial* (1947), *The Jackboot Mutiny* (1955).

MARCEL PAGNOL (1895–) This extremely popular French playwright and theatre producer turned film director–producer in the early 30's when he had Alexander Korda direct *Marius* (1931), the first part of his triology on peasant life. Marc Allegret directed the second part, *Fanny* (1932), while he did the third, *César* (1936), himself. **Films include:** *Un Direct au Coeur* (debut, 1933), *Angèle* (1934), *La Femme du Boulanger* (1938), *La Belle Meunière* (1948), *Topaze* (1951).

ALAN J. PAKULA (1928–) Although he is primarily a producer, Pakula did direct two popular films, the screen adaptation of *The Sterile Cuckoo* (1969), starring Liza Minnelli, and the excellent suspense melodrama *Klute* (1970), starring Jane Fonda and Donald Sutherland.

Alan J. Pakula's Klute *(1971)*

ROBERT PARRISH (1916–) He was an actor and worked as a film editor before settling down to the combined roles of director and producer. Most of Parrish's films are routine action adventures. **Credits include:** *Cry Danger* (1951), *Saddle the Wind* (1958), *Up From the Beach* (1965), *Doppelganger* (1969).

PIER PAOLO PASOLINI (1922–) Poet, novelist and screenplay writer of the 50's, Pasolini has emerged as one of Italy's foremost film-makers. A Marxist and staunch opponent of the Catholic Church, Pasolini has used his dense and often enigmatic films to lampoon political and religious dogma and to delve into the various realms of myth. **Credits include:** *Accattone* (debut, 1961), *Comizi d'Amore* (1964), *The Gospel According to St. Matthew* (1964), *Oedipus Rex* (1967), *Theorem* (1968), *Medea* (1969), *The Decameron* (1971), *The Canterbury Tales* (1972).

Sam Peckinpah's Straw Dogs *(1971)*

SAM PECKINPAH (1926–) The acknowledged contemporary master of the film Western, Peckinpah served his apprenticeship to film-making as a TV scriptwriter (for *Zane Grey Theatre*) and then as writer-director of *Gunsmoke* (1957) and creator of *The Rifleman* (1958) and *The Westerner* (1961). His best films to date are *Ride the High Country* (debut, 1961) and *The Wild Bunch* (1969), his first commercial success. In the early 70's Peckinpah's work suffered from too-slick handling and stomach-turning violence. **Credits include:** *The Deadly Companions* (1962), *Major Dundee* (1965), *Straw Dogs* (1971), *Junior Bonner* (1972), *The Getaway* (1973), *Pat Garrett and Billy the Kid* (1973).

ARTHUR PENN (1922–) Two of his most successful films have examined some of America's most durable and romantic myths—*Bonnie and Clyde* (1967) focused on a pair of dashing bank robbers and *Little Big Man* (1971) gave the Indian's point of view of the settling of the West. Penn was a television and stage director before he began working in films. **His credits include:** *The Left-Handed Gun* (1958), *The Miracle Worker* (1962), *Mickey One* (1965), *The Chase* (1966), *Alice's Restaurant* (1969).

Arthur Penn's Bonnie and Clyde *(1967)*

Sydney Pollack's They Shoot Horses, Don't They? *(1969)*

Otto Preminger's Anatomy of a Murder *(1958)*

Jean Renoir's La Grande Illusion *(1937)*

FRANK PERRY (1930–   ) He made his name with a sensitive film about mentally disturbed youngsters, *David and Lisa* (1963). It received wide attention not only because the subject matter was unusual but also because Perry produced it independently and on a very small budget. **Subsequent films include:** *Ladybug, Ladybug* (1964), *The Swimmer* (1968), *Diary of a Mad Housewife* (1970), *Doc* (1971), *Play It As It Lays* (1972).

JOSEPH PEVNEY (1920–   ) Director of scores of second features during more than 20 years in Hollywood, Pevney, a former actor, has also turned out a few lightweight star vehicles like *Tammy and the Bachelor* (1957) and *Cash McCall* (1960). He directed the 1957 tribute to Lon Chaney, *Man of a Thousand Faces*. **Films include:** *Shakedown* (1950), *Desert Legion* (1953), *Congo Crossing* (1956), *Night of the Grizzly* (1966).

IRVING PICHEL (1891–1954) Character actor Pichel played scores of film roles, including that of Fagin in the first sound version of *Oliver Twist* (1933). Between acting assignments Pichel took up directing and turned out a wide variety of pictures. **Screen highlights:** *The Sheik Steps Out* (1937), *The Moon Is Down* (1943), *Tomorrow Is Forever* (1946), *Sante Fe* (1951), *Martin Luther* (1953).

ROMAN POLANSKI (1933–   ) A master of the chilling and the bizarre, Polanski began making motion pictures in his native Poland. He attracted international attention with the short *Two Men in a Wardrobe* (1958) and was lauded for his first feature, *Knife in the Water* (1962). Later films were shot in England and the United States and include the popular success *Rosemary's Baby* (1968). **Other credits:** *Repulsion* (1965), *Cul-de-Sac* (1966), *Dance of the Vampires* (1967), *Macbeth* (1971).

SYDNEY POLLACK (1930–   ) After several minor films this former stage and TV actor attracted wide attention as the director of *They Shoot Horses, Don't They?* (1969), a sensitive and grueling study of desperate young people during the depression of the 30's. He later scored an even bigger success with the Streisand–Redford tearjerker *The Way We Were* (1973). **Other films include:** *The Slender Thread* (1965), *This Property Is Condemned* (1966), *The Scalphunters* (1968).

ABRAHAM POLONSKY (1910–   ) He is a talented screenwriter, novelist and director whose screen career has only just recovered from his being blacklisted during the days of Senator Joseph McCarthy's Communist witchhunt in the early 50's. **Films include:** *Force of Evil* (1948), *Tell Them Willie Boy Is Here* (1969), *Romance of a Horse Thief* (1971).

GILLO PONTEVORVO (1919–   ) He is best known as the scenarist-director of the shattering and brilliant *The Battle of Algiers* (1966), the story of the struggle to end French rule in Algeria, which he filmed on location with a cast of non-professionals. He had done documentary work in his native Italy and directed two features earlier in his career. **Credits include:** *La Grande Strada Azzura* (1957), *Kapò* (1960), *Queimada!* (1970).

H. C. POTTER (1904–   ) His heydey was the 30's and 40's, when he directed some of Hollywood's most memorable comedies. In addition to his work in films, Potter directs for the Broadway stage. **Films include:** *Beloved Enemy* (1936), *The Cowboy and the Lady* (1938), *Blackmail* (1939), *Hellzapoppin!* (1941), *Mr. Lucky* (1943), *Mr. Blandings Builds His Dream House* (1948), *Top Secret Affair* (1957).

MICHAEL POWELL (1905–   ) Active in films as an editor, assistant director and scriptwriter from the mid-20's, Britisher Powell emerged from six years of obscurity as a director of "B"'s with *The Edge of the World* (1938). Most of his most interesting work was done in collaboration with Emeric Pressburger between 1942 and 1957. **Film highlights:** *The Thief of Bagdad* (1940), *One of Our Aircraft Is Missing* (1942), *Colonel Blimp* (1945), *The Red Shoes* (1948), *The Tales of Hoffmann* (1951), *Peeping Tom* (1959), *Sebastian* (1968).

OTTO PREMINGER (1906–   ) His flamboyant personality has helped him achieve a celebrity status few director-producers enjoy. Born in Vienna, Preminger worked there for Max Reinhardt as an actor and director before moving to America in 1934. He worked primarily as a producer and director for the stage before turning to the screen in the mid-40's. Since then his works have ranged from tense dramas to light comedies and screen adaptations of popular novels like *Anatomy of a Murder* (1958), *Exodus* (1960) and *Advise and Consent* (1962). Preminger has scored two important Hollywood firsts—he released *The Moon Is Blue* (1953) without the approval of the Hollywood Production Code and made one of the first films about drug addiction, *The Man With the Golden Arm* (1955). **Highlights of more than 35 films:** *Under Your Spell* (U.S. debut, 1936), *Laura* (1944), *Forever Amber* (1947), *The Thirteenth Letter* (1951), *Carmen Jones* (1954), *Bonjour Tristesse* (1958), *Hurry Sundown* (1967), *Such Good Friends* (1972).

VSEVOLOD ILARIONOVICH PUDOVKIN (1893–1953) The director of several of the Russian silent classics, Pudovkin holds a place among the top ranks of cinema innovators and theoreticians. In 1920 he abandoned a career in chemistry to work in the infant Soviet film industry as an actor, writer and director. His first film, *Mother* (1926), is considered a masterpiece. Although he continued to make films into the early 50's, his sound films only rarely equaled his early work. **Other films include:** *Mechanics of the Brain* (1926), *The End of St. Petersburg* (1927), *Storm Over Asia* (1928), *Deserter* (1931), *Suvorov* (1940), *The Harvest* (1953).

Q

RICHARD QUINE (1920–   ) An actor-scriptwriter turned director, he began making thrillers in the 50's. His best work, however, has been on lively Hollywood comedies like *My Sister Eileen* (1955) and *The Solid Gold Cadillac* (1956). His later forays into melodrama have met with less success. **Films include:** *Drive a Crooked Road* (1954), *Bell, Book and Candle* (1958), *The World of Susie Wong* (1960), *How to Murder Your Wife*

(1965), *Hotel* (1967), *A Talent for Loving* (1969), *The Moonshine War* (1970).

R

BOB RAFELSON (1938–   ) Rafelson wrote, directed and produced a 1968 film, *Head,* but had to wait two years before achieving recognition as a promising new Hollywood talent with his *Five Easy Pieces* (1970). The picture won an Academy Award nomination for the year's best picture.

IRVING RAPPER (1898–   ) In more than 20 years in Hollywood, English-born Rapper has built up a list of screen credits that includes such successes as *Now, Voyager* (1942) and *The Corn Is Green* (1946). **Other credits:** *Shining Victory* (1941), *Rhapsody in Blue* (1945), *The Glass Menagerie* (1950), *Marjorie Morningstar* (1958), *The Miracle* (1959).

NICHOLAS RAY (1911–   ) Critics were enthusiastic about Ray's early work, particularly his first film, the low-budget *They Live by Night* (1949), the off-beat Western *Johnny Guitar* (1954) and his sympathetic portrait of troubled youngsters, *Rebel Without a Cause* (1955). Later Ray work proved disappointing. **Screen credits include:** *In a Lonely Place* (1950), *The True Story of Jesse James* (1957), *Bitter Victory* (1957), *Wind Across the Everglades* (1958), *55 Days at Peking* (1963).

SATYAJIT RAY (1921–   ) Ray achieved international recognition when his first film, *Pather Panchali* (1955), won the award for best documentary at the Cannes Film Festival. Ray is India's foremost director, and although his films are based on life in his native land, their perception and simplicity give them a wide appeal that attracts audiences throughout the world. His pictures generally are studies of deprivation and glimpses of everyday life, but Ray has also attempted slapstick comedy and examinations of political and social issues. **Films include:** *The Unvanquished* (1956), *The World of Apu* (1958), *The Music Room* (1958), *Parashpatar* (1958), *Devi* (1961), *Kanchenjunga* (1962), *The Rival* (1971).

SIR CAROL REED (1906–   ) One of England's most respected directors, Reed has turned out a wide variety of films, from low-key studies of working-class life made during the 30's and early 40's to the ebullient *Oliver!* (1968), for which he won an Academy Award. His best film, however, is the taut spy drama *The Third Man* (1949). **Credits include:** *Midshipman Easy* (debut, 1934), *The Stars Look Down* (1939), *The Fallen Idol* (1948), *Trapeze* (1956), *Our Man in Havana* (1959), *The Agony and the Ecstasy* (1965).

KAREL REISZ (1926–   ) A onetime critic and writer, Czech-born Reisz has worked exclusively in England. He began his directing career when he collaborated with Tony Richardson on the documentary *Momma Don't Allow* (1955). His first solo feature was *Saturday Night, Sunday Morning* (1960), the picture that started the British trend in realistic studies of the working class. **Other films include:** *Night Must Fall* (1963), *Morgan!* (1966), *Isadora* (1968).

JEAN RENOIR (1894–   ) The son of artist Auguste Renoir, he is the elder statesman of French films, with a long and distinguished career that dates back to the mid-20's. Although he has made several notable films during the later portion of his career, Renoir was at his best as the young master of poetic realism in pre-World War II France. His memorable films of that period include the bitter-sweet look at the Great War, *La Grande Illusion* (1937) and the biting satire *La Règle du Jeu* (1939). Renoir lived in self-imposed exile from France between 1939 and 1954. He worked in Hollywood for a while, then in India and Italy, before returning home and making the brilliant *French Cancan* (1954). **Highlights:** *Nana* (1926), *La Chienne* (1931), *Le Crime de Monsieur Lange* (1936), *La Vie Est à Nous* (1936), *The Southerner* (1945), *The Diary of a Chambermaid* (1946), *The River* (1950), *Le Petit Théâtre de Jean Renoir* (1971).

ALAIN RESNAIS (1922–   ) Former stage actor and documentary-maker, French director Renais made an auspicious debut as a director of feature films with *Hiroshima, Mon Amour* (1959), a skillful blending of love and war themes that brought him an enthusiastic international following. Most of Resnais' films examine time, memory, human behavior and the shaping and growth of personality. **They include:** *Last Year at Marienbad* (1961), *Muriel* (1963), *La Guerre Est Finie* (1966), *Je t' Aime Je t' Aime* (1968).

TONY RICHARDSON (1928–   ) As one of England's leading directors Richardson has scored hit after hit with films ranging in style from the dramatic screen adaptation of *Look Back in Anger* (1958) to the lush and lively *Tom Jones* (1963). Richardson has directed for both the stage and television, and in order to encourage the experimental work of young film directors, he established Woodfall Films in association with John Osborne. **His films include:** *A Taste of Honey* (1961), *The Loneliness of the Long Distance Runner* (1963), *Hamlet* (1969), *The Charge of the Light Brigade* (1968), *Ned Kelly* (1970).

HANS RICHTER (1888–   ) Berliner Richter began experimenting with films in Zurich during the 20's and made a name for himself with abstract films made by painting directly on film strips. He is considered an avant-garde director who has specialized in art films, including a series made in the United States, featuring the work of some of the world's most celebrated artists. **Films include:** *Rhythmus 21* (1921), *Filmstudy* (1926), *Everyday* (1929), *Dreams That Money Can Buy* (1945–47).

MARTIN RITT (1919–   ) Meticulous attention to detail characterizes Ritt's work, as does his feel for the time and place in which the stories he films are set. He worked in television and directed for the stage before establishing himself in Hollywood. **Films include:** *Edge of the City* (debut, 1956), *The Long Hot Summer* (1958), *Hud* (1962), *The Spy Who Came in From the Cold* (1965), *Hombre* (1967), *The Molly Maguires* (1969), *The Great White Hope* (1970), *Pete 'n' Tillie* (1973).

MARK ROBSON (1913–   ) He was a film editor and a director of horror films before winning assignments to handle some of Hollywood's slickest commercial successes. The best of Robson's work is considered to be *Home of the Brave* (1949).

Alain Resnais' Last Year at Marienbad *(1961)*

Tony Richardson's Tom Jones *(1963)*

Martin Ritt's The Long Hot Summer *(1958)*

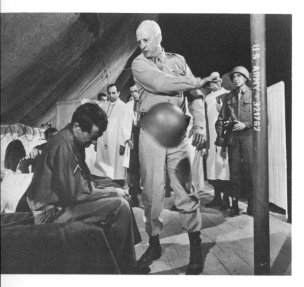

Franklin Schaffner's Patton *(1969)*

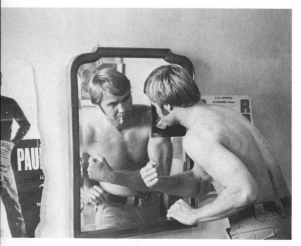

John Schlesinger's Midnight Cowboy *(1969)*

George Seaton's Miracle on 34th Street *(1947)*

Films include: *The Seventh Victim* (1943), *Bedlam* (1946), *The Bridges at Toko-Ri* (1954), *Peyton Place* (1958), *Von Ryan's Express* (1965), *Valley of the Dolls* (1967), *Happy Birthday, Wanda June* (1972).

ERIC ROHMER (1920–   ) French director Rohmer has a reputation for intellectual films—features that rely heavily on the sophisticated conversations of the leading characters. He was a writer and critic before making his first feature film, *Le Signe du Lion* (1960), in Paris. His work since has been concentrated in his "*Six Contes Moraux,*" a series of films that includes *La Collectionneuse* (1967), *Ma Nuit Chez Maud* (1969), *Claire's Knee* (1970), and *Chloe in the Afternoon* (1972).

STUART ROSENBERG (1925–   ) Although he is primarily a TV director, Rosenberg has made several feature films. **Credits include:** *Murder, Inc.* (1960), *Cool Hand Luke* (1967), *The April Fools* (1969), *Hall of Mirrors* (1969).

ROBERTO ROSSELLINI (1906–   ) Over the years Rossellini's work has evolved from documentaries to realistic features based on war themes, studies of individuals and of moral problems and then back to stark examinations of history. His first feature was *La Nave Bianca* (with De Robertis, 1941), which he followed with several films that reflected the trauma of World War II. With these films Rossellini became the recognized leader of Italian neo-realism. **Credits include:** *Open City* (1945), *Stromboli* (1949), *Viaggio in Italia* (1953), *India* (1958), *Illibatezza* (1962).

ROBERT ROSSEN (1908–1966) Rossen started out in Hollywood as a screenwriter and had to his credit several important films, including *A Walk in the Sun* (1945). Two years after his directorial debut with *Johnny O'Clock* (1947) Rossen won an Academy Award for *All the King's Men* (1949). He was considered at his best with films that dealt with success and its pitfalls. **Credits include:** *Body and Soul* (1947), *The Brave Bulls* (1950), *They Came to Cordura* (1959), *The Hustler* (1961), *Lilith* (1964).

S

MALCOLM ST. CLAIR (1897–1952) His work includes some of the most successful silent comedies, and at the peak of his career in 1927 St. Clair was rated only after Ernst Lubitsch and Erich von Stroheim as the best of American directors. St. Clair started out with the Mack Sennett Studios as a gag man, directed his first short, *Rip and Stitch, Tailors* (1919), and later found his forte to be subtle and sophisticated comedy. He continued to direct until 1948, but his career flagged with the coming of sound. **Highlights:** *George Washington* (feature debut, 1923), *The Show-Off* (1926), *The Grand Duchess and the Waiter* (1926), *Gentlemen Prefer Blondes* (1928), *Crack-Up* (1937), *The Bullfighters* (1945).

FRANKLIN J. SCHAFFNER (1920–   ) A TV director of some note whose credits include *Person to Person* and *Playhouse 90,* Schaffner turned to the screen and established a reputation as an astute and meticulous film director. In 1969 he won an Academy Award for *Patton.* **Films include:** *The Best Man* (1964), *The War Lord* (1965), *Planet of the Apes* (1968), *Nicholas and Alexandra* (1971).

JOHN SCHLESINGER (1926–   ) Although he is British and directs principally in England, it was an American picture, *Midnight Cowboy* (1969), that won Schlesinger an Academy Award. He was an actor and a television director before making his first feature film, *A Kind of Loving* (1962). **Films include:** *Billy Liar* (1963), *Darling* (1965), *Far From the Madding Crowd* (1967), *Sunday, Bloody Sunday* (1971).

MARTIN SCORSESE (1940–   ) His first commercial film, *Mean Streets* (1973), was selected for the New York Film Festival and carved a niche for him among promising young American film-makers.

GEORGE SEATON (1911–   ) Seaton began his career as a stage actor and producer, moved to Hollywood, where he was a scriptwriter for MGM, and then broke into directing in the 40's. He continues to script most of his films and has two Academy Awards to his credit for the screenplays of *Miracle on 34th Street* (1947) and *The Country Girl* (1954), both of which he directed. **Films include:** *Coney Island* (1943), *The Shocking Miss Pilgrim* (1947), *Teacher's Pet* (1958), *36 Hours* (1965), *Airport* (1969).

GEORGE B. SEITZ (1888–1944) A writer and director of silent serials, he directed many episodes of the *Perils of Pauline* series and turned out altogether more than 100 pictures, both silent and sound. In the late 30's and early 40's he found a successful niche directing many films in the *Andy Hardy* series. **Credits include:** *The Fatal Ring* (1917), *The Women in His Life* (1934), *Andy Hardy Meets a Debutante* (1940), *Kit Carson* (1940), *China Caravan* (1942).

GEORGE SIDNEY (1911–   ) Some of the brightest musical comedies of the 40's are among Sidney's screen credits. He is a onetime child actor, vaudeville performer and musician who got his start in Hollywood directing shorts. In addition to musicals, Sidney has directed some lively costume pictures, including *The Three Musketeers* (1948) and *Scaramouche* (1952). **Films include:** *Free and Easy* (feature debut, 1941), *The Harvey Girls* (1946), *Annie Get Your Gun* (1950), *Showboat* (1951), *The Eddie Duchin Story* (1956), *Bye Bye Birdie* (1962), *Half a Sixpence* (1967).

DON SIEGEL (1912–   ) Preceding his career as a director of tough crime dramas, Siegel won Academy Awards for two short subjects, *Hitler Lives* (1945). and *Star in the Night* (1945). The work he did directing second features brought favorable notice from film critics, and in subsequent bigger-budget films he has maintained his early reputation for excellence. **Films include:** *The Verdict* (feature debut, 1946), *Riot in Cell Block 11* (1954), *Baby Face Nelson* (1957), *Hell Is for Heroes* (1962), *Madigan* (1967), *Dirty Harry* (1971).

ELIOT SILVERSTEIN (c. 1925–   ) Primarily a TV director, Silverstein has directed for the screen occasionally, scoring his biggest success with the comic Western *Cat Ballou* (1965). **Credits include:** *Belle Sommers* (1962), *The Happening* (1967), *A Man Called Horse* (1969).

ROBERT SIODMAK (1900–) The American-born but European-trained Siodmak is considered a master of chilling suspense pictures and hard-hitting crime stories. He began directing in Germany in 1929 with *People on Sunday* (with Wilder and Zinnemann) but moved to Hollywood when Hitler came to power. He stayed for nearly 20 years directing what critics consider to be his best films, including *The Spiral Staircase* (1945) and *Cry of the City* (1949). **Films include:** *The Killers* (1946), *The Suspect* (1944), *The Dark Mirror* (1946), *The Crimson Pirate* (1952), *Le Grand Jeu* (1953), *Escape From East Berlin* (1962).

VILGOT SJOMAN (1924–) Few films have received the attention lavished on Sjoman's *I Am Curious Yellow* (1967), a cinema landmark only because of the legal controversy that surrounded it. *Curious*, a Swedish picture, broke through the censor's barriers against explicit sex and frontal nudity in films in the United States. Critics generally agreed that the film's artistic merits didn't warrant all the fuss. **Other films include:** *"491"* (1966), *I Am Curious Blue* (1967).

VICTOR SJOSTROM (1879–1960) One of the giants of the Swedish film industry, Sjostrom made his mark as a director and as an actor. Most of the films he directed were silents and illustrate his understanding of the Swedish character and how it is shaped by the elements of nature. Sjostrom's most famous film is, perhaps, *The Phantom Carriage* (1921). He went to Hollywood to direct some of the most memorable American silents. During the sound era he concentrated on acting and made one of his last appearances in Ingmar Bergman's *Wild Strawberries* (1957). **Films include:** *Ingeborg Holm* (1913), *He Who Gets Slapped* (1924), *The Scarlet Letter* (1926), *The Wind* (1928).

JOHN STAHL (1886–1950) This former stage actor arrived in Hollywood in 1914 and began his directing career in the silent teens. It was in the early sound era, however, that he found his niche with popular tearjerkers, including *Back Street* (1932), *Imitation of Life* (1934) and *Magnificent Obsession* (1935). **Credits include:** *Husband and Lovers* (1924), *The Keys of the Kingdom* (1944), *The Foxes of Harrow* (1947).

GEORGE STEVENS (1904–) Former cameraman and scriptwriter Stevens began directing in the early 30's, making some of the liveliest comedies of that and the next decade. In the 50's he turned to more dramatic vehicles, directing the classic *Shane* (1953) and winning two Academy Awards for *A Place in the Sun* (1951) and *Giant* (1956). In recent years his films have been less successful, though *The Only Game in Town* (1969) was highly praised. **Credits include:** *Alice Adams* (1935), *Woman of the Year* (1941), *The Diary of Anne Frank* (1959), *The Greatest Story Ever Told* (1964).

ROBERT STEVENSON (1905–) The British-born Stevenson has done much of his work for the Walt Disney studios and is responsible for some of its most popular comedies, including *Mary Poppins* (1964) and *The Love Bug* (1969). He directed a few films in England before moving to Hollywood and in his pre-Disney days turned out a well-received version of *Jane Eyre* (1943). **Films include:** *Tudor Rose* (1936), *To the Ends of the Earth* (1948), *The Absent-Minded Professor* (1960), *That Darn Cat* (1965).

MAURITZ STILLER (1883–1928) Although he is considered one of the great directors of early Swedish films, Helsinki-born Stiller is primarily remembered as the discoverer of superstar Greta Garbo. His films ranged from thrillers and sophisticated comedy to epiclike studies of man and his environment. He caught the attention of Hollywood's Louis B. Mayer with his *The Atonement of Gösta Berling*, and Stiller and his protegé, Garbo, were drawn to California, where Garbo's career blossomed and his was destroyed. His health failed, and he returned to Sweden, where he died shortly thereafter. **Credits include:** *The Black Masks* (1912), *Love and Journalism* (1916), *Herr Arne's Treasure* (1919), *Hotel Imperial* (1927).

JOHN STURGES (1911–) He has a flair for action pictures and has turned out some of Hollywood's most memorable Westerns, including *Bad Day at Black Rock* (1954). Sturges worked as a film cutter and editor before directing his first picture, *The Man Who Dared* (1946). **Films include:** *Gunfight at the OK Corral* (1957), *The Magnificent Seven* (1960), *The Old Man and the Sea* (1958), *The Great Escape* (1963), *Ice Station Zebra* (1968), *Marooned* (1969).

PRESTON STURGES (1898–1959) During the 40's Sturges mocked contemporary manners and morals in a series of screen comedies that include his classic *The Lady Eve* (1941). He was a playwright who went to Hollywood after one of his plays became a Broadway hit. His later films were considered no match for the pictures he made in the early 40's. **Films include:** *Sullivan's Travels* (1941), *The Palm Beach Story* (1942), *Hail the Conquering Hero* (1944), *The Diary of Major Thompson* (1955).

T

JACQUES TATI See entry on page 464.

NORMAN TAUROG (1899–) Taurog progressed from two-reel comedies to some of the most popular films of the 30's and 40's, winning an early Academy Award for *Skippy* (1931). Among his more popular films of that period were *The Adventures of Tom Sawyer* (1938), *Young Tom Edison* (1940) and *Girl Crazy* (1942). He directed many musicals throughout his career with such stars as Bing Crosby, Deanna Durbin, Judy Garland, Mario Lanza and, later, Elvis Presley. **Credits include:** *If I Had a Million* (1932), *Boys Town* (1938), *The Hoodlum Saint* (1946), *Living It Up* (1954), *Tickle Me* (1965).

MAURICE TOURNEUR (1878–1961) The French director of prestigious American silents, Tourneur was considered on a par with D. W. Griffith and was one of the first directors to stress film-making as art rather than mere photography. He began as a stage and screen actor, started directing for Eclair studios in France and was sent by them to manage their Tucson studios in the United States. The work he did in the U. S. brought him instant recognition. He made some classic films throughout the 20's and returned to France only when his style began to look dated in America. **Films include:** *The Blue Bird* (1918), *The Last of the Mohicans* (1922), *Aloma of the South Seas* (1926), *Impasse des Deux Anges* (1949).

George Stevens' A Place in the Sun *(1951)*

Robert Stevenson's Jane Eyre *(1943)*

John Sturges' The Old Man and the Sea *(1958)*

François Truffaut's Jules et Jim *(1961)*

King Vidor's Stella Dallas *(1937)*

Josef von Sternberg's Blonde Venus *(1932)*

JAN TROELL (1931–) Swede Jan Troell turned his youthful hobby into his adult vocation when he entered the film world photographing Widerberg's *The Pram* (1963). He soon turned to directing warm and sensitive studies of individuals and their ability to cope with their problems. He is probably best known for his recent two-part film, *The Emigrants* (U.S., 1972) and *The New Land* (U.S., 1973), a chronicle of a 19th-century Swedish family's move to America. **Films include:** *Here Is Your Life* (1966), *Who Saw Him Die?* (1967), *Zandy's Bride* (1974).

FRANÇOIS TRUFFAUT (1932–) French director Truffaut first achieved recognition of his formidable talents at the age of 27 with the semi-autobiographical film *400 Blows* (1959), the story of a misunderstood youth. It is still considered to be one of his best works. Truffaut has continued to turn out memorable films, including *Day for Night* (1973), winner of the New York Film Critics' best-picture award and an Oscar for Best Foreign Film. The highly personal style of his films have attracted an international following of admirers. **Films include:** *Shoot the Piano Player* (1960), *Jules et Jim* (1961), *Fahrenheit 451* (1966), *The Bride Wore Black* (1967), *L'Enfant Sauvage* (1970), *Two English Girls* (1971).

V

ROGER VADIM (1928–) Though he is a director of some merit, Parisian Vadim is probably better known as the mentor and former husband of Brigitte Bardot, and, later, of Jane Fonda. His first film, *And God Created Woman* (1956), brought him and his star, Bardot, immediate recognition. Subsequent films, such as *Les Liaisons Dangereuses* (1959) and *La Ronde* (1964), have emphasized the merit of his work, but too often in other pictures the commercial and erotic elements have overshadowed the artistic worth. **Credits include:** *Vice and Virtue* (1962), *The Game Is Over* (1966), *Pretty Maids All in a Row* (1970), *Hellé* (1972).

W. S. VAN DYKE (1887–1944) As a director for MGM during the 30's, Van Dyke handled a wide range of studio assignments, including the popular *Thin Man* series and that all-time favorite *San Francisco* (1936), starring Jeanette MacDonald and Clark Gable. Van Dyke got his start during the silent days as an assistant to D. W. Griffith and directed scores of Westerns, including those starring Buck Jones and Tim McCoy. Later he directed Johnny Weissmuller in the first Tarzan sound film, *Tarzan, the Ape Man* (1932). **Other screen credits include:** *White Shadows of the South Seas* (1928), *Marie Antoinette* (1938), *Sweethearts* (1938), *I Married an Angel* (1942), *Journey for Margaret* (1942).

CHARLES VIDOR (1900–1959) Particularly noted for his flair for combining music and drama in the same picture, Vidor directed Rita Hayworth in one of her most popular films, *Gilda* (1946), and Doris Day in *Love Me or Leave Me* (1955), the story of torch singer Ruth Etting. He was born in Hungary and studied film-making in Europe before immigrating to the United States. **Films include:** *The Mask of Fu Manchu* (1932), *A Song to Re-*

member (1945), *Hans Christian Andersen* (1952), *The Swan* (1956), *The Joker Is Wild* (1957).

KING VIDOR (1894–) During the silent era Vidor emerged as a bold new director who broke taboos when he filmed *The Big Parade* (1925), about World War I, despite the Hollywood conviction that the public didn't want to see war pictures, and *The Crowd* (1928), a rare silent about ordinary people instead of sheiks and sirens. *The Crowd* is still regarded as his best work and as the most notable example of his technique. After the advent of sound Vidor remained on the scene as director of big-budget prestige pictures. **His films include:** *Northwest Passage* (1940), *Duel in the Sun* (1947), *War and Peace* (1956), *Solomon and Sheba* (1959).

JEAN VIGO (1905–1934) Regarded as one of France's most promising directors before his death at age 29, Vigo was an innovator whose first film, *À Propos de Nice* (1930), a study of the idle rich on the Riviera, was enthusiastically received. He made only three other films, one of which, *Zéro de Conduite* (1933), was banned because of its harsh representation of the French educational system. His last film was *L'Atalante* (1934), an insightful love story about a barge sailor.

LUCHINO VISCONTI (1906–) Although his output of films has been relatively small, Visconti is considered one of Italy's most influential directors. He is an Italian aristocrat of Communist sympathies who also directs for the theatre and the opera. He created a stir with his first film, *Ossessione* (1942), which he based on James Cain's *The Postman Always Rings Twice*. It was banned for a time after its realease, as was his second picture, *La Terra Trema* (1948). The film that made Visconti's international reputation was *Rocco and His Brothers* (1960). **Other films include:** *Bellissima* (1951), *The Leopard* (1963), *The Stranger* (1967), *The Damned* (1967), *Death in Venice* (1970).

JOSEF VON STERNBERG (1894–1969) Von Sternberg was born in Austria but came to the United States when quite young. He began working in the film industry in 1914 and directed his first film, *The Salvation Hunters* (1924), ten years later. It was not until he introduced the gangster film to the cinema repertory with the silent *Underworld* (1927) that he attained recognition. One of the highlights of his career was also the beginning of his downfall—*The Blue Angel* (1930), made in Germany. It was with this film that he introduced Marlene Dietrich to the moviegoer and began a long string of films with her as the star. These films increased Dietrich's stature but somehow lessened Von Sternberg's. From the late 30's his career declined. **Credits include:** *An American Tragedy* (1931), *The Scarlet Empress* (1934), *Crime and Punishment* (1935), *Macao* (1952).

ERICH VON STROHEIM See entry on page 484.

W

ANDRZEJ WAJDA (1926–) The early films of this Polish director reflect the dilemma of his people and his homeland during the Second World War and the years of political turmoil that followed. Wajda's first film, *A Generation* (1954), is about a young man serving in the Polish resistance. The themes of war and resistence recur in most of Wajda's early films. Later, his pictures treated more varied subjects. **Films include:** *Kanal* (1957), *Ashes and Diamonds* (1957), *The Siberian Lady Macbeth* (1961), *The Birchwood* (1970).

RAOUL WALSH (1892–   ) He was a stage and screen actor who played John Wilkes Booth in the epic *The Birth of a Nation* (1915). In the mid-teens he turned to direction (working for a time as an assistant to D. W. Griffith). He made more than 200 Hollywood features—most of them action adventures, Westerns or gangster pictures. **His screen credits include:** *Carmen* (1915), *Kindred of the Dust* (1923), *What Price Glory?* (1926), *Me and My Gal* (1932), *They Drive by Night* (1940), *High Sierra* (1941), *The Naked and the Dead* (1958), *A Distant Trumpet* (1964).

CHARLES WALTERS (1911–   ) Once a dancer himself, Walters served as a dance director on 40's MGM musicals before winning assignments to handle pictures like the classics *Easter Parade* (1948) and *The Barkleys of Broadway* (1949). His later work included light comedies and musicals, among them *Lili* (1953), *The Tender Trap* (1955), *High Society* (1956), *Don't Go Near the Water* (1957), *Please Don't Eat the Daisies* (1960), *The Unsinkable Molly Brown* (1964).

ORSON WELLES (1915–   ) Multi-talented actor-director-writer Welles began his career acting in Dublin with the Gate Theatre. He performed on the U.S. stage, appeared on radio and in 1937 established the repertory Mercury Theatre in New York. In 1938 he directed his first film, *Too Much Johnson*, and two years later wrote, directed and starred in the now classic *Citizen Kane*, introducing in the film technical innovations that have since become part of film-making technique. His easily recognizable portrait of William Randolph Hearst in *Kane* won him a formidable enemy who wielded his great influence to curtail distribution of the film and virtually to ruin Welles' career in Hollywood. Welles returned to radio and to acting on stage and screen. In 1947 he directed the unpopular (in Hollywood) *Lady from Shanghai* and thereafter did most of his work in Europe. **Credits include:** *Journey Into Fear* (1942), *The Stranger* (1946), *Touch of Evil* (1958), *The Immortal Story* (1968).

WILLIAM WELLMAN (1896–   ) Although one of Wellman's biggest successes was the tearjerker *A Star Is Born* (1937), he is best known for Westerns and action melodramas. He was an actor before directing his first silent, *The Man Who Won* (1923). Many of his films reflect his interest in flying, among them his major silent work, *Wings* (1927), and *Lafayette Escadrille* (1958). **Major credits include:** *Public Enemy* (1931), *Call of the Wild* (1935), *The Ox-Bow Incident* (1943), *The Track of the Cat* (1954), *The High and the Mighty* (1954).

LINA WERTMULLER (c. 1930–   ) Although she had been directing films in her native Italy for more than ten years, Wertmuller did not make her mark on the international film scene until 1974 with *Love and Anarchy*. She had worked as a scriptwriter in films, television and the theatre and served as an assistant director to Federico Fellini on *8½* (1963). In 1974 she also directed *Everything's Set*.

BO WIDERBERG (1930–   ) He was a well-known writer in his native Sweden before he directed his first feature film, *The Pram* (1963). Widerberg's films, especially his most famous, *Elvira Madigan* (1967), reflect a romantic outlook that some critics feel mars the seriousness of his work. A frequent Widerberg theme concerns the socialist movement in Sweden. **Films include:** *Love '65* (1965), *Thirty Times Your Money* (1966), *The Ballad of Joe Hill* (1971).

HERBERT WILCOX (1891–   ) His wife, actress Anna Neagle, was the star of early Wilcox pictures during the 30's. They included several biographical films based on the lives of Queen Victoria, Nell Gwynn and Edith Cavell. Later, Wilcox directed many light comedies, including *Piccadilly Incident* (1946), starring Neagle and Michael Wilding. His career flourished during the 30's, 40's and early 50's and then faltered. **Films include:** *Goodnight Vienna* (1932), *Victoria the Great* (1937), *Odette* (1951), *The Lady With the Lamp* (1952).

BILLY WILDER (1906–   ) Some of Hollywood's most memorable comedies have been the work of Wilder, a Vienna-born director who worked as a scriptwriter for films in Germany and the United States before directing *The Major and the Minor* (1942). He is a two-time Academy Award winner for the drama *The Lost Weekend* (1945) and the tragicomedy *The Apartment* (1960). Wilder also has to his credits the classic *Sunset Boulevard* (1950). **Credits include:** *Double Indemnity* (1944), *Stalag 17* (1953), *Sabrina* (1954), *Witness for the Prosecution* (1958), *Some Like It Hot* (1959), *One, Two, Three* (1961), *The Fortune Cookie* (1966).

ROBERT WISE (1914–   ) Wise first worked as a film editor on such prestigious assignments as Welles' *Citizen Kane* (1940) and *The Magnificent Ambersons* (1942). He later turned to directing and won critical praise for such film dramas as *Executive Suite* (1954) and *I Want to Live!* (1958). He has also achieved recognition for his musicals, winning Academy Awards for *West Side Story* (with Jerome Robbins, 1961) and *The Sound of Music* (1965). **Other credits include:** *Somebody Up There Likes Me* (1956), *Run Silent, Run Deep* (1958), *Two for the Seesaw* (1962), *The Sand Pebbles* (1966), *Star!* (1968), *The Andromeda Strain* (1970), *Two People* (1973).

SAM WOOD (1883–1949) Director of some of Hollywood's biggest studio-produced hits of the 30's and 40's, Wood made more than 100 pictures during both the silent and sound eras. They ranged from sophisticated comedies to tear-jerkers, drama and Marx Brothers romps. **Films include:** *Peck's Bad Boy* (1921), *A Night at the Opera* (1935), *A Day at the Races* (1937), *Goodbye Mr. Chips* (1939), *King's Row* (1942), *For Whom the Bell Tolls* (1943), *Command Decision* (1948), *Ambush* (1950).

WILLIAM WYLER (1902–   ) One of Hollywood's most versatile film-makers, Wyler has proven adept at directing a range of pictures, including screen adaptations of prestigious plays and novels, romantic comedies, musicals and epic Westerns. In association with Samuel Goldwyn, Wyler directed *Dodsworth* (1936), *Wuthering Heights* (with Howard Hawks, 1939) and *The Little Foxes* (with Hawks, 1941), among many others. He has won Academy Awards three times—for

Robert Wise's The Sound of Music *(1965)*

William Wellman's The Ox-Bow Incident *(1943)*

Billy Wilder's Sunset Boulevard *(1950)*

William Wyler's Dodsworth *(1936)*

Franco Zeffirelli's Romeo and Juliet *(1968)*

Fred Zinnemann's From Here to Eternity (1953)

Mrs. Miniver (1942), *The Best Years of Our Lives* (1956) and *Ben Hur* (1959). **Highlights:** *Jezebel* (1938), *Roman Holiday* (1953), *The Desperate Hours* (1955), *The Collector* (1965), *Funny Girl* (1968), *The Liberation of L. B. Jones* (1970).

Y

PETER YATES (1929–   ) A British director who made his name in Hollywood, Yates is best known for the action-packed detective film *Bullitt* (1968), the Steve McQueen picture with the famous auto chase sequence. He started out as a film cutter but switched to directing in 1962 with *Summer Holiday.* **Films include:** *One Way Pendulum* (1964), *John and Mary* (1969), *Murphy's War* (1971), *The Hot Rock* (1973).

BUD YORKIN (1926–   ) During the 60's Yorkin switched from television to film directing and subsequently made several offbeat comedies, including *Come Blow Your Horn* (1963), *Never Too Late* (1965), *Divorce American Style* (1967), *Inspector Clouseau* (1968), *The Thief Who Came to Dinner* (1973).

TERENCE YOUNG (1915–   ) Most of his films are suspense stories or fast-paced thrillers like some of the James Bond series Young directed in the mid-60's. A departure was the romantic *Mayerling* (1968). **Films include:** *Corridor of Mirrors* (1949), *From Russia With Love* (1963), *Thunderball* (1965), *Wait Until Dark* (1967), *The Poppy Is Also a Flower* (1967).

Z

FRANCO ZEFFIRELLI (1923–   ) After directing primarily for the Italian stage and opera, Zeffirelli took on the film version of *The Taming of the Shrew* (1967) with Richard Burton and Elizabeth Taylor. His next picture was another Shakespearean adaptation, *Romeo and Juliet* (1968). Zeffirelli's films are visually lush but have not appealed to critics as much as they have to audiences. His only other screen credit is *Brother Sun, Sister Moon.*

MAI ZETTERLING See entry on page 505.

FRED ZINNEMANN (1907–   ) One of the most respected of Hollywood directors, Zinnemann has won three Academy Awards—for a short, *That Mothers Might Live* (1938), for *From Here to Eternity* (1953) and for *A Man for All Seasons* (1966). He was born in Vienna and arrived in Hollywood in 1930 as an actor. From the beginning of his directorial career Zinnemann's films have reflected his concern for individuals as they struggle with personal dilemmas. **Films include:** *Kid Glove Killer* (1942), *The Seventh Cross* (1944), *High Noon* (1952), *Oklahoma!* (1955), *The Nun's Story* (1958), *The Day of the Jackal* (1973).

INDEX
To the people
in this book.

A

Abbott, Bud, 9, 80, 82, 107, 391, 518
Abbott, George, 9
Abbott, John, 9
Abel, Walter, 9
Acuff, Eddie, 9
Adams, Edie, 9, 305
Adams, Nick, 10
Adler, Buddy, 329
Adler, Luther, 10
Adler, Stella, 60
Adorée, Renée, 10
Adrian, Iris, 10
Aherne, Brian, 10, 47, 83
Ahn, Philip, 10–11
Aimée, Anouk, 11, 166, 474
Alberghetti, Anna Maria, 11
Alberni, Luis, 11
Albert, Eddie, 11, 180
Albertson, Frank, 12
Albertson, Jack, 12
Albright, Hardie, 12
Albright, Lola, 12
Alda, Alan, 12
Alda, Robert, 12
Aldrich, Robert, 506
Alexander, Ben, 13
Alexander, Katherine, 13
Allégret, Marc, 34, 506, 521
Allégret, Yves, 506
Allen, Elizabeth, 13
Allen, Gracie, 13, 48, 70
Allen, Rex, 394
Allen, Woody, 13, 88, 291, 292 314
Allgood, Sara, 14
Allison, May, 484
Allister, Claude, 14
Allyson, June, 14,112, 282, 398
Altman, Robert, 295, 497, 503, 506
Alvardo, Don, 14
Ameche, Don, 15, 248, 438
Ames, Leon, 15
Anderson, Eddie (Rochester), 15
Anderson, Dame Judith, 16

Anderson, Lindsay, 220, 348 , 418, 506
Anderson, Michael, 506
Anderson, Richard, 16
Anderson, Warner, 16
Andersson, Bibi, 16, 507
Andress, Ursula, 16, 132
Andrews, Dana, 17, 346
Andrews, Harry, 17
Andrews, Julie, 17, 249, 263, 292, 361, 480
Andrews Sisters, 18, 107
Angel, Heather, 18, 262
Angeli, Pier, 18
Ankers, Evelyn, 18
Ankrum, Morris, 18
Annabella, 18, 19
Annakin, Ken, 506
Ann-Margret, 19
Anspach, Susan, 19, 305
Antonioni, Michelangelo, 248, 362, 413, 483, 506
Arbuckle, Roscoe "Fatty," 19, 88, 291
Arden, Eve, 20
Arkin, Alan, 20
Arlen, Richard, 20, 154, 422, 501
Arletty, 20
Arliss, George, 20, 21, 124, 285, 365, 389
Armendariz, Pedro, 21
Armetta, Henry, 21
Armstrong, Louis, 21–22
Armstrong, Robert, 22, 73
Arnaz, Desi, 31, 118
Arness, James, 22, 203
Arno, Sig, 22, 23
Arnold, Jack, 506
Arnold, Edward, 23
Arnt, Charles, 23
Arthur, George K., 23
Arthur, Jean, 23–24, 82, 455
Ashley, Elizabeth, 24
Asquith, Anthony, 506
Astaire, Adele, 25
Astaire, Fred, 24, 25, 50, 54, 90, 109, 184, 199, 411, 417, 422, 423
Asther, Nils, 25
Astor, Mary, 25–26, 38, 179, 328
Ates, Roscoe, 26
Attenborough, Richard, 26, 27
Atwill, Lionel, 26, 488
Auer, Mischa, 27, 190
Aumont, Jean-Pierre, 27, 359
Autant-Lara, Claude, 507
Autry, Gene, 27, 69, 423

Avalon, Frankie, 27, 268
Aylmer, Felix, 27
Ayres, Agnes, 28
Ayres, Lew, 28, 51, 391, 502
Aznavour, Charles, 28

B

Bacall, Lauren, 29, 56, 98, 135, 420, 432
Bacharach, Burt, 135
Backus, Jim, 29, 433
Bacon, Irving, 29
Bacon, Lloyd, 507
Baddeley, Hermione, 29–30
Bailey, Pearl, 30, 202
Bain, Barbara, 311
Bainter, Fay, 30
Baker, Bob, 302
Baker, Carroll, 30, 31, 149, 471
Baker, Diane, 30
Baker, Joe Don, 222
Baker, Kenny, 355
Baker, Stanley, 31
Bakewell, William, 31
Ball, Lucille, 31, 177, 447, 451
Balsam, Martin, 32, 420
Bancroft, Anne, 32, 145, 255
Bancroft, George, 32
Bankhead, Tallulah, 32–33, 103, 156, 260, 390, 435
Banks, Leslie, 33
Banky, Vilma, 33, 99, 314
Bannen, Ian, 33
Bara, Theda, 33–34, 63, 135, 215, 308, 367
Barbier, George, 34
Bardot, Brigitte, 34, 326
Bari, Lynn, 34, 35
Barker, Lex, 34, 109, 286
Barnes, Binnie, 35
Barnett, Vince, 35
Barrat, Robert, 35
Barrault, Jean-Louis, 35
Barrie, Mona, 36
Barrie, Wendy, 36
Barrier, Edgar, 36
Barriscale, Bessie, 299
Barrymore, Ethel, 36, 217, 265, 274
Barrymore, John, 25, 36–37, 86, 98, 107, 168, 169, 181, 249, 265, 274, 285, 289, 326, 340, 399, 410, 504

540